THE
ARLINGTON READER

Contexts and Connections

Third Edition

Lynn Z. Bloom
University of Connecticut

Louise Z. Smith
University of Massachusetts—Boston

Bedford/St. Martin's
Boston ◆ New York

For Bedford/St. Martin's

Executive Editor: John E. Sullivan III
Senior Production Editor: Anne Noonan
Production Supervisor: Ashley Chalmers
Senior Marketing Manager: Molly Parke
Editorial Assistant: Shannon Walsh
Copy Editor: Jacqueline Rebisz
Photo Researcher: Naomi Kornhauser
Permissions Manager: Kalina Ingham Hintz
Text Design: Jean Hammond
Cover Design: Donna Dennison
Cover Art: Untitled (*Woman in Green*), Daniel Korty
Composition: Glyph International
Printing and Binding: RR Donnelley & Sons Company

President: Joan E. Feinberg
Editorial Director: Denise B. Wydra
Editor in Chief: Karen S. Henry
Director of Marketing: Karen R. Soeltz
Director of Production: Susan W. Brown
Associate Director, Editorial Production: Elise S. Kaiser
Managing Editor: Elizabeth M. Schaaf

Library of Congress Control Number: 2010936228

Manufactured in the United States of America.

6   5   4   3   2   1
f   e   d   c   b   a

For information, write: Bedford/St. Martin's, 75 Arlington Street, Boston, MA 02116
(617-399-4000)

ISBN: 978-0-312-60565-0

Acknowledgments

Acknowledgments and copyrights are continued at the back of the book on page 654, which constitute an extension of the copyright page. It is a violation of the law to reproduce these selections by any means whatsoever without the written permission of the copyright holder.

Preface for Instructors

WHY THIS BOOK?

This new edition of *The Arlington Reader* presents a mix of class-tested and cutting-edge essays and graphic images designed not only to encourage discussion but also to provoke and address controversy. We hope to engage first-year composition students with topics that matter to them and to the world.

The revisions to *The Arlington Reader* are based on our extensive experience as researchers, writing teachers, and discriminating readers of contemporary writing. This blend of wide reading, theory, research, and practical expertise governs the book's philosophy and pedagogy. *The Arlington Reader* aims to

- teach students how to read, write, and think critically at the college level.
- help students respond actively to written texts and illustrations, with reflection, critique, dialogue, and debate.
- enable students to read selected essays in their original cultural and intellectual contexts rather than as bodies of words floating free of time and place.
- teach students to differentiate and make connections among important ideas.
- introduce students to a wide range of excellent modern and contemporary prose writers and major thinkers whose works are central to a liberal education.
- acquaint students with what professionals in various disciplines think, value, and argue about as critically important in our contemporary world.
- help newcomers to American culture respect their own traditions and values while they are learning new ones.
- enable all students, irrespective of birth and background, to share in America's ever-changing multicultural values and viewpoints.

CRITERIA FOR INCLUSION IN *THE ARLINGTON READER*

To be included in *The Arlington Reader*, an essay must first and foremost be teachable; it must contribute to the intellectual, political, and rhetorical balance of the whole book; and it must serve as a good illustration of professional or literary writing, in substance and in style.

An essay's *teachability* is determined in part by its *accessibility*. How much do teachers have to know or learn in order to teach the work? Will students understand its concepts and vocabulary, with or without much explanation in class? Is it intellectually appropriate for them? Is it too technical, too allusive, too arty for students to stick with it? Is the essay short enough to be discussed in one or two class periods?

An essay's *balance with the rest of the book* is reflected in the ways that its topic, point of view, and moral and ethical stance contribute to the kinds of dialogue, debate, and critical thinking *The Arlington Reader* hopes to engender. Will it enlarge the students' understanding of the world or of a particular issue? Does the essay represent views and values that students should consider, confront, and either challenge or adopt? Does the author's reputation, stand on issues, ethnicity, or gender contribute to the anthology's balanced perspective?

An essay's *aesthetic qualities* are related to form and style. Is its *form* a good example of narration or description or definition or comparison and contrast and the rest? Are these rhetorical patterns woven into an argument in a compelling way (since, it could be argued, every text is some kind of argument)? Is the essay clearly organized? Is its *style* rich in sentence rhythms, vocabulary, figurative language, tone, even wit? Does the author "make it new," enabling readers to see the subject afresh?

FEATURES

Readings. *The Arlington Reader* includes a mix of class-tested and contemporary essays. Numerous *classic authors*, spanning the centuries but primarily from the twentieth and twenty-first centuries, provide continuity and intellectual solidity in this collection of significant writing. Among them are Charles Darwin, Henry David Thoreau, Stephen Jay Gould, Alice Walker, Martin Luther King Jr., Virginia Woolf, and Annie Dillard. Distinguished *fresh voices* include Matthew B. Crawford, Brian Doyle, Joseph Fuller, and Sandra Postel. *The Arlington Reader* also includes many women and multicultural authors, among them Sherman Alexie, Gloria Anzaldúa, Leslie Silko, Amy Tan, and Alice Walker, who bring alternative views and contemporary voices to the classroom.

Reflecting the needs of today's instructors and the interests of today's students, *The Arlington Reader* offers essays that are excellent models of good writing in style and technique and that illustrate one or more significant rhetorical concerns such as argument, comparison and contrast, and narrative. The essays range from three to fifteen pages long, so they're brief enough to be taught in one or two class periods but substantial enough to elicit serious discussion and writing.

Thematic orientation across disciplines. Eight thematic chapters address important areas of intellectual inquiry and controversy, intended to appeal to contemporary student writers. The chapters include (1) Speaking, Reading, and Writing; (2) Identity; (3) Relationships; (4) Education; (5) Technology; (6) Science; (7) Ethics; and (8) The Environment. The chapters are broad and flexible enough to encompass a variety of topics, and the range of disciplines allows students to work across a number of academic subject areas. An alternative *Rhetorical Table of Contents* allows this book to be easily adapted to individual instructors' needs.

Distinctive contextual materials. Throughout *The Arlington Reader*, contextual materials reveal authors' and readers' changing understandings of the essays. In each chapter, a classic, often-taught piece is followed by a five- to seven-page cluster of related materials that allows instructors and students alike to understand these time-tested selections in greater depth. For instance, the context for Richard Rodriguez's classic "Aria: Memoir of a Bilingual Childhood," includes excerpts from two interviews with the author (1994, 1999); photographs of the author; Rodriguez's 1993 Op-Ed essay, "Slouching towards Los Angeles," which argues that America was founded on Protestant individualism—a tradition Rodriguez shares; Octavio Paz's "The Labyrinth of Solitude," which analyzes the cultural tradition of masculine silence; Richard Hoggart's "The Uses of Literacy," which addresses "the friction point of two cultures," that of the wealthy and another composed of those who are not; and Paul Zweig's "The Child of Two Cultures," which points out that "the essential function of education . . . is to change the student, extract him from his intimate circumstance—family, ghetto, minority community—and give him access to the public world." Contextual materials add depth, freshness, and new perspectives to essays, and students see the sources, motives, and circumstances of an important piece of writing. These correlated readings also enable teachers to encourage student dialogues with the works they read, and to experiment with various forms of writing, gaining "textual power" as Robert Scholes recommends, by creating "a text in response to a text."

Photographs. Each chapter contains two or more photographs, many by well-known photographers, supplemented, at times, by cartoons and graphic essays. The accompanying commentary is designed to help students learn to analyze images with the thoughtful, critical attention that leads to new insights. For example, in looking at Dorothea Lange's "Migrant Mother," the photograph that gave a human face to America's Great Depression in the 1930s, students are encouraged to consider humanitarian issues on a large as well as individual scale and to consult the Smithsonian Web site to see Lange's additional photographs of destitute Florence Owens Thompson and her seven hungry children.

Apparatus. Informative yet unobtrusive editorial commentary helps students move from critical reading to thoughtful writing and revising.

- *A unique two-part introduction* contains advice on critical reading to help students fully engage with the selections as well as advice on writing essays in a variety of genres. It guides students through the process of turning analytical reading into thoughtful writing.

- *Headnotes* supply a substantial biographical note about the author of each essay and provide historical, cultural, and rhetorical contexts for essays.
- *Questions for discussion and writing* follow each essay, "Linked Readings" pair, and photograph. They include open-ended suggestions for discussion, interpretation, commentary, or dissent. These questions help students to read, think, and write about the essay's content, style, and rhetorical strategies and to make connections with other readings in the book and with issues outside the text, as well.

NEW TO THIS EDITION

New up-to-the-minute readings throughout. Fourty four selections are new to the third edition. For instance, Esther Dyson examines new media pitfalls in "Reflections on Privacy 2.0," and Gregory Orr looks back to a haunting civil rights era scare in "Return to Hayneville" to see just how far we've come since then.

Two new edgy chapters, focus on current, controversial issues. The essays in these chapters, as with all the chapters, speak to one another, in dialogue, in disagreement, but in common concern with — as Sherry Turkle puts it — "social, moral, and political" issues.

Chapter 5, "Wired — Be Careful What You Wish For: What Are the Consequences of Life in the High-Tech Fast Lane?" is concerned with issues of technology. For example, Nicholas Carr's "Is Google Making Us Stupid?" focuses on major changes in the way we read materials on the Internet; do we all "zip along the surface like a guy on a Jet Ski" rather than diving deeply into a sea of print? And in "How Computers Change the Way We Think," Sherry Turkle addresses "word processing vs. thinking," "taking things at interface value," and "simulation and its discontents."

Chapter 8, "The Environment: Will We Save It or Lose It? Will This Be the End of the World As We Know It?" also has many new readings, and raises equally profound social, moral, and political issues. For instance, two international leaders and Nobel Peace Prize winners, Al Gore ("A Planetary Emergency," 583) and Wangari Maathai ("The Green Belt Movement"), reinforced by former Czech president Vaclav Havel ("Our Moral Footprint") explain why no nation is an environmentally isolated ecosystem. Jared Diamond's "The World as a Polder" (632) offers a scenario even grimmer. If humans do not quickly address the world's current hot-button environmental problems — all interrelated — such as the destruction of natural habitats (forests, wetlands, coral reefs), animals and plants, and the depletion of soil and energy sources, the world will succumb to "warfare, genocide, starvation, disease epidemics, and collapses of societies"? Will this be the end of the world as we know it?

Streamlined and affordable. Now briefer, *The Arlington Reader* provides top-notch pedagogy and readings but has a net price $10–15 lower than most other readers.

New photographs exhibit a point of view, tell stories, and implicitly argue for understanding, action, or both. Among these are Simon McComb's "Education in Open Air"—a lovely scene of the ocean viewed by a writer on the beach—that may be juxtaposed with two other environmentally sensitive photographs: "Satellite Image of Haiti and the Dominican Republic" (one arid, the other lush) and "Kangerlua Glacier Melting."

Increased connections among the readings. In addition to paired readings, chapters are designed to emphasize thematic connections throughout, and there are now more questions that connect selections so that students can compare ideas and see how they resonate.

YOU GET MORE DIGITAL CHOICES FOR *THE ARLINGTON READER*

The Arlington Reader doesn't stop with a book. Online, you'll find both free and affordable premium resources to help students get even more out of the book and your course. You'll also find convenient instructor resources, such as downloadable sample syllabi, classroom activities, and even a nationwide community of teachers. To learn more about or order any of the products below, contact your Bedford/St. Martin's sales representative, e-mail sales support (sales_support@ bfwpub.com), or visit the Web site at bedfordstmartins.com/Arlington/catalog.

Student resources. Send students to free and open resources, upgrade to an expanding collection of innovative digital content, or package a standalone CD-ROM for free with *The Arlington Reader*.

Re:Writing, the best free collection of online resources for the writing class, offers clear advice on citing sources in *Research and Documentation Online* by Diana Hacker, 30 sample papers and designed documents, and over 9,000 writing and grammar exercises with immediate feedback and reporting in *Exercise Central*. Updated and redesigned, *Re:Writing* also features five free videos from *VideoCentral* and three new visual tutorials from our popular *ix visual exercises* by Cheryl Ball and Kristin Arola. *Re:Writing* is completely free and open (no codes required) to ensure access to all students. Visit bedfordstmartins.com/ rewriting.

VideoCentral is a growing collection of videos for the writing class that captures real-world, academic, and student writers talking about how and why they write. Writer and teacher Peter Berkow interviewed hundreds of people—from Michael Moore to Cynthia Selfe—to produce 50 brief videos about topics such as revising and getting feedback. *VideoCentral* can be packaged for free with *The Arlington Reader*. An activation code is required. To learn more, visit bedfordstmartins.com/videocentral. To order *VideoCentral* packaged with the print book, use ISBN 0-312-58333-8 or 978-0-312-58333-0.

Re:Writing Plus gathers all of Bedford/St. Martin's premium digital content for composition into one online collection. It includes hundreds of model documents, the first ever peer review game, and *VideoCentral. Re:Writing Plus* can be purchased separately or packaged with the print book at a significant discount. An activation code is required. To learn more, visit bedfordstmartins .com/rewriting. To order *Re:Writing Plus* packaged with the print book, use ISBN 0-312-58337-0 or 978-0-312-58337-8.

i-series on CD-ROM presents multimedia tutorials in a flexible format — because there are things you can't do in a book. To learn more, visit at bedfordstmartins.com/arlington/catalog.

- *ix visual exercises* helps students put into practice key rhetorical and visual concepts. To order *ix visual exercises* packaged with the print book, use ISBN 0-312-58336-2 or 978-0-312-58336-1.
- *i-claim: visualizing argument* offers a new way to see argument — with 6 tutorials, an illustrated glossary, and over 70 multimedia arguments. To order *i-claim: visualizing argument* packaged with the print book, use ISBN 0-312-58335-4 or 978-0-312-58335-4.
- *i-cite: visualizing sources* brings research to life through an animated introduction, four tutorials, and hands-on source practice. To order *i-claim: visualizing argument* packaged with the print book, use ISBN 0-312-58334-6 or 978-0-312-58334-7.

Instructor resources. You have a lot to do in your course. Bedford/St. Martin's wants to make it easy for you to find the support you need — and to get it quickly. To find everything available with *The Arlington Reader*, visit bedfordstmartins .com/arlington/catalog.

The *Instructor's Manual for The Arlington Reader* is available in PDF that can be downloaded from the Bedford/St. Martin's online catalog at bedfordstmartins .com/arlington/catalog. In addition to overviews of each of the assignments, the Instructor's Manual includes teaching tips, sample syllabi, alternative thematic groupings, and suggestions for classroom activities.

Teaching Central offers the entire list of Bedford/St. Martin's print and online professional resources in one place. You'll find landmark reference works, sourcebooks on pedagogical issues, award-winning collections, and practical advice for the classroom — all free for instructors. See bedfordstmartins.com/ teaching central.

Bits collects creative ideas for teaching a range of composition topics in an easily searchable blog. A community of teachers — leading scholars, authors, and editors — discuss revision, research, grammar and style, technology, peer review, and much more. Take, use, adapt, and pass the ideas around. Then, come back to the site to comment or share your own suggestion. See bedfordbits.com.

Content cartridges for the most common course management systems — Blackboard, WebCT, Angel, and Desire2Learn — allow you to easily download digital materials from Bedford/St. Martin's for your course. See bedfordstmartins .com/cms.

ACKNOWLEDGMENTS

We thank the following instructors who responded to our questionnaire: Karen Amano-Tompkins, Los Angeles Harbor College; Vickie L. Beam, Belmont Abbey College; James Burns, University of Delaware; Anthony Daly, Saddleback College; John Dean, Texas State University-San Marcos; Christopher Dowd, Manchester Community College; Benjamin Engel, Texas State University-San Marcos; LaToya Faulk, Michigan State University; Charlene Gill, Texas State University-San Marcos; Lisa Gring-Pemble, George Mason University; Dick Heaberlin, Texas State University-San Marcos; Lisa Drnec Kerr, Western New England College; Annette March, California State University-Monterey Bay; Marigrace Miller, Manchester Community College; Sarah Jane Morrison, Texas State University-San Marcos; David A. Roberts, Ohio Northern University; Linda Rosekrans, SUNY College at Cortland; Rene Scheys, Fullerton College; Suzanne Scott, George Mason University; Jennifer Viereck, Midlands Technical College; John M. Withers IV, Belmont Abbey College; and Laura E. Young, Texas State University-San Marcos.

We also thank the following reviewers: David Calonne, Eastern Michigan University; Theresa James, South Florida Community College; Audrey Kerr, Southern Connecticut State University; Thomas McConnell, University of South Carolina Upstate; Ivan Dale McDaniel, South Florida Community College; Charlotte Pressler, South Florida Community College; and Mark Sanders, Stephen F. Austin State University. We are grateful as well to those reviewers who chose to remain anonymous.

In the first edition, Chuck Christensen, Joan Feinberg, and Nancy Perry were instrumental in the conception and evolution of *The Arlington Reader*. Ning Yu brought his multicultural, Asian American scholar's perspective to a number of the headnotes and study questions and to the Instructor's Manual. Mark Gallaher and Matthew Simpson scrutinized our headnotes and questions and wrote some new ones, as did Kathrine Adeylott, crack researcher. George W. Smith gave quiet encouragement.

For the second and third editions, Denise M. Lovett, a novelist of distinction, has made significant revisions to the apparatus, as well as prepared the new material for the instructor's guide. Sandy Schechter oversaw text permissions, and Naomi Kornhauser cleared permissions for art. Lori Corsini-Nelson helped with manuscript preparation on all three editions, aided on the third by the invaluable efforts of Scott Allison, Tina Parziale, and Stuart Ziarnik, often on short notice. Anne Noonan supervised the book's production. Shannon Walsh handled innumerable details with good humor and patience. On all editions, John Sullivan coordinated the entire project, keeping track of details great and small, and keeping the work on target and on time with grace, good answers, and good will.

Our students over the years have been emphatic about what works and what doesn't; their experiences reverberate throughout *The Arlington Reader*. Martin Bloom, philosopher and social psychologist, has contributed his expertise and a parodist's intolerance of the banal and trivial, an attitude he shares with our students.

Contents

1   Speaking, Reading, Writing: How Does Language Make Us Human?   27

4.   Education and the American Character: What Do We Teach? What Do We Learn? And Why Does This Matter?   241

is essential that consent forms be written in plain language that research subjects can understand."

5   Wired—Be Careful What We Wish For: What Are the Consequences of Life in the High-Tech Fast Lane?   326

7 Ethics: What Principles Do—and Should—We Live By? 479

Introduction:
Reading and Writing in Context

READING IN CONTEXT

For each chapter's context essay, *The Arlington Reader* provides Context readings. You can think of the Contexts as a room with many groups of people in conversation, each group discussing a series of questions and answers. Someone entering the room listens for a while to the conversations, identifies the question others are talking about (anywhere from "Which film will win the Academy Award for Best Picture?" to "How can the United States foster peace in the Middle East?"), finds something relevant to say about it, and thus evokes others' answers. Likewise, every piece of writing enters into conversation with others; it has its say and is answered by later writing. Every text — from a grocery list to a political speech to a sonnet — answers a question even as it raises other questions. Interpretation depends on readers' answers to questions the text is raising, sometimes many answers to many questions. The contextualized essays, widely reprinted and often beloved, remain central because they raise a multitude of fundamental questions ("What is the meaning of truth, beauty, justice, life itself?") even as they provide a wealth of answers that many generations of readers find useful. Writers work not in a vacuum but in a world of words — other people's speaking and writing as well as their own. Therefore, writers always have other texts (their questions and answers) in mind when they sit down to write a new piece, and they expect some of their readers to have some of those texts in mind, too.

Sometimes writers explicitly signal such expectations. For instance, Richard Rodriguez opens the prologue to his *Hunger of Memory* (see "Aria" p. 275) with "I have taken Caliban's advice. I have stolen their books. I will have some run of this isle." In one stroke, Rodriguez tells readers that he expects us to share his knowledge of at least some of the following things about Caliban.

- He is the character in *The Tempest* whom Shakespeare describes as "savage and deformed."
- He lives alone on his island until Prospero, the highly educated Duke of Milan, arrives, enslaves him, and teaches him to talk.

- He represents "natural man" to some people.
- He represents native peoples oppressed by imperialism to others.

This sort of reference, in which a word or phrase calls forth a whole cluster of information and associations in the readers whom a writer imagines addressing, is called *allusion*. Some readers will recognize Caliban, and others won't. That is how writers establish solidarity with some readers and, just as important, how they set themselves apart from others. Even if we don't recognize Caliban, Rodriguez expects that as we read we will pick up enough clues from other things he says about Caliban to keep us going as we seek and construct meaning. As we read the "Aria," we'll gradually understand what Caliban's having "stolen their books" has to do with Rodriguez.

Most of the time, however, writers are much less explicit about which works they assume readers already know or know about. Neither in "Why I Write" (p. 60) nor in "On Keeping a Notebook" (p. 54) does Joan Didion explicitly mention the kind of reporting that she helped to invent — and that these two essays illustrate: the 1960s' New Journalism. Yet works by Didion and other New Journalists (such as Tom Wolfe, p. 62) form the contemporary context that helps us understand "On Keeping a Notebook" much better than if we read it simply as a statement of Didion's personal interests. By reading her essays on other writers, reviews of her books, and other texts (including ads, films, and news reports) that were part of the conversation she was participating in, we can infer the contemporary context of her works. By inferring, we can imaginatively enter her world to some extent, though never entirely: as readers, each of us always has to stand in our own historical and cultural moment. There is no such thing as a static reader, a timeless and universal being whose reaction to a text is always predictably the same. As time ceaselessly moves on, our readings of necessity change to accommodate whatever is relevant at the time in the world, in our own lives.

Besides paying attention to earlier contexts (like *The Tempest* for Rodriguez) and to contemporary contexts (like the New Journalism for Didion), we also need to look at the ways people who read a text long after it was written view it. As you already know, a work becomes canonical when generations of readers have found it useful. However, later readers don't all use it the same way. For example, 1940s readers used E. B. White's "Once More to the Lake" (p. 163) to find pleasure in its elegant, gently witty style and to find comfort during wartime in its portrayal of a prewar world (the Nazis had occupied Paris since June 1940 and by June 1941 had widened World War II by invading the Soviet Union). In fact, some readers even thought that White's essay encapsulated the very way of life that American G.I.s were fighting to protect and yearning to come home to. In the postwar period — indeed, throughout the rest of the twentieth century — this essay has maintained its role as a model of style for college writers. But readers also found new uses for it. In the 1980s, some used the essay to examine mythic and psychoanalytic elements in a father's confronting his own mortality through his son's unawareness of death. In the 1990s, some used the essay to represent white, male, middle-class complacency about differences in race, gender, and class. They criticized White for not addressing issues he could not have anticipated when he was writing half a century earlier. As "multiculturalism" and "diversity" increasingly displaced "style" in college composition courses, "Once More to the Lake" began to disappear from composition textbooks. Some day it may return, however, if readers find other relevant meanings, as happened when people stopped reading Louisa May Alcott's *Little Women* (1868) entirely as a children's classic and began using it to document feminist arguments about gender roles and women's education. In contrast, the technology essays in Chapter 5 represent such rapidly changing technology that the specific information must be continually updated, even though the ethical issues—of privacy, intimacy, empathy, representation, intellectual property—remain perennial and unresolved.

A multitude of other readings from many perspectives, far too many to represent in this book, forms the contexts for each of *The Arlington Reader*'s eight contextualized essays. (Moreover, as you realize by now, *every* piece of writing has its contexts.) Each writing in the context cluster focuses on the theme, topic, or background of the lead essay.

Reading Interpretively

How else would you read?

If that was your first reaction to our heading, then you're already doing it. That is, a voice in your head is already conversing with the voice on the page, asking, "What does 'interpretively' say that 'reading' doesn't already say?" or "Is there some kind of 'reading' that's not 'interpretive'?" As you talk back—reacting, questioning, and constructing responses—you are creating meaning. That's interpretation: a creative conversation between the voice on the page and the voice in your head. Just as we all sometimes tune out of conversations, so we sometimes find ourselves passing our eyes along the page while our minds are somewhere else. At these times, we are not reading interpretively. Then we have to backtrack to where we began just going through the motions. We pick up the dropped threads of attention and move forward, back-stepping to fit new passages into what we already read and reminding ourselves of how we got to where we are now, looking for repetitions and variations, listening to personal associations, considering how we might put this piece to use. Not simply *on* or *off,* interpretation involves acts of mind—feeling, reasoning, remembering, predicting, associating, applying—that overlap and tumble and zigzag, each from moment to moment playing greater or lesser roles in the conversation.

Readers call on all these activities to answer *interpretive questions*—that is, questions to which reasonably well-informed readers of a text might give differing answers. Interpretive questions call on more than simple recall. "What is Marjane Satrapi's ethnicity?" is not an interpretive question, but a matter of fact. Readers of

"The Convocation" (p. 312) must answer, "Iranian." In contrast, "How does ethnicity affect Satrapi's relationships with boyfriends?" or "How does it affect her relationships with college administrators?" are interpretive questions. Well-informed readers would give different answers depending on which aspects of her memorable cartoon sequence they found most significant or vivid or lasting or ambivalent. And so on.

General Strategies for Interpretive Reading

Why Are You Reading? For fun? The fun results from interpretation you're already doing, so go for it! To satisfy a college assignment (which also could be fun)? Then keep in mind what the assignment asks you to do. Are you merely supposed to know what the piece is about? If so, then reading the introduction may suffice. To summarize? Then you can skim the introduction, conclusion, and paragraph beginnings and get the gist. Are you supposed to recall detailed information from an economics or biology textbook? Does this piece march along, posing a question, marshaling arguments and evidence, and advocating a belief or action? Are you supposed to explain why you agree or disagree? Or does the piece circle around an idea or experience, looking at it in various ways without even trying to reach a definitive conclusion? Are you supposed to relate it to your personal experience? To other things you have read? Each of these purposes requires a somewhat different kind of reading.

How Does It Relate to You? What is the title? What do you already know about the subject, and how do you know it? What are your related experiences, opinions, and feelings? How does it fit in with lectures, discussions, and other readings in your course? What do you know about the author's qualifications to write on this subject? What are you required to do with it? Pass an exam? Follow its directions? Write a personal essay? Incorporate it with other texts in a long paper?

How Does the Format Help You? The editors of some textbooks, such as those for biology and economics, employ typographical features—such as centered and left-justified headings, different type fonts, and colors—that highlight the main ideas and show how each part relates to the other parts. The headings, for instance, make up a rough outline; all of the elements can suggest what questions to keep in mind as you're reading and what information to acquire for the exam.

If the reading at hand doesn't have many headings or other special features, like most of the selections in this book, then the marks you make—commenting in the margins, for example, or circling key words—gradually create the picture, showing what you noticed and what you'll come back to later. No two readers' marks will be quite the same, and yours won't be the same next month or next year as they are today. Thus, no two readers will create the same picture of a text, and you won't create the same picture twice. But what's important is that you do create a picture, that it is *your* picture, and that you will risk setting it beside another picture. The only way to become an active learner and an interpretive reader, not just a parrot of others' learning, is to start marking up what you're reading—one of the best reasons for reading a work in hard copy. Next we'll say more about how to make the marks of creative reading.

What Are You Marking—and Why? Let's assume you *are* marking your texts. Readers who aren't doing so fail to get the most out of what they read. In class, you refer to your marks and quickly spot passages that raise interesting questions, support or challenge a view that is emerging from class discussion, or open up a whole new approach. Meanwhile, readers who don't mark are flipping pages or scrolling up and down screens, knowing they saw just the right thing—but where? By the time they've found it, the discussion has moved on to something else. At exam and paper-writing time, you're reviewing your marks while they're spending time rereading everything—or not. So, the question is not whether to mark, but how.

Marking a book you own multiplies both its value and the efficiency of your reading time. Marking does not deface a book, as some believe (inheriting attitudes from the days of costly clothbound books), unless it's a library volume whose readers should not be obliged to work with—or around—your interpretations. Artist Chuck Close observes of his time in Yale's School of Art, "You could always tell who Richard [Serra] had been studying when you'd go to the library and find a book all stuck together with paint." Rather, marking honors a book with your active engagement, bringing you more nearly face-to-face with the writers' voices on the page. If your book is new, you haven't yet left any traces of your conversations with the author(s). If you lost it the same day you bought it, you'd lose money. But if you lost it in a few months, after your markings have made many parts of the book *really* yours, that would cost far more—months of your own thinking, responding, generating new ideas. So mark up this book as you wish; you can even use Post-its to comment on key spots.

When to mark? Active, independent-minded readers mark while reading and afterward. That way, they are making their own observations, picking up names and definitions, noticing patterns, forming questions: all the things strong readers do. More timid readers, fearing that they won't notice or question the "right" things, may postpone marking until class discussion, when other readers (and the instructor) call attention to passages which then, *ipso facto,* become the "right" ones. Unfortunately, those less confident readers are merely recording other people's readings, and—like auditing an aerobics class—that doesn't strengthen the body of their own ideas. Instead, they should stop worrying about whether they're reading "right" and instead ask, "What do *I* notice? What meanings can *I* make of that?" There's only one wrong answer to those questions: "Nothing." When you mark up your reading before class, then you're all set to ask questions, offer evidence, and contrast your reaction with someone else's: then *your* reading becomes the "right" stuff.

What to write? The traces previous owners have left in your used books can help answer that. You may have wondered:

- "Why did you color almost this whole page with a green highlighter?"
- "Why did you underline this phrase and write 'Ha!'?"
- "Why did you write 'steers ~ shoes'?"

Noticing the Structure. The headings in a biology or economics book show a chapter's structure at a glance. A text without headings often puts a paragraph's main idea at or near the beginning, and it uses transitions to show its structure. A writer who promises to explain three steps or kinds or reasons may enumerate them with transitions like *first* (or *in the first place*), *second*, and *third*, or *to begin with*, *next*, and *finally*. You would write in the margin, "three reasons for . . ." followed by paragraphs numbered 1, 2, 3, plus a phrase or sentence to label each (like "steers ~ shoes"). To signal that a new paragraph is adding something similar to what was just said, you would use transitions such as *and, in addition, likewise,* and *moreover*. In contrast, transitions like *but, however, in contrast,* and *whereas* to signal a subtraction, as it were, a different, if not opposite, direction in thinking. *Because, as a result, thus, so,* and *therefore* signal cause-and-effect thinking.

More speculative, meandering pieces often send more subtle connective signals, linking paragraphs by repeating a name or key word, by using a pronoun (*it, he, they*) to refer to a term (*antecedent*) in the previous paragraph's last sentence, or by using comparative terms like *more* and *less*. Thus, repetitions such as these signal a more "meandering" paragraph, in contrast to the more tightly logical writing described in the preceding paragraph. Sometimes even the repetition of an image, or variations of a sound or an image (say, a lighthouse beam in one paragraph, headlights in the next), is enough to link thought to thought.

Paragraph middles often include colorful details or anecdotes that exemplify or illustrate the paragraph's main point. Likewise, a section of several paragraphs often includes some details that give examples and illustrations. In fact, everything we've said about paragraph structure applies to sections of essays. Sometimes writers call attention to their illustrations with *for example*, but not always. So don't mistake these details for main ideas; that is, keep your attention on what the illustration illustrates. Keep asking, "Why are you telling me this?"

Noticing Surprises. Suppose while reading through a series of long, winding, complicated sentences you are suddenly hit with a short one. *Pow!*—a fragment. These sentences are using formal, even esoteric, language, but then the writer says, "*Pow!*" You are reading about Homeric heroes, but then you see Superman's name. You may notice that the meaning of a key term changes little by little each time the writer uses it. Or, to take an example from Martin Luther King's "Letter from Birmingham Jail" (p. 494), you are reading one sentence many lines long that builds and builds through ten situations each beginning with "when" and leading up to a thunderclap: "then you will understand" (paragraph 14). These surprising changes—respectively, in *syntax* (word order), *register* (the degree of formality in word choice), *domain* (the area referred to, in this case classical literature or modern U.S. comic books), *definition*, and *rhythm*—create emphases. You can legitimately ask (but seldom answer with certainty), "Why are you telling me this *this* way?" You can describe with certainty how such surprises affect you as a reader.

Using What You've Read. You may ask of your reading, almost automatically, "What does this have to do with my experience?" You may also ask what assumptions a writer expects you to share. For example, what must you assume about the role of art institutions in defining what constitutes "art" in order to share Alice Walker's views of the quilt in the Smithsonian, of blues singers, and of her mother's garden (p. 192)? What must you assume or learn about cultural meanings of silence among Mexican men in order to understand the silence of Richard Rodriguez's father (p. 275)? Another important question you may ask is, "What must I do, or not do, if I accept what this writer is saying?" What must you teach your child if you accept N. Scott Momaday's (p. 118) or E. B. White's (p. 163) view of parenthood? In asking "How can I use this essay?" you enter the stream of conversation among the generations of readers who constitute its contexts. Welcome (again)!

WRITING IN CONTEXT

How do I know what I think until I see what I've said?
—E. M. FORSTER

Imagine your entire life—past, present, and maybe even future—being projected before you on a large computer screen. You can see any part of it by zooming in for a close-up of any thought, experience, belief, or understanding you've ever had. The close-up can help you review anything you've ever known, wondered about, or investigated—with or without answers. Or, you can zoom out to get enlarged views of the world you've been living in—people and places you know or have read about at home and abroad; theories, philosophies, and political systems—not only in your own community, state, or country but around the world.

As a writer, you can draw on your whole life, everything you've experienced or imagined, thought or read about, and bring it to bear on the work at hand. When you begin to bring your vast background into the foreground of your consciousness, you'll be surprised to find that the sharpened focus reveals how much more you know than you thought you knew. Vague and fuzzy ideas can gain new clarity—and your job as a writer is to expand and translate these ideas into prose others can understand. *The Arlington Reader* aims to enlarge the context, the universe of your reading, and the ways and means to translate that reading into writing.

Writing in College

A writing course for first-year college students is a common requirement in the United States. Because good writing is essential to learning and communicating throughout your college experience—and indeed, throughout the rest of your life—writing courses are designed to help you not only learn to write but also write to learn, in ways that are effective, efficient, and enjoyable. No matter what your career plan, even as a stockbroker or a Web designer, your life is inescapably bound up in writing, as it is in reading. When using a computer, you're awash in e-mail, instant messaging, chat rooms, and reading—and responding to—material on an exuberant explosion of Web sites. You write notes, in longhand or electronically; make lists to put your day—or your life—in order; give advice and directions; complain, criticize—and say "thank you"; tell stories or jokes (and sometimes write them down); explain processes—how things work (or don't), the nature of a natural or scientific phenomenon; interpret maps, diagrams, charts; take a stand through a letter to the editor or your legislator, or an op-ed piece for the school paper; or write privately to yourself in a journal or tweet friends—and thus revisit the significance of notes, messages, and, yes, love letters and letters to the world. You may already have been writing for work—memos, instructions, reports, project proposals, research designs, product manuals. Or you've written for more personal reasons (perhaps a combination of work and play) to convey a record of your experience, your family, or your culture, or as a witness to events of historical or political significance (on and beyond September 11, 2001). *The Arlington Reader* provides readings that will help expand your vision of the world and of the ways to become a meaningful part of it through your writing.

In college, much of your writing necessarily has an academic focus. You write to understand the dimensions of a particular subject or field: what its key terms and concepts are; its scope, dimensions, major issues, points of agreement and controversy, changes and developments. You're learning the language, general and specific, and one or more ways of looking at an issue or the field it's embedded in. To make the subject your own, you need to understand it well enough to take into account the perspectives of others, explain them in your own language, weigh the evidence, and come to your own informed opinions. As you gather information and evidence for your papers, you may also become a sophisticated user of Internet and library information sources and of ways to evaluate their utility and worth. To be able to do all these things is to write with the authority you'll be developing throughout your college career and the rest of your life. The information on the following pages is designed to help you write with authority, power, and pleasure; the checklists throughout highlight the issues addressed.

Learning to Write with Ease, Effectiveness, and Efficiency

The Best Place. You'll write better if you have an agreeable place to work—a comfortable chair, good light, space free from distractions where you can leave your equipment out, ready for use. Your computer will have access to a dictionary, encyclopedia, and the Internet (and music!); you may have most of what you need readily at hand, including many specialized books (much of the entire world's library!) and journals available through your college's Internet subscription; photographs or other renderings of art, sculpture, ancient and modern artifacts and manuscripts. If your computer is a laptop and your home or dorm room is noisy, you can easily move to a quieter spot.

The Best Time, Schedule, and Frame of Mind. The best time for writing is when you're most alert. If you haven't discovered when this is, try writing at different times of the day or night to discover a predictable pattern—that is, the time when you get the most done with the greatest pleasure. Try to build your schedule around this optimum time, even if it means getting up early or staying up late to capture the best stretch of time. A half hour or more of quality time adds up. Then, when you're away from your desk—reading, walking, sleeping—your ideas will continue to percolate. You also need to determine a writing schedule, perhaps with your teacher's help, that will allow adequate time for investigating your subject, drafting your paper, and revising and editing your work. If you start the process early and schedule your work in blocks, even short ones, over a period of days, you'll avoid last-minute panic and unrealistic all-nighters.

Ask yourself these questions:

- When and where do I do my best writing? How can I (re)arrange my schedule and my space to get my work done efficiently?
- What else will help me enjoy the process? Food? Music? Exercise? Working on the assignment with a friend or trusted reader to help talk it over?
- After you've finished one paper, ask What worked best for me? What will I change the next time?

Audience. The purpose(s) of your writing is (are) intimately related to the audience you're writing for. Although your immediate readers are your teacher and fellow students, it's useful to think of a target group of readers beyond your classroom—strangers who may become friends, even converts to your point of view. Because your assignments and reasons for writing will vary, you are likely to be writing different papers for different audiences—an op-ed article for newspaper readers, a how-to essay for fellow cooks, a research report for a biology class or lab job, a term paper for a course but also for readers in the professional field, a résumé and application letter for prospective employers. Although you can reasonably expect your readers to have common sense and share a fund of common knowledge, your sense of audience will help you decide whether to write in a manner general or specific, simple or complicated; what language to use; which terms to define; and how much background information to provide.

Audience Checklist

- Do I have a specific group or groups of readers in mind—my family, parents of teenagers, churchgoers, legislators, or scientists?
- What aspects of their age range, ethnicity or nationality, gender, and levels of education and income do I need to consider?
- What opinions and values do they probably share that are relevant to my topic? Are they likely to agree with one another? With me?
- Do they know more, or less, than I do about the subject? What do I need to learn in order to address this audience?
- How simple or technical should my language be? What terms or concepts will I need to define, explain, or illustrate?
- What are the most useful and relevant links to recommend to my readers?
- What do I want to accomplish in writing this? To teach my readers something? Convince them of my point of view? Move them to action—or to tears? Entertain them?

Developing an Effective Writing Process

College writing is as varied as college writers and the disciplines they write in. And just as there is a wide range of essays in *The Arlington Reader,* there is a wide range of ways to write them (pp. 16–26). The information and checklists that follow apply to college writing in general; your instructor can suggest adaptations to specific assignments. For clarity, this discussion presents the writing process as a sequence of stages—inventing and planning, drafting, revising, and editing. However, in reality, while you're working on a paper, the process may resemble a series of loops rather than a straight line. The process of writing stimulates new ideas, new ways of handling what you've already written—a process ideally adapted to writing on a computer, where you can easily add, delete, and move material without destroying the parts you want to save and build on. Moreover, the process of writing different types of papers can vary considerably. If you're writing a lab report, you can slot the information discovered in the lab into a prescribed format; writing an argument can involve a lot more variation (p. 17).

Writing Assignments

Most writing assignments allow some latitude of topic and perhaps of form and style. Once you know the purpose of the assignment, you can begin exploring relevant topics. The stronger your interest in a particular topic—human rights, international terrorism, creativity—the more incentive you'll have to write about it. Because of your interest, you may already know enough about the subject to think of different ways of looking at it. Thus you could imagine a series of questions, such as "How can identity theft be prevented?" "What's the best way to do this?" and "What preventive measures can the United States take?" Be sure to capture these questions in writing so that they won't escape you later on. When you arrive at an appealing topic, find an angle of vision that allows you to narrow your focus and make the topic manageable to write about in the time allotted to do so. For example, you could ask "What measures can the United States take to prevent identity theft without curtailing the civil liberties guaranteed under the Constitution?" You could further restrict the topic to a single type of identity theft (say, theft of social security numbers) and a single civil liberty (such as freedom of the press).

Writing Assignment Checklist

- What is the purpose of the assignment?
- How can I find a subject and focus that mean a great deal to me? (The more you care about your writing, the better it's likely to be.)
- What kind of a paper am I going to write? What key words (words that identify main or key concepts, such as *explain, analyze, define,* and *argue*) or other instructions indicate this?
- What steps do I have to go through to write it? (When in doubt, ask the instructor.)
- Is this a major or minor assignment? How much time should I expect to spend on it, and over what period of time? One week? Two weeks? A month?

Invention: Developing Your Ideas

When you begin a paper, it's a good idea to take an inventory of what you already know about your subject—from your participation in a job or activity, from the people and places you know, and from your reading and life experiences. Talk to friends, relatives, and specialists—perhaps by means of interviews or a listserv. As you list your areas of knowledge, the gaps will also show up, and you can focus your reading and Internet and library searches on the sorts of information you need to find out. Unless you're writing a research paper, two or three reliable, up-to-date sources (books, research articles, or Web sites) are probably enough. Beware of sources such as Wikipedia that are not always reliable. Don't forget the value of facts and figures, illustrations, maps, graphs, and charts. But be selective; if you discover as you write that you need more information, you can always include more later. Keeping your limited focus in mind, resist the impulse to download everything you can find on the Internet or to quote long blocks in your paper. Be sure to indicate where you found the items you're likely to use; that way you can locate them again and acknowledge the sources as your paper develops.

Invention Checklist

- What are the main points, crucial information, and essential definitions in each of my sources? Where do they agree or disagree with other sources?
- Are my sources up-to-date?
- What clusters of ideas are emerging as I investigate the subject? What's missing? List the major ideas by key words or phrases.

- Where do I agree and disagree with my sources? Why?
- Do the ideas cluster around a central point that identifies a subject and my attitude toward it? Could this be my trial thesis? Is it interesting to me? To my audience? Is it worth writing about?
- What arrangements of my list of ideas are possible? Which one do I like best for its logic? Organization? Dialogue among sources? Sense of play?
- What is the visible structure or skeleton of my preferred arrangement? Where do the major elements—those in the most prominent places, occupying the most space—and the minor ones fall?
- Do I need to make a more formal outline? Will the longer sentences and greater detail help me develop my ideas?

Drafting

Now it's time to start writing. To get started, you might want to dash off a focused freewriting on your general topic, or a "zero draft"—a throwaway version that roughs out some of the ideas you've found. Let a trial thesis emerge, and post it where you can see it as you write; if you get off the track, you can either change the thesis to fit what you're saying or tailor your discussion to fit the thesis. Trust your taste and intuition (what looks as if it will work best?) to decide what to include, what to emphasize, and what to omit. Your common sense can help you counteract myths that produce writer's block if you take as your motto, "I'm going to do the best I can in the time I have to work on this paper." Your writing does not have to be perfect right from the outset. Or ever. Your early draft may be enough for one day's work, but let the ideas steep so that when you return you'll have something to build on.

When you revisit your paper you'll have two main tasks: to develop the material you started with and to find a design—or pattern of organization—that best fits the type of paper you're writing. Your paper will begin to grow before your eyes as you write short sections—on a single word, concept, or subsection of the larger paper. When you get enough pieces, separate or loosely related, you can begin to put them together, clustering each around a central concept embedded in a key word or phrase. Your key words should emphasize the main points and signal the major divisions, clues to your paper's emerging structure and rhetorical type (for instance, exposition, narration, description, argument—see p. 16). If you see an essay in this book of the rhetorical type that does what you'd like to do, you can use it as a model or select those parts that apply. The Rhetorical Index (pp. 661–669) identifies specific selection titles under their rhetorical headings.

When drafting, you don't have to begin at the beginning and march through to the end. If a workable introduction doesn't emerge after a few minutes, move on to another section—what you know or like best—and write that first. That should lead to another section and then another. You can even write the introduction last. If you decide not to write the whole paper in a single sitting, try to draft a section—say, one or two pages—before you take a break. Writing on a computer makes it easy to move the parts around and reassemble them when you're through. But save—don't discard—the false starts and paragraphs you decided to omit; you might like them better later, or you might decide to use them in some other piece of writing.

Thoughtful responses to your writing—from yourself, a writing group, your instructor—can be particularly valuable after you've completed your first draft. Set it aside for at least a day to gain perspective, then be especially tough-minded. It's easy to be seduced by the crisp appearance of a paper fresh from your printer, but don't be fooled by that pretty face. Ask the following questions instead—of yourself, your peer group, your instructor, or all three. The checklist can also be used to guide peer-group discussions.

Drafting Checklist

- What's the "heart"—the center of gravity—of my material? Does my draft concentrate on this?
- What works best in this draft? Why?
- How can the rest of the paper be changed to come up to this standard?

You could stop right there, and the discussion would be profitable. Or you could continue with the following questions; and even try them out on real people:

- What don't my readers (or I) understand that needs to be explained? Where do I need to add information, illustrations (in words or images), or more analysis?
- What bores or annoys me, or my readers, in this draft? Do I need to delete warm-up attempts or other material that's off the point?

Re-vision and Revision

Revision is central to the writing process. It doesn't occur only when you've finished drafting; you may be revising continually as you compose to make what emerges on paper more closely match what's going on in your mind. This is particularly true if you get new ideas as you write and see your subject from new angles. Although the specifics of how and what you revise depend on what you did in the earlier draft(s), be prepared, if necessary, to make big changes. You may need to frame a new thesis or drastically revise your current one. You may need to reorganize your work according to a different format or arrangement. You may need more information or more material from more reliable and up-to-date sources in order to write with greater authority. In revision, rewrite to enhance the strongest aspects of your writing, and discard irrelevant material and the weakest sections. If, however, you've hit a home run with an early draft, you can concentrate on matters of style, usage, and documentation as you do the final edit.

Revision Checklist

- If my paper has an explicit thesis, does it reflect what I am really trying to say? Do I need to change the thesis to make it fit my subject better? (Some papers—such as one concentrating on telling a story, a character sketch, or an extended description—won't necessarily have an unexplicit thesis, though one may be implicit.)

- Is each major point developed sufficiently to make it compelling? (One clue: Is the paper long enough to do the job I set out to do?)
- Do comparable points receive equal development and emphasis?
- What pattern of organization best fits my material?
- Do the section and paragraph headings (if any) and breaks reflect my emphasis? Do transitional words or phrases signal where the essay has been—and where it's going?
- What proportion of the work does my introduction occupy? (If it takes up more than 20 percent, it's probably too long.) Does it encourage readers to continue? Does it contain key words and concepts that signal what follows?
- Does the conclusion follow logically or otherwise appropriately from what precedes it?

Style and Editing

"Style is organic to the person doing the writing," says writer William Zinsser (*On Writing Well*, New York: Harper, 1998), "as much a part of him as his hair, or, if he is bald, his lack of it. Trying to add style is like adding a toupee." All writing, like all writers, has some sort of intrinsic style, whether it's dull and boring, clear and straightforward, or lively and engaging. Yet while you're in the early or middle stages of drafting and revising a paper, it's uneconomical to spend much effort on the length and rhythm of your sentences, on the variety and felicity of your words, or even on spelling and grammatical correctness. There's no point in polishing parts of a paper that may ultimately be cut out. But after you've settled on the content, you'll need to pay attention to these matters of style. They make the difference between a casual paper and one dressed to go on a job interview, where you know you'll be judged, in part, on your language, appearance, polish, ease—and character.

The style you write in should suit you, your subject, and the type of essay you're writing. Your style—like the writer it portrays—should be appealing to your readers, attracting them to your subject, your point of view, and your character and credibility that inevitably emerge through your writing. Don't be afraid to come out as a human being. If you find your subject fascinating, exciting, or enraging, you'll have an incentive to write with compelling conviction—and metaphor and symbol, wit and humor, when they fit. You'll want to avoid clichés (often the first figurative language that comes to mind, such as "pretty as a picture")—stale language that clogs your writing like hair plugging a drain.

In most papers for a first-year composition course or an audience of non-specialists, you'll probably aim for a slightly more formal version of the language you use in conversation—a middle range that's neither slangy nor stuffy but that allows you to write in the first person and to use contractions. If you're writing on technical issues you'll need some technical vocabulary. Thus, in a paper on a legal issue, *domicile* might well be one of your words, instead of "house," which you'd use in a less formal paper. In a technical paper you might also have to use *habeas corpus* and other legal terms for which there is no exact English equivalent. Likewise, your sentences and paragraphs will probably land in the middle range. This means that although your sentences can range from short to very long, they'll average out to between fifteen words (slightly longer than sentences in newspaper editorials) and twenty-five to thirty words (the average for professional academic writing). For easy reading, newspapers often put breaks at every column inch, but your paragraphs will be somewhat longer than these. In academic writing, paragraph breaks are dictated not by the eye but by the amount of development required for the ideas you're expressing. In fact, the appearance of a lot of short paragraphs (except in dialogue) in your essay may signal that your ideas need greater elaboration.

The best way to tell how your writing sounds is to read it aloud — to yourself or, better yet, to someone from your target group of readers. Go with the flow. If you have to pause (even gasp!) for breath as you read a sentence, consider breaking it up or using more punctuation. If you have a lot of short, choppy sentences, combine some. Repetition may be necessary for emphasis, as in Caesar's boast: "I came, I saw, I conquered." Nevertheless, if you're repeating yourself — too many words or too many of the same words that drone on and on — vary your vocabulary (synonyms abound in your dictionary and spell-check) and cut out the excess. But beware: Don't use spell-check or dictionary words unless you're familiar with them or can see them used in context, for not all synonyms are equivalent. How would Caesar's boast sound as "I came, I saw, I trounced"? Or "thrashed"? Or "subdued"? "Steamrolled" would, of course, be impossible, even if your dictionary allows it.

Style and Editing Checklist

Title and Thesis

- Is the title specific? Accurate? Witty, provocative, or otherwise appealing?
- Is my thesis (overt or implied) clear? (Not every paper needs an explicitly stated thesis. The central point or emphasis of character sketches, descriptions, and satires, for instance, may be implied.) Does everything in the paper have relevance to this?

Words

- Do I use strong, emphatic, active verbs ("My research team wrote the report" rather than "The report was written by my research team")? Have I used the passive voice to imply passivity ("The World Trade Center was destroyed...")?
- Are verb tenses congruent? If there are shifts between present and past tenses, are they intentional?
- Are pronoun references clear? (If I say *it* or *that*, will readers know what I'm referring to?)

- Is my vocabulary appropriate to the subject, the audience, and the paper's degree of technicality?
- Have I omitted vague words and unnecessary repetitions?
- Have I defined key concepts and words used in specialized or unfamiliar ways?

Sentences

- Do my sentences have an emphasis and variety that reinforce their meaning?
- Does the paper contain sentence fragments? Can these phrases—punctuated with a period but lacking a subject or verb—really stand alone, or should they be incorporated into other sentences?
- Have I treated comparable concepts and grammatical structures in parallel ways ("I came, I saw, I conquered")?

Spelling, Mechanics, and Citations

- Have I acknowledged sources—including Web links—accurately and completely (with sufficient information to send readers to the exact spot)? Are they in the appropriate note and citation form?
- Have I integrated quotations, paraphrases, and summaries smoothly into my own text?
- Have I checked all spelling and issues of grammar and usage that gave me trouble in this paper? (Use a reliable handbook to double-check your spell- and grammar-checks.)

Finally . . .

- Is there anything I should have done on this paper that I haven't yet done? If so, why not do it now, rather than face another revision?

Writing in a Universe of Nonfiction

This section illustrates some of the common types of writing you'll find in *The Arlington Reader,* various forms of short nonfiction prose that you'll be reading and responding to. It identifies the general characteristics of each rhetorical type as well as strategies for talking or writing about a specific piece or the type it represents. You can use these illustrations (listed below in alphabetical order) for ideas and as examples of types of writing—in class discussion, in person or online, in writing groups, or on your own.

Although this discussion highlights characteristics of each rhetorical type of writing (for example, definition or description), in the real world, most writing is a hybrid of forms, perhaps with one type dominating. For instance, E. B. White's "Once More to the Lake" (p. 163) is a *personal essay* that develops and interprets ideas in relation to the author's experience, *narrating* the story of a father's return to a summer camp in Maine with his young son. It also includes *comparison and contrast* (between past and present, father—now and earlier—and son), *description* of the setting, *explanation* in the form of *process analysis* (how they spent their summer vacation), and *illustration* (of an idyllic summer), which also serves as a *definition* of a loving father–son relationship. The entire piece can also be read as a historical document; or as an *implied argument* in favor of both rural vacations and parents and children spending long, lazy times together. When you're writing, don't worry about trying to separate out the types or even about identifying them. No matter what you're concentrating on—say, an argument—other types will simply emerge as you write and become absorbed in your main focus.

Analysis.   *Analysis* involves dividing something into its component parts and scrutinizing each part for its intrinsic merit and its relationship to the whole. It's usually easier to understand the subject in smaller parts than it is to try to make sense of a complicated whole all at once. Consequently, when you're reading printed material—whether it's an essay, a novel, a poem, a play, a textbook chapter, or a Web site—it's useful to consider the elements in the following list. You can use the same questions—and answers—to govern your analytic writing about essays, fiction, and other forms of literature when you're writing criticism or a review.

Analysis Checklist
- What is (are) the writer's purpose(s) or multiple purposes? Do these reinforce one another, or do they conflict?
- What's the thesis, or main point, and significant subpoints? Are they presented logically? Accurately? Where do we agree, and where will I (or others) dispute the author?
- What evidence does the writer use to support these claims? Are they logical? Appropriate?
- Who is the intended audience—primary (the immediate readers, such as teachers and fellow students) and secondary (others who might read the paper, such as newspaper readers of a letter to the editor initially written for class)? What knowledge—and biases—does each bring to the subject? What do they need to know? What biases have to be cultivated (such as understanding another culture) or overcome (male chauvinism, for instance)?
- How does the writer's purpose and imagined audience influence the choice of language, organization (what comes first, in the middle, last—and why?), illustrations, and tone?
- In what context—time, place, culture—and with what political, economic, and social issues in mind was this work written? What significant changes have occurred between the original context and the context in which you are now reading this?

Argument.   *Argument* dominates academic writing—indeed, any writing in which the author is doing what Joan Didion says all writers do: "Listen to me, see it my way, change your mind." An argument seeks to convince readers of the truth or merits of an idea and often hopes to discredit alternative views. An argument may be a call to action—(Martin Luther King Jr.'s "Letter from

Birmingham Jail," pp. 494–507) — intended to change readers' minds or behavior, to right a wrong, or to effect reform.

Direct arguments require evidence, good reasons, and a logical way to dispel disagreements. Scientific papers, critical articles, position papers, and many other types of academic writing are based on considerations such as the following:

- At the outset, do I expect my readers to agree with my position? To be neutral? To oppose my point of view? Given this starting point, what do I need to do to ensure their agreement?
- What is my strongest (and perhaps most controversial) point? If the audience agrees with this point, the discussion belongs at the beginning. But if the audience is hostile, it's better to identify points of agreement and lead up to the major controversy gradually — near the end. Usually the most controversial points warrant the most detailed discussion.
- What are my best sources of evidence? Personal experience — my own or that of others? Judgment from experts in the field? Scientific evidence, statistical data, historical records, or case histories?
- How can I evaluate the evidence? (Just because something appears on a Web site or in print doesn't make it reliable.) For starters, it should be authoritative, up-to-date, taken from a reputable source, and representative enough to permit generalizations.
- Even if I can't convince my readers, what language and tone will best compel their thoughtful attention to my point of view? Sincere or sarcastic? Cool or passionate? Angry or conciliatory? Something else? What can I do to make sure they'll hear me out and not stop paying attention partway through? (Here's a good place to ask your writing group for suggestions.)

Indirect arguments promote their case through ethics — trust in the writer and the writer's values — and appeals to emotion as well as facts. Implied or indirect arguments are present in many varieties of writing, including personal writing, eyewitness accounts, stories, character sketches, case histories (such as accounts of "poster children"), and satires (Sherman Alexie's "What Sacagawea Means to Me," p. 115). Indirect arguments, through means such as these, are often incorporated into direct arguments as well; the more extensively ethical and emotional appeals are used, the more likely the argument is to be made through indirect rather than direct means. The essence of an emotional appeal is passion ("I have a dream"; "We shall overcome"). Yet because academic culture prefers understatement to overkill, it's better to present revealing facts and telling narratives and to let your readers interpret these for themselves — as Lynda Barry does in "Hate" (p. 522) — rather than harangue them. If you can put them in your shoes, they're likely to walk your walk.

Argument Checklist

- How can I best convince my readers that my judgment and character are sound (judgment and character together equal *authorial ethos*) and qualify me to make my case? ("I am a genius" won't work.)

- To reinforce my ethical appeals and authorial ethos, what's the best evidence I can use? Examples from my own life? Others' experiences? References to literature, statistics, and scientific research?
- How can I be sure my readers will react the way I want them to (with sympathy, anger, or resolve to change things)? Can I trust my examples to speak for themselves? What language and details will reinforce the examples without being preachy? (Test the reactions of people unfamiliar with your examples. Do they get the point? Are they moved?)

Definition.   *Definitions* essentially answer the question "What is *X*?" They identify something as a member of a class (sports cars) and then specify what distinguishes it from all other members of that class (2010 Mazda RX 8). Any definition of a class must include all of its members. *Negative definitions* explain what is excluded from a given class and why (why the Volkswagen Passat 3.6 is not a sports car). Definitions are necessary in much academic writing, either to explain unfamiliar terms or to tell readers how you're interpreting a controversial or ambiguous term used in an argument that follows. Many definitions reflect cultural and other biases; what connotations do "rural area," "small town," and "big city" (and is that the same as "teeming metropolis"?) have for you? Definitions can employ a variety of techniques, such as analogy, comparison and contrast, and division and classification.

Definition Checklist
- *Explanatory definitions* interpret things according to their purpose: What is *X* for? What does *X* do?
- *Descriptive definitions* focus on individuality — for instance, a person's (Deirdre McCloskey's "Yes, Ma'am," p. 151) or a group's (Eric Liu's "Notes of a Native Speaker," p. 93).
- *Essential or existential definitions* ask: What is the essence or fundamental nature of *X* (an abstraction such as truth, beauty, or play)? Or what does it mean to be *X* (Bobbie Ann Mason, "Being Country," p. 105) or to live as an *X* or in a state of *X*?
- *Logical definitions,* common in scientific and philosophical writing, identify the term as a member of a more general class (for example, intelligence), and then specify the features that make it different from all other members of that class (as Howard Gardner does with different kinds of intelligence — such as emotional and artistic — in "Who Owns Intelligence?" p. 298).
- *Process definitions,* often used in how-to and scientific writing, consider such questions as: How is *X* produced? How does it work? What does it do or not do? With what effects? (See Nicholas Carr, "Is Google Making Us Stupid?" p. 336.)

Description.   *Description* aims to bring a scene, an event, or a person to life by conveying a sensory impression, by creating a mood, or both. It re-creates a particular context. Drawing heavily on sensory information, description tells how a subject looks, sounds, smells, tastes, acts, and feels, as in N. Scott

Momaday's "The Way to Rainy Mountain," (p. 118). Although it's tempting to think of description as a series of snapshots in adventure pieces (George Orwell's "Shooting an Elephant," p. 516) or snapshot-like travel accounts, description is really much broader than that; Orwell, for instance, is presenting a political and ethical argument. Details about how people live—their characteristic behavior, values, companions, possessions, beliefs, fears—can present vivid portraits, as Barbara Ehrenreich does in anatomizing a waitress's life in "Serving in Florida," p. 206). Nonsensory details help describe an abstraction, such as a psychological moment or state of mind—for instance, happiness or terror. Images and analogies ("My love is like a red, red rose") also help. You are never a neutral observer; everything you decide to include or omit reveals your attitude toward the subject and will influence your readers.

Description Checklist
- From what perspective do I want to present this information? Distant? Close up? As a series of snapshots or vignettes? With admiration or as a critique?
- How will I organize my description?
- Have I let the heavy-duty words—nouns and verbs—bear the weight of the description and thereby avoided piles of adjectives that would bury the subject?

Editorials and Op-Eds.   The placement of these short "think pieces" on a newspaper's editorial pages tells readers they can expect expressions of opinion—commentary, discussion, argument, reflection—often in dialogue with other pieces on the same pages or in previous issues of the paper. Although these brief essays (of between five hundred and eight hundred words) often address current events, the best convey the columnist's distinctive style, quality of mind, and point of view in memorable writing that transcends time (see the essays by Elie Wiesel [p. 73], Václav Havel [p. 591], Anna Quindlen [p. 158], and Peter Singer [p. 557]). For suggestions on how to write these essays, pick the type that best fits what you want to say (such as analysis, argument, definition, or satire) and consult that category.

Exposition.   As its name indicates, *exposition* exposes information through explaining, defining, or otherwise interpreting its subject. This broad term encompasses most of the essays in this book. Expository writing, the all-purpose utility vehicle of academia, includes most research reports, critical analyses, literature reviews, case histories, exam answers (which you can think of as mini-essays), and term papers. Expository writing can incorporate many techniques used in other sorts of writing as well: definition, illustration, comparison and contrast, cause and effect, division and classification, and analogy. For suggestions on writing, see the other categories.

Parody and Satire.   *Parody* and *satire* make fun of their subject, exaggerating or otherwise distorting the subject, values, style, language, characters (who, in a satire, correspond directly to people in real life), or other features of an author, work, or prevailing philosophy. Satire is always critical of the people or groups it's attacking, aiming for improvement and reform (see Alexie's "What Sacagawea Means to Me," p. 115). In Art Spiegelman's "Mein Kampf" (p. 109) and Roz Chast's "The I.M.s of Romeo and Juliet" (p. 326), satire is visual as well as verbal. Whereas satire may be comical or bitter, parody always aims to make people laugh. For either type to succeed, readers must recognize the correspondence between the target and the wit of the writer's presentation. You're not trying to win hearts and minds through sweet reason; satire and parody allow enough latitude for you to gross out your readers and still expect them to stick with you to the end.

Parody and Satire Checklist

- What annoys, provokes, angers, or strikes me as sufficiently ridiculous (or boring) to be a fit subject for satire or parody?
- Will my readers recognize the subject, even after my distortions?
- What can I do to ensure that my readers will take my side, directing their own laughter or scorn at the object of my witty imitation (or attack)? Have I checked out my peers' reactions to the features I'm exaggerating: the subject's typical manner of speech (vocabulary, expressions, sentence patterns, jargon), gestures, behavior, dress, mental or moral qualities, activities, and so on?
- Is my piece short? Satire and parody depend on a fast pace; prolong the humor and the punch loses its fizz.

Interviews.   Encouraging people to talk about themselves in *interviews* is a fairly simple way to do original research. Almost anyone — expert or amateur, friend or stranger — can be informative or engaging to an interviewer with a lively curiosity and a sympathetic ear. Take notes — quoting in particular proper names, key words, colorful language — even if you're taping at the same time. That will eliminate the need, and the time, to make a long transcript. When you write up what you've heard, you can highlight the key words and group similar ideas by topic. Your write-up will probably salvage the most quotable 10 percent of the interview's "pure gold," as interviewer Studs Terkel calls it.

Interview Checklist

- Set up the appointment in advance, identifying who you are and why you'd like to talk with this person.
- Keep your purpose in mind. Do you want to focus on the subject's entire life or just part of it? Obtain information about something the subject knows (how to write well), can do (how to sculpt in stone or wood), has invented (Apple computers), or has experienced, such as a historical period (the 1970s), a significant event (September 11), or an unusual opportunity (Peace Corps service).

- Do your homework. Learn enough about your topic beforehand so that you won't waste time on the trivial or the obvious.
- Begin with low-key, factual questions, and then move gradually toward more complicated ones about issues and matters of opinion. Prepare a number of open-ended questions that can't be answered with a laconic "yes" or "no."
- Talk as little as necessary, and keep the focus on the person you're interviewing, not on yourself.
- Write up and amplify your notes as soon as possible, while the interview is still fresh in your mind.

Lists.   A *list* may start out as a random assemblage of notes jotted down as you try to decide on your next paper topic. Yet as you move the items around you'll discover that each list has its own logic and that each reconfiguration of the items embeds new possibilities. You can also group like items and move the groups around—as you might in making a grocery list, which you would ultimately arrange to match your circuit through the grocery store—fruits, vegetables, meat, baking ingredients, dairy. If you add numbers, a list can be the basis of an outline; if you draw in connections, a list can become a diagram in linear or cluster form. Lists can metamorphose into no-nonsense statements of commandments or rules (see the United Nations' "Universal Declaration of Human Rights," p. 488). Common patterns of organization are listed below. Each pattern can also be reversed.

- From farthest away in space or time to nearest. (Common in historical accounts. Travel writing usually reverses this, starting at home and moving away.)
- Most important, urgent, or necessary to least important, urgent, or necessary. (A common pattern in argument.)
- Points of agreement (in order of importance), followed by points of disagreement.
- Most intimate (human relationship) to most distant.
- Highly dominant (largest, strongest, loudest) to least conspicuous (smallest, weakest, softest).
- Most to least familiar or interesting.
- Most to least ethical, political, social, or costly in terms of resources or consequences.

Narration.   "We tell ourselves stories in order to live," says Joan Didion. Indeed, *narratives* form the basis of stories both true and fictional—autobiography and many personal essays; history; newspaper accounts of breaking events, from sports to murder to terrorism-in-progress; accounts of travel and adventure; short stories and novels; jokes, fables, and other cautionary tales. Narratives recount the action of an event or series of interrelated events, often in a chronological sequence—how to get from there to here, sometimes with flashbacks or flash-forwards that anticipate the ending. For shifts between past, more remote past, and present see E. B. White, "Once More to the Lake" (p. 163). Essential questions to ask include the following:

Narration Checklist

- Why am I telling this story—for its own sake, to convey information, or to make a larger point about its subject? What does it mean to me? To my readers?
- What background information will I need to supply for readers who haven't been there; haven't done that; or don't know the people, the history, or the culture they represent?

Narratives answer some or all of the journalist's basic questions—which are also fundamental to analyzing a *process* and explaining a *cause-and-effect* relationship:

- *Who* participated? What were their motives?
- *What* happened?
- *Why* did this event or phenomenon happen?
- *When* did it happen? Would it make sense—or good drama—to discuss this in flashbacks?
- *Where* did it happen? Should I describe the scene?
- *How* did it happen? Under what circumstances?

Writing about People.   "I like man, but not men," said essayist Ralph Waldo Emerson, perhaps anticipating Mark Twain's observation that "Man is the only animal that blushes. Or needs to." People write about people (including themselves), more than any other subject. People are the focus of portraits, character sketches, interviews, personal narratives, and human-interest vignettes; all of these can be freestanding or incorporated into longer essays or works of history, social analysis, scientific discovery—writing of all sorts on virtually any subject. Writers focus on human subjects because they're intrinsically fascinating, antagonizing, repellent, problem-causing and problem-solving, inspiring, and evocative of a host of other reactions, as the contents of the entire *Arlington Reader* reveal. We will take a close look at particular people and cultures in Chapter 2, "Identity with Attitude." Even when the focus is on a topic other than specific people (such as science or social issues), it's humans who are interpreting it, and it's writing that will help determine how people will understand the subject years, even centuries, later—as essays in Chapter 4 by Jonathan Kozol (p. 252) and Linda Simon (p. 320) reveal (not by chance is this chapter titled "Education and the American Character." How do we know or decide what it means?"). So varied are writings about people, interpreted globally, that all the suggestions in this list are applicable in some circumstances. If you're concentrating on an individual, consider the following questions.

Writing about People Checklist

- Do I know this person well enough to write about him or her? From personal acquaintance or experience (say, watching the subject's public performance on stage, TV, film, the Internet, or in the news)?

- Do I have a reliable sense of the subject's inner as well as outer selves? From what sources have I gotten information? (Beware of press releases, blogs, personal Web sites, and other biased news sources.) How do I decide among conflicting sources?
- What am I emphasizing—character or personality, philosophy, values, roles or relationships, decisions or actions, contributions or failings, or some combination?
- Can I convey the actual or potential long-term significance of whatever aspects of the subject I'm concentrating on?

Writing about Places.   Places don't proclaim their significance, people do—in the course of interpreting Indian pueblos, Walden Pond, and toxic-waste dumps. Scientists write about the *natural world,* including matters of ecology (Rachel Carson, p. 612), natural history (Terry Tempest Williams, p. 576), and the physical sciences (Stephen Jay Gould, p. 437), whereas other writers find spiritual inspiration in the same settings (Henry David Thoreau, p. 594; Leslie Marmon Silko, p. 39). Social analysts interpret places as the sites of social or political history (N. Scott Momaday, p. 118) or criticism (George Orwell, p. 516). Roving correspondents and people on the move write about places as contexts for adventure and exploration—the more grungy or harrowing, the better the story. Aim for understatement; let telling details, vignettes, and dialogue demonstrate the significance of the place rather than belabor your interpretations. For writing, the suggestions under "Description," "Lists," and "Narration" earlier in this chapter will help you avoid predictable, postcard-pretty shots. Also consider the following questions.

Writing about Places Checklist

- Do I have original observations about this place or an unusual perspective to view it from? What can I include to keep my commentary about a familiar place fresh to readers who already know it well?
- Should I use photographs or other illustrations? It's your call as to whether they will stimulate or stunt your readers' imaginative understanding.
- What kind of character do I (as participant-author) appear to be in this writing? Authoritative scientist? Humble wayfaring sojourner? Stranger in a strange land? Cool adventurer?

Writing about Processes.   Accounts of how things are done, accomplished, made, or played or performed abound in a wide variety of writings. How-to-do (or not do) it, steps to success, recipes, plans, and rules all interpret processes for individuals, disciplines, and whole societies to get things done. They focus on attaining a maximum of success with a minimum of struggle. Those in *The Arlington Reader* concern writing and other forms of creative processes (Chapter 1), education (Chapter 4), technology (Chapter 5), and ethics (Chapter 7, also Chapters 5 and 8). Analyses of how things work and develop in nature abound in science writing (Chapter 6, "Science—Discovery, Invention,

Controversy," and Chapter 8, "The Environment"). Most process writings follow a logical sequence from the beginning of the process to the end, dividing the process into steps according to what has to be done first, second, third, and so on. Dr. Spock's advice on bringing up children—"Trust yourself. You know more than you think you do."—offers a good beginning: Take stock of what you (and your readers) know, and build from there. The more complicated the process—like rearing a child—the more varied the explanation of how to do it may be, though what you emphasize and in how much detail, and what you can skip, depend on how much your readers already know and can tolerate. Both amateurs and experts may want to know a lot more about the process at hand, but whereas novices need the basics, experts may crave the esoteric.

Writing about Processes Checklist

- Is my knowledge of the process derived from intimate knowledge? Mine or someone else's? Is it up-to-date?
- Why have I chosen this particular means to an end? Am I aware of other ways (worse? better?) to do it?
- Will a typical reader be able to follow my directions successfully and with relative ease? If a test audience gets confused, what do I need to provide to untangle the process? More information? Specific details? Diagrams or photographs? Citations of books or links to relevant Web sites?

Research Reports.   *Research reports* may take a variety of forms, particularly in the humanities. In the physical or social sciences; engineering, computer science, or other technology; and business or industry, each context for writing (lab, journal, subspecialty) may have its own form. Nevertheless, the following model represents a common format employed in scientific papers and lab reports: (1) Statement of the problem, incorporating the proposition(s) to be tested and definitions of key terms; (2) review of major research articles and books on the topic to be investigated, to provide an intellectual and sometimes methodological context into which the current research fits; (3) step-by-step description of the research design, method, equipment, procedure (see "Writing about Processes," above), and ways of measuring the results; (4) statement of research results, often combined with (5) analysis of these. The results/analysis section is often (but not always) the longest; many of the pieces in Chapters 5 ("Technology") and 6 ("Science") deal with the results of "Discovery, Invention, and Controversy," (6) conclusion and suggestions for additional research. When you're writing, ask yourself, your instructor, and your peer group whatever questions pertain from the following list.

Research Report Checklist

- Do I have enough information on hand (say, from lab investigation or others' research) to write about this subject? Is my information up-to-date? State-of-the-art?

- Am I writing for specialists who know more than I do about the subject? For a general audience, who may know less? In either case, how will I adapt my material—definitions, references to others' work, explanations of my process—to my readers' level of understanding and interest? What will they take for granted that I don't need to elaborate on at all?
- Is my writing organized clearly, according to the logical (and expected) pattern of a process, a research sequence, or the development of a phenomenon over time?
- Do I need to use supporting illustrations, such as facts, figures, case histories, graphs, statistics, maps, or photographs? (See "Replaceable You," p. 410.)
- Does my writing embed extended definition, explanation, or narrative? Does it argue for my view of the subject—and oppose other interpretations? Or some combination of these?

Writer's Notebook or Journal.   Keeping a *writer's notebook* or *journal* can be a good way to jump-start your writing. Whether you write with pencil, pen, or word processor, you can freewrite—following an idea or key word to see where it leads, perhaps as a response to a writing assignment. You can doodle, make lists, draw pictures, or paste in citations or articles. You're not providing a record of your daily life; you're including material that you might want to write about someday (see Joan Didion, "On Keeping a Notebook," p. 54). What's in the notebook is private, intended only for yourself, so you may not have to elaborate on fragmentary notes or ideas—just put in enough to jog your memory when you revisit the scene. It's helpful to date each entry, or even identify it by topic, so that you can find it easily if you want to consult it when you're writing a paper. Your entries might include some of the following:

Writer's Notebook Checklist

- Reactions to your reading, or provocative quotations from it. Be sure to identify your sources for return visits.
- Commentary on notable, puzzling, or problematic events—current or past; local (college, hometown), national, or international.
- Good (or even bad) ideas—your own or those of others.
- Problems or puzzles—of an academic or human nature—to solve.
- Sketches of people who are intrinsically memorable or associated with interesting events, professions, activities, or lifestyles.
- Photographs, drawings, maps, diagrams, graphs, or charts.
- Jokes; cartoons; funny, weird, or unusual names of people, places, pets, or businesses.
- Titles of or key words from articles, books, films, songs or albums, or TV shows.
- Web sites.

CHAPTER 1

Speaking, Reading, Writing: How Does Language Make Us Human?

PAULA SCHER, FOGELSON-LUBLINER, AND NEVILLE BRODY AND JEFF KNOWLES

Better Signs of Trouble

In the coming days, a Homeland Security task force is to recommend whether to keep, revise or scrap the color-coded terrorism-alert system that has for years alternately panicked and befuddled Americans. The Op-Ed editors asked four graphic designers for their own ideas for an improved warning system.

C=Caution   **A=Alert**

The threat of terrorism will forever be with us. We will always need to be cautious in airports, train stations and other public spaces. Therefore, our everyday condition is one of "caution," symbolized by the letter C.

In certain rare instances there will be evidence, based on reliable intelligence, that a terrorist attack of some sort is likely to occur. In these situations, Americans would be put on "alert," symbolized by the letter A. "Alert" means that people should follow the safety instructions and recommendations of the appropriate authorities.

— *PAULA SCHER*

Instead of relying on scary language and irrelevant colors, our system takes advantage of people's innate ability to read emotions in the eyes of those around us. The eyes introduce an approachable human element to a potentially frightening message, and also remind us that even when there is no imminent danger we should still be aware of our surroundings. Alerts can be animated on mobile phones, Web sites and TV, and printed in the newspaper.

— FOGELSON-LUBLINER

>c> :-)

>c> :-|

>c> :-(

>c> :-@

An effective alert system should take advantage of readily available distribution methods as well as commonly used symbols and language. Via e-mail and text messages sent from an official protocol (to avoid hoaxes), these simple alerts could be easily and urgently sent out to hundreds of millions of Americans; just as effortlessly and quickly, these messages would be blogged about on the Internet, shared on social networks and forwarded from one person to another.

— NEVILLE BRODY and JEFF KNOWLES

QUESTIONS FOR DISCUSSION AND WRITING

1. Do you know what the Homeland Security's current system of terrorism-alert warnings is? Where can you find the current information? How long did it take you to locate this? On a day-to-day basis, are you aware of the current alert level? Whether or not you know what it is, does the alert level influence your behavior? If so, in what ways? If not, why not?

2. Examine the alternative proposals and "read" the symbols the graphic designers have proposed. Which, if any, conveys terrorism alerts the most clearly and unambiguously? Why? Rank these three options according to how clearly they communicate danger. If none of these designs works, what are their communication problems?

3. Would you like terrorism-alert warnings to be communicated via your mobile phone and/or e-mail and text messages? Would you read them? Every day, or only under extreme circumstances? What determines whether you read or delete any given message? Have text messages changed your way of reading? If so, in what ways?

4. Design your own terrorism-alert warning and explain why it's better than—or at least equivalent to—those depicted here.

EUDORA WELTY

Listening

Born in Jackson, Mississippi, Eudora Welty (1909–2001) devoted most of her life to reading, writing, and gardening in the house her parents built in the 1920s. Her one extended departure from the South took her to the University of Wisconsin (B.A., 1929) and then to Columbia University in New York. She soon returned, however, traveling through "Depression-worn" Mississippi towns as a part-time journalist and photographer for the Works Progress Administration. Her fiction—short stories such as "Why I Live at the P.O." and "Death of a Traveling Salesman" as well as novels such as Delta Wedding *(1946),* The Ponder Heart *(1952), and* The Optimist's Daughter *(1972)—reflects the rural and small-town southern life she came to know during the first half of the twentieth century. Her work has received a Pulitzer Prize (1972) and numerous other awards, including the Presidential Medal of Freedom. Welty died in Jackson on July 23, 2001.*

Welty's experience of language largely involved listening—even to the words she read. Welty reflects on her own literary skill in her autobiographical account of her development as a writer, One Writer's Beginnings *(1983). An excerpt from the chapter titled "Listening" follows, taking as its motif Welty's observation that "Ever since I was first read to, then started reading to myself, there has never been a line read that I didn't hear."*

I learned from the age of two or three that any room in our house, at any time of day, was there to read in, or to be read to. My mother read to me. She'd read to me in the big bedroom in the mornings, when we were in her rocker together, which ticked in rhythm as we rocked, as though we had a cricket accompanying the story. She'd read to me in the diningroom on winter afternoons in front of the coal fire, with our cuckoo clock ending the story with "Cuckoo," and at night when I'd got in my own bed. I must have given her no peace. Sometimes she read to me in the kitchen while she sat churning, and the churning sobbed along with *any* story. It was my ambition to have her read to me while I churned; once she granted my wish, but she read off my story before I brought her butter. She was an expressive reader. When she was reading "Puss in Boots," for instance, it was impossible not to know that she distrusted *all* cats.

It had been startling and disappointing to me to find out that story books had been written by *people*, that books were not natural wonders, coming up of themselves like grass. Yet regardless of where they came from, I cannot remember a time when I was not in love with them—with the books themselves, cover and binding and the paper they were printed on, with their smell and their weight and with their possession in my arms, captured and carried off to myself. Still illiterate, I was ready for them, committed to all the reading I could give them.

Neither of my parents had come from homes that could afford to buy many books, but though it must have been something of a strain on his salary, as the youngest officer in a young insurance company, my father was all the while carefully selecting and ordering away for what he and Mother thought we children should grow up with. They bought first for the future.

Besides the bookcase in the livingroom, which was always called "the library," there were the encyclopedia tables and dictionary stand under windows in our diningroom. Here to help us grow up arguing around the diningroom table were the Unabridged Webster, the Columbia Encyclopedia, Compton's Pictured Encyclopedia, the Lincoln Library of Information, and later the Book of Knowledge. And the year we moved into our new house, there was room to celebrate it with the new 1925 edition of the Britannica, which my father, his face always deliberately turned toward the future, was of course disposed to think better than any previous edition.

In "the library," inside the mission-style bookcase with its three diamond- ⁵ latticed glass doors, with my father's Morris chair and the glass-shaded lamp on its table beside it, were books I could soon begin on—and I did, reading them all alike and as they came, straight down their rows, top shelf to bottom. There was the set of Stoddard's Lectures, in all its late nineteenth-century vocabulary and vignettes of peasant life and quaint beliefs and customs, with matching halftone illustrations: Vesuvius erupting, Venice by moonlight, gypsies glimpsed by their campfires. I didn't know then the clue they were to my father's longing to see the rest of the world. I read straight through his other love-from-afar: the Victrola Book of the Opera, with opera after opera in synopsis, with portraits in costume of Melba, Caruso, Galli-Curci, and Geraldine Farrar, some of whose voices we could listen to on our Red Seal records.

My mother read secondarily for information; she sank as a hedonist into novels. She read Dickens in the spirit in which she would have eloped with him. The novels of her girlhood that had stayed on in her imagination, besides those of Dickens and Scott and Robert Louis Stevenson, were *Jane Eyre, Trilby, The*

Woman in White, Green Mansions, King Solomon's Mines. Marie Corelli's name would crop up but I understood she had gone out of favor with my mother, who had only kept *Ardath* out of loyalty. In time she absorbed herself in Galsworthy, Edith Wharton, above all in Thomas Mann of the *Joseph* volumes.

St. Elmo was not in our house; I saw it often in other houses. This wildly popular Southern novel is where all the Edna Earles in our population started coming from. They're all named for the heroine, who succeeded in bringing a dissolute, sinning roué and atheist of a lover (St. Elmo) to his knees. My mother was able to forgo it. But she remembered the classic advice given to rose growers on how to water their bushes long enough: "Take a chair and *St. Elmo.*"

To both my parents I owe my early acquaintance with a beloved Mark Twain. There was a full set of Mark Twain and a short set of Ring Lardner in our bookcase, and those were the volumes that in time united us all, parents and children.

Reading everything that stood before me was how I came upon a worn old book without a back that had belonged to my father as a child. It was called *Sanford and Merton.* Is there anyone left who recognizes it, I wonder? It is the famous moral tale written by Thomas Day in the 1780s, but of him no mention is made on the title page of this book; here it is *Sanford and Merton in Words of One Syllable* by Mary Godolphin. Here are the rich boy and the poor boy and Mr. Barlow, their teacher and interlocutor, in long discourses alternating with dramatic scenes—danger and rescue allotted to the rich and the poor respectively. It may have only words of one syllable, but one of them is "quoth." It ends with not one but two morals, both engraved on rings: "Do what you ought, come what may," and "If we would be great, we must first learn to be good."

This book was lacking its front cover, the back held on by strips of pasted 10 paper, now turned golden, in several layers, and the pages stained, flecked, and tattered around the edges; its garish illustrations had come unattached but were preserved, laid in. I had the feeling even in my heedless childhood that this was the only book my father as a little boy had had of his own. He had held onto it, and might have gone to sleep on its coverless face: he had lost his mother when he was seven. My father had never made any mention to his own children of the book, but he had brought it along with him from Ohio to our house and shelved it in our bookcase.

My mother had brought from West Virginia that set of Dickens; those books looked sad, too—they had been through fire and water before I was born, she told me, and there they were, lined up—as I later realized, waiting for *me.*

I was presented, from as early as I can remember, with books of my own, which appeared on my birthday and Christmas morning. Indeed, my parents could not give me books enough. They must have sacrificed to give me on my sixth or seventh birthday—it was after I became a reader for myself—the ten-volume set of Our Wonder World. These were beautifully made, heavy books I would lie down with on the floor in front of the diningroom hearth, and more often than the rest volume 5, *Every Child's Story Book*, was under my eyes. There were the fairy tales—Grimm, Andersen, the English, the French, "Ali Baba and the Forty Thieves"; and there was Aesop and Reynard the Fox; there were the myths and legends, Robin Hood, King Arthur, and St. George and the Dragon, even the history of Joan of Arc; a whack of *Pilgrim's Progress* and a long piece of *Gulliver*. They all carried their classic illustrations. I located myself in these pages and could go straight to the stories and pictures I loved; very often "The Yellow Dwarf" was first choice, with Walter Crane's Yellow Dwarf in full color making his terrifying appearance flanked by turkeys. Now that volume is as worn and backless and hanging apart as my father's poor *Sanford and Merton*. The precious page with Edward Lear's "Jumblies" on it has been in danger of slipping out for all these years. One measure of my love for Our Wonder World was that for a long time I wondered if I would go through fire and water for it as my mother had done for Charles Dickens; and the only comfort was to think I could ask my mother to do it for me.

I believe I'm the only child I know of who grew up with this treasure in the house. I used to ask others, "Did you have Our Wonder World?" I'd have to tell them the Book of Knowledge could not hold a candle to it.

I live in gratitude to my parents for initiating me—and as early as I begged for it, without keeping me waiting—into knowledge of the word, into reading and spelling, by way of the alphabet. They taught it to me at home in time for me to begin to read before starting to school. I believe the alphabet is no longer considered an essential piece of equipment for traveling through life. In my day it was the keystone to knowledge. You learned the alphabet as you learned to count to ten, as you learned "Now I lay me" and the Lord's Prayer and your father's and mother's name and address and telephone number, all in case you were lost.

My love for the alphabet, which endures, grew out of reciting it but, before that, out of seeing the letters on the page. In my own story books, before I could read them for myself, I fell in love with various winding, enchanted-looking initials drawn by Walter Crane at the heads of fairy tales. In "Once upon a time," an "O" had a rabbit running it as a treadmill, his feet upon flowers. When the day came, years later, for me to see the Book of Kells, all the wizardry of letter, initial, and word swept over me a thousand times over, and the illumination, the gold, seemed a part of the word's beauty and holiness that had been there from the start.

My mother always sang to her children. Her voice came out just a little bit in the minor key. "Wee Willie Winkie's" song was wonderfully sad when she sang the lullabies.

"Oh, but now there's a record. She could have her own record to listen to," my father would have said. For there came a Victrola record of "Bobby Shafftoe" and "Rock-a-Bye Baby," all of Mother's lullabies, which could be played to take her place. Soon I was able to play her my own lullabies all day long.

Our Victrola stood in the diningroom. I was allowed to climb onto the seat of a diningroom chair to wind it, start the record turning, and set the needle playing. In a second I'd jumped to the floor, to spin or march around the table as the music called for—now there were all the other records I could play too. I skinned back onto the chair just in time to lift the needle at the end, stop the record and turn it over, then change the needle. That brass receptacle with a hole in the lid gave off a metallic smell like human sweat, from all the hot needles that were fed it. Winding up, dancing, being cocked to start and stop the record, was of course all in one the act of *listening*—to "Overture to *Daughter of the Regiment*," "Selections from *The Fortune Teller*," "Kiss Me Again," "Gypsy Dance from *Carmen*," "Stars and Stripes Forever," "When the Midnight Choo-Choo Leaves for Alabam," or whatever came next. Movement must be at the very heart of listening.

Ever since I was first read to, then started reading to myself, there has never been a line read that I didn't *hear*. As my eyes followed the sentence, a voice was saying it silently to me. It isn't my mother's voice, or the voice of any person I can identify, certainly not my own. It is human, but inward, and it is inwardly that I listen to it. It is to me the voice of the story or the poem itself. The cadence, whatever it is that asks you to believe, the feeling that resides in the printed word, reaches me through the reader-voice. I have supposed, but never found out, that this is the case with all readers—to read as listeners—and with all writers, to write as listeners. It may be part of the desire to write. The sound of what falls on the page begins the process of testing it for truth, for me. Whether I am right to trust so far I don't know. By now I don't know whether I could do either one, reading or writing, without the other.

My own words, when I am at work on a story, I hear too as they go, in the same voice that I hear when I read in books. When I write and the sound of it comes back to my ears, then I act to make my changes. I have always trusted this voice.   20

QUESTIONS FOR DISCUSSION AND WRITING

1. What connections does Welty make among listening, reading, and writing? Explain why Welty devotes so much space to her childhood *reading* in her essay on "Listening." Why are the people, places, and objects around which her reading took place so important?

2. With a partner, take turns reading aloud sentences or paragraphs from this essay or another essay of your choice. Notice where the emphasis in each sentence falls, where you have to pause for breath, the characteristic sounds of the words and cadence of the sentences. Repeat words, phrases, and whole sentences to understand their feeling and their meaning. Then try the same with your own writing and your partner's. What does your experience of close listening teach you about writing? What strikes you when you listen that you didn't notice when you read these silently?

3. Compare Welty's experiences as one who loves reading and books with Sherman Alexie's in "The Joy of Reading and Writing" (p. 45). Not every avid reader becomes a writer. What enabled these people to move from childhood reading to careers as writers?

AMY TAN

Mother Tongue

Amy Tan's first novel, The Joy Luck Club *(1989), an integrated suite of stories about mothers and daughters, was a finalist for the National Book Award. Tan earned a bachelor's degree in English (1973) and a master's degree in linguistics (1974) at San Jose State University. Her second novel,* The Kitchen God's Wife *(1991), is based on her mother's life in China before she immigrated to the United States after World War II. Her third book,* The Hundred Secret Senses *(1995), examines marriage and the meanings of motherhood and sisterhood in two cultures.* The Bonesetter's Daughter *(2001) returns to the complex relationship of Chinese mothers and their American-born daughters. Her most recent novel,* Saving Fish from Drowning *(2005), departs from her usual themes depicting mother–daughter relationships to an adventure story that recounts the kidnapping of eleven American tourists in Burma by natives who mistake the fifteen-year-old among them for a "god."*

In "Mother Tongue," first published in the Threepenny Review *(Fall 1990), Tan discusses "all the Englishes I grew up with"—the "simple" English "I spoke to my mother," the "broken" English "she used with me," her "'watered down'" translation of her mother's Chinese, and "her internal language," or what Tan "imagined to be her translation of her Chinese if she could speak in perfect English."*

I am not a scholar of English or literature. I cannot give you much more than personal opinions on the English language and its variations in this country or others.

I am a writer. And by that definition, I am someone who has always loved language. I am fascinated by language in daily life. I spend a great deal of my time thinking about the power of language—the way it can evoke an emotion, a visual image, a complex idea, or a simple truth. Language is the tool of my trade. And I use them all—all the Englishes I grew up with.

Recently, I was made keenly aware of the different Englishes I do use. I was giving a talk to a large group of people, the same talk I had already given to half a dozen other groups. The nature of the talk was about my writing, my life, and my book, *The Joy Luck Club.* The talk was going along well enough, until I remembered one major difference that made the whole talk sound wrong. My mother was in the room. And it was perhaps the first time she had heard me give a lengthy speech, using the kind of English I have never used with her. I was saying things like, "The intersection of memory upon imagination" and "There is an aspect of my fiction that relates to thus-and-thus"—a speech filled with carefully wrought grammatical phrases, burdened, it suddenly seemed to me, with nominalized forms, past perfect tenses, conditional phrases, all the forms of standard

English that I had learned in school and through books, the forms of English I did not use at home with my mother.

Just last week, I was walking down the street with my mother, and I again found myself conscious of the English I was using, the English I do use with her. We were talking about the price of new and used furniture and I heard myself saying this: "Not waste money that way." My husband was with us as well, and he didn't notice any switch in my English. And then I realized why. It's because over the twenty years we've been together I've often used that same kind of English with him, and sometimes he even uses it with me. It has become our language of intimacy, a different sort of English that relates to family talk, the language I grew up with.

So you'll have some idea of what this family talk I heard sounds like, I'll quote what my mother said during a recent conversation which I videotaped and then transcribed. During this conversation, my mother was talking about a political gangster in Shanghai who had the same last name as her family's, Du, and how the gangster in his early years wanted to be adopted by her family, which was rich by comparison. Later, the gangster became more powerful, far richer than my mother's family, and one day showed up at my mother's wedding to pay his respects. Here's what she said in part:

"Du Yusong having business like fruit stand. Like off the street kind. He is Du like Du Zong—but not Tsung-ming Island people. The local people call putong, the river east side, he belong to that side local people. That man want to ask Du Zong father take him in like become own family. Du Zong father wasn't look down on him, but didn't take seriously, until that man big like become a mafia. Now important person, very hard to inviting him. Chinese way, came only to show respect, don't stay for dinner. Respect for making big celebration, he shows up. Mean give lots of respect. Chinese custom. Chinese social life that way. If too important won't have to stay too long. He come to my wedding. I didn't see, I heard it. I gone to boy's side, they have YMCA dinner. Chinese age I was nineteen."

You should know that my mother's expressive command of English belies how much she actually understands. She reads the *Forbes* report, listens to *Wall Street Week,* converses daily with her stockbroker, reads all of Shirley MacLaine's books with ease—all kinds of things I can't begin to understand. Yet some of my friends tell me they understand 50 percent of what my mother says. Some say they understand 80 to 90 percent. Some say they understand none of it, as if she were speaking pure Chinese. But to me, my mother's English is perfectly clear, perfectly natural. It's my mother tongue. Her language, as I hear it, is vivid, direct, full of observation and imagery. That was the language that helped shape the way I saw things, expressed things, made sense of the world.

Lately, I've been giving more thought to the kind of English my mother speaks. Like others, I have described it to people as "broken" or "fractured" English. But I wince when I say that. It has always bothered me that I can think of no way to describe it other than "broken," as if it were damaged and needed to be fixed, as if it lacked a certain wholeness and soundness. I've heard other terms used, "limited English," for example. But they seem just as bad, as if everything is limited, including people's perceptions of the limited English speaker.

I know this for a fact, because when I was growing up, my mother's "limited" English limited *my* perception of her. I was ashamed of her English. I believed that her English reflected the quality of what she had to say. That is, because she expressed them imperfectly her thoughts were imperfect. And I had plenty of empirical evidence to support me: the fact that people in department stores, at banks, and at restaurants did not take her seriously, did not give her good service, pretended not to understand her, or even acted as if they did not hear her.

My mother has long realized the limitations of her English as well. When I was   10 fifteen, she used to have me call people on the phone to pretend I was she. In this guise, I was forced to ask for information or even to complain and yell at people who had been rude to her. One time it was a call to her stockbroker in New York. She had cashed out her small portfolio and it just happened we were going to go to New York the next week, our very first trip outside California. I had to get on the phone and say in an adolescent voice that was not very convincing, "This is Mrs. Tan."

And my mother was standing in the back whispering loudly, "Why he don't send me check, already two weeks late. So mad he lie to me, losing me money."

And then I said in perfect English, "Yes, I'm getting rather concerned. You had agreed to send the check two weeks ago, but it hasn't arrived."

Then she began to talk more loudly. "What he want, I come to New York tell him front of his boss, you cheating me?" And I was trying to calm her down, make her be quiet, while telling the stockbroker, "I can't tolerate any more excuses. If I don't receive the check immediately, I am going to have to speak to your manager when I'm in New York next week." And sure enough, the following week there we were in front of this astonished stockbroker, and I was sitting there red-faced and quiet, and my mother, the real Mrs. Tan, was shouting at his boss in her impeccable broken English.

We used a similar routine just five days ago, for a situation that was far less humorous. My mother had gone to the hospital for an appointment, to find out about a benign brain tumor a CAT scan had revealed a month ago. She said she had spoken very good English, her best English, no mistakes. Still, she said, the hospital did not apologize when they said they had lost the CAT scan and she had come for nothing. She said they did not seem to have any sympathy when she told them she was anxious to know the exact diagnosis, since her husband and son had both died of brain tumors. She said they would not give her any more information until the next time and she would have to make another appointment for that. So she said she would not leave until the doctor called her daughter. She wouldn't budge. And when the doctor finally called her daughter, me, who spoke in perfect English—lo and behold—we had assurances the CAT scan would be found, promises that a conference call on Monday would be held, and apologies for any suffering my mother had gone through for a most regrettable mistake.

I think my mother's English almost had an effect on limiting my possibili- 15 ties in life as well. Sociologists and linguists probably will tell you that a person's developing language skills are more influenced by peers. But I do think that the language spoken in the family, especially in immigrant families which are more insular, plays a large role in shaping the language of the child. And I believe that it affected my results on achievement tests, IQ tests, and the SAT. While my English skills were never judged as poor, compared to math, English could not be considered my strong suit. In grade school I did moderately well, getting perhaps B's, sometimes B-pluses, in English and scoring perhaps in the sixtieth or seventieth percentile on achievement tests. But those scores were not good enough to override the opinion that my true abilities lay in math and science, because in those areas I achieved A's and scored in the ninetieth percentile or higher.

This was understandable. Math is precise; there is only one correct answer. Whereas, for me at least, the answers on English tests were always a judgment call, a matter of opinion and personal experience. Those tests were constructed around items like fill-in-the-blank sentence completion, such as, "Even though Tom was _____, Mary thought he was _____." And the correct answer always seemed to be the most bland combinations of thoughts, for example "Even though Tom was shy, Mary thought he was charming," with the grammatical structure "even though" limiting the correct answer to some sort of semantic opposites, so you wouldn't get answers like, "Even though Tom was foolish, Mary thought he was ridiculous." Well, according to my mother, there were very few limitations as to what Tom could have been and what Mary might have thought of him. So I never did well on tests like that.

The same was true with word analogies, pairs of words in which you were supposed to find some sort of logical, semantic relationship — for example, "*Sunset* is to *nightfall* as _____ is to _____." And here you would be presented with a list of four possible pairs, one of which showed the same kind of relationship: *red* is to *spotlight, bus* is to *arrival, chills* is to *fever, yawn* is to *boring*. Well, I could never think that way. I knew what the tests were asking, but I could not block out of my mind the images already created by the first pair, "*sunset* is to *nightfall*" — and I would see a burst of colors against a darkening sky, the moon rising, the lowering of a curtain of stars. And all the other pairs of words — red, bus, spotlight, boring — just threw up a mass of confusing images, making it impossible for me to sort out something as logical as saying: "A sunset precedes nightfall" is the same as "a chill precedes a fever." The only way I would have gotten that answer right would have been to imagine an associative situation, for example, my being disobedient and staying out past sunset, catching a chill at night, which turns into feverish pneumonia as punishment, which indeed did happen to me.

I have been thinking about all this lately, about my mother's English, about achievement tests. Because lately I've been asked, as a writer, why there are not more Asian Americans represented in American literature. Why are there few Asian Americans enrolled in creative writing programs? Why do so many Chinese students go into engineering? Well, these are broad sociological questions I can't begin to answer. But I have noticed in surveys—in fact, just last week—that Asian students, as a whole, always do significantly better on math achievement tests than in English. And this makes me think that there are other Asian American students whose English spoken in the home might also be described as "broken" or "limited." And perhaps they also have teachers who are steering them away from writing and into math and science, which is what happened to me.

Fortunately, I happen to be rebellious in nature and enjoy the challenge of disproving assumptions made about me. I became an English major my first year in college, after being enrolled as pre-med. I started writing nonfiction as a free-lancer the week after I was told by my former boss that writing was my worst skill and I should hone my talents toward account management.

But it wasn't until 1985 that I finally began to write fiction. And at first I 20 wrote using what I thought to be wittily crafted sentences, sentences that would finally prove I had mastery over the English language. Here's an example from the first draft of a story that later made its way into *The Joy Luck Club*, but without this line: "That was my mental quandary in its nascent state." A terrible line, which I can barely pronounce.

Fortunately, for reasons I won't get into today, I later decided I should envision a reader for the stories I would write. And the reader I decided upon was my mother, because these were stories about mothers. So with this reader in mind—and in fact she did read my early drafts—I began to write stories using all the Englishes I grew up with: the English I spoke to my mother, which for lack of a better term might be described as "simple"; the English she used with me, which for lack of a better term might be described as "broken"; my translation of her Chinese, which could certainly be described as "watered down"; and what I imagined to be her translation of her Chinese if she could speak in perfect English, her internal language, and for that I sought to preserve the essence, but neither an English nor a Chinese structure. I wanted to capture what language ability tests can never reveal: her intent, her passion, her imagery, the rhythms of her speech, and the nature of her thoughts.

Apart from what any critic had to say about my writing, I knew I had succeeded where it counted when my mother finished reading my book and gave me her verdict: "So easy to read."

QUESTIONS FOR DISCUSSION AND WRITING

1. What connections does Tan make throughout the essay between speaking and writing? In which English has Tan written "Mother Tongue"? Why?

2. How do the "Englishes" spoken by Tan and her mother help them communicate their personalities, intelligence, and relationship with one another?

3. What differences are there between language used for family or home and language for public use?

4. With family, friends, teammates, or colleagues at school or work, tape (video or audio) a conversation that involves more than one "language"—formal, informal, slang, specialized for the task at hand, or bilingual. Then analyze the tape and write a paper identifying the conspicuous features of the languages involved. How do the speakers know which language(s) to use under what circumstances?

5. Present to an audience of college-educated Americans an argument for or against the necessity of speaking (or writing) in Standard English. (What, in your estimation, are the conspicuous features of Standard English?) Are there times and places where you'd allow for exceptions?

LESLIE MARMON SILKO

Language and Literature from a Pueblo Indian Perspective

Of Pueblo, Laguna, Mexican, and white ancestry, Leslie Marmon Silko (b. 1948) grew up on the Laguna Pueblo reservation before earning a bachelor's degree from the University of New Mexico in 1969. Her citation as the 2004 honoree of Women's History Month reads, "The family house sat on the fringe of Laguna Pueblo—not quite excluded, not quite included. It became a metaphor for Silko's life" and work, "anchored to the traditions and stories of Laguna Pueblo on one side with Anglo mainstream on the other." Silko writes fiction (Ceremony, *1977;* Almanac of the Dead, *1991; and* Gardens in the Dunes: A Novel, *1999), poetry* (Laguna Woman: Poems, *1974), and nonfiction* (Yellow Woman and the Beauty of the Spirit, *1997). She won a MacArthur "genius" fellowship (1983). Silko's concern for understanding and sharing Pueblo culture on its own terms pervades her work, leading her to examine the interaction between Native American and Western cultures.*

For the Pueblo peoples, geographical, historical, and personal identities are bound up in a web of storytelling that appends tradition to modern reality. In "Language and Literature from a Pueblo Indian Perspective" (in Leslie A. Fiedler and Houston A. Baker, eds., English Literature: Opening Up the Canon, *Baltimore: Johns Hopkins UP, 1979), Silko explains how this oral tradition serves a unifying cultural function: Pueblo Indians learn and rehearse a vast repertoire of oral narratives covering everything from the creation of the world to family stories. Whereas Western anthropologists would create a hierarchy of Pueblo narratives, Silko explains that each Pueblo story—each word, in fact—is a passageway to another story in a seamless nonlinear unity.*

Where I come from, the words most highly valued are those spoken from the heart, unpremeditated and unrehearsed. Among the Pueblo people, a written speech or statement is highly suspect because the true feelings of the speaker remain hidden as she reads words that are detached from the occasion and the audience. I have intentionally not written a formal paper because I want you to *hear* and to experience English in a structure that follows patterns from the oral tradition. For those of you accustomed to being taken from point A to point B to point C, this presentation may be somewhat difficult to follow. Pueblo expression resembles something like a spider's web — with many little threads radiating from the center, crisscrossing each other. As with the web, the structure emerges as it is made and you must simply listen and trust, as the Pueblo people do, that meaning will be made.

My task is a formidable one: I ask you to set aside a number of basic approaches that you have been using, and probably will continue to use, and instead, to approach language from the Pueblo perspective, one that embraces the whole of creation and the whole of history and time.

What changes would Pueblo writers make to English as a language for literature? I have some examples of stories in English that I will use to address this question. At the same time, I would like to explain the importance of storytelling and how it relates to a Pueblo theory of language.

So, I will begin, appropriately enough, with the Pueblo Creation story, an all-inclusive story of how life began. In this story, Tséitsínako, Thought Woman, by thinking of her sisters, and together with her sisters, thought of everything that is. In this way, the world was created. Everything in this world was a part of the original creation; the people at home understood that far away there were other human beings, also a part of this world. The Creation story even includes a prophecy, which describes the origin of European and African peoples and also refers to Asians.

This story, I think, suggests something about why the Pueblo people are 5 more concerned with story and communication and less concerned with a particular language. There are at least six, possibly seven, distinct languages among the twenty pueblos of the southwestern United States, for example, Zuñi and Hopi. And from mesa to mesa there are subtle differences in language. But the particular language being spoken isn't as important as what a speaker is trying to say, and this emphasis on the story itself stems, I believe, from a view of narrative particular to the Pueblo and other Native American peoples — that is, that language *is* story.

I will try to clarify this statement. At Laguna Pueblo, for example, many individual words have their own stories. So when one is telling a story, and one is using words to tell the story, each word that one is speaking has a story of its own, too. Often the speakers or tellers will go into these word-stories, creating an elaborate structure of stories-within-stories. This structure, which becomes very apparent in the actual telling of a story, informs contemporary Pueblo writing and storytelling as well as the traditional narratives. This perspective on narrative — of story within story, the idea that one story is only the beginning of many stories, and the sense that stories never truly end — represents an important contribution of Native American cultures to the English language.

Many people think of storytelling as something that is done at bedtime, that it is something done for small children. But when I use the term *storytelling*, I'm talking about something much bigger than that. I'm talking about something that comes out of an experience and an understanding of that original view of creation—that we are all part of a whole; we do not differentiate or fragment stories and experiences. In the beginning, Tséitsínako, Thought Woman, thought of all things, and all of these things are held together as one holds many things together in a single thought.

So in the telling (and you will hear a few of the dimensions of this telling) first of all, as mentioned earlier, the storytelling always includes the audience, the listeners. In fact, a great deal of the story is believed to be inside the listener; the storyteller's role is to draw the story out of the listeners. The storytelling continues from generation to generation.

Basically, the origin story constructs our identity—within this story, we know who we are. We are the Lagunas. This is where we come from. We came this way. We came by this place. And so from the time we are very young, we hear these stories, so that when we go out into the world, when one asks who we are, or where we are from, we immediately know: we are the people who came from the north. We are the people of these stories.

In the Creation story, Antelope says that he will help knock a hole in   10
the earth so that the people can come up, out into the next world. Antelope tries and tries; he uses his hooves, but is unable to break through. It is then that Badger says, "Let me help you." And Badger very patiently uses his claws and digs a way through, bringing the people into the world. When the Badger clan people think of themselves, or when the Antelope people think of themselves, it is as people who are of *this* story, and this is *our* place, and we fit into the very beginning when the people first came, before we began our journey south.

Within the clans there are stories that identify the clan. One moves, then, from the idea of one's identity as a tribal person into clan identity, then to one's identity as a member of an extended family. And it is the notion of "extended family" that has produced a kind of story that some distinguish from other Pueblo stories, though Pueblo people do not. Anthropologists and ethnologists have, for a long time, differentiated the types of stories the Pueblos tell. They tended to elevate the old, sacred, and traditional stories and to brush aside family stories, the family's account of itself. But in Pueblo culture, these family stories are given equal recognition. There is no definite, present pattern for the way one will hear the stories of one's own family, but it is a very critical part of one's childhood, and the storytelling continues throughout one's life. One will hear stories of importance to the family—sometimes wonderful stories—stories about the time a maternal uncle got the biggest deer that was ever seen and brought it back from the mountains. And so an individual's identity will extend from the identity constructed around the family—"I am from the family of my uncle who brought in this wonderful deer and it was a wonderful hunt."

Family accounts include negative stories, too; perhaps an uncle did something unacceptable. It is very important that one keep track of all these stories—both positive and not so positive—about one's own family and other families. Because even when there is no way around it—old Uncle Pete *did* do a terrible thing—by knowing the stories that originate in other families, one is able to deal with terrible sorts of things that might happen within one's own family. If a member of the family does something that cannot be excused, one always knows stories about similar inexcusable things done by a member of another family. But this knowledge is not communicated for malicious reasons. It is very important to understand this. Keeping track of all the stories within the community gives us all a certain distance, a useful perspective, that brings incidents down to a level we can deal with. If others have done it before, it cannot be so terrible. If others have endured, so can we.

The stories are always bringing us together, keeping this whole together, keeping this family together, keeping this clan together. "Don't go away, don't isolate yourself, but come here, because we have all had these kinds of experiences." And so there is this constant pulling together to resist the tendency to run or hide or separate oneself during a traumatic emotional experience. This separation not only endangers the group but the individual as well—one does not recover by oneself.

Because storytelling lies at the heart of Pueblo culture, it is absurd to attempt to fix the stories in time. "When did they tell the stories?" or "What time of day does the storytelling take place?"—these questions are nonsensical from a Pueblo perspective, because our storytelling goes on constantly: as some old grandmother puts on the shoes of a child and tells her the story of a little girl who didn't wear her shoes, for instance, or someone comes into the house for coffee to talk with a teenage boy who has just been in a lot of trouble, to reassure him that someone else's son has been in that kind of trouble, too. Storytelling is an ongoing process, working on many different levels.

Here's one story that is often told at a time of individual crisis (and I want 15 to remind you that we make no distinctions between types of story—historical, sacred, plain gossip—because these distinctions are not useful when discussing the Pueblo *experience* of language). There was a young man who, when he came back from the war in Vietnam, had saved up his army pay and bought a beautiful red Volkswagen. He was very proud of it. One night he drove up to a place called the King's Bar right across the reservation line. The bar is notorious for many reasons, particularly for the deep *arroyo* located behind it. The young man ran in to pick up a cold six-pack, but he forgot to put on his emergency brake. And his little red Volkswagen rolled back into the *arroyo* and was all smashed up. He felt very bad about it, but within a few days everybody had come to him with stories about other people who had lost cars and family members to that *arroyo*, for instance, George Day's station wagon, with his mother-in-law and kids inside. So everybody was saying, "Well, at least your mother-in-law and kids weren't in the car when it rolled in," and one can't argue with that kind of story. The story of the young man and his smashed-up Volkswagen was now joined with all the other stories of cars that fell into that *arroyo*. . . .

There are a great many parallels between Pueblo experiences and those of African and Caribbean peoples — one is that we have all had the conqueror's language imposed on us. But our experience with English has been somewhat different in that the Bureau of Indian Affairs schools were not interested in teaching us the canon of Western classics. For instance, we never heard of Shakespeare. We were given Dick and Jane, and I can remember reading that the robins were heading south for the winter. It took me a long time to figure out what was going on. I worried for quite a while about our robins in Laguna because they didn't leave in the winter, until I finally realized that all the big textbook companies are up in Boston and *their* robins do go south in the winter. But in a way, this dreadful formal education freed us by encouraging us to maintain our narratives. Whatever literature we were exposed to at school (which was damn little), at home the storytelling, the special regard for telling and bringing together through the telling, was going on constantly.

And as the old people say, "If you can remember the stories, you will be all right. Just remember the stories." . . .

One of the other advantages that we Pueblos have enjoyed is that we have always been able to stay with the land. Our stories cannot be separated from their geographical locations, from actual physical places on the land. We were not relocated like so many Native American groups who were torn away from their ancestral land. And our stories are so much a part of these places that it is almost impossible for future generations to lose them — there is a story connected with every place, every object in the landscape.

Dennis Brutus has talked about the "yet unborn" as well as "those from the past," and how we are still *all* in *this* place, and language — the storytelling — is our way of passing through or being with them, or being together again. When Aunt Susie told her stories, she would tell a younger child to go open the door so that our esteemed predecessors might bring in their gifts to us. "They are out there," Aunt Susie would say. "Let them come in. They're here, they're here with us *within* the stories."

A few years ago, when Aunt Susie was 106, I paid her a visit, and while I was there she said, "Well, I'll be leaving here soon. I think I'll be leaving here next week, and I will be going over to the Cliff House." She said, "It's going to be real good to get back over there." I was listening, and I was thinking that she must be talking about her house at Paguate Village, just north of Laguna. And she went on, "Well, my mother's sister (and she gave her Indian name) will be there. She has been living there. She will be there and we will be over there, and I will get a chance to write down these stories I've been telling you." Now you must understand, of course, that Aunt Susie's mother's sister, a great storyteller herself, has long since passed over into the land of the dead. But then I realized, too, that

Aunt Susie wasn't talking about death the way most of us do. She was talking about "going over" as a journey, a journey that perhaps we can only begin to understand through an appreciation for the boundless capacity of language that, through storytelling, brings us together, despite great distances between cultures, despite great distances in time.

QUESTIONS FOR DISCUSSION AND WRITING

1. "Where I come from, the words most highly valued are those spoken from the heart, unpremeditated and unrehearsed. Among the Pueblo people, a written speech or statement is highly suspect because the true feelings of the speaker remain hidden as she reads words that are detached from the occasion and the audience" (paragraph 1). What is the relation between speaking and writing in the Pueblo culture, as Silko explains it?

2. What is the relation between speaking and writing in your own culture (or in the various subcultures to which you belong—for instance, your classes, your family, social or special interest groups of which you are a member)? Are there circumstances under which one is more important than the other? In your own communication, do speech and writing reinforce one another often? In what ways?

3. Why does a Pueblo story have many stories within it (see paragraphs 5–6)? Is there a sense of unity, common elements in a story that is so closely connected with many other stories? How so? When you're telling a true story—about your life, your family, your hometown, a life-changing experience or insight—are you ever cognizant of its relation to other people's stories? What connections do these have in common?

4. Why does Silko think that having been able to "stay with the land" (paragraph 18) is an advantage for the Pueblos in developing their unique views of language, literature, and life? Silko's argument about the close connection between the Pueblo stories and their "geographical locations" suggests that every life in every place is unique. If so, how can storytellers—orally or in writing—communicate meaningfully with people unfamiliar with the places their stories come from?

5. Silko says, "Within the clans there are stories that identify the clan" (paragraph 11). Examine the stories of two or three of the following authors to determine how they reflect on minority experience in the United States: Silko, Sherman Alexie (p. 45), Eric Liu (p. 93), Esmeralda Santiago (p. 99), James Baldwin (p. 134), Richard Rodriguez (p. 275), Lynda Barry (p. 522). How do these stories handle issues such as exclusion, prejudice, stereotyping, culture clashes, and dual identity? What information do the writers have to include to ensure that a majority audience understands what they're saying? Do they have to write in Standard English rather than in another language or dialect in order to reinforce their points? If you identify with a particular racial, ethnic, or cultural heritage, incorporate your own story into your analysis.

SHERMAN ALEXIE

The Joy of Reading and Writing:
Superman and Me

For author Sherman Alexie, Native American identity is a challenge to be met with imaginative writing. In over a dozen novels and collections of stories and poems, Alexie uses stories to deal with the tragic depression, stultifying normalcy, and quirky comedy of Indian life on and off the reservation. Unlike some authors, however, Alexie is impatient with mythical stereotypes. As he wryly informed a Cineaste *magazine interviewer, "I've never seen an Indian turn into a deer. I mean, I know thousands of Indians, I've been an Indian my whole life, and I've yet to see an Indian turn into an animal!" A descendent of Spokane and Coeur d'Alene tribal ancestors, Alexie was born in 1966 on the Spokane Indian Reservation in Wellpinit, Washington. He attended Gonzaga University and finished his degree at Washington State University (B.A., 1991). A year after graduation his first book,* The Business of Fancydancing: Stories and Poems, *appeared. Other work includes the screenplay for the film* Smoke Signals *(1998), based on his story collection* The Lone Ranger and Tonto Fistfight in Heaven *(1993). His story collection* Ten Little Indians *appeared in 2003. His first young adult novel,* The Absolutely True Diary of a Part-Time Indian *(2007), deals with disability in addition to Alexie's familiar themes of poverty and ethnicity; it captivates with its mixture of raucous humor and true grit.*

"The Joy of Reading and Writing: Superman and Me" (first published in The Most Wonderful Books, *1997) discloses the excitement, stimulation, and power that being immersed in books, literally and figuratively, can convey to readers, novice and sophisticated alike. As a child, Alexie understood their many messages, which together meant "I refused to fail."*

I learned to read with a *Superman* comic book. Simple enough, I suppose. I cannot recall which particular *Superman* comic book I read, nor can I remember which villain he fought in that issue. I cannot remember the plot, nor the means by which I obtained the comic book. What I can remember is this: I was three years old, a Spokane Indian boy living with his family on the Spokane Indian Reservation in eastern Washington state. We were poor by most standards, but one of my parents usually managed to find some minimum-wage job or another, which made us middle-class by reservation standards. I had a brother and three sisters. We lived on a combination of irregular paychecks, hope, fear, and government surplus food.

My father, who is one of the few Indians who went to Catholic school on purpose, was an avid reader of westerns, spy thrillers, murder mysteries, gangster epics, basketball player biographies, and anything else he could find. He bought his books by the pound at Dutch's Pawn Shop, Goodwill, Salvation Army, and Value Village. When he had extra money, he bought new novels at supermarkets, convenience stores, and hospital gift shops. Our house was filled with books. They were stacked in crazy piles in the bathroom, bedrooms, and living room. In a fit of unemployment-inspired creative energy, my father built a set of bookshelves and soon filled them with a random assortment of books about the Kennedy assassination, Watergate, the Vietnam War, and the entire twenty-three-book series of the Apache westerns. My father loved books, and since I loved my father with an aching devotion, I decided to love books as well.

I can remember picking up my father's books before I could read. The words themselves were mostly foreign, but I still remember the exact moment when I first understood, with a sudden clarity, the purpose of a paragraph. I didn't have the vocabulary to say "paragraph," but I realized that a paragraph was a fence that held words. The words inside a paragraph worked together for a common purpose. They had some specific reason for being inside the same fence. This knowledge delighted me. I began to think of everything in terms of paragraphs. Our reservation was a small paragraph within the United States. My family's house was a paragraph, distinct from the other paragraphs of the LeBrets to the north, the Fords to our south, and the Tribal School to the west. Inside our house, each family member existed as a separate paragraph but still had genetics and common experiences to link us. Now, using this logic, I can see my changed family as an essay of seven paragraphs: mother, father, older brother, the deceased sister, my younger twin sisters, and our adopted little brother.

At the same time I was seeing the world in paragraphs, I also picked up the *Superman* comic book. Each panel, complete with picture, dialogue, and narrative, was a three-dimensional paragraph. In one panel, Superman breaks through a door. His suit is red, blue, and yellow. The brown door shatters into many pieces. I look at the narrative above the picture. I cannot read the words, but I assume it tells me that "Superman is breaking down the door." Aloud, I pretend to read the words and say, "Superman is breaking down the door." Words, dialogue, also float out of Superman's mouth. Because he is breaking down the door, I assume he says, "I am breaking down the door." Once again, I pretend to read the words and say aloud, "I am breaking down the door." In this way, I learned to read.

This might be an interesting story all by itself. A little Indian boy teaches ⁵ himself to read at an early age and advances quickly. He reads *Grapes of Wrath* in kindergarten when other children are struggling through Dick and Jane. If he'd been anything but an Indian boy living on the reservation, he might have been called a prodigy. But he is an Indian boy living on the reservation and is simply an oddity. He grows into a man who often speaks of his childhood in the third-person, as if it will somehow dull the pain and make him sound more modest about his talents.

A smart Indian is a dangerous person, widely feared and ridiculed by Indians and non-Indians alike. I fought with my classmates on a daily basis. They wanted me to stay quiet when the non-Indian teacher asked for answers, for volunteers, for help. We were Indian children who were expected to be stupid. Most lived up to those expectations inside the classroom but subverted them on the outside. They struggled with basic reading in school but could remember how to sing a few dozen powwow songs. They were monosyllabic in front of their non-Indian teachers but could tell complicated stories and jokes at the dinner table. They submissively ducked their heads when confronted by a non-Indian adult but would slug it out with the Indian bully who was ten years older. As Indian children, we were expected to fail in the non-Indian world. Those who failed were ceremonially accepted by other Indians and appropriately pitied by non-Indians.

I refused to fail. I was smart. I was arrogant. I was lucky. I read books late into the night, until I could barely keep my eyes open. I read books at recess, then during lunch, and in the few minutes left after I had finished my classroom assignments. I read books in the car when my family traveled to powwows or basketball games. In shopping malls, I ran to the bookstores and read bits and pieces of as many books as I could. I read the books my father brought home from the pawnshops and secondhand. I read the books I borrowed from the library. I read the backs of cereal boxes. I read the newspaper. I read the bulletins posted on the walls of the school, the clinic, the tribal offices, the post office. I read junk mail. I read auto-repair manuals. I read magazines. I read anything that had words and paragraphs. I read with equal parts joy and desperation. I loved those books, but I also knew that love had only one purpose. I was trying to save my life.

Despite all the books I read, I am still surprised I became a writer. I was going to be a pediatrician. These days, I write novels, short stories, and poems. I visit schools and teach creative writing to Indian kids. In all my years in the reservation school system, I was never taught how to write poetry, short stories, or novels. I was certainly never taught that Indians wrote poetry, short stories, and novels. Writing was something beyond Indians. I cannot recall a single time that a guest teacher visited the reservation. There must have been visiting teachers. Who were they? Where are they now? Do they exist? I visit the schools as often as possible. The Indian kids crowd the classroom. Many are writing their own poems, short stories, and novels. They have read my books. They have read many other books. They look at me with bright eyes and arrogant wonder. They are trying to save their lives. Then there are the sullen and already defeated Indian kids who sit in the back rows and ignore me with theatrical precision. The pages of their notebooks are empty. They carry neither pencil nor pen. They stare out the window. They refuse and resist. "Books," I say to them. "Books," I say. I throw my weight against their locked doors. The door holds. I am smart. I am arrogant. I am lucky. I am trying to save our lives.

QUESTIONS FOR DISCUSSION AND WRITING

1. Elaborate — in discussion or in a paper — on Alexie's observations that "A smart Indian is a dangerous person" and "I refused to fail. I was smart. I was arrogant. I was lucky. I read books late into the night" (paragraphs 6 and 7). Why is a "smart Indian . . . widely feared and ridiculed by Indians and non-Indians alike" (paragraph 6)? What threats does an independent-minded Indian (or anyone) pose to complacent or powerful people or to society in general?

2. Compare and contrast Welty's "Listening" (p. 29) and Alexie's "Joy of Reading and Writing." Using the Questions for Discussion and Writing following Welty (p. 33), examine the connections each makes between the acts of reading and writing. Have your experiences with e-mail, Twitter, and other social media influenced this answer? If so, in what ways?

3. Write a paper, either individually or with a partner, on reading as a source of empowerment for the reader. Draw on your experiences as a reader, as well as those of Alexie and Welty.

RICHARD WRIGHT

From *Fighting Words*

Richard Wright, son of sharecroppers, was born in Mississippi in 1908. He grew up in a household impoverished in body, soul, and spirit and dominated by a fundamentalist grandmother who forbade reading anything but the Bible. His autobiography, Black Boy *(1945), chronicles the discrimination, despair, and anger that impelled Wright to move to Chicago and, ultimately, to Paris, where he lived until his death in 1960. His internationally distinguished reputation puts him in the ranks of the celebrated authors he cites in paragraph 45 of "Fighting Words," an excerpt from* Black Boy.

I stood at a counter [in the bank lobby] and picked up the Memphis *Commercial Appeal* and began my free reading of the press. I came finally to the editorial page and saw an article dealing with one H. L. Mencken. I knew by hearsay that he was the editor of the *American Mercury*, but aside from that I knew nothing about him. The article was a furious denunciation of Mencken, concluding with one, hot, short sentence: Mencken is a fool.

I wondered what on earth this Mencken had done to call down upon him the scorn of the South. . . . Undoubtedly he must be advocating ideas that the South did not like. Were there, then, people other than Negroes who criticized the South? . . .

Now, how could I find out about this Mencken? There was a huge library near the riverfront, but I knew that Negroes were not allowed to patronize its shelves any more than they were the parks and playgrounds of the city. I had gone into the library several times to get books for the white men on the job. Which of them would now help me to get books? And how could I read them without causing concern to the white men with whom I worked? . . .

One morning I paused before the [desk of a] Catholic fellow [who was hated by white Southerners].

"I want to ask you a favor," I whispered to him.   5

"What is it?"

"I want to read. I can't get books from the library. I wonder if you'd let me use your card?"

He looked at me suspiciously.

"My card is full most of the time," he said.

"I see," I said and waited, posing my question silently.

"You're not trying to get me into trouble, are you, boy?" he asked, staring at me.

"Oh, no, sir."

"What book do you want?"

"A book by H. L. Mencken."

"Which one?"

"I don't know. Has he written more than one?"

"He has written several."

"I didn't know that."

"What makes you want to read Mencken?"

"Oh, I just saw his name in the newspaper," I said.

"It's good of you to want to read," he said. "But you ought to read the right things."

I said nothing. Would he want to supervise my reading?

"Let me think," he said. "I'll figure out something."

I turned from him and he called me back. He stared at me quizzically.

"Richard, don't mention this to the other white men," he said.

"I understand," I said. "I won't say a word."

A few days later he called me to him.

"I've got a card in my wife's name," he said. "Here's mine."

"Thank you, sir."

"Do you think you can manage it?"

"I'll manage fine," I said.

"If they suspect you, you'll get in trouble," he said.

"I'll write the same kind of notes to the library that you wrote when you sent me for books," I told him. "I'll sign your name."

He laughed.

"Go ahead. Let me see what you get," he said.

That afternoon I addressed myself to forging a note. Now, what were the names of books written by H. L. Mencken? I did not know any of them. I finally wrote what I thought would be a foolproof note: *Dear Madam: Will you please let this nigger boy*—I used the word "nigger" to make the librarian feel that I could not possibly be the author of the note—*have some books by H. L. Mencken?* I forged the white man's name.

I entered the library as I had always done when on errands for whites, but I felt that I would somehow slip up and betray myself. I doffed my hat, stood a respectful distance from the desk, looked as unbookish as possible, and waited for the white patrons to be taken care of. When the desk was clear of people, I still waited. The white librarian looked at me.

"What do you want, boy?"

As though I did not possess the power of speech, I stepped forward and simply handed her the forged note, not parting my lips.

"What books by Mencken does he want?" she asked.   40

"I don't know, ma'am," I said, avoiding her eyes. . . .

"You're not using these books, are you?" she asked pointedly.

"Oh, no, ma'am. I can't read." . . .

I said nothing. She stamped the card and handed me the books.

That night in my rented room . . . I opened *A Book of Prefaces* and began to   45
read. I was jarred and shocked by the style, the clear, clean, sweeping sentences. . . .
Yes, this man was fighting, fighting with words. He was using words as a weapon,
using them as one would use a club. Could words be weapons? Well, yes, for here
they were. Then, maybe, perhaps, I could use them as a weapon? No. It frightened
me. I read on and what amazed me was not what he said, but how on earth anybody had the courage to say it.

Occasionally I glanced up to reassure myself that I was alone in the room.
Who were these men about whom Mencken was talking so passionately? Who was
Anatole France? Joseph Conrad? Sinclair Lewis, Sherwood Anderson, Dostoevski,
George Moore, Gustave Flaubert, Maupassant, Tolstoy, Frank Harris, Mark Twain,
Thomas Hardy, Arnold Bennett, Stephen Crane, Zola, Norris, Gorky, Bergson,
Ibsen, Balzac, Bernard Shaw, Dumas, Poe, Thomas Mann, O. Henry, Dreiser, H. G.
Wells, Gogol, T. S. Eliot, Gide, Baudelaire, Edgar Lee Masters, Stendhal, Turgenev,
Huneker, Nietzsche, and scores of others? Were these men real? Did they exist or
had they existed? . . . I concluded the book with the conviction that I had somehow
overlooked something terribly important in life. I had once tried to write, had once
reveled in feeling, had let my crude imagination roam, but the impulse to dream
had been slowly beaten out of me by experience. Now it surged up again and I hun-
gered for books, new ways of looking and seeing. It was not a matter of believing or
disbelieving what I read, but of feeling something new, of being affected by something that made the look of the world different.

QUESTIONS FOR DISCUSSION AND WRITING

1. Why did Wright have to lie to take out library books he wanted to read in the
   segregated South? He had to use a white man's library card (paragraphs 10–
   40), since none was available to him, and he lied to the librarian who asked,
   "You're not using those books, are you?". . . "On, no, ma'am. I can't read"
   (paragraphs 42 and 43). Why were African Americans denied access to books
   at that time?

2. Judging from the experiences of Welty (p. 29), Alexie (p. 45), and Wright, why do you suppose that some people who love to read become writers, while many do not?

3. Many autobiographers and other authors write of their excitement at learning to read or of discovering particular authors with a wide range of possibilities, power, and perspective opening before them. As Wright explains in his concluding paragraph (paragraph 46), his encounters with the universe of major authors, ranging from Anatole France and Joseph Conrad to Turgenev and Nietzsche, gave him "new ways of looking and seeing . . . of feeling something new, of being affected by something that made the look of the world different." Have you ever been excited, electrified by something you read in print or online? At school or on your own? What was this reading? In what ways has it shaped your current thinking, expanded your understanding of the world? If nothing you've ever read has affected you in this dramatic way, make a list of the characteristics a piece would need to have in order to make an indelible impression on you.

4. Writing as an instrumental medium—producing, for instance, directions, operators' manuals, records of meetings, contracts and other legal documents—forms the foundation of many transactions and professions, including advertising, the law, and many aspects of engineering and computer programming. In contrast, Welty, Alexie, Wright and other creative writers view writing as a means of exploring oneself, one's gender, and one's culture, and as a form of storytelling that provides insight as well as entertainment. Write a brief paper in two parts, perhaps defining a favorite topic (work, love, ethics) or explaining how to do something you enjoy doing. One part should reflect an instrumental approach to the subject; the other should be a narrative disclosing your passion for the subject and/or the process.

SCOTT McCLOUD

Reading the Comics

*Scott McCloud (b. 1960) is a cartoonist (*Zot! *1984). Since the publication of* Understanding Comics: The Invisible Art *in 1993 (itself written as a comic), he has been internationally acknowledged as a leading theorist of comics. His works, notably* Reinventing Comics *(2000) and* Making Comics *(2006), analyze the genre of comics as an artistic and literary form in addition to telling readers how to write, draw, and read comics.*

THE CLOSURE OF *ELECTRONIC* MEDIA IS *CONTINUOUS*, LARGELY *INVOLUNTARY* AND *VIRTUALLY IMPERCEPTIBLE*.

BUT CLOSURE IN **COMICS** IS *FAR* FROM CONTINUOUS AND *ANYTHING* BUT *INVOLUNTARY*!

NOW YOU *DIE*!!

NO!
NO!

EEYAA!!

EVERY ACT COMMITTED TO PAPER BY THE COMICS ARTIST IS *AIDED* AND *ABETTED* BY A *SILENT* ACCOMPLICE.

AN *EQUAL PARTNER IN CRIME* KNOWN AS *THE READER*.

I MAY HAVE DRAWN AN *AXE* BEING *RAISED* IN THIS EXAMPLE, BUT I'M NOT THE ONE WHO LET IT *DROP* OR DECIDED HOW *HARD* THE BLOW, OR *WHO* SCREAMED, OR *WHY*.

NOW YOU *DIE*!!

NO!
NO!

EEYAA!!

THAT, DEAR READER, WAS *YOUR SPECIAL CRIME*, EACH OF YOU COMMITTING IT IN YOUR OWN *STYLE*.

ALL OF YOU *PARTICIPATED* IN THE MURDER. ALL OF YOU *HELD THE AXE* AND *CHOSE YOUR SPOT*.

QUESTIONS FOR DISCUSSION AND WRITING

1. Read the words and images in McCloud's first three panels to explain how he arrives at his definition of comics in the fourth: "Comics **is** closure!" How does the reader participate in making meaning and attainimg closure (panels 5–9)? Look at any of the illustrations in *The Arlington Reader*, such as "The Damm Family in Their Car" (p. 224), "Migrant Mother" (p. 556), or "Education in Open Air" (p. 241), and "read" them to provide a satisfactory interpretation for yourself before examining the accompanying commentaries. Did your reading provide satisfying "closure"? Why or why not?

2. Now examine "Better Signs of Trouble" (p. 27), "Picturing the Past Ten Years" (p. 79), and "Nobody Knows I'm Gay" (p. 148), two diagrams and a photograph that combine words and images. "Read" some of the images without the words. Then reread them with the words. What changes? What new meanings emerge? Without knowing the words, would you have interpreted the visual elements as the visual artists did? Identify some points of discrepancy and show why the interpretations differ.

3. Write a brief analysis of "Nobody Knows I'm Gay" (p. 148). Then erase that message from the T-shirt and put a new message there. It should be witty, ambiguous, and perhaps satiric. Keep a list of your rejected attempts. What did you finally come up with? Now, write a brief analysis of your new message. Did you provide the "closure" that McCloud identifies?

4. Draw a brief cartoon sequence, as McCloud has done, to explain an abstract concept.

JOAN DIDION

On Keeping a Notebook

Born in 1934 and reared on a ranch near Sacramento, California, Didion graduated from the University of California, Berkeley (1956). Winning Vogue's *Prix de Paris writing contest enabled her to start near the top, working in New York as a* Vogue *copywriter and editor for the next eight years. In 1964 she married John Gregory Dunne and moved to Los Angeles, where the couple, both novelists and nonfiction writers, began a long career of collaborating on screenplays until his death in 2003. Among their films are* Panic in Needle Park *(1973) and* A Star Is Born *(1976). Their screenplay for* Up Close and Personal *(1996) took eight years, twenty-seven drafts, and three hundred additional revisions. "We were each the person the other trusted," Didion explains in* The Year of Magical Thinking *(2005), a meditation on "marriage and children and memory" prompted by*

Dunne's death in December 2003 and interwoven with their daughter Quintana's mysterious mortal illness.

Didion's novels, including A Book of Common Prayer (1977) and Democracy (1984), have been praised for their elegant prose and distinctive voice—precise, controlled, and concise. These qualities also characterize her essays, particularly those collected in Slouching Towards Bethlehem (1968) and The White Album (1979). Many are cynical commentaries on the erosion of traditional American pioneer values expressed in strong family and social structures. In "On Keeping a Notebook" (Holiday, 1966), Didion discusses what a notebook means for someone who writes, or wants to—not to provide "an accurate factual record of what I have been doing or thinking" but a way to demonstrate "how it felt to me." Thus the notebook collects an "indiscriminate and erratic assemblage" of facts, names, events, oddities, all filtered through the writer's consciousness and imagination, the "images that shimmer around the edges" (as she explains in "Why I Write," page 60)—"You just lie low and let them develop."

"'That woman Estelle,'" the note reads, "'is partly the reason why George Sharp and I are separated today.' Dirty crepe-de-Chine wrapper, hotel bar, Wilmington RR, 9:45 a.m. August Monday morning."

Since the note is in my notebook, it presumably has some meaning to me. I study it for a long while. At first I have only the most general notion of what I was doing on an August Monday morning in the bar of the hotel across from the Pennsylvania Railroad station in Wilmington, Delaware (waiting for a train? missing one? 1960? 1961? why Wilmington?), but I do remember being there. The woman in the dirty crepe-de-Chine wrapper had come down from her room for a beer, and the bartender had heard before the reason why George Sharp and she were separated today. "Sure," he said, and went on mopping the floor. "You told me." At the other end of the bar is a girl. She is talking, pointedly, not to the man beside her but to a cat lying in the triangle of sunlight cast through the open door. She is wearing a plaid silk dress from Peck & Peck, and the hem is coming down.

Here is what it is: the girl has been on the Eastern Shore, and now she is going back to the city, leaving the man beside her, and all she can see ahead are the viscous summer sidewalks and the 3 a.m. long-distance calls that will make her lie awake and then sleep drugged through all the steaming mornings left in August (1960? 1961?). Because she must go directly from the train to lunch in New York, she wishes that she had a safety pin for the hem of the plaid silk dress, and she also wishes that she could forget about the hem and the lunch and stay in the cool bar that smells of disinfectant and malt and make friends with the woman in the crepe-de-Chine wrapper. She is afflicted by a little self-pity, and she wants to compare Estelles. That is what that was all about.

Why did I write it down? In order to remember, of course, but exactly what was it I wanted to remember? How much of it actually happened? Did any of it?

Why do I keep a notebook at all? It is easy to deceive oneself on all those scores. The impulse to write things down is a peculiarly compulsive one, inexplicable to those who do not share it, useful only accidentally, only secondarily, in the way that any compulsion tries to justify itself. I suppose that it begins or does not begin in the cradle. Although I have felt compelled to write things down since I was five years old, I doubt that my daughter ever will, for she is a singularly blessed and accepting child, delighted with life exactly as life presents itself to her, unafraid to go to sleep and unafraid to wake up. Keepers of private notebooks are a different breed altogether, lonely and resistant rearrangers of things, anxious malcontents, children afflicted apparently at birth with some presentiment of loss.

My first notebook was a Big Five tablet, given to me by my mother with the sensible suggestion that I stop whining and learn to amuse myself by writing down my thoughts. She returned the tablet to me a few years ago; the first entry is an account of a woman who believed herself to be freezing to death in the Arctic night, only to find, when day broke, that she had stumbled onto the Sahara Desert, where she would die of the heat before lunch. I have no idea what turn of a five-year-old's mind could have prompted so insistently "ironic" and exotic a story, but it does reveal a certain predilection for the extreme which has dogged me into adult life; perhaps if I were analytically inclined I would find it a truer story than any I might have told about Donald Johnson's birthday party or the day my cousin Brenda put Kitty Litter in the aquarium.

So the point of my keeping a notebook has never been, nor is it now, to have an accurate factual record of what I have been doing or thinking. That would be a different impulse entirely, an instinct for reality which I sometimes envy but do not possess. At no point have I ever been able successfully to keep a diary; my approach to daily life ranges from the grossly negligent to the merely absent, and on those few occasions when I have tried dutifully to record a day's events, boredom has so overcome me that the results are mysterious at best. What is this business about "shopping, typing piece, dinner with E, depressed"? Shopping for what? Typing what piece? Who is E? Was this "E" depressed, or was I depressed? Who cares?

In fact I have abandoned altogether that kind of pointless entry; instead I tell what some would call lies. "That's simply not true," the members of my family frequently tell me when they come up against my memory of a shared event. "The party was *not* for you, the spider was *not* a black widow, *it wasn't that way at all.*" Very likely they are right, for not only have I always had trouble distinguishing between what happened and what merely might have happened, but I remain unconvinced that the distinction, for my purposes, matters. The cracked crab that I recall having for lunch the day my father came home from Detroit in 1945 must certainly be embroidery, worked into the day's pattern, to lend verisimilitude; I was ten years old and would not now remember the cracked crab. The day's events did not turn on cracked crab. And yet it is precisely that fictitious crab that makes me see the afternoon all over again, a home movie run all too often, the father bearing gifts, the child weeping, an exercise in family love and guilt. Or that is what it was to me. Similarly, perhaps it never did snow that August in Vermont; perhaps there never were flurries in the night wind, and maybe no one else felt the ground hardening and summer already dead even as we pretended to bask in it, but that was how it felt to me, and it might as well have snowed, could have snowed, did snow.

How it felt to me: that is getting closer to the truth about a notebook. I sometimes delude myself about why I keep a notebook, imagine that some thrifty virtue derives from preserving everything observed. See enough and write it down, I tell myself, and then some morning when the world seems drained of wonder, some day when I am only going through the motions of doing what I am supposed to do, which is write—on that bankrupt morning I will simply open my notebook and there it will all be, a forgotten account with accumulated interest, paid passage back to the world out there: dialogue overheard in hotels and elevators and at the hat-check counter in Pavillon (one middle-aged man shows his hat check to another and says, "That's my old football number"); impressions of Bettina Aptheker and Benjamin Sonnenberg and Teddy ("Mr. Acapulco") Stauffer; careful *aperçus* about tennis bums and failed fashion models and Greek shipping heiresses, one of whom taught me a significant lesson (a lesson I could have learned from F. Scott Fitzgerald, but perhaps we all must meet the very rich for ourselves) by asking, when I arrived to interview her in her orchid-filled sitting room on the second day of a paralyzing New York blizzard, whether it was snowing outside.

I imagine, in other words, that the notebook is about other people. But of course it is not. I have no real business with what one stranger said to another at the hat-check counter in Pavillon; in fact I suspect that the line "That's my old football number" touched not my own imagination at all, but merely some memory of something once read, probably "The Eighty-Yard Run." Nor is my concern with a woman in a dirty crepe-de-Chine wrapper in a Wilmington bar. My stake is always, of course, in the unmentioned girl in the plaid silk dress. *Remember what it was to be me:* that is always the point.

It is a difficult point to admit. We are brought up in the ethic that others, any 10 others, all others, are by definition more interesting than ourselves; taught to be diffident, just this side of self-effacing. ("You're the least important person in the room and don't forget it," Jessica Mitford's governess would hiss in her ear on the advent of any social occasion; I copied that into my notebook because it is only recently that I have been able to enter a room without hearing some such phrase in my inner ear.) Only the very young and the very old may recount their dreams at breakfast, dwell upon self, interrupt with memories of beach picnics and favorite Liberty lawn dresses and the rainbow trout in a creek near Colorado Springs. The rest of us are expected, rightly, to affect absorption in other people's favorite dresses, other people's trout.

And so we do. But our notebooks give us away, for however dutifully we record what we see around us, the common denominator of all we see is always, transparently, shamelessly, the implacable "I." We are not talking here about the kind of notebook that is patently for public consumption, a structural conceit for binding together a series of graceful *pensées*; we are talking about something private, about bits of the mind's string too short to use, an indiscriminate and erratic assemblage with meaning only for its maker.

And sometimes even the maker has difficulty with the meaning. There does not seem to be, for example, any point in my knowing for the rest of my life that, during 1964, 720 tons of soot fell on every square mile of New York City, yet there it is in my notebook, labeled "FACT." Nor do I really need to remember that Ambrose Bierce liked to spell Leland Stanford's name "£eland $tanford" or that "smart women almost always wear black in Cuba," a fashion hint without much potential for practical application. And does not the relevance of these notes seem marginal at best?:

> In the basement museum of the Inyo County Courthouse in Independence, California, sign pinned to a mandarin coat: "This MANDARIN COAT was often worn by Mrs. Minnie S. Brooks when giving lectures on her TEAPOT COLLECTION."
> Redhead getting out of car in front of Beverly Wilshire Hotel, chinchilla stole, Vuitton bags with tags reading:
>
> MRS LOU FOX
>
> HOTEL SAHARA
>
> VEGAS

Well, perhaps not entirely marginal. As a matter of fact, Mrs. Minnie S. Brooks and her MANDARIN COAT pull me back into my own childhood, for although I never knew Mrs. Brooks and did not visit Inyo County until I was thirty, I grew up in just such a world, in houses cluttered with Indian relics and bits of gold ore and ambergris and the souvenirs my Aunt Mercy Farnsworth brought back from the Orient. It is a long way from that world to Mrs. Lou Fox's world, where we all live now, and is it not just as well to remember that? Might not Mrs. Minnie S. Brooks help me to remember what I am? Might not Mrs. Lou Fox help me to remember what I am not?

But sometimes the point is harder to discern. What exactly did I have in mind when I noted down that it cost the father of someone I know $650 a month to light the place on the Hudson in which he lived before the Crash? What use was I planning to make of this line by Jimmy Hoffa: "I may have my faults, but being wrong ain't one of them"? And although I think it interesting to know where the girls who travel with the Syndicate have their hair done when they find themselves on the West Coast, will I ever make suitable use of it? Might I not be better off just passing it on to John O'Hara? What is a recipe for sauerkraut doing in my notebook? What kind of magpie keeps this notebook? *"He was born the night the*

Titanic went down." That seems a nice enough line, and I even recall who said it, but is it not really a better line in life than it could ever be in fiction?

But of course that is exactly it: not that I should ever use the line, but that I should remember the woman who said it and the afternoon I heard it. We were on her terrace by the sea, and we were finishing the wine left from lunch, trying to get what sun there was, a California winter sun. The woman whose husband was born the night the *Titanic* went down wanted to rent her house, wanted to go back to her children in Paris. I remember wishing that I could afford the house, which cost $1,000 a month. "Someday you will," she said lazily. "Someday it all comes." There in the sun on her terrace it seemed easy to believe in someday, but later I had a low-grade afternoon hangover and ran over a black snake on the way to the supermarket and was flooded with inexplicable fear when I heard the checkout clerk explaining to the man ahead of me why she was finally divorcing her husband. "He left me no choice," she said over and over as she punched the register. "He has a little seven-month-old baby by her, he left me no choice." I would like to believe that my dread then was for the human condition, but of course it was for me, because I wanted a baby and did not then have one and because I wanted to own the house that cost $1,000 a month to rent and because I had a hangover.

It all comes back. Perhaps it is difficult to see the value in having one's self back in that kind of mood, but I do see it; I think we are well advised to keep on nodding terms with the people we used to be whether we find them attractive company or not. Otherwise they turn up unannounced and surprise us, come hammering on the mind's door at 4 a.m. of a bad night and demand to know who deserted them, who betrayed them, who is going to make amends. We forget all too soon the things we thought we could never forget. We forget the loves and the betrayals alike, forget what we whispered and what we screamed, forget who we were. I have already lost touch with a couple of people I used to be; one of them, a seventeen-year-old, presents little threat, although it would be of some interest to me to know again what it feels like to sit on a river levee drinking vodka-and-orange-juice and listening to Les Paul and Mary Ford and their echoes sing "How High the Moon" on the car radio. (You see I still have the scenes, but I no longer perceive myself among those present, no longer could even improvise the dialogue.) The other one, a twenty-three-year-old, bothers me more. She was always a good deal of trouble, and I suspect she will reappear when I least want to see her, skirts too long, shy to the point of aggravation, always the injured party, full of recriminations and little hurts and stories I do not want to hear again, at once saddening me and angering me with her vulnerability and ignorance, an apparition all the more insistent for being so long banished.

It is a good idea, then, to keep in touch, and I suppose that keeping in touch is what notebooks are all about. And we are all on our own when it comes to keeping those lines open to ourselves: your notebook will never help me, nor mine you. *"So what's new in the whiskey business?"* What could that possibly mean to you? To me it means a blonde in a Pucci bathing suit sitting with a couple of fat men by the pool at the Beverly Hills Hotel. Another man approaches, and they all regard one another in silence for a while. "So what's new in the whiskey business?" one of the fat men finally says by way of welcome, and the blonde stands up, arches one foot and dips it in the pool, looking all the while at the cabaña where Baby Pignatari is talking on the telephone. That is all there is to that, except that several years later I saw the blonde coming out of Saks Fifth Avenue in New York with her California complexion and a voluminous mink coat. In the harsh wind that day she looked old and irrevocably tired to me, and even the skins in the mink coat were not worked the way they were doing them that year, not the way she would have wanted them done, and there is the point of the story. For a while after that I did not like to look in the mirror, and my eyes would skim the newspapers and pick out only the deaths, the cancer victims, the premature coronaries, the suicides, and I stopped riding the Lexington Avenue IRT because I noticed for the first time that all the strangers I had seen for years—the man with the seeing-eye dog, the spinster who read the classified pages every day, the fat girl who always got off with me at Grand Central—looked older than they once had.

It all comes back. Even that recipe for sauerkraut: even that brings it back. I was on Fire Island when I first made that sauerkraut, and it was raining, and we drank a lot of bourbon and ate the sauerkraut and went to bed at ten, and I listened to the rain and the Atlantic and felt safe. I made the sauerkraut again last night and it did not make me feel any safer, but that is, as they say, another story.

CONTEXTS FOR "ON KEEPING A NOTEBOOK"

JOAN DIDION

Why I Write

In "Why I Write," first published in the New York Times Book Review *(1976), Didion confesses that she "stole the title" from George Orwell's manifesto, in which he identifies the writer's purposes as egoistical, historical, aesthetic, and political. Didion's own writings reflect these, as well. In "Why I Write" she concentrates on the aesthetic and the spiritual, trying to make each word and sentence represent precisely each "physical fact" in "the pictures in [her] mind."*

From Joan Didion, "Why I Write," *New York Times Book Review,* December 5, 1976.

Of course I stole the title for this talk from George Orwell. One reason I stole it was that I like the sound of the words: *Why I Write*. There you have three short unambiguous words that share a sound, and the sound they share is this:

I

I

I

In many ways writing is the act of saying *I*, of imposing oneself upon other people, of saying *listen to me, see it my way, change your mind.* It's an aggressive, even a hostile act. You can disguise its aggressiveness all you want with veils of subordinate clauses and qualifiers and tentative subjunctives, with ellipses and evasions — with the whole manner of intimating rather than claiming, of alluding rather than stating — but there's no getting around the fact that setting words on paper is the tactic of a secret bully, an invasion, an imposition of the writer's sensibility on the reader's most private space.

I stole the title not only because the words sounded right but because they seemed to sum up, in a no-nonsense way, all I have to tell you. Like many writers I have only this one "subject," this one "area": the act of writing. I can bring you no reports from any other front. I may have other interests: I am "interested," for example, in marine biology, but I don't flatter myself that you would come out to hear me talk about it. I am not a scholar. I am not in the least an intellectual, which is not to say that when I hear the word "intellectual" I reach for my gun, but only to say that I do not think in abstracts. During the years when I was an undergraduate at Berkeley I tried, with a kind of hopeless late-adolescent energy, to buy some temporary visa into the world of ideas, to forge for myself a mind that could deal with the abstract.

In short I tried to think. I failed. My attention veered inexorably back to the specific, to the tangible, to what was generally considered, by everyone I knew then and for that matter have known since, the peripheral. I would try to contemplate the Hegelian dialectic and would find myself concentrating instead on a flowering pear tree outside my window and the particular way the petals fell on my floor. I would try to read linguistic theory and would find myself wondering instead if the lights were on in the bevatron up the hill. When I say that I was wondering if the lights were on in the bevatron you might immediately suspect, if you deal in ideas at all, that I was registering the bevatron as a political symbol, thinking in shorthand about the military-industrial complex and its role in the university community, but you would be wrong. I was only wondering if the lights were on in the bevatron, and how they looked. A physical fact.

Why have the night lights in the bevatron burned in my mind for twenty years? 5 *What is going on in these pictures in my mind?*

When I talk about pictures in my mind I am talking, quite specifically, about images that shimmer around the edges. There used to be an illustration in every elementary psychology book showing a cat drawn by a patient in varying stages of schizophrenia. This cat had a shimmer around it. You could see the molecular structure breaking down at the very edges of the cat: the cat became the background and the background the cat, everything interacting, exchanging ions. People on hallucinogens describe the same perception of objects. I'm not a schizophrenic, nor do I take hallucinogens, but certain images do shimmer for me. Look hard enough, and you can't miss the shimmer. It's there. You can't think too much about these pictures that shimmer. You just lie low and let them develop. You stay quiet. You don't talk to many people and you keep your nervous system from shorting out and you try to locate the cat in the shimmer, the grammar in the picture.

Just as I meant "shimmer" literally I mean "grammar" literally. Grammar is a piano I play by ear, since I seem to have been out of school the year the rules were mentioned. All I know about grammar is its infinite power. To shift the structure of a sentence alters the meaning of that sentence, as definitely and inflexibly as the position of a camera alters the meaning of the object photographed. Many people know about camera angles now, but not so many know about sentences. The arrangement of the words matters, and the arrangement you want can be found in the picture in your mind. The picture dictates the arrangement. The picture dictates whether this will be a sentence with or without clauses, a sentence that ends hard or a dying-fall sentence, long or short, active or passive. The picture tells you how to arrange the words and the arrangement of the words tells you, or tells me, what's going on in the picture. *Nota bene:*

It tells you.

You don't tell it.

TOM WOLFE

The New Journalism

To use writing as a way to "remember how it was to be me" — *the purpose Didion identifies in* "On Keeping a Notebook" — *inspired the New Journalists of the 1960s. Didion, Truman Capote* (In Cold Blood, *1966), George Plimpton* (Paper Lion, *1966), Hunter Thompson* (Hell's Angels, *1967), Norman Mailer* (Armies of the Night, *1968), and others abandoned traditional* "objective," "voiceless" *reportage and instead immersed themselves in events and in the language people actually spoke. By representing their own physical and emotional experiences of events, the New Journalists produced feature articles that sounded like novels. Tom Wolfe, in such books as* The Electric Kool-Aid Acid Test *(1968), and* The Right Stuff *(1979), revitalized* "objective" *reporting with New Journalism's* "personality, energy, drive, bravura . . . style, in a*

From Tom Wolfe, *The New Journalism*, ed. Tom Wolfe and E. W. Johnson (New York: Harper, 1973).

word." In this excerpt from Wolfe's The New Journalism *(1973), he identifies four novelistic elements of that art form: scene-by-scene construction; fully recorded dialogue; the witnessing of each scene through the eyes of an individual character, whom the journalist interviews; and the inclusion of objects, gestures, and styles through which people express their "status life," or "position in the world."*

If you follow the progress of the New Journalism closely through the 1960s, you see an interesting thing happening. You see journalists learning the techniques of realism—particularly of the sort found in Fielding, Smollett, Balzac, Dickens and Gogol—from scratch. By trial and error, by "instinct" rather than theory, journalists began to discover the devices that gave the realistic novel its unique power, variously known as its "immediacy," its "concrete reality," its "emotional involvement," its "gripping" or "absorbing" quality.

This extraordinary power was derived mainly from just four devices, they discovered. The basic one was scene-by-scene construction, telling the story by moving from scene to scene and resorting as little as possible to sheer historical narrative. Hence the sometimes extraordinary feats of reporting that the new journalists undertook: so that they could actually witness the scenes in other people's lives as they took place—and record the dialogue in full, which was device No. 2. Magazine writers, like the early novelists, learned by trial and error something that has since been demonstrated in academic studies: namely, that realistic dialogue involves the reader more completely than any other single device. It also establishes and defines character more quickly and effectively than any other single device. (Dickens has a way of fixing a character in your mind so that you have the feeling he has described every inch of his appearance—only to go back and discover that he actually took care of the physical description in two or three sentences; the rest he has accomplished with dialogue.) Journalists were working on dialogue of the fullest, most completely revealing sort in the very moment when novelists were cutting back, using dialogue in more and more cryptic, fey and curiously abstract ways.

The third device was the so-called "third-person point of view," the technique of presenting every scene to the reader through the eyes of a particular character, giving the reader the feeling of being inside the character's mind and experiencing the emotional reality of the scene as he experiences it. Journalists had often used the first-person point of view—"I was there"—just as autobiographers, memoirists and novelists had. This is very limiting for the journalist, however, since he can bring the reader inside the mind of only one character—himself—a point of view that often proves irrelevant to the story and irritating to the reader. Yet how could a journalist, writing nonfiction, accurately penetrate the thoughts of another person?

The answer proved to be marvelously simple: interview him about his thoughts and emotions, along with everything else. This was what I had done in *The Electric Kool-Aid Acid Test*, what John Sack did in *M* and what Gay Talese did in *Honor Thy Father*.

The fourth device has always been the least understood. This is the recording of 5
everyday gestures, habits, manners, customs, styles of furniture, clothing, decora-
tion, styles of traveling, eating, keeping house, modes of behaving toward children,
servants, superiors, inferiors, peers, plus the various looks, glances, poses, styles
of walking and other symbolic details that might exist within a scene. Symbolic of
what? Symbolic, generally, of people's *status life*, using that term in the broad sense
of the entire pattern of behavior and possessions through which people express
their position in the world or what they think it is or what they hope it to be. The
recording of such details is not mere embroidery in prose. It lies as close to the center of the power of realism as any other device in literature.

JOAN DIDION

Last Words

*Here Didion describes how, by studying Hemingway's stripped-down sentences, she
learned to style her own. For Didion, as for Hemingway and Orwell (p. 516), words
are "the manifest expression of personal honor."*

> In the late summer of that year we lived in a house in a village that looked
> across the river and the plain to the mountains. In the bed of the river there
> were pebbles and boulders, dry and white in the sun, and the water was clear
> and swiftly moving and blue in the channels. Troops went by the house and
> down the road and the dust they raised powdered the leaves of the trees.
> The trunks of the trees too were dusty and the leaves fell early that year and
> we saw the troops marching along the road and the dust rising and leaves,
> stirred by the breeze, falling and the soldiers marching and afterward the
> road bare and white except for the leaves.

So goes the famous first paragraph of Ernest Hemingway's *A Farewell to Arms*,
which I was moved to reread by the recent announcement that what was said to
be Hemingway's last novel would be published posthumously next year. That
paragraph, which was published in 1929, bears examination: four deceptively
simple sentences, one hundred and twenty-six words, the arrangement of which
remains as mysterious and thrilling to me now as it did when I first read them, at
twelve or thirteen, and imagined that if I studied them closely enough and practiced hard enough I might one day arrange one hundred and twenty-six such
words myself. Only one of the words has three syllables. Twenty-two have two.
The other hundred and three have one. Twenty-four of the words are "the," fifteen are "and." There are four commas. The liturgical cadence of the paragraph

From Joan Didion, "Last Words," *The New Yorker*, November 9, 1998, 74–80.

derives in part from the placement of the commas (their presence in the second and fourth sentences, their absence in the first and third), but also from that repetition of "the" and of "and," creating a rhythm so pronounced that the omission of "the" before the word "leaves" in the fourth sentence ("and we saw the troops marching along the road and the dust rising and leaves, stirred by the breeze, falling") casts exactly what it was meant to cast, a chill, a premonition, a foreshadowing of the story to come, the awareness that the author has already shifted his attention from late summer to a darker season. The power of the paragraph, offering as it does the illusion but not the fact of specificity, derives precisely from this kind of deliberate omission, from the tension of withheld information. In the late summer of *what* year? *What* river, *what* mountains, *what* troops?

JOAN DIDION

Interview (1999)

Joan Didion's writing itself hinges on the main thrust of her writing process: to keep on writing. Like professional writers of poems, plays, fiction, and nonfiction, student writers also need purposes and persistence.

LBF: What advice would you give to beginning writers?

JD: The most important and hardest thing for any writer to learn is the discipline of sitting down and writing even when you have to spend three days writing bad stuff before the fourth day, when you write something better. If you've been away from what you've been working on even for a day and a half, you have to put in those three days of bad writing to get to the fourth, or you lose the thread, you lose the rhythm. When you are a young writer, those three days are so unpleasant that you tend to think, "I'll go away until the mood strikes me." Well, you're out of the mood because you're not sitting there, because you haven't had that period of trying to push through till the fourth day when the rhythm comes.

From Lewis Burke Frumkes, "A Conversation with Joan Didion," *The Writer*, March 1999, 14–15.

KATHERINE ANNE PORTER

You Do Not Create a Style. You Work . . .

Katherine Anne Porter (1890–1981) was born in Indian Creek, Texas. She concealed in later life the poverty that caused her to receive little formal education and to make an early, abusive, and brief marriage. Her writing career began as a journalist during the two years spent in a tuberculosis sanatorium. After recovery, in the 1920s she lived alternately in New York City and Mexico, the site of some of her best essays and short stories collected in Flowering Judas *(1930). Her short novel* Pale Horse, Pale Rider *(1938) was based on her near-fatal bout of influenza in 1919.* Ship of Fools *(1962), Porter's only full-length novel, brought her financial and popular success. This excerpt from a* Paris Review *interview (1963) reveals Porter's understanding that style is integral to the writer, just as symbols are integral to the work.*

INTERVIEWER: You are frequently spoken of as a stylist. Do you think a style can be cultivated, or at least refined?

PORTER: I've been called a stylist until I really could tear my hair out. And I simply don't believe in style. The style is you. Oh, you can cultivate a style, I suppose, if you like. But I should say it remains a cultivated style. It remains artificial and imposed, and I don't think it deceives anyone. A cultivated style would be like a mask. Everybody knows it's a mask, and sooner or later you must show yourself—or at least, you show yourself as someone who could not afford to show himself, and so created something to hide behind. Style is the man, Aristotle said it first, as far as I know, and everybody has said it since, because it is one of those unarguable truths. You do not create a style. You work, and develop yourself; your style is an emanation from your own being. Symbolism is the same way. I never consciously took or adopted a symbol in my life. I certainly did not say, "This blooming tree upon which Judas is supposed to have hanged himself is going to be the center of my story." I named "Flowering Judas" after it was written, because when reading back over it I suddenly saw the whole symbolic plan and pattern of which I was totally unconscious while I was writing. There's a pox of symbolist theory going the rounds these days in American colleges in the writing courses. Miss Mary McCarthy, who is one of the wittiest and most acute and in some ways the worst-tempered woman in American letters, tells about a little girl who came to her with a story. Now Miss McCarthy is an extremely good critic, and she found this to be a good story, and she told the girl that it was—that she considered it a finished work, and that she could with a clear conscience go on to something else. And the little girl said, "But Miss McCarthy, my writing teacher said, 'Yes, it's a good piece of work, but now we must go back and put in the symbols!'" I think that's an amusing story, and it makes my blood run cold.

Katherine Anne Porter, "You Do Not Create a Style. You Work . . . ." Excerpt from *The Paris Review,* Winter–Spring, 1963.

QUESTIONS FOR DISCUSSION AND WRITING

1. Make a list of all the ways you use writing and another list of all the ways people in your household use writing. Include everything from tweets, twitters, and blogs to love letters to legal documents. Compare your lists with those of others in your class. What is distinctive about your lists? What factors do you think might account for the differences in the composition and style of your and your peers' lists?

2. In her 1999 interview, Didion advises beginning writers to learn "the discipline of sitting down and writing" (paragraph 2). What methods help you keep writing even when you write "bad stuff " (paragraph 2)?

3. In "Why I Write," Didion uses repetition to emphasize the "aggressiveness" of the act of writing (paragraph 2). What phrases does she repeat? What is the effect on you as a reader? How do these differ from or resemble the effect she feels as a reader of Hemingway (see "Last Words," p. 64).

4. Observe an ordinary event—people taking seats on a bus, sharing a meal, waiting in an office. Write "just the facts" you see objectively, withholding your attitudes and judgments. Then rewrite the account from your perspective, adding and changing language in order to express your eyewitness experience. What does this exercise suggest about telling the truth and telling lies, one of Didion's major concerns in "On Keeping a Notebook"? How does this revision reflect your personal style?

5. In the excerpt from "The New Journalism" (p. 62), Tom Wolfe explains that some writers use details to let readers know their "*status life*," or "position in the world" (paragraph 5). What details and word choices does Didion use to express her "status life"? What other stylistic gestures do other writers in Chapter 1 use to embody their "status lives"?

6. For what purposes do you revise your writing?

PETER ELBOW

Freewriting

Peter Elbow (b. 1935) grew up in New Jersey and was educated at Williams College, Oxford, Harvard, and Brandeis. Known for his innovative methods of teaching writing, Elbow taught and directed writing programs at MIT, Evergreen State College, SUNY–Stony Brook, and the University of Massachusetts at Amherst, from which he retired in 2000. In 2001 Elbow received an award from the National Council of Teachers of English for his "transforming influence and lasting intellectual contribution to the English profession," derived primarily from his numerous articles and two books that have become contemporary classics, Writing with Power *(1986) and* Writing without Teachers *(Oxford UP 1973), in which "Freewriting" appears.*

This manifesto of "power to the people"—in Elbow's view, writing students, most likely those in Freshman English—liberates students from teachers and grammar books in urging them to listen to their own voices, "the only source of power," a natural sound, texture, and rhythm "that will make a reader listen." To do this, writers have to listen to their own voices—sssssh! Try it.

The most effective way I know to improve your writing is to do freewriting exercises regularly. At least three times a week. They are sometimes called "automatic writing," "babbling," or "jabbering" exercises. The idea is simply to write for ten minutes (later on, perhaps fifteen or twenty). Don't stop for anything. Go quickly without rushing. Never stop to look back, to cross something out, to wonder how to spell something, to wonder what word or thought to use, or to think about what you are doing. If you can't think of a word or a spelling, just use a squiggle or else write, "I can't think of it." Just put down something. The easiest thing is just to put down whatever is in your mind. If you get stuck it's fine to write "I can't think what to say, I can't think what to say" as many times as you want; or to repeat the last word you wrote over and over again; or anything else. The only requirement is that you *never* stop.

What happens to a freewriting exercise is important. It must be a piece of writing which, even if someone reads it, doesn't send any ripples back to you. It is like writing something and putting it in a bottle in the sea. The teacherless class helps your writing by providing maximum feedback. Freewritings help you by providing no feedback at all. When I assign one, I invite the writer to let me read it. But I also tell him to keep it if he prefers. I read it quickly and make no comments at all and I do not speak with him about it. The main thing is that a freewriting must never be evaluated in any way; in fact there must be no discussion or comment at all.

Here is an example of a fairly coherent exercise (sometimes they are very incoherent, which is fine):

> I think I'll write what's on my mind, but the only thing on my mind right now is what to write for ten minutes. I've never done this before and I'm not prepared in any way—the sky is cloudy today, how's that? now I'm afraid I won't be able to think of what to write when I get to the end of the sentence—well, here I am at the end of the sentence—here I am again, again, again, at least I'm still writing—Now I ask is there some reason to be happy that I'm still writing—ah yes! Here comes the question again—What am I getting out of this? What point is there in it? It's almost obscene to always ask it but I seem to question everything that way and I was gonna say something else pertaining to that but I got so busy writing down the first part that I forgot what I was leading into. This is kind of fun oh don't stop writing—cars and trucks speeding by somewhere out the window, pens clittering across peoples' papers. The sky is still cloudy—is it symbolic that I should be mentioning it? Huh? I dunno. Maybe I should try colors, blue,

red, dirty words—wait a minute—no can't do that, orange, yellow, arm tired, green pink violet magenta lavender red brown black green—now that I can't think of any more colors—just about done—relief? maybe.

Freewriting may seem crazy but actually it makes simple sense. Think of the difference between speaking and writing. Writing has the advantage of permitting more editing. But that's its downfall too. Almost everybody interposes a massive and complicated series of editings between the time words start to be born into consciousness and when they finally come off the end of the pencil or typewriter onto the page. This is partly because schooling makes us obsessed with the "mistakes" we make in writing. Many people are constantly thinking about spelling and grammar as they try to write. I am always thinking about the awkwardness, wordiness, and general mushiness of my natural verbal product as I try to write down words.

But it's not just "mistakes" or "bad writing" we edit as we write. We also edit 5 unacceptable thoughts and feelings, as we do in speaking. In writing there is more time to do it so the editing is heavier: when speaking, there's someone right there waiting for a reply and he'll get bored or think we're crazy if we don't come out with *something*. Most of the time in speaking, we settle for the catch-as-catch-can way in which the words tumble out. In writing, however, there's a chance to try to get them right. But the opportunity to get them right is a terrible burden: you can work for two hours trying to get a paragraph "right" and discover it's not right at all. And then give up.

Editing, *in itself*, is not the problem. Editing is usually necessary if we want to end up with something satisfactory. The problem is that editing goes on *at the same time* as producing. The editor is, as it were, constantly looking over the shoulder of the producer and constantly fiddling with what he's doing while he's in the middle of trying to do it. No wonder the producer gets nervous, jumpy, inhibited, and finally can't be coherent. It's an unnecessary burden to try to think of words and also worry at the same time whether they're the right words.

The main thing about freewriting is that it is *nonediting*. It is an exercise in bringing together the process of producing words and putting them down on the page. Practiced regularly, it undoes the ingrained habit of editing at the same time you are trying to produce. It will make writing less blocked because words will come more easily. You will use up more paper, but chew up fewer pencils.

Next time you write, notice how often you stop yourself from writing down something you were going to write down. Or else cross it out after it's written. "Naturally," you say, "it wasn't any good." But think for a moment about the occasions when you spoke well. Seldom was it because you first got the beginning just right. Usually it was a matter of a halting or even garbled beginning, but you kept going and your speech finally became coherent and even powerful. There is a lesson here for writing: trying to get the beginning just right is a formula for failure—and probably a secret tactic to make yourself give up writing. Make some words, whatever they are, and then grab hold of that line and reel in as hard as you can. Afterwards you can throw away lousy beginnings and make new ones. This is the quickest way to get into good writing.

The habit of compulsive, premature editing doesn't just make writing hard. It also makes writing dead. Your voice is damped out by all the interruptions, changes, and hesitations between the consciousness and the page. In your natural way of producing words there is a sound, a texture, a rhythm—a voice—which is the main source of power in your writing. I don't know how it works, but this voice is the force that will make a reader listen to you, the energy that drives the meanings through his thick skull. Maybe you don't *like* your voice; maybe people have made fun of it. But it's the only voice you've got. It's your only source of power. You better get back into it, no matter what you think of it. If you keep writing in it, it may change into something you like better. But if you abandon it, you'll likely never have a voice and never be heard.

Freewritings are vacuums. Gradually you will begin to carry over into your 10 regular writing some of the voice, force, and connectedness that creep into those vacuums.

QUESTIONS FOR DISCUSSION AND WRITING

1. What is freewriting (paragraph 1)? What does Elbow suggest if no ideas come to mind? What differences does he find between the processes of speaking and writing (paragraphs 4 and 5)?

2. Elbow says that "compulsive, premature editing doesn't just make writing hard. It also makes writing dead" (paragraph 9). What does he mean by "editing"? What does he mean by "compulsive, premature editing"? When in the writing process is it appropriate to edit one's work?

3. How, in Elbow's view, does freewriting serve as an antidote to "compulsive, premature editing"? Is he right?

4. In your experience, what other factors might make writing dead? Are these different for your own writing than for "dead" writing you might be required to read? What can you do to bring life to your own writing? To your reading?

5. What does Elbow mean by "voice" (paragraph 9)—a notoriously difficult term to define? Why should it be so hard to define voice when, in good writers as in good speakers, it is as clear and distinctive as a fingerprint?

6. Try freewriting for ten or fifteen minutes a day for a week, following Elbow's suggestions. Experiment by writing in different settings, at different times of the day or night, and, if you wish, in different tones, modes, media. Are any of these writings useful warm-ups for longer pieces—either academic essays or stories—poetry, creative nonfiction? If freewriting works for you, keep it up!

STEPHEN KING

Write or Die

One of the most popular and prolific authors of our time, Stephen King (also writ-ing as Richard Bachman and John Swithen) began writing because he loved read-ing; the range of authors whom he cites as models includes H. P. Lovecraft, Ernest Hemingway, Elmore Leonard, Joyce Carol Oates, Graham Greene, and T. S. Eliot. Born in 1947, King began submitting stories to magazines and collecting rejection slips when he was twelve. He published his first story at age nineteen. Growing up in rural Maine, he helped his mother support the family with a number of tough jobs, including janitor, mill hand, and laundry laborer. After graduating from the University of Maine (B.A., 1970), King taught high school English while work-ing on his extremely popular first novel, Carrie *(1974). A rush of best-sellers fol-lowed:* Salem's Lot *(1975),* The Shining *(1977),* The Stand *(1978),* The Dead Zone *(1979),* Firestarter *(1980), and* Cujo *(1981). After his novella "The Body" (from the collection* Different Seasons, *1982) was turned into the coming-of-age film* Stand by Me, *King's reputation grew beyond his core fans of horror, fantasy, and science fiction. His most recent novels include* Cell *(2006) (cell phone users gone amok),* Under the Dome *(2009) (with overtones of 9/11), and* Ur *(2009)—about the unspeakable unleashed on a Kindle reader (and available only on Kindle).*

King is a compulsive writer, having published, since 1974, over seventy novels in addition to short stories and nonfiction—two books a year, sometimes more, writing through, in, and around major complications in his life, as he explains in On Writing: A Memoir of the Craft *(2000).* On Writing *is part autobiography, part writing manual. "Write or Die," an excerpt from* On Writing, *discusses two key influences on his writing—a guidance counselor at the end of his rope with the young King and a ruthlessly honest newspaper editor.*

Hardly a week after being sprung from detention hall, I was once more invited to step down to the principal's office. I went with a sinking heart, wondering what new shit I'd stepped in.

It wasn't Mr. Higgins who wanted to see me, at least; this time the school guidance counselor had issued the summons. There had been discussions about me, he said, and how to turn my "restless pen" into more constructive channels. He had enquired of John Gould, editor of Lisbon's weekly newspaper, and had discovered Gould had an opening for a sports reporter. While the school couldn't *insist* that I take this job, everyone in the front office felt it would be a good idea. *Do it or die,* the G.C.'s eyes suggested. Maybe that was just paranoia, but even now, almost forty years later, I don't think so.

I groaned inside. I was shut of *Dave's Rag*, almost shut of *The Drum*, and now here was the Lisbon *Weekly Enterprise*. Instead of being haunted by waters, like Norman Maclean in *A River Runs Through It*, I was as a teenager haunted by newspapers. Still, what could I do? I rechecked the look in the guidance counselor's eyes and said I would be delighted to interview for the job.

Gould — not the well-known New England humorist or the novelist who wrote *The Greenleaf Fires* but a relation of both, I think — greeted me warily but with some interest. We would try each other out, he said, if that suited me.

Now that I was away from the administrative offices of Lisbon High, I felt   5 able to muster a little honesty. I told Mr. Gould that I didn't know much about sports. Gould said, "These are games people understand when they're watching them drunk in bars. You'll learn if you try."

He gave me a huge roll of yellow paper on which to type my copy — I think I still have it somewhere — and promised me a wage of half a cent a word. It was the first time someone had promised me wages for writing.

The first two pieces I turned in had to do with a basketball game in which an LHS player broke the school scoring record. One was a straight piece of reporting. The other was a sidebar about Robert Ransom's record-breaking performance. I brought both to Gould the day after the game so he'd have them for Friday, which was when the paper came out. He read the game piece, made two minor corrections, and spiked it. Then he started in on the feature piece with a large black pen.

I took my fair share of English Lit classes in my two remaining years at Lisbon, and my fair share of composition, fiction, and poetry classes in college, but John Gould taught me more than any of them, and in no more than ten minutes. I wish I still had the piece — it deserves to be framed, editorial corrections and all — but I can remember pretty well how it went and how it looked after Gould had combed through it with that black pen of his. Here's an example:

> Last night, in the ~~well-loved~~ gymnasium of Lisbon High School, partisans and Jay Hills fans alike were stunned by an athletic performance unequalled in school history. Bob Ransom, ~~known as "Bullet" Bob for both his size and accuracy,~~ scored thirty-seven points. Yes, you heard me right. ~~Plus~~ he did it with grace, speed . . . and with an odd courtesy as well, committing only two personal fouls in his ~~knight-like~~ quest for a record
> which has eluded Lisbon ~~thinclads~~ players since ~~the years of Korea~~ 1953 . . .

Gould stopped at "the years of Korea" and looked up at me. "What year was the last record made?" he asked.

Luckily, I had my notes. "1953," I said. Gould grunted and went back to work.   10 When he finished marking my copy in the manner indicated above, he looked up and saw something on my face. I think he must have mistaken it for horror. It wasn't; it was pure revelation. Why, I wondered, didn't English teachers ever do this? It was like the Visible Man Old Raw Diehl had on his desk in the biology room.

"I only took out the bad parts, you know," Gould said. "Most of it's pretty good."

"I know," I said, meaning both things: yes, most of it was good—okay anyway, serviceable—and yes, he had only taken out the bad parts. "I won't do it again."

He laughed. "If that's true, you'll never have to work for a living. You can do this instead. Do I have to explain any of these marks?"

"No," I said.

"When you write a story, you're telling yourself the story," he said. "When you rewrite, your main job is taking out all the things that are *not* the story."   15

Gould said something else that was interesting on the day I turned in my first two pieces: write with the door closed, rewrite with the door open. Your stuff starts out being just for you, in other words, but then it goes out. Once you know what the story is and get it right—as right as you can, anyway—it belongs to anyone who wants to read it. Or criticize it. If you're very lucky (this is my idea, not John Gould's, but I believe he would have subscribed to the notion), more will want to do the former than the latter. . . .

ELIE WIESEL

Why I Write: Making No Become Yes

Elie Wiesel devotes his life to serving as the world's conscience of the Holocaust. He was born in 1929 in Sighet, Hungary, "which no longer exists except in the memory of those it expelled." During World War II, he survived harrowing experiences in the concentration camps of Auschwitz and Buchenwald. Members of his family were killed there, among the six million Jews systematically exterminated in Europe. As a teenager, he was liberated from Buchenwald in 1945 and sent to Paris, where he studied philosophy before immigrating to New York in 1956. Wiesel has devoted his life to writing over fifty-seven books of fiction, nonfiction, poetry, and drama on the Holocaust theme, including Night *(1961),* The Accident *(1962),* The Trial of God *(1978),* All Rivers Run to the Sea *(1995), and* A Mad Desire to Dance *(2009). As one critic writes, in Wiesel's writing, "the Holocaust looms as the shadow, the central but unspoken mystery in the life of his protagonists. Even pre-Holocaust events are seen as warnings of impending doom." Wiesel's literary and humanitarian efforts have been acknowledged with a host of awards worldwide, including the Nobel Peace Prize in 1986.*

On receiving the Congressional Gold Medal (1984), Wiesel explained his philosophy of writing: "I have learned that suffering confers no privileges: it depends on what one does with it. That is why survivors have tried to teach their contemporaries

how to build on ruins; how to invent hope in a world that offers none; how to pro-
claim faith to a generation that has seen it shamed and mutilated." He elaborates on
this theme in "Why I Write: Making No Become Yes," an essay originally published
in the New York Times Book Review *(April 14, 1986).*

Why do I write?

Perhaps in order not to go mad. Or, on the contrary, to touch the bottom of madness. Like Samuel Beckett, the survivor expresses himself "en désespoir de cause"—out of desperation.

Speaking of the solitude of the survivor, the great Yiddish and Hebrew poet and thinker Aaron Zeitlin addresses those—his father, his brother, his friends—who have died and left him: "You have abandoned me," he says to them. "You are together, without me. I am here. Alone. And I make words."

So do I, just like him. I also say words, write words, reluctantly.

There are easier occupations, far more pleasant ones. But for the survivor, writ-   5
ing is not a profession, but an occupation, a duty. Camus calls it "an honor." As he puts it: "I entered literature through worship." Other writers have said they did so through anger, through love. Speaking for myself, I would say—through silence.

It was by seeking, by probing silence that I began to discover the perils and power of the word. I never intended to be a philosopher, or a theologian. The only role I sought was that of witness. I believed that, having survived by chance, I was duty-bound to give meaning to my survival, to justify each moment of my life. I knew the story had to be told. Not to transmit an experience is to betray it. This is what Jewish tradition teaches us. But how to do this? "When Israel is in exile, so is the word," says the Zohar. The word has deserted the meaning it was intended to convey—impossible to make them coincide. The displacement, the shift, is irrevocable.

This was never more true than right after the upheaval. We all knew that we could never, never say what had to be said, that we could never express in words, coherent, intelligible words, our experience of madness on an absolute scale. The walk through flaming night, the silence before and after the selection, the monotonous praying of the condemned, the Kaddish of the dying, the fear and hunger of the sick, the shame and suffering, the haunted eyes, the demented stares. I thought that I would never be able to speak of them. All words seemed inadequate, worn, foolish, lifeless, whereas I wanted them to be searing.

Where was I to discover a fresh vocabulary, a primeval language? The language of night was not human, it was primitive, almost animal—hoarse shouting, screams, muffled moaning, savage howling, the sound of beating. A brute strikes out wildly, a body falls. An officer raises his arm and a whole community walks toward a common grave. A soldier shrugs his shoulders, and a thousand families are torn apart, to be reunited only by death. This was the concentration camp language. It negated all other language and took its place. Rather than a link, it became a wall. Could it be surmounted? Could the reader be brought to the other side? I knew the answer was negative, and yet I knew that "no" had to become "yes." It was the last wish of the dead.

The fear of forgetting remains the main obsession of all those who have passed through the universe of the damned. The enemy counted on people's incredulity and forgetfulness. How could one foil this plot? And if memory grew hollow, empty of substance, what would happen to all we had accumulated along the way? Remember, said the father to his son, and the son to his friend. Gather the names, the faces, the tears. We had all taken an oath: "If, by some miracle, I emerge alive, I will devote my life to testifying on behalf of those whose shadow will fall on mine forever and ever."

That is why I write certain things rather than others—to remain faithful.   10

Of course, there are times of doubt for the survivor, times when one gives in to weakness, or longs for comfort. I hear a voice within me telling me to stop mourning the past. I too want to sing of love and of its magic. I too want to celebrate the sun, and the dawn that heralds the sun. I would like to shout, and shout loudly: "Listen, listen well! I too am capable of victory, do you hear? I too am open to laughter and joy! I want to stride, head high, my face unguarded, without having to point to the ashes over there on the horizon, without having to tamper with facts to hide their tragic ugliness. For a man born blind, God himself is blind, but look, I see, I am not blind." One feels like shouting this, but the shout changes to a murmur. One must make a choice; one must remain faithful. A big word, I know. Nevertheless, I use it, it suits me. Having written the things I have written, I feel I can afford no longer to play with words. If I say that the writer in me wants to remain loyal, it is because it is true. This sentiment moves all survivors; they owe nothing to anyone, but everything to the dead.

I owe them my roots and my memory. I am duty-bound to serve as their emissary, transmitting the history of their disappearance, even if it disturbs, even if it brings pain. Not to do so would be to betray them, and thus myself. And since I am incapable of communicating their cry by shouting, I simply look at them, I see them and write.

While writing, I question them as I question myself. I believe I have said it before, elsewhere. I write to understand as much as to be understood. Will I succeed one day? Wherever one starts, one reaches darkness. God? He remains the God of darkness. Man? The source of darkness. The killers' derision, their victims' tears, the onlookers' indifference, their complicity and complacency—the divine role in all that I do not understand. A million children massacred—I shall never understand.

Jewish children—they haunt my writings. I see them again and again. I shall always see them. Hounded, humiliated, bent like the old men who surround them as though to protect them, unable to do so. They are thirsty, the children, and there is no one to give them water. They are hungry, but there is no one to give them a crust of bread. They are afraid, and there is no one to reassure them.

They walk in the middle of the road, like vagabonds. They are on the way to   15
the station, and they will never return. In sealed cars, without air or food, they

travel toward another world. They guess where they are going, they know it, and they keep silent. Tense, thoughtful, they listen to the wind, the call of death in the distance.

All these children, these old people, I see them. I never stop seeing them. I belong to them.

But they, to whom do they belong?

People tend to think that a murderer weakens when facing a child. The child reawakens the killer's lost humanity. The killer can no longer kill the child before him, the child inside him.

But with us it happened differently. Our Jewish children had no effect upon the killers. Nor upon the world. Nor upon God.

I think of them. I think of their childhood. Their childhood is a small Jewish 20 town, and this town is no more. They frighten me; they reflect an image of myself, one that I pursue and run from at the same time—the image of a Jewish adolescent who knew no fear, except the fear of God, whose faith was whole, comforting, and not marked by anxiety.

No, I do not understand. And if I write, it is to warn the reader that he will not understand either. "You will not understand, you will never understand," were the words heard everywhere during the reign of night. I can only echo them. You, who never lived under a sky of blood, will never know what it was like. Even if you read all the books ever written, even if you listen to all the testimonies ever given, you will remain on this side of the wall, you will view the agony and death of a people from afar, through the screen of a memory that is not your own.

An admission of impotence and guilt? I do not know. All I know is that Treblinka and Auschwitz cannot be told. And yet I have tried. God knows I have tried.

Have I attempted too much or not enough? Among some twenty-five volumes, only three or four penetrate the phantasmagoric realm of the dead. In my other books, through my other books, I have tried to follow other roads. For it is dangerous to linger among the dead, they hold on to you and you run the risk of speaking only to them. And so I have forced myself to turn away from them and study other periods, explore other destinies and teach other tales—the Bible and the Talmud, Hasidism and its fervor, the shtetl and its songs, Jerusalem and its echoes, the Russian Jews and their anguish, their awakening, their courage. At times, it has seemed to me that I was speaking of other things with the sole purpose of keeping the essential—the personal experience—unspoken. At times I have wondered: And what if I was wrong? Perhaps I should not have heeded my own advice and stayed in my own world with the dead.

But then, I have not forgotten the dead. They have their rightful place even in the works about the Hasidic capitals Ruzhany and Korets, and Jerusalem. Even in my biblical and Midrashic tales, I pursue their presence, mute and motionless. The presence of the dead then beckons in such tangible ways that it affects even the most removed characters. Thus they appear on Mount Moriah, where Abraham is about to sacrifice his son, a burnt offering to their common God. They appear on Mount Nebo, where Moses enters solitude and death. They appear in

Hasidic and Talmudic legends in which victims forever need defending against forces that would crush them. Technically, so to speak, they are of course elsewhere, in time and space, but on a deeper, truer plane, the dead are part of every story, of every scene.

"But what is the connection?" you will ask. Believe me, there is one. After 25 Auschwitz everything brings us back to Auschwitz. When I speak of Abraham, Isaac and Jacob, when I invoke Rabbi Yohanan ben Zakkai and Rabbi Akiba, it is the better to understand them in the light of Auschwitz. As for the Maggid of Mezeritch and his disciples, it is in order to encounter the followers of their followers that I reconstruct their spellbound, spellbinding universe. I like to imagine them alive, exuberant, celebrating life and hope. Their happiness is as necessary to me as it was once to themselves.

And yet—how did they manage to keep their faith intact? How did they manage to sing as they went to meet the Angel of Death? I know Hasidim who never vacillated—I respect their strength. I know others who chose rebellion, protest, rage—I respect their courage. For there comes a time when only those who do not believe in God will not cry out to him in wrath and anguish.

Do not judge either group. Even the heroes perished as martyrs, even the martyrs died as heroes. Who would dare oppose knives to prayers? The faith of some matters as much as the strength of others. It is not ours to judge, it is only ours to tell the tale.

But where is one to begin? Whom is one to include? One meets a Hasid in all my novels. And a child. And an old man. And a beggar. And a madman. They are all part of my inner landscape. The reason why? Pursued and persecuted by the killers, I offer them shelter. The enemy wanted to create a society purged of their presence, and I have brought some of them back. The world denied them, repudiated them, so I let them live at least within the feverish dreams of my characters.

It is for them that I write, and yet the survivor may experience remorse. He has tried to bear witness; it was all in vain.

After the liberation, we had illusions. We were convinced that a new world 30 would be built upon the ruins of Europe. A new civilization would see the light. No more wars, no more hate, no more intolerance, no fanaticism. And all this because the witnesses would speak. And speak they did, to no avail.

They will continue, for they cannot do otherwise. When man, in his grief, falls silent, Goethe says, then God gives him the strength to sing his sorrows. From that moment on, he may no longer choose not to sing, whether his song is heard or not. What matters is to struggle against silence with words, or through another form of silence. What matters is to gather a smile here and there, a tear here and there, a word here and there, and thus justify the faith placed in you, a long time ago, by so many victims.

Why do I write? To wrench those victims from oblivion. To help the dead vanquish death.

Translated from the French by Rosette C Lamont.

QUESTIONS FOR DISCUSSION AND WRITING

1. Why do you suppose King initially regarded writing for a newspaper as a punishment rather than an opportunity?

2. How does King's reproduction of Gould's editing illustrate his advice to the young writer? Explain Gould's distinction between writing "with the door closed" and rewriting "with the door open" (paragraph 16). Why are both important?

3. Wiesel says, "The only role I sought [as a writer] was that of witness" (paragraph 6). What does he mean by "witness"? Could any—or all—of the other writers in this book be considered "witnesses" to their beliefs and values? Explain your answer with references to the writers' works. In what ways does writing as a witness require the reader to "open the door," as King says (paragraph 16)?

4. What does Wiesel mean by "[n]ot to transmit an experience is to betray it" (paragraph 6)? Why is it important to twenty-first-century readers that the experience of the Holocaust, which occurred over seventy years ago, be kept fresh in memory? What does Wiesel expect his readers to do with this knowledge?

5. Pick a cultural, social, or political issue that you feel profoundly invested in, and then write an essay in which you play the role of "witness," explaining why you think this issue should be kept alive and treated seriously. Write it first for yourself—"with the door shut," as King would say. Then, open that door. Think of classmates or other people you know who aren't particularly invested in this issue, and write your essay to them, seeking to change their minds and perhaps move them to action. Discuss the subject with them first, in order to determine the points to emphasize in your argument.

6. In "On Keeping a Notebook" (p. 54) Joan Didion asserts that the "impulse to write things down is a peculiarly compulsive one" (paragraph 4). Although a compulsion could be seen as a type of aberrant behavior, Wiesel (who as of 2009 had written fifty-seven books and scores of speeches and articles) uses writing to bear moral witness, over and over, to remind the world to behave in a moral way, with justice and compassion. A quick Internet search will reveal that Stephen King (p. 71) is likewise a compulsive author, providing entertainment, social commentary, and food for thought for millions. Comment on the connections among compulsivity, creativity, and commitment of Wiesel and King. Are these essentially positive connections?

7. Wiesel and King write all the time, in and out of disaster, displacement, devastation, and in happier times, as well. Have you become a compulsive writer on social media—Twitter, Facebook, e-mail, and/or a blog? If so, with what consequences? Have these been as productive for you as they have been for Wiesel and King? If not, what can you do to transform the negatives into positives? Write your own essay in response to Wiesel's "Why I Write" or King's "Write or Die."

PHILLIP NIEMEYER

Picturing the Past 10 Years

	2000	2001	2002	2003	2004	2005	2006	2007	2008	2009
IT!	Florida Recount	9/11	Flag Pins	Bring 'em on. (Iraq)	Abu Ghraib	Katrina	Watching TV on Computers	Baby Boom	The Election	The Economy
NEWISH	Tiniest Phone	Airport Security	Guantánamo	Friendster / MySpace	Wiretaps	Self-Portraits	Tsunami	Rock Bands	Moms on Facebook	Iran on Twitter
BUSINESS	Rolling Blackouts	Dot-Com Crash	$650 / 1BR, A/C, WIFI, W/D, RR, NO-FEE, COZY (Craigslist)	Credit-Default Swaps	GOOG 85.00 (Google I.P.O.)	Blackwater	¥ China	TRP this HOUSE (Housing Boom)	PLEASE BUY THIS HOUSE (Foreclosures)	Stimulus
FEAR	More Is Not Enough	Anthrax	Snipers	Everything	SEVERE HIGH ELEVATED GUARDED LOW (It's Too Late)	I.E.D.'s	H5N1 (Avian Flu)	$322\frac{9}{10}$ (Peak Oil)	Credit Freeze	H1N1 (Swine Flu)
MAVERICK	John McCain	NO (Russ Feingold)	Al Jazeera	We're ashamed the president... is from Texas (Dixie Chicks)	AIR AMERICA (Al Franken)	George Bush doesn't care about black people. (Kanye West)	Sincere Beards	T. Boone Pickens	REVOLUTION (Ron Paul)	Goldman Sachs
CHAMPION	Shaq & Kobe	Dale Earnhardt Sr.	Patriots	Steroids	Mia Hamm	Lance Armstrong	Barbaro	Tiger Woods	Michael Phelps	27 (Yankees, Again)
CULTURE	Pokémon	Wikipedia! *According to Wikipedia	"American Idol"	HEY YA! (OutKast)	Camera Phones	M.M.O.R.P.G.'s	yummo! (Rachael Ray)	Writers' Strike	The Art Market	Lady Gaga
COUPLE	Carrie & Mr. Big	Harry Potter & Voldemort	Europe & Money	★☆☆☆☆ Gigli (Bennifer)	Demi Moore & Ashton Kutcher	Tom Cruise & Oprah Winfrey	I can't quit you. (Heath Ledger & Jake Gyllenhaal)	Brangelina & Family	Federer & Nadal	+8÷2 (Not Jon & Kate)
FAD	Going Viral	Oprah's Book Club	Collagen	Tuscany	Brownie & BigTime & Rummy & BoyGenius & Condi. (Nicknames)	Movies in the Mail	Ironic Mustaches	Crocs	I'm NOT A Plastic Bag (Canvas Totes)	V V (Vampires)
LOGO	Lattes	FDNY NYPD (First Responders)	BADA BING! (HBO)	O (Oprah)	W04 (Dubya)	CNN FOX NEWS (News vs. News)	Apple	LUKOIL (Russian Moguls)	Obama	citi
NOUN	glitch	news cycle	freedom fries	spider hole	friendly fire	truthiness	chatter	surge	hope	Auto-Tune
VERB	I.M.	outsource	download	punk'd	Swift boat	Google	text	blog	go rogue	crowd-source
	2000	2001	2002	2003	2004	2005	2006	2007	2008	2009

QUESTIONS FOR DISCUSSION AND WRITING

1. Which references in this chart do you understand immediately? Which require more thought? Which escape you completely (after all, how old were you eight or ten years ago)? Is it only your age that causes some references to mean more than others? What else strongly influences your cultural memory?

2. Show this chart to your parents or, better yet, your grandparents. Which references do they understand? Have to think about? Miss entirely? Chart the respective generational responses and write an essay that summarizes, then interprets, your findings.

3. Construct a chart of your own for another year or two—say 2010 or 2011, and write a commentary justifying (and if necessary explaining) why you've included those particular entries.

MARJORIE AGOSÍN

Always Living in Spanish

Writer and human rights activist Marjorie Agosín was born in 1955 into a Jewish family that resided in Chile, having left Europe under the shadow of the Holocaust. At the age of sixteen, Agosín was uprooted from her girlhood in Santiago de Chile when the Socialist government of Salvador Allende was overthrown. Her family immigrated to the United States, where she attended the University of Georgia (B.A., 1976) and earned advanced degrees at Indiana University (M.A., 1977; Ph.D., 1982). Currently a professor of Spanish at Wellesley, Agosín is the author of several volumes of poetry and autobiography, including Dear Anne Frank *(English edition, 1998). Her literary criticism and nonfiction are about women and other groups targeted for discrimination in third-world countries, including* Invisible Dreamer: Memory, Judaism, and Human Rights *(2001). Among her numerous literary honors is the Latino Literature Prize for Poetry (1995) for* Toward the Splendid City *(1994).*

"Always Living in Spanish" explores the link between language and identity, from the personal to the ethnic to the geographic versions of the self. Each of Agosín's languages evokes a different set of images and feelings; writing in her native Spanish connects her to her formative experiences.

In the evenings in the northern hemisphere, I repeat the ancient ritual that I observed as a child in the southern hemisphere: going out while the night is still warm and trying to recognize the stars as it begins to grow dark silently. In the sky of my country, Chile, that long and wide stretch of land that the poets blessed and dictators abused, I could easily name the stars: the three Marias, the Southern Cross, and the three Lilies, names of beloved and courageous women.

But here in the United States, where I have lived since I was a young girl, the solitude of exile makes me feel that so little is mine, that not even the sky has the same constellations, the trees and the fauna the same names or sounds, or the rubbish the same smell. How does one recover the familiar? How does one name the unfamiliar? How can one be another or live in a foreign language? These are the dilemmas of one who writes in Spanish and lives in translation.

Since my earliest childhood in Chile I lived with the tempos and the melodies of a multiplicity of tongues: German, Yiddish, Russian, Turkish, and many

Latin songs. Because everyone was from somewhere else, my relatives laughed, sang, and fought in a Babylon of languages. Spanish was reserved for matters of extreme seriousness, for commercial transactions, or for illnesses, but everyone's mother tongue was always associated with the memory of spaces inhabited in the past: the shtetl, the flowering and vast Vienna avenues, the minarets of Turkey, and the Ladino whispers of Toledo. When my paternal grandmother sang old songs in Turkish, her voice and body assumed the passion of one who was there in the city of Istanbul, gazing by turns toward the west and the east.

Destiny and the always ambiguous nature of history continued my family's enforced migration, and because of it I, too, became one who had to live and speak in translation. The disappearances, torture, and clandestine deaths in my country in the early seventies drove us to the United States, that other America that looked with suspicion at those who did not speak English and especially those who came from the supposedly uncivilized regions of Latin America. I had left a dangerous place that was my home, only to arrive in a dangerous place that was not: a high school in the small town of Athens, Georgia, where my poor English and my accent were the cause of ridicule and insult. The only way I could recover my usurped country and my Chilean childhood was by continuing to write in Spanish, the same way my grandparents had sung in their own tongues in diasporic sites.

The new and learned English language did not fit with the visceral emotions 5 and themes that my poetry contained, but by writing in Spanish I could recover fragrances, spoken rhythms, and the passion of my own identity. Daily I felt the need to translate myself for the strangers living all around me, to tell them why we were in Georgia, why we are different, why we had fled, why my accent was so thick, and why I did not look Hispanic. Only at night, writing poems in Spanish, could I return to my senses, and soothe my own sorrow over what I had left behind.

This is how I became a Chilean poet who wrote in Spanish and lived in the southern United States. And then, one day, a poem of mine was translated and published in the English language. Finally, for the first time since I had left Chile, I felt I didn't have to explain myself. My poem, expressed in another language, spoke for itself . . . and for me.

Sometimes the austere sounds of English help me bear the solitude of knowing that I am foreign and so far away from those about whom I write. I must admit I would like more opportunities to read in Spanish to people whose language and culture is also mine, to join in our common heritage and in the feast of our sounds. I would also like readers of English to understand the beauty of the spoken word in Spanish, that constant flow of oxytonic and paroxytonic syllables (*Vérde qué té quiéro vérde*),[1] the joy of writing—of dancing—in another

---

[1]Oxytonic places the main stress on a word's last or only syllable. Paroxytonic stress occurs on a word's next to last syllable. *Vérde qué té quiéro vérde* "Green how I want you green" is the opening line of a poem by Federico García Lorca that illustrates this stress pattern.

language. I believe that many exiles share the unresolvable torment of not being able to live in the language of their childhood.

I miss that undulating and sensuous language of mine, those baroque descriptions, the sense of being and feeling that Spanish gives me. It is perhaps for this reason that I have chosen and will always choose to write in Spanish. Nothing else from my childhood world remains. My country seems to be frozen in gestures of silence and oblivion. My relatives have died, and I have grown up not knowing a young generation of cousins and nieces and nephews. Many of my friends were disappeared, others were tortured, and the most fortunate, like me, became guardians of memory. For us, to write in Spanish is to always be in active pursuit of memory. I seek to recapture a world lost to me on that sorrowful afternoon when the blue electric sky and the Andean cordillera bade me farewell. On that, my last Chilean day, I carried under my arm my innocence recorded in a little blue notebook I kept even then. Gradually that diary filled with memoranda, poems written in free verse, descriptions of dreams and of the thresholds of my house surrounded by cherry trees and gardenias. To write in Spanish is for me a gesture of survival. And because of translation, my memory has now become a part of the memory of many others.

Translators are not traitors, as the proverb says, but rather splendid friends in this great human community of language.

QUESTIONS FOR DISCUSSION AND WRITING

1. How many sources of identity does Agosín mention in this essay? Consider dimensions of the self such as languages, locations, time periods, and ethnicity. Do you think her struggle to reconnect or stay connected to these parts of herself is atypical, or does everyone experience this struggle? Give examples to support your answers.

2. This essay expresses Agosín's feelings about her native Spanish and her feelings about English. What is the main difference between the two languages for her? What different feelings and ideas does each language evoke? Can Agosín's writing in English — for an English-speaking audience — adequately convey her feelings and thoughts about writing in Spanish? Or can only Spanish do justice to this subject? What does Agosín say to evoke a sympathetic understanding from even monolingual readers?

3. If you speak a second language — fluently or as a beginner — have you noticed that you associate different feelings, thoughts, or parts of your identity with that language? Write about the sensual, geographic, ethnic, or life-history aspects of your "first" compared with your "second" language. Alternatively, you could discuss within your family or circle of friends how various forms of language such as slang, sarcasm, or acronyms (used in text messaging) shape and express identity.

4. Write about the problem of being expected to function in a culture different from the one you grew up in — one of the central issues in Agosín's essay. Discuss how you, or someone you know, dealt with being placed in an unfamiliar environment — perhaps through emigration or a move, extended travel, a new job, or study abroad — where differences of language or culture presented a major challenge. In what ways did this experience compare to the experiences that Agosín describes, such as longing for the familiar or trying to reconnect with one's past? Draw some general conclusions about the way people cope with living "'in translation'" (paragraph 2).

DAVID BROWN

Science Reporting and Evidence-Based Journalism

David Brown (born 1951 in Framingham, Massachusetts) graduated from Amherst (B.A., 1973) and the Medical College of Pennsylvania (M.D., 1987). While in medical school, he occasionally contributed to National Public Radio and won the 1987 William Carlos Williams Poetry Competition. In 1991, after a three-year residency at the University of Maryland Hospital, he became a staff writer on medicine and science for the Washington Post, *on topics ranging from the AIDS epidemic to health care. In his 2008 remarks at the University of Iowa Project on Rhetoric of Inquiry, "Science Reporting and Evidence-Based Journalism" (reprinted here), Brown reflects on the possibilities and problems of science journalism as well as its reliance on factual evidence as support.*

What does science journalism have that makes it a model for good journalism as a whole? Quite a few things, I think. But the most important thing it has is evidence. Science is built on speculative ideas — hypotheses — and the evidence that either confirms them, challenges them, or occasionally overthrows them.

Scientific evidence in a form that is explicable, even if boiled down, should be a part of almost every story about a discovery, a new insight, a revised theory, a more precise diagnostic strategy, a better therapy. Science reporting, in fact, should be the model for evidence-based journalism.

So what is evidence? For starters, evidence usually involves numbers. Science requires measuring things, and numbers are the language of measurement. So, numbers in a news story are important. But they alone don't constitute evidence. Too often, numbers in news stories are used to garland and decorate what is treated as the real news — namely, someone telling you how great something is, what it all means, and all the ways it's going to change our world. But of course, that isn't evidence.

In science, there is a natural tension between evidence and opinion, and evidence always wins. Unfortunately, in a lot of science reporting, as in a lot of reporting in general, that isn't the case. Take a look sometime at a science story in the daily news. Say a story about the effectiveness of a new cancer treatment, or the discovery of a skull that may revise our view of human history, or environmental changes suggesting a faster rate of global warming, or experiments showing that bisphenol A damages health.

Read the story. Then notice how much space is devoted to describing the [5] evidence for what is purportedly new in this news, and how much is devoted to someone telling you what to think about it. Ask yourself whether there is enough information in the story to permit you to reach your *own* opinion about its newsworthiness.

I think you'll be surprised. If there isn't enough information to give you, the reader, a fighting chance to decide for yourself whether something is important, then somebody isn't doing his or her job.

The reporter has two tasks. (And I will say parenthetically this is all reporters; it's just a clearer assignment when the subject is science.) The first is to provide enough information so a reader can judge the strength of a claim. The second is to describe how the news fits into what's already known about the subject. How much of a breakthrough is this new study that found that statin drugs can reverse atherosclerosis? How plausible are these descriptions of Gulf War syndrome the Senate committee is hearing? Is the so-called ABC (abstinence, be faithful, use condoms) approach to AIDS prevention in Africa a success or a failure? Are standardized tests changing public school curriculums, as this critic claims?

All of these are questions for which there is an "evidence base" that has a life quite apart from the Yes or No answers people may offer when the question is put to them. Any story that wants to engage these questions—and thousands more like them—needs to seek out that evidence and present at least a bit of it to the reader.

This seems like a tall order—and it is. That's because it isn't always easy to boil down research findings to a few numbers that capture the essence of what happened in an experiment or a study. And it isn't always possible to find out how a new piece of knowledge fits into what's already known about a subject. Sometimes it just can't be done, or can't be done by deadline.

On the first task—knowing how much to boil something down without [10] making the final dish indigestible—that's a big part of the fun of being a science reporter. And on the second task, we have technology on our side. Thanks to the Internet and e-mail, search engines like PubMed and Google Scholar, and data bases like the Cochrane Library, we can round up information faster and more systematically than anyone could have imagined even 10 years ago.

When I say this is a tall order I don't mean to imply nobody is doing it. There is lots of great daily reporting on the flood of scientific knowledge and discovery that daily washes over us. But as a rule, this "evidence-based paradigm" hasn't caught on in the reporting of scientific and technical subjects to the extent one might hope.

I have a few theories why it hasn't. First, the people who are in charge of American journalism tend to be intimidated by science and scientists. They are often unwilling to bring their own natural (and legendary) skepticism to scientific topics. Few had anything other than the minimum number of science courses required in college. They tend to think of science as a realm of priestly knowledge where the thinking, logic and judgment of ordinary people fear to tread. This last misconception is particularly unfortunate, in my opinion. And I hasten to add, in Albert Einstein's, as well.

Einstein said, in 1936, "The whole of science is nothing more than a refinement of everyday thinking." He probably should have added, "except for quantum mechanics." Nevertheless, I think this is a profound, and profoundly democratic, assertion. Every executive editor should have it taped to his or her computer.

Second, most editors—and here I'm talking about managing editors and executive editors, not science editors—don't understand that science is iterative and conditional. It moves in small steps and those steps are sometimes in the wrong direction. Like most Americans, editors were weaned on the notion that American science (and especially medicine) is one breakthrough after another, interrupted by the occasional scandalous failure. Furthermore, there is the notion that things are either right or wrong. Look at how the word "flawed" is thrown around by the press. It's wielded like some sort of wand that freezes a piece of research or a report in its tracks. Someone asserts a study is "flawed" and the assumption is the conversation is over. In science, though, calling something "flawed" says nothing. It starts the conversation, not ends it.

How is the study flawed? Do the flaws invalidate it? Do the flaws give it less   15 credibility even though it retains some? Is there any way to compensate for the flaws? Every piece of scientific research, like every human being, has some flaw if you look hard enough. The question is: How serious is the flaw, and what is its effect?

Third, the press tends to be very interested in what authority figures say about an event in the news. This, I think, is an important and overlooked fact. It explains why many editors, faced with a scientific assertion in the news, are more likely to say to a reporter: "Find out what other people think about this" than to ask: "Well, what does the evidence say about this claim?"

In politics, diplomacy, popular culture, and even economics—the subjects that editors are most conversant with—what authority figures have to say actually *is* evidence much of the time. What Larry Sabato of the University of Virginia says about the latest doings of the presidential candidates is evidence. His opinion—or, more precisely, the press's opinion of his opinion—can change minds and alter the perception of things. The same is true, although to a lesser extent, of what the chairman of the Federal Reserve says about the economy. In politics and economics, a changed perception can mean a changed reality.

But that's not true with science and medicine. Until about 20 years ago, pep-tic ulcers were a disease of the high-strung, the impatient, the worried. And when they weren't caused by stress, they were caused by spicy food. This is what every authority said for a century. But it turns out 90 percent of ulcers are caused by a bacterium called *Helicobacter pylori*. That discovery won Australian physicians Barry Marshall and Robin Warren a Nobel Prize in 2005.

This means that all those years when men in gray flannel suits came home to their attentive wives to consume suppers of milk toast and bouillon didn't do anything to change the fact that a bacterium was sitting in their duodenums eroding their intestinal mucosa. Nor did the surgical procedures that presumed to cure the disease mean much. Nor did the assertions of full professors of medi-cine who proclaimed the truth of these therapies.

What authority figures have to say about findings in science is ultimately 20
irrelevant. When all is said and done, all that counts is the evidence. So, to give more space to the commentary than to the evidence probably isn't a good idea. And yet that's often the case.

Here is one recent example. In the summer of 2008, the United States Preventive Services Task Force released a new recommendation that men over 75 years of age not be given prostate specific antigen, or PSA, blood tests as a screen for prostate cancer. The task force, which is assembled by the U.S. Public Health Service, is strictly evidence-based, examining every study on a subject and rating the strength of its recommendations based on the strength of the evidence reviewed.

The 1,000-word news story contained these statements:

"There is this idea that more is always better, and if a test is available we should use it," said Howard A. Brody, a professor of family medicine at the Uni-versity of Texas Medical Branch at Galveston. "A lot of times, we're doing more harm than good."

E. David Crawford, a professor of surgery at the University of Colorado at Denver: "You have to individualize treatment. If a 75-year-old man is found to have high-grade prostate cancer, it's going to kill him, and we can intervene and do something for him."

And then there was J. Brantley Thrasher, chairman of the urology depart- 25
ment at the University of Kansas and a spokesman for the American Urological Association, who said: "We have seen a dramatic drop in mortality. They're not paying attention to that."

What the story didn't contain was any data on the relationship between PSA testing and cancer mortality in older men, what kind of studies the task force drew upon, and what the most credible of them showed. It also provided no data on younger men, for whom (according to the article) there may be some benefits of testing. And this got on Page 1, which is pricey real estate in the newspaper world.

Giving the reader the evidence, rather than the words of an expert telling him what to think, is also the democratic thing to do. I find it curious that the press—the great defender of the people's right to know—often doesn't give the reader enough information to make a decision about how important something is.

The fourth reason the "evidence-based paradigm" hasn't caught on is that some version of a narrative—with a protagonist, emotional engagement, conflict and resolution—is the archetypal journalistic form. It exists only occasionally in long narrative stories. Nevertheless, it suffuses journalism, and is even captured in what we in the trade call anecdotal ledes—the two- or three-paragraph vignette, usually featuring one person, that starts a story. It often, too, is apparent when the writer returns to that person at the end of the story, the kicker.

There is a lot to be said for narrative, and even for the overdone anecdotal lede. But for science writing, it is a hazardous form.

Why? Because the narrative form makes an anecdote evidence. That's okay, 30 as long as the anecdote is representative of the body of evidence and that body is adequately described. However, problems arise when the anecdote, or often three or four anecdotes, become all the evidence there is. All the evidence, that is, except for the opinions of people interpreting the anecdotes as evidence.

This is what happened with Gulf War syndrome. Gulf War syndrome was built largely from the empathetic recounting of soldiers' stories, even though when they were investigated rigorously there was little or no evidence that any new illness arose from the United States first war against Iraq.

This phenomenon is also what led to the demonization of insurance companies in the 1990s when there was uncertainty over whether high-dose chemotherapy, followed by bone marrow transplantation, was the best strategy for treating breast cancer. Needy vulnerable patients, and heartless penny-pinching insurers, battling each other while cancer slowly killed one of the combatants—this was the story line in hundreds of news stories. What many stories failed to mention was that the evidence base for this unusually painful, expensive and dangerous treatment was extremely weak. In fact, when randomized clinical trials were finally performed—which was after some state legislatures made it illegal for insurers to refuse to pay for this treatment—they showed that bone marrow transplant did *not* lead to better survival than standard treatment. In the meantime, 48,000 women had undergone it.

The fifth and most troubling reason we don't see more evidence in a lot of science stories is that often it is not in the interest of reporters or editors to tell a story completely. We in the media live in a time of incredible competition for readers' attention—from television, radio, magazines both real and online, the gigantic blogosphere, and sometimes even our own websites. At the same time, getting on Page 1 is almost all that counts. It has always been important. Reporters who wrote accounts of the Battle of Gettysburg I am sure wanted them on the front of their oversize, gray, art-free, and barely readable newspapers. But today Page 1 is a Golden Calf we worship obscenely.

Science stories, and especially medical stories, have a really good shot of getting out on Page 1. They are inherently interesting and they appeal to what might be termed, somewhat cynically, as the narcissism of the reader. But that often isn't enough to get them on the front page. To get there, the story must emphasize novelty, potency, and certainty in a way that, as a general rule, rarely exists in a piece of scientific research. That truth is why so many medical stories only mention the magnitude of change that occurs with a new diagnostic test or treatment, and not the *absolute* change it brings about.

Consider, as an example, a hypothetical innovation that increases the diagnosis of a certain illness by 50 percent, or triples the survival duration of patients with specific disease. That sounds like big news—and of course it may be. However, if a condition is diagnosed in time to cure it in only 5 percent of cases, and the new test increases that to 7.5 percent of cases, that may not be such a breakthrough—although of course, it *is* an improvement of 50 percent. Same with a disease, such as liver cancer, in which the survival after diagnosis is roughly six months. Tripling it to 18 months is not a trivial improvement, but is probably not what a reader thinks of when he reads that a new treatment "triples the life expectancy" of someone with liver cancer. The *absolute* risk of an outcome, and not just the *relative* risk of it, should be *absolutely* required of any story about a medical innovation.

But it isn't, and part of the reason is that saying that the likelihood of an event (such as a cure) goes from 5 percent to 10 percent, instead of saying that there was a 100 percent improvement in cure rate, tends to deflate the perceived news value of a story. Consequently, it isn't surprising that it's almost never said the first way, and almost always said the second way.

I would like to give you an example of some of these forces in play. The story I have chosen is a disposable one. The inaccurate reporting surrounding it didn't cause much outrage at the time, and by now has been forgotten by just about everyone. A lot of people might not even consider what I will now describe to be a problem. Which, to me, frames the problem perfectly. In 2006, at the American College of Cardiology conference, a study was presented showing that when patients with blockages in their coronary arteries were given high doses of a statin—the family of drugs that millions of Americans take for their cholesterol—the blockages actually shrunk in size.

This was presented as a breakthrough—a new path leading to a cure for coronary heart disease, the leading cause of death in the United States. The study was led by a prominent cardiologist who was the incoming president of the organization at whose meeting it was presented. At a press conference, this man told reporters that previous studies had "shown slowing of coronary disease, but not regression." The pharmaceutical company that makes the drug used in the study, and the American College of Cardiology, each put out press releases saying the study demonstrated regression of coronary disease "for the first time."

This news literally went around the world. It was on Page 1 of the *Daily Mail* in London, where the story asserted the study showed the "first conclusive evidence" the drugs could reduce coronary plaque. It was on Page 1 of the

West Australian in Perth, under the headline "Miracle drug to stop heart attacks." It was on the front page of *USA Today*, in the *Wall Street Journal*, and on NPR— each time with claims that this was the *first time* that drugs had reversed coronary artery disease.

The only trouble was it wasn't the first. It wasn't the second. It wasn't even 40 the fifth. The reporters and editors should have smelled something funny when they were told a dramatic effect like this had burst forth fully formed 19 years after the first of these drugs arrived on the market. Science just doesn't work that way. Science moves in small steps. Something unusual is noticed in a few people and then an astute researcher explores what is noticed by magnifying the conditions under which it occurred (assuming this can be done ethically) to get a better look at it. That is exactly what happened with statins and the shrinking of coronary artery blockages.

The first drug in this family, a compound called lovastatin, was approved in 1987. Three years later, in 1990, a study appeared in the *New England Journal of Medicine* that described how out of about 150 patients taking lovastatin, 32 percent showed regression of coronary blockages compared to 11 percent of patients not getting the drug. That was the first signal that a statin could reverse coronary artery disease. There followed about a dozen more that reproduced, refined, and magnified the finding. The study presented in 2006 at the American College of Cardiology by its incoming president was the latest refinement. It wasn't even remotely the first.

But we in the press love "firsts." We are total suckers for "firsts." "Firsts" get stories on Page 1. "Betters" don't ever get stories on Page 1. The researchers, the American College of Cardiology, the medical reporters, and their editors know this. The ironic thing is that there *was* a "first" in this study. It was the first time that the majority of patients getting an extremely aggressive dose of statins showed a shrinkage of their coronary blockages. But somebody judged that wasn't quite good enough. The news had to be juiced to be the first time it *ever* happened.

So you ask, who cares? What damage is done? Especially if the story gets doctors and patients to think about using statins at higher doses—blockage-shrinking doses. The trouble is that it's an exaggeration. And exaggerations at some point—it's hard to say exactly at what point—become lies. But the sad truth is that people, as a rule, don't complain about exaggerations. Nobody is damaged by them, and many people actually benefit from them. Only truth is damaged by a "first" that didn't actually happen first.

Which is why exaggerations do more damage to the credibility of science— and I think to all of society—than outright lies or mistakes. They float by, and eventually people come to expect them. It's like inflation. It creeps up and one day words—like dollars—just aren't worth what they used to be.

Is the assertion that in 2006, statin drugs were shown to shrink coronary 45 blockages for the first time any different from the assertion by Sarah Palin that she stopped the "Bridge to Nowhere," or Barack Obama's assertion that John McCain is willing to have the Iraq war go on another 100 years? I don't think so.

We live in a time when saying something over and over makes it true, or at least gives what's said some of the heft and power of truth. As Tommy Smothers said at the Emmy Awards the other night, "Truth is that you believe what I told you." We also live in a time where—with blogs, zines, and blast e-mails—everyone can buy ink by the barrel (at least metaphorically speaking), even if almost nobody can afford to run a newspaper.

In this new world, science reporting—done without exaggeration, and with an eye to giving the reader enough information to make up his own mind—can be a model for intelligent discourse. It can be an exercise in truth-telling and democracy. And what could be better than that?

QUESTIONS FOR DISCUSSION AND WRITING

1. Brown spends the first ten paragraphs defining "evidence-based" journalism. What is his definition?

2. Brown says that one of the science reporter's two tasks is "to provide enough information so a reader can judge the strength of a claim"(paragraph 7). Why is it so hard to perform this first task—"knowing how much to boil something down without making the final dish indigestible" (paragraph 10)? Why does Brown, an experienced science reporter, consider this "fun"?

3. The science reporter's second task is "to describe how the news fits into what's already known about the subject" (paragraph 7). Given the vast amount of information available on many scientific subjects, how can a reporter, or a student in the process of discovering a subject, accomplish this task without becoming overwhelmed not only by the amount of information but by its technicality? Consider some of the examples Brown cites throughout his essay in preparing your answer, augmented by information you know from other sources, perhaps your own investigations.

4. In Brown's estimation, what's wrong with using the opinions of authority figures to comment on "a scientific assertion in the news." Many editors, Brown says, "are more likely to say to a reporter: 'Find out what other people think about this' than to ask: 'Well, what does the evidence say about this claim?'" (paragraph 16). What are the significant differences between opinion and evidence? How can Brown so confidently assert that "what authority figures have to say about findings in science is ultimately irrelevant" (paragraph 20)? Isn't that ultimately disrespectful of a reporter's sources?

5. What's the problem with using narrative, "the archetypal journalistic form"—"with a protagonist, emotional engagement, conflict and resolution" (paragraph 28) as the basis for scientific reporting?

6. Brown says that "the fifth and most troubling reason we don't see more evidence in a lot of science stories is that often it is not in the interest of reporters or editors to tell a story completely" (paragraph 33). What evidence does he give to support this claim? In what ways does Natasha Singer and Duff Wilson's "Medical Editors Push for Ghostwriting Crackdown" (p. 570) corroborate what Brown is saying?

7. Find a scientific article in a respected newspaper and subject it to the five-pronged analysis Brown explains in "Science Reporting and Evidence-Based Journalism." How well does it do? Or, try writing an essay based on solid evidence and see how hard it is to avoid the pitfalls Brown identifies. What makes such reporting so difficult to do responsibly?

CHAPTER 2

Identity with Attitude: Who Am I, and Why Does It Matter?

FRANZ BOAS AND GEORGE HUNT

An "Authentic" Indian

QUESTIONS FOR DISCUSSION AND WRITING

1. This photograph (from around 1900) shows anthropologist Franz Boas (*left*) and photographer George Hunt (*right*) creating an artificial backdrop to make their Kwakiutl Native Peoples subject appear more "authentic" than she would look if posed against the real-life background of a picket fence or columned building.

What does this staging say about the construction and reading of ethnicity? How does this photograph serve as a visual metaphor for Alexie's "What Sacagawea Means to Me" (p. 115)? Might it also have relevance for Momaday's "The Way to Rainy Mountain" (p. 118)?

2. How much of what you see on television reality shows or on social media Web sites such as Facebook is a true picture of reality? Rate the visual imagery of the presentations of "reality" that you have chosen on a continuum of totally (well, mostly) true to essentially false. How can you tell what's really true and what has been altered? Are you responding to visual clues? People's behavior? Your knowledge of people and particular contexts? Is there virtue in such fakery? Why not present the truth? What are some of the short- and long-range consequences of such presentations, true or false?

ERIC LIU

Notes of a Native Speaker

Eric Liu was born in Poughkeepsie, New York, in 1968. "My own assimilation began long before I was born," writes Liu, whose parents came to the United States from Taiwan in the late 1950s. His father was an IBM executive, and his mother worked as a computer programmer. Liu and his sister grew up with the photos and pilot stories of their grandfather, a general in the Nationalist Chinese air force during World War II. "Shadow-dancing" with his identity as a "Renaissance boy" or an "Asian overachiever," Liu graduated summa cum laude with a bachelor's degree in history from Yale (1990). He interned with Senator Daniel Patrick Moynihan one summer and spent two other summers in Marine Officer Candidate School in Quantico, Virginia. At age twenty-five, Liu became President Bill Clinton's youngest speechwriter. He attended Harvard Law School and then, in 2000, returned to the White House as deputy domestic policy adviser. He is a political commentator on CNN as well as a teacher at the Evans School of Public Affairs at the University of Washington.

The title of Liu's memoir, The Accidental Asian: Notes of a Native Speaker *(1998), is a multiracial reference to Anne Tyler's* The Accidental Tourist *(1985), James Baldwin's essay "Notes of a Native Son" (1955), and Richard Wright's* Native Son *(1940). Although Liu grew up speaking a mixture of English and Mandarin, English is his native language. Refusing to look at ten million Americans of Asian descent as an ethnic group, Liu focuses on the diversity of Asian American heritage and downplays race.*

Here are some of the ways you could say I am "white":

> I listen to National Public Radio.
> I wear khaki Dockers.

I own brown suede bucks.
I eat gourmet greens.
I have few close friends "of color."
I married a white woman.
I am a child of the suburbs.
I furnish my condo à la Crate & Barrel.
I vacation in charming bed-and-breakfasts.
I have never once been the victim of blatant discrimination.
I am a member of several exclusive institutions.
I have been in the inner sanctums of political power.
I have been there as something other than an attendant.
I have the ambition to return.
I am a producer of the culture.
I expect my voice to be heard.
I speak flawless, unaccented English.
I subscribe to *Foreign Affairs.*
I do not mind when editorialists write in the first person plural.
I do not mind how white television casts are.
I am not too ethnic.
I am wary of minority militants.
I consider myself neither in exile nor in opposition.
I am considered "a credit to my race."

I never asked to be white. I am not literally white. That is, I do not have white skin or white ancestors. I have yellow skin and yellow ancestors, hundreds of generations of them. But like so many other Asian Americans of the second generation, I find myself now the bearer of a strange new status: white, by acclamation. Thus it is that I have been described as an "honorary white," by other whites, and as a "banana," by other Asians. Both the honorific and the epithet take as a given this idea: to the extent that I have moved away from the periphery and toward the center of American life, I have become white inside. *Some are born white, others achieve whiteness, still others have whiteness thrust upon them.* This, supposedly, is what it means to assimilate.

There was a time when assimilation did quite strictly mean whitening. In fact, well into the first half of this century, mimicry of the stylized standards of the WASP gentry was the proper, dominant, perhaps even sole method of ensuring that your origins would not be held against you. You "made it" in society not only by putting on airs of anglitude, but also by assiduously bleaching out the marks of a darker, dirtier past. And this bargain, stifling as it was, was open to European immigrants almost exclusively; to blacks, only on the passing occasion; to Asians, hardly at all.

Times have changed, and I suppose you could call it progress that a China-man, too, may now aspire to whiteness. But precisely because the times have changed, that aspiration—and the *imputation* of the aspiration—now seems astonishingly outmoded. The meaning of "American" has undergone a revolution in the twenty-nine years I have been alive, a revolution of color, class, and culture. Yet the vocabulary of "assimilation" has remained fixed all this time: fixed in whiteness, which is still our metonym for power; and fixed in shame, which is what the colored are expected to feel for embracing the power.

I have assimilated. I am of the mainstream. In many ways I fit the psychological profile of the so-called banana: imitative, impressionable, rootless, eager to please. As I will admit in this essay, I have at times gone to great lengths to downplay my difference, the better to penetrate the "establishment" of the moment. Yet I'm not sure that what I did was so cut-and-dried as "becoming white." I plead guilty to the charges above: achieving, learning the ways of the upper middle class, distancing myself from radicals of any hue. But having confessed, I still do not know my crime.

To be an accused banana is to stand at the ill-fated intersection of class and race. And because class is the only thing Americans have more trouble talking about than race, a minority's climb up the social ladder is often willfully misnamed and wrongly portrayed. There is usually, in the portrayal, a strong whiff of betrayal: the assimilist is a traitor to his kind, to his class, to his own family. He cannot gain the world without losing his soul. To be sure, something *is* lost in any migration, whether from place to place or from class to class. But something is gained as well. And the result is always more complicated than the monochrome language of "whiteness" and "authenticity" would suggest. . . .

I recently dug up a photograph of myself from freshman year of college that made me smile. I have on the wrong shoes, the wrong socks, the wrong checkered shirt tucked the wrong way into the wrong slacks. I look like what I was: a boy sprung from a middlebrow burg who affected a secondhand preppiness. I look nervous. Compare that image to one from my senior-class dinner: now I am attired in a gray tweed jacket with a green plaid bow tie and a sensible button-down shirt, all purchased at the Yale Co-op. I look confident, and more than a bit contrived.

What happened in between those two photographs is that I experienced, then overcame, what the poet Meena Alexander has called "the shock of arrival." When I was deposited at the wrought-iron gates of my residential college as a freshman, I felt more like an outsider than I'd thought possible. It wasn't just that I was a small Chinese boy standing at a grand WASP temple; nor simply that I was a hayseed neophyte puzzled by the refinements of college style. It was *both*: color and class were all twisted together in a double helix of felt inadequacy.

For a while I coped with the shock by retreating to a group of my own kind—not fellow Asians, but fellow marginal public-school grads who resented the rah-rah Yalies to whom everything came so effortlessly. Aligning myself this way was bearable—I was hiding, but at least I could place myself in a long tradition of underdog exiles at Yale. Aligning myself by race, on the other hand, would have seemed too inhibiting.

I know this doesn't make much sense. I know also that college, in the multicultural era, is supposed to be where the deracinated minority youth discovers the "person of color" inside. To a point, I did. I studied Chinese, took an Asian American history course, a seminar on race politics. But ultimately, college was where the unconscious habits of my adolescent assimilation hardened into self-conscious strategy.

I still remember the moment, in the first week of school, when I came upon   10
a table in Yale Station set up by the Asian American Student Association. The upperclassman staffing the table was pleasant enough. He certainly did not strike me as a fanatic. Yet, for some reason, I flashed immediately to a scene I'd witnessed days earlier, on the corner outside. Several Lubavitcher Jews, dressed in black, their faces bracketed by dangling side curls, were looking for fellow travelers at this busy crossroads. Their method was crude but memorable. As any vaguely Jewish-looking male walked past, the zealots would quickly approach, extend a pamphlet, and ask, "Excuse me, sir, are you Jewish?" Since most were not, and since those who weren't about to stop, the result was a frantic, nervous, almost comical buzz all about the corner: Excuse me, are you Jewish? Are you Jewish? Excuse me. Are you Jewish?

I looked now at the clean-cut Korean boy at the AASA table (I think I can distinguish among Asian ethnicities as readily as those Hasidim thought they could tell Gentile from Jew), and though he had merely offered an introductory hello and was now smiling mutely at me, in the back of my mind I heard only this: *Excuse me, are you Asian? Are you Asian? Excuse me. Are you Asian?* I took one of the flyers on the table, even put my name on a mailing list, so as not to appear impolite. But I had already resolved not to be active in any Asians-only group. I thought then: I would never *choose* to be so pigeonholed.

This allergic sensitivity to "pigeonholing" is one of the unhappy hallmarks of the banana mentality. What does the banana fear? That is, what did *I* fear? The possibility of being mistaken for someone more Chinese. The possibility of being known only, or even primarily, for being Asian. The possibility of being written off by whites as a self-segregating ethnic clumper. These were the threats—unseen and, frankly, unsubstantiated—that I felt I should keep at bay.

I didn't avoid making Asian friends in college or working with Asian classmates; I simply never went out of my way to do so. This distinction seemed important—it marked, to my mind, the difference between self-hate and self-respect. That the two should have been so proximate in the first place never struck me as odd, or telling. Nor did it ever occur to me that the reasons I gave myself for dissociating from Asians as a group—that I didn't want to be part of a clique, that I didn't want to get absorbed and lose my individuality—were the very developments that marked my own assimilation. I simply hewed to my ideology of race neutrality and self-reliance. I didn't need that crutch, I told myself nervously, that crutch of racial affinity. What's more, I was vaguely insulted by the presumption that I might.

But again: Who was making the presumption? Who more than I was taking the mere existence of Korean volleyball leagues or Taiwanese social sets or pan-Asian student clubs to mean that *all* people of Asian descent, myself included, needed such quasi-kinship groups? And who more than I interpreted this need as infirmity, as a failure to fit in? I resented the faintly sneering way that some whites regarded Asians as an undifferentiated mass. But whose sneer, really, did I resent more than my own?

I was keenly aware of the unflattering mythologies that attach to Asian 15 Americans: that we are indelibly foreign, exotic, math and science geeks, numbers people rather than people people, followers and not leaders, physically frail but devious and sneaky, unknowable and potentially treacherous. These stereotypes of Asian otherness and inferiority were like immense blocks of ice sitting before me, challenging me to chip away at them. And I did, tirelessly. All the while, though, I was oblivious to rumors of my *own* otherness and inferiority, rumors that rose off those blocks like a fog, wafting into my consciousness and chilling my sense of self.

As I had done in high school, I combated the stereotypes in part by trying to disprove them. If Asians were reputed to be math and science geeks, I would be a student of history and politics. If Asians were supposed to be feeble subalterns, I'd lift weights and go to Marine officer candidate school. If Asians were alien, I'd be ardently patriotic. If Asians were shy and retiring, I'd try to be exuberant and jocular. If they were narrow-minded specialists, I'd be a well-rounded generalist. If they were perpetual outsiders, I'd join every establishment outfit I could and show that I, too, could run with the swift.

I overstate, of course. It wasn't that I chose to do all these things with no other purpose than to cut against a supposed convention. I was neither so Pavlovian nor so calculating that I would simply remake myself into the opposite of what people expected. I actually *liked* history, and wasn't especially good at math. As the grandson of a military officer, I *wanted* to see what officer candidates school would be like, and I enjoyed it, at least once I'd finished. I am *by nature* enthusiastic and allegiant, a joiner, and a bit of a jingo.

At the same time, I was often aware, sometimes even hopeful, that others might think me "exceptional" for my race. I derived satisfaction from being the "atypical" Asian, the only Chinese face at OCS or in this club or that.

The irony is that in working so duteously to defy stereotype, I became a slave to it. For to act self-consciously against Asian "tendencies" is not to break loose from the cage of myth and legend; it is to turn the very key that locks you inside. What spontaneity is there when the value of every act is measured, at least in part, by its power to refute a presumption about why you act? The *typical Asian* I imagined, and the *atypical Asian* I imagined myself to be, were identical in this sense: neither was as much a creature of free will as a human being ought to be.

Let me say it plainly, then: I am not proud to have had this mentality. I 20 believe I have outgrown it. And I expose it now not to justify it but to detoxify it, to prevent its further spread.

Yet it would be misleading, I think, to suggest that my education centered solely on the discomfort caused by race. The fact is, when I first got to college I felt deficient compared with people of *every* color. Part of why I believed it so necessary to achieve was that I lacked the connections, the wealth, the experience, the sophistication that so many of my classmates seemed to have. I didn't get the jokes or the intellectual references. I didn't have the canny attitude. So in addition to all my coursework, I began to puzzle over this, the culture of the influential class.

Over time, I suppose, I learned the culture. My interests and vocabulary became ever more worldly. I made my way onto what Calvin Trillin once described as the "magic escalator" of a Yale education. Extracurriculars opened the door to an alumni internship, which brought me to Capitol Hill, which led to a job and a life in Washington after commencement. Gradually, very gradually, I found that I was not so much of an outsider anymore. I found that by almost any standard, but particularly by the standards of my younger self, I was actually beginning to "make it."

It has taken me until now, however, to appraise the thoughts and acts of that younger self. I can see now that the straitening path I took was not the only or even the best path. For while it may be possible to transcend race, *it is not always necessary to try.* And while racial identity is sometimes a shackle, it is not *only* a shackle. I could have spared myself a great deal of heartache had I understood this earlier, that the choice of race is not simply "embrace or efface."

I wonder sometimes how I would have turned out had I been, from the start, more comfortable in my own skin. What did I miss by distancing myself from race? What friendships did I forgo, what self-knowledge did I defer? Had certain accidents of privilege been accidents of privation or exclusion, I might well have developed a different view of the world. But I do not know just how my view would have differed.

What I know is that through all those years of shadow-dancing with my identity, something happened, something that had only partially to do with color. By the time I left Yale I was no longer the scared boy of that freshman photo. I had become more sure of myself and of my place—sure enough, indeed, to perceive the folly of my fears. And in the years since, I have assumed a sense of expectation, of access and *belonging,* that my younger self could scarcely have imagined. All this happened incrementally. There was no clear tipping point, no obvious moment of mutation. The shock of arrival, it would seem, is simply that I arrived.

25

QUESTIONS FOR DISCUSSION AND WRITING

1. In the opening paragraph, how does Liu intend for his list to portray the essence of "whiteness"? Explain why this list is an effective definition of whiteness—or why it fails to define whiteness—for you.

2. Liu says "college was where the unconscious habits of my . . . assimilation hardened into self-conscious strategy" (paragraph 9). Describe the strategy of assimilation that he developed. What did it consist of? What stages did it go through? What did it accomplish for him?

3. Considering the focus on self-definition in this essay, do you find that it cele-brates self-centeredness? Does Liu say too much about himself and not enough about others? What does he gain and what does he lose by focusing on himself? Write an essay in which you either defend or criticize Liu's focus on himself. Include references to yourself, if they fit.

4. Have you ever felt that you had to assimilate yourself into a group? Write about your experience of assimilation, stressing any stages that you went through and explaining the positive or negative aspects of the process. Or, write about some-one else's assimilation into a group. Does the desire to assimilate ever justify deception, withholding information, or other forms of manipulating evidence or other people?

ESMERALDA SANTIAGO

Jíbara

Born in Puerto Rico in 1948, the eldest daughter of a poor laboring family, Esmeralda Santiago divided her early years between a small village in the rural countryside and a suburb near San Juan. When she was thirteen, her mother left Santiago's father and moved her daughter and nine other children to Brooklyn, New York. There Santiago attended public junior high school and later graduated from the High School of Per-forming Arts in Manhattan. She attended community college part-time before trans-ferring to Harvard, where she earned a bachelor's degree in film production in 1976. Her literary career developed from her work as a writer and producer of documentary films. Her first book, the memoir When I Was Puerto Rican, *was published to criti-cal acclaim in 1993. Santiago followed this in 1996 with a novel,* America's Dream, *about a Puerto Rican housekeeper who flees an abusive husband to work in the United States. A second memoir,* Almost a Woman, *appeared in 1998, and a third,* The Turkish Lover, *in 2004.*

In this opening chapter from When I Was Puerto Rican, *Santiago recalls her early childhood in rural Puerto Rico, where her family lived like jíbaros, or country people, even though their roots were in the city. Santiago says the book was a reac-tion to her sense of displacement upon first returning to Puerto Rico as an adult: "I felt as Puerto Rican as when I left the island, but to those who had never left, I was contaminated by Americanisms, and, therefore, had become less than Puerto Rican. Yet, in the United States, my darkness, my accented speech, my frequent lapses into the confused silence between English and Spanish identified me as foreign, non-American. In writing the book I wanted to get back to that feeling of Puertoricanness I had before I came here."*

Al jíbaro nunca se le quita la mancha de plátano.
A jíbaro can never wash away the stain of the plantain.

We came to Macún when I was four, to a rectangle of rippled metal sheets on stilts hovering in the middle of a circle of red dirt. Our home was a giant version of the lard cans used to haul water from the public fountain. Its windows and doors were also metal, and, as we stepped in, I touched the wall and burned my fingers.

"That'll teach you," Mami scolded. "Never touch a wall on the sunny side."

She searched a bundle of clothes and diapers for her jar of Vick's VapoRub to smear on my fingers. They were red the rest of the day, and I couldn't suck my thumb that night. "You're too big for that anyway," she said.

The floor was a patchwork of odd-shaped wooden slats that rose in the middle and dipped toward the front and back doors, where they butted against shiny, worn thresholds. Papi nailed new boards under Mami's treadle sewing machine, and under their bed, but the floor still groaned and sagged to the corners, threatening to collapse and bring the house down with it.

"I'll rip the whole thing out," Papi suggested. "We'll have to live with a dirt 5 floor for a while. . . ."

Mami looked at her feet and shuddered. A dirt floor, we'd heard, meant snakes and scorpions could crawl into the house from their holes in the ground. Mami didn't know any better, and I had yet to learn not everything I heard was true, so we reacted in what was to become a pattern for us: what frightened her I became curious about, and what she found exciting terrified me. As Mami pulled her feet onto the rungs of her rocking chair and rubbed the goose bumps from her arms, I imagined a world of fascinating creatures slithering underfoot, drawing squiggly patterns on the dirt.

The day Papi tore up the floor, I followed him holding a can into which he dropped the straight nails, still usable. My fingers itched with a rust-colored powder, and when I licked them, a dry, metallic taste curled the tip of my tongue. Mami stood on the threshold scratching one ankle with the toes of the other foot.

"Negi, come help me gather kindling for the fire."

"I'm working with Papi," I whined, hoping he'd ask me to stay. He didn't turn around but continued on his knees, digging out nails with the hammer's claw, muttering the words to his favorite *chachachá*.

"Do as I say!" Mami ordered. Still, Papi kept his back to us. I plunked the can 10 full of nails down hard, willing him to hear and tell me to stay, but he didn't. I dawdled after Mami down the three steps into the yard. Delsa and Norma, my younger sisters, took turns swinging from a rope Papi had hung under the mango tree.

"Why can't they help with the kindling?" I pouted.

Mami swatted the side of my head. "Don't talk back," she said. "You girls keep away from the house while your father is working," she warned as we walked by my sisters having fun.

She led the way into a thicket behind the latrine. Twigs crackled under my bare feet, stinging the soles. A bananaquit flew to the thorny branch of a lemon tree and looked from side to side. Dots of sun danced on the green walls of the shady grove above low bushes weighted with pigeon peas, the earth screened with twigs, sensitive *moriviví* plants, and french weed studded with tiny blue flowers. Mami hummed softly, the yellow and orange flowers of her dress blending into the greenness: a miraculous garden with legs and arms and a melody. Her hair, choked at the nape with a rubber band, floated thick and black to her waist, and as she bent over to pick up sticks, it rained across her shoulders and down her arms, covering her face and tangling in the twigs she cradled. A red butterfly circled her and flew close to her ear. She gasped and swatted it into a bush.

"It felt like it was going right into my brain," she muttered with an embarrassed smile.

Delsa and Norma toddled through the underbrush. "Mami, come see what I 15 found," Delsa called.

A hen had scratched out a hollow and carpeted its walls and floor with dry grass. She had laid four eggs, smaller and not as white as the ones our neighbor Doña Lola gave us from time to time.

"Can we eat them?" Delsa asked.

"No."

"But if we leave them here a snake will get them," I said, imagining a serpent swallowing each egg whole. Mami shuddered and rubbed her arms where tiny bumps had formed making the fine hairs stand straight up. She gave me a look, half puzzled, half angry, and drew us to her side.

"All right, let's get our sticks together and bring them to the kitchen." As 20 she picked hers up, she looked carefully around.

"One, two, three, four," she chanted. "One, two, three, four."

We marched single file into our yard, where Papi stacked floorboards.

"Come look," he said.

The dirt was orange, striped in places where crumbs had slipped through the cracks when Mami swept. Papi had left a few boards down the center of the room and around his and Mami's bed, to stand on until the ground was swept and flattened. Mami was afraid to come into the house. There were small holes in the dirt, holes where snakes and scorpions hid. She turned around swiftly and threw herself off balance so that she skipped toward the kitchen shed.

"Let's go make supper!" She singsang to make it sound like fun. Delsa and 25 Norma followed her skirt, but I stared at the dirt, where squiggly lines stretched from one wall to the other. Mami waited for me.

"Negi, come help in the kitchen."

I pretended not to hear but felt her eyes bore holes in the back of my head. Papi stepped between us.

"Let her stay. I can use the help."

I peered between his legs and saw her squint and pucker her lips as if she were about to spit. He chuckled, "Heh, heh," and she whirled toward the kitchen shed, where the fire in the *fogón* was almost out.

"Take these boards and lay them on the pile for the cooking fire," Papi said. 30 "Careful with the splinters."

I walked a broad circle around Mami, who looked up from her vegetable chopping whenever I went by. When I passed carrying a wide board, Mami asked to see it. Black bugs, like ants, but bigger and blacker, crawled over it in a frenzy.

"Termites!" she gasped.

I was covered with them. They swarmed inside my shirt and panties, into my hair, under my arms. Until Mami saw them, I hadn't felt them sting. But they bit ridges into my skin that itched and hurt at the same time. Mami ran me to the washtub and dunked me among my father's soaking shirts.

"Pablo!" she called, "Oh, my God! Look at her. She's being eaten alive!"

I screamed, imagining my skin disappearing in chunks into the invisible   35 mouths of hundreds of tiny black specks creeping into parts of my body I couldn't even reach. Mami pulled off my clothes and threw them on the ground. The soap in the washtub burned my skin, and Mami scrubbed me so hard her fingernails dug angry furrows into my arms and legs. She turned me around to wash my back and I almost fell out of the tub.

"Be still," she said. "I have to get them all."

She pushed and shoved and turned me so fast I didn't know what to do with my body, so I flailed, seeming to resist, while in fact I wanted nothing more than to be rid of the creepy crawling things that covered me. Mami wrapped me in a towel and lifted me out of the tub with a groan. Hundreds of black bugs floated between the bubbles.

She carried me to the house pressed against her bosom, fragrant of curdled milk. Delsa and Norma ran after us, but Papi scooped them up, one on each arm, and carried them to the rope swing. Mami balanced on the floorboards to her bed, lay me beside her, held me tight, kissed my forehead, my eyes, and murmured, "It's all right. It's over. It's all right."

I wrapped my legs around her and buried my face under her chin. It felt good to have Mami so close, so warm, swathed by her softness, her smell of wood smoke and oregano. She rubbed circles on my back and caressed the hair from my face. She kissed me, brushed my tears with her fingertips, and dried my nose with the towel, or the hem of her dress.

"You see," she murmured, "what happens when you don't do as I say?"   40

I turned away from her and curled into a tight ball of shame. Mami rolled off the bed and went outside. I lay on her pillow, whimpering, wondering how the termites knew I'd disobeyed my mother.

We children slept in hammocks strung across the room, tied to the beams in sturdy knots that were done and undone daily. A curtain separated our side of the room from the end where my parents slept in a four-poster bed veiled with mosquito netting. On the days he worked, Papi left the house before dawn and sometimes joked that he woke the roosters to sing the *barrio* awake. We wouldn't see him again until dusk, dragging down the dirt road, his wooden toolbox pulling on his arm, making his body list sideways. When he didn't work, he and Mami rustled behind the flowered curtain, creaked the springs under their mattress, their voices a murmur that I strained to hear but couldn't.

I was an early riser but was not allowed out until the sun shot in through the crack near Mami's sewing machine and swept a glistening stripe of gold across the dirt floor.

The next morning, I turned out of the hammock and ran outside as soon as the sun streaked in. Mami and Papi sat by the kitchen shed sipping coffee. My arms and belly were pimpled with red dots. The night before, Mami had bathed me in *alcoholado*, which soothed my skin and cooled the hot itch.

"*Ay bendito*," Mami said, "here's our spotty early riser. Come here, let me look." She turned me around, rubbing the spots. "Are you itchy?"

"No, it doesn't itch at all."

"Stay out of the sun today so the spots don't scar."

Papi hummed along with the battery-operated radio. He never went anywhere without it. When he worked around the house, he propped it on a rock, or the nearest fence post, and tuned it to his favorite station, which played romantic ballads, *chachachás*, and a reading of the news every half hour. He delighted in stories from faraway places like Russia, Madagascar, and Istanbul. Whenever the newscaster mentioned a country with a particularly musical name, he'd repeat it or make a rhyme of it. "*Pakistán. Sacristán. ¿Dónde están?*" he sang as he mixed cement or hammered nails, his voice echoing against the walls.

Early each morning the radio brought us a program called "The Day Breaker's Club," which played the traditional music and poetry of the Puerto Rican country dweller, the *jíbaro*. Although the songs and poems chronicled a life of struggle and hardship, their message was that *jíbaros* were rewarded by a life of independence and contemplation, a closeness to nature coupled with a respect for its intractability, and a deeply rooted and proud nationalism. I wanted to be a *jíbara* more than anything in the world, but Mami said I couldn't because I was born in the city, where *jíbaros* were mocked for their unsophisticated customs and peculiar dialect.

"Don't be a *jíbara*," she scolded, rapping her knuckles on my skull, as if to waken the intelligence she said was there.

I ducked away, my scalp smarting, and scrambled into the oregano bushes. In the fragrant shade, I fretted. If we were not *jíbaros*, why did we live like them? Our house, a box squatting on low stilts, was shaped like a *bohío*, the kind of house *jíbaros* lived in. Our favorite program, "The Day Breaker's Club," played the traditional music of rural Puerto Rico and gave information about crops, husbandry, and the weather. Our neighbor Doña Lola was a *jíbara*, although Mami had warned us never to call her that. Poems and stories about the hardships and joys of the Puerto Rican *jíbaro* were required reading at every grade level in school. My own grandparents, whom I was to respect as well as love, were said to be *jíbaros*. But I couldn't be one, nor was I to call anyone a *jíbaro*, lest they be offended. Even at the tender age when I didn't yet know my real name, I was puzzled by the hypocrisy of celebrating a people everyone looked down on. But there was no arguing with Mami, who, in those days, was always right.

On the radio, the newscaster talked about submarines, torpedoes, and a place called Korea, where Puerto Rican men went to die. His voice faded as Papi carried him into the house just as Delsa and Norma came out for their oatmeal.

Delsa's black curly hair framed a heart-shaped face with tiny pouty lips and round eyes thick with lashes. Mami called her *Muñequita*, Little Doll. Norma's hair was the color of clay, her yellow eyes slanted at the corners, and her skin glowed the same color as the inside of a yam. Mami called her *La Colorá*, the red girl. I thought I had no nickname until she told me my name wasn't Negi but Esmeralda.

"You're named after your father's sister, who is also your godmother. You know her as Titi Merín."

"Why does everyone call me Negi?"   55

"Because when you were little you were so black, my mother said you were a *negrita*. And we all called you *Negrita*, and it got shortened to Negi."

Delsa was darker than I was, nutty brown, but not as sun ripened as Papi. Norma was lighter, rust colored, and not as pale as Mami, whose skin was pink. Norma's yellow eyes with black pupils looked like sunflowers. Delsa had black eyes. I'd never seen my eyes, because the only mirror in the house was hung up too high for me to reach. I touched my hair, which was not curly like Delsa's, nor *pasita*, raisined, like Papi's. Mami cut it short whenever it grew into my eyes, but I'd seen dark brown wisps by my cheeks and near my temples.

"So *Negi* means I'm black?"

"It's a sweet name because we love you, *Negrita*." She hugged and kissed me.

"Does anyone call Titi Merín Esmeralda?"   60

"Oh, sure. People who don't know her well — the government, her boss. We all have our official names, and then our nicknames, which are like secrets that only the people who love us use."

"How come you don't have a nickname?"

"I do. Everyone calls me Monín. That's my nickname."

"What's your real name?"

"Ramona."   65

"Papi doesn't have a nickname."

"Yes he does. Some people call him Pablito."

It seemed too complicated, as if each one of us were really two people, one who was loved and the official one who, I assumed, was not.

QUESTIONS FOR DISCUSSION AND WRITING

1. How would you characterize Santiago's parents in terms of their relationship both to each other and to their children? How would you characterize Santiago's feelings for her parents?

2. Santiago writes that *jíbaros*, the poor country people of Puerto Rico, are both celebrated for their struggle and independence and mocked for their lack of sophistication. What qualities does this contradiction attribute to Puerto Ricans? What, if any, groups within your culture are likewise celebrated and scorned? Examine some other readings in this book, such as Lynda Barry's cartoon rendering of

multicultural poverty (p. 522) and W. E. B. Du Bois's definition of "The 'Veil' of Self-Consciousness" (p. 144), which Sherman Alexie's "What Sacagawea Means to Me" (p. 115) satirically illustrates.

3. Santiago writes at some length about the nicknames her family members had for one another. In what ways might such nicknames, beginning in childhood, have a role in shaping one's identity? Why, as Santiago suggests, might family nicknames create a conflict of identity? You might consider this question in terms of the language of family and the language of the outside world that Richard Rodriguez writes about in "Aria: A Memoir of a Bilingual Childhood" (p. 275).

4. Part of the charm of this memoir lies in Santiago's description of her and her sisters' mischievous behavior and her mother's response to it. In an essay, narrate some mischievous behavior from your childhood—innocent or not so innocent—that brought the wrath of a parent or other authority figure. To what extent was that angry response justified?

BOBBIE ANN MASON

Being Country

Born (1940) in Mayfield, Kentucky, Bobbie Ann Mason grew up on a dairy farm, and in Clear Springs: A Memoir *(1999), she describes her family's "independence, stability, authenticity" along with their "crippling social isolation." She earned a bachelor's degree at the University of Kentucky (1962), a master's at the State University of New York at Binghamton (1966), and a doctorate at the University of Connecticut (1972). She contributes regularly to* Mother Jones, The Atlantic Monthly, *and* The New Yorker. *Her novel* In Country *(1984) was made into a film in 1989. Other works include* Shiloh and Other Stories *(1983) and* Feather Crowns *(1994). Her themes are often the encroachment of modern life—television, fast food, shopping malls, the Vietnam War—into traditional rural life; her characters, farmers and working-class people, try to cope with change and balance their individual needs with those of their families.*

Mason's writing style, unsentimental and spare, echoes the language of rural western Kentuckians. She uses names—places, roads, brand names, popular musicians, and TV characters—to portend changes to rural life, changes that have already become commonplace elsewhere. In "Being Country" from Clear Springs, *Mason uses physical images from her youth, the routines and rhythms of farm life, and a constant concern for food—home-grown, home-cooked food—to illustrate rural experience.*

One day Mama and Granny were shelling beans and talking about the proper method of drying apples. I was nearly eleven and still entirely absorbed with the

March girls in *Little Women*. Drying apples was not in my dreams. Beth's death was weighing darkly on me at that moment, and I threw a little tantrum—what Mama called a hissy fit.

"Can't y'all talk about anything but food?" I screamed.

There was a shocked silence. "Well, what else is there?" Granny asked.

Granny didn't question a woman's duties, but I did. I didn't want to be hulling beans in a hot kitchen when I was fifty years old. I wanted to *be* somebody, maybe an airline stewardess. Also, I had been listening to the radio. I had notions.

Our lives were haunted by the fear of crop failure. We ate as if we didn't know 5 where our next meal might come from. All my life I have had a recurrent food dream: I face a buffet or cafeteria line, laden with beautiful foods. I spend the entire dream choosing the foods I want. My anticipation is deliciously agonizing. I always wake up just as I've made my selections but before I get to eat.

Working with food was fraught with anxiety and desperation. In truth, no one in memory had missed a meal—except Peyton Washam on the banks of Panther Creek wistfully regarding his seed corn. But the rumble of poor Peyton's belly must have survived to trouble our dreams. We were at the mercy of nature, and it wasn't to be trusted. My mother watched the skies at evening for a portent of the morrow. A cloud that went over and then turned around and came back was an especially bad sign. Our livelihood—even our lives—depended on forces outside our control.

I think this dependence on nature was at the core of my rebellion. I hated the constant sense of helplessness before vast forces, the continuous threat of failure. Farmers didn't take initiative, I began to see; they reacted to whatever presented itself. I especially hated women's part in the dependence.

My mother allowed me to get spoiled. She never even tried to teach me to cook. "You didn't want to learn," she says now. "You were a lady of leisure, and you didn't want to help. You had your nose in a book."

I believed progress meant freedom from the field and the range. That meant moving to town, I thought.

Because we lived on the edge of Mayfield, I was acutely conscious of being 10 country. I felt inferior to people in town because we grew our food and made our clothes, while they bought whatever they needed. Although we were self-sufficient and resourceful and held clear title to our land, we lived in a state of psychological poverty. As I grew older, this acute sense of separation from town affected me more deeply. I began to sense that the fine life in town— celebrated in magazines, on radio, in movies—was denied us. Of course we weren't poor at all. Poor people had too many kids, and they weren't landowners; they rented decrepit little houses with plank floors and trash in the yard. "Poor people are wormy and eat wild onions," Mama said. We weren't poor, but we were country.

We had three wardrobes—everyday clothes, school clothes, and Sunday clothes. We didn't wear our school clothes at home, but we could wear them to town. When we got home from church, we had to change back into everyday clothes before we ate Mama's big Sunday dinner.

"Don't eat in your good clothes!" Mama always cried. "You'll spill something on them."

Mama always preferred outdoor life, but she was a natural cook. At harvest time, after she'd come in from the garden and put out a wash, she would whip out a noontime dinner for the men in the field—my father and grandfather and maybe some neighbors and a couple of hired hands: fried chicken with milk gravy, ham, mashed potatoes, lima beans, field peas, corn, slaw, sliced tomatoes, fried apples, biscuits, and peach pie. This was not considered a banquet, only plain hearty food, fuel for work. All the ingredients except the flour, sugar, and salt came from our farm—the chickens, the hogs, the milk and butter, the Irish potatoes, the beans, peas, corn, cabbage, apples, peaches. Nothing was processed, except by Mama. She was always butchering and plucking and planting and hoeing and shredding and slicing and creaming (scraping cobs for the creamed corn) and pressure-cooking and canning and freezing and thawing and mixing and shaping and baking and frying.

We would eat our pie right on the same plate as our turnip greens so as not to mess up another dish. The peach cobbler oozed all over the turnip-green juice and the pork grease. "It all goes to the same place," Mama said. It was boarding-house reach, no "Pass the peas, please." Conversation detracted from the sensuous pleasure of filling yourself. A meal required meat and vegetables and dessert. The beverages were milk and iced tea ("ice-tea"). We never used napkins or ate tossed salad. Our salads were Jell-O and slaw. We ate "poke salet" and wilted lettuce. Mama picked tender, young pokeweed in the woods in the spring, before it turned poison, and cooked it a good long time to get the bitterness out. We liked it with vinegar and minced boiled eggs. Wilted lettuce was tender new lettuce, shredded, with sliced radishes and green onions, and blasted with hot bacon grease to blanch the rawness. "Too many fresh vegetables in summer gives people the scours," Daddy said.

Food was better in town, we thought. It wasn't plain and everyday. The centers of pleasure were there—the hamburger and barbecue places, the movie shows, all the places to buy things. Woolworth's, with the pneumatic tubes overhead rushing money along a metallic mole tunnel up to a balcony; Lochridge & Ridgway, with an engraved sign on the third-story cornice: STOVES, APPLIANCES, PLOWS. On the mezzanine at that store, I bought my first phonograph records, brittle 78s of big-band music—Woody Herman and Glenn Miller, and Glen Gray and his Casa Loma Orchestra playing "No Name Jive." A circuit of the courthouse square took you past the grand furniture stores, the two dime stores, the shoe stores, the men's stores, the ladies' stores, the banks, the drugstores. You'd walk past the poolroom and an exhaust fan would blow the intoxicating smell of hamburgers in your face. Before she bought a freezer, Mama stored meat in a rented food locker in town, near the ice company. She stored the butchered calf there, and she fetched hunks of him each week to fry. But hamburgers in town were better. They were greasier, and they came in waxed-paper packages.

At the corner drugstore, on the square, Mama and Janice and I sat at fili-greed wrought-iron tables on a black-and-white mosaic tile floor, eating pepper-mint ice cream. It was very cold in there, under the ceiling fans. The ice cream was served elegantly, in paper cones sunk into black plastic holders. We were uptown.

The A&P grocery, a block away, reeked of the rich aroma of ground coffee. Daddy couldn't stand the smell of coffee, but Mama loved it. Daddy retched and scoffed in his exaggerated fashion. "I can't stand that smell!" Granny perked coffee, and Granddaddy told me it would turn a child black. I hated coffee. I wouldn't touch it till I was thirty. We savored store-bought food—coconuts, pineapples, and Vienna sausages and potted meat in little cans that opened with keys. We rarely went to the uptown A&P. We usually traded at a small mom-and-pop grocery, where the proprietors slapped the hands of black children who touched the candy case. I wondered if they were black from coffee.

QUESTIONS FOR DISCUSSION AND WRITING

1. Mason says she "wanted to *be* somebody" (paragraph 4), particularly someone who is not preoccupied with food. Judging by the essay, to what extent does she succeed? What passages support your view?

2. Although town food is touted as more sophisticated and desirable than farm food, is Mason working a subtle irony in the juxtaposition? Homemade "gravy, ham, mashed potatoes" were ordinary, but town hamburgers "were better. They were greasier, and they came in waxed-paper packages" (paragraph 15). If there is an irony here, what is it, and how might Mason have intended for it to work?

3. Mason uses lists to describe Mama's work with food. How do these lists affect you as a reader? What difference would it make if Mason had chosen to break them up into shorter sentences?

4. Compare and contrast Mason's lists with the list that opens Eric Liu's "Notes of a Native Speaker" (p. 93). Write an essay that includes a description of some activity with which you are very familiar, using lists to convey the movements and sensations—sight, sound, smell, touch, taste—that accompany the activity. See if you can make your reader experience the same things you experience.

5. In your upbringing, did you ever yearn, as Mason did, for fundamentally different surroundings? For example, did you ever wish you could live a different sort of life? Explain why you were attracted to a different place or different people—or even different foods. If you eventually got to experience these things, describe what the experience was like and discuss whether it met your expectations.

ART SPIEGELMAN

Mein Kampf (My Struggle)

Art Spiegelman was born in Stockholm, Sweden, in 1948 to Nazi concentration camp survivors, and grew up in Queens, New York. The legacy of Spiegelman's family, his American Jewish identity, and his dedication to sequential art shaped his Pulitzer Prize–winning graphic novel Maus, A Survivor's Tale *(two volumes, 1986 and 1992).* Maus, *which was translated into twenty languages, gave the world new metaphors for the Holocaust, portraying Jews as mice and Nazis as predatory cats, an idea that came to Spiegelman when he noticed parallels between the mice in cat-and-mouse cartoons and racist stereotypes in films. Spiegelman graduated from New York's High School of Art and Design and from Harpur College. In 1971 he joined the counterculture comic book scene of San Francisco, California. He subsequently taught at the School of Visual Arts in New York City, married sequential artist and editor Françoise Mouly, and collaborated with her on the magazine* Raw, *in which episodes of* Maus *were first serialized. More recently, Spiegelman has authored* In the Shadow of No Towers *(2004), which deals with the September 11, 2001, attacks from the perspective of a New York City dweller, and* Breakdowns: Portrait of the Artist as a Young%@&*! *(2008) that combines his 1970 classics with autobiographical sketching of his growth as a comic artist.*

"Mein Kampf" (My Struggle), published in the New York Times Magazine *in 1996, is both a twisted reference to the Holocaust and a study of creative crisis. Spiegelman copies the title of Adolf Hitler's autobiographical political manifesto, but he explores career issues instead of genocidal theories. The piece gives a new meaning to the term "victim of his own success," as the artist is stalked by his own creation.*

QUESTIONS FOR DISCUSSION AND WRITING

1. What does Spiegelman mean when he writes, "now I feel like there's a 5,000-pound mouse breathing down my neck!" (panel 4)? What does this mouse, an obvious reference to Spiegelman's graphic novel *Maus*, symbolize? In what ways does Spiegelman intertwine the personal and the political in this autobiographical account? Identify recurrent images, characters, language.

2. Graphic novels are closely allied with comic strips; both can present serious subject manner in an apparently humorous format. In "Mein Kampf" Spiegelman uses humor to address grave issues of genocide, human survival, family relationships, and artistic representations of these, as well as his own creative crisis and his problems with memory. What does the graphic art format accomplish that might be hard to achieve in a poem or a novel? What advantages might poetry or fiction have? (It will be helpful to have a specific work of literature in mind when you answer this.)

3. In the last few panels, the artist's son appears. How does this add to or extend the meaning of "Mein Kampf"? In what way is the ending a satisfactory resolution to the piece? Are any questions or problems left unresolved?

4. Write an analysis of the way "Mein Kampf" tells a story and develops a set of ideas. With a partner or in a team, working through each frame in order, explain what you learn as you move from one frame to the next (in addition to what the dialogue balloons express). What subtle as well as obvious interactions do you see between the words and the images that contribute to the overall message and emotional tone?

5. Compare "Mein Kampf" with Lynda Barry's graphic treatment of "Hate" (p. 522) in their autobiographical approach to issues of ethnic, racial, and cultural stereotypes, prejudices, and hate. Are there positives to counteract the negatives? If you like one better than the other, explain why.

MAXINE HONG KINGSTON

On Discovery

Maxine Hong Kingston (b. 1940) attended the University of California at Berkeley (B.A., 1962) and then taught school in Hawaii as she pursued her writing career. Her alma mater designated her a Chancellor's Distinguished Professor (1990), and the state of Hawaii named her a National Treasure. Her first book, The Woman Warrior: Memoir of a Girlhood among Ghosts *(1976), received the National Book Critics Circle Award and became instantly popular and widely taught. Kingston's other works include* China Men *(1980), the novel* Tripmaster Monkey: His Fake Book *(1989), and* The Fifth Book of Peace *(2003). In these works she mixes autobiography and fiction, history and fantasy. She explores the influence of cultural stories, both from China, where her father was a scholar and her mother was a doctor, and from Stockton, California, where her immigrant parents ran a laundry business.*

"On Discovery" is the opening chapter of China Men, *Kingston's nonfiction analysis of the fate of Chinese men who went to America, at first as laborers on the transcontinental railroad, later as immigrants facing many difficulties of cultural displacement and assimilation. "On Discovery" is a parable, a story with a moral, and a reminder to readers not to take gender for granted, as a settled, immutable category or fixed way of looking at either men or women. "Gold Mountain" is the name that prospective immigrants who had not seen the country applied to the United States, another proverbial (although sometimes mythical) Utopia. (Remember, utopia means "nowhere," "out of place.")*

Once upon a time, a man, named Tang Ao, looking for the Gold Mountain, crossed an ocean, and came upon the Land of Women. The women immediately captured him, not on guard against ladies. When they asked Tang Ao to come along, he followed; if he had had male companions, he would've winked over his shoulder.

"We have to prepare you to meet the queen," the women said. They locked him in a canopied apartment equipped with pots of makeup, mirrors, and a woman's clothes. "Let us help you off with your armor and boots," said the women. They slipped his coat off his shoulders, pulled it down his arms, and shackled his wrists behind him. The women who kneeled to take off his shoes chained his ankles together.

A door opened, and he expected to meet his match, but it was only two old women with sewing boxes in their hands. "The less you struggle, the less it'll hurt," one said, squinting a bright eye as she threaded her needle. Two captors sat on him while another held his head. He felt an old woman's dry fingers trace his ear; the long nail on her little finger scraped his neck. "What are you doing?" he asked. "Sewing your lips together," she joked, blackening needles in a candle flame. The ones who sat on him bounced with laughter. But the old women did not sew his lips together. They pulled his earlobes taut and jabbed a needle through each of them. They had to poke and probe before puncturing the layers of skin correctly, the hole in the front of the lobe in line with the one in back, the layers of skin sliding about so. They worked the needle through — a last jerk for the needle's wide eye ("needle's nose" in Chinese). They strung his raw flesh with silk threads; he could feel the fibers.

The women who sat on him turned to direct their attention to his feet. They bent his toes so far backward that his arched foot cracked. The old ladies squeezed each foot and broke many tiny bones along the sides. They gathered his toes, toes over and under one another like a knot of ginger root. Tang Ao wept with pain. As they wound the bandages tight and tighter around his feet, the women sang footbinding songs to distract him: "Use aloe for binding feet and not for scholars."

During the months of a season, they fed him on women's food: the tea was ₅ thick with white chrysanthemums and stirred the cool female winds inside his body; chicken wings made his hair shine; vinegar soup improved his womb. They drew the loops of thread through the scabs that grew daily over the holes in his earlobes. One day they inserted gold hoops. Every night they unbound his feet, but his veins had shrunk, and the blood pumping through them hurt so much, he begged to have his feet re-wrapped tight. They forced him to wash his used bandages, which were embroidered with flowers and smelled of rot and cheese. He hung the bandages up to dry, streamers that dropped and draped wall to wall. He felt embarrassed; the wrappings were like underwear, and they were his.

One day his attendants changed his gold hoops to jade studs and strapped his feet to shoes that curved like bridges. They plucked out each hair on his face, powdered him white, painted his eyebrows like a moth's wings, painted his cheeks and lips red. He served a meal at the queen's court. His hips swayed and his shoulders swiveled because of his shaped feet. "She's pretty, don't you agree?" the diners said, smacking their lips at his dainty feet as he bent to put dishes before them.

In the Women's Land there are no taxes and no wars. Some scholars say that the country was discovered during the reign of Empress Wu (A.D. 694–705), and some earlier than that, A.D. 441, and it was in North America.

QUESTIONS FOR DISCUSSION AND WRITING

1. How do you know that you're reading a parable and not a true story? Does this matter?

2. What is done to Tang Ao to transform him from a man into a woman? Why are these changes brought about by women, in "the Land of Women"? For what purposes?

3. Why is Tang Ao so passive, allowing many painful things to be done to him? Given the fact that he is ashamed and embarrassed—as well as in pain—why doesn't he resist? Rebel?

4. Is "'She's pretty, don't you agree'" (paragraph 6) a compliment? A commentary on Tang Ao's servile degradation? Both?

5. Is it possible to change a person's identity by changing their external appearance? Discuss, with relation to "makeovers," weight loss, and other conspicuous physical changes. Are there comparable psychological changes that also occur? Changes in the ways others react to such transformations?

6. In what ways, if any, does Tang Ao's transformation relate to deliberate "passing" by members of various racial, ethnic, and cultural groups? People whose sexual preference is ambiguous or not apparent? People with disabilities?

SHERMAN ALEXIE

What Sacagawea Means to Me

For Alexie's biographical information, see page 45. "What Sacagawea Means to Me,"
originally published in Time *(2002), uses the ultra-American image of the theme*
park as a springboard for creative cultural analysis. Alexie raises questions about eth-
nicity, gender, and social class in relation to Sacagawea, a Native American woman
who, in 1804, was drafted into Lewis and Clark's expedition and lived out a complex
relationship to the conquering race.

In the future, every U.S. citizen will get to be Sacagawea for fifteen minutes. For
the low price of admission, every American, regardless of race, religion, gender,
and age, will climb through the portal into Sacagawea's Shoshone Indian brain.
In the multicultural theme park called Sacagawea Land, you will be kidnapped
as a child by the Hidatsa tribe and sold to Toussaint Charbonneau, the French-
Canadian trader who will take you as one of his wives and father two of your
children. Your first child, Jean-Baptiste, will be only a few months old as you
carry him during your long journey with Lewis and Clark. The two captains will
lead the adventure, fighting rivers, animals, weather, and diseases for thousands
of miles, and you will march right beside them. But you, the aboriginal multitasker, will also breastfeed. And at the end of your Sacagawea journey, you will be
shown the exit and given a souvenir T-shirt that reads, IF THE U.S. IS EDEN, THEN
SACAGAWEA IS EVE.

Sacagawea is our mother. She is the first gene pair of the American DNA.
In the beginning, she was the word, and the word was possibility. I revel in the
wondrous possibilities of Sacagawea. It is good to be joyous in the presence of her
spirit, because I hope she had moments of joy in what must have been a grueling life. This much is true: Sacagawea died of some mysterious illness when she
was only in her twenties. Most illnesses were mysterious in the nineteenth century, but I suspect that Sacagawea's indigenous immune system was defenseless
against an immigrant virus. Perhaps Lewis and Clark infected Sacagawea. If that
is true, then certain postcolonial historians would argue that she was murdered
not by germs but by colonists who carried those germs. I don't know much about
the science of disease and immunities, but I know enough poetry to recognize
that individual human beings are invaded and colonized by foreign bodies, just
as individual civilizations are invaded and colonized by foreign bodies. In that
sense, colonization might be a natural process, tragic and violent to be sure, but
predictable and ordinary as well, and possibly necessary for the advance, however
constructive and destructive, of all civilizations.

After all, Lewis and Clark's story has never been just the triumphant tale of two
white men, no matter what the white historians might need to believe. Sacagawea
was not the primary hero of this story either, no matter what the Native American

historians and I might want to believe. The story of Lewis and Clark is also the story of the approximately forty-five nameless and faceless first- and second-generation European Americans who joined the journey, then left or completed it, often without monetary or historical compensation. Considering the time and place, I imagine those forty-five were illiterate, low-skilled laborers subject to managerial whims and nineteenth-century downsizing. And it is most certainly the story of the black slave York, who also cast votes during this allegedly democratic adventure. It's even the story of Seaman, the domesticated Newfoundland dog who must have been a welcome and friendly presence and who survived the risk of becoming supper during one lean time or another. The Lewis and Clark Expedition was exactly the kind of multicultural, trigenerational, bigendered, animal-friendly, government-supported, partly French-Canadian project that should rightly be celebrated by liberals and castigated by conservatives.

In the end, I wonder if colonization might somehow be magical. After all, Miles Davis is the direct descendant of slaves and slave owners. Hank Williams is the direct descendant of poor whites and poorer Indians. In 1876 Emily Dickinson was writing her poems in an Amherst attic while Crazy Horse was killing Custer on the banks of the Little Big Horn. I remain stunned by these contradictions, by the successive generations of social, political, and artistic mutations that can be so beautiful and painful. How did we get from there to here? This country somehow gave life to Maria Tallchief and Ted Bundy, to Geronimo and Joe McCarthy, to Nathan Bedford Forrest and Toni Morrison, to the Declaration of Independence and Executive Order No. 1066, to César Chávez and Richard Nixon, to theme parks and national parks, to smallpox and the vaccine for smallpox.

As a Native American, I want to hate this country and its contradictions. I   5 want to believe that Sacagawea hated this country and its contradictions. But this country exists, in whole and in part, because Sacagawea helped Lewis and Clark. In the land that came to be called Idaho, she acted as diplomat between her long-lost brother and the Lewis and Clark party. Why wouldn't she ask her brother and her tribe to take revenge against the men who had enslaved her? Sacagawea is a contradiction. Here in Seattle, I exist, in whole and in part, because a half-white man named James Cox fell in love with a Spokane Indian woman named Etta Adams who gave birth to my mother. I am a contradiction; I am Sacagawea.

QUESTIONS FOR DISCUSSION AND WRITING

1. The opening paragraph of Alexie's essay places the reader in the frame of the story with sentences such as "You will be kidnapped as a child by the Hidatsa tribe and sold to Toussaint Charbonneau." Why does Alexie change the reader's identity? What ideas is he trying to convey, and what connections is he attempting to create? For example, when he writes "you, the aboriginal multitasker, will

also breastfeed," how is he trying to affect you as a male or female Indian or non-Indian reader?

2. Alexie states that "Lewis and Clark's story has never been just the triumphant tale of two white men, no matter what the white historians might need to believe" (paragraph 3). Why would white historians "need to believe" a different account from what Alexie offers? In what ways is Alexie's tale *nontriumphant* or *nonwhite*? Make a list of the ways Alexie attempts to modify, contradict, or update the story told by traditional historians. You could extend this discussion by bringing to class some traditional accounts of the Lewis and Clark Expedition or writing a research paper on contrasting interpretations of the Lewis and Clark Expedition.

3. Although Alexie is a Native American author deeply concerned with the effects of colonization on his ancestors, he also discusses the "forty-five nameless and faceless first- and second-generation European Americans who joined the journey" (paragraph 3), who are white. Why does he draw attention to this group?

4. In the last two paragraphs of "What Sacagawea Means to Me," Alexie discusses contradictions. Write a paper about one or more of these contradictions in which you explain its meaning or try to resolve it, or both. For example, what should we make of the fact that Emily Dickinson was composing classic American poetry at the same time that Crazy Horse was battling Custer? Are these activities equivalent? Does one cancel out the other? Do they represent a larger contradiction in American society? How can one nation (the "United" States) embody such differences? Or consider the following question: What does America *stand for* if it can produce both Geronimo and Joe McCarthy, both the Declaration of Independence and Executive Order No. 1066 (which provided for the internment of Japanese Americans during World War II)?

5. Compare Alexie's way of discussing the problems experienced by nonwhites in America to that of Leslie Marmon Silko's in "Language and Literature from a Pueblo Indian Perspective" (p. 39) and Alice Walker's "In Search of Our Mothers' Gardens" (p. 192). Which writer's approach to the problem of nonwhite existence and identity is more effective, in your opinion? Why? By yourself or with a partner, write an essay in which you explain which of the two essays is more likely to change readers' perceptions about the experience of being nonwhite in America.

N. SCOTT MOMADAY

The Way to Rainy Mountain

N. Scott Momaday (b. 1934) in Lawton, Oklahoma, grew up on an Indian reservation in the Southwest, where his Cherokee-Caucasian mother and Kiowa father were both teachers. After earning his doctorate at Stanford University (1963), where he was a student of essayist and novelist Wallace Stegner, Momaday taught English at the University of California at Santa Barbara, and at Berkeley, Stanford, and the University of Arizona. For Momaday, identity is "a moral idea, for it accounts for the way in which [a man] reacts to other men and to the world in general." Primarily a poet (Angle of Geese, 1974; The Gourd Dancer, 1976), Momaday has also written two novels—the Pulitzer Prize–winning House Made of Dawn *(1968), which launched a renaissance in Native American writing, and* The Ancient Child *(1989), as well as* The Names: A Memoir *(1976). Like his earlier books, Momaday's recent collections—*In the Presence of the Sun: Stories and Poems *(1992),* The Man Made of Words: Essays, Stories, Passages *(1997), and* In the Bear's House *(1999)—combine story, poem, prose poem, dialogue, ethnography, history, and personal history.*

In "The Way to Rainy Mountain," which became the prologue to Momaday's book of the same title, Momaday preserves and validates the Native American oral tradition, retelling Kiowa legends, tracing the history of the Kiowas' migration, lyrically describing the landscape of their journey, and placing himself and his family within that matrix. The Context readings following this essay explore how stories "take place," how a storyteller listens to others' stories and creates several storytelling voices, and how listeners understand a story in terms of other stories they know and create.

A single knoll rises out of the plain in Oklahoma, north and west of the Wichita Range. For my people, the Kiowas, it is an old landmark, and they gave it the name Rainy Mountain. The hardest weather in the world is there. Winter brings blizzards, hot tornadic winds arise in the spring, and in summer the prairie is an anvil's edge. The grass turns brittle and brown, and it cracks beneath your feet. There are green belts along the rivers and creeks, linear groves of hickory and pecan, willow and witch hazel. At a distance in July or August the steaming foliage seems almost to writhe in fire. Great green and yellow grasshoppers are everywhere in the tall grass, popping up like corn to sting the flesh, and tortoises crawl about on the red earth, going nowhere in the plenty of time. Loneliness is an aspect of the land. All things in the plain are isolate; there is no confusion of objects in the eye, but *one* hill or *one* tree or *one* man. To look upon that landscape in the early morning, with the sun at your back, is to lose the sense of proportion. Your imagination comes to life, and this, you think, is where Creation was begun.

I returned to Rainy Mountain in July. My grandmother had died in the spring, and I wanted to be at her grave. She had lived to be very old and at last infirm. Her only living daughter was with her when she died, and I was told that in death her face was that of a child.

I like to think of her as a child. When she was born, the Kiowas were living the last great moment of their history. For more than a hundred years they had controlled the open range from the Smoky Hill River to the Red, from the headwaters of the Canadian to the fork of the Arkansas and Cimarron. In alliance with the Comanches, they had ruled the whole of the southern Plains. War was their sacred business, and they were among the finest horsemen the world has ever known. But warfare for the Kiowas was preeminently a matter of disposition rather than of survival, and they never understood the grim, unrelenting advance of the U.S. Cavalry. When at last, divided and ill-provisioned, they were driven onto the Staked Plains in the cold rains of autumn, they fell into panic. In Palo Duro Canyon they abandoned their crucial stores to pillage and had nothing then but their lives. In order to save themselves, they surrendered to the soldiers at Fort Sill and were imprisoned in the old stone corral that now stands as a military museum. My grandmother was spared the humiliation of those high gray walls by eight or ten years, but she must have known from birth the affliction of defeat, the dark brooding of old warriors.

Her name was Aho, and she belonged to the last culture to evolve in North America. Her forebears came down from the high country in western Montana nearly three centuries ago. They were a mountain people, a mysterious tribe of hunters whose language has never been positively classified in any major group. In the late seventeenth century they began a long migration to the south and east. It was a journey toward the dawn, and it led to a golden age. Along the way the Kiowas were befriended by the Crows, who gave them the culture and religion of the Plains. They acquired horses, and their ancient nomadic spirit was suddenly free of the ground. They acquired Tai-me, the sacred Sun Dance doll, from that moment the object and symbol of their worship, and so shared in the divinity of the sun. Not least, they acquired the sense of destiny, therefore courage and pride. When they entered upon the southern Plains they had been transformed. No longer were they slaves to the simple necessity of survival; they were a lordly and dangerous society of fighters and thieves, hunters and priests of the sun. According to their origin myth, they entered the world through a hollow log. From one point of view, their migration was the fruit of an old prophecy, for indeed they emerged from a sunless world.

Although my grandmother lived out her long life in the shadow of Rainy 5 Mountain, the immense landscape of the continental interior lay like memory in her blood. She could tell of the Crows, whom she had never seen, and of the Black Hills, where she had never been. I wanted to see in reality what she had seen more perfectly in the mind's eye, and traveled fifteen hundred miles to begin my pilgrimage.

Yellowstone, it seemed to me, was the top of the world, a region of deep lakes and dark timber, canyons and waterfalls. But, beautiful as it is, one might have the sense of confinement there. The skyline in all directions is close at hand, the high wall of the woods and deep cleavages of shade. There is a perfect freedom in the mountains, but it belongs to the eagle and the elk, the badger and the bear. The

Kiowas reckoned their stature by the distance they could see, and they were bent and blind in the wilderness.

Descending eastward, the highland meadows are a stairway to the plain. In July the inland slope of the Rockies is luxuriant with flax and buckwheat, stonecrop and larkspur. The earth unfolds and the limit of the land recedes. Clusters of trees, and animals grazing far in the distance, cause the vision to reach away and wonder to build upon the mind. The sun follows a longer course in the day, and the sky is immense beyond all comparison. The great billowing clouds that sail upon it are shadows that move upon the grain like water, dividing light. Farther down, in the land of the Crows and Blackfeet, the plain is yellow. Sweet clover takes hold of the hills and bends upon itself to cover and seal the soil. There the Kiowas paused on their way; they had come to the place where they must change their lives. The sun is at home on the plains. Precisely there does it have the certain character of a god. When the Kiowas came to the land of the Crows, they could see the dark lees of the hills at dawn across the Bighorn River, the profusion of light on the grain shelves, the oldest deity ranging after the solstices. Not yet would they veer southward to the caldron of the land that lay below; they must wean their blood from the northern winter and hold the mountains a while longer in their view. They bore Tai-me in procession to the east.

A dark mist lay over the Black Hills, and the land was like iron. At the top of a ridge I caught sight of Devil's Tower upthrust against the gray sky as if in the birth of time the core of the earth had broken through its crust and the motion of the world was begun. There are things in nature that engender an awful quiet in the heart of man; Devil's Tower is one of them. Two centuries ago, because they could not do otherwise, the Kiowas made a legend at the base of the rock. My grandmother said:

> Eight children were there at play, seven sisters and their brother. Suddenly the boy was struck dumb; he trembled and began to run upon his hands and feet. His fingers became claws, and his body was covered with fur. Directly there was a bear where the boy had been. The sisters were terrified; they ran, and the bear after them. They came to the stump of a great tree, and the tree spoke to them. It bade them climb upon it, and as they did so it began to rise into the air. The bear came to kill them, but they were just beyond its reach. It reared against the tree and scored the bark all around with its claws. The seven sisters were borne into the sky, and they became the stars of the Big Dipper.

From that moment, and so long as the legend lives, the Kiowas have kinsmen in the night sky. Whatever they were in the mountains, they could be no more. However tenuous their well-being, however much they had suffered and would suffer again, they had found a way out of the wilderness.

My grandmother had a reverence for the sun, a holy regard that now is all but gone out of mankind. There was a wariness in her, and an ancient awe. She was a Christian in her later years, but she had come a long way about, and she never forgot her birthright. As a child she had been to the Sun Dances; she had taken part in those annual rites, and by then she had learned the restoration of her people in the presence of Tai-me. She was about seven when the last Kiowa Sun Dance was held in 1887 on the Washita River above Rainy Mountain Creek. The buffalo were gone. In order to consummate the ancient sacrifice—to impale the head of a buffalo bull upon the medicine tree—a delegation of old men journeyed into Texas, there to beg and barter for an animal from the Goodnight herd. She was ten when the Kiowas came together for the last time as a living Sun Dance culture. They could find no buffalo; they had to hang an old hide from the sacred tree. Before the dance could begin, a company of soldiers rode out from Fort Sill under orders to disperse the tribe. Forbidden without cause the essential act of their faith, having seen the wild herds slaughtered and left to rot upon the ground, the Kiowas backed away forever from the medicine tree. That was July 20, 1890, at the great bend of the Washita. My grandmother was there. Without bitterness, and for as long as she lived, she bore a vision of deicide.

Now that I can have her only in memory, I see my grandmother in the sev-   10
eral postures that were peculiar to her: standing at the wood stove on a winter morning and turning meat in a great iron skillet; sitting at the south window, bent above her beadwork, and afterwards, when her vision failed, looking down for a long time into the fold of her hands; going out upon a cane, very slowly as she did when the weight of age came upon her; praying. I remember her most often at prayer. She made long, rambling prayers out of suffering and hope, having seen many things. I was never sure that I had the right to hear, so exclusive were they of all mere custom and company. The last time I saw her she prayed standing by the side of her bed at night, naked to the waist, the light of a kerosene lamp moving upon her dark skin. Her long, black hair, always drawn and braided in the day, lay upon her shoulders and against her breasts like a shawl. I do not speak Kiowa, and I never understood her prayers, but there was something inherently sad in the sound, some merest hesitation upon the syllables of sorrow. She began in a high and descending pitch, exhausting her breath to silence; then again and again—and always the same intensity of effort, of something that is, and is not, like urgency in the human voice. Transported so in the dancing light among the shadows of her room, she seemed beyond the reach of time. But that was illusion; I think I knew then that I should not see her again.

Houses are like sentinels in the plain, old keepers of the weather watch. There, in a very little while, wood takes on the appearance of great age. All colors wear soon away in the wind and rain, and then the wood is burned gray and the grain appears and the nails turn red with rust. The windowpanes are black and opaque; you imagine there is nothing within, and indeed there are many ghosts, bones given up to the land. They stand here and there against the sky, and you approach them for a longer time than you expect. They belong in the distance; it is their domain.

Once there was a lot of sound in my grandmother's house, a lot of coming and going, feasting and talk. The summers there were full of excitement and reunion. The Kiowas are a summer people; they abide the cold and keep to themselves, but when the season turns and the land becomes warm and vital they cannot hold still; an old love of going returns upon them. The aged visitors who came to my grandmother's house when I was a child were made of lean and leather, and they bore themselves upright. They wore great black hats and bright ample shirts that shook in the wind. They rubbed fat upon their hair and wound their braids with strips of colored cloth. Some of them painted their faces and carried the scars of old and cherished enmities. They were an old council of warlords, come to remind and be reminded of who they were. Their wives and daughters served them well. The women might indulge themselves; gossip was at once the mark and compensation of their servitude. They made loud and elaborate talk among themselves, full of jest and gesture, fright and false alarm. They went abroad in fringed and flowered shawls, bright beadwork and German silver. They were at home in the kitchen, and they prepared meals that were banquets.

There were frequent prayer meetings, and great nocturnal feasts. When I was a child I played with my cousins outside, where the lamplight fell upon the ground and the singing of the old people rose up around us and carried away into the darkness. There were a lot of good things to eat, a lot of laughter and surprise. And afterwards, when the quiet returned, I lay down with my grandmother and could hear the frogs away by the river and feel the motion of the air.

Now there is a funeral silence in the rooms, the endless wake of some final word. The walls have closed in upon my grandmother's house. When I returned to it in mourning, I saw for the first time in my life how small it was. It was late at night, and there was a white moon, nearly full. I sat for a long time on the stone steps by the kitchen door. From there I could see out across the land; I could see the long row of trees by the creek, the low light upon the rolling plains, and the stars of the Big Dipper. Once I looked at the moon and caught sight of a strange thing. A cricket had perched upon the handrail, only a few inches away from me. My line of vision was such that the creature filled the moon like a fossil. It had gone there, I thought, to live and die, for there, of all places, was its small definition made whole and eternal. A warm wind rose up and purled like the longing within me.

The next morning I awoke at dawn and went out on the dirt road to Rainy 15 Mountain. It was already hot, and the grasshoppers began to fill the air. Still, it was early in the morning, and the birds sang out of the shadows. The long yellow grass on the mountain shone in the bright light, and a scissortail hied above the land. There, where it ought to be, at the end of a long and legendary way, was my grandmother's grave. Here and there on the dark stones were ancestral names. Looking back once, I saw the mountain and came away.

CONTEXTS FOR
"THE WAY TO RAINY MOUNTAIN"

Stories often open by establishing a location and its atmosphere. Because his stories are rooted in history and biography, Momaday's choice of location is somewhat limited: The Kiowas actually lived here, *migrated* there. *Nevertheless, he is free to choose the places from which his storyteller tells those events: Of all the places where the Kiowas lived, he chooses Rainy Mountain and its nearby cemetery, and that choice governs what his storyteller can see and tell or not tell.*

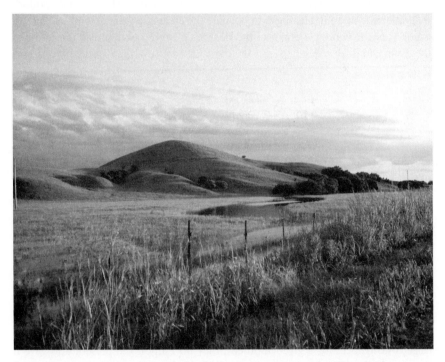

"Rainy Mountain. Many of my relatives lie in the cemetery nearby. The grasshoppers are innumerable."

N. SCOTT MOMADAY
East of My Grandmother's House

In section 24 of The Way to Rainy Mountain, *N. Scott Momaday reflects on the way place can inspire imagination.*

East of my grandmother's house the sun rises out of the plain. Once in his life a man ought to concentrate his mind upon the remembered earth, I believe. He ought to give himself up to a particular landscape in his experience, to look at it from as many angles as he can, to wonder about it, to dwell upon it. He ought to imagine that he touches it with his hands at every season and listens to the sounds that are made upon it. He ought to imagine the creatures there and all the faintest motions of the wind. He ought to recollect the glare of noon and all the colors of the dawn and dusk.

N. SCOTT MOMADAY
I Invented History

In one short paragraph of his memoir, The Names *(1976), N. Scott Momaday explains that as the past ("tracks" beneath his feet) and the future (the "infinite promise" of childhood's horizon) bear upon the present moment in a particular place, they gradually shape one's identity.*

I invented history. In April's thin white light, in the white landscape of the Staked Plains, I looked for tracks among the tufts of coarse, brittle grass, amid the stones, beside the tangle of dusty hedges. When I look back upon those days—days of infinite promise and steady adventure and the certain sanctity of childhood—I see how much was there in the balance. The past and the future were simply the large contingencies of a given moment; they bore upon the present and gave it shape. One does not pass through time, but time enters upon him, in his place. As a child, I knew this surely, as a matter of fact; I am not wise to doubt it now. Notions of the past and future are essentially notions of the present. In the same way an idea of one's ancestry and posterity is really an idea of the self. About this time I was formulating an idea of myself.

From N. Scott Momaday, *The Way to Rainy Mountain* (Albuquerque: University of New Mexico Press, 1969), 83.

From N. Scott Momaday, *The Names: A Memoir* (New York: Harper, 1976), 101–102.

N. SCOTT MOMADAY

Disturbing the Spirits:
Indian Bones Must Stay in the Ground

In this op-ed piece, occasioned by the discovery of a 9,300-year-old skeleton near the Columbia River in Washington State, N. Scott Momaday explains that "Native American creationism—which holds that the Indians sprang from the spirit world around us"—underlies the historical and spiritual attitudes that prompt Native Americans to oppose scientific research of archaeological sites and exhumed skeletons.

It might appear that the battle between evolutionists and creationists has broken out again in the case of a 9,300-year-old skeleton recently discovered near the Columbia River in Washington State. But because these remains were found on the sacred land of an Indian tribe, the Umatilla in nearby Oregon, it is not quite as simple as that. There is also history to consider and vindication. . . .

Reason, naturally is on the side of science. Indian creationists, like creationists in general, assume unreasonable attitudes. "We did not come from Asia," said a Hopi friend who opposes research on our origins. "We did not come from elsewhere. We were always here."

Even as intelligent a man as Vine Deloria Jr., a prominent Indian historian, dismisses as "scientific folklore" the discovery that Indians arrived in North America by crossing a land bridge across the Bering Strait. Yet there is solid evidence that people migrated that way from Asia to North America some 20,000 years ago.

There is no question that the arguments in favor of scientific inquiry are legitimate. Science has unlocked countless doors, has allowed human beings to see themselves with a clarity not available to our forebears.

The problem is this: Archeologists and anthropologists, especially, have given   5 science a bad name in the Indian world. For hundreds of years, the remains of American Indians have been taken from the earth and deposited in museums. The scientists involved have often acted without respect, much less reverence, toward these remains.

The violation of burial sites and the confiscation of human remains have been shameful and unprofessional. The boxes of human bones stacked in the Smithsonian Institution, often unidentified, virtually forgotten, are a sad reminder of this disrespect.

To many Native Americans, the theft of what is sacred to their community stands as the greatest of all the crimes perpetrated upon them. Wounds to the spirit are considered eminently more serious than wounds to the body. Indians have endured massacres, alcoholism, disease, poverty. The desecration of spiritual life has been no less an assault. Because the scientific scrutiny of human remains

From N. Scott Momaday, "Disturbing the Spirits," *New York Times*, 2 November 1996, p. 23.

once interred in sacred ground is indelibly associated with this painful history, Native Americans will resist. They feel they must. At stake is their identity, their dignity and their spirit.

N. SCOTT MOMADAY
The Native Voice

There are different kinds of stories. The basic story is one that centers upon an event. In American Indian oral tradition stories range from origin myths through trickster and hero tales to prophecy. With the exception of epic matter and certain creation myths, they are generally short. Concentration is a principle of their structure. Stories are formed. The form of the story is particular and perceptible.

Stories are true. They are true to our common experience, actual or imagined; they are statements that concern the human condition. To the extent that the human condition involves moral considerations, stories have moral implications. Beyond that, stories are true in that they are established squarely upon belief. In the oral tradition stories are told not merely to entertain or to instruct; they are told to be believed. Stories are not subject to the imposition of such questions as true or false, fact or fiction. Stories are realities lived and believed. In this sense they are indisputably true.

The storyteller is he who tells the story. To say this is to say that the storyteller is preeminently *entitled* to tell the story. He is original and creative. He creates the storytelling experience and himself and his audience in the process. He exists in the person of the storyteller for the sake of telling the story. When he is otherwise occupied, he is someone other than the storyteller. His telling of the story is a unique performance. The storyteller creates himself in the sense that the mask he wears for the sake of telling the story is of his own making, and it is never the same. He creates his listener in the sense that he determines the listener's existence within, and in relation to, the story, and it is never the same. The storyteller says in effect: "On this occasion I am, for I imagine that I am; and on this occasion you are, for I imagine that you are. And this imagining is the burden of the story, and indeed it is the story."

I have lived with the Kiowa story of the arrowmaker all my life. I have literally no memory that is older than that of hearing my father tell it to me when I was a small child. Such things take precedence in the mind. I set the story down in writing for the first time, and I have expressed my thoughts concerning it. I have told the story many times to many people in many parts of the world, and I believe that I have not yet found out its whole meaning.

From N. Scott Momaday, "The Native Voice," in *Columbia Literary History of the United States*, ed. Emory Elliott (New York: Columbia University Press, 1988), 5–15.

N. SCOTT MOMADAY

The Whole Journey and Three Voices

The preceding passage from "The Native Voice" helps us understand Momaday's explanation of Rainy Mountain *as a "whole journey," though not in linear form (first this happened, then that . . .). The author braids together three complementary storytelling voices (visually signaled by a different font or typeface): the mythical, the historical, and the immediately personal. In "The Man Made of Words" (1970), Momaday elaborates on the Prologue to* Rainy Mountain: *Every human being, he says, is "made of words" in the sense that language is "the element in which we think and dream and act, in which we live our daily lives." To answer the question "What is an American Indian?" Momaday retells passages from* Rainy Mountain. *Knowledge passes from one generation to another, he says, through "racial memory" expressed in the workings of imagination: When "imagination is superimposed upon historical event . . . [i]t becomes a story . . . deeply invested with meaning." He describes the "three voices" of* Rainy Mountain *as the voice of myth, the voice of history, and the voice of immediacy.*

THE WHOLE JOURNEY

Three hundred years ago the Kiowa lived in the mountains of what is now western Montana, near the headwaters of the Yellowstone River. Near the end of the 17th century they began a long migration to the south and east. They passed along the present border between Montana and Wyoming to the Black Hills and proceeded southward along the eastern slopes of the Rockies to the Wichita Mountains in the Southern Plains (Southwestern Oklahoma).

I mention this old journey of the Kiowas because it is in a sense definitive of the tribal mind; it is essential to the way in which the Kiowas think of themselves as a people. The migration was carried on over a course of many generations and many hundreds of miles. When it began, the Kiowas were a desperate and divided people, given up wholly to a day-by-day struggle for survival. When it ended, they were a race of centaurs, a lordly society of warriors and buffalo hunters. Along the way they had acquired horses, a knowledge and possession of the open land, and a sense of destiny. In alliance with the Comanches, they ruled the southern plains for a hundred years.

That migration — and the new golden age to which it led — is closely reflected in Kiowa legend and lore. Several years ago I retraced the route of that migration, and when I came to the end, I interviewed a number of Kiowa elders and obtained

From N. Scott Momaday, "The Man Made of Words," in *Indian Voices: The First Convocation of American Indian Scholars*, ed. Rupert Costo et al. (San Francisco: Indian Historian Press, 1970), 49–52, 58–59.

from them a remarkable body of history and learning, fact and fiction — all of it in the oral tradition and all of it valuable in its own right and for its own sake.

THREE VOICES

There are three distinct narrative voices in *The Way to Rainy Mountain* — the mythical, the historical, and the immediate. Each of the translations is followed by two kinds of commentary; the first is documentary and the second is privately reminiscent. Together, they serve, hopefully, to validate the oral tradition to an extent that might not otherwise be possible. The commentaries are meant to provide a context in which the elements of oral tradition might transcend the categorical limits of prehistory, anonymity, and archaeology in the narrow sense.

All of this is to say that I believe there is a way (first) in which the elements 5 of oral tradition can be shown, dramatically, to exist within the framework of a literary continuance, a deeper and more vital context of language and meaning than that which is generally taken into account; and (secondly) in which those elements can be located, with some precision on an evolutionary scale.

The device of the journey is peculiarly appropriate to such a principle of narration as this. And *The Way to Rainy Mountain* is a whole journey, intricate with notion and meaning; and it is made with the whole memory, that experience of the mind which is legendary as well as historical, personal as well as cultural.

PAULA GUNN ALLEN

Voice of the Turtle:
American Indian Literature, 1900–1970

UCLA Professor Paula Gunn Allen rejects the notion that Native American literary history is "'evolutionary,' as a white materialist-determinist notion that has no vital part in the Native Narrative Tradition. History is, rather, an account of how the transitory and the enduring interact." Just as Momaday tells the "whole journey" of the Kiowas by braiding together three storytelling voices, so Allen adopts weaving, rather than linear progress, as her metaphor for literary transformation.

A number of factors contributed to the sudden silencing of Native voices in publishing circles, the most important of these being the Great Depression and World War Two. The very influential work of the American historian Frederick B. Turner played a large role in the redefinition of Native people as forever beyond the pale of "civilized" culture, as did a dramatic rise in xenophobia, cultural chauvinism,

From Paula Gunn Allen, *Voice of the Turtle: American Indian Literature, 1900–1970* (New York: Ballantine, 1994), 4–8.

Portrait of N. Scott Momaday

and white supremacist thought that culminated in the establishment of the Third Reich in Germany but was by no means confined to that unhappy nation.

In the bland and blinding white cocoon of the 1950s, with its Red Scare, Cold War, and suburban fixations, a reawakened consciousness stirred in the United States. As a result, the nation returned to its former self in the 1960s, as though recovering from profound shock. In the ferment of the sixties, via Hippies, Civil Rights, the Peace Movement, Kennedy's Manpower Act, Johnson's War on Poverty, and especially the GI Bill that educated thousands of Native vets from the Second World War and the Korean and Vietnam Wars, Native writers began to publish fiction once again. The signal events of those years were the publication of N. Scott Momaday's *House Made of Dawn* in 1968 and John Milton's anthology, *The American Indian Speaks* which was published in 1969 — the year Momaday was awarded the Pulitzer Prize for fiction. In a sense, 1970 marked the end of literary and cultural dispossession. As the last quarter of the century has unfolded, the tiny trickle of fiction begun by Native writers during the first seventy years has become a broad and stately river.

Modern people think of change as progress, and that is the primary organizing principle — motivating force and raison d'être — of modern life. But Native people see change as the fundamental sacred process, as Transformation, as Ritual, as intrinsic to all of existence whenever and wherever, in whatever form or style it takes. Transformation: to change someone or something from one state or condition to another. Magic. What mages, wise ones, shamans do. Also what all peoples, human or otherwise, participate in. The wise are conscious of the process of Ritual Transformation in every facet of life.

Native American fiction in the twentieth century has two sides: the Oral Tradition of the Native Nations, and Western fiction and its antecedents. As does the Bible for the thought and literature of the West, ceremonial texts provide a major source of the symbols, allusions, and philosophical assumptions that inform our world and thus our work. It is a mistake to believe that ceremonial texts are "dated" and thus irrelevant to the work of modern writers. Which of these is inhalation, sine, and which exhalation, cosine, is impossible to say. They interact, as wings of a bird in flight interact. They give shape to our experience. They *signify.*

QUESTIONS FOR DISCUSSION AND WRITING

1. If you were to tell a grandchild or another youngster about a place in your childhood that shaped your character, what place would it be? Make a long list of everything you can remember about the place; then sort your list into clusters of things—maybe the atmosphere, the physical qualities, the personal associations that certain physical qualities evoke, whatever works. Think about what made this place special for you and in what ways its special quality became an important part of who you are.

   Read the "Writing about Places" section of the introduction (p. 24), and then write a sketch—complemented by photographs or drawings if you like—that shows your special place to others in your class.

2. Momaday says "I invented history" (p. 124). His writings in the Context readings address several dimensions of history: natural, personal, social, and cultural. In what ways does the special place you wrote about in question 1 fit into the past and the future? How and to what extent does it connect with various dimensions of history? In what ways do Sherman Alexie's (p. 115) and Gloria Anzaldúa's (p. 149) interpretations corroborate or alter Momaday's views of cultural history?

3. Read the "Narration" section of the introduction (p. 22), and then reflect on a story you were told as a child. What, if any, was the moral of the story? How explicit was it? Write about this story, and share your writing with your classmates, reflecting with them on how your story connects with stories they recall. As Momaday does, write about how that childhood story helps shape a story you now tell about yourself as an adult.

4. Reread Momaday's "The Native Voice" (p. 126); then reflect on a storytelling performance that has significance for you. Who told the story? How would you describe the scene of the storytelling? Try writing down as much of the story as you can in the language you recall. Considering *The Way to Rainy Mountain's* "three voices"—and mythic, historical, and immediate—explain which "voice" your story already embodies, and write companion pieces for it that embody the other two voices.

5. The final section of the Context readings explains how stories evoke other stories in order to persuade people to take action. To whom might you retell your story from question 4, and what action might that person or persons take in response? What other familiar stories do you want them to keep in mind? Rewrite your story, including references to related stories, as a call to a particular audience to take a particular action. On the basis of your story, what should they do?

6. Sherman Alexie says, "I always want to be on the edge of offending somebody." Thus he has criticized the "Mother Earth Father Sky" clichés that he claims are perpetuated by Indian authors such as Momaday. Compare and contrast Alexie's satiric interpretation of an iconic Indian woman, Sacagawea (p. 115) with Momaday's depiction of his grandmother in "The Way to Rainy Mountain" (p. 118). Is Alexie's criticism of Momaday justified? Has Momaday offered any defense of his depiction of his ancestors and their native land in any of the readings in this chapter?

HEATHER KING

The Closest to Love We Ever Get

Heather King, a devout Catholic, grew up on the New Hampshire coast. She gradu- ated from the University of New Hampshire (1977) and Boston's Suffolk Law School (1984) before working as an attorney in Beverly Hills. Two memoirs deal with her lifelong struggles with alcoholism. Parched *(2005) is a "tragicomic memoir about alcoholism as spiritual thirst"; aided by her family, she discovers—as many have before her—that "suffering leads to redemption." Her second memoir,* Redeemed: A Spiritual Misfit Stumbles toward God, Marginal Sanity, and the Peace That Passes All Understanding *(2008), follows her journey through her "holy" phase of recov- ery, in which religion offers strength as she copes with marital difficulties, divorce, her father's death, and breast cancer. King currently lives in Los Angeles, California, and is a commentator for NPR's* All Things Considered. *"The Closest to Love We Ever Get," first published in* Portland *magazine in 2007, weaves the major strands of her life into a seamless, spiritual whole. "How," she asks, "can you deal with this cease- lessly pulsing aorta of life with anything but spirituality?"*

I'm a person who craves quiet and solitude, yet I've lived in the crowded, noisy Los Angeles neighborhood of Koreatown for eleven years. I tell myself it's because I have a spacious, beautiful apartment and a gated courtyard filled with hibiscus and pomegranates. I tell myself it's because I pay only $760 a month—half as much as almost anywhere else in the city. But the longer I stay, the more I see it's not just the apartment that keeps me here: it's the challenges, the dilemmas, the paradoxes. People blast *ranchera* music at three in the morning but they also prune bougainvillea into glories of cascading blooms. They spray-paint gang slogans on my garage door by night and scrub the sidewalks clean by day. As I hang out my clothes on the line by the lemon tree, my back is to a busted washing machine; across the alley, a brand-new down comforter, still in its package, sits on top of a dumpster.

Part of my impulse living here is to hide out from the rest of the city—from the cell phones and SUVs, the hipsters, the people writing screenplays in too-cool-to-care coffeehouses—but in Koreatown I can't hide out from myself. Here I come face to face every day with the cross of my irritation, my anger, my racism, my fear. Here I am plunged into the deepest contradictions: between abundance and scarcity, community and solitude, sin and grace, my longing for wholeness and my resistance to it.

Here, I have no voice, no particular power. At Mass at St. Basil's, at 24-Hour Fitness, at Charlie Chan's Printing, at Ralph's Grocery, at the Vietnamese shop where I get my pedicures, I am often the only white person present. When I call out my window to Jung, the kid next door, to keep it down, he yells back: "We were here first! Why don't *you* move?" His nine-year-old face contorted by hate; hurt and fury rising in my own throat; I don't have to read the headlines on Iraq to know how wars start, how the battle lines are drawn.

I have driven from Koreatown to Death Valley, to Anza Borrego, to the East Mojave. I am pulled to the desert as if by a magnet; I'm forever scheming to escape there for a week, or two, or a month; I devour books about the desert, and yet I am uneasy with the nature writers who leave human beings out, who see us as a blight on the landscape. As a human being, and a Catholic, I see the cross everywhere: in actual deserts and, in the middle of one of the most densely populated sections of Los Angeles, in the desert of my own conflicted heart. Living in Koreatown has fortified my sense of apartness, allowed me to be in the city but not always of it, shaped me as a writer. But a writer has to be fully engaged: emotionally, spiritually, physically; has to mingle his or her body and blood with the rest of the world, the people in it, the page; has to find a way to cherish that world even as he or she struggles to endure it—Flannery O'Connor's phrase—which is perhaps the best definition of the cross I know. How can you be Catholic? people ask, and I want to ask back, but am afraid to, How can you write unless in some sense you have died and been resurrected and, in one way or another, are burning to tell people about it? How can you bear the sorrow of a world in which every last thing passes away without knowing that Christ is right up there on the cross with you? How can you be spiritual in LA? someone from back East once asked and, as a car alarm blared, a leaf blower blasted, and I looked out my window at the children hanging out the windows of the six-story apartment building across the street and screaming, I thought, *How can you deal with this ceaselessly pulsing aorta of life with anything but spirituality?*

Sometimes I have coffee with my friend Joan, who waitresses at Langer's 5 Deli, or my friend Larry, a janitor at Kaiser. Here is what feeds me: sitting on the corner of Wilshire and Serrano with traffic streaming by while Joan tells me about her troubles with the cook at work, or while Larry, who did time at every mental health facility from Camarillo to Norwalk before he stopped drinking, reminisces about his "nuthouse romances." What feeds me is the miracle of flesh-and-blood, of stories, of the daily struggles that "break, blow, burn" and make us new, as John Donne put it, that give us compassion for the struggles of others.

Inching out into Oxford Avenue on foot, headed to the library, I can barely make it across, there are so many cars barreling down from either direction: honking, cutting each other off, jostling for space. It's so easy to feel besieged, so easy to think *Why are there so many of them?* instead of realizing I'm one of "them" myself; that nobody else likes being crowded either. *How can a person live a life of love?* I ask myself as I reach the opposite curb: not love tacked on, added as an afterthought, but shot through every second; flaming out, "like shining from shook foil," as Gerard Manley Hopkins described the grandeur of God.

Wending my way home with my books, my vision temporarily transformed, I'm not seeing the refrigerators abandoned on the sidewalk, the triple-parked ice cream trucks, the overflowing trash cans. I'm seeing flashes of colorful Mexican tile, the 98-cent-store mural of waltzing Ajax cans and jitterbugging mops, my favorite flowers: the heliotrope on Ardmore, the wisteria near Harvard, the lemon on Mariposa. Or maybe it's not that I'm seeing one group of things instead of another but, for one fleeting moment, all simultaneously: the opposites held in balance a paradigm for the terrible tension and ambiguity of the human condition; the dreadful reality that we can never quite be sure which things we have done and which things we have failed to do, the difference between how we long for the world to be and how it must be a kind of crucifixion in the darkest, most excruciating depths of which we discover — the rear windows of the parked cars I'm walking by now covered with jacaranda blossoms — it's not that there's not enough beauty; it's that there's so much it can hardly be borne.

Monday morning, putting out the garbage as the sky turns pink above the salmon stucco façades, I bend my face to the gardenia in the courtyard, knowing that every shabby corner, every bird and flower and blade of grass, every honking horn and piece of graffitti, every pain and contradiction, deserves a song of praise. *O sacrament most holy, o sacrament divine . . . ,* we sang at Mass yesterday. The kids are coming in droves now, making their way to Hobart Middle School — pushing, yelling, throwing their candy wrappers on the sidewalk — and that is a kind of hymn, too. We're all doing our part, their exuberant shouts mingling with the thoughts I'll shape into an essay, all drifting like incense, raised aloft and offered up to the smoggy air above Koreatown. Maybe that's exactly as it should be. Maybe I need their noise and they need my silence; maybe the song we make together — all of us — is the closest to love we ever get.

"What are we here for?" Annie Dillard asks in *The Writing Life*. "*Propter chorum*, the monks say: for the sake of the choir."

QUESTIONS FOR DISCUSSION AND WRITING

1. Why does King choose to live in the Koreatown neighborhood of Los Angeles, where she is "often the only white person present" (paragraph 3)?

2. "As a human being, and a Catholic, I see the cross everywhere: in actual deserts and, in the middle of one of the most densely populated sections of Los Angeles, in the desert of my own conflicted heart" (paragraph 4). In what ways do King's locations influence her spirituality?

3. How does King answer her own question, "How can you deal with this cease-lessly pulsing aorta of life with anything but spirituality?" (paragraph 4)? What connections does she make between spirituality and living "*a life of love*" (paragraph 6)?

4. What is the meaning of King's title, "The Closest to Love We Ever Get"? Cite specific examples from the essay in your answer.

5. Spirituality is hard to put into words. If you consider yourself a spiritual person, try to explain your spirituality, using five or six key words. Or explain your own or another's spirituality in relation to a particular place, as King does. For instance, you could compare the descriptions of place in this essay with the relation of geography to human life and values in N. Scott Momaday's "The Way to Rainy Mountain" (p. 118) and/or E. B. White's "Once More to the Lake" (p. 163).

PAIRED READINGS: DOUBLE CONSCIOUSNESS

JAMES BALDWIN

Stranger in the Village

Through his fiction, James Baldwin (1924–1987) undertook to arouse the conscience of America during a time of social strife and racial polarization. Born in Harlem, he supplemented his education with intensive and obsessive reading. Baldwin's work would draw extensively on his Harlem youth—especially his struggle with a step-father who called him ugly and refused to recognize his talent. Editing school news-papers, writing stories, and publishing articles, Baldwin entered literary circles but, disgusted by racial encounters and an unsatisfactory personal life, moved to Paris in 1948. During a sojourn in Switzerland he completed his first novel, Go Tell It on the Mountain *(1953). The novels that followed center on family relations, homo-sexual love, and race; the best known are* Giovanni's Room *(1956) and* Another Country *(1962). Two of his plays,* The Amen Corner *(1955) and* Blues for Mister Charlie *(1964), have been produced on Broadway. Baldwin's two best-selling essay collections,* Notes of a Native Son *(1955) and* The Fire Next Time *(1963), give voice to the urgent emotional and spiritual dangers of racism. Essayist Phillip Lopate calls*

Baldwin "the greatest American essayist in the second half of the twentieth century." Baldwin retained his U.S. citizenship but lived primarily in France until his death, returning to the United States several times to lend his support to civil rights marches with Martin Luther King Jr., Stokely Carmichael, and Malcolm X.

In "Stranger in the Village," from Notes of a Native Son *(1955), Baldwin's account of his experience as the only black person living in a Swiss village leads into a meditation on blackness, whiteness, and the unique challenge of an American identity.*

From all available evidence no black man had ever set foot in this tiny Swiss village before I came. I was told before arriving that I would probably be a "sight" for the village; I took this to mean that people of my complexion were rarely seen in Switzerland, and also that city people are always something of a "sight" outside of the city. It did not occur to me—possibly because I am an American—that there could be people anywhere who had never seen a Negro.

It is a fact that cannot be explained on the basis of the inaccessibility of the village. The village is very high, but it is only four hours from Milan and three hours from Lausanne. It is true that it is virtually unknown. Few people making plans for a holiday would elect to come here. On the other hand, the villagers are able, presumably, to come and go as they please—which they do: to another town at the foot of the mountain, with a population of approximately five thousand, the nearest place to see a movie or go to the bank. In the village there is no movie house, no bank, no library, no theater; very few radios, one jeep, one station wagon; and at the moment, one typewriter, mine, an invention which the woman next door to me here had never seen. There are about six hundred people living here, all Catholic—I conclude this from the fact that the Catholic church is open all year round, whereas the Protestant chapel, set off on a hill a little removed from the village, is open only in the summertime when the tourists arrive. There are four or five hotels, all closed now, and four or five *bistros*, of which, however, only two do any business during the winter. These two do not do a great deal, for life in the village seems to end around nine or ten o'clock. There are a few stores, butcher, baker, *épicerie*, a hardware store, and a money-changer—who cannot change travelers' checks, but must send them down to the bank, an operation which takes two or three days. There is something called the *Ballet Haus*, closed in the winter and used for God knows what, certainly not ballet, during the summer. There seems to be only one schoolhouse in the village, and this for the quite young children; I suppose this to mean that their older brothers and sisters at some point descend from these mountains in order to complete their education—possibly, again, to the town just below. The landscape is absolutely forbidding, mountains towering on all four sides, ice and snow as far as the eye can reach. In this white wilderness, men and women and children move all day, carrying washing, wood, buckets of milk or water, sometimes skiing on Sunday afternoons. All week long boys and young men are to be seen shoveling snow off the rooftops, or dragging wood down from the forest in sleds.

The village's only real attraction, which explains the tourist season, is the hot spring water. A disquietingly high proportion of these tourists are cripples, or semi-cripples, who come year after year—from other parts of Switzerland, usually—to take the waters. This lends the village, at the height of the season, a rather terrifying air of sanctity, as though it were a lesser Lourdes. There is often something beautiful, there is always something awful, in the spectacle of a person who has lost one of his faculties, a faculty he never questioned until it was gone, and who struggles to recover it. Yet people remain people, on crutches or indeed on deathbeds; and wherever I passed, the first summer I was here, among the native villagers or among the lame, a wind passed with me—of astonishment, curiosity, amusement, and outrage. That first summer I stayed two weeks and never intended to return. But I did return in the winter, to work; the village offers, obviously, no distractions whatever and has the further advantage of being extremely cheap. Now it is winter again, a year later, and I am here again. Everyone in the village knows my name, though they scarcely ever use it, knows that I come from America—though, this, apparently, they will never really believe: black men come from Africa—and everyone knows that I am the friend of the son of a woman who was born here, and that I am staying in their chalet. But I remain as much a stranger today as I was the first day I arrived, and the children shout *Neger! Neger!* as I walk along the streets.

It must be admitted that in the beginning I was far too shocked to have any real reaction. In so far as I reacted at all, I reacted by trying to be pleasant—it being a great part of the American Negro's education (long before he goes to school) that he must make people "like" him. This smile-and-the-world-smiles-with-you routine worked about as well in this situation as it had in the situation for which it was designed, which is to say that it did not work at all. No one, after all, can be liked whose human weight and complexity cannot be, or has not been, admitted. My smile was simply another unheard-of phenomenon which allowed them to see my teeth—they did not, really, see my smile and I began to think that, should I take to snarling, no one would notice any difference. All of the physical characteristics of the Negro which had caused me, in America, a very different and almost forgotten pain were nothing less than miraculous—or infernal—in the eyes of the village people. Some thought my hair was the color of tar, that it had the texture of wire, or the texture of cotton. It was jocularly suggested that I might let it all grow long and make myself a winter coat. If I sat in the sun for more than five minutes some daring creature was certain to come along and gingerly put his fingers on my hair, as though he were afraid of an electric shock, or put his hand on my hand, astonished that the color did not rub off. In all of this, in which it must be conceded there was the charm of genuine wonder and in which there was certainly no element of intentional unkindness, there was yet no suggestion that I was human: I was simply a living wonder.

I knew that they did not mean to be unkind, and I know it now; it is necessary, nevertheless, for me to repeat this to myself each time that I walk out of the chalet. The children who shout *Neger!* have no way of knowing the echoes this sound raises in me. They are brimming with good humor and the more daring swell with pride when I stop to speak with them. Just the same, there are days when I cannot pause and smile, when I have no heart to play with them; when, indeed, I mutter sourly to myself, exactly as I muttered on the streets of a city these children have never seen, when I was no bigger than these children are now: *Your* mother *was a nigger.* Joyce is right about history being a nightmare—but it may be the nightmare from which no one *can* awaken. People are trapped in history and history is trapped in them.

There is a custom in the village—I am told it is repeated in many villages—of "buying" African natives for the purpose of converting them to Christianity. There stands in the church all year round a small box with a slot for money, decorated with a black figurine, and into this box the villagers drop their francs. During the *carnaval* which precedes Lent, two village children have their faces blackened—out of which bloodless darkness their blue eyes shine like ice—and fantastic horsehair wigs are placed on their blond heads; thus disguised, they solicit among the villagers for money for the missionaries in Africa. Between the box in the church and the blackened children, the village "bought" last year six or eight African natives. This was reported to me with pride by the wife of one of the *bistro* owners and I was careful to express astonishment and pleasure at the solicitude shown by the village for the souls of black folks. The *bistro* owner's wife beamed with a pleasure far more genuine than my own and seemed to feel that I might now breathe more easily concerning the souls of at least six of my kinsmen.

I tried not to think of these so lately baptized kinsmen, of the price paid for them, or the peculiar price they themselves would pay, and said nothing about my father, who having taken his own conversion too literally never, at bottom, forgave the white world (which he described as heathen) for having saddled him with a Christ in whom, to judge at least from their treatment of him, they themselves no longer believed. I thought of white men arriving for the first time in an African village, strangers there, as I am a stranger here, and tried to imagine the astounded populace touching their hair and marveling at the color of their skin. But there is a great difference between being the first white man to be seen by Africans and being the first black man to be seen by whites. The white man takes the astonishment as tribute, for he arrives to conquer and to convert the natives, whose inferiority in relation to himself is not even to be questioned; whereas I, without a thought of conquest, find myself among a people whose culture controls me, has even, in a sense, created me, people who have cost me more in anguish and rage than they will ever know, who yet do not even know of my existence. The astonishment with which I might have greeted them, should they have stumbled into my African village a few hundred years ago, might have rejoiced their hearts. But the astonishment with which they greet me today can only poison mine.

And this is so despite everything I may do to feel differently, despite my friendly conversations with the *bistro* owner's wife, despite their three-year-old son who has at last become my friend, despite the *saluts* and *bonsoirs*[1] which I exchange with people as I walk, despite the fact that I know that no individual can be taken to task for what history is doing, or has done. I say that the culture of these people controls me—but they can scarcely be held responsible for European culture. America comes out of Europe, but these people have never seen America, nor have most of them seen more of Europe than the hamlet at the foot of their mountain. Yet they move with an authority which I shall never have; and they regard me, quite rightly, not only as a stranger in their village but as a suspect latecomer, bearing no credentials, to everything they have—however unconsciously—inherited.

For this village, even were it incomparably more remote and incredibly more primitive, is the West, the West onto which I have been so strangely grafted. These people cannot be, from the point of view of power, strangers anywhere in the world; they have made the modern world, in effect, even if they do not know it. The most illiterate among them is related, in a way that I am not, to Dante, Shakespeare, Michelangelo, Aeschylus, Da Vinci, Rembrandt, and Racine; the cathedral at Chartres says something to them which it cannot say to me, as indeed would New York's Empire State Building, should anyone here ever see it. Out of their hymns and dances come Beethoven and Bach. Go back a few centuries and they are in their full glory—but I am in Africa, watching the conquerors arrive.

The rage of the disesteemed is personally fruitless, but it is also absolutely   10 inevitable; this rage, so generally discounted, so little understood even among the people whose daily bread it is, is one of the things that makes history. Rage can only with difficulty, and never entirely, be brought under the domination of the intelligence and is therefore not susceptible to any arguments whatever. This is a fact which ordinary representatives of the *Herrenvolk*,[2] having never felt this rage and being unable to imagine, quite fail to understand. Also, rage cannot be hidden, it can only be dissembled. This dissembling deludes the thoughtless, and strengthens rage and adds, to rage, contempt. There are, no doubt, as many ways of coping with the resulting complex of tensions as there are black men in the world, but no black man can hope ever to be entirely liberated from this internal warfare—rage, dissembling, and contempt having inevitably accompanied his first realization of the power of white men. What is crucial here is that, since white men represent in the black man's world so heavy a weight, white men have for black men a reality which is far from being reciprocal; and hence all black men have toward all white men an attitude which is designed, really, either to rob the white man of the jewel of his naïveté, or else to make it cost him dear.

The black man insists, by whatever means he finds at his disposal, that the white man cease to regard him as an exotic rarity and recognize him as a human being. This is a very charged and difficult moment, for there is a great deal of will power involved in the white man's naïveté. Most people are not naturally

---

[1]"Hellos" and "good evenings."

[2]Master race.

reflective any more than they are naturally malicious, and the white man prefers to keep the black man at a certain human remove because it is easier for him thus to preserve his simplicity and avoid being called to account for crimes committed by his forefathers, or his neighbors. He is inescapably aware, nevertheless, that he is in a better position in the world than black men are, nor can he quite put to death the suspicion that he is hated by black men therefore. He does not wish to be hated, neither does he wish to change places, and at this point in his uneasiness he can scarcely avoid having recourse to those legends which white men have created about black men, the most usual effect of which is that the white man finds himself enmeshed, so to speak, in his own language which describes hell, as well as the attributes which lead one to hell, as being as black as night.

Every legend, moreover, contains its residuum of truth, and the root function of language is to control the universe by describing it. It is of quite considerable significance that black men remain, in the imagination, and in overwhelming numbers in fact, beyond the disciplines of salvation; and this despite the fact that the West has been "buying" African natives for centuries. There is, I should hazard, an instantaneous necessity to be divorced from this so visibly unsaved stranger, in whose heart, moreover, one cannot guess what dreams of vengeance are being nourished; and, at the same time, there are few things on earth more attractive than the idea of the unspeakable liberty which is allowed the unredeemed. When, beneath the black mask, a human being begins to make himself felt one cannot escape a certain awful wonder as to what kind of human being it is. What one's imagination makes of other people is dictated, of course, by the laws of one's own personality and it is one of the ironies of black-white relations that, by means of what the white man imagines the black man to be, the black man is enabled to know who the white man is.

I have said, for example, that I am as much a stranger in this village today as I was the first summer I arrived, but this is not quite true. The villagers wonder less about the texture of my hair than they did then, and wonder rather more about me. And the fact that their wonder now exists on another level is reflected in their attitudes and in their eyes. There are the children who make those delightful, hilarious, sometimes astonishingly grave overtures of friendship in the unpredictable fashion of children; other children, having been taught that the devil is a black man, scream in genuine anguish as I approach. Some of the older women never pass without a friendly greeting, never pass, indeed, if it seems that they will be able to engage me in conversation; other women look down or look away or rather contemptuously smirk. Some of the men drink with me and suggest that I learn how to ski—partly, I gather, because they cannot imagine what I would look like on skis—and want to know if I am married, and ask questions about my *métier*. But some of the men have accused *le sale nègre*[3]—behind my back—of stealing wood and there is already in the eyes of some of them that peculiar, intent, paranoiac malevolence which one sometimes surprises in the

---

[3]The dirty Negro.

eyes of American white men when, out walking with their Sunday girl, they see a Negro male approach.

There is a dreadful abyss between the streets of this village and the streets of the city in which I was born, between the children who shout *Neger!* today and those who shouted *Nigger!* yesterday — the abyss is experience, the American experience. The syllable hurled behind me today expresses, above all, wonder: I am a stranger here. But I am not a stranger in America and the same syllable riding on the American air expresses the war my presence has occasioned in the American soul.

For this village brings home to me this fact: that there was a day, and not really a very distant day, when Americans were scarcely Americans at all but discontented Europeans, facing a great unconquered continent and strolling, say, into a marketplace and seeing black men for the first time. The shock this spectacle afforded is suggested, surely, by the promptness with which they decided that these black men were not really men but cattle. It is true that the necessity on the part of the settlers of the New World of reconciling their moral assumptions with the fact — and the necessity — of slavery enhanced immensely the charm of this idea, and it is also true that this idea expresses, with a truly American bluntness, the attitude which to varying extents all masters have had toward all slaves.

But between all former slaves and slave-owners and the drama which begins for Americans over three hundred years ago at Jamestown, there are at least two differences to be observed. The American Negro slave could not suppose, for one thing, as slaves in past epochs had supposed and often done, that he would ever be able to wrest the power from his master's hands. This was a supposition which the modern era, which was to bring about such vast changes in the aims and dimensions of power, put to death; it only begins, in unprecedented fashion, and with dreadful implications, to be resurrected today. But even had this supposition persisted with undiminished force, the American Negro slave could not have used it to lend his condition dignity, for the reason that this supposition rests on another: that the slave in exile yet remains related to his past, has some means — if only in memory — of revering and sustaining the forms of his former life, is able, in short, to maintain his identity.

This was not the case with the American Negro slave. He is unique among the black men of the world in that his past was taken from him, almost literally, at one blow. One wonders what on earth the first slave found to say to the first dark child he bore. I am told that there are Haitians able to trace their ancestry back to African kings, but any American Negro wishing to go back so far will find his journey through time abruptly arrested by the signature on the bill of sale which served as the entrance paper for his ancestor. At the time — to say nothing of the circumstances — of the enslavement of the captive black man who was to become the American Negro, there was not the remotest possibility that he would ever take power from his master's hands. There was no reason to suppose that his situation would ever change, nor was there, shortly, anything to indicate that his situation had ever been different. It was his necessity, in the words of E. Franklin

Frazier, to find a "motive for living under American culture or die." The identity of the American Negro comes out of this extreme situation, and the evolution of this identity was a source of the most intolerable anxiety in the minds and the lives of his masters.

For the history of the American Negro is unique also in this: that the question of his humanity, and of his rights therefore as a human being, became a burning one for several generations of Americans, so burning a question that it ultimately became one of those used to divide the nation. It is out of this argument that the venom of the epithet *Nigger!* is derived. It is an argument which Europe has never had, and hence Europe quite sincerely fails to understand how or why the argument arose in the first place, why its effects are frequently disastrous and always so unpredictable, why it refuses until today to be entirely settled. Europe's black possessions remained—and do remain—in Europe's colonies, at which remove they represented no threat whatever to European identity. If they posed any problem at all for the European conscience it was a problem which remained comfortingly abstract: in effect, the black man, as a *man* did not exist for Europe. But in America, even as a slave, he was an inescapable part of the general social fabric and no American could escape having an attitude toward him. Americans attempt until today to make an abstraction of the Negro, but the very nature of these abstractions reveals the tremendous effects the presence of the Negro has had on the American character.

When one considers the history of the Negro in America it is of the greatest importance to recognize that the moral beliefs of a person, or a people, are never really as tenuous as life—which is not moral—very often causes them to appear; these create for them a frame of reference and a necessary hope, the hope being that when life has done its worst they will be enabled to rise above themselves and to triumph over life. Life would scarcely be bearable if this hope did not exist. Again, even when the worst has been said, to betray a belief is not by any means to have put oneself beyond its power; the betrayal of a belief is not the same thing as ceasing to believe. If this were not so there would be no moral standards in the world at all. Yet one must also recognize that morality is based on ideas and that all ideas are dangerous—dangerous because ideas can only lead to action and where the action leads no man can say. And dangerous in this respect: that confronted with the impossibility of remaining faithful to one's beliefs, and the equal impossibility of becoming free of them, one can be driven to the most inhuman excesses. The ideas on which American beliefs are based are not, though Americans often seem to think so, ideas which originated in America. They came out of Europe. And the establishment of democracy on the American continent was scarcely as radical a break with the past as was the necessity, which Americans faced, of broadening this concept to include black men.

This was, literally, a hard necessity. It was impossible, for one thing, for 20 Americans to abandon their beliefs, not only because these beliefs alone seemed able to justify the sacrifices they had endured and the blood that they had spilled, but also because these beliefs afforded them their only bulwark against a moral chaos as absolute as the physical chaos of the continent it was their destiny to conquer. But in the situation in which Americans found themselves, these beliefs threatened an idea which, whether or not one likes to think so, is the very warp and woof of the heritage of the West, the idea of white supremacy.

Americans have made themselves notorious by the shrillness and the brutality with which they have insisted on this idea, but they did not invent it; and it has escaped the world's notice that those very excesses of which Americans have been guilty imply a certain, unprecedented uneasiness over the idea's life and power, if not, indeed, the idea's validity. The idea of white supremacy rests simply on the fact that white men are the creators of civilization (the present civilization, which is the only one that matters; all previous civilizations are simply "contributions" to our own) and are therefore civilization's guardians and defenders. Thus it was impossible for Americans to accept the black man as one of themselves, for to do so was to jeopardize their status as white men. But not so to accept him was to deny his human reality, his human weight and complexity, and the strain of denying the overwhelmingly undeniable forced Americans into rationalizations so fantastic that they approached the pathological.

At the root of the American Negro problem is the necessity of the American white man to find a way of living with the Negro in order to be able to live with himself. And the history of this problem can be reduced to the means used by Americans—lynch law and law, segregation and legal acceptance, terrorization and concession—either to come to terms with this necessity, or to find a way around it, or (most usually) to find a way of doing both these things at once. The resulting spectacle, at once foolish and dreadful, led someone to make the quite accurate observation that "the Negro-in-America is a form of insanity which overtakes white men."

In this long battle, a battle by no means finished, the unforeseeable effects of which will be felt by many future generations, the white man's motive was the protection of his identity; the black man was motivated by the need to establish an identity. And despite the terrorization which the Negro in America endured and endures sporadically until today, despite the cruel and totally inescapable ambivalence of his status in his country, the battle for his identity has long ago been won. He is not a visitor to the West, but a citizen there, an American; as American as the Americans who despise him, the Americans who fear him, the Americans who love him—the Americans who became less than themselves, or rose to be greater than themselves by virtue of the fact that the challenge he represented was inescapable. He is perhaps the only black man in the world whose relationship to white men is more terrible, more subtle, and more meaningful than the relationship of bitter possessed to uncertain possessors. His survival depended, and his development depends, on his ability to turn his peculiar status in the Western world to his own advantage and, it may be, to the very great advantage of that world. It remains for him to fashion out of his experience that which will give him sustenance, and a voice.

The cathedral at Chartres, I have said, says something to the people of this village which it cannot say to me; but it is important to understand that this cathedral says something to me which it cannot say to them. Perhaps they are struck by the power of the spires, the glory of the windows; but they have known God, after all, longer than I have known him, and in a different way, and I am terrified by the slippery bottomless well to be found in the crypt, down which heretics were hurled to death, and by the obscene, inescapable gargoyles jutting out of the stone and seeming to say that God and the devil can never be divorced. I doubt that the villagers think of the devil when they face a cathedral because they have never been identified with the devil. But I must accept the status which myth, if nothing else, gives me in the West before I can hope to change the myth.

Yet, if the American Negro has arrived at his identity by virtue of the abso- 25 luteness of his estrangement from his past, American white men still nourish the illusion that there is some means of recovering the European innocence, of returning to a state in which black men do not exist. This is one of the greatest errors Americans can make. The identity they fought so hard to protect has, by virtue of that battle, undergone a change: Americans are as unlike any other white people in the world as it is possible to be. I do not think, for example, that it is too much to suggest that the American vision of the world—which allows so little reality, generally speaking, for any of the darker forces in human life, which tends until today to paint moral issues in glaring black and white—owes a great deal to the battle waged by Americans to maintain between themselves and black men a human separation which could not be bridged. It is only now beginning to be borne in on us—very faintly, it must be admitted, very slowly, and very much against our will—that this vision of the world is dangerously inaccurate, and perfectly useless. For it protects our moral high-mindedness at the terrible expense of weakening our grasp of reality. People who shut their eyes to reality simply invite their own destruction, and anyone who insists on remaining in a state of innocence long after that innocence is dead turns himself into a monster.

The time has come to realize that the interracial drama acted out on the American continent has not only created a new black man, it has created a new white man, too. No road whatever will lead Americans back to the simplicity of this European village where white men still have the luxury of looking on me as a stranger. I am not, really, a stranger any longer for any American alive. One of the things that distinguishes Americans from other people is that no other people has ever been so deeply involved in the lives of black men, and vice versa. This fact faced, with all its implications, it can be seen that the history of the American Negro problem is not merely shameful, it is also something of an achievement. For even when the worst has been said, it must also be added that the perpetual challenge posed by this problem was always, somehow, perpetually met. It is precisely this black-white experience which may prove of indispensable value to us in the world we face today. This world is white no longer, and it will never be white again.

W. E. B. DU BOIS
The "Veil" of Self-Consciousness

This essay, first published in the Atlantic Monthly *(1897), helped introduce the Harvard-educated black sociologist W. E. B. Du Bois (1868–1963) to a national audience and went on to become the opening chapter of his classic* The Souls of Black Folk *(1903). Du Bois argued that, given the opportunity to educate themselves, American blacks would emerge from behind what he referred to as their "veil" of self-conscious "differentness."*

Between me and the other world there is ever an unasked question: unasked by some through feelings of delicacy; by others through the difficulty of rightly framing it. All, nevertheless, flutter round it. They approach me in a half-hesitant sort of way, eye me curiously or compassionately, and then, instead of saying directly, How does it feel to be a problem? they say, I know an excellent colored man in my town; or I fought at Mechanicsville; or, Do not these Southern outrages make your blood boil? At these I smile, or am interested, or reduce the boiling to a simmer, as the occasion may require. To the real question, How does it feel to be a problem? I answer seldom a word . . .

After the Egyptian and Indian, the Greek and Roman, the Teuton and Mongolian, the Negro is a sort of seventh son, born with a veil, and gifted with second-sight in this American world,—a world which yields him no self-consciousness, but only lets him see himself through the revelation of the other world. It is a peculiar sensation, this double-consciousness, this sense of always looking at one's self through the eyes of others, of measuring one's soul by the tape of a world that looks on in amused contempt and pity. One ever feels his two-ness,—an American, a Negro; two souls, two thoughts, two unreconciled strivings; two warring ideals in one dark body, whose dogged strength alone keeps it from being torn asunder. The history of the American Negro is the history of this strife,—this longing to attain self-conscious manhood, to merge his double self into a better and truer self. In this merging he wishes neither of the older selves to be lost. He does not wish to Africanize America, for America has too much to teach the world and Africa; he does not wish to bleach his Negro blood in a flood of white Americanism, for he believes—foolishly, perhaps, but fervently—that Negro blood has yet a message for the world. He simply wishes to make it possible for a man to be both a Negro and an American without being cursed and spit upon by his fellows, without losing the opportunity of self-development.

This is the end of his striving: to be a co-worker in the kingdom of culture, to escape both death and isolation, and to husband and use his best powers.

QUESTIONS FOR DISCUSSION AND WRITING

1. The "physical characteristics of the Negro" cause James Baldwin problems in Europe as well as in the United States (paragraph 4), as they did for Du Bois fifty years earlier. What are these problems? Does Baldwin, too, experience a "veil of self-consciousness"? What are the differences between the problems he experiences on either side of the Atlantic? What are some of the similarities? How does Baldwin respond to them?

2. What is Baldwin's attitude toward the villagers' practice of "'buying' African natives for the purpose of converting them to Christianity" (paragraph 6)? What is the villagers' attitude toward it? Does Baldwin understand the villagers' "reason" to feel that way? Do they understand his reason not to? Why or why not?

3. Du Bois, an African American intellectual writing in *The Souls of Black Folk* (1903), refers to the question he is often asked, "How does it feel to be a problem?" Baldwin, writing half a century later, analyzes the "root of the American Negro problem" (paragraph 22). What does Baldwin consider the basis of "the problem"? In what ways has American society changed in the half century since Baldwin wrote that could cause a different judgment today? Is the election of Barack Obama as U.S. president in itself a sufficient indicator of major social changes? Explain your answer with particular reference to education, economics, and politics.

4. The rest of the essays in this chapter, by Sojourner Truth (1850), Gloria Anzaldúa (writing in 2002 about the 1980s–90s), and Deirdre McCloskey (1999), address issues in which gender identity and sexual preference were also seen as "problems" in the culture they lived in and during the time they wrote. The motto on the T-shirt in the photograph on p. 148, "Nobody Knows I'm Gay," also provides a witty comment on gender-related "problems." Analyze one or more of these pieces in relation to the issues raised by Du Bois and Baldwin.

5. Have you ever felt like a "stranger in a strange land," displaced or alien in an unfamiliar culture—of a school, town, state or region, country? What was the nature of this experience? Did you like being an "outsider"? Why or why not? Whether or not you liked it, did you learn or grow from this, and if so, in what ways? Does this estrangement still continue? If so, with what effects? Or have you gotten beyond this, and if so, with what consequences, for better or for worse? Do you know of others in comparable situations, anywhere in the world? Write an analysis, even if it's inconclusive.

SOJOURNER TRUTH

Ain't I a Woman?

Born Isabella Van Wagener to a family of slaves in Ulster County, New York, Sojourner Truth (1797–1883) grew up the property of various masters who abused her physically and sexually, until she fled and found refuge in 1827. A religious vision- ary since childhood, she devoted herself to evangelical work in New York City while raising two children and doing domestic work. In 1843 she heeded a call to "travel up and down the land," changed her name to Sojourner Truth, and embarked on a mission to preach. At a utopian community in Northampton, Massachusetts, she embraced the cause of abolition, eventually taking her message to the Midwest, where her charismatic oratory attracted a large following. In 1850 Truth took on the cause of women's rights and began to fight oppression on two fronts. Her autobiography, The Narrative of Sojourner Truth (1850)—which she dictated to Olive Gilbert, a sym- pathetic white woman—sold enough copies to provide a source of income.

Nell Irvin Painter's Sojourner Truth: A Life, a Symbol (1996) questions whether Truth's quintessential feminist statement—"Ain't I a Woman?"—is entirely her own creation. She did deliver an effective speech at the 1851 Ohio Women's Rights Con- vention, but it appears to have been embellished by later biographers. Regardless, this incendiary speech is a model of persuasive oratory.

Well, children, where there is so much racket there must be something out of kil- ter. I think that 'twixt the negroes of the South and the women at the North, all talking about rights, the white men will be in a fix pretty soon. But what's all this here talking about?

That man over there says women need to be helped into carriages, and lifted over ditches, and to have the best place everywhere. Nobody ever helps me into car- riages, or over mud-puddles, or gives me any best place! And ain't I a woman? Look at me! Look at my arm! I have ploughed and planted, and gathered into barns, and no man could head me! And ain't I a woman? I could work as much and eat as much as a man—when I could get it—and bear the lash as well! And ain't I a woman? I have borne thirteen children, and seen them most all sold off to slavery, and when I cried out with my mother's grief, none but Jesus heard me! And ain't I a woman?

Then they talk about this thing in the head; what's this they call it? [Intellect, someone whispers.] That's it, honey. What's that got to do with women's rights or negro's rights? If my cup won't hold but a pint, and yours holds a quart, wouldn't you be mean not to let me have my little half-measure full?

Then that little man in black there, he says women can't have as much rights as men, 'cause Christ wasn't a woman! Where did your Christ come from? Where did your Christ come from? From God and a woman! Man had nothing to do with Him.

If the first woman God ever made was strong enough to turn the world 5 upside down all alone, these women together ought to be able to turn it back, and get it right side up again! And now they is asking to do it, the men better let them.

Obliged to you for hearing me, and now old Sojourner ain't got nothing more to say.

QUESTIONS FOR DISCUSSION AND WRITING

1. How does Sojourner Truth establish her authority to speak on the topic of women's rights? How does she paint a picture of herself that makes the audience sympathetic to her cause?

2. How does the repeated phrase "ain't I a woman?" work in this speech to move the audience and convey Truth's ideas? What would the speech be like if that phrase were absent? What types of rhetorical moves in this piece show that it is a speech and not a written essay?

3. Do you think women have achieved equality in U.S. society since Truth gave her speech? Are there areas in which advances still need to be made? Write a short essay—or perhaps a short speech—designed to convince people of your point of view.

4. How does Truth's self-presentation compare to Alice Walker's description, in "In Search of Our Mothers' Gardens" (p. 192), of the women Jean Toomer met in the 1920s? Does Truth's speech support Moynihan's assertion that "destroying the Negro family under slavery [. . .] broke the will of the Negro people" (p. 203, paragraph 8)?

BOB DAEMMRICH

Nobody Knows I'm Gay

QUESTIONS FOR DISCUSSION AND WRITING

1. "Meaning in context"—is there any other kind? How do you "read" the message on the T-shirt? Though amusing, is it serious? Is the wearer blowing his "cover"? What messages on the subject is he sending to his readers?

2. Suppose the wearer is actually not gay. Are there any clues in the picture about the sexual orientations of this man or his two companions? Does your interpretation change if you know that this photograph was taken on October 11, 2003, National Coming Out Day, at a gay rights rally at the University of Texas at Austin?

3. Suppose the T-shirt was plain white. How would that affect your interpretation of the people in the photograph? Would you even remember it?

GLORIA ANZALDÚA

From *Beyond Traditional Notions of Identity*

Gloria Anzaldúa, among the first openly lesbian Chicana authors, was born in 1942 in southwest Texas, a borderland between the United States and Mexico that she considers "una herida abierta," an open wound, where "the Third World grates against the First and bleeds." The daughter of a sharecropper and a field worker, she labored in the fields weekends and summers throughout high school and college, before graduating with a bachelor's degree from Pan American University in 1969. She earned a master's degree in English and education from the University of Texas in Austin (1972) and a doctorate from the University of California at Santa Cruz. Her work, such as This Bridge Called My Back: Writings by Radical Women of Color *(co-edited with Cherríe Moraga, 1981) and* Borderlands/La Frontera, The New Mestiza *(1987), powerfully addresses—in two English and six Spanish dialects—issues of poverty, racism, and gender. Anzaldúa died in 2004. "Beyond Traditional Notions of Identity," revisiting* Borderlands *after two decades, was published in the* Chronicle of Higher Education *October 11, 2002.*

More than two decades ago, Cherríe Moraga and I edited a multigenre collection giving voice to radical women of color, *This Bridge Called My Back: Writings by Radical Women of Color*. Every generation that reads *This Bridge Called My Back* rewrites it. Like the trestle bridge, and other things that have reached their zenith, it will decline unless we attach it to new growth or append new growth to it. In a new collection of writings and art, *this bridge we call home: radical visions for transformation*, AnaLouise Keating and I, together with our contributors, attempt to continue the dialogue of the past 21 years, rethink the old ideas, and germinate new theories. We move from focusing on what has been done to us (victimhood) to a more extensive level of agency, one that questions what we're doing to each other, to those in distant countries, and to the earth's environment.

Twenty-one years ago we struggled with the recognition of difference within the context of commonality. Today we grapple with the recognition of commonality within the context of difference. While *This Bridge Called My Back* displaced whiteness, *this bridge we call home* carries that displacement further. It questions the terms *white* and *women of color* by showing that whiteness may not be applied to all whites, because some possess women-of-color consciousness, just as some women of color bear white consciousness. We intend to change notions of identity, viewing it as part of a more complex system covering a larger terrain, and demonstrating that the politics of exclusion based on traditional categories diminishes our humanness.

Today categories of race and gender are more permeable and flexible than they were for those of us growing up before the 1980s. Today we need to move beyond separate and easy identifications, creating bridges that cross race and other classifications among different groups via intergenerational dialogue. Rather than legislating and restricting racial identities, we hope to make them more pliant.

We must learn to incorporate additional underrepresented voices; we must attempt to break the impasse between women of color and other groups. By including women and men of different "races," nationalities, classes, sexualities, genders, and ages in our discussions, we complicate the debates within feminist theory both inside and outside the academy and inside and outside the United States.

Our goal is not to use differences to separate us from others, but neither   5
is it to gloss over those differences. Many of us identify with groups and social positions not limited to our ethnic, racial, religious, class, gender, and national classifications. Though most people self-define by what they exclude, we define who we are by what we include — what I call the new tribalism. I fear that many *mujeres de color* will not want whites or men to join the dialogue. We risk the displeasure of those women. There are no safe spaces. "Home" can be unsafe and dangerous because it bears the likelihood of intimacy and thus thinner boundaries.

QUESTIONS FOR DISCUSSION AND WRITING

1. Anzaldúa explains that two decades earlier her work had "struggled with the recognition of difference within the context of commonality" but that now "we grapple with the recognition of commonality within the context of difference" (paragraph 2). Explain how this perspective applies to Eric Liu's "Notes of a Native Speaker" (p. 93), Sherman Alexie's "What Sacagawea Means to Me" (p. 115), and Richard Rodriguez's "Aria" (p. 275).

2. What does Anzaldúa mean by "Today categories of race and gender are more permeable and flexible than they were for those of us growing up before the 1980s" (paragraph 3)? Consider such essays as those by Kingston, "On Discovery" (p. 112), and McCloskey, "Yes, Ma'am" (p. 151) in your answer.

3. "Today," says Anzaldúa, "we need to . . . [create] bridges that cross race and other classifications among different groups via intergenerational dialogue" (paragraph 3). With a partner, preferably one of a racial or ethnic group different from yours and possibly of another generation, write an essay expanding on this idea.

DEIRDRE N. McCLOSKEY
Yes, Ma'am

Deirdre N. McCloskey was born Donald McCloskey in 1942, in Ann Arbor, Michigan. As Donald, McCloskey earned undergraduate and graduate degrees in economics at Harvard University and became a professor at the University of Chicago and the University of Iowa as well as a scholar noted for taking a sometimes controversial cross-disciplinary approach that combined economic theory and practice with history, philosophy, and rhetoric. In the mid-1990s, after years of internal struggle, McCloskey—who had been married for three decades and had two children—began the process of a gender change, resulting in complete gender reassignment surgery in 1996 and a new identity as Deirdre N. McCloskey.

Since 2000 Deirdre McCloskey has been Distinguished Professor of Economics, History, English, and Communication at the University of Illinois at Chicago and was Visiting Tinbergen Professor (2002–2006) of Philosophy, Economics, and Art and Cultural Studies at Erasmus University of Rotterdam. Her most recent (of fourteen) books include How to Be Human—Though an Economist *(2001),* The Bourgeois Virtues: Ethics for an Age of Capitalism *(2006), and* The Cult of Statistical Significance: How the Standard Error Costs Us Jobs, Justice, and Lives *(with Stephen Ziliak, 2008). Describing herself as a "postmodern free-market quantitative Episcopalian feminist Aristotelian," McCloskey has also published some 360 articles on economic theory, economic history, philosophy, rhetoric, feminism, ethics, and law. Her highly personal* Crossing: A Memoir *appeared in 1999 to much critical acclaim.*

Clients contemplating a sex change are generally required by their physicians to live life as a member of the opposite sex for a year or more before gender reassignment surgery, and even after surgery they must continue to adapt physically to their new identity. In the following chapter from Crossing, *McCloskey describes her early attempts to assume a physical identity that strangers would accept as that of a woman. She also considers the gestural differences between women and men and the hostility directed at those perceived to be cross-gendered.*

It's hard to pass. You just try it, Dee would say. I mean really try to pass as the opposite gender, not just put on a joke dress and a lampshade hat for the Lions picnic. You'll be surprised at how many gender clues there are and how easy it is to get them wrong. Scores of them, natural and unnatural, genetic and socially constructed.

No, hundreds. Women stand and sit at angles. Men offer their hands to shake. Women put their hands to their chests when speaking of themselves. Men barge through. Women look frequently at nonspeaking participants in a conversation. Men don't look at each other when talking. Women carry papers and books clutched to their midriffs, men balance things on their hips. Women smile at other women when entering their space. Men never smile at male strangers. Women put their hands on their hips with fingers pointing backward. Men use wide gestures. Women frequently fold their hands together in their laps. Men walk from their shoulders, women from their hips. And on and on.

Dee watched other women in her culture for characteristic gestures and practiced them on the spot. *The way the hands gesture together, as though in a little dance. The way the fingers lie up the arm when the arms are crossed. Standing with feet in a ballet pose. Pulling your hair from under a coat just put on.* (It was some time before her hair was long enough to make that feminine gesture useful.) Years into her transition she could amuse herself in a dull moment in a mall or airport by breaking down other women's gestures and trying them out. Like square dancing: hundreds of calls.

Rest one elbow on the back of the other hand, laid horizontally across your middle, the free hand stretching vertically to frame your face from the bottom, palm out. In touching your face, which you should do frequently, hold the hand in a graceful pose. For situations such as display at the dinner table, learn the hand pose used in ballet—fingers arched and separated, middle finger almost touching the thumb. Pinky up, but not too much, since it's an obvious parody of the ladylike. Overacting evokes the theatrical tradition of drag. Try to create a somewhat splayed effect with the fingers, angled up, instead of masculine cupping. When shaking hands—don't be the first to offer—use no strong grip, and place your hand sideward into the other person's. Check your hair frequently. Play idly with your jewelry. Check your clothing (a set of gestures that women's clothes require more often than men's, or else you stride out of the ladies' room with the back of your skirt up around your behind). Always stand more on one foot than the other. Stand with your legs crossed (a youngish gesture, this). Never stand manlike with feet parallel and legs spread wide. Angle your feet when you stop at the corner before crossing. Rest with hands together, not sprawled all over like a man's. When sitting cross your legs, either knee over knee angled to one side (never lower leg crossed horizontally over the knee, like the Greek boy in the statue removing a splinter) or to one side beneath the chair ankle over ankle. Never slouch when you sit. Stick your rear end solidly into the back of the chair, and never stretch your legs out, crossed at the ankles. Keep your knees together when you sit—"close the gates of hell" used to be the misogynist joke about it—which is easier if your knees are naturally angled inward, as girls' and especially women's are. If your feet are not crossed when sitting, keep your legs together from feet to knees. "Take up less space" is one formula; another is "keep your wrists loose," and still another "keep your elbows close to your body," this one imitating the effect of a female angle in the elbow, a piece of biology. But the formulas are hard to apply, like formal grammatical rules. Imitate, imitate, the way girls learn it. Deirdre was congratulated three years into full time: "Last year your motions were a little abrupt; now they are convincingly feminine." The gesture language is probably imitated with the same ease and at the same age as the spoken language, and like the spoken language it is hard to learn as an adult.

Little girls act different from little boys, independent of the slight structural differences in their bodies. By age ten many girls even know the secret smile.

Much of behavior is gendered. A lot of it is culturally specific and variable from person to person. European men cross their legs in a way that in America is coded as feminine. American soldiers in Vietnam would sneer at what they read as femininity in their Vietnamese allies and enemies: "They're all queer, you know." Mediterranean and Middle Eastern women make broader gestures, not the little dance of hands that upper-middle-class women in America use. The gender clues figure in any culture in an abundance that only a gender crosser or Dustin Hoffman preparing for *Tootsie* can grasp.

Of course if you are *aiming* to be funny then you want to be read, even if you are skillful at giving appropriate gender clues. Passing is not at issue. The Australian comedian who has developed the character "Dame Edna" is good at it. Without a leer or a nudge, he simply *is* the absurd Dame and sometimes spends hours in character, yet of course his audience knows. Miss Piggy of the Muppets is similar. She is gloriously who she is, yet everyone knows it's cross-speaking—her voice is always that of a man using falsetto. Getting read is part of the joke.

If you are not trying to be funny, you do not want to get read. Really, you don't. A sincere but detected attempt to jump the gender border from male to female—and no joking about it—creates anxiety in men, to be released by laughter if they can handle it or by a length of steel pipe if they can't. A 1997 survey claimed that 60 percent of cross-gendered people had been assaulted. Deirdre knew a gender crosser who had been beaten by four young men outside a bar even in peaceful Iowa City. The director of Gender PAC noted that "RuPaul is funny so long as she stays in a television studio. But try walking to the subway and she'll be a grease spot on the sidewalk before she makes it home." (If a female-to-male crosser was read by men maybe he would be regarded as cute, or rational: after all, it's rational to prefer to be a man, isn't it? Like the daily prayer by Orthodox Jewish men thanking God for not making them women. On the other hand, Brandon Teena, a pre-op female-to-male thief outed by the Falls City, Nebraska, police department was raped, complained about it to the police, who did nothing, and the next week in 1993 was murdered. Not by women.)

The anxiety is weirdly strong. A standard routine in the movies is that two men are forced to sleep with each other by circumstances (oh, sure), and then one of them dreams that he's sleeping with a woman. The other man, horrified by the amorous advances, rejects them violently, and the awakened dreamer is ashamed. The routine enacts over and over again the male anxiety about being homosexual, much less being a woman, and the violent reaction the anxiety arouses. With this threat of violence in mind, Donald's sister had given him her own pepper spray. The pepper spray, though, wouldn't be much good against a steel pipe.

Women who read a cross-dresser are not violent, but frightened and indignant. Who is this guy? What's he up to? Deirdre knew from being a woman on trains late at night in Holland or walking by Dutch cafés in the summertime or living later in the less demonstrative but more dangerous environment of America that women have daily experiences of men in fact being up to something, often something sexual, often enough something dangerous. At first it was flattering, the knocking on windows of the *eetcafé* as she went by, the propositions to come into the jazz club and have a drink. Then it was tedious or frightening. Women experience dangerous men all day long and are on the alert. The alertness is not male bashing, merely prudence in the company of people with greater upper-body strength and the inclination to use it, intoxicated by lethal fantasies about What She Really Wants. Women who read a gender crosser are putting her in this category of dangerous men. To be read by women is utterly demoralizing. After all, the gender crosser is trying to join the women, to pass as one, and instead they are treating her like a man, maybe nuts, probably dangerous, definitely another one of those bloody *men.*

On all counts it is better for a gender crosser to pass rapidly to the other side,   10 and making the crossing rapid ought to be the purpose of medical intervention, such as facial surgery, and social intervention, such as counseling on gender clues. Women acquainted with a gender crosser sometimes think of her interest in facial surgery as vanity. Natural-born women have no problem passing as women. "You're silly to want operations," says a woman out of a face with pointed chin, no brow-ridges, high cheekbones. Deirdre's mother declared that getting electrolysis, which she regarded as merely temporary, was "vain." But a nose job or a facelift or electrolysis that will make a gender crosser passable will also make her less likely to be scorned or raped or killed—at any rate at no more than the shocking rates for genetic women. Deirdre knew a not very passable gender crosser in tolerant Holland who had been raped three times. It is merely prudent to pass.

Some radical feminists object to gender crossing. They complain of the gender crosser that she (when they have the ruth to call her "she") is adopting oppressive stereotypes about women and therefore contributing to society's discrimination. The gender crosser, they claim, is pulling women back to the 1950s, white gloves and pillbox hats, lovely garden parties, and a *Leave It to Beaver* vision of a woman's life.

There is little truth in the stereotype argument. The crossphobe who uses it ordinarily doesn't know any gender crossers. A gender crosser with a job or career outside the home tries to keep it and does not in practice dissolve into a 1950s heaven of full-time cookie baking and teatime gossip. Far from becoming passive and stereotypically feminine, the gender crossers Deirdre knew often retained much of their masculine sides. The crossphobes mix up gender crossers with drag queens or female impersonators, whose shtick is indeed a parody of women—sometimes demeaning and stereotypical, though often enough loving and amusing. In 1958 the sociologist Harold Garfinkel described a gender crosser named Agnes. Latter-day crossphobes attack Agnes as "displaying rigidly traditional ideas of what a woman is" or having "stereotypical views of femininity" or "constructing an extremely narrow and constricted view of womanhood." Agnes was nineteen, a typist, at the height of the feminine mystique. But no allowances:

"I don't support you in your effort to have an operation, because you have stereo-typical views of what it means to be a woman." Unlike all the other nineteen-year-old typists in 1958. (Agnes had the operation, and was fine, because Garfinkel and a psychiatrist named Stoller did support her.)

A gender crosser trying to be a woman must reproduce enough of the char-acteristic gestures to escape being read, and often—especially in voice—this is difficult. It becomes second nature, and a comfort to oneself even when alone. But if you fail you are classed with people stereotyping women. Or murdered. The crossphobe radical feminists are allies in hatred with the gay-bashing mur-derers of Matthew Shephard.

The complaint about stereotyping will be delivered by a genetic woman whose every gesture and syllable is stereotypically feminine. At seminars in which Deirdre was attacked for stereotyping she would reply with the same stereotypi-cally feminine gestures or turns of phrase just used by the crossphobe—who had been practicing them since she was a little girl. This was Garfinkel's point, that gender is something "done," a performance, not an essence springing from genitals or chromosomes. Deirdre would say, "Of course I [putting her hand to her chest in the feminine way of referring to oneself, just used by the cross-phobe] would never [doing a deprecating double flap with her hands in the style of American middle-class women] want to damage women by *stereotyp-ing* [raising her voice in the falsetto of emphasis stereotypical of women, for instance the crossphobe attacking the genuineness of gender crossers]."

The passing worked better, slowly, each month, if she dressed carefully and   15
worked at it. Each little acceptance delighted her. The signal was being called "mevrouw" in Holland, "ma'am" in America, "madame" in France, "madam" in England. *Yes: call me madam.*

She is getting up to leave a Dutch tram at Oostzeedijk, intent on how to make the transfer to the subway. *Let's see: across there and down. Remember to watch for the bicycles.* The tram has almost stopped and she is pressing the exit button when she hears finally through her English thoughts and the haze of a foreign tongue, *"Mevrouw! Mevrouw!" It's me they're calling,* she thinks. *Oh. I've left a package.* She smiles in thanks and snatches up the package, slip-ping out the door as it closes, still smiling. They see her as "ma'am."

At the grocery store she is accosted by a woman giving out samples of a Dutch delicacy. It doesn't look very good. The woman babbles at Dee in Dutch, and Dee catches only the blessed "mevrouw." She smiles and shakes her head no thank you and pushes the cart toward the canned goods.

In May in Paris with an economist friend, Nancy, who is visiting there for a year, she walks out of a hat store, wearing the lovely lace floppy number just pur-chased. An elegant Frenchman goes by and says with a smile, "Un beau chapeau, madame!" Deirdre's French is poor, and she is still wondering if he could have said what she thought he had said when he politely repeats it in English over his shoulder as he walks on, "A beautiful hat, madame!" She would say when telling the story, "I could have kissed him. If he had proposed, I would have married him on the spot. Even though he was shorter."

A month later she wears the hat (which can be worn only in Paris or at special events) to a daylong concert of classical music in the park in Rotterdam. Sitting at luncheon on the grass with some members of her women's group, she feels particularly lovely. A Dutchman passes by and makes in Dutch the same remark the Frenchman had made, "A beautiful hat, mevrouw!"

The women's group meets at a restaurant in Rotterdam. It is a year since she abandoned the male role. The waiter asks the *"dames"* (DAH-mez) what they want, including Deirdre without notice or comment. ***One of the dames. Yes.*** 20

QUESTIONS FOR DISCUSSION AND WRITING

1. In her opening paragraphs, McCloskey observes a number of "gender clues," distinctions between the physical behavior and gestures of women and men. Are these distinctions borne out by your own observations?

2. At the end of paragraph 4, McCloskey claims that children early on learn gendered behavior through imitation. In paragraph 5, she makes the further point that gender-identified behavior differs from culture to culture. What do these ideas suggest about her views on gender?

3. McCloskey writes that both men and women respond negatively when they detect in someone a "sincere . . . attempt to jump the gender border from male to female," but in different ways (paragraphs 7–9). How does she account for these different negative reactions?

4. McCloskey refers to herself throughout this essay in the third person—as "she," "Dee," "Deirdre," and even "Donald" (her pre-crossing name). Why might she have chosen to do this? What is its effect on you as a reader?

5. "Some radical feminists object to gender crossing," McCloskey writes at the beginning of paragraph 11. Starting with McCloskey's elaboration of this point, write an essay in which you explore your views about gendered behavior, as described in paragraphs 4–5, and gender stereotypes, such as the female homemakers and garden clubbers and the male breadwinners and sports enthusiasts depicted in popular films and television. Expand your perspective with references to Kingston (p. 112) and Anzaldúa (p. 149).

CHAPTER 3

Relationships and Life Choices: Life, Love, Work, Play— What's the Best Balance?

KIM WARP

Rising Sea Levels — An Alternative Theory

Rising Sea Levels — An Alternative Theory

QUESTIONS FOR DISCUSSION AND WRITING

1. What is the butt of the joke in this cartoon and its caption? Might Kim Warp, the cartoonist, be attacking two problems with a single drawing? Is obesity a fit subject for humor? Why or why not?

2. How are the people presented in this cartoon? Do they fit stereotypes? Are they caricatures, or do they appear to be drawn from life as we know it?

3. Current estimates are that 66 percent of Americans are moderately to severely obese, and that childhood obesity has more than tripled in the past thirty years, from 6.5 percent in 1980 to 19.6 percent in 2008. Major health risks for both adults and children include type 2 diabetes, heart disease, high blood pressure, stroke, some types of cancer, pulmonary hypertension, and cardiac arrhythmia (National Center for Chronic Disease Prevention and Health Promotion). Is obesity a lifestyle choice? If so, should society be expected to pay for the medical consequences? Why or why not?

4. Write one or more alternative captions for this cartoon. If you wish, consult some of the Internet entries under "Fat Rights" or under "Fat Acceptance."

ANNA QUINDLEN

Anniversary

Anna Quindlen (b. 1952) became a New York Times *reporter within three years of graduating from Barnard (B.A., 1974). In 1992 her* New York Times *column, "Public and Private," won the Pulitzer Prize for Commentary as well as the accolade that she was "the unintended voice of the baby boom generation." Between 1999 and 2009 she wrote a bimonthly column for* Newsweek, *to which she continues to contribute in semiretirement. Her columns, focusing on "the rocky emotional terrain of marriage, parenthood, secret desires and self-doubts," as* Newsweek *says, have been collected in* Living Out Loud *(1988) and* Thinking Out Loud *(1994). Her novels also focus on the complications of family life:* Object Lessons *(1991), on the "dislocations of growing up";* One True Thing *(1995), on right-to-die issues;* Black and Blue *(1998), on domestic violence. "Anniversary," first published in* Newsweek *(1997), addresses familiar mother–daughter issues that transcend time. Indeed, the essay itself is timeless.*

I needed my mother again the other day. This time it was a fairly serious matter, a question from my doctor about our family medical history. Most of the time what I want is more trivial: the name of the family that lived next to us on Kenwood Road, the fate of that black wool party dress with the killer neckline, curiosity about whether those tears were real or calculated to keep all five of us in line. "When Mom cried, man," my brother Bob said not long ago. "That's what I really couldn't handle."

I've needed my mother many many times over the last twenty-five years, but she has never been there, except in my mind, where she tells me to buy quality, keep my hair off my face, and give my father the benefit of the doubt. When Bob's wife was dying of cancer several years ago, we made her make video- and audiotapes for her children because our little sister, who was eight when our own mother died, cannot remember what Prudence Marguerite Pantano Quindlen looked or sounded like. I remember. I remember everything. I was nineteen; I was older. I am older now by five years than my mother was when she died. Her death transformed my life.

We're different, those of us whose mothers have gone and left us to fend for ourselves. For that is what we wind up doing, no matter how good our fathers, or family, or friends: On some deep emotional level, we fend for ourselves. The simplest way to say it is also the most true—we are the world's grown-ups. "No girl becomes a woman until her mother dies" goes an old proverb. No matter what others may see, or she herself thinks, we believe down to our bones that our mother's greatest calling was us; with that fulcrum to our lives gone, we become adults overnight.

This makes some of us hard, sometimes, and driven, too. We perform for a theater of empty seats: Look at me, Ma, I did good, I'm okay, I'll get by. It was no surprise to me to discover that Madonna's mother died when she was a child. Rosie O'Donnell used to watch the old talk shows, Mike Douglas, Merv Griffin, with her mom before her mom died when she was a kid. I don't know Rosie O'Donnell, but I know whom she thinks of every time she steps through those curtains and onto that stage and hears the applause. Maybe she hears the sound of two hands clapping, the two that are not there, the only ones that count.

The funny thing is that the loss makes us good and happy people in some 5 ways, too, in love with life because we know how fleeting and how precious it can be. We have our priorities straight.

QUESTIONS FOR DISCUSSION AND WRITING

1. What sorts of advice do you seek from your parents (or parent surrogates)? Big questions, like the meaning of life? Matters of value? Is the advice conveyed explicitly or implicitly to you? By what means? Can you—and do you—count on your parents for their opinions on more trivial matters, such as those Quindlen mentions in paragraph 1? Why are even the small, seemingly insignificant matters actually important? How do you know?

2. What does Quindlen mean by '"No girl becomes a woman until her mother dies"' (paragraph 3)? How does your mother's presence in your life influence your answer, whether she is alive and present, absent, or dead? Would you give the same answer concerning your father? Explain.

3. Quindlen concludes this short tribute to her mother with an acknowledgment of the understanding that many come to when they have experienced a medical crisis or death: "The funny thing is that the loss makes us good and happy people in

some ways, too, in love with life because we know how fleeting and how precious it can be." What does she mean by this? Is even to mention it sentimental?

4. As a culture, Americans tend to prefer satire to sentimentality, even (or especially) when discussing people and matters dear to our hearts. Is "Anniversary" a sentimental essay? Why or why not? Is it all right to admit that you like it even if it is indeed sentimental? Or do you prefer to avoid sentimentality at all costs? In what ways can you tell a parent or person in an equivalent relationship that you love them without the expression becoming either mechanical and routine or saccharine? Do actions speak louder than words?

5. Analyze your answers with a classmate, and compare the similarities and differences in your responses to your respective parents. In what ways do the presence of other adults in your life — stepparents, close adult friends of the family — affect your relationships with your parents? Can you generalize from your answers?

BRIAN DOYLE

Joyas Voladoras

Brian Doyle, editor of Portland Magazine *(University of Portland, in Oregon) has published nine collections of essays, including* Two Voices: A Father and Son Discuss Family and Faith, *coauthored with his father, Jim Doyle (1996);* Credo *(1999);* Saints Passionate & Peculiar *(2002); and* Leaping: Revelations and Epiphanies *(2003). Doyle's essays have appeared in the* American Scholar, *the* Atlantic Monthly, *and* Harper's. *His award-winning work has been included in the* Best American Essays *anthologies of 1998, 1999, 2003, and 2009. "Joyas Voladoras," originally published in the* American Scholar *(2004), represents Doyle at his characteristic best: short (six paragraphs), ranging from earth to heaven and back again through precise, evocative details that get at the heart of the matter—in this case, the human heart and its endurance through the experiences, common yet profound, that connect all creatures small and great.*

Consider the hummingbird for a long moment. A hummingbird's heart beats ten times a second. A hummingbird's heart is the size of a pencil eraser. A hummingbird's heart is a lot of the hummingbird. *Joyas voladoras,* flying jewels, the first white explorers in the Americas called them, and the white men had never seen such creatures, for hummingbirds came into the world only in the Americas, nowhere else in the universe, more than three hundred species of them whirring and zooming and nectaring in hummer time zones nine times removed from ours, their hearts hammering faster than we could clearly hear if we pressed our elephantine ears to their infinitesimal chests.

Each one visits a thousand flowers a day. They can dive at sixty miles an hour. They can fly backwards. They can fly more than five hundred miles without pausing to rest. But when they rest they come close to death: on frigid nights, or when they are starving, they retreat into torpor, their metabolic rate slowing to a fifteenth of their normal sleep rate, their hearts sludging nearly to a halt, barely beating, and if they are not soon warmed, if they do not soon find that which is sweet, their hearts grow cold, and they cease to be. Consider for a moment those hummingbirds who did not open their eyes again today, this very day, in the Americas: bearded helmetcrests and booted racket-tails, violet-tailed sylphs and violet-capped woodnymphs, crimson topazes and purple-crowned fairies, red-tailed comets and amethyst woodstars, rainbow-bearded thornbills and glittering-bellied emeralds, velvet-purple coronets and golden-bellied star-frontlets, fiery-tailed awlbills and Andean hillstars, spatuletails and pufflegs, each the most amazing thing you have never seen, each thunderous wild heart the size of an infant's fingernail, each mad heart silent, a brilliant music stilled.

Hummingbirds, like all flying birds but more so, have incredible enormous immense ferocious metabolisms. To drive those metabolisms they have racecar hearts that eat oxygen at an eye-popping rate. Their hearts are built of thinner, leaner fibers than ours. Their arteries are stiffer and more taut. They have more mito-chondria in their heart muscles—anything to gulp more oxygen. Their hearts are stripped to the skin for the war against gravity and inertia, the mad search for food, the insane idea of flight. The price of their ambition is a life closer to death; they suf-fer more heart attacks and aneurysms and ruptures than any other living creature. It's expensive to fly. You burn out. You fry the machine. You melt the engine. Every creature on earth has approximately two billion heartbeats to spend in a lifetime. You can spend them slowly, like a tortoise, and live to be two hundred years old, or you can spend them fast, like a hummingbird, and live to be two years old.

The biggest heart in the world is inside the blue whale. It weighs more than seven tons. It's as big as a room. It *is* a room, with four chambers. A child could walk around in it, head high, bending only to step through the valves. The valves are as big as the swinging doors in a saloon. This house of a heart drives a creature a hundred feet long. When this creature is born it is twenty feet long and weighs four tons. It is waaaaay bigger than your car. It drinks a hundred gallons of milk from its mama every day and gains two hundred pounds a day, and when it is seven or eight years old it endures an unimaginable puberty and then it essentially disappears from human ken, for next to nothing is known of the mating habits, travel pat-terns, diet, social life, language, social structure, diseases, spirituality, wars, stories, despairs, and arts of the blue whale. There are perhaps ten thousand blue whales in the world, living in every ocean on earth, and of the largest mammal who ever lived we know nearly nothing. But we know this: the animals with the largest hearts in the world generally travel in pairs, and their penetrating moaning cries, their pierc-ing yearning tongue, can be heard underwater for miles and miles.

Mammals and birds have hearts with four chambers. Reptiles and turtles 5 have hearts with three chambers. Fish have hearts with two chambers. Insects and mollusks have hearts with one chamber. Worms have hearts with one chamber, although they may have as many as eleven single-chambered hearts. Unicellular bacteria have no hearts at all; but even they have fluid eternally in motion, washing from one side of the cell to the other, swirling and whirling. No living being is without interior liquid motion. We all churn inside.

So much held in a heart in a lifetime. So much held in a heart in a day, an hour, a moment. We are utterly open with no one, in the end—not mother and father, not wife or husband, not lover, not child, not friend. We open windows to each but we live alone in the house of the heart. Perhaps we must. Perhaps we could not bear to be so naked, for fear of a constantly harrowed heart. When young we think there will come one person who will savor and sustain us always; when we are older we know this is the dream of a child, that all hearts finally are bruised and scarred, scored and torn, repaired by time and will, patched by force of character, yet fragile and rickety forevermore, no matter how ferocious the defense and how many bricks you bring to the wall. You can brick up your heart as stout and tight and hard and cold and impregnable as you possibly can and down it comes in an instant, felled by a woman's second glance, a child's apple breath, the shatter of glass in the road, the words "I have something to tell you," a cat with a broken spine dragging itself into the forest to die, the brush of your mother's papery ancient hand in a thicket of your hair, the memory of your father's voice early in the morning echoing from the kitchen where he is making pancakes for his children.

QUESTIONS FOR DISCUSSION AND WRITING

1. The essay's title, "Joyas Voladoras," means "flying jewels," the name the first explorers of the Americas gave to hummingbirds, says Doyle (paragraph 1). What characteristics of hummingbirds does each of the first three paragraphs focus on?

2. Doyle connects the two halves of his essay with "Every creature on earth has approximately two billion heartbeats to spend in a lifetime" (paragraph 3). What themes are common to both halves of the essay? What features unify hummingbirds, whales, humans?

3. Explain the significance of the last two sentences in paragraph 5, "No living being is without interior liquid motion. We all churn inside," in relation to the final paragraph. What sorts of "churning" does paragraph 6 identify?

4. Doyle writes that "all hearts finally are bruised and scarred, scored and torn, repaired by time and will, patched by force of character, yet fragile and rickety forevermore" (paragraph 6). Based on your own understanding of family relationships and life choices, is Doyle right? Explain.

5. Write an interpretive essay on one of the photographs in *The Arlington Reader* (such as "The Damm Family in Their Car," p. 224; "Replaceable You," p. 410; "Migrant Mother," p. 556; "Nobody Knows I'm Gay," p. 148; or a photograph of your choice. To guide your interpretation, use some of the considerations of human relationships Doyle raises in the last paragraph of "Joyas Voladoras."

E. B. WHITE

Once More to the Lake

E. B. (Elwyn Brooks) White (1899–1985) is beloved for his children's books —Stuart Little (1945), Charlotte's Web (1952), and The Trumpet of the Swan (1970) —and famous for his distinguished essays. He grew up in Mount Vernon, New York, a place of ponds and spacious yards and amateur musicales; and his family spent August at Belgrade Lake, Maine. In later years, White humorously reflected that his childhood lacked the deprivation and loneliness often thought to be essential to becoming a writer. After graduating from Cornell, where he edited the Daily Sun, in 1926 White joined the staff of the country's most sophisticated and politically astute magazine, The New Yorker. White wrote the "Talk of the Town" and "Notes and Comment" columns for thirty years. Between 1938 and 1943, he also wrote the "One Man's Meat" column for Harper's. The essays from these three columns were collected in One Man's Meat (1942) and The Points of My Compass (1962). In 1937 White helped his former English professor at Cornell, William Strunk Jr., to revise The Elements of Style (originally published in 1918). Now known as "Strunk and White," this classic handbook for writers advocates clarity, precision, and simple elegance.

"Once More to the Lake" (Harper's, August 1941) became a staple of the essay canon because of the elegant simplicity of White's style. With sophistication, light irony, and gentle common sense, White examines the humorous and serious sides of ordinary life —and human relationships, here just on the brink of World War II.

One summer, along about 1904, my father rented a camp on a lake in Maine and took us all there for the month of August. We all got ringworm from some kittens and had to rub Pond's Extract on our arms and legs night and morning, and my father rolled over in a canoe with all his clothes on; but outside of that the vacation was a success and from then on none of us ever thought there was any place in the world like that lake in Maine. We returned summer after summer —always on August 1 for one month. I have since become a saltwater man, but sometimes in summer there are days when the restlessness of the tides and the fearful cold of the sea water and the incessant wind that blows across the afternoon and into the evening make me wish for the placidity of a lake in the woods. A few weeks ago this feeling got so strong I bought myself a couple of bass hooks and a spinner and returned to the lake where we used to go, for a week's fishing and to revisit old haunts.

I took along my son, who had never had any fresh water up his nose and who had seen lily pads only from train windows. On the journey over to the lake I began to wonder what it would be like. I wondered how time would have marred this unique, this holy spot —the coves and streams, the hills that the sun set behind, the camps and the paths behind the camps. I was sure that the tarred road would have found it out, and I wondered in what other ways it would be desolated. It is strange how much you can remember about places like that once you allow your mind to return into the grooves that lead back. You remember one thing, and that suddenly reminds you of another thing. I guess I remembered clearest of all the early mornings, when the lake was cool and motionless, remembered how the bedroom smelled of the lumber it was made of and of the wet woods whose scent entered through the screen. The partitions in the camp were thin and did not extend clear to the top of the rooms, and as I was always the first up I would dress softly so as not to wake the others, and sneak out into the sweet outdoors and start out in the canoe, keeping close along the shore in the long shadows of the pines. I remembered being very careful never to rub my paddle against the gunwale for fear of disturbing the stillness of the cathedral.

The lake had never been what you would call a wild lake. There were cottages sprinkled around the shores, and it was in farming country although the shores of the lake were quite heavily wooded. Some of the cottages were owned by nearby farmers, and you would live at the shore and eat your meals at the farmhouse. That's what our family did. But although it wasn't wild, it was a fairly large and undisturbed lake and there were places in it that, to a child at least, seemed infinitely remote and primeval.

I was right about the tar: it led to within half a mile of the shore. But when I got back there, with my boy, and we settled into a camp near a farmhouse and into the kind of summertime I had known, I could tell that it was going to be pretty much the same as it had been before—I knew it, lying in bed the first morning smelling the bedroom and hearing the boy sneak quietly out and go off along the shore in a boat. I began to sustain the illusion that he was I, and therefore, by simple transposition, that I was my father. This sensation persisted, kept cropping up all the time we were there. It was not an entirely new feeling, but in this setting it grew much stronger. I seemed to be living a dual existence. I would be in the middle of some simple act, I would be picking up a bait box or laying down a table fork, or I would be saying something and suddenly it would be not I but my father who was saying the words or making the gesture. It gave me a creepy sensation.

We went fishing the first morning. I felt the same damp moss covering the 5 worms in the bait can, and saw the dragonfly alight on the tip of my rod as it hovered a few inches from the surface of the water. It was the arrival of this fly that convinced me beyond any doubt that everything was as it always had been, that the years were a mirage and that there had been no years. The small waves were the same, chucking the rowboat under the chin as we fished at anchor, and the boat was the same boat, the same color green and the ribs broken in the same places, and under the floorboards the same fresh water leavings and débris—the dead hellgrammite, the wisps of moss, the rusty discarded fishhook, the dried blood from yesterday's catch. We stared silently at the tips of our rods, at the dragonflies that came and went. I lowered the tip of mine into the water, tentatively, pensively dislodging the fly, which darted two feet away, poised, darted two feet back, and came to rest again a little farther up the rod. There had been no years between the ducking of this dragonfly and the other one—the one that was part of memory. I looked at the boy, who was silently watching his fly, and it was my hands that held his rod, my eyes watching. I felt dizzy and didn't know which rod I was at the end of.

We caught two bass, hauling them in briskly as though they were mackerel, pulling them over the side of the boat in a businesslike manner without any landing net, and stunning them with a blow on the back of the head. When we got back for a swim before lunch, the lake was exactly where we had left it, the same number of inches from the dock, and there was only the merest suggestion of a breeze. This seemed an utterly enchanted sea, this lake you could leave to its own devices for a few hours and come back to, and find that it had not stirred, this constant and trustworthy body of water. In the shallows, the dark, water-soaked sticks and twigs, smooth and old, were undulating in clusters on the bottom against the clean ribbed sand, and the track of the mussel was plain. A school of minnows swam by, each minnow with its small individual shadow, doubling the attendance, so clear and sharp in the sunlight. Some of the other campers were in swimming, along the shore, one of them with a cake of soap, and the water felt thin and clear and unsubstantial. Over the years there had been this person with the cake of soap, this cultist, and here he was. There had been no years.

Up to the farmhouse to dinner through the teeming dusty field, the road under our sneakers was only a two-track road. The middle track was missing, the one with the marks of the hooves and the splotches of dried, flaky manure. There had always been three tracks to choose from in choosing which track to walk in; now the choice was narrowed down to two. For a moment I missed terribly the middle alternative. But the way led past the tennis court, and something about the way it lay there in the sun reassured me; the tape had loosened along the backline, the alleys were green with plantains and other weeds, and the net (installed in June and removed in September) sagged in the dry noon, and the whole place steamed with midday heat and hunger and emptiness. There was a choice of pie for dessert, and one was blueberry and one was apple, and the waitresses were the same country girls, there having been no passage of time, only the illusion of it as in a dropped curtain — the waitresses were still fifteen; their hair had been washed, that was the only difference — they had been to the movies and seen the pretty girls with the clean hair.

Summertime, oh, summertime, pattern of life indelible with fade-proof lake, the wood unshatterable, the pasture with the sweetfern and the juniper forever and ever, summer without end; this was the background, and the life along the shore was the design, the cottages with their innocent and tranquil design, their tiny docks with the flagpole and the American flag floating against the white clouds in the blue sky, the little paths over the roots of the trees leading from camp to camp and the paths leading back to the outhouses and the can of lime for sprinkling, and at the souvenir counters at the store the miniature birch-bark canoes and the postcards that showed things looking a little better than they looked. This was the American family at play, escaping the city heat, wondering whether the newcomers in the camp at the head of the cove were "common" or "nice," wondering whether it was true that the people who drove up for Sunday dinner at the farmhouse were turned away because there wasn't enough chicken.

It seemed to me, as I kept remembering all this, that those times and those summers had been infinitely precious and worth saving. There had been jollity and peace and goodness. The arriving (at the beginning of August) had been so big a business in itself, at the railway station the farm wagon drawn up, the first smell of the pine-laden air, the first glimpse of the smiling farmer, and the great importance of the trunks and your father's enormous authority in such matters, and the feel of the wagon under you for the long ten-mile haul, and at the top of the last long hill catching the first view of the lake after eleven months of not see-ing this cherished body of water. The shouts and cries of the other campers when they saw you, and the trunks to be unpacked, to give up their rich burden. (Arriv-ing was less exciting nowadays, when you sneaked up in your car and parked it under a tree near the camp and took out the bags and in five minutes it was all over, no fuss, no loud wonderful fuss about trunks.)

Peace and goodness and jollity. The only thing that was wrong now, really, 10
was the sound of the place, an unfamiliar nervous sound of the outboard motors. This was the note that jarred, the one thing that would sometimes break the illusion and set the years moving. In those other summertimes all motors were inboard; and when they were at a little distance, the noise they made was a seda-tive, an ingredient of summer sleep. They were one-cylinder and two-cylinder engines, and some were make-and-break and some were jump-spark, but they all made a sleepy sound across the lake. The one-lungers throbbed and flut-tered, and the twin-cylinder ones purred and purred, and that was a quiet sound, too. But now the campers all had outboards. In the daytime, in the hot morn-ings, these motors made a petulant, irritable sound; at night in the still evening when the afterglow lit the water, they whined about one's ears like mosquitoes. My boy loved our rented outboard, and his great desire was to achieve single-handed mastery over it, and authority, and he soon learned the trick of choking it a little (but not too much), and the adjustment of the needle valve. Watching him I would remember the things you could do with the old one-cylinder engine with the heavy flywheel, how you could have it eating out of your hand if you got really close to it spiritually. Motorboats in those days didn't have clutches, and you would make a landing by shutting off the motor at the proper time and coasting in with a dead rudder. But there was a way of reversing them, if you learned the trick, by cutting the switch and putting it on again exactly on the final dying revolution of the flywheel, so that it would kick back against compression and begin reversing. Approaching a dock in a strong following breeze, it was dif-ficult to slow up sufficiently by the ordinary coasting method, and if a boy felt he had complete mastery over his motor, he was tempted to keep it running beyond its time and then reverse it a few feet from the dock. It took a cool nerve, because if you threw the switch a twentieth of a second too soon you would catch the flywheel when it still had speed enough to go up past center, and the boat would leap ahead, charging bull-fashion at the dock.

We had a good week at the camp. The bass were biting well and the sun shone endlessly, day after day. We would be tired at night and lie down in the accumulated heat of the little bedrooms after the long hot day and the breeze would stir almost imperceptibly outside and the smell of the swamp drift in through the rusty screens. Sleep would come easily and in the morning the red squirrel would be on the roof, tapping out his gay routine. I kept remembering everything, lying in bed in the mornings—the small steamboat that had a long rounded stern like the lip of a Ubangi, and how quietly she ran on the moonlight sails, when the older boys played their mandolins and the girls sang and we ate doughnuts dipped in sugar, and how sweet the music was on the water in the shining night, and what it had felt like to think about girls then. After breakfast we would go up to the store and the things were in the same place—the minnows in a bottle, the plugs and spinners disarranged and pawed over by the youngsters from the boys' camp, the Fig Newtons and the Beeman's gum. Outside, the road was tarred and cars stood in front of the store. Inside, all was just as it had always been, except there was more Coca-Cola and not so much Moxie and root beer and birch beer and sarsaparilla. We would walk out with the bottle of pop apiece and sometimes the pop would backfire up our noses and hurt. We explored the streams, quietly, where the turtles slid off the sunny logs and dug their way into the soft bottom; and we lay on the town wharf and fed worms to the tame bass. Everywhere we went I had trouble making out which was I, the one walking at my side, the one walking in my pants.

One afternoon while we were at that lake a thunderstorm came up. It was like the revival of an old melodrama that I had seen long ago with childish awe. The second-act climax of the drama of the electrical disturbance over a lake in America had not changed in any important respect. This was the big scene, still the big scene. The whole thing was so familiar, the first feeling of oppression and heat and a general air around camp of not wanting to go very far away. In mid-afternoon (it was all the same) a curious darkening of the sky, and a lull in everything that had made life tick; and then the way the boats suddenly swung the other way at their moorings with the coming of a breeze out of the new quarter, and the premonitory rumble. Then the kettle drum, then the snare, then the bass drum and cymbals, then crackling light against the dark, and the gods grinning and licking their chops in the hills. Afterward the calm, the rain steadily rustling in the calm lake, the return of light and hope and spirits, and the campers running out in joy and relief to go swimming in the rain, their bright cries perpetuating the deathless joke about how they were getting simply drenched, and the children screaming with delight at the new sensation of bathing in the rain, and the joke about getting drenched linking the generations in a strong indestructible chain. And the comedian who waded in carrying an umbrella.

When the others went swimming my son said he was going in, too. He pulled his dripping trunks from the line where they had hung all through the shower and wrung them out. Languidly, and with no thought of going in, I watched him, his hard little body, skinny and bare, saw him wince slightly as he pulled up around his vitals the small, soggy, icy garment. As he buckled the swollen belt, suddenly my groin felt the chill of death.

E. B. White and brother Stanley paddling a canoe at Belgrade Lake, 1910.

QUESTIONS FOR DISCUSSION AND WRITING

1. Explain Brian Doyle's observation in relation to "Once More to the Lake." In your own experience, is his an accurate observation of the human condition? Would you accept all of what he says? If not, explain how you would modify this statement: "When young we think there will come one person who will savor and sustain us always; when we are older we know this is the dream of a child, that all hearts finally are bruised and scarred, scored and torn, repaired by time and will, patched by force of character, yet fragile and rickety forevermore, no matter how ferocious the defense and how many bricks you bring to the wall."

2. Although Tolstoy has famously said, "All happy families are alike," Quindlen, White, and Alice Walker (p. 192) offer snapshots of happy families, and each is different. What characteristics have they in common? In what ways do they differ? Write a definition of a happy family, based on these readings and your own family (happy or not) and those of others. How does the ideal compare with the reality? Is it consistent over time or often changing?

3. Is there any hint of problems to come in E. B. White's commentary on idyllic three-generation family relationships in "Once More to the Lake"? In what ways does White remind readers of both the presence and passing of time?

4. Children learn from the adults around them, for better and for worse. Identify some of the values, as well as skills, that White's son learned from his father, just as White had learned from his own father. What values and skills did Quindlen and Alice Walker (p. 192) learn from their parents? In what ways have the values they learned as children influenced the adults they have become? Under what circumstances do children learn the truth of Doyle's observations quoted in question 1?

5. After discussion with a classmate, good friend, or relative, write an essay in which you address Doyle's comment: "We are utterly open with no one, in the end—not mother and father, not wife or husband, not lover, not child, not friend. We open windows to each other but we live alone in the house of the heart."

GREGORY ORR

Return to Hayneville

Gregory Orr (b. 1947) grew up in New York's Hudson Valley. He received a B.A. from Antioch College (1969) and an M.F.A. from Columbia University (1972). While hunting, when he was twelve, he accidentally shot and killed his younger brother; soon thereafter his mother died suddenly, and his father became addicted to amphetamines. The searing experiences of his childhood have been the subject of much of his writing. Orr began to write poetry to "process experience" into "lucid meaning." In his essay, "The Making of Poems," Orr said, "I believe in poetry as a way of surviving the emotional chaos, spiritual confusions and traumatic events that come with being alive." He is the author of eleven collections of poetry, including Burning the Empty Nests *(1973),* Gathering the Bones Together *(1975),* City of Salt *(1995),* Concerning the Book That Is the Body of the Beloved *(2005), and* How Beautiful the Beloved *(2009). From 1978 to 2003 he was the poetry editor of* Virginia Quarterly Review. *He has also published a memoir,* The Blessing *(2002), and three books of essays, including* Poetry As Survival *(2002). He lives with his wife and two daughters in Charlottesville, Virginia, and teaches at the University of Virginia, where in 1975 he founded the MFA Program in Writing.*

In "Return to Hayneville" (Alabama), from the Virginia Quarterly Review *(2008), Orr recounts the terrifying events of the Freedom Summer of 1965. While trying to register African Americans to vote, he was kidnapped at gunpoint and held in solitary confinement for eight disorienting, dangerous days and endless nights.*

I was born and raised in rural upstate New York, but who I am began with a younger brother's death in a hunting accident when I was twelve and he was eight. I held the gun that killed him. But if my life began at twelve with my brother's sudden, violent death, then my end, determined by the trajectory of that harsh beginning, could easily have taken place a scant six years later, when, in June 1965, I was kidnapped at gunpoint by vigilantes near the small town of Hayneville, Alabama.

When I was sixteen, in my senior year of high school, I became involved in the civil rights movement partly because I hoped I could lose myself in that worthwhile work. I became a member of CORE (Congress of Racial Equality) and canvassed door-to-door in poorer neighborhoods in the nearby city of Kingston. I traveled down to Atlantic City with a carload of CORE members to picket the Democratic National Convention in August 1964. Earlier that summer, the Mississippi Freedom Democratic Party—another civil rights group—had chosen a slate of racially integrated delegates to challenge Mississippi's all-white official Democratic Party delegates for seats at the convention. The goal was to put Lyndon Johnson and the whole liberal wing of the party on the spot—testing their commitment to change. I was one of about twenty or so people parading in a small circle on the dilapidated boardwalk outside the convention hall. We carried signs urging on the drama inside: SUPPORT THE FREEDOM DELEGATION and ONE MAN, ONE VOTE. I felt confused and thrilled and purposeful all at the same time.

Three marchers carried poles, each bearing a huge charcoal portrait of a different young man. Their larger-than-life faces gazed down at us as we walked our repetitive circle. They were renditions of Andrew Goodman, James Chaney, and Michael Schwerner, SNCC (Student Nonviolent Coordinating Committee) volunteers who had been missing for months, whose bodies had only recently been discovered. They had last been seen alive on June 21, driving away from the Neshoba County sheriff's office in Philadelphia, Mississippi. When an informer led investigators to the spot where their tortured bodies had been bulldozed into a clay dam, the mystery of their whereabouts ended abruptly and they began a second life—the life of martyrs to a cause. Those three faces mesmerized us as we circled the boardwalk, singing and trying to ignore the heckling from bystanders. The artist who had drawn them had resolved their faces into a few bold lines that gave them a subtle dignity. They seemed at peace, all their uncertainties and inner complexities over. I longed to be like them, to transcend my confusions and the agonies of my past and be taken up into some noble simplicity beyond change. I longed to sacrifice myself and escape myself—to become a martyr for the movement. If it took death to gain access to the grandeur of meaning, so be it. And thus are young soldiers born.

I was too young, only seventeen, to go to Mississippi that summer, but a year later I was on my way. I drove south, alone, in a '56 Ford my father had bought me for the trip. And so it commenced—my instruction in the grim distance between the myth of the martyr and the intimate reality of violence.

Cut to November 2006—more than forty years have passed since my late- 5
adolescent misadventures in the Deep South. I'm a poet and a professor—that's
how I've spent my life. One of the happier perquisites of my profession is that
I'm sometimes asked to read my poems at various colleges and universities. One
such invitation has come my way: a former student of mine, a poet named Chris,
is teaching at Auburn University and has invited me down. I'm reading that
same week in Atlanta, and as I look over my Rand McNally, I see that I can not
only drive from Atlanta to Auburn, but proceed an hour or so farther and drive
straight through time and into my own past. I decide to go back to Hayneville,
the tiny town that has been so long lodged like a sliver in my memory.

Chris says he'll take the trip with me, and he brings Brian, a former student
of his own. I'm glad of the company. Three poets from three generations: I'll turn
sixty within the year, Chris is in his early forties, Brian in his mid-twenties. As we
leave town in my rented, economy-size Hyundai, pulling onto the interstate in the
late-afternoon drizzle, Brian asks where we're headed. For several days, I've felt a
quiet tension about this trip, and suddenly it seems I can release some of the tension by telling Brian and Chris the story of that long-ago summer. At first, I try
to talk about what happened to me in Hayneville itself, but I quickly see that I'll
have to start further back in order to make a coherent story of it.

As we drive down the highway toward Montgomery, I feel like one of those
pilgrims in Chaucer, challenged by my travel companions to entertain them on
the journey. Brian's in the back seat, and as I begin my story, I occasionally turn
my head slightly as if acknowledging I'm aware of him as an audience, but soon
I'll become so caught up in the narrative that I'll lose all sense of my companions
and of time and distance passing. I'll drive steadily toward Hayneville, as though
the story and the highway were a single, fused flowing.

It was late May 1965. After brief training, another volunteer, a man from Pittsburgh named Steve, and I were assigned to work in Bolivar County, Mississippi—
the Delta region, where COFO (Council of Federated Organizations) was trying to gain momentum for a strike of field workers. The going wage was $4 a
day—dawn to dusk, hoeing the cotton by hand, everyone from seven-year-old
kids to octogenarians. We'd been in Bolivar only a week or so, helping out at the
office. Suddenly there was a summons from headquarters: everyone who could be
mustered and spared from their local work—any new volunteers and all the local
residents who could be persuaded—should report to the state capital in Jackson.
The governor of Mississippi had called a secret session of the legislature, and the
movement was organizing a mass demonstration to draw national attention to
what it suspected was serious political skullduggery.

At ten in the morning on June 14, about five hundred of us—men, women,
teenagers, old folks—assembled in Jackson. We walked two abreast down the sidewalk toward the capitol. Our leaders told us we'd be stopped by the police and
warned we could not parade without a permit. At that point, we would have to
choose to be arrested or to disperse. We were urged to let ourselves be arrested—the

plan was to fill the jail to overflowing and apply the steady pressure of media and economics (they'll have to feed and house us at city expense). The powers that be had learned to present a sanitized image to the media, so our arrest was very polite. Journalists and photographers there watched each of us being ushered onto a truck by two city policemen, who held us by both arms, firmly but calmly. The trucks themselves were large, enclosed vehicles, the kind you'd use to transport chairs for a rally or municipal lawnmowers. They packed about thirty of us inside, then closed the doors. And we were off—each truck with its own motorcycle escort gliding through red lights, heading, we presumed, toward the city jail. But the actual destination was our first big surprise. We activists may have had a plan to demonstrate, but the State of Mississippi and the City of Jackson had their own plan. We were taken to the county fairgrounds—twenty or so fenced acres of clear-cut land set with half a dozen long, low, tin-roofed barns. Another thing we didn't know: when each truck entered the fairgrounds, the gate swung shut behind it, and police turned back anyone else who tried to enter.

The truck I was on stopped, backed up, then came to a final halt. When the   10
doors opened and our eyes adjusted to the flood of light, we saw that we weren't at the jail at all but in a narrow alley between two barns. A score of uniformed officers were gathered there, wearing the uniforms of motorcycle cops—tall leather boots, mirrored sunglasses, and blue helmets with the black ear-flaps pulled down. Each tanned face was almost indistinguishable under its partial disguise—only the nose and mouth showing—some already grinning at the joke of our surprise and what was in store for us. Each of them had his nightstick out, some tapping their clubs rhythmically in the palms of their hands, others just standing there expectantly with the stick held at each end. I didn't notice until I was up close, and even then, in my confusion, didn't comprehend, that the lower half of each officer's silver badge, where the identifying number should have been displayed, was neatly covered with black tape. An officer ordered us to climb down, and when some of us didn't, two officers climbed up and pushed us to the edge where others pulled us down. And it began. They swung their clubs right and left, randomly but thoroughly, for about ten minutes. It made no difference what you did, whether you screamed or were silent—you were struck again and again and, if you fell to the ground, kicked. It hurts to be beaten over the head or back or shoulders with a wooden club. It's also terrifying. Then an order came and the clubbing stopped. We were told to get up. One kid couldn't and was dragged away somewhere, his leg too damaged to stand on.

We filed through a door into one of the barns. Inside, there was a calm that felt surreal after the violence outside. In the middle of the empty concrete floor, five card tables had been set up in a row, each with a typewriter and a city policeman seated in a folding chair. At the far end of the barn, half hidden in shadow, was a milling cluster of frightened women and girls who, their initial beating and processing over, had been told to assemble there. Our dazed group lined up, and each of us in turn was formally processed and charged. The women from our truck were sent to join the other women at the far end of the barn. I was told to go out one of the side doors to the next barn, where the men were being confined. Just as I was about to go through the door, an officer told me to take my straw hat off and carry it in my hands. I emerged into the outdoors and the bright sunlight and saw them—two lines of about fifteen highway patrolmen on either side. I was ordered to walk, not run, between them. Again I was beaten with nightsticks, but this time more thoroughly, as I was the only target. When I covered my head with raised arms to ward off the first blow from the officer on my right, I was jabbed in the ribs with a club from the other side. Instinctively, I pivoted in that direction, only to be left vulnerable in the other. I heard blows and felt sharp pokes or slaps fall flat and hard across my ribs and back from both directions. Whether they were simultaneous or alternating, it made no difference; my defense was hopeless. By the time I neared the end of this gantlet, I was cringing from feinted blows, the humiliation of my fear and their laughter far worse than the physical pain.

Inside the other barn, men and boys were assembled in a dense clump surrounded by a loose ring of officers. Later that afternoon we would go through another ritually structured set of beatings. When anyone tried to sit down or move out to the edge of the impacted group to get some air, two or three officers dashed across the small, intervening space and beat him with clubs. This technique was designed to make us prisoners panic and fight one another to get to the safer center of the mass. But it didn't work. We tried to protect ourselves as best we could and keep the most vulnerable, especially the children, safe in the middle. A bearded young man in our group was noticeably defiant, and at a certain point an officer ran in and deftly struck him with a slicing motion of the blunt end of his nightstick in such a way that the taut skin of his forehead split and blood streamed down over the whole of his face. To see an individual human face suddenly turned into a mask of blood is to witness the eradication of the personal, and, if you're standing nearby as I was, to be sickened and unnerved.

The hours went by as more prisoners were processed and our group continued to grow—there were more than 150 men and boys in the barn. Evening fell. We were ordered to sit in rows on the concrete floor, three feet apart, three feet between the rows. We didn't know it, but we were waiting for mattresses to be delivered. We were told to sit bolt upright and not move; officers walked up and down the rows. If you leaned a hand down to rest or shifted your weight, a shouting patrolman rushed up with his club raised.

A black kid of maybe ten or twelve sat next to me. We'd been there for an hour and things were pretty quiet when a state patrolman stopped in front of the boy. He looked him over for a minute, then ordered him to take off the pin he was wearing—one of those movement buttons that said FREEDOM NOW or ONE MAN, ONE VOTE. No safety clasp, just an open pin. The guard told the kid to pull the pin off his shirt. He did. "Put it in your mouth," the guard said. I turned my head to the right and saw the boy place it in his mouth. "Swallow it," the guard said, his voice menacing, but not loud. If the kid tried to swallow it, the pin would choke him or pierce his throat and lodge there until he bled to death in agony.

Watching the scene, I felt murderous rage fill my whole being, geysering up   15
in the single second it took to see what seemed about to happen. I became nothing but the impulse to scramble to my feet, grab the guard's pistol before he knew what was happening, and shoot him as many times as possible. Nothing but that intense impulse and a very small voice inside me that said: "You don't stand a chance. It would take longer than you imagine—long enough for him to turn on you, for his buddies to rush up and grab you. And then what? You would be their sudden and absolute target."

How long did that moment last? How long did the guard loom over the boy with his threats? How long did the boy sit there with the pin in his mouth, tasting its metallic bitterness but refusing to swallow, or unable to swallow? It could have been five minutes; it could have been less. The guard repeated his command several times, along with profanities. And then other officers were there, urging him to give it up, persuading him to move on, to move away.

The mattresses finally arrived, and each of us dragged one off to his place in a row. We were officially segregated according to the laws of the sovereign state of Mississippi—a vigilantly patrolled lane separated two imaginary cellblocks, one for blacks and one for whites. We lay down to sleep. The pounding of nightsticks on the concrete floor woke us at dawn, and we realized the highway patrolmen who had abused us with such relish and impunity the previous day were nowhere in sight. They'd been replaced by Fish and Game wardens, who looked altogether more rustic and thoughtful (some had mustaches) and made no effort to conceal their badge numbers and even wore nametags. Later that morning, a plainclothes officer entered our barn and announced that the FBI had arrived and that if anyone had complaints about their treatment, they should step forward to be interviewed. I did so and was ushered out into the same alley where we'd first been greeted and beaten. The narrow lane had been rigged at one end with an awning for shade. Under the awning, four FBI agents sat at small desks. When my turn came, I told my narrative about the beatings, but how could I identify the perpetrators? The agent asked if I could specify hair or eye color or badge number. I couldn't. Could I point out now, in person, any of the officers who had beaten me? They weren't there, of course; they'd left in the middle of the night. The agent recorded my story of the previous day's beatings and violence and thanked me for my time. If they had actually wanted to protect us, the FBI could easily have arrived anytime the preceding day. Many in the movement already knew what was inconceivable to me at the time—that events like this were stage-managed and that the FBI wasn't a friend or even a neutral ally of the civil rights movement.

For the next ten days, we lay each morning on our mattresses until breakfast—grits and a molasses syrup and powdered milk so watered down I could see all the way to the bottom of the fifty-gallon pot that held it. After breakfast, we rolled up our mattresses and either sat all day on the concrete floor or paced the imaginary confines of our collective cell. Twice a day, we were lined up for the bathroom—it was then or never as we stood pressed up against one another, waiting for our brief turn in one of the five stinking stalls. No showers, no chance to wash at all, the same reeking clothes day after day. Hot as hell once the sun heated the tin roof, but chill at night when we huddled, blanketless, in the dark on our bare mattresses. The mosquito fogger sprayed around the outside of the barn each evening, sending its toxic cloud in under the closed doors to set us all coughing. Boredom, stench, heat.

Word came from outside: we could, at any time, be released by posting a $50 bond that the movement would provide, but the plan called for as many as possible to stay inside for as long as we could. There was hope that we would seriously inconvenience the state by staying, that another demonstration in support of us might take place—there was even talk of Martin Luther King Jr. himself showing up for it. Rumors and hope, and a request to persevere. Most of us stayed, though some of the youngest and oldest chose to leave. The violence mostly gone; if it occurred, it was sporadic and spontaneous and ended quickly without major consequence. Exhausted by the lack of substantial food, worn down by boredom and discomfort, I gradually lost heart. I had dreamed of meaningful work and even heroic martyrdom, but here I was merely cannon fodder. I held a place, I counted, but only as an integer in the calculus of a complex political game playing out in rooms far above me. And close up, as close as the arc of a swung billy club, I had discovered that for every martyr whose life was resolved into a meaningful death, there were hundreds of others who were merely beaten, terrorized, humiliated. As I sank into depression and brooded in the stifling heat of that jail-barn, I was learning that I wanted to live.

On the tenth day there, my name was called and I was led outside and taken 20 to a pay phone attached to a post near our barn. Picking up the receiver, I heard the voice of my father's lawyer, who was calling from upstate New York. We'd met only once; I hardly knew him. He began by saying he couldn't stand me or any of the causes I believed in, but my father was his dear friend and was frantic with worry. My fine had been paid. I was to leave now and drive back north immediately if I cared a damn about my family. End of story. His tongue-lashing eliminated the last of my resolve. The officer standing beside me took me in a patrol car to where I'd left the Ford ten days ago, as if the whole thing had been prearranged.

I should have called the COFO office and told them I was leaving, heading north that very day, but I was ashamed. I was deserting—a frightened and confused teenager. The map told me my quickest route north was by state roads from Jackson to Selma, Alabama, and then on to Montgomery, where the interstate began. When I passed through Selma it was early evening and I was starved (we'd been fed nothing but vegetables and grits for ten days), but I was too afraid to stop for dinner.

It was dusk on U.S. 80, past Selma and within fifteen miles of Montgomery, when I heard a siren. A white car pulled up close behind me, flashing its lights. I thought it was a police car and pulled over, but the two men who jumped out, one tall and rather thin, the other shorter and stout, wore no uniforms. They did each wear holsters, and as they approached, one on each side of my car, they drew their pistols. I rolled up my windows and locked my doors. Rap of a pistol barrel on the window two inches from my head: "Get out, you son of a bitch, or I'll blow your head off."

I got out and stood on the road's shoulder, beside my car. They prodded me with their guns and told me they were going to kill me. They searched my car and found SNCC pamphlets in the trunk. They were sure I was an agitator rumored to be coming to their town—my New York license plates had been a strong clue that the pamphlets confirmed. The men made two promises about my immediate future. The first was that they would kill me and dump my body in the swamp. The second, made a few moments later, was that they were going to take me to a jail where I would rot. With those two contradictory threats left floating in the air, they took my wallet and went back to their vehicle, ordering me to follow them in my own car. They pulled onto the highway and zoomed off. I started my car and followed them. We hadn't driven more than a mile when they signaled and turned off to the right, onto a smaller road. I hesitated, uncertain what to do, then made the turn and followed.

I pause in this story I'm telling Chris and Brian when I realize we've reached the green sign marking the turnoff for Hayneville. I'd been so caught up in telling it that I hardly noticed we'd passed through Montgomery and were speeding down Route 80 toward Selma. Suddenly I realize the old story and my present journey are eerily coinciding at this forlorn intersection. It's as if my ghost Ford from forty years ago is approaching the turnoff from the west, coming from Selma, at the same moment that my shiny white rental reaches that same turn from the direction of Montgomery. The terrified boy in the ghost Ford drives right into us, and for a moment we and the story are one and the same. Now I'm driving slowly down that back road toward Hayneville, telling Chris and Brian what it felt like the first time I took this road, alone, following the car driven by my would-be killers.

Their car was newer than mine and faster. It sped up. A voice in my head 25 started screaming: "What are you doing? You are obligingly speeding to your own death—driving to your own grave! Turn around and make a run for it!" But how could I? They had my wallet with my license and all my money. It was pitch-dark now. The road was so narrow there was no place to turn around; there were swamps on either side. If I tried to make a getaway, their car could easily overtake mine, and they would surely shoot me. This hysterical dialogue raged in my head for the ten long minutes of that ride, and then we emerged out of the dark into Hayneville. We passed the courthouse, pulled into a narrow street, and stopped in back of a small jail.

Even as I describe that terrifying drive, I see that the wooded swamps are gone. (Or were they imagined in the dark so long ago?) It's mostly fields and pasture, with a pond here and there gleaming like oil in the deepening gloom. And now we're arriving in the town itself. Again, as with the first time I was here, it's almost completely dark under the overarching trees, only a glimpse of a gray sky from which all trace of light is gone. I recognize things: there is the courthouse—no wonder it stood out—white and two stories high on its tree-filled lawn in a town of twenty or so tiny houses and bungalows. And there is something completely new in town, the only new thing as far as I can see: a BP convenience store, where I stop for gas. The station is shiny and all lit up, its blue-green signs glowing intensely in the dark like those roadside stores in Edward Hopper paintings, gleaming forlornly against the primeval dark of rural Anywhere, America. I'm trembling with a kind of giddy excitement as I pump the gas. Even here I can see changes—the man behind the counter in the station, whom I take to be the owner, is black, and so are most of his customers. Back then, whites owned everything. As I pull my car out of the station across from the courthouse, I see that the sheriff's car, just now parking beside the small police bungalow behind the courthouse, is driven by a black officer.

When we got to the jail forty years ago, I felt relieved. At least the terrifying drive was over. But my torment was only entering another phase. I'd be held there in solitary confinement, without charges, for eight days. I was kept on the second floor the entire time, separate from all other prisoners and personnel, seeing and talking to no one except the silent trusty who brought me food twice a day and took away my empty tray. Why was I so isolated from the rest of the prisoners? It was possible they didn't want people to know where I was, as they waited to find out if anyone was aware that I was "missing." Ever since the murders of Goodman, Schwerner, and Chaney, volunteers were under strict orders to check in with headquarters before traveling any distance, to record their destination and expected arrival time, so that if anything went wrong an alert could be sent out for an immediate search. I hadn't called, so no one knew I was in Hayneville's jail.

Four days into my incarceration, my father's lawyer called the DA in Jackson, Mississippi, to ask if he knew why I hadn't arrived home. The DA didn't know; they'd let me go. Then he tried the state attorney general's office in Montgomery, which was run at the time by Richmond Flowers, a racial moderate. His office made inquiries and learned I was being held in Hayneville, but they couldn't offer any help. They told Dad's lawyer that Lowndes County resisted all outside interference, even from Alabama state authorities. On my fifth day there, my father's lawyer managed to call the jail and was told (by the sheriff himself, slyly posing as a deputy) that indeed a young man named Greg Orr was there and was at that moment playing checkers with the sheriff.

Of course this was a lie. I had no knowledge of the call, no sense that anyone in the world knew where I was. Each day I spent in that cell was an eternity. I was unmoored from structures except food and the alternation of day and night. I didn't know when my spell in solitary would end. If someone had said to me, "You'll be kept alone in a small cell with no one to speak to for eight days," I could have tried to organize the ordeal in my mind—I could have, for starters, kept track of the days and known that each one passing brought me closer to the end. But there was no known end point, and so no measurement—it was wholly arbitrary and made me more aware of my own powerlessness. Already depressed and disoriented by the ten days in "jail" in Jackson, I was even more frightened in Hayneville. I had a better sense of how dangerous my situation was, and my imagination took over from there.

In the middle of my eighth day the sheriff came to my cell, unlocked it, and   30 told me I was free to go. That was it: no apology, no formal charges, no anything. I was taken to my car, told to get out of town. I was set free as abruptly and mysteriously as I had been captured and incarcerated. I got in my car and drove. I drove and drove. I have one memory of stopping in some rest area in South Carolina in the middle of the night and trying to wash and shave, but my hands were shaking too much to control the razor. I slept whenever I couldn't drive any longer, pulling into parking lots and climbing into the back seat. By the time I reached New Jersey, I was hallucinating huge rats running across the highway in front of my headlights. And then I was home, back in the Hudson River valley town I'd left only a month or so earlier.

I spent July in my hometown, but in early August I took a job in New York with a small film company, synchronizing sound and picture. On my way home from work one August day, I bought a *New York Times* to read on the subway. When I looked at the front page, I saw a story about a murder that had just taken place in Hayneville. I turned to the inner page to finish the article and was stunned to see a photograph of one of the men who had kidnapped me on the highway. The news article related that he had shotgunned Jonathan Daniels, an Episcopal seminary student and civil rights volunteer, in broad daylight on the courthouse lawn, in front of half a dozen witnesses. From what I could tell, the victim and the others with him might have been the "outside agitators" whom I had been mistaken for. According to the newspaper, they, like me, had been arbitrarily arrested and held without charges for days in the jail and then suddenly released. But unlike me, they had no car. They spent several hours desperately trying to find someone to drive them to Montgomery, while the murderer, a friend of the sheriff's and a "special unpaid deputy," became more and more agitated. He found the released organizers near the courthouse and aimed his shotgun at a young black woman, Ruby Sales. The seminary student pushed her aside and stood in front just as the gun went off.

Though the sheriff's friend was charged with murder, the verdict, given by a local, all-white jury in that very courthouse, was not guilty on the basis of self-defense. The same courthouse later saw the trial of the killers of Viola Liuzzo, the Detroit housewife who, three months before my arrival in town, had participated in the Selma-to-Montgomery march. On the evening of March 25, she was killed by gunfire while ferrying marchers in her car on Route 80. Her slayers, quickly apprehended, were also found not guilty by another all-white Hayneville jury, even though eyewitness prosecution testimony was given by one of the four Klansmen (a paid FBI informer) present that night in the murder car.

My situation in Hayneville resembled the seminary student's: arbitrary arrest, jail time without arraignment or trial, and then sudden release. But I had a car, and timing mattered: the *New York Times* article stressed that the killer had been upset about the passage of the Voting Rights Act—as if part of his motivation was a kind of crazed act of political protest. When I was apprehended and jailed, the status quo in Hayneville seemed secure—if my presence there was a sign of change, it was the sort of change the town felt it could easily contain and control.

Two others died there: a murder in March, another in August. And in between, in late June, my own narrow escape, as I slipped through the same violent landscape. "Slipped through" makes me sound like a fish that found a hole in the net, but surely I was trapped in it, surely it was luck that pulled me from its entanglements and casually tossed me back into the sea.

And here I am again, forty-one years later, approaching the jail, that brick edifice in which all my emotions and memories of Hayneville are concentrated. Not the memory or idea of jail, but this dingy incarnation of incarceration—a building full of little cages where people are captive. I've been monologuing until now, spewing out nonstop the whole story that brought me here, but as we travel the last few blocks, I go silent with anticipation. Chris and Brian are also quiet but excited. Now that we're in the town itself, certain key nouns connect to real things. There is the courthouse pretty much as I described it. And here, down this little lane a half block past the courthouse, is the jail itself, that brick, L-shaped building I've been talking about. But how different it is from what I remembered and described! It's an empty husk. Boarded up—from the looks of it, abandoned a number of years ago. Deserted, dilapidated, the mortar rotted out between the grimy bricks. The only thing not in utter disrepair is a small exercise yard attached to the back, behind a chain-link fence topped with razor wire.

When I stop in the cinder parking lot and hop out of the car I feel like a kid who has arrived at a playground. I'm surprised by my responses. Here, at a place that was a locus of some of the most intense misery I've ever known, I'm feeling curiously happy. Chris and Brian have also climbed out. I can see they're glad, too, pleased to have found some real, palpable thing at the end of a tunnel of words burrowing from the distant past. Chris has a camera and begins to take pictures, though it's night now and there's no way of knowing if anything will register. The doors to the building are locked, but Brian, exploring the fence's gate, finds it's open, and we're able to enter the yard. We climb some rusty steps to a second-floor landing; from there I can point to the window that was across the corridor from my cell and that I peered out of after shinnying up my cell door's bars and craning my neck. That giddiness I felt when I first set my feet on the parking lot has been growing more intense. I'm laughing now, and when I'm not laughing, I'm unable to stop grinning. Earlier, in the car, telling the stories of my long-ago misadventures, the words had zipped directly from my brain's private memory to my tongue in a kind of nonstop narrative that mostly bypassed my emotions. Now my brain has stopped functioning almost entirely, and I'm taken over by this odd laughter that's bubbling up from some wordless source far down in my body—some deep, cellular place.

Brian and Chris poke around the weed-grown yard, looking for anything interesting, some rusty artifact to point to or pick up and ponder. I'm ordinarily a person who likes souvenirs—a shell from a beach, a rock from a memorable walk in the woods—but I have no wish to take anything physical from this place. Even a pebble would weigh me down, and the truth is I feel weightless right now, as if I'm a happy spirit moving through a scene of desolation.

My beginning was a rifle shot and someone innocent suddenly dead. My end might well have been something eerily similar: perhaps a pistol shot, my own death in this tiny town so far from my home—a beginning and end so close to each other as to render the life cryptic and tragic by way of its brevity. Only, Hayneville *wasn't* my end. It was a place where my life could have ended but didn't, and now, almost half a century later, I stand beside that closed-down, dilapidated jail, laughing. But laughing at what, at whom? Not at the confused and earnest kid I was all those years ago, the one who blundered through and escaped thanks to blind luck. What is this laughter that's fountaining up through me?

As we're leaving and I pause in the cindery parking lot with one hand on my car-door handle, taking a last look at the old jail, a single word comes to me: *joy*. It's joy I'm feeling—joy is at the heart of this peculiar laughter. Joy is my body's primal response to the enormity of the gift it has been given—a whole life! A whole life was there waiting for me the day I left this town. A life full of joys I couldn't imagine back then: a long, deeply satisfying marriage to a woman I love, two wonderful daughters, forty years of writing poems and teaching the craft of poetry. Laughing to think that the kid I was had gone south seeking the dark blessing of death in a noble cause, but had instead been given the far more complex blessing of life, given his whole existence and all the future struggle to sort it out and make it significant—to himself and, if he was lucky as a writer, to others also. Laughing at how my life went on past this town and blossomed into its possibilities, one of which (shining in the dark) was love.

QUESTIONS FOR DISCUSSION AND WRITING

1. Compare and contrast Orr's return to Hayneville with E. B. White's return as an adult to the lake where he had spent happy summers as a child. Why would Orr voluntarily return to the site of the place where, forty years earlier, he was beaten, terrorized, "kidnapped at gunpoint by vigilantes," jailed, and could have been killed?

2. Orr is writing about a historical event that happened forty years ago—the Civil Rights Movement in the deep South in 1965. For him (though not necessarily for his readers) this is living history. Does he explain enough about the historical background to enable a contemporary audience to understand its significance? What does he emphasize about his own participation? What relation does it have to the historical aspects? Did he make a difference in the voting rights of African Americans in the segregated South?

3. Midway through the essay, Orr says, "Close up, as close as the arc of a swung billy club, I had discovered that for every martyr whose life was resolved into a meaningful death, there were hundreds of others who were merely beaten, terrorized, humiliated. As I sank into depression . . . in the stifling heat of that jail-barn, I was learning that I wanted to live" (paragraph 19). Why does this realization come at the essay's midpoint? What had Orr believed about his values before that realization? How does this new understanding influence his behavior and state of mind thereafter? What, if any, were the long-lasting effects of Orr's participation on himself as a person? On his development as a writer?

4. This essay reads like a mystery story even though at the outset we realize that Orr survived. What elements contribute to the plot, conflict, and suspense?

5. We often find that some activity or relationship that seems very simple at the outset unfolds in ways far more complicated than we had anticipated, for better or for worse. Identify such an activity (such as participation in a sport or club, community service, human rights activity) or relationship (your role as a son or daughter, friend, employee, spouse, parent) and tell its true story, as Orr has done. Be sure to characterize one or two of the main participants and the principal activities in order to disclose their implications. If your story is ongoing, it may not yet have an ending.

SCOTT RUSSELL SANDERS

Under the Influence: Paying the Price of My Father's Booze

Scott Russell Sanders, an English professor at Indiana University from 1971 until 2009, has published more than a dozen collections of essays focusing on human and spiritual ties to families, towns, the land, and "the practical problems of living on a small planet." Many of his essays deal with the varied facets of parent-child relationships, enduring and ever complicated.

Guilt, shame, rage, and fear, along with the specter of insanity and abandonment, represent the legacy of alcoholism for Scott Russell Sanders, whose father died at the age of sixty-four from drinking. For Sanders, alcohol "turned a key" in his father's head, transforming him into another person—a person who had to be disavowed, hidden from neighbors and relatives, hidden from oneself.

Taken from Sanders's essay collection entitled Secrets of the Universe: Scenes from the Journey Home *(1991), "Under the Influence" does not compete with tales of suffering. "Other people have keener sources of grief: poverty, racism, rape, war," writes Sanders. "I am only trying to understand the corrosive mixture of helplessness, responsibility, and shame that I learned to feel as the son of an alcoholic." He depicts this ordeal in clear images that accumulate until reality is unmistakable. Childhood perception, adult realization, biblical analogies, and family ritual combine with bittersweet humor—perhaps the key to survival—to create a disturbing yet compelling human testament.*

My father drank. He drank as a gut-punched boxer gasps for breath, as a starving dog gobbles food—compulsively, secretly, in pain and trembling. I use the past tense not because he ever quit drinking but because he quit living. That is how the story ends for my father, age sixty-four, heart bursting, body cooling, slumped and forsaken on the linoleum of my brother's trailer. The story continues for my brother, my sister, my mother, and me, and will continue as long as memory holds.

In the perennial present of memory, I slip into the garage or barn to see my father tipping back the flat green bottles of wine, the brown cylinders of whiskey, the cans of beer disguised in paper bags. His Adam's apple bobs, the liquid gurgles, he wipes the sandy-haired back of a hand over his lips, and then, his bloodshot gaze bumping into me, he stashes the bottle or can inside his jacket, under the workbench, between two bales of hay, and we both pretend the moment has not occurred.

"What's up, buddy?" he says, thick-tongued and edgy.

"Sky's up," I answer, playing along.

"And don't forget prices," he grumbles. "Prices are always up. And taxes."   5

In memory, his white 1951 Pontiac with the stripes down the hood and the Indian head on the snout lurches to a stop in the driveway; or it is the 1956 Ford station wagon, or the 1963 Rambler shaped like a toad, or the sleek 1969 Bonneville that will do 120 miles per hour on straightaways; or it is the robin's-egg-blue pickup, new in 1980, battered in 1981, the year of his death. He climbs out, grinning dangerously, unsteady on his legs, and we children interrupt our game of catch, our building of snow forts, our picking of plums, to watch in silence as he weaves past us into the house, where he drops into his overstuffed chair and falls asleep. Shaking her head, our mother stubs out a cigarette he has left smoldering in the ashtray. All evening, until our bedtimes, we tiptoe past him, as past a snoring dragon. Then we curl fearfully in our sheets, listening. Eventually he wakes with a grunt, Mother slings accusations at him, he snarls back, she yells, he growls, their voices clashing. Before long, she retreats to their bedroom, sobbing—not from the blows of fists, for he never strikes her, but from the force of his words.

Left alone, our father prowls the house, thumping into furniture, rummaging in the kitchen, slamming doors, turning the pages of the newspaper with a savage crackle, muttering back at the late-night drivel from television. The roof might fly off, the walls might buckle from the pressure of his rage. Whatever my brother and sister and mother may be thinking on their own rumpled pillows, I lie there hating him, loving him, fearing him, knowing I have failed him. I tell myself he drinks to ease the ache that gnaws at his belly, an ache I must have caused by disappointing him somehow, a murderous ache I should be able to relieve by doing all my chores, earning A's in school, winning baseball games, fixing the broken washer and the burst pipes, bringing in the money to fill his empty wallet. He would not hide the green bottles in his toolbox, would not sneak off to the barn with a lump under his coat, would not fall asleep in the daylight, would not roar and fume, would not drink himself to death, if only I were perfect.

I am forty-four, and I know full well now that my father was an alcoholic, a man consumed by disease rather than by disappointment. What had seemed to me a private grief is in fact, of course, a public scourge. In the United States alone, some ten or fifteen million people share his ailment, and behind the doors they slam in fury or disgrace, countless other children tremble. I comfort myself with such knowledge, holding it against the throb of memory like an ice pack against a bruise. Other people have keener sources of grief: poverty, racism, rape, war. I do not wish to compete to determine who has suffered most. I am only trying to understand the corrosive mixture of helplessness, responsibility, and shame that I learned to feel as the son of an alcoholic. I realize now that I did not cause my father's illness, nor could I have cured it. Yet for all this grownup knowledge, I am still ten years old, my own son's age, and as that boy I struggle in guilt and confusion to save my father from pain.

Consider a few of our synonyms for *drunk*: tipsy, tight, pickled, soused, and plowed; stoned and stewed, lubricated and inebriated, juiced and sluiced; three sheets to the wind, in your cups, out of your mind, under the table; lit up, tanked up, wiped out; besotted, blotto, bombed, and buzzed; plastered, polluted, putrefied; loaded or looped, boozy, woozy, fuddled, or smashed; crocked and shit-faced, corked and pissed, snockered and sloshed.

It is a mostly humorous lexicon, as the lore that deals with drunks—in jokes   10 and cartoons, in plays, films and television skits—is largely comic. Aunt Matilda nips elderberry wine from the sideboard and burps politely during supper. Uncle Fred slouches to the table glassy-eyed, wearing a lampshade for a hat and murmuring, "Candy is dandy, but liquor is quicker." Inspired by cocktails, Mrs. Somebody recounts the events of her day in a fuzzy dialect, while Mr. Somebody nibbles her ear and croons a bawdy song. On the sofa with Boyfriend, Daughter Somebody giggles, licking gin from her lips, and loosens the bows in her hair. Junior knocks back some brews with his chums at the Leopard Lounge and stumbles home to the wrong house, wonders foggily why he cannot locate his pajamas, and crawls naked into bed with the ugliest girl in school. The family dog slurps from a neglected martini and wobbles to the nursery, where he vomits in Baby's shoe.

It is all great fun. But if in the audience you notice a few laughing faces turn grim when the drunk lurches onstage, don't be surprised, for these are the children of alcoholics. Over the grinning mask of Dionysus, the leering face of Bacchus, these children cannot help seeing the bloated features of their own parents. Instead of laughing, they wince, they mourn. Instead of celebrating the drunk as one freed from constraints, they pity him as one enslaved. They refuse to believe *in vino veritas*, having seen their befuddled parents skid away from truth toward folly and oblivion. And so these children bite their lips until the lush staggers into the wings.

My father, when drunk, was neither funny nor honest; he was pathetic, frightening, deceitful. There seemed to be a leak in him somewhere, and he poured in booze to keep from draining dry. Like a torture victim who refuses to squeal, he would never admit that he had touched a drop, not even in his last year, when he seemed to be dissolving in alcohol before our very eyes. I never knew him to lie about anything, ever, except about this one ruinous fact. Drowsy, clumsy, unable to fix a bicycle tire, balance a grocery sack, or walk across a room, he was stripped of his true self by drink. In a matter of minutes, the contents of a bottle could transform a brave man into a coward, a buddy into a bully, a gifted athlete and skilled carpenter and shrewd businessman into a bumbler. No dictionary of synonyms for *drunk* would soften the anguish of watching our prince turn into a frog.

Father's drinking became the family secret. While growing up, we children never breathed a word of it beyond the four walls of our house. To this day, my brother and sister rarely mention it, and then only when I press them. I did not confess the ugly, bewildering fact to my wife until his wavering and slurred speech forced me to. Recently, on the seventh anniversary of my father's death, I asked my mother if she ever spoke of his drinking to friends. "No, no, never," she replied hastily. "I couldn't bear for anyone to know."

The secret bores under the skin, gets in the blood, into the bone, and stays there. Long after you have supposedly been cured of malaria, the fever can flare up, the tremors can shake you. So it is with the fevers of shame. You swallow the bitter quinine of knowledge, and you learn to feel pity and compassion toward the drinker. Yet the shame lingers and, because of it, anger.

For a long stretch of my childhood we lived on a military reservation in Ohio, an   15 arsenal where bombs were stored underground in bunkers and vintage airplanes burst into flames and unstable artillery shells boomed nightly at the dump. We had the feeling, as children, that we played within a minefield, where a heedless footfall could trigger an explosion. When Father was drinking, the house, too, became a minefield. The least bump could set off either parent.

The more he drank, the more obsessed Mother became with stopping him. She hunted for bottles, counted the cash in his wallet, sniffed at his breath. Without meaning to snoop, we children blundered left and right into damning evidence. On afternoons when he came home from work sober, we flung ourselves at him for hugs and felt against our ribs the telltale lump in his coat. In the barn we tumbled on the hay and heard beneath our sneakers the crunch of broken glass. We tugged open a drawer in his workbench, looking for screwdrivers or crescent wrenches, and spied a gleaming six-pack among the tools. Playing tag, we darted around the house just in time to see him sway on the rear stoop and heave a finished bottle into the woods. In his goodnight kiss we smelled the cloying sweetness of Clorets, the mints he chewed to camouflage his dragon's breath.

I can summon up that kiss right now by recalling Theodore Roethke's lines about his own father:

> The whiskey on your breath
> Could make a small boy dizzy;
> But I hung on like death:
> Such waltzing was not easy.

Such waltzing was hard, terribly hard, for with a boy's scrawny arms I was trying to hold my tipsy father upright.

For years, the chief source of those incriminating bottles and cans was a grimy store a mile from us, a cinderblock place called Sly's, with two gas pumps outside and a mangy dog asleep in the window. Inside, on rusty metal shelves or in wheezing coolers, you could find pop and Popsicles, cigarettes, potato chips, canned soup, raunchy postcards, fishing gear, Twinkies, wine, and beer. When Father drove anywhere on errands, Mother would send us along as guards, warning us not to let him out of our sight. And so with one or more of us on board, Father would cruise up to Sly's, pump a dollar's worth of gas or plump the tires with air, and then, telling us to wait in the car, he would head for the doorway.

Dutiful and panicky, we cried, "Let us go with you!"

"No," he answered. "I'll be back in two shakes."   20

"Please!"

"No!" he roared. "Don't you budge or I'll jerk a knot in your tails!"

So we stayed put, kicking the seats, while he ducked inside. Often, when he had parked the car at a careless angle, we gazed in through the window and saw Mr. Sly fetching down from the shelf behind the cash register two green pints of Gallo wine. Father swigged one of them right there at the counter, stuffed the other in his pocket, and then out he came, a bulge in his coat, a flustered look on his reddened face.

Because the mom and pop who ran the dump were neighbors of ours, living just down the tar-blistered road, I hated them all the more for poisoning my father. I wanted to sneak in their store and smash the bottles and set fire to the place. I also hated the Gallo brothers, Ernest and Julio, whose jovial faces beamed from the labels of their wine, labels I would find, torn and curled, when I burned the trash. I noted the Gallo brothers' address in California and studied the road atlas to see how far that was from Ohio, because I meant to go out there and tell Ernest and Julio what they were doing to my father, and then, if they showed no mercy, I would kill them.

While growing up on the back roads and in the country schools and cramped   25
Methodist churches of Ohio and Tennessee, I never heard the word *alcoholic,*
never happened across it in books or magazines. In the nearby towns, there were no addiction-treatment programs, no community mental-health centers, no Alcoholics Anonymous chapters, no therapists. Left alone with our grievous secret, we had no way of understanding Father's drinking except as an act of will, a deliberate folly or cruelty, a moral weakness, a sin. He drank because he chose to, pure and simple. Why our father, so playful and competent and kind when sober, would choose to ruin himself and punish his family we could not fathom.

Our neighborhood was high on the Bible, and the Bible was hard on drunkards. "Woe to those who are heroes at drinking wine and valiant men in mixing strong drink," wrote Isaiah. "The priest and the prophet reel with strong drink, they are confused with wine, they err in vision, they stumble in giving judgment.

For all tables are full of vomit, no place is without filthiness." We children had seen those fouled tables at the local truck stop where the notorious boozers hung out, our father occasionally among them. "Wine and new wine take away the understanding," declared the prophet Hosea. We had also seen evidence of that in our father, who could multiply seven-digit numbers in his head when sober but when drunk could not help us with fourth-grade math. Proverbs warned: "Do not look at wine when it is red, when it sparkles in the cup and goes down smoothly. At the last it bites like a serpent and stings like an adder. Your eyes will see strange things, and your mind utter perverse things." Woe, woe.

Dismayingly often, these biblical drunkards stirred up trouble for their own kids. Noah made fresh wine after the flood, drank too much of it, fell asleep without any clothes on, and was glimpsed in the buff by his son Ham, whom Noah promptly cursed. In one passage—it was so shocking we had to read it under our blankets with flashlights—the patriarch Lot fell down drunk and slept with his daughters. The sins of the fathers set their children's teeth on edge.

Our ministers were fond of quoting St. Paul's pronouncement that drunkards would not inherit the kingdom of God. These grave preachers assured us that the wine referred to in the Last Supper was in fact grape juice. Bible and sermons and hymns combined to give us the impression that Moses should have brought down from the mountain another stone tablet, bearing the Eleventh Commandment: Thou shalt not drink.

The scariest and most illuminating Bible story apropos of drunkards was the one about the lunatic and the swine. We knew it by heart: When Jesus climbed out of his boat one day, this lunatic came charging up from the graveyard, stark naked and filthy, frothing at the mouth, so violent that he broke the strongest chains. Nobody would go near him. Night and day for years, this madman had been wailing among the tombs and bruising himself with stones. Jesus took one look at him and said, "Come out of the man, you unclean spirits!" for he could see that the lunatic was possessed by demons. Meanwhile, some hogs were conveniently rooting nearby. "If we have to come out," begged the demons, "at least let us go into those swine." Jesus agreed, the unclean spirits entered the hogs, and the hogs raced straight off a cliff and plunged into a lake. Hearing the story in Sunday school, my friends thought mainly of the pigs. (How big a splash did they make? Who paid for the lost pork?) But I thought of the redeemed lunatic, who bathed himself and put on clothes and calmly sat at the feet of Jesus, restored—so the Bible said—to "his right mind."

When drunk, our father was clearly in his wrong mind. He became a stranger, 30 as fearful to us as any graveyard lunatic, not quite frothing at the mouth but fierce enough, quick-tempered, explosive; or else he grew maudlin and weepy, which frightened us nearly as much. In my boyhood despair, I reasoned that maybe he wasn't to blame for turning into an ogre: Maybe, like the lunatic, he was possessed by demons.

If my father was indeed possessed, who would exorcise him? If he was a sinner, who would save him? If he was ill, who would cure him? If he suffered, who would ease his pain? Not ministers or doctors, for we could not bring ourselves to confide in them; not the neighbors, for we pretended they had never seen him drunk; not Mother, who fussed and pleaded but could not budge him; not my brother and sister, who were only kids. That left me. It did not matter that I, too, was only a child, and a bewildered one at that. I could not excuse myself.

On first reading a description of delirium tremens—in a book on alcoholism I smuggled from a university library—I thought immediately of the frothing lunatic and the frenzied swine. When I read stories or watched films about grisly metamorphoses—Dr. Jekyll and Mr. Hyde, the mild husband changing into a werewolf, the kindly neighbor inhabited by a brutal alien—I could not help but see my own father's mutation from sober to drunk. Even today, knowing better, I am attracted by the demonic theory of drink, for when I recall my father's transformation, the emergence of his ugly second self, I find it easy to believe in being possessed by unclean spirits. We never knew which version of Father would come home from work, the true or the tainted, nor could we guess how far down the slope toward cruelty he would slide.

How far a man *could* slide we gauged by observing our back-road neighbors—the out-of-work miners who had dragged their families to our corner of Ohio from the desolate hollows of Appalachia, the tightfisted farmers, the surly mechanics, the balked and broken men. There was, for example, whiskey-soaked Mr. Jenkins, who beat his wife and kids so hard we could hear their screams from the road. There was Mr. Lavo the wino, who fell asleep smoking time and again, until one night his disgusted wife bundled up the children and went outside and left him in his easy chair to burn; he awoke on his own, staggered out coughing into the yard, and pounded her flat while the children looked on and the shack turned to ash. There was the truck driver, Mr. Sampson, who tripped over his son's tricycle one night while drunk and got mad, jumped into his semi, and drove away, shifting through the dozen gears, and never came back. We saw the bruised children of these fathers clump onto our school bus, we saw the abandoned children huddle in the pews at church, we saw the stunned and battered mothers begging for help at our doors.

Our own father never beat us, and I don't think he beat Mother, but he threatened often. The Old Testament Yahweh was not more terrible in His rage. Eyes blazing, voice booming, Father would pull out his belt and swear to give us a whipping, but he never followed through, never needed to, because we could imagine it so vividly. He shoved us, pawed us with the back of his hand, not to injure, just to clear a space. I can see him grabbing Mother by the hair as she cowers on a chair during a nightly quarrel. He twists her neck back until she gapes up at him, and then he lifts over her skull a glass quart bottle of milk, and milk spilling down his forearm, and he yells at her, "Say just one more word, one goddamn word, and I'll shut you up!" I fear she will prick him with her sharp tongue, but she is terrified into silence, and so am I, and the leaking bottle quivers in the air, and milk seeps through the red hair of my father's uplifted arm, and the entire scene is there to this moment, the head jerked back, the club raised.

When the drink made him weepy, Father would pack, kiss each of us chil-   35
dren on the head, and announce from the front door that he was moving out.
"Where to?" we demanded, fearful each time that he would leave for good, as Mr.
Sampson had roared away for good in his diesel truck. "Someplace where I won't
get hounded every minute," Father would answer, his jaw quivering. He stabbed
a look at Mother, who might say, "Don't run into the ditch before you get there,"
or "Good riddance," and then he would slink away. Mother watched him go with
arms crossed over her chest, her face closed like the lid on a box of snakes. We
children bawled. Where could he go? To the truck stop, that den of iniquity? To
one of those dark, ratty flophouses in town? Would he wind up sleeping under a
railroad bridge or on a park bench or in a cardboard box, mummied in rags like
the bums we had seen on our trips to Cleveland and Chicago? We bawled and
bawled, wondering if he would ever come back.

He always did come back, a day or a week later, but each time there was a
sliver less of him.

In Kafka's *Metamorphosis,* which opens famously with Gregor Samsa waking up
from uneasy dreams to find himself transformed into an insect, Gregor's family keep reassuring themselves that things will be just fine again "when he comes
back to us." Each time alcohol transformed our father we held out the same
hope, that he would really and truly come back to us, our authentic father, the
tender and playful and competent man, and then all things would be fine. We
had grounds for such hope. After his tearful departures and chapfallen returns,
he would sometimes go weeks, even months, without drinking. Those were glad
times. Every day without the furtive glint of bottles, every meal without a fight,
every bedtime without sobs encouraged us to believe that such bliss might go on
forever.

Mother was fooled by such a hope all during the forty-odd years she knew
Greeley Ray Sanders. Soon after she met him in a Chicago delicatessen on the
eve of World War II and fell for his butter-melting Mississippi drawl and his
wavy red hair, she learned that he drank heavily. But then so did a lot of men.
She would soon coax or scold him into breaking the nasty habit. She would
point out to him how ugly and foolish it was, this bleary drinking, and then he
would quit. He refused to quit during their engagement, however, still refused
during the first years of marriage, refused until my older sister came along. The
shock of fatherhood sobered him, and he remained sober through my birth at
the end of the war and right on through until we moved in 1951 to the Ohio
arsenal. The arsenal had more than its share of alcoholics, drug addicts, and
other varieties of escape artists. There I turned six and started school and woke
into a child's flickering awareness, just in time to see my father begin sneaking
swigs in the garage.

He sobered up again for most of a year at the height of the Korean War, to
celebrate the birth of my brother. But aside from that dry spell, his only breaks
from drinking before I graduated from high school were just long enough to raise

and then dash our hopes. Then during the fall of my senior year—the time of the Cuban Missile Crisis, when it seemed that the nightly explosions at the munitions dump and the nightly rages in our household might spread to engulf the globe—Father collapsed. His liver, kidneys, and heart all conked out. The doctors saved him, but only by a hair. He stayed in the hospital for weeks, going through a withdrawal so terrible that Mother would not let us visit him. If he wanted to kill himself, the doctors solemnly warned him, all he had to do was hit the bottle again. One binge would finish him.

Father must have believed them, for he stayed dry the next fifteen years. It 40 was an answer to prayer, Mother said, it was a miracle. I believe it was a reflex of fear, which he sustained over the years through courage and pride. He knew a man could die from drink, for his brother Roscoe had. We children never laid eyes on doomed Uncle Roscoe, but in the stories Mother told us he became a fairy-tale figure, like a boy who took the wrong turn in the woods and was gobbled up by the wolf.

The fifteen-year dry spell came to an end with Father's retirement in the spring of 1978. Like many men, he gave up his identity along with his job. One day he was a boss at the factory, with a brass plate on his door and a reputation to uphold; the next day he was a nobody at home. He and Mother were leaving Ontario, the last of the many places to which his job had carried them, and they were moving to a new house in Mississippi, his childhood stomping ground. As a boy in Mississippi, Father sold Coca-Cola during dances while the moonshiners peddled their brew in the parking lot; as a young blade, he fought in bars and in the ring, winning a state Golden Gloves championship; he gambled at poker, hunted pheasant, raced motorcycles and cars, played semiprofessional baseball, and, along with all his buddies—in the Black Cat Saloon, behind the cotton gin, in the woods—he drank hard. It was a perilous youth to dream of recovering.

After his final day of work, Mother drove on ahead with a car full of begonias and violets, while Father stayed behind to oversee the packing. When the van was loaded, the sweaty movers broke open a six-pack and offered him a beer.

"Let's drink to retirement!" they crowed. "Let's drink to freedom! to fishing! hunting! loafing! Let's drink to a guy who's going home!"

At least I imagine some such words, for that is all I can do, imagine, and I see Father's hand trembling in midair as he thinks about the fifteen sober years and about the doctors' warning, and he tells himself, *Goddamnit, I am a free man,* and *Why can't a free man drink one beer after a lifetime of hard work?* and I see his arm reaching, his fingers closing, the can tilting to his lips. I even supply a label for the beer, a swaggering brand that promises on television to deliver the essence of life. I watch the amber liquid pour down his throat, the alcohol steal into his blood, the key turn in his brain.

Soon after my parents moved back to Father's treacherous stomping ground, my 45 wife and I visited them in Mississippi with our four-year-old daughter. Mother had been too distraught to warn me about the return of the demons. So when I climbed out of the car that bright July morning and saw my father napping in the hammock, I felt uneasy, and when he lurched upright and blinked his bloodshot eyes and greeted us in a syrupy voice, I was hurled back into childhood.

"What's the matter with Papaw?" our daughter asked.

"Nothing," I said. "Nothing!"

Like a child again, I pretended not to see him in his stupor, and behind my phony smile I grieved. On that visit and on the few that remained before his death, once again I found bottles in the workbench, bottles in the woods. Again his hands shook too much for him to run a saw, to make his precious miniature furniture, to drive straight down back roads. Again he wound up in the ditch, in the hospital, in jail, in the treatment center. Again he shouted and wept. Again he lied. "I never touched a drop," he swore. "Your mother's making it up."

I no longer fancied I could reason with the men whose names I found on the bottles—Jim Beam, Jack Daniel's—but I was able now to recall the cold statistics about alcoholism: ten million victims, fifteen million, twenty. And yet, in spite of my age, I reacted in the same blind way as I had in childhood, by vainly seeking to erase through my efforts whatever drove him to drink. I worked on their place twelve and sixteen hours a day, in the swelter of Mississippi summers, digging ditches, running electrical wires, planting trees, mowing grass, building sheds, as though what nagged at him was some list of chores, as though by taking his worries upon my shoulders I could redeem him. I was flung back into boyhood, acting as though my father would not drink himself to death if only I were perfect.

I failed of perfection; he succeeded in dying. To the end, he considered himself not sick but sinful. "Do you want to kill yourself?" I asked him. "Why not?" he answered. "Why the hell not? What's there to save?" To the end, he would not speak about his feelings, would not or could not give a name to the beast that was devouring him.

In silence, he went rushing off to the cliff. Unlike the biblical swine, however, he left behind a few of the demons to haunt his children. Life with him and the loss of him twisted us into shapes that will be familiar to other sons and daughters of alcoholics. My brother became a rebel, my sister retreated into shyness, I played the stalwart and dutiful son who would hold the family together. If my father was unstable, I would be a rock. If he squandered money on drink, I would pinch every penny. If he wept when drunk—and only when drunk—I would not let myself weep at all. If he roared at the Little League umpire for calling my pitches balls, I would throw nothing but strikes. Watching him flounder and rage, I came to dread the loss of control. I would go through life without making anyone mad. I vowed never to put in my mouth or veins any chemical that would banish my everyday self. I would never make a scene, never lash out at the ones I loved, never hurt a soul. Through hard work, relentless work, I would achieve something dazzling—in the classroom, on the basketball court, in the science lab, in the pages of books—and my achievement would distract the world's eyes from his humiliation. I would become a worthy sacrifice, and the smoke of my burning would please God.

It is far easier to recognize these twists in my character than to undo them. Work has become an addiction for me, as drink was an addiction for my father. Knowing this, my daughter gave me a placard for the wall: WORKAHOLIC. The labor is endless and futile, for I can no more redeem myself through work than I could redeem my father. I still panic in the face of other people's anger, because his drunken temper was so terrible. I shrink from causing sadness or disappointment even to strangers, as though I were still concealing the family shame. I still notice every twitch of emotion in those faces around me, having learned as a child to read the weather in faces, and I blame myself for their least pang of unhappiness or anger. In certain moods I blame myself for everything. Guilt burns like acid in my veins.

I am moved to write these pages now because my own son, at the age of ten, is taking on himself the griefs of the world, and in particular the griefs of his father. He tells me that when I am gripped by sadness, he feels responsible; he feels there must be something he can do to spring me from depression, to fix my life, and that crushing sense of responsibility is exactly what I felt at the age of ten in the face of my father's drinking. My son wonders if I, too, am possessed. I write, therefore, to drag into the light what eats at me—the fear, the guilt, the shame—so that my own children may be spared.

I still shy away from nightclubs, from bars, from parties where the solvent is alcohol. My friends puzzle over this, but it is no more peculiar than for a man to shy away from the lions' den after seeing his father torn apart. I took my own first drink at the age of twenty-one, half a glass of burgundy. I knew the odds of my becoming an alcoholic were four times higher than for the children of nonalcoholic fathers. So I sipped warily.

I still do—once a week, perhaps, a glass of wine, a can of beer, nothing 55 stronger, nothing more. I listen for the turning of a key in my brain.

QUESTIONS FOR DISCUSSION AND WRITING

1. What is the price that Sanders has paid, and is still paying, for his father's drinking problem? What evidence does Sanders provide to demonstrate that alcoholism is a social problem rather than an isolated, individual matter?

2. What was the father like when he was sober? What was he like when drunk? What examples are the most powerful, the most painful, or the most pleasant in this essay?

3. For what audience is Sanders writing? His mother, siblings, and children? Other alcoholics and their families? People who know little about alcoholism? Himself? What is the relation of alcohol to each of these audiences?

ALICE WALKER

In Search of Our Mothers' Gardens

Author of the Pulitzer Prize–winning novel The Color Purple *(1982), Alice Walker is a poet, novelist, essayist, and civil rights activist. She was born (1944) and raised in segregated Eatonton, Georgia, where her parents, Willie Lee and Minnie Walker, were sharecroppers. Walker graduated from Sarah Lawrence (B.A., 1965). During the civil rights movement, she was a voter registration worker in Georgia and a Head Start worker in Mississippi, before teaching at various colleges, including Tougaloo, Wellesley, and her alma mater. Walker addresses the human implications of social issues in her essay collections, including* Living by the Word *(1988) and* Anything We Love Can Be Saved: A Writer's Activism *(1997); short-story collections, such as* In Love and Trouble *(1973) and* You Can't Keep a Good Woman Down *(1981); and novels, including* Meridian *(1976) and* Possessing the Secret of Joy *(1992). Walker's poetry includes* Revolutionary Petunias, and Other Poems *(1973), where "In Search of Our Mothers' Gardens" first appeared under the title "Women"; and* Her Blue Body Everything We Know: Earthling Poems, 1965–1990 *(1991). Her four children's books include* Why War Is Never a Good Idea *(2007).*

Walker wrote "In Search of Our Mothers' Gardens" for a 1973 Radcliffe symposium on "The Black Woman: Myths and Realities." In 1974 she revised the speech, which was published in Ms. *and later collected in* In Search of Our Mothers' Gardens: Womanist Prose *(1983), coining* womanist *to denote her philosophical and political commitment to "the survival and wholeness of entire people, male and female." The essay combines historical analysis, literary criticism, and autobiography to explore the "creative spirit" of generations of African American women. Walker urges readers to recognize that many such women expressed their "creative spirit" through quilting, gardening, blues singing, storytelling, and poetry. The Contexts that follow examine Walker's rhetorical relationships with her various audiences.*

I

I described her own nature and temperament. Told how they needed a larger life for their expression. . . . I pointed out that in lieu of proper channels, her emotions had overflowed into paths and dissipated them. I talked beautifully I thought, about an art that would be born, an art that would open the way for women the likes of her. I asked her to hope, and build up an inner life against the coming of that day. . . . I sang, with a strange quiver in my voice, a promise song.

—"Avey," Jean Toomer, *Cane*

The poet speaking to a prostitute who falls asleep while he's talking—

When the poet Jean Toomer walked through the South in the early twenties, he discovered a curious thing: Black women whose spirituality was so intense, so deep, so *unconscious*, they were themselves unaware of the richness they held. They stumbled blindly through their lives: creatures so abused and mutilated in body, so dimmed and confused by pain, that they considered themselves unworthy even of hope. In the selfless abstractions their bodies became to the men who used them, they became more than "sexual objects," more even than mere women: they became Saints. Instead of being perceived as whole persons, their bodies became shrines; what was thought to be their minds became temples suitable for worship. These crazy "Saints" stared out at the world, wildly, like lunatics—or quietly, like suicides; and the "God" that was in their gate was as mute as a great stone.

Who were these "Saints"? These crazy, loony, pitiful women?

Some of them without a doubt, were our mothers and grandmothers.

In the still heat of the post-Reconstruction South, this is how they seemed to 5 Jean Toomer: exquisite butterflies trapped in an evil honey, toiling away their lives in an era, a century, that did not acknowledge them, except as "the *mule* of the world." They dreamed dreams that no one knew—not even themselves, in any coherent fashion—and saw visions no one could understand. They wandered or sat about the countryside crooning lullabies to ghosts, and drawing the mother of Christ in charcoal on courthouse walls.

They forced their minds to desert their bodies and their striving spirits sought to rise, the frail whirlwinds from the hard red clay. And when those frail whirlwinds fell, in scattered particles, upon the ground, no one mourned. Instead, men lit candles to celebrate the emptiness that remained, as people do who enter a beautiful but vacant space to resurrect a God.

Our mothers and grandmothers, some of them: moving to music not yet written. And they waited.

They waited for a day when the unknown thing that was in them would be made known; but guessed, somehow in their darkness, that on the day of their revelation they would be long dead. Therefore to Toomer they walked, and even ran, in slow motion. For they were going nowhere immediate, and the future was not yet within their grasp. And men took our mothers and grandmothers, "but got no pleasure from it." So complex was their passion and their calm.

To Toomer, they lay vacant and fallow as autumn fields, with harvest time never in sight: and he saw them enter loveless marriages, without joy; and become prostitutes, without resistance; and become mothers of children without fulfillment.

For these grandmothers and mothers of ours were not "Saints," but Artists; 10 driven to a numb and bleeding madness by the springs of creativity in them for which there was no release. They were Creators, who lived lives of spiritual waste, because they were so rich in spirituality—which is the basis of Art—that the strain of enduring their unused and unwanted talent drove them insane. Throwing away this spirituality was their pathetic attempt to lighten the soul to a weight their work-worn, sexually abused bodies could bear.

What did it mean for a Black woman to be an artist in our grandmothers' time? In our great-grandmothers' day? It is a question with an answer cruel enough to stop the blood.

Did you have a genius of a great-great-grandmother who died under some ignorant and depraved white overseer's lash? Or was she required to bake biscuits for a lazy backwater tramp, when she cried out in her soul to paint watercolors of sunsets, or the rain falling on the green and peaceful pasturelands? Or was her body broken and forced to bear children (who were more often than not sold away from her) — eight, ten, fifteen, twenty children — when her one joy was the thought of modeling heroic figures of Rebellion, in stone or clay?

How was the creativity of the Black woman kept alive, year after year and century after century, when for most of the years Black people have been in America, it was a punishable crime for a Black person to read or write? And the freedom to paint, to sculpt, to expand the mind with action, did not exist. Consider, if you can bear to imagine it, what might have been the result if singing, too, had been forbidden by law. Listen to the voices of Bessie Smith, Billie Holiday, Nina Simone, Roberta Flack, and Aretha Franklin, among others, and imagine those voices muzzled for life. Then you may begin to comprehend the lives of our "crazy," "Sainted" mothers and grandmothers. The agony of the lives of women who might have been Poets, Novelists, Essayists, and Short Story Writers (over a period of centuries), who died with their real gifts stifled within them.

And, if this were the end of the story, we would have cause to cry out in my paraphrase of Okot p'Bitek's great poem:

O, my clanswomen
Let us all cry together!
Come,
Let us mourn the death of our mother,
The death of a Queen
The ash that was produced
By a great fire!
O this homestead is utterly dead
Close the gates
With *lacari* thorns,
For our mother
The creator of the Stool is lost!
And all the young women
Have perished in the wilderness.[1]

But this is not the end of the story, for all the young women — our mothers and grandmothers, *ourselves* — have not perished in the wilderness. And if we ask ourselves why, and search for and find the answer, we will know beyond all efforts to erase it from our minds, just exactly who, and of what, we Black American women are.

---

[1]Okot p'Bitek, *Song of Lawino: An Africa Lament* (Nairobi: East African Publishing House, 1966). [Editors' note.]

One example, perhaps the most pathetic, most misunderstood one, can provide a backdrop for our mothers' work: Phillis Wheatley, a slave in the 1700s.

Virginia Woolf, in her book, *A Room of One's Own*, wrote that in order for a woman to write fiction she must have two things, certainly: a room of her own (with a key and lock) and enough money to support herself.

What then are we to make of Phillis Wheatley, a slave, who owned not even herself? This sickly, frail, Black girl who required a servant of her own at times—her health was so precarious—and who, had she been white, would have been easily considered the intellectual superior of all the women and most of the men in the society of her day.

Virginia Woolf wrote further, speaking of course not of our Phillis, that "any woman born with a great gift in the sixteenth century [insert *eighteenth century*, insert *Black woman*, insert *born or made a slave*] would certainly have gone crazed, shot herself, or ended her days in some lonely cottage outside the village, half witch, half wizard [insert *Saint*], feared and mocked at. For it needs little skill and psychology to be sure that a highly gifted girl who had tried to use her gift for poetry would have been so thwarted and hindered by contrary instincts [add *chains, guns, the lash, the ownership of one's body by someone else, submission to an alien religion*] that she must have lost her health and sanity to a certainty."

The key words, as they relate to Phillis, are "contrary instincts." For when we 20 read the poetry of Phillis Wheatley—as when we read the novels of Nella Larsen or the oddly false-sounding autobiography of that freest of all Black women writers, Zora Hurston—evidence of "contrary instincts" is everywhere. Her loyalties were completely divided, as was, without question, her mind.

But how could this be otherwise? Captured at seven, a slave of wealthy, doting whites who instilled in her the "savagery" of the Africa they "rescued" her from . . . one wonders if she was even able to remember her homeland as she had known it, or as it really was.

Yet, because she did try to use her gift for poetry in a world that made her a slave, she was "so thwarted and hindered by . . . contrary instincts that she . . . lost her health. . . ." In the last years of her brief life, burdened not only with the need to express her gift but also with a penniless, friendless "freedom" and several small children for whom she was forced to do strenuous work to feed, she lost her health, certainly. Suffering from malnutrition and neglect and who knows what mental agonies, Phillis Wheatley died.

So torn by "contrary instincts" was Black, kidnapped, enslaved Phillis that her description of "the Goddess"—as she poetically called the Liberty she did not have—is ironically, cruelly humorous. And, in fact, has held Phillis up to ridicule for more than a century. It is usually read prior to hanging Phillis's memory as that of a fool. She wrote:

The Goddess comes, she moves divinely fair,
Olive and laurel binds her *golden* hair:

Wherever shines this native of the skies,
Unnumber'd charms and recent graces rise.

[Emphasis mine]

It is obvious that Phillis, the slave, combed the "Goddess's" hair every morning; prior, perhaps, to bringing in the milk, or fixing her mistress's lunch. She took her imagery from the one thing she saw elevated above all others.

With the benefit of hindsight we ask, "How could she?"   25

But at last, Phillis, we understand. No more snickering when your stiff, struggling, ambivalent lines are forced on us. We know now that you were not an idiot nor a traitor; only a sickly little Black girl, snatched from your home and country and made a slave; a woman who still struggled to sing the song that was your gift, although in a land of barbarians who praised you for your bewildered tongue. It is not so much what you sang, as that you kept alive, in so many of our ancestors, the notion of song.

II

Black women are called, in the folklore that so aptly identifies one's status in society, "the *mule* of the world," because we have been handed the burdens that everyone else—*everyone* else—refused to carry. We have been called "Matriarchs," "Superwomen," and "Mean and Evil Bitches." Not to mention "Castrators" and "Sapphire's Mama." When we have pleaded for understanding, our character has been distorted; when we have asked for simple caring, we have been handed empty inspirational appellations, then stuck in the farthest corner. When we have asked for love, we have been given children. In short, even our plainer gifts, our labors of fidelity and love, have been knocked down our throats. To be an Artist and a Black woman, even today, lowers our status in many respects, rather than raises it: and yet, Artists we will be.

Therefore we must fearlessly pull out of ourselves and look at and identify with our lives the living creativity some of our great-grandmothers were not allowed to know. I stress *some* of them because it is well known that the majority of our great-grandmothers knew, even without "knowing" it, the reality of their spirituality, even if they didn't recognize it beyond what happened in the singing at church—and they never had any intention of giving it up.

How they did it: those millions of Black women who were not Phillis Wheatley, or Lucy Terry or Frances Harper or Zora Hurston or Nella Larsen or Bessie Smith—nor Elizabeth Catlett, nor Katherine Dunham, either—brings me to the title of this essay, "In Search of Our Mothers' Gardens," which is a personal account that is yet shared, in its theme and its meaning, by all of us. I found, while thinking about the far-reaching world of the creative Black woman, that often the truest answer to a question that really matters can be found very close.

In the late 1920s my mother ran away from home to marry my father. Mar-   30
riage, if not running away, was expected of seventeen-year-old girls. By the time she was twenty, she had two children and was pregnant with a third. Five children

later, I was born. And this is how I came to know my mother: she seemed a large, soft, loving-eyed woman who was rarely impatient in our home. Her quick, violent temper was on view only a few times a year, when she battled with the white landlord who had the misfortune to suggest to her that her children did not need to go to school.

She made all the clothes we wore, even my brothers' overalls. She made all the towels and sheets we used. She spent the summers canning vegetables and fruits. She spent the winter evenings making quilts enough to cover all our beds.

During the "working" day, she labored beside—not behind—my father in the fields. Her day began before sunup, and did not end until late at night. There was never a moment for her to sit down, undisturbed, to unravel her own private thoughts; never a time free from interruption—by work or the noisy inquiries of her many children. And yet, it is to my mother—and all our mothers who were not famous—that I went in search of the secret of what has fed that muzzled and often mutilated, but vibrant, creative spirit that the Black woman has inherited, and that pops out in wild and unlikely places to this day.

But when, you will ask, did my overworked mother have time to know or care about feeding the creative spirit?

The answer is so simple that many of us have spent years discovering it. We have constantly looked high, when we should have looked high—and low.

For example: in the Smithsonian Institution in Washington, D.C., there 35 hangs a quilt unlike any other in the world. In fanciful, inspired, and yet simple and identifiable figures, it portrays the story of the Crucifixion. It is considered rare, beyond price. Though it follows no known pattern of quiltmaking, and though it is made of bits and pieces of worthless rags, it is obviously the work of a person of powerful imagination and deep spiritual feelings. Below this quilt I saw a note that says it was made by "an anonymous Black woman in Alabama, a hundred years ago."

If we could locate this "anonymous" Black woman from Alabama, she would turn out to be one of our grandmothers—an artist who left her mark in the only materials she could afford, and in the only medium her position in society allowed her to use.

As Virginia Woolf wrote further, in *A Room of One's Own*:

"Yet genius of a sort must have existed among women as it must have existed among the working class. [Change this to *slaves* and *the wives and daughters of sharecroppers*.] Now and again an Emily Brontë or a Robert Burns [change this to *a Zora Hurston or a Richard Wright*] blazes out and proves its presence. But certainly it never got itself on to paper. When, however, one reads of a witch being ducked, of a woman possessed by devils [or *Sainthood*], of a wise woman selling herbs [our rootworkers], or even a very remarkable man who had a mother, then I think we are on the track of a suppressed poet, of some mute and inglorious Jane Austen. . . . Indeed, I would venture to guess that Anon, who wrote so many poems without singing them, was often a woman. . . ."

And so our mothers and grandmothers have, more often than not anonymously, handed on the creative spark, the seed of the flower they themselves never hoped to see: or like a sealed letter they could not plainly read.

And so it is, certainly, with my own mother. Unlike Ma Rainey's songs, 40 which retained their creator's name even while blasting forth from Bessie Smith's mouth, no song or poem will bear my mother's name. Yet so many of the stories that I write, that we all write, are my mother's stories. Only recently did I fully realize this: that through years of listening to my mother's stories of her life, I have absorbed not only the stories themselves, but something of the manner in which she spoke, something of the urgency that involves the knowledge that her stories—like her life—must be recorded. It is probably for this reason that so much of what I have written is about characters whose counterparts in real life are so much older than I am.

But the telling of these stories, which came from my mother's lips as naturally as breathing, was not the only way my mother showed herself as an artist. For stories, too, were subject to being distracted, to dying without conclusion. Dinners must be started, and cotton must be gathered before the big rains. The artist that was and is my mother showed itself to me only after many years. This is what I finally noticed:

Like Mem, a character in *The Third Life of Grange Copeland,* my mother adorned with flowers whatever shabby house we were forced to live in. And not just your typical straggly country stand of zinnias, either. She planted ambitious gardens—and still does—with over fifty different varieties of plants that bloom profusely from early March until late November. Before she left home for the fields, she watered her flowers, chopped up the grass, and laid out new beds. When she returned from the fields she might divide clumps of bulbs, dig a cold pit, uproot and replant roses, or prune branches from her taller bushes or trees—until night came and it was too dark to see.

Whatever she planted grew as if by magic, and her fame as a grower of flowers spread over three counties. Because of her creativity with her flowers, even my memories of poverty are seen through a screen of blooms—sunflowers, petunias, roses, dahlias, forsythia, spirea, delphiniums, verbena . . . and on and on.

And I remember people coming to my mother's yard to be given cuttings from her flowers; I hear again the praise showered on her because whatever rocky soil she landed on, she turned into a garden. A garden so brilliant with colors, so original in its design, so magnificent with life and creativity, that to this day people drive by our house in Georgia—perfect strangers and imperfect strangers—and ask to stand or walk among my mother's art.

I notice that it is only when my mother is working in her flowers that she is 45 radiant, almost to the point of being invisible—except as Creator: hand and eye. She is involved in work her soul must have. Ordering the universe in the image of her personal conception of Beauty.

Her face, as she prepares the Art that is her gift, is a legacy of respect she leaves to me, for all that illuminates and cherishes life. She had handed down respect for the possibilities—and the will to grasp them.

For her, so hindered and intruded upon in so many ways, being an artist has still been a daily part of her life. This ability to hold on, even in very simple ways, is work Black women have done for a very long time.

This poem is not enough, but it is something, for the woman who literally covered the holes in our walls with sunflowers:

> They were women then
> My mama's generation
> Husky of voice—Stout of
> Step
> With fists as well as
> Hands
> How they battered down
> Doors
> And ironed
> Starched white
> Shirts
> How they led
> Armies
> Headragged Generals
> Across mined
> Fields
> Booby-trapped
> Ditches
> To discover books
> Desks
> A place for us
> How they knew what we
> *Must* know
> Without knowing a page
> Of it
> Themselves.

Guided by my heritage of love and beauty and a respect for strength—in search of my mother's garden, I found my own.

And perhaps in Africa over two hundred years ago, there was just such a mother; perhaps she painted vivid and daring decorations in oranges and yellows and greens on the walls of her hut; perhaps she sang—in a voice like Roberta Flack's—*sweetly* over the compounds of her village; perhaps she wove the most stunning mats or told the most ingenious stories of all the village story-tellers.

Perhaps she was herself a poet—though only her daughter's name is signed to the poems that we know.

Perhaps Phillis Wheatley's mother was also an artist.

Perhaps in more than Phillis Wheatley's biological life is her mother's signature made clear.

CONTEXTS FOR "IN SEARCH OF OUR MOTHERS' GARDENS"

JAMES BALDWIN
Autobiographical Notes

For a biography see p. 134.

I know, in any case, that the most crucial time in my own development came when I was forced to recognize that I was a kind of bastard of the West; when I followed the line of my past I did not find myself in Europe but in Africa. And this meant that in some subtle way, in a really profound way, I brought to Shakespeare, Bach, Rembrandt, to the stones of Paris, to the cathedral at Chartres, and to the Empire State Building, a special attitude. These were not really my creations, they did not contain my history; I might search in them in vain forever for any reflection of myself. I was an interloper; this was not my heritage. At the same time I had no other heritage which I could possibly hope to use—I had certainly been unfitted for the jungle or the tribe. I would have to appropriate these white centuries, I would have to make them mine—I would have to accept my special attitude, my special place in this scheme—otherwise I would have no place in *any* scheme. What was the most difficult was the fact that I was forced to admit something I had always hidden from myself, which the American Negro has had to hide from himself as the price of his public progress; that I hated and feared white people. This did not mean that I loved black people; on the contrary, I despised them, possibly because they failed to produce Rembrandt. In effect, I hated and feared the world. And this meant, not only that I thus gave the world an altogether murderous power over me, but also that in such a self-destroying limbo I could never hope to write.

One writes out of one thing only—one's own experience. Everything depends on how relentlessly one forces from this experience the last drop, sweet

From James Baldwin, "Autobiographical Notes," in *Notes of a Native Son* (Boston: Beacon Press, 1955), 6–7.

or bitter, it can possibly give. This is the only real concern of the artist, to recreate out of the disorder of life that order which is art. The difficulty then, for me, of being a Negro writer was the fact that I was, in effect, prohibited from examining my own experience too closely by the tremendous demands and the very real dangers of my social situation....

AMIRI BARAKA

The Myth of Negro Literature

Poet and playwright Amiri Baraka was born Everett LeRoi Jones in Newark, New Jersey, in 1934. In the 1960s Baraka and other artists sought to define Negritude— that is, the particular artistic quality that expressed the African American experience most authentically. In this excerpt from his address to the American Society of African Culture (1962), Baraka identifies "Negro music" as an authentic expression and insists, since the idea was then controversial, on "calling Negro music Art" with a capital A to emphasize its importance.

Negro music alone, because it drew its strengths and beauties out of the depth of the black man's soul, and because to a large extent its traditions could be carried on by the lowest classes of Negroes, has been able to survive the constant and willful dilutions of the black middle class. Blues and jazz have been the only consistent exhibitors of "Negritude" in informal American culture simply because the bearers of its tradition maintained their essential identities as Negroes; in no other art (and I will persist in calling Negro music Art) has this been possible.

DANIEL PATRICK MOYNIHAN

The Negro Family: The Case for National Action

Then assistant secretary of labor Daniel Patrick Moynihan (1927–2003) issued The Moynihan Report *in 1965, which drew on research by African American sociologists Kenneth Clark and E. Franklin Frazier to trace the economic and social consequences of racial oppression on black families. However, by linking the "black matriarchy" with*

From Amiri Baraka, "The Myth of Negro Literature," in *Home, Social Essays* (New York: William Morrow, 1966), 107.

From Daniel Patrick Moynihan, *The Negro Family: The Case for National Action* (Washington, D.C.: U.S. Department of Labor, 1965).

"social pathology" in the black community, the report, entitled The Negro Family: The Case for National Action, *from which "The Tangle of Pathology" is excerpted, sparked a searing controversy. Among black leaders, radicals responded with indignation, while conservatives organized "citizenship clinics" and acknowledged Moynihan's record of supporting civil rights.*

THE TANGLE OF PATHOLOGY

That the Negro American has survived at all is extraordinary—a lesser people might simply have died out, as indeed others have. That the Negro community has not only survived, but in this political generation has entered national affairs as a moderate, humane, and constructive national force is the highest testament to the healing powers of the democratic ideal and the creative vitality of the Negro people.

But it may not be supposed that the Negro American community has not paid a fearful price for the incredible mistreatment to which it has been subjected over the past three centuries.

In essence, the Negro community has been forced into a matriarchal structure which, because it is so out of line with the rest of the American society, seriously retards the progress of the group as a whole, and imposes a crushing burden on the Negro male and, in consequence, on a great many Negro women as well. . . .

Ours is a society which presumes male leadership in private and public affairs. The arrangements of society facilitate such leadership and reward it. A sub-culture, such as that of the Negro American, in which this is not the pattern, is placed at a distinct disadvantage.

Here an earlier word of caution should be repeated. There is much evidence 5 that a considerable number of Negro families have managed to break out of the tangle of pathology and to establish themselves as stable, effective units, living according to patterns of American society in general. E. Franklin Frazier has suggested that the middle-class Negro American family is, if anything, more patriarchal and protective of its children than the general run of such families. Given equal opportunities, the children of these families will perform as well or better than their white peers. They need no help from anyone, and ask none. . . .

It might be estimated that as much as half of the Negro community falls into the middle class. However, the remaining half is in desperate and deteriorating circumstances. Moreover, because of housing segregation it is immensely difficult for the stable half to escape from the cultural influences of the unstable one. The children of middle-class Negroes often as not must grow up in, or next to the slums, an experience almost unknown to white middle-class children. They are therefore constantly exposed to the pathology of the disturbed group and constantly in danger of being drawn into it. It is for this reason that the propositions put forth in this study may be thought of as having a more or less general application.

Obviously, not every instance of social pathology afflicting the Negro community can be traced to the weakness of family structure. If, for example, organized crime in the Negro community were not largely controlled by whites, there would be more capital accumulation among Negroes, and therefore probably more Negro business enterprises. If it were not for the hostility and fear many whites exhibit towards Negroes, they in turn would be less afflicted by hostility and fear and so on. There is no one Negro community. There is no one Negro problem. There is no one solution. Nonetheless, at the center of the tangle of pathology is the weakness of the family structure. Once or twice removed, it will be found to be the principal source of most of the aberrant, inadequate, or antisocial behavior that did not establish, but now serves to perpetuate the cycle of poverty and deprivation.

It was by destroying the Negro family under slavery that white America broke the will of the Negro people. Although that will has reasserted itself in our time, it is a resurgence doomed to frustration unless the viability of the Negro family is restored.

Matriarchy

A fundamental fact of Negro American family life is the often reversed roles of husband and wife.

Robert O. Blood Jr. and Donald M. Wolfe, in a study of Detroit families, note that "Negro husbands have unusually low power,"[1] and while this is characteristic of all low income families, the pattern pervades the Negro social structure: "the cumulative result of discrimination in jobs . . . , the segregated housing, and the poor schooling of Negro men."[2] In 44 percent of the Negro families studied, the wife was dominant, as against 20 percent of white wives. "Whereas the majority of white families are equalitarian, the largest percentage of Negro families are dominated by the wife."[3]

The matriarchal pattern of so many Negro families reinforces itself over the generations. This process begins with education. Although the gap appears to be closing at the moment, for a long while, Negro females were better educated than Negro males, and this remains true today for the Negro population as a whole.

NOTES

1. Robert O. Blood Jr., and Donald M. Wolfe, *Husbands and Wives: The Dynamics of Married Living* (Illinois: The Free Press of Glencoe, 1960), p. 34.

2. Ibid., p. 35.

3. Ibid.

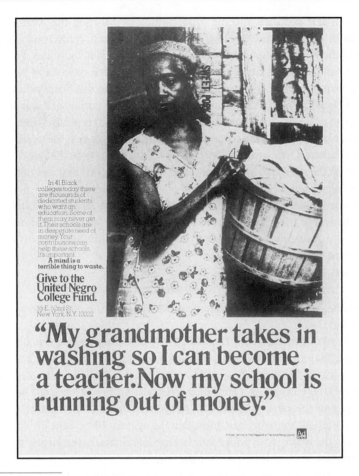

Courtesy: United Negro College Fund Advertisement from *Ms.* (July 1975, p. 103).

ALICE WALKER

Interview (1983)

In this 1983 interview, Walker explains her wish to expand her audience by encouraging reading in the African American community. Twenty years later, Oprah Winfrey's book club was a direct result of efforts like Walker's.

In any case, I think anybody can *only write.* Writing or not writing is not dependent on what the market is—whether your work is going to sell or not. If it were, there is not a black woman who would write. And that includes Phillis Wheatley. Think of *her* antagonistic market! I mean if you really thought about the market, you would

From Alice Walker, Interview, in *Black Women Writers at Work,* ed. Claudia Tate (New York: Continuum, 1983), 175–187.

probably just take a job canning fish. Even the most successful black women writers don't make a lot of money, compared to what white male and female writers earn just routinely. We live in a society that is racist and white. That is one problem. Another is, we don't have a large black readership; I mean, black people, generally speaking, don't read. That is our *main* problem. Instead of attacking each other, we could try to address that problem by doing whatever we can to see that more black works get out into the world . . . and by stimulating an interest in literature among black people. Black women writers seem to be trying to do just that, and that's really commendable.

. . . Black women instinctively feel a need to connect with their reading audience, to be direct, to build a readership for us all, but more than that, to build *independence*. None of us will survive except in very distorted ways if we have to depend on white publishers and white readers forever. And white critics. [. . .]

TONI MORRISON

The Pain of Being Black

Sixteen years after Alice Walker addressed the Radcliffe symposium, the "myths" it aimed to dispel remained. Winner of the 1993 Nobel Prize in Literature and the 1988 Pulitzer Prize for Beloved, *Toni Morrison, in a* Time *magazine interview, rejects* The Moynihan Report's *link between "black matriarchy" and "social pathology."*

Well, neither [unwed teenage pregnancies nor single-parent households] seems to me a debility. I don't think a female running a house is a problem, a broken family. It's perceived as one because of the notion that a head is a man.

Two parents can't raise a child any more than one. You need a whole community—everybody—to raise a child. The notion that the head is the one who brings in the most money is a patriarchal notion, that a woman—and I have raised two children, alone—is somehow lesser than a male head. Or that I am incomplete without the male. This is not true. And the little nuclear family is a paradigm that just doesn't work. It doesn't work for white people or for black people. Why we are hanging onto it, I don't know. It isolates people into little units—people need a larger unit.

QUESTIONS FOR DISCUSSION AND WRITING

1. How do *you* recognize a work of art? What counts as art? What role do institutions such as the Smithsonian play in defining what counts—for others and for you—as a work of art? How can one distinguish "art" from the "Art" Amiri Baraka describes? What passages from Walker's essay support your analysis?

From an interview with Bonnie Angelo, *Time*, 22 May 1989, 120–23.

2. In "Autobiographical Notes," Baldwin describes the role of white culture in his development as a black artist. What does he mean by "white culture"? Who represents "white culture" in Walker's essay, and what is the role of white culture in Walker's development?

3. What role does gender play in Baldwin's and Walker's definitions of what counts as art? How does Walker redefine art by considering women's production of it?

4. Basing your explanation on the readings included here, explain who "the black woman" is. What are the various elements of myth, history, and culture that comprise her identity? In what ways—and to what extent—does Walker's mother embody "the black woman"? What passages from these readings support your explanation?

5. Write a conversation among Morrison, Moynihan, and Walker about the costs and benefits of black women's roles in the family.

6. What definition of *creativity* does Walker provide in "In Search of Our Mothers' Gardens," and how do her examples help you understand its meaning? What is the value of Walker's parenthetical revision of the short passage by Virginia Woolf (paragraph 37)? How does Woolf comment on the nature of imagination?

PAIRED READINGS: WORKING WITH YOUR HANDS

BARBARA EHRENREICH
Serving in Florida

Social commentator and critic Barbara Ehrenreich (b. 1941) has for most of her writing life brought a liberal viewpoint to many contemporary political and social issues. She grew up in Butte, Montana, in a working-class family. After earning a doctorate in biology at Rockefeller University (1968), Ehrenreich soon began writing for general audiences. Her books include Fear of Falling: The Inner Life of the Middle Class *(1989),* The Worst Years of Our Lives: Irreverent Notes on a Decade of Greed *(1990);* Bait and Switch *(2005), and* Bright-sided: How Relentless Promotion of Positive Thinking Has Undermined America *(2009).*

In Nickel and Dimed: On (Not) Getting By in America *(2001) Ehrenreich reports on the plight of the working poor in the United States. To research the book, she moved to various parts of the country and tried to live as cheaply as possible on the income she could make working as a housecleaner, a nursing home aide, a Wal-Mart sales clerk and—in the excerpt below, as a server in a series of Florida restaurants. She learned that "one job is not enough; you need at least two if you intend to live indoors."*

I could drift along like this, in some dreamy proletarian idyll, except for two things. One is management. If I have kept this subject to the margins so far it is because I still flinch to think that I spent all those weeks under the surveillance of men (and later women) whose job it was to monitor my behavior for signs of sloth, theft, drug abuse, or worse. Not that managers and especially "assistant managers" in low-wage settings like this are exactly the class enemy. Mostly, in the restaurant business, they are former cooks still capable of pinch-hitting in the kitchen, just as in hotels they are likely to be former clerks, and paid a salary of only about $400 a week. But everyone knows they have crossed over to the other side, which is, crudely put, corporate as opposed to human. Cooks want to prepare tasty meals, servers want to serve them graciously, but managers are there for only one reason—to make sure that money is made for some theoretical entity, the corporation, which exists far away in Chicago or New York, if a corporation can be said to have a physical existence at all. Reflecting on her career, Gail tells me ruefully that she swore, years ago, never to work for a corporation again. "They don't cut you no slack. You give and you give and they take."

Managers can sit—for hours at a time if they want—but it's their job to see that no one else ever does, even when there's nothing to do, and this is why, for servers, slow times can be as exhausting as rushes. You start dragging out each little chore because if the manager on duty catches you in an idle moment he will give you something far nastier to do. So I wipe, I clean, I consolidate catsup bottles and recheck the cheesecake supply, even tour the tables to make sure the customer evaluation forms are all standing perkily in their places—wondering all the time how many calories I burn in these strictly theatrical exercises. In desperation, I even take the desserts out of their glass display case and freshen them up with whipped cream and bright new maraschino cherries; anything to look busy. When, on a particularly dead afternoon, Stu finds me glancing at a *USA Today* a customer has left behind, he assigns me to vacuum the entire floor with the broken vacuum cleaner, which has a handle only two feet long, and the only way to do that without incurring orthopedic damage is to proceed from spot to spot on your knees.

On my first Friday at Hearthside there is a "mandatory meeting for all restaurant employees," which I attend, eager for insight into our overall marketing strategy and the niche (your basic Ohio cuisine with a tropical twist?) we aim to inhabit. But there is no "we" at this meeting. Phillip, our top manager except for an occasional "consultant" sent out by corporate headquarters, opens it with a sneer: "The break room—it's disgusting. Butts in the ashtrays, newspapers lying around, crumbs." This windowless little room, which also houses the time clock for the entire hotel, is where we stash our bags and civilian clothes and take our half-hour meal breaks. But a break room is not a right, he tells us, it can be taken away. We should also know that the lockers in the break room and whatever is in them can be searched at any time. Then comes gossip; there has been gossip; gossip (which seems to mean employees talking among themselves) must stop. Off-duty employees are henceforth barred from eating at the restaurant, because "other servers gather around them and gossip." When Phillip has exhausted his agenda of rebukes, Joan complains about the condition of the ladies' room and I throw in my two bits about the vacuum cleaner. But I don't see any backup coming from my fellow servers, each of whom has slipped into her own personal funk; Gail, my role model, stares sorrowfully at a point six inches from her nose. The meeting ends when Andy, one of the cooks, gets up, muttering about breaking up his day off for this almighty bullshit.

Just four days later we are suddenly summoned into the kitchen at 3:30 P.M., even though there are live tables on the floor. We all—about ten of us—stand around Phillip, who announces grimly that there has been a report of some "drug activity" on the night shift and that, as a result, we are now to be a "drug-free" workplace, meaning that all new hires will be tested and possibly also current employees on a random basis. I am glad that this part of the kitchen is so dark because I find myself blushing as hard as if I had been caught toking up in the ladies' room myself: I haven't been treated this way—lined up in the corridor, threatened with locker searches, peppered with carelessly aimed accusations— since at least junior high school. Back on the floor, Joan cracks, "Next they'll be telling us we can't have *sex* on the job." When I ask Stu what happened to inspire the crackdown, he just mutters about "management decisions" and takes the opportunity to upbraid Gail and me for being too generous with the rolls. From now on there's to be only one per customer and it goes out with the dinner, not with the salad. He's also been riding the cooks, prompting Andy to come out of the kitchen and observe—with the serenity of a man whose customary implement is a butcher knife—that "Stu has a death wish today."

Later in the evening, the gossip crystallizes around the theory that Stu is   5 himself the drug culprit, that he uses the restaurant phone to order up marijuana and sends one of the late servers out to fetch it for him. The server was caught and she may have ratted out Stu, at least enough to cast some suspicion on him, thus accounting for his pissy behavior. Who knows? Personally, I'm ready to believe anything bad about Stu, who serves no evident function and presumes too much on our common ethnicity, sidling up to me one night to engage in a little nativism directed at the Haitian immigrants: "I feel like I'm the foreigner here. They're taking over the country." Still later that evening, the drug in question escalates to crack. Lionel, the busboy, entertains us for the rest of the shift by standing just behind Stu's back and sucking deliriously on an imaginary joint or maybe a pipe.

The other problem, in addition to the less-than-nurturing management style, is that this job shows no sign of being financially viable. You might imagine, from a comfortable distance, that people who live, year in and year out, on $6 to $10 an hour have discovered some survival stratagems unknown to the middle class. But no. It's not hard to get my coworkers talking about their living situations, because housing, in almost every case, is the principal source of disruption in their lives, the first thing they fill you in on when they arrive for their shifts. After a week, I have compiled the following survey:

Gail is sharing a room in a well-known downtown flophouse for $250 a week. Her roommate, a male friend, has begun hitting on her, driving her nuts, but the rent would be impossible alone.

Claude, the Haitian cook, is desperate to get out of the two-room apartment he shares with his girlfriend and two other, unrelated people. As far as I can determine, the other Haitian men live in similarly crowded situations.

Annette, a twenty-year-old server who is six months pregnant and abandoned by her boyfriend, lives with her mother, a postal clerk.

Marianne, who is a breakfast server, and her boyfriend are paying $170 a week for a one-person trailer.

Billy, who at $10 an hour is the wealthiest of us, lives in the trailer he owns, paying only the $400-a-month lot fee.

The other white cook, Andy, lives on his dry-docked boat, which, as far as I can tell from his loving descriptions, can't be more than twenty feet long. He offers to take me out on it once it's repaired, but the offer comes with inquiries as to my marital status, so I do not follow up on it.

Tina, another server, and her husband are paying $60 a night for a room in the Days Inn. This is because they have no car and the Days Inn is in walking distance of the Hearthside. When Marianne is tossed out of her trailer for subletting (which is against trailer park rules), she leaves her boyfriend and moves in with Tina and her husband.

Joan, who had fooled me with her numerous and tasteful outfits (hostesses wear their own clothes), lives in a van parked behind a shopping center at night and showers in Tina's motel room. The clothes are from thrift shops.[1]

It strikes me, in my middle-class solipsism, that there is gross improvidence in some of these arrangements. When Gail and I are wrapping silverware in napkins—the only task for which we are permitted to sit—she tells me she is thinking of escaping from her roommate by moving into the Days Inn herself. I am astounded: how she can even think of paying $40 to $60 a day? But if I was afraid of sounding like a social worker, I have come out just sounding like a fool. She squints at me in disbelief: "And where am I supposed to get a month's rent and a month's deposit for an apartment?" I'd been feeling pretty smug about my $500 efficiency, but of course it was made possible only by the $1,300 I had allotted myself for start-up costs when I began my low-wage life: $1,000 for the first month's rent and deposit, $100 for initial groceries and cash in my pocket, $200

---

[1] I could find no statistics on the number of employed people living in cars or vans, but according to a 1997 report of the National Coalition for the Homeless, "Myths and Facts about Homelessness," nearly one-fifth of all homeless people (in twenty-nine cities across the nation) are employed in full- or part-time jobs.

stuffed away for emergencies. In poverty, as in certain propositions in physics, starting conditions are everything.

There are no secret economies that nourish the poor; on the contrary, there are a host of special costs. If you can't put up the two months' rent you need to secure an apartment, you end up paying through the nose for a room by the week. If you have only a room, with a hot plate at best, you can't save by cooking up huge lentil stews that can be frozen for the week ahead. You eat fast food or the hot dogs and Styrofoam cups of soup that can be microwaved in a convenience store. If you have no money for health insurance—and the Hearthside's niggardly plan kicks in only after three months—you go without routine care or prescription drugs and end up paying the price. Gail, for example, was doing fine, healthwise anyway, until she ran out of money for estrogen pills. She is supposed to be on the company health plan by now, but they claim to have lost her application form and to be beginning the paperwork all over again. So she spends $9 a pop for pills to control the migraines she wouldn't have, she insists, if her estrogen supplements were covered. Similarly, Marianne's boyfriend lost his job as a roofer because he missed so much time after getting a cut on his foot for which he couldn't afford the prescribed antibiotic.

My own situation, when I sit down to assess it after two weeks of work, would not be much better if this were my actual life. The seductive thing about waitressing is that you don't have to wait for payday to feel a few bills in your pocket, and my tips usually cover meals and gas, plus something left over to stuff into the kitchen drawer I use as a bank. But as the tourist business slows in the summer heat, I sometimes leave work with only $20 in tips (the gross is higher, but servers share about 15 percent of their tips with the busboys and bartenders). With wages included, this amounts to about the minimum wage of $5.15 an hour. The sum in the drawer is piling up but at the present rate of accumulation will be more than $100 short of my rent when the end of the month comes around. Nor can I see any expenses to cut. True, I haven't gone the lentil stew route yet, but that's because I don't have a large cooking pot, potholders, or a ladle to stir with (which would cost a total of about $30 at Kmart, somewhat less at a thrift store), not to mention onions, carrots, and the indispensable bay leaf. I do make my lunch almost every day—usually some slow-burning, high-protein combo like frozen chicken patties with melted cheese on top and canned pinto beans on the side. Dinner is at the Hearthside, which offers its employees a choice of BLT, fish sandwich, or hamburger for only $2. The burger lasts longest, especially if it's heaped with gut-puckering jalapeños, but by midnight my stomach is growling again.

So unless I want to start using my car as a residence, I have to find a second or an alternative job. I call all the hotels I'd filled out housekeeping applications at weeks ago—the Hyatt, Holiday Inn, Econo Lodge, HoJo's, Best Western, plus a half dozen locally run guest houses. Nothing. Then I start making the rounds again, wasting whole mornings waiting for some assistant manager to show up, even dipping into places so creepy that the front-desk clerk greets you from behind bullet-proof glass and sells pints of liquor over the counter. But either someone has exposed my real-life housekeeping habits—which are, shall we say, mellow—or I am at the wrong end of some infallible ethnic equation: most, but by no means all, of the working housekeepers I see on my job searches are African Americans, Spanish-speaking, or refugees from the Central European post-Communist world, while servers are almost invariably white and monolingually English-speaking. When I finally get a positive response, I have been identified once again as server material. Jerry's—again, not the real name—which is part of a well-known national chain and physically attached here to another budget hotel, is ready to use me at once. The prospect is both exciting and terrifying because, with about the same number of tables and counter seats, Jerry's attracts three or four times the volume of customers as the gloomy old Hearthside.

Picture a fat person's hell, and I don't mean a place with no food. Instead there is everything you might eat if eating had no bodily consequences—the cheese fries, the chicken-fried steaks, the fudge-laden desserts—only here every bite must be paid for, one way or another, in human discomfort. The kitchen is a cavern, a stomach leading to the lower intestine that is the garbage and dishwashing area, from which issue bizarre smells combining the edible and the offal: creamy carrion, pizza barf, and that unique and enigmatic Jerry's scent, citrus fart. The floor is slick with spills, forcing us to walk through the kitchen with tiny steps, like Susan McDougal in leg irons. Sinks everywhere are clogged with scraps of lettuce, decomposing lemon wedges, water-logged toast crusts. Put your hand down on any counter and you risk being stuck to it by the film of ancient syrup spills, and this is unfortunate because hands are utensils here, used for scooping up lettuce onto the salad plates, lifting out pie slices, and even moving hash browns from one plate to another. The regulation poster in the single unisex rest room admonishes us to wash our hands thoroughly, and even offers instructions for doing so, but there is always some vital substance missing—soap, paper towels, toilet paper—and I never found all three at once. You learn to stuff your pockets with napkins before going in there, and too bad about the customers, who must eat, although they don't realize it, almost literally out of our hands.

The break room summarizes the whole situation: there is none, because there are no breaks at Jerry's. For six to eight hours in a row, you never sit except to pee. Actually, there are three folding chairs at a table immediately adjacent to the bathroom, but hardly anyone ever sits in this, the very rectum of the gastro-architectural system. Rather, the function of the peri-toilet area is to house the ashtrays in which servers and dishwashers leave their cigarettes burning at all times, like votive candles, so they don't have to waste time lighting up again when they dash back here for a puff. Almost everyone smokes as if their pulmonary well-being depended on it—the multinational mélange of cooks; the dishwashers, who are all Czechs here; the servers, who are American natives—creating an atmosphere in which oxygen is only an occasional pollutant. My first morning at Jerry's, when the hypoglycemic shakes set in, I complain to one of my fellow servers that I don't understand how she can go so long without food. "Well, I don't understand how *you* can go so long without a cigarette," she responds in a tone of reproach. Because work is what you do for others; smoking is what you do for yourself. I don't know why the antismoking crusaders have never grasped the element of defiant self-nurturance that makes the habit so endearing to its victims—as if, in the American workplace, the only thing people have to call their own is the tumors they are nourishing and the spare moments they devote to feeding them.

Now, the Industrial Revolution is not an easy transition, especially, in my experience, when you have to zip through it in just a couple of days. I have gone from craft work straight into the factory, from the air-conditioned morgue of the Hearthside directly into the flames. Customers arrive in human waves, sometimes disgorged fifty at a time from their tour buses, peckish and whiny. Instead of two "girls" on the floor at once, there can be as many as six of us running around in our brilliant pink-and-orange Hawaiian shirts. Conversations, either with customers or with fellow employees, seldom last more than twenty seconds at a time. On my first day, in fact, I am hurt by my sister servers' coldness. My mentor for the day is a supremely competent, emotionally uninflected twenty-three-year-old, and the others, who gossip a little among themselves about the real reason someone is out sick today and the size of the bail bond someone else has had to pay, ignore me completely. On my second day, I find out why. "Well, it's good to see *you* again," one of them says in greeting. "Hardly anyone comes back after the first day." I feel powerfully vindicated—a survivor—but it would take a long time, probably months, before I could hope to be accepted into this sorority.

I start out with the beautiful, heroic idea of handling the two jobs at once, and for two days I almost do it: working the breakfast/lunch shift at Jerry's from 8:00 till 2:00, arriving at the Hearthside a few minutes late, at 2:10, and attempting to hold out until 10:00. In the few minutes I have between jobs, I pick up a spicy chicken sandwich at the Wendy's drive-through window, gobble it down in the car, and change from khaki slacks to black, from Hawaiian to rust-colored polo. There is a problem, though. When, during the 3:00–4:00 o'clock dead time, I finally sit down to wrap silver, my flesh seems to bond to the seat. I try to refuel with a purloined cup of clam chowder, as I've seen Gail and Joan do dozens of times, but Stu catches me and hisses "No *eating*!" although there's not a customer around to be offended by the sight of food making contact with a server's lips. So I tell Gail I'm going to quit, and she hugs me and says she might just follow me to Jerry's herself.

But the chances of this are minuscule. She has left the flophouse and her 15 annoying roommate and is back to living in her truck. But, guess what, she reports to me excitedly later that evening, Phillip has given her permission to park overnight in the hotel parking lot, as long as she keeps out of sight, and the parking lot should be totally safe since it's patrolled by a hotel security guard! With the Hearthside offering benefits like that, how could anyone think of leaving? This must be Phillip's theory, anyway. He accepts my resignation with a shrug, his main concern being that I return my two polo shirts and aprons.

Gail would have triumphed at Jerry's, I'm sure, but for me it's a crash course in exhaustion management. Years ago, the kindly fry cook who trained me to waitress at a Los Angeles truck stop used to say: Never make an unnecessary trip; if you don't have to walk fast, walk slow; if you don't have to walk, stand. But at Jerry's the effort of distinguishing necessary from unnecessary and urgent from whenever would itself be too much of an energy drain. The only thing to do is to treat each shift as a one-time-only emergency: you've got fifty starving people out there, lying scattered on the battlefield, so get out there and feed them! Forget that you will have to do this again tomorrow, forget that you will have to be alert enough to dodge the drunks on the drive home tonight—just burn, burn, burn! Ideally, at some point you enter what servers call a "rhythm" and psychologists term a "flow state," where signals pass from the sense organs directly to the muscles, bypassing the cerebral cortex, and a Zen-like emptiness sets in. I'm on a 2:00–10:00 P.M. shift now, and a male server from the morning shift tells me about the time he "pulled a triple"—three shifts in a row, all the way around the clock—and then got off and had a drink and met this girl, and maybe he shouldn't tell me this, but they had sex right then and there and it was like *beautiful.*

MALCOLM GLADWELL

The Physical Genius

Born in 1963 in England of English and Jamaican parents, Malcolm Gladwell grew up in Ontario and attended the University of Toronto (B.A., 1984). For a decade, he was a business and science writer for the Washington Post; *since 1996 he has been a staff writer for* The New Yorker. *His writing often deals with the unexpected implications of social science research for politics, technology, and consumer behavior.*

His published works include countless New Yorker *essays and four books:* The Tipping Point: How Little Things Can Make a Big Difference *(2000);* Blink: The Power of Thinking without Thinking *(2005);* Outliers: The Story of Success *(2008); and* What the Dog Saw *(2009). Typically, Gladwell postulates an unusual, perhaps unlikely cause-and-effect connection between seemingly unlike phenomena and exploits the consequences. Thus, in* Outliers *he explores the thesis that "the lives of outliers—people whose achievements fall outside normal experience—follow a peculiar and unexpected logic," determined by "generation, family, culture, class"—and the likelihood that if someone spends ten thousand hours to practice a skill, they'll excel at it.*

Gladwell's New Yorker *essay "The Physical Genius" (August 1999) emphasizes the human drama of brain surgery through his description of Charlie Wilson—an ace neurosurgeon—and through it, the larger topic: Why do some people excel at disciplines that involve the perfection of physical movement?*

Early one recent morning, while the San Francisco fog was lifting from the surrounding hills, Charlie Wilson performed his two thousand nine hundred and eighty-seventh transsphenoidal resection of a pituitary tumor. The patient was a man in his sixties who had complained of impotence and obscured vision. Diagnostic imaging revealed a growth, eighteen millimeters in diameter, that had enveloped his pituitary gland and was compressing his optic nerve. He was anesthetized and covered in blue surgical drapes, and one of Wilson's neurosurgery residents—a tall, slender woman in her final year of training—"opened" the case, making a small incision in his upper gum, directly underneath his nose. She then tunnelled back through his nasal passages until she reached the pituitary, creating a cavity several inches deep and about one and a half centimetres in diameter.

Wilson entered the operating room quickly, walking stiffly, bent slightly at the waist. He is sixty-nine—a small, wiry man with heavily muscled arms. His hair is cut very close to his scalp, so that, as residents over the years have joked, he might better empathize with the shaved heads of his patients. He is part Cherokee Indian and has high, broad cheekbones and large ears, which stick out at almost forty-five-degree angles. He was wearing Nike cross-trainers, and surgical scrubs marked with the logo of the medical center he has dominated for the past thirty years—Moffitt Hospital, at the University of California, San Francisco. When he was busiest, in the nineteen-eighties, he would routinely do seven or eight brain surgeries in a row, starting at dawn and ending at dusk, lining up patients in adjoining operating rooms and striding from one to the other like a conquering general. On this particular day, he would do five, of which the transsphenoidal was the first, but the rituals would be the same. Wilson believes that neurosurgery is best conducted in silence, with a scrub nurse who can anticipate his every step, and a resident who does not have to be told what to do, only shown. There was no music in the O.R. To guard against unanticipated disturbances, the door was locked. Pagers were set to "buzz," not beep. The phone was put on "Do Not Disturb."

Wilson sat by the patient in what looked like a barber's chair, manipulating a surgical microscope with a foot pedal. In his left hand he wielded a tiny suction tube, which removed excess blood. In his right he held a series of instruments in steady alternation: Cloward elevator, Penfield No. 2, Cloward rongeur, Fulton rongeur, conchatome, Hardy dissector, Kurze scissors, and so on. He worked quickly, with no wasted motion. Through the microscope, the tumor looked like a piece of lobster flesh, white and fibrous. He removed the middle of it, exposing the pituitary underneath. Then he took a ring curette—a long instrument with a circular scalpel perpendicular to the handle—and ran it lightly across the surface of the gland, peeling the tumor away as he did so.

It was, he would say later, like running a squeegee across a windshield, except that in this case the windshield was a surgical field one centimetre in diameter, flanked on either side by the carotid arteries, the principal sources of blood to the brain. If Wilson were to wander too far to the right or to the left and nick either artery, the patient might, in the neurosurgical shorthand, "stroke." If he were to push too far to the rear, he might damage any number of critical nerves. If he were not to probe aggressively, though, he might miss a bit of tumor and defeat the purpose of the procedure entirely. It was a delicate operation, which called for caution and confidence and the ability to distinguish between what was supposed to be there and what wasn't. Wilson never wavered. At one point, there was bleeding from the right side of the pituitary, which signalled to Wilson that a small piece of tumor was still just outside his field of vision, and so he gently slid the ring curette over, feeling with the instrument as if by his fingertips, navigating around the carotid, lifting out the remaining bit of tumor. In the hands of an ordinary neurosurgeon, the operation—down to that last bit of blindfolded acrobatics—might have taken several hours. It took Charlie Wilson twenty-five minutes.

Neurosurgery is generally thought to attract the most gifted and driven of   5
medical-school graduates. Even in that rarefied world, however, there are surgeons who are superstars and surgeons who are merely very good. Charlie Wilson is one of the superstars. Those who have trained with him say that if you showed them a dozen videotapes of different neurosurgeons in action—with the camera focussed just on the hands of the surgeon and the movements of the instruments—they could pick Wilson out in an instant, the same way an old baseball hand could look at a dozen batters in silhouette and tell you which one was Willie Mays. Wilson has a distinctive fluidity and grace.

There are thousands of people who have played in the National Hockey League over the years, but there has been only one Wayne Gretzky. Thousands of cellists play professionally all over the world, but very few will ever earn comparison with Yo-Yo Ma. People like Gretzky or Ma or Charlie Wilson all have an affinity for translating thought into action. They're what we might call physical geniuses. But what makes them so good at what they do?

The temptation is to treat physical genius in the same way that we treat intellectual genius—to think of it as something that can be ascribed to a single factor, a physical version of I.Q. When professional football coaches assess the year's crop of college prospects, they put them through drills designed to measure what they regard as athleticism: How high can you jump? How many pounds can you bench press? How fast can you sprint? The sum of the scores on these tests is considered predictive of athletic performance, and every year some college player's stock shoots up before draft day because it is suddenly discovered that he can run, say, 4.4 seconds in the forty-yard dash as opposed to 4.6 seconds. This much seems like common sense. The puzzling thing about physical genius, however, is that the closer you look at it the less it can be described by such cut-and-dried measures of athleticism.

Consider, for example, Tony Gwynn, who has been one of the best hitters in baseball over the past fifteen years. We would call him extraordinarily coordinated, by which we mean that in the course of several hundred milliseconds he can execute a series of perfectly synchronized muscular actions—the rotation of the shoulder, the movement of the arms, the shift of the hips—and can regulate the outcome of those actions so that his bat hits the ball with exactly the desired degree of force. These are abilities governed by specific neurological mechanisms. Timing, for example, appears to be controlled by the cerebellum....

What sets physical geniuses apart from other people, then, is not merely being able to do something but knowing what to do—their capacity to pick up on subtle patterns that others generally miss. This is what we mean when we say that great athletes have a "feel" for the game, or that they "see" the court or the field or the ice in a special way. Wayne Gretzky, in a 1981 game against the St. Louis Blues, stood behind the St. Louis goal, laid the puck across the blade of his stick, then bounced it off the back of the goalie in front of him and into the net. Gretzky's genius at that moment lay in seeing a scoring possibility where no one had seen one before. "People talk about skating, puck-handling, and shooting," Gretzky told an interviewer some years later, "but the whole sport is angles and caroms, forgetting the straight direction the puck is going, calculating where it will be diverted, factoring in all the interruptions." Neurosurgeons say that when the very best surgeons operate they always know where they are going, and they mean that the Charlie Wilsons of this world possess that same special feel—an ability to calculate the diversions and to factor in the interruptions when faced with a confusing mass of blood and tissue.

When Charlie Wilson came to U.C. San Francisco, in July of 1968, his first   10
case concerned a woman who had just had a pituitary operation. The previous surgeon had done the one thing that surgeons are not supposed to do in pituitary surgery—tear one of the carotid arteries. Wilson was so dismayed by the outcome that he resolved he would teach himself how to do the transsphenoidal, which was then a relatively uncommon procedure. He carefully read the medical literature. He practiced on a few cadavers. He called a friend in Los Angeles who was an expert at the procedure, and had him come to San Francisco and perform two operations while Wilson watched. He flew to Paris to observe Gérard Guiot, who was one of the great transsphenoidal surgeons at the time. Then he flew home. It was the equivalent of someone preparing for a major-league tryout by watching the Yankees on television and hitting balls in an amusement-arcade batting cage. "Charlie went slowly," recalls Ernest Bates, a Bay-area neurosurgeon who scrubbed with Wilson on his first transsphenoidal, "but he knew the anatomy and, boom, he was there. I thought, My God, this was the first? You'd have thought he had done a hundred. Charlie has a skill that the rest of us just don't have."

This is the hard part about understanding physical genius, because the source of that special skill—that "feel"—is still something of a mystery. "Sometimes during the course of an operation, there'll be several possible ways of doing something, and I'll size them up and, without having any conscious reason, I'll just do one of them," Wilson told me. He speaks with a soft, slow drawl, a remnant of Neosho, Missouri, the little town where he grew up, and where his father was a pharmacist, who kept his store open from 7 A.M. to 11 P.M., seven days a week. Wilson has a plainspoken, unpretentious quality. When he talks about his extraordinary success as a surgeon, he gives the impression that he is talking about some abstract trait that he is neither responsible for nor completely able to understand. "It's sort of an invisible hand," he went on. "It begins almost to seem mystical. Sometimes a resident asks, 'Why did you do that?' and I say"—here Wilson gave a little shrug—"'Well, it just seemed like the right thing.'"

There is a neurosurgeon at Columbia Presbyterian Center, in Manhattan, by the name of Don Quest, who served two tours in Vietnam flying A-1s off the *U.S.S. Kitty Hawk*. Quest sounds like the kind of person who bungee jumps on the weekend and has personalized license plates that read "Ace." In fact, he is a thoughtful, dapper man with a carefully trimmed mustache, who plays the trombone in his spare time and quite cheerfully describes himself as compulsive. "When I read the *New York Times*, I don't speed-read it," Quest told me. "I read it carefully. I read everything. It drives my wife crazy." He was wearing a spotless physician's coat and a bow tie. "When I'm reading a novel—and there are so many novels I want to read—even if it's not very good I can't throw it away. I stick with it. It's quite frustrating, because I don't really have time for garbage." Quest talked about what it was like to repair a particularly tricky aneurysm compared to what it was like to land at night in rough seas and a heavy fog when you are running out of fuel and the lights are off on the carrier's landing strip, because the skies are full of enemy aircraft. "I think they are similar," he said, after some thought, and what he meant was that they were both exercises in a certain kind of exhaustive and meticulous preparation. "There is a checklist, before you take off, and this was drilled into us," Quest said. "It's on the dashboard with all the things you need to do. People forget to put the hook down, and you can't land on an aircraft carrier if the hook isn't down. Or they don't put the wheels down. One of my friends, my roommate, landed at night on the aircraft carrier with the wheels up. Thank God, the hook caught, because his engine stopped. He would have gone in the water." Quest did not seem like the kind of person who would forget to put the wheels down. "Some people are much more compulsive than others, and it shows," he went on to say. "It shows in how well they do their landing on the aircraft carrier, how many times they screw up, or are on the wrong radio frequency, or get lost, or their ordinances aren't accurate in terms of dropping a bomb. The ones who are the best are the ones who are always very careful."

Quest isn't saying that fine motor ability is irrelevant. One would expect him to perform extremely well on tests of the sort Ivry and Keele might devise. And, like Tony Gwynn, he's probably an adept and swift decision maker. But these abilities, Quest is saying, are of little use if you don't have the right sort of personality. Charles Bosk, a sociologist at the University of Pennsylvania, once conducted a set of interviews with young doctors who had either resigned or been fired from neurosurgery-training programs, in an effort to figure out what separated the unsuccessful surgeons from their successful counterparts. He concluded that, far more than technical skills or intelligence, what was necessary for success was the sort of attitude that Quest has—a practical-minded obsession with the possibility and the consequences of failure. "When I interviewed the surgeons who were fired, I used to leave the interview shaking," Bosk said. "I would hear these horrible stories about what they did wrong, but the thing was that they didn't *know* that what they did was wrong. In my interviewing, I began to develop what I thought was an indicator of whether someone was going to be a good surgeon or not. It was a couple of simple questions: Have you ever made a mistake? And, if so, what was your worst mistake? The people who said, 'Gee, I haven't really had one,' or, 'I've had a couple of bad outcomes but they were due to things outside my control'—invariably those were the worst candidates. And the residents who said, 'I make mistakes all the time. There was this horrible thing that happened just yesterday and here's what it was.' They were the best. They had the ability to rethink everything that they'd done and imagine how they might have done it differently."

What this attitude drives you to do is practice over and over again, until even the smallest imperfections are ironed out. After doing poorly in a tournament just prior to this year's Wimbledon, Greg Rusedski, who is one of the top tennis players in the world, told reporters that he was going home to hit a thousand practice serves. One of the things that set Rusedski apart from lesser players, in other words, is that he is the kind of person who is willing to stand out in the summer sun, repeating the same physical movement again and again, in single-minded pursuit of some fractional improvement in his performance. Wayne Gretzky was the same way. He would frequently stay behind after practice, long after everyone had left, flipping pucks to a specific spot in the crease, or aiming shot after shot at the crossbar or the goal post.

And Charlie Wilson? In his first few years as a professor at U.C.S.F., he [15] would disappear at the end of the day into a special laboratory to practice his craft on rats: isolating, cutting, and then sewing up their tiny blood vessels, and sometimes operating on a single rat two or three times. He would construct an artificial aneurysm using a vein graft on the side of a rat artery, then manipulate the aneurysm the same way he would in a human being, toughening its base with a gentle coagulating current—and return two or three days later to see how successful his work had been. Wilson sees surgery as akin to a military campaign. Training with him is like boot camp. He goes to bed somewhere around eleven at night and rises at 4:30 A.M. For years, he ran upward of eighty miles a week, competing in marathons and hundred-mile ultra-marathons. He quit only after he had a hip replacement and two knee surgeries and found himself operating in a cast. Then he took up rowing. On his days in the operating room, at the height of his career, Wilson would run his morning ten or twelve miles, conduct medical rounds, operate steadily until six or seven in the evening, and, in between, see patients, attend meetings, and work on what now totals six hundred academic articles. . . . [T]o Wilson the perfect operation requires a particular grace and rhythm. "In every way, it is analogous to the routine of a concert pianist," he says. "If you were going to do a concert and you didn't practice for a week, someone would notice that, just as I notice if one of my scrub nurses has been off for a week. There is that fraction-of-a-second difference in the way she reacts."

"Wilson has a certain way of positioning the arm of the retractor blade"—an instrument used to hold brain tissue in place—"so that the back end of the retractor doesn't stick up at all and he won't accidentally bump into it," Michon Morita told me. "Every once in a while, though, I'd see him when he didn't quite put it in the position he wanted to, and bumped it, which caused a little bit of hemorrhage on the brain surface. It wasn't harming the patient, and it was nothing he couldn't handle. But I'd hear 'That was stupid,' and I'd immediately ask myself, What did I do wrong? Then I'd realize he was chastising himself. Most people would say that if there was no harm done to the patient it was no big deal. But he wants to be perfect in everything, and when that perfection is broken he gets frustrated."

This kind of obsessive preparation does two things. It creates consistency. Practice is what enables Greg Rusedski to hit a serve at a hundred and twenty-five miles per hour again and again. It's what enables a pianist to play Chopin's double-thirds Étude at full speed, striking every key with precisely calibrated force. More important, practice changes the *way* a task is perceived. A chess master, for example, can look at a game in progress for a few seconds and then perfectly reconstruct that same position on a blank chessboard. That's not because chess masters have great memories (they don't have the same knack when faced with a random arrangement of pieces) but because hours and hours of chess playing have enabled them to do what psychologists call "chunking." Chunking is based on the fact that we store familiar sequences—like our telephone number or our bank-machine password—in long-term memory as a single unit, or chunk. If I told you a number you'd never heard before, though, you would be able to store it only in short-term memory, one digit at a time, and if I asked you to repeat it back to me you might be able to remember only a few of those digits—maybe the first two or the last three. By contrast, when the chess masters see the board from a real game, they are able to break the board down into a handful of chunks—two or three clusters of pieces in positions that they have encountered before.

In "The Game of Our Lives," a classic account of the 1980–81 season of the Edmonton Oilers hockey team, Peter Gzowski argues that one of the principal explanations for the particular genius of Wayne Gretzky was that he was hockey's greatest chunker. Gretzky, who holds nearly every scoring record in professional hockey, baffled many observers because he seemed to reverse the normal laws of hockey. Most great offensive players prefer to keep the rest of the action on the ice behind them—to try to make the act of scoring be just about themselves and the goalie. Gretzky liked to keep the action in front of him. He would set up by the side of the rink, or behind the opposing team's net, so that the eleven other players on the ice were in full view, and then slide the perfect pass to the perfect spot. He made hockey look easy, even as he was playing in a way that made it more complicated. Gzowski says that Gretzky could do that because, like master chess players, he wasn't seeing all eleven other players individually; he was seeing only chunks. Here is Gzowski's conclusion after talking to Gretzky about a game he once played against the Montreal Canadiens. It could as easily serve as an explanation for Charlie Wilson's twenty-five-minute transsphenoidal resection:

> What Gretzky perceives on a hockey rink is, in a curious way, more simple than what a less accomplished player perceives. He sees not so much a set of moving players as a number of situations. . . . Moving in on the Montreal blueline, as he was able to recall while he watched a videotape of himself, he was aware of the position of all the other players on the ice. The pattern they formed was, to him, one fact, and he reacted to that fact. When he sends a pass to what to the rest of us appears an empty space on the ice, and when a teammate magically appears in that space to collect the puck, he has in reality simply summoned up from his bank account of knowledge the fact that in a particular situation, someone is likely to be in a particular spot, and if he is not there now he will be there presently.

. . . "A good [tennis] player knows where the ball is going," [Charlie] Wilson says. "He anticipates it. He is there. I just wasn't." What Wilson is describing is a failure not of skill or of resolve but of the least understood element of physical genius—imagination. For some reason, he could not make the game come alive in his mind.

When psychologists study people who are expert at motor tasks, they find that almost all of them use their imaginations in a very particular and sophisticated way. Jack Nicklaus, for instance, has said that he has never taken a swing that he didn't first mentally rehearse, frame by frame. Yo-Yo Ma told me that he remembers riding on a bus, at the age of seven, and solving a difficult musical problem by visualizing himself playing the piece on the cello. Robert Spetzler, who trained with Wilson and is widely considered to be the heir to Wilson's mantle, says that when he gets into uncharted territory in an operation he feels himself transferring his mental image of what ought to happen onto the surgical field. Charlie Wilson talks about going running in the morning and reviewing each of the day's operations in his head—visualizing the entire procedure and each potential outcome in advance. "It was a virtual rehearsal," he says, "so when I was actually doing the operation, it was as if I were doing it for the second time." Once, he says, he had finished a case and taken off his gloves and was walking down the hall away from the operating room when he suddenly stopped, because he realized that the tape he had been playing in his head didn't match the operation that had unfolded before his eyes. "I was correlating everything—what I saw, what I expected, what the X-rays said. And I just realized that I had not pursued one particular thing. So I turned around, scrubbed, and went back in, and, sure enough, there was a little remnant of tumor that was just around the corner. It would have been a disaster."

The Harvard University psychologist Stephen Kosslyn has shown that this power to visualize consists of at least four separate abilities, working in combination. The first is the ability to generate an image—to take something out of long-term memory and reconstruct it on demand. The second is what he calls "image inspection," which is the ability to take that mental picture and draw inferences from it. The third is "image maintenance," the ability to hold that picture steady. And the fourth is "image transformation," which is the ability to take that image and manipulate it. If I asked you whether a frog had a tail, for example, you would summon up a picture of a frog from your long-term memory (image generation), hold it steady in your mind (image maintenance), rotate the frog around until you see his backside (image transformation), and then look to see if there was a tail there (image inspection). These four abilities are highly variable. Kosslyn once gave a group of people a list of thirteen tasks, each designed to test a different aspect of visualization, and the results were all over the map. You could be very good at generation and maintenance, for example, without being good at transformation, or you could be good at transformation without necessarily being adept at inspection and maintenance. Some of the correlations, in fact, were negative, meaning that sometimes being good at one of those four things meant that you were likely to be bad at another. Bennett Stein, a former chairman of neurosurgery at Columbia Presbyterian Center, says that one of the reasons some neurosurgery residents fail in their training is that they are incapable of making the transition between the way a particular problem is depicted in an X-ray or an M.R.I., and how the problem looks when they encounter it in real life. These are people whose capacities for mental imaging simply do not match what's required for dealing with the complexities of brain surgery. Perhaps these people can generate an image but are unable to transform it in precisely the way that is necessary to be a great surgeon; or perhaps they can transform the image but they cannot maintain it. . . .

"Certain aneurysms at the base of the brain are surrounded by very important blood vessels and nerves, and the typical neurosurgeon will make that dissection with a set of micro-instruments that are curved, each with a blunt end," Craig Yorke, who trained with Wilson and now practices neurosurgery in Topeka, recalls. "The neurosurgeon will sneak up on them. Charlie would call for a No. 11 blade, which is a thin, very low-profile scalpel, and would just cut down to where the aneurysm was. He would be there in a quarter of the time." The speed and the audacity of Wilson's maneuvers, Yorke said, would sometimes leave him breathless. "Do you know about Gestalt psychology?" he continued. "If I look at a particular field—tumor or aneurysm—I will see the gestalt after I've worked on it for a little while. He would just glance at it and see it. It's a conceptual, a spatial thing. His use of the No. 11 blade depended on his ability to construct a gestalt of the surgical field first. If just anybody had held up the eleven blade in that way it might have been a catastrophe. He could do it because he had the picture of the whole anatomy in his head when he picked up the instrument."

If you think of physical genius as a pyramid, with, at the bottom, the raw components of coordination, and, above that, the practice that perfects those particular movements, then this faculty of imagination is the top layer. This is what separates the physical genius from those who are merely very good. Michael Jordan and Karl Malone, his longtime rival, did not differ so much in their athletic ability or in how obsessively they practiced. The difference between them is that Jordan could always generate a million different scenarios by which his team could win, some of which were chunks stored in long-term memory, others of which were flights of fancy that came to him, figuratively and literally, in midair. Jordan twice won championships in the face of unexpected adversity: once, a case of the flu, and, the second time, a back injury to his teammate Scottie Pippen, and he seemed to thrive on these obstacles, in a way Karl Malone never could.

Yo-Yo Ma says that only once, early in his career, did he try for a technically perfect performance. "I was seventeen," he told me. "I spent a year working on it. I was playing a Brahms sonata at the 92nd Street Y. I remember working really hard at it, and in the middle of the performance I thought, I'm bored. It would have been nothing for me to get up from the stage and walk away. That's when I decided I would always opt for expression over perfection." It isn't that Ma doesn't achieve perfection; it's that he finds striving for perfection to be banal. He says that he sometimes welcomes it when he breaks a string, because that is precisely the kind of thing (like illness or an injury to a teammate) that you cannot prepare for — that you haven't chunked and, like some robot, stored neatly in long-term memory. The most successful performers improvise. They create, in Ma's words, "something living." Ma says he spends ninety per cent of his time "looking at the score, figuring it out — who's saying this, who wrote this and why," letting his mind wander, and only ten per cent on the instrument itself. Like Jordan, his genius originates principally in his imagination. If he spent less time dreaming and more time playing, he would be Karl Malone.

Here is the source of the physical genius's motivation. After all, what is this sensation — this feeling of having what you do fit perfectly into the dimensions of your imagination — but the purest form of pleasure? Tony Gwynn and Wayne Gretzky and Charlie Wilson and all the other physical geniuses are driven to greatness because they have found something so compelling that they cannot put it aside. Perhaps this explains why a great many top neurosurgeons are also highly musical. . . . Wilson . . . is a cellist and, when he was a student in New Orleans, he would play jazz piano at Pat O'Brien's, in the French Quarter. Music is one of the few vocations that offer a kind of sensory and cognitive immersion similar to surgery: the engagement of hand and eye, the challenge of sustained performance, the combination of mind and motion — all of it animated by the full force of the imagination. Once, in an E-mail describing his special training sessions on rats, Wilson wrote that he worked on them for two years and "then trailed off when I finally figured that I was doing it for fun, not for practice." For fun! When someone chooses to end a twelve-hour day alone in a laboratory, inducing aneurysms in the arteries of rats, we might call that behavior obsessive. But that is an uncharitable word. A better explanation is that, for some mysterious and wonderful reason, Wilson finds the act of surgery irresistible, in the way that musicians find pleasure in the sounds they produce on their instruments, or in the way Tony Gwynn gets a thrill every time he strokes a ball cleanly through the infield. Before he was two years old, it is said, Wayne Gretzky watched hockey games on television, enraptured, and slid his stockinged feet on the linoleum in imitation of the players, then cried when the game was over, because he could not understand how something so sublime should have to come to an end. This was long before Gretzky was any good at the game itself, or was skilled in any of its aspects, or could create even the smallest of chunks. But what he had was what the physical genius must have before any of the other layers of expertise fall into place: he had stumbled onto the one thing that, on some profound aesthetic level, made him happy. . . .

QUESTIONS FOR DISCUSSION AND WRITING

1. Ehrenreich identifies several problems low-wage restaurant workers face, including inadequate housing and health insurance. With a partner or team, identify the factors Ehrenreich implies underlie these conditions. In a paper or oral presentation, suggest ways that working conditions in such a low-wage industry might be improved.

2. In describing the restaurant she designates as "Jerry's," Ehrenreich uses terms like "lower intestine" and "rectum" (paragraphs 11 and 12). How does this metaphor of the restaurant as the entrails of the human body serve as a larger statement about American laborers? Why does Ehrenreich follow her description of the kitchen and rest room with her description of smoking as "defiant self-nurturance" (paragraph 12)?

3. Write an essay about the worst job you've ever held. Did you feel, like Ehrenreich, that you could "drift along" except for "the less-than-nurturing management style" (paragraph 6) and the low pay? Did you ever discuss specific problems with your manager(s) or co-worker(s)? If so, what was the outcome?

4. Have you been trained, in classrooms or sports programs or on the job, to use your imagination? If imagination is key to success in various fields, consider what kind of education you have received in using the four visualization skills discussed in paragraph 21 of "The Physical Genius." Would imagination make a waitstaff or similar job such as those Ehrenreich addresses in "Serving in Florida" any easier? More pleasant?

5. Gladwell focuses on the physical genius's ability to "feel" his or her way through a chosen activity, an intuitive ability that is difficult to explain. Consider what kinds of activities you associate with intuitive or unconventional approaches. For example, if you play a musical instrument or sing, you might contrast such an activity with writing or with caring for an animal or repairing a machine, such as a car.

MARY ELLEN MARK

The Damm Family in Their Car, Los Angeles, 1987

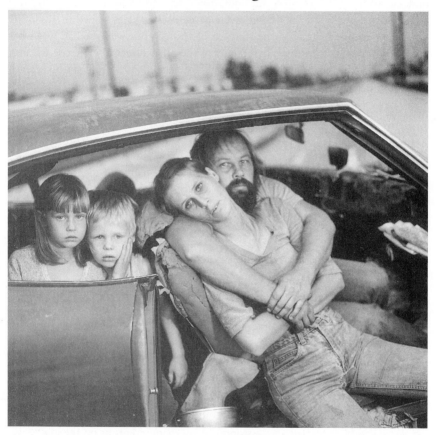

QUESTIONS FOR DISCUSSION AND WRITING

1. Analyze this photograph of a homeless family in their car. What do you understand from each element of the photograph: the figures? Their expressions, postures, apparent nutrition level, clothing? The condition of the car? The road and the rest of the background? If you hadn't been told that this family was homeless, would you have known from the details?

2. "Read" the people in this picture. What stories does this picture tell? Would each family member tell the same story? To whom? Why do you think the Damm family would have allowed Mark, a professional photographer, to take their picture?

3. What message(s) does this picture send? To whom? Is there any expectation of hope? Or change? What are viewers supposed to think or to do as a consequence of seeing this picture?

MATTHEW B. CRAWFORD

The Case for Working with Your Hands

After earning a B.S. in physics from the University of California and a Ph.D. in political philosophy from the University of Chicago (2000), Matthew Crawford opened Shockoe Moto, a motorcycle repair shop in Richmond, Virginia. His experience there provided both the real-world knowledge and the philosophical and ethical under- standing to write Shop Class as Soulcraft: An Inquiry into the Value of Work *(2009), which takes a second look at America's celebration of white-collar work and the consequent devaluing of manual labor. Crawford reiterates these beliefs in his* New York Times *article "The Case for Working with Your Hands" (2009). Here he questions the conventionally accepted importance of education as a means to a "good job," which "academic credentials do not guarantee." Instead he cites his life experi- ence as proof that the manual trades are more satisfying than the cubicle alternatives for which schools typically prepare students.*

The television show "Deadliest Catch" depicts commercial crab fishermen in the Bering Sea. Another, "Dirty Jobs," shows all kinds of grueling work; one episode featured a guy who inseminates turkeys for a living. The weird fascination of these shows must lie partly in the fact that such confrontations with material real- ity have become exotically unfamiliar. Many of us do work that feels more surreal than real. Working in an office, you often find it difficult to see any tangible result from your efforts. What exactly have you accomplished at the end of any given day? Where the chain of cause and effect is opaque and responsibility diffuse, the experience of individual agency can be elusive. "Dilbert," "The Office" and similar portrayals of cubicle life attest to the dark absurdism with which many Americans have come to view their white-collar jobs.

Is there a more "real" alternative (short of inseminating turkeys)?

High-school shop-class programs were widely dismantled in the 1990s as educators prepared students to become "knowledge workers." The imperative of the last 20 years to round up every warm body and send it to college, then to the cubicle, was tied to a vision of the future in which we somehow take leave of material reality and glide about in a pure information economy. This has not come to pass. To begin with, such work often feels more enervating than gliding. More fundamentally, now as ever, somebody has to actually do things: fix our cars, unclog our toilets, build our houses.

When we praise people who do work that is straightforwardly useful, the praise often betrays an assumption that they had no other options. We idealize them as the salt of the earth and emphasize the sacrifice for others their work may entail. Such sacrifice does indeed occur—the hazards faced by a lineman restoring power during a storm come to mind. But what if such work answers as well to a basic human need of the one who does it? I take this to be the suggestion of Marge

Piercy's poem "To Be of Use," which concludes with the lines "the pitcher longs for water to carry/and a person for work that is real." Beneath our gratitude for the lineman may rest envy.

This seems to be a moment when the useful arts have an especially compel- 5 ling economic rationale. A car mechanics' trade association reports that repair shops have seen their business jump significantly in the current recession: people aren't buying new cars; they are fixing the ones they have. The current downturn is likely to pass eventually. But there are also systemic changes in the economy, arising from information technology, that have the surprising effect of making the manual trades—plumbing, electrical work, car repair—more attractive as careers. The Princeton economist Alan Blinder argues that the crucial distinction in the emerging labor market is not between those with more or less education, but between those whose services can be delivered over a wire and those who must do their work in person or on site. The latter will find their livelihoods more secure against outsourcing to distant countries. As Blinder puts it, "You can't hammer a nail over the Internet." Nor can the Indians fix your car. Because they are in India.

If the goal is to earn a living, then, maybe it isn't really true that 18-year-olds need to be imparted with a sense of panic about getting into college (though they certainly need to learn). Some people are hustled off to college, then to the cubicle, against their own inclinations and natural bents, when they would rather be learning to build things or fix things. One shop teacher suggested to me that "in schools, we create artificial learning environments for our children that they know to be contrived and undeserving of their full attention and engagement. Without the opportunity to learn through the hands, the world remains abstract and distant, and the passions for learning will not be engaged."

A gifted young person who chooses to become a mechanic rather than to accumulate academic credentials is viewed as eccentric, if not self-destructive. There is a pervasive anxiety among parents that there is only one track to success for their children. It runs through a series of gates controlled by prestigious institutions. Further, there is wide use of drugs to medicate boys, especially, against their natural tendency toward action, the better to "keep things on track." I taught briefly in a public high school and would have loved to have set up a Ritalin fogger in my classroom. It is a rare person, male or female, who is naturally inclined to sit still for 17 years in school, and then indefinitely at work.

The trades suffer from low prestige, and I believe this is based on a simple mistake. Because the work is dirty, many people assume it is also stupid. This is not my experience. I have a small business as a motorcycle mechanic in Richmond, Va., which I started in 2002. I work on Japanese and European motorcycles, mostly older bikes with some "vintage" cachet that makes people willing to spend money on them. I have found the satisfactions of the work to be very much bound up with the intellectual challenges it presents. And yet my decision to go into this line of work is a choice that seems to perplex many people.

After finishing a Ph.D. in political philosophy at the University of Chicago in 2000, I managed to stay on with a one-year postdoctoral fellowship at the university's Committee on Social Thought. The academic job market was utterly bleak. In a state of professional panic, I retreated to a makeshift workshop I set up in the basement of a Hyde Park apartment building, where I spent the winter tearing down an old Honda motorcycle and rebuilding it. The physicality of it, and the clear specificity of what the project required of me, was a balm. Stumped by a starter motor that seemed to check out in every way but wouldn't work, I started asking around at Honda dealerships. Nobody had an answer; finally one service manager told me to call Fred Cousins of Triple O Service. "If anyone can help you, Fred can."

I called Fred, and he invited me to come to his independent motorcycle- 10 repair shop, tucked discreetly into an unmarked warehouse on Goose Island. He told me to put the motor on a certain bench that was free of clutter. He checked the electrical resistance through the windings, as I had done, to confirm there was no short circuit or broken wire. He spun the shaft that ran through the center of the motor, as I had. No problem: it spun freely. Then he hooked it up to a battery. It moved ever so slightly but wouldn't spin. He grasped the shaft, delicately, with three fingers, and tried to wiggle it side to side. "Too much free play," he said. He suggested that the problem was with the bushing (a thick-walled sleeve of metal) that captured the end of the shaft in the end of the cylindrical motor housing. It was worn, so it wasn't locating the shaft precisely enough. The shaft was free to move too much side to side (perhaps a couple of hundredths of an inch), causing the outer circumference of the rotor to bind on the inner circumference of the motor housing when a current was applied. Fred scrounged around for a Honda motor. He found one with the same bushing, then used a "blind hole bearing puller" to extract it, as well as the one in my motor. Then he gently tapped the new, or rather newer, one into place. The motor worked! Then Fred gave me an impromptu dissertation on the peculiar metallurgy of these Honda starter-motor bushings of the mid-'70s. Here was a scholar.

Over the next six months I spent a lot of time at Fred's shop, learning, and put in only occasional appearances at the university. This was something of a regression: I worked on cars throughout high school and college, and one of my early jobs was at a Porsche repair shop. Now I was rediscovering the intensely absorbing nature of the work, and it got me thinking about possible livelihoods.

As it happened, in the spring I landed a job as executive director of a policy organization in Washington. This felt like a coup. But certain perversities became apparent as I settled into the job. It sometimes required me to reason backward, from desired conclusion to suitable premise. The organization had taken certain positions, and there were some facts it was more fond of than others. As its figurehead, I was making arguments I didn't fully buy myself. Further, my boss seemed intent on retraining me according to a certain cognitive style — that of the corporate world, from which he had recently come. This style demanded that I project an image of rationality but not indulge too much in actual reasoning.

As I sat in my K Street office, Fred's life as an independent tradesman gave me an image that I kept coming back to: someone who really knows what he is doing, losing himself in work that is genuinely useful and has a certain integrity to it. He also seemed to be having a lot of fun.

Seeing a motorcycle about to leave my shop under its own power, several days after arriving in the back of a pickup truck, I don't feel tired even though I've been standing on a concrete floor all day. Peering into the portal of his helmet, I think I can make out the edges of a grin on the face of a guy who hasn't ridden his bike in a while. I give him a wave. With one of his hands on the throttle and the other on the clutch, I know he can't wave back. But I can hear his salute in the exuberant "bwaaAAAAP!" of a crisp throttle, gratuitously revved. That sound pleases me, as I know it does him. It's a ventriloquist conversation in one mechanical voice, and the gist of it is "Yeah!"

After five months at the think tank, I'd saved enough money to buy some tools I needed, and I quit and went into business fixing bikes. My shop rate is $40 per hour. Other shops have rates as high as $70 per hour, but I tend to work pretty slowly. Further, only about half the time I spend in the shop ends up being billable (I have no employees; every little chore falls to me), so it usually works out closer to $20 per hour—a modest but decent wage. The business goes up and down; when it is down I have supplemented it with writing. The work is sometimes frustrating, but it is never irrational.

And it frequently requires complex thinking. In fixing motorcycles you come   15
up with several imagined trains of cause and effect for manifest symptoms, and you judge their likelihood before tearing anything down. This imagining relies on a mental library that you develop. An internal combustion engine can work in any number of ways, and different manufacturers have tried different approaches. Each has its own proclivities for failure. You also develop a library of sounds and smells and feels. For example, the backfire of a too-lean fuel mixture is subtly different from an ignition backfire.

As in any learned profession, you just have to know a lot. If the motorcycle is 30 years old, from an obscure maker that went out of business 20 years ago, its tendencies are known mostly through lore. It would probably be impossible to do such work in isolation, without access to a collective historical memory; you have to be embedded in a community of mechanic-antiquarians. These relationships are maintained by telephone, in a network of reciprocal favors that spans the country. My most reliable source, Fred, has such an encyclopedic knowledge of obscure European motorcycles that all I have been able to offer him in exchange is deliveries of obscure European beer.

There is always a risk of introducing new complications when working on old motorcycles, and this enters the diagnostic logic. Measured in likelihood of screw-ups, the cost is not identical for all avenues of inquiry when deciding which hypothesis to pursue. Imagine you're trying to figure out why a bike won't start. The fasteners holding the engine covers on 1970s-era Hondas are Phillips head, and they are almost always rounded out and corroded. Do you really want to check the condition of the starter clutch if each of eight screws will need to be drilled out and extracted, risking damage to the engine case? Such impediments have to be taken into account. The attractiveness of any hypothesis is determined in part by physical circumstances that have no logical connection to the diagnostic problem at hand. The mechanic's proper response to the situation cannot be anticipated by a set of rules or algorithms.

There probably aren't many jobs that can be reduced to rule-following and still be done well. But in many jobs there is an attempt to do just this, and the perversity of it may go unnoticed by those who design the work process. Mechanics face something like this problem in the factory service manuals that we use. These manuals tell you to be systematic in eliminating variables, presenting an idealized image of diagnostic work. But they never take into account the risks of working on old machines. So you put the manual away and consider the facts before you. You do this because ultimately you are responsible to the motorcycle and its owner, not to some procedure.

Some diagnostic situations contain a lot of variables. Any given symptom may have several possible causes, and further, these causes may interact with one another and therefore be difficult to isolate. In deciding how to proceed, there often comes a point where you have to step back and get a larger gestalt. Have a cigarette and walk around the lift. The gap between theory and practice stretches out in front of you, and this is where it gets interesting. What you need now is the kind of judgment that arises only from experience; hunches rather than rules. For me, at least, there is more real thinking going on in the bike shop than there was in the think tank.

Put differently, mechanical work has required me to cultivate different intel- 20 lectual habits. Further, habits of mind have an ethical dimension that we don't often think about. Good diagnosis requires attentiveness to the machine, almost a conversation with it, rather than assertiveness, as in the position papers produced on K Street. Cognitive psychologists speak of "metacognition," which is the activity of stepping back and thinking about your own thinking. It is what you do when you stop for a moment in your pursuit of a solution, and wonder whether your understanding of the problem is adequate. The slap of worn-out pistons hitting their cylinders can sound a lot like loose valve tappets, so to be a good mechanic you have to be constantly open to the possibility that you may be mistaken. This is a virtue that is at once cognitive and moral. It seems to develop because the mechanic, if he is the sort who goes on to become good at it, internalizes the healthy functioning of the motorcycle as an object of passionate concern. How else can you explain the elation he gets when he identifies the root cause of some problem?

This active concern for the motorcycle is reinforced by the social aspects of the job. As is the case with many independent mechanics, my business is based entirely on word of mouth. I sometimes barter services with machinists and metal fabricators. This has a very different feel than transactions with money; it situates me in a community. The result is that I really don't want to mess up anybody's motorcycle or charge more than a fair price. You often hear people complain about mechanics and other tradespeople whom they take to be dishonest or incompetent. I am sure this is sometimes justified. But it is also true that the mechanic deals with a large element of chance.

I once accidentally dropped a feeler gauge down into the crankcase of a Kawasaki Ninja that was practically brand new, while performing its first scheduled valve adjustment. I escaped a complete tear-down of the motor only through an operation that involved the use of a stethoscope, another pair of trusted hands and the sort of concentration we associate with a bomb squad. When finally I laid my fingers on that feeler gauge, I felt as if I had cheated death. I don't remember ever feeling so alive as in the hours that followed.

Often as not, however, such crises do not end in redemption. Moments of elation are counterbalanced with failures, and these, too, are vivid, taking place right before your eyes. With stakes that are often high and immediate, the manual trades elicit heedful absorption in work. They are punctuated by moments of pleasure that take place against a darker backdrop: a keen awareness of catastrophe as an always-present possibility. The core experience is one of individual responsibility, supported by face-to-face interactions between tradesman and customer.

Contrast the experience of being a middle manager. This is a stock figure of ridicule, but the sociologist Robert Jackall spent years inhabiting the world of corporate managers, conducting interviews, and he poignantly describes the "moral maze" they feel trapped in. Like the mechanic, the manager faces the possibility of disaster at any time. But in his case these disasters feel arbitrary; they are typically a result of corporate restructurings, not of physics. A manager has to make many decisions for which he is accountable. Unlike an entrepreneur with his own business, however, his decisions can be reversed at any time by someone higher up the food chain (and there is always someone higher up the food chain). It's important for your career that these reversals not look like defeats, and more generally you have to spend a lot of time managing what others think of you. Survival depends on a crucial insight: you can't back down from an argument that you initially made in straightforward language, with moral conviction, without seeming to lose your integrity. So managers learn the art of provisional thinking and feeling, expressed in corporate doublespeak, and cultivate a lack of commitment to their own actions. Nothing is set in concrete the way it is when you are, for example, pouring concrete.

Those who work on the lower rungs of the information-age office hierarchy face their own kinds of unreality, as I learned some time ago. After earning a master's degree in the early 1990s, I had a hard time finding work but eventually landed a job in the Bay Area writing brief summaries of academic journal articles, which were then sold on CD-ROMs to subscribing libraries. When I got the phone call offering me the job, I was excited. I felt I had grabbed hold of the passing world—miraculously, through the mere filament of a classified ad — and reeled myself into its current. My new bosses immediately took up residence in my imagination, where I often surprised them with my hidden depths. As I was shown to my cubicle, I felt a real sense of being honored. It seemed more than spacious enough. It was my desk, where I would think my thoughts — my unique contribution to a common enterprise, in a real company with hundreds of employees. The regularity of the cubicles made me feel I had found a place in the order of things. I was to be a knowledge worker.

But the feel of the job changed on my first day. The company had gotten its start by providing libraries with a subject index of popular magazines like *Sports Illustrated*. Through a series of mergers and acquisitions, it now found itself offering not just indexes but also abstracts (that is, summaries), and of a very different kind of material: scholarly works in the physical and biological sciences, humanities, social sciences and law. Some of this stuff was simply incomprehensible to anyone but an expert in the particular field covered by the journal. I was reading articles in Classical Philology where practically every other word was in Greek. Some of the scientific journals were no less mysterious. Yet the categorical difference between, say, *Sports Illustrated* and *Nature Genetics* seemed not to have impressed itself on the company's decision makers. In some of the titles I was assigned, articles began with an abstract written by the author. But even in such cases I was to write my own. The reason offered was that unless I did so, there would be no "value added" by our product. It was hard to believe I was going to add anything other than error and confusion to such material. But then, I hadn't yet been trained.

My job was structured on the supposition that in writing an abstract of an article there is a method that merely needs to be applied, and that this can be done without understanding the text. I was actually told this by the trainer, Monica, as she stood before a whiteboard, diagramming an abstract. Monica seemed a perfectly sensible person and gave no outward signs of suffering delusions. She didn't insist too much on what she was telling us, and it became clear she was in a position similar to that of a veteran Soviet bureaucrat who must work on two levels at once: reality and official ideology. The official ideology was a bit like the factory service manuals I mentioned before, the ones that offer procedures that mechanics often have to ignore in order to do their jobs.

My starting quota, after finishing a week of training, was 15 articles per day. By my 11th month at the company, my quota was up to 28 articles per day (this was the normal, scheduled increase). I was always sleepy while at work, and I think this exhaustion was because I felt trapped in a contradiction: the fast pace demanded complete focus on the task, yet that pace also made any real concentration impossible. I had to actively suppress my own ability to think, because the more you think, the more the inadequacies in your understanding of an author's argument come into focus. This can only slow you down. To not do justice to an author who had poured himself into the subject at hand felt like violence against what was best in myself.

The quota demanded, then, not just dumbing down but also a bit of moral re-education, the opposite of the kind that occurs in the heedful absorption of mechanical work. I had to suppress my sense of responsibility to the article itself, and to others—to the author, to begin with, as well as to the hapless users of the database, who might naïvely suppose that my abstract reflected the author's work. Such detachment was made easy by the fact there was no immediate consequence for me; I could write any nonsense whatever.

Now, it is probably true that every job entails some kind of mutilation. I 30 used to work as an electrician and had my own business doing it for a while. As an electrician you breathe a lot of unknown dust in crawl spaces, your knees get bruised, your neck gets strained from looking up at the ceiling while installing lights or ceiling fans and you get shocked regularly, sometimes while on a ladder. Your hands are sliced up from twisting wires together, handling junction boxes made out of stamped sheet metal and cutting metal conduit with a hacksaw. But none of this damage touches the best part of yourself.

You might wonder: Wasn't there any quality control? My supervisor would periodically read a few of my abstracts, and I was sometimes corrected and told not to begin an abstract with a dependent clause. But I was never confronted with an abstract I had written and told that it did not adequately reflect the article. The quality standards were the generic ones of grammar, which could be applied without my supervisor having to read the article at hand. Rather, my supervisor and I both were held to a metric that was conjured by someone remote from the work process—an absentee decision maker armed with a (putatively) profit-maximizing calculus, one that took no account of the intrinsic nature of the job. I wonder whether the resulting perversity really made for maximum profits in the long term. Corporate managers are not, after all, the owners of the businesses they run.

At lunch I had a standing arrangement with two other abstracters. One was from my group, a laconic, disheveled man named Mike whom I liked instantly. He did about as well on his quota as I did on mine, but it didn't seem to bother him too much. The other guy was from beyond the partition, a meticulously groomed Liberian named Henry who said he had worked for the C.I.A. He had to flee Liberia very suddenly one day and soon found himself resettled near the office parks of Foster City, Calif. Henry wasn't going to sweat the quota. Come 12:30, the three of us would hike to the food court in the mall. This movement was always thrilling. It involved traversing several "campuses," with ponds frequented by oddly real seagulls, then the lunch itself, which I always savored. (Marx writes that under conditions of estranged labor, man "no longer feels himself to be freely active in any but his animal functions.") Over his burrito, Mike would recount the outrageous things he had written in his abstracts. I could see my own future in such moments of sabotage—the compensating pleasures of a cubicle drone. Always funny and gentle, Mike confided one day that he was doing quite a bit of heroin. On the job. This actually made some sense.

How was it that I, once a proudly self-employed electrician, had ended up among these walking wounded, a "knowledge worker" at a salary of $23,000? I had a master's degree, and it needed to be used. The escalating demand for academic credentials in the job market gives the impression of an ever-more-knowledgeable society, whose members perform cognitive feats their unschooled parents could scarcely conceive of. On paper, my abstracting job, multiplied a millionfold, is precisely what puts the futurologist in a rapture: we are getting to be so smart! Yet my M.A. obscures a more real stupidification of the work I secured with that credential, and a wage to match. When I first got the degree, I felt as if I had been inducted to a certain order of society. But despite the beautiful ties I wore, it turned out to be a more proletarian existence than I had known as an electrician. In that job I had made quite a bit more money. I also felt free and active, rather than confined and stultified.

A good job requires a field of action where you can put your best capacities to work and see an effect in the world. Academic credentials do not guarantee this.

Nor can big business or big government—those idols of the right and the   35
left—reliably secure such work for us. Everyone is rightly concerned about economic growth on the one hand or unemployment and wages on the other, but the character of work doesn't figure much in political debate. Labor unions address important concerns like workplace safety and family leave, and management looks for greater efficiency, but on the nature of the job itself, the dominant political and economic paradigms are mute. Yet work forms us, and deforms us, with broad public consequences.

The visceral experience of failure seems to have been edited out of the career trajectories of gifted students. It stands to reason, then, that those who end up making big decisions that affect all of us don't seem to have much sense of their own fallibility, and of how badly things can go wrong even with the best of intentions (like when I dropped that feeler gauge down into the Ninja). In the boardrooms of Wall Street and the corridors of Pennsylvania Avenue, I don't think you'll see a yellow sign that says "Think Safety!" as you do on job sites and in many repair shops, no doubt because those who sit on the swivel chairs tend to live remote from the consequences of the decisions they make. Why not encourage gifted students to learn a trade, if only in the summers, so that their fingers will be crushed once or twice before they go on to run the country?

There is good reason to suppose that responsibility has to be installed in the foundation of your mental equipment—at the level of perception and habit. There is an ethic of paying attention that develops in the trades through hard experience. It inflects your perception of the world and your habitual responses to it. This is due to the immediate feedback you get from material objects and to the fact that the work is typically situated in face-to-face interactions between tradesman and customer.

An economy that is more entrepreneurial, less managerial, would be less subject to the kind of distortions that occur when corporate managers' compensation is tied to the short-term profit of distant shareholders. For most entrepreneurs, profit is at once a more capacious and a more concrete thing than this. It is a calculation in which the intrinsic satisfactions of work count—not least, the exercise of your own powers of reason.

Ultimately it is enlightened self-interest, then, not a harangue about humility or public-spiritedness, that will compel us to take a fresh look at the trades. The good life comes in a variety of forms. This variety has become difficult to see; our field of aspiration has narrowed into certain channels. But the current perplexity in the economy seems to be softening our gaze. Our peripheral vision is perhaps recovering, allowing us to consider the full range of lives worth choosing. For anyone who feels ill suited by disposition to spend his days sitting in an office, the question of what a good job looks like is now wide open.

QUESTIONS FOR DISCUSSION AND WRITING

1. Malcolm Gladwell, in "The Physical Genius" (p. 213), emphasizes the physical genius's ability to "pick up on subtle patterns" (paragraph 9) in order to excel at the work at hand. Crawford emphasizes how important it is to get the big picture, to understand the "gap between theory and practice" necessary to do good work with one's hands, an "ethical dimension" that leads to "the kind of judgment that arises only from experience; hunches rather than rules" (paragraphs 19–20). What similarities and differences are there between working with your brain and working with your hands? What similarities and differences are there between Gladwell's and Crawford's conceptions of the way people do their best work? Might these be differences of emphasis, rather than actual qualitative differences?

2. Barbara Ehrenreich, throughout "Serving in Florida" (p. 206), and Crawford (paragraphs 25–29) describe jobs that are demeaning, dull, and disheartening. What makes them such bad jobs? Are the problems inherent in the nature of the work itself? Could they be made better? If so, in what ways? Are these negotiable by the workers themselves, or do the bosses and managers have to figure out possible improvements?

3. Write an essay defending or arguing against Crawford's proposition that "[a] good job requires a field of action where you can put your best capacities to work and see an effect in the world. Academic credentials do not guarantee this." Feel free to draw on the essays by Ehrenreich, Malcolm Gladwell, Crawford, and Virginia Woolf in your discussion.

VIRGINIA WOOLF

Professions for Women

Virginia Woolf (1882–1941) was a significant figure in London literary society in the 1920s–30s. As a prolific writer of novels, essays, short stories, letters, and diaries, she—along with James Joyce—changed the face of modern literature, in part by exploring human consciousness from the inside out, as "stream of consciousness," rather than the outside in. Although the plots of her novels may seem uneventful and the subjects commonplace, Woolf's experimental techniques and inventive style transform the ordinary into world-class beauty and brilliance. Thus, a day in the life of Mrs. Dalloway *(1925), who is giving a party, encapsulates Mrs. Dalloway's life history and that of modern England, as well, in characteristically precise, diamond-edged language. In* To the Lighthouse *(1927), depicting a day of the Ramsay family's seaside summer vacation, Woolf's imaginative perspective invites readers into the mind of Mrs. Ramsay, an unerring interpreter of her cantankerous husband, her brood of rambunctious and romantic children, and a flock of guests—all of whom receive her tender, loving care and a critical eye. The central character in* Orlando *(1928) is transformed from a Renaissance man (self-confident, assertive) into a late nineteenth-century woman (demure and flirtatious, in accord with the values of the time).*

Woolf's book-length essay A Room of One's Own *(1929), concludes that "a woman must have money and a room of her own if she is to write fiction," a feminist point of view reflected, as well, in "Professions for Women." This was originally delivered as a speech to the Women's Service League in 1931 and then published in* The Death of the Moth and Other Essays *(1942). Here Woolf continues to explore the multiple barriers that women must overcome to attain autonomy and professional success in male-dominated society. To do this women have to kill off "The Angel in the House," the embodiment of the nurturing, self-effacing feminine ideal.*

When your secretary invited me to come here, she told me that your Society is concerned with the employment of women and she suggested that I might tell you something about my own professional experiences. It is true I am a woman; it is true I am employed; but what professional experiences have I had? It is difficult to say. My profession is literature; and in that profession there are fewer experiences for women than in any other, with the exception of the stage—fewer, I mean, that are peculiar to women. For the road was cut many years ago—by Fanny Burney, by Aphra Behn, by Harriet Martineau, by Jane Austen, by George Eliot—many famous women, and many more unknown and forgotten, have been before me, making the path smooth, and regulating my steps. Thus, when I came to write, there were very few material obstacles in my way. Writing was a reputable and harmless occupation. The family peace was not broken by the scratching of a pen. No demand was made upon the family purse. For ten and sixpence one can buy paper enough to write all the plays of Shakespeare—if one has a mind that way. Pianos and models, Paris, Vienna and Berlin, masters and mistresses, are not needed by a writer. The cheapness of writing paper is, of course, the reason why women have succeeded as writers before they have succeeded in the other professions.

But to tell you my story—it is a simple one. You have only got to figure to yourselves a girl in a bedroom with a pen in her hand. She had only to move that pen from left to right—from ten o'clock to one. Then it occurred to her to do what is simple and cheap enough after all—to slip a few of those pages into an envelope, fix a penny stamp in the corner, and drop the envelope into the red box at the corner. It was thus that I became a journalist; and my effort was rewarded on the first day of the following month—a very glorious day it was for me—by a letter from an editor containing a cheque for one pound ten shillings and sixpence. But to show you how little I deserve to be called a professional woman, how little I know of the struggles and difficulties of such lives, I have to admit that instead of spending that sum upon bread and butter, rent, shoes and stockings, or butcher's bills, I went out and bought a cat—a beautiful cat, a Persian cat, which very soon involved me in bitter disputes with my neighbors.

What could be easier than to write articles and to buy Persian cats with the profits? But wait a moment. Articles have to be about something. Mine, I seem to remember, was about a novel by a famous man. And while I was writing this review, I discovered that if I were going to review books I should need to do battle with a certain phantom. And the phantom was a woman, and when I came to know her better I called her after the heroine of a famous poem, The Angel in the House. It was she who used to come between me and my paper when I was writing reviews. It was she who bothered me and wasted my time and so tormented me that at last I killed her. You who come of a younger and happier generation may not have heard of her—you may not know what I mean by the Angel in the House. I will describe her as shortly as I can. She was intensely sympathetic. She was immensely charming. She was utterly unselfish. She excelled in the difficult arts of family life. She sacrificed herself daily. If there was a chicken, she took the leg; if there was a draught she sat in it—in short she was so constituted that she never had a mind or a wish of her own, but preferred to sympathize always with the minds and wishes of others. Above all—I need not say it—she was pure. Her purity was supposed to be her chief beauty—her blushes, her great grace. In those days—the last of Queen Victoria—every house had its Angel. And when I came to write I encountered her with the very first words. The shadow of her wings fell on my page; I heard the rustling of her skirts in the room. Directly, that is to say, I took my pen in hand to review that novel by a famous man, she slipped behind me and whispered: "My dear, you are a young woman. You are writing about a book that has been written by a man. Be sympathetic; be tender; flatter; deceive; use all the arts and wiles of our sex. Never let anybody guess that you have a mind of your own.

Above all, be pure." And she made as if to guide my pen. I now record the one act for which I take some credit to myself, though the credit rightly belongs to some excellent ancestors of mine who left me a certain sum of money—shall we say five hundred pounds a year?—so that it was not necessary for me to depend solely on charm for my living. I turned upon her and caught her by the throat. I did my best to kill her. My excuse, if I were to be had up in a court of law, would be that I acted in self-defense. Had I not killed her she would have killed me. She would have plucked the heart out of my writing. For, as I found, directly I put pen to paper, you cannot review even a novel without having a mind of your own, without expressing what you think to be the truth about human relations, morality, sex. And all these questions, according to the Angel in the House, cannot be dealt with freely and openly by women; they must charm, they must conciliate, they must—to put it bluntly—tell lies if they are to succeed. Thus, whenever I felt the shadow of her wing or the radiance of her halo upon my page, I took up the inkpot and flung it at her. She died hard. Her fictitious nature was of great assistance to her. It is far harder to kill a phantom than a reality. She was always creeping back when I thought I had dispatched her. Though I flatter myself that I killed her in the end, the struggle was severe; it took much time that had better have been spent upon learning Greek grammar; or in roaming the world in search of adventures. But it was a real experience; it was an experience that was bound to befall all women writers at that time. Killing the Angel in the House was part of the occupation of a woman writer.

But to continue my story. The Angel was dead; what then remained? You may say that what remained was a simple and common object—a young woman in a bedroom with an inkpot. In other words, now that she had rid herself of falsehood, that young woman had only to be herself. Ah, but what is "herself"? I mean, what is a woman? I assure you, I do not know. I do not believe that you know. I do not believe that anybody can know until she has expressed herself in all the arts and professions open to human skill. That indeed is one of the reasons why I have come here—out of respect for you, who are in process of showing us by your experiments what a woman is, who are in process of providing us, by your failures and successes, with that extremely important piece of information.

But to continue the story of my professional experiences. I made one [5] pound ten and six by my first review; and I bought a Persian cat with the proceeds. Then I grew ambitious. A Persian cat is all very well, I said; but a Persian cat is not enough. I must have a motor car. And it was thus that I became a novelist—for it is a very strange thing that people will give you a motor car if you will tell them a story. It is a still stranger thing that there is nothing so delightful in the world as telling stories. It is far pleasanter than writing reviews of famous novels. And yet, if I am to obey your secretary and tell you my professional experiences as a novelist, I must tell you about a very strange experience that befell me as a novelist. And to understand it you must try first to imagine a novelist's state of mind. I hope I am not giving away professional secrets if I say that a novelist's chief desire is to be as unconscious as possible. He has to induce in himself a state of perpetual lethargy. He wants life to proceed with the utmost quiet and regularity. He wants to see the same faces, to read the same books, to do the same things day after day, month after month, while he is writing, so that nothing may break the illusion in which he is living — so that nothing may disturb or disquiet the mysterious nosings about, feelings round, darts, dashes and sudden discoveries of that very shy and illusive spirit, the imagination. I suspect that this state is the same both for men and women. Be that as it may, I want you to imagine me writing a novel in a state of trance. I want you to figure to yourselves a girl sitting with a pen in her hand, which for minutes, and indeed for hours, she never dips into the inkpot. The image that comes to my mind when I think of this girl is the image of a fisherman lying sunk in dreams on the verge of a deep lake with a rod held out over the water. She was letting her imagination sweep unchecked round every rock and cranny of the world that lies submerged in the depths of our unconscious being. Now came the experience, the experience that I believe to be far commoner with women writers than with men. The line raced through the girl's fingers. Her imagination had rushed away. It had sought the pools, the depths, the dark places where the largest fish slumber. And then there was a smash. There was an explosion. There was foam and confusion. The imagination had dashed itself against something hard. The girl was roused from her dream. She was indeed in a state of the most acute and difficult distress. To speak without figure she had thought of something, something about the body, about the passions which it was unfitting for her as a woman to say. Men, her reason told her, would be shocked. The consciousness of what men will say of a woman who speaks the truth about her passions had roused her from her artist's state of unconsciousness. She could write no more. The trance was over. Her imagination could work no longer. This I believe to be a very common experience with women writers — they are impeded by the extreme conventionality of the other sex. For though men sensibly allow themselves great freedom in these respects, I doubt that they realize or can control the extreme severity with which they condemn such freedom in women.

These then were two very genuine experiences of my own. These were two of the adventures of my professional life. The first — killing the Angel in the House — I think I solved. She died. But the second, telling the truth about my own experiences as a body, I do not think I solved. I doubt that any woman has solved it yet. The obstacles against her are still immensely powerful — and yet they are very difficult to define. Outwardly, what is simpler than to write books? Outwardly, what obstacles are there for a woman rather than for a man? Inwardly, I think, the case is very different; she has still many ghosts to fight, many prejudices to overcome. Indeed it will be a long time still, I think, before a woman can sit down to write a book without finding a phantom to be slain, a rock to be dashed against. And if this is so in literature, the freest of all professions for women, how is it in the new professions which you are now for the first time entering?

Those are the questions that I should like, had I time, to ask you. And indeed, if I have laid stress upon these professional experiences of mine, it is because I believe that they are, though in different forms, yours also. Even when the path is nominally open—when there is nothing to prevent a woman from being a doctor, a lawyer, a civil servant—there are many phantoms and obstacles, as I believe, looming in her way. To discuss and define them is I think of great value and importance; for thus only can the labour be shared, the difficulties be solved. But besides this, it is necessary also to discuss the ends and the aims for which we are fighting, for which we are doing battle with these formidable obstacles. Those aims cannot be taken for granted; they must be perpetually questioned and examined. The whole position, as I see it—here in this hall surrounded by women practising for the first time in history I know not how many different professions—is one of extraordinary interest and importance. You have won rooms of your own in the house hitherto exclusively owned by men. You are able, though not without great labour and effort, to pay the rent. You are earning your five hundred pounds a year. But this freedom is only a beginning; the room is your own, but it is still bare. It has to be furnished; it has to be decorated; it has to be shared. How are you going to furnish it, how are you going to decorate it? With whom are you going to share it, and upon what terms? These, I think, are questions of the utmost importance and interest. For the first time in history you are able to ask for them; for the first time you are able to decide for yourselves what the answers should be. Willingly would I stay and discuss those questions and answers—but not tonight. My time is up; and I must cease.

QUESTIONS FOR DISCUSSION AND WRITING

1. What does Woolf mean by "The Angel in the House" (paragraph 3)?

2. "I did my best to kill [The Angel in the House]. . . . Had I not killed her she would have killed me. She would have plucked the heart out of my writing" (paragraph 3). Explain this conflict and the struggle it took for Woolf to succeed as a professional writer. What other claims did society and family make on a woman's time and efforts?

3. Woolf originally delivered "Professions for Women" as a talk in 1931. Have conditions for women's education and professional expectations changed so much in the subsequent eighty years as to make Woolf's analysis irrelevant today? Why or why not?

4. Consider the lives of the women Barbara Ehrenreich describes in "Serving in Florida" (or in *Nickeled and Dimed*, the larger book from which this is taken).

How can they be expected to fulfill the duties of wives, mothers, nurturers of a family while they are working all day (or night) at very tiring, minimum-wage jobs?

5. Write an essay in which you examine what would be the ideal conditions for anyone—man or woman—to lead fulfilling lives that combined multiple roles, as spouses, parents, workers? What sorts of jobs and support systems would best promote this ideal?

CHAPTER 4

Education and the American Character: What Do We Teach? What Do We Learn? And Why Does This Matter?

SIMON McCOMB

Education in Open Air

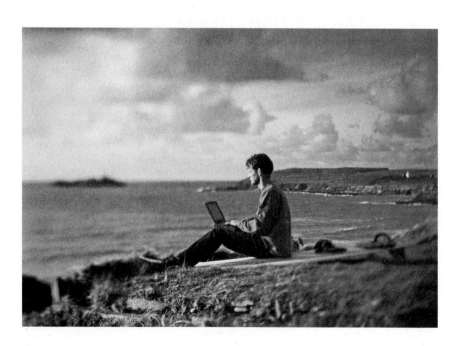

QUESTIONS FOR DISCUSSION AND WRITING

1. We often think of learning as taking place in classrooms, conventionally recognized as sites of formal instruction between teacher and students. Yet as this photograph reminds us, education can take place anywhere, much of it driven by the learners themselves. What sorts of learning might be going on as represented in this photograph? (Note what this young man is sitting on.)

2. How might the setting be influencing the participant's experience? His understanding of and appreciation of the environment? Is this far more beautiful, more tranquil than the ordinary learning environment? Or can any setting, natural or otherwise, become conducive to an education? Explain with specific reference to the settings you like best and to those settings you find the least conducive. In uncongenial settings, what inhibits or otherwise interferes with learning?

3. Would you have answered question 2 differently if the principal figure had been a college-age woman rather than a man? Someone not white?

4. Why are substantially fewer men than women attending college throughout the United States (except in urban areas)? In what ways, if any, is this photograph a commentary on that fact?

STANLEY FISH, GERALD GRAFF, JAMES MacGREGOR BURNS, AND NANCY HOPKINS

College Advice, From People Who Have Been There Awhile

Stanley Fish is a professor of law at Florida International University and Liberal Arts Dean Emeritus at the University of Illinois, Chicago (see also Fish, p. 460). Gerald Graff is a professor of English and education at the University of Illinois, Chicago, as well as associate liberal arts dean of curriculum and instruction. James MacGregor Burns is emeritus professor of government at Williams College and a Pulitzer Prize–winning presidential biographer. Nancy Hopkins is a professor of biology at the Massachusetts Institute of Technology, where her research focuses on gene development in fish. Herewith, their advice. Although intended for incoming students, this advice can serve as a useful reminder to more advanced students as well.

STANLEY FISH

The Hunt for a Good Teacher

I would give entering freshmen two pieces of advice. First, find out who the good teachers are. Ask your adviser; poll older students; search the Internet; and consult the teacher-evaluation guides available at most colleges. (As a professor, I am against those guides; too often they are the vehicles of petty grievances put forward by people who have no long-term stake in the enterprise. But if I were a student, I would take advantage of them.)

To some extent your options will be limited by distribution requirements (in colleges that still have them) and scheduling. But within these limits you should do everything you can to get a seat in the class of a professor known for both his or her knowledge of the material and the ability to make it a window on the larger universe. Years later you may not be able to recall the details of lectures and discussions, but the benefits of being in the company of a challenging mind will be yours forever.

Second, I would advise students to take a composition course even if they have tested out of it. I have taught many students whose SAT scores exempted them from the writing requirement, but a disheartening number of them couldn't write and an equal number had never been asked to. They managed to get through high-school without learning how to write a clean English sentence, and if you can't do that you can't do anything.

I give this advice with some trepidation because too many writing courses today teach everything but the craft of writing and are instead the vehicles of the instructor's social and political obsessions. In the face of what I consider a dereliction of pedagogical duty, I can say only, "Buyer beware." If your writing instructor isn't teaching writing, get out of that class and find someone who is.

GERALD GRAFF

An Argument Worth Having

Freshmen are often overwhelmed by the intellectual challenge of college—so many subjects to be covered, so many facts, methods and philosophical isms to sort out, so many big words to assimilate. As if that weren't enough, what your different instructors tell you may be flatly contradictory.

Students understandably cope with this cognitive dissonance by giving each of their teachers in turn whatever he or she seems to want. Students learn to be free-market capitalists in one course and socialists in the next, universalists in the morning and relativists after lunch. This tactic has got many a student through college, but the trouble is that, even when each course is excellent in itself, jumping through a series of hoops doesn't add up to a real socialization into the ways of intellectual culture.

What the most successful college students do, in my experience, is cut through the clutter of jargons, methods and ideological differences to locate the common practices of argument and analysis hidden behind it all. Contrary to the cliché that no "one size fits all" educational recipe is possible, successful academics of all fields and intellectual persuasions make some key moves that you can emulate:

1. Recognize that knowing a lot of stuff won't do you much good unless you can do something with what you know by turning it into an argument.
2. Pay close attention to what others are saying and writing and then summarize their arguments and assumptions in a recognizable way. Work especially on summarizing the views that go most against your own.
3. As you summarize, look not only for the thesis of an argument, but for who or what provoked it—the points of controversy.
4. Use these summaries to motivate what you say and to indicate why it needs saying. Don't be afraid to give your own opinion, especially if you can back it up with reasons and evidence, but don't disagree with anything without carefully summarizing it first.

It's too often a secret that only a minority of high achievers figure out, but the better you get at entering the conversation by summarizing it and putting in your own oar, the more you'll get out of your college education.

JAMES MacGREGOR BURNS

Off-Campus Life

Try to read a good newspaper every day—at bedtime or at breakfast or when you take a break in the afternoon. If you are interested in art, literature or music, widen your horizons by poring over the science section. In the mood for spicy scandals? Read the business pages. Want to impress your poli sci prof? Read columnists.

The newspaper will be your path to the world at large. At Williams College, where I was a student in the 1930s, we read the alarming reports in *The Times* about Germany's brutal onslaught against peaceful nations. In the spring of 1938, we burned Hitler in effigy—and made Page 11 of *The Times*! In June 1940, as France fell to Nazi troops, hundreds of graduating seniors urged compulsory military training, and provided another Williams story to the paper.

In addition, a great newspaper will teach you how to write: most articles are models of clarity and substance—with no academic jargon! Pay attention to the writer's vocabulary, see how many active verbs are used, file away striking new words for future use. Study how articles are structured—how the first paragraph tells the reader simply and clearly the subject and main points. Take a look at the last paragraph; it will often show you how to conclude an essay with a pithy phrase or a telling quotation.

A great newspaper will help you in the classroom—and it will be your conduit to the real world outside the classroom. Become addicted.

Another way to stay connected with the real world: get to know your teach-   5 ers outside of class. Chat and engage with them, perhaps on the walk away from class. Ask them not only about the coursework but also about their own intellectual interests and research. Equally important to maintaining that lifeline to the universe beyond college is getting to know the janitors and housekeepers in your dorm, the security staff on the campus, the people who work in the cafeteria. Talk to them, ask them questions and thank them.

NANCY HOPKINS

My Crush on DNA

Fall in love! Not with that attractive person sitting three rows in front of you in calculus class, but with an intellectual vision of the future you probably can't even imagine at the moment. A millennium or so ago I entered Harvard wanting to major in math. But in my junior year I heard a biology lecture by James D. Watson, the scientist who co-discovered the double-helical structure of DNA, the molecule that genes are made of. By the end of that lecture I was a goner—in love with DNA. Until then I had not known that a new science, called molecular biology and based on DNA, had already begun to unravel the secret of life.

Listening to Dr. Watson's lecture I could even imagine that molecular biologists might one day answer all the important questions I had about humans: How do you make a hand? Why do I look like my mother? How does a cell become cancerous? What is memory? I staggered breathlessly out of that classroom and started down the long unpredictable path to becoming a professor of molecular biology at M.I.T. What I have learned is that passion, along with curiosity, drives science. Passion is the mysterious force behind nearly every scientific breakthrough. Perhaps it's because without it you might never be able to tolerate the huge amount of hard work and frustration that scientific discovery entails. But if you have it, you're in luck. Today, 45 years after Watson's lecture, new discoveries in biology still take my breath away.

For the next four years you will get to poke around the corridors of your college, listen to any lecture you choose, work in a lab. The field of science you fall in love with may be so new it doesn't even have a name yet. You may be the person who constructs a new biological species, or figures out how to stop global warming, or aging. Maybe you'll discover life on another planet. My advice to you is this: Don't settle for anything less.

QUESTIONS FOR DISCUSSION AND WRITING

1. These four seasoned professors offer good advice, not only to new college students but to all undergraduates. This includes, "find out who the good teachers are" and take their courses (Fish); "take a composition course" (Fish); summarize the existing conversation in a given discipline and then join in with your own thoughts, backed up with "reasons and evidence" (Graff); "read a good newspaper every day" (Burns); and "[f]all in love . . . with an intellectual vision of the future you probably can't even imagine at the moment" (Hopkins). Which advice strikes you as most useful for a new student? For a more experienced student? Is any of it inappropriate? Impossible to accomplish? Prioritize the advice and explain your answer.

2. Now or nearer to the end of the semester, write your own "College Advice" to incoming students. This can be straightforward, or a parody in the manner of David Sedaris's "What I Learned and What I Said at Princeton" (p. 246).

3. Or, write a draft of your own "College Advice" now, and then revise it near the end of the semester. Provide a rationale for the major additions, deletions, and changes you've made.

4. None of these professors offers advice for relations among fellow students. Provide "College Advice" for getting along with roommates, eating groups, social networking groups on- and offline.

DAVID SEDARIS

What I Learned and What I Said at Princeton

David Sedaris was born in Raleigh, North Carolina, in 1957. He dropped out of Kent State University in 1977 and ten years later graduated from the Art Institute of Chicago. His career as a humorist began unexpectedly, with his first reading from "SantaLand Diaries" on National Public Radio in 1992, a self-satirizing account of his career as a Santa's elf during Christmas season that focused on the backstage seediness of playing Crumpet the elf. In recent years his biting satirical tone has softened somewhat in stories about living in Paris with his life's companion, Hugh, as in Me Talk Pretty One Day *(2000), or about his dysfunctional family, in* Dress Your Family in Corduroy and Denim *(2004). Nevertheless,* When You are Engulfed in Flames *(2008) does include essays on chimpanzees at a typing school and hostility toward a paraplegic.*

Despite the claims of his baccalaureate address delivered at Princeton in June 2006 (New Yorker, June 26, 2006), Sedaris did not attend the university of which he speaks so fondly: "This chapel, for instance—I remember when it was just a clearing, cordoned off with sharp sticks. Prayer was compulsory back then, and you couldn't just fake it by moving your lips. . . . I'm dating myself, but this was before Jesus Christ."

It's been interesting to walk around campus this afternoon, as when *I* went to Princeton things were completely different. This chapel, for instance—I remember when it was just a clearing, cordoned off with sharp sticks. Prayer was compulsory back then, and you couldn't just fake it by moving your lips; you had to know the words, and really mean them. I'm dating myself, but this was before Jesus Christ. We worshipped a God named Sashatiba, who had five eyes, including one right here, on the Adam's apple. None of us ever met him, but word had it that he might appear at any moment, so we were always at the ready. *Whatever you do, don't look at his neck,* I used to tell myself.

It's funny now, but I thought about it a lot. Some people thought about it a little too much, and it really affected their academic performance. Again, I date myself, but back then we were on a pass-fail system. If you passed, you got to live, and if you failed you were burned alive on a pyre that's now the Transgender Studies Building. Following the first grading period, the air was so thick with smoke you could barely find your way across campus. There were those who said that it smelled like meat, no different from a barbecue, but I could tell the difference. I mean, really. Since when do you grill hair? Or those ugly, chunky shoes we all used to wear?

It kept you on your toes, though, I'll say that much. If I'd been burned alive because of bad grades, my parents would have killed me, especially my father, who meant well but was just a little too gung ho for my taste. He had the whole outfit: Princeton breastplate, Princeton nightcap; he even got the velvet cape with the tiger head hanging like a rucksack from between the shoulder blades. In those days, the mascot was a sabretooth, so you can imagine how silly it looked, and how painful it was to sit down. Then, there was his wagon, completely covered with decals and bumper stickers: "I hold my horses for Ivy League schools," "My son was accepted at the best university in the United States and all I got was a bill for a hundred and sixty-eight thousand dollars." On and on, which was just so . . . *wrong.*

One of the things they did back then was start you off with a modesty seminar, an eight-hour session that all the freshmen had to sit through. It might be different today, but in my time it took the form of a role-playing exercise, my classmates and I pretending to be graduates, and the teacher assuming the part of an average citizen: the soldier, the bloodletter, the whore with a heart of gold.

"Tell me, young man. Did you attend a university of higher learning?"   5

To anyone holding a tool or a weapon, we were trained to respond, "What? Me go to college?" If, on the other hand, the character held a degree, you were allowed to say, "Sort of," or, sometimes, "I think so."

"So where do you sort of think you went?"

And it was the next bit that you had to get just right. Inflection was everything, and it took the foreign students forever to master it.

"Where do you sort of think you went?"

And we'd say, "Umm, Princeton?"—as if it were an oral exam, and we weren't   10 quite sure that this was the correct answer.

"Princeton, my goodness," the teacher would say. "That must have been quite something!"

You had to let him get it out, but once he started in on how brilliant and committed you must be it was time to hold up your hands, saying, "Oh, it isn't that hard to get into."

Then he'd say, "Really? But I heard—"

"Wrong," you'd tell him. "You heard wrong. It's not that great of a school."

This was the way it had to be done—you had to play it down, which wasn't   15 easy when your dad was out there, reading your acceptance letter into a bullhorn.

I needed to temper my dad's enthusiasm a bit, and so I announced that I would be majoring in patricide. The Princeton program was very strong back then, the best in the country, but it wasn't the sort of thing your father could get too worked up about. Or, at least, most fathers wouldn't. Mine was over the moon. "Killed by a Princeton graduate!" he said. "And my own son, no less."

My mom was actually jealous. "So what's wrong with matricide?" she asked. "What, I'm not good enough to murder?"

They started bickering, so in order to make peace I promised to consider a double major.

"And how much more is that going to cost us?" they said.

Those last few months at home were pretty tough, but then I started my   20 freshman year, and got caught up in the life of the mind. My idol-worship class was the best, but my dad didn't get it. "What the hell does that have to do with patricide?" he asked.

And I said, "Umm. *Everything*?"

He didn't understand that it's all connected, that one subject leads to another and forms a kind of chain that raises its head and nods like a cobra when you're sucking on a bong after three days of no sleep. On acid it's even wilder, and appears to eat things. But, not having gone to college, my dad had no concept of a well-rounded liberal-arts education. He thought that all my classes should be murder-related, with no lunch breaks or anything. Fortunately, it doesn't work that way.

In truth, I had no idea what I wanted to study, so for the first few years I took everything that came my way. I enjoyed pillaging and astrology, but the thing that ultimately stuck was comparative literature. There wasn't much of it to compare back then, no more than a handful of epic poems and one novel about a lady detective, but that's part of what I liked about it. The field was new, and full of possibilities, but try telling that to my parents.

"You mean you *won't* be killing us?" my mother said. "But I told everyone you were going for that double major."

Dad followed his "I'm so disappointed" speech with a lecture on career op-   25 portunities. "You're going to study literature and get a job doing *what*?" he said. "*Literaturizing*?"

We spent my entire vacation arguing; then, just before I went back to school, my father approached me in my bedroom. "Promise me you'll keep an open mind," he said. And, as he left, he slipped an engraved dagger into my book bag.

I had many fine teachers during my years at Princeton, but the one I think of most often was my fortune-telling professor—a complete hag with wild gray hair, warts the size of new potatoes, the whole nine yards. She taught us to forecast the weather up to two weeks in advance, but ask her for anything weightier and you were likely to be disappointed.

The alchemy majors wanted to know how much money they'd be making after graduation. "Just give us an approximate figure," they'd say, and the professor would shake her head and cover her crystal ball with a little cozy given to her by one of her previous classes. When it came to our futures, she drew the line, no matter how hard we begged—and, I mean, we really tried. I was as let down as the next guy, but, in retrospect, I can see that she acted in our best interests. Look at yourself on the day that you graduated from college, then look at yourself today. I did that recently, and it was, like, "What the hell happened?"

The answer, of course, is life. What the hag chose not to foretell—and what we, in our certainty, could not have fathomed—is that stuff comes up. Weird doors open. People fall into things. Maybe the engineering whiz will wind up brewing cider, not because he has to but because he finds it challenging. Who knows? Maybe the athlete will bring peace to all nations, or the class moron will go on to become the President of the United States—though that's more likely to happen at Harvard or Yale, schools that will pretty much let in anybody.

There were those who left Princeton and soared like arrows into the bosoms 30 of power and finance, but I was not one of them. My path was a winding one, with plenty of obstacles along the way. When school was finished, I went back home, an Ivy League graduate with four years' worth of dirty laundry and his whole life ahead of him. "What are you going to do now?" my parents asked.

And I said, "Well, I was thinking of washing some of these underpants."

That took six months. Then I moved on to the shirts.

"Now what?" my parents asked.

And, when I told them I didn't know, they lost what little patience they had left. "What kind of a community-college answer is that?" my mother said. "You went to the best school there is—how can you not know something?"

And I said, "I don't know."   35

In time, my father stopped wearing his Princeton gear. My mother stopped talking about my "potential," and she and my dad got themselves a brown-and-white puppy. In terms of intelligence, it was just average, but they couldn't see that at all. "Aren't you just the smartest dog in the world?" they'd ask, and the puppy would shake their hands just like I used to do.

My first alumni weekend cheered me up a bit. It was nice to know that I wasn't the only unemployed graduate in the world, but the warm feeling evaporated when I got back home and saw that my parents had given the dog my bedroom. In place of the Princeton pennant they'd bought for my first birthday was a banner reading, "Westminster or bust."

I could see which way the wind was blowing, and so I left, and moved to the city, where a former classmate, a philosophy major, got me a job on his rag-picking crew.

When the industry moved overseas—this the doing of *another* former classmate—I stayed put, and eventually found work skinning hides for a ratcatcher, a thin, serious man with the longest beard I had ever seen.

At night, I read and reread the handful of books I'd taken with me when I left home, and eventually, out of boredom as much as anything else, I started to write myself. It wasn't much, at first: character sketches, accounts of my day, parodies of articles in the alumni newsletter. Then, in time, I became more ambitious, and began crafting little stories about my family. I read one of them out loud to the ratcatcher, who'd never laughed at anything but roared at the description of my mother and her puppy. "My mom was just the same," he said. "I graduated from Brown, and two weeks later she was raising falcons on my top bunk!" The story about my dad defecating in his neighbor's well pleased my boss so much that he asked for a copy, and sent it to his own father.

This gave me the confidence to continue, and in time I completed an entire book, which was subsequently published. I presented a first edition to my parents, who started with the story about our neighbor's well, and then got up to close the drapes. Fifty pages later, they were boarding up the door and looking for ways to disguise themselves. Other people had loved my writing, but these two didn't get it at all. "What's wrong?" I asked. 40

My father adjusted his makeshift turban, and sketched a mustache on my mother's upper lip. "What's wrong?" he said. "I'll tell you what's wrong: you're killing us."

"But I thought that's what you wanted?"

"We did," my mother wept, "but not this way."

It hadn't occurred to me until that moment, but I seemed to have come full circle. What started as a dodge had inadvertently become my life's work, an irony I never could have appreciated had my extraordinary parents not put me through Princeton.

QUESTIONS FOR DISCUSSION AND WRITING

1. Sedaris actually delivered this commencement address at Princeton (June 2006). Despite his opening claim, "when *I* went to Princeton things were completely different" (paragraph 1), he never attended Princeton. At what point does he expect his audience to know this? Why is it important to recognize that Sedaris is writing a satire? Identify at least ten aspects of college that he is satirizing. Write your own satire on the topic that most appeals to you.

2. Why have you enrolled in the college you're attending? How did you choose it? In either a satire or a straightforward paper, discuss your criteria, and highlight the major issues influencing your decision. Which issues pertained to the actual education you expected to receive and to your understanding of its quality? If you've been there long enough to assess the accuracy of your predictions, include these assessments.

3. Can all students' parents be expected to be as proud of their child's acceptance as Sedaris's dad allegedly was, "reading [his] acceptance letter into a bullhorn" (paragraph 15)? Or is this pride reserved essentially for parents and students in elitist schools? Where does Sedaris critique this? How would he expect his audience of newly minted Princeton graduates to react?

4. Sedaris satirizes parents' relations with their college student children, both while the children are in college and after they have graduated and moved back home (paragraph 30 and following). Do you think most college graduates' expectations are fulfilled by their undergraduate experiences? What do you expect to occur as a consequence of earning a college degree? What evidence have you that your expectations will be fulfilled? Or not? Write a paper analyzing this.

5. Or, discuss the ideas raised in question 4 with your parents (or others who have a stake in your education) and write a dialogue that captures the essence of this conversation. What are the major points of agreement? Disagreement? What can you do to ensure that your expectations will be fulfilled (see Fish, Graff, Burns, and Hopkins, p. 242)?

CHARLES M. SCHULZ

Peanuts: *Slow Reading*

QUESTIONS FOR DISCUSSION AND WRITING

1. "Mixed brain dominance" as a term applying to ADHD and various other types of conditions related to attention span has appeared in educational and psychological professional literature for over half a century, about the same length of time since this *Peanuts* cartoon was first published (in 1962, and reprinted — most recently — in 2009). Check out some Web sites to see whether Linus's explanation is accurate.

2. Why not consult an eye doctor to see whether a child slow to read might in fact need glasses? What other factors might contribute to "slow reading"? Consider the explanations implied in Richard Rodriguez, "Aria: Memoir of a Bilingual

Childhood" (p. 275) and in Jonathan Kozol's "The Human Cost of an Illiterate Society" (p. 252).

3. "Stupidity," Lucy's knee-jerk answer, blames the victim—and, judging from people's blogs, is an explanation many are willing to accept concerning their own behavior. Why is this explanation humorous but not necessarily accurate? What factors in society, and in educational systems you're familiar with, contribute to making people "stupid"? Smart?

4. Consider the difficulties in reading that Jonathan Kozol (p. 252) and Deborah Franklin (p. 260) point out, and analyze "Slow Reading" (p. 251) in light of what you've found.

JONATHAN KOZOL

The Human Cost of an Illiterate Society

Jonathan Kozol (b. 1936) grew up in Newton, Massachusetts, graduated from Harvard (B.A., 1958), and received a Rhodes scholarship but abandoned it to spend four years in Paris writing a novel, The Fume of Poppies *(1958). Moved by the murders of civil rights activists in the South, he returned to the United States to become deeply involved in the civil rights movement and issues of social justice, to which he has devoted the rest of his life as an author, educator, and activist. Kozol's first book,* Death at an Early Age: The Destruction of the Hearts and Minds of Negro Children in the Boston Public Schools *(1967), won a National Book Award. Other award-winning books include* Rachel and Her Children: Homeless Families in America *(1988),* Savage Inequalities: Children in America's Schools *(1991), and* Amazing Grace: The Lives of Children and the Conscience of a Nation *(1995). His most recent book is* Letters to a Young Teacher *(2007).*

"The Human Cost of an Illiterate Society," a chapter from Illiterate America *(1985), shows how illiteracy degrades people's quality of life, makes them vulnerable to others' interpretations of the written word, and prevents their full participation in democratic society.*

PRECAUTIONS. READ BEFORE USING.

Poison: Contains sodium hydroxide (caustic soda-lye).

Corrosive: Causes severe eye and skin damage, may cause blindness.

Harmful or fatal if swallowed.

If swallowed, give large quantities of milk or water.

Do not induce vomiting.

Important: Keep water out of can at all times to prevent contents from violently erupting. . . .

–Warning on a Can of Drāno

We are speaking here no longer of the dangers faced by passengers on Eastern Airlines or the dollar costs incurred by U.S. corporations and taxpayers. We are speaking now of human suffering and of the ethical dilemmas that are faced by a society that looks upon such suffering with qualified concern but does not take those actions which its wealth and ingenuity would seemingly demand.

Questions of literacy, in Socrates' belief, must at length be judged as matters of morality. Socrates could not have had in mind the moral compromise peculiar to a nation like our own. Some of our Founding Fathers did, however, have this question in their minds. One of the wisest of those Founding Fathers (one who may not have been most compassionate but surely was more prescient than some of his peers) recognized the special dangers that illiteracy would pose to basic equity in the political construction that he helped to shape.

"A people who mean to be their own governors," James Madison wrote, "must arm themselves with the power knowledge gives. A popular government without popular information or the means of acquiring it, is but a prologue to a farce or a tragedy, or perhaps both."

Tragedy looms larger than farce in the United States today. Illiterate citizens seldom vote. Those who do are forced to cast a vote of questionable worth. They cannot make informed decisions based on serious print information. Sometimes they can be alerted to their interests by aggressive voter education. More frequently, they vote for a face, a smile, or a style, not for a mind or character or body of beliefs.

The number of illiterate adults exceeds by 16 million the entire vote cast 5 for the winner in the 1980 presidential contest. If even one third of all illiterates could vote, and read enough and do sufficient math to vote in their self-interest, Ronald Reagan would not likely have been chosen president. There is, of course, no way to know for sure. We do know this: Democracy is a mendacious term when used by those who are prepared to countenance the forced exclusion of one third of our electorate. So long as 60 million people are denied significant participation, the government is neither of, nor for, nor by, the people. It is a government, at best, of those two thirds whose wealth, skin color, or parental privilege allows them opportunity to profit from the provocation and instruction of the written word.

The undermining of democracy in the United States is one "expense" that sensitive Americans can easily deplore because it represents a contradiction that endangers citizens of all political positions. The human price is not so obvious at first.

Since I first immersed myself within this work I have often had the following dream: I find that I am in a railroad station or a large department store within a city that is utterly unknown to me and where I cannot understand the printed words. None of the signs or symbols is familiar. Everything looks strange: like mirror writing of some kind. Gradually I understand that I am in the Soviet Union. All the letters on the walls around me are Cyrillic. I look for my pocket dictionary but I find that it has been mislaid. Where have I left it? Then I recall that I forgot to bring it with me when I packed my bags in Boston. I struggle to remember the name of my hotel. I try to ask somebody for directions. One person stops and looks at me in a peculiar way. I lose the nerve to ask. At last I reach into my wallet for an ID card. The card is missing. Have I lost it? Then I remember that my card was confiscated for some reason, many years before. Around this point, I wake up in a panic.

This panic is not so different from the misery that millions of adult illiterates experience each day within the course of their routine existence in the U.S.A.

Illiterates cannot read the menu in a restaurant.

They cannot read the cost of items on the menu in the *window* of the restau- 10
rant before they enter.

Illiterates cannot read the letters that their children bring home from their teachers. They cannot study school department circulars that tell them of the courses that their children must be taking if they hope to pass the SAT exams. They cannot help with homework. They cannot write a letter to the teacher. They are afraid to visit in the classroom. They do not want to humiliate their child or themselves.

Illiterates cannot read instructions on a bottle of prescription medicine. They cannot find out when a medicine is past the year of safe consumption; nor can they read of allergenic risks, warnings to diabetics, or the potential sedative effect of certain kinds of nonprescription pills. They cannot observe preventive health care admonitions. They cannot read about "the seven warning signs of cancer" or the indications of blood-sugar fluctuations or the risks of eating certain foods that aggravate the likelihood of cardiac arrest.

Illiterates live, in more than literal ways, an uninsured existence. They cannot understand the written details on a health insurance form. They cannot read the waivers that they sign preceding surgical procedures. Several women I have known in Boston have entered a slum hospital with the intention of obtaining a tubal ligation and have emerged a few days later after having been subjected to a hysterectomy. Unaware of their rights, incognizant of jargon, intimidated by the unfamiliar air of fear and atmosphere of ether that so many of us find oppressive in the confines even of the most attractive and expensive medical facilities, they have signed their names to documents they could not read and which nobody, in the hectic situation that prevails so often in those overcrowded hospitals that serve the urban poor, had even bothered to explain.

Childbirth might seem to be the last inalienable right of any female citizen within a civilized society. Illiterate mothers, as we shall see, already have been cheated of the power to protect their progeny against the likelihood of demolition in deficient public schools and, as a result, against the verbal servitude within which they themselves exist. Surgical denial of the right to bear that child in the first place represents an ultimate denial, an unspeakable metaphor, a final darkness that denies even the twilight gleamings of our own humanity. What greater violation of our biological, our biblical, our spiritual humanity could possibly exist than that which takes place nightly, perhaps hourly these days, within such overburdened and benighted institutions as the Boston City Hospital? Illiteracy has many costs; few are so irreversible as this.

Even the roof above one's head, the gas or other fuel for heating that pro- 15 tects the residents of northern city slums against the threat of illness in the winter months become uncertain guarantees. Illiterates cannot read the lease that they must sign to live in an apartment which, too often, they cannot afford. They cannot manage check accounts and therefore seldom pay for anything by mail. Hours and entire days of difficult travel (and the cost of bus or other public transit) must be added to the real cost of whatever they consume. Loss of interest on the check accounts they do not have, and could not manage if they did, must be regarded as another of the excess costs paid by the citizen who is excluded from the common instruments of commerce in a numerate society.

"I couldn't understand the bills," a woman in Washington, D.C., reports, "and then I couldn't write the checks to pay them. We signed things we didn't know what they were."

Illiterates cannot read the notices that they receive from welfare offices or from the IRS. They must depend on word-of-mouth instruction from the welfare worker—or from other persons whom they have good reason to mistrust. They do not know what rights they have, what deadlines and requirements they face, what options they might choose to exercise. They are half-citizens. Their rights exist in print but not in fact.

Illiterates cannot look up numbers in a telephone directory. Even if they can find the names of friends, few possess the sorting skills to make use of the yellow pages; categories are bewildering and trade names are beyond decoding capabilities for millions of nonreaders. Even the emergency numbers listed on the first page of the phone book—"Ambulance," "Police," and "Fire"—are too frequently beyond the recognition of nonreaders.

Many illiterates cannot read the admonition on a pack of cigarettes. Neither the Surgeon General's warning nor its reproduction on the package can alert them to the risks. Although most people learn by word of mouth that smoking is related to a number of grave physical disorders, they do not get the chance to read the detailed stories which can document this danger with the vividness that turns concern into determination to resist. They can see the handsome cowboy or the slim Virginia lady lighting up a filter cigarette; they cannot heed the words that tell them that this product is (not "may be") dangerous to their health. Sixty million men and women are condemned to be the unalerted, high-risk candidates for cancer.

Illiterates do not buy "no-name" products in the supermarkets. They must 20 depend on photographs or the familiar logos that are printed on the packages of brand-name groceries. The poorest people, therefore, are denied the benefits of the least costly products.

Illiterates depend almost entirely upon label recognition. Many labels, however, are not easy to distinguish. Dozens of different kinds of Campbell's soup appear identical to the nonreader. The purchaser who cannot read and does not dare to ask for help, out of the fear of being stigmatized (a fear which is unfortunately realistic), frequently comes home with something which she never wanted and her family never tasted.

Illiterates cannot read instructions on a pack of frozen food. Packages sometimes provide an illustration to explain the cooking preparations; but illustrations are of little help to someone who must "boil water, drop the food—*within* its plastic wrapper—in the boiling water, wait for it to simmer, instantly remove."

Even when labels are seemingly clear, they may be easily mistaken. A woman in Detroit brought home a gallon of Crisco for her children's dinner. She thought that she had bought the chicken that was pictured on the label. She had enough Crisco now to last a year—but no more money to go back and buy the food for dinner.

Recipes provided on the packages of certain staples sometimes tempt a semiliterate person to prepare a meal her children have not tasted. The longing to vary the uniform and often starchy content of low-budget meals provided to the family that relies on food stamps commonly leads to ruinous results. Scarce funds have been wasted and the food must be thrown out. The same applies to distribution of food-surplus produce in emergency conditions. Government inducements to poor people to "explore the ways" by which to make a tasty meal from tasteless noodles, surplus cheese, and powdered milk are useless to nonreaders. Intended as benevolent advice, such recommendations mock reality and foster deeper feelings of resentment and of inability to cope. (Those, on the other hand, who cautiously refrain from "innovative" recipes in preparation of their children's meals must suffer the opprobrium of "laziness," "lack of imagination. . . .")

Illiterates cannot travel freely. When they attempt to do so, they encounter 25 risks that few of us can dream of. They cannot read traffic signs and, while they often learn to recognize and to decipher symbols, they cannot manage street names which they haven't seen before. The same is true for bus and subway stops. While ingenuity can sometimes help a man or woman to discern directions from familiar landmarks, buildings, cemeteries, churches, and the like, most illiterates are virtually immobilized. They seldom wander past the streets and neighborhoods they know. Geographical paralysis becomes a bitter metaphor for their entire existence. They are immobilized in almost every sense we can imagine. They can't move up. They can't move out. They cannot see beyond. Illiterates may take an oral test for drivers' permits in most sections of America. It is a questionable concession. Where will they go? How will they get there? How will they get home? Could it be that some of us might like it better if they stayed where they belong?

Travel is only one of many instances of circumscribed existence. Choice, in almost all of its facets, is diminished in the life of an illiterate adult. Even the printed TV schedule, which provides most people with the luxury of preselection, does not belong within the arsenal of options in illiterate existence. One consequence is that the viewer watches only what appears at moments when he happens to have time to turn the switch. Another consequence, a lot more common, is that the TV set remains in operation night and day. Whatever the program offered at the hour when he walks into the room will be the nutriment that he accepts and swallows. Thus, to passivity, is added frequency—indeed, almost uninterrupted continuity. Freedom to select is no more possible here than in the choice of home or surgery or food.

"You don't choose," said one illiterate woman. "You take your wishes from somebody else." Whether in perusal of a menu, selection of highways, purchase of groceries, or determination of affordable enjoyment, illiterate Americans must trust somebody else: a friend, a relative, a stranger on the street, a grocery clerk, a TV copywriter.

"All of our mail we get, it's hard for her to read. Settin' down and writing a letter, she can't do it. Like if we get a bill . . . we take it over to my sister-in-law . . . My sister-in-law reads it."

Billing agencies harass poor people for the payment of the bills for purchases that might have taken place six months before. Utility companies offer an agreement for a staggered payment schedule on a bill past due. "You have to trust them," one man said. Precisely for this reason, you end up by trusting no one and suspecting everyone of possible deceit. A submerged sense of distrust becomes the corollary to a constant need to trust. "They are cheating me . . . I have been tricked . . . I do not know . . ."

Not knowing: This is a familiar theme. Not knowing the right word for the right thing at the right time is one form of subjugation. Not knowing the world that lies concealed behind those words is a more terrifying feeling. The longitude and latitude of one's existence are beyond all easy apprehension. Even the hard, cold stars within the firmament above one's head begin to mock the possibilities for self-location. Where am I? Where did I come from? Where will I go?

"I've lost a lot of jobs," one man explains. "Today, even if you're a janitor, there's still reading and writing . . . They leave a note saying, 'Go to room so-and-so . . .' You can't do it. You can't read it. You don't know."

"The hardest thing about it is that I've been places where I didn't know where I was. You don't know where you are . . . You're lost."

"Like I said: I have two kids. What do I do if one of my kids starts choking? I go running to the phone . . . I can't look up the hospital phone number. That's if we're at home. Out on the street, I can't read the sign. I get to a pay phone. 'Okay, tell us where you are. We'll send an ambulance.' I look at the street sign. Right there, I can't tell you what it says. I'd have to spell it out, letter for letter. By that time, one of my kids would be dead . . . These are the kinds of fears you go with, every single day . . ."

"Reading directions, I suffer with. I work with chemicals . . . That's scary to begin with . . ."

"You sit down. They throw the menu in front of you. Where do you go from there? Nine times out of ten you say, 'Go ahead. Pick out something for the both of us.' I've eaten some weird things, let me tell you!"

Menus. Chemicals. A child choking while his mother searches for a word she does not know to find assistance that will come too late. Another mother speaks about the inability to help her kids to read: "I can't read to them. Of course that's leaving them out of something they should have. Oh, it matters. You *believe* it matters! I ordered all these books. The kids belong to a book club. Donny wanted me to read a book to him. I told Donny: 'I can't read.' He said: 'Mommy, you sit down. I'll read it to you.' I tried it one day, reading from the pictures. Donny looked at me. He said, 'Mommy, that's not right.' He's only five. He knew I couldn't read . . ."

A landlord tells a woman that her lease allows him to evict her if her baby cries and causes inconvenience to her neighbors. The consequence of challenging his words conveys a danger which appears, unlikely as it seems, even more alarming than the danger of eviction. Once she admits that she can't read, in the desire to maneuver for the time in which to call a friend, she will have defined herself in terms of an explicit impotence that she cannot endure. Capitulation in this case is preferable to self-humiliation. Resisting the definition of oneself in terms of what one cannot do, what others take for granted, represents a need so great that other imperatives (even one so urgent as the need to keep one's home in winter's cold) evaporate and fall away in face of fear. Even the loss of home and shelter, in this case, is not so terrifying as the loss of self.

"I come out of school. I was sixteen. They had their meetings. The directors meet. They said that I was wasting their school paper. I was wasting pencils . . ."

Another illiterate, looking back, believes she was not worthy of her teacher's time. She believes that it was wrong of her to take up space within her school. She believes that it was right to leave in order that somebody more deserving could receive her place.

Children choke. Their mother chokes another way: on more than chicken bones.   40

People eat what others order, know what others tell them, struggle not to see themselves as they believe the world perceives them. A man in California speaks about his own loss of identity, of self-location, definition:

"I stood at the bottom of the ramp. My car had broke down on the freeway. There was a phone. I asked for the police. They was nice. They said to tell them where I was. I looked up at the signs. There was one that I had seen before. I read it to them: ONE WAY STREET. They thought it was a joke. I told them I couldn't read. There was other signs above the ramp. They told me to try. I looked around for somebody to help. All the cars was going by real fast. I couldn't make them understand that I was lost. The cop was nice. He told me: 'Try once more.' I did my best. I couldn't read. I only knew the sign above my head. The cop was trying to be nice. He knew that I was trapped. 'I can't send out a car to you if you can't tell me where you are.' I felt afraid. I nearly cried. I'm forty-eight years old. I only said: 'I'm on a one-way street . . .'"

Perhaps we might slow down a moment here and look at the realities described above. This is the nation that we live in. This is a society that most of us did not create but which our President and other leaders have been willing to sustain by virtue of malign neglect. Do we possess the character and courage to address a problem which so many nations, poorer than our own, have found it natural to correct?

The answers to these questions represent a reasonable test of our belief in the democracy to which we have been asked in public school to swear allegiance.

QUESTIONS FOR DISCUSSION AND WRITING

1. Quoting Socrates, Kozol argues that questions of literacy are ultimately "matters of morality" (paragraph 2) and that illiteracy is a threat to democracy. How does he support this argument?

2. Kozol opens his chapter on the cost of illiteracy with the warning on a can of Drāno. Why does he include the warning without further explanation about its significance to the chapter? Writing about the human cost of illiteracy, Kozol faces a dilemma that is innate to his subject and medium: One must first be literate to read his book, so those he wants to help have no access to his written message. To what extent does his medium limit the effectiveness of his message?

3. Kozol repeats the same phrase ("Illiterates cannot") to introduce his topic sentences. What is the effect of this repetition? What could be some of the advantages and risks for Kozol in using this rhetorical design? Why does he choose the negative pattern for the repeated opening phrase?

4. Kozol's argument is true for people who have to live in a civilization based on the power of the written word. Yet it is possible to challenge Kozol and perhaps ourselves from a different perspective. Drawing on Henry David Thoreau (p. 594), Leslie Marmon Silko (p. 39), and Richard Rodriguez (p. 275), imagine that you are a member of an ancient yet highly advanced oral civilization, and write an essay with a title such as "The Human Cost of a Literate Society."

5. In the years before informed consent guidelines were adopted (see Deborah Franklin, p. 260, and the Guidelines for Informed Consent, p. 262), people such as those characterized in Kozol's "The Human Cost of an Illiterate Society" were often used as subjects in medical research projects—without their consent, and sometimes with notorious results. Examine the critiques of such practices (see, for instance, commentary on the Tuskegee Syphilis Study, 1932–72; or Rebecca Skloot's *The Immortal Life of Henrietta Lacks*, 2010) from medical, ethical, legal, and political perspectives. Report your findings.

DEBORAH FRANKLIN

"Informed Consent"—What Information? What Consent?

Deborah Franklin is a journalist, based in San Francisco, whose work focuses on sci-ence and medicine. She has published regularly in Health *and in* Fortune. *In this article, which originally appeared in the* New York Times *(January 24, 2006), she defines "informed consent" and demonstrates why signing a consent form should be a thoughtful process in which the signer feels free to ask questions—and get good answers—rather that being an automatic act.*

The guidelines provided by the United States Government and the American Psychological Association in "Tips on Informed Consent" provide rational, sensible, ethical procedures for researchers to follow in preparing informed consent forms. We, as research subjects—or medical patients—could use these tips to make certain that we understand the purpose of the research, what we're being asked to do, what the procedures will be, what the potential risks are, and how the information will be used. Our very lives could depend on such vigilance.

Anybody up for a spinal tap? How about a needle through your ribs to siphon fluid from around your lungs?

Patients in hospitals and clinics face these sorts of invasive and somewhat risky but potentially lifesaving procedures every day, and in each case, a doctor must decide how much to tell a patient beforehand about the pros, cons and alternatives.

This disclosure is legally known as informed consent for the test or treatment and, except for emergencies, it ideally starts with a candid, unhurried conversa-tion between doctor and patient and ends in a shared decision. Unfortunately, according to researchers who have been tracking the ways the process unravels, that sort of helpful discussion is too often replaced with a clipboard of legalese and a pen.

"Some people act as if informed consent is a piece of paper with somebody's name on it. But that's just the last step," said Dr. Constantine Manthous, a pul-monary and critical care specialist who teaches Yale medical students and treats patients in the intensive care unit at Bridgeport Hospital in Bridgeport, Conn.

"Getting truly informed consent means you have explained what the proce-   5 dure is, and the risks, benefits and alternatives," Dr. Manthous said. "Then you ask the patient to replay it: 'Could you tell me in your own words so that I can make sure you've got it?' Only then should you be giving them a piece of paper to sign."

Dr. Dean Schillinger, a health literacy specialist at the University of Califor-nia, San Francisco, urges doctors to take the discussion a step further. "You want to say something like, 'I don't know much about your particular concerns, but what keeps you up at night about this procedure?'" he said, adding, "That's when you'll start to hear the worries about sexual dysfunction and the like."

Dr. Clarence Braddock III, an internist and bioethicist at Stanford who is also looking for ways to improve the process, says it doesn't help that the language of the written permission slips is usually either too broad or amounts to a lawyer-driven list of everything that could possibly go wrong.

In practice, the relative risks and benefits can be very different for each patient depending on age, health and other factors. These differences can readily be spelled out in a conversation, but not in a one-size-fits-all form, Dr. Braddock said.

Sometimes, the consent form sends a patient running. Several years ago, when Cécile Lelièvre, an information technology specialist in San Francisco, needed minor surgery, a doctor told her that he could perform the repair in his office but that he would be better able to control her pain in the local hospital clinic. "That sounded good to me," Ms. Lelièvre said. "I certainly didn't want to hurt. He didn't say more about the anesthesia, and I didn't ask."

But when she showed up in the clinic on the day of the procedure, among 10 the several pages of fine print the receptionist handed her to read and sign was a consent to a type of conscious anesthesia commonly known as an epidural. All the common and remote risks that an epidural entails were listed—from temporary nausea and severe headache to persistent nerve damage and cardiac arrest—without any specifics about how rarely such complications occur.

"If the doctor had mentioned the epidural ahead of time, and helped me weigh the risks, I think I would have gone with it," Ms. Lelièvre said. "But I knew somebody who'd had a bad experience with an epidural when she had her baby, and I was scared to death. I just walked away. I told them, 'I'm sorry, I'm not doing this today.'"

A few months later, suddenly in excruciating pain, Ms. Lelièvre needed emergency surgery to repair an aggravation of the same problem under general anesthesia—arguably an even riskier undertaking.

If doctors' overreliance on consent forms is bad for patients who can read well, it is a disaster for the 21 percent of adults in the United States who read at a sixth-grade level or below, and for an additional 27 percent who, according to the National Adult Literacy Survey, lack the proficiency needed to navigate the health care system easily.

Unless they pay close attention, doctors may miss the signs that a patient is a poor reader, said Toni Cordell, a literacy advocate who graduated from high school reading at a fifth-grade level. "We're often ashamed, and we get really good at hiding it," she said.

At the University of Michigan, Dr. Alan Tait has been working with col- 15 leagues in the department of anesthesiology to develop an improved consent form aimed at parents with low literacy skills whose children are facing surgery.

"Using simpler, friendlier language is just the first step," Dr. Tait said. The form in one experimental survey of 305 parents was vastly preferred by those who read well in addition to those with low literacy skills. It also used a larger typeface, shorter paragraphs, illustrations and bulleted points to help clarify the message.

Elsewhere, health literacy specialists are working on audio or video consent forms—interactive audiotapes or DVD's that can be navigated at a patient's own pace via a telephone keypad, a touch-screen kiosk or an inexpensive DVD player.

Most rely on live-action vignettes and colorful images instead of dense blocks of text to explain complicated concepts like the risks and benefits of different types of blood pressure medicines or asthma inhalers or the ins and outs of glucose monitors used for diabetes.

The new forms, aids and devices may eventually supplement or even replace some existing forms. But none can or should be expected to replace the bond of trust between doctor and patient that is crucial to good care and is forged only during the give and take of a good conversation.

QUESTIONS FOR DISCUSSION AND WRITING

1. Consider your most recent experiences with "informed consent" forms. Did you read them? Understand them? Sign them in haste, or after delibration? What do you believe will be done as a consequence of your "informed consent"? Were you really informed? Why or why not?

2. According to Franklin, who should bear the responsibility for providing appropriate information to the patient?

3. Look up your college or university's ethical guidelines for informed consent for research projects—required by the federal government for all federally funded research involving human subjects. What are they? Where can you find them? What compliance measures does your school use to ensure that these guidelines are followed?

SOCIAL PSYCHOLOGY NETWORK

Tips on Informed Consent

Included here are guidelines for informed consent from socialpsychology.org. One of the most important ethical rules governing research on humans is that participants must give their informed consent before taking part in a study.

UNITED STATES GOVERNMENT GUIDELINES

According to the U.S. Office for Human Research Protections (OHRP), the Code of Federal Regulations (CFR) requires that certain information be provided to research subjects before they participate in a study, including:

- A statement that the study involves research, an explanation of the purposes of the research and the expected duration of the subject's participation, a description of the procedures to be followed, and identification of any procedures which are experimental

- A description of any reasonably foreseeable risks or discomforts to the subject
- A description of any benefits to the subject or to others which may reasonably be expected from the research
- A disclosure of appropriate alternative procedures or courses of treatment, if any, that might be advantageous to the subject
- A statement describing the extent, if any, to which confidentiality of records identifying the subject will be maintained
- For research involving more than minimal risk, an explanation as to whether there are any treatments or compensation if injury occurs and, if so, what they consist of, or where further information may be obtained (Note: A risk is considered "minimal" when the probability and magnitude of harm or discomfort anticipated in the proposed research are not greater, in and of themselves, than those ordinarily encountered in daily life or during the performance of routine physical or psychological examinations or tests)
- An explanation of whom to contact for answers to pertinent questions about the research and research subjects' rights, and whom to contact in the event of a research-related injury to the subject
- A statement that participation is voluntary, refusal to participate will involve no penalty or loss of benefits to which the subject is otherwise entitled, and the subject may discontinue participation at any time without penalty or loss of benefits to which the subject is otherwise entitled

Note: It is essential that consent forms be written in plain language that research subjects can understand. In addition, the consent form should not contain any exculpatory language. That is, subjects should not be asked to waive (or appear to waive) any of their legal rights, nor should they be asked to release the investigator, sponsor, or institution (or its agents) from liability for negligence.

AMERICAN PSYCHOLOGICAL ASSOCIATION GUIDELINES

According to Sections 3.10, 8.02, and 8.04 of the American Psychological Association's "Ethical Principles of Psychologists and Code of Conduct," there are several essential elements of informed consent. These elements include telling participants clearly about:

1. The purpose of the research, expected duration, and procedures;
2. Their right to decline to participate and to withdraw from the research once participation has begun;
3. The foreseeable consequences of declining or withdrawing;
4. Reasonably foreseeable factors that may be expected to influence their willingness to participate such as potential risks, discomfort, or adverse effects;
5. Any prospective research benefits;
6. Limits of confidentiality;
7. Incentives for participation; and
8. Whom to contact for questions about the research and research participants' rights.

Informed consent also provides an opportunity for prospective participants to ask questions and receive answers.

In addition, the following guidelines apply to special populations:

- When psychologists conduct research with clients/patients, students, or subordinates as participants, psychologists take steps to protect the prospective participants from adverse consequences of declining or withdrawing from participation.
- When research participation is a course requirement or an opportunity for extra credit, the prospective participant is given the choice of equitable alternative activities.
- For persons who are legally incapable of giving informed consent, psychologists nevertheless (1) provide an appropriate explanation, (2) seek the individual's assent, (3) consider such persons' preferences and best interests, and (4) obtain appropriate permission from a legally authorized person, if such substitute consent is permitted or required by law.

ADDITIONAL SPN GUIDELINES FOR WEB-BASED STUDIES

In the case of web-based studies that have a link in Social Psychology Network, informed consent can be "documented" by requiring participants to click on a link or image that (1) indicates acceptance of the consent form, and (2) advances participants to an online study web page that is otherwise inaccesible to visitors. The consent form should also clearly identify the institutional review board that approved the study (e.g., the Wesleyan University Institutional Review Board), state the name and email address of the principal investigator (or faculty supervisor if the study is a student project), and include information on who participants can contact if they wish to bring a complaint or get further information (e.g., the name and telephone number of a departmental chairperson, Institutional Review Board, or Ethics Committee).

In addition, studies linked in Social Psychology Network should not exceed minimal risk (i.e., the level of risk found in daily life) or involve deception, and consent forms should inform participants that responses transmitted over the World Wide Web may not be secure (unless the study is using a secure server with https rather than http).

QUESTIONS FOR DISCUSSION AND WRITING

1. On what points do the U. S. Government and American Psychological Association guidelines for informed consent agree? Are there any significant points of disagreement? Are Franklin's implied recommendations in "'Informed Consent'—What Information? What Consent?" (p. 260) in agreement with the guidelines provided by the U. S. Government and the APA?

2. Have you ever been a subject in a research study? Were the guidelines printed here or comparable guidelines used in the research in which you participated? How could you tell?

DAVE LEONHARDT

The College Dropout Boom

Dave Leonhardt grew up in New York and graduated from Yale in 1994 with a B.S. in applied mathematics. After writing for Business Week *and the* Washington Post, *in 2000 he began writing for the* New York Times, *where he publishes a weekly column. In addition, he writes for* Economic Scene *and the Economix blog. "The College Dropout Boom" was originally published in the* New York Times *on May 24, 2005. Here Leonhardt uses the case history of Andy Blevins of Chilhowie, Virginia, to illustrate his sobering analysis of the following information: "Many people [who drop out of college] plan to return to get their degrees, even if few actually do. Almost one in three Americans in their mid-20's now fall into this group, up from one in five in the late 1960's. . . . Most come from poor and working-class families."*

In fact, Andy Blevins defied Leonhardt's prediction. Inspired in part by Leonhardt's interview process, which took place over six months before the article was published, Blevins enrolled in Virginia Highlands Community College, where he received an associate's degree before completing a bachelor's in education at Virginia Intermont College in May 2008, working full-time while taking sixteen credit hours each semester. "I was so busy there wasn't much time for fun, but once I went back I loved it," he said in a phone interview on February 17, 2010. He now teaches full-time in a middle school and coaches basketball, juggling child care with his wife, who also returned to college for a degree in physical therapy. "I have a job where I enjoy going to work," he says. He plans to earn a master's degree.

One of the biggest decisions Andy Blevins has ever made, and one of the few he now regrets, never seemed like much of a decision at all. It just felt like the natural thing to do.

In the summer of 1995, he was moving boxes of soup cans, paper towels and dog food across the floor of a supermarket warehouse, one of the biggest buildings here in southwest Virginia. The heat was brutal. The job had sounded impossible when he arrived fresh off his first year of college, looking to make some summer money, still a skinny teenager with sandy blond hair and a narrow, freckled face.

But hard work done well was something he understood, even if he was the first college boy in his family. Soon he was making bonuses on top of his $6.75 an hour, more money than either of his parents made. His girlfriend was around, and so were his hometown buddies. Andy acted more outgoing with them, more relaxed. People in Chilhowie noticed that.

It was just about the perfect summer. So the thought crossed his mind: maybe it did not have to end. Maybe he would take a break from college and keep working. He had been getting C's and D's, and college never felt like home, anyway.

"I enjoyed working hard, getting the job done, getting a paycheck," Mr.   5
Blevins recalled. "I just knew I didn't want to quit."

So he quit college instead, and with that, Andy Blevins joined one of the largest and fastest-growing groups of young adults in America. He became a college dropout, though nongraduate may be the more precise term.

Many people like him plan to return to get their degrees, even if few actually do. Almost one in three Americans in their mid-20's now fall into this group, up from one in five in the late 1960's, when the Census Bureau began keeping such data. Most come from poor and working-class families.

The phenomenon has been largely overlooked in the glare of positive news about the country's gains in education. Going to college has become the norm throughout most of the United States, even in many places where college was once considered an exotic destination—places like Chilhowie (pronounced chill-HOW-ee), an Appalachian hamlet with a simple brick downtown. At elite universities, classrooms are filled with women, blacks, Jews and Latinos, groups largely excluded two generations ago. The American system of higher learning seems to have become a great equalizer.

In fact, though, colleges have come to reinforce many of the advantages of birth. On campuses that enroll poorer students, graduation rates are often low. And at institutions where nearly everyone graduates—small colleges like Colgate, major state institutions like the University of Colorado and elite private universities like Stanford—more students today come from the top of the nation's income ladder than they did two decades ago.

Only 41 percent of low-income students entering a four-year college man-   10
aged to graduate within five years, the Department of Education found in a study last year, but 66 percent of high-income students did. That gap had grown over recent years. "We need to recognize that the most serious domestic problem in the United States today is the widening gap between the children of the rich and the children of the poor," Lawrence H. Summers, the president of Harvard, said last year when announcing that Harvard would give full scholarships to all its lowest-income students. "And education is the most powerful weapon we have to address that problem."

There is certainly much to celebrate about higher education today. Many more students from all classes are getting four-year degrees and reaping their benefits. But those broad gains mask the fact that poor and working-class students have nevertheless been falling behind; for them, not having a degree remains the norm.

That loss of ground is all the more significant because a college education matters much more now than it once did. A bachelor's degree, not a year or two of courses, tends to determine a person's place in today's globalized, computerized economy. College graduates have received steady pay increases over the past two decades, while the pay of everyone else has risen little more than the rate of inflation.

As a result, despite one of the great education explosions in modern history, economic mobility — moving from one income group to another over the course of a lifetime — has stopped rising, researchers say. Some recent studies suggest that it has declined over the last generation.

Put another way, children seem to be following the paths of their parents more than they once did. Grades and test scores, rather than privilege, determine success today, but that success is largely being passed down from one generation to the next. A nation that believes that everyone should have a fair shake finds itself with a kind of inherited meritocracy.

In this system, the students at the best colleges may be diverse — male and female and of various colors, religions and hometowns — but they tend to share an upper-middle-class upbringing. An old joke that Harvard's idea of diversity is putting a rich kid from California in the same room as a rich kid from New York is truer today than ever; Harvard has more students from California than it did in years past and just as big a share of upper-income students. [15]

Students like these remain in college because they can hardly imagine doing otherwise. Their parents, understanding the importance of a bachelor's degree, spent hours reading to them, researching school districts and making it clear to them that they simply must graduate from college.

Andy Blevins says that he too knows the importance of a degree, but that he did not while growing up, and not even in his year at Radford University, 66 miles up the Interstate from Chilhowie. Ten years after trading college for the warehouse, Mr. Blevins, 29, spends his days at the same supermarket company. He has worked his way up to produce buyer, earning $35,000 a year with health benefits and a 401(k) plan. He is on a path typical for someone who attended college without getting a four-year degree. Men in their early 40's in this category made an average of $42,000 in 2000. Those with a four-year degree made $65,000.

Still boyish-looking but no longer rail thin, Mr. Blevins says he has many reasons to be happy. He lives with his wife, Karla, and their year-old son, Lucas, in a small blue-and-yellow house at the end of a cul-de-sac in the middle of a stunningly picturesque Appalachian valley. He plays golf with some of the same friends who made him want to stay around Chilhowie.

But he does think about what might have been, about what he could be doing if he had the degree. As it is, he always feels as if he is on thin ice. Were he to lose his job, he says, everything could slip away with it. What kind of job could a guy without a college degree get? One night, while talking to his wife about his life, he used the word "trapped."

"Looking back, I wish I had gotten that degree," Mr. Blevins said in his soft- [20] spoken lilt. "Four years seemed like a thousand years then. But I wish I would have just put in my four years."

THE BARRIERS

Why so many low-income students fall from the college ranks is a question without a simple answer. Many high schools do a poor job of preparing teenagers for college. Many of the colleges where lower-income students tend to enroll have limited resources and offer a narrow range of majors, leaving some students disenchanted and unwilling to continue.

Then there is the cost. Tuition bills scare some students from even applying and leave others with years of debt. To Mr. Blevins, like many other students of limited means, every week of going to classes seemed like another week of losing money—money that might have been made at a job.

"The system makes a false promise to students," said John T. Casteen III, the president of the University of Virginia, himself the son of a Virginia shipyard worker.

Colleges, Mr. Casteen said, present themselves as meritocracies in which academic ability and hard work are always rewarded. In fact, he said, many working-class students face obstacles they cannot overcome on their own.

For much of his 15 years as Virginia's president, Mr. Casteen has focused on   25 raising money and expanding the university, the most prestigious in the state. In the meantime, students with backgrounds like his have become ever scarcer on campus. The university's genteel nickname, the Cavaliers, and its aristocratic sword-crossed coat of arms seem appropriate today. No flagship state university has a smaller proportion of low-income students than Virginia. Just 8 percent of undergraduates last year came from families in the bottom half of the income distribution, down from 11 percent a decade ago.

That change sneaked up on him, Mr. Casteen said, and he has spent a good part of the last year trying to prevent it from becoming part of his legacy. Starting with next fall's freshman class, the university will charge no tuition and require no loans for students whose parents make less than twice the poverty level, or about $37,700 a year for a family of four. The university has also increased financial aid to middle-income students.

To Mr. Casteen, these are steps to remove what he describes as "artificial barriers" to a college education placed in the way of otherwise deserving students. Doing so "is a fundamental obligation of a free culture," he said.

But the deterrents to a degree can also be homegrown. Many low-income teenagers know few people who have made it through college. A majority of the nongraduates are young men, and some come from towns where the factory work ethic, to get working as soon as possible, remains strong, even if the factories themselves are vanishing. Whatever the reasons, college just does not feel normal.

"You get there and you start to struggle," said Leanna Blevins, Andy's older sister, who did get a bachelor's degree and then went on to earn a Ph.D. at Virginia studying the college experiences of poor students. "And at home your parents are trying to be supportive and say, 'Well, if you're not happy, if it's not right for you, come back home. It's O.K.' And they think they're doing the right thing. But they don't know that maybe what the student needs is to hear them say, 'Stick it out just one semester. You can do it. Just stay there. Come home on the weekend, but stick it out.'"

Today, Ms. Blevins, petite and high-energy, is helping to start a new college 30 a few hours' drive from Chilhowie for low-income students. Her brother said he had daydreamed about attending it and had talked to her about how he might return to college.

For her part, Ms. Blevins says, she has daydreamed about having a life that would seem as natural as her brother's, a life in which she would not feel like an outsider in her hometown. Once, when a high-school teacher asked students to list their goals for the next decade, Ms. Blevins wrote, "having a college degree" and "not being married."

"I think my family probably thinks I'm liberal," Ms. Blevins, who is now married, said with a laugh, "that I've just been educated too much and I'm gettin' above my raisin'."

Her brother said that he just wanted more control over his life, not a new one. At a time when many people complain of scattered lives, Mr. Blevins can stand in one spot—his church parking lot, next to a graveyard—and take in much of his world. "That's my parents' house," he said one day, pointing to a sliver of roof visible over a hill. "That's my uncle's trailer. My grandfather is buried here. I'll probably be buried here."

TAKING CLASS INTO ACCOUNT

Opening up colleges to new kinds of students has generally meant one thing over the last generation: affirmative action. Intended to right the wrongs of years of exclusion, the programs have swelled the number of women, blacks and Latinos on campuses. But affirmative action was never supposed to address broad economic inequities, just the ones that stem from specific kinds of discrimination.

That is now beginning to change. Like Virginia, a handful of other colleges 35 are not only increasing financial aid but also promising to give weight to economic class in granting admissions. They say they want to make an effort to admit more low-income students, just as they now do for minorities and children of alumni.

"The great colleges and universities were designed to provide for mobility, to seek out talent," said Anthony W. Marx, president of Amherst College. "If we are blind to the educational disadvantages associated with need, we will simply replicate these disadvantages while appearing to make decisions based on merit."

With several populous states having already banned race-based preferences and the United States Supreme Court suggesting that it may outlaw such programs in a couple of decades, the future of affirmative action may well revolve around economics. Polls consistently show that programs based on class backgrounds have wider support than those based on race.

The explosion in the number of nongraduates has also begun to get the attention of policy makers. This year, New York became one of a small group of states to tie college financing more closely to graduation rates, rewarding colleges more for moving students along than for simply admitting them. Nowhere is the stratification of education more vivid than here in Virginia, where Thomas Jefferson once tried, and failed, to set up the nation's first public high schools. At a modest high school in the Tidewater city of Portsmouth, not far from Mr. Casteen's boyhood home, a guidance office wall filled with college pennants does not include one from rarefied Virginia. The colleges whose pennants are up — Old Dominion University and others that seem in the realm of the possible — have far lower graduation rates.

Across the country, the upper middle class so dominates elite universities that high-income students, on average, actually get slightly more financial aid from colleges than low-income students do. These elite colleges are so expensive that even many high-income students receive large grants. In the early 1990's, by contrast, poorer students got 50 percent more aid on average than the wealthier ones, according to the College Board, the organization that runs the SAT entrance exams.

At the other end of the spectrum are community colleges, the two-year institutions that are intended to be feeders for four-year colleges. In nearly every one are tales of academic success against tremendous odds: a battered wife or a combat veteran or a laid-off worker on the way to a better life. But over all, community colleges tend to be places where dreams are put on hold. 40

Most people who enroll say they plan to get a four-year degree eventually; few actually do. Full-time jobs, commutes and children or parents who need care often get in the way. One recent national survey found that about 75 percent of students enrolling in community colleges said they hoped to transfer to a four-year institution. But only 17 percent of those who had entered in the mid-1990's made the switch within five years, according to a separate study. The rest were out working or still studying toward the two-year degree.

"We here in Virginia do a good job of getting them in," said Glenn Dubois, chancellor of the Virginia Community College System and himself a community college graduate. "We have to get better in getting them out."

"I WEAR A TIE EVERY DAY"

College degree or not, Mr. Blevins has the kind of life that many Americans say they aspire to. He fills it with family, friends, church and a five-handicap golf game. He does not sit in traffic commuting to an office park. He does not talk wistfully of a relocated brother or best friend he sees only twice a year. He does not worry about who will care for his son while he works and his wife attends community college to become a physical therapist. His grandparents down the street watch Lucas, just as they took care of Andy and his two sisters when they were children. When Mr. Blevins comes home from work, it is his turn to play with Lucas, tossing him into the air and rolling around on the floor with him and a stuffed elephant.

Mr. Blevins also sings in a quartet called the Gospel Gentlemen. One member is his brother-in-law; another lives on Mr. Blevins's street. In the long white van the group owns, they wend their way along mountain roads on their way to singing dates at local church functions, sometimes harmonizing, sometimes ribbing one another or talking about where to buy golf equipment.

Inside the churches, the other singers often talk to the audience between 45 songs, about God or a grandmother or what a song means to them. Mr. Blevins rarely does, but his shyness fades once he is back in the van with his friends.

At the warehouse, he is usually the first to arrive, around 6:30 in the morning. The grandson of a coal miner, he takes pride, he says, in having moved up to become a supermarket buyer. He decides which bananas, grapes, onions and potatoes the company will sell and makes sure that there are always enough. Most people with his job have graduated from college.

"I'm pretty fortunate to not have a degree but have a job where I wear a tie every day," he said.

He worries about how long it will last, though, mindful of what happened to his father, Dwight, a decade ago. A high school graduate, Dwight Blevins was laid off from his own warehouse job and ended up with another one that paid less and offered a smaller pension.

"A lot of places, they're not looking that you're trained in something," Andy Blevins said one evening, sitting on his back porch. "They just want you to have a degree."

Figuring out how to get one is the core quandary facing the nation's col- 50 lege nongraduates. Many seem to want one. In a *New York Times* poll, 43 percent of them called it essential to success, while 42 percent of college graduates and 32 percent of high-school dropouts did. This in itself is a change from the days when "college boy" was an insult in many working-class neighborhoods. But once students take a break — the phrase that many use instead of drop out — the ideal can quickly give way to reality. Family and work can make a return to school seem even harder than finishing it in the first place.

After dropping out of Radford, Andy Blevins enrolled part-time in a community college, trying to juggle work and studies. He lasted a year. From time to time in the decade since, he has thought about giving it another try. But then he has wondered if that would be crazy. He works every third Saturday, and his phone rings on Sundays when there is a problem with the supply of potatoes or apples. "It never ends," he said. "There's a never a lull."

To spend more time with Lucas, Mr. Blevins has already cut back on his singing. If he took night classes, he said, when would he ever see his little boy? Anyway, he said, it would take years to get a degree part-time. To him, it is a tug of war between living in the present and sacrificing for the future.

FEW BREAKS FOR THE NEEDY

The college admissions system often seems ruthlessly meritocratic. Yes, children of alumni still have an advantage. But many other pillars of the old system — the polite rejections of women or blacks, the spots reserved for graduates of Choate and Exeter — have crumbled.

This was the meritocracy Mr. Casteen described when he greeted the parents of freshman in a University of Virginia lecture hall late last summer. Hailing from all 50 states and 52 foreign countries, the students were more intelligent and better prepared than he and his classmates had been, he told the parents in his quiet, deep voice. The class included 17 students with a perfect SAT score.

If anything, children of privilege think that the system has moved so far from   55
its old-boy history that they are now at a disadvantage when they apply, because colleges are trying to diversify their student rolls. To get into a good college, the sons and daughters of the upper middle class often talk of needing a higher SAT score than, say, an applicant who grew up on a farm, in a ghetto or in a factory town. Some state legislators from Northern Virginia's affluent suburbs have argued that this is a form of geographic discrimination and have quixotically proposed bills to outlaw it.

But the conventional wisdom is not quite right. The elite colleges have not been giving much of a break to the low-income students who apply. When William G. Bowen, a former president of Princeton, looked at admissions records recently, he found that if test scores were equal a low-income student had no better chance than a high-income one of getting into a group of 19 colleges, including Harvard, Yale, Princeton, Williams and Virginia. Athletes, legacy applicants and minority students all got in with lower scores on average. Poorer students did not.

The findings befuddled many administrators, who insist that admissions officers have tried to give poorer applicants a leg up. To emphasize the point, Virginia announced this spring that it was changing its admissions policy from "need blind"—a term long used to assure applicants that they would not be punished for seeking financial aid—to "need conscious." Administrators at Amherst and Harvard have also recently said that they would redouble their efforts to take into account the obstacles students have overcome.

"The same score reflects more ability when you come from a less fortunate background," Mr. Summers, the president of Harvard, said. "You haven't had a chance to take the test-prep course. You went to a school that didn't do as good a job coaching you for the test. You came from a home without the same opportunities for learning."

But it is probably not a coincidence that elite colleges have not yet turned this sentiment into action. Admitting large numbers of low-income students could bring clear complications. Too many in a freshman class would probably lower the college's average SAT score, thereby damaging its ranking by *U.S. News & World Report*, a leading arbiter of academic prestige. Some colleges, like Emory University in Atlanta, have climbed fast in the rankings over precisely the same period in which their percentage of low-income students has tumbled. The math is simple: when a college goes looking for applicants with high SAT scores, it is far more likely to find them among well-off teenagers.

More spots for low-income applicants might also mean fewer for the   60
children of alumni, who make up the fund-raising base for universities. More

generous financial aid policies will probably lead to higher tuition for those students who can afford the list price. Higher tuition, lower ranking, tougher admission requirements: they do not make for an easy marketing pitch to alumni
clubs around the country. But Mr. Casteen and his colleagues are going ahead,
saying the pendulum has swung too far in one direction.

That was the mission of John Blackburn, Virginia's easy-going admissions
dean, when he rented a car and took to the road recently. Mr. Blackburn thought
of the trip as a reprise of the drives Mr. Casteen took 25 years earlier, when he was
the admissions dean, traveling to churches and community centers to persuade
black parents that the university was finally interested in their children.

One Monday night, Mr. Blackburn came to Big Stone Gap, in a mostly poor
corner of the state not far from Andy Blevins's town. A community college there
was holding a college fair, and Mr. Blackburn set up a table in a hallway, draping
it with the University of Virginia's blue and orange flag.

As students came by, Mr. Blackburn would explain Virginia's new admissions
and financial aid policies. But he soon realized that the Virginia name might have
been scaring off the very people his pitch was intended for. Most of the students
who did approach the table showed little interest in the financial aid and expressed little need for it. One man walked up to Mr. Blackburn and introduced
his son as an aspiring doctor. The father was an ophthalmologist. Other doctors
came by, too. So did some lawyers.

"You can't just raise the UVa flag," Mr. Blackburn said, packing up his materials at the end of the night, "and expect a lot of low-income kids to come out."

When the applications started arriving in his office this spring, there seemed   65
to be no increase in those from low-income students. So Mr. Blackburn extended
the deadline two weeks for everybody, and his colleagues also helped some applicants with the maze of financial aid forms. Of 3,100 incoming freshmen, it now
seems that about 180 will qualify for the new financial aid program, up from 130
who would have done so last year. It is not a huge number, but Virginia administrators call it a start.

A BIG DECISION

On a still-dark February morning, with the winter's heaviest snowfall on the
ground, Andy Blevins scraped off his Jeep and began his daily drive to the supermarket warehouse. As he passed the home of Mike Nash, his neighbor and fellow
gospel singer, he noticed that the car was still in the driveway. For Mr. Nash, a
school counselor and the only college graduate in the singing group, this was a
snow day.

Mr. Blevins later sat down with his calendar and counted to 280: the number
of days he had worked last year. Two hundred and eighty days—six days a week
most of the time—without ever really knowing what the future would hold.

"I just realized I'm going to have to do something about this," he said,
"because it's never going to end."

In the weeks afterward, his daydreaming about college and his conversations about it with his sister Leanna turned into serious research. He requested his transcripts from Radford and from Virginia Highlands Community College and figured out that he had about a year's worth of credits. He also talked to Leanna about how he could become an elementary school teacher. He always felt that he could relate to children, he said. The job would take up 180 days, not 280. Teachers do not usually get laid off or lose their pensions or have to take a big pay cut to find new work.

So the decision was made. On May 31, Andy Blevins says, he will return to 70 Virginia Highlands, taking classes at night; the Gospel Gentlemen are no longer booking performances. After a year, he plans to take classes by video and on the Web that are offered at the community college but run by Old Dominion, a Norfolk, Va., university with a big group of working-class students.

"I don't like classes, but I've gotten so motivated to go back to school," Mr. Blevins said. "I don't want to, but, then again, I do."

He thinks he can get his bachelor's degree in three years. If he gets it at all, he will have defied the odds.

QUESTIONS FOR DISCUSSION AND WRITING

1. Identify the essay's main points that explain the meaning of Leonhardt's title, "The College Dropout Boom." Are you convinced that "'the most serious domestic problem in the United States today is the widening gap between the children of the rich and the children of the poor'" (paragraph 10)? Why or why not?

2. Compare and contrast the educational and career paths of Andy Blevins, described in the article as a high school graduate, and his sister Leanna, who earned a Ph.D. from the University of Virginia and is currently the associate director of the New College Institute (Martinsville, Virginia), dedicated to helping low-income students from southern Virginia find and complete college degree programs (check their Web site). What advice might Leanna have offered her brother? How does the biographical update influence your answer?

3. What does Leonhardt mean by "the future of affirmative action may well revolve around economics" (paragraph 37)? What was the major focus of affirmative action in the past (before, say, 2000; paragraph 34)? Why has the focus changed since 2000?

4. What are the major reasons in the twenty-first century that people who start college drop out? Why are wealthier students more likely to complete college than low-income students? Interview two students from very different economic backgrounds and write an essay on your findings, drawing on your own experience, as well. Use Barbara Ehrenreich's "Serving in Florida" (p. 206), Malcolm Gladwell's "The Physical Genius" (p. 213), and Matthew B. Crawford's "The Case for Working with Your Hands" (p. 225), as desired, to reinforce your points.

5. Leonhardt's essay assumes that having a college degree provides benefits that are not likely without one. Identify and explain some of these alleged advantages, preferably with relation to your chosen profession (Web sites can provide information about educational criteria, pay, and job opportunities). Yet Matthew Crawford makes an excellent "The Case for Working with Your Hands" (p. 225) and prior to completing a degree, Andy Blevins himself had a job and a life that he enjoyed (paragraphs 43–52). Weigh the evidence, pro and con, and convince an audience of skeptics of the merits of your position.

RICHARD RODRIGUEZ

Aria: A Memoir of a Bilingual Childhood

Richard Rodriguez, born in San Francisco in 1944, is the author of Days of Obligation: An Argument with My Mexican Father *(1993) and* Brown: An Erotic History of the Americas *(2002). His memoir,* Hunger of Memory: The Education of Richard Rodriguez *(1982), is a moving and provocative account of growing up bilingual and bicultural as the son of Mexican immigrants in a largely white neighborhood in Sacramento. The book became a focal point in the 1980s' national debate about bilingual education, a debate that continues into the twenty-first century with various "English-only" initiatives.*

In his memoir's opening chapter, "Aria," Rodriguez reflects on the difficult transition from his private, Spanish-speaking world to the public, English-speaking one. Although the English-only classroom brought estrangement from his family and heritage, Rodriguez nevertheless argues in Hunger of Memory *against both bilingual education and affirmative action—programs he acknowledges having benefited from as a scholarship student at both Stanford (B.A., 1967) and Columbia (M.A., 1969) and as a doctoral student in English at the University of California at Berkeley.*

How does Rodriguez as a memoirist weigh his individuality against the public dimensions of his experience? How he defines his individual "self" within cultural traditions, social structures, and political agendas are issues addressed in the Contexts following "Aria."

I remember, to start with, that day in Sacramento, in a California now nearly thirty years past, when I first entered a classroom—able to understand about fifty stray English words. The third of four children, I had been preceded by my older brother and sister to a neighborhood Roman Catholic school. But neither of them had revealed very much about their classroom experiences. They left each morning and returned each afternoon, always together, speaking Spanish as they climbed the five steps to the porch. And their mysterious books, wrapped in brown shopping-bag paper, remained on the table next to the door, closed firmly behind them.

An accident of geography sent me to a school where all my classmates were white and many were the children of doctors and lawyers and business executives. On that first day of school, my classmates must certainly have been uneasy to find themselves apart from their families, in the first institution of their lives. But I was astonished. I was fated to be the "problem student" in class.

The nun said, in a friendly but oddly impersonal voice: "Boys and girls, this is Richard Rodriguez." (I heard her sound it out: *Rich-heard Road-ree-guess.*) It was the first time I had heard anyone say my name in English. "Richard," the nun repeated more slowly, writing my name down in her book. Quickly I turned to see my mother's face dissolve in a watery blur behind the pebbled-glass door.

Now, many years later, I hear of something called "bilingual education"—a scheme proposed in the late 1960s by Hispanic-American social activists, later endorsed by a congressional vote. It is a program that seeks to permit non-English-speaking children (many from lower-class homes) to use their "family language" as the language of school. Such, at least, is the aim its supporters announce. I hear them, and am forced to say no: It is not possible for a child, any child, ever to use his family's language in school. Not to understand this is to misunderstand the public uses of schooling and to trivialize the nature of intimate life.

Memory teaches me what I know of these matters. The boy reminds the 5 adult. I was a bilingual child, but of a certain kind: "socially disadvantaged," the son of working-class parents, both Mexican immigrants.

In the early years of my boyhood, my parents coped very well in America. My father had steady work. My mother managed at home. They were nobody's victims. When we moved to a house many blocks from the Mexican-American section of town, they were not intimidated by those two or three neighbors who initially tried to make us unwelcome. ("Keep your brats away from my sidewalk!") But despite all they achieved, or perhaps because they had so much to achieve, they lacked any deep feeling of ease, of belonging in public. They regarded the people at work or in crowds as being very distant from us. Those were the others, *los gringos.* That term was interchangeable in their speech with another, even more telling: *los americanos.*

I grew up in a house where the only regular guests were my relations. On a certain day, enormous families of relatives would visit us, and there would be so many people that the noise and the bodies would spill out to the backyard and onto the front porch. Then for weeks no one would come. (If the doorbell rang, it was usually a salesman.) Our house stood apart—gaudy yellow in a row of white bungalows. We were the people with the noisy dog, the people who raised chickens. We were the foreigners on the block. A few neighbors would smile and wave at us. We waved back. But until I was seven years old, I did not know the name of the old couple living next door or the names of the kids living across the street.

In public, my father and mother spoke a hesitant, accented, and not always grammatical English. And then they would have to strain, their bodies tense, to catch the sense of what was rapidly said by *los gringos.* At home, they returned to Spanish. The language of their Mexican past sounded in counterpoint to the English spoken in public. The words would come quickly, with ease. Conveyed through those sounds was the pleasing, soothing, consoling reminder that one was at home.

During those years when I was first learning to speak, my mother and father addressed me only in Spanish; in Spanish I learned to reply. By contrast, English (*inglés*) was the language I came to associate with gringos, rarely heard in the house. I learned my first words of English overhearing my parents speaking to strangers. At six years of age, I knew just enough words for my mother to trust me on errands to stores one block away—but no more.

I was then a listening child, careful to hear the very different sounds of Spanish and English. Wide-eyed with hearing, I'd listen to sounds more than to words. First, there were English (*gringo*) sounds. So many words still were unknown to me that when the butcher or the lady at the drugstore said something, exotic polysyllabic sounds would bloom in the midst of their sentences. Often the speech of people in public seemed to me very loud, booming with confidence. The man behind the counter would literally ask, "What can I do for you?" But by being so firm and clear, the sound of his voice said that he was a gringo; he belonged in public society. There were also the high, nasal notes of middle-class American speech—which I rarely am conscious of hearing today because I hear them so often, but could not stop hearing when I was a boy. Crowds at Safeway or at bus stops were noisy with the birdlike sounds of *los gringos*. I'd move away from them all—all the chirping chatter above me.

My own sounds I was unable to hear, but I knew that I spoke English poorly. My words could not extend to form complete thoughts. And the words I did speak I didn't know well enough to make distinct sounds. (Listeners would usually lower their heads to hear better what I was trying to say.) But it was one thing for *me* to speak English with difficulty; it was more troubling to hear my parents speaking in public: their high-whining vowels and guttural consonants; their sentences that got stuck with "eh" and "ah" sounds; the confused syntax; the hesitant rhythm of sounds so different from the way gringos spoke. I'd notice, moreover, that my parents' voices were softer than those of gringos we would meet.

I am tempted to say now that none of this mattered. (In adulthood I am embarrassed by childhood fears.) And, in a way, it didn't matter very much that my parents could not speak English with ease. Their linguistic difficulties had no serious consequences. My mother and father made themselves understood at the county hospital clinic and at government offices. And yet, in another way, it mattered very much. It was unsettling to hear my parents struggle with English. Hearing them, I'd grow nervous, and my clutching trust in their protection and power would be weakened.

There were many times like the night at a brightly lit gasoline station (a blaring white memory) when I stood uneasily hearing my father talk to a teenage attendant. I do not recall what they were saying, but I cannot forget the sounds my father made as he spoke. At one point his words slid together to form one long word—sounds as confused as the threads of blue and green oil in the puddle next to my shoes. His voice rushed through what he had left to say. Toward the end, he reached falsetto notes, appealing to his listener's understanding. I looked away at the lights of passing automobiles. I tried not to hear any more. But I heard only too well the attendant's reply, his calm, easy tones. Shortly afterward, headed for home, I shivered when my father put his hand on my shoulder. The very first chance that I got, I evaded his grasp and ran on ahead into the dark, skipping with feigned boyish exuberance.

But then there was Spanish: *español*, the language rarely heard away from the house; *español*, the language which seemed to me therefore a private language, my family's language. To hear its sounds was to feel myself specially recognized as one of the family, apart from *los otros*. A simple remark, an inconsequential comment could convey that assurance. My parents would say something to me and I would feel embraced by the sounds of their words. Those sounds said: *I am speaking with ease in Spanish. I am addressing you in words I never use with los gringos. I recognize you as someone special, close, like no one outside. You belong with us. In the family. Ricardo.*

At the age of six, well past the time when most middle-class children no lon- 15 ger notice the difference between sounds uttered at home and words spoken in public, I had a different experience. I lived in a world compounded of sounds. I was a child longer than most. I lived in a magical world, surrounded by sounds both pleasing and fearful. I shared with my family a language enchantingly private—different from that used in the city around us.

Just opening or closing the screen door behind me was an important experi-ence. I'd rarely leave home all alone or without feeling reluctance. Walking down the sidewalk, under the canopy of tall trees, I'd warily notice the (suddenly) silent neighborhood kids who stood warily watching me. Nervously, I'd arrive at the grocery store to hear there the sounds of the gringo, reminding me that in this so-big world I was a foreigner. But if leaving home was never routine, neither was coming back. Walking toward our house, climbing the steps from the sidewalk, in summer when the front door was open, I'd hear voices beyond the screen door talking in Spanish. For a second or two I'd stay, linger there listening. Smiling, I'd hear my mother call out, saying in Spanish, "Is that you, Richard?" Those were her words, but all the while her sounds would assure me: *You are home now. Come closer inside. With us. "Sí,"* I'd reply.

Once more inside the house, I would resume my place in the family. The sounds would grow harder to hear. Once more at home, I would grow less con-scious of them. It required, however, no more than the blurt of the doorbell to alert me all over again to listen to sounds. The house would turn instantly quiet while my mother went to the door. I'd hear her hard English sounds. I'd wait to hear her voice turn to soft-sounding Spanish, which assured me, as surely as did the clicking tongue of the lock on the door, that the stranger was gone.

Plainly it is not healthy to hear such sounds so often. It is not healthy to dis-tinguish public from private sounds so easily. I remained cloistered by sounds, timid and shy in public, too dependent on the voices at home. And yet I was a very happy child when I was at home. I remember many nights when my father would come back from work, and I'd hear him call out to my mother in Spanish, sounding relieved. In Spanish, his voice would sound the light and free notes that he never could manage in English. Some nights I'd jump up just hearing his voice. My brother and I would come running into the room where he was with our mother. Our laughing (so deep was the pleasure!) became screaming. Like others who feel the pain of public alienation, we transformed the knowledge of our public separateness into a consoling reminder of our intimacy. Excited, our voices joined in a celebration of sounds. *We are speaking now the way we never speak out in public—we are together*, the sounds told me. Some nights no one seemed willing to loosen the hold that sounds had on us. At dinner we invented new words that sounded Spanish, but made sense only to us. We pieced together new words by taking, say, an English verb and giving it Spanish endings. My mother's instructions at bedtime would be lacquered with mock-urgent tones. Or a word like *sí*, sounded in several notes, would convey added measures of feeling. Tongues lingered around the edges of words, especially fat vowels, and we happily sounded that military drum roll, the twirling roar of the Spanish *r*. Family language, my family's sounds: the voices of my parents and sisters and brother. Their voices insisting: *You belong here. We are family members. Related. Special to one another. Listen!* Voices singing and sighing, rising and straining, then surging, teeming with pleasure which burst syllables into fragments of laughter. At times it seemed there was steady quiet only when, from another room, the rustling whispers of my parents faded and I edged closer to sleep.

Supporters of bilingual education imply today that students like me miss a great deal by not being taught in their family's language. What they seem not to recognize is that, as a socially disadvantaged child, I regarded Spanish as a private language. It was a ghetto language that deepened and strengthened my feeling of public separateness. What I needed to learn in school was that I had the right, and the obligation, to speak the public language. The odd truth is that my first-grade classmates could have become bilingual, in the conventional sense of the word, more easily than I. Had they been taught early (as upper-middle-class children often are taught) a "second language" like Spanish or French, they could have regarded it simply as another public language. In my case, such bilingualism could not have been so quickly achieved. What I did not believe was that I could speak a single public language.

Without question, it would have pleased me to have heard my teachers address   20 me in Spanish when I entered the classroom. I would have felt much less afraid. I would have imagined that my instructors were somehow "related" to me; I would indeed have heard their Spanish as my family's language. I would have trusted them and responded with ease. But I would have delayed—postponed for how long?—having to learn the language of public society. I would have evaded—and for how long?—learning the great lesson of school: that I had a public identity.

Fortunately, my teachers were unsentimental about their responsibility. What they understood was that I needed to speak public English. So their voices would search me out, asking me questions. Each time I heard them I'd look up in surprise to see a nun's face frowning at me. I'd mumble, not really meaning to answer. The nun would persist. "Richard, stand up. Don't look at the floor.

Speak up. Speak to the entire class, not just to me!" But I couldn't believe English could be my language to use. (In part, I did not want to believe it.) I continued to mumble. I resisted the teacher's demands. (Did I somehow suspect that once I learned this public language my family life would be changed?) Silent, waiting for the bell to sound, I remained dazed, diffident, afraid.

Because I wrongly imagined that English was intrinsically a public language and Spanish was intrinsically private, I easily noted the difference between class-room language and the language at home. At school, words were directed to a general audience of listeners. ("Boys and girls . . .") Words were meaningfully ordered. And the point was not self-expression alone, but to make oneself understood by many others. The teacher quizzed: "Boys and girls, why do we use that word in this sentence? Could we think of a better word to use there? Would the sentence change its meaning if the words were differently arranged? Isn't there a better way of saying much the same thing?" (I couldn't say. I wouldn't try to say.)

Three months passed. Five. A half year. Unsmiling, ever watchful, my teachers noted my silence. They began to connect my behavior with the slow progress my brother and sisters were making. Until, one Saturday morning, three nuns arrived at the house to talk to our parents. Stiffly they sat on the blue living-room sofa. From the doorway of another room, spying on the visitors, I noted the incongruity, the clash of two worlds, the faces and voices of school intruding upon the familiar setting of home. I overheard one voice gently wondering, "Do your children speak only Spanish at home, Mrs. Rodriguez?" While another voice added, "That Richard especially seems so timid and shy."

That Rich-heard!

With great tact, the visitors continued, "Is it possible for you and your husband   25
to encourage your children to practice their English when they are home?" Of course my parents complied. What would they not do for their children's well-being? And how could they question the Church's authority which those women represented? In an instant they agreed to give up the language (the sounds) which had revealed and accentuated our family's closeness. The moment after the visitors left, the change was observed. "*Ahora*, speak to us only *en inglés*," my father and mother told us.

At first, it seemed a kind of game. After dinner each night, the family gathered together to practice "our" English. It was still then *inglés*, a language foreign to us, so we felt drawn to it as strangers. Laughing, we would try to define words we could not pronounce. We played with strange English sounds, often overanglicizing our pronunciations. And we filled the smiling gaps of our sentences with familiar Spanish sounds. But that was cheating, somebody shouted, and everyone laughed.

In school, meanwhile, like my brother and sisters, I was required to attend a daily tutoring session. I needed a full year of this special work. I also needed my teachers to keep my attention from straying in class by calling out, "*Rich-heard*"—their English voices slowly loosening the ties to my other name, with its three notes, *Ri-car-do*. Most of all, I needed to hear my mother and father speak to me in a moment of seriousness in "broken"—suddenly heartbreaking—English. This scene was inevitable.

One Saturday morning I entered the kitchen where my parents were talking, but I did not realize that they were talking in Spanish until, the moment they saw me, their voices changed and they began speaking English. The gringo sounds they uttered startled me. Pushed me away. In that moment of trivial misunderstanding and profound insight, I felt my throat twisted by unsounded grief. I simply turned and left the room. But I had no place to escape to where I could grieve in Spanish. My brother and sisters were speaking English in another part of the house.

Again and again in the days following, as I grew increasingly angry, I was obliged to hear my mother and father encouraging me: "Speak to us *en inglés.*" Only then did I determine to learn classroom English. Thus, sometime afterward it happened: One day in school, I raised my hand to volunteer an answer to a question. I spoke out in a loud voice and I did not think it remarkable when the entire class understood. That day I moved very far from being the disadvantaged child I had been only days earlier. Taken hold at last was the belief, the calming assurance, that I *belonged* in public.

Shortly after, I stopped hearing the high, troubling sounds of *los gringos.* A more and more confident speaker of English, I didn't listen to how strangers sounded when they talked to me. With so many English-speaking people around me, I no longer heard American accents. Conversations quickened. Listening to persons whose voices sounded eccentrically pitched, I might note their sounds for a few seconds, but then I'd concentrate on what they were saying. Now when I heard someone's tone of voice — angry or questioning or sarcastic or happy or sad — I didn't distinguish it from the words it expressed. Sound and word were thus tightly wedded. At the end of each day I was often bemused, and always relieved, to realize how "soundless," though crowded with words, my day in public had been. An eight-year-old boy, I finally came to accept what had been technically true since my birth: I was an American citizen.

But diminished by then was the special feeling of closeness at home. Gone was 30 the desperate, urgent, intense feeling of being at home among those with whom I felt intimate. Our family remained a loving family, but one greatly changed. We were no longer so close, no longer bound tightly together by the knowledge of our separateness from *los gringos.* Neither my older brother nor my sisters rushed home after school any more. Nor did I. When I arrived home, often there would be neighborhood kids in the house. Or the house would be empty of sounds.

Following the dramatic Americanization of their children, even my parents grew more publicly confident — especially my mother. First she learned the names of all the people on the block. Then she decided we needed to have a telephone in our house. My father, for his part, continued to use the word *gringo,* but it was no longer charged with bitterness or distrust. Stripped of any emotional content, the word simply became a name for those Americans not of Hispanic descent. Hearing him, sometimes, I wasn't sure if he was pronouncing the Spanish word *gringo,* or saying gringo in English.

There was a new silence at home. As we children learned more and more English, we shared fewer and fewer words with our parents. Sentences needed to be spoken slowly when one of us addressed our mother or father. Often the parent wouldn't understand. The child would need to repeat himself. Still the parent misunderstood. The young voice, frustrated, would end up saying, "Never mind"—the subject was closed. Dinners would be noisy with the clinking of knives and forks against dishes. My mother would smile softly between her remarks; my father, at the other end of the table, would chew and chew his food while he stared over the heads of his children.

My mother! My father! After English became my primary language, I no longer knew what words to use in addressing my parents. The old Spanish words (those tender accents of sound) I had earlier used—*mamá* and *papá*—I couldn't use any more. They would have been all-too-painful reminders of how much had changed in my life. On the other hand, the words I heard neighborhood kids call their parents seemed equally unsatisfactory. "Mother" and "father," "ma," "papa," "pa," "dad," "pop" (how I hated the all-American sound of that last word)—all these I felt were unsuitable terms of address for *my* parents. As a result, I never used them at home. Whenever I'd speak to my parents, I would try to get their attention by looking at them. In public conversations, I'd refer to them as my "parents" or my "mother" and "father."

My mother and father, for their part, responded differently, as their children spoke to them less. My mother grew restless, seemed troubled and anxious at the scarceness of words exchanged in the house. She would question me about my day when I came home from school. She smiled at my small talk. She pried at the edges of my sentences to get me to say something more. ("What . . . ?") She'd join conversations she overheard, but her intrusions often stopped her children's talking. By contrast, my father seemed to grow reconciled to the new quiet. Though his English somewhat improved, he tended more and more to retire into silence. At dinner he spoke very little. One night his children and even his wife helplessly giggled at his garbled English pronunciation of the Catholic "Grace Before Meals." Thereafter he made his wife recite the prayer at the start of each meal, even on formal occasions when there were guests in the house.

Hers became the public voice of the family. On official business it was she, not my father, who would usually talk to strangers on the phone or in stores. We children grew so accustomed to his silence that years later we would routinely refer to his "shyness." (My mother often tried to explain: Both of his parents died when he was eight. He was raised by an uncle who treated him as little more than a menial servant. He was never encouraged to speak. He grew up alone—a man of few words.) But I realized my father was not shy whenever I'd watch him speaking Spanish with relatives. Using Spanish, he was quickly effusive. Especially when talking with other men, his voice would spark, flicker, flare alive with varied sounds. In Spanish he expressed ideas and feelings he rarely revealed when speaking English. With firm Spanish sounds he conveyed a confidence and authority that English would never allow him.

The silence at home, however, was not simply the result of fewer words passing between parents and children. More profound for me was the silence

35

created by my inattention to sounds. At about the time I no longer bothered to listen with care to the sounds of English in public, I grew careless about listening to the sounds made by the family when they spoke. Most of the time I would hear someone speaking at home and didn't distinguish his sounds from the words people uttered in public. I didn't even pay much attention to my parents' accented and ungrammatical speech—at least not at home. Only when I was with them in public would I become alert to their accents. But even then their sounds caused me less and less concern. For I was growing increasingly confident of my own public identity.

I would have been happier about my public success had I not recalled, sometimes, what it had been like earlier, when my family conveyed its intimacy through a set of conveniently private sounds. Sometimes in public, hearing a stranger, I'd hark back to my lost past. A Mexican farm worker approached me one day downtown. He wanted directions to some place. "*Hijito*, . . . " he said. And his voice stirred old longings. Another time I was standing beside my mother in the visiting room of a Carmelite convent, before the dense screen which rendered the nuns shadowy figures. I heard several of them speaking Spanish in their busy, singsong, overlapping voices, assuring my mother that, yes, yes, we were remembered, all our family was remembered, in their prayers. Those voices echoed faraway family sounds. Another day a dark-faced old woman touched my shoulder lightly to steady herself as she boarded a bus. She murmured something to me I couldn't quite comprehend. Her Spanish voice came near, like the face of a never-before-seen relative in the instant before I was kissed. That voice, like so many of the Spanish voices I'd hear in public, recalled the golden age of my childhood.

Bilingual educators say today that children lose a degree of "individuality" by becoming assimilated into public society. (Bilingual schooling is a program popularized in the seventies, that decade when middle-class "ethnics" began to resist the process of assimilation—the "American melting pot.") But the bilingualists oversimplify when they scorn the value and necessity of assimilation. They do not seem to realize that a person is individualized in two ways. So they do not realize that, while one suffers a diminished sense of *private* individuality by being assimilated into public society, such assimilation makes possible the achievement of *public* individuality.

Simplistically again, the bilingualists insist that a student should be reminded of his difference from others in mass society, of his "heritage." But they equate mere separateness with individuality. The fact is that only in private—with intimates—is separateness from the crowd a prerequisite for individuality; an intimate "tells" me that I am unique, unlike all others, apart from the crowd. In public, by contrast, full individuality is achieved, paradoxically, by those who are able to consider themselves members of the crowd. Thus it happened for me. Only when I was able to think of myself as an American, no longer an alien in gringo society, could I seek the rights and opportunities necessary for full public individuality. The social and political advantages I enjoy as a man began on the day I came to believe that my name is indeed *Rich-heard Road-ree-guess*. It is true that my public society today is often impersonal; in fact, my public society is usually mass society. But despite the anonymity of the crowd, and despite the fact that the individuality I achieve in public is often tenuous—because it depends on my being one in a crowd—I celebrate the day I acquired my new name. Those middle-class ethnics who scorn assimilation seem to me filled with decadent self-pity, obsessed by the burden of public life. Dangerously, they romanticize public separateness and trivialize the dilemma of those who are truly socially disadvantaged.

If I rehearse here the changes in my private life after my Americanization, it is 40 finally to emphasize a public gain. The loss implies the gain. The house I returned to each afternoon was quiet. Intimate sounds no longer greeted me at the door. Inside there were other noises. The telephone rang. Neighborhood kids ran past the door of the bedroom where I was reading my schoolbooks—covered with brown shopping-bag paper. Once I learned the public language, it would never again be easy for me to hear intimate family voices. More and more of my day was spent hearing words, not sounds. But that may only be a way of saying that on the day I raised my hand in class and spoke loudly to an entire roomful of faces, my childhood started to end.

CONTEXTS FOR "ARIA: A MEMOIR OF A BILINGUAL CHILDHOOD"

Richard Rodriguez at age eighteen

RICHARD RODRIGUEZ

Interview Excerpt

In this excerpt from a 1994 interview, Richard Rodriguez briefly reflects on Hunger of Memory *as a youthful work.*

RODRIGUEZ: If you ask me about these individual [minority] students, I think they are required to think of themselves as representing a cause. Their admission is in the name of a larger population for whom they feel responsible, and they do claim to have a kind of communal voice to speak in the name of the people. If you have a different opinion, then you are not of the people.

Multiculturalism, as it is expressed in the platitudes of the American campus, is not multiculturalism. It is an idea about culture that has a specific genesis, a specific history, and a specific politics. What people mean by multiculturalism is different hues of themselves. They don't mean Islamic fundamentalists or skinheads. They mean other brown and black students who share opinions like theirs. It isn't diversity. It's a pretense to diversity. And this is an exposure of it—they can't even tolerate my paltry opinion.

REASON: *Days of Obligation* got a friendlier response than *Hunger of Memory*, partly because it was more Mexican.

RODRIGUEZ: I think of it as more Catholic rather than more Mexican. An older man is writing this book. I thought of my earlier book as a more deeply Protestant book: my objection to the popular ideology of that time; my insistence that *I am this man,* contrary to what you want to make me; my declaration of myself, of my profession—political and personal; my defiance of my mother's wishes in publishing this memoir. It seemed to me very Protestant and very self-assertive—in the best sense. . . .

RICHARD RODRIGUEZ

Slouching towards Los Angeles

To understand what Rodriguez might mean by calling Hunger of Memory *a "Protestant" work, this opinion piece (1993) argues that America was founded on Protestant individualism; ironically, by emphasizing his individuality, Rodriguez places himself in the historically dominant group.*

From Virginia I. Postrel and Nick Gillespie, "The New, New World: Richard Rodriguez on Culture and Assimilation," *Reason: Free Minds and Free Markets*, August/September 1994, 35–41.

From Richard Rodriguez, "Slouching towards Los Angeles," *Los Angeles Times*, 11 April 1993.

I have been traveling recently across America, visiting colleges and making happy-talk appearances on morning television. On airplanes and in classrooms, I have been hearing Americans say what many say in Los Angeles—that America doesn't exist anymore as a unified culture.

So what else is new? Americans have always said that. We Americans have never easily believed in ourselves as a nation. What traditionally we share is the belief that we share nothing in common at all with people on the other side of town. Who is more American, after all, than today's brown and black neo-nationalists in Los Angeles?

America is a Puritan country, Protestant baptized. It was Protestantism that taught Americans to fear the crowd and to believe in individualism. Nineteenth-century nativists feared that Catholics and Jews would undermine the Protestant idea of America. But it was, paradoxically, American Protestantism that allowed for an immigrant nation. Lacking a communal sense, how could Americans resist the coming of strangers? The immigrant country of the nineteenth century became a country of tribes and neighborhoods more truly than a nation of solitary individuals. Then, as today, Americans trusted diversity, not uniformity. Americans trusted the space between us more than we liked any notion of an American melting pot that might turn us into one another.

Our teachers used to be able to tell us this; the schoolmarm used to be subversive of American individuality. Our teachers used to be able to pose the possibility of a national culture—a line connecting Thomas Jefferson, the slave owner, to Malcolm X. Our teachers used to be able to tell us why all of us speak Black English.

Richard Rodriguez photographed as a mask.

Or how the Mexican farmworkers in Delano were related to the Yiddish-speaking grandmothers who worked the sweatshops of the Lower East Side. America may not have wanted to listen. But our teachers used to insist that there was something called an American culture, a common history.

All over America, in identical hotels, there are weekend conferences for busi- 5 ness executives on multiculturalism. But any immigrant kid could tell you that America exists. There *is* a culture. There is a shared accent, a shared defiance of authority, a shared skepticism about community. There is a stance, a common impatience at the fast-food counter. Moreover, though executives who attend multicultural seminars do not want to hear it, the deepest separation between us derives not from race or ethnicity but from class.

OCTAVIO PAZ

The Labyrinth of Solitude

Mexican diplomat, poet, essayist, translator, and literary and cultural historian Octavio Paz (1914–1998) won the Nobel Prize for literature in 1990. He analyzed the Mexican man's love of silence and privacy in The Labyrinth of Solitude *(1959). The following passage from "Mexican Masks," the second chapter, helps us understand the cultural tradition underlying Rodriguez's father's habitual silence and reticence.*

> *Impassioned heart,*
> *disguise your sorrow . . .*
> *—Popular song*

The Mexican, whether young or old, *criollo* or *mestizo*,[1] general or laborer or lawyer, seems to me to be a person who shuts himself away to protect himself: his face is a mask and so is his smile. In his harsh solitude, which is both barbed and courteous, everything serves him as a defense: silence and words, politeness and disdain, irony and resignation. He is jealous of his own privacy and that of others, and he is afraid even to glance at his neighbor, because a mere glance can trigger the rage of these electrically charged spirits. He passes through life like a man who has been flayed; everything can hurt him, including words and the very suspicion of words. His language is full of reticences, of metaphors and allusions, of unfinished phrases, while his silence is full of tints, folds, thunderheads, sudden rainbows, indecipherable threats. Even in a quarrel he prefers veiled expressions

From Octavio Paz, *The Labyrinth of Solitude*, trans. Lysander Kemp (New York: Grove, 1961), 29–30.

[1]*Criollo*: a person of pure Spanish blood living in the Americas.—*Tr.*

Mestizo: a person of mixed Spanish and Indian blood.—*Tr.*

to outright insults: "A word to the wise is sufficient." He builds a wall of indifference and remoteness between reality and himself, a wall that is no less impenetrable for being invisible. The Mexican is always remote, from the world and from other people. And also from himself.

The speech of our people reflects the extent to which we protect ourselves from the outside world: the ideal of manliness is never to "crack," never to back down. Those who "open themselves up" are cowards. Unlike other people, we believe that opening oneself up is a weakness or a betrayal. The Mexican can bend, can bow humbly, can even stoop, but he cannot back down, that is, he cannot allow the outside world to penetrate his privacy. The man who backs down is not to be trusted, is a traitor or a person of doubtful loyalty; he babbles secrets and is incapable of confronting a dangerous situation. Women are inferior beings because, in submitting, they open themselves up. Their inferiority is constitutional and resides in their sex, their submissiveness, which is a wound that never heals.

Hermeticism is one of the several recourses of our suspicion and distrust. It shows that we instinctively regard the world around us to be dangerous. This reaction is justifiable if one considers what our history has been and the kind of society we have created. The harshness and hostility of our environment, and the hidden, indefinable threat that is always afloat in the air, oblige us to close ourselves in, like those plants that survive by storing up liquid within their spiny exteriors. But this attitude, legitimate enough in its origins, has become a mechanism that functions automatically. Our response to sympathy and tenderness is reserve, since we cannot tell whether those feelings are genuine or simulated. In addition, our masculine integrity is as much endangered by kindness as it is by hostility. Any opening in our defenses is a lessening of our manliness.

Our relationships with other men are always tinged with suspicion. Every time a Mexican confides in a friend or acquaintance, every time he opens himself up, it is an abdication. He dreads that the person in whom he has confided will scorn him. Therefore confidences result in dishonor, and they are as dangerous for the person to whom they are made as they are for the person who makes them.

RICHARD HOGGART

The Uses of Literacy

Part of Rodriguez's self-definition involves his emergence from working-class life, an emergence signaled by the title of his prologue to Hunger of Memory: *"Middle-Class Pastoral." As the memoir's second chapter explains, Rodriguez read Richard Hoggart's treatise (published in 1957) on the experience of the working-class student,*

From Richard Hoggart, *The Uses of Literacy: Aspects of Working-Class Life, with Special Reference to Publications and Entertainments* (London: Chatto, 1957), 239–41.

or "scholarship boy," attending English schools for upper-class and aristocratic boys. A "scholarship boy," writes Hoggart, is "at the friction-point of two cultures," always anxiously adjusting his family's ways—their reading, table manners, vocabulary and pronunciation, conversational topics and gestures, and countless other markers of social class—to those of wealthier boys and their families. Rodriguez read Hoggart's book when he traveled to London's British Museum to research his doctoral dissertation on English Renaissance literature. The book changed his life. Recognizing in himself a Mexican American version of the "scholarship boy," he abandoned his dissertation—and with it his assured career as a university professor—in order to write Hunger of Memory. *The following passage from Hoggart's book is reflected in Rodriguez's "Aria."*

Almost every working-class boy who goes through the process of further education by scholarships finds himself chafing against his environment during adolescence. He is at the friction-point of two cultures; the test of his real education lies in his ability, by about the age of twenty-five, to smile at his father with his whole face and to respect his flighty young sister and his slower brother. I shall be concerned with those for whom the uprooting is particularly troublesome, not because I under-estimate the gains which this kind of selection gives, nor because I wish to stress the more depressing features in contemporary life, but because the difficulties of some people illuminate much in the wider discussion of cultural change. Like transplanted stock, they react to a widespread drought earlier than those who have been left in their original soil.

I am sometimes inclined to think that the problem of self-adjustment is, in general, especially difficult for those working-class boys who are only moderately endowed, who have talent sufficient to separate them from the majority of their working-class contemporaries, but not to go much farther. I am not implying a correlation between intelligence and lack of unease; intellectual people have their own troubles: but this kind of anxiety often seems most to afflict those in the working-classes who have been pulled one stage away from their original culture and yet have not the intellectual equipment which would then cause them to move on to join the "declassed" professionals and experts. In one sense, it is true, no one is ever "declassed"; and it is interesting to see how this occasionally obtrudes (particularly today, when ex-working-class boys move in all the managing areas of society)—in the touch of insecurity, which often appears as an undue concern to establish "presence" in an otherwise quite professorial professor, in the intermittent rough homeliness of an important executive and committee-man, in the tendency to vertigo which betrays a lurking sense of uncertainty in a successful journalist.

But I am chiefly concerned with those who are self-conscious and yet not self-aware in any full sense, who are as a result uncertain, dissatisfied and gnawed by self-doubt. Sometimes they lack will, though they have intelligence, and "it takes will to cross this waste." More often perhaps, though they have as much will as the majority, they have not sufficient to resolve the complex tensions which their uprooting, the peculiar problems of their particular domestic settings, and the uncertainties common to the time create.

As childhood gives way to adolescence and that to manhood, this kind of boy tends to be progressively cut off from the ordinary life of his group. He is marked out early: and here I am thinking not so much of his teachers in the "elementary" school as of fellow-members of his family. "'E's got brains," or "'E's bright," he hears constantly; and in part the tone is one of pride and admiration. He is in a way cut off by his parents as much as by his talent which urges him to break away from his group. Yet on their side this is not altogether from admiration: "'E's got brains," yes, and he is expected to follow the trail that opens. But there can also be a limiting quality in the tone with which the phrase is used; character counts more. Still, he has brains—a mark of pride and almost a brand; he is heading for a different world, a different sort of job. . . .

PAUL ZWEIG

The Child of Two Cultures

Memoir intrinsically involves its writer in maintaining a balance between private and public selves. By 1994, when Rodriguez insisted "I am this man," he desperately wanted to escape the grasp of political groups who used his name and memoir as mere bumper stickers. In the prologue to Hunger of Memory, *Rodriguez had foreseen this risk:*

> My book is necessarily political, in the conventional sense, for public issues—editorials and ballot stubs, petitions and placards, faceless formulations of greater and lesser good by greater and lesser minds—have bisected my life and changed its course. And, in some broad sense, my writing is political because it concerns my movement away from the company of family and into the city. This was my coming of age: I became a man by becoming a public man.

Paul Zweig places Hunger of Memory *within an American tradition of autobiographical writing that is "as personal as possible so as to be as public as possible." As Zweig points out, if the memoir were entirely individual ("I am this man"), few readers would be interested in it; instead, Rodriguez's achievement is to "identify [the] universal labor of growing up in his own particular experience."*

Advocates of bilingual education are wrong, [Rodriguez] insists, in supposing that the values of home life are embodied in language, not persons. If students at school can learn in their home language, it is claimed, they will be less disoriented,

From Paul Zweig, "The Child of Two Cultures," *New York Times Book Review*, 28 February 1982, 1, 26.

better able to attend to the business of schooling. But the business of schooling is to take children out of the home and thrust upon them a new set of demands. Education, to work, must change children. That is its function, according to Richard Rodriguez. It must teach them a new voice, indeed a new language, less charged with intimate feelings than the old language, less comfortable, but appropriate to the impersonal world in which self-respect, success, money, culture are won. To win is also to lose, yes; but this can't be avoided, shouldn't be avoided.

Here is the political point Mr. Rodriguez wants to drive home. The struggle for social justice begun 20 years ago with the civil rights movement in the South and expanded since to include all "minority" groups—Hispanics, Chicanos, Haitians, but also gays and women—has taken a wrong turn in the matter of education. Affirmative action and bilingual school programs; the demand for ethnic studies in the university, for relevance; the attempt to legitimize black ghetto English—all ignore the essential function of education, which is to change the student, extract him from his intimate circumstance—family, ghetto, minority community—and give him access to the public world, which in the United States is negotiated in standard English, embodied by a set of attitudes, a voice, which is everywhere recognized as a passport to all the larger ambitions the public world makes possible.

The failure of educators and social activists alike to know this, according to Mr. Rodriguez, reflects the larger failure of American education, which rarely succeeds in changing anyone. Its greatest success comes with those children born in closest proximity to the public world, for whom, therefore, the change is smallest: children of the upper middle classes. Mr. Rodriguez offers himself as an example of the long labor of change: its costs, about which he is movingly frank, its loneliness, but also its triumphs.

RICHARD RODRIGUEZ
Interview (1999)

A "self" naturally changes with time, and a tougher, hipper Rodriguez surmises in this 1999 interview excerpt that his former "Bambi" self might now hold little appeal for young Chicano males.

RODRIGUEZ: I must tell you that I am not sure that I would like Richard Rodriguez were I not he. At some very simple level I can tell you that I don't like the voice. I don't even like the tenderness of *Hunger of Memory*; frankly, it's

From Timothy S. Sedore, "Violating the Boundaries: An Interview with Richard Rodriguez," *Michigan Quarterly Review* (Summer 1999): 425–46.

too soft for men. It's not Latino enough, it's a little too feminine, a little too American. He looks like Bambi on the cover. I'm not sure I like this guy. He whimpers too much. He's too soft. He's not what I want.

As a young Mexican American male in the city, I would want something tougher: I would want something more robust. When I think of the Chicano movement in its most wonderful forms I think of my friend Tony who died a few weeks ago. Tony was an artist, and he was a writer. He wasn't a great writer, but he was Chicano in the sense that he was a rebel. He tried to undo society in a wonderfully comic way. He belonged to a group called Culture Clash, and they began a movement about twenty years ago. Tony ultimately became a muralist instead of a performer, but he was always into adolescent forms of rebellion against the gringo society. He was like, "I'm doing the emblems, I'm doing the iconography." He mocked the culture by parodying it. He was constantly playing at the edges of the American culture.

Maybe that's what I would have wanted. I wanted a Rich Rodriguez with more guts, someone who was tougher. I think to myself, if I'm a Chicano and all of my life I've been stuck with losers, then I want somebody who's tough. I want somebody who represents us as a contender. Richard Rodriguez grew up in a little, close, white neighborhood with the Anglos. He's not what I would have in mind as a Chicano. He doesn't have the spirit.

QUESTIONS FOR DISCUSSION AND WRITING

1. In his 1994 interview, Rodriguez examines the "pretense to diversity," an idea he elaborates on in his 1999 interview. What do you think "pretense to diversity" means? Which passages from "Aria" describe qualities that Rodriguez would consider "Chicano" or "non-Chicano"? Make a list of qualities that define each term. Which qualities in each list does he apply to himself? Which describe the qualities of "Bambi," the self-deprecating label he adopts in the 1999 interview? In what ways does Rodriguez represent Chicanos as a group? What motivates him to reject a Chicano identity? To accept it?

2. In Chapter 2, N. Scott Momaday suggests that we understand a story in terms of other stories we already know (p. 118). Which of the stories that Rodriguez tells in "Aria" seem to you to advocate the individualism he describes in "Slouching towards Los Angeles"? Which seem to challenge that individualism?

3. Which passages in Rodriguez's "Aria" are most closely related to Octavio Paz's account of masks? In each passage, who wears a mask? For what motives? Looking closely at the passages in "Aria" where Rodriguez represents differing languages, describe the effects of each representation on you as a reader. What do you think is gained and lost through representations of language variation?

4. Divide a sheet of paper into four quadrants, labeling the two columns "Richard Hoggart" and "Richard Rodriguez" and the two rows "Similar" and "Different." In each row, write pairs of passages from *The Uses of Literacy* and "Aria." On the basis of your evidence, explain to what extent social class—rather than ethnicity—is the key to the identity of a "scholarship boy." In what ways is Rodriguez a "scholarship boy," and in what ways is he not?

5. One reason that a piece of writing is reread over time is that various generations of writers find it useful for furthering various political agendas. With a partner, consider the selection on the politics of bilingual education, "The Child of Two Cultures." What do writers try to accomplish by citing Rodriguez's *Hunger of Memory*? In the library or on the Internet, locate some contemporary debates about bilingual and ESL (English as a Second Language) curricula. What differences between these two curricula can you identify? Which passages from "Aria" could be used to support bilingual, ESL, or "English-only" agendas today?

WILL COUNTS

Central High School, Little Rock, Arkansas, September 4, 1957

QUESTIONS FOR DISCUSSION AND WRITING

1. The Associated Press has designated this photograph, taken by Will Counts in 1957, as one of the top one hundred photographs of the twentieth century. Read the picture as if you were innocent of its historical context or significance. What's going on? Where are these people going? Who is the most conspicuous figure? Can you read her expression? Why are so many of the people so angry? Why are helmeted soldiers present?

2. Now, read the picture again with this information in mind. Elizabeth Eckford (b. 1941) was one of nine black students, "The Little Rock Nine," designated by

the federal courts to desegregate Little Rock's Central High School in September 1957. Her family had no phone, so she didn't learn of a change of meeting place for the nine, and arrived alone at the school. Twice she tried to enter the school, surrounded by an angry mob chanting "Two, four, six, eight, we ain't gonna integrate," and was turned back by Arkansas National Guard troops, ordered by Governor Orval Faubus. Because all Little Rock high schools were closed the following year, Eckford had to complete her high school education by correspondence and night courses. In what ways, if any, does this information alter your understanding of the picture? You may use this as the springboard to a paper on some aspect of school desegregation, if you wish.

3. Time marches on, and history changes. Eckford (with the other eight) was awarded the prestigious Spingarn Medal by the National Association for the Advancement of Colored People in 1958 and the Congressional Gold Medal, presented by President Bill Clinton in 1999. In 1997 Hazel Bryan Massery (the girl immediately behind Eckford, with segregationist mouth wide open—the very picture of "hate assailing grace") apologized to Eckford at a reconciliation rally in Little Rock in 1997, and the two subsequently made speeches together. In what ways does this additional information affect your understanding of the changed racial climate in the United States, as represented by the actions of these two former adversaries, now allies?

PAIRED READINGS: KNOWING THE WORLD

PLATO

The Allegory of the Cave

Born in Athens (c. 428–347 B.C.E.), Plato was the most famous pupil of Socrates. Together with Aristotle, these three thinkers are the philosophical forebears of Western thought. The dialogues of Plato display the Socratic method of philosophical exploration, in which Socrates poses step-by-step questions about concepts of "good," "justice," and "piety." Each question has a simple answer, but cumulatively they reveal contradictions, ambiguities, and other barriers to understanding. For this reason, Plato's The Republic *argues that a just government should be guided by statesmen whose learning—attained through dialogue rather than through the senses—makes them both persuasive and wise.*

"The Allegory of the Cave," from The Republic, *tells of prisoners who understand life only through shadows flickering on the wall of their cave. Like all allegories, this story conveys abstract ideas through more concrete representation, in this case, Plato's belief that "ideas," or pure forms, exist only in the spiritual realm. Before birth, we see ideas perfectly, but on earth our memories fade and our senses perceive*

only unreliable shadows of those ideas. Plato's allegory thus suggests that, like the prisoners, people on earth understand life only through sense perceptions similar to shadows; as a result, they know reality only incompletely. Be prepared to compare this with the following essay, Howard Gardner's "Who Owns Intelligence?" (p. 298).

Next, said I, here is a parable to illustrate the degrees in which our nature may be enlightened or unenlightened. Imagine the condition of men living in a sort of cavernous chamber underground, with an entrance open to the light and a long passage all down the cave. Here they have been from childhood, chained by the leg and also by the neck, so that they cannot move and can see only what is in front of them, because the chains will not let them turn their heads. At some distance higher up is the light of a fire burning behind them; and between the prisoners and the fire is a track with a parapet built along it, like the screen at a puppet-show, which hides the performers while they show their puppets over the top.

I see, said he.

Now behind this parapet imagine persons carrying along various artificial objects, including figures of men and animals in wood or stone or other materials, which project above the parapet. Naturally, some of these persons will be talking, others silent.

It is a strange picture, he said, and a strange sort of prisoners.

Like ourselves, I replied; for in the first place prisoners so confined would   5
have seen nothing of themselves or of one another, except the shadows thrown by the fire-light on the wall of the Cave facing them, would they?

Not if all their lives they had been prevented from moving their heads.

And they would have seen as little of the objects carried past.

Of course.

Now, if they could talk to one another, would they not suppose that their words referred only to those passing shadows which they saw?

Necessarily.   10

And suppose their prison had an echo from the wall facing them? When one of the people crossing behind them spoke, they could only suppose that the sound came from the shadow passing before their eyes.

No doubt.

In every way, then, such prisoners would recognize as reality nothing but the shadows of those artificial objects.

Inevitably.

Now consider what would happen if their release from the chains and the   15
healing of their unwisdom should come about in this way. Suppose one of them were set free and forced suddenly to stand up, turn his head, and walk with eyes lifted to the light; all these movements would be painful, and he would be too dazzled to make out the objects whose shadows he had been used to see. What do you think he would say, if someone told him that what he had formerly seen

was meaningless illusion, but now, being somewhat nearer to reality and turned towards more real objects, he was getting a truer view? Suppose further that he were shown the various objects being carried by and were made to say, in reply to questions, what each of them was. Would he not be perplexed and believe the objects now shown him to be not so real as what he formerly saw?

Yes, not nearly so real.

And if he were forced to look at the fire-light itself, would not his eyes ache, so that he would try to escape and turn back to the things which he could see distinctly, convinced that they really were clearer than these other objects now being shown to him?

Yes.

And suppose someone were to drag him away forcibly up the steep and rugged ascent and not let him go until he had hauled him out into the sunlight, would he not suffer pain and vexation at such treatment, and, when he had come out into the light, find his eyes so full of its radiance that he could not see a single one of the things that he was now told were real?

Certainly he would not see them all at once.   20

He would need, then, to grow accustomed before he could see things in that upper world. At first it would be easiest to make out shadows, and then the images of men and things reflected in water, and later on the things themselves. After that, it would be easier to watch the heavenly bodies and the sky itself by night, looking at the light of the moon and stars rather than the Sun and the Sun's light in the day-time.

Yes, surely.

Last of all, he would be able to look at the Sun and contemplate its nature, not as it appears when reflected in water or any alien medium, but as it is in itself in its own domain.

No doubt.

And now he would begin to draw the conclusion that it is the Sun that pro- 25
duces the seasons and the course of the year and controls everything in the visible world, and moreover is in a way the cause of all that he and his companions used to see.

Clearly he would come at last to that conclusion.

Then if he called to mind his fellow prisoners and what passed for wisdom in his former dwelling-place, he would surely think himself happy in the change and be sorry for them. They may have had a practice of honoring and commending one another, with prizes for the man who had the keenest eye for the passing shadows and the best memory for the order in which they followed or accompanied one another, so that he could make a good guess as to which was going to come next. Would our released prisoner be likely to covet those prizes or to envy the men exalted to honor and power in the Cave? Would he not feel like Homer's Achilles, that he would far sooner 'be on earth as a hired servant in the house of a landless man' or endure anything rather than go back to his old beliefs and live in the old way?

Yes, he would prefer any fate to such a life.

Now imagine what would happen if he went down again to take his former seat in the Cave. Coming suddenly out of the sunlight, his eyes would be filled with darkness. He might be required once more to deliver his opinion on those shadows, in competition with the prisoners who had never been released, while his eyesight was still dim and unsteady; and it might take some time to become used to the darkness. They would laugh at him and say that he had gone up only to come back with his sight ruined; it was worth no one's while even to attempt the ascent. If they could lay hands on the man who was trying to set them free and lead them up, they would kill him.

Yes, they would.   30

Every feature in this parable, my dear Glaucon, is meant to fit our earlier analysis. The prison dwelling corresponds to the region revealed to us through the sense of sight, and the fire-light within it to the power of the Sun. The ascent to see the things in the upper world you may take as standing for the upward journey of the soul into the region of the intelligible; then you will be in possession of what I surmise, since that is what you wish to be told. Heaven knows whether it is true; but this, at any rate, is how it appears to me. In the world of knowledge, the last thing to be perceived and only with great difficulty is the essential Form of Goodness. Once it is perceived, the conclusion must follow that, for all things, this is the cause of whatever is right and good; in the visible world it gives birth to light and to the lord of light, while it is itself sovereign in the intelligible world and the parent of intelligence and truth. Without having had a vision of this Form no one can act with wisdom, either in his own life or in matters of state.

HOWARD GARDNER

Who Owns Intelligence?

Howard Gardner was born in Scranton, Pennsylvania, in 1943. As a boy, he was a gifted pianist. He attended Harvard University (B.A., 1965; Ph.D., 1971) and, as a Harvard professor, has researched normal and gifted children's creativity. Brain Damage: Gateway to the Mind (1975) reports on his research with aphasic adults—those unable to process language. Recipient of a 1981 MacArthur "genius" fellowship, Gardner soon turned his attention to the theory of intelligence used in the social sciences and standardized testing. His conclusion—that people possess more than one type of intelligence—inspired his enduring book Frames of Mind: The Theory of Multiple Intelligences *(1983), first published in 1983; 25th anniversary edition, 2008. Here he categorizes intelligence as "object-related" (math and logic), "object-free" (music and language), and "personal" (our perceptions of ourselves and of others). Other books build on his earlier research:* Multiple Intelligences: The

Theory in Practice *(1993), and* Intelligence Reframed: Multiple Intelligences for the Twenty-first Century *(1999);* Changing Minds: The Art and Science of Changing Our Own and Other People's Minds *(2004); and* Five Minds for the Future *(2007).* The Disciplined Mind: Beyond Facts and Standardized Tests *(2000) counters E. D. Hirsch Jr.'s emphasis on acquisition of factual knowledge in* Cultural Literacy *(1987) and instead argues for deep understanding of a few traditional disciplines.*

Gardner summarizes current theory and his own beliefs in "Who Owns Intelligence?" (Atlantic 1999). After first reviewing the history of the IQ test, the first measure of intellectual potential to be developed by modern psychology, he surveys current theories of intelligence, arguing that several schools of "experts are competing for the 'ownership' of intelligence in the next century."

Almost a century ago Alfred Binet, a gifted psychologist, was asked by the French Ministry of Education to help determine who would experience difficulty in school. Given the influx of provincials to the capital, along with immigrants of uncertain stock, Parisian officials believed they needed to know who might not advance smoothly through the system. Proceeding in an empirical manner, Binet posed many questions to youngsters of different ages. He ascertained which questions when answered correctly predicted success in school, and which questions when answered incorrectly foretold school difficulties. The items that discriminated most clearly between the two groups became, in effect, the first test of intelligence.

Binet is a hero to many psychologists. He was a keen observer, a careful scholar, an inventive technologist. Perhaps even more important for his followers, he devised the instrument that is often considered psychology's greatest success story. Millions of people who have never heard Binet's name have had aspects of their fate influenced by instrumentation that the French psychologist inspired. And thousands of psychometricians — specialists in the measurement of psychological variables — earn their living courtesy of Binet's invention.

Although it has prevailed over the long run, the psychologists' version of intelligence is now facing its biggest threat. Many scholars and observers — and even some iconoclastic psychologists — feel that intelligence is too important to be left to the psychometricians. Experts are extending the breadth of the concept — proposing many intelligences, including emotional intelligence and moral intelligence. They are experimenting with new methods of ascertaining intelligence, including some that avoid tests altogether in favor of direct measures of brain activity. They are forcing citizens everywhere to confront a number of questions: What is intelligence? How ought it to be assessed? And how do our notions of intelligence fit with what we value about human beings? In short, experts are competing for the "ownership" of intelligence in the next century.

The outline of the psychometricians' success story is well known. Binet's colleagues in England and Germany contributed to the conceptualization and instrumentation of intelligence testing — which soon became known as IQ tests.

(An IQ, or intelligence quotient, designates the ratio between mental age and chronological age. Clearly we'd prefer that a child in our care have an IQ of 120, being smarter than average for his or her years, than an IQ of 80, being older than average for his or her intelligence.) Like other Parisian fashions of the period, the intelligence test migrated easily to the United States. First used to determine who was "feeble-minded," it was soon used to assess "normal" children, to identify the "gifted," and to determine who was fit to serve in the Army. By the 1920s the intelligence test had become a fixture in educational practice in the United States and much of Western Europe.

Early intelligence tests were not without their critics. Many enduring con-   5 cerns were first raised by the influential journalist Walter Lippmann, in a series of published debates with Lewis Terman, of Stanford University, the father of IQ testing in America. Lippmann pointed out the superficiality of the questions, their possible cultural biases, and the risks of trying to determine a person's intellectual potential with a brief oral or paper-and-pencil measure.

Perhaps surprisingly, the conceptualization of intelligence did not advance much in the decades following Binet's and Terman's pioneering contributions. Intelligence tests came to be seen, rightly or wrongly, as primarily a tool for selecting people to fill academic or vocational niches. In one of the most famous—if irritating—remarks about intelligence testing, the influential Harvard psychologist E. G. Boring declared, "Intelligence is what the tests test." So long as these tests did what they were supposed to do (that is, give some indication of school success), it did not seem necessary or prudent to probe too deeply into their meaning or to explore alternative views of the human intellect.

Psychologists who study intelligence have argued chiefly about three questions. The first: Is intelligence singular, or does it consist of various more or less independent intellectual faculties? The purists—ranging from the turn-of-the-century English psychologist Charles Spearman to his latter-day disciples Richard J. Herrnstein and Charles Murray (of *The Bell Curve* fame)—defend the notion of a single overarching "g," or general intelligence. The pluralists—ranging from L. L. Thurstone, of the University of Chicago, who posited seven vectors of the mind, to J. P. Guilford, of the University of Southern California, who discerned 150 factors of the intellect—construe intelligence as composed of some or even many dissociable components. In his much cited *The Mismeasure of Man* (1981) the paleontologist Stephen Jay Gould argued that the conflicting conclusions reached on this issue reflect alternative assumptions about statistical procedures rather than the way the mind is. Still, psychologists continue the debate, with a majority sympathetic to the general-intelligence perspective.

The public is more interested in the second question: Is intelligence (or are intelligences) largely inherited? This is by and large a Western question. In the Confucian societies of East Asia individual differences in endowment are assumed to be modest, and differences in achievement are thought to be due largely to effort. In the West, however, many students of the subject sympathize with the view—defended within psychology by Lewis Terman, among others—that intelligence is inborn and one can do little to alter one's intellectual birthright.

Studies of identical twins reared apart provide surprisingly strong support for the "heritability" of psychometric intelligence. That is, if one wants to predict someone's score on an intelligence test, the scores of the biological parents (even if the child has not had appreciable contact with them) are more likely to prove relevant than the scores of the adoptive parents. By the same token, the IQs of identical twins are more similar than the IQs of fraternal twins. And, contrary to common sense (and political correctness), the IQs of biologically related people grow closer in the later years of life. Still, because of the intricacies of behavioral genetics and the difficulties of conducting valid experiments with human child-rearing, a few defend the proposition that intelligence is largely environmental rather than heritable, and some believe that we cannot answer the question at all.

Most scholars agree that even if psychometric intelligence is largely inher- 10 ited, it is not possible to pinpoint the sources of differences in average IQ between groups, such as the fifteen-point difference typically observed between African-American and white populations. That is because in our society the contemporary—let alone the historical—experiences of these two groups cannot be equated. One could ferret out the differences (if any) between black and white populations only in a society that was truly color-blind.

One other question has intrigued laypeople and psychologists: Are intelligence tests biased? Cultural assumptions are evident in early intelligence tests. Some class biases are obvious—who except the wealthy could readily answer a question about polo? Others are more subtle. Suppose the question is what one should do with money found on the street. Although ordinarily one might turn it over to the police, what if one had a hungry child? Or what if the police force were known to be hostile to members of one's ethnic group? Only the canonical response to such a question would be scored as correct.

Psychometricians have striven to remove the obviously biased items from such measures. But biases that are built into the test situation itself are far more difficult to deal with. For example, a person's background affects his or her reaction to being placed in an unfamiliar locale, being instructed by someone dressed in a certain way, and having a printed test booklet thrust into his or her hands. And as the psychologist Claude M. Steele has argued . . . , the biases prove even more acute when people know that their academic potential is being measured and that their racial or ethnic group is widely considered to be less intelligent than the dominant social group.

The idea of bias touches on the common assumption that tests in general, and intelligence tests in particular, are inherently conservative instruments—tools of the establishment. It is therefore worth noting that many testing pioneers thought of themselves as progressives in the social sphere. They were devising instruments that could reveal people of talent even if those people came from "remote and apparently inferior backgrounds," to quote from a college catalogue of the 1950s. And occasionally the tests did discover intellectual diamonds in the rough. More often, however, they picked out the privileged. The still unresolved question of the causal relationship between IQ and social privilege has stimulated many a dissertation across the social sciences.

Paradoxically, one of the clearest signs of the success of intelligence tests is that they are no longer widely administered. In the wake of legal cases about the propriety of making consequential decisions about education on the basis of IQ scores, many public school officials have become test-shy. By and large, the testing of IQ in the schools is restricted to cases involving a recognized problem (such as a learning disability) or a selection procedure (determining eligibility for a program that serves gifted children).

Despite this apparent setback, intelligence testing and the line of thinking that   15 underlies it have actually triumphed. Many widely used scholastic measures, chief among them the SAT (renamed the Scholastic Assessment Test a few years ago), are thinly disguised intelligence tests that correlate highly with scores on standard psychometric instruments. Virtually no one raised in the developed world today has gone untouched by Binet's seemingly simple invention of a century ago.

MULTIPLE INTELLIGENCES

The concept of intelligence has in recent years undergone its most robust challenge since the days of Walter Lippmann. Some who are informed by psychology but not bound by the assumptions of the psychometricians have invaded this formerly sacrosanct territory. They have put forth their own ideas of what intelligence is, how (and whether) it should be measured, and which values should be invoked in considerations of the human intellect. For the first time in many years the intelligence establishment is clearly on the defensive—and the new century seems likely to usher in quite different ways of thinking about intelligence.

One evident factor in the rethinking of intelligence is the perspective introduced by scholars who are not psychologists. Anthropologists have commented on the parochialism of the Western view of intelligence. Some cultures do not even have a concept called intelligence, and others define intelligence in terms of traits that we in the West might consider odd—obedience, good listening skills, or moral fiber, for example. Neuroscientists are skeptical that the highly differentiated and modular structure of the brain is consistent with a unitary form of intelligence. Computer scientists have devised programs deemed intelligent; these programs often go about problem solving in ways quite different from those embraced by human beings or other animals.

Even within the field of psychology the natives have been getting restless. Probably the most restless is the Yale psychologist Robert J. Sternberg. A prodigious scholar, Sternberg, who is forty-nine, has written dozens of books and hundreds of articles, the majority of them focusing in one or another way on intelligence. Sternberg began with the strategic goal of understanding the actual mental processes mobilized by standard test items, such as the solving of analogies.

But he soon went beyond standard intelligence testing by insisting on two hitherto neglected forms of intelligence: the "practical" ability to adapt to varying contexts (as we all must in these days of divorcing and downsizing), and the capacity
to automate familiar activities so that we can deal effectively with novelty and
display "creative" intelligence.

Sternberg has gone to greater pains than many other critics of standard intelligence testing to measure these forms of intelligence with the paper-and-pencil
laboratory methods favored by the profession. And he has found that a person's
ability to adapt to diverse contexts or to deal with novel information can be differentiated from success at standard IQ-test problems. His efforts to create a new
intelligence test have not been crowned with easy victory. Most psychometricians
are conservative—they like the tests that have been in use for decades, and if new
ones are to be marketed, these must correlate well with existing instruments. So
much for openness to novelty within psychometrics.

Others in the field seem less bound by its strictures. The psychologist and jour- 20
nalist Daniel Goleman has achieved worldwide success with his book *Emotional
Intelligence* (1995). Contending that this new concept (sometimes nicknamed EQ)
may matter as much as or more than IQ, Goleman draws attention to such pivotal
human abilities as controlling one's emotional reactions and "reading" the signals
of others. In the view of the noted psychiatrist Robert Coles, author of *The Moral
Intelligence of Children* (1997), among many other books, we should prize character
over intellect. He decries the amorality of our families, hence our children; he shows
how we might cultivate human beings with a strong sense of right and wrong, who
are willing to act on that sense even when it runs counter to self-interest. Other,
frankly popular accounts deal with leadership intelligence (LQ), executive intelligence (EQ or ExQ), and even financial intelligence.

Like Coles's and Goleman's efforts, my work on "multiple intelligences" eschews
the psychologists' credo of operationalization and test-making. I began by asking
two questions: How did the human mind and brain evolve over millions of years?
and How can we account for the diversity of skills and capacities that are or have
been valued in different communities around the world?

Armed with these questions and a set of eight criteria, I have concluded
that all human beings possess at least eight intelligences: linguistic and logical-
mathematical (the two most prized in school and the ones central to success on
standard intelligence tests), musical, spatial, bodily-kinesthetic, naturalist, interpersonal, and intrapersonal.

I make two complementary claims about intelligence. The first is universal.
We all possess these eight intelligences—and possibly more. Indeed, rather than
seeing us as "rational animals," I offer a new definition of what it means to be a
human being, cognitively speaking: *Homo sapiens sapiens* is the animal that possesses these eight forms of mental representation.

My second claim concerns individual differences. Owing to the accidents of
heredity, environment, and their interactions, no two of us exhibit the same intelligences in precisely the same proportions. Our "profiles of intelligence" differ from

one another. This fact poses intriguing challenges and opportunities for our education system. We can ignore these differences and pretend that we are all the same; historically, that is what most education systems have done. Or we can fashion an education system that tries to exploit these differences, individualizing instruction and assessment as much as possible.

INTELLIGENCE AND MORALITY

As the century of Binet and his successors draws to a close, we'd be wise to take stock of, and to anticipate, the course of thinking about intelligence. Although my crystal ball is no clearer than anyone else's (the species may lack "future intelligence"), it seems safe to predict that interest in intelligence will not go away.   25

To begin with, the psychometric community has scarcely laid down its arms. New versions of the standard tests continue to be created, and occasionally new tests surface as well. Researchers in the psychometric tradition churn out fresh evidence of the predictive power of their instruments and the correlations between measured intelligence and one's life chances. And some in the psychometric tradition are searching for the biological basis of intelligence: the gene or complex of genes that may affect intelligence, the neural structures that are crucial for intelligence, or telltale brain-wave patterns that distinguish the bright from the less bright.

Beyond various psychometric twists, interest in intelligence is likely to grow in other ways. It will be fed by the creation of machines that display intelligence and by the specific intelligence or intelligences. Moreover, observers as diverse as Richard Herrnstein and Robert B. Reich, President Clinton's first Secretary of Labor, have agreed that in coming years a large proportion of society's rewards will go to those people who are skilled symbol analysts—who can sit at a computer screen (or its technological successor), manipulate numbers and other kinds of symbols, and use the results of their operations to contrive plans, tactics, and strategies for enterprises ranging from business to science to war games. These people may well color how intelligence is conceived in decades to come—just as the need to provide good middle-level bureaucrats to run an empire served as a primary molder of intelligence tests in the early years of the century.

Surveying the landscape of intelligence, I discern three struggles between opposing forces. The extent to which, and the manner in which, these various struggles are resolved will influence the lives of millions of people. I believe that the three struggles are interrelated; that the first struggle provides the key to the other two; and that the ensemble of struggles can be resolved in an optimal way.

The first struggle concerns the breadth of our definition of intelligence. One camp consists of the purists, who believe in a single form of intelligence—one that basically predicts success in school and in school-like activities. Arrayed against the purists are the progressive pluralists, who believe that many forms of intelligence exist. Some of these pluralists would like to broaden the definition of intelligence considerably, to include the abilities to create, to lead, and to stand out in terms of emotional sensitivity or moral excellence.

The second struggle concerns the assessment of intelligence. Again, one read- 30 ily encounters a traditional position. Once chiefly concerned with paper-and-pencil tests, the traditionally oriented practitioner is now likely to use computers to provide the same information more quickly and more accurately. But other positions abound. Purists disdain psychological tasks of any complexity, preferring to look instead at reaction time, brain waves, and other physiological measures of intellect. In contrast, simulators favor measures closely resembling the actual abilities that are prized. And skeptics warn against the continued expansion of testing. They emphasize the damage often done to individual life chances and self-esteem by a regimen of psychological testing, and call for less technocratic, more humane methods—ranging from self-assessment to the examination of portfolios of student work to selection in the service of social equity.

The final struggle concerns the relationship between intelligence and the qualities we value in human beings. Although no one would baldly equate intellect and human worth, nuanced positions have emerged on this issue. Some (in the *Bell Curve* mold) see intelligence as closely related to a person's ethics and values; they believe that brighter people are more likely to appreciate moral complexity and to behave judiciously. Some call for a sharp distinction between the realm of intellect on the one hand, and character, morality, or ethics on the other. Society's ambivalence on this issue can be discerned in the figures that become the culture's heroes. For every Albert Einstein or Bobby Fischer who is celebrated for his intellect, there is a Forrest Gump or a Chauncey Gardiner[1] who is celebrated for human—and humane—traits that would never be captured on any kind of intelligence test.

Thanks to the work of the past decade or two, the stranglehold of the psychometricians has at last been broken. This is a beneficent development. Yet now that the psychometricians have been overcome, we risk deciding that anything goes—that emotions, morality, creativity, must all be absorbed into the "new (or even the New Age) intelligence." The challenge is to chart a concept of intelligence that reflects new insights and discoveries and yet can withstand rigorous scrutiny.

An analogy may help. One can think of the scope of intelligence as represented by an elastic band. For many years the definition of intelligence went unchallenged, and the band seemed to have lost its elasticity. Some of the new definitions expand the band, so that it has become taut and resilient; and yet earlier work on intelligence is still germane. Other definitions so expand the band that it is likely finally to snap—and the earlier work on intelligence will no longer be of use.

---

[1]Chauncey Gardiner is the hero of Jerzy Kosinski's novel *Being There* (1971), who begins as Chauncey, an actual gardener, and becomes a U.S. president; understanding nothing, he talks about the only thing he knows—gardening—but is hailed as a genius who uses the garden to describe the world situation. [Editors' note.]

Until now the term "intelligence" has been limited largely to certain kinds of problem-solving involving language and logic—the skills at a premium in the bureaucrat or the law professor. However, human beings are able to deal with numerous kinds of content besides words, numbers, and logical relations—for example, space, music, the psyches of other human beings. Like the elastic band, definitions of intelligence need to be expanded to include human skill in dealing with these diverse contents. And we must not restrict attention to solving problems that have been posed by others; we must consider equally the capacity of individuals to fashion products—scientific experiments, effective organizations— that draw on one or more human intelligences. The elastic band can accommodate such broadening as well.

So long as intelligences are restricted to the processing of contents in the world, we avoid epistemological problems—as we should. "Intelligence" should not be expanded to include personality, motivation, will, attention, character, creativity, and other important and significant human capacities. Such stretching is likely to snap the band.

Let's see what happens when one crosses one of these lines—for example, when one attempts to conflate intelligence and creativity. Beginning with a definition, we extend the descriptor "creative" to those people (or works or institutions) who meet two criteria: they are innovative, and their innovations are eventually accepted by a relevant community.

No one denies that creativity is important—and, indeed, it may prove even more important in the future, when nearly all standard (algorithmic) procedures will be carried out by computers. Yet creativity should not be equated with intelligence. An expert may be intelligent in one or more domains but not necessarily inclined toward, or successful in, innovation. Similarly, although it is clear that the ability to innovate requires a certain degree of intelligence, we don't find a significant correlation between measures of intellect and of creativity. Indeed, creativity seems more dependent on a certain kind of temperament and personality— risk-taking, tough-skinned, persevering, above all having a lust to alter the status quo and leave a mark on society—than on efficiency in processing various kinds of information. By collapsing these categories together we risk missing dimensions that are important but separate; and we may think that we are training (or selecting) one when we are actually training (or selecting) the other.

Next consider what happens when one stretches the idea of intelligence to include attitudes and behaviors—and thus confronts human values within a culture. A few values can be expressed generically enough that they command universal respect: the Golden Rule is one promising candidate. Most values, however, turn out to be specific to certain cultures or subcultures—even such seeming unproblematic ones as the unacceptability of killing or lying. Once one conflates morality and intelligence, one needs to deal with widely divergent views of what is good or bad and why. Moreover, one must confront the fact that people who score high on tests of moral reasoning may act immorally outside the test situation—even as courageous and self-sacrificing people may turn out to be unremarkable on formal tests of moral reasoning or intelligence. It is far preferable to construe intelligence itself as morally neutral and then decide whether a given use of intelligence qualifies as moral, immoral, or amoral in context.

As I see it, no intelligence is moral or immoral in itself. One can be gifted in language and use that gift to write great verse, as did Johann Wolfgang von Goethe, or to foment hatred, as did Joseph Goebbels. Mother Teresa and Lyndon Johnson, Mohandas Gandhi and Niccolò Machiavelli, may have had equivalent degrees of interpersonal intelligence, but they put their skills to widely divergent uses.

Perhaps there is a form of intelligence that determines whether or not a   40
situation harbors moral consideration or consequences. But the term "moral intelligence" carries little force. After all, Adolf Hitler and Joseph Stalin may well have had an exquisite sense of which situations contained moral considerations. However, either they did not care or they embraced their own peculiar morality according to which eliminating Jews was the moral thing to do in quest of a pure Aryan society, or wiping out a generation was necessary in the quest to establish a communist state.

THE BORDERS OF INTELLIGENCE

Writing as a scholar rather than as a layperson, I see two problems with the notion of emotional intelligence. First, unlike language or space, the emotions are not contents to be processed; rather, cognition has evolved so that we can make sense of human beings (self and others) that possess and experience emotions. Emotions are part and parcel of all cognition, though they may well prove more salient at certain times or under certain circumstances: they accompany our interactions with others, our listening to great music, our feelings when we solve — or fail to solve — a difficult mathematical problem. If one calls some intelligences emotional, one suggests that other intelligences are not — and that implication flies in the face of experience and empirical data.

The second problem is the conflation of emotional intelligence and a certain preferred pattern of behavior. This is the trap that Daniel Goleman sometimes falls into in his otherwise admirable *Emotional Intelligence*. Goleman singles out as emotionally intelligent those people who use their understanding of emotions to make others feel better, to solve conflicts, or to cooperate in home or work situations. No one would dispute that such people are wanted. However, people who understand emotion may not necessarily use their skills for the benefit of society.

For this reason I prefer the term "emotional sensitivity" — a term (encompassing my interpersonal and intrapersonal intelligences) that could apply to people who are sensitive to emotions in themselves and in others. Presumably, clinicians and salespeople excel in sensitivity to others, poets and mystics in sensitivity to themselves. And some autistic or psychopathological people seem completely insensitive to the emotional realm. I would insist, however, on a strict distinction between emotional sensitivity and being a "good" or "moral" person.

A person may be sensitive to the emotions of others but use that sensitivity to manipulate or to deceive them, or to create hatred.

I call, then, for a delineation of intelligence that includes the full range of contents to which human beings are sensitive, but at the same time designates as off limits such valued but separate human traits as creativity, morality, and emotional appropriateness. I believe that such a delineation makes scientific and epistemological sense. It reinvigorates the elastic band without stretching it to the breaking point. It helps to resolve the two remaining struggles: how to assess, and what kinds of human beings to admire.

Once we decide to restrict intelligence to human information-processing and product-making capacities, we can make use of the established technology of assessment. That is, we can continue to use paper-and-pencil or computer-adapted testing techniques while looking at a broader range of capacities, such as musical sensitivity and empathy with others. And we can avoid ticklish and possibly unresolvable questions about the assessment of values and morality that may well be restricted to a particular culture and that may well change over time.

Still, even with a limited perspective on intelligence, important questions remain about which assessment path to follow — that of the purist, the simulator, or the skeptic. Here I have strong views. I question the wisdom of searching for a "pure" intelligence — be it general intelligence, musical intelligence, or interpersonal intelligence. I do not believe that such alchemical intellectual essences actually exist; they are a product of our penchant for creating terminology rather than determinable and measurable entities. Moreover, the correlations that have thus far been found between supposedly pure measures and the skills that we actually value in the world are too modest to be useful.

What does exist is the use of intelligences, individually and in concert, to carry out tasks that are valued by a society. Accordingly, we should be assessing the extent to which human beings succeed in carrying out tasks of consequence that presumably involve certain intelligences. To be concrete, we should not test musical intelligence by looking at the ability to discriminate between two tones or timbres; rather, we should be teaching people to sing songs or play instruments or transform melodies and seeing how readily they master such feats. At the same time, we should abjure a search for pure emotional sensitivity — for example, a test that matches facial expressions to galvanic skin response. Rather, we should place (or observe) people in situations that call for them to be sensitive to the aspirations and motives of others. For example, we could see how they handle a situation in which they and colleagues have to break up a fight between two teenagers, or persuade a boss to change a policy of which they do not approve.

Here powerful new simulations can be invoked. We are now in a position to draw on technologies that can deliver realistic situations or problems and also record the success of subjects in dealing with them. A student can be presented with an unfamiliar tune on a computer and asked to learn that tune, transpose it, orchestrate it, and the like. Such exercises would reveal much about the student's intelligence in musical matters.

Turning to the social (or human, if you prefer) realm, subjects can be presented with simulated interactions and asked to judge the shifting motivations of each actor. Or they can be asked to work in an interactive hypermedia production with unfamiliar people who are trying to accomplish some sort of goal, and to respond to their various moves and countermoves. The program can alter responses in light of the moves of the subject. Like a high-stakes poker game, such a measure should reveal much about the interpersonal or emotional sensitivity of a subject.

A significant increase in the breadth—the elasticity—of our concept of in- 50
telligence, then, should open the possibility for innovative forms of assessment far more realistic than the classic short-answer examinations. Why settle for an IQ or an SAT test, in which the items are at best remote proxies for the ability to design experiments, write essays, critique musical performances, and so forth? Why not instead ask people actually (or virtually) to carry out such tasks? And yet by not opening up the Pandora's box of values and subjectivity, one can continue to make judicious use of the insights and technologies achieved by those who have devoted decades to perfecting mental measurement.

To be sure, one can create a psychometric instrument for any conceivable human virtue, including morality, creativity, and emotional intelligence in its several senses. Indeed, since the publication of Daniel Goleman's book dozens of efforts have been made to create tests for emotional intelligence. The resulting instruments are not, however, necessarily useful. Such instruments are far more likely to satisfy the test maker's desire for reliability (a subject gets roughly the same score on two separate administrations of the test) than the need for validity (the test measures the trait that it purports to measure).

Such instruments-on-demand prove dubious for two reasons. First, beyond some platitudes, few can agree on what it means to be moral, ethical, a good person: consider the differing values of Jesse Helms and Jesse Jackson, Margaret Thatcher and Margaret Mead. Second, scores on such tests are much more likely to reveal test-taking savvy (skills in language and logic) than fundamental character.

In speaking about character, I turn to a final concern: the relationship between intelligence and what I will call virtue—those qualities that we admire and wish to hold up as examples for our children. No doubt the desire to expand intelligence to encompass ethics and character represents a direct response to the general feeling that our society is lacking in these dimensions; the expansionist view of intelligence reflects the hope that if we transmit the technology of intelligence to these virtues, we might in the end secure a more virtuous population.

I have already indicated my strong reservations about trying to make the word "intelligence" all things to all people—the psychometric equivalent of the true, the beautiful, and the good. Yet the problem remains: how, in a post-Aristotelian, post-Confucian era in which psychometrics looms large, do we think about the virtuous human being?

My analysis suggests one promising approach. We should recognize that intel- 55
ligences, creativity, and morality—to mention just three desiderata—are separate. Each may require its own form of measurement or assessment, and some will prove

far easier to assess objectively than others. Indeed, with respect to creativity and morality, we are more likely to rely on overall judgments by experts than on any putative test battery. At the same time, testing prevents us from looking for people who combine several of these attributes—who have musical and interpersonal intelligence, who are psychometrically intelligent and creative in the arts, who combine emotional sensitivity and a high standard of moral conduct.

Let me introduce another analogy at this point. In college admissions much attention is paid to scholastic performance, as measured by College Board examinations and grades. However, other features are also weighed, and sometimes a person with lower test scores is admitted if he or she proves exemplary in terms of citizenship or athletics or motivation. Admissions officers do not confound these virtues (indeed, they may use different scales and issue different grades), but they recognize the attractiveness of candidates who exemplify two or more desirable traits.

We have left the Eden of classical times, in which various intellectual and ethical values necessarily commingled, and we are unlikely ever to re-create it. We should recognize that these virtues can be separate and will often prove to be remote from one another. When we attempt to aggregate them, through phrases like "emotional intelligence," "creative intelligence," and "moral intelligence," we should realize that we are expressing a wish rather than denoting a necessary or even a likely coupling.

We have an aid in converting this wish to reality: the existence of powerful examples—people who succeed in exemplifying two or more cardinal human virtues. To name names is risky—particularly when one generation's heroes can become the subject of the next generation's pathographies. Even so, I can without apology mention Niels Bohr, George C. Marshall, Rachel Carson, Arthur Ashe, Louis Armstrong, Pablo Casals, Ella Fitzgerald.

In studying the lives of such people, we discover human possibilities. Young human beings learn primarily from the examples of powerful adults around them—those who are admirable and also those who are simply glamorous. Sustained attention to admirable examples may well increase the future incidence of people who actually do yoke capacities that are scientifically and epistemologically separate.

In one of the most evocative phrases of the century the British novelist E. M. Forster counseled us, "Only connect." I believe that some expansionists in the territory of intelligence, though well motivated, have prematurely asserted connections that do not exist. But I also believe that as human beings, we can help to forge connections that may be important for our physical and psychic survival. 60

Just how the precise borders of intelligence are drawn is a question we can leave to scholars. But the imperative to broaden our definition of intelligence in a responsible way goes well beyond the academy. Who "owns" intelligence promises to be an issue even more critical in the next century than it has been in this era of the IQ test.

QUESTIONS FOR DISCUSSION AND WRITING

1. Visualize Plato's parable by means of an outline or a drawing. How many stages are there in the process through which "our nature may be enlightened or unenlightened" (paragraph 1)? In what sequence are these stages arranged? Why does Plato choose this order? Try drawing a comparable diagram for Gardner's "eight intelligences" (paragraph 22).

2. Identify and examine Gardner's "eight intelligences": "linguistic and logical-mathematical . . . musical, spatial, bodily-kinesthetic, naturalist, interpersonal, and intrapersonal" (paragraph 22). Does Plato's "Allegory of the Cave" address any of these? If so, which sorts of intelligence?

3. In Plato, and in Gardner, which kinds of intelligence are primary? Why? If Gardner considers each kind of intelligence equivalent to every other kind, does he make a different case for the importance of each? On what grounds? Do you agree with him? If so, explain why. If not, make a case for a hierarchical arrangement of the different kinds of intelligence Gardner identifies. Does your hierarchy depend on, for example, a person's choice of profession or passionate involvement? For instance, a person with high musical intelligence might or might not have equally high bodily-kinesthetic intelligence, and this could lead to a differential expenditure of time, energy, and talent in one area or the other. Yet good musicians need excellent muscular coordination and good timing, among other things, just as good athletes do. So don't oversimplify your discussion. Draw on your own experience and that of people you know.

4. What is "alchemy"? What does Gardner mean by speaking of "pure intelligence" as "alchemical" (paragraph 46)?

5. What are Gardner's reasons for differentiating intelligence from creativity and from morality? Illustrate your answer with examples you have seen in action.

6. Do Plato and Gardner challenge the ways you think about thinking? About understanding the world? After discussion, write an essay in which you define what you mean by thinking, and illustrate this with examples. In your estimation, does "thinking" equal "intelligence"? What can thinking in itself accomplish? Then, examine some of the different types of intelligence Gardner discusses to question your original definition.

7. Imagine you're a teacher (in a specific field that you know a lot about), a coach, a chef, a musician—someone giving instruction to a person who doesn't know much about the subject at hand but is eager to learn. How could you best teach this novice the fundamentals? How could you decide whether or not that person had sufficient "intelligence" in that area to make it worth proceeding for more advanced instruction? Work out a plan of action and, if time permits, try it out on an actual pupil. After you've tested this out, what refinements in the initial plan would you make?

8. Why does Plato use the prisoners in a cave (almost a dungeon) as a metaphor of people in search of knowledge? What can we learn from this metaphor about

Plato's evaluation of knowledge and the human capacity for acquiring knowledge? Can human beings acquire complete and certain knowledge? Why or why
not? Now bring Gardner's analysis into the mix and see whether you arrive at the
same answers. Does Gardner use any conspicuous metaphors or other figures of
speech to reinforce his analysis?

9. Describe the characteristics of the Socratic dialogue based on specific details
   from "The Allegory of the Cave." Who talks most often? Who responds with brief
   phrases? What problems does the unequal use of language reveal about the form
   of the Socratic dialogue? What possible truths does this format discourage us
   from discovering?

MARJANE SATRAPI

The Convocation

*Marjane Satrapi was born in Rasht, Iran, in 1969 and earned two college degrees,
including an M.A. in visual communication from Islamic Azad University. She is
a graphic illustrator currently writing in Paris. Her signature style employs "almost
childlike drawings which take on the stark expressiveness of block prints" (Publisher's
Weekly, Oct. 3, 2006). These characterize her animated films as well as her books.
When she was a child in Iran, her liberal family experienced growing oppression
during times of great political unrest, which included the Revolution, the fall of the
Shah, the establishment of the Ayatollah Khomeini's regime, and the beginning of
the Iran-Iraq War. Many of these events are limned in* Persepolis, *Satrapi's critically
acclaimed, graphic autobiography (Part 1, 2003; Part 2, 2004; film, 2007).* Persepolis
*itself, declared a United Nations World Heritage site in 1979, was the ancient
Persian capital (c. 515 B.C.E.), so Satrapi's title invites us to read of contemporary
events through this classical lens.*

*As the Khomeini regime became more oppressive, Satrapi's parents sent her to
the Lycée Français de Vienne at fourteen. In their attempt to ensure educational freedom, Satrapi—away from parental wisdom and nurturing–experienced isolation
and alienation, and made many mistakes of adolescent misjudgment. Nevertheless,
Satrapi's tumultuous childhood through her college years inspired* Persepolis; *the
animated film version concentrates on her experiences in those turbulent times.
Other Iranian-based works include* Embroideries *(2005) and* Chicken with Plums
(2006). "The Convocation" comes near the end of Persepolis, *when Marjane has returned to Tehran to enter college where, as a new student, she opposes the administration's sexist policies that constrain women's dress and behavior.*

THE CONVOCATION

[1]Reza, also a new student, is the man she will marry in two years. [Editor's note.]

MANY OF THE STUDENTS KNEW ONE ANOTHER ALREADY. IN LISTENING TO THEM, I UNDERSTOOD THAT THEY'D TAKEN THE PREPARATORY CLASSES TOGETHER. OUR FIRST LESSON WAS "ART HISTORY."

WHAT IS GENERALLY KNOWN AS ARAB ART AND ARCHITECTURE SHOULD IN FACT BE CALLED THE ART OF THE ISLAMIC EMPIRE, WHICH STRETCHED FROM CHINA TO SPAIN. THIS ART IS A CROSS BETWEEN INDIAN, PERSIAN, AND MESOPOTAMIAN ART. THOSE WHOM WE CONSIDER, LIKE AVICENNA, TO BE "ARAB SCHOLARS" ARE FOR THE MOST PART ANYTHING BUT ARABS. EVEN THE FIRST BOOK OF ARABIC GRAMMAR WAS WRITTEN BY AN IRANIAN.

IT WAS FUNNY TO SEE TO WHAT EXTENT THE ISLAMIC REPUBLIC WAS NOT ABLE TO PUT AN END TO OUR CHAUVINISM. TO THE CONTRARY! PEOPLE OFTEN COMPARED THE OBSCURANTISM OF THE NEW REGIME TO THE ARAB INVASION. ACCORDING TO THIS LOGIC, "BEING PERSIAN" MEANT "NOT BEING A FANATIC." BUT THIS PARALLEL WENT ONLY SO FAR CONSIDERING THE FACT THAT OUR GOVERNMENT WASN'T COMPOSED OF ARAB INVADERS BUT PERSIAN FUNDAMENTALISTS.

AT LUNCH TIME.

THE PROFESSOR IS VERY INTERESTING, BUT OH MY! DOES HIS MOUTH SMELL. EVEN THIRTY FEET AWAY YOU CAN SMELL HIS JACKAL'S BREATH!

AMONG THE GUYS, A FEW EVEN HAVE HAIR CUTS!!! MY GOD!

HA! HA! HA!

DESPITE THEIR UPTIGHT APPEARANCE, THE GIRLS IN MY CLASS SEEMED TO BE QUITE THE COMEDIANS.

HEY! LOOK, THE GUY IN THE BLUE SHIRT... HE'S REALLY NOT BAD!

THEY WERE TALKING ABOUT REZA. I SUDDENLY FOUND THEM A LOT LESS FUNNY.

HI, I'M SHOUKA.

AND I'M NIYOOSHA.

NICE TO MEET YOU. I'M MARJANE.

NIYOOSHA HAD VERY GREEN EYES WHICH MADE HER THE MOST SOUGHT AFTER GIRL AT THE COLLEGE. (THE MAJORITY OF IRANIANS HAVE BLACK EYES.)

YOU'VE LIVED ABROAD?

YES, HOW DID YOU KNOW?

BECAUSE OF YOUR MAGHNAEH.* YOU WEAR IT LIKE A BEGINNER.

SHOUKA WAS VERY FUNNY. UNFORTUNATELY, WHEN SHE GOT MARRIED TWO YEARS LATER, HER HUSBAND FORBADE HER FROM ASSOCIATING WITH ME. TO HIM, I WAS AN AMORAL PERSON.

*HOODED HEAD-SCARF

IT'S TRUE THAT WEARING THE VEIL WAS A REAL SCIENCE. YOU HAD TO MAKE A SPECIAL FOLD, LIKE THIS:

NOT A HAIR SHOWS IN PROFILE.

BUT YOU SEE TUFTS FROM THE FRONT.

NEVERTHELESS, THINGS WERE EVOLVING... YEAR BY YEAR, WOMEN WERE WINNING AN EIGHTH OF AN INCH OF HAIR AND LOSING AN EIGHTH OF AN INCH OF VEIL.

WITH PRACTICE, EVEN THOUGH THEY WERE COVERED FROM HEAD TO FOOT, YOU GOT TO THE POINT WHERE YOU COULD GUESS THEIR SHAPE, THE WAY THEY WORE THEIR HAIR AND EVEN THEIR POLITICAL OPINIONS. OBVIOUSLY, THE MORE A WOMAN SHOWED, THE MORE PROGRESSIVE AND MODERN SHE WAS.

COMING HOME THAT EVENING.

HI EVERYONE!

HI.

SO, HOW WAS YOUR FIRST DAY?

LOOK WHAT GRANDMA BROUGHT FOR YOU.

GRANDMA?

EVER SINCE MY COWARDLY ACT MY GRANDMA HADN'T BEEN SPEAKING TO ME.[2]

WHAT'S THIS?

IT'S A COTTON HEAD-SCARF!

THIS WAY YOUR HEAD CAN BREATHE. OTHERWISE YOU'LL BE BALD IN NO TIME.

SHE HAD GIVEN ME A GIFT, SHE HAD THOUGHT OF MY HAIR, SHE WAS TALKING TO ME ...

... WHEW! SHE HAD FORGIVEN ME.

OH, GRANDMA! THANK YOU!!

FINE, FINE, IT'S OKAY!

I HAD FORGOTTEN HER EXTREME INTRANSIGENCE.

---

[2]The police, observing Marjane and Reza on the street, questioned them about their relationship. To protect herself and to deflect attention from Reza, Marjane blames an innocent man, whom the police arrest — claiming he's homosexual — and beat, breaking his nose and causing him to limp. When telling her beloved grandmother about this incident, Marjane laughs, and her grandmother becomes irate at her granddaughter's insensitivity: "Have you forgotten who your grandfather was? He spent a third of his life in prison for having defended some innocents." [Editor's note.]

AFTER THE LECTURE.

YOU'RE REALLY COURAGEOUS.

BRAVO! WHAT FRANK SPEAKING!

THANKS.

SATRAPI!

YOU'VE BEEN SUMMONED BY THE ISLAMIC COMMISSION...GOOD LUCK!

IS IT SERIOUS?

I REALLY DON'T KNOW.

THE DIRECTOR OF OUR COLLEGE HAD STUDIED IN THE UNITED STATES AND REMAINED QUITE SECULAR.

WHAT IS IT?

I'VE BEEN SUMMONED BY THE ISLAMIC COMMISSION!

OH SHIT!

WISH ME LUCK!

IT WAS AS IF I WERE GOING TO MEET MY EXECUTIONER.

...BUT TO MY PLEASANT SUR-PRISE, MY EXECUTIONER PROVED TO BE THE "TRUE RELIGIOUS" MAN, THE ONE WHO HAD PASSED ME ON THE IDEOLOGICAL TEST.

SO MISS SATRAPI... ALWAYS SAYING WHAT YOU THINK... IT'S GOOD! YOU'RE HONEST, BUT YOU ARE LOST.

YES.

READ THE SACRED TEXT. YOU'LL SEE THAT WEARING THE VEIL IS SYNONYMOUS WITH EMANCIPATION.

IF YOU SAY SO.

IT IS NOT I WHO SAYS IT, IT'S GOD... I'M GOING TO GIVE YOU A SECOND CHANCE. THIS TIME, YOU'RE NOT EXPELLED. IN EXCHANGE, I AM ASKING YOU TO IMAGINE THE UNIFORM ADAPTED TO THE NEEDS OF THE STUDENTS IN YOUR COLLEGE. NOTHING EXTRAVAGANT, YOU UNDERSTAND.

OF COURSE.

I APPLIED MYSELF. DESIGNING THE "MODEL" THAT WOULD PLEASE BOTH THE ADMINISTRA-TION AND THE INTERESTED PARTIES WASN'T EASY. I MADE DOZENS OF SKETCHES.

THIS WAS THE RESULT OF MY RESEARCH.

SHORT HEAD-SCARF

WIDE TROUSERS

THOUGH SUBTLE, THESE DIFFER-ENCES MEANT A LOT TO US.

THIS LITTLE REBELLION RECON-CILED MY GRANDMOTHER AND ME.

IT'S FEAR THAT MAKES US LOSE OUR CONSCIENCE. IT'S ALSO WHAT TRANSFORMS US INTO COWARDS. YOU HAD GUTS! I'M PROUD OF YOU!

AND THIS IS HOW I RECOVERED MY SELF-ESTEEM AND MY DIGNITY. FOR THE FIRST TIME IN A LONG TIME, I WAS HAPPY WITH MYSELF.

QUESTIONS FOR DISCUSSION AND WRITING

1. What evidence does Satrapi present of a repressive university administration? How do the Iranian students, like students everywhere, manage to subvert the administration?

2. Given that all the women are dressed alike, in veils and identical garments that cover their entire bodies, in what ways does Satrapi individualize them so readers can tell them apart?

3. What characterizes Satrapi herself—not only her appearance, but her beliefs, behavior, and personality? Is she likable? Explain your answer.

4. Why does Satrapi devote an entire page to the single panel in which the administrator, lecturing on the theme of "Moral and Religious Conduct," tells the "young ladies" to "wear less-wide trousers and longer head-scarves" to "cover your hair well, not wear makeup . . ."?

5. Satrapi defends women's dress: "Is religion defending our physical integrity or is it just opposed to fashion?" And she criticizes the sexism of these edicts: "Why is it that I, as a woman, am expected to feel nothing when watching these men with their clothes sculpted on but they, as men, can get excited by two inches less of my head-scarf?" Why isn't she punished for this?

6. How does this "little rebellion" enable her to reconcile with her grandmother?

7. If you're an artist, represent a significant incident in your life, preferably one in which you stood up for something important, in cartoon form. What will you choose to emphasize about yourself, physically and temperamentally? Or tell the story of the same incident in words.

LINDA SIMON

The Naked Source

Linda Simon (b. 1946) earned a doctorate in English and American literature from Brandeis University in 1983, and is currently associate professor of English at Skidmore College. She has written several biographical studies, including The Biography of Alice B. Toklas *(1977),* Of Virtue Rare: Margaret Beaufort, Matriarch of the House of Tudor *(1982),* Genuine Reality: A Life of William James *(1998), and* Dark Light: Electricity and Anxiety from the Telegraph to the X-Ray *(2004), making her an authority on the interpretation of primary data that underpins biographical and historical writing.*

"The Naked Source," originally published in the Michigan Quarterly Review *(1998), is a manifesto for revamping historical education. Primary sources—naked data—wait for us to interpret them and render them into coherent narratives by using our curiosity, imagination, intuition, and perseverance. History is more than stuff to learn for a test—it's a way of making sense of the world.*

It is true that my students do not know history. That annals of the American past, as students tell it, are compressed into a compact chronicle: John Kennedy and Martin Luther King flourish just a breath away from FDR and Woodrow Wilson, who themselves come right on the heels of Jefferson and Lincoln. The far and distant past is more obscure still.

Some, because they are bright and inquisitive, have learned names, dates, and the titles of major events. But even these masters of Trivial Pursuit often betray their ignorance of a real sense of the past. Teachers all have favorite oneliners that point to an abyss in historical knowledge. Mine is: Sputnik *who*?

There is no debate here. Students do not know history. Students should learn history. There is less agreement about what they should know, why they should know it, and far less agreement about how they should pursue this study of the past.

When I ask my students why they need to know history, they reply earnestly: We need to learn history because those who do not know history are doomed to repeat the mistakes of the past. They have heard this somewhere, although no one can attribute the remark. And if they are told that George Santayana said it, they know not who Santayana was, although if you care to inform them they will dutifully record his name, dates (1863–1952), and the title of the work (*The Life of Reason*) in which the remark was made.

Is that so? I ask. What will not be repeated? 5

Inevitably they respond emotionally with the example of the Holocaust. Some have watched an episode of a PBS series. Some have seen the film *The Diary of Anne Frank*. Such genocide, they reply, will not be repeated because we know about it. Undaunted by examples of contemporary genocide, they remain firm in their conviction. Genocide, they maintain. And the Great Depression.

The Great Depression has made a big impact on the adolescent imagination. Given any work of literature written at any time during the 1930s, some students will explain it as a direct response to the Great Depression. Wasn't everyone depressed, after all? And aren't most serious works of literature grim, glum, dark, and deep. There you have it.

But now we know about the Great Depression. And so it will not, cannot, happen again.

I am not persuaded that requiring students to read Tacitus or Thucydides, Carl Becker or Francis Parkman, Samuel Eliot Morison or Arnold Toynbee will remedy this situation, although I believe that students, and we, might well benefit from these writers' illumination. What students lack, after all, is a sense of historical-mindedness, a sense that lives were lived in a context, a sense that events (the Battle of Barnet, for example) had consequences (if men were slain on the battlefield, they could not return to the farm), a sense that answers must generate questions, more questions, and still more subtle questions.

As it is, students learning history, especially in the early grades, are asked 10 prescribed questions and are given little opportunity to pursue their own inquiry or satisfy their own curiosity. The following questions are from current high school texts:

> Has the role of the present United Nations proved that the hopes and dreams of Woodrow Wilson were achievable? If so, how? If not, why?

> What were the advantages of an isolationist policy for the United States in the nineteenth century? Were there disadvantages?

Questions such as these perpetuate the idea that history is a body of knowledge on which students will be tested. The first question, in other words, asks students: Did you read the section in the text on the role of the United Nations? Did you read the section on Wilson's aims in proposing the League of Nations? Can you put these two sections together?

The second question asks students: Did you understand the term *isolationist*? Did you read the section on U.S. foreign relations in the nineteenth century? Can you summarize the debate that the authors of the textbook recount?

Questions such as these perpetuate the idea that history can uncover "facts" and "truth," that history is objective, and that students, if only they are diligent, can recover "right answers" about the past. Questions such as these ignore the role of historians. Even those bright students who can recall dates and events rarely can recall the name of a historian, much less any feeling about who this particular man or woman was. For many students, historical facts are things out there, like sea shells or autumn leaves, and it hardly matters who fetches them. The sea shell will look the same whether it is gathered in Charles Beard's pocket or Henri Pirenne's.

What students really need to learn, more than "history," is a sense of the historical method of inquiry. They need to know what it is that historians do and how they do it. They need to understand the role of imagination and intuition in the telling of histories, they need to practice, themselves, confronting sources, making judgments, and defending conclusions.

When I ask my freshmen what they think historians do, they usually offer 15 me some lofty phrases about "influencing the course of future events." But what I mean is: what do historians do after breakfast? That is a question few of my students can answer. And they are surprised when I read them the following passage by British historian A. L. Rowse from his book *The Use of History.*

> You might think that in order to learn history you need a library of books to begin with. Not at all: that only comes at the end. What you need at the beginning is a pair of stout walking shoes, a pencil and a notebook; perhaps I should add a good county guide covering the area you mean to explore . . . and a map of the country . . . that gives you field footpaths and a wealth of things of interest, marks churches and historic buildings and ruins, wayside crosses and holy wells, prehistoric camps and dykes, the sites of battles. When you can't go for a walk, it is quite a good thing to study the map and plan where you would like to go. I am all in favor of the open-air approach to

history; the most delightful and enjoyable, the most imaginative and informative, and—what not everybody understands—the best training.

It is the best training because it gives the would-be historian an encounter with the things that all historians look at and puzzle over: primary sources about the past. Historians look at battlefields and old buildings, read letters and diaries and documents, interview eyewitnesses or participants in events. And they ask questions of these sources. Gradually, after asking increasingly sophisticated questions, they make some sense, for themselves, of what once happened.

What professional historians do, however, is not what most students do when they set out to learn history within the confines of a course. Instead of putting students face to face with primary sources, instructors are more likely to send them to read what other people say about the past. Students begin with a library of books of secondary sources, or they may begin with a text. But that, cautions Rowse, should come "at the end." Instead of allowing students to gain experience in weighing evidence and making inferences, the structures of many courses encourage them to amass information. "I found it!" exclaim enthusiastic students. They need to ask, "But what does it mean?"

They need to ask that question of the kinds of sources that historians actually use. Instead of reading Morison's rendering of Columbus's voyages, for example, students might read Columbus himself: his journal, his letters to the Spanish monarchs. Then they can begin to decide for themselves what sort of man this was and what sort of experience he had. Morison—as excellent a historian as he is—comes later. With some sense of the sources that Morison used, students can begin to evaluate his contribution to history, to understand how he drew conclusions from the material available to him, to see how "facts" are augmented by historical intuition. They can begin to understand, too, that the reconstruction of the past is slow and painstaking work.

Courses that cover several decades or even millennia may give students a false impression of historical inquiry. Historians, like archaeologists or epidemiologists, move slowly through bumpy and perilous terrain. They are used to travelling for miles only to find themselves stranded at a dead end. Once, in the archives of Westminster Abbey, I eagerly awaited reading a fragment of a letter from King Henry VI (after all, that is how it was described in the card catalog), only to lift out of an envelope the corner of a page, about an inch across, with the faintest ink-mark the only evidence that it had, five hundred years before, been a letter at all.

Slowly the historian assembles pieces of the past. A household expense 20 record might be the only artifact proving that a certain medieval woman existed. How much can be known about her? How much can be known by examining someone's checkbook today? Yet historians must make do with just such odd legacies: wills and land deeds, maps and drawings, family portraits or photographs. Can you imagine the excitement over the discovery of a diary or a cache of letters? At last, a text. But the diary may prove a disappointment, a frustration.

William James recorded the title of a book he may have been reading or the name of a visitor. Didn't he understand that a historian or biographer would need the deep, reflective ruminations of which we know he was more than capable?

Students have not had these experiences. When they are asked to write, they write *about* history. The research paper or the term paper seems to many of them another form of test — this time a take-home drawn out over weeks. Even if they have learned that "voice" and "audience" are important for a writer, they see history papers as different. They must be objective; they must learn proper footnoting and documentation. They must compile an impressive bibliography. Most important, they must find something out. The research paper produces nothing so much as anxiety, and the student often feels overwhelmed by the project.

They might, instead, be asked to write history as historians do it. They might be introduced to archives — in their college, in their community, in their state capital. They might be encouraged to interview people, and to interview them again and again until they begin to get the kind of information that will enlighten them about a particular time or event. They might be encouraged to read newspapers on microfilm or the bound volumes of old magazines that are yellowing in the basement of their local library. And then they might be asked to write in that most challenging form: the historical narrative.

"I can recall experiencing upon the completing of my first work of history," George Kennan wrote once, ". . . a moment of panic when the question suddenly presented itself to me: What is it that I have done here? Perhaps what I have written is not really history but rather some sort of novel, the product of my own imagination, — an imagination stimulated, inspired and informed, let us hope, by the documents I have been reading, but imagination nevertheless." Most historians share Kennan's reaction.

Students, of course, can never discover the boundary between "fact" and imaginative construction unless they have contact with primary sources. They cannot know where the historian has intervened to analyze the information he or she has discovered. "Most of the facts that you excavate," Morison wrote in "History as a Literary Art," "are dumb things; it is for you to make them speak by proper selection, arrangement, and emphasis." Morison suggested that beginning historians look to such writers as Sherwood Anderson and Henry James for examples of the kind of palpable description and intense characterization that can make literature — historical or fictional — come alive.

Students need to be persuaded that they are writing literature, not taking a 25 test, when they set out to be historians. Their writing needs to be read and evaluated not only for the facts that they have managed to compile, but for the sense of the past that they have conveyed. They need to discover that the past was not only battles and elections, Major Forces and Charismatic Leaders, but ordinary people, growing up, courting, dancing to a different beat, camping by a river that has long since dried up, lighting out for a territory that no longer exists. Except in the imagination of historians, as they confront the naked source, unaided.

QUESTIONS FOR DISCUSSION AND WRITING

1. Do you agree with Simon that "[t]here is no debate here. Students do not know history" (paragraph 3)? Consider your experience with history classes. Have you studied the past in the way that Simon recommends, or have you merely amassed dates and names to repeat back on tests?

2. Simon asserts that well-written history is a type of literature — not merely a compilation of facts. The historian actually interprets the primary data and makes up a plausible story. How does this image of the historian at work match your experience as a reader of history? How does Robert Pearce's interest in George Orwell's writings illustrate Simon's view of the historian at work? Would Simon consider Orwell a historian?

3. Write a historical narrative based on primary sources like those discussed by Simon. Investigate a person or an event from your local history — your family or hometown, for example. Use: diaries, old news reports, town records, archives, or photographs. You might also interview people who know about the subject of your study.

4. Explore an aspect of history that intrigues you by writing a two-part essay sequence. First, write a short essay in which you describe a period, an event, or a person that you would like to learn more about; also explain why this subject interests you. Include a list of questions about your subject that you would like to answer. Next, find several sources of information — history books, encyclopedias, videos, Web sites — and write a second, longer essay about your subject. Explain what you learned, what surprises you encountered, and how closely the historical record matches what you expected to find. Were you able to answer all of your questions? Why or why not? Where could you turn to find the answers?

CHAPTER 5

Wired — Be Careful What We Wish For: What Are the Consequences of Life in the High-Tech Fast Lane?

ROZ CHAST

The I.M.s of Romeo and Juliet

QUESTIONS FOR DISCUSSION AND WRITING

1. What characteristics of instant messaging does this dialogue between Romeo and Juliet illustrate? How do these messages depart from Standard English? Is this real writing or a form of shorthand or code?

2. Are Romeo and Juliet typical American teenagers? What electronic equipment, clothing, books, and food reinforce your opinion? Why are these strewn so messily on the floor?

3. Do readers need to be familiar with Shakespeare's *Romeo and Juliet* to understand the humor of "The I.M.s of Romeo and Juliet"? To provide "closure" (see McCloud, p. 51)? In either case, why or why not?

DENNIS BARON

The New Technologies of the Word

Dennis Baron (b. 1944) earned three degrees in English—B.A. (Brandeis, 1965), M.A. (Columbia, 1968), Ph.D. (University of Michigan, 1971)—and has spent most of his career as a professor of English and linguistics at the University of Illinois at Urbana–Champaign. His wide-ranging publications address such topics as language legislation, policy, and reform; minority languages and dialects; linguistic rights; reading, writing, and other aspects of literacy; and technologies of communication. These are addressed in such books as Grammar and Gender *(1986) and* The English Only Question: An Official Language for Americans? *(1990). "The New Technologies of the Word" (originally a talk for the International Association of World Englishes, 2002), reprinted here, was a precursor to Baron's most recent book,* A Better Pencil: Reading, Writing and the Digital Revolution *(2009). He explains that this book "puts our complex, still-evolving hate-love relationship with computers and the Internet into perspective, describing how the digital revolution influences our reading and writing practices, and how the latest technologies differ from what came before."*

"The New Technologies of the Word" examines the way new communication methods spawned by computers and cell phones, currently 4.6 billion in use for a worldwide population of 6.8 billion (in 2010), influence not only writing but a myriad of other behaviors. In particular, Baron argues that e-mail and cell phones produce new modes of communication, and "watching these new genres arise and evolve is like being present at the birth of stars." Indeed, with Wi-Fi and fiber optics promising broadband speeds 100 times faster than the current digital subscriber lines or cable, Baron's discussion of technological advances may require daily updating!

I am going to talk specifically about how electronic technologies are introducing major changes in the practice of American English: the computer has altered the ways we write and read significantly in the past 20 years, and the cell phone is changing spoken interaction in ways that continue to evolve. Both technologies are reconfiguring our notions of public and private language, and both are calling our attention increasingly to what is being called the "digital divide" between haves and have nots—and that is what brings us back to language policy both on the national and the global scale.

I think that the new technologies of the word, as I call them, are reinforcing two trends that we may all be observing in what is going on with English around the world. One is the continued spread of English as a world language (with the caveat so nicely articulated by [scholars] many years ago that world languages, like world empires, come and go). But this accent on global English is balanced by what I see as a new emphasis on the local: both local varieties of English set against the umbrella of World Englishes. And also a renewed emphasis on local languages and varieties in tandem with and in resistance to dominant world and national languages. The new technologies of the word are the tools of the globalizers, working for standardization. But what they produce after their initial spread is often a surprising reinforcement of the local.

Not so long ago the claim was going unquestioned that English was the language of the World Wide Web, and that the web itself embodied a kind of digital imperialism increasing the domination by English of the communication pathways. After all, it was argued, computers were limited in their ability to represent non-Roman alphabets, and anyway it was felt that everyone who had anything important to say was saying it in English. How could we be so naïve—and so colonialist—in what we envision as an increasingly postcolonial world? In any case it has become clear that many languages are now claiming their own space in a cyberspace that is perfectly able to stretch to fit them, and that the effects of technology on language practice apply not just to speakers and writers of English, but to users of any language. What is true across languages is true as well within them: the standard language imposed top down by governments, schools, and cultural norms is everywhere met by the infinite variety of local forms and practices. The computer can transmit norms downward from the top, but it can also empower individuals "at the bottom" as it were to take control of authorship: nowadays you don't have to seize the radio stations and the mimeograph machines to support the revolution. Instead, in this age of digital reproduction, you can simply fire up your PC and send your manifesto into cyberspace.

TECHNOLOGY

Language, both written and spoken, depends heavily on technology for its transmission. I would argue that speech itself is a technology, as is writing. And the means we use to transmit speech and writing are technological as well.

Today we tend to think of technology as referring primarily to computers, 5 and when I speak of the new technologies of the word I too will consider the impact of digital technology on our communication practices. But we shouldn't lose sight of the fact that there are other technologies—old technologies of the word, if you will—that remain even today more prevalent than computers—that mediate our communication.

For example, there's the humble wood pencil [hold up pencil], which as Henry Petroski [author of *The Pencil*, 2002] has shown, is a complex technology. True it has no electronics, nor any moving parts, and it costs only a few cents to manufacture and purchase in this age of mechanical reproduction. But a pencil is complex enough that you could not easily replicate one in a home workshop, and even if you could master the technologies of woodworking, chemistry, mineralogy, painting and engineering necessary to make a do-it-yourself pencil, the materials would cost you something on the order of $50, not a few cents per unit. . . .

[Henry David] Thoreau . . . was an engineer and entrepreneur who took a marginal [family] business which churned out a cheap, low-quality product and turned it profitable. Thoreau may have written idealistically, but he spent six months in the Harvard College library researching European pencil technology in an effort to make the Thoreau pencil better and more expensive than any import. And the man who invented civil disobedience, refusing to pay taxes being used to finance an unjust war, used his marketing skills to sell his pencils. . . .

NOSTALGIA FOR THE OLD WAYS

Socrates warned that the new technology of writing would work to the detriment of the old technology of memory. We remember this, of course, because Plato wrote it down. One of the common complaints we hear today is that computers signal the death of handwriting. Penmanship, as it was once called in American schools, is no longer practiced with any rigor, except by those few diehards who want to bring back the fountain pen.

Perhaps copying all the letters in a big round hand, as the Ruler of the Queen's Navee did to gain advancement, is a lost art for most of us, but standardized handwriting was a literacy technology just as computer writing is today. From a purely practical standpoint, uniform script was once enforced for scribes and clerks to ensure legibility in documents destined to have multiple readers. Indeed, a copperplate-perfect handwriting in the nineteenth century was a class marker. The rich didn't need a nice round hand, for they didn't work in offices and could afford to allow their handwriting to express their individuality. Once the press freed us from a dependence on hand-copied manuscripts, and the typewriter liberated the office from the tyranny of the inkwell, it was inevitable that handwriting would become a lost art, revived from time to time by people who feel trapped in the present.

THE BIRTH OF GENRES

OK, enough about the old technologies of the word. Let's take a look at the new. 10
In the last decade or two, three new written genres have emerged: email, the web page, and instant messaging now form a significant slice of writing practice in the

United States and at least email and the web page are gaining importance around the globe as well. In addition, the mobile phone is now a major factor influencing spoken communication. Watching these new genres arise and evolve is like being present at the birth of stars: we have the unusual opportunity to observe these linguistic genres spin off from older ways of doing things with words, starting out as one sort of communication practice and winding up as something completely different, developing their own conventions of style and usage, of appropriateness and correctness, of grammaticality and acceptability. . . .

Email started out in the emerging computer companies of the 1960s and 1970s for in-house electronic memos. In addition, programmers sent email to one another to pass the time while their programs were compiling—much as telegraphers in the early days of electronic communication sent personal messages to one another, and played games, while they waited for paying customers. The first email users were techies, and the mainframe computer systems they sent their email on were not user-friendly. Those computers were designed for number-crunching, not word-processing. Even programmers didn't program on the machines: they wrote out their code on pads of paper—and they probably used no. 2 pencils to write with. Line editors were cumbersome to work with, and initially computer keyboards only allowed working in one case, upper or lower.

This technology was so unforgiving that only a few diehards saw the possibilities that computers offered writers. Many of the early computer writers were a ragged and persistent gang, and as a result, in the early days of email, a frontier mystique developed around computer writing: it wasn't something for the faint of heart. Because correcting text was so difficult, and perhaps also because programmers wanted to give the impression that they had more important things to do than submit to the niceties of writing conventional prose, emailers were lawless—at least when it came to observing the laws of spelling, grammar, and usage that constrain writers using conventional technologies. They typed their email quickly, without concern for form or style: it was their version of shooting from the hip. They wore incorrectness as a badge of authority. They keyed their messages in lower case. They rejected linguistic conventionality and wrapped themselves in the mantle of Thoreau.

But as it is with all communication, an initially chaotic system began to self-organize. Plus, the early chaos of email may have been more myth than reality. Anecdotal evidence supports a claim that there was plenty of concern for linguistic correctness when computer writing was young. And even those writers of emails who openly derided the schoolmarm approach to grammar developed conventions early on. For one thing, writers were using computers to send conventional messages—memos, reports, notices of meetings—at the same time that what I will call the "desperado email" was emerging. . . .

As with the early days of writing itself, digital literacy was limited to a class of scribes, or programmers, who had mastered the steep learning curve of the technology and who could, if necessary, mediate the literacy technology for the uninitiated. For digital writing to spread beyond this small group of adepts a number of things had to happen: the practice had to become easier to learn (both the hardware and the software needed to be made more writer-friendly); and computers had to become less expensive if more people were to have access to them.

In fact both of these things started to happen, first with the success of the per- 15 sonal computer in the early 1980s. Then in the later 1980s, graphical user interfaces and black-on-white screens allowed for text display approximating an actual typed or printed document. This, combined with significantly lower costs, led more people both to be able to afford the machine and to see that it could allow them to produce the kinds of documents they were already used to producing.

As more people adopted the technology, they brought with them their conventional concerns. The new converts to digital writing, like typists and pen-men before them, wanted to know how to do it right: how to write a business letter; how to write a report; how to write a personal letter, and they brought their concern for this medieval *ars dictaminis*, as updated for the modern office, to the newly emerging genres of email and newsgroups. The electronic frontier was suddenly becoming settled and urbanized, and there arose a sometimes not-so-subtle distinction between newcomers and old-timers. The old-timers clung to their lawlessness as a badge of authority. They were there first, after all: they invented the wheel. Newcomers asked silly questions like, "Should an email have a greeting?" And newcomers to the discourse show an inordinate fondness for spell-checking.

Soon manuals on correct electronic communication, or netiquette, began to surface. There are numerous on-line lists of do's and don'ts for email. . . . One sure sign that conventionality has come into play once and for all, that the electronic frontier is finally becoming civilized, is the appearance of chapters on electronic communication in every major college writing textbook.

THE CHARGE AGAINST EMAIL

While it is heralded by its proponents as the best thing since sliced bread, technology also seems often to generate suspicion. Critics of email view it as a leading force in the inevitable decline and fall of the English language.

Located somewhere between the traditional letter and the phone call, email continues to carve out its own communication space. True, there are junk emails that replicate conventional technology's junk mail. And there are email confidence schemes that are as intrusive as the soliciting phone calls timed to coincide with dinner. Email seems private but is in fact very public: it is discoverable in court, and if you use email at work, it is the property of your employer, who may spy on your email as well as your phone calls at will.

But the main charge against email is that it is too informal. By 'too informal' 20 critics tend to mean that, despite the prevalence of usage guides, emailers do not evince enough concern for spelling and usage. They use too many shortcuts: acronyms like IMHO or BTW, and emoticons. There's too much slang. In short, the language of Shakespeare, Addison and Steele, and Hemingway gets no respect from emailers. And emoticons have become our newest punctuation marks.

Of course emails vary in their degree of formality, and in their observance of stylistic niceties, the way any text may. The speed of email, compared to the post office, may take some getting used to. And so perhaps the most common complaint of emailers themselves doesn't concern error or slang, it's the experience many of us have had of sending off an email before we are really ready. It may be an angry email, or an incomplete one. Or we may have sent it to the wrong recipient. . . .

Nonetheless email has made inroads in our communication practice. Once you start down the email path, there's no going back. See what happens when the computers go down in an office. People don't immediately switch over to the phone, or walk down the corridor for a chat. Initially, at least, they sit around staring at their screens, wondering how they're going to get anything done today.

INSTANT MESSAGING

Instant messaging [IM] is an even newer genre than email, popular with college students as well as the teen and pre-teen set. It differs from email in that it is a real-time exchange, a digital conversation among two or more selected participants, the so-called "buddy list," that seems to thrive on short turns, rapid turn-taking, with participants dropping in and out of the conversation with regularity. . . .

From what I can tell by looking at transcripts of IM sessions among the seventh-grade set, IM is mostly phatic communication. "I'm here. Are you there?" "I'm here." "Silly joke, silly joke." "Acronym, acronym." "G2G." "TTFN." If Monty Python were still going strong, they'd surely do an IM skit. . . .

IM is more than a written conference call, with images and sounds to 25 accompany its staccato exchanges. It is already thriving beyond the teen set in offices everywhere: it provides an easier switch than email does between onscreen work and chatting with a friend, since the IM screen can remain open alongside the spreadsheet or word processing document. It seems safe to predict that IM will develop more fully just as email has done, and that it too, while remaining reasonably informal, will develop rules and conventions of the kind every speech community seems to form.

CELL PHONES

IM, even when only two buddies converse, seems to be private discourse carried on in a public electronic space. Both email and Instant Messaging are skewing our ideas of public and private language. But cell phones warp the contexts of public and private even more noticeably. Consider these scenarios:

- In a crowded gate area at O'Hare Airport in Chicago, a man who looks like he's been sleeping in his clothes marches up and down amidst the clumps of weary passengers huddled with their luggage. There's a scowl on his face and his arms saw the air as he talks loudly and angrily to himself. Terrorist? Psychotic off his meds? Neither, actually: he's a frustrated business traveler talking on his hands-free cell phone, squeezing in some work while he waits for his long-delayed flight to board. . . .

- It's the first day of my "Literacy and Technology" class at the University of Illinois, and just as I begin my soliloquy on how the new technologies are changing the ways we communicate, a tinkling melody emanates from a backpack. Without any embarrassment, a student digs out her phone, answers the call, carries on a short conversation, then hangs up. I say, pointedly, "As I was saying . . . ," though only some of the students see the irony: what just happened was exactly the point I was trying to make, that mobile telephony changes conditions for more people than just the caller and the called. Subsequent in-class phone calls are less well-timed to coincide with the syllabus. Despite my requests that students turn their phones off before coming into the room — requests there was no need to make only a semester earlier — it takes the class a while to get into the habit. Then one day my own phone rings while I am teaching. I answer the call, have a short, embarrassed conversation while the class giggles and strains to hear what I am whispering, then go back to teaching. We have no more interruptions that semester, but I notice that students now turn their phones back on even before they close their books and stow them away — the traditional signal to the instructor that my fifty minutes is up. . . .

Cell phones have come a long way in a few short years. In 1994, . . . perhaps 10 million Americans had cell phones. Today [2002] more than 100 million Americans have them[1] and some people are giving up their land phones entirely. They are changing both the nature of telephone interaction and the way people behave in public. . . .

More and more I see people walking together in an animated group, but each person is talking on a phone to someone else. At least I presume they're talking to someone else. There is, after all, that scene in the movie "Clueless" where Cher strolls alongside her best friend, Dionne, and they are chattering to one another on their cell phones.

Before cell phones, people in a group could talk to one another face to face, and people alone could give full attention to their immediate surroundings: looking at the scenery, driving the car, perusing the menu, observing the *comédie humaine*. Now the cell phone connects us across space, freeing us from our local context just as the land phone did when it first came on the scene.

Cell phones used in public can create an instant audience, albeit a sometimes unwilling one. This morning at the local coffee bar, a woman came in already talking loudly on her phone, and while she was ordering her latte she took a second call and switched deftly between her two callers and the barista, at times

30

---

[1] But see the Baron headnote (p. 327). [Editor's note.]

involving all three in what seemed to be a single conversation. But the rest of us in the coffee line were also auditors, for talking on a cell phone seems to bring out an emotive voice. People bare half a conversation to an audience of strangers, a conversation that is sometimes uncomfortably personal for those within earshot, though it is even more often boring (who cares what your mother ate for lunch?) or simply distracting (I can't hear the person I'm with because the cell phone talker is so loud). . . .

When telephones first came on the scene, in the 1880s, whispering was not an option. Neither was privacy. Phones were rare, and when households or businesses got their first phones, they were placed in a central location: a first-floor hallway or a front desk or counter. Speaking on the telephone meant there was no place to hide, and it took some time before extensions became available that allowed callers to retreat into bedrooms or back offices, or phone cords became long enough for teenagers to haul the phone into a closet or bathroom for privacy. Not only bystanders listened in to phone calls. Telephone operators were required to check in on conversations to determine whether the line was still in use, since the connection was not automatically broken when a caller hung up the phone. But soon enough operators took on the role of conversation monitors, occasionally threatening to suspend the phone privileges of callers who used vulgar language and profanity. Privacy was further compromised in rural areas by party lines, where members of other households on the same phone line could eavesdrop.

Early telephone technology was poor by today's standards, too. Voice reproduction was so unnatural, and line noise so common, that in many cases speakers had to shout or speak very loudly in order to be heard. And speakers shouted as well in response to the room noise that occasionally made it hard for them to hear their callers. This same attempt to overcome background noise from traffic, machinery, and other talkers nearby, may lie behind the tendency of cell phone users to speak more loudly on the phone than they would to someone who is right next to them.

CONCLUSIONS

New technologies of communication often get their big break by duplicating older ones. When writing emerged in the ancient Mediterranean as an inventory device, it was useful to merchants. But once someone realized that writing could duplicate speech, there was no turning back. Cabinet makers invented the wood pencil in the sixteenth century to mark measurements in wood without gouging the wood. Once someone realized they were perfect portable writing and drawing instruments, freeing writers from their dependence on the inkwell, pencils became the first laptops. Computers began life as number crunchers (the name *computer* was first used to refer to human beings doing repetitive computations). They still crunch numbers, it's true, but most of us now depend on our computers as writing tools, not calculators.

Our communication practices have been permanently altered by electronic technologies, and that should surprise no one, nor should it be the cause of lamentation. The computer allows more people to become authors, if by authors we mean any writer who sends a creation out into the world of readers. By doing that, the computer allows more authorial languages to claim public space and authority they might not otherwise have had.

But at the same time, as authorship and linguistic prominence shift from 35 older technologies to the computer, this democratization of the public word reinforces the divide between those who have computers and those who don't, and it further distances those who have literacy from those who don't.

But even as we worry about access to computers, equating that, perhaps mistakenly, with access to literacy, the technology is moving in new ways that may cause us once again to rethink what we mean by literacy, and to re-evaluate the interactions of language practice and technology. Already mobile phones are becoming more computer-like, and there is some chance that computers will become more like telephones. If the next big development in the digital world is the perfection of speech-to-text software, then writers will no longer key in their texts, they'll speak them, and their words will magically appear on screen.

If this actually works, and it's probably still a long time coming, it will signal a change in writing practice: we will all be dictating our text to our computers. More important, it will mark a change in our thinking about literacy. Computers can already turn text to speech efficiently enough to eliminate our dependence on the visual processing of text. Link speech to text with text to speech and you eliminate the middle terms: writing and reading could conceivably be reconfigured in such a way that they become an invisible part of the communication.

At the very least, this will cause traditionalists to lament the decline in the keyboarding skills of the young. But in fact the implications of speech to text for reconfiguring literacy are staggering. However there's no need to see the library going the way of the 8-track tape, or the quill pen. Even though my cell phone can receive email messages, for now speech to text still belongs in the realm of science fiction, like cold fusion or, dare I say, machine translation?

QUESTIONS FOR DISCUSSION AND WRITING

1. Baron begins his discussion of technology with the pencil, manufactured (and used) by Henry David Thoreau, and the importance of handwriting in America in the nineteenth and twentieth centuries (paragraphs 6–10). What, if anything, do you write by hand? Under what circumstances? Were you taught penmanship in school? When did you learn to use a computer or other electronic communication device(s)? Did you teach yourself or learn by trial and error? Note that Baron skips completely over typewriters, the mainstay of American offices throughout most of the twentieth century. Why?

2. Based on the examples that Baron supplies (paragraph 26), do you agree that electronic technologies such as e-mail, cell phones, message boards, and blogs are causing "major changes in the practice of American English" (paragraph 1)? How are these changes creating written or unwritten guidelines for using e-mail, cell phones, smartphones, and instant messaging? What is the basis of rules such as those imposed by Internet discussion lists on behaviors such as "flaming" and "spamming," by colleges and high schools on in-class cell phone use, and by some states on using a cell phone while driving? To what extent are these rules justified as matters of privacy, etiquette, safety, or ethics?

3. Baron writes about the way the World Wide Web and language affect each other, arguing that the Web could be both an agent of language "imperialism" and a way to empower individuals "at the bottom" to "take control of authorship" (paragraph 3). By yourself or with a group, write a paper about language "imperialism" or language liberation involving the Web, using research and your own experience. Focus on a case in which individuals, or relatively powerless groups, used the Internet to gain power or a case in which institutions or governments used the Internet to dominate others.

NICHOLAS CARR

Is Google Making Us Stupid?

Technology author Nicholas Carr (b. 1959) earned a B.A. from Dartmouth and an M.A. from Harvard. Carr has been a columnist for the Guardian *and the* Industry Standard; *his writing on technology has appeared in the* New York Times Magazine, Wired, *the* Financial Times, *and* Die Zeit. *Carr's blog (since 2005), Rough Type, focuses on the impact of information technologies on people, society, business, the world. This orientation is reflected in* Does IT Matter? *(2004) and* The Shallows: What the Internet Is Doing to Our Brains *(2010). Likewise, in* The Big Switch: Rewiring the World from Edison to Google *(2008), he demonstrates how and why "[T]he interplay of technological and economic forces rarely produces the results we at first expect. . . . [T]he economic forces that the World Wide Computer is unleashing . . . the replacement of skilled as well as unskilled workers with software, the global trade in knowledge work, and the ability of companies to aggregate volunteer labor and harvest its economic value—we're left with a prospect that is far from Utopian. The erosion of the middle class may well accelerate, as the divide widens between a relatively small group of extraordinarily wealthy people—the digital elite—and a very large set of people who face eroding fortunes and a persistent struggle to make ends meet. In the YouTube economy, everyone is free to play, but only a few reap the rewards."*

"Is Google Making Us Stupid?" (Atlantic, 2008) was a precursor to Carr's The Shallows: What the Internet Is Doing to Our Brains (2010). The essay was included in The Best American Science and Nature Writing, The Best Technology Writing, *and* The Best Spiritual Writing. *In this triple-winner, Carr argues that "media are not just passive channels of information. They supply the stuff of thought, but they also shape the process of thought. And what the Net seems to be doing is chipping away my capacity for concentration and contemplation. My mind now expects to take in information the way the Net distributes it: in a swiftly moving stream of particles." Carr's essay thoughtfully explores the high price of "zipping among lots of bits of information"—the "loss of depth in our thinking."*

"Dave, stop. Stop, will you? Stop, Dave. Will you stop, Dave?" So the supercomputer HAL pleads with the implacable astronaut Dave Bowman in a famous and weirdly poignant scene toward the end of Stanley Kubrick's *2001: A Space Odyssey*. Bowman, having nearly been sent to a deep-space death by the malfunctioning machine, is calmly coldly disconnecting the memory circuits that control its artificial brain. "Dave, my mind is going," HAL says, forlornly. "I can feel it. I can feel it."

I can feel it, too. Over the past few years I've had an uncomfortable sense that someone, or something, has been tinkering with my brain, remapping the neural circuitry, reprogramming the memory. My mind isn't going—so far as I can tell—but it's changing. I'm not thinking the way I used to think. I can feel it most strongly when I'm reading. Immersing myself in a book or a lengthy article used to be easy. My mind would get caught up in the narrative or the turns of the argument, and I'd spend hours strolling through long stretches of prose. That's rarely the case anymore. Now my concentration often starts to drift after two or three pages. I get fidgety, lose the thread, begin looking for something else to do. I feel as if I'm always dragging my wayward brain back to the text. The deep reading that used to come naturally has become a struggle.

I think I know what's going on. For more than a decade now, I've been spending a lot of time online, searching and surfing and sometimes adding to the great databases of the Internet. The Web has been a godsend to me as a writer. Research that once required days in the stacks or periodical rooms of libraries can now be done in minutes. A few Google searches, some quick clicks on hyperlinks, and I've got the telltale fact or pithy quote I was after. Even when I'm not working, I'm as likely as not to be foraging in the Web's info-thickets—reading and writing e-mails, scanning headlines and blog posts, watching videos and listening to podcasts, or just tripping from link to link to link. (Unlike footnotes, to which they're sometimes likened, hyperlinks don't merely point to related works; they propel you toward them.)

For me, as for others, the Net is becoming a universal medium, the conduit for most of the information that flows through my eyes and ears and into my mind. The advantages of having immediate access to such an incredibly rich store of information are many, and they've been widely described and duly applauded. "The perfect recall of silicon memory," *Wired*'s Clive Thompson has written, "can be an enormous boon to thinking." But that boon comes at a price. As the media theorist Marshall McLuhan pointed out in the 1960s, media are not just passive channels of information. They supply the stuff of thought, but they also shape the process of thought. And what the Net seems to be doing is chipping away my capacity for concentration and contemplation. My mind now expects to take in information the way the Net distributes it: in a swiftly moving stream of particles. Once I was a scuba diver in the sea of words. Now I zip along the surface like a guy on a Jet Ski.

I'm not the only one. When I mention my troubles with reading to friends   5 and acquaintances—literary types, most of them—many say they're having similar experiences. The more they use the Web, the more they have to fight to stay focused on long pieces of writing. Some of the bloggers I follow have also begun mentioning the phenomenon. Scott Karp, who writes a blog about online media, recently confessed that he has stopped reading books altogether. "I was a lit major in college, and used to be [a] voracious book reader," he wrote. "What happened?" He speculates on the answer: "What if I do all my reading on the web not so much because the way I read has changed, i.e. I'm just seeking convenience, but because the way I THINK has changed?"

Bruce Friedman, who blogs regularly about the use of computers in medicine, also has described how the Internet has altered his mental habits. "I now have almost totally lost the ability to read and absorb a longish article on the web or in print," he wrote earlier this year. A pathologist who has long been on the faculty of the University of Michigan Medical School, Friedman elaborated on his comment in a telephone conversation with me. His thinking, he said, has taken on a "staccato" quality, reflecting the way he quickly scans short passages of text from many sources online. "I can't read *War and Peace* anymore," he admitted. "I've lost the ability to do that. Even a blog post of more than three or four paragraphs is too much to absorb. I skim it."

Anecdotes alone don't prove much. And we still await the long-term neurological and psychological experiments that will provide a definitive picture of how Internet use affects cognition. But a recently published study of online research habits, conducted by scholars from University College London, suggests that we may well be in the midst of a sea change in the way we read and think. As part of the five-year research program, the scholars examined computer logs documenting the behavior of visitors to two popular research sites, one operated by the British Library and one by a U.K. educational consortium, that provide access to journal articles, e-books, and other sources of written information. They found that people using the sites exhibited "a form of skimming activity," hopping from one source to another and rarely returning to any source they'd already visited. They typically read no more than one or two pages of an article or book before they would "bounce" out to another site. Sometimes they'd save a long article, but there's no evidence that they ever went back and actually read it. The authors of the study report:

> It is clear that users are not reading online in the traditional sense; indeed there are signs that new forms of "reading" are emerging as users "power browse" horizontally through titles, contents pages and abstracts going for quick wins. It almost seems that they go online to avoid reading in the traditional sense.

Thanks to the ubiquity of text on the Internet, not to mention the popularity of text-messaging on cell phones, we may well be reading more today than we did in the 1970s or 1980s, when television was our medium of choice. But it's a different kind of reading, and behind it lies a different kind of thinking—perhaps even a new sense of the self. "We are not only *what* we read," says Maryanne Wolf, a developmental psychologist at Tufts University and the author of *Proust and the Squid: The Story and Science of the Reading Brain.* "We are *how* we read." Wolf worries that the style of reading promoted by the Net, a style that puts "efficiency" and "immediacy" above all else, may be weakening our capacity for the kind of deep reading that emerged when an earlier technology, the printing press, made long and complex works of prose commonplace. When we read online, she says, we tend to become "mere decoders of information." Our ability to interpret text, to make the rich mental connections that form when we read deeply and without distraction, remains largely disengaged.

Reading, explains Wolf, is not an instinctive skill for human beings. It's not etched into our genes the way speech is. We have to teach our minds how to translate the symbolic characters we see into the language we understand. And the media or other technologies we use in learning and practicing the craft of reading play an important part in shaping the neural circuits inside our brains. Experiments demonstrate that readers of ideograms, such as the Chinese, develop a mental circuitry for reading that is very different from the circuitry found in those of us whose written language employs an alphabet. The variations extend across many regions of the brain, including those that govern such essential cognitive functions as memory and the interpretation of visual and auditory stimuli. We can expect as well that the circuits woven by our use of the Net will be different from those woven by our reading of books and other printed works.

Sometime in 1882, Friedrich Nietzsche bought a typewriter—a Malling-Hansen   10 Writing Ball, to be precise. His vision was failing, and keeping his eyes focused on a page had become exhausting and painful, often bringing on crushing headaches. He had been forced to curtail his writing, and he feared that he would soon have to give it up. The typewriter rescued him, at least for a time. Once he had mastered touch-typing, he was able to write with his eyes closed, using only the tips of his fingers. Words could once again flow from his mind to the page.

But the machine had a subtler effect on his work. One of Nietzsche's friends, a composer, noticed a change in the style of his writing. His already terse prose had become even tighter, more telegraphic. "Perhaps you will through this instrument even take to a new idiom," the friend wrote in a letter, noting that, in his own work, his "'thoughts' in music and language often depend on the quality of pen and paper."

"You are right," Nietzsche replied, "our writing equipment takes part in the forming of our thoughts." Under the sway of the machine, writes the German media scholar Friedrich A. Kittler, Nietzsche's prose "changed from arguments to aphorisms, from thoughts to puns, from rhetoric to telegram style."

The human brain is almost infinitely malleable. People used to think that our mental meshwork, the dense connections formed among the 100 billion or so neurons inside our skulls, was largely fixed by the time we reached adulthood. But brain researchers have discovered that that's not the case. James Olds, a professor of neuroscience who directs the Krasnow Institute for Advanced Study at George Mason University, says that even the adult mind "is very plastic." Nerve cells routinely break old connections and form new ones. "The brain," according to Olds, "has the ability to reprogram itself on the fly, altering the way it functions."

As we use what the sociologist Daniel Bell has called our "intellectual technologies"—the tools that extend our mental rather than our physical capacities—we inevitably begin to take on the qualities of those technologies. The mechanical clock, which came into common use in the 14th century, provides a compelling example. In *Technics and Civilization,* the historian and cultural critic Lewis Mumford described how the clock "disassociated time from human events and helped create the belief in an independent world of mathematically measurable sequences." The "abstract framework of divided time" became "the point of reference for both action and thought."

The clock's methodical ticking helped bring into being the scientific mind and the scientific man. But it also took something away. As the late MIT computer scientist Joseph Weizenbaum observed in his 1976 book, *Computer Power and Human Reason: From Judgment to Calculation,* the conception of the world that emerged from the widespread use of timekeeping instruments "remains an impoverished version of the older one, for it rests on a rejection of those direct experiences that formed the basis for, and indeed constituted, the old reality." In deciding when to eat, to work, to sleep, to rise, we stopped listening to our senses and started obeying the clock.

The process of adapting to new intellectual technologies is reflected in the changing metaphors we use to explain ourselves to ourselves. When the mechanical clock arrived, people began thinking of their brains as operating "like clockwork." Today, in the age of software, we have come to think of them as operating "like computers." But the changes, neuroscience tells us, go much deeper than metaphor. Thanks to our brain's plasticity, the adaptation occurs also at a biological level.

The Internet promises to have particularly far-reaching effects on cognition. In a paper published in 1936, the British mathematician Alan Turing proved that a digital computer, which at the time existed only as a theoretical machine, could be programmed to perform the function of any other information-processing device. And that's what we're seeing today. The Internet, an immeasurably powerful computing system, is subsuming most of our other intellectual technologies. It's becoming our map and our clock, our printing press and our typewriter, our calculator and our telephone, and our radio and TV.

When the Net absorbs a medium, that medium is re-created in the Net's image. It injects the medium's content with hyperlinks, blinking ads, and other digital gewgaws, and it surrounds the content with the content of all the other media it has absorbed. A new e-mail message, for instance, may announce its arrival as we're glancing over the latest headlines at a newspaper's site. The result is to scatter our attention and diffuse our concentration.

The Net's influence doesn't end at the edges of a computer screen, either. As people's minds become attuned to the crazy quilt of Internet media, traditional media have to adapt to the audience's new expectations. Television programs add text crawls and pop-up ads, and magazines and newspapers shorten their articles, introduce capsule summaries, and crowd their pages with easy-to-browse info-snippets. When, in March of this year, *The New York Times* decided to devote the second and third pages of every edition to article abstracts, its design director, Tom Bodkin, explained that the "shortcuts" would give harried readers a quick "taste" of the day's news, sparing them the "less efficient" method of actually turning the pages and reading the articles. Old media have little choice but to play by the new-media rules.

Never has a communications system played so many roles in our lives—or   20 exerted such broad influence over our thoughts—as the Internet does today. Yet, for all that's been written about the Net, there's been little consideration of how, exactly, it's reprogramming us. The Net's intellectual ethic remains obscure.

About the same time that Nietzsche started using his typewriter, an earnest young man named Frederick Winslow Taylor carried a stopwatch into the Midvale Steel plant in Philadelphia and began a historic series of experiments aimed at improving the efficiency of the plant's machinists. With the approval of Midvale's owners, he recruited a group of factory hands, set them to work on various metalworking machines, and recorded and timed their every movement as well as the operations of the machines. By breaking down every job into a sequence of small, discrete steps and then testing different ways of performing each one, Taylor created a set of precise instructions—an "algorithm," we might say today—for how each worker should work. Midvale's employees grumbled about the strict new regime, claiming that it turned them into little more than automatons, but the factory's productivity soared.

More than a hundred years after the invention of the steam engine, the Industrial Revolution had at last found its philosophy and its philosopher. Taylor's tight industrial choreography—his "system," as he liked to call it—was embraced by manufacturers throughout the country and, in time, around the world. Seeking maximum speed, maximum efficiency, and maximum output, factory owners used time-and-motion studies to organize their work and con-figure the jobs of their workers. The goal, as Taylor defined it in his celebrated 1911 treatise, *The Principles of Scientific Management*, was to identify and adopt, for every job, the "one best method" of work and thereby to effect "the gradual substitution of science for rule of thumb throughout the mechanic arts." Once his system was applied to all acts of manual labor, Taylor assured his followers, it would bring about a restructuring not only of industry but of society, creating a utopia of perfect efficiency. "In the past the man has been first," he declared; "in the future the system must be first."

Taylor's system is still very much with us; it remains the ethic of industrial manufacturing. And now, thanks to the growing power that computer engineers and software coders wield over our intellectual lives, Taylor's ethic is beginning to govern the realm of the mind as well. The Internet is a machine designed for the efficient and automated collection, transmission, and manipulation of information, and its legions of programmers are intent on finding the "one best method"—the perfect algorithm—to carry out every mental movement of what we've come to describe as "knowledge work."

Google's headquarters, in Mountain View, California—the Googleplex—is the Internet's high church, and the religion practiced inside its walls is Taylorism. Google, says its chief executive, Eric Schmidt, is "a company that's founded around the science of measurement," and it is striving to "systematize everything" it does. Drawing on the terabytes of behavioral data it collects through its search engine and other sites, it carries out thousands of experiments a day, according to the *Harvard Business Review,* and it uses the results to refine the algorithms that increasingly control how people find information and extract meaning from it. What Taylor did for the work of the hand, Google is doing for the work of the mind.

The company has declared that its mission is "to organize the world's infor- 25 mation and make it universally accessible and useful." It seeks to develop "the perfect search engine," which it defines as something that "understands exactly what you mean and gives you back exactly what you want." In Google's view, information is a kind of commodity, a utilitarian resource that can be mined and processed with industrial efficiency. The more pieces of information we can "access" and the faster we can extract their gist, the more productive we become as thinkers.

Where does it end? Sergey Brin and Larry Page, the gifted young men who founded Google while pursuing doctoral degrees in computer science at Stanford, speak frequently of their desire to turn their search engine into an artificial intelligence, a HAL-like machine that might be connected directly to our brains. "The ultimate search engine is something as smart as people—or smarter," Page said in a speech a few years back. "For us, working on search is a way to work on artificial intelligence." In a 2004 interview with *Newsweek,* Brin said, "Certainly if you had all the world's information directly attached to your brain, or an artificial brain that was smarter than your brain, you'd be better off." Last year, Page told a convention of scientists that Google is "really trying to build artificial intelligence and to do it on a large scale."

Such an ambition is a natural one, even an admirable one, for a pair of math whizzes with vast quantities of cash at their disposal and a small army of computer scientists in their employ. A fundamentally scientific enterprise, Google is motivated by a desire to use technology, in Eric Schmidt's words, "to solve problems that have never been solved before," and artificial intelligence is the hardest problem out there. Why wouldn't Brin and Page want to be the ones to crack it?

Still, their easy assumption that we'd all "be better off" if our brains were supplemented, or even replaced, by an artificial intelligence is unsettling. It suggests a belief that intelligence is the output of a mechanical process, a series of discrete steps that can be isolated, measured, and optimized. In Google's world, the world we enter when we go online, there's little place for the fuzziness of contemplation. Ambiguity is not an opening for insight but a bug to be fixed. The human brain is just an outdated computer that needs a faster processor and a bigger hard drive.

The idea that our minds should operate as high-speed data-processing machines is not only built into the workings of the Internet, it is the network's reigning business model as well. The faster we surf across the Web—the more links we click and pages we view—the more opportunities Google and other companies gain to collect information about us and to feed us advertisements. Most of the proprietors of the commercial Internet have a financial stake in collecting the crumbs of data we leave behind as we flit from link to link—the more crumbs, the better. The last thing these companies want is to encourage leisurely reading or slow, concentrated thought. It's in their economic interest to drive us to distraction.

Maybe I'm just a worrywart. Just as there's a tendency to glorify technological 30 progress, there's a countertendency to expect the worst of every new tool or machine. In Plato's *Phaedrus,* Socrates bemoaned the development of writing. He feared that, as people came to rely on the written word as a substitute for the knowledge they used to carry inside their heads, they would, in the words of one of the dialogue's characters, "cease to exercise their memory and become forgetful." And because they would be able to "receive a quantity of information without proper instruction," they would "be thought very knowledgeable when they are for the most part quite ignorant." They would be "filled with the conceit of wisdom instead of real wisdom." Socrates wasn't wrong—the new technology did often have the effects he feared—but he was shortsighted. He couldn't foresee the many ways that writing and reading would serve to spread information, spur fresh ideas, and expand human knowledge (if not wisdom).

The arrival of Gutenberg's printing press, in the 15th century, set off another round of teeth gnashing. The Italian humanist Hieronimo Squarciafico worried that the easy availability of books would lead to intellectual laziness, making men "less studious" and weakening their minds. Others argued that cheaply printed books and broadsheets would undermine religious authority, demean the work of scholars and scribes, and spread sedition and debauchery. As New York University professor Clay Shirky notes, "Most of the arguments made against the printing press were correct, even prescient." But, again, the doomsayers were unable to imagine the myriad blessings that the printed word would deliver.

So, yes, you should be skeptical of my skepticism. Perhaps those who dismiss critics of the Internet as Luddites or nostalgists will be proved correct, and from our hyperactive, data-stoked minds will spring a golden age of intellectual discovery and universal wisdom. Then again, the Net isn't the alphabet, and although it may replace the printing press, it produces something altogether different. The kind of deep reading that a sequence of printed pages promotes is valuable not just for the knowledge we acquire from the author's words but for the intellectual vibrations those words set off within our own minds. In the quiet spaces opened up by the sustained, undistracted reading of a book, or by any other act of contemplation, for that matter, we make our own associations, draw our own inferences and analogies, foster our own ideas. Deep reading, as Maryanne Wolf argues, is indistinguishable from deep thinking.

If we lose those quiet spaces, or fill them up with "content," we will sacrifice something important not only in our selves but in our culture. In a recent essay, the playwright Richard Foreman eloquently described what's at stake:

> I come from a tradition of Western culture, in which the ideal (my ideal) was the complex, dense and "cathedral-like" structure of the highly educated and articulate personality—a man or woman who carried inside themselves a personally constructed and unique version of the entire heritage of the West. [But now] I see within us all (myself included) the replacement of complex inner density with a new kind of self—evolving under the pressure of information overload and the technology of the "instantly available."

As we are drained of our "inner repertory of dense cultural inheritance," Foreman concluded, we risk turning into "'pancake people—spread wide and thin as we connect with that vast network of information accessed by the mere touch of a button."

I'm haunted by that scene in *2001*. What makes it so poignant, and so weird, is the computer's emotional response to the disassembly of its mind: its despair as one circuit after another goes dark, its childlike pleading with the astronaut—"I can feel it. I can feel it. I'm afraid"—and its final reversion to what can only be called a state of innocence. HAL's outpouring of feeling contrasts with the emotionlessness that characterizes the human figures in the film, who go about their business with an almost robotic efficiency. Their thoughts and actions feel scripted, as if they're following the steps of an algorithm. In the world of *2001*, people have become so machinelike that the most human character turns out to be a machine. That's the essence of Kubrick's dark prophecy: as we come to rely on computers to mediate our understanding of the world, it is our own intelligence that flattens into artificial intelligence.

QUESTIONS FOR DISCUSSION AND WRITING

1. In paragraphs 2 and 3 Carr explains how the fact that he reads so many materials on the Internet is "remapping the neural circuitry, reprogrammed the memory. . . . I'm not thinking the way I used to think." What is his explanation for how continuous exposure to the Internet shapes "the process of thought" and is "chipping away my capacity for concentration and contemplation" (paragraph 4)? Is his explanation convincing? Why or why not?

2. Do the positive features of reading online (such as ease of locating and accessing millions of documents, worldwide) outweigh the losses Carr identifies, such as becoming "'mere decoders of information'" and disengagement from the process of making "the rich mental connections that form when we read deeply and without distraction" (paragraph 8)?

3. Carr says that the "Internet, an immeasurably powerful computing system, is subsuming most of our other intellectual technologies. It's becoming our map and our clock, our printing press and our typewriter, our calculator and our telephone, and our radio and TV" (paragraph 17). Does your use of the Internet verify Carr's assertion of its functions? (If so, today do you access these technologies via computer or cell phone?) He continues the analysis, explaining how the presence of "hyperlinks, blinking ads, and other digital gewgaws . . . scatter our attention and diffuse our concentration" (paragraph 18). Pick an article of interest to you, perhaps on the Internet version of the *New York Times,* and as you read it keep track of all the electronic distractions that occur during your reading. What effects do these distractions have on your ability to understand, remember, process, and store the information in the article? Has this experience been typical?

4. Is Carr accurate in claiming that Google really wants our minds to "operate as high-speed data processing machines" for the financial benefit of the advertisers whose "economic interest [is] to drive us to distraction" (paragraph 29)? Carr quotes Richard Foreman, who says that "we risk turning into 'pancake people'—spread wide and thin as we connect with that vast network of information accessed by the mere touch of a button'" (paragraph 33). Is this pessimistic conclusion justified? Why or why not?

5. If you and your peers are considerably younger than Carr, who was born in 1959, do you, on occasion, dive deep into the text as Carr used to, "a scuba diver in the sea of words" (paragraph 4)? Or have you always read in the way that he now reads, zipping "along the surface like a guy on a Jet Ski" (paragraph 4)? If so, in what ways have your experiences of reading—in print or online—differed from Carr's? Are these differences significant? Discuss alternative styles of reading—in print and on the Internet—with classmates and make a chart of the similarities and differences. Analyze your observations.

RAY KURZWEIL

Frontiers

Ray Kurzweil (b. 1948) has been called the successor and "rightful heir to Thomas Edison" by Inc. *magazine because of his numerous significant electronic and technological inventions;* Forbes *magazine calls him "the ultimate thinking machine." As a high school senior he won first prize in the Westinghouse Science Talent Search by inventing computer software that could compose and play classical music. As an MIT sophomore, he invented the Select College Consulting Program, which analyzed thousands of criteria to match college applicants with appropriate schools. Other notable inventions include the first text-to-speech synthesizer and the first CCD flat-bed scanner, which in combination provided the technological basis for the first print-to-speech reading machine for the blind—the Kurzweil Reading Machine. Among Kurzweil's countless other inventions are sophisticated music synthesizers and voice-recognition software that enables speech to text conversion and vice versa. These inventions are of enormous aid to people with visual impairments or learning disabilities such as ADD and dyslexia. He received the National Medal of Technology in 1999, was inducted into the National Inventors Hall of Fame in 2002, and in 2009 was presented with the Arthur C. Clarke Lifetime Achievement Award.*

Through recent works such as The Singularity Is Near: When Humans Transcend Biology *(2006), Kurzweil has examined futurist perspectives of technology's development, human biology, and the possibility of immortality. According to Kurzweil, "The common wisdom is to think linearly, to assume that the current pace of change will continue indefinitely. But this attitude is gradually changing, as more and more people understand the exponential perspective and how explosive an exponential can be. That is the true nature of these technology trends," as echoed in his brief comments here from the* Atlantic *(November 2007).*

The American idea is to push beyond frontiers, whether in geography (Manifest Destiny), science (splitting the atom, DNA), invention (the telephone, the lightbulb, the airplane, the Internet), industry (mass production), music (jazz, rock and roll), or popular culture (Hollywood).

The means of creativity have now been democratized. For example, anyone with an inexpensive high-definition video camera and a personal computer can create a high-quality, full-length motion picture. A musician in her dorm room commands the resources once available only in a multimillion-dollar recording studio. Just a few years ago, a couple of students at Stanford University wrote some software on their personal computers that revolutionized Web searches and became the basis of a company now worth $150 billion. Individuals now have the tools to break new ground in every field.

These information tools are more than doubling their power in terms of price-performance and capacity every year, which means multiplying by a thousand in less than a decade, by a billion in 25 years. Every decade, according to my models, we are also shrinking the size of these technologies by a factor of about 100. Today you can e-mail movies and sound recordings and books. In about 20 years, you will be able to e-mail three-dimensional products; they will be "printed" in 3-D using tabletop nanotechnology assembly devices, which will rearrange molecules from inexpensive input material into complex products. So you will be able to e-mail a blouse, for instance, or a computer, or a toaster—or the toast. That will democratize the means of production, so we'll finally be able to bury Karl Marx.

This exponential growth of information technology is not limited to electronics; it also includes our biology. This biotechnology revolution is also doubling its power each year, and will ultimately bring great gains to human longevity. That is not a new story. Life expectancy was only about 40 years in 1857, when *The Atlantic Monthly* was founded. It was 47 years in 1900. It is now pushing 80, but this increase will go into high gear in about a decade.

Despite well-publicized obstructions, the American drive to push beyond 5 frontiers is alive and well, and represents the dominant philosophy in the world today, with continued exponential advance on the horizon.

QUESTIONS FOR DISCUSSION AND WRITING

1. What does Kurzweil mean by declaring, "The means of creativity have now been democratized" (paragraph 2)?

2. Are you or anyone you know about hoping to make a revolutionary software discovery during your college years or thereafter? What would someone need to know and what characteristics of mind and personality would they need to possess in order to help bring that dream to reality? How much financial backing do you think would be necessary?

3. What are some of the major technological inventions or breakthroughs during your lifetime?

4. What connections does Kurzweil make between exponentially increasing technology and exponentially increasing life expectancy (paragraphs 3 and 4)?

SHERRY TURKLE

How Computers Change the Way We Think

Sherry Turkle, a clinical psychologist, sociologist, and media commentator on the effects of technology, is Abby Rockefeller Mauzé Professor of the Social Studies of Science and Technology at the Massachusetts Institute of Technology and director of the MIT Initiative on Technology and Self, a center of research and reflection on the evolving connections between people and artifacts. She was born in 1948, and earned from Harvard a B.A. (1970), and a Ph.D. in sociology and personality psychology (1976). Her research and writing often focus on the cultural and psychological implications of computer technology, for she regards "computers as carriers of culture, as objects that give rise to new metaphors, to new relationships between people and machines, between different people, and most significantly between people and their ways of thinking about themselves." Turkle is the author of The Second Self: Computers and the Human Spirit *(1984; revised 2005); and* Life on the Screen: Identity in the Age of the Internet *(1997). She has edited four collections on the relationships between things and thinking, including* Evocative Objects: Things We Think With *(2007) and* Simulation and Its Discontents *(2009), and is currently at work on a book on robots and the human spirit. "How Computers Change the Way We Think" was first published in the* Chronicle of Higher Education *(2004).*

The tools we use to think change the ways in which we think. The invention of written language brought about a radical shift in how we process, organize, store, and transmit representations of the world. Although writing remains our primary information technology, today when we think about the impact of technology on our habits of mind, we think primarily of the computer.

My first encounters with how computers change the way we think came soon after I joined the faculty at the Massachusetts Institute of Technology in the late 1970s, at the end of the era of the slide rule and the beginning of the era of the personal computer. At a lunch for new faculty members, several senior professors in engineering complained that the transition from slide rules to calculators had affected their students' ability to deal with issues of scale. When students used slide rules, they had to insert decimal points themselves. The professors insisted that that required students to maintain a mental sense of scale, whereas those who relied on calculators made frequent errors in orders of magnitude. Additionally, the students with calculators had lost their ability to do "back of the envelope" calculations, and with that, an intuitive feel for the material.

That same semester, I taught a course in the history of psychology. There, I experienced the impact of computational objects on students' ideas about their emotional lives. My class had read Freud's essay on slips of the tongue, with its famous first example: The chairman of a parliamentary session opens a meeting by declaring it closed. The students discussed how Freud interpreted such errors as revealing a person's mixed emotions. A computer-science major disagreed with Freud's approach. The mind, she argued, is a computer. And in a computational dictionary—like we have in the human mind—"closed" and "open" are designated by the same symbol, separated by a sign for opposition. "Closed" equals "minus open." To substitute "closed" for "open" does not require the notion of ambivalence or conflict.

"When the chairman made that substitution," she declared, "a bit was dropped; a minus sign was lost. There was a power surge. No problem."

The young woman turned a Freudian slip into an information-processing error. An explanation in terms of meaning had become an explanation in terms of mechanism.

Such encounters turned me to the study of both the instrumental and the subjective sides of the nascent computer culture. As an ethnographer and psychologist, I began to study not only what the computer was doing *for* us, but what it was doing *to* us, including how it was changing the way we see ourselves, our sense of human identity.

In the 1980s, I surveyed the psychological effects of computational objects in everyday life—largely the unintended side effects of people's tendency to project thoughts and feelings onto their machines. In the 20 years since, computational objects have become more explicitly designed to have emotional and cognitive effects. And those "effects by design" will become even stronger in the decade to come. Machines are being designed to serve explicitly as companions, pets, and tutors. And they are introduced in school settings for the youngest children.

Today, starting in elementary school, students use e-mail, word processing, computer simulations, virtual communities, and PowerPoint software. In the process, they are absorbing more than the content of what appears on their screens. They are learning new ways to think about what it means to know and understand.

What follows is a short and certainly not comprehensive list of areas where I see information technology encouraging changes in thinking. There can be no simple way of cataloging whether any particular change is good or bad. That is contested terrain. At every step we have to ask, as educators and citizens, whether current technology is leading us in directions that serve our human purposes. Such questions are not technical; they are social, moral, and political. For me, addressing that subjective side of computation is one of the more significant challenges for the next decade of information technology in higher education. Technology does not determine change, but it encourages us to take certain directions. If we make those directions clear, we can more easily exert human choice.

THINKING ABOUT PRIVACY

Today's college students are habituated to a world of online blogging, instant messaging, and Web browsing that leaves electronic traces. Yet they have had little experience with the right to privacy. Unlike past generations of Americans, who grew up with the notion that the privacy of their mail was sacrosanct, our children are accustomed to electronic surveillance as part of their daily lives. 10

I have colleagues who feel that the increased incursions on privacy have put the topic more in the news, and that this is a positive change. But middle-school and high-school students tend to be willing to provide personal information online with no safeguards, and college students seem uninterested in violations of privacy and in increased governmental and commercial surveillance. Professors find that students do not understand that in a democracy, privacy is a right, not merely a privilege. In 10 years, ideas about the relationship of privacy and government will require even more active pedagogy. (One might also hope that increased education about the kinds of silent surveillance that technology makes possible may inspire more active political engagement with the issue.)

AVATARS OR A SELF?

Chat rooms, role-playing games, and other technological venues offer us many different contexts for presenting ourselves online. Those possibilities are particularly important for adolescents because they offer what Erik Erikson described as a moratorium, a time out or safe space for the personal experimentation that is so crucial for adolescent development. Our dangerous world—with crime, terrorism, drugs, and AIDS—offers little in the way of safe spaces. Online worlds can provide valuable spaces for identity play.

But some people who gain fluency in expressing multiple aspects for self may find it harder to develop authentic selves. Some children who write narratives for their screen avatars may grow up with too little experience of how to share their real feelings with other people. For those who are lonely yet afraid of intimacy, information technology has made it possible to have the illusion of companionship without the demands of friendship.

FROM POWERFUL IDEAS TO POWERPOINT

In the 1970s and early 1980s, some educators wanted to make programming part of the regular curriculum for K–12 education. They argued that because information technology carries ideas, it might as well carry the most powerful ideas that computer science has to offer. It is ironic that in most elementary schools today, the ideas being carried by information technology are not ideas from computer science like procedural thinking, but more likely to be those embedded in productivity tools like PowerPoint presentation software.

PowerPoint does more than provide a way of transmitting content. It carries 15 its own way of thinking, its own aesthetic—which not surprisingly shows up in the aesthetic of college freshmen. In that aesthetic, presentation becomes its own powerful idea.

To be sure, the software cannot be blamed for lower intellectual standards. Misuse of the former is as much a symptom as a cause of the latter. Indeed, the culture in which our children are raised is increasingly a culture of presentation, a corporate culture in which appearance is often more important than reality. In contemporary political discourse, the bar has also been lowered. Use of rhetorical devices at the expense of cogent argument regularly goes without notice. But it is precisely because standards of intellectual rigor outside the educational sphere have fallen that educators must attend to how we use, and when we introduce, software that has been designed to simplify the organization and processing of information.

In "The Cognitive Style of PowerPoint" (Graphics Press, 2003), Edward R. Tufte suggests that PowerPoint equates bulleting with clear thinking. It does not teach students to begin a discussion or construct a narrative. It encourages presentation, not conversation. Of course, in the hands of a master teacher, a PowerPoint presentation with few words and powerful images can serve as the jumping-off point for a brilliant lecture. But in the hands of elementary-school students, often introduced to PowerPoint in the third grade, and often infatuated with its swooshing sounds, animated icons, and flashing text, a slide show is more likely to close down debate than open it up.

Developed to serve the needs of the corporate boardroom, the software is designed to convey absolute authority. Teachers used to tell students that clear exposition depended on clear outlining, but presentation software has fetishized the outline at the expense of the content.

Narrative, the exposition of content, takes time. PowerPoint, like so much in the computer culture, speeds up the pace.

WORD PROCESSING VS. THINKING

The catalog for the Vermont Country Store advertises a manual typewriter, which the advertising copy says "moves at a pace that allows time to compose your thoughts." As many of us know, it is possible to manipulate text on a computer screen and see how it looks faster than we can think about what the words mean.

Word processing has its own complex psychology. From a pedagogical point of view, it can make dedicated students into better writers because it allows them to revise text, rearrange paragraphs, and experiment with the tone and shape of an essay. Few professional writers would part with their computers; some claim that they simply cannot think without their hands on the keyboard. Yet the ability to quickly fill the page, to see it before you can think it, can make bad writers even worse.

A seventh grader once told me that the typewriter she found in her mother's attic is "cool because you have to type each letter by itself. You have to know what you are doing in advance or it comes out a mess." The idea of thinking ahead has become exotic.

TAKING THINGS AT INTERFACE VALUE

We expect software to be easy to use, and we assume that we don't have to know how a computer works. In the early 1980s, most computer users who spoke of transparency meant that, as with any other machine, you could "open the hood" and poke around. But only a few years later, Macintosh users began to use the term when they talked about seeing their documents and programs represented by attractive and easy-to-interpret icons. They were referring to an ability to make things work without needing to go below the screen surface. Paradoxically, it was the screen's opacity that permitted that kind of transparency. Today, when people say that something is transparent, they mean that they can see how to make it work, not that they know how it works. In other words, transparency means epistemic opacity.

The people who built or bought the first generation of personal computers understood them down to the bits and bytes. The next generation of operation systems were more complex, but they still invited that old-time reductive understanding. Contemporary information technology encourages different habits of mind. Today's college students are already used to taking things at (inter) face value; their successors in 2014 will be even less accustomed to probing below the surface.

SIMULATION AND ITS DISCONTENTS

Some thinkers argue that the new opacity is empowering, enabling anyone to use the most sophisticated technological tools and to experiment with simulation in complex and creative ways. But it is also true that our tools carry the message that they are beyond our understanding. It is possible that in daily life, epistemic opacity can lead to passivity.

I first became aware of that possibility in the early 1990s, when the first generation of complex simulation games were introduced and immediately became popular for home as well as school use. SimLife teaches the principles of evolution by getting children involved in the development of complex ecosystems; in that sense it is an extraordinary learning tool. During one session in which I played SimLife with Tim, a 13-year-old, the screen before us flashed a message: "Your orgot is being eaten up." "What's an orgot?" I asked. Tim didn't know. "I just ignore that," he said confidently. "You don't need to know that kind of stuff to play."

For me, that story serves as a cautionary tale. Computer simulations enable their users to think about complex phenomena as dynamic, evolving systems. But they also accustom us to manipulating systems whose core assumptions we may not understand and that may not be true.

We live in a culture of simulation. Our games, our economic and political systems, and the ways architects design buildings, chemists envisage molecules, and surgeons perform operations all use simulation technology. In 10 years the degree to which simulations are embedded in every area of life will have increased exponentially. We need to develop a new form of media literacy: readership skills for the culture of simulation.

We come to written text with habits of readership based on centuries of civilization. At the very least, we have learned to begin with the journalist's traditional questions: who, what, when, where, why, and how. Who wrote these words, what is their message, why were they written, and how are they situated in time and place, politically and socially? A central project for higher education during the next 10 years should be creating programs in information-technology literacy, with the goal of teaching students to interrogate simulations in much the same spirit, challenging their built-in assumptions.

Despite the ever-increasing complexity of software, most computer environ-   30 ments put users in worlds based on constrained choices. In other words, immersion in programmed worlds puts us in reassuring environments where the rules are clear. For example, when you play a video game, you often go through a series of frightening situations that you escape by mastering the rules—you experience life as a reassuring dichotomy of scary and safe. Children grow up in a culture of video games, action films, fantasy epics, and computer programs that all rely on that familiar scenario of almost losing but then regaining total mastery: There is danger. It is mastered. A still-more-powerful monster appears. It is subdued. Scary. Safe.

Yet in the real world, we have never had a greater need to work our way out of binary assumptions. In the decade ahead, we need to rebuild the culture around information technology. In that new socio-technical culture, assumptions about the nature of mastery would be less absolute. The new culture would make it easier, not more difficult, to consider life in shades of gray, to see moral dilemmas in terms other than a battle between Good and Evil. For never has our world been more complex, hybridized, and global. Never have we so needed to have many contradictory thoughts and feelings at the same time. Our tools must help us accomplish that, not fight against us.

Information technology is identity technology. Embedding it in a culture that supports democracy, freedom of expression, tolerance, diversity, and complexity of opinion is one of the next decade's greatest challenges. We cannot afford to fail.

When I first began studying the computer culture, a small breed of highly trained technologists thought of themselves as "computer people." That is no longer the case. If we take the computer as a carrier of a way of knowing, a way of seeing the world and our place in it, we are all computer people now.

CONTEXTS FOR "HOW COMPUTERS CHANGE THE WAY WE THINK"

SHERRY TURKLE

The Human Spirit in a Computer Culture

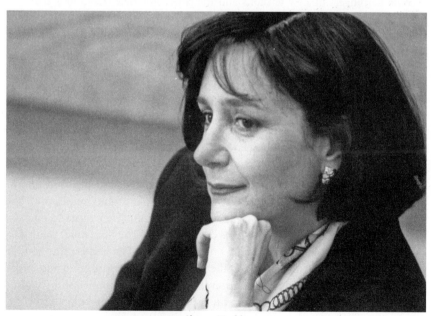

Sherry Turkle

Ours has been called a culture of narcissism.[1] The label is apt but can be misleading. It reads colloquially as selfishness and self-absorption. But these images do not capture the anxiety behind our search for mirrors. We are insecure in our understanding of ourselves, and this insecurity breeds a new preoccupation with the question of who we are. We search for ways to see ourselves. The computer is a new mirror, the first psychological machine. Beyond its nature as an analytical engine lies its second nature as an evocative object.

I have described groups of people chosen for the intensity of their involvement with computers, where the computer's second nature—as reflective medium and as philosophical provocateur—is writ plain. Some of them were involved with the computer professionally, but many were not. They came to the computer on their own, or perhaps it is better to say that the computer came to them. For what is new in the 1980s is that intense involvement with computers, largely confined to computer subcultures when I began my study in 1976, has become a popular phenomenon. Today, when computer companies project their sales of personal computers, they think in tens of millions. This means that for middle-class Americans, and soon for their counterparts in much of the world, if you don't have a computer at home you have a friend or colleague or neighbor who does. We are living in a culture that invites us all to interact with computers in ways that permit us to become intimate with their second nature. And as this happens, the relationships between people and machines that we have seen in the computer subcultures become harbingers of new tensions and the search for new resolutions that will mark our culture as a whole in the almost immediate future.

For example, the computer offers hackers something for which many of us are hungry. Hysteria, its roots in sexual repression, was the neurosis of Freud's time. Today we suffer not less but differently. Terrified of being alone, yet afraid of intimacy, we experience widespread feelings of emptiness, of disconnection, of the unreality of self. And here the computer, a companion without emotional demands, offers a compromise. You can be a loner, but never alone. You can interact, but need never feel vulnerable to another person.

The hackers illustrate another facet of our emerging relationships with machines. Their response to the computer is artistic, even romantic. They want their programs to be beautiful and elegant expressions of their uniqueness and genius. They recognize one another not because they belong to the same "profession," but because they share an urgency to create in their medium. They relate to one another not just as technical experts, but as creative artists. The Romantics wanted to escape rationalist egoism by becoming one with nature. The hackers find soul in the machine—they lose themselves in the idea of mind building mind and in the sense of merging their minds with a universal system. When nineteenth-century Romantics looked for an alternative to the mechanism and competition of society,

From Sherry Turkle, *The Second Self: Computers and the Human Spirit* (1984).

[1] See Christopher Lasch, *The Culture of Narcissism* (New York: Norton, 1979).

they looked to a perfect society of two, "perfect friendship," or "perfect love." This desire for fusion has its echo today, although in a new and troubling form. Instead of a quest for an idealized person, now there is the computer as a second self. . . .

SHERRY TURKLE

"Logins R Us"

On a WELL discussion group about online personae (subtitled "boon or bête-noire") participants shared a sense that their virtual identities were evocative objects for thinking about the self. For several, experiences in virtual space compelled them to pay greater attention to what they take for granted in the real. "The persona thing intrigues me," said one. "It's a chance for all of us who aren't actors to play [with] masks. And think about the masks we wear every day."[1]

In this way, online personae have something in common with the self that emerges in a psychoanalytic encounter. It, too, is significantly virtual, constructed within the space of the analysis, where its slightest shifts can come under the most intense scrutiny.[2]

What most characterized the WELL discussion about online personae was the way many of the participants expressed the belief that life on the WELL introduced them to the many within themselves. One person wrote that through participating in an electronic bulletin board and letting the many sides of ourselves show, "We start to resemble little corporations, 'Logins R Us,' and like any company, we each have within us the bean-counter, the visionary, the heart-throb, the fundamentalist, and the wild child. Long may they wave."[3] Other participants responded to this comment with enthusiasm. One, echoing the social psychologist Kenneth Gergen,[4] described identity as a "pastiche of personalities" in which "the test of competence is not so much the integrity of the whole but the apparent correct representation appearing at the right time, in the right context, not to the detriment of the rest of the internal 'collective.'"[5] Another said that he thought of his ego "as a hollow tube, through which, one at a time, the 'many' speak through at the appropriate moment. . . . I'd like to hear more . . . about the possibilities surrounding the notion that what we perceive as 'one' in any context is, perhaps, a conglomerate of 'ones.'" This writer went on:

> Hindu culture is rooted in the "many" as the root of spiritual experience. A person's momentary behavior reflects some influence from one of hundreds of gods and/or goddesses. I am interested in . . . how this natural assumption of the "many" creates an alternative psychology.[6]

From Sherry Turkle, *Life on the Screen: Identity and the Age of the Internet* (1995).

Another writer concurred:

Did you ever see that cartoon by R. Crumb about "Which is the real R. Crumb?" He goes through four pages of incarnations, from successful businessman to street beggar, from media celebrity to gut-gnawing recluse, etc. etc. Then at the end he says, "Which is the real one?" . . . "It all depends on what mood I'm in!"

We're all like that on-line.[7]

Howard Rheingold, the member of the WELL who began the discussion topic, also referred to Gergen's notion of a "saturated self," the idea that communication technologies have caused us to "colonize each other's brains." Gergen describes us as saturated with the many "voices of humankind—both harmonious and alien." He believes that as "we absorb their varied rhymes and reasons, they become part of us and we of them. Social saturation furnishes us with a multiplicity of incoherent and unrelated languages of the self." With our relationships spread across the globe and our knowledge of other cultures relativizing our attitudes and depriving us of any norm, we "exist in a state of continuous construction and reconstruction; it is a world where anything goes that can be negotiated. Each reality of self gives way to reflexive questioning, irony, and ultimately the playful probing of yet another reality. The center fails to hold."[8]

Although people may at first feel anguish at what they sense as a breakdown 5 of identity, Gergen believes they may come to embrace the new possibilities. Individual notions of self vanish "into a stage of relatedness. One ceases to believe in a self independent of the relations in which he or she is embedded."[9] "We live in each other's brains, as voices, images, words on screens," said Rheingold in the online discussion. "We are multiple personalities and we include each other."[10] . . .

IDENTITY AND MULTIPLICITY

Without any principle of coherence, the self spins off in all directions. Multiplicity is not viable if it means shifting among personalities that cannot communicate. Multiplicity is not acceptable if it means being confused to a point of immobility.[11] How can we be multiple and coherent at the same time? In *The Protean Self*, Robert Jay Lifton tries to resolve this seeming contradiction. He begins by assuming that a unitary view of self corresponded to a traditional culture with stable symbols, institutions, and relationships. He finds the old unitary notion no longer viable because traditional culture has broken down and identifies a range of responses. One is a dogmatic insistence on unity. Another is to return to systems of belief, such as religious fundamentalism, that enforce conformity. A third is to embrace the idea of a fragmented self.[12] Lifton says this is a dangerous option that may result in a "fluidity lacking in moral content and sustainable inner form." But Lifton sees another possibility, a healthy protean self. It is capable, like Proteus, of fluid transformations but is grounded in coherence and a moral outlook. It is multiple but integrated.[13] You can have a sense of self without being one self.

Lifton's language is theoretical. Experiences in MUDs,[14] on the WELL, on local bulletin boards, on commercial network services, and on the World Wide Web are bringing his theory down to earth. On the Web, the idiom for constructing a "home" identity is to assemble a "home page" of virtual objects that correspond to one's interests. One constructs a home page by composing or "pasting" on it words, images, and sounds, and by making connections between it and other sites on the Internet or the Web. Like the agents in emergent AI, one's identity emerges from whom one knows, one's associations and connections. People link their home page to pages about such things as music, paintings, television shows, cities, books, photographs, comic strips, and fashion models. As I write this book I am in the process of constructing my own home page. It now contains links to the text of my curriculum vitae, to drafts of recent papers (one about MUDs, one about French psychoanalysis), and to the reading lists for the two courses I shall teach next fall. A "visitor" to my home page can also click a highlighted word and watch images of Michel Foucault and Power Rangers "morph," one into the other, a visual play on my contention that children's toys bring postmodernism down to earth. This display, affectionately referred to as "The Mighty Morphin' Michel Foucault," was a present from my assistant at MIT, Cynthia Col. A virtual home, like a real one, is furnished with objects you buy, build, or receive as gifts. . . .

I am not limited in the number of links I can create. If we take the home page as a real estate metaphor for the self, its decor is postmodern. Its different rooms with different styles are located on computers all over the world. But through one's efforts, they are brought together to be of a piece. . . .

Through the fragmented selves presented by patients and through theories that stress the decentered subject, contemporary psychology confronts what is left out of theories of the unitary self. Now it must ask, What is the self when it functions as a society?[15] What is the self when it divides its labors among its constituent "alters"?[16] Those burdened by posttraumatic dissociative disorders suffer these questions; here I have suggested that inhabitants of virtual communities play with them.

Ideas about mind can become a vital cultural presence when they are carried by evocative objects-to-think-with.[17] I said earlier that these objects need not be material. For example, dreams and slips of the tongue were objects-to-think-with that brought psychoanalytic ideas into everyday life. People could play with their own and others' dreams and slips. Today, people are being helped to develop ideas about identity as multiplicity by a new practice of identity as multiplicity in online life. Virtual personae are objects-to-think-with.

When people adopt an online persona they cross a boundary into highly-charged territory. Some feel an uncomfortable sense of fragmentation, some a sense of relief. Some sense the possibilities for self-discovery, even self-transformation. Serena, a twenty-six-year-old graduate student in history, says, "When I log on to a new MUD and I create a character and know I have to start typing my description, I always feel a sense of panic. Like I could find out something I don't want to know." Arlie, a twenty-year-old undergraduate, says, "I am always very self-conscious when I create a new character. Usually, I end up creating someone I wouldn't want my parents to know about. It takes me, like three hours. But that someone is part of me." In these ways and others, many more of us are experimenting with multiplicity than ever before.

With this last comment, I am not implying that MUDs or computer bulletin boards are causally implicated in the dramatic increase of people who exhibit symptoms of multiple personality disorder (MPD), or that people on MUDs have MPD, or that MUDding is like having MPD. What I am saying is that the many manifestations of multiplicity in our culture, including the adoption of on-line personae, are contributing to a general reconsideration of traditional, unitary notions of identity.

NOTES

1. mcdee, The WELL, conference on virtual communities (vc.20.17), 18 April 1992.
2. The sentiment that life online could provide a different experience of self was seconded by a participant who described himself as a man whose conversational abilities as an adult were impaired by having been a stutterer as a child. Online he was able to discover the experience of participating in the flow of a conversation.

   I echo [the previous contributor] in feeling that my online persona differs greatly from my persona offline. And, in many ways, my online persona is more "me." I feel a lot more freedom to speak here. Growing up, I had a severe stuttering problem. I couldn't speak a word without stuttering, so I spoke only when absolutely necessary. I worked through it in my early 20s and you wouldn't even notice it now (except when I'm stressed out), but at 37 I'm still shy to speak. I'm a lot more comfortable with listening than with talking. And when I do speak I usually feel out of sync: I'll inadvertently step on other people's words, or lose people's attention, or talk through instead of to. I didn't learn the dynamic of conversation that most people take for granted, I think. Here, though, it's completely different: I have a feel for the flow of the "conversations," have the time to measure my response, don't have to worry about the balance of conversational space—we all make as much space as we want just by pressing "r" to respond. It's been a wonderfully liberating experience for me. (Anonymous)

3. spoonman, The WELL, conference on virtual communities (vc.20.65), 11 June 1992.
4. Kenneth Gergen, *The Saturated Self: Dilemmas of Identity in Contemporary Life* (New York: Basic Books, 1991).
5. bluefire (Bob Jacobson), The WELL, conference on virtual reality (vr.85.146), 15 August 1993.
6. The WELL, conference on virtual reality (vr.85.148), 17 August 1993.
7. Art Kleiner, The WELL, conference on virtual reality (vr.47.41), 2 October 1990.
8. Gergen, *The Saturated Self,* p. 6.
9. Gergen, *The Saturated Self,* p. 17.
10. hlr (Howard Rheingold), The WELL, conference on virtual reality (vr.47.351), 2 February 1993.

11. James M. Glass, *Shattered Selves: Multiple Personality in a Postmodern World* (Ithaca, N.Y.: Cornell University Press, 1993).

12. Robert Jay Lifton, *The Protean Self: Human Resilience in an Age of Fragmentation* (New York: Basic Books, 1993), p. 192.

13. Lifton, *The Protean Self*, pp. 229–32.

14. A MUD is a multi-user dungeon, a text-based virtual world.

15. See, for example, Marvin Minsky, *The Society of Mind* (New York: Simon & Schuster, 1985).

16. See, for example, Colin Ross, *Multiple Personality Disorder: Diagnosis, Clinical Features, and Treatment* (New York: John Wiley & Sons, 1989).

17. Claude Lévi-Strauss, *The Savage Mind* (Chicago: University of Chicago Press, 1960).

LARRY WILLIAMS

Multitasking Man

SHERRY TURKLE

Inner History: Collection and Recollection in the Digital Archive

The essayists in this collection consider devices that come supplied with sanctioned ways of understanding them. The authors take time to go further, often not knowing what they are looking for. . . .

Computer and Internet pioneer Gordon Bell has immersed himself in the project of creating a full digital life archive. In 1998, he began the process of scanning books, cards, letters, memos, posters, and photographs—even the logos of his coffee mugs and T-shirts—into a digital archive. He then moved on to movies, videotaped lectures, and voice recordings. Faced with the question of how to organize and retrieve this mass of data, Bell began to work with a team from Microsoft. The MyLifeBits project was born. Bell and his colleague Jim Gemmel describe the process of data collection:

> The system records his [Bell's] telephone calls and the programs playing on radio and television. When he is working at his PC, MyLifeBits automatically stores a copy of every Web page he visits and a transcript of every instant message he sends or receives. It also records the files he opens, the songs he plays and the searches he performs. The system even monitors which windows are in the foreground of his screen at any time and how much mouse and keyboard activity is going on. . . .
>
> To obtain a visual record of his day, Bell wears the SenseCam, a camera developed by Microsoft Research that automatically takes pictures when its sensors indicate that the user might want a photograph. For example, if the SenseCam's passive infrared sensor detects a warm body nearby, it photographs the person. If the light level changes significantly—a sign that the user has probably moved in or out of a room and entered a new setting—the camera takes another snapshot.[1]

What compels the architects of this program is the idea of a complete, digitally accessible life. To be sure, there are medical applications ("your physician would have access to a detailed, ongoing health record, and you would no longer have to rack your brain to answer questions such as 'When did you first feel this way?'"), but most of all, the authors speak of posterity, of MyLifeBits as a way for people to "tell their life stories to their descendants."[2] But what is it that future generations want to know of our lives?

In the collection *Evocative Objects,* architect Susan Yee describes her visit 5 to the Le Corbusier archive in Paris on the day its materials were digitized.[3] Yee began her relationship to Le Corbusier through the physicality of his drawings.

From Sherry Turkle, *The Inner History of Devices* (Cambridge: MIT Press, 2008).

The master's original blueprints, sketches, and plans were brought to her in long metal boxes. Le Corbusier's handwritten notes in the margins of his sketches, the traces of his fingerprints, the smudges, the dirt—Yee was thrilled by all of these. One morning, Yee has all of this in her hands, but by the afternoon, she has only digital materials to work with. Yee experiences a loss of connection to Le Corbusier: "It made the drawings feel anonymous," she says. More important, Yee says that the digitized archives made her feel anonymous.

When working in the physical archive, Yee was on a kind of pilgrimage. She did not pause in her work, so completely was she immersed in the touch and feel of Le Corbusier's artifacts. But once the material was on the screen, there was a disconnect. Yee found herself switching screens, moving from the Le Corbusier materials to check her email back at MIT. More than a resource, the digitized archive becomes a state of mind.

MyLifeBits is the ultimate tool for data collection. But what of recollection in the fully archived life? Speaking of photography, Susan Sontag writes that "travel becomes a strategy for accumulating photographs."[4] In digital culture, does life become a strategy for establishing an archive?[5] When we know that everything in our lives is captured, will we begin to live the life we hope to have archived?

The fantasy of a complete record for all time—a kind of immortality—is part of the seduction of digital capture. But memoir, clinical writing, and ethnography are not only about capturing events but about remembering and forgetting, choice and interpretation. The complete digital archive gives equal weight to every person, every change of venue. The digital archive follows chronologies and categories. The human act of remembrance puts events into shifting camps of meaning. When Bell and Gemmell consider the quantity of information on MyLifeBits, they talk about the "pesky problem of photograph labeling."[6] The program is going to use face-recognition technology to label most photographs automatically. In reading this, I recall childhood times with my mother in which she wrote funny things, silly poems, or sentimental inscriptions on the backs of family photographs. She liked putting them in a big drawer, so that, in a way, picking a photo out of the drawer, almost at random, was finding a surprise. Moments around the photograph drawer were moments of recollection in laughter, regret, sometimes mourning. Now automated for a steady stream of photographs over a lifetime, photograph labeling is just a technical problem. Bell and Gemmell sum it up by saying that "most of us do not want to be the librarians of our digital archives—we want the computer to be the librarian!"[7] In this new context, reviewing your life becomes managing the past. Subtly, attitudes toward one's own life shift; my mother, happily annotating her messy drawer of snapshots, never saw herself as a librarian.

Of course, the digital archive is only a resource; it remains for us to take its materials as the basis for the deeply felt enterprise of recollection. But one wonders if the mere fact of the archive will not make us feel that the job is already done.

NOTES

1. C. Gordon Bell and Jim Gemmell, "A Digital Life," *Scientific American* 296, no. 3 (March 2007): 63. http://sciam.com/print_version.cfm?articleID=CC50D7BF-E7F2-99DF-34DA5FF0B0A22B50 (accessed August 7, 2007).

2. Ibid., 58, 60.

3. Susan Yee, "The Archive," in *Evocative Objects: Things We Think With,* ed. Sherry Turkle (Cambridge, Mass.: MIT Press, 2007), 32–36.

4. Susan Sontag, *On Photography* (New York: Dell, 1978), 9.

5. Bell and Gemmell discuss the burdens of having a digital shadow. They anticipate that other people captured by the SenseCam may need to be pixellated so as not to invade their privacy; data would have to be stored "offshore" to protect it from loss and/or illegal seizure; there is danger from "identity thieves, gossipmongers, or an authoritarian state." Bell and Gemmell admit that despite all problems, "for us the excitement far outweighs the fear." Bell and Gemmell, "A Digital Life," 64, 65.

6. Ibid., 63.

7. Ibid., 65.

JAMES GLEICK

From "Cyber-Neologoliferation"

Writer James Gleick (b. 1954) earned a B.A. in English from Harvard in 1976. For a decade he was a technology reporter at the New York Times, *writing the Fast Forward column. Much of his work focuses on the cultural ramifications of science and technology. His books include* Chaos: Making a New Science *(1987);* Faster: The Acceleration of Just About Everything *(1999); and* Isaac Newton *(2003).*

The *OED*[1] is a historical dictionary, providing citations meant to show the evolution of every word, beginning with the earliest known usage. So a key task, and a popular sport for thousands of volunteer word aficionados, is antedating: finding earlier citations than those already known. This used to be painstakingly slow and chancy. When [editor Bernadette] Paton started in new words, she found herself struggling with *headcase*. She had current citations, but she says she felt sure it must be older, and books were of little use. She wandered around the office muttering *headcase, headcase, headcase.* Suddenly one of her colleagues started singing: "My name is Bill, and I'm a *headcase* / They practice making up on my face." She perked up.

"What date would that be?" she asked.

"I don't know, it's a Who song," he said, "1966 probably, something like that."

From the *New York Times,* 6 November 2006.

[1]The OED is the *Oxford English Dictionary*.

So "I'm a Boy," by P. Townshend, became the *OED*'s earliest citation for *headcase.*

Antedating is entirely different now: online databases have opened the flood- 5 gates. Lately Paton has been looking at words starting with *pseudo-*. Searching through databases of old newspapers and historical documents has changed her view of them. "I tended to think of *pseudo-* as a prefix that just took off in the sixties and seventies, but now we find that a lot of them go back much earlier than we thought." Also in the P's, *poison pen* has just been antedated with a 1911 headline in the *Evening Post* in Frederick, Maryland. "You get the sense that this sort of language seeps into local newspapers first," she says. "We would never in a million years have sent a reader to read a small newspaper like that."

The job of a new-words editor felt very different precyberspace, Paton says: "New words weren't proliferating at quite the rate they have done in the last ten years. Not just the Internet, but text messaging and so on has created lots and lots of new vocabulary." Much of the new vocabulary appears online long before it will make it into books. Take *geek*. It was not till 2003 that *OED3* caught up with the main modern sense: "a person who is extremely devoted to and knowledgeable about computers or related technology." Internet chitchat provides the earliest known reference, a posting to a Usenet newsgroup, net.jokes, on February 20, 1984.

The scouring of the Internet for evidence — the use of cyberspace as a language lab — is being systematized in a program called the Oxford English Corpus. This is a giant body of text that begins in 2000 and now contains more than 1.5 billion words, from published material but also from Web sites, Weblogs, chat rooms, fanzines, corporate home pages, and radio transcripts. The corpus sends its home-built Web crawler out in search of text, raw material to show how the language is really used. . . .

It is clear that the English of the *OED* is no longer the purely written language, much less a formal or respectable English, the diction recommended by any authority. [Peter] Gilliver, a longtime editor who also seems to be the *OED*'s resident historian, points out that the dictionary feels obliged to include words that many would regard simply as misspellings. No one is particularly proud of the new entry as of December 2003 for *nucular,* a word not associated with high standards of diction. "Bizarrely, I was amazed to find that the spelling n-u-c-u-l-a-r has decades of history," Gilliver says. "And that is not to be confused with the quite different word *nucular,* meaning 'of or relating to a nucule.'" There is even a new entry for *miniscule;* it has citations going back more than one hundred years.

Yet the very notion of correct and incorrect spelling seems under attack. In Shakespeare's day there was no such thing: no right and wrong in spelling, no dictionaries to consult. The word *debt* could be spelled det, dete, dett, dette, or dept, and no one would complain.

Then spelling crystallized, with the spread of printing. Now, with mass com- 10 munication taking another leap forward, spelling may be diversifying again, spellcheckers notwithstanding. The *OED* so far does not recognize *straight-laced*, but the Oxford English Corpus finds it outnumbering *strait-laced*. Similarly for *just desserts*.

To explain why cyberspace is a challenge for the *OED* as well as a godsend, Gilliver uses the phrase "sensitive ears."

"You know we are listening to the language," he says. "When you are listening to the language by collecting pieces of paper, that's fine, but now it's as if we can hear everything said anywhere. Members of some tiny English-speaking community anywhere in the world just happen to commit their communications to the Web: there it is. You thought some word was obsolete? Actually, no, it still survives in a very small community of people who happen to use the Web—we can hear about it."

In part, it's just a problem of too much information: a small number of lexicographers with limited time. But it's also that the *OED* is coming face to face with the language's boundlessness.

The universe of human discourse always has backwaters. The language spoken in one valley was a little different from the language of the next valley and so on. There are more valleys now than ever, but they are not so isolated. They find one another in chat rooms and on blogs. When they coin a word, anyone may hear.

Neologisms can be formed by committee: *transistor*, Bell Laboratories, 1948. Or by wags: *booboisie*, H. L. Mencken, 1922. But most arise through spontaneous generation, organisms appearing in a petri dish, like *blog* (c. 1999). If there is an ultimate limit to the sensitivity of lexicographers' ears, no one has yet found it. The rate of change in the language itself—particularly the process of neologism—has surely shifted into a higher gear now, but away from dictionaries, scholars of language have no clear way to measure the process. When they need quantification, they look to the dictionaries.

"An awful lot of neologisms are spur-of-the-moment creations, whether it's literary effect or it's conversational effect," says Naomi S. Baron, a linguist at American University, who studies these issues. "I could probably count on the fingers of a hand and a half the serious linguists who know anything about the Internet. That hand and a half of us are fascinated to watch how the Internet makes it possible not just for new words to be coined but for neologisms to spread like wildfire."

It's partly a matter of sheer intensity. Cyberspace is an engine driving change in the language. "I think of it as a saucepan under which the temperature has been turned up," Gilliver says. "Any word, because of the interconnectedness of the English-speaking world, can spring from the backwater. And they are still backwaters, but they have this instant connection to ordinary, everyday discourse." Like the printing press, the telegraph, and the telephone before it, the Internet is transforming the language simply by transmitting information differently. And what makes cyberspace different from all previous information technologies is its intermixing of scales from the largest to the smallest without prejudice, broadcasting to the millions, narrowcasting to groups, instant messaging one to one.

So anyone can be an *OED* author now. And, by the way, many try. "What people love to do is send us words they've invented," Bernadette Paton says, guiding me through a windowless room used for storage of old word slips. *Will you put the word I have invented into one of your dictionaries?* is a question in the AskOxford.com FAQ. All the submissions go into the files, and until there is evidence for some general usage, that's where the wannabes remain.

Don't bother sending in *FAQ*. Don't bother sending in *wannabes*.

They're not even particularly new. For that matter, don't bother sending in anything you find via Google. "Please note," the *OED*'s Web site warns solemnly, "it is generally safe to assume that examples found by searching the Web, using search engines such as Google, will have already been considered by *OED* editors." 20

JOHN HOCKENBERRY

From "The Blogs of War"

John Hockenberry (b. 1956) is an award-winning journalist who has been a correspondent for National Public Radio, and for NBC (1996–2005). Moving Violations: War Zones, Wheelchairs, and Declarations of Independence *(1995) is an account of the automobile accident in 1976 that left him a paraplegic and his subsequent career as a wheelchair-bound journalist at Mount Saint Helens and in the Middle East, interwoven with a critique of contemporary culture's treatment of people with disabilities. He writes, "On the 21st-century battlefield, the campfire glow comes from a laptop. It's a real-time window on life behind the lines—and suddenly the Pentagon is on the defensive."*

The snapshots of Iraqi prisoners being abused at Abu Ghraib were taken by soldiers and shared in the digital military netherworld of Iraq. Their release to the world in May last year detonated a media explosion that rocked a presidential campaign, cratered America's moral high ground, and demonstrated how even a superpower could be blitzkrieged by some homemade downloadable porn. In the middle of it all, a lone reservist sergeant stationed on the Iraqi border posed a simple question:

I cannot help but wonder upon reflection of the circumstances, how much longer we will be able to carry with us our digital cameras, or take photographs and document the experiences we have had.

The writer was 24-year-old Chris Missick, a soldier with the Army's 319th Signal Battalion and author of the blog A Line in the Sand. While balloon-faced cable pundits shrieked about the scandal, Missick was posting late at night in his

From *Wired*, August 2005.

Army-issue "blacks," with a mug of coffee and a small French press beside him, his laptop blasting Elliot Smith's "Cupid's Trick" into his headphones. He quickly seized on perhaps the most profound and crucial implication of Abu Ghraib:

Never before has a war been so immediately documented, never before have sentiments from the front scurried their way to the home front with such ease and precision. Here I sit, in the desert, staring daily at the electric fence, the deep trenches and the concertina wire that separates the border of Iraq and Kuwait, and write home and upload my daily reflections and opinions on the war and my circumstances here, as well as some of the pictures I have taken along the way. It is amazing, and empowering, and yet the question remains, should I as a lower enlisted soldier have such power to express my opinion and broadcast to the world a singular soldier's point of view? To those outside the uniform who have never lived the military life, the question may seem absurd, and yet, as an example of what exists even in the small following of readers I have here, the implications of thought expressed by soldiers daily could be explosive.

His sober assessments of the potential of free speech in a war zone began   5
attracting a wider following, eventually logging somewhere north of 100,000 pageviews. No blogging record, but rivaling the wonkish audience for the Pentagon's daily briefing on C-Span or DOD [Department of Defense] press releases.

Missick is just one voice—and a very pro-Pentagon one at that—in an oddball online Greek chorus narrating the conflict in Iraq. It includes a core group of about 100 regulars and hundreds more loosely organized activists, angry contrarians, jolly testosterone fuckups, self-appointed pundits, and would-be poets who call themselves milbloggers, as in military bloggers. Whether posting from inside Iraq on active duty, from noncombat bases around the world, or even from their neighborhoods back home after being discharged—where they can still follow events closely and deliver their often blunt opinions—milbloggers offer an unprecedented real-time real-life window on war and the people who wage it. Their collective voice competes with and occasionally undermines the DOD's elaborate message machine and the much-loathed mainstream media, usually dismissed as MSM.

WILLIAM DERESIEWICZ

From "Faux Friendship"

William Deresiewicz (b. 1964) was an assistant professor, then associate professor of English at Yale from 1998 to 2008. His provocative essays and reviews have appeared in a variety of publications, including the Nation, *the* American Scholar, *the* London Review of Books, *and the* New York Times.

From *The Chronicle of Higher Education*, 6 December 2009.

We live at a time when friendship has become both all and nothing at all. . . . What, in our brave new mediated world, is friendship becoming? The Facebook phenomenon, so sudden and forceful a distortion of social space, needs little elaboration. Having been relegated to our screens, are our friendships now anything more than a form of distraction? When they've shrunk to the size of a wall post, do they retain any content? If we have 768 "friends," in what sense do we have any? Facebook isn't the whole of contemporary friendship, but it sure looks a lot like its future. Yet Facebook—and MySpace, and Twitter, and whatever we're stampeding for next—are just the latest stages of a long attenuation. They've accelerated the fragmentation of consciousness, but they didn't initiate it. They have reified the idea of universal friendship, but they didn't invent it. In retrospect, it seems inevitable that once we decided to become friends with everyone, we would forget how to be friends with anyone. We may pride ourselves today on our aptitude for friendship—friends, after all, are the only people we have left—but it's not clear that we still even know what it means. . . .

With the social-networking sites of the new century—Friendster and MySpace were launched in 2003, Facebook in 2004—the friendship circle has expanded to engulf the whole of the social world, and in so doing, destroyed both its own nature and that of the individual friendship itself. Facebook's very premise—and promise—is that it makes our friendship circles visible. There they are, my friends, all in the same place. Except, of course, they're not in the same place, or, rather, they're not my friends. They're simulacra of my friends, little dehydrated packets of images and information, no more my friends than a set of baseball cards is the New York Mets.

I remember realizing a few years ago that most of the members of what I thought of as my "circle" didn't actually know one another. One I'd met in graduate school, another at a job, one in Boston, another in Brooklyn, one lived in Minneapolis now, another in Israel, so that I was ultimately able to enumerate some 14 people, none of whom had ever met any of the others. To imagine that they added up to a circle, an embracing and encircling structure, was a belief, I realized, that violated the laws of feeling as well as geometry. They were a set of points, and I was wandering somewhere among them. Facebook seduces us, however, into exactly that illusion, inviting us to believe that by assembling a list, we have conjured a group. Visual juxtaposition creates the mirage of emotional proximity. "It's like they're all having a conversation," a woman I know once said about her Facebook page, full of posts and comments from friends and friends of friends. "Except they're not."

Friendship is devolving, in other words, from a relationship to a feeling—from something people share to something each of us hugs privately to ourselves in the loneliness of our electronic caves, rearranging the tokens of connection like a lonely child playing with dolls. The same path was long ago trodden by community. As the traditional face-to-face community disappeared, we held on to what we had lost—the closeness, the rootedness—by clinging to the word, no matter how much we had to water down its meaning. Now we speak of the Jewish "community" and the medical "community" and the "community" of readers, even though none of them actually is one. What we have, instead of community, is, if we're lucky, a "sense" of community—the feeling without the structure; a private emotion, not a collective experience. And now friendship, which arose to its present importance as a replacement for community, is going the same way. We have "friends," just as we belong to "communities." Scanning my Facebook page gives me, precisely, a "sense" of connection. Not an actual connection, just a sense.

What purpose do all those wall posts and status updates serve? On the first   5 beautiful weekend of spring this year, a friend posted this update from Central Park: "[So-and-so] is in the Park with the rest of the City." The first question that comes to mind is, if you're enjoying a beautiful day in the park, why don't you give your iPhone a rest? But the more important one is, why did you need to tell us that? We have always shared our little private observations and moments of feeling—it's part of what friendship's about, part of the way we remain present in one another's lives—but things are different now. Until a few years ago, you could share your thoughts with only one friend at a time (on the phone, say), or maybe with a small group, later, in person. And when you did, you were talking to specific people, and you tailored what you said, and how you said it, to who they were—their interests, their personalities, most of all, your degree of mutual intimacy. "Reach out and touch someone" meant someone in particular, someone you were actually thinking about. It meant having a conversation. Now we're just broadcasting our stream of consciousness, live from Central Park, to all 500 of our friends at once, hoping that someone, anyone, will confirm our existence by answering back. We haven't just stopped talking to our friends as individuals, at such moments, we have stopped thinking of them as individuals. We have turned them into an indiscriminate mass, a kind of audience or faceless public. We address ourselves not to a circle, but to a cloud. . . .

Perhaps I need to surrender the idea that the value of friendship lies precisely in the space of privacy it creates: not the secrets that two people exchange so much as the unique and inviolate world they build up between them, the spider web of shared discovery they spin out, slowly and carefully, together. There's something faintly obscene about performing that intimacy in front of everyone you know, as if its real purpose were to show what a deep person you are. Are we really so hungry for validation? So desperate to prove we have friends?

But surely Facebook has its benefits. Long-lost friends can reconnect, far-flung ones can stay in touch. I wonder, though. Having recently moved across the country, I thought that Facebook would help me feel connected to the friends I'd left behind. But now I find the opposite is true. Reading about the mundane details of their lives, a steady stream of trivia and ephemera, leaves me feeling both empty and unpleasantly full, as if I had just binged on junk food, and precisely because it reminds me of the real sustenance, the real knowledge, we exchange by e-mail or phone or face-to-face. And the whole theatrical quality of the business, the sense that my friends are doing their best to impersonate themselves, only makes it worse. The person I read about, I cannot help feeling, is not quite the person I know. . . .

Finally, the new social-networking Web sites have falsified our understanding of intimacy itself, and with it, our understanding of ourselves. The absurd idea, bruited about in the media, that a MySpace profile or "25 Random Things About Me" can tell us more about someone than even a good friend might be aware of is based on desiccated notions about what knowing another person means: First, that intimacy is confessional—an idea both peculiarly American and peculiarly young, perhaps because both types of people tend to travel among strangers, and so believe in the instant disgorging of the self as the quickest route to familiarity. Second, that identity is reducible to information: the name of your cat, your favorite Beatle, the stupid thing you did in seventh grade. Third, that it is reducible, in particular, to the kind of information that social-networking Web sites are most interested in eliciting, consumer preferences. Forget that we're all conducting market research on ourselves. Far worse is that Facebook amplifies our long-standing tendency to see ourselves ("I'm a Skin Bracer man!") in just those terms. We wear T-shirts that proclaim our brand loyalty, pique ourselves on owning a Mac, and now put up lists of our favorite songs. "15 movies in 15 minutes. Rule: Don't take too long to think about it."

So information replaces experience, as it has throughout our culture. But when I think about my friends, what makes them who they are, and why I love them, it is not the names of their siblings that come to mind, or their fear of spiders. It is their qualities of character. This one's emotional generosity, that one's moral seriousness, the dark humor of a third. Yet even those are just descriptions, and no more specify the individuals uniquely than to say that one has red hair, another is tall. To understand what they really look like, you would have to see a picture. And to understand who they really are, you would have to hear about the things they've done. Character, revealed through action: the two eternal elements of narrative. In order to know people, you have to listen to their stories.

But that is precisely what the Facebook page does not leave room for, or 500   10 friends, time for. Literally does not leave room for. E-mail, with its rapid-fire etiquette and scrolling format, already trimmed the letter down to a certain acceptable maximum, perhaps a thousand words. Now, with Facebook, the box is shrinking even more, leaving perhaps a third of that length as the conventional limit for a message, far less for a comment. (And we all know the deal on Twitter.) The 10-page missive has gone the way of the buggy whip, soon to be followed, it seems, by the three-hour conversation. Each evolved as a space for telling stories, an act that cannot usefully be accomplished in much less. Posting information is like pornography, a slick, impersonal exhibition. Exchanging stories is like making love: probing, questing, questioning, caressing. It is mutual. It is intimate. It takes patience, devotion, sensitivity, subtlety, skill—and it teaches them all, too.

They call them social-networking sites for a reason. Networking once meant something specific: climbing the jungle gym of professional contacts in order to advance your career. The truth is that Hume and Smith were not completely right. Commercial society did not eliminate the self-interested aspects of making friends and influencing people, it just changed the way we went about it. Now, in the age of the entrepreneurial self, even our closest relationships are being pressed onto this template. A recent book on the sociology of modern science describes a networking event at a West Coast university: "There do not seem to be any single-tons—disconsolately lurking at the margins—nor do dyads appear, except fleetingly." No solitude, no friendship, no space for refusal—the exact contemporary paradigm. At the same time, the author assures us, "face time" is valued in this "community" as a "high-bandwidth interaction," offering "unusual capacity for interruption, repair, feedback and learning." Actual human contact, rendered "unusual" and weighed by the values of a systems engineer. We have given our hearts to machines, and now we are turning into machines. The face of friendship in the new century.

QUESTIONS FOR DISCUSSION AND WRITING

1. Turkle begins her list of areas where information technology encourages "changes in thinking" with the observation, "There can be no simple way of cataloging whether any particular change is good or bad. That is contested terrain. At every step we have to ask . . . whether current technology is leading us in directions that serve our human purposes" (paragraph 9). Make a list of some of the major technological tools and technologies that you use regularly and identify their positives and negatives. What are their best and worst features? Could you do without any (word processor, Internet and its many ramifications, including social networking sites, and more—and others, such as a cell phone, that Turkle doesn't discuss), on either a permanent or temporary basis? Why or why not?

2. In what ways do the new technologies Turkle discusses here reflect the views of Dennis Baron in "The New Technologies of the Word" (p. 327)? Are these new technologies changing the ways people think, and write and read—as Nicholas Carr argues in "Is Google Making Us Stupid?" (p. 336)? How does Gleick's discussion of "Cyber-Neologoliferation" (p. 362), concerning the ease and frequency with which words can arise and be added to the lexicon, influence your views? How does the fact that embedded journalists or combatants themselves can communicate directly from military sites (including battles), as Hockenberry illustrates in "The Blogs of War" (p. 365) contribute to this dialogue? What are some of the ethical as well as intellectual issues underlying this conversation?

3. At the end of "How Computers Change the Way We Think" Turkle concludes that current computing habits and software may undermine "democracy, freedom of expression, tolerance, diversity, and complexity of opinion" (paragraph 32). Does Turkle's "The Human Spirit in a Computer Culture" (p. 353) reinforce or change this view? Can you supplement the evidence Turkle offers with information derived from your own experiences? Is she right? Are there positive features, also embedded in technology, that can counteract the negatives? Identify some and show how these might work.

4. In "Faux Friendship," William Deresiewicz laments the "distortion of social space" (paragraph 1) that Facebook and other social networking sites provide. When friendships have "shrunk to the size of a wall post, do they retain any content? If we have 768 'friends,' in what sense do we have any" (paragraph 1)? How does Michael J. Bugeja's discussion, "Facing the Facebook" (p. 399), influence your answer? What do Turkle's observations in "Logins R Us" (p. 355) and "Inner History" (p. 360) add to this discussion? Where do you find your friends—in real life and on the Internet? Discuss with classmates—who may also be "friends"—what elements these friendships have in common. In what ways are they different? Do both serve important purposes? Are these purposes the same or different? Compile your main points in a manifesto about the nature of friendship and how it is enhanced or degraded by social networking.

5. Turkle raises privacy issues (paragraphs 10 and 11) that Esther Dyson, in "Reflections on Privacy 2.0" (p. 378); Daniel J. Solove, in "The End of Privacy?" (p. 384); and Michael J. Bugeja, in "Facing the Facebook" (p. 399), also discuss at length. Which are the most significant? Are you coming of age in a time when privacy is no longer a concern? Or do you expect privacy issues and violations to influence—even haunt—you for the rest of your life? These authors do not discuss identity theft, invasion of private banking and other accounts, and other encroachments on one's personal life, but you may include these if you wish. Illustrate your answers and explain. Are you worried? Should you be? Which of the aspects of privacy might "inspire more active political engagement," as Turkle hopes (paragraph 11)?

6. None of the authors in this chapter is suggesting anything as radical and Luddite as doing away with the Internet or the technological applications of computers and other electronic media, yet many point out major problems. Rank order the problems from worst to mildest, pick one that most immediately affects you (or to which you may even be contributing), analyze it, and propose a solution.

7. The photograph "Multitasking Man" (p. 359) can be read in a variety of ways, depending on its context. In what ways does it address any of the issues in the Context readings accompanying Turkle's "How Computers Change the Way We Think"? Write alternative captions for this picture as if it were embedded in each of the following works: Nicholas Carr, "Is Google Making Us Stupid?" (p. 336); G. Anthony Gorry, "Empathy in the Virtual World" (p. 372); Daniel J. Solove, "The End of Privacy?" (p. 378); Cathy Guisewite, "We Saw Paris" (p. 391); Joseph Fuller, "The Terminator Comes to Wall Street" (p. 404). Are all of these equally good matches?

G. ANTHONY GORRY

Empathy in the Virtual World

G. Anthony Gorry is a preeminent authority on the way technology and information processing affects our institutions, culture, and values. Gorry is a professor of management and computer science at Rice University, where he directs the W. M. Keck Center for Computational Biology and the Center for Technology in Teaching and Learning. A graduate of Yale (B.A., 1962), he did graduate work at the University of California at Berkeley (M.S., 1963) and MIT (Ph.D., 1967). In addition to applying artificial intelligence—sophisticated computer algorithms that can mimic human decision processes—to the practice of medicine and management, Gorry has written extensively on other issues in applied computation in organizations and educational settings.

In "Empathy in the Virtual World" (originally published in the Chronicle of Higher Education *in 2009), Gorry addresses the social consequences of the new technologies, in which online immersion replaces actual face-to-face contact in the real world. Like the chained prisoners in Plato's cave, Gorry asserts, people mistake the "shadows on the wall" for reality—"a sorry scene . . . a pale imitation of what life should be," particularly when it leads to a loss of empathy. Is such a loss inevitable? he asks.*

We live increasingly "on the screen," deeply engaged with the patterns of light and energy upon which so much of modern life depends. At work we turn our backs to our coworkers, immersing ourselves in the flood of information engendered by countless computers. At the end of the workday, computers tag along with us in cellphones and music players. Still others, embedded in video displays, wait at home. They are all parts of an enormous electronic web woven on wires or only air. We marvel at what we can do with this technology. We turn less attention, however, to what the technology may be doing to us.

Recall Plato's allegory of the cave, in which Socrates tells of prisoners who are rigidly chained in a cave, facing a wall with a fire burning brightly behind them. Between the fire and the prisoners, people carry vessels, statues of animals made of wood and stone, and other things back and forth on a walkway. Held fast, the prisoners see only shadows on the wall and hear only echoes of the voices behind them. Mistaking these for reality, the prisoners vie with one another to name the shadowy shapes, and they judge one another by their facility for quickly recognizing the images.

A sorry scene, we say—a pale imitation of what life should be, a cruel punishment. We do not need philosophers or scientists to tell us that without social interaction, we would not be human. But what has the prisoners' plight to do with us? We are not in chains. We have many face-to-face engagements with others. And the centuries between that cave and the present have seen monumental developments in human consciousness: the emergence of language and imagination, and the invention of tools of communication that have enabled rhapsodes, scribes, and novelists to thrust us into lives real and invented. Today digital technology extends that reach, making possible ever-beguiling fabrications for entertainment and escape. It has put us at the gate of a magical garden crowded with many others who, from the flickers on a screen, clamor for our attention and concern.

If Socrates could wander the halls of our workplaces or visit our homes, he would be amazed by the advance of our multimedia computers over the primitive technology of his cave with its statues and firelight. Technology, however, never bestows its bounty freely, and Socrates might make us a bit uncomfortable with questions about the role that machines play in modern life: Do they bind us in subtle ways? Are they drawing us into such intimacy that life on the screen will soon replace the face-to-face community as the primary setting for social interaction? If so, at what cost?

I fear that we will pay for our entry into the magical garden of cyberspace   5 with a loss of empathy—that our devotion to ephemeral images will diminish our readiness to care for those around us. We might hope, of course, for an increase in understanding, tolerance, and perhaps even empathy as technology makes more permeable the boundaries that presently divide communities and nations. Such benefits would surely be a boon to our troubled world. But as technology exposes us to the pain and suffering of so many others, it might also numb our emotions, distance us from our fellow humans, and attenuate our empathetic responses to their misfortunes. In our life on the screen, we might know more and more about others and care less and less about them.

What is the source of our feelings for others—the "pity for the sorrowful, anguish for the miserable, joy for the successful" that Adam Smith called fellow feeling? Perhaps it is simply in our nature to respond emotionally to those around us. Indeed, our emotional responses arise swiftly and unbidden, particularly in the presence of those bearing the weight of injury, loss, fear, or despair. We might, therefore, expect our natural sympathy and compassion to be impervious to corrosion by modern life. Yet for every heartwarming account of compassion, aid, and sacrifice, the daily news offers a story of indifference, hatred, or abuse that illuminates a second aspect of our nature: a willingness to advance our individual interests at others' expense.

Evolutionary theory and neuroscience both seem to confirm the view of those who attribute humans' compassionate acts to strict social controls—including laws, mores, teachings, and taboos—that alone keep our brutish self-interest in check. If that is so, then changes in the way we interact, and particularly the loss of those social controls, could undermine our caring for one another. Natural selection shaped the brains and behavior of our primate forebears to serve both self and others. By grouping, they could better meet environmental challenges and promote their reproductive success. Individuals still cared most for their own prospects and those of their kin, but increasing social integration demanded care for the interests of the community. Natural selection, therefore, favored primates that could sense the intentions and needs of others of their kind. In time, they became sensitive to the emotions and behavior of others. Our ancestors responded instinctively to body language—not only gross actions, but the twitch of an eye, tremor of a hand, tensing of a leg, and the dilation of a pupil, all subtle indicators of the intent of the brain within the body observed. Thus primates could forge alliances, exchange favors, achieve status, and even deceive. Those who were particularly skilled in "working the crowd" gained added advantages for themselves and their offspring. Because of those advantages, primate sociability became a powerful adjunct to a fierce focus on self.

Genetic adaptations to the demands of that long-ago time still influence our culture, and ancient emotional centers in our brains affect many of our social interactions. But the emergence of imagination set us on the path to what J. K. Rowling characterized as understanding without having experienced, to thinking ourselves into other people's minds and places. One hundred years ago, Joseph Conrad noted that there is a permanently enduring part of our being "which is not dependent on wisdom . . . which is a gift and not an acquisition." The artist speaks to that part of us, for through it, "one may perchance attain to such clearness of sincerity that at last the presented vision of regret or pity, of terror or mirth, shall awaken in the hearts of the beholders that feeling of unavoidable solidarity; of the solidarity in mysterious origin, in toil, in joy, in hope, in uncertain fate, which binds men to each other and all mankind to the visible world."

For hundreds of years, novels have engaged our empathetic faculties with the lives of imagined others. We learn to read through practice, shaping our brains to accommodate the linearity and fixity of text. Literacy repays that effort by introducing us to a multitude of fictional others whose lives can entertain and edify us. Today, as our brains acclimate to digital technology, a computer screen is increasingly our window to the world. Technology crowds our lives with others' experiences, each claiming a bit of our attention and concern. Some readers of novels say that by introducing us to fictional others, stories make us more sensitive to the feelings of real people. With its jumble of streaming video, elaborate games, social networks, news reports, fiction, and gossip, cyberspace could coax us to greater regard for the unfortunate and oppressed. The widespread grief that followed the death of Princess Diana is a vivid example of the power of technology's Muses to extend the reach of another's mythical life into our own. As digital technology increases its hold on our imaginations, perhaps it will do what novels are said to do: make us a more compassionate, "nicer" species.

Hesiod observed that the Muses have the power to make false things seem   10 true. That, of course, is how they sustain fiction. Today's technology offers new ways to engage our imaginations. Movies, television advertising, and pictures in magazines depict tantalizing, unreal worlds that offer us, if we will suspend our disbelief, what Sontag called "knowledge at bargain prices—a semblance of knowledge, a semblance of wisdom." Even when we know that what we see cannot be, the falsity of our experience may not reduce our empathetic response, which is more automatic than considered. Our brains, seeking stimulation rather than knowledge, may find more engagement in a montage of simulated joys and agonies than in the lives of real people and events.

In the movie theater, for example, watching the *Titanic* slowly sink, we suffer with its desperate passengers and fear for their fate. We know the images we see are an amalgamation of the real and artificial. But our brains care little about the way technology weds fact and fiction; we care about the experience, not analysis, and for a few minutes, the sinking is real.

Of course, artists have drawn us into imaginative worlds for thousands of years. But when their performances were finished, their books read, or their movies seen, we returned to our everyday lives—and to our friends and neighbors. Now digital technology is erasing the boundary between the magic and the mundane. Computers give us not only a diversion or a lesson, but a fantastic life in which we can indulge our interests with the click of a link, where we can be any place at any time, where we can be who we want to be.

Technology is replacing the traditional social structures of the face-to-face community with more-fluid electronic arenas for gossip, preening, and posturing. Facebook and MySpace members "strut their stuff" with embellished self-descriptions and accumulations of "friends" from far and wide. Those affectations would mean little if we were not so sensitive to trappings of rank, so irresistibly drawn to judge and categorize others. Repeated encounters with those who present themselves as a blend of the actual and the fantasized alter our expectations of trustworthiness and reciprocity. Absent the accountability of face-to-face interaction, there seems little need to adhere to social conventions of the past. Users are free to invent themselves without regard for the concerns or needs of others.

John Updike said the Internet is chewing up books, casting fragments adrift on an electronic flood. We might say the same of lives; technology is cutting out pieces and offering them isolated from their natural context. Just as a dismembered novel loses accountability and intimacy, so too does a person who appears only in fragments. Other people's experiences are reduced to grist for the mill of our emotions, where our inclinations, histories, prejudices, and aesthetic preferences grind them to our liking. With technology as a remote control, we can tune in the emotional stimulation we crave and tune out what we find unpleasant or disturbing. As we shuttle from e-mail to hyperlinks to phone calls, we may find little time or inclination to uncover real suffering in the chaotic mix of the actual and the invented.

A century ago, in "The Machine Stops," E. M. Forster envisioned a time when   15
a powerful Machine would mediate all experience. His Machine had woven an electronic garment that "had seemed heavenly at first." Over time, however, technology had imprisoned humanity in an electronic cave where the body had become "white pap, the home of ideas as colorless, last sloshy stirrings of a spirit that had grasped the stars." The sudden failure of the Machine doomed its dependents, who knew no other life but that on the screen.

Many cultures have used art and its technologies to promote social well-being. But now the very fullness of life on the screen may thwart that intent. Multitudinous and multifaceted appeals to our emotions may so absorb us that we have no energy to devote to others. We want the frightened to be comforted, the sick to be healed, and the defenseless to be protected, but in the virtual world, actions that have consequences are few. Feelings without deeds may be the colorless, sloshing stirrings derided by Forster. If natural selection endowed us with a limited capacity to empathize with others, then technology's parade of fragmented lives may sap us of feeling. Like profligate shoppers who have squandered our money on trinkets that please our fancy, we may have nothing left to spend for anything truly worthy.

Because our biology drives our venture into cyberspace, we can expect a deepening intimacy with our digital machines. They give today's Muses new ways to meet our brains' incessant demands for emotional stimulation—to forge fetters that bind us to our electronic environments. If our technology remains robust, we may avoid the catastrophic failure imagined by Forster. But what of empathy?

Socrates argued that poetry, through its power to stir our emotions and appeal to our baser inclinations, undermines understanding. So he proposed to exclude it from the education of the elite in his ideal community. For them, philosophy—an arduous but ultimately more-reliable mode of thinking— would be the path to understanding.

Today our increasingly seductive technologies would alarm him even more; he would surely limit the engagement of his elite with multimedia fabrications. Socrates recognized, however, that art is the vehicle through which society guides the many to good citizenship. He anticipated the arguments of later advocates of novel reading in the promotion of empathy: The right artistic creations—the right fictions—will raise aspirations, enhance fellow feeling, and improve behavior. So despite his reservations, Socrates might see new opportunities for artists and teachers to encourage sympathy and compassion.

Digital technology has fostered a radical egalitarianism that has displaced the [20] authorities that were traditionally empowered to cultivate and guide our feelings for one another. It has made Muses of us all. In turn, we have created the cacophony of the Internet that conveys not a single tradition but a flood of fragments, which can inform us of much but can teach us little.

In this chaos, we may sense an unsettling possibility. Natural selection embedded our dogged pursuit of our own interests in a matrix of sociability. Once we live disembodied lives, in which identity is largely an imaginative construction, will falsehood predominate? Will false identities free us to conceal our intentions, to pursue our own selfish interests more aggressively? It would be deeply distressing if digital technology, which offers so many opportunities for liberation, liberated some of our worst inclinations and behaviors from existing social restraints.

On the other hand, stories of the imagined lives of others have guided empathy for thousands of years. Over time, different modes of communication—songs, poems, and novels—have elevated some ways of understanding over others. Reading pre-empted oral performance, and now multimedia are pushing reading aside. At each transition, masters of the older mode scorned the new and vigorously but fruitlessly resisted it. Those who embraced the new found powerful ways to convey their imaginative conceptions.

Now technology is dramatically changing the path to Conrad's "permanently enduring" part of our being. If we would foster empathy, we must change as well. We may have to jettison old habits of thought and avoid a debilitating yearning for the past. As McLuhan argued, we cannot drive into the future looking in the rearview mirror. But we can remember the road we have traveled. Our traditions embody much from our past that is important to our society, and we should find them anchors in the digital flood.

QUESTIONS FOR DISCUSSION AND WRITING

1. In what ways does Plato's allegory of the cave represent "[a] sorry scene—a pale imitation of what life should be, a cruel punishment" (paragraph 3)? Does Gorry make legitimate connections between contemporary users of the Internet and the experiences of prisoners viewing not real life but "only shadows on the wall" (paragraphs 1–4)? Explain.

2. Why does Gorry fear that "our devotion to ephemeral images will diminish our readiness to care for those around us" (paragraph 5)? What evidence does he cite that Internet use leads to such "loss of empathy"?

3. Do you still read books off-line? If so, what do you read? What determines whether you read something on- or off-line? Do you ever read fiction? If so, drawing on your own experience, comment on Gorry's observation that literature introduces us "to a multitude of fictional others whose lives can entertain and edify us" (paragraph 9). Does technology do the same, making us "a more compassionate, 'nicer' species" (paragraph 9)?

4. Discuss with several classmates what sort of "strict social controls—including laws, mores, teachings, and taboos" (paragraph 7)—influence your own behavior with regard to other people. Make a list of the positive and negative controls; then rearrange the list, beginning with the most important factors and proceeding down to the least. Then analyze how and why the three most important factors, both positive and negative, are so powerful.

5. Is Gorry accurate in his claim that "[r]epeated encounters with those who present themselves as a blend of the actual and the fantasized [in Facebook and MySpace] alter our expectations of trustworthiness and reciprocity" (paragraph 13)? Do users really "invent themselves without regard for the concerns or needs of others" (paragraph 13)? "Once we live disembodied lives, in which identity is largely an imaginative construction, will falsehood predominate" (paragraph 21)? Address these questions with regard to your own experiences and those of your peers. Is there a viable alternative to Gorry's pessimistic interpretations?

6. Gorry's essay is full of analogies and metaphors. Find several, beginning with Plato's allegory of the cave. Are these a good way to make his point?

ESTHER DYSON

Reflections on Privacy 2.0

Esther Dyson (b. 1951) is the daughter of physicist Freeman Dyson and mathematician Verena Huber-Dyson. Her family background, education (a B.A. in economics from Harvard), and early career as a reporter at Forbes *magazine have contributed to her endeavors for over thirty years as technology guru and entrepreneur. Longtime CEO of EDVenture Holdings, she has invested in a variety of start-ups, particularly in online services (Flickr), health care/genetics (23andMe), and space travel (Space Adventures, Zero Gravity Corporation)—for which she has also completed training to become a space tourist. Questioning whether digital technology "enables us to find meaning, or whether it reduces meaningfulness by turning everything into numbers," Dyson chairs both ICANN, which assigns Internet domain names, and the Electronic Frontier Foundation (EFF), advocating rights in our digital age. She told Nick Bilton of the* New York Times *(February 26, 2010), "I have a short attention span. I couldn't stay doing the same thing for 30 years. My life is like a series of comic strips, which is why I like investing: I really like new stuff. I often like to quote what the math professors say: 'The remainder of the proof is an exercise left to the reader.'"*

In "Reflections on Privacy 2.0," the keynote essay in Scientific American's *special issue on the future of privacy (September 2008), Dyson lays the groundwork by analyzing the phenomenon that "many issues posing as questions of privacy can turn out to be matters of security, health policy, insurance or self-presentation," complicated by easy Internet access. Daniel J. Solove's "The End of Privacy?" that follows this selection, addresses some of the issues Dyson raises here. Questions for Discussion and Writing follow Solove (p. 384).*

Privacy is a public Rorschach test: say the word aloud, and you can start any number of passionate discussions. One person worries about governmental abuse of power; another blushes about his drug use and sexual history; a third vents outrage about how corporations collect private data to target their ads or how insurance companies dig through personal medical records to deny coverage to certain people. Some fear a world of pervasive commercialization, in which data are used to sort everyone into one or another "market segment"—the better to cater to people's deepest desires or to exploit their most frivolous whims. Others fret over state intrusion and social strictures.

Such fears are typically presented as trade-offs: privacy versus effective medical care, privacy versus free (advertising-driven) content, privacy versus security. Those debates are all well worn, but they are now returning to the fore in a way they did not when specialists, insiders and die-hard privacy advocates were the only ones paying attention.

On the one hand, the erosion of privacy is unmistakable. Most Americans are online today, and most of us have probably had one or more "Now how did they know that?" experiences. The U.S. administration is breaching people's privacy right and left, while conducting more and more of its operations in obscurity. It has become hard to act anonymously if someone—particularly the government—makes any effort to find out who you are.

On the other hand, new and compelling reasons have arisen for people to disclose private information. Personalized medicine is on the threshold of reality. Detailed and accurate health and genetic information from private medical histories, both to treat individuals and to analyze epidemiological statistics across populations, has enormous potential for enhancing the general social welfare. Many people take pleasure in sharing personal information with others on social-networking Web sites. More darkly, the heightened threat of terrorism has led many to give up private information for illusory promises of safety and security.

Much of the privacy that people took for granted in the past was a by-product of friction in finding and assembling information. That friction is mostly gone. Everyone lives like a celebrity, their movements watchable, their weight gains or bad hair days the subject of comment, questions once left unspoken now explicitly asked: Was that lunch together a "date"? Which of my friends is a top friend?

BOUNDARY CONDITIONS

This issue of *Scientific American* [September 2008] focuses mostly on technologies that erode privacy and technologies that preserve it. But to help frame the discussion I'd like to lay out three orthogonal points.

First, in defining some disclosure of information as a breach of privacy, it is useful to distinguish any objective harms arising from the disclosure—fraud, denial of a service, denial of freedom—from any subjective privacy harms, in which the mere knowledge by a second or third party of one's private information is experienced as an injury. In many cases, what is called a breach of privacy is actually a breach of security or a financial harm: if your Social Security number is disclosed and misused—and I probably give mine out several times a month—that's not an issue of privacy; it's an issue of security. As for breaches of *privacy*, the "harm" a person feels is subjective and personal. Rather than attempting to define privacy for all, society should give individuals the tools to control the use and spread of their data. The balance between secrecy and disclosure is an individual preference, but the need for tools and even laws to implement that preference is general.

Second, as the borders between private and public are redrawn, people must retain the right to bear witness. When personal privacy is increasingly limited in a friction-free world of trackable data, the right of individuals to track and report on the activities of powerful organizations, whether governments or big businesses, is key to preserving freedom and to balancing the interests of individuals and institutions.

The third point elaborates on the first: in assessing the changes in the expectations people have about privacy, it is important to recognize the granularity of personal control of data. Privacy is not a one-size-fits-all condition: Different people at different times have different preferences about what happens to their personal information and who gets to see it. They may not have the right or ability to set such conditions in coercive relationships—in dealing with a government entity, for instance, or with an organization such as an employer or an insurance company from which they want something in return. But people often have a better bargaining position than they realize. Now they are gaining the tools and knowledge to exploit that position.

OBJECTIVE HARMS

Security is not the only public issue posing as privacy. Many issues of medical and 10
genetic privacy, for instance, are really issues of money and insurance. Should people in poor health be compelled to pay more for their care? If you think they should not, you might feel forced to conclude that they should tacitly be allowed to lie. This conclusion is often misleadingly positioned as the protection of privacy. The real issue, however, is not privacy but rather the business model of the insurance industry in the U.S. People would not care about medical privacy so much if revealing the truth about their health did not expose them to costly medical bills and insurance premiums.

Genetic data seem to present a particularly troubling example of the potential for discrimination. One fear is that insurance companies will soon require genetic tests of applicants—and will deny insurance to any applicant with a genetic risk. A genome does indeed carry a fair amount of information; it can uniquely identify anyone except an identical twin, and it can reveal family relationships that may have been hidden. Some rare diseases can be diagnosed by the presence of certain genetic markers.

But genes are only one factor in a person's life. Genes tell little about family dynamics, and they cannot say what a person has done with inherited abilities. Genes typically make themselves felt through complex interactions with upbringing, behavior, environment and sheer chance.

And genetic discrimination may soon be against the law anyway. This past May [2008], President George W. Bush signed into law the Genetic Information Nondiscrimination Act (GINA), which outlaws discrimination in insurance and employment on the basis of genetic tests.

Nevertheless, the coming flood of medical and genetic information is likely to change the very nature of health insurance. With better liquidity of health information about a broad population and with better tracking of the outcomes of treatments and diseases, accurate prediction on the basis of statistical studies becomes progressively easier. But if individuals can be assigned to so-called cost buckets with reasonable accuracy, insuring people against high medical costs is no longer a matter of community rating—that is, pooling collective assets against unknown individual risks. Rather it is a matter of mandating subsidies paid by society to provide affordable insurance to those whose high health risks would otherwise make their insurance premiums or treatment prohibitively expensive.

As a consequence, society will have to decide, clearly and openly, which kinds 15 of discrimination are acceptable and which are not. All of us will be forced to confront ethical choices crisply rather than hiding behind the confusion of information opacity. If insurance companies are asked to administer subsidies, they will demand clear rules about which individual health costs, and what proportion of them, society wants—and will pay—to provide. (The trick, as ever, is to make sure the insurers and health care providers keep costs down by providing good care and maintaining their customers' health rather than by limiting care. Increased information about health risks and treatment outcomes that I mentioned earlier will help measure the effectiveness of care and make that happen.)

THE RIGHT TO BEAR WITNESS

People really need rules about privacy when one party is in a position to demand data from another. The most important example is the government's power to collect and use (or misuse) personal data. That power needs to be limited.

What is the best way to limit government power? Not so much by rules that protect the privacy of individuals, which the government may decline to observe or enforce, but by rules that limit the privacy of the government and of government officials. The public must retain the right to know and to bear witness.

A primary instrument for ensuring that right has traditionally been the media. But the Internet is giving people the tools and the platform to take things into their own hands. Every camera and video recorder can bear public witness to acts of oppression, as the Rodney King video showed dramatically back in 1991 and as the Abu Ghraib photographs showed in 2004. The Internet is the platform that gives everyone instant access to a potentially worldwide audience. Reports from nongovernmental organizations (NGOs) and from private citizens around the globe are distributed on the Internet via social-networking and file-sharing sites and as cell phone text messages.

Ironically, perhaps the best model for what citizens should require of government is the kind of information that government requires of business. Business disclosure rules are tightening all the time—about labor practices, financial results, everything a business does. Investors have a right to know about the company they own, and customers have a right to know about the ingredients in the products they buy and how those products were made.

By the same token, citizens have a right to know about the job-related 20 behavior of the people we elect and pay. We have a right to know about conflicts of interest and what public servants do with their (our) time. We should have the same rights vis-à-vis government that shareholders and customers (and, for that matter, the U.S. Securities and Exchange Commission) have vis-à-vis a publicly traded company. In fact, I would argue, citizens have extra rights with respect to government precisely because we are coerced into giving governments so much data. We should be able to monitor what the government does with our personal data and to audit (through representatives) the processes for managing the data and keeping them secure. The Sunlight Foundation (www.sunlightfoundation .com), of which I am a trustee, is encouraging people to find out and post information about their congressional representatives and, ultimately, about all public servants.

SUNSHINE FOR BUSINESSES

As for businesses' privacy rights, they don't (and shouldn't) have many. True, they have a right to record their own transactions with customers—and transactions done on credit typically require customers to prove their creditworthiness by giving up private information. But just as a company can refuse to sell on credit, a consumer can refuse to do business with a company that asks for too much data. Beyond that, everything should be negotiable. Customers can demand to know what companies are doing with their data, and if the customers don't like the response, they can move on. What the law needs to enforce is that companies actually follow the practices they disclose.

As with disclosures by government (and especially by politicians when they run for office), disclosure about businesses is going beyond what is required by regulation. In every sphere of activity, the little guy is biting back. All kinds of Web sites are devoted to ratings, discussions and other user-generated content about services—hotels, doctors, and the like—as well as products. To be sure, many of the hotel reviews are posted by the hotels themselves or by their competitors. (To discourage such tactics, some sites require user biographies and encourage users to rate the credibility of the other users and reviewers.) Patients can check out doctors and hospitals on a variety of sites, from HealthGrades.com (a paid service) to a number of sites funded by advertising.

For user information about physical products, consider a proposed new service called Barcode Wikipedia (www.sicamp.org/?page_id=21). This service will enable users to post whatever they know or can find out about a product—its ingredients or components, where it was manufactured or assembled, the labor practices of the maker, its environmental impact or side effects, and so on. Companies are free to post on the site as well, telling their side of the story. With such open access, of course, postings are likely to include exaggerations and untruths as well as useful information. Yet with time—as Wikipedia itself has demonstrated—users will police other users, and the truth, more or less, will emerge.

PUBLIC LIVES

Until recently, privacy for most people was afforded (though not guaranteed) by information friction: Information about what you did in private didn't travel too far unless you were famous or went to extreme lengths to be public about your activities. Now the concept of privacy itself is changing. Many adults are appalled at what they find on Facebook or MySpace. Some adolescents are aware of the risks of using social-networking Web sites but don't take them seriously—a teenage shortcoming from time immemorial. And it's likely that some kind of statute of limitations on foolish behavior will emerge: Most employers (who can search the Web pages of job applicants as well as anybody) will simply lower their standards and keep hiring, though some may remain stricter. Just think of tattoos: 20 years ago adults warned kids against getting them. Now every second woman in my health-club locker room seems to have a tattoo, and I assume it's the same proportion or more for the men.

Kids still have a sense of privacy, and they can still be hurt by the opinions of others. It's just that more of them are used to living more of their lives in public than their parents are. I think that's a real change. But the 20th century was also a change from the 19th century. In the 19th century few people slept alone: children slept together in one room, if not with their parents. Some rich people had rooms of their own, but they also had servants to take out their chamber pots, help dress them and take care of their most intimate needs. Our 20th-century notions of physical privacy are quite new. 25

For centuries before that, most people in most villages knew a great deal about one another. Yet little was explicit. What was different in the past is that Juan could not go online and see what Alice was saying. Juan might have guessed what Alice knew, but he didn't have to face the fact that Alice knew it. Likewise, Juan could easily avoid Alice. Today if Juan is Alice's ex-boyfriend, he can torment himself by watching her flirt online. Is there such a concept as privacy from one's own desires?

MY DATA, MYSELF

A second major change in personal privacy is that people are learning to exert some control over which of their data others can see. Facebook has given millions of people the tools—and, somewhat inadvertently, practice in using them. Last year Facebook annoyed some of its users with Beacon, a service that tracked their off-site purchases and informed their friends. The practice had been disclosed, but not effectively, and as a result many users discovered the privacy settings they had previously ignored. (Facebook subsequently rejiggered things to a more sensible approach, and the fuss died down.) Now many members change their privacy settings, both for incoming news from their friends (do you really want to know every time Matt goes on a date?) and for outgoing news to your friends (do you really want to tell everyone about your sales trip to Redmond, Wash.?). Users can share photographs within private groups or post them for all to see.

Flickr, a Web site for sharing photographs, enables users to control who sees them, albeit in a limited way. (Full disclosure: I was an investor in Flickr.) But those controls are likely to get more precise. Now, if you want, you can define a closed group, but that's not quite the same as being able to make selective disclosures to specific friends. For example, you might want to create two intersecting family groups: one comprising your full siblings and your mother; the other comprising all your siblings plus your father and your stepmother but not your mother. Other people might create other family subsets—a father and his children, for instance, but not his new wife—the mere existence of which may call for privacy.

The blogger and social-networking expert danah boyd (yes, all lowercase), who is a nonresident fellow at Harvard University's Berkman Center for Internet & Society, recently waxed eloquent about users' desire to control exactly who sees their posts and what ads accompany those posts. In other words, what matters is not the ads I see; it's the ads my friends see on "my" Web page. The issue for boyd—and for many other people—is not privacy so much as presentation of self (including, in boyd's case, her own name). People know they cannot control everything others say about them, but they will flock to online-community services that enable them to control how they present themselves online, as well as who can see which of those presentations.

That kind of control will extend, I believe, to the notion of "friending" ven- 30 dors. Alice is happy for the vendor that sold her a size 42 red sweater to know her purchasing habits, but she doesn't want her friends, her current boyfriend or other vendors to have access to that information. Of course, Alice has no control over what other people say or know about her. If Juan continues wearing the red sweater even after their breakup, some may notice. And they can combine that information in lots of ways.

Nevertheless, transparency doesn't make things simple. These new social tools make services and things, lives and relationships, appear exactly as complicated as they are—or perhaps as complicated as anyone cares to uncover. And the reality is that no single truth—or simple list of who is allowed to know what—exists. Ambiguity is a constant of history and novels, political campaigns and contract negotiations, sales pitches, thank-you letters and compliments, to say nothing of divorces, lawsuits, employee resignations and halfhearted invitations to lunch. Adding silicon and software won't make the ambiguity go away.

DANIEL J. SOLOVE

The End of Privacy?

Daniel Solove (b. 1973) earned a B.A. in English from Washington University (St. Louis) in 1994 and a J.D. from Yale in 1997. Since 2000, after two legal clerkships and a year at a prestigious law firm, he has been a professor, first at Seton Hall, and since 2004, at George Washington University Law School. His international reputation on privacy rights has been established by three books as well as numerous professional articles and a textbook, Information Privacy Law *(third edition, 2009). In* The Digital Person: Technology and Privacy in the Information Age *(2004) Solove says, I "explored how business and the government were threatening individual privacy by collecting massive digital dossiers of information about people," thereby jeopardizing their "free-dom and well-being." In* The Future of Reputation: Gossip, Rumor, and Privacy on the internet *(2007) Solove investigates the clash of values that occur when "gossip and rumor" are spread on the Internet. He says: "We're invading each other's privacy . . . and our own privacy by exposures of information we later come to regret. . . . Protecting privacy can come into tension with safeguarding free speech, and I cherish both values" (vii). In* Understanding Privacy *(2009), Solove provides a framework for understanding privacy, "one of the most important concepts of our time, yet . . . one of the most elusive," as he addresses issues of "surveillance, data mining, identity theft, state involvement in reproductive and marital decisions," and other hot-button issues. "The End of Privacy?" like Esther Dyson's "Reflections on Privacy 2.0," was first published in* Scientific American's *special issue on the future of privacy (September 2008). In it Solove examines the phenomenon of "social-networking Web sites [which] may be radically realigning what is considered public and private."*

He has a name, but most people just know him as "the Star Wars Kid." In fact, he is known around the world by tens of millions of people. Unfortunately, his noto-riety is for one of the most embarrassing moments in his life.

In 2002, as a 15-year-old, the Star Wars Kid videotaped himself waving around a golf-ball retriever while pretending it was a lightsaber. Without the help of the expert choreographers working on the *Star Wars* movies, he stumbled around awkwardly in the video.

The video was found by some of the boy's tormentors, who uploaded it to an Internet video site. It became an instant hit with a multitude of fans. All across the blogosphere, people started mocking the boy, making fun of him for being pudgy, awkward and nerdy.

Several remixed videos of the Star Wars Kid started popping up, adorned with special effects. People edited the video to make the golf-ball retriever glow like a lightsaber. They added *Star Wars* music to the video. Others mashed it up with other movies. Dozens of embellished versions were created. The Star Wars Kid appeared in a video game and on the television shows *Family Guy* and *South Park*. It is one thing to be teased by classmates in school, but imagine being ridi-culed by masses the world over. The teenager dropped out of school and had to seek counseling. What happened to the Star Wars Kid can happen to anyone, and it can happen in an instant. Today collecting personal information has become second nature. More and more people have cell phone cameras, digital audio recorders, Web cameras and other recording technologies that readily capture details about their lives.

For the first time in history nearly anybody can disseminate information 5 around the world. People do not need to be famous enough to be interviewed by the mainstream media. With the Internet, anybody can reach a global audience.

Technology has led to a generational divide. On one side are high school and college students whose lives virtually revolve around social-networking sites and blogs. On the other side are their parents, for whom recollection of the past often remains locked in fading memories or, at best, in books, photographs and videos. For the current generation, the past is preserved on the Internet, potentially forever. And this change raises the question of how much privacy people can expect—or even desire—in an age of ubiquitous networking.

GENERATION GOOGLE

The number of young people using social-networking Web sites such as Facebook and MySpace is staggering. At most college campuses, more than 90 percent of students maintain their own sites. I call the people growing up today "Generation Google." For them, many fragments of personal information will reside on the Internet forever, accessible to this and future generations through a simple Google search.

That openness is both good and bad. People can now spread their ideas everywhere without reliance on publishers, broadcasters or other traditional gatekeepers. But that transformation also creates profound threats to privacy and reputations. The *New York Times* is not likely to care about the latest gossip at Dubuque Senior High School or Oregon State University. Bloggers and others communicating online may care a great deal. For them, stories and rumors about friends, enemies, family members, bosses, co-workers and others are all prime fodder for Internet postings.

Before the Internet, gossip would spread by word of mouth and remain within the boundaries of that social circle. Private details would be confined to diaries and kept locked in a desk drawer. Social networking spawned by the Internet allows communities worldwide to revert to the close-knit culture of preindustrial society, in which nearly every member of a tribe or a farming hamlet knew everything about the neighbors. Except that now the "villagers" span the globe.

College students have begun to share salacious details about their school-   10 mates. A Web site called JuicyCampus serves as an electronic bulletin board that allows students nationwide to post anonymously and without verification a sordid array of tidbits about sex, drugs and drunkenness. Another site, Don't Date Him Girl, invites women to post complaints about the men they have dated, along with real names and actual photographs.

Social-networking sites and blogs are not the only threat to privacy. . . . Companies collect and use our personal information at every turn. Your credit-card company has a record of your purchases. If you shop online, merchants keep tabs on every item you have bought. Your Internet service provider has information about how you surf the Internet. Your cable company has data about which television shows you watch.

The government also compromises privacy by assembling vast databases that can be searched for suspicious patterns of behavior. The National Security Agency listens and examines the records of millions of telephone conversations. Other agencies analyze financial transactions. Thousands of government bodies at the federal and state level have records of personal information, chronicling births, marriages, employment, property ownership and more. The information is often stored in public records, making it readily accessible to anyone—and the trend toward more accessible personal data continues to grow as more records become electronic.

THE FUTURE OF REPUTATION

Broad-based exposure of personal information diminishes the ability to protect reputation by shaping the image that is presented to others. Reputation plays an important role in society, and preserving private details of one's life is essential to it. We look to people's reputations to decide whether to make friends, go on a date, hire a new employee or undertake a prospective business deal.

Some would argue that the decline of privacy might allow people to be less inhibited and more honest. But when everybody's transgressions are exposed, people may not judge one another less harshly. Having your personal information may fail to improve my judgment of you. It may, in fact, increase the likelihood that I will hastily condemn you. Moreover, the loss of privacy might inhibit freedom. Elevated visibility that comes with living in a transparent online world means you may never overcome past mistakes.

People want to have the option of "starting over," of reinventing themselves 15 throughout their lives. As American philosopher John Dewey once said, a person is not "something complete, perfect, [or] finished," but is "something moving, changing, discrete, and above all initiating instead of final." In the past, episodes of youthful experimentation and foolishness were eventually forgotten, giving us an opportunity to start anew, to change and to grow. But with so much information online, it is harder to make these moments forgettable. People must now live with the digital baggage of their pasts.

This openness means that the opportunities for members of Generation Google might be limited because of something they did years ago as wild teenagers. Their intimate secrets may be revealed by other people they know. Or they might become the unwitting victim of a false rumor. Like it or not, many people are beginning to get used to having a lot more of their personal information online.

WHAT IS TO BE DONE?

Can we prevent a future in which so much information about people's private lives circulates beyond their control? Some technologists and legal scholars flatly say no. Privacy, they maintain, is just not compatible with a world in which information flows so freely. As Scott McNealy of Sun Microsystems once famously declared: "You already have zero privacy. Get over it." Countless books and articles have heralded the "end," "death" and "destruction" of privacy.

Those proclamations are wrongheaded at best. It is still possible to protect privacy, but doing so requires that we rethink outdated understandings of the concept. One such view holds that privacy requires total secrecy: once information is revealed to others, it is no longer private. This notion of privacy is unsuited to an online world. The generation of people growing up today understands privacy in a more nuanced way. They know that personal information is routinely shared with countless others, and they also know that they leave a trail of data wherever they go.

The more subtle understanding of privacy embraced by Generation Google recognizes that a person should retain some control over personal information that becomes publicly available. This generation wants a say in how private details of their lives are disseminated.

The issue of control over personal information came to the fore in 2006, 20 when Facebook launched a feature called News Feeds, which sent a notice to people's friends registered with the service when their profile was changed or updated. But to the great surprise of those who run Facebook, many of its users reacted with outrage. Nearly 700,000 of them complained. At first blush, the outcry over News Feeds seems baffling. Many of the users who protested had profiles completely accessible to the public. So why did they think it was a privacy violation to alert their friends to changes in their profiles?

Instead of viewing privacy as secrets hidden away in a dark closet, they considered the issue as a matter of accessibility. They figured that most people would not scrutinize their profiles carefully enough to notice minor changes and updates. They could make changes inconspicuously. But Facebook's News Feeds made information more widely noticeable. The privacy objection, then, was not about secrecy; it was about accessibility.

In 2007 Facebook again encountered another privacy outcry when it launched an advertising system with two parts, called Social Ads and Beacon. With Social Ads, whenever users wrote something positive about a product or a movie, Facebook would use their names, images and words in advertisements sent to friends in the hope that an endorsement would induce other users to purchase a product more than an advertisement might. With Beacon, Facebook made data-sharing deals with a variety of other commercial Web sites. If a person bought a movie ticket on Fandango or an item on another site, that information would pop up in that person's public profile.

Facebook rolled out these programs without adequately informing its users. People unwittingly found themselves shilling products on their friends' Web sites. And some people were shocked to see their private purchases on other Web sites suddenly displayed to the public as part of their profiles that appeared on the Facebook site.

The outcry and an ensuing online petition called for Facebook to reform its practices—a document that quickly attracted tens of thousands of signatures and that ultimately led to several changes. As witnessed in these instances, privacy does not always involve sharing of secrets. Facebook users did not want their identities used to endorse products with Social Ads. It is one thing to write about how much one enjoys a movie or CD; it is another to be used on a billboard to pitch products to others.

CHANGING THE LAW

Canada and most European countries have more stringent privacy statutes than 25
the U.S., which has resisted enacting all-encompassing legislation. Privacy laws
elsewhere recognize that revealing information to others does not extinguish
one's right to privacy. Increasing accessibility of personal information, however,
means that U.S. law also should begin recognizing the need to safeguard a degree
of privacy in the public realm.

In some areas, U.S. law has a well-developed system of controlling information. Copyright recognizes strong rights for public information, protecting a wide
range of works, from movies to software. Procuring copyright protection does
not require locking a work of intellect behind closed doors. You can read a copy-
righted magazine, make a duplicate for your own use and lend it to others. But
you cannot do whatever you want: for instance, photocopying it from cover to
cover or selling bootleg copies in the street. Copyright law tries to achieve a balance between freedom and control, even though it still must wrestle with the
ongoing controversies in a digital age.

The closest U.S. privacy law comes to a legal doctrine akin to copyright is the
appropriation tort, which prevents the use of someone else's name or likeness for
financial benefit. Unfortunately, the law has developed in a way that is often inef-
fective against the type of privacy threats now cropping up. Copyright primarily
functions as a form of property right, protecting works of self-expression, such
as a song or painting. To cope with increased threats to privacy, the scope of the
appropriation tort should be expanded. The broadening might actually embody
the original early 20th-century interpretation of this principle of common law,
which conceived of privacy as more than a means to protect property: "The right
to withdraw from the public gaze at such times as a person may see fit . . . is
embraced within the right of personal liberty," declared the Georgia Supreme
Court in 1905. Today, however, the tort does not apply when a person's name or
image appears in news, art, literature, or on social-networking sites. At the same
time the appropriation tort protects against using someone's name or picture
without consent to advertise products, it allows these representations to be used
in a news story. This limitation is fairly significant. It means that the tort would
rarely apply to Internet-related postings.

Any widening of the scope of the appropriation tort must be balanced
against the competing need to allow legitimate news gathering and dissemination
of public information. The tort should probably apply only when photographs
and other personal information are used in ways that are not of public concern—a criterion that will inevitably be subject to ongoing judicial deliberation.

Appropriation is not the only common-law privacy tort that needs an overhaul to become more relevant in an era of networked digital communications. We
already have many legal tools to protect privacy, but they are currently crippled
by conceptions of privacy that prevent them from working effectively. A broader
development of the law should take into account problematic uses of personal
information illustrated by the Star Wars Kid or Facebook's Beacon service.

It would be best if these disputes could be resolved without recourse to the 30
courts, but the broad reach of electronic networking will probably necessitate
changes in common law. The threats to privacy are formidable, and people are
starting to realize how strongly they regard privacy as a basic right. Toward this
goal, society must develop a new and more nuanced understanding of public and
private life—one that acknowledges that more personal information is going to
be available yet also protects some choice over how that information is shared
and distributed.

QUESTIONS FOR DISCUSSION AND WRITING

1. Explain and expand on Dyson's assertion that "[p]rivacy is not a one-size-fits-
   all condition: Different people at different times have different preferences about
   what happens to their personal information and who gets to see it" (paragraph 9).
   How do you define *privacy*? In what ways does your definition respond to
   Dyson's identification of "boundary conditions" for privacy (paragraphs 6–9)?

2. What are some major consequences of the fact that "[t]he Internet is the platform
   that gives everyone instant access to a potentially worldwide audience" (Dyson,
   paragraph 18; echoed by Solove in paragraph 5 of "The End of Privacy?")?

3. If you use social-networking Web sites such as Facebook or MySpace, in what
   ways do you select, edit, or otherwise control the information you put online?
   Do you consider yourself a member of what Solove calls "Generation Google"
   (paragraph 7)? With what consequences?

4. Do you or people you know well (family members, friends) believe that others
   know a great deal more about you than you've told them or you want them to
   know? How do you know what others know about you: your credit rating? Your
   medical history? Your genetic makeup? Your criminal record? What are some of the
   major consequences of dissemination of such personal information over the Internet, which might pertain to your ability to obtain health insurance or personalized
   medicine, or conduct personal relationships (see Dyson paragraphs 1–5; Solove
   passim)? Do either Dyson or Solove suggest ways in which a private individual can
   control access to such information, particularly if "many fragments of personal
   information will reside on the Internet forever, accessible to this and future generations through a simple Google search (Solove paragraph 7)?

5. Dyson concludes: "[T]ransparency doesn't make things simple. These new social
   tools make services and things, issues and relationships, appear exactly as complicated as they are—or perhaps as complicated as anyone cares to uncover.
   And the reality is that no single truth—or simple list of who is allowed to know
   what—exists" (paragraph 31). Solove addresses these complications, taking issue
   with the view that "'[y]ou already have zero privacy. Get over it'" (paragraph 17)
   to assert that "Generation Google recognizes that a person should retain some
   control over personal information that becomes publicly available" (paragraph 19).

With a discussion group, write a position paper explaining the ideal amount of control over dissemination of personal information, what sorts, and to whom and under what circumstances it should be disclosed. Feel free to consult other articles in the *Scientific American* September 2008 issue, and elsewhere, in addition to your own experience.

CATHY GUISEWITE

We *Saw Paris*

QUESTIONS FOR DISCUSSION AND WRITING

1. What's the point of a vacation? What should an ideal travel experience be? How does the trip this character has taken compare with the ideal?

2. What has complicated the trip for the narrator? What point is Guisewite, the cartoonist, making about technology? About the values of travelers who would spend thirty-six hours of a ten-day trip finding the right technology to record and send their vacation photos?

3. Who really saw Paris? Why does this claim "*We saw Paris*" bore the listeners?

AMITAI ETZIONI WITH RADHIKA BHAT

Social Chances, Social Forgiveness, and the Internet

Sociologist and public intellectual Amitai Etzioni was born in Germany in 1929 and spent his childhood in Palestine to escape Nazi persecution. After earning B.A. and M.A. degrees from Hebrew University in Jerusalem, he completed his Ph.D. in sociology at the

University of California, Berkeley, in 1958. He served as a senior advisor on domestic affairs to the Carter White House (1979–80); taught at Columbia University for twenty years and also at the Harvard Business School; and is currently University Professor at the George Washington University. There he directs the Institute for Communitarian Policy Studies, a "nonpartisan research organization dedicated to finding constructive solutions to social problems through morally informed policy analysis and open moral dialogue." (CPS Web site, July 10, 2010). His recent books include The New Golden Rule *(1996),* The Limits of Privacy *(1999),* The Monochrome Society *(2001),* My Brother's Keeper *(2003), and* Security First: For a Muscular, Moral Foreign Policy *(2007), an argument for a U.S. foreign policy that emphasizes security rather than democratization.*

Radhika Bhat is a research and outreach assistant at the Institute for Communitarian Policy Studies. "Second Chances, Social Forgiveness, and the Internet," originally published in the American Scholar *(2009), asks whether the Internet, with its instant ability to transmit information worldwide about a person's criminal acts (as well as everything else, for better and for worse) is really "destroying second chances" for convicted criminals to make a fresh start, creating an unforgiving society, and "hindering the possibility for rehabilitation and even redemption."*

A young man in upstate New York drinks too much and gets a little rowdy, picks a fight, smashes up the bar, and is arrested. When he gets into trouble again a short time later, the judge sends him to jail for a week. After his release, he gets fired and cannot find a new job because he has a record. The local newspaper carries a story about his misconduct. The merchants on Main Street refuse to sell him anything on credit. The young women gossip about him and refuse to date him. One day he has had enough. He packs his meager belongings, leaves without a good-bye, and moves to a small town in Oregon. Here, he gains a new start. Nobody knows about his rowdy past, and he has learned his lesson. He drinks less, avoids fights, works in a lumberyard, and soon marries a nice local woman, has three kids, and lives happily ever after. Cue the choir of angels singing in the background.

The idea that people deserve a second chance is an important American value. Perhaps it grows out of our history, in which those who got into trouble in Europe (whether it was their fault or not) moved to the United States to start a new life. And as the American West was settled, many easterners and midwesterners found a place there for a second beginning. More profoundly, the belief in a new beginning is a tenet of Christianity, which allows sinners to repent and be fully redeemed, to be reborn. In a similar vein, the secular, progressive, optimistic, therapeutic culture of today's America rejects the notion that there are inherently bad people. As individuals, we seek insights into our failings so we can learn to overcome them and achieve a new start. From a sociological perspective, people are thrown off course by their social conditions—because they are poor, for instance, and subject to discrimination. But these conditions can be altered, and then these people will be able to lead good lives. Under the right conditions, criminals can pay their debt to society and be rehabilitated, sex offenders can be reformed, and others who have flunked out can pass another test. Just give them a second chance.

The latest chapter of this deeply entrenched narrative introduces a big bad wolf, the Internet. It stands charged with killing the opportunity for people to have that much-deserved second chance. By computerizing local public records, the Internet casts the shadow of people's past far and fast; like a curse they cannot undo, their records now follow them wherever they go. True, even in the good old days, arrest records, criminal sentences, bankruptcy filings, and even divorce records were public. Some were listed in blotters kept in police stations, others in courthouses; anyone who wished to take the trouble could go there and read them. But most people did not. Above all, there was no way for people in distant communities to find these damning facts without going to inordinate lengths.

The first sign of trouble due to technological changes came about in the late 19th century when newspapers started publishing this sort of information. In 1890, after newspapers printed social gossip about the family of Boston lawyer Samuel D. Warren, he and his law partner, the future Supreme Court Justice Louis D. Brandeis, published in the *Harvard Law Review* what is considered the most seminal law review article ever written, one that became the foundation of the American right to privacy. In it, they asserted that an individual has the right to keep certain information hidden from others. Warren and Brandeis were not trying to stop gossip. (Although people often find gossip annoying, sociologists view it as an important part of the informal social controls that nudge people to be better than they would otherwise be, thus minimizing the role for policing. Hence the great concern with the breakdown of communities—where people know each other and gossip—and the quest for new soft tools to advance social order.) But Warren and Brandeis correctly saw that a major change takes place once gossip is spread to a large community, as it is via the print media, to people who do not personally know those who are being gossiped about, and who are therefore unaware of the special circumstances, of the "whole story." This change was a harbinger of things to come.

In recent decades, online databases have dramatically increased the size of the audience that has access to public information and the ease with which it can be examined. Several companies have started compiling criminal records, making them available to everyone in the country and indeed the world. For instance, PeopleFinders, a company based in Sacramento, recently introduced CriminalSearches.com, a free service to access public criminal records, which draws data from local courthouses. A similar thing is happening to many other types of public records, ranging from birth records to divorces.

These developments disturb privacy advocates and anyone who is keen on ensuring that people have the opportunity for a new start. Beth Givens, director of the Privacy Rights Clearinghouse, says that Internet databases cause a "loss of 'social forgiveness.'" For instance, a person's "conviction of graffiti vandalism at age 19 will still be there at age 29 when [he's] a solid citizen trying to get a job and raise a family"—and the conviction will be there for anyone to see. Furthermore, as companies "rely on background checks to screen workers, [they] risk impos- ing unfair barriers to rehabilitated criminals," wrote reporters Ann Zimmerman and Kortney Stringer in *The Wall Street Journal*. In short, as journalist Brad Stone wrote in *The New York Times*, by allowing the producers of databases to remove "the obstacles to getting criminal information," we are losing "a valuable, ignorance- fueled civil peace."

But hold on for just a minute. Is the Internet age really destroying second chances, making us less forgiving and hindering the possibility for rehabilitation and even redemption? The sad fact is that most convicted criminals in the pre-digital age did not use the second chance that their obscurity gave them, nor did they use their third or fourth chances. Convincing data show that most criminal offenders— especially those involved in violent crimes—are not rehabilitated; they commit new crimes. And many commit numerous crimes before they are caught again. Thus, while obscurity may well help a small percentage of criminals get a second chance, it helps a large percentage of them strike again.

Take the case of James Webb (not the U.S. Senator from Virginia of the same name). He had served 20 years in prison for raping six women when, on August 16, 1995, he was released on parole. But rather than look for a new start, he raped another woman the day after he was released. Then he raped three more women in the next few months. He was re-arrested in December 1995, after he committed the fourth rape. Or consider the case of James Richardson, a New York resident who served 20 years of a life term for raping and murdering a 10-year-old girl. After he was paroled in 1992, he committed three bank rob- beries before being re-incarcerated. Both cases happened before the advent of databanks of criminal convictions.

These two are typical cases. In its most recent study on recidivism in the United States, the Justice Department's Bureau of Justice Statistics tracked two- thirds of the prisoners released in 15 states in 1994. It found that within three years of their release, 67.5 percent of them were re-arrested for a new offense. In short, most people who commit crimes are more likely to commit crimes in the future than to make good use of a second chance. This was true long before the digitization of criminal data and the loss of obscurity.

Moreover, just because only two-thirds of the prisoners were re-arrested 10 does not mean that the other third did not commit any crimes. Many crimes are never solved and their perpetrators never caught. Studies found that the majority of rapists and child molesters had been convicted more than once for a sexual assault—and committed numerous offenses before they were caught again. On average, these offenders admitted to having committed *two to five times* as many sex crimes as were officially documented. That is, not only did they fail to use their second chances to start a new life, they used obscurity to their advantage.

In short, the image of a young person who goes astray, and who would return to the straight and narrow life if just given a second chance, does not fit most offenders. Indeed, prisons are considered colleges for crime; they harden those sentenced to spend time in them, making them *more* disposed to future criminal behavior upon release. Social scientists differ about whom to blame for the limited success of rehabilitation. Some fault "the system," or poor social conditions, or lack of job training. Others place more blame on the character of those involved. In any case, obscurity hardly serves to overcome strong factors that agitate against rehabilitation.

Online databases also display the records of physicians who do not live up to the Hippocratic oath; these doctors do harm, and plenty of it. The National Practitioner Data Bank allows state licensing boards, hospitals, and other health-care entities to find out whether the license of a doctor has been revoked recently in another state or if the doctor has been disciplined. Doctors' licenses are generally revoked only if they commit very serious offenses, such as repeated gross negligence, criminal felonies, or practicing while under the influence of drugs or alcohol.

If these databases had been used as intended in the late 1990s and early 2000s, they could have tracked Pamela L. Johnson, a physician who was forced to leave Duke University Medical Center after many of her patients suffered from unusual complications. In response, Johnson moved to New Mexico and lied about her professional history in order to obtain a medical license there and continue practicing. After three patients in New Mexico filed lawsuits alleging that she was negligent or had botched surgical procedures, she moved again and set up shop in Michigan.

Similarly, Joseph S. Hayes, a medical doctor licensed in Tennessee, was convicted of drug abuse and assault, including choking a patient, actions which resulted in the revocation of his Tennessee license in 1991. But his license was reinstated in 1993. When he was charged with fondling a female patient in 1999, he simply moved to South Carolina to continue practicing medicine. Similar stories could be told about scores of other doctors. (The exploits of one of the most notorious of these doctors are laid out in a new book, *Charlatan*, by Pope Brock.)

Beyond assuming that Internet databases do little harm to those who are not 15 likely to reform themselves, we can show real benefits from the widespread dissemination of information about wrongdoers—for their potential victims. Few doctors are hired by hospitals these days without first being checked through the digitized data sources. Before you hire an accountant, such data makes it possible to discover whether he or she has a record of embezzlement. A community can find out if a new school nurse is a sex offender. Employers may direct ex-offenders to other jobs, or they may still hire them but provide extra oversight, or just decide that they are willing to take the risk. But they do so well informed—and thus warned—rather than ignorant of the sad facts.

Registration and notification laws for sex offenders provide a good case in point. The Washington State Institute for Public Policy conducted a study in 2005 that evaluated the effectiveness of the state's community notification laws. In 1990, Washington passed the Community Protection Act, a law that requires sex offenders to register with their county sheriff and authorizes law enforcement to release information to the public. The study found that by 1999 the recidivism rate among felony sex offenders in the state had dropped 70 percent from the pre-1990 level, in part due to communities' awareness of the sex offenders in their neighborhoods. In addition, offenders subject to community notification were arrested for new crimes much more quickly than offenders who were released without notification.

True, online databases increase the size of the community that has access to information, but these technological developments merely help communities catch up with other social developments. People do business over greater distances and move around much more, and much farther, than they did in earlier eras. Our travel and transactions are no longer limited to the county store and local diner. Our access to data needs to expand to match the new scope of our lives.

All of this is not to deny that we face a moral dilemma. Although most offenders are not rehabilitated, some are. It is incorrect to assume that "once a criminal, always a criminal." Take the case of Mike Kolomichuk, who in 1979 pleaded guilty to two counts of battery after having an altercation with an undercover police officer in a bar in Florida. As punishment, he received unsupervised probation, during which he conducted himself well. Kolomichuk eventually moved to Ohio, where almost 30 years later he ran as a write-in candidate for mayor of the village of Lakemore and won. His criminal past was not an issue in the election because his record was unknown in the village of 2,500 people. When his criminal history came out a few months later, there was talk of the need for a new election, but it soon subsided. Today, Kolomichuk remains mayor and is continuing his efforts to revitalize the community. In this case, obscurity may well have helped.

The argument can be made, then, that just as we believe it is better to let a hundred guilty people walk free than to condemn one innocent person, we should let a hundred criminals benefit from obscurity in order to provide a chance at rehabilitation for the few who put obscurity to good use. But there are ways, although imperfect, for allowing second chances for offenders while still allowing a community to protect itself by using online databases.

What is needed is a mixture of technological and legal means to replace the mea- 20
sures that were once naturally woven into the fabric of communities with measures that can satisfy the needs of a large, complex, and mobile society.

For example, where the inefficiency of paper records once ensured that information would not travel far, we now must introduce into the digitized world barriers for information that should not be spread. Formerly, in smaller communities, if a person was arrested, his neighbors would learn whether he had been exonerated or convicted. The community might even have had a sense of whether a person who was released had in fact committed the crime, or whether the arrest was unjustified. These days, an arrest record may travel across the globe in nanoseconds, but it is difficult to find out if it was justified. Either arrest records should not be made public (although they might be available to police in other jurisdictions) or they must be accompanied with information about the outcome of the case.

In addition, a criminal record could be sealed both locally and in online databases, say after seven years, if the person has not committed a new crime. There is considerable precedent for such a move. For instance, information about juvenile offenders and presentations to grand juries are often sealed.

Another measure could limit access to certain databanks to those who are trained to understand the limitations of these databanks. For instance, several states allow only police authorities and educational institutions to access databases on sex offenders.

One other major concern is that lawbreakers who have paid their debt to society will face discrimination in hiring and housing. Protections against such discrimination are already in place, but others might be added. For instance, employers cannot, as a general rule, legally maintain a policy of refusing to hire people merely because they are ex-cons, whether the employer gets this information from a police blotter or a computer.

Internet databases should be held accountable for the information they pro- 25 vide. If they rely on public records, then they should be required to keep up with the changes in these records. They should also provide mechanisms for filing complaints if the online data are erroneous, and they should make proper corrections in a timely fashion, the way those who keep tabs on credit records are expected to do.

These are a few examples of measures that provide obscurity equivalents in the digital age. Still, let's remember the importance of gossip fueled by public records. As a rule, we care deeply about the approval of others. In most communities, being arrested is a source of major humiliation, and people will go to great pains to avoid ending up in jail. In such cases, the social system does not work if the information is not publicly available. This holds true for the digitized world, where the need for a much wider-ranging "informal social communication," as sociologists call gossip, applies not merely to criminals, sexual predators, and disgraced physicians. It holds for people who trade on eBay, sell used books on Amazon, or distribute loans from e-banks. These people are also eager to maintain their reputation—not just locally but globally. If we cannot find ways to deal in cyberspace with those who deceive and cheat, then our ability to use the Internet for travel, trade, investment, and much else will be severely set back.

This need is served in part by user-generated feedback and ratings, which inform others who may do business via the Internet—much like traditional community gossip would. The ability of people to obscure their past in pre-Internet days made it all too easy for charlatans, quacks, and criminal offenders to hurt more people by simply switching locations. The new, digitized transparency is one major means of facilitating deals between people who do not know each other. With enough effort, its undesirable side effects can be curbed, and people can still gain a second chance.

QUESTIONS FOR DISCUSSION AND WRITING

1. Does everybody who has made a mistake, particularly one leading to a criminal conviction, deserve a second chance? Why is this opportunity such a pervasive and "important American value" in today's "progressive, optimistic, therapeutic culture" (paragraph 2)? Analyze the reasons Etzioni and Bhat offer in paragraph 2 for this culture of forgiveness. Should these always be operative?

2. What concepts of privacy discussed by Dyson and Solove are applicable to people with criminal convictions?

3. Why is the Internet the "big bad wolf," capable of "killing the opportunity for people to have that much-deserved second chance" (paragraph 3)? In what ways does the Internet contribute to "the breakdown of communities—where people know each other and gossip" (paragraph 4) by spreading gossip "to people who do not personally know those who are being gossiped about, and who are therefore unaware of the . . . 'whole story'" (paragraph 4)?

4. "But hold on", say Etzioni and Bhat. "The sad fact is that most convicted criminals in the pre-digital age did not use the second chance that their obscurity gave them, nor did they use their third or fourth chances"—they committed new crimes (paragraph 7). Does the evidence concerning wrongdoers in paragraphs 7–17 convince you that "Internet databases do little harm to those who are not likely to reform themselves" and there are "real benefits from the widespread dissemination of information about wrongdoers—for their potential victims" (paragraph 15)? Why or why not? If you personally know of a criminal conviction, see what you can find out about the person and the case via an Internet search. How easy was it to find the information? How does the availability of the information affect your opinion?

5. Do Etzioni and Bhat offer any solutions to the possibility that, if convicted, you may run but you can't hide? Should access to "certain databanks" be limited "to those who are trained to understand the limitations of these databanks," thereby allowing "only police authorities and educational institutions to access databases on sex offenders" (paragraph 24)?

6. Discuss the impact of the availability on the Internet of any and all information about a person from a combination of perspectives—social, ethical, moral, legal, psychological. Formulate a policy statement that you believe should govern Internet dissemination of such information. What would it take to implement your proposed policy?

MICHAEL J. BUGEJA

Facing the Facebook

Poet, professor, ethicist, and academic administrator Michael J. Bugeja (pronounced "boo-shay-ah") was born in 1952. He earned a B.A. (1974) from St. Peter's College, New Jersey, and a Ph.D. from Oklahoma State University in 1985. He worked for United Press International before becoming a journalism professor. Bugeja is currently director of the Greenlee School of Journalism and Communication at Iowa State University. An author of several books of poetry and a regular contributor to literary magazines, Bugeja is also a prolific nonfiction writer. Culture's Sleeping Beauty: Essays on Poetry, Prejudice, and Belief *(1992) is about literature and spirituality, while* Academic Socialism: Merit and Moral in Higher Education *(1994) and* Living Ethics: Developing Values in Mass Communication *(1996), updated in 2007 as* Living Ethics Across Media Platforms, *are concerned with value systems and institutions.* Interpersonal Divide: The Search for Community in a Technological Age *(2005), deals with the interpersonal dimensions of our computerized society.*

"Facing the Facebook," first published in the Chronicle of Higher Education *(January 2006), surveys one of the most popular online student identity networks. This virtual subculture absorbs thousands of student-hours, yet many professors are unaware of its existence. Bugeja argues that the ethical and educational consequences of the time students spend online need more attention. Colleges like to invest in technology, but technology could be undermining their educational goal, which is "to inspire critical thinking in learners rather than multitasking."*

Information technology in the classroom was supposed to bridge digital divides and enhance student research. Increasingly, however, our networks are being used to entertain members of "the Facebook Generation" who text-message during class, talk on their cell phones during labs, and listen to iPods rather than guest speakers in the wireless lecture hall.

That is true at my institution, Iowa State University. With a total enrollment of 25,741, Iowa State logs 20,247 registered users on *Facebook*, which bills itself as "an online directory that connects people through social networks at schools." While I'd venture to say that most of the students on any campus are regular visitors to Facebook.com, many professors and administrators have yet to hear about Facebook, let alone evaluate its impact.

On many levels, Facebook is fascinating—an interactive, image-laden directory featuring groups that share lifestyles or attitudes. Many students find it addictive, as evidenced by discussion groups with names like "Addicted to the Facebook," which boasts 330 members at Iowa State. Nationwide, Facebook tallies 250 million hits every day and ranks ninth in overall traffic on the Internet.

That kind of social networking affects all levels of academe:

- Institutions seeking to build enrollment learn that "technology" rates higher than "rigor" or "reputation" in high-school focus groups. That may pressure provosts and deans to continue investing in technology rather than in tenure-track positions.
- Professors and librarians encounter improper use of technology by students, and some of those cases go to judiciary officials enforcing the student code.
- Career and academic advisers must deal with employers and parents who have screened Facebook and discovered what users have been up to in residence halls.
- Finally, academics assessing learning outcomes often discover that technology is as much a distraction in the classroom as a tool.

To be sure, classroom distractions have plagued teachers in less technologi-   5 cal times. In my era, there was the ubiquitous comic book hidden in a boring text. A comic book cannot compare with a computer, of course. Neither did it require university money at the expense of faculty jobs.

John W. Curtis, research director at the American Association of University Professors, believes that investment in technology is one of several factors responsible for the well-documented loss of tenured positions in the past decade. "We often hear the assertion that rising faculty salaries drive the cost of tuition," he says, but data over 25 years show that is not the case. "One of the several sources behind rising tuition rates is investment in technology."

Facebook is not the sole source for those woes. However, it is a Janus-faced symbol of the online habits of students and the traditional objectives of higher education, one of which is to inspire critical thinking in learners rather than multitasking. The situation will only get worse as freshmen enter our institutions weaned on high-school versions of the Facebook and equipped with gaming devices, cell phones, iPods, and other portable technologies.

Michael Tracey, a journalism professor at the University of Colorado, recounts a class discussion during which he asked how many people had seen the previous night's *NewsHour* on PBS or read that day's *New York Times*. "A couple of hands went up out of about 140 students who were present," he recalls. "One student chirped: 'Ask them how many use Facebook.' I did. Every hand in the room went up. She then said: 'Ask them how many used it today.' I did. Every hand in the room went up. I was amazed."

Christine Rosen, a fellow at the Ethics and Public Policy Center in Washington, believes experiences like that are an example of what she calls "egocasting, the thoroughly personalized and extremely narrow pursuit of one's personal taste."

"Facebook is an interesting example of the egocasting phenomenon," she   10 says, "because it encourages egocasting even though it claims to further 'social networking' and build communities." Unlike real communities, however, most interactions in online groups do not take place face-to-face. "It would be more accurate to call it 'Imagebook' rather than 'Facebook,'" Rosen says, "because users first see an image of a face, not the face itself, and identities are constructed and easily manipulated (and often not truthful)." It's no surprise, she says, that "people who use networks like Facebook have a tendency to describe themselves like products."

To test that, I registered on the Iowa State Facebook and noticed that the discussion groups looked a lot like direct mailing lists. Some, in fact, are the same or barely distinguishable from mailing lists compiled in *The Lifestyle Market Analyst*, a reference book that looks at potential audiences for advertisers. For instance, "Baseball Addicts" and "Kick Ass Conservatives" are Facebook groups while "Baseball Fanatics" and "Iowa Conservatives" are the names of commercial mailing lists. You can find "PC Gamers," "Outdoor Enthusiasts," and advocates for and against gun control on both Facebook and in marketing directories. Several Facebook groups resemble advertisements for products or lifestyles such as "Apple Macintosh Users," "Avid Sweatpants Users," or "Brunettes Having More Fun."

"It is ironic," Rosen said, "that the technologies we embrace and praise for the degree of control they give us individually also give marketers and advertisers the most direct window into our psyche and buying habits they've ever had."

Online networks like Facebook allow high levels of surveillance, she adds, and not just for marketers. "College administrators are known to troll the profiles on Facebook for evidence of illegal behavior by students," she said. "Students might think they are merely crafting and surfing a vast network of peers, but because their Facebook profile is, in essence, a public diary, there is nothing to stop anyone else—from marketers, to parents, to college officials—from reading it as well."

Her comments bear out. For instance, a panel at the University of Missouri at Columbia has been formed to educate students on Facebook content that may violate student-conduct policies or local laws. A Duquesne University student was asked to write a paper because the Facebook group he created was deemed homophobic. Students at Northern Kentucky University were charged with code violations when a keg was seen in a dorm-room picture online, and a University of Oklahoma student was visited by the Secret Service because of assassination references in comments regarding President Bush.

My concerns are mostly ethical. In my field, I know of students who showcase 15 inappropriate pictures of partners or use stereotypes to describe themselves and others on Facebook. What does that mean in terms of taste, sensitivity, and bias?

I know of online disclosures of substance abuse that have come back to haunt students under investigation for related offenses. I know of fictitious Facebook personae that masquerade as administrators, including college presidents. Such inventions mirror the fabricated sources and situations used by Stephen Glass in articles for *The New Republic* and other publications before his deceptions were exposed in 1998.

Facebook forbids such fabrications. According to Chris Hughes, a spokesman, misrepresentation is against the "Terms of Service." "In other words," he says, "you can't create a profile for Tom Cruise using your account. When users report a profile, we take a look and decide if the content seems authentic. If not, we'll remove the user from the network."

Shortly after interviewing Hughes, I heard from Michael Tracey, the Colorado journalism professor, who learned that an account had been opened in his name on MySpace, another networking site, "with photos and all kinds of weird details." He suspects one of the students from the course he spoke with me about is behind the ruse.

Unless we reassess our high-tech priorities, issues associated with insensitivity, indiscretion, bias, and fabrication will consume us in higher education. Potential solutions will challenge core beliefs concerning digital divides, pedagogies, budget allocations, and, above all, our duty to instill critical thinking in multitaskers.

Christine Rosen believes that "those who run institutions of higher learning have embraced technology as a means of furthering education. But they have failed to realize that the younger generation views technology largely as a means of delivering entertainment—be it music, video games, Internet access, or television—and secondarily, as a means of communicating." 20

"Technology," she adds, "also provides new and unusual ways to isolate oneself from opinions or ideas that make us uncomfortable, from people who we would rather not have to know, from those often-awkward social interactions with strangers in public spaces. In the college context this is more worrisome since part of the purpose of a liberal education is to expose students to ideas that challenge them to think in new ways and expose them to things that they hadn't known about before."

What can we do in the short term about the misuse of technology, especially in wireless locales? The Facebook's spokesman, Hughes, is not overly concerned. He notes that students who use computers in classrooms and labs routinely perform "a host of activities online while listening to lectures," like checking their e-mail, sending instant messages, or reading the news. "Usage of Facebook during class," he says, "doesn't strike me as being that different than usage of any of those other tools. If professors don't want their students to have access to the Internet during class," Hughes adds, "they can remove wireless installations or ask their students not to bring computers to class."

Some less-drastic measures include clauses in syllabi warning against using Facebook or other nonassigned Internet sites during class. Some professors punish students who violate such rules and reward those who visit the library. Still others have stopped using technology in the classroom, forcing students to listen, debate, and otherwise hone their interpersonal skills.

A few institutions are assessing how to respond to Facebook and similar digital distractions. Last fall the University of New Mexico blocked access to Facebook because of security concerns. My preference is not to block content but to instill in students what I call "interpersonal intelligence," or the ability to discern when, where, and for what purpose technology may be appropriate or inappropriate.

That, alas, requires critical thinking and suggests that we have reached a point 25
where we must make hard decisions about our investment in technology and our
tradition of high standards. Because the students already have.

QUESTIONS FOR DISCUSSION AND WRITING

1. Although colleges spend millions of dollars on computer technology for their
   students' use, many professors are unaware of the amount of time students spend
   on networks such as Facebook, argues Bugeja. What problems does he attribute
   to the use of this online community? What does Facebook have to do with ethical questions such as surveillance, illegal behavior, insensitivity, and homophobia
   (see Dyson [p. 378] and Solove [p. 384] as well)?

2. University administrators are obviously patrolling the Facebook community in
   some colleges—students have been disciplined for posting content that violates
   conduct policies, as in the case where a keg appeared in a dorm-room picture
   online. To what extent do administrators have the right to use Facebook as a surveillance tool? Are students' rights being violated in such cases? Why or why not?

3. Ask two people—a professor or college administrator and yourself or another
   student—the following questions and write a paper on your findings, addressing the role of Facebook or comparable phenomena in college culture. Do you
   think that Internet services such as Facebook have a predominantly positive or
   negative effect on our culture? What is the predominant type of information exchanged or learned via these networks? What would change, in your life or in
   college culture in general, if Facebook and MySpace became unavailable? Would
   these changes be for the better or for worse? Is there any consensus among those
   polled? On what do your respondents agree? Disagree? Explain why. Do you
   know anyone who has sworn off Facebook? Why have thay done so?

4. As a class project, write a collaborative paper on Facebook, explaining this
   social and technological phenomenon to the uninitiated. Include an explanation
   of what Facebook is and what it does, why students use it, what typical ways it is
   used, and any important issues or problems connected with Facebook activities
   (see Dyson [p. 378] and Solove [p. 384]). You might want to interview students
   in or outside the class, using a questionnaire to gather quantitative data (e.g.,
   hours spent using Facebook, types of use, number of Facebook "friends" listed).
   You could also structure this project around a particular issue, such as Internet
   addiction or whether Facebook is a community-building technology.

JOSEPH FULLER

The Terminator Comes to Wall Street

Joseph Fuller (b. 1957), is a graduate of Harvard University and the Harvard Business School. He is a co-founder and chief executive officer of Monitor Group, an international management consulting firm headquartered in Cambridge, Massachusetts. He joined Monitor at its inception in 1983 and currently oversees the firm's consulting operations in twenty-seven offices worldwide, focusing on life sciences and telecommunications. In person and in print he also addresses corporate governance and organizational dynamics. His articles have appeared in the Wall Street Journal, *the* Financial Times, *the* Washington Post, *and the* Harvard Business Review. *In "The Terminator Comes to Wall Street," first published in the* American Scholar *(2009), Fuller explains how "computer based modeling and trading programs developed for Wall Street" worsened the financial crisis of 2008. He then analyzes what can be done to prevent future disasters—exacerbated if not generated by computers.*

You've seen this story in countless Hollywood science-fiction movies, from *The Terminator* to *War Games*. Scientists develop a sophisticated computer or robot to assure the nation's security, but something goes wrong and the technology itself mutates into a catastrophic threat. Unfortunately, the U.S. economic system now finds itself crippled by a real-life technology-gone-wrong story line. In this case, the culprit is not a Pentagon fighting machine, but rather the computer-based modeling and trading programs developed for Wall Street over the last quarter century.

Business models—whether they are models for analyzing market trends or running a major auto manufacturer—typically assume that history provides a guide to future outcomes. Such an assumption is usually reliable, but whenever events fall outside historical norms, the results can be catastrophic. Against this background, consider the introduction of computer-based program trading, arguably the most important change in global investing since the founding of the first mutual fund—the Massachusetts Investors Trust—in 1924. Over the past 20 years on Wall Street, computer-based models have gradually replaced human networks of strategists and traders. Quantitative analysts ("Quants") trained in mathematics and physics have used sophisticated data analytics and modeling skills to evaluate securities and develop portfolio-management theories. The advent of Quants has allowed firms of all stripes to trade ever-larger volumes of securities and to extend their activities to new and exotic instruments. Using either mathematical or statistical models, firms have also been able to trade huge volumes of securities globally. In many cases, the computers didn't just provide advice, they actually executed stock trades. By the end of September 2008, the global stock exchange NYSE Euronext reported that so-called program trading, in which computers execute trades based on programs developed by Quants without specific human intervention, represented almost 17 percent of trades—more than 900 million shares per day.

Since the data that feed these analytical formulas come from the past, the models can have trouble responding to extraordinary or unprecedented events. When credit markets began to seize up in mid-2008 and the securities markets went into free fall, the models tried to figure out a suitable response. They had been programmed to avoid volatility by moving out of securities and into cash. Of course, when many models trading hundreds of millions of shares all tried to liquidate investments and move into cash, they only increased the stock declines, leading to further volatility and thus to more selling. The models had not been programmed to understand a scenario in which everyone might try to move to cash at the same time. The effect was like a panicked crowd trying to escape from a burning theater.

Any good movie gives its audience clues early in the action that foreshadow subsequent events. For the stock market in this current economic crisis, the 1997 death of Long Term Capital Management (LTCM) was the clue that went unheeded by the Quants. LTCM was a U.S. hedge fund that used high leverage and complex mathematics-based trading strategies to rack up big profits in the mid-1990s. In 1998, a lethal combination of losses on major investments mixed with the Russian financial crisis, coming on the heels of a financial crisis in Asia in 1997, put LTCM under immense pressure. As LTCM sold off assets in a frantic effort to cover its debts, its massive selling further depressed the market value of those assets, leading to a classic flight-to-liquidity, in which concerned investors seek to exit a troubled investment firm's vehicles, exacerbating the problem they are trying to escape. A chain reaction doomed the company itself and shook the capital markets. The Federal Reserve Bank of New York organized a bailout led by commercial banks to prevent LTCM's problems from infecting the broader market.

If the need for a bailout sounds familiar to us today, Wall Street and its regulators did not pick up the echo from LTCM as soon as they should have. They failed to perceive the vulnerability to volatility of trading models such as those that LTCM employed. More important, they ascribed the firm's collapse to a defective trading strategy rather than to a toxic mix of an aggressive strategy funded by high leverage (in LTCM's case, $25 in debt for every dollar of invested capital). Indeed, within two years, the Clinton administration had completed the dismantling of the Glass-Steagall Act, eliminating the distinction between investment and commercial banks and allowing investment banks to take on even more leverage to fund their trading strategies. Had regulators seen LTCM as an omen instead of an anomaly, they might have imposed stricter limitations on the use of leverage or enacted more exacting reporting requirements for the industry.

Computer models have three inherent problems. The first problem is that those who created the models don't understand the markets. Modelers are experts in math, computer science, or physics. They are *not* generally experts in stocks, bonds, markets, or psychology. Modelers like to think of markets as efficient abstractions, but these abstractions can never fully account for the messy and irrational actions that humans take for emotional reasons. Moreover, as we have seen, they construct their models or programs based on a study of historical market data. They test them by showing how well the model would have performed in a given historical situation. Because their programs must have some parameters, modelers necessarily have to exclude unprecedented circumstances like the current simultaneous volatility in global debt, equity, currency, and commodity markets.

The second problem is that managers don't understand the modelers. Most of the current generation of senior executives on Wall Street lack the technical background to understand the models (or the algorithms that underlie them) that power their own firms' trading strategies. Because they are unable to speak the same language as the people creating the models, the managers have difficulty framing the questions necessary to comprehend how the models might respond to different situations. The problem here goes beyond comprehension. Even if the executives were Quants, they might well not understand as much as they would like about the programs running their businesses. The models themselves—and particularly the interaction among models—has grown so complex that it may have become impossible for any human to fully grasp the types and volumes of derivatives traded in this way or to predict how the models will interact with each other.

The third problem is that the models don't "understand" each other. Each model executes its own strategy based on its calculus for maximizing value in a given market. But individual models are not able to take into account the role other models play in driving the markets. As a result, each program reacts almost in real time to the actions of other programs, potentially compounding volatility and leading to wild market swings. As we have seen, this happened recently when a set of models analyzing market data led their respective firms to liquidate assets and maximize their cash positions. The cumulative effect intensified the resulting selloff.

In horror and science-fiction movies, the threat rarely dies easily. Barred from entering a police station, the Terminator utters its famous "I'll be back" line before smashing through the door in a car. How can regulators avoid the model-driven volatility of the 2008 market? It won't be easy. Computer-based trading programs have become too integrated into the way the stock markets work to simply shut them off. But there are steps that companies and regulators can take to reduce future model-driven volatility.

First, bank executives must manage their company's models. During the recent crisis, executives and board members of troubled institutions protested that they didn't fully understand the risks their firms had incurred. The trading positions were so massive and the models that governed them so complex that they defied anyone's ability to understand them. That explanation should evoke little sympathy now and none in the future. Financial institutions don't need to elevate math Ph.D.'s to the highest echelons of top management, but they must build the capability to ensure that executives understand the nature of the risks underlying their trading strategies. In short, they need risk managers who can explain in plain English not only the firm's trading positions, but also the logic of the models driving them. Managers need to be equipped to ask the Quants the right questions: Which past events were used to create the model? What are the five or 10 most important differences between those past events and the current economic situation? How will the model attempt to account for those differences?

Companies must also overhaul their internal-governance systems. First, executives familiar with the day-to-day workings of the market, who understand the human factors that so strongly influence the financial industry, need to oversee the work of modelers. They must assemble people who have sweated through trading highs and lows and have them sit down with the math guys who are building the models. If a financial firm already has such a system in place, it should work on making it better. There's room for improvement throughout the industry.

Boards of directors should also insist that the compensation system for publicly traded financial institutions be changed. As recent events have proven all too conclusively, strategies that yield short-term gains can lead to intermediate-term disasters. Companies should place substantial percentages of the bonuses of traders and their bosses in bonus "banks" that pay out over multi-year periods. That will help ensure a pay-for-actual-performance culture and instill more discipline in the investing process. Investors in private investment firms should demand the same protections.

Boards should also devote more time to understanding the trading strategies of the firms they oversee. Audit and risk-management committees should extend their writ to include a review of the logic embedded in the models being employed to trade major positions. It is no longer sufficient for boards to rely on the risk-management department to understand the firm's overall investment posture. Board members must roll up their sleeves and understand how those positions are constructed and how vulnerable their positions are to unexpected events.

As regulators and legislators design new regulatory structures to prevent future financial calamities, they must take into account the pervasive role that models play in making global markets work. Models enable great market liquidity and permit firms to achieve a high level of productivity. It will not work for regulators to adopt some Luddite point of view seeking to curb the use of models. Nor will it work for regulators to rely on accurate reporting of an institution's risk exposure. Those exposures change constantly; retrospective reporting would provide investors only limited insight into the risk positions of major firms. Likewise, legislators cannot demand that managers cease to take imprudent risks if, in fact, the risks are being taken and magnified by the interplay of computers.

However, regulators can hold managers and boards to a higher degree of 15
accountability. The regulators must establish new rules that stipulate the responsibilities of management and boards for overseeing trading risk. Those rules must
be framed by experienced financial professionals and reflect the predominance of
models in the trading strategies of financial institutions.

They must also find ways to dial down the volatility in markets. Regulators
in the United States and in other major markets must revisit the use of market
"circuit breakers." In recent months, circuit breakers that suspended trading
when markets fell too fast were employed repeatedly worldwide. As we move to
harmonize financial regulations globally, regulators must themselves use models
to understand how program trading drives volatility and how to test alternative
regulatory mechanisms.

While regulators will not be able to suppress individual models, they *can*
change the rules that drive the behavior of the companies that employ them. For
example, they can change the leverage ratios that companies are allowed, in order
to reduce the use of aggressive trading strategies. Such a regulation would limit
investors' borrowing to a multiple of their equity, like forcing home buyers to pay
at least a certain percentage of the home price as their down payment. Less leverage reduces the capacity of firms to take on risk, therefore reducing the possibility
that a few bad investment decisions will compel a firm to sell assets rapidly to
cover its debts, roiling the markets.

Investment firms will wrangle with the challenge of tying their models to a better understanding of market behaviors. Regulators will struggle to adjust market
rules to curtail the explosive effects of existing models. Meanwhile, new types of
computer-based trading programs will emerge as technologies driving them continue to evolve. At the cutting edge of modeling science, researchers are trying to
move away from relatively crude rules-based models toward models that approximate the processes of human reason.

Such artificially intelligent models might be able to consider numerous different data streams, interpret them, and look for patterns rather than simply trying to fit market behavior into a fixed algorithm. Given the torrid pace at which
both processing power and data storage continue to improve, some of the technological barriers to such advanced models should fall in the coming years.

Given the extent to which the government has helped support the banking 20
system, regulators will have a small window of opportunity in which to influence
compensation practices. These regulators may wish to consider the compensation
practices for the Quants who build the trading models. If the compensation for
modelers depended on the long-term performance of their models, the Quants
might very well develop models that prized steady growth over short-term dazzle.

With more oversight and better management at the investment firms, and
more intelligent regulation, it's possible to create an environment in which the
Quants and their programs enable liquidity and productivity, with reduced volatility. We don't need any more real-life technology-gone-wrong scenarios.

QUESTIONS FOR DISCUSSION AND WRITING

1. Fuller asserts, "The U.S. economic system now finds itself crippled by a real-life technology-gone-wrong story line. . . . Business models . . . typically assume that history provides a guide to future outcomes. Such an assumption is usually reliable, but whenever events fall outside historical norms, the results can be catastrophic" (paragraphs 1 and 2). What is that story line? Follow this line through to its conclusion.

2. What is "computer-based program trading" and why is it so important (paragraph 2)? Are computers to blame for our country's economic problems? How is it possible to blame the computers rather than the quantitative analysts who use "sophisticated data analytics and modeling skills to evaluate securities and develop portfolio management theories" (paragraph 2)? Or the managers who hire the modelers?

3. Fuller identifies "three inherent problems" with computer models. "The first problem is that those who created the models don't understand the markets. Modelers are experts in math, computer science, or physics. They are not generally experts in stocks, bonds, markets, or psychology." What problems has this disconnect between the modelers' "abstractions" and the "messy and irrational actions that humans take" led to (paragraph 6)?

4. "The second problem is that managers don't understand the modelers," says Fuller. They "lack the technical background to understand the models . . . that power their own firms' trading strategies" (paragraph 7). With what consequences?

5. "The third problem," writes Fuller, "is that the models don't 'understand' each other. Each model executes its own strategy based on its calculus for maximizing value in a given market. But individual models are not able to take into account the role other models play in driving the markets" (paragraph 8). Again, with what consequences?

6. Fuller devotes the last half of the article to solutions, with each point clearly identified in the first sentence of each paragraph, 10–17, as in: "First, bank executives must manage their company's models" (paragraph 10). In combination, to the extent of your knowledge, are these likely to be successful?

7. This article, clear and concise, is written for a general, educated audience. Has Fuller succeeded in explaining "[h]ow computer modeling [has] worsened the financial crisis and what we ought to do about it"? Does he justify his conclusion that the solution is not to eliminate "artificially intelligent models" but to improve them (paragraph 19)?

CHAPTER 6

Science—Discovery, Invention, Controversy: If We're So Smart, Why Don't We Live in Utopia?

HENRY GROSKINSKY

Replaceable You

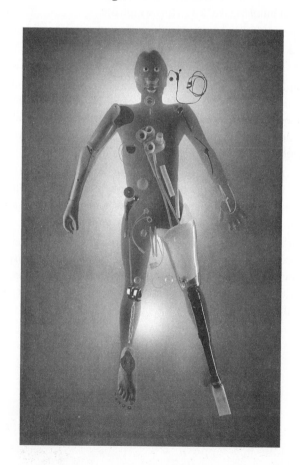

QUESTIONS FOR DISCUSSION AND WRITING

1. The twenty-six artificial body parts are glass eye, cheek implant, teeth, ear, chin, voice box, heart, pacemaker, shoulder, elbow, wrist, finger joints, insulin dispenser, hip, blood vessels, arm and hand, experimental hand, bladder, sphincter, testicle (nonfunctional), penile implant, tendon, knee, ligament, leg and foot, foot and toe joints. What does this image say about the impact of technology on our lives? How close could, or should, someone come to being bionic?

2. This image was constructed in 1989. What replacement body parts are now available to humans that were unavailable two decades ago? Can you think of any negative consequences to the individual or to society? Consider, for instance, the potential total cost of such replacements. Or are there only positive benefits? What are some of these?

ELLEN GOODMAN

Cure or Quest for Perfection?

Ellen Goodman (b. 1941) graduated from Radcliffe in 1963 and began her career in journalism as a researcher for Newsweek, *then as a reporter at the* Detroit Free Press. *A columnist at the* Boston Globe *since 1974, she received a Pulitzer Prize for Distinguished Commentary in 1980. Among her six volumes of collected columns are* Close to Home *(1979),* Making Sense *(1989),* Value Judgments *(1993), and* Paper Trail *(2004).* Turning Points *(1979) addresses the contemporary roles of women; Goodman and Patricia O'Brien have collaborated on* I Know Just What You Mean: The Power of Friendship in Women's Lives *(2000). Although "Cure or Quest for Perfection?" was originally published in the* Boston Globe *in January 2002, it remains particularly relevant in light of the ongoing controversy over stem cell research.*

As someone who scraped through the college science requirement with a physics-for-poets course, I should be pleased that the President's Council on Bioethics opened its first session on a literary note.

The required reading for the panel assembled to grapple with 21st-century problems was a 19th-century short story. "The Birthmark," written by Nathaniel Hawthorne in 1843, is a tale of a young scientist who emerged from his grimy lab, "washed the stain of acids from his fingers and persuaded a beautiful woman to become his wife."

No sooner were they wed than he became obsessed with her one small flaw, a tiny hand-shaped birthmark on her pale cheek. Eventually, the scientist created a potion to remove the birthmark. Alas, it also removed his wife.

There are several ways to interpret this story. (Is there a marriage counselor in the room?) But Leon Kass, the assigning professor and chair of the president's panel, meant it as a cautionary moral tale about scientific hubris. The tale, he said, "allows us to reflect deeply on the human aspiration to eliminate all defects, the aspiration for perfection."

The aspiration for perfection? Did this critic stack the literary and public   5 policy deck?

The first bioethics debate before the council and the country is human cloning. The House of Representatives has already passed a total ban. Soon the issue will come before the Senate in two forms. One bill backs the total ban supported by the president. The other would ban cloning to make genetic replicas of people but allow cloning to treat disease. This is the distinction supported by the National Academy of Sciences.

Today, no responsible scientist or public policy maker is in favor of reproductive cloning. There's no compelling reason that justifies the risks or the results. But therapeutic cloning—creating very early human embryos in the quest to cure diseases—is another story. A story that doesn't fit Hawthorne's plot or Kass's lit-crit.

Just imagine what parents of a child born with a devastating disease such as Fanconi anemia would make of having it compared to this "birthmark." Cystic fibrosis, for that matter, is not a little blemish on a perfect cheek. And curing Parkinson's disease is not the hubristic pursuit of perfection.

There are indeed some serious moral arguments about what is a "defect." But is anyone ready to argue that Alzheimer's disease should be protected from the mad hand of a scientist?

As Dartmouth bioethicist Ron Green says: "The people who are trying to   10 develop the new tools of genetic science and cell research are not seeking perfection. They are, like scientists and physicians for the past 200 years, seeking to reduce the burden of human suffering."

The plot thickens because this promising line of research entails early-stage embryos. Every scientific inquiry and bioethical conversation about cloning runs into the propeller of religion and prolife politics.

The fundamental question is not about the moral status of the scientist but the moral status of the embryo. Is an embryo an "unborn child"? Does this cluster of cells have equal or greater moral weight than a suffering adult? Says Green, "I believe that the cloning issue is being used as a pretext to impose a radical right-to-life agenda on scientific research."

Last summer [2001] President Bush signed on to a political compromise that allowed government funding of research for some existing stem cells. But he opposes cloning on the grounds that life begins at conception. And on Tuesday, the 29th anniversary of *Roe v. Wade*, the president again declared that "unborn children should be welcomed in life and protected in law." But what are the implications of that for, say, in vitro fertilization? And what will happen now that Britain allows therapeutic cloning? Can we ban importing cures based on cloning?

Philip Kitcher, who argues forcefully for democratic checks on science in "Science, Truth, and Democracy," nevertheless says, "When religion enters the public sphere, then all of a sudden claims held very firmly go unchallenged and we reach a stalemate."

In the bioethics debate that goes on inside our own heads, most Americans 15 sense that the embryo is neither a child nor a mere piece of tissue. We should be wary watchdogs over scientists or manufacturers who would deal with embryos as commodities. But using these clusters of cells to cure suffering of existing humans passes the moral threshold test.

As for aspiring to perfection? If Hawthorne's scientist had simply cured his wife's birthmark, I imagine he would have found fault with her cooking. In my own required reading, I keep a jaundiced eye on progress, but somehow I'm glad medicine didn't stop "aspiring" in 1843.

QUESTIONS FOR DISCUSSION AND WRITING

1. Goodman employs several rhetorical questions, for example, in her title and in the text, to suggest a counterargument. To what other purposes does she employ such questions? Do you find this tactic effective? Why or why not?

2. Explain what Goodman means by "the moral threshold test" (paragraph 15). Does Hawthorne's story suggest a threshold? What are Goodman's objections to "The Birthmark" as a metaphor for the bioethics issues she raises?

3. Goodman positions herself as a mainstream American when she writes that "most Americans sense that an embryo is neither a child nor a mere piece of tissue" (paragraph 15). Identify other ways in which she garners the reader's support for her stance. On what basis does she argue that political radicalism in the bioethics debate is inappropriate?

BILL McKIBBEN

Designer Genes

Born in Palo Alto, California, in 1960, Bill McKibben earned a bachelor's degree from Harvard (1982) and soon began his writing career as a staff writer and editor for the New Yorker. *His work for the past two decades has been mainly about environmental issues, from a serious yet hopeful perspective.* The End of Nature *(1989) concerns the impact of human behavior on the planet.* Hope, Human and Wild: True Stories of Living Lightly on the Earth *(1995), focuses on some recent positive outcomes of environmentalism.* Eaarth *(2010), a call to change the way humans treat the earth, focuses on climate change and population growth. In* Maybe One: A Case for Smaller Families *(1998), McKibben offers a father's perspective on overpopulation, arguing that an only child often has many advantages over a child with siblings. Moreover, the world's current population growth rate will lead to species extinction, soil erosion, and food shortages.*

Bioethics—making informed choices about the impact of science on human life—is the topic of McKibben's Staying Human in an Engineered Age *(2003). One chapter, "Designer Genes," ponders the consequences of enhancing children's genes. Advances in genetic engineering may soon offer parents ways to increase their off-spring's intelligence and physical strength, but, as McKibben points out, we should consider the unintended—and undesirable—outcomes.*

I grew up in a household where we were very suspicious of dented cans. Dented cans were, according to my mother, a well-established gateway to botulism, and botulism was a bad thing, worse than swimming immediately after lunch. It was one of those bad things measured in extinctions, as in "three tablespoons of botulism toxin could theoretically kill every human on Earth." Or something like that.

So I refused to believe the early reports, a few years back, that socialites had begun injecting dilute strains of the toxin into their brows in an effort to temporarily remove the vertical furrow that appears between one's eyes as one ages. It sounded like a Monty Python routine, some clinic where they daubed your soles with plague germs to combat athlete's foot. But I was wrong to doubt. As the world now knows, Botox has become, in a few short years, a staple weapon in the cosmetic arsenal—so prevalent that, in the words of one writer, "it is now rare in certain social enclaves to see a woman over the age of thirty-five with the ability to look angry." With their facial muscles essentially paralyzed, actresses are having trouble acting; since the treatment requires periodic booster shots, doctors "warn that you could marry a woman (or a man) with a flawlessly even face and wind up with someone who four months later looks like a Shar-Pei." But never mind—now you can get Botoxed in strip mall storefronts and at cocktail parties.

People, in other words, will do fairly far out things for less than pressing causes. And more so all the time: public approval of "aesthetic surgery" has grown 50 percent in the United States in the last decade. But why stop there? Once you accept the idea that our bodies are essentially plastic and that it's okay to manipulate that plastic, there's no reason to think that consumers would balk because "genes" were involved instead of, say, "toxins." Especially since genetic engineering would not promote your own vanity, but instead be sold as a boon to your child.

The vision of genetic engineers is to do to humans what we have already done to salmon and wheat, pine trees and tomatoes. That is, to make them *better* in some way; to delete, modify, or add genes in developing embryos so that the cells of the resulting person will produce proteins that make them taller and more muscular, or smarter and less aggressive, maybe handsome and possibly straight. Even happy. As early as 1993, a March of Dimes poll found that 43 percent of Americans would engage in genetic engineering "simply to enhance their children's looks or intelligence."

Ethical guidelines promulgated by the scientific oversight boards so far pro- 5
hibit actual attempts at human genetic engineering, but researchers have walked
right to the line, maybe even stuck their toes a trifle over. In the spring of 2001, for
instance, a fertility clinic in New Jersey impregnated fifteen women with embryos
fashioned from their own eggs, their partner's sperm, and a small portion of an egg
donated by a second woman. The procedure was designed to work around defects
in the would-be mother's egg—but in at least two of the cases, tests showed the
resulting babies carried genetic material from all three "parents."

And so the genetic modification of humans is not only possible, it's coming
fast; a mix of technical progress and shifting mood means it could easily happen in the next few years. Consider what happened with plants. A decade ago,
university research farms were growing small plots of genetically modified grain
and vegetables. Sometimes activists who didn't like what they were doing would
come and rip the plants up, one by one. Then, all of a sudden in the mid-1990s,
before anyone had paid any real attention, farmers had planted half the corn and
soybean fields in America with transgenic seed.

Every time you turn your back this technology creeps a little closer. Gallops,
actually, growing and spreading as fast as the Internet. One moment you've sort
of heard of it; the next moment it's everywhere. But we haven't done it yet. For
the moment we remain, if barely, a fully human species. And so we have time yet
to consider, to decide, to act. This is arguably the biggest decision humans will
ever make.

Right up until this decade, the genes that humans carried in their bodies were
exclusively the result of chance—of how the genes of the sperm and the egg, the
father and the mother, combined. The only way you could intervene in the process was by choosing who you would mate with—and that was as much wishful
thinking as anything else, as generation upon generation of surprised parents have
discovered.

But that is changing. We now know two different methods to change human
genes. The first, and less controversial, is called somatic gene therapy. Somatic
gene therapy begins with an existing individual—someone with, say, cystic fibrosis. Researchers try to deliver new, modified genes to some of her cells, usually
by putting the genes aboard viruses they inject into the patient, hoping that the
viruses will infect the cells and thereby transmit the genes. Somatic gene therapy
is, in other words, much like medicine. You take an existing patient with an existing condition, and you in essence try and convince her cells to manufacture the
medicine she needs.

Germline genetic engineering, on the other hand, is something very novel 10
indeed. "Germ" here refers not to microbes, but to the egg and sperm cells, the germ
cells of the human being. Scientists intent on genetic engineering would probably
start with a fertilized embryo a week or so old. They would tease apart the cells of
that embryo, and then, selecting one, they would add to, delete, or modify some
of its genes. They could also insert artificial chromosomes containing predesigned

genes. They would then take the cell, place it inside an egg whose nucleus had been removed, and implant the resulting new embryo inside a woman. The embryo would, if all went according to plan, grow into a genetically engineered child. His genes would be pushing out proteins to meet the particular choices made by his parents and by the companies and clinicians they were buying the genes from. Instead of coming solely from the combination of his parents, and thus the combination of their parents, and so on back through time, those genes could come from any other person, or any other plant or animal, or out of the thin blue sky. And once implanted, they will pass to his children and on into time.

But all this work will require one large change in our current way of doing business. Instead of making babies by making love, we will have to move conception to the laboratory. You need to have the embryo out there where you can work on it—to make the necessary copies, try to add or delete genes, and then implant the one that seems likely to turn out best. Gregory Stock, a researcher at the University of California and an apostle of the new genetic technologies, says that "the union of egg and sperm from two individuals . . . would be too unpredictable with intercourse." And once you've got the embryo out on the lab bench, gravity disappears altogether. "Ultimately," says Michael West, CEO of Advanced Cell Technology, the firm furthest out on the cutting edge of these technologies, "the dream of biologists is to have the sequence of DNA, the programming code of life, and to be able to edit it the way you can a document on a word processor."

Does it sound far-fetched? We began doing it with animals (mice) in 1978, and we've managed the trick with most of the obvious mammals, except one. Some of the first germline interventions might be semi-medical. You might, say some advocates, start by improving "visual and auditory acuity," first to eliminate nearsightedness or prevent deafness, then to "improve artistic potential." But why stop there? "If something has evolved elsewhere, then it is possible for us to determine its genetic basis and transfer it into the human genome," says Princeton geneticist Lee Silver—just as we have stuck flounder genes into strawberries to keep them from freezing, and jellyfish genes into rabbits and monkeys to make them glow in the dark.

But would we actually do this? Is there any real need to raise these questions as more than curiosities, or will the schemes simply fade away on their own, ignored by the parents who are their necessary consumers?

Anyone who has entered a baby supply store in the last few years knows that even the soberest parents can be counted on to spend virtually unlimited sums in pursuit of successful offspring. What if the "Baby Einstein" video series, which immerses "learning-enabled" babies in English, Spanish, Japanese, Hebrew, German, Russian, and French, could be bolstered with a little gene tweaking to improve memory? What if the Wombsongs prenatal music system, piping in Brahms to your waiting fetus, could be supplemented with an auditory upgrade? One sociologist told the *New York Times* we'd crossed the line from parenting to "product development," and even if that remark is truer in Manhattan than elsewhere, it's not hard to imagine what such attitudes will mean across the affluent world.

Here's one small example. In the 1980s, two drug companies were awarded 15
patents to market human growth hormone to the few thousand American children suffering from dwarfism. The PDA thought the market would be very small,
so HGH was given "orphan drug status," a series of special market advantages
designed to reward the manufacturers for taking on such an unattractive business. But within a few years, HGH had become one of the largest selling drugs
in the country, with half a billion dollars in sales. This was not because there'd
been a sharp increase in the number of dwarves, but because there'd been a sharp
increase in the number of parents who wanted to make their slightly short children taller. Before long the drug companies were arguing that the children in the
bottom 5 percent of their normal height range were in fact in need of three to five
shots a week of HGH. Take eleven-year-old Marco Oriti. At four foot one, he was
about four inches shorter than average, and projected to eventually top out at five
foot four. This was enough to convince his parents to start on a six-day-a-week
HGH regimen, which will cost them $150,000 over the next four years. "You want
to give your child the edge no matter what," said his mother.

A few of the would-be parents out on the current cutting edge of the reproduction revolution—those who need to obtain sperm or eggs for in vitro fertilization—
exhibit similar zeal. Ads started appearing in Ivy League college newspapers a
few years ago: couples were willing to pay $50,000 for an egg, provided the donor
was at least five feet, ten inches tall, white, and had scored 1400 on her SATs.
There is, in other words, a market just waiting for the first clinic with a catalogue
of germline modifications, a market that two California artists proved when they
opened a small boutique, Gene Genies Worldwide, in a trendy part of Pasadena.
Tran Kim-Trang and Karl Mihail wanted to get people thinking more deeply
about these emerging technologies, so they outfitted their store with petri dishes
and models of the double helix and printed up brochures highlighting traits with
genetic links: creativity, extroversion, thrill-seeking criminality. When they opened
the doors, they found people ready to shell out for designer families (one man
insisted he wanted the survival ability of a cockroach). The "store" was meant to
be ironic, but the irony was lost on a culture so deeply consumeristic that this
land of manipulation seems like the obvious next step. "Generally, people refused
to believe this store was an art project," says Tran. And why not? The next store in
the mall could easily have been a Botox salon.

But say you're not ready. Say you're perfectly happy with the prospect of a
child who shares the unmodified genes of you and your partner. Say you think
that manipulating the DNA of your child might be dangerous, or presumptuous, or icky. How long will you be able to hold that line if the procedure begins
to spread among your neighbors? Maybe not so long as you think. If germline
manipulation actually does begin, it seems likely to set off a kind of biological
arms race. "Suppose parents could add thirty points to their child's IQ?" asks MIT
economist Lester Thurow. "Wouldn't you want to do it? And if you don't, your
child will be the stupidest in the neighborhood." That's precisely what it might
feel like to be the parent facing the choice. Individual competition more or less

defines the society we've built, and in that context love can almost be defined as giving your kids what they need to make their way in the world. Deciding not to soup them up . . . well, it could come to seem like child abuse.

Of course, the problem about arms races is that you never really get anywhere. If everyone's adding thirty IQ points, then having an IQ of one hundred fifty won't get you any closer to Stanford than you were at the outset. The very first athlete engineered to use twice as much oxygen as the next guy will be unbeatable in the Tour de France—but in no time he'll merely be the new standard. You'll have to do what he did to be in the race, but your upgrades won't put you ahead, merely back on a level playing field. You might be able to argue that society as a whole was helped, because there was more total brainpower at work, but your kid won't be any closer to the top of the pack. All you'll be able to do is guarantee she won't be left hopelessly far behind.

In fact, the arms race problem has an extra ironic twist when it comes to genetic manipulation. The United States and the Soviet Union could, and did, keep adding new weapons to their arsenals over the decades. But with germline manipulation, you get only one shot; the extra chromosome you stick in your kid when he's born is the one he carries throughout his life. So let's say baby Sophie has a state-of-the-art gene job: her parents paid for the proteins discovered by, say, 2005 that on average yield ten extra IQ points. By the time Sophie is five, though, scientists will doubtless have discovered ten more genes linked to intelligence. Now anyone with a platinum card can get twenty IQ points, not to mention a memory boost and a permanent wrinkle-free brow. So by the time Sophie is twenty-five and in the job market, she's already more or less obsolete—the kids coming out of college plainly just have better hardware.

"For all his billions, Bill Gates could not have purchased a single genetic [20] enhancement for his son Rory John," writes Gregory Stock at the University of California. "And you can bet that any enhancements a billion dollars can buy Rory's child in 2030 will seem crude alongside those available for modest sums in 2060." It's not, he adds, "so different from upgraded software. You'll want the new release."

The vision of one's child as a nearly useless copy of Windows 95 should make parents fight like hell to make sure we never get started down this path. But the vision gets lost easily in the gushing excitement about "improving" the opportunities for our kids.

Beginning the hour my daughter came home from the hospital, I spent part of every day with her in the woods out back, showing her trees and ferns and chipmunks and frogs. One of her very first words was "birch," and you couldn't have asked for a prouder papa. She got her middle name from the mountain we see out the window; for her fifth birthday she got her own child-sized canoe; her school wardrobe may not be relentlessly up-to-date, but she's never lacked for hiking boots. As I write these words, she's spending her first summer at sleepaway camp, one we chose because the kids sleep in tents and spend days in the mountains. All of which is to say that I have done everything in my power to try to mold her into a lover of the natural world. That is where my deepest satisfactions lie, and I want the same for her. It seems benign enough, but it has its drawbacks; it means less time and money and energy for trips to the city and music lessons and so forth. As time goes on and she develops stronger opinions of her own, I yield more and more, but I keep trying to stack the deck, to nudge her in the direction that's meant something to me. On a Saturday morning, when the question comes up of what to do, the very first words out of my mouth always involve yet another hike. I can't help myself.

In other words, we already "engineer" our offspring in some sense of the word: we do our best, and often our worst, to steer them in particular directions. And our worst can be pretty bad. We all know people whose lives were blighted trying to meet the expectations of their parents. We've all seen the crazed devotion to getting kids into the right schools, the right professions, the right income brackets. Parents try to pass down their prejudices, their politics, their attitude toward the world ("we've got to toughen that kid up—he's going to get walked all over"). There are fathers who start teaching the curveball at the age of four, and sons made to feel worthless if they don't make the Little League traveling team. People move house so that their kids can grow up with the right band of schoolmates. They threaten to disown them for marrying African Americans, or for not marrying African Americans. No dictator anywhere has ever tried to rule his subjects with as much attention to detail as the average modern parent.

Why not take this just one small step further? Why not engineer children to up the odds that all that nudging will stick? In the words of Lee Silver, a Princeton geneticist, "Why not seize this power? Why not control what has been left to chance in the past? Indeed, we control all other aspects of our children's lives and identities through powerful social and environmental influences. . . . On what basis can we reject positive genetic influences on a person's essence when we accept the rights of parents to benefit their children in every other way?" If you can buy your kid three years at Deerfield, four at Harvard, and three more at Harvard Law, why shouldn't you be able to turbocharge his IQ a bit?

But most likely the answer has already occurred to you as well. Because 25 you know plenty of people who managed to rebel successfully against whatever agenda their parents laid out for them, or who took that agenda and bent it to fit their own particular personality. In our society that's often what growing up is all about—the sometimes excruciatingly difficult, frequently liberating break with the expectations of your parents. The decision to join the Peace Corps (or, the decision to leave the commune where you grew up and go to business school). The discovery that you were happiest davening in an Orthodox shul three hours a day, much to the consternation of your good suburban parents who almost always made it to Yom Kippur services; the decision that, much as you respected the Southern Baptist piety of your parents, the Bible won't be your watchword.

Without the grounding offered by tradition, the search for the "authentic you" can be hard; our generations contain the first people who routinely shop religions, for instance. But the sometimes poignant difficulty of finding yourself merely underscores how essential it is. Silver says the costs of germline engineering and a college education might be roughly comparable; in both cases, he goes on, the point is to "increase the chances the child will become wiser in some way, and better able to achieve success and happiness." But that's half the story, at best. College is where you go to be exposed to a thousand new influences, ideas that should be able to take you in almost any direction. It's where you go to get out from under your parents' thumb, to find out that you actually don't have to go to law school if you don't want to. As often as not, the harder parents try to wrench their kids in one direction, the harder those kids eventually fight to determine their own destiny. I am as prepared as I can be for the possibility—the probability—that Sophie will decide she wants to live her life in the concrete heart of Manhattan. It's her life (and perhaps her kids will have a secret desire to come wander in the woods with me).

We try to shape the lives of our kids—to "improve" their lives, as we would measure improvement—but our gravity is usually weak enough that kids can break out of it if and when they need to. (When it isn't, when parents manage to bend their children to the point of breaking, we think of them as monstrous.) "Many of the most creative and valuable human lives are the result of particularly difficult struggles" against expectation and influence, writes the legal scholar Martha Nussbaum.

That's not how a genetic engineer thinks of his product. He works to ensure absolute success. Last spring an Israeli researcher announced that he had managed to produce a featherless chicken. This constituted an improvement, to his mind, because "it will be cheaper to produce since its lack of feathers means there is no need to pluck it before it hits the shelves." Also, poultry farmers would no longer have to ventilate their vast barns to keep their birds from overheating. "Feathers are a waste," the scientist explained. "The chickens are using feed to produce something that has to be dumped, and the farmers have to waste electricity to overcome that fact." Now, that engineer was not trying to influence his chickens to shed their feathers because they'd be happier and the farmer would be happier and everyone would be happier. He was inserting a gene that created a protein that made good and certain they would not be producing feathers. Just substitute, say, an even temperament for feathers, and you'll know what the human engineers envision.

"With reprogenetics," writes Lee Silver, "parents can gain *complete control* [emphasis mine] over their destiny, with the ability to guide and enhance the characteristics of their children, and their children's children as well." Such parents would not be calling their children on the phone at annoying frequent intervals to suggest that it's time to get a real job; instead, just like the chicken guy, they would be inserting genes that produced proteins that would make their child behave in certain ways throughout his life. You cannot rebel against the production of that protein. Perhaps you can still do everything in your power to defeat the wishes of your parents, but that protein will nonetheless be pumped out relentlessly into your system, defining who you are. You won't grow feathers, no matter how much you want them. And maybe they can engineer your mood enough that your lack of plumage won't even cross your mind.

Such children will, in effect, be assigned a goal by their programmers: "intel- 30 ligence," "even temper," "athleticism." (As with chickens, the market will doubtless lean in the direction of efficiency. It may be hard to find genes for, say, dreaminess.) Now two possibilities arise. Perhaps the programming doesn't work very well, and your lad spells poorly, or turns moody, or can't hit the inside fastball. In the present world, you just tell yourself that that's who he is. But in the coming world, he'll be, in essence, a defective product. Do you still accept *him* unconditionally? Why? If your new Jetta got thirty miles to the gallon instead of the forty it was designed to get, you'd take it back. You'd call it a lemon. If necessary, you'd sue.

Or what if the engineering worked pretty well, but you decided, too late, that you'd picked the wrong package, hadn't gotten the best features? Would you feel buyer's remorse if the kid next door had a better ear, a stronger arm?

Say the gene work went a little awry and left you with a kid who had some serious problems; what kind of guilt would that leave you with? Remember, this is not a child created by the random interaction of your genes with those of your partner, this is a child created with specific intent. Does *Consumer Reports* start rating the various biotech offerings?

What if you had a second child five years after the first, and by that time the upgrades were undeniably improved: how would you feel about the first kid? How would he feel about his new brother, the latest model?

The other outcome—that the genetic engineering works just as you had hoped—seems at least as bad. Now your child is a product. You can take precisely as much pride in her achievements as you take in the achievements of your dish-washing detergent. It was designed to produce streak-free glassware, and she was designed to be sweet-tempered, social, and smart. And what can she take pride in? Her good grades? She may have worked hard, but she'll always know that she was spec'ed for good grades. Her kindness to others? Well, yes, it's good to be kind—but perhaps it's not much of an accomplishment once the various genes with some link to sociability have been catalogued and manipulated. I have no doubt that these qualms would be one of the powerful psychological afflictions of the future—at least until someone figures out a fix that keeps the next generations from having such bad thoughts.

Britain's chief rabbi, Jonathan Sacks, was asked a few years ago about the 35 announcement that Italian doctors were trying to clone humans. "If there is a mystery at the heart of human condition, it is otherness: the otherness of man and woman, parent and child. It is the space we make for otherness that makes love something other than narcissism." I remember so well the feeling of walking into the maternity ward with Sue, and walking out with Sue and Sophie: where there had been two there were now, somehow, three, each of us our own person, but now commanded to make a family, a place where we all could thrive. She was so mysterious, that Sophie, and in many ways she still is. There are times when, like every parent, I see myself reflected in her, and times when I wonder if she's even related. She's ours to nurture and protect, but she is who *she is.* That's the mystery and the glory of any child.

Mystery, however, is not one of the words that thrills engineers. They try to deliver solid bridges, unyielding dams, reliable cars. We wouldn't want it any other way. The only question is if their product line should be expanded to include children.

Right now both the genes, and the limits that they set on us, connect us with every human that came before. Human beings can look at rock art carved into African cliffs and French caves thirty thousand years ago and feel an electric, immediate kinship. We've gone from digging sticks to combines, and from drum circles to symphony orchestras (and back again to drum circles), but we still hear in the same range and see in the same spectrum, still produce adrenaline and dopamine in the same ways, still think in many of the same patterns. We are, by and large, the same people, more closely genetically related to one another than we may be to our engineered grandchildren.

These new technologies show us that human meaning dangles by a far thinner thread than we had thought. If germline genetic engineering ever starts, it will accelerate endlessly and unstoppably into the future, as individuals make the calculation that they have no choice but to equip their kids for the world that's being made. The first child whose genes come in part from some corporate lab, the first child who has been "enhanced" from what came before—that's the first child who will glance back over his shoulder and see a gap between himself and human history.

These would be mere consumer decisions—but that also means that they would benefit the rich far more than the poor. They would take the gap in power, wealth, and education that currently divides both our society and the world at large, and write that division into our very biology. A sixth of the American population lacks health insurance of any kind—they can't afford to go to the doctor for a *check-up.* And much of the rest of the world is far worse off. If we can't afford the fifty cents per person it would take to buy bed nets to protect most of Africa from malaria, it is unlikely we will extend to anyone but the top tax bracket these latest forms of genetic technology. The injustice is so obvious that even the strongest proponents of genetic engineering make little attempt to deny it. "Anyone who accepts the right of affluent parents to provide their children with an expensive private school education cannot use 'unfairness' as a reason for rejecting the use of reprogenetic technologies," says Lee Silver.

These new technologies, however, are not yet inevitable. Unlike global warm- 40 ing, this genie is not yet out of the bottle. But if germline genetic engineering is going to be stopped, it will have to happen now, before it's quite begun. It will have to be a political choice, that is—one we make not as parents but as citizens, not as individuals but as a whole, thinking not only about our own offspring but about everyone.

So far the discussion has been confined to a few scientists, a few philosophers, a few ideologues. It needs to spread widely, and quickly, and loudly. The stakes are absurdly high, nothing less than the meaning of being human. And given the seductions that we've seen — the intuitively and culturally delicious prospect of a *better* child — the arguments against must be not only powerful but also deep. They'll need to resonate on the same intuitive and cultural level. We'll need to feel in our gut the reasons why, this time, we should tell Prometheus thanks, but no thanks.

QUESTIONS FOR DISCUSSION AND WRITING

1. "Individual competition more or less defines the society we've built," argues McKibben, discussing a potential "arms race" resulting from the genetic enhancement of children (paragraphs 17 and 18). What evidence does McKibben give that parents already are in a race to enhance their children? Consider his points about baby supply stores, HGH, and egg donations (paragraphs 14–16). To what extent do you agree with McKibben's predictions about a competition in genetic child enhancement?

2. Do you agree with McKibben that, in our society, growing up is often "the sometimes excruciatingly difficult, frequently liberating break with the expectations of your parents" (paragraph 25)? In what ways would germline genetic engineering of children interfere with maturation (paragraphs 26–29)? How important is it for an individual's maturation to have to make one's own decisions and to be independent?

3. Write a paper on McKibben's concerns about economic inequality and genetic engineering. Consider the consequences of genetically engineering children, given the fact that wealth would determine whose children received the most enhancements (paragraphs 38–39). What would happen to the world of sports, for example, if the offspring of rich children had the best genetic modifications of their strength and stamina genes? How would the world of academia change if wealthy children were engineered for intelligence, while poorer children were not? Would these changes be essentially positive or negative for America?

FREEMAN DYSON

Our Biotech Future

Freeman Dyson, physicist and futurist, was born in Crowthorne, Berkshire, England, in 1923. After World War II service in the R.A.F. Bomber Command, he earned a B.A. in math at Cambridge University (1945). Although he never earned a Ph.D., his brilliance as a physicist enabled him to study and then teach at Cornell (1947–53), and then to accept a prestigious appointment at Princeton in 1953, with which he is still affiliated. His discoveries in quantum electrodynamics, nuclear pulse propulsion (on NASA's Orion Project, 1957–61), and the stability of bulk matter have led to numerous honors. In his first (of nine) books, Disturbing the Universe *(1979) Dyson, "scientist, citizen, student, parent," focuses on issues of disarmament and "expansion of our frontiers into the galaxy." In his characteristically reader-friendly language, he articulates this hope for a peaceful future in* Weapons and Hope *(1984). The essays in* A Many-Colored Glass: Reflections on the Place of Life in the Universe *(2007), in which the essay below appears, reiterate Dyson's career-long concerns, focusing on the "human and ethical consequences of biotechnology; the place of life in the universe; and the implications of biology for philosophy and religion."*

It has become part of the accepted wisdom to say that the twentieth century was the century of physics and the twenty-first century will be the century of biology. Two facts about the coming century are agreed on by almost everyone. Biology is now bigger than physics, as measured by the size of budgets, by the size of the workforce, or by the output of major discoveries; and biology is likely to remain the biggest part of science through the twenty-first century. Biology is also more important than physics, as measured by its economic consequences, its ethical implications, or its effects on human welfare.

These facts raise an interesting question. Will the domestication of high technology, which we have seen marching from triumph to triumph with the advent of personal computers and GPS receivers and digital cameras, soon be extended from physical technology to biotechnology? I believe that the answer to this question is yes. Here I am bold enough to make a definite prediction. I predict that the domestication of biotechnology will dominate our lives during the next fifty years at least as much as the domestication of computers has dominated our lives during the past fifty years.

I see a close analogy between John von Neumann's blinkered vision of computers as large centralized facilities and the public perception of genetic engineering today as an activity of large pharmaceutical and agribusiness corporations such as Monsanto. The public distrusts Monsanto because Monsanto likes to put genes for poisonous pesticides into food crops, just as we distrusted von Neumann because he liked to use his computer for designing hydrogen bombs secretly at midnight. It is likely that genetic engineering will remain unpopular and controversial so long as it remains a centralized activity in the hands of large corporations.

I see a bright future for the biotechnology industry when it follows the path of the computer industry, the path that von Neumann failed to foresee, becoming small and domesticated rather than big and centralized. The first step in this direction was taken recently when genetically modified tropical fish with new and brilliant colors appeared in pet stores. For biotechnology to become domesticated, the next step is to become user-friendly. I recently spent a happy day at the Philadelphia Flower Show, the biggest indoor flower show in the world, where flower breeders from all over the world show off the results of their efforts. I have also visited the reptile show in San Diego, an equally impressive show displaying the work of another set of breeders. Philadelphia excels in orchids and roses, San Diego excels in lizards and snakes. The main problem for a grandparent visiting the reptile show with a grandchild is to get the grandchild out of the building without actually buying a snake.

Every orchid or rose or lizard or snake is the work of a dedicated and   5 skilled breeder. There are thousands of people, amateurs and professionals, who devote their lives to this business. Now imagine what will happen when the tools of genetic engineering become accessible to these people. There will be do-it-yourself kits for gardeners, who will use genetic engineering to breed new varieties of roses and orchids. Also kits for lovers of pigeons and parrots and lizards and snakes to breed new varieties of pets. Breeders of dogs and cats will have their kits too.

Domesticated biotechnology, once it gets into the hands of housewives and children, will give us an explosion of diversity of new living creatures rather than the monoculture crops that the big corporations prefer. New lineages will proliferate to replace those that monoculture farming and deforestation have destroyed. Designing genomes will be a personal thing, a new art form as creative as painting or sculpture.

Few of the new creations will be masterpieces, but a great many will bring joy to their creators and variety to our fauna and flora. The final step in the domestication of biotechnology will be biotech games, designed like computer games for children down to kindergarten age but played with real eggs and seeds rather than with images on a screen. Playing such games, kids will acquire an intimate feeling for the organisms that they are growing. The winner could be the kid whose seed grows the prickliest cactus or the kid whose egg hatches the cutest dinosaur. These games will be messy and possibly dangerous. Rules and regulations will be needed to make sure that our kids do not endanger themselves and others. The dangers of biotechnology are real and serious.

If domestication of biotechnology is the wave of the future, five important questions need to be answered. First, can it be stopped? Second, ought it to be stopped? Third, if stopping it is either impossible or undesirable, what are the appropriate limits that our society must impose on it? Fourth, how should the limits be decided? Fifth, how should the limits be enforced, nationally and internationally? I do not attempt to answer these questions here. I leave it to our children and grandchildren to supply the answers.

A NEW BIOLOGY FOR A NEW CENTURY

Carl Woese is the world's greatest expert in the field of microbial taxonomy, the classification and understanding of microbes. He explored the ancestry of microbes by tracing the similarities and differences between their genomes. He discovered the large-scale structure of the tree of life, with all living creatures descended from three primordial branches. Before Woese, the tree of life had two main branches, called prokaryotes and eukaryotes, the prokaryotes composed of cells without nuclei and the eukaryotes composed of cells with nuclei. All kinds of plants and animals, including humans, belonged to the eukaryote branch. The prokaryote branch contained only microbes. Woese discovered, by studying the anatomy of microbes in detail, that there are two fundamentally different kinds of prokaryotes, which he called bacteria and archea. So he constructed a new tree of life with three branches: bacteria, archea, and eukaryotes. Most of the well-known microbes are bacteria. The archea were at first supposed to be rare and confined to extreme environments such as hot springs, but they are now known to be abundant and widely distributed over the planet. Woese recently published two provocative and illuminating articles with the titles "A New Biology for a New Century" and, with Nigel Goldenfeld, "Biology's Next Revolution."

Woese's main theme is the obsolescence of reductionist biology as it has been 10 practiced for the last hundred years, with its assumption that biological processes can be understood by studying genes and molecules. What is needed instead is a new synthetic biology based on emergent patterns of organization. Aside from his main theme, he raises another important question. When did Darwinian evolution begin? By Darwinian evolution he means evolution as Darwin understood it, based on the competition for survival of noninterbreeding species. He presents evidence that Darwinian evolution does not go back to the beginning of life. When we compare genomes of ancient lineages of living creatures, we find evidence of numerous transfers of genetic information from one lineage to another. In early times, horizontal gene transfer, the sharing of genes between unrelated species, was prevalent. It becomes more prevalent the further back you go in time.

Whatever Carl Woese writes, even in a speculative vein, needs to be taken seriously. In his "New Biology" article, he is postulating a golden age of pre-Darwinian life, when horizontal gene transfer was universal and separate species did not yet exist. Life was then a community of cells of various kinds, sharing their genetic information so that clever chemical tricks and catalytic processes invented by one creature could be inherited by all of them. Evolution was a communal affair, the whole community advancing in metabolic and reproductive efficiency as the genes of the most efficient cells were shared. Evolution could be rapid, as new chemical devices could be evolved simultaneously by cells of different kinds working in parallel and then reassembled in a single cell by horizontal gene transfer.

But then one evil day, a cell resembling a primitive bacterium happened to find itself one jump ahead of its neighbors in efficiency. That cell, anticipating Bill Gates by 3 billion years, separated itself from the community and refused to share. Its offspring became the first species of bacteria—and the first species of any kind—to reserve their intellectual property for their own private use. With their superior efficiency, the bacteria continued to prosper and to evolve separately, while the rest of the community continued its communal life. Some millions of years later, another cell separated itself from the community and became the ancestor of the archea. Sometime after that, a third cell separated itself and became the ancestor of the eukaryotes. And so it went on, until nothing was left of the community and all life was divided into species. The Darwinian interlude had begun.

The Darwinian interlude has lasted for 2 or 3 billion years. It probably slowed down the pace of evolution considerably. The basic biochemical machinery of life had evolved rapidly during the few hundreds of millions of years of the pre-Darwinian era, and it changed very little in the next 2 billion years of microbial evolution. Darwinian evolution is slow because individual species, once established, evolve very little. With rare exceptions, Darwinian evolution requires established species to become extinct so that new species can replace them.

Now, after 3 billion years, the Darwinian interlude is over. It was an interlude between two periods of horizontal gene transfer. The epoch of Darwinian evolution based on competition between species ended about 10,000 years ago, when a single species, *Homo sapiens,* began to dominate and reorganize the biosphere. Since that time, cultural evolution has replaced biological evolution as the main driving force of change. Cultural evolution is not Darwinian. Cultures spread by horizontal transfer of ideas more than by genetic inheritance. Cultural evolution is running a thousand times faster than Darwinian evolution, taking us into a new era of cultural interdependence, which we call globalization. And now, as *Homo sapiens* domesticates the new biotechnology, we are reviving the ancient pre-Darwinian practice of horizontal gene transfer, moving genes easily from microbes to plants and animals, blurring the boundaries between species. We are moving rapidly into the post-Darwinian era, when species other than our own will no longer exist, and the rules of open-source sharing will be extended from the exchange of software to the exchange of genes. Then the evolution of life will once again be communal, as it was in the good old days before separate species and intellectual property were invented.

I would like to borrow Carl Woese's vision of the future of biology and 15 extend it to the whole of science. Here is his metaphor for the future of science:

> Imagine a child playing in a woodland stream, poking a stick into an eddy in the flowing current, thereby disrupting it. But the eddy quickly reforms. The child disperses it again. Again it reforms, and the fascinating game goes on. There you have it! Organisms are resilient patterns in a turbulent flow— patterns in an energy flow . . . It is becoming increasingly clear that to understand living systems in any deep sense, we must come to see them not materialistically, as machines, but as stable, complex, dynamic organization.

This picture of living creatures as patterns of organization rather than collections of molecules applies not only to bees and bacteria, butterflies and rain forests, but also to sand dunes and snowflakes, thunderstorms and hurricanes. The nonliving universe is as diverse and dynamic as the living universe and is also dominated by patterns of organization that are not yet understood. The reductionist physics and reductionist molecular biology of the twentieth century will continue to be important in the twenty-first century, but they will not be dominant. The big problems, the evolution of the universe as a whole, the origin of life, the nature of human consciousness, and the evolution of Earth's climate, cannot be understood by reducing them to elementary particles and molecules. New ways of thinking and new ways of organizing large databases will be needed.

GREEN TECHNOLOGY

The domestication of biotechnology in everyday life may also be helpful in solving practical economic and environmental problems. Once a new generation of children has grown up, as familiar with biotech games as our grandchildren are now with computer games, biotechnology will no longer seem weird and alien. In the era of open-source biology, the magic of genes will be available to anyone with the skill and imagination to use it. The way will be open for biotechnology to move into the mainstream of economic development, to help us solve some of our urgent social problems and ameliorate the human condition all over Earth. Open-source biology could be a powerful tool, giving us access to cheap and abundant solar energy.

A plant is a creature that uses the energy of sunlight to convert water and carbon dioxide and other simple chemicals into roots and leaves and flowers. To live, it needs to collect sunlight. But it uses sunlight with low efficiency. The most efficient crop plants, such as sugar cane or maize, convert about 1 percent of the sunlight that falls onto them into chemical energy. Artificial solar collectors made of silicon can do much better. Silicon solar cells can convert sunlight into electrical energy with 15 percent efficiency, and electrical energy can be converted into chemical energy without much loss. We can imagine that in the future, when we have mastered the art of genetically engineering plants, we may breed new crop plants that have leaves made of silicon, converting sunlight into chemical energy with ten times the efficiency of natural plants. These artificial crop plants would reduce the area of land needed for biomass production by a factor of ten. They would allow solar energy to be used on a massive scale without taking up too much land. They would look like natural plants except that their leaves would be black, the color of silicon, instead of green, the color of chlorophyll. The question I am asking is, how long will it take us to grow plants with silicon leaves?

If the natural evolution of plants had been driven by the need for high efficiency of utilization of sunlight, then the leaves of all plants would have been black. Black leaves would absorb sunlight more efficiently than leaves of any other color. Obviously plant evolution was driven by other needs, and in particular by the need for protection against overheating. For a plant growing in a hot climate, it is advantageous to reflect as much as possible of the sunlight that is not used for growth. There is plenty of sunlight, and it is not important to use it with maximum efficiency. The plants have evolved with chlorophyll in their leaves to absorb the useful red and blue components of sunlight and to reflect the green. That is why it is reasonable for plants in tropical climates to be green. But this logic does not explain why plants in cold climates where sunlight is scarce are also green. We could imagine that in a place like Iceland, overheating would not be a problem, and plants with black leaves using sunlight more efficiently would have an evolutionary advantage. For some reason that we do not understand, natural plants with black leaves never appeared. Why not? Perhaps we shall not understand why nature did not travel this route until we have traveled it ourselves.

After we have explored this route to the end, when we have created new forests of black-leaved plants that can use sunlight ten times more efficiently than natural plants, we shall be confronted by a new set of environmental problems. Who shall be allowed to grow the black-leaved plants? Will black-leaved plants remain an artificially maintained cultivar, or will they invade and permanently change the natural ecology? What shall we do with the silicon trash that these plants leave behind them? Shall we be able to design a whole ecology of silicon-eating microbes and fungi and earthworms to keep the black-leaved plants in balance with the rest of nature and to recycle their silicon? The twenty-first century will bring us powerful new tools of genetic engineering with which to manipulate our farms and forests. With the new tools will come new questions and new responsibilities.

Rural poverty is one of the great evils of the modern world. The lack of jobs and   20 economic opportunities in villages drives millions of people to migrate from villages into overcrowded cities. The continuing migration causes immense social and environmental problems in the major cities of poor countries. The effects of poverty are most visible in the cities, but the causes of poverty lie mostly in the villages. What the world needs is a technology that directly attacks the problem of rural poverty by creating wealth and jobs in the villages. A technology that creates industries and careers in villages would give the villagers a practical alternative to migration. It would give them a chance to survive and prosper without uprooting themselves.

The shifting balance of wealth and population between villages and cities is one of the main themes of human history over the last 10,000 years. The shift from villages to cities is strongly coupled with a shift from one kind of technology to another. I find it convenient to call the two kinds of technology green and gray. The adjective "green" has been appropriated and abused by various political movements, especially in Europe, so I need to explain clearly what I have in mind when I speak of green and gray. Green technology is based on biology; gray technology, on physics and chemistry.

Roughly speaking, green technology is the technology that gave birth to village communities 10,000 years ago, starting with the domestication of plants and animals, the invention of agriculture, the breeding of goats and sheep and horses and cows and pigs, the manufacture of textiles and cheese and wine. Gray technology is the technology that gave birth to cities and empires 5,000 years later, starting with the forging of bronze and iron, the invention of wheeled vehicles and paved roads, the building of ships and war chariots, the manufacture of swords and guns and bombs. Gray technology also produced the steel plows, tractors, reapers, and processing plants that made agriculture more productive and transferred much of the resulting wealth from village-based farmers to city-based corporations.

For the first 5,000 of the 10,000 years of human civilization, wealth and power belonged to villages with green technology, and for the second 5,000 years wealth and power belonged to cities with gray technology. Beginning about 500 years ago, gray technology became increasingly dominant, as we learned to build machines that used power from wind and water and steam and electricity. In the last hundred years, wealth and power were even more heavily concentrated in cities as gray technology raced ahead. As cities became richer, rural poverty deepened.

This sketch of the last 10,000 years of human history puts the problem of rural poverty into a new perspective. If rural poverty is a consequence of the unbalanced growth of gray technology, it is possible that a shift in the balance back from gray to green might cause rural poverty to disappear. That is my dream. During the last fifty years we have seen explosive progress in the scientific understanding of the basic processes of life, and in the last twenty years this new understanding has given rise to explosive growth of green technology. The new green technology allows us to breed new varieties of animals and plants as our ancestors did 10,000 years ago, but now a hundred times faster. It now takes us a decade instead of a millennium to create new crop plants, such as the herbicide-resistant varieties of maize and soybeans that allow weeds to be controlled without plowing and greatly reduce the erosion of topsoil by wind and rain. Guided by a precise understanding of genes and genomes instead of by trial and error, we can within a few years modify plants so as to give them improved yield, improved nutritive value, and improved resistance to pests and diseases.

Within a few more decades, as the continued exploring of genomes gives 25 us better knowledge of the architecture of living creatures, we shall be able to design new species of microbes and plants according to our needs. The way will then be open for green technology to do more cheaply and cleanly many of the things that gray technology can do, and also to do many things that gray technology has failed to do. Green technology could replace most of our existing chemical industries and a large part of our mining and manufacturing industries. Genetically engineered earthworms could extract common metals such as aluminum and titanium from clay, and genetically engineered seaweed could extract magnesium or gold from seawater. Green technology could also achieve more extensive recycling of waste products and worn-out machines, with great benefit to the environment. An economic system based on green technology could come much closer to the goal of sustainability, using sunlight instead of fossil fuels as the primary source of energy. New species of termites could be engineered to chew up derelict automobiles instead of houses, and new species of tree could be engineered to convert carbon dioxide and sunlight into liquid fuels instead of cellulose.

Before genetically modified termites and trees can be allowed to help solve our economic and environmental problems, great arguments will rage over the possible damage they may do. Many of the people who call themselves green are passionately opposed to green technology. But in the end, if the technology is developed carefully and deployed with sensitivity to human feelings, it is likely to be accepted by most of the people who will be affected by it, just as the equally unnatural and unfamiliar green technologies of milking cows and plowing soils and fermenting grapes were accepted by our ancestors long ago. I am not saying that the political acceptance of green technology will be quick or easy. I say only that green technology has enormous promise for preserving the balance of nature on this planet as well as for relieving human misery. Future generations of people raised from childhood with biotech toys and games will probably accept it more easily than we do. Nobody can predict how long it may take to try out the new technology in a thousand different ways and measure its costs and benefits.

What has this dream of a resurgent green technology to do with the problem of rural poverty? In the past, green technology has always been rural, based in farms and villages rather than in cities. In the future it will pervade cities as well as countryside, factories as well as forests. It will not be entirely rural. But it will still have a large rural component. After all, the cloning of Dolly occurred in a rural animal-breeding station in Scotland, not in an urban laboratory in Silicon Valley. Green technology will use land and sunlight as its primary sources of raw materials and energy. Land and sunlight cannot be concentrated in cities but are spread more or less evenly over the planet. When industries and technologies are based on land and sunlight, they will bring employment and wealth to rural populations.

In a country like India with a large rural population, bringing wealth to the villages means bringing jobs other than farming. Most of the villagers must cease to be subsistence farmers and become shopkeepers or schoolteachers or bankers or engineers or poets. In the end the villages must become gentrified, as they are today in England, with the old farm workers' cottages converted into garages, and the few remaining farmers converted into highly skilled professionals. It is fortunate that sunlight is most abundant in tropical countries, where a large fraction of the world's people live and where rural poverty is most acute. Since sunlight is distributed more equitably than coal and oil, green technology can be a great equalizer, helping to narrow the gap between rich and poor countries.

My book *The Sun, the Genome, and the Internet* (1999) describes a vision of green technology enriching villages all over the world and halting the migration from villages to megacities. The three components of the vision are all essential: the sun to provide energy where it is needed, the genome to provide plants that can convert sunlight into chemical fuels cheaply and efficiently, the Internet to end the intellectual and economic isolation of rural populations. With all three components in place, every village in Africa could enjoy its fair share of the blessings of civilization. People who prefer to live in cities would still be free to move from villages to cities, but they would not be compelled to move by economic necessity.

QUESTIONS FOR DISCUSSION AND WRITING

1. Dyson opens with the striking claim, "I predict that the domestication of biotechnology will dominate our lives during the next fifty years at least as much as the domestication of computers has dominated our lives during the past fifty years" (paragraph 2). What does he mean by "the domestication of biotechnology"? How does "the domestication of computers" explain this analogous concept? In what ways have computers been "domesticated" during your lifetime (see chapter 5)?

2. Based on the information Dyson provides in this essay, with a partner or your class, discuss the answer(s) to one or more of the questions he asks (but doesn't answer): "If the domestication of biotechnology is the wave of the future . . . First, can it be stopped? Second, ought it to be stopped? Third, if stopping it is either impossible or undesirable, what are the appropriate limits that our society must impose on it? Fourth, how should the limits be decided? Fifth, how should the limits be enforced, nationally and internationally" (paragraph 8)? Write a paper that incorporates the main principles of your reasoning.

3. "Now, after 3 billion years, the Darwinian interlude is over," says Dyson. "The new green technology allows us to breed new varieties of animals and plants as our ancestors did ten thousand years ago, but now a hundred times faster" (paragraphs 14 and 24). At various points in the essay Dyson talks about the implications of "domesticated biotechnology, once it gets into the hands of housewives and children" (paragraph 6). What are some of the new breeds that ordinary people might produce, and for what purposes could these be created? What leads Dyson to believe that "open source" biotech sharing and creation would result in beneficial biotech creations and not monsters and mutants?

4. What is "green technology" (paragraphs 17 and 18)? If "green" is so good, why does Dyson lament that the more energy-efficient "black" didn't evolve? Could—and should—genetic technology create "black-leaved plants" (paragraph 19)? If so, how could their impact on the "natural ecology" be predicted in advance, for better and, perhaps, for worse (see the questions Dyson asks in paragraph 19), as people "manipulate our farms and forests." What would the advantages and disadvantages of such genetic engineering be in comparison with the "manipulation" of these environments that goes on as a result of slash-and-burn farming, clearcutting, and other current destructive practices?

5. Dyson distinguishes between "green" and "gray" technology (paragraphs 21–23). What does he mean by each of these terms? How does "the unbalanced growth of gray technology" cause rural poverty? What would have to happen for green technology to shift the balance back? What's the best proportion of green/gray technology for the part of the world in which you live? For the world in general?

6. Write, with a partner who knows science, if possible, an essay in which you explain what Dyson means by the claim that "biology is likely to remain the biggest part of science through the twenty-first century . . . as measured by its economic consequences, its ethical implications, or its effects on human welfare"

(paragraph 1). You can focus on a single claim of Dyson's, and on examining the significant implications of a single development of bio-technology.

LEWIS THOMAS

The Technology of Medicine

Lewis Thomas (1913–1993) established his scientific reputation on the basis of some two hundred research papers on immunology and experimental pathology. He graduated from Harvard Medical School (1937), served in the South Pacific during World War II, did research on rheumatic fever at Tulane and the University of Minnesota, taught at Johns Hopkins, the School of Medicine at New York University where he transformed immunology into a clinical science, and Yale Medical School. From 1973 to 1980 he was president of Memorial Sloan-Kettering Cancer Center, leading it into international research distinction. His contributions in research and administration led him to be called "the father of modern immunology and experimental pathology."

Although he wrote his scientific papers in "the relentlessly flat style required for absolute unambiguity," beginning in 1971 his monthly essays in the New England Journal of Medicine *were witty, graceful commentaries on science, medicine, philosophy, and life itself for general readers. He published collections of these columns,* The Lives of a Cell: Notes of a Biology Watcher *(1972),* The Medusa and the Snail *(1979), and* Late Night Thoughts on Listening to Mahler's Ninth Symphony *(1983); and his autobiography,* The Youngest Science: Notes of a Medicine-Watcher *(1983). "The Technology of Medicine," from* The Lives of a Cell, *offers an enduring categorization of three levels of medical technology (supportive, halfway, and preventive) and uses this classification to argue that "the real high technology of medicine . . . comes as the result of genuine understanding of disease mechanisms" and—in contrast to flashy machinery and elaborate procedures—is "relatively inexpensive and relatively easy to deliver."*

Technology assessment has become a routine exercise for the scientific enterprises on which the country is obliged to spend vast sums for its needs. Brainy committees are continually evaluating the effectiveness and cost of doing various things in space, defense, energy, transportation, and the like, to give advice about prudent investments for the future.

Somehow medicine, for all the $80-odd billion that it is said to cost the nation, has not yet come in for much of this analytical treatment. It seems taken for granted that the technology of medicine simply exists, take it or leave it, and the only major technologic problem which policy-makers are interested in is how to deliver today's kind of health care, with equity, to all the people.

When, as is bound to happen sooner or later, the analysts get around to the technology of medicine itself, they will have to face the problem of measuring the relative cost and effectiveness of all the things that are done in the management of disease. They make their living at this kind of thing, and I wish them well, but I imagine they will have a bewildering time. For one thing, our methods of managing disease are constantly changing—partly under the influence of new bits of information brought in from all corners of biologic science. At the same time, a great many things are done that are not so closely related to science, some not related at all.

In fact, there are three quite different levels of technology in medicine, so unlike each other as to seem altogether different undertakings. Practitioners of medicine and the analysts will be in trouble if they are not kept separate.

1. First of all, there is a large body of what might be termed "nontechnology," 5 impossible to measure in terms of its capacity to alter either the natural course of disease or its eventual outcome. A great deal of money is spent on this. It is valued highly by the professionals as well as the patients. It consists of what is sometimes called "supportive therapy." It tides patients over through diseases that are not, by and large, understood. It is what is meant by the phrases "caring for" and "standing by." It is indispensable. It is not, however, a technology in any real sense, since it does not involve measures directed at the underlying mechanism of disease.

It includes the large part of any good doctor's time that is taken up with simply providing reassurance, explaining to patients who fear that they have contracted one or another lethal disease that they are, in fact, quite healthy.

It is what physicians used to be engaged in at the bedside of patients with diphtheria, meningitis, poliomyelitis, lobar pneumonia, and all the rest of the infectious diseases that have since come under control.

It is what physicians must now do for patients with intractable cancer, severe rheumatoid arthritis, multiple sclerosis, stroke, and advanced cirrhosis. One can think of at least twenty major diseases that require this kind of supportive medical care because of the absence of an effective technology. I would include a large amount of what is called mental disease, and most varieties of cancer, in this category.

The cost of this nontechnology is very high, and getting higher all the time. It requires not only a great deal of time but also very hard effort and skill on the part of physicians; only the very best of doctors are good at coping with this kind of defeat. It also involves long periods of hospitalization, lots of nursing, lots of involvement of nonmedical professionals in and out of the hospital. It represents, in short, a substantial segment of today's expenditures for health.

2. At the next level up is a kind of technology best termed "halfway technol- 10 ogy." This represents the kinds of things that must be done after the fact, in efforts to compensate for the incapacitating effects of certain diseases whose course one is unable to do very much about. It is a technology designed to make up for disease, or to postpone death.

The outstanding examples in recent years are the transplantations of hearts, kidneys, livers, and other organs, and the equally spectacular inventions of artificial organs. In the public mind, this kind of technology has come to seem like the equivalent of the high technologies of the physical sciences. The media tend to present each new procedure as though it represented a breakthrough and therapeutic triumph, instead of the makeshift that it really is.

In fact, this level of technology is, by its nature, at the same time highly sophisticated and profoundly primitive. It is the kind of thing that one must continue to do until there is a genuine understanding of the mechanisms involved in disease. In chronic glomerulonephritis, for example, a much clearer insight will be needed into the events leading to the destruction of glomeruli by the immunologic reactants that now appear to govern this disease, before one will know how to intervene intelligently to prevent the process, or turn it around. But when this level of understanding has been reached, the technology of kidney replacement will not be much needed and should no longer pose the huge problem of logistics, cost, and ethics that it poses today.

An extremely complex and costly technology for the management of coronary heart disease has evolved — involving specialized ambulances and hospital units, all kinds of electronic gadgetry, and whole platoons of new professional personnel — to deal with the end results of coronary thrombosis. Almost everything offered today for the treatment of heart disease is at this level of technology, with the transplanted and artificial hearts as ultimate examples. When enough has been learned to know what really goes wrong in heart disease, one ought to be in a position to figure out ways to prevent or reverse the process, and when this happens the current elaborate technology will probably be set to one side.

Much of what is done in the treatment of cancer, by surgery, irradiation, and chemotherapy, represents halfway technology, in the sense that these measures are directed at the existence of already established cancer cells, but not at the mechanisms by which cells become neoplastic.

It is a characteristic of this kind of technology that it costs an enormous amount of money and requires a continuing expansion of hospital facilities. There is no end to the need for new, highly trained people to run the enterprise. And there is really no way out of this, at the present state of knowledge. If the installation of specialized coronary-care units can result in the extension of life for only a few patients with coronary disease (and there is no question that this technology is effective in a few cases), it seems to me an inevitable fact of life that as many of these as can be will be put together, and as much money as can be found will be spent. I do not see that anyone has much choice in this. The only thing that can move medicine away from this level of technology is new information, and the only imaginable source of this information is research.

3. The third type of technology is the kind that is so effective that it seems to attract the least public notice; it has come to be taken for granted. This is the genuinely decisive technology of modern medicine, exemplified best by modern methods for immunization against diphtheria, pertussis, and the childhood virus diseases, and the contemporary use of antibiotics and chemotherapy for bacterial infections. The capacity to deal effectively with syphilis and tuberculosis represents a milestone in human endeavor, even though full use of this potential has not yet been made. And there are, of course, other examples: the treatment of endocrinologic disorders with appropriate hormones, the prevention of hemolytic

disease of the newborn, the treatment and prevention of various nutritional disorders, and perhaps just around the corner the management of Parkinsonism and sickle-cell anemia. There are other examples, and everyone will have his favorite candidates for the list, but the truth is that there are nothing like as many as the public has been led to believe.

The point to be made about this kind of technology—the real high technology of medicine—is that it comes as the result of a genuine understanding of disease mechanisms, and when it becomes available, it is relatively inexpensive, and relatively easy to deliver.

Offhand, I cannot think of any important human disease for which medicine possesses the outright capacity to prevent or cure where the cost of the technology is itself a major problem. The price is never as high as the cost of managing the same diseases during the earlier stages of no-technology or halfway technology. If a case of typhoid fever had to be managed today by the best methods of 1935, it would run to a staggering expense. At, say, around fifty days of hospitalization, requiring the most demanding kind of nursing care, with the obsessive concern for details of diet that characterized the therapy of that time, with daily laboratory monitoring, and, on occasion, surgical intervention for abdominal catastrophe, I should think $10,000 would be a conservative estimate for the illness, as contrasted with today's cost of a bottle of chloramphenicol and a day or two of fever. The halfway technology that was evolving for poliomyelitis in the early 1950s, just before the emergence of the basic research that made the vaccine possible, provides another illustration of the point. Do you remember Sister Kenny, and the cost of those institutes for rehabilitation, with all those ceremonially applied hot fomentations, and the debates about whether the affected limbs should be totally immobilized or kept in passive motion as frequently as possible, and the masses of statistically tormented data mobilized to support one view or the other? It is the cost of that kind of technology, and its relative effectiveness, that must be compared with the cost and effectiveness of the vaccine.

Pulmonary tuberculosis had similar episodes in its history. There was a sudden enthusiasm for the surgical removal of infected lung tissue in the early 1950s, and elaborate plans were being made for new and expensive installations for major pulmonary surgery in tuberculosis hospitals, and then INH and streptomycin came along and the hospitals themselves were closed up.

It is when physicians are bogged down by their incomplete technologies, by the innumerable things they are obliged to do in medicine when they lack a clear understanding of disease mechanisms, that the deficiencies of the health-care system are most conspicuous. If I were a policy-maker, interested in saving money for health care over the long haul, I would regard it as an act of high prudence to give high priority to a lot more basic research in biologic science. This is the only way to get the full mileage that biology owes to the science of medicine, even though it seems, as used to be said in the days when the phrase still had some meaning, like asking for the moon.

QUESTIONS FOR DISCUSSION AND WRITING

1. Why is "nontechnology" so valued by professionals and patients? Why is it so expensive, in human and in economic costs? (See paragraphs 5–9.)

2. Why does Thomas consider "halfway technology" (paragraph 10) "halfway"? Why does he consider it, despite media claims of "breakthrough" and "therapeutic triumph" (paragraph 11), to be "at the same time highly sophisticated and profoundly primitive" (paragraphs 12–15)? Why is "halfway technology" so costly?

3. If the "genuinely decisive technology of modern medicine" (paragraph 16), "the real, high technology of medicine" (paragraph 17), is inexpensive and effective, why is so little emphasis, attention, and policy directed toward "basic research in biological science" (paragraph 20) in comparison with the huge amounts of money and effort spent on nontechnology and halfway technology? Thomas made this argument in 1971; have there been significant changes in resource allocation since then? Explain.

4. Both Freeman Dyson (pp. 423–31) and Thomas are writing, as experts, for nonspecialized general readers. Both make assertions about and claims for science, based on their expertise. Yet Thomas is much easier to understand than Dyson is. Why? Consider in your answer the way each defines terms, the average length of sentences and paragraphs, and the sorts of evidence each scientist uses in making his argument. Because Thomas's writing is more accessible, are his arguments more or less compelling than Dyson's? Or is each equally convincing? Why or why not?

5. Write an essay for taxpayers arguing that Thomas's assertion that basic research in biological science should be more heavily supported than applied technological research, as the major way to keep health care costs manageable and at the same time to maintain effective quality of treatment.

STEPHEN JAY GOULD

Evolution as Fact and Theory

Stephen Jay Gould (1941–2002) was born in New York City, attended Antioch College (B.A., 1963) and Columbia University (Ph.D., 1967), and taught zoology at Harvard for thirty-five years. A MacArthur "genius" Fellow (1981–1986), his wide-ranging knowledge of the liberal arts enabled him to bridge scientific and humanistic learning and thus to make complex scientific concepts understandable to nonscientists. Gould's witty "This View of Life" columns in Natural History *are full of literary, musical, and historical learning. Collections of these columns include* The Panda's Thumb *(1980),* The Flamingo's Smile *(1985),* Bully for Brontosaurus *(1991), and* The Mismeasure of Man *(1981) on fallacies and abuses of intelligence testing. In* Full House: The Spread of Excellence from Plato to Darwin *(1996), he wrote that the "suppression of human arrogance [is] the common achievement of great scientific revolutions." An example of that arrogance, Gould often argues, is the belief that human beings are superior to all other creatures.*

"Evolution as Fact and Theory" first appeared in Discover *(May 1981). The readings following "Evolution as Fact and Theory" explore how scientists form definitions and how definitions can function politically, especially in the debate about creationism.*

Kirtley Mather, who died last year at age 89, was a pillar of both science and the Christian religion in America and one of my dearest friends. The difference of half a century in our ages evaporated before our common interests. The most curious thing we shared was a battle we each fought at the same age. For Kirtley had gone to Tennessee with Clarence Darrow to testify for evolution at the Scopes trial of 1925. When I think that we are enmeshed again in the same struggle for one of the best documented, most compelling and exciting concepts in all of science, I don't know whether to laugh or cry.

According to idealized principles of scientific discourse, the arousal of dormant issues should reflect fresh data that give renewed life to abandoned notions. Those outside the current debate may therefore be excused for suspecting that creationists have come up with something new, or that evolutionists have generated some serious internal trouble. But nothing has changed; the creationists have not a single new fact or argument. Darrow and Bryan were at least more entertaining than we lesser antagonists today. The rise of creationism is politics, pure and simple; it represents one issue (and by no means the major concern) of the resurgent evangelical right. Arguments that seemed kooky just a decade ago have re-entered the mainstream.

CREATIONISM IS NOT SCIENCE

The basic attack of the creationists falls apart on two general counts before we even reach the supposed factual details of their complaints against evolution. First, they play upon a vernacular misunderstanding of the word "theory" to convey the false impression that we evolutionists are covering up the rotten core of our edifice. Second, they misuse a popular philosophy of science to argue that they are behaving scientifically in attacking evolution. Yet the same philosophy demonstrates that their own belief is not science, and that "scientific creationism" is therefore meaningless and self-contradictory, a superb example of what Orwell called "newspeak."

In the American vernacular, "theory" often means "imperfect fact" — part of a hierarchy of confidence running downhill from fact to theory to hypothesis to guess. Thus the power of the creationist argument: evolution is "only" a theory, and intense debate now rages about many aspects of the theory. If evolution is less than a fact, and scientists can't even make up their minds about the theory, then what confidence can we have in it? Indeed, President Reagan echoed this argument before an evangelical group in Dallas when he said (in what I devoutly hope was campaign rhetoric): "Well, it is a theory. It is a scientific theory only, and it has in recent years been challenged in the world of science — that is, not believed in the scientific community to be as infallible as it once was."

Well, evolution *is* a theory. It is also a fact. And facts and theories are different
things, not rungs in a hierarchy of increasing certainty. Facts are the world's data.
Theories are structures of ideas that explain and interpret facts. Facts do not go away
when scientists debate rival theories to explain them. Einstein's theory of gravitation
replaced Newton's, but apples did not suspend themselves in mid-air pending the
outcome. And human beings evolved from apelike ancestors whether they did so by
Darwin's proposed mechanism or by some other, yet to be discovered.

Moreover, "fact" does not mean "absolute certainty." The final proofs of logic
and mathematics flow deductively from stated premises and achieve certainty
only because they are *not* about the empirical world. Evolutionists make no claim
for perpetual truth, though creationists often do (and then attack us for a style
of argument that they themselves favor). In science, "fact" can only mean "confirmed to such a degree that it would be perverse to withhold provisional assent."
I suppose that apples might start to rise tomorrow, but the possibility does not
merit equal time in physics classrooms.

Evolutionists have been clear about this distinction between fact and theory from the very beginning, if only because we have always acknowledged how
far we are from completely understanding the mechanisms (theory) by which
evolution (fact) occurred. Darwin continually emphasized the difference between
his two great and separate accomplishments: establishing the fact of evolution,
and proposing a theory—natural selection—to explain the mechanism of evolution. He wrote in *The Descent of Man*: "I had two distinct objects in view; firstly,
to show that species had not been separately created, and secondly, that natural
selection had been the chief agent of change. . . . Hence if I have erred in . . . having exaggerated its [natural selection's] power . . . I have at least, as I hope, done
good service in aiding to overthrow the dogma of separate creations."

Thus Darwin acknowledged the provisional nature of natural selection while
affirming the fact of evolution. The fruitful theoretical debate that Darwin initiated has never ceased. From the 1940s through the 1960s, Darwin's own theory
of natural selection did achieve a temporary hegemony that it never enjoyed in
his lifetime. But renewed debate characterizes our decade, and, while no biologist
questions the importance of natural selection, many now doubt its ubiquity. In
particular, many evolutionists argue that substantial amounts of genetic change
may not be subject to natural selection and may spread through populations at
random. Others are challenging Darwin's linking of natural selection with gradual, imperceptible change through all intermediary degrees; they are arguing that
most evolutionary events may occur far more rapidly than Darwin envisioned.

Scientists regard debates on fundamental issues of theory as a sign of
intellectual health and a source of excitement. Science is—and how else can I
say it?—most fun when it plays with interesting ideas, examines their implications, and recognizes that old information may be explained in surprisingly new
ways. Evolutionary theory is now enjoying this uncommon vigor. Yet amidst all
this turmoil no biologist has been led to doubt the fact that evolution occurred;
we are debating *how* it happened. We are all trying to explain the same thing: the

tree of evolutionary descent linking all organisms by ties of genealogy. Creationists pervert and caricature this debate by conveniently neglecting the common conviction that underlies it, and by falsely suggesting that we now doubt the very phenomenon we are struggling to understand.

Using another invalid argument, creationists claim that "the dogma of separate creations," as Darwin characterized it a century ago, is a scientific theory meriting equal time with evolution in high school biology curricula. But a prevailing viewpoint among philosophers of science belies this creationist argument. Philosopher Karl Popper has argued for decades that the primary criterion of science is the falsifiability of its theories. We can never prove absolutely, but we can falsify. A set of ideas that cannot, in principle, be falsified is not science.

The entire creationist argument involves little more than a rhetorical attempt to falsify evolution by presenting supposed contradictions among its supporters. Their brand of creationism, they claim, is "scientific" because it follows the Popperian model in trying to demolish evolution. Yet Popper's argument must apply in both directions. One does not become a scientist by the simple act of trying to falsify another scientific system; one has to present an alternative system that also meets Popper's criterion—it too must be falsifiable in principle.

"Scientific creationism" is a self-contradictory, nonsense phrase precisely because it cannot be falsified. I can envision observations and experiments that would disprove any evolutionary theory I know, but I cannot imagine what potential data could lead creationists to abandon their beliefs. Unbeatable systems are dogma, not science. Lest I seem harsh or rhetorical, I quote creationism's leading intellectual, Duane Gish, Ph.D., from his recent (1978) book *Evolution? The Fossils Say No!* "By creation we mean the bringing into being by a supernatural Creator of the basic kinds of plants and animals by the process of sudden, or fiat, creation. We do not know how the Creator created, what processes He used, *for He used processes which are not now operating anywhere in the natural universe* [Gish's italics]. This is why we refer to creation as special creation. We cannot discover by scientific investigations anything about the creative processes used by the Creator." Pray tell, Dr. Gish, in the light of your last sentence, what then is "scientific" creationism?

THE FACT OF EVOLUTION

Our confidence that evolution occurred centers upon three general arguments. First, we have abundant, direct, observational evidence of evolution in action, from both the field and the laboratory. It ranges from countless experiments on change in nearly everything about fruit flies subjected to artificial selection in the laboratory to the famous British moths that turned black when industrial soot darkened the trees upon which they rest. (The moths gain protection from sharp-sighted bird predators by blending into the background.) Creationists do not deny these observations; how could they? Creationists have tightened their act. They now argue that God only created "basic kinds," and allowed for limited evolutionary meandering within them. Thus toy poodles and Great Danes come from the dog kind and moths can change color, but nature cannot convert a dog to a cat or a monkey to a man.

The second and third arguments for evolution—the case for major changes—do not involve direct observation of evolution in action. They rest upon inference, but are no less secure for that reason. Major evolutionary change requires too much time for direct observation on the scale of recorded human history. All historical sciences rest upon inference, and evolution is no different from geology, cosmology, or human history in this respect. In principle, we cannot observe processes that operated in the past. We must infer them from results that still survive: living and fossil organisms for evolution, documents and artifacts for human history, strata and topography for geology.

The second argument—that the imperfection of nature reveals evolution— 15 strikes many people as ironic, for they feel that evolution should be most elegantly displayed in the nearly perfect adaptation expressed by some organisms— the chamber of a gull's wing, or butterflies that cannot be seen in ground litter because they mimic leaves so precisely. But perfection could be imposed by a wise creator or evolved by natural selection. Perfection covers the tracks of past history. And past history—the evidence of descent—is our mark of evolution.

Evolution lies exposed in the *imperfections* that record a history of descent. Why should a rat run, a bat fly, a porpoise swim, and I type this essay with structures built of the same bones unless we all inherited them from a common ancestor? An engineer, starting from scratch, could design better limbs in each case. Why should all the large native mammals of Australia be marsupials, unless they descended from a common ancestor isolated on this island continent? Marsupials are not "better," or ideally suited for Australia; many have been wiped out by placental mammals imported by man from other continents. This principle of imperfection extends to all historical sciences. When we recognize the etymology of September, October, November, and December (seventh, eighth, ninth, and tenth, from the Latin), we know that two additional items (January and February) must have been added to an original calendar of ten months.

The third argument is more direct: transitions are often found in the fossil record. Preserved transitions are not common—and should not be, according to our understanding of evolution (see next section)—but they are not entirely wanting, as creationists often claim. The lower jaw of reptiles contains several bones, that of mammals only one. The non-mammalian jawbones are reduced, step by step, in mammalian ancestors until they become tiny nubbins located at the back of the jaw. The "hammer" and "anvil" bones of the mammalian ear are descendants of these nubbins. How could such a transition be accomplished? the creationists ask. Surely a bone is either entirely in the jaw or in the ear. Yet paleontologists have discovered two transitional lineages or therapsids (the so-called mammal-like reptiles) with a double jaw joint—one composed of the old quadrate and articular bones (soon to become the hammer and anvil), the other of the squamosal and dentary bones (as in modern mammals). For that matter, what better transitional form could we desire than the oldest human, *Australopithecus afarensis*, with its apelike palate, its human upright stance, and a cranial capacity larger than any ape's of the same body size but a full 1,000 cubic centimeters below ours? If God made each of the half dozen human species discovered in ancient rocks, why did he create in an unbroken temporal sequence of progressively more modern features—increasing cranial capacity, reduced face and teeth, larger body size? Did he create to mimic evolution and test our faith thereby?

AN EXAMPLE OF CREATIONIST ARGUMENT

Faced with these facts of evolution and the philosophical bankruptcy of their own position, creationists rely upon distortion and innuendo to buttress their rhetorical claim. If I should sound sharp or bitter, indeed I am—for I have become a major target of these practices.

I count myself among the evolutionists who argue for a jerky, or episodic, rather than a smoothly gradual, pace of change. In 1972 my colleague Niles Eldredge and I developed the theory of punctuated equilibrium. We argued that two outstanding facts of the fossil record—geologically "sudden" origin of new species and failure to change thereafter (stasis)—reflect the predictions of evolutionary theory, not the imperfections of the fossil record. In most theories, small isolated populations are the source of new species, and the process of speciation takes thousands or tens of thousands of years. This amount of time, so long when measured against our lives, is a geological microsecond. It represents much less than 1 percent of the average life span for a fossil invertebrate species—more than 10 million years. Large, widespread, and well-established species, on the other hand, are not expected to change very much. We believe that the inertia of large populations explains the stasis of most fossil species over millions of years.

We proposed the theory of punctuated equilibrium largely to provide a differ- 20 ent explanation for pervasive trends in the fossil record. Trends, we argued, cannot be attributed to gradual transformation within lineages, but must arise from the differential success of certain kinds of species. A trend, we argued, is more like climbing a flight of stairs (punctuations and stasis) than rolling up an inclined plane.

Since we proposed punctuated equilibria to explain trends, it is infuriating to be quoted again and again by creationists—whether through design or stupidity, I do not know—as admitting that the fossil record includes no transitional forms. Transitional forms are generally lacking at the species level, but are abundant between larger groups. The evolution from reptiles to mammals, as mentioned earlier, is well documented. Yet a pamphlet entitled "Harvard Scientists Agree Evolution Is a Hoax" states: "The facts of punctuated equilibrium which Gould and Eldredge . . . are forcing Darwinists to swallow fit the picture that Bryan insisted on, and which God has revealed to us in the Bible."

Continuing the distortion, several creationists have equated the theory of punctuated equilibrium with a caricature of the beliefs of Richard Goldschmidt, a great early geneticist. Goldschmidt argued, in a famous book published in 1940, that new groups can arise all at once through major mutations. He referred to these suddenly transformed creatures as "hopeful monsters." (I am attracted to some aspects of the non-caricatured version, but Goldschmidt's theory still has nothing to do with punctuated equilibrium.) Creationist Luther Sunderland talks of the "punctuated equilibrium hopeful monster theory" and tells his hopeful readers that "it amounts to tacit admission that anti-evolutionists are correct in asserting there is no fossil evidence supporting the theory that all life is connected to a common ancestor." Duane Gish writes, "According to Goldschmidt, and now apparently according to Gould, a reptile laid an egg from which the first bird, feathers and all, was produced." Any evolutionist who believed such nonsense would rightly be laughed off the intellectual stage; yet the only theory that could ever envision such a scenario for the evolution of birds is creationism—God acts in the egg.

CONCLUSION

I am both angry at and amused by the creationists; but mostly I am deeply sad. Sad for many reasons. Sad because so many people who respond to creationist appeals are troubled for the right reason, but venting their anger at the wrong target. It is true that scientists have often been dogmatic and elitist. It is true that we have often allowed the white-coated, advertising image to represent us—"Scientists say that Brand X cures bunions ten times faster than . . ." We have not fought it adequately because we derive benefits from appearing as a new priesthood. It is also true that faceless bureaucratic state power intrudes more and more into our lives and removes choices that should belong to individuals and communities. I can understand that requiring that evolution be taught in schools might be seen as one more insult on all these grounds. But the culprit is not, and cannot be, evolution or any other fact of the natural world. Identify and fight your legitimate enemies by all means, but we are not among them.

I am sad because the practical result of this brouhaha will not be expanded coverage to include creationism (that would also make me sad), but the reduction or excision of evolution from high school curricula. Evolution is one of the half dozen "great ideas" developed by science. It speaks to the profound issues of genealogy that fascinate all of us—the "roots" phenomenon writ large. Where did we come from? Where did life arise? How did it develop? How are organisms related? It forces us to think, ponder, and wonder. Shall we deprive millions of this knowledge and once again teach biology as a set of dull and unconnected facts, without the thread that weaves diverse material into a supple unity?

But most of all I am saddened by a trend I am just beginning to discern among 25 my colleagues. I sense that some now wish to mute the healthy debate about theory that has brought new life to evolutionary biology. It provides grist for creationist mills, they say, even if only by distortion. Perhaps we should lie low and rally round the flag of strict Darwinism, at least for the moment—a kind of old-time religion on our part.

But we should borrow another metaphor and recognize that we too have to tread a straight and narrow path, surrounded by roads to perdition. For if we ever begin to suppress our search to understand nature, to quench our own intellectual excitement in a misguided effort to present a united front where it does not and should not exist, then we are truly lost.

CONTEXTS FOR "EVOLUTION AS FACT AND THEORY"

THOMAS HENRY HUXLEY
Evolution and Ethics

Man, the animal, in fact, has worked his way to the headship of the sentient world, and has become the superb animal which he is, in virtue of his success in the struggle for existence. The conditions having been of a certain order, man's organization has adjusted itself to them better than that of his competitors in the cosmic strife. In the case of mankind, the self-assertion, the unscrupulous seizing upon all that can be grasped, the tenacious holding of all that can be kept, which constitute the essence of the struggle for existence, have answered. For his successful progress, throughout the savage state, man has been largely indebted to those qualities which he shares with the ape and the tiger; his exceptional physical organization; his cunning, his sociability, his curiosity, and his imitativeness; his ruthless and ferocious destructiveness when his anger is roused by opposition.

But, in proportion as men have passed from anarchy to social organization, and in proportion as civilization has grown in worth, these deeply ingrained serviceable qualities have become defects. After the manner of successful persons, civilized man would gladly kick down the ladder by which he has climbed. He would be only too pleased to see "the ape and tiger die." But they decline to suit his convenience; and the unwelcome intrusion of these boon companions of his hot youth into the ranged existence of civil life adds pains and griefs, innumerable and immeasurably great, to those which the cosmic process necessarily brings on the mere animal. In fact, civilized man brands all these ape and tiger promptings with the name of sins; he punishes many of the acts which flow from them as crimes; and, in extreme cases, he does his best to put an end to the survival of the fittest of former days by axe and rope.

DEFINING "THEORY"

As Gould explains in paragraphs 10 and 11 of "Evolution as Fact and Theory," the feature that differentiates scientific theory from theory in other fields is its "falsifiability." In the sixteenth century, Sir Francis Bacon argued that a scientific theory is confirmed by accumulated empirical evidence in its favor. This positive empirical evidence is only half the story, however, as the twentieth-century philosopher Karl Popper argues in *The Logic of Scientific Discovery* (1959), a translation of *Logik der Forschung* (1935). The other half is counterevidence, which scientists must also seek in order to discover where a theory breaks down. This counterevidence may consist of newly available empirical evidence, anomalies newly

From Thomas Henry Huxley, "Evolution and Ethics," in *Evolution and Ethics and Other Essays* (New York: Appleton, 1893), 50–52.

detected in the old evidence, or changes in what scientists agree "counts" as evidence. A scientific revolution begins when an old theory is increasingly questioned and a new theory gradually gains scientists' acceptance. The new agreement is what Thomas Kuhn, in his well-known 1962 article "The Historical Structure of Scientific Discovery," calls a "paradigm shift." Thus, what we consider scientific knowledge is only a set of beliefs that we have not yet been able to break or "falsify." What counts as scientific knowledge, then, does go through changes, and evolution is no exception.

Paleontologists acknowledge that there are "gaps" in the physical evidence for the evolution of certain species—that is, not all of the fossil remains that demonstrate a steady change in a species have been found. Thus, paleontologists must infer the existence of certain structures at various stages of a species' development, as Gould notes in "Evolution and the Triumph of Homology" (1986), where he further explains that Darwin's scientific methodology was also historical (in the sense that, in the absence of a full documentary record, historians infer connections from one event to another). The "gaps" in the fossil record are not, however, to be confused with the "gaps" or flaws in scientific reasoning.

Theories in fields other than science are not "falsifiable" in the same sense. Positive evidence may be found to support them, and counterevidence may break them. But that evidence is not entirely empirical. For example, historians may explain events through Marxist theory (which rests only in part on "hard" economic data) or "great man" theory, but evidence for either theory does not "break" the other. The two theories can coexist. The social sciences (anthropology, economics, psychology, and sociology), as their name implies, may be more or less scientific, depending on the falsifiability of particular claims. However, cultural elements prevent the social sciences from being as scientific, or as "falsifiable," as the natural sciences. Religious belief rests on sacred texts such as Genesis, which some believers take to be literally the word of God. There may be positive empirical evidence for some passages in sacred texts, but the belief that they are the word of the divine is just that: belief, not empirically falsifiable fact. Gould calls these entirely separate yet authoritative teachings "Nonoverlapping Magisteria" (1997). (A *magisterium* is an authoritative teaching.) Neither teaching "breaks" the other, yet one is empirical and the other is moral.

PHILLIP E. JOHNSON

The Unraveling of Scientific Materialism

Creationist Phillip E. Johnson, professor of law at the University of California at Berkeley, argues in this essay that paleontologists lack proof of evolution because the fossil record is incomplete, a fact paleontologists readily acknowledge. Johnson does not, however,

From Phillip E. Johnson, "The Unraveling of Scientific Materialism," *First Things: A Monthly Journal of Religion and Public Life* 77 (November 1997): 22–25.

dispute the positive evidence through which paleontologists infer developmental stages from the fossil records that are available. Rather, Johnson rejects Gould's argument in "Nonoverlapping Magisteria" because, he writes, Gould denies religion's "power to determine the facts" or to "make an independent judgment about the evidence that supports the 'facts.'"

Not even the strictest biblical literalists deny the bred varieties of dogs, the variation of finch beaks, and similar instances within types. The more controversial claims of large-scale evolution are what arouse skepticism. Scientists may think they have good reasons for believing that living organisms evolved naturally from nonliving chemicals, or that complex organs evolved by the accumulation of micromutations through natural selection, but having reasons is not the same as having proof. I have seen people, previously inclined to believe whatever "science says," become skeptical when they realize that the scientists actually do seem to think that variations in finch beaks or peppered moths, or the mere existence of fossils, proves all the vast claims of "evolution." It is as though the scientists, so confident in their answers, simply do not understand the question.

The reason for opposition to scientific accounts of our origins, according to [Richard C.] Lewontin, is not that people are ignorant of facts, but that they have not learned to think from the right starting point. In his words, "The primary problem is not to provide the public with the knowledge of how far it is to the nearest star and what genes are made of. . . . Rather, the problem is to get them to reject irrational and supernatural explanations of the world, the demons that exist only in their imaginations, and to accept a social and intellectual apparatus, Science, as the only begetter of truth." What the public needs to learn is that, like it or not, "We exist as material beings in a material world, all of whose phenomena are the consequences of material relations among material entities." In a word, the public needs to accept materialism, which means that they must put God (whom Lewontin calls the "Supreme Extraterrestrial") in the trash can of history where such myths belong.

Although Lewontin wants the public to accept science as the only source of truth, he freely admits that mainstream science itself is not free of the hokum that Sagan so often found in fringe science. . . .

Lewontin laments that even scientists frequently cannot judge the reliability of scientific claims outside their fields of speciality, and have to take the word of recognized authorities on faith. . . .

Lewontin is brilliantly insightful, but too crankily honest to be as good a manipu- 5
lator as his Harvard colleague Stephen Jay Gould. Gould displays both his talent and his unscrupulousness in an essay in the March 1997 issue of *Natural History*, entitled "Nonoverlapping Magisteria" and subtitled "Science and religion are not in conflict, for their teachings occupy distinctly different domains." With a subtitle like that, you can be sure that Gould is out to reassure the public that

evolution leads to no alarming conclusions. True to form, Gould insists that the only dissenters from evolution are "Protestant fundamentalists who believe that every word of the Bible must be literally true." Gould also insists that evolution (he never defines the word) is "both true and entirely compatible with Christian belief." Gould is familiar with nonliteralist opposition to evolutionary naturalism, but he blandly denies that any such phenomenon exists. . . .

The centerpiece of Gould's essay is an analysis of the complete text of Pope John Paul's statement of October 22, 1996, to the Pontifical Academy of Sciences endorsing evolution as "more than a hypothesis." He fails to quote the Pope's crucial qualification that "theories of evolution which, in accordance with the philosophies inspiring them, consider the spirit as emerging from the forces of living matter or as a mere epiphenomenon of this matter, are incompatible with the truth about man." Of course, a theory based on materialism assumes by definition that there is no "spirit" active in this world that is independent of matter. Gould knows this perfectly well, and he also knows, just as Richard Lewontin does, that the evidence doesn't support the claims for the creative power of natural selection made by writers such as Richard Dawkins. That is why the philosophy that really supports the theory has to be protected from critical scrutiny.

Gould's essay is a tissue of half-truths aimed at putting the religious people to sleep, or luring them into a "dialogue" on terms set by the materialists. Thus Gould graciously allows religion to participate in discussions of morality or the meaning of life, because science does not claim authority over such questions of value, and because "Religion is too important to too many people for any dismissal or denigration of the comfort still sought by many folks from theology." Gould insists, however, that all such discussion must cede to science the power to determine the *facts*, and one of the facts is an evolutionary process that is every bit as materialistic and purposeless for Gould as it is for Lewontin or Dawkins. If religion wants to accept a dialogue on those terms, that's fine with Gould—but don't let those religious people think they get to make an independent judgment about the evidence that supposedly supports the "facts." And if the religious people are gullible enough to accept materialism as one of the facts, they won't be capable of causing much trouble.

POLITICAL DIMENSIONS OF DEFINITION

The term *newspeak* (which Gould mentions in paragraph 3 of "Evolution as Fact and Theory") was coined by George Orwell in his novel *Nineteen Eighty-Four* (1949) to contrast with oldspeak (or Standard English). Orwell defined it, in part, as the practice of stripping words of certain meanings that do not serve the particular political beliefs of Ingsoc, or "English Socialism":

> The purpose of Newspeak was not only to provide a medium of expression for the world view and mental habits proper to the devotees of Ingsoc,

but to make all other modes of thought impossible. It was intended that when Newspeak had been adopted once and for all and Oldspeak forgotten, a heretical thought—that is, a thought diverged from the principles of Ingsoc—should be literally unthinkable . . .

Gould calls "scientific creationism" an example of newspeak. Creationism's argument that evolution is "just a theory" involves stripping two essential meanings—empirically grounded and falsifiable—from the scientific definition of theory. Hence, *scientific creationism* is a contradiction in terms. Similarly, creationism's argument that a gap in the fossil record constitutes a gap in the theory of evolution blurs two distinct definitions: absence and logical flaw.

JAMES GLEICK

Stephen Jay Gould: Breaking Tradition with Darwin

A decade ago, [Gould] and Niles Eldredge, a fellow paleontologist at the American Museum of Natural History in New York, broke with orthodox Darwinism by proposing a new model for the pace of evolutionary change. The traditional view was, and is, that big changes are made gradually, by the accumulation of many tiny changes over eons. Gould and Eldredge, joined now by many other American and British paleontologists, argue for a theory of fits and starts. Most important change, they believe, takes place in the geological instant when a new species is born—a long instant, to be sure, lasting perhaps 5,000 to 50,000 years, but virtually no time at all compared to the millions of years most species survive. After that first burst of change comes a long period of stability.

The fits-and-starts theory—known as punctuated equilibrium, or, familiarly, as "punk eke"—addresses one of the great nuisances of evolutionary theory, the fossil record. As creationists love to point out, the evidence preserved in the earth's rocks shows many species virtually unchanged throughout their histories, with precious few transitional stages between them. Darwin and his successors have had to argue that the fossil record is incomplete by its very nature, preserving only a tiny fraction of organisms and preserving them at unreliable intervals. Gould and Eldredge ask whether the rocks might not after all be telling a true story. Perhaps transitional stages rarely appear because their existence really was brief.

This initial break with Neo-Darwinism, now accepted by many in the field, gave the modern debates their shape, but its implications have remained poorly understood except by specialists.

From James Gleick, "Stephen Jay Gould: Breaking Tradition with Darwin," *New York Times Magazine,* November 20, 1983, 54–56.

One piece of evolutionary theory that has firmly established itself in the way we think about human origins is the idea that we descended from our primate ancestors by continuously improving features such as brain size. Gould and Eldredge challenge that, suggesting that the important history of human ancestors is not a matter of gradual improvement, but of new humanlike species splitting off from the old. Our evolutionary history is more like a copiously branching bush than a ladder toward perfection. The new species probably formed quickly in small, geographically isolated populations and from then on, Gould and Eldredge argue, they remained more or less static.

"So that at any one time," Eldredge suggests, "you might have two or three   5 species of various brain sizes, and the long-term winners of their competition would be the bigger-brained species. It's an analogue of natural selection at the species level."

A major area of contention to flow from punctuated equilibrium is just this suggestion—that individuals are not the only players on the evolutionary stage. Perhaps species or local populations or even genes can be targets of natural selection. That is the basis of the hierarchical model of evolution that Gould and others are building—a model meant to explain the great events, the birth and death of species and the reshaping of ecosystems.

Whether natural selection is sorting individuals or species, it is still a process of adaptation—and the traditional view remains that what we are, what we have made ourselves, arises from usefulness in survival and reproduction. Gould challenges that as well.

"I don't doubt for a moment that there was a conventional selective reason for our large brain," he said. "That reason's probably complex—there are a whole host of interrelated advantages of large brains. What I do want to say very strongly is that most of what our brains do—most of what is essential to our considering of ourselves as being human—is not directly selected for, is not a product of natural selection, but arises as a nonadaptive structural consequence of building a computer so powerful as the human brain.

"To give just one example: The most terrible fact that the evolution of the large brain allowed us to learn is the fact of our personal mortality. Think of how much of the architecture of human culture and cultural traditions, how much of human religion, for example, arises and attempts to deal with that terrible fact, which we have come to learn as a result of the complex structure of our brain. You can't argue the brain became large *so that* we would learn the fact of our coming personal mortality."

QUESTIONS FOR DISCUSSION AND WRITING

1. In "Evolution as Fact and Theory," Gould distinguishes between "the mechanisms (theory) by which evolution (fact) occurred" (paragraph 7). How does this definition serve Gould's purpose?

2. After reading these selections, write an essay on the media's role in the development of science. How does Gould view scientific endeavor and the public role of the scientist? How does public debate shape scientific disagreement and consensus?

3. Huxley writes in "Evolution and Ethics" that "civilized man brands all these ape and tiger promptings with the name of sins" (paragraph 2). How might Huxley and Gould define sin? What might each argue are the social purposes of his definition of sin?

4. Edward O. Wilson explains that "success by organisms can ultimately be disastrous for their species" ("Microbes 3, Humans 2," p. 476, paragraph 3). In view of Gould's theory of "punctuated equilibrium" (see Gleick's "Stephen Jay Gould: Breaking Tradition with Darwin"), what implications might Gould draw from the observation that an organism's success can jeopardize the survival of its species?

5. Gould writes in "Evolution as Fact and Theory" that science is "most fun when it plays with interesting ideas [and] examines their implications" (paragraph 9). On what basis, then, does Gould exclude creationism from this set of "interesting ideas"?

6. After reading the selections in this chapter, including Darwin's "Understanding Natural Selection" (p. 451), write an essay on the process through which "facts" become accepted as such.

7. In *Darwin Loves You: Natural Selection and the Re-enchantment of the World* (2006), George Levine claims that through his literary style Darwin expressed "almost mystical awe at the sheer existence of life in the universe; Darwin disenchanted believers in Heaven, but he reënchanted lovers of Earth" (Adam Gopnik, "Rewriting Nature," *New Yorker*, October 23, 2006, p. 59). In what ways is this enchantment manifested in the essays by Gould and Darwin included here?

MARISA ACOCELLA MARCHETTO

How Chemo Works

QUESTIONS FOR DISCUSSION AND WRITING

1. Charts, diagrams, models, and cartoons—such as "Better Signs of Trouble" (by Scher, Fogelson-Lubliner, Brody and Knowles; Henry Groskinsky's "Replaceable You" (p. 410); Scott McCloud's "Reading the Comics" (p. 51), and Marchetto's "How Chemo Works"—are often used to provide explanations of complicated phenomena. Is one picture worth a thousand words? Always? Necessarily? Which of the visual representations above is the clearest? The wittiest? Which, if any, needs more explanation?

2. Marchetto's cartoon panel, one small element of a two-hundred-page cartoon autobiography, *Cancer Vixen* (Knopf 2006), is more of a commentary than a scientific explanation. This cartoon is in keeping with Marchetto's irreverent, witty, in-your-face attitude toward her treatment for breast cancer. What facts and explanation of a process does she provide? What else do you need to know?

3. If you needed a scientific explanation of "How Chemo Works," what scientific sources would be good to consult?

CHARLES DARWIN

Understanding Natural Selection

Charles Darwin (1809–1882) was the first to establish the concept of evolution by natural selection, the biological process through which species change and adapt over time. Born in Shrewsbury, England, Darwin was always more interested in direct observation and specimen collecting than in his formal studies, whether in medical school at the University of Edinburgh or divinity school at Cambridge University (B.A., 1831). In 1831 to 1836, he voyaged to South America and the South Pacific aboard the HMS Beagle, *recording in his journal his meticulous observations of flora and fauna, from trees to insects. Published in 1839, this journal remains a classic of natural history. After taking careful notes and collecting specimens, Darwin began to work privately on his hypothesis that within species "favorable variations would tend to be preserved, and unfavorable ones to be destroyed," leading to the gradual formation of new species. His theory, published as* On the Origin of Species by Means of Natural Selection *(1859), is the source of the following excerpt.*

In "Understanding Natural Selection," Darwin explains that variations within a species endure if those variations aid in survival or enhance reproduction. Through genetic mutation, some members of a species will be more likely to produce offspring who will increase in number compared to those of less well-adapted members, and a new species may arise.

Although natural selection can act only through and for the good of each being, yet characters and structures, which we are apt to consider as of very trifling importance, may thus be acted on. When we see leaf-eating insects green, and bark-feeders mottled-grey; the alpine ptarmigan white in winter, the red-grouse the color of heather, and the black-grouse that of peaty earth, we must believe that these tints are of service to these birds and insects in preserving them from danger. Grouse, if not destroyed at some period of their lives, would increase in countless numbers; they are known to suffer largely from birds of prey; and hawks are guided by eyesight to their prey—so much so, that on parts of the Continent persons are warned not to keep white pigeons, as being the most liable to destruction. Hence I can see no reason to doubt that natural selection might be most effective in giving the proper color to each kind of grouse, and in keeping that color, when once acquired, true and constant. Nor ought we to think that the occasional destruction of an animal of any particular color would produce little effect: we should remember how essential it is in a flock of white sheep to destroy every lamb with the faintest trace of black. In plants the down on the fruit and the color of the flesh are considered by botanists as characters of the most trifling importance: yet we hear from an excellent horticulturist, Downing, that in the United States smooth-skinned fruits suffer far more from a beetle, a curculio, than those with down; that purple plums suffer far more from a certain disease than yellow plums; whereas another disease attacks yellow-fleshed peaches far more than those with other colored flesh. If, with all the aids of art, these slight differences make a great difference in cultivating the several varieties, assuredly, in a state of nature, where the trees would have to struggle with other trees and with a host of enemies, such differences would effectually settle which variety, whether a smooth or downy, a yellow or purple fleshed fruit, should succeed.

In looking at many small points of difference between species, which, as far as our ignorance permits us to judge, seem to be quite unimportant, we must not forget that climate, food, and so on probably produce some slight and direct effect. It is, however, far more necessary to bear in mind that there are many unknown laws of correlation to growth, which, when one part of the organization is modified through variation, and the modifications are accumulated by natural selection for the good of the being, will cause other modifications, often of the most unexpected nature.

As we see that those variations which under domestication appear at any particular period of life, tend to reappear in the offspring of the same period; for instance, in the seeds of the many varieties of our culinary and agricultural plants; in the caterpillar and cocoon stages of the varieties of the silkworm; in the eggs of poultry, and in the color of the down of their chickens; in the horns of our sheep and cattle when nearly adult; so in a state of nature, natural selection will be enabled to act on and modify organic beings at any age, by the accumulation of profitable variations at that age, and by their inheritance at a corresponding age. If it profit a plant to have its seeds more and more widely disseminated by the wind, I can see no greater difficulty in this being effected through natural selection, than in the cotton-planter increasing and improving by selection the down in the pods on his cotton-trees. Natural selection may modify and adapt the larva of an insect to a score of contingencies, wholly different from those which concern the mature insect. These modifications will no doubt affect, through the laws of correlation, the structure of the adult; and probably in the case of those insects which live only for a few hours, and which never feed, a large part of their structure is merely the correlated result of successive changes in the structure of their larvae. So, conversely, modifications in the adult will probably often affect the structure of the larva; but in all cases natural selection will ensure that modifications consequent on other modifications at a different period of life, shall not be in the least degree injurious: for if they became so, they would cause the extinction of the species.

Natural selection will modify the structure of the young in relation to the parent, and of the parent in relation to the young. In social animals it will adapt the structure of each individual for the benefit of the community; if each in consequence profits by the selected change. What natural selection cannot do, is to modify the structure of one species, without giving it any advantage, for the good of another species; and though statements to this effect may be found in works of natural history, I cannot find one case which will bear investigation. A structure used only once in an animal's whole life, if of high importance to it, might be modified to any extent by natural selection; for instance, the great jaws possessed by certain insects, and used exclusively for opening the cocoon — or the hard tip to the beak of nestling birds, used for breaking the egg. It has been asserted, that of the best short-beaked tumbler pigeons more perish in the egg than are able to get out of it; so that fanciers assist in the act of hatching.

Now, if nature had to make the beak of a full-grown pigeon very short for the bird's own advantage, the process of modification would be very slow, and there would be simultaneously the most rigorous selection of the young birds within the egg, which had the most powerful and hardest beaks, for all with weak beaks would inevitably perish: or, more delicate and more easily broken shells might be selected, the thickness of the shell being known to vary like every other structure.

SEXUAL SELECTION

Inasmuch as peculiarities often appear under domestication in one sex and become   5 hereditarily attached to that sex, the same fact probably occurs under nature, and if so, natural selection will be able to modify one sex in its functional relations to the other sex, or in relation to wholly different habits of life in the two sexes, as is sometimes the case with insects. And this leads me to say a few words on what I call sexual selection. This depends, not on a struggle for existence, but on a struggle between the males for possession of the females; the result is not death to the unsuccessful competitor, but few or no offspring. Sexual selection is, therefore, less rigorous than natural selection. Generally, the most vigorous males, those which are best fitted for their places in nature, will leave most progeny. But in many cases, victory will depend not on general vigor, but on having special weapons, confined to the male sex. A hornless stag or spurless cock would have a poor chance of leaving offspring. Sexual selection by always allowing the victor to breed might surely give indomitable courage, length to the spur, and strength to the wing to strike in the spurred leg, as well as the brutal cock-fighter, who knows well that he can improve his breed by careful selection of the best cocks. How low in the scale of nature this law of battle descends, I know not; male alligators have been described as fighting, bellowing, and whirling round, like Indians in a war dance, for the possession of the females; male salmons have been seen fighting all day long; male stag beetles often bear wounds from the huge mandibles of other males. The war is, perhaps, severest between the males of polygamous animals, and these seem oftenest provided with special weapons. The males of carnivorous animals are already well armed; though to them and to others, special means of defence may be given through means of sexual selection, as the mane to the lion, the shoulder-pad to the boar, and the hooked jaw to the male salmon, for the shield may be as important for victory, as the sword or spear.

Amongst birds, the contest is often of a more peaceful character. All those who have attended to the subject, believe that there is the severest rivalry between the males of many species to attract by singing to the females. The rock-thrush of Guiana, birds of Paradise, and some others, congregate; and successive males display their gorgeous plumage and perform strange antics before the females, which standing by as spectators, at last choose the most attractive partner. Those who have closely attended to birds in confinement well know that they often take individual preferences and dislikes: thus Sir R. Heron has described how one pied peacock was eminently attractive to all his hen birds. It may appear childish to attribute any effect to such apparently weak means: I cannot here enter on the details necessary to support this view; but if man can in a short time give elegant carriage and beauty to his bantams, according to his standard of beauty, I can see no good reason to doubt that female birds, by selecting, during thousands of generations, the most melodious or beautiful males, according to their standard of beauty, might produce a marked effect. I strongly suspect that some well-known laws with respect to the plumage of male and female birds, in comparison with the plumage of the young, can be explained on the view of plumage having been chiefly modified by sexual selection, acting when the birds have come to the breeding age or during the breeding season; the modifications thus produced being inherited at corresponding ages or seasons, either by the males alone, or by the males and females; but I have not space here to enter on this subject.

Thus it is, as I believe, that when the males and females of any animal have the same general habits of life, but differ in structure, color, or ornament, such differences have been mainly caused by sexual selection; that is, individual males have had, in successive generations, some slight advantage over other males, in their weapons, means of defence, or charms; and have transmitted these advantages to their male offspring. Yet, I would not wish to attribute all such sexual differences to this agency: for we see peculiarities arising and becoming attached to the male sex in our domestic animals (as the wattle in male carriers, horn-like protuberances in the cocks of certain fowls, and so on), which we cannot believe to be either useful to the males in battle, or attractive to the females. We see analogous cases under nature, for instance, the tuft of hair on the breast of the turkey-cock, which can hardly be either useful or ornamental to this bird; indeed, had the tuft appeared under domestication, it would have been called a monstrosity.

ILLUSTRATION OF THE ACTION
OF NATURAL SELECTION

... Let us take the case of a wolf, which preys on various animals, securing some by craft, some by strength, and some by fleetness; and let us suppose that the fleetest prey, a deer for instance, had from any change in the country increased in numbers, or that other prey had decreased in numbers, during that season of the year when the wolf is hardest pressed for food. I can under such circumstances see no reason to doubt that the swiftest and slimmest wolves would have the best chance of surviving, and so be preserved or selected—provided always that they retain strength to master their prey at this or at some other period of the year, when they might be compelled to prey on other animals. I can see no more reason to doubt this, than that man can improve the fleetness of his greyhounds by careful and methodical selection, or by that unconscious selection which results from each man trying to keep the best dogs without any thought of modifying the breed.

Even without any change in the proportional numbers of the animals on which our wolf preyed, a cub might be born with an innate tendency to pursue certain kinds of prey. Nor can this be thought very improbable; for we often observe great differences in the natural tendencies of our domestic animals; one cat, for instance, taking to catch rats, another mice; one cat . . . bringing home winged game, another hares or rabbits, and another hunting on marshy ground and almost nightly catching woodcocks or snipes. The tendency to catch rats rather than mice is known to be inherited. Now, if any slight innate change of habit or of structure benefited an individual wolf, it would have the best chance of surviving and of leaving offspring. Some of its young would probably inherit the same habits or structure, and by the repetition of this process, a new variety might be formed which would either supplant or coexist with the parent-form of wolf. Or, again, the wolves inhabiting a mountainous district, and those frequenting the lowlands, would naturally be forced to hunt different prey; and from the continued preservation of the individuals best fitted for the two sites, two varieties might slowly be formed. . . .

QUESTIONS FOR DISCUSSION AND WRITING

1. What is "natural selection"? Why, according to Darwin, is it difficult for people to see natural selection at work?

2. What is the effect of subtle variations within a species, according to Darwin?

3. What does Darwin mean by "sexual selection" (paragraph 5)? How does it help explain variations among males and among females of a species? How does sexual selection differ from natural selection?

4. What examples does Darwin use to support his argument for natural selection? Do you find some examples more persuasive than others? If so, which ones? Read Stephen Jay Gould's "Evolution as Fact and Theory" (p. 437) for a fuller understanding of this subject. How does Gould help you understand Darwin's argument?

5. Did you find any of Darwin's writing difficult to follow? If so, what parts? What might account for their difficulty?

Instructor's Manual
for

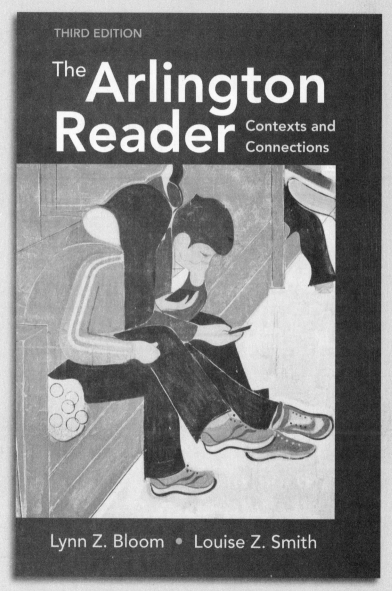

THIRD EDITION

The **Arlington Reader**
Contexts and Connections

Lynn Z. Bloom • Louise Z. Smith

Carole Center • Denise M. Lovett
Matthew Simpson • Ning Yu

INSTRUCTOR'S MANUAL
FOR

THE
ARLINGTON READER

INSTRUCTOR'S MANUAL
FOR

THE
ARLINGTON READER

Contexts and Connections

Third Edition

Prepared by

Carole Center
University of Massachusetts–Boston

Denise M. Lovett
University of Connecticut

Matthew Simpson
University of Connecticut

Ning Yu
Western Washington University

Bedford/St. Martin's
Boston ◆ New York

Preface

The Instructor's Manual for *The Arlington Reader: Contexts and Connections* is designed not so much to provide "standard answers" to the study questions following each essay in *The Arlington Reader* as to offer an overview of the rich materials included in the text and its unique organization. We are aware that each instructor has his or her own agenda in the classroom as informed by the needs of students, yet we'd like to note that the conception and structure of *The Arlington Reader* itself suggest ways of maximizing its benefits to student writers. They are the emphases on Contexts and Connections, as revealed in the subtitle.

We provide four sample syllabi to help instructors plan day-to-day schedules for in-class activities, reading and writing assignments, and independent projects. These syllabi include (1) an introductory semester-long composition course, (2) an introductory composition course for freshman students in the quarter system, (3) an upper-division writing course emphasizing contextuality and research (including library research and field notes) for the semester system, and (4) a similar course for the quarter system. These syllabi only begin to suggest the text's versatility and the vast possibilities for instructors to use it creatively.

The bulk of this manual is composed of sample responses to the Questions for Discussion and Writing that follow each essay in the text. We designed these deliberately open-ended questions to stimulate independent thinking and generate further exploration of issues under discussion. Therefore, this manual provides possible responses rather than definitive answers to the study questions. For the writing assignments and research questions, we trust individual instructors will find the best ways to use them according to the specific needs and skills of their students. Many of these questions give students opportunities to connect their reading and writing experience with their personal lives and their views on social issues, thereby encouraging them to become mature, independent, and responsible thinkers, critics, and co-makers of the canons and of our culture.

Contents

2   Identity with Attitude: Who am I, and why does it matter?   46

3   Relationships and Life Choices: Life, love, work, play— what's the best balance?   66

4 **Education and the American Character: What do we teach? What do we learn? And why does this matter? 84**

5 **Wired—Be Careful What We Wish For: What are the consequences of life in the high-tech fast lane? 105**

SAMPLE SYLLABI

SAMPLE SYLLABUS 1

First-Semester Expository Writing Course
(15-week semester, three 50-minute classes per week)

Introduction

> How can I know what I think until I see what I say?—E. M. Forster

This course is based on two assumptions: (1) Writing is a recursive process of discovery that circles around the phases of planning, drafting, revising, and editing; and therefore (2) the secret to good writing is rewriting. Good expository writing in college evolves out of the sustained process embedded in the first assumption. Through assigned reading, class discussion, individual thinking, and personal experience, you will engage a variety of topics, developing a personal and informed point of view and taking into account the views of others. In other words, you will learn to engage in an ongoing conversation on a wide range of topics that directly concern your everyday life, using formal written English. You will also learn that reading, thinking, and writing are inseparable aspects of a complex process of meaning making and intellectual discovery.

You will find the complex process of reading, thinking, writing, and rewriting both challenging and rewarding, for it goes beyond the specific task of developing writing skills and leads you toward a more general goal of acculturating yourself to the disciplines, values, and orientation of the academy and the liberal arts. Through this expository writing course, you will learn to be a sophisticated and conscientious critical thinker, for you will write to understand what *you* think about writing itself, about your identity, about your education, about the place where you live, about work and play, and about creative expression, among other topics. At first you may think you know too little about these topics to write or even to start thinking about them. Yet through reading, writing, and revision, you will be surprised by what you already know and what you are capable of knowing.

Since this is your first college writing course, you will have a lot of in-class time to write with your peers. Know that help is available when you need it. Turn the pages. Hit the keyboard. Have fun watching yourself think—in words.

Requirements
- Read the assignments carefully, and prepare to respond to the thought-provoking questions offered at the end of each essay.
- Submit five essays that add up to a minimum of twenty-five pages of typed, double-spaced, finished prose with one-inch margins and 12-point type.

- Provide with each completed, typed essay at least one rough draft, which may be handwritten. Keep all your rough drafts and final drafts in a folder organized in chronological sequence. I will collect them at the middle and the end of the semester. These drafts will not be graded.
- Participate in class discussion.
- Engage actively in peer groups and conferences.

Week 1

1. *Course introduction and self-portrayal:* What are the goals of this course, and how do we work together effectively?
2. *Work due:* Read Joan Didion's "On Keeping a Notebook," and prepare to respond to Question 1.

Week 2

1. *Work due:* Respond to Didion Questions 2, 3, and 5.
2. Whole-class discussion of "writer's block." Peer-group discussion of your responses to Questions 3 and 5.
3. *Work due:* Respond to Welty Question 1.

   Lecture on the process of writing and the function of freewriting. You are encouraged to ask questions during the lecture, drawing on your newly gained knowledge from reading Didion and Welty. Peer-group discussion of Welty Question 1. Ten minutes of free writing.

4. *Work due:* Read Richard Wright's "Fighting Words" and write notes in response to Questions 2 and 3. Be prepared to discuss your relationship with books.

   Class discussion of Question 2. Group discussion of Question 3. Feel free to draw on your notes. Twenty minutes of in-class guided planning of Essay 1, "My Relationship with Books," a personal narrative with a focus on your experience as a reader.

Week 3

1. *Work due:* Read Marjorie Agosín's "Always Living in Spanish," and prepare to discuss Questions 1 and 2. Rough draft of Essay 1.

   Group discussion of Questions 1 and 2. As a group, create a list of sources of personal identity. Incorporate into the list your experiences of reading and writing. Drawing on Welty, Wright, and Agosín, describe how the physical experiences of reading and writing formed your relationship with books. Work out an outline that will give your draft greater cohesion and a more vivid texture.

2. *Work due:* Second draft of Essay 1. Read Peter Elbow, "Freewriting" (p. 67). Notebook entries done as freewrites about "automatic writing" and "feedback."

Class discussion of your draft and notes. How has thinking about freewriting made you more conscious of the writing process? What is your greatest gain from this consciousness? Group discussion of your second draft and ways to improve it.

3. *Work due:* Third draft of Essay 1. Read Katherine Anne Porter's "You Do Not Create a Style. You Work . . ." (p. 66).

   Peer editing. In-class final revision of Essay 1, making your sentences resonant—at least in the first paragraph. Submit the paper before you leave class.

Week 4

1. *Work due:* Read the Context essays (pp. 123–30) in Chapter 2 carefully, and write notes in response to Question 1 (pp. 130–31). Make that list as long as you can, focusing on your emotional involvement with the place, its influence on you, and your memory of it. Be prepared to discuss Questions 3 and 4. Class discussion of Questions 3 and 4.

   Group discussion of your list. Ask one another questions so that more details of that place emerge.

2. *Work due:* Read Bobbie Ann Mason's "Being Country" in Chapter 2 and write notes in response to Question 5.

   Class discussion of Question 5. Twenty-five-minute group discussion, comparing and contrasting your answers with your list for Question 1 of the Context essays. What do you want to add to your old list? Revise the list for your place accordingly.

3. *Work due:* Read E. B. White's "Once More to the Lake" in Chapter 3, and write notes comparing and contrasting the stories that E. B. White's Maine lake evokes and the stories N. Scott Momaday's Rainy Mountain evokes. What do these stories tell us about the two writers?

   Class discussion. Open-ended writing (not freewriting) guided by your revised notes on place. Try to incorporate as many details as you can, organizing them in relevant clusters but drawing no conclusions about your place.

Week 5

1. *Work due:* Read Leslie Marmon Silko's "Language and Literature from a Pueblo Indian Perspective" in Chapter 1, and write notes in response to Questions 1–3. Instructor's comments on Essay 1, focusing on sentence-level issues but also covering strengths and weaknesses at the paragraph and essay levels. Group discussion of Questions 1–3.

   In-class writing: Using your notes in response to Question 3, discuss whether the stories within stories that White's "Once More to the Lake" evokes are connected to the land in the same way that Silko finds in Pueblo narratives.

2. *Work due:* Reread White's essay; write notes in response to Question 3. Be prepared to discuss how your understanding of White's essay has changed since your first reading.

   Group discussion on two issues: (1) What kinds of stories does Silko's place tell? What kinds of stories does White's lake tell? What do they tell us about the two cultures? (2) What stories does your preliminary writing from last week tell? What do you want your place stories to say about you as a person? About your culture? How do you plan to do it?

3. *Work due:* Write analytical notes, incorporating ideas gathered from the previous class discussion. These notes provide you with a "point" about your place and your place stories, while the lists compiled earlier provide copious details.

   In-class planning: Combine these two sets of information into a meaningful outline for Essay 2, a description of your place that is rich in physical details and descriptive of your personal involvement with it. As soon as your outline is ready, start working on your first draft. Are you surprised how smoothly your writing can go?

Week 6

1. *Work due:* Rough draft of Essay 2. Read Henry David Thoreau's "Where I Lived, and What I Lived For" in Chapter 8 in class, and write notes in response to Questions 1 and 2.

   Class discussion: How do you avoid sounding egocentric while describing a place with which you're intimately involved? How does Thoreau handle this problem?

2. *Work due:* Read William Rees's "Life in the Lap of Luxury as Ecosystems Collapse" in Chapter 8. Write notes in response to Question 3 on Thoreau and Questions 1 and 2 on Rees.

   Class discussion of the relevance of Thoreau's idea of a "simple life" to Rees's notion of an "ecological footprint."

3. *Work due:* Second draft of Essay 2. Peer editing of the second draft.

   Class discussion of what we can do and what we want to do to reduce our "ecological footprint," as inspired by our writing about special places.

Week 7

1. *Work due:* Essay 2. All drafts of both essays. Read the Context essay in Chapter 4, and write notes in response to Questions 1–3.

   Class discussion of the effects of language variation on you as a reader. Group discussion: Tell stories about people you know who speak with unusual accents.

2. *Work due:* Read Amy Tan's "Mother Tongue" in Chapter 1. Write notes in response to Questions 1–3.

   Class discussion of Questions 1 and 2. Group discussion of Question 3.

3. *Work due:* Do the project described in Tan Question 4. Group discussion and sharing of the result of your projects.

Week 8

1. *Work due:* Read Gloria Anzaldúa's "Beyond Traditional Notions of Identity" in Chapter 2. Write notes in response to Questions 1 and 2.

   Class discussion of Questions 1 and 2. Instructor's comments on Essay 2, focusing on paragraph-level issues but also covering strengths and weaknesses at the sentence and essay levels.

2. *Work due:* Reread Anzaldúa. Expand on notes in response to Questions 1 and 2. Class discussion of these questions.

3. *Work due*: Reread the Rodriguez essay and the Context readings for "Aria." Write lengthy notes in response to Question 3. This will evolve into your third essay. Class discussion of this question.

Week 9

1. *Work due:* Review your notes on Tan, Anzaldúa, Silko, and Rodriguez. Expand the writing topic described in Rodriguez Question 3 to include ideas gathered from all of your notes.

   Class discussion of these authors' treatment of variations of English.

   In-class planning: Work out an outline for an essay that classifies these few authors' uses of variations of English.

2. *Work due:* First rough draft of Essay 3, your classification essay. Read Eric Liu's "Notes of a Native Speaker" in Chapter 2 and write notes in response to Questions 1 and 3.

   Class discussion of these questions. Group discussion of your first draft.

3. *Work due:* Second draft of Essay 3.

   Group discussion of draft, focusing on the clarity and appropriateness of classification. In-class rewriting.

Week 10

1. *Work due:* Essay 3. Read the Context essay (Martin Luther King) in Chapter 7 (p. 514) and write notes in response to Questions 1–3. Be especially thorough in examining the arguments in each of the Context essays. Brief lecture on induction and deduction.

Class discussion of these questions; take notes on what you and your peers have to say.

2. *Work due:* Read George Orwell's "Shooting an Elephant" in Chapter 7.

   In-class writing: Drawing on the notes you collected while reading George Orwell's "Shooting an Elephant" and Martin Luther King's "Letter from Birmingham Jail," write a deductive argument in response to Question 6 under "Shooting an Elephant." Imitate the tone and structure of either essay.

3. *Work due:* Read Howard Gardner's "Who Owns Intelligence?" in Chapter 4, and write notes in response to Questions 2 and 3. Read Sojourner Truth's "Ain't I a Woman?" and Deirdre N. McCloskey's "Yes, Ma'am," both in Chapter 2.

   In-class writing: Drawing on the notes you collected while reading "Shooting an Elephant" and Martin Luther King's "Letter from Birmingham Jail," write an inductive argument in response to Question 6 under "Shooting an Elephant." Imitate the intimate and sarcastic tones of the two pieces you just read.

Week 11

1. *Work due:* Reread Gardner's "Who Owns Intelligence?" in Chapter 4, and write notes in response to Questions 4 and 5.

   Instructor's comments on Essay 3, focusing on the overall structure of the essay. Discussion of Gardner Question 4.

2. *Work due:* Read Linda Simon's "The Naked Source" in Chapter 4, and write copious notes in response to Questions 2 and 4. Simon's emphasis on the "imaginative construction" of history (24) through reading primary sources suggests that good history requires the simultaneous application of what Gardner calls "capacities that are scientifically and epistemologically separate" (59). How is the idea that history is a type of literature compatible with Gardner's notion of "cardinal human virtues" (58)?

   Group discussion and sharing of these notes. Note the similarities and differences.

3. *Work due:* Expanded notes on Simon Question 4.

   In-class writing: Group discussion of notes. In-class rewriting.

Week 12

1. *Work due:* Read Sherman Alexie's "What Sacagawea Means to Me" in Chapter 2, and write notes in response to Questions 1–3.

   Group discussion of these questions and the possible audience(s) for your history essay.

2. *In-class writing:* Revise your history draft according to the new sense of audience gained from the previous class discussion.

3. *Peer editing.* Final touching up. Submit the history essay.

Week 13

1. *Work due:* Read Maxine Hong Kingston's "On Discovery" in Chapter 2, and write notes to help explain how Tang Ao is transformed into a woman. Be prepared to discuss Questions 2–4.

   Group discussion.

   In-class writing: Do you have a voice? What is it like? Since when have you been conscious of this voice? What was it like before you developed your own voice? What is the relationship between your voice and your sense of identity?

2. *Work due:* Read Art Spiegelman's "Mein Kampf" in Chapter 2. Write notes in response to Questions 1–3. Read Elie Wiesel's "Why I Write" in Chapter 1.

   Group discussion of Questions 1–3.

   In-class writing: Compare Spiegelman and Wiesel.

3. *Work due:* Read the Context essays for Alice Walker in Chapter 3. Write notes in response to Questions 1 and 2 as well as about your experiences of ethnic stereotyping.

   Instructor's comments on Essay 4. Group discussion on the questions.

   In-class writing: Contrast Spiegelman's or Alexie's narratives with your family's history.

Week 14

1. *Work due:* Reread Wiesel and write copious notes in response to Question 6.

   Group discussion of Question 6.

   In-class writing: Compare and contrast the different responses to Question 6.

2. *Work due:* Reread Anzaldúa's essay in Chapter 2 and write notes in response to Question 3 about "intergenerational dialogue." Reread Kingston's essay in Chapter 2. Group discussion of Wiesel's notion of his role as a "witness" (6) and how women's writing redefines their history.

   In-class writing: Compare and contrast treatments of history by Alexie and Spiegelman.

Week 15

1. Now you have compared and contrasted the narratives of Alexie, Kingston, Spiegelman, Wiesel, and Anzaldúa. Choose one pair and start drafting, developing your exercise into a five-page comparison/contrast essay.

2. *Work due:* First draft of Essay 5. Group discussion of your first draft. In-class rewriting.

3. Peer editing of the second draft of Essay 5. Final touching up. Submit the paper in class.

SAMPLE SYLLABUS 2

First-Quarter Expository Writing Course
(10-week quarter, five 50-minute classes per week)

Introduction

How can I know what I think until I see what I say? — E. M. Forster

This course is based on two assumptions: (1) Writing is a recursive process of discovery that circles around the phases of planning, drafting, revising, and editing; and therefore (2) the secret to good writing is rewriting. Good expository writing in college evolves out of the sustained process embedded in the first assumption. Through assigned reading, class discussion, individual thinking, and personal experience, you will engage a variety of topics, developing a personal and informed point of view and taking into account the views of others. In other words, you will learn to engage in an ongoing conversation on a wide range of topics that directly concern your everyday life, using formal written English. You will also learn that reading, thinking, and writing are inseparable aspects of a complex process of meaning making and intellectual discovery.

You will find the complex process of reading, thinking, writing, and rewriting both challenging and rewarding, for it goes beyond the specific task of developing writing skills and leads you toward a more general goal of acculturating yourself to the disciplines, values, and orientation of the academy and the liberal arts. Through this expository writing course, you will learn to be a sophisticated and conscientious critical thinker, for you will write to understand what *you* think about writing itself, about your identity, about your education, about the place where you live, about work and play, and about creative expression, among many other topics. At first you may think you know too little about these topics to write or even to start thinking about them. Yet through reading, writing, and revision, you will be surprised by what you already know and what you are capable of knowing.

Since this is your first college writing course, we will have a lot of in-class time to write with your peers. Know that help is available when you need it. Turn the pages. Hit the keyboard. Have fun watching yourself think—in words.

Requirements

- Read the assignments carefully, and prepare to respond to the thought-provoking questions offered at the end of each essay.
- Submit five essays that add up to a minimum of twenty-five pages of typed, double-spaced, finished prose with one-inch margins and 12-point type.
- Provide with each completed, typed essay at least one rough draft, which may be handwritten. Keep all your rough drafts and final drafts in a folder organized in chronological sequence. I will collect them at the middle and the end of the semester. These drafts will not be graded.
- Participate in class discussion.
- Engage actively in peer groups and conferences.

Week 1

1. *Course introduction and self-portrayal:* What are the goals of this course, and how do we work together effectively?

2. *Work due:* Respond to Joan Didion's "On Keeping a Notebook." Prepare to respond to Question 1.

3. *Work due:* Respond to Didion Questions 2, 3, and 5.

   Class discussion of "writer's block." Peer-group discussion of your responses to Questions 3 and 5.

4. *Work due:* Respond to Welty Question 1.

   Lecture on the process of writing and the function of freewriting. You are encouraged to ask questions during the lecture, drawing on your newly gained knowledge from reading Didion and Welty. Peer-group discussion of Welty Question 1. Ten minutes of freewriting.

Week 2

1. *Work due:* Read Richard Wright's "Fighting Words" and write notes in response to Questions 2 and 3. Be prepared to discuss your relationship with books.

   Class discussion of Question 2. Group discussion of Question 3. Feel free to draw on your notes. Twenty minutes of in-class guided planning of Essay 1, "My Relationship with Books," a personal narrative with a focus on your experience as a reader.

2. *Work due:* Read Marjorie Agosín's "Always Living in Spanish" in Chapter 1 and prepare to discuss Questions 1 and 2 in class.

Group discussion of Questions 1 and 2. As a group, create a list of sources of personal identity. Incorporate into the list your experiences of reading and writing. Drawing on Welty, Didion, and Wright, describe how the physical experiences of reading and writing formed your relationship with books. Twenty-minute in-class writing session. Using the list from group discussion for additional and/or alternative details, work out an outline.

3. *In-class writing:* First draft of Essay 1, fleshing out the outline.

4. *Work due:* Class discussion of your draft and the notes about drafting. How has early revision made you more conscious of the writing process? What is your greatest gain from this consciousness?

   In-class writing: Second draft of Essay 1.

5. *Work due:* Read Katherine Anne Porter's "You Do Not Create a Style. You Work . . . " in Chapter 1.

   In-class final revision of Essay 1, making your sentences resonant—at least in the first paragraph. Submit the paper.

Week 3

1. *Work due:* Read the Context essays (pp. 123–30) in Chapter 2 carefully, and write notes in response to Study Question 1 (p. 130). Make that list as long as you can, focusing on your emotional involvement with the place, its influence on you, and your memory of it. Be prepared to discuss Questions 3 and 4. Class discussion of Questions 3 and 4.

   Group discussion of your list. Ask one another questions so that more details of that place emerge.

2. *Work due:* Read Bobbie Ann Mason's "Being Country" in Chapter 2, and write notes (lists) in response to Question 5.

   Class discussion of Question 5. Group discussion, comparing and contrasting your answers with your list for Question 1 of the Context essay. What do you want to add to your old list? Revise the list for your place accordingly.

3. *Work due:* Read E. B. White's "Once More to the Lake" in Chapter 3, and write notes comparing and contrasting the stories that E. B. White's Maine lake evokes and the stories N. Scott Momaday's Rainy Mountain evokes. What do these stories tell us about the two writers?

   Class discussion. Open-ended writing (not freewriting) guided by your revised notes on place. Try to incorporate as many details from the list as you can, organizing them in relevant clusters but drawing no conclusions about your place.

4. *Work due:* Read Leslie Marmon Silko's "Language and Literature from a Pueblo Indian Perspective" and write notes in response to Questions 1–3. Instructor's comments on Essay 1, focusing on sentence-level issues but also covering strengths and weaknesses at the paragraph and essay levels.

   Group discussion of Questions 1–3.

   In-class writing: Using your notes in response to Question 3, discuss whether the stories within stories that White's "Once More to the Lake" evokes are connected to the land in the same way that Silko finds in Pueblo narratives.

5. *Work due:* Reread White's essay; write notes in response to Question 3. Be prepared to discuss how your understanding of White's essay has changed since your first reading.

   Group discussion on two issues: (1) What kinds of stories does Silko's place tell? What kinds of stories does White's lake tell? What do they tell us about the two cultures? (2) What stories does your preliminary writing from last week tell? What do you want your place stories to say about you as a person? About your culture? How do you plan to do it?

Week 4

1. *Work due:* Write analytical notes, incorporating ideas gathered from the previous class discussion. These notes provide you with a "point" about your place and your place stories, while the lists compiled earlier provide copious details.

   In-class planning: Combine these two sets of information into a meaningful outline for Essay 2, a description of your place that is rich in physical details and descriptive of your personal involvement with it. As soon as your outline is ready, start working on your first draft. Are you surprised how smoothly your writing can go?

2. *In-class writing:* Rough draft of Essay 2.

3. *Work due:* Rough draft of Essay 2. Read Henry David Thoreau's "Where I Lived, and What I Lived For" in Chapter 8 in class, and write notes in response to Questions 1 and 2.

   Class discussion: How do you avoid sounding egocentric while describing a place with which you're intimately involved? How does Thoreau handle this problem?

4. *Work due:* Read William Rees's "Life in the Lap of Luxury as Ecosystems Collapse" in Chapter 8. Write notes in response to Question 3 on Thoreau and Questions 1 and 2 on Rees.

Class discussion of the relevance of Thoreau's idea of a "simple life" to Rees's notion of an "ecological footprint."

5. *Work due:* Second draft of Essay 2. Peer editing of the second draft.

Class discussion of what we can do and what we want to do to reduce our "ecological footprint," as inspired by our writing about special places.

Week 5

1. *Work due:* Essay 2. All drafts of both essays. Read the Context essay in Chapter 4 and write notes in response to Questions 1–3.

Class discussion of the effects of language variation on you as a reader. In groups, tell stories about people you know who speak with unusual accents.

2. *Work due:* Read Amy Tan's "Mother Tongue" in Chapter 1. Write notes in response to Questions 1–3.

Class discussion of Questions 1 and 2. Group discussion of Question 3.

3. *Work due:* Do the project described in Tan Question 4. Group discussion and sharing of what you have achieved in your projects.

4. *Work due:* Read Gloria Anzaldúa's "Beyond Traditional Notions of Identity" in Chapter 2. Write notes in response to Questions 1 and 2.

Class discussion of Questions 1 and 2. Instructor's comments on Essay 2, focusing on paragraph-level issues but also covering strengths and weaknesses at the sentence and essay levels.

5. *Work due:* Reread Anzaldúa. Expand on notes in response to Questions 1 and 2. Class discussion of these questions.

Week 6

1. *Work due:* Reread the Rodriguez essay and the Contexts for "Aria." Write lengthy notes in response to Question 5. This will evolve into your third essay. Class discussion of this question.

2. *Work due:* Review your notes on Tan, Anzaldúa, Silko, and Rodriguez. Expand the writing topic described in Rodriguez Question 3 to include ideas gathered from all of your notes.

Class discussion of these authors' treatment of variations of English.

In-class planning: Work out an outline for an essay that classifies these four authors' uses of variations of English.

3. *In-class writing:* First rough draft of Essay 3, your classification essay.

4. *Work due:* Read Eric Liu's "Notes of a Native Speaker" in Chapter 2, and write notes in response to Questions 1 and 3.

Class discussion of these questions. Group discussion of your first draft.

5. *Work due:* Second draft of Essay 3.

Group discussion of draft, focusing on the clarity and appropriateness of classification. In-class rewriting.

Week 7

1. *Work due:* Essay 3. Read the Context essay (Martin Luther King) in Chapter 7 (p. 514) and write notes in response to Questions 1–3. Be especially thorough in examining the arguments in each of the Context essays. Brief lecture on induction and deduction.

Class discussion of these questions; take notes on what you and your peers have to say.

2. *Work due:* Read George Orwell's "Shooting an Elephant" in Chapter 7.

In-class writing: Drawing on the notes you collected while reading George Orwell's "Shooting an Elephant" and Martin Luther King's "Letter from Birmingham Jail," write a deductive argument in response to Question 6 under "Shooting an Elephant." Imitate the tone and structure of either essay.

3. *Work due:* Read Howard Gardner's "Who Owns Intelligence?" in Chapter 4, and write notes in response to Questions 2 and 3. Read Sojourner Truth's "Ain't I a Woman?" and Deirdre N. McCloskey's "Yes, Ma'am," both in Chapter 2.

In-class writing: Drawing on the notes you collected while reading "Shooting an Elephant" and Martin Luther King's "Letter from Birmingham Jail," write an inductive argument in response to Question 6 under "Shooting an Elephant."

4. *Work due:* Reread Gardner's "Who Owns Intelligence?" in Chapter 4, and write notes in response to Questions 4 and 5.

Instructor's comments on Essay 3, focusing on the overall structure of the essay. Discussion of Gardner Question 4.

5. *Work due:* Read Linda Simon's "The Naked Source" in Chapter 4, and write copious notes in response to Questions 2 and 4. Simon's emphasis on the "imaginative construction" of history (24) through reading primary sources suggests that good history requires the application of what Gardner calls "capacities that are scientifically and epistemologically separate" (59). How is the idea that history is a type of literature compatible with Gardner's notion of "cardinal human virtues" (58)?

Group discussion and sharing of these notes. Note the similarities and differences.

Week 8

1. *Work due:* Expanded notes on Simon Question 4.

   In-class writing: Group discussion of notes. In-class rewriting.

2. *Work due:* Read Sherman Alexie's "What Sacagawea Means to Me" in Chapter 2, and write notes in response to Question 1–3.

   Group discussion of these questions and the possible audience(s) for your history essay.

3. *In-class writing:* Revise your history draft according to the new sense of audience gained from the previous class discussion.

4. Peer editing. Final touching up. Submit the history essay.

5. *Work due:* Read Read Maxine Hong Kingston's "On Discovery" in Chapter 2, and write notes to help explain how Tang Ao is transformed into a woman. Be prepared to discuss Questions 2–4.

   Group discussion.

Week 9

1. *In-class writing:* Do you have a voice? What is it like? Since when have you been conscious of this voice? What was it like before you developed your own voice? What is the relationship between your voice and your sense of identity?

2. *Work due:* Read Art Spiegelman's "Mein Kampf" in Chapter 2. Write notes in response to Questions 1–3. Read Elie Wiesel's "Why I Write" in Chapter 1.

   Group discussion of Questions 1–3.

   In-class writing: Compare Spiegelman and Wiesel.

3. *Work due:* Read the Contexts for Alice Walker in Chapter 3. Write notes in response to Questions 1–3 as well as about your own experiences of ethnic stereotyping.

   Instructor's comments on Essay 4. Group discussion on the questions.

   In-class writing: Contrast Spiegelman's or Alexie's narrative with your family's history.

4. *Work due:* Reread Wiesel, and write copious notes in response to Question 6.

   Group discussion of Question 6.

   In-class writing: Compare and contrast the different responses to Question 6.

5. *Work due:* Reread Anzaldúa's essay in Chapter 2, and write notes in response to Question 3 about "intergenerational dialogue." Reread Kingston's essay in

Chapter 2. Group discussion of Wiesel's notion of his role as a "witness" (6) and how women's writing redefines their history.

Week 10

1. *In-class writing:* Compare and contrast treatments of history by Alexie and Spiegelman.

2. Now you have compared and contrasted the experiences of narratives of Alexie, Kingston, Spiegelman, Wiesel, and Anzaldúa. Choose one pair and start drafting, developing your exercise into a five-page comparison/contrast essay.

3. *Work due:* First draft of Essay 5. Group discussion of your first draft. In-class rewriting.

4. Peer editing of the second draft of Essay 5. Final touching up. Submit the paper in class.

SAMPLE SYLLABUS 3

Upper-Division Writing Proficiency Course for the Semester System
(15-week semester, two 65-minute classes per week)

Introduction

How can I know what I think until I see what I say?—E. M. Forster

This course is based on several assumptions: Writing is part of a continuous process of thinking, reading, rethinking, researching, evaluating, discovering, testing, and organizing thinking through written words. The process is recursive and demands intensive and sustained engagement. As an upper-division student, you have mastered useful basic writing skills, yet you will find in this course that even for professional writers, good writing is hardly ever done in one sitting. Therefore, it is helpful for you to remember this at the very start: The secret to good writing is rewriting, going back and forth over the phases of planning, researching, drafting, revising, and editing. Good research writing at the college level requires a certain degree of originality and extensive contextualization—positioning yourself in relation to other writers who have discussed the issues that you plan to work on. Thus, you are entering an ongoing conversation held among careful thinkers. Your successful approach to this kind of writing is via discovery rather than preconception. Enjoy reading, thinking, researching, and writing as inseparable aspects of a complex process of meaning making and intellectual discovery. You will come out of this course a more sophisticated, conscious, and conscientious critical thinker.

Requirements

- Attend class regularly and participate in class activities.
- Submit three five-page essays and two ten-page research papers, double-spaced, in finished prose with one-inch margins and 12-point type.
- Submit essays with drafts (though drafts will not be graded).
- Engage actively in peer groups and conferences.

Week 1

1. Course introduction.

   In-class reading: Joan Didion's "Why I Write," and the 1999 interview.

   In-class writing: "Why I write and what I write about."

2. *Work due:* Read Didion's "On Keeping a Notebook" in Chapter 1, and write notes in response to the Questions for that essay.

   Class discussion of Didion.

   In-class writing: Response to Questions 2 and 5.

Week 2

1. *Work due:* Read Richard Wright's "Fighting Words" and Stephen King's "Write or Die" in Chapter 1. Write notes in response to the Questions following each essay.

   Class discussion of what motivates these authors to write. Compare and contrast their motives with those of Didion.

2. *Work due:* Read N. Scott Momaday's "The Way to Rainy Mountain," Eric Liu's "Notes of a Native Speaker," and Sherman Alexie's "What Sacagawea Means to Me" in Chapter 2.

   Class discussion of the authors' motives for writing.

   In-class writing: "Why Writers Write." Drawing on the details collected about the writers, make a general argument about what motivates people to write.

Week 3

1. *Work due:* First draft of Essay 1. Group discussion of the first draft.

   In-class writing: Second draft of Essay 1.

2. *Work due:* Read Plato's "The Allegory of the Cave" and Howard Gardner's "Who Owns Intelligence?" in Chapter 4. Write notes in response to the Questions following each essay.

Class discussion of the Questions. Peer editing. Submit Essay 1 with at least two drafts. Lecture on two basic methods of research: systematic reading and observation.

Week 4

1. *Work due:* Read Alice Walker's "In Search of Our Mothers' Gardens" in Chapter 3 and Context essays. Write notes in response to the questions that follow the essay.

   Class discussion of the Questions.

   In-class writing: "From what sources spring creative ideas?"

2. *Work due:* First draft of Essay 2. Reread Momaday's "The Way to Rainy Mountain" and write notes in response to the Questions (pp. 130–31).

   Discuss Momaday's essays in class. Discuss drafts in groups.

   In-class writing: Incorporate into your draft new ideas acquired from reading and discussing Momaday's essays.

Week 5

1. *Work due:* Second draft of Essay 2.

   Instructor's comments on Essay 1. Peer editing. Final touching up. Submit Essay 2 with at least two rough drafts. Lecture on two additional research methods: experimentation and interviewing.

2. You have written two essays, which are actually short, guided research papers. Now is the time to start a longer project.

   Work due: Read Bobbie Ann Mason's "Being Country" in Chapter 2, E. B. White's "Once More to the Lake" in Chapter 3, and Henry David Thoreau's "Where I Lived, and What I Lived For" in Chapter 8. Write notes in response to the Questions following each essay.

   Class discussion: How do Mason, White, and Thoreau suggest that we are defined by where we live? Support your discussion with details gathered from your reading notes.

Week 6

1. *Work due:* Read Leslie Marmon Silko's "Language and Literature from a Pueblo Indian Perspective" in Chapter 1. What kind of knowledge does Silko learn from tribal stories? What role does native knowledge of place play in negotiating human-nature relations? Write notes in response to the Questions on Silko (p. 44).

   Class discussion of these questions.

In-class writing: List elements of place in the essays by White, Thoreau, Momaday, and Silko. The more detailed your list is, the more useful it will be for your research project.

2. *Work due:* Read Rachel Carson's "The Obligation to Endure" and William E. Rees's "Life in the Lap of Luxury as Ecosystems Collapse" in Chapter 8. Write notes in response to the questions following each essay.

   Class discussion: What's the significance of the kind of "global" knowledge discussed in these two essays? How does this kind of knowledge compare to White's, Thoreau's, Momaday's, and Silko's knowledge? "Think globally, act locally": Is this just a cliché or true practical wisdom?

Week 7

1. *Work due:* Read Sandra Postel's "Troubled Waters" in Chapter 8 and Stephen Jay Gould's "Evolution as Fact and Theory" and Charles Darwin's "Understanding Natural Selection" in Chapter 6. Write notes in response to the Questions following each essay.

   Instructor's comments on Essay 2. Discuss the questions, and review the significance of global knowledge, especially in relation to these essays. Make a detailed list of your responses.

2. Guided library tour. Start conducting research in the library and on the Internet for environmental protection cases that show some degree of success. Look for evidence that local knowledge and global knowledge together play a positive role in protecting the environment.

Week 8

1. Independent research in the library or on the Internet. Independent drafting.

2. *Work due:* First draft of Research Paper 1.

   Group discussion of the draft. In class discussion, each group reports on two exciting cases in which combined knowledge of local and global issues plays an important role. Lecture on MLA style and the works-cited list.

Week 9

1. In-class revising.

2. *Work due:* Read Bobbie Ann Mason's "Being Country" and James Baldwin's "Stranger in the Village" in Chapter 2, and Virginia Woolf's "Profession for Women" in Chapter 3. Write notes in response to the Questions following each essay. Submit Research Paper 1, together with all drafts.

   Discuss the Questions in class.

   In-class writing: Think of details leading to an explanation of how individuality is constructed socially, in relation to Mason, Baldwin, and Woolf.

Week 10

1. *Work due:* Reread Liu's "Notes of a Native Speaker" and Alice Walker's "In Search of Our Mothers' Gardens" in Chapter 3. Write notes in response to the Questions following Liu. Be prepared to discuss Walker's definitions of creativity.

   Discuss the Questions. Continue last week's in-class writing, adding new ideas from this week's reading.

2. *In-class writing:* Essay 3.

Week 11

1. *Work due:* Rough draft of Essay 3.

   Instructor's comments on Research Paper 1. Group discussion of draft. In-class revising.

2. *Work due:* Second draft of Essay 3.

   Group discussion of second draft. In-class revising.

Week 12

1. *Work due:* Essay 3. Read Amy Tan's "Mother Tongue" and Marjorie Agosín's "Always Living in Spanish" in Chapter 1. Write notes in response to the Questions following each essay.

   Group discussion of the Questions. In class discussion, compare and contrast the linguistic bias that works against and for Tan and Agosín.

2. *Work due:* Read Dennis Baron's "The New Technologies of the Word" in Chapter 5 and Lynda Barry's "Hate" in Chapter 7.

   Discuss how minority groups and nonnative English speakers in the United States negotiate the English language with respect to their culture or "storytelling."

   In-class writing: Contrast the role of storytelling in minority cultures and mainstream cultures.

Week 13

1. *Work due:* Reread Silko's "Language and Literature from a Pueblo Indian Perspective" in Chapter 1. Read Richard Rodriguez's "Aria: A Memoir of a Bilingual Childhood" and the Contexts essays in Chapter 4. Write notes in response to the Questions.

   Group discussion of the Questions.

   In-class writing: Continue the project from last week.

2. *Independent project:* Interview someone you know whose native language is not English, focusing on the tremendous linguistic disadvantages that he or

she has to overcome in order to advance in education, career, social status, and so on.

Week 14

1. Independent research in the library and on the Internet.

2. Instructor's comments on Essay 3.

   In-class writing: Research Paper 2.

Week 15

1. *Work due:* First draft of Research Paper 2. Group discussion of draft. In-class revising.

2. *Work due:* Second draft of Research Paper 2. Group discussion of draft. In-class revising. Submit Research Paper 2.

SAMPLE SYLLABUS 4

Upper-Division Writing Proficiency Course for the Quarter System
(10-week quarter, three 65-minute classes per week)

Introduction

How can I know what I think until I see what I say? — E. M. Forster

This course is based on several assumptions: Writing is part of a continuous process of thinking, reading, rethinking, researching, evaluating, discovering, testing, and organizing thinking through written words. The process is recursive and demands intensive and sustained engagement. As an upper-division student, you have mastered useful basic writing skills, yet you will find in this course that even for professional writers, good writing is hardly ever done in one sitting. Therefore, it is helpful for you to remember this at the very start: The secret to good writing is rewriting, going back and forth over the phases of planning, researching, drafting, revising, and editing. Good research writing at the college level requires a certain degree of originality and extensive contextualization — positioning yourself in relation to other writers who have discussed the issues that you plan to work on. Thus, you are entering an ongoing conversation held among careful thinkers. Your successful approach to this kind of writing is via discovery rather than preconception. Enjoy reading, thinking, researching, and writing as inseparable aspects of a complex process of meaning making and intellectual discovery. You will come out of this course a more sophisticated, conscious, and conscientious critical thinker.

Requirements

- Attend class regularly and participate in class activities.
- Submit three five-page essays and two ten-page research papers, double-spaced, in finished prose with one-inch margins and 12-point type.
- Submit essays with drafts (though drafts will not be graded).
- Engage actively in peer groups and conferences.

Week 1

1. Course introduction.

   In-class reading: Joan Didion's "Why I Write," and the 1977 and 1999 interviews.

   In-class writing: "Why I write and what I write about."

2. *Work due:* Read Didion's "On Keeping a Notebook" in Chapter 1, and write notes in response to the Questions for that essay.

   Class discussion of Didion.

   In-class writing: Response to Question 1.

3. *Work due:* Read Richard Wright's "Fighting Words" and Stephen King's "Write or Die" in Chapter 1. Write notes in response to the Questions following each essay.

   Class discussion of what motivates these authors to write. Compare and contrast their motives with those of Didion.

Week 2

1. *Work due:* Read N. Scott Momaday's "The Way to Rainy Mountain," Eric Liu's "Notes of a Native Speaker," and Sherman Alexie's "What Sacagawea Means to Me" in Chapter 2.

   Class discussion of the authors' motives for writing.

   In-class writing: "Why Writers Write." Drawing on the details collected about these writers, make a general argument about what motivates people to write.

2. *Work due:* First draft of Essay 1. Group discussion of the first draft.

   In-class writing: Second draft of Essay 1.

3. *Work due:* Read Plato's "The Allegory of the Cave" and Howard Gardner's "Who Owns Intelligence?" in Chapter 4. Write notes in response to the Questions following each essay.

   Class discussion of the Questions. Peer editing. Submit Essay 1 with at least two drafts. Lecture on two basic methods of research: systematic reading and observation.

Week 3

1. *Work due:* Read Alice Walker's "In Search of Our Mothers' Gardens" in Chapter 3. Write notes in response to the Questions that follow the essay.

   Class discussion of the Questions.

   In-class writing: "From what sources spring creative ideas?"

2. *Work due:* First draft of Essay 2. Reread Momaday's "The Way to Rainy Mountain" in Chapter 2 and write notes in response to the Questions (pp. 130–31).

   Discuss Momaday's essays in class. Discuss drafts in groups.

   In-class writing: Incorporate into your draft new ideas acquired from reading and discussing Momaday's essays.

3. *Work due:* Second draft of Essay 2.

   Instructor's comments on Essay 1. Peer editing. Final touching up. Submit Essay 2 with at least two rough drafts. Lecture on two additional research methods: experimentation and interviewing.

Week 4

1. You have written two essays, which are actually short, guided research papers. Now it's time to start a longer project.

   Work due: Read Bobbie Ann Mason's "Being Country" in Chapter 2, E. B. White's "Once More to the Lake" in Chapter 3, and Henry David Thoreau's "Where I Lived, and What I Lived For" in Chapter 8. Write notes in response to the Questions following each essay.

   Class discussion: How do Mason, White, and Thoreau suggest that we are defined by where we live?

2. *Work due:* Read Leslie Marmon Silko's "Language and Literature from a Pueblo Indian Perspective" in Chapter 1. What kind of knowledge does Silko learn from tribal stories? What role does native knowledge of place play in negotiating human-nature relations? Write notes in response to the Questions on Silko (p. 44).

   Class discussion of these questions.

   In-class writing: List elements of local geographies as displayed in the essays by White, Thoreau, Momaday, and Silko. The more detailed your list is, the more useful it will be for your research project.

3. *Work due:* Read Rachel Carson's "The Obligation to Endure" and William E. Rees's "Life in the Lap of Luxury as Ecosystems Collapse" in Chapter 8. Write notes in response to the Questions following each essay.

Class discussion: What's the significance of the kind of "global" knowledge discussed in these two essays? How does this kind of knowledge compare to White's, Thoreau's, Momaday's, and Silko's knowledge? "Think globally, act locally": Is this just a cliché or true practical wisdom?

Week 5

1. *Work due:* Read Sandra Postel's "Troubled Waters" in Chapter 8 and Stephen Jay Gould's "Evolution as Fact and Theory" and Charles Darwin's "Understanding Natural Selection" in Chapter 6. Write notes in response to the Questions following each essay.

   Instructor's comments on Essay 2. Discuss the Questions, and review the significance of global knowledge, especially in relation to these two essays. Make a detailed list of your responses.

2. Guided library tour. Start conducting research in the library and on the Internet for environmental protection cases that show some degree of success. Look for evidence that local knowledge and global knowledge together play a positive role in protecting the environment.

3. Independent research in the library or on the Internet. Independent drafting.

Week 6

1. *Work due:* First draft of Research Paper 1.

   Group discussion of the draft. In class discussion, each group reports on two exciting cases in which combined knowledge of local and global issues plays an important role. Lecture on MLA style and the works-cited list.

2. In-class revising.

3. *Work due:* Read Bobbie Ann Mason's "Being Country" and James Baldwin's "Stranger in the Village" in Chapter 2, and Virginia Woolf's "Professions for Women" in Chapter 3. Write notes in response to the Questions following each essay. Submit Research Paper 1, together with all drafts.

   Discuss the Questions in class.

   In-class writing: Think of details leading to an explanation of how individuality is constructed socially, in relation to Mason, Baldwin, and Woolf.

Week 7

1. *Work due:* Reread Liu's "Notes of a Native Speaker" and Alice Walker's "In Search of Our Mothers' Gardens" in Chapter 3. Write notes in response to the Questions following Liu and Walker. Be prepared to discuss self-definition.

2. *In-class writing:* Essay 3.

3. *Work due:* Rough draft of Essay 3.

Instructor's comments on Research Paper 1. Group discussion of draft. In-class revising.

Week 8

1. *Work due:* Second draft of Essay 3.

   Group discussion of second draft. In-class revising.

2. *Work due:* Essay 3. Read Amy Tan's "Mother Tongue" and Marjorie Agosín's "Always Living in Spanish" in Chapter 1. Write notes in response to the Questions following each essay.

   Group discussion of the Questions. In class discussion, compare and contrast the linguistic bias that works against and for Tan and Agosín.

3. *Work due:* Read Dennis Baron's "The New Technologies of the Word" in Chapter 5 and Lynda Barry's "Hate" in Chapter 7.

   Discuss how minority groups and nonnative English speakers in the United States negotiate the English language with respect to their culture or "story-telling."

   In-class writing: Contrast the role of storytelling in minority cultures and mainstream cultures.

Week 9

1. *Work due:* Reread Silko's "Language and Literature from a Pueblo Indian Perspective" in Chapter 1. Read Richard Rodriguez's "Aria: A Memoir of a Bilingual Childhood" and the Contexts in Chapter 4. Write notes in response to the Questions.

   Group discussion of the Questions.

   In-class writing: Continue the project from last week.

2. *Independent project:* Interview someone you know whose native language is not English, focusing on the tremendous linguistic disadvantages that he or she has to overcome in order to advance in education, career, social status, and so on.

3. Independent research in the library and on the Internet.

Week 10

1. Instructor's comments on Essay 3.

   In-class writing: Research Paper 2.

2. *Work due:* First draft of Research Paper 2. Group discussion of draft. In-class revising.

3. *Work due:* Second draft of Research Paper 2. Group discussion of draft. In-class revising. Submit Research Paper 2.

Alternative Thematic Clusters

Selections That Focus on Language(s)

Amy Tan, "Mother Tongue" (Chapter 1)
Marjorie Agosín, "Always Living in Spanish" (Chapter 1)
N. Scott Momaday, "The Way to Rainy Mountain" (Chapter 2)
Richard Rodriguez, "Aria: A Memoir of a Bilingual Childhood" (Chapter 4)
Dennis Baron, "The New Technologies of the Word" (Chapter 5)
Stanley Fish, "Academic Cross-Dressing: How Intelligent Design Gets Its Arguments from the Left" (Chapter 6)
Lynda Barry, "Hate" (Chapter 7)
Kelly Ritter, "The Economics of Authorship: Online Paper Mills, Student Writers, and First-Year Composition" (Chapter 7)
Annie Dillard, "Heaven and Earth in Jest" (Chapter 8)

Selections That Focus on the Environment

Leslie Marmon Silko, "Language and Literature from a Pueblo Indian Perspective" (Chapter 1)
E. B. White, "Once More to the Lake" (Chapter 3)
Charles Darwin, "Understanding Natural Selection" (Chapter 6)
Edward O. Wilson, "Microbes 3, Humans 2" (Chapter 6)
George Orwell, "Shooting an Elephant" (Chapter 7)
Henry David Thoreau, "Where I Lived, and What I Lived For" (Chapter 8)
Rachel Carson, "The Obligation to Endure" (Chapter 8)
William E. Rees, "Life in the Lap of Luxury as Ecosystems Collapse" (Chapter 8)
Sandra Postel, "Troubled Waters" (Chapter 8)
Annie Dillard, "Heaven and Earth in Jest" (Chapter 8)
Henry David Thoreau, "Journal" (Contexts in Chapter 8)
Vaclav Havel, "Our Moral Footprint" (Chapter 8)

Selections That Focus on Ethnicity and Multiculturalism

Amy Tan, "Mother Tongue" (Chapter 1)
Leslie Marmon Silko, "Language and Literature from a Pueblo Indian Perspective" (Chapter 1)
Gloria Anzaldúa, "Beyond Traditional Notions of Identity" (Chapter 2)
N. Scott Momaday, "The Way to Rainy Mountain" (Chapter 2)
Contexts in Chapter 2
Sojourner Truth, "Ain't I a Woman?" (Chapter 2)
Eric Liu, "Notes of a Native Speaker" (Chapter 2)
James Baldwin, "Stranger in the Village" (Chapter 2)

Alice Walker, "In Search of Our Mothers' Gardens" (Chapter 3)
Martin Luther King Jr., "Letter from Birmingham Jail" (Chapter 7)
Contexts in Chapter 3
Richard Rodriguez, "Aria: A Memoir of a Bilingual Childhood" (Chapter 4)
Contexts in Chapter 4

Selections That Focus on Women and Gender Issues

Deirdre N. McCloskey, "Yes, Ma'am" (Chapter 2)
Sojourner Truth, "Ain't I a Woman?" (Chapter 2)
Gloria Anzaldúa, "Beyond Traditional Notions of Identity" (Chapter 2)
Maxine Hong Kingston, "On Discovery" (Chapter 2)
Alice Walker, "In Search of Our Mothers' Gardens" (Chapter 3)
Natalie Angier, "Men, Women, Sex, and Darwin" (Chapter 6)

Selections That Focus on Knowledge, Ideas, and Intelligence

David Brown, "Science Reporting and Evidence-Based Journalism" (Chapter 1)
Richard Wright, "Fighting Words" (Chapter 1)
Sojourner Truth, "Ain't I a Woman?" (Chapter 2)
Malcolm Gladwell, "The Physical Genius" (Chapter 3)
Matthew B. Crawford, "The Case for Working with Your Hands" (Chapter 3)
Howard Gardner, "Who Owns Intelligence?" (Chapter 4)
Plato, "The Allegory of the Cave" (Chapter 4)
Stephen Jay Gould, "Evolution as Fact and Theory" (Chapter 6)
Freeman Dyson, "Our Biotech Future" (Chapter 6)
Stanley Fish, "Academic Cross-Dressing: How Intelligent Design Gets Its
    Arguments from the Left" (Chapter 6)
Contexts in Chapter 6
Wendell Berry, "Faustian Economics" (Chapter 8)

1 SPEAKING, READING, WRITING: HOW DOES LANGUAGE MAKE US HUMAN?

Paula Scher, Fogelson-Lubliner, and Neville Brody and Jeff Knowles, *Better Signs of Trouble* (p. 27)

1. Students can find current information about terrorism alerts on Homeland Security's Web site www.dhs.gov/index.shtm. They will find a "National Threat Advisory," which is based on the color-coded Homeland Security Advisory System. The links "Check the Threat Level" and "Preparedness, Response, Recovery" provide information about the level of risk of a terrorist attack and ways that the public can respond to the current alert level. The instructor might ask students to investigate whether Homeland Security's terrorism-alert system is available on a day-to-day basis through other Web sites or media and to consider whether a color-coded system is informative and practical. Students can explore specifically how an alert level might alter their behavior, for example, while traveling domestically or internationally and on land or in the air, and whether an alert might encourage them to prepare an emergency plan and kit or subscribe to e-mail updates.

2. Each of these proposed warning systems has advantages and drawbacks. Scher's has the advantage of simplicity, but the letters do not rely on universal signs and so may not convey their intended messages to a non-English speaker. The instructor may want to develop with the class a set of criteria through which to evaluate the different warning systems, including factors such as simplicity, flexibility, ease of interpretation by different populations, and suitability to different channels of distribution. The three alternative sign systems illustrate that communication is multidimensional and contextual. A warning system designed to reach a large, diverse population needs to not only communicate information quickly, but to be adaptable to different modes of communication—electronic and print. The instructor might ask students to consider the advantages and drawbacks of a system that does not depend on color and whether each of these alternative systems is more or less likely to panic or inform the public.

3. Michael J. Bugeja, in "Facing the Facebook," and Cathy Guisewite, in "We Saw Paris" (Chapter 5), each make the point that electronic communication shapes our perceptions of what is "real." Many people rely on portable electronic devices for information more than any other source because they are rarely without them and often access that information selectively. Students should consider how the opportunity to delete messages unread, selecting the information they read and the people with whom they communicate, shapes their communication practices. Students may consider whether electronic warnings might lose their

urgency with repetition and over time and how electronic communication habits can affect the government's ability to communicate with the public.

4. The instructor should encourage students to explore various ways of using graphics and text, alone or interactively. As Nicholas Carr points out in "Is Google Making Us Stupid?" (Chapter 5), "As people's minds become attuned to the crazy quilt of Internet media, traditional media have to adapt to the audience's new expectations" with "text crawls," "pop-up ads," and "easy-to-browse info-snippets" (19). Students might incorporate the many ways electronic media can capture users' attention and direct them to sources of information, creating a more interactive and animated system than the examples in "Better Signs of Trouble" or one that relies more on globally recognizable images and less on text.

Eudora Welty, *Listening* (p. 29)

1. For Eudora Welty, the act of listening is never isolated. Listening to the family Victrola, for instance, includes climbing onto a chair, winding and starting the record, setting the needle, jumping down to the floor, dancing or marching to the music, and "being cocked to start and stop the record. . . ." Movement, among other things, "must be at the very heart of listening" (18). Listening is closely connected with writing and therefore directly affects Welty as a writer.

Listening is inseparable from reading. Before Welty could read by herself, she listened intensely to her mother, who read to her everywhere in the house and whenever time allowed. "My mother read to me . . . in the big bedroom in the mornings, when we were in her rocker together. . . . She'd read to me in the diningroom on winter afternoons in front of the coal fire, with our cuckoo clock ending the story with 'Cuckoo,' and at night when I'd got in my own bed. . . . She was an expressive reader" (1). Listening to her mother's expressive reading helped Welty develop a sense of voice, a vitally important quality for a writer. "Ever since I was first read to, then started reading to myself, there has never been a line read that I didn't *hear*. As my eyes followed the sentence, a voice was saying it silently to me. It isn't my mother's voice, or the voice of any person I can identify, certainly not my own. It is human, but inward. . . . It is to me the voice of the story or the poem itself" (19).

An avid reader, she remembers not only the content of the books she read in her childhood, but also the contexts in which she read those books. In "Listening" she describes the contexts of her early reading vividly, thereby illustrating the intimate relation between reading and physical experience and emphasizing the intimate relation between the imaginary world (of words) and the real world (of children's actual memory of their physical life).

2. This exercise helps students understand Welty's emphasis on writing as physical experience. Ask students to take notes on the differences in the meaning and sounds of words as they read, speak, and listen to their own and their partners' sentences. Encourage students to understand how the "feeling that resides in the printed word" (19) emerges through its vocalization.

3. For both Welty and Alexie, the love of books represents a connection between members of a family and between the reader and the physical and psychic experience of reading. Welty remembers her mother reading as her rocking chair "ticked in rhythm as we rocked" (1), the rooms where the family's books lived (4–5), the places where she read, and how she "located" herself within her books (11). Similarly, Alexie's love of books grew out of his "aching devotion" to his father, who built shelves for the books that sprawled across their home (2). Through reading, both Welty and Alexie gained glimpses of their parents' inner lives. Welty's father's reading hinted at his "longing to see the rest of the world" and introduced her to his love of opera (5), whereas her mother's reading illustrated her "hedonistic" streak (6). Alexie's father's wide-ranging tastes and the "crazy piles" of books around their home paint a portrait of a man with a voracious appetite for life (2).

Both Welty and Alexie consider reading and writing inseparable from life itself, and perhaps this deep connection led each to become a writer. For Welty, writers are born through the habit of reading "as listeners" and the desire "to write as listeners": "[T]he sound of what falls on the page" is the test of the truth of the written word (19). Alexie's experience of growing up on a reservation in which a prodigious reader is "an oddity" (5) suggests that reading and writing both defined his life and separated him from his culture. His discovery that "a paragraph was a fence that held words" (3) acts as a larger metaphor for his life: In acquiring the knowledge that would enable him to "save [his] life" (7), he also sets himself apart by becoming "a smart Indian" (6). Both learned to trust the writing voice. Welty writes by listening for her "reader-voice" (19), whereas Alexie has created a self that rejects the perception that "Writing was something beyond Indians" (7). The "arrogant wonder" that he observes in teaching creative writing to "Indian kids" seems to have been the source of stamina that enabled him to develop that self-confidence (7).

Amy Tan, *Mother Tongue* (p. 34)

1. Amy Tan believes that spoken Englishes empower written English: A writer should draw on "all the Englishes [she] grew up with" (2, 21), including all variations of the spoken English "in this country or others" (1). The rhythm and vitality of Tan's mother's English provide Tan with a powerful "mother tongue" that eventually helps her write her first successful book, *The Joy Luck Club*.

However, in "Mother Tongue," Tan mainly uses grammatically correct Standard English because it is accessible to a large audience of people who might understand little or none of her mother's version of English. At the same time, in order to illustrate her mother's powerful English for her large audience, Tan provides examples of her "mother's tongue" and the contexts in which it is used. Tan is thus able to educate a large number of people about the great variety of Englishes that contribute to our culture.

2. Out of ignorance, some have called Tan's "mother tongue" "broken," "fractured," or "limited English" (8), and treated the immigrant mother rudely out of linguistic bias. The adverse linguistic situation has repeatedly frustrated Mrs. Tan but never broken her spirit. To the contrary, Mrs. Tan's character, intelligence, and willpower are conveyed through her unique version of English. A fine example is when she is "whispering loudly" (11) to her daughter, complaining about a stockbroker who had been rude and unprofessional to Mrs. Tan: "Why he don't send me check, already two weeks late. So mad he lie to me, losing me money" (11). As her daughter translates her "impeccable broken English" (13) into a polite, "standard" English, she gets louder and louder in her dictation: "What he want, I come to New York tell him front of his boss, you cheating me?" (13). Her smart, no-nonsense attitude is conveyed much more efficiently and vividly by her "broken" English than her daughter's polite translation.

As her mother's spokesperson, the adolescent Tan reveals her intelligence, education, mastery of English, and devotion to her family through her polite translation of "mother tongue" into a "standard" version of English meant for people outside of her immediate family. Catching her mother's authoritative tone, the young Tan firmly asserts on behalf of her mother: "I can't tolerate any more excuses. If I don't receive the check immediately, I am going to have to speak to your manager when I'm in New York next week" (13).

Mrs. Tan's adverse linguistic experience bonds mother and daughter more closely. Mrs. Tan learns through her experience that she can trust her daughter fully, and Tan, acting as her mother's spokesperson, comes to understand the frustration and hardship of the immigrant generation. She thereby develops a powerfully balanced version of written English that successfully depicts the linguistic genius of immigrants thought to speak only "broken" or "limited" English. As a writer, Tan acts not only as the spokesperson of her mother but also of all Chinese Americans, all Asian Americans, and indeed, all immigrant mothers and daughters.

3. This question is an indirect answer to the second half of Question 1. To her husband, Tan speaks a "mother tongue" that is grammatically "incorrect" and filled with phrases such as "Not waste money that way." This version of English has become their "language of intimacy, a different sort of English that relates to family talk . . ." (4). While the particular phrase quoted here lacks an auxiliary verb (*do*) and therefore might be regarded as "broken" or "fractured," most people can still understand its meaning.

Phrases from Tan's mother's "family talk," however, may puzzle general readers: "The local people call putong, the river east side, he belong to that side local people" (6). Although most readers can "correct" her grammar by replacing "he belong to" with "he belongs to," they lack the cultural background to know the exact meaning of the first half of the sentence. Her brief paraphrase of putong, "river east side," doesn't help much, for the phrase "East Side" may conjure up different connotations for people from different U.S. cities, yet none of those applies to putong. "Putong" means the east side of Huangpu River, which used to separate Shanghai City from its poor rural outskirt. Putong local people, ironically, are the Shanghai equivalent in social status of the residents of our inner-city ghettos. Small wonder then that Mr. Du Yusong later became the head of a major gang in Shanghai. This kind of language is powerful but accessible to a fairly limited audience, an intimate circle rather than the general public.

In writing "Mother Tongue," Tan uses mainly Standard written English to reach general readers. However, she carefully contextualizes passages from her mother's speech so that their power and freshness are apparent even to readers who may find them hard to understand but who are likely to be sympathetic to the linguistic predicament of immigrants. "Mother tongue" and Standard English are suited to different audiences and different purposes, which is why Tan feels awkward when her mother walks into the room where Tan is giving a talk in Standard English.

4. For this exercise, students should concentrate on analyzing the context in which communication takes place and how that context shapes communication. For example, the speakers may be more or less known to one another, be of different ages or ethnicities, or have different socioeconomic or educational backgrounds. The purpose of the conversation might be to carry out a specific task, create intimacy, foster social bonds, or simply fill time. The phrases, gestures, and vocabulary each speaker uses will depend on this context.

5. This presentation should take an argumentative form. The student might introduce the topic with a short narrative or a definition of "Standard English." The student might take into account the various forms of English used on Internet sites, blogs, and streaming radio and in print, and consider how the content and audience shape each. Because English is a dynamic, international language with a rich and eclectic history and has spawned countless dialects, students should be challenged to consider how "standard" forms of language come to be spoken, how they evolve, and what purposes they serve.

Leslie Marmon Silko, *Language and Literature from a Pueblo Indian Perspective* (p. 39)

1. Speaking, for Silko, is a more authentic form of communication than writing because the audience cannot hear the writer's "true feelings" when she reads from a prepared text (1). Because Pueblo storytelling is an oral tradition and Pueblo narratives resemble "a spider's web" of "crisscrossing" threads rather than a linear structure (1), the storyteller spontaneously creates "an elaborate structure of stories-within-stories" (6) that builds on this tradition. Thus, the meaning that emerges from a story is a specifically oral experience inseparable from the storyteller's presentation (6) and her relationship to the audience (8). Silko suggests that in contrast to Pueblo stories, which "never truly end" (6), a written story would give an inauthentic sense of finality to a fundamentally oral tradition and activity (6). The interconnected and holistic nature of storytelling, Silko argues, is essential to the Pueblo identity and culture (11).

2. Students might begin by listing different types of spoken and written communication they observe and engage in among friends, family, classmates, and colleagues. Forms of communication might range from the fleeting and informal, such as jokes, grocery lists, notations on a calendar, or texting, to the more formal, such as chaired meetings, study groups, study guides, assignments, or lectures. Students might identify how oral and written communication creates bonds among friends and family and discuss the importance of texting and e-mail in maintaining social ties. Examples of speech and writing that interact and reinforce one another include class presentations with supporting documents and taking notes in class. This assignment gives students an opportunity to explore how both writing and speaking reinforce learning as they hear and reiterate what they have learned in classroom discussion or peer-group work.

3. Pueblo stories connect to other stories because an oral tradition lends itself to creating unexpected thematic connections. The unity of Pueblo storytelling is grounded in the culture's cosmological view of creation as an "all-inclusive story" (4): "Everything in this world was a part of the original creation," so everything in the world is linked (4). Silko points out that Pueblo storytelling "goes on constantly" (14), an observation that characterizes the human experience generally. By noting how one's stories link to the stories of others, students become aware that all narratives have deep cultural connections. Their stories about their families or personal experiences may evince close connections with fairy tales or Shakespearean dramas or Homeric epics. Heroism, tragedy, generational conflict, sibling rivalry—stories are all patterned after life, even if each story is unique because each storyteller is unique.

4. Silko writes that "there is a story connected with every place, every object in the landscape" (18). Storytellers need to ground their stories in specific places, landscapes, and interiors that contribute to the meanings of a story. The storyteller who speaks to an unfamiliar audience is challenged to communicate the importance of place. This question asks students to imagine how to convey place by using the senses. How can a listener or reader imagine an unfamiliar place? Imagery is key here, so students should be encouraged to use figurative language in their answers.

5. Each of these authors uses different modes and stylistic techniques to explore the minority experience. This question asks the student to consider how each writer conveys that experience while presenting it so that the reader can understand it and empathize. Baldwin's emphasis on relations between Europeans and Africans and their descendents contextualizes his experience of cultural isolation in a Swiss village. Santiago uses vivid descriptions of place and family to chronicle her experience of two cultures and two names. Barry uses a child's perspective to depict the experience of learning to distinguish between raw emotion and the kind of hate that fuels prejudice. Rodriguez, Liu, and Alexie each describe experiences of cultural assimilation by a member of a minority group. Silko describes the sociolinguistic differences between her native culture and that of the conquering culture. In each essay, the writer uses examples of nonstandard

English or non-English phraseology to convey a flavor of his or her minority culture and also provides contextual information through which the reader can understand the writer's experience of difference.

Sherman Alexie, *The Joy of Reading and Writing: Superman and Me* (p. 45)

1. Alexie's connection between Superman's power and the act of teaching himself to read by interpreting Superman's actions with words suggests that reading allows the reader to identify, name, and ultimately enact his own fantasies of power. The "smart Indian" is, through such self-empowerment, one who defies expectations and risks community rejection. Alexie benefited from having a father who was an obsessive reader and whose reading illustrated the connection between power and literacy: His father moved from "westerns, spy thrillers, murder mysteries, gangster epics, [and] basketball player biographies" to "books about the Kennedy assassination, Watergate, the Vietnam War," and the imaginative reconstruction of Native American history—"the entire twenty-three-book series of the Apache westerns" (2). Alexie suggests that the act of reading represents both personal and political empowerment: Just as Alexie once interpreted Superman's acts as "breaking down the door" (4), the adult Alexie visits reservation classrooms in order to "save lives" by metaphorically throwing his weight against "their locked doors" (8).

2. For Alexie, as for Welty, reading is a physical experience. Just as books dominated Welty's childhood, Alexie's home was "filled with books," which "were stacked in crazy piles" (2). In addition, Alexie emphasizes reading as a way of exploring the community: He reads books in bookstores and from the library, and he reads newspapers, cereal boxes, bulletins posted on the walls of public places, junk mail, and magazines (7). Both Welty and Alexie link their sensory awareness of words to the material world. Welty regards listening, reading, and writing as interconnected aspects of one comprehensive process, while Alexie first understands a paragraph as "a fence that held words" and begins to "think of everything in terms of paragraphs" (3).

Just as Alexie's and Welty's experiences of reading and writing are shaped by where they read and what they read, e-mail, Twitter, and other electronic forms of communication are shaping reading and writing practices and the relationship between reading and writing. For example, the speed of electronic media encourages the development of shorthand phonetic writing, as Roz Chast illustrates in "The I.M.s of Romeo and Juliet" (Chapter 5). The instructor might ask students to compare the experience of reading electronic texts, including on Kindles and iPads, with Alexie's and Welty's experiences of reading.

3. Students might respond to this question by focusing on how reading has illuminated for them their ethnic or historical heritage, helped them develop their political and social identity, or more generally contributed to their intellectual development.

The student might consider, as Welty does, how family culture develops different attitudes toward reading and writing. Welty's family viewed reading as pleasurable as well as educational and books as companions as well as sources of knowledge. Alexie's father set an influential example without, it seems, voicing particular expectations that his son emulate him. However, his father's influence must have been significant, for Alexie's experience of school suggests that formal education discouraged his fellow Native American students from viewing literacy as empowering. The instructor might ask students to expand on this question by discussing Wiesel's treatment of writing as a moral duty (Chapter 1) or Kozol's description of the costs of illiteracy (Chapter 4).

Richard Wright, From *Fighting Words* (p. 48)

1. Alexie's assertion that "a smart Indian is a dangerous person" (6) in "The Joy of Reading and Writing: Superman and Me" (Chapter 1) might apply to Wright's description of his younger self's realization that an author can use "words as a weapon" (45). Wright also suggests that a literate African American is a dangerous person. Wright's quest to obtain a library card and check out books to read illustrates his dawning realization that reading is a political act. He begins his quest by making a connection between an editor who denounces Mencken for, apparently, "advocating ideas that the South did not like" (2) and the possibility that "people other than Negroes" might also criticize the South (2). By worrying that reading might cause "concern to the white men with whom I worked" (3), Wright suggests that literacy represents a challenge to the segregated South. Judging from the behavior of a white librarian, many whites actively enforced these exclusionary rules. By the time he has read Mencken, Wright has reconnected with his former "impulse to dream," equates illiteracy with passivity and helplessness, and realizes that reading offers "new ways of looking and seeing" (46).

2. Welty, Alexie, and Wright share a sense of amazement and wonder at the power of writing, and all become writers as a way to empower themselves. Welty's writing is an extension of the reading that fed her development as a child: She writes by listening to her "reader-voice" (19). Alexie's reading, which was his way of "trying to save [his] life" (7), transforms into a life of writing; he sees himself in his students who write in an effort "to save their lives" (8). Wright is struck by the power of writers to command the passion Mencken feels toward them. By asking "Were these men real?" (46), he suggests that such power is hard for him to grasp even as it creates "new ways of looking and seeing" (46). This power, Wright implies, offers the possibility that he might develop an authentic self that contrasts with his life as an African American in the segregated South. In a revealing passage, Wright worries that he might "betray myself" to the white librarian and strives to look "as unbookish as possible" (36), linking his self-betrayal to illiteracy. If the writers Mencken discusses are "real," Wright implies, he too might find a "real" self as a writer.

3. Wright's list of writers (46) represents a range of genres, languages, and eras, from novels to drama to philosophy to social commentary. The instructor can encourage students to consider this question as widely as possible by extending this list to other texts, such as graphic novels and music lyrics, for example. To list the characteristics required for a piece of writing to make an electrifying impression on the reader is to consider the aesthetics of stylistic techniques such as characterization, description, clarity, voice, and formality. The instructor can use this question to start a classroom discussion about what constitutes "good" writing.

4. This assignment asks students to write in two modes: process and narrative. The instructor might ask students to write each section for a different audience: the first part for a reader who wants to learn about a topic and the second for a close friend or an audience of fellow aficionados. The student should make his or her expectations of the audience explicit, perhaps by addressing the reader directly. The instructor may ask students to incorporate images into their essays in order to discuss how image and text interact, as Scott McCloud explores in "Reading the Comics" (Chapter 1). The instructor should emphasize that as students explore the relationship of writer to reader, they should also consider how the purpose of the text—to instruct, define, or narrate—shapes the writer's choice of vocabulary, sentence and overall structure, and tone. The exercise should encourage the student to see writing as contextual and multidimensional.

Scott McCloud, *Reading the Comics* (p. 51)

1. McCloud theorizes that the reader of comics must actively join the individual panels together to create meaning: The reader "mentally construct[s] a continuous, unified reality" (panel 2) based on his or her experience. Thus, the reader is complicit in constructing the action that the comic illustrates by filling in the implied actions that occur between the panels. The reader's desire to understand the action illustrated in the comics impels him or her to impose the "grammar" of closure on the comic's visual elements, its "visual iconography" (panel 3). Thus, even though the form of comics contains, and indeed is founded on, gaps in meaning, it requires the reader to finalize their meaning, or to provide "closure" in order to be understood.

For the second part of this question, students should consider how interpreting these three photographs from *The Arlington Reader* can both "open up" meaning and produce "closure." The themes suggested by "Education in Open Air" (Chapter 4) include the relationships between nature and technology, learner and environment, and the sublime and the analytical, as well as the observer's perception of the gendered, racially defined subject—any of which could "fix" or "open up" a reading. A "closed" reading of "Migrant Mother" (p. 556) might focus on the subject's despair or endurance, while an "open" reading might lead the observer to investigate the relationships between photographer, location, historical context, and subject. Reading "The Damm Family in

Their Car" as a portrait of passive hopelessness provides "closure," whereas an "open" interpretation might take into account the ironic symbolism of the car in American culture, the metaphor of the highway, the association of masculinity with power, and the frailty of the family as a social unit.

McCloud's argument that closure is "*anything* but *involuntary*" (panel 4) and that "every act committed to paper by the comics artist is *aided* and *abetted* by a *silent accomplice*" (panel 5) might form the basis of a class discussion on how interpretive reading imposes meaning on a text, an act of closure that McCloud describes as the reader's "special crime"—the termination of the process of interpretation and the finalization of meaning.

2. This exercise helps students understand how a reader interprets the relationship between text and image within a cultural context to produce meaning. For example, the reader could not easily interpret the image of the shoeless foot as Niemeyer intends in "Picturing the Past 10 Years" without the words "Airport Security" or without knowing that increased airport security measures in 2001 required passengers to take their shoes off to be x-rayed. The words "Nobody Knows I'm Gay" on the central figure's T-shirt invites the reader to embark on a process of open-ended interpretation. The words ironically deny what they simultaneously declare. While the text invites the observer to read the photographed figures as making a defiant statement against cultural prohibitions on or personal anxieties about "coming out," one might also read the text as an ironic "cover" over the wearer's sexual orientation. The text both guides the interpretation of the photograph and lends ambiguity to the sexual orientation of the three figures, who might or might not be gay. The visual elements of "Better Signs of Trouble" each use text in a specific way. Scher's warning system requires the reader to understand the textual definitions below the symbols; Fogel–Lubliner's text is intended to reinforce the emotional content of the images, and the reader of Brody and Knowles's system must understand that textual symbols create images that represent states of alertness or concern.

3. This assignment works best with a message that is ambiguous, defiant, or subverts its own meaning. Students should be encouraged to use the context of the photograph as much as possible in creating a new message, including the gender, age, ethnicities, and arrangement of the figures and the background and time of day. Students may want to recontextualize the photograph to support a new message. The instructor might ask students to describe a "closed" and an "open" interpretation of the new message.

4. For this exercise, students should examine McCloud's representations of "experience" (panel 1), "jagged, staccato rhythm" (panel 2), "continuous" closure (panel 5), and a "silent accomplice" (panels 7 and 9) as examples of abstract ideas represented visually. Students might use abstract or specific imagery, as McCloud does, respectively, in panels 2 and 7. This assignment works best when the student has an investment in the concept, so the instructor should encourage students to

use concepts and images from a recent assignment, perhaps from another course, that the students found particularly enjoyable or challenging.

Joan Didion, *On Keeping a Notebook* and Contexts (p. 54)

1. This assignment asks students to consider the context of writing, the purposes different forms of writing serve, and the many social practices it embodies. For example, the life of a text may be ephemeral (a grocery list), private (a love letter), public (a power of attorney), an expression of the deepest recesses of the self (a diary), a formalization of economic relationships (a last will and testament), a social gesture (an invitation), or the embodiment of social or familial relations (a scrapbook of memorabilia) or history (a family tree). Didion points out that "the act of saying *I*, of imposing oneself upon other people," is "an aggressive, even a hostile act" (2); writing might also be explored as a way of imposing oneself on the world or of endowing a relationship with materiality. This exercise could form the basis of a classroom discussion on how writing defines the self in the world as well as family relations, everyday life, and cultural practices. Who would we be without writing?

2. In the 1999 interview, Didion advises writers to learn "the discipline of sitting down and writing even when you have to spend three days writing bad stuff before the fourth day, when you write something better" (2). Students can't afford to sit in a room for three days to start writing. But the gist of her advice—perseverance—is relevant to student writers and professional writers alike.

Student responses to this question will vary. However, students might explore this question by comparing their views of "bad stuff" with Elbow's discussion of "bad writing" (5) in "Freewriting" (Chapter 1). The instructor might ask students who incline toward self-censorship to write as if speaking when, as Elbow describes, "there's someone right there waiting for a reply and he'll get bored or think we're crazy if we don't come up with *something*" (5). Simply writing —anything—will do the trick.

3. In "Why I Write" (p. 60), Didion employs a chanting repetition to emphasize that she is always more curious about specific matters in life than about abstract ideas or theories:

> I would try to read linguistic theory and would find myself wondering instead if the lights were on in the bevatron up the hill. When I say that I was wondering if the lights were on in the bevatron you might immediately suspect, if you deal in ideas at all, that I was registering the bevatron as a political symbol, thinking in shorthand about the military-industrial complex and its role in the university community, but you would be wrong. I was only wondering if the lights were on in the bevatron, and how they looked. A physical fact. (4)

Her deliberate repetition of *wondering* and *bevatron* brings two images to mind: her wondering look and the particle accelerator on top of the hill. Thus she prepares readers for the final sentence, or sentence fragment, at the end of the paragraph—"A physical fact"—driving home the message that she is keen on specifics but dubious on the hidden meaning of the bevatron as a symbol of political, technological, or military power.

4. Writing "just the facts" encourages students to observe carefully and to apply the oft-quoted advice to "show rather than tell." By rewriting the "factual" account to incorporate and develop the observer's experience, the student will learn what Didion means by *"How it felt to me"* in "Keeping a Notebook" (8). The instructor might also point out that Didion's explanation of grammar in "Why I Write" makes a similar point: An observable object such as a cat becomes the writer's "picture" through the grammar of a sentence (6–7). As Didion explains in "On Keeping a Notebook," writing invariably portrays the experience of the observer and participant. The observer's experience dictates its "truth." A "lie"—that which only "might have happened"—might be the very image that recreates the experience the writer seeks to capture (7). The instructor should ask students to analyze the stylistic and substantive transformations their writing undergoes when turning a factual account into a narrative of personal experience.

5. For Tom Wolfe, "the least understood" device of New Journalism is the use of the symbol of one's *"status life,"* which can be "the entire pattern of behavior and possessions through which people express their position in the world or what they think it is or what they hope it to be" (5). In "On Keeping a Notebook," Didion reveals her "status life" in a series of questions about why she was taking notes "in the bar of the hotel across from the Pennsylvania Railroad station in Wilmington, Delaware" (2). Was she "waiting for a train? Missing one? 1960? 1961? Why Wilmington?" (2). Readers learn from these remarks that the speaker is well educated, curious, and middle class or higher. She must be middle class or higher because she stayed in a hotel rather than a motel; she must be a sophisticated traveler for she can't even remember why or when she was at a certain place. While this technique is effective, it doesn't belong to New Journalists exclusively; in other essays in Chapter 1 we can find many examples of this technique. Why does Amy Tan open "Mother Tongue" with a lecture she was giving in highly educated English and then convey the uneasy feeling her mother's entrance to the scene caused her? Readers get an idea about her status life: She is from a modest immigrant family whose "mother tongue" is a special version of English that some people would call "broken" or "limited."

Peter Elbow, *Freewriting* (p. 67)

1. For Elbow, freewriting impedes the "ingrained habit of editing at the same time you are trying to produce" (6) and opens the floodgates of the writer's mind. By writing "whatever is in your mind" (1), the writer overrides any tendency to evaluate his or her writing. Elbow encourages writers to "[j]ust put down something" (1) when faced with a dearth of ideas. Elbow characterizes speaking as a

more informal, relaxed process than writing: Writers may worry about "spelling and grammar" as they write; in contrast, when speaking, "we settle for the catch-as-catch-can way in which the words tumble out" (5). Elbow's example suggests that even writing about the difficulty of writing will eventually produce ideas.

2. Elbow defines editing as a "massive and complicated series" of steps that interpose themselves between the conscious awareness of words and their appearance on the page (4). Freewriting is intended to eliminate these steps and allow the writer to explore the "texture" and "rhythm" of his or her voice and the "energy" that "drives the meanings" that the writer wants to commit to paper (9). "[C]ompulsive, premature editing" (9) deadens this voice, while freewriting creates a place for it to speak without criticism or censorship. Elbow suggests that editing is a different process than producing (6), implying that editing should follow the production of a draft.

3. Because freewriting is *"nonediting"* (7), it should "make writing less blocked because words will come more easily" (7). Students who are unused to freewriting may find it initially uncomfortable or nonproductive. The instructor might encourage students to freewrite daily for a set period and then analyze the results before arguing whether Elbow is right or not.

4. This exercise might form the basis of a classroom discussion on the qualities that make writing "dead" or "alive." Students could compare two illustrative texts and consider how sentence structure and word choice can animate writing or drag it down, how literary allusions or cultural references can enliven writing or make it obscure, and how tone can elicit the reader's interest and empathy or create distance and even hostility. This assignment should help students see that "dead" writing shuts down the reader's engagement with a text, whereas strong writing invites the reader to hear the writer's voice.

5. For Elbow, voice is "the force that will make a reader listen to you" (9). The writer's voice emerges when the writer is not "nervous, jumpy, inhibited" (6), is free from "interruptions, changes, and hesitations between the consciousness and the page" (9), and when his or her words "come more easily" (7). Sometimes "a halting or even garbled beginning" (8) is precisely what the writer needs to become "coherent and even powerful" because "trying to get the beginning just right is a formula for failure" (8).

6. The instructor may want to encourage students to record these various experiments in a journal. Students should try writing in a variety of modes and analyze the outcomes of each attempt. For example, students might write as a Pueblo storyteller, using Silko's nonlinear model of narration (Chapter 1), as a reporter according to Tom Wolfe's description of New Journalism (Chapter 1), or as a science journalist according to David Brown's idea of "evidence-based journalism" (Chapter 1). For each mode of writing, the student should record whether his or her voice changed, became more coherent and powerful, or acquired a particular "texture" or "rhythm" (9).

Stephen King, *Write or Die* (p. 71)

Elie Wiesel, *Why I Write: Making No Become Yes* (p. 73)

1. The young Stephen King regarded the guidance counselor's suggestion to write for a local newspaper as a punishment for two reasons. First, he was just released from detention hall and expected some milder continuation of the punishment. That's why he read the counselor's look as *"Do it or die"* (2). The offer appeared to be anything but an opportunity.

The second reason is more specifically connected with his nascent writing experience. Known for his less-than-constructive but "restless pen" (2), King had worked for two other local newspapers, *Dave's Rag* and *The Drum,* but was unsuccessful with both. Consequently, he became a teenager "haunted by newspapers" (3). Knowing little about sports but feeling compelled by the expectation of the school authority to take a writing job with another local newspaper, he seemed doomed to repeat his previous failures, which, of course, appeared to him to be punishment rather than an opportunity.

2. John Gould drove home the lesson of having a sharp focus by practicing what he preached. His approach was simple and direct—getting out what is not the story. It must have worked extremely well for the dubious teenager, because forty years later King could reproduce that piece from memory. As that brief but razor-sharp reproduction demonstrates, Gould made three deletions "with a large black pen" (7) and changed two phrases. The piece was about a basketball game in which "an LHS player broke the school scoring record" (9). That the hometown high school's gymnasium was "well-loved" and the record-breaking player's nickname and size were not immediately relevant. That player just broke the record; therefore, to say that he was "known for his accuracy" was redundant. The word "plus" was a mere filler, so Gould crossed it off. The word "thinclads" originally referred to everybody who was "clad" in thin clothes, and later specifically referred to track athletes. It did not contribute to the clarity of the piece and was replaced by the plain word "player." The phrase "since the years of Korea" was vague as it referred to a number of years rather than to a single year and Gould simply replaced it with the year 1953. "I only took out the bad parts" (11), said Gould.

3. As an established writer reviewing a turning point in his adolescent life and a moment of epiphany in his nascent writing career, King intentionally or unintentionally covers both the writing product and its process. Gould's editorial corrections (9) illustrate the difference between a good writing product and one that needs improvement; King's recounting of what Gould said about writing and rewriting directs readers' attention to the complex process through which that product is actually created.

Writing in this context means the specific stage of drafting, especially when the writer starts to discover his or her ideas with the help of pen and paper —

including early revision. At this stage, writers often physically shut themselves up in a small room and focus on nothing but their ideas and feelings. This stage is concerned with developing ideas and with making initial decisions about what form will best convey those ideas. Gould translated that idea into plainer words for King: "When you write a story, you're telling yourself the story" (15).

At the rewriting stage, the door must be open because writers prepare to send their work to be read by others who may be critical of it. Composition scholars call this stage the crucial transitional phase; if successful, it transforms the writer-based essay into a reader-based one that is interesting not only for the author but also for a wide range of readers (who may or may not share with the author some important assumptions about the subject matter).

4. Wiesel uses the term "witness" (6) in a moral and religious sense: "I believed that, having survived by chance, I was duty-bound to give meaning to my survival, to justify each moment of my life. I knew the story had to be told. Not to transmit an experience is to betray it" (6). The source of his belief is "Jewish tradition" (6). To write as a witness, for Wiesel, is to "remain faithful" to the memory and experiences of victims of the Nazi concentration camps (8–10), to "remain loyal" to their sufferings (11), and to try to understand the horror of genocide and of the massacre of Jewish children (15–22). "Why I Write" describes the process of writing as witnessing; for example, Wiesel describes the challenge of finding "a fresh vocabulary" that would allow him to convey "concentration camp language" (8). Many of the essays from *The Arlington Reader* demonstrate their writers' belief in witnessing as a moral act, including Richard Wright's description of segregation in "Fighting Words" in Chapter 1, and, in Chapter 3, Barbara Ehrenreich's investigation of the working poor ("Serving in Florida"), Alice Walker's testament to the creative life of African American women ("In Search of Our Mothers' Gardens), and Virginia Woolf's statement on women's struggle for intellectual and economic autonomy ("Professions for Women"). The instructor should encourage students to define the underlying beliefs and values of the writer in question, even if those beliefs and values are not as explicit as Wiesel makes his. King's advice to "open the door" applies to any writer who wants the reader to understand and engage with the acts the writer has witnessed. As King points out, writing with the "door open" reminds the writer that writing is not "just for you" but also for the reader (15).

5. Wiesel suggests that failing to transmit an experience will "exile" it from human experience; the words that can convey the meanings of an experience become irreparably displaced from that experience (6). For example, Wiesel writes, "After Auschwitz everything brings us back to Auschwitz" (25): To witness is to remind his readers of the literal and symbolic meaning of Auschwitz and thus to keep the individual and collective experience of the Holocaust alive in the consciousness—and conscience—of the world. Wiesel writes that the reader

who has "never lived under a sky of blood" can never "know what it was like" (21), and yet he is compelled to try to "tell the tale" (27) to defy the world's denial of the humanity of those murdered in the camps. Wiesel expects his reader to understand the moral force of his "struggle against silence" (31) and thus to also understand the morality of the act of writing as witnessing.

6. This assignment asks students to adopt Wiesel's commitment to "make no become yes" by transforming experience into language and persuading the reader to experience it as the writer does. The challenge to the writer is to etch that experience into the minds of his readers. The instructor should encourage the student to review King's advice about writing with the door "closed" and then "open" to remember that the writer's passion must translate into an experience the reader can imaginatively share.

7. Both Wiesel and King imply that compulsive creativity produces a range of psychic experiences, from the liberating to the agonizing. King implies that his guidance counselor's determination to turn King's "restless pen" into "constructive channels" (2) was a response to King's tendencies to explore the dark parts of his psyche — an exploration that fuels many of his horror and fantasy novels. Wiesel finds writing disturbing, frustrating, and uncertain, but also essential to his being: Transmitting the history of the dead is a duty, "even if it disturbs, even if it brings pain" (12). Although he writes "to understand," he "shall never understand" (14); at times he hears "a voice within [him] telling [him] to stop mourning the past" (11) even as he can "never stop seeing [the murdered children]" (16). Both writers depict writing as an action that transcends the positive or negative experiences it engenders because it represents a passionate vocation.

8. This assignment asks students to explore the values they transmit and embody in their writing and to consider how electronic writing shapes those values. The instructor might ask students to compare the results of this assignment with their responses to Question 6. Does the energy they invest in social networking and writing for their peers translate into academic writing? In what ways did their responses for these two assignments differ?

Phillip Niemeyer, *Picturing the Past Ten Years* (p. 79)

1. Niemeyer's chart invites the reader to interpret the images and text by using cultural references. Part of the fun of deciphering the chart lies in remembering and locating oneself in relation to the context that the images and text represent. Thus, through this process of interpretation, students understand how contextual knowledge and experience support the production of meaning. Students may remember specific events or language that became an important part of their lives, or influenced their parents' or family's lives and so became a part of family culture, or created a media sensation. Other events may seem obscure,

and some of the language may appear dated or, in contrast, have become fully assimilated into contemporary culture.

2. By involving parents and grandparents in reading Niemeyer's chart, students can learn how much background information they need to make interpretation possible. Some cultural references are difficult to explain to somebody who does not remember the circumstances in which they appeared; others require minimal contextual information. This assignment invites students to examine how their own lives are shaped by popular culture and topical events and to explore how each generation defines itself in a particular historical moment.

3. By constructing their own chart, students can apply the knowledge they have gained through Questions 2 and 3 and define crucial events that have shaped their lives. This exercise can form the basis of a classroom activity and discussion.

Marjorie Agosín, *Always Living in Spanish* (p. 80)

1. Agosín mentions the role of landscape, of smells and sounds, of the melodies and rhythms of language, and of songs and writing in the formation of her identity. Her struggle to connect to her new home and to reconnect to her childhood in Chile leads her to become highly conscious of these sources of identity. Ask students to consider the ways in which their experiences of culture and family have developed around sources of identity such as food, music, and the local environment.

2. Agosín describes English as "austere" (7), while she finds Spanish "undulating and sensuous" (8). To some extent, the richness Agosín associates with Spanish is linked to her diverse cultural heritage, for example, to the "multiplicity of tongues" that characterized her childhood and the "memory of spaces" those languages connoted (3). In contrast, her life in the United States seemed to her culturally impoverished and linguistically limited. While it is only in Spanish that Agosín can express the "visceral emotions and themes" of her poetry, she also implies that a poem can be "itself" (6) in either Spanish or English. For this reason, she calls translators "splendid friends" (8). Monolingual readers might interpret Agosín's description of the "torment of not being able to live in the language of [...] childhood" (6) as a universal, if also experientially unique, condition. From childhood experiences that fuel the development of personal identity we are all exiled, as well as from the linguistic intimacy and connectedness Agosín describes—although her experience was perhaps more acute as a result of her geographical displacement.

3. and 4. These questions allow students to expand on issues of identity and language and apply them to their own experiences.

David Brown, *Science Reporting and Evidence-Based Journalism* (p. 83)

1. For Brown, evidence is the foundation of scientific thought: Evidence confirms, challenges, or overthrows the hypotheses that science sets out to examine (1).

Evidence includes information that can be measured (3), but more importantly, evidence is information that allows the reader to "judge the strength of a claim" (7). Brown's definition is fundamental to his argument because he considers unsupported opinion (5, 20), simplistic notions of good and "flawed" science (14), and anecdote-based narrative (27–29) poor substitutes for evidence. Evidence allows the reader "to make a decision about how important something is" (26).

2. Providing relevant contextual information in a way that allows the reader to judge "the strength of a claim" is difficult because there are many forces working against this "evidence-based paradigm" (11). The editors who manage the flow of information from the journalist to the reader tend "to be intimidated by science and scientists" (12). Brown claims that editors do not fully appreciate that science is an ongoing, dynamic learning process and that scientific knowledge is inherently flawed because science does not constitute a "realm of priestly knowledge" based on esoteric logic and judgment (12). Rather, scientific research is an extension of "everyday thinking" (12–13), and its flaws can be examined and analyzed (15). It is difficult for journalists to follow an "evidence-based" paradigm, Brown argues, because science journalism tends to be driven by experts' opinions (16) and to follow a narrative form (27–29). In addition, journalists face pressure to emphasize novelty at the expense of evidence (33). Brown clearly finds the challenge of evidence-based reporting fun because he loves science and believes that when writing about science, "all that counts is the evidence" (20).

3. Brown uses Gulf War syndrome as an example of a new illness for which "there was little or no evidence" (30). Brown suggests a reporter's first step in sifting through the vast amount of information on a particular subject such as this is to examine the evidence on which experts base their opinions (8) and apply his or her natural "skepticism" (12). Brown implies that asking the right questions is essential (7, 15) when evaluating information. This assignment might form the basis of a classroom discussion on evaluating information sources, particularly considering how the very technological resources that Brown mentions (10) can also overwhelm the writer.

4. As Brown points out, expert opinion does not allow the reader to evaluate the strength of a scientific claim because it does not constitute evidence. His stance implies that such a practice does not treat the reader with sufficient respect: "Giving the reader the evidence, rather than the words of an expert telling him what to think, is also the democratic thing to do" (26). Brown distinguishes evidence from opinion by characterizing evidence as information that can be measured and contextualized within a larger body of knowledge (3, 7). He argues that experts' pronouncements are "ultimately irrelevant" because "when all is said and done, all that counts is the evidence" (20). Brown illustrates the unreliability of opinion through his example of the study of statins' effects on coronary heart disease (36–40). He suggests that the sources of scientific news—in this case, a cardiolo-

gist, a pharmaceutical company, and the American College of Cardiology—each contributed, perhaps unwittingly, to the perception that the study was a significant breakthrough, and this perception led to exaggerated claims in the media about the study's results.

5. Narrative, Brown argues, "makes an anecdote evidence" and thus gives the impression that anecdotal evidence suffices to establish the credibility of a claim (29). The paradigm of narrative encourages dramatic conflict at the expense of evidence. Because narrative relies on a protagonist who elicits the reader's involvement in an emotional conflict, articles written in a narrative form tend to work toward dramatic outcomes. For example, the question about whether high-dose chemotherapy and bone marrow transplants were "the best strategy for beating breast cancer" (31) became a media drama of patients victimized by demonic insurance companies—rather than reportage based on evidence. Brown points out the impact of such anecdotal evidence used irresponsibly: Thousands of women underwent a "painful, expensive, and dangerous treatment" and did not enjoy improved survival rates (31).

6. Brown uses his experience to support his argument that reporters and editors do not have an incentive "to tell a story completely" (32), writing from the point of view of a journalist competing to get his story on page 1 (32). Singer and Wilson point to some of the dangers of writing about science without rigorously scrutinizing the evidence backing scientific claims. Some drug makers participate in the writing of scientific articles, turning them into "marketing vehicles for their products" (3). Such articles may present skewed research results (9) and influence the direction of new research and medical practices (26). Singer and Wilson's article corroborates Brown's point that exaggerations, mistakes, and lies degrade the quality of journalism and public discourse (Brown 43–46).

7. The five criteria that define Brown's "evidence-based" model are: (1) an approach characterized by "natural" skepticism (12); (2) an understanding that science is "iterative and conditional" and that flaws "start the conversation" about scientific progress rather than end it (14); (3) a greater emphasis on evidence relative to commentary (20); (4) a preponderance of evidence rather than narrative and anecdote (27–29); and (5) an emphasis on completeness of the story rather than novelty and certainty (32–33). As Brown points out, science writing may not always accomplish the twofold task of providing enough information to allow the reader to "judge the strength of a claim" and to describe "what's already known about the subject" (7). Students will find this dual goal, as Brown observes, "a tall order" (9). Nevertheless, students will benefit by exploring how writers rely on shortcuts such as using experts' opinions. By reflecting on the difficulty of writing about science without resorting to exaggeration or distortion, students can begin to explore what Brown means by "a model for intelligent discourse" (46).

2   IDENTITY WITH ATTITUDE: WHO AM I, AND WHY DOES IT MATTER?

Franz Boas and George Hunt, *An "Authentic" Indian* (p. 92)

1. The dark backdrop Franz Boas and George Hunt hold literally veils the presence of the immigrants who conquered indigenous peoples such as this Kwakiutl woman. The photograph suggests that the artifice of the staging itself will ultimately be concealed, since the two white men will be omitted from the final photograph of the subject and the artifacts that accompany her. Thus, the two white men, an anthropologist and a photographer, consciously construct the image of an "authentic" Indian by carefully partitioning her from the history that allows them to define her ethnicity.

Students can compare this visual orchestration of an "authentic" Indian to Sherman Alexie's imaginary theme-park experience of an indigenous American woman's life. In "What Sacagawea Means to Me" (p. 115), Alexie identifies similar ways in which white Americans conceal historical facts to construct a particular version of history and image of ethnicity. For example, Alexie points out that others accompanied Sacagawea and Lewis and Clark on the journey, including York, a black slave. The construction of the Lewis and Clark journey as "the triumphant tale of two white men" (3), like the staged photograph of the "authentic" Indian, conceals the artificiality of its construction. Concealing the historical relationship between European immigrants and indigenous natives, Alexie argues, allows the conquerors to deny the complexity and violence of that history.

The staged photograph also detaches the subject from her own landscape and history and thus metaphorically replicates what Momaday characterizes in "Disturbing the Spirits" as "crimes" (7) against Native Americans. In "East of My Grandmother's House," Momaday imagines a deep physical connection between personal experience and landscape: "Once in his life a man ought to concentrate his mind upon the remembered earth, I believe. He ought to give himself up to a particular landscape in his experience [...]. He ought to imagine that he touches it with his hands at every season and listens to the sounds that are made upon it" (1). "The Way to Rainy Mountain" explores the landscape's power to awaken the spirit: "To look upon that landscape in the early morning, with the sun at your back, is to lose the sense of proportion. Your imagination comes to life, and this, you think, is where Creation was begun" (1). From this perspective, the photograph of the Kwakiutl subject robs her spiritually and diminishes her cultural identity. Ask students to consider what kind of story this photograph tells, particularly in light of Momaday's observation in "The Native Voice" that the "storyteller creates the storytelling experience and himself and his audience in the process" (2).

2. Boaz and Hunt's photograph can help students explore the construction of meaning by considering how visual clues, framing, and modes of presentation create the depicted subject. As Michael J. Bugeja argues in "Facing the Facebook" (Chapter 5), the identities of those who use Facebook resemble marketing categories or "advertisements for products or lifestyles" (11), suggesting that Facebook users appear to one another as a collection of marketable attributes. The instructor may want to challenge students to define the ways that television reality shows create "reality," whether the "truth" of any experience can be conveyed to others without shaping it, and whether there is a definitive boundary between omission and distortion. Elie Wiesel's "Why I Write" (Chapter 1) describes the daunting struggle to convey the truth of experience and might be an instructive companion text.

Eric Liu, *Notes of a Native Speaker* (p. 93)

1. Eric Liu tries to define "the essence of whiteness" in terms of cultural preference, clothing, diet, location of residence, interior design, travel, marriage, social and political position, sociolinguistic position, interest in international affairs from an American perspective, sense of ethnicity, racial attitude, self-confidence, and a sense of merit. On closer scrutiny, however, the "whiteness" he portrays includes only a small circle of white people near the center of power. It is revealing that this small group should be regarded as the "essence" or "mainstream" of white, or even all, America: "I am a member of several exclusive institutions. I have been in the inner sanctums of political power. I have been there as something other than an attendant. I have the ambition to return. I expect my voice to be heard. I consider myself neither in exile nor in opposition" (p. 94).

This small circle excludes half of humanity, be it white or "colored" — "I married a white woman." This circle includes only the upper-middle class — "I own brown suede bucks. I eat gourmet greens. I am a child of the suburbs. I furnish my condo à la Crate & Barrel." This circle, of course, is privileged in terms of racial, ethnic, and other cultural areas: "I have never once been the victim of blatant discrimination. I am not too ethnic. I am wary of minority militants. I am a producer of the culture." This circle even may exclude upper-middle-class whites from certain geographical regions of the United States: "I speak flawless, unaccented English." This circle pretends to go beyond America and to be interested in the affairs of the world, yet from a definitely U.S.-centered perspective: "I subscribe to *Foreign Affairs*." Liu intends to portray the essence of whiteness as privilege. Many white students may think that Liu's list fails to define whiteness, but these students should be aware that Liu offers this list "not to justify it but to detoxify it, to prevent its further spread" (20).

2. Liu's "self-conscious," developed at Yale, is basically "race neutrality and self-reliance" (13). He thought he didn't need the "crutch" of Asian support groups and clubs. Although he didn't avoid making Asian friends in college or

working with Asian classmates, "[he] simply never went out of [his] way to do so" (13). He didn't need to emphasize his Asian background to climb the "'magic escalator' of a Yale education" (22). He concentrated all of his energy on combatting the "stereotypes [of Asians] by trying to disprove them" (16). Consequently, he became "the only Chinese face at OCS or in this club or that" (18). Gradually, he was no longer an outsider in mainstream America: An alumni internship took him to Capitol Hill, which "led to a job and a life in Washington after commencement. . . .[B]y almost any standard, but particularly by the standards of my younger self, I was actually beginning to 'make it'" (22). The instructor may want students to compare Liu's experience of assimilation with that Richard Rodriguez describes in "Aria" (p. 275). For Liu, assimilation represents "[moving] away from the periphery and toward the center of American life" (1); Rodriguez makes a similar argument about learning English as moving away from the private circle to the public world. For both, assimilation is an act of self-empowerment, yet each essayist also suggests that a price must be paid for cultural status and financial success through assimilation. Students might also compare Liu's experience of cultural adaptation with Amy Tan's in "Mother Tongue" (p. 34) and describe each writer's treatment of new immigrants. Does one or the other seem truer to the American spirit?

3. While Liu indeed focuses on self-definition, he does not argue for egocentrism. Instead, he describes the personal struggle of an Asian American to find his identity in a society that still holds upper-middle-class, white male values as the essence of America. Compare Liu's piece with Richard Rodriguez's "Aria" and Amy Tan's "Mother Tongue," both of which put the search for identity at the center of their contemplation of racial issues in society. These authors do not argue for themselves alone but for many others who have been placed in similar situations against their will.

4. Liu describes his youthful perception of racial identity as a choice between "'embrace or efface'" and of his subsequent experience of assimilation as "the straitening path" (23). Liu realizes that as he focused on learning "the culture of the influential class" (21), he may have also missed out on friendships and "self-knowledge" as a result of "distancing" himself from his race (23). In contrast, Amy Tan characterizes her experience as a Chinese American as one formed by multiple Englishes, and her adaptation as less mainstream than Liu's: Her mother's "broken" English limited her perception of her mother's qualities and "almost had an effect on limiting my possibilities in life" (15). Tan might agree with Liu that "while it may be possible to transcend race, *it is not always necessary to try*" (23). Richard Rodriguez describes his experience of speaking English as learning "public language," which implies the loss of "intimate family voices" (40). Students may want to approach this assignment by building on their responses to Question 3. Ask them to consider how personal struggles articulate larger social issues: How does the desire of the individual to succeed in a culture place him, in Liu's words, "at the ill-fated intersection of class and race" (5)?

Esmeralda Santiago, *Jíbara* (p. 99)

1. In "Aria," the Context essay for Chapter 4, Richard Rodriguez describes the intimate sounds of the Spanish language spoken at home and several times openly refers to his family as "very loving." Esmeralda Santiago, however, chooses to represent the loving bonds in an indirect and perhaps more effective way. Santiago, for instance, depicts the close bond between mother and daughter through small incidents of tension: The mother wants the daughter to help "gather kindling for the fire" (8), but the daughter wants to work with her father, who is not, at first, supportive. However, as the domestic drama unfolds, readers soon see the indirect expression of mutual warm feelings: Despite all her tough words, the mother is especially afraid of snakes, and the daughters tease her about it; after Negi returns from gathering kindling, the father helps her avoid working in the kitchen and lets her stay and work with him. Then, after Negi is stung by hundreds of termites, her mother shows profound care for and love of her daughter through her actions and through her unique way of scolding. In short, Santiago doesn't tell us but *shows* us that her parents are warmhearted people who love their children and each other deeply.

2. As a child, Santiago is "puzzled by the hypocrisy of celebrating" the *jíbaros*, a people "everyone looked down on" (51). Although urban Puerto Ricans respect the *jíbaros* for their pride, nationalism, and independence, the country dwellers are also "mocked for their unsophisticated customs and their peculiar dialect" (49). Santiago seems to share her fellow Puerto Ricans' contradictory feelings about the *jíbaros*. On the one hand, the *jíbaros* represent "traditional music and poetry" (49), which she associates with her father and his beloved radio. Yet, living in the country brings worries: The floor sags, "threatening to collapse and bring the house down with it" (4), leaving a dirt floor, which "meant snakes and scorpions could crawl into the house" (6). This contradictory celebration and scorn suggests that Santiago, like other Puerto Ricans, experiences some cultural anxiety about the very "closeness to nature" and "proud nationalism" that she admires. Closeness to nature can also suggest poverty, while nationalism may be associated with both emotional security and provincialism.

The second part of this question asks students to refer to other readings in the book to explore how their perceptions of groups in their own cultures are formed. For example, Eric Liu describes his resistance to the "unflattering mythologies that attach to Asian Americans: that we are indelibly foreign, exotic, math and science geeks, numbers people rather than people people, followers and not leaders, physically frail but devious and sneaky, unknowable and potentially treacherous" (15). Such stereotypes might, Gloria Anzaldúa suggests, result from "traditional categories" of race and gender, which sustain a "politics of exclusion" that "diminishes our humanness" (2). Similarly, Deirdre N. McCloskey argues that gender itself is "culturally specific" (5), and that gendered behavior is learned much the same way as spoken language. By exploring their own perceptions of other cultures and ethnicities, students can also examine how such perceptions contribute to the formation of their cultural identities.

3. Although this question is text-based, the instructor would do well to encourage students to draw from their own experience in their responses, beginning with a review of the clues provided in both texts. Does Santiago's younger sister Delsa behave like a little doll because her mother calls her *muñequita*? How would her other younger sister, Norma, respond to her own skin that "glowed the same color as the inside of a yam," growing up answering the nickname "the red girl" (*la colora*)? While nicknames are often terms of endearment, they can also mislead or confuse children about who they are, depending on the implication of the nicknames. Santiago herself, for instance, had never seen her own face in a mirror and was thereby confused about her own skin color: "So *Negi* means I'm black?" (58). Having a private language of endearment at home, according to Rodriguez, has a similar effect on the children: On the one hand, they feel loved and accepted at home; on the other hand, the private language becomes a barrier between themselves and the outside world that uses a different, public language. Drawing from their own experience, students may see the two-sided nature of many issues. This question can thus lead them to think critically about how language forms perceptions and constructs meaning.

4. This question allows students to explore the process of personal development through the recollection of childhood experience. The instructor should encourage the student to use some of the techniques Santiago employs effectively, including

- dialogue;
- sensory experience ("a dry, metallic taste" [7], "stinging the soles" [13]);
- detailed description (13);
- metaphor ("nutty brown," "rust colored," "black pupils [. . .] like sunflowers" [57]);
- the child's perspective ("I imagined a world of fascinating creatures" [6], "wondering how the termites knew I'd disobeyed my mother [41]);
- embedded contextual information ("Poems and stories about the hardships and joys of the Puerto Rican *jíbaro* were required reading" [51]).

Reflecting on an adult's angry response to childish mischief is an opportunity to make sense of the past, as Santiago does when she writes, "I had yet to learn not everything I heard was true, so we reacted in what was to become a pattern for us: what frightened her I became curious about, and what she found exciting terrified me" (6).

Bobbie Ann Mason, *Being Country* (p. 105)

1. In certain passages of "Being Country," Bobbie Ann Mason does seem to have transcended the harsh reality of life on a farm, with food always a concern. At the very opening of this excerpt, she presents her eleven-year-old self as "entirely absorbed" with reading a nineteenth-century American novel and irritated by

the food-centered conversation on a twentieth-century American farm. Unlike her grandmother, who regards food as the sole purpose of a farm life, the young Mason is concerned with issues far beyond the subject of food. She "questions a woman's duties" (4) and her dislike for farm life is based on a higher reason than its "inferior" food: "We were at the mercy of nature, and it wasn't to be trusted. . . . Our livelihood—even our lives—depended on forces outside our control. . . . I especially hated women's part in the dependence" (6, 7). Yet, as she recounts her youthful fascination with town life, Mason also reveals how her early preoccupation with food has endured and shaped her writing and her memories of childhood. For example, she describes a recurrent dream of a "buffet or cafeteria line, laden with beautiful foods" from which she wakes up before getting to eat (5). She also enjoys utilizing many and varied verbs in her description of her mother's food preparation: "butchering and plucking and planting and hoeing and shredding and slicing and creaming (scraping cobs for the creamed corn) and pressure-cooking and canning and freezing and thawing and mixing and shaping and baking and frying" (13).

2. The first clue to the irony of that statement is in its syntax: "Food was better in town, we thought" (15). The phrase "we thought," positioned as an afterthought, reveals the unreliability of the thoughts of an eleven-year-old narrator. Other clues come in the second statement about the superiority of food in town: "But hamburgers in town were better. They were greasier, and they came in waxed-paper packages" (15). The hamburgers are neither more nutritious nor more tasty than country food, but simply "greasier." What kind of superiority is that? The only thing that hamburgers in town have that her mother's country food doesn't is the wax-paper package. Mason's irony is further sharpened by her seemingly random description of the busy streets in town: the A&P "reeked of the rich aroma of ground coffee" (17); the "exhaust fan would blow the intoxicating smell of hamburgers in your face" (15). In contrast, back on the farm, "[n]othing was processed, except by Mama" (13).

3. Mason's lists reveal the abundance of the farm: the "chickens, the hogs, the milk and butter, the Irish potatoes, the beans, peas, corn, cabbage, apples, [and] peaches" all come from the family's farm (13). The narrator tells the reader that this abundance did not come easily, as nature is an unreliable ally for the farmer and the food only comes from hard, continuous work. If Mason had broken her lists into shorter sentences, they would not as effectively capture for the reader the diligence of the farmer's wife or illustrate the healthier, if harder, lifestyle of rural people compared to that of city dwellers.

4. For a discussion of Liu's list of the traits that define "whiteness," see Question 1 under Liu in the *Instructor's Manual*. Liu's list defines the preferences of the dominant culture and himself as a participant in that culture, while Mason's lists in paragraphs 13, 15, and 17 evoke the narrator's memories of a childhood in rural and small-town Kentucky. Ask students to keep the purpose of their lists in mind as they write. For example, a list could describe the complexity of an activity (such as working on a car engine) or a range of experiences (such as those that occur while travelling).

5. The instructor may ask students to compare Mason's childhood ambivalence toward her home and upbringing with Alice Walker's more idealizing portrait of her mother in "In Search of Our Mothers' Gardens" (Chapter 3) to explore both the longing to leave home behind and create a new self and the desire to preserve and recapture certain aspects of childhood. New experiences can disappoint and evoke nostalgia for the familiar. The willingness to explore ambivalence is key to this assignment, so ask students to be open to the paradoxes of longing and to the complexities of its fulfillment.

Art Spiegelman, *Mein Kampf (My Struggle)* (p. 109)

1. A metaphor that combines Spiegelman's political and personal material, the five-thousand-pound mouse embodies both the memory of the Holocaust and the success of Spiegelman's graphic novel *Maus*. He is thus haunted by his creation of "Jewish mice and Nazi cats" (panel 3) as much as by the memories his creation represents: "remembering those who remembered the death camps is a hard act to follow" (panel 4). The act of remembering is central to the artist's work; the word "memories" appears in the background in several panels accompanied by modifiers: "repressed" (panel 5), "erotic" and "neurotic" (panel 6), and "intrauterine" and "childhood" (panel 7). In another telling repetition, Spiegelman uses the phrase "I was just another baby-boom boy" in panels 1 and 9, a deliberately banal statement that contrasts with his references to the Holocaust and suggests that his inability to remember speaks to the desire to free himself of memory, to be "just another baby-boom boy." The statements "My parents survived Auschwitz" and "Two of their grandparents survived Auschwitz" in the second and last panels correspond to the dual imagery of father and son dressed up in fantasy clothing. That both father and son rip their play outfits at the knee suggests that the artist's son's life will follow a pattern similar to his father's — that is, Dash will also be burdened by memories. The son's wish in the final panel that King Kong "just **ate** the girl" alludes to the same kind of memory haunting the father — that of historical violence and its fictional counterpart. The father's assurance to his son that "it was only a **story**" represses the link between fiction and historical memory and his own haunted memories and suggests that fear, memory, fantasy, and denial are part of the legacy the artist leaves to his reader and his children.

2. The graphic art form allows the author to combine visual as well as textual clues in the construction of a narrative and to focus the reader's attention on the interaction of text and image. Students might refer to other texts in this chapter to compare the graphic art form with purely textual forms. For example, Deirdre N. McCloskey's "Yes, Ma'am" concerns itself largely with describing visual imagery. On the other hand, texts such as James Baldwin's "Stranger in the Village" and N. Scott Momaday's "The Way to Rainy Mountain" portray the writers as inheritors of history, narrative, and perceptions of ethnicity in a way that is perhaps less amenable to a graphic art format.

3. The appearance of the author's son extends the artist's act of remembering to the generation growing up in America after the Holocaust and yet still marked by it. The statement "Two of their grandparents survived Auschwitz" in the final panel appears in parentheses, as though the family's history is receding into the background. Despite the son's distance from the Holocaust, his anguish at the death of King Kong suggests that he experiences as keenly as his father the metaphoric possibilities of graphic art. Immediately following Dash's expressed desire that King Kong "just **ate** the girl" so that "then there wouldn't be any trouble" is the second reference to the Holocaust, suggesting that Dash wants to rewrite King Kong's history, perhaps to recast the role of the victim by blaming him for failing to act (to eat the girl).

4. This exercise asks students to explore the tension between Spiegelman's creative struggle and the problem of historical memory in terms of the interaction between imagery and text. For example, following the photograph of the artist as a boy in play clothes (panel 9), the artist examines its source, the family album, and tosses it aside: His rejection implies that historical documents are of limited use in the act of remembering. Another example of the thematic intersection of image and text occurs in the panels of the adult artist bursting out of the play outfit of his childhood. When his son interrupts his soliloquy, and brings him back into the present, the artist resumes his original outfit and offers the reader a dated photograph of his son Dashiell in his Superman outfit. Like his father, Dash also rips the knee of his play outfit. The similar experiences of father and son suggest that while both outgrow their childhood fantasies, Dash may find himself as haunted as his father by history and memory.

5. This question asks students to compare Spiegelman's use of graphic art as a political and personal medium to explore his history and creative sources with Barry's depiction of the raw emotions that children experience in the process of socialization (p. 522). Both graphic essays touch on the hypocrisy of adults who want to deny the reality and power of children's emotions. The sole voice of honesty in Barry's graphic essay, the substitute teacher, is punished for acknowledging her students' feelings. The substitute teacher distinguishes between the impersonal hatred of those "we don't know" (panel 17), which constitutes "the kind of hate that has destructive intent" and the kind of hate that is "a response to something destructive" (panel 18). When the artist tries to explain this distinction to her mother, her mother responds with prejudice: "This teacher is a Beatnik" (panel 18). In both essays, the children find a way of coping with their feelings: Dash revises the King Kong story by suggesting that he should have eaten the girl, while Lynda expresses her gratitude for "finally being understood" by writing a love note to the teacher (panel 19).

Maxine Hong Kingston, *On Discovery* (p. 112)

1. "On Discovery" employs a traditional fairy-tale beginning: "Once upon a time." Kingston follows this clause with the hero's name, who is, simply, "a man";

she does not give him any distinctive traits. Tang Ao's experiences before reaching the Land of Women are not germane to the story, so the narrator summarizes the journey in the first sentence: "[L]ooking for the Gold Mountain, [he] crossed an ocean, and came upon the Land of Women" (1). The "Gold Mountain" is an emblem for a utopia of wealth. In the same sentence, the "Gold Mountain" is juxtaposed with his unexpected discovery, "the Land of Women," suggesting that Tang Ao will not find what he seeks and that a moral tale will follow. What will Tang Ao find instead of gold? The instructor should encourage students to read the first sentence aloud and hear how its regular rhythm creates a traditional storytelling tone for the tale.

2. The women set out to "prepare" Tang Ao "to meet the Queen" (2), which he does, although not in the way he expects. He has his earlobes pierced (3); his feet bound (4–5); his body shaped through diet (5); gold hoops put through his ears (5); his facial hair plucked (6); and his face painted (6). By the time Tang Ao is prepared to "[serve] a meal at the queen's court" (6), his appearance and manner of walking have been transformed to conform to a highly artificial model of femininity.

3. At first Tang Ao does not resist his capture because he is "not on guard against ladies" (1). His innocence of the women's intentions might be read as comparable to the state of a young girl who has not yet learned of the cultural expectations that will be imposed on her. Tang Ao is locked up, shackled, and chained before he realizes what awaits him. After enduring the pain of foot binding (4), he can no longer bear not to have his feet wrapped tight (5) and so cooperates in the practice that entraps him. The shame he feels from his used bandages reinforces his degraded condition (5). Physically and psychologically, Tang Ao loses his sense of self, which stifles his capacity to resist.

4. The diners' comment, "She's pretty," reinforces Tang Ao's loss of identity and degradation. The feminine pronoun "she" denies Tang Ao his name, ignores his individuality, and defines him solely through his gender. The adjective "pretty" diminishes him by implying that he is ornamental and "compliments" him on his successful transformation from an autonomous individual to an object of scorn.

5. Tang Ao's external transformation is accompanied by psychological changes: He experiences bodily pain, shame, and embarrassment as the result of the changes to his body, and is reduced to begging for the very treatment that has degraded him (5). External transformation, Kingston suggests, is tantamount to a change of identity. Students might explore the types of psychological changes that accompany weight loss, makeovers, temporary and permanent hair removal, and plastic surgery. Such changes might be disturbing or liberating or even both. Students may also want to explore the boundary between self-creation and changes made under pressure to conform to particular notions of gender or beauty.

6. Tang Ao appears to "pass" successfully as a woman, although Kingston's parable suggests that the diners are perfectly aware that he is, biologically, a man. His performance as a woman is not his choice; rather, it enslaves him. In contrast, "passing" in the form of cultural assimilation can offer real benefits, as Eric Liu (Chapter 2) and Richard Rodriguez (Chapter 4) suggest. Deirdre N. McCloskey (Chapter 2) describes the struggle to pass as an act of personal empowerment. Ask students to consider whether passing is a form of coercion or of self-creation.

Sherman Alexie, *What Sacagawea Means to Me* (p. 115)

1. With the invitation to "climb through the portal into Sacagawea's Shoshone Indian brain," Alexie asks the reader to transcend his or her own identity and question the received version of Lewis and Clark's journey as "the triumphant tale of two white men" (3). His emphasis on Sacagawea's maternity, and his juxtaposition of the verb "breastfeed" with his description of the "adventure, fighting rivers, animals, weather, and diseases for thousands of miles" (1) underscores one of Alexie's main themes: that European and African Americans along with indigenous peoples produced "successive generations of social, political, and artistic mutations that can be so beautiful and painful" (4). By describing Sacagawea as "our mother" (2), Alexie links indigenous peoples with the various ethnic groups who immigrated to North America and together produced a culture of "contradictions," which are nevertheless "magical" (4).

2. Alexie suggests that traditional historical accounts of Lewis and Clark's journey revise the narrative of colonization from that of a "natural process, tragic and violent to be sure, but predictable and ordinary as well" (2). This revised version of history, one that "white historians might need to believe," tends to minimize the role of certain ethnic groups, such as African Americans, and conceal the violence of colonization: "individual human beings are invaded and colonized by foreign bodies, just as individual civilizations are invaded and colonized by foreign bodies" (2). Although this process is "possibly necessary for the advance, however constructive and destructive, of all civilizations" (2), it offers a less comfortable narrative than some traditional accounts and challenges the primacy and autonomy of the white male explorer.

3. Alexie emphasizes the diversity of the expedition as part of his challenge to the traditional version of Lewis and Clark's journey: In addition to the forty-five unnamed European Americans, he draws the reader's attention to York, a black slave, who accompanied Sacagawea and the explorers, and even to Seaman, a Newfoundland dog. That the expedition was neither as independent nor as solitary as the traditional story portrays and that it involved a variety of people, some of whom "joined the journey, then left or completed it, often without monetary or historical compensation" (3) suggests that history itself cannot be easily summed up by a neat and definitive narrative.

4. Alexie joins unlikely pairs of American personalities and historical figures and events, including Nathan Bedford Forrest, a Confederate general, with Toni Morrison, the Nobel Prize–winning African American scholar and writer; Maria Tallchief, a Native American ballerina and teacher, with Ted Bundy, a serial murderer; and Geronimo, the Apache leader, with Joe McCarthy, the senator who instigated investigations of communist sympathizers in the U.S. government. This exercise asks students to explore the complex tensions in American culture and values through these unlikely pairs.

5. In "Language and Literature from a Pueblo Indian Perspective," Silko emphasizes the distinctive features of the Pueblo storytelling tradition and its importance to sustaining Pueblo culture. Silko implies that "Pueblo expression" (1) and "perspective" (2) are part of an ongoing experience separate from the dominant European culture that colonized North America. Silko minimizes the influence of European culture on Pueblo traditions and distances them from the similar experiences of "African and Caribbean peoples": Although "we have all had the conqueror's language imposed on us," the "dreadful formal education" devised by the Bureau of Indian Affairs "freed us by encouraging us to maintain our narratives" (16). She also claims that the Pueblo enjoy a particular continuity of tradition: "We were not relocated like so many Native American groups that were torn away from their ancestral land" (18) and, as a result, "our stories are so much a part of these places that it is almost impossible for future generations to lose them" (18). In "In Search of Our Mothers' Gardens," Walker represents African American women's experience in the context of and as inseparable from American history and culture: "[I]n the heat of the post-Reconstruction South," women "dreamed dreams that no one knew" and "saw visions that no one could understand" because they were trapped in "an era, a century, that did not acknowledge them, except as 'the *mule* of the world'" (5). Walker sees African American women's creativity as inseparable from the history and legacy of slavery. For example, Walker argues that Phillis Wheatley's poetry can only be understood by recognizing that she "struggled to sing the song that was your gift [...] in a land of barbarians" (20–26). Students might consider the effectiveness of each writer's approach in relation to his or her purpose. Silko seeks to preserve the Pueblo storytelling tradition; Walker wants to incorporate into African American history the unacknowledged creativity of her female ancestors; and Alexie suggests, through the device of the theme park, that Native American culture has become a relic of American history, a fantasy of white heroism, and an integral part of modern America.

N. Scott Momaday, *The Way to Rainy Mountain* and Contexts (p. 118)

1. Inexperienced students may not know how to take full advantage of open-ended questions like this one. Excited about the freedom offered by such an

assignment, students may forget to apply the useful details they've just learned from the readings. You can help students by asking them questions closely tied to the specifics of Momaday's essays. For instance, how does Momaday describe the Rainy Mountain landscape? When he introduces the seasons on the Oklahoma plain, why does he give winter and spring each a brief phrase but summer the rest of the paragraph? Why is fall left out of the introduction? When students write about their own place, which seasons do they choose to highlight and why?

You might arrange a space and time for students to read one another's essays about a place. Focus not just on physical place, but also on how it is perceived or represented by the imagination of the author. Students can share with one another how they decided to include certain details while leaving out others, what made them arrange their paragraphs in the order they appear, and what alternative orders they could use and to what effects.

2. As this question suggests, the response should be a continuation of students' responses to Question 1. To help students grasp the significance of this open-ended assignment, you may want to explore the interrelation of history and story as well as the questionable dichotomy between the subjective and objective. Students may want to ask themselves how the process of writing about a place becomes writing about one's own history. What is the role of place in personal and local history narratives? What can be the effects of human narrative on the natural evolution of a given landscape? Does a landscape free from human impact exist? What are the storyteller's responsibility to the land that sustains him or her? What contribution does the land make to the storyteller's (or any person's) identity? Momaday defines identity as "a moral idea, for it accounts for the way in which [a man] reacts to other men and to the world in general" (p. 118). How do students define the term *identity*? How do they define their own identity in relation to the place essay that they write? Students can compare Momaday's treatment of history with Sherman Alexie's in "What Sacagawea Means to Me" (p. 115), which considers an iconic Native American figure in the context of the European conquest and argues that the interaction of immigrant and indigenous peoples produced "successive generations of social, political, and artistic mutations" that are "beautiful and painful" (4).

3. A storyteller begins by listening to others' stories. Momaday, for instance, begins by listening to Kiowa storytellers, such as his grandmother. This is the gist of what it means to write in context. Writers don't create a text *ex nihilo;* they do so by reading other texts. Ask students to think about how their childhood stories have shaped both their identities and the stories they tell. They may also want to ask: To what extent is our identity shaped by the stories we tell? From this insider's (a fellow storyteller's) perspective, students may better understand what Momaday means by "I invented history . . . in the same way an idea of one's ancestry and posterity is really an idea of the self" (p. 124).

4. and 5. For these assignments the instructor needs to encourage students to recognize that they have an innate ability to master the art of storytelling. Students can then explore their own "unique performance" of storytelling, through

which they create themselves. Experimenting with voices means experimenting with identities. This assignment encourages students to compare and contrast their stories with other essays in this book. For example, in Chapter 1, Eudora Welty tells about her love of books in "Listening" (p. 29); and Amy Tan tells stories in different versions of English in "Mother Tongue" (p. 34).

6. In "The Way to Rainy Mountain," Momaday celebrates the mythology of the Kiowa and emphasizes the symbolic importance of the landscape and animal life in Kiowa culture. Momaday's portrayal of Kiowa history is tied to his theory of storytelling: He argues in "East of My Grandmother's House" (p. 124) that "a man" should "give himself up to a particular landscape in his experience" and "imagine the creatures there" and "all the colors of the dawn and dusk" (1). Thus, for Momaday, the art of storytelling is inextricable from the natural world. The criticism that writers such as Momaday perpetuate "Mother Earth Father Sky" clichés implies that such writers sustain a mythic and mystical image of indigenous Americans while detaching their experience from the history of European colonization. In a sense, Alexie suggests that writers such as Momaday reject the "veil of self-consciousness" that W. E. B. Du Bois and James Baldwin describe—the sense that one's identity is formed through others' perceptions. Momaday might respond to such a criticism that identity is intimately linked to his ancestry: in "I Invented History" (p. 124), he states that "an idea of one's ancestry and posterity is really an idea of the self" (1). For example, in "The Whole Journey" (p. 127) Momaday remarks that the seventeenth-century migration of the Kiowa to the Southern Plains "is essential to the way in which the Kiowa think of themselves as people" (2). For Momaday, oral tradition, the legend and lore of the Kiowa, is "valuable in its own right and for its own sake" (3), suggesting that his primary concern is not to place the Kiowa experience in the context of European conquest, but to animate and sustain it. In contrast, Alexie explores the historical fictions that American culture has produced. The instructor should encourage students to keep in mind that both writers use their different perceptions of history imaginatively and for specific purposes. Ask students to support their comparison with concrete examples from each text.

Heather King, *The Closest to Love We Ever Get* (p. 131)

1. King finds "the challenges, the dilemmas, the paradoxes" of life in Koreatown fascinating, and at the same time feels the need to confront "the cross of my irritation, my anger, my racism, my fear" (2). Life in Koreatown plunges her "into the deepest contradictions: between abundance and scarcity, community and solitude, sin and grace, my longing for wholeness and my resistance to it" (2). In this diverse neighborhood, King has "no voice, no particular power" (3), by which she means that she is "often the only white person" (3) in the local shops and in the local church. Thus, King implies that the challenges of living in an urban, ethnically nonwhite neighborhood offer opportunities for spiritual growth.

2. Despite her love of the desert, and of books about the desert, King is "uneasy with the nature writers who leave human beings out, who see us as a blight on the landscape" (4). For King, the spiritual life, which coincides with her writing life, requires total engagement with "the rest of the world, the people in it, the page" (4). Life in Los Angeles, and in Koreatown in particular, reinforces King's sense that her spiritual path lies in making her way through the everyday struggles of humanity: "It's so easy to feel besieged" by the teeming crowds of the city, and, at the same time, the "ceaselessly pulsing aorta of life" (4) is the test of her spirituality, because it is the human condition.

3. For King, the spiritually engaged life is one in which the individual mingles "his or her body and blood with the rest of the world" and finds "a way to cherish that world even as he or she struggles to endure it" (4). King's image of the "ceaselessly pulsating aorta" (4) suggests an intimate connection between life, love, and spirituality: It conveys the miraculous nature of life, its relentlessness, and its endurance. When King writes, "What feeds me is the miracle of flesh-and-blood stories" (5), she implies that the "daily struggles" of everyday life (5) enrich her spirit just as the heart pumps blood through the body. Thus, spirituality is for King the state of loving the world and living imbued with the knowledge of Christ's death and resurrection (4). This state transcends the apparent contradictions she sees around her: To love is to see "opposites held in balance [in] a paradigm for the terrible tension and ambiguity of the human condition" (7). To love does not mean to love only that which is conventionally beautiful, but to see that there is beauty everywhere, "so much it can hardly be borne" (7).

4. King suggests that the state of love is an experience in which one sees "for one fleeting moment, all simultaneously" (7). Consequently, "the closest to love we ever get" is a state of uncertainty in which the observer accepts "the difference between how we long for the world to be and how it must be a kind of crucifixion in the darkest, most excruciating depths" (7). For King, in this state "*ranchera* music" coexists with bougainvillea (1) and the "colorful Mexican tile" with "overflowing trash cans" (7) and "every shabby corner" "deserves a song of praise" (8).

5. This assignment works best when students use concrete settings to explore spiritual experiences. For example, E. B. White's metaphors of the lake and woods as a "holy spot" and "cathedral" (2) are grounded in the specificity of the location, including its "coves and streams, the hills that the sun set behind, the camps and the paths behind the campus" (2). He links the spiritual experience of the lake to these specific traits: "It is strange how much you can remember about places like that once you allow your mind to return into the grooves that lead back" (2). Thus, the transformations within the self are part of the physical experience of walking down the paths around the lake. Self-discovery, memory, and transcendence are inseparable, as when White experiences himself becoming his father and watching his son as if the latter "was I." (4). For Momaday, the landscape is infused with history and culture. Questions 2 and 6 under Momaday's "The Way

to Rainy Mountain" and Context readings in the *Instructor's Manual* explore this relationship.

James Baldwin, *Stranger in the Village* (p. 134)
W. E. B. Du Bois, *The "Veil" of Self-Consciousness* (p. 144)

1. Because of his physical appearance—his skin color, hair, teeth, and so on—James Baldwin is regarded by white men on both sides of the Atlantic as "an exotic rarity" (11), rather than as just another human being. In the small mountain village, the Swiss children call him "*Neger*" out of a sense of "genuine wonder" in which "there was . . . no suggestion that I was human" (4). But there is a major difference, he realizes, between the pain he feels now and the pain he suffered back in the United States: "There is a dreadful abyss between the streets of this village and the streets of the city in which I was born . . . the abyss is experience, the American experience" (14), and "the same syllable riding on the American air expresses the war my presence has occasioned in the American soul" (14). Baldwin sounds more forgiving to the Swiss villagers than to the people who uttered the word "nigger" to him but he still experiences in Europe the "veil of self-consciousness"that Du Bois describes. For Du Bois, this "double-conscious-ness" is a sense of seeing himself "through the eyes of others" and of "measuring one's soul by the tape of a world that looks on in amused contempt and pity" (2). As a result, Du Bois experiences his "two-ness,—an American, a Negro" as "two warring ideals in one dark body" (2). Similarly, Baldwin suspects that the Swiss villagers do not believe that he is an American since "black men come from Africa" (3). For Baldwin, the consciousness that white culture resists recognizing the human being "beneath the black mask" (12) makes him a stranger in a world onto which he has been "grafted" (9). Whiteness is the cultural norm in the West: "white men have for black men a reality which is far from reciprocal" (10). Yet, paradoxically, white culture makes itself known through its construction of black-ness: "it is one of the ironies of black-white relations that, by means of what the white man imagines the black man to be, the black man is enabled to know who the white man is" (12). Thus, for Baldwin, "double-consciousness" is more than a sense of seeing the self through others' eyes; it is also a sense of how "the black man" has become "an inescapable part of the general social fabric" (18).

2. The villagers are proud of the practice of "'buying' African natives for the purpose of converting them to Christianity." Baldwin feigns "astonish-ment and pleasure at the solicitude shown by the village for the souls of black folks" (6). Although in his heart he understands the practice as another case of people being trapped in history and history in them, he can't help wondering at "the peculiar price" those African natives have to pay. He knows well that his father, "who having taken his own conversion too literally never, at bottom, forgave the white world (which he described as heathen) for having saddled him with a Christ in whom, to judge at least from their treatment of him, they

themselves no longer believed" (7). The Swiss villagers cannot understand this sense of history.

3. According to Baldwin, the root of the problem is "the necessity of the American white man to find a way of living with the Negro in order to be able to live with himself" (22). Again, Baldwin's explanation is rooted in his theory of history being trapped in people and people trapped in history. The white man is unable to live with himself at this "very charged and difficult moment" (11) because he is trapped by the history he has created and is probably still perpetuating. The institution of slavery and the unconscious mentality of racism deny the humanity of the African Americans. In reaction, the black man "insists, by whatever means he finds at his disposal, that the white man . . . recognize him as a human being" (11).

Thus, for Baldwin, the "identity of the American Negro" is inseparable from the fact of his enslavement: Because the American slave had his history "taken from him" (16), "the question" of his very humanity and rights "as a human being" came to divide the nation (17). In the wake of this "burning" question, "the strain of denying the overwhelming undeniable [fact of the black man's humanity] forced Americans into rationalizations so fantastic that they approached the pathological" (21). Students should consider how American society now deals with the legacy of slavery. Students might compare some of the race-related issues President Obama raised during his campaign with those that took center stage during the civil rights movement as described in Martin Luther King's "Letter from Birmingham Jail" (Chapter 7). The instructor may want to ask students to consider the ways in which African American music, food, linguistic patterns, and other cultural practices have become integral to mainstream American culture. Does cultural integration diminish Du Bois's notion of "two-ness" (2) for African Americans?

4. Baldwin and Du Bois each discuss the experience of being a nonwhite American. For Du Bois, a "double-consciousness," or the "sense of always looking at one's self through the eyes of others" (2) creates "two warring ideals in one dark body," that of "an American" and of "a Negro" (2). For Baldwin, "the Negro in America" has an indisputable identity, one that represents an "inescapable" challenge to white America (23). Can gender identity and sexual preference also create this sense of "double-consciousness" or of representing an "inescapable" challenge to the dominant culture? McCloskey implies as much, for those who cross gender boundaries face a serious risk of assault (7). Baldwin experiences difference as degrees of cultural confidence: The Swiss he observes "move with an authority which I shall never have" (8). Not only is he different because he is not native to this village, but also he feels that he has been "strangely grafted" onto Western culture (9). Similarly, McCloskey describes how difficult it is to mimic the "scores of [...] natural and unnatural, genetic and socially constructed" gender clues that are involved in passing (1).

Sojourner Truth and Gloria Anzaldúa both suggest that the blurring of gender and ethnic boundaries poses a threat to the dominant culture. Truth points out that "'twixt the Negroes of the South and the women at the North, all talking about rights, the white men will be in a fix pretty soon" (1). Anzaldúa argues that "creating bridges that cross race and other classifications" implies, not that "[t]here are no safe spaces," but instead there is a greater "likelihood of intimacy and thus thinner boundaries" (5). Similarly, Du Bois imagines the American "Negro" as a "co-worker in the kingdom of culture" (3). The instructor may ask students to use some of the specific ideas these writers employ, including McCloskey's use of performance and passing, Du Bois's image of "warring ideals," (2), Baldwin's analysis of the role of history in the creation of identity, or Anzaldúa's discussion of the intersection between "consciousness" and identity (2).

5. The instructor can ask the students to use the readings in this chapter as a platform from which to explore the experience of alienation and the challenge of constructing and sustaining an identity rooted in gender, ethnicity, spirituality, language, or location. Encourage students to avoid the temptation to simplify complex experiences and instead to explore the implications of a lack of closure.

Sojourner Truth, *Ain't I a Woman?* (p. 146)

1. Sojourner Truth establishes her voice first by addressing the audience as "children," as if she is a mother to them all, and she speaks with a motherly authority. This initial voice is later reinforced by her status as the mother of thirteen children and references to Eve as the mother of the human race and to the Virgin Mary, the mother of Christ. Truth thereby establishes the authority of all women.

2. The repetition of this question conveys to the audience two things — first, that half of the freed slaves are women, and second, because women have ploughed, planted, and harvested like men, there is no reason to assume they are weak. In addition, the repetition creates a cadence like that of a blues singer, such that it holds the audience spellbound. Without this repeated question, her speech would lose power.

Truth uses colloquialism, omission, imperfect grammar, and asides to enhance the direct effect of spoken words on her audience. Rather than "Am I not a woman?" she deliberately uses the colloquial word *Ain't* to highlight that this is a real-life working woman with little education expressing her feelings, not a calculated written deliberation. She also drops the first syllable in the word *because* to highlight the oral nature of her communication and uses grammatical structures that standard written English avoids: "What's all this here talking about?" (1). Her use of asides also contributes to the conversational tone: "Then they talk about this thing in the head; what's this they call it?" (3). The combined effect of these rhetorical devices is to distinguish her communication from the written essay and thereby to give her speech a sense of immediacy that written communication often lacks.

3. The instructor might ask students to consider how Deirdre N. McCloskey's discussion of gender as performance illustrates the persistence of misogynistic tendencies in contemporary society. There is still, McCloskey observes, a great

deal of hostility toward women: "Women experience dangerous men all day long and are on the alert. The alertness is not male bashing, merely prudence in the company of people with greater upper-body strength and the inclination to use it, intoxicated by lethal fantasies about What She Really Wants" (9). McCloskey's observations of "male anxiety about being homosexual, much less being a woman" (8) and of female fear and indignation toward cross-dressers (9) indicate that women are, and see themselves as, beleaguered.

4. Jean Toomer, according to Walker, discovered in black women a "spirituality [...] so intense, so deep, so *unconscious*, they were themselves unaware of the richness they held. They stumbled blindly through their lives: creatures so abused [...] that they considered themselves unworthy even of hope" (1). In contrast, Truth presents herself as an astute and self-aware speaker with a clear mission. Truth's speech is a powerful counterargument to Moynihan's stance that slavery destroyed the Negro family and thus "broke the will of the Negro people" (8): While Truth certainly points out that slavery damaged the African American family by separating children from their parents, its will has quite clearly not been broken.

Bob Daemmrich, *Nobody Knows I'm Gay* (p. 148)

1. The statement "Nobody Knows I'm Gay" acquires its particular meaning in this context through the appearance of the letters, which are large, capitalized, and printed in a bold font, and through its defiant and public placement on a T-shirt. The man wearing the shirt makes the implicit claim that being gay is a state of being that cannot be read or deciphered as easily as some social categories, like ethnicity, and so by publicly declaring his sexuality he rejects the ease with which he could disguise it. By blowing his cover, the wearer rejects the idea of concealing his authentic self and deliberately refutes the secrecy and shame the statement would suggest in another context.

2. and 3. These questions ask students to consider how visual clues guide the interpretation of an image. Without the statement on the T-shirt, the viewer might not consider the sexuality of the three young people in the photograph, or might assume that they are heterosexual. With the information that the photograph was taken at a gay rights rally, the viewer might assume that the wearer and his companions are gay, or that the two people flanking the central figure are friends and supporters of gay rights, or that the wearer himself is not gay but is demonstrating solidarity with the gay community.

Gloria Anzaldúa, *Beyond Traditional Notions of Identity* (p. 149)

1. In describing "commonality within the context of difference" (2), Anzaldúa is referring to a sense of consciousness that transcends "separate and easy identifications" (3). She argues that "ethnic, racial, religious, class, gender,

and national classifications" (5) do not fully describe identity and thus identities based on such classifications should become "more pliant" (3). For example, "some women of color bear white consciousness" (2), by which Anzaldúa means that "consciousness" of ethnicity is as important in the formation of identity as the physical or cultural characteristics of that ethnicity. As a young man, Eric Liu saw the choice of racial identity as either "embrace or efface" (23) and thus saw assimilation as the adoption of the consciousness of mainstream, white America: He became white "by acclimation" (1). Sherman Alexie, on the other hand, sees an inevitable overlapping of the consciousnesses of the various ethnicities comprising American culture: As the descendent of "a half-white man named James Cox" and "a Spokane Indian woman named Etta Adams," Alexie considers himself "a contradiction" (5). Richard Rodriguez argues that assimilation is necessary to achieve "public individuality" (38): "[F]ull individuality is achieved, paradoxically, by those who are able to consider themselves members of the crowd" (39). Anzaldúa speaks more explicitly to the issue of gender than do Liu, Alexie, and Rodriguez, although Liu and Alexie suggest that mainstream American culture tends to be defined not only as white, but also as masculine.

2. Anzaldúa argues that today racial and gender categories are less clearly determinants of identity than before the 1980s. "Twenty-one years ago, we struggled with the recognition of difference within the context of commonality" (2). She implies that at that time "women of color" sought recognition of their distinctive experience from mainstream white culture. Now, she argues, "additional underrepresented voices" should form part of a "dialogue" that revises the experience of "victimhood" and focuses on "agency" (1). As part of this larger dialogue, Anzaldúa considers that nationality, class, sexuality, gender, and age should be incorporated into "feminist theory" (4) from which a "new tribalism" (5) will emerge. This new sense of identity creates "bridges that cross race and other classifications" (2).

McCloskey examines the idea that gender is a fluid classification by tracing the subtleties of gender performance through gestures, posture, and clothing (2–4) and physical alterations (10). And, McCloskey argues that much of gendered behavior is "culturally specific" (5). At the same time, McCloskey argues that conformity to gendered behavior is essential to survival, for to fail to behave according to culturally accepted notions of gender is to risk being raped and murdered (7, 10, 13). Kingston's parable illustrates the enormous amount of work required to instill gendered behavior in an individual and the psychic costs of performing that behavior.

3. This assignment asks students to use the readings to explore the classifications that determine identity and examine how they contribute to their perceptions of their own identities and those of other groups. A good place to start might be Eric Liu's list of "the ways you could say I am white" (p. 93), McCloskey's discussion of gender (p. 151), and Amy Tan's essay on the different forms of English she speaks (p. 34).

Deirdre N. McCloskey, *Yes, Ma'am* (p. 151)

1. Although responses will vary, be sure to have students ground their observations in McCloskey's text, particularly in paragraphs 2–4. McCloskey pays attention to hand gestures; the positioning of the body, face, and fingers; the manner of shaking hands; the arrangement of hair, jewelry, and clothing; and the placement of legs, knees, and feet (2–4). Students may not have reflected closely on the multiplicity and subtlety of the "gender clues" McCloskey describes; ask them to observe their own and others' behavior, perhaps of individuals of different ages and ethnicities, and to explore how subtle differences in behavior elicit particular responses in an observer as well as judgments about the sexuality and sexual behavior of the observed.

2. Through her observations, McCloskey notices that "[l]ittle girls act different from little boys independent of the slight structural differences in their bodies" (4). For her, the biological foundation for gender difference is negligible: The "structural differences" are "slight," and the difference in gender behavior is "independent" of those differences. She seems to accept the theory of sociologist Harold Garfinkel that "gender is something 'done,' a performance, not an essence springing from genitals or chromosomes" (14). This explains why, as a gender crosser, McCloskey takes so much time to observe, analyze, and then "reproduce enough of the characteristic gestures" in order to first pass as a woman and then successfully cross to the realm of femininity.

3. According to McCloskey, a "sincere . . . attempt to jump the gender border from male to female," when detected, creates in men a "weirdly strong" anxiety "about being homosexual" (8). Their reaction, therefore, is often violent and dangerous. She gives both statistics and anecdotal evidence to prove her point: "A 1997 survey claimed that 60 percent of cross-gendered people had been assaulted" (7), and McCloskey knows "a gender crosser who had been beaten by four young men outside a bar even in peaceful Iowa City" (7).

A gender crosser also creates anxiety among women. However, these women "are not violent, but frightened and indignant" (9). Having successfully crossed the gender border, McCloskey knows "from being a woman on trains late at night in Holland or walking by Dutch cafes in summertime or living later in the less demonstrative but more dangerous environment of America that women have daily experiences of men in fact being up to something [bad]" (9). McCloskey seems to be more sympathetic to women because their anxiety is based on a more realistic ground.

4. McCloskey's reluctance to use personal pronouns is based on her own history. The word *Dee* seems to be an idiosyncratic abbreviation for both her male and female names. Preserving a certain degree of neutrality, it can be used to refer to Donald when discussing her pre-crossing life or to Deirdre when discussing her post-crossing life. Her manipulation of pronouns and names is in keeping with her general view about gender as a cultural-specific performance, rather than biological given. She seems to suggest that enlightened readers should experience, through her manipulation of those words, the instability of gender identity and

the arbitrariness of gender definition and gender border. People have the freedom to move from one side of the border to the other, as McCloskey has done. Even if most readers are not willing or able to do so themselves, she should at least give them a vicarious experience of that freedom and mobility, through her writing.

5. McCloskey elaborates on this point by arguing that those who object to gender crossing on the grounds that it perpetuates "oppressive stereotypes" "ordinarily [don't] know any gender crossers" (11–12). McCloskey distinguishes between gender crossers and "drag queens or female impersonators" who parody women (12): Gender crossers seek "to escape being read" (13). McCloskey also attacks female "crossphobes" who are themselves "stereotypically feminine" (14). This assignment invites students to explore their own feelings toward and views of gender, gendered behavior, and behaviors that breach or challenge gender norms. The instructor can encourage the student to explore his or her own fears, anxieties, and even hostility toward cross-gendered behavior—attitudes, McCloskey points out, that can lead to violence. In addition, the instructor should ask students to consider how popular culture reinforces gender norms and how those norms are internalized. Why is gender so crucial to identity? The student can consider how Kingston's "On Discovery" suggests that those who enforce gendered norms also express contempt for that behavior: The diners at the queen's court dismiss Tang Ao with the comment "She's pretty," thereby denying Tang Ao his individuality and defining him solely in terms of his gendered performance (6). Anzaldúa alludes to the resistance people feel when the identity boundaries that define them are blurred: "Many *mujeres de color* will not want whites or men to join the dialogue" (5). She implies that, for many, being female and nonwhite is so central to their identity that they can neither experience nor expect anybody else to experience a consciousness that is not based on categories of gender and ethnicity. Students should be encouraged to explore how gendered norms can be a form of safety, as McCloskey suggests: Gendered behavior situates individuals within a group and so always implies both inclusion and exclusion. Stereotyped images of men and women perpetuate gender norms and reinforce anxieties toward breaches of gender roles.

3   RELATIONSHIPS AND LIFE CHOICES: LIFE, LOVE, WORK, PLAY—WHAT'S THE BEST BALANCE?

Kim Warp, *Rising Sea Levels—An Alternative Theory* (p. 157)

1. Warp's cartoon gets unexpected and humorous mileage out of the relationship between an immersed object and the fluid it displaces: Increasingly obese sea bathers displace more water. The cartoon's joke hinges on a nonsensical, and

yet comically logical, link between a social and health problem, obesity, and a scientific problem, climate change and its impact on sea levels. The cartoon does not take aim at the overweight, but rather invites the reader to enjoy how an apparently simple logical relationship can produce a far-fetched theory. Humor often works by manipulating the audience's expectations; the reader who thinks that obesity is a serious problem or who is overweight can nevertheless enjoy Warp's cartoon as an absurd twist on the empirically observable relationship between cause and effect. Moreover, Warp leaves the "alternative theory" unstated, which heightens the reader's participation and enjoyment.

2. Warp's overweight characters include three men and four women. Two appear to be young and all are white. The two central figures are caricatures in that they are both consuming high-calorie items, presumably a soda and ice cream on a cone. Warp does not make her characters lifelike; they are drawn simply and their facial features are similar. Because the characters all appear to be enjoying their day at the beach rather than worrying about their health or rising sea levels, they might be interpreted as caricatures of complacency.

3. This question asks students to debate the difficulty of determining how much control an individual has over his or her health and how to manage the social costs of individual choices. An individual's obesity may be linked to numerous factors, some of which may be easier to control than others. The social costs of obesity are not borne only by the obese, for medical costs affect the whole health care system.

4. Encourage students to make unexpected or absurd connections between image and text to make this a fun exercise. Humor often depends on the readers' involvement, so students should create a caption that asks them to fill in the implied blank, as Warp's original caption does.

Anna Quindlen, *Anniversary* (p. 158)

1. Quindlen describes how parents convey important messages to children in matters of everyday life. For example, she characterizes "the fate of that black wool party dress" (1) as a "trivial" matter, but she also links that memory to her mother's reminder "to buy quality" (2), and so the dress symbolizes her mother's values for Quindlen. Ask students to explore how their memories connect to such larger messages. Sometimes these larger messages are difficult for children to interpret, even in hindsight. Quindlen has come to see the seemingly insignificant matter of whether her mother's tears "were real or calculated to keep all five of us in line" (2) as symbolic of the mystery of her mother's emotional life. Were those tears an indictor of her mother's deep emotional investment in her children? Was she her mother's "greatest calling" (3)? Quindlen suggests that becoming an adult, which a woman does only upon her mother's death, involves an acceptance that such questions cannot be answered.

2. Quindlen argues that "those of us whose mothers have gone" must "fend for ourselves" (3). A woman whose mother dies must become the "fulcrum" of her own life (3). Encourage students to explore their experience of a mother's role in the family. Is a mother always or even necessarily a "fulcrum" (3)? In the student's experience, do many people imagine that they must "perform" for their mothers (4)? These questions can form the basis of a classroom discussion on gender roles in the family, the various cultural constructions of motherhood, and the dynamics of mother-son and mother-daughter relations. For example, are either sons or daughters "naturally" closer to their mothers? How do parents' relationships with their own parents and siblings shape their relationships with their children?

3. Quindlen's final paragraph takes a sudden turn from her previous discussion of loss. By using simple, rather conventional phrases ("good and happy" and "how fleeting and how precious" [5]), she concludes on an optimistic note. The final sentence provides balance to this sentimentality: Death becomes a way to reset "priorities" (5). Students might discuss whether this final paragraph is effective. Does it indicate that Quindlen has acquired self-understanding as a result of examining her memories and feelings of loss? Do discussions of death require a comforting conclusion?

4. This question invites students to consider whether sentimentality conceals the complexities and conflicts that characterize intimate relationships. Ask students to define the "sentimental" in their own words as a starting point, and encourage them to use specific examples. What is particularly embarrassing about sentimental actions or words? Does familial love necessarily imply sentimentality? Quindlen suggests that actions speak louder than words when she refers to Madonna and Rosie O'Donnell: She sees each woman's professional choices and performance as, in part, an extension of her relationship with her mother. Such choices, for Quindlen, appear to testify more profoundly to the nature of the mother-daughter relationship than expressions of affection.

5. Ask students to explore how their relationships with adults who are not their parents have offered them particular insights into an older generation's world. Quindlen's comment that those who have lost their mothers "fend for ourselves" (3) suggests that only with a mother's death do children relinquish their emotional expectations of her. Relationships with other adults may allow the young to see parental figures as people with emotional demands and needs separate from their children.

Brian Doyle, *Joyas Voladoras* (p. 160)

1. Doyle's first three paragraphs convey the immense range of features and colors of the more than three hundred different species of hummingbirds. Each species has particularly formed tails, heads, and bills, and its own distinctive and

brilliant hues. Doyle emphasizes that in the midst of this diversity, hummingbirds all have tiny hearts, are amazingly fast and maneuverable in flight, and share a "ferocious" metabolism (3) and a lifespan of two years (3).

2. The motion of the heart, which pumps fluid through the body, links every living creature on earth. By pointing out that all living things have "approximately two billion heartbeats to spend in a lifetime" (3), Doyle emphasizes the heart's central role in the experience of life: In terms of heart beats, every living creature has a comparable lifespan. Thus, one theme that links the two halves of the essay is the connectedness of earth's diverse life forms. Hearts vary in the number of chambers (5), in speed (3), and in size (4), but they all beat approximately the same number of times (3), and they all pump fluid (5). Despite their differences, hummingbirds, whales, and humans share a fundamental trait: They all have four-chamber hearts.

3. Doyle uses the verb "churn" to suggest two kinds of agitation: movement and emotion. We churn at the knowledge that "we live alone," and as a result of our experiences of love, pain, and loss (6). That we all "churn" captures for Doyle the sense that life is a miraculous, tumultuous condition.

4. Doyle's description of the strength and frailty of the many different types of hearts suggests that it is the nature of life to experience love and loss and to endure those experiences despite their intensity and the scars they leave. Ask students to explore particular experiences that they consider both difficult and formative, such as the loss of a beloved person or animal or an event that led to a painful, if clarifying, epiphany.

5. Encourage students to ground their discussion in the details of the photo-graph. For example, "The Damm Family in Their Car" includes several elements that emphasize stasis; "Replaceable You" shows the replacement of body parts with plastic, metal, and glass in the form of mechanical devices and solid implants; "Migrant Mother" offers the viewer access to the mother but not to her children; and the relationship between text and image in "Nobody Knows I'm Gay" implies the difficulty of "reading" others. Doyle's portrait of the fullness and solitude of the living heart offers the student various ways to consider human relationships as, on the one hand, enduring, enriching, and intimate, and on the other, fragile, separate, and incomprehensible. Encourage students to examine Doyle's effective use of metaphors: "your mother's papery ancient hand," "a child's apple breath," "house of the heart," "brick up your heart," and "thicket of your hair" (all from 6); "the war against gravity and inertia" and "racecar hearts" (both from 3), "as big as a room" (4); and "we all churn" (5).

E. B. White, *Once More to the Lake* (p. 163)

1. Although student responses will vary, the instructor can provide guidance by pointing out connections between the E. B. White and Context essays and

Doyle's observations (p. 160). For example, while White longs for a "pattern of life indelible with fade-proof lake, the wood unshatterable, the pasture with the sweetfern and the juniper forever and ever, summer without end" (8), he ends his essay with "the chill of death" (13), suggesting the inevitability of decay and resignation. Similarly, Doyle concludes with the juxtaposition of death and life: "[Y]our mother's papery ancient hand" is followed by the image of a father "making pancakes for his children" (6). The essays are dissimilar in that Doyle uses the image of the "bruised and scarred" heart to suggest how childish illusions gradually erode over a lifetime, whereas White's essay emphasizes the fleeting moments that make up the passage of time.

2. Quindlen characterizes her experience of family as one of everyday intimacy, stability, and the longing for response and approval. For White, family life is based on fleeting moments of transcendent beauty and awareness: the sight of a dragonfly (5), catching fish (6), or walking up the road (7). Walker describes a large family with hard-working parents: Her mother made her children's clothes, canned vegetables and fruits, and made quilts and worked alongside her husband in the fields (31–32). Walker considers the stories her mother told (40) and her mother's gift for gardening a "heritage of love and beauty and respect for strength" (49) and central to her development. All three writers find beauty and happiness in memories of everyday life.

3. White notes that although the lake had never been "wild," a feeling of "primeval" remoteness has been lost by the extension of the tar road to within a half-mile of the shore (3). He also notes the new, louder outboard motors on boats (10). Despite these changes, White describes the lake as a "constant and trustworthy body of water" (6), so much so that he gets the eerie feeling that he is the boy "walking at my side" (11). The continuity of present and past paradoxically remind the narrator of time forever lost. This sense of time passing brings to the narrator's consciousness the inevitability of death.

4. White's son learns from his father the pleasures of "the placidity of a lake in the woods" (1) and of freshwater fishing, although, as White makes clear, his son learns as much from his own experience of the lake as he does from his father. Just as White had done as a boy, his son rises early to canoe along the lake shore (2, 4). And, the arrival of a thunderstorm gives White's son the same opportunity he had of watching "a curious darkening of the sky, and a lull in everything that had made life tick," of "the premonitory rumble," and the "crackling light against the dark" (12). Afterward, his son joins the others who "delight at the new sensation of bathing in the rain" (12) just as the narrator himself once had. From these experiences, White's son learns, as did White as a boy, that certain times are "infinitely precious and worth saving" (9).

Quindlen learned from her mother "to buy quality, keep my hair off my face, and give my father the benefit of the doubt" (2). She also learned from her mother's death how it feels to be propelled into adulthood. Walker learns from her mother that education is worth fighting for when her mother "battled with the white landlord who had the misfortune to suggest to her that her children did not need to go to school" (30). Observing her mother's industriousness and artistry in the garden, Walker realized that even a woman with several children and no time "to unravel her own private thoughts" (32) has "creative spirit" (32). Quindlen seems to have found her mother instrumental in her own decision to become a writer. Because Quindlen imagines that Rosie O'Donnell performs for her mother every time she steps "onto that stage" (4), she may also imagine herself telling her mother "I'm okay" with every piece of writing she publishes.

Children learn of their aloneness from the first moments that they begin to realize that their mothers are distinct people from themselves. This sense of aloneness is both healthy and painful. Perhaps the first bruises on the heart that Doyle imagines are those of the toddler who must defy her mother to establish her autonomy, a necessary development that also frightens her. Throughout childhood and adolescence, the individual discovers the joys and fears of developing into an autonomous person and learns that development necessarily involves moments of anguish.

5. This assignment asks students to consider the limits to intimacy—to pose the question, how well can we really know another person? The instructor should encourage students to use the readings by comparing how each writer portrays the relations between parent and child and suggests limits to intergenerational intimacy.

Gregory Orr, *Return to Hayneville* (p. 169)

1. Both White and Orr narrate the experience of returning to a place of youth where life and death intersect in a climactic epiphany. White returns to again experience "the placidity of a lake in the woods" (1) and to give his son the experience of "fresh water up his nose," "lily pads," and the scent of "wet woods" (2). There, watching his son, he feels "the chill of death" (13). Orr has the opportunity to return to Hayneville by chance—he will be giving a reading at nearby Auburn University. His experiences in Hayneville are "lodged like a sliver in my memory" (5), suggesting that he has never examined them. Having the company of two men to make a party of "[t]hree poets from three generations" (6) gives Orr the opportunity to tell his story and make sense of it "like one of those pilgrims in Chaucer, challenged by my travel companions to entertain them on the journey" (7). The compulsion to tell a story for an audience also serves the storyteller's need to tell his story. The drive itself is the literal and metaphorical vehicle Orr requires to revisit his memories, for as he tells his tale, it seems "as though the story and the highway were a single, fused flowing" (7).

2. Orr begins his story with a brief description of the Democratic National Convention in 1964. This beginning provides the reader with historical context and explains Orr's relationship to the events he witnessed and participated in: "I was one of about twenty or so people parading in a small circle on the dilapidated

boardwalk [...]. I felt confused and thrilled and purposeful all at the same time" (1). Thus, Orr suggests that he was a small part of a much larger political movement. The three SNCC volunteers who were murdered in the segregated South illustrate the real dangers that the movement entailed. This setting dovetails with Orr's own history. The gun accident that led to his brother's death (1) motivates his young self to long "to transcend my confusions and the agonies of my past and be taken up into some noble simplicity beyond change" (3) and even "to sacrifice myself and escape myself—to become a martyr for the movement" (3). When Orr is arrested for participating in the protest in Jackson, Mississippi (9), he is caught up in events that will force him to reexamine these desires. Although Orr's involvement did not make a direct impact on the situation in Mississippi, his story suggests that the sacrifices that every participant made were all significant in the confrontation with injustice.

3. Orr's epiphany that his life was worth living comes at the moment that he has become disillusioned with his youthful fantasies: "I gradually lost heart. I had dreamed of meaningful work and even heroic martyrdom, but here I was merely cannon fodder" (19). This realization follows a brutal education in the exercise of gratuitous power. He does not, at first, realize the significance of the fact that the officers have disguised themselves and covered their badge numbers (10). His second beating leaves him "hopeless," "cringing," and humiliated (12). Then, Orr watches a guard demand that a young boy swallow the button pinned to his shirt (14), an act that instills him with "murderous rage" (15). Slowly he is worn down by poor food and sanitary conditions, "[b]oredom, stench, and heat" (18).

At the depth of his depression and realization that he is one of "hundreds [...] who were merely beaten, terrorized, humiliated" (19) in the name of a cause, Orr changes from a young man with dreams of heroism into one simply trying to survive. His realization that he wanted to live probably helped him endure his subsequent eight-day incarceration in solitary confinement in Hayneville (29). Orr's values before these events were largely abstract; the value of his own life becomes real and tangible as he realizes, paradoxically, the abstract value of his participation in the movement: He was only "an integer in the calculus of a complex game playing out in rooms above me" (19).

Perhaps the most significant moment after his ordeal was seeing in the *New York Times* the story of a seminary student who died to save a woman from being murdered by the same man who had kidnapped him in Hayneville (31). That he, by sheer luck, "slipped through the same violent landscape" (34) left him, he implies, with a weight not unlike that he felt after his brother's death. After telling his story and revisiting Hayneville, Orr feels "weightless" (37). He interprets his escape as an enormous "gift," that of "my whole life" (38). He realizes that he "had gone south seeking the dark blessing of death" but had been given an entire existence "to sort it out and make it significant" (38). That life he chose to spend writing, teaching, and having a family (38).

4. Orr includes several conflicts, including one between racism and justice and those experienced by his young self struggling to come to terms with his brother's death and by his older self seeking to understand the past. The narrative's two interwoven plots, Orr's youthful journey and his return to Hayneville, each have a separate mystery and climax centered on Orr's survival and personal development. Orr's story does not offer a neat resolution, and he leaves unexplained many threads that contribute to its suspense, including the stories of those who he was detained with, those who died, those who persecuted the volunteers, and his own family.

5. This question asks the student to explore the complex conflicts that human relations inevitably produce and to examine their impact on individual personal development. Encourage students to avoid the temptation to wrap up their story in a single, enclosed meaning. Orr's narrative has several climatic moments, including his realization that he "wanted to live" (19), his sense that his "narrow escape" from danger has also "trapped" him in his memories (34), and his experience of "joy" upon returning to Hayneville. He does not try to summarize his experiences in the South and those experiences are necessarily conflicted. His personal narrative is his own, but also part of a larger social and political landscape.

Scott Russell Sanders, *Under the Influence: Paying the Price of My Father's Booze* (p. 181)

1. Scott Russell Sanders has paid a huge price for his father's alcoholism. When he was a child, he had to play along with the lies his father told to hide his drinking problem (2–4). When his parents bickered, Sanders lay in bed with feelings of rage, fear, and devastating guilt: "I lie there hating him, loving him, fearing him, knowing I have failed him. I tell myself he drinks to ease the ache that gnaws at his belly, an ache I must have caused by disappointing him somehow, a murderous ache I should be able to relieve by doing all my chores, earning A's in school, winning baseball games, fixing the broken washer and the burst pipes" (7).

Seven years after his father died of a heart attack triggered by his alcoholism, Sanders is still "paying the price for his father's booze." Guilt keeps gnawing at his heart, and driven by the urge to redeem himself he has become what his daughter calls a "workaholic." More seriously, his guilt seems to have been passed on to his son, who "takes on himself the griefs of the world, and in particular the griefs of his father" (53). Sanders is a very sober and self-disciplined man. He didn't taste his first wine until age twenty-one; nevertheless, guilt and fear burn "like acid in [his] veins" (52). Even though he drinks only moderate amounts of alcohol—"once a week, perhaps, a glass of wine, a can of beer, nothing stronger, nothing more" (55)—there lurks in him a fear of being possessed by the demon that destroyed his father. As he takes his weekly glass of wine, he listens "for the turning of a key in [his] brain" (55), because years ago he had seen "the amber liquid pour down [father's] throat, the alcohol steal into his blood, the key turn in his brain" (44).

Although his family is connected through hand tools, it has been torn apart by alcohol: "My brother became a rebel, my sister retreated into shyness, I played the stalwart and dutiful son who would hold the family together" (51). Moreover, he knows that alcoholism is a social problem rather than an isolated, individual woe for his family, for he knows family members of other alcoholics, has seen "countless other children tremble" (8), and understands that "a private grief is in fact, of course, a public scourge" (8). He has observed his "back-road neighbors" (33) and offers statistics about tens of millions who suffer from alcoholism.

2. Sanders's father's "mutation from sober to drunk" (32) could be triggered by a single drink, as in the case of his first beer after staying "dry" for fifteen years, when he moved back to Mississippi after he retired. He was two different people. When sober, his father "could multiply seven-digit numbers in his head . . . but when drunk could not help us with fourth-grade math" (26). When sober, he lovingly taught his son how to hit a nail on its head with a treasured family hammer. Yet when drunk, he would snarl at his wife, snore like a dragon, and "threaten . . . often" to beat his wife and children. Most painfully, alcohol made him a chronic liar. Not even attempting to hide his blood-shot eyes and dragon breath from his four-year-old granddaughter, he would shout and weep and lie in his son's face: "I never touched a drop. . . . Your mother's making it up" (48).

Perhaps one of the most painful moments that Sanders recalls is when he is confronted with his boyish helplessness: He decides that he will "tell Ernest and Julio [Gallo] what they were doing to my father, and then, if they showed no mercy, I would kill them" (24). In a narrative of almost unremitting pain, Sanders's experiences of normality are fleeting and inversely related to his father's drinking. He was a good student, played baseball, but did so with a terrible burden of guilt. His home was like a "minefield" (15) in which "a heedless footfall could trigger an explosion" (15).

3. Sanders seems to have written this essay for a varied audience. First and foremost, he is writing for himself: "My son wonders if I, too, am possessed. I write, therefore, to drag into the light what eats at me—the fear, the guilt, the shame—so that my own children may be spared" (53). As this quotation indicates, Sanders's family, especially his children, are also part of his audience: "I am moved to write these pages because my own son, at the age of ten, is taking on himself the griefs of the world, and in particular the griefs of his father" (53). In addition, his audience includes other alcoholics and their families. He criticizes American culture for trivializing the devastation of alcoholism:

> [I]n jokes and cartoons, in plays, films and television skits [drinking is] all great fun. But if in the audience you notice a few laughing faces turn grim when the drunk lurches onstage, don't be surprised, for these are the children of alcoholics. Over the grinning mask of Dionysus, the leering face of Bacchus, these children cannot help seeing the bloated features of their own parents. Instead of laughing, they wince, they mourn. Instead of celebrating the drunk as one freed from constraints, they pity him as one enslaved. (10–11)

As cultural criticism, the essay also reaches the general reading public. It condemns the alcohol industry and challenges show business for glorifying suffering and victimization.

4. This assignment, which resembles writing in a diary or freewriting, helps students to discover what Peter Elbow calls "voice, force, and connectedness" (10). Encourage students to freewrite this assignment as Stephen King recommends—"with the door closed" (16). Then, students who decide to revise the piece, perhaps to share with the class, can revise "with the door open" (16).

5. Sanders opens his essay with an angry tone, as the images in the first paragraph indicate: "My father drank. He drank as a gut-punched boxer gasps for breath, as a dog gobbles food — compulsively, secretly, in pain and trembling" (1). He compares the father to a loser and to a sneaky and perhaps mean-spirited animal. But Sanders's rage is partly directed at his father, partly at the source of his father's problem, the alcohol business, and partly at the enormous damage alcoholism wreaks on society: He reflects on his childhood fantasy of killing the Gallo brothers, "I no longer fancied I could reason with the men whose names I found on the bottles—Jim Beam, Jack Daniel's—but I was able now to recall the cold statistics about alcoholism: ten million victims, fifteen million, twenty" (49). Toward the end of the essay, he frankly states the negative effect that his father's drinking problem has had on himself and his siblings: "Life with him and the loss of him twisted us into shapes that will be familiar to other sons and daughters of alcoholics" (51). Sanders becomes almost desperate when he tells us that "it is far easier to recognize these twists in my character than to undo them" (52).

Expressing anger at his father's drinking habit, Sanders avoids self-pity by controlling his tone. Although his psyche has been twisted by the early traumatic experience of having an alcoholic father, under the influence of his own son, he is writing about and trying to deal with his problems. His focus is on the problem rather than himself, and rather than self-pity, he reveals a large heart full of sympathy and love. He writes for other children of alcoholics, keeping readers' attention on the effects of alcoholism.

6. Quindlen's memories of her mother's voice provide the support she needs to manage her life. These memories connect Quindlen to her mother even as they cut her off from her source of family information, common sense, and everyday wisdom. Quindlen's mother's early death left a sense in her daughter that she must always "fend" for herself (3) and that she is performing for the mother who is not there (4). Sanders's father's legacy to his son, which Sanders passes onto his own son, is a "crushing sense of responsibility" (53)—in Sanders's case, for his father's alcoholism, and in his son's, for Sanders's "depression" (53). In addition, Sanders feels his father's influence in his self-imposed immersion in "hard, relentless work" out of a dread of "the loss of control" (51) and a fear of "causing sadness of disappointment, even to strangers, as though I were still concealing the family shame" (52). Students can compare the ways that families transmit psychic damage, such as the feelings of fear and loss Sanders and Quindlen explore, with the

life-affirming values that Amy Tan describes: Her mother gave her the legacy of "her intent, her passion, her imagery, the rhythms of her speech, and the nature of her thoughts" (22). Tan's mother also showed her daughter how to stand up to others by confronting her stockbroker (13) and the hospital staff and doctor when her CAT scan was misplaced (14).

7. The positive aspects of loss that Quindlen refers to include her response to her sister-in-law's imminent death, which was to help make videotapes for her children. Quindlen also reflects her love of life in her feelings of camaraderie with others who have lost their mothers. When she writes that "[w]e have our priorities straight" (5), she suggests that those who know that life is "fleeting" and "precious" make an effort to achieve their goals. Sanders expresses his respect for life in part by denouncing the "humorous [...] lore that deals with drunks" (10), which trivializes and conceals the "truth" of alcoholism (11). Sanders also suggests that life is both precious and powerful when he describes how his father's spells of sobriety followed the births of his children and, similarly, his own hopes that by "[dragging] into the light what eats at me—the fear, the guilt, the shame" (53), his children "may be spared" (53) this pain.

The student should ground this discussion in specific detail, as Quindlen and Sanders do. Ask the student to use techniques such as dialogue and descriptive examples to convey how an experience of loss has acted as a reminder that life is "fleeting and precious." For example, Sanders's detailed description of stopping at Sly's and watching his father go inside to buy wine (18–25) employs dialogue, description ("a cinderblock place"), a list ("pop and Popsicles, cigarettes, potato chips, canned soup, raunchy postcards, fishing gear, Twinkies, wine, and beer"), active verbs ("swigged," "stuffed," "smash"), and visual detail ("a mangy dog asleep in the window"). Remind students that concrete language and tangible details bring narrative to life.

Alice Walker, *In Search of Our Mothers' Gardens* and Contexts (p. 192)

1. For Alice Walker, art is the expression of spiritual impulses, the creative talents that all of us have and all of us want to use. Art, with a capital A, Baraka suggests, is the product of that expression when others, especially such arbiters of culture as museum directors, recognize it as worthy of attention. Walker claims this status for black women's "muzzled" (13, 32) creativity by naming them "Artists" (10). Both in the past, when oppression made expression impossible, and in the present, when expression for black women is becoming possible, Walker declares for all black women that "Artists we will be" (28). Part of the process by which expression becomes possible is the belated acknowledgment of "the far-reaching world of the creative Black woman" (29) expressed through domestic arts, including sewing, quilting, cooking, and gardening, when they are the work of "a person of powerful imagination and deep spiritual feelings" (35). Whether

or not such artistic products are given the imprimatur of Art by being hung in the Smithsonian, Walker claims them as such.

In having students explore the question "What counts as art?" the instructor might initiate classroom discussion by asking students to identify and debate the criteria Walker, Baldwin, and Baraka use to define art. For example, Baraka claims for "Negro music"—blues and jazz—the status of Art as it grows "out of the depth of the black man's soul" and from those who "maintained their essential identities as Negroes." Authenticity of experience also counts for Walker: The "vibrant, creative spirit" (32) lives, in her mother's case, through stories she hands down and the gardens she creates. Because she "is involved in work her soul must have" (41), "being an artist has [...] been a daily part of her life" (43).

2. Baldwin's examples of white culture include exemplars of traditional European (white male) high art from Shakespeare to the architectural grandeur of Chartres. His list in "A Stranger in the Village" (p. 134) is similar. Baldwin's relationship to white culture is highly conflicted. He has had to work himself out of a "self-destroying limbo" of resentment toward white culture for its achievements and toward black culture for its oppression in order to define himself as a black artist ("Autobiographical Notes" 1).

Walker appears less conflicted than Baldwin. She is of the next generation, born twenty years later than Baldwin, and has inherited the fruits of his struggle. She has European high art (represented by Virginia Woolf) at her command when she wants to use that tradition. She knows African poetry and can imagine an African ancestor, whereas Baldwin seems to shy away from a tribal past. She easily claims African American artistic roots, in both music (the one African American art that was not successfully suppressed) and literature—through Wheatley, Zora Neale Hurston, and the other black female writers she names (29). Readers who notice that the European artist Walker references is a woman may wonder if Walker's comfort with white culture extends to white male artists.

3. James Baldwin defines Art, white or black, as male. In his listing of European artists in "Autobiographical Notes," Baldwin focuses on arts that were particularly exclusive of women: narrative poetry, playwriting, architecture, oil painting, sculpture. Walker's project is to call attention to the contribution of black women artists. By listing significant black women musicians in paragraph 13, for example, she makes explicit the female contribution to blues and jazz. Walker herself is largely responsible for the rediscovery of Zora Neale Hurston, an important female artist who participated in the Harlem Renaissance. As part of her project, Walker opens the definition of art to include domestic arts, which are often dismissed as everyday tasks rather than as creative productions. Walker points out that "we have constantly looked high [for art] when we should have looked high—and low" (34). In reclaiming this "lost" art, Walker is placing contemporary black women artists in an ongoing tradition of black female art; they

are not *sui generis* but are inspired, nurtured, and "guided by [a] heritage of love and beauty and a respect for strength" (49).

4. Walker offers a number of images of the black woman. Black women are crazed saints, driven to madness by the lack of an outlet for expressing their feelings and insights and by physical and sexual abuse. Black woman are "the *mule* of the world" (5), recalling Sojourner Truth's declaration that "I have ploughed and planted, and gathered into barns, and no man could head me!" (2). Black women are "Artists"—Walker's mother is both Artist and mule, creating beautiful, "ambitious" (42) gardens *and* laboring with her husband in the fields *and* raising children *and* maintaining a home.

Walker lists a number of other stereotypes about black women, including "'Matriarchs,' 'Superwomen,' and 'Mean and Evil Bitches'" (27). The term "matriarch" is immediately suggestive of Daniel Patrick Moynihan's "The Negro Family," in which he argues that families headed by women are the cause of much of the social pathology afflicting lower-class blacks. The image of the laundress in the United Negro College Fund advertisement (p. 204) exemplifies "the mule of the world" but with the difference that this woman's labor has enabled her granddaughter to work toward a professional career.

5. Moynihan argues that black matriarchs disempower black men. In terms of the stereotypes that Walker lists, successful black women can be constructed by their critics as "Superwomen" and as "Mean and Evil Bitches" (27) grabbing success at the expense of black men. Walker's "Looking to the Side, and Back" denounces the position that it is "the responsibility of the black woman . . . to support the black man; *whatever* he does" (5). The matriarch stereotype highlights the achievements of superwomen who support the family financially, raise the children, and run the household, ignoring the costs of such an effort. The stereotype also ignores the subjugation of black women, by whites and by black men, that Walker references in "In Search of Our Mothers' Gardens": Women are "abused and mutilated in body" by overwork, too many children, and violence (2). In her portrayal of her mother, Walker includes some of the elements of the matriarch stereotype, emphasizing her mother's contributions in all areas of the family's life, including sewing all the clothes, towels, sheets, and quilts. However, her mother worked with her father, not in his place. Walker describes one example of black women who are not superwomen in "Looking to the Side, and Back": black women oppressed by black men.

Toni Morrison supports alternatives to the nuclear family: Successful families do not have to consist of a father, mother, and children. In fact, Morrison argues, successful child rearing is a community, and not a family, responsibility: "[P]eople need a larger unit" (2). Moynihan argues that the traditional nuclear family paradigm is "stable" and "effective" (5) and that black families without such a structure are at a disadvantage. Walker looks at the functioning of a family rather than its structure. The nuclear family that consists of a woman "required to bake biscuits for a lazy backwater tramp" (12) is not healthy just because there are two parents present. Neither is the nuclear family in which the woman is compelled to bear too many children (12). For Walker, the health of a family is dependent on all family members having an opportunity to develop their talents and express their creativity. When such opportunities are absent, the family is pathological no matter what its structure.

6. Walker defines creativity as an expression of spirituality, "of powerful imagination and deep spiritual feelings" (35). Creativity is an active entity, prone to popping "out in wild and unlikely places" (32) and is suppressed with difficulty and at great cost. Walker's revision of Virginia Woolf's comment on repressed creativity is an extension of the idea that genius exists among those not recognized as artists—those who could not, in Walker's words, develop "the creative spark" (39). Walker adds to Woolf's discussion black and enslaved women and "daughters of sharecroppers" (38) and reinterprets Woolf's list of unsuppressed geniuses to exemplify black artists such as Zora Neale Hurston and Richard Wright. She also revises the perception of creativity as demonic possession to its manifestation as spirituality, or "Sainthood" (38). Thus, Walker extends and reshapes Woolf's comment on the nature of imagination by including African American culture.

You might ask students to make a full list of those "unsuppressed geniuses" noted by Walker. In addition to Hurston and Wright, students may pick up on references to Phillis Wheatley, Virginia Woolf, Roberta Flack, Bessie Smith, and her own mother. Some students may even suggest Walker herself. You can ask students to consider what these references might mean to Walker. Of course, students are not likely to be familiar with many of these names, so you'll first have to ask them to go to the library or to the Internet to research them.

Once students have a handle on who these people are, they can then turn to questions about why Walker included them in her essay: What purpose do these references serve? What kinds of examples do they make for readers? How does understanding the context of Walker's essay help to answer these questions? Your students could pursue these question further as a research project; they might also ask what other figures Walker could have included in her essay.

Barbara Ehrenreich, *Serving in Florida* (p. 206)

Malcolm Gladwell, *The Physical Genius* (p. 213)

1. The factors Ehrenreich identifies as underlying the conditions facing these restaurant workers include low wages, housing costs, including the up-front costs of moving into an apartment (security deposit and a month's rent in advance), lack of access to health insurance, and prescription costs. The cycle of poverty is difficult to break: "starting conditions are everything" (7). To answer the second part of this

question, students might do some research on homelessness and on the debate on health care reform and its likely impact on poor and low-income groups.

2. Ehrenreich's word choice indicates the disgust she feels at the conditions in the kitchen at Jerry's. Her metaphors from the human digestive system suggest offensive odors, horrible textures, and constipation. She also makes a connection between the need for good hygiene to prevent the spread of diseases from human wastes, the filthy kitchen, and the workers' inability to wash their hands. By drawing a parallel between the restaurant, where food is prepared and served, to the internal body, where it is processed, Ehrenreich suggests that low-wage workers laboring in unsanitary and inequitable conditions are the "fuel" driving the American economy. The problems that these workers face are transferred onto unsuspecting consumers: The restaurant's customers "eat, although they don't realize it, almost literally out of our hands" (11).

3. Student responses will vary, but the instructor should encourage students to use the techniques Ehrenreich employs to describe her working experience, including dialogue (with her co-workers), description (especially by appealing to sight, touch, and smell), analogy (comparing the restaurant to the internal body), and anecdotal evidence (wage rates and tips, and housing and prescription costs).

4. According to Gladwell (21), the four visualization skills in Stephen Kosslyn's formulation are generating an image, "image inspection" (inferring from the image), "image maintenance" (holding the image in mind), and "image transformation" (manipulating the image). Encourage students to translate these skills, which act as a mental "rehearsal" (20), into their own experiences in the classroom, playing sports, working, or pursuing a hobby. Notably, each of Gladwell's examples is a person who has the time and privacy needed to engage his imaginative faculties: Jack Nicklaus has found the time to "mentally rehearse, frame by frame" a particular swing; Yo Yo Ma solved a "difficult musical problem" when he was riding on a bus, presumably undisturbed by background noise; and Charlie Wilson reviews his day's upcoming surgeries while running (20). In contrast, Ehrenreich describes a workplace with no privacy and relentless activity, and workers who struggle simply to survive. For example, while working at Jerry's, she spends "weeks under the surveillance of men (and later women) whose job it was to monitor my behavior for signs of sloth, theft, drug abuse, or worse" (1). Gladwell's discussion of genius emphasizes the imagination as a problem-solving organ rather than as one of evasion. Perhaps the only way a worker in Ehrenreich's position at Jerry's could use her imagination to make the work easier or more pleasant would be to imagine herself elsewhere. Ehrenreich suggests that with practice a worker might be able to enter "a 'flow state'" in which "a Zen-like emptiness sets in" (16), but this condition does not allow the individual to produce satisfying work, merely to endure demeaning conditions.

5. Gladwell's description of the process of visualization suggests that it can produce the "fluidity and grace" that Charlie Wilson achieves in surgery in other

activities. An athlete has "a 'feel' for the game" (9) just as Wilson has a "feel" that he uses "without having any conscious reason" (11). Practice is essential to the pursuit of perfection, as Gladwell illustrates in his discussion of Greg Rusedksi (14) and Wilson (15). Thus, an intuitive "feel" combined with relentless practice can improve any activity. Students who play music or a sport, create artistic works, repair bicycles or cars, or communicate naturally with animals may immediately understand this. Some students may need to be encouraged to see how visualization might be brought to such activities.

Mary Ellen Mark, *The Damm Family in Their Car, Los Angeles, 1987* (p. 224)

1. The photograph creates dissonance between the symbols of mobility—the car and the open road—and the family's immobility. The car is off the road, not traveling down it toward an optimistic future. The family members are in a car, but are not mobile, not moving forward in their lives. The overall impression is of a family that is off the highway of opportunity and progress.

2. and 3. Each family member is a portrait of distress and despair. The son seems to be in pain whereas the daughter's face conveys extreme passivity and hopelessness. The mother leans back and is held by her husband in a pose reminiscent of Michelangelo's *Pieta*, the dead Christ held in his mother's arms. The father appears protective, wary, and perhaps defensive.

The four characters stare directly at the camera with wide-opened eyes. Their gaze is unflinching and almost confrontational. They appear to be close to the edge of their resources; they look desperate and deeply distressed. The photograph implicitly challenges the viewer to acknowledge the fact of the Damms' homelessness as well as the possibility that there may be, for these people, no hope of change. In responding to these questions, students might consider the various types of impoverishment discussed in the essays in this book and the ways in which the United Nations' "Universal Declaration of Human Rights" addresses the sources of poverty (Chapter 7). The instructor might direct students to Barbara Ehrenreich's "Serving in Florida (p. 206), Jonathan Kozol's "The Human Cost of an Illiterate Society" (p. 252), and Alice Walker's "In Search of Our Mothers' Gardens" (p. 192) to explore the issues the working poor face and how illiteracy and racism perpetuate poverty.

Matthew B. Crawford, *The Case for Working with Your Hands* (p. 225)

1. Gladwell argues that the physical genius's ability to "calculate the diversions and to factor in the interruptions" (9) helps create a "feel" for an activity, and he shows that visualization and practice are central to perfecting this skill. Similarly, Crawford describes a process of using "the judgment that arises only

from experience" (19). He imagines this "larger gestalt" as a way of "thinking about your own thinking" (19–20), a process that may correspond to Gladwell's description of the capacity to "pick up on subtle patterns" (9). Crawford's assertion that "to be a good mechanic you have to be constantly open to the possibility that you may be mistaken" (20) also seems similar to Gladwell's analysis of creativity. When Crawford writes that a good mechanic "internalizes the healthy functioning of the motorcycle" (20), he refers to a similar kind of physical and mental immersion in an activity that Gladwell describes among athletes and surgeons. Both Gladwell and Crawford emphasize that the brain and the hands work together in the performance of a physical activity and both define the ideal form of work as a seamless intersection of mind and body.

2. Ehrenreich describes jobs that are demeaning because the employees are treated with little respect. She observes, and is subjected to, being monitored by others (1), arbitrary orders by managers (2), rebukes (3), threats of arbitrary drug testing (4), and filthy conditions (11). Ehrenreich does not suggest that serving food is innately disheartening work; rather, the low-cost restaurant industry operates on the basis of cheap labor and its workers have little power to negotiate the terms of employment. She also suggests that the management structure is so far removed from the day-to-day business that improvement is highly unlikely.

Crawford distinguishes between the acquisition of knowledge and the reality of being a knowledge worker. His work violated rather than employed his knowledge: He wrote abstracts of scholarly works "without understanding the text" and thus performed work that "felt like violence against what was best in [him]self" (28). Crawford describes a business model that required speedy writing, and thus placed little importance on quality. Crawford's description suggests that the work is "confined and stultified" (33) because "mutilation" (30) is an inherent part of the job.

3. Crawford's comment does not suggest that academic credentials are not important, but that the experience of manual work can be enriching and fulfilling. Because knowledge workers often "live remote from the consequences of the decisions they make" (36), they should "learn a trade, if only in the summers, so that their fingers will be crushed once or twice before they go on to run the country" (36). Ehrenreich emphasizes the experience of the working poor, who have little opportunity to test their "capacities," while Gladwell's subjects are unusual in that they are extremely talented in a particular area. Virginia Woolf's speech addresses the prejudices faced by the professional woman writer and all women who strive to achieve. These women cannot fulfill their potential, she argues, when they are impeded by "extreme conventionality" (5). Similarly, Crawford describes the convention that everybody, to succeed, must be "hustled off to college, then to a cubicle, against their own inclinations and natural bents, when they would rather be learning to build things or fix things" (6). Encourage students to examine a particular "field of action" and explore whether higher education has

direct or indirect benefits in developing the individual's professional and personal lives. Crawford suggests that his life as a mechanic is richer and more rewarding because he is educated; his interest in working with his hands does not diminish the value he places on knowledge.

Virgina Woolf, *Professions for Women* (p. 235)

1. The "Angel in the House" is the imaginative embodiment of Victorian and early-twentieth-century femininity. The image of the "Angel" represents an impossible ideal: She is "charming," "unselfish," and "pure" (3). She is also a "phantom" that haunts and hinders the woman writer, for "you cannot even review a novel without having a mind of your own, without expressing what you think to be the truth" (3). This "Angel" does not have a mind of her own because she prefers "to sympathize always with the minds and wishes of others," (3) and so, Woolf argues, the woman who aspires to write must kill her (3).

2. Good writing, Woolf argues, tells "the truth about human relations, morality, sex," and the "Angel" dictates that such matters "cannot be dealt with freely and openly by women" (3). The feminine ideal that the "Angel" embodies discourages truthfulness in women: "[T]hey must charm, they must conciliate, they must—to put it bluntly—tell lies if they are to succeed" (3). Woolf describes a society in which the "consciousness of what men will say of a woman who speaks the truth about her passions" (5) stifles the female imagination. The "phantoms and obstacles" that stop a woman from achieving are those that prevent her from using her time to develop her talents and that impose the expectation that she must be "sympathetic," "charming," "unselfish," and "pure" (3).

3. Woolf is careful to set her development as a woman writer in the past: "In those days—the last of Queen Victoria—every house had its Angel. [The struggle to kill the Angel] was an experience that was bound to befall all women writers at that time" (3). She also describes the young women to whom she speaks as facing their own challenges: "[T]here are many phantoms and obstacles . . . looming" in the way of the woman who wants to be "a doctor, a lawyer, a civil servant" (7). Students may need reminding that while twenty-first-century Western women find professions such as law and medicine open to them and that women are highly active in government affairs, there is still a gap in power and salaries in many occupations. Students may want to examine the articles in the U.N.'s "Universal Declaration of Human Rights" that address gender discrimination and consider how for many women in the world today, Woolf's analysis may still resonate.

4. Ehrenreich's analysis suggests the working poor whose lives she describes are barely able to survive, much less care for children. Many live in sub-standard housing, in motels, boats, and cars, and are on the verge of homelessness (6). Students can use this assignment to explore the problems of child care and working mothers as well as the tensions created by cultural expectations of mothers.

5. This assignment asks students to consider the social context in which families and individuals live and work. The instructor should ask students to consider how the extended family, health insurance and access to health care, access to child care, workers' ability to take maternity or paternity leave, the costs and stresses of commuting, housing costs, and environmental issues all contribute to overall living conditions. Remind students that individuals' and families' needs change over the cycle of their lives as young children become teenagers and college students. In addition, the instructor may want to remind students that factors outside of an individual's control, such as employment prospects, the costs of an education, the return on investments, mortgage rates, and health issues, can have a major impact on life choices.

4   EDUCATION AND THE AMERICAN CHARACTER: WHAT DO WE TEACH? WHAT DO WE LEARN? AND WHY DOES THIS MATTER?

Simon McComb, *Education in Open Air* (p. 241)

1. McComb's photograph captures multiple interactions, including technology and nature, learner and environment, reader and writer, individual and community, the life of the mind, and the life of the body. The instructor might use this assignment to remind students that where and how we learn are as much a part of the learning process as what we learn. Students might respond to McComb's photograph by discussing what kind of learning takes place outside the classroom, how technology and electronic communication make distance learning possible, and how technology changes the individual's interaction with his or her environment. Is there a conflict between the apparently undisturbed beauty of the photograph and the technology and consumer products the man uses? Does the surfboard suggest that physical activity is integral to intellectual development? How do students reconcile their personal needs in the context of an academic life that may leave little time for contemplation or reflection?

2. Many of the essays in *The Arlington Reader* explore the relationship between individual and environment. For example, Momaday's "The Way to Rainy Mountain" (Chapter 2) represents landscape as an inseparable part of the human experience, whereas Annie Dillard in "Heaven and Earth in Jest" (Chapter 8) explores the capacity for spirituality through nature, and Heather King, in "The Closest to Love We Ever Get" (Chapter 2), finds spirituality within the human community. The instructor might ask students to explore learning environments with reference to Malcolm Gladwell's "The Physical Genius" and Matthew B. Crawford's "The Case

for Working with Your Hands" (both in Chapter 3), both of which suggest that some of the most important learning experiences are hands-on.

The instructor should encourage students to examine the relationship between types of learning and different environments. For example, might McComb's photograph convey a stage in the process of learning such as brainstorming or integrating information or exploring a problem through writing? Does the photograph suggest that traditional higher education may not suit all dispositions? After all, learning is a lifelong process that can take place in many different types of environments. Does the photograph represent a democratic view of learning or, on the contrary, suggest that learning is a privileged activity confined to those with the leisure to enjoy it?

3. This question asks students to consider the relationships among gender, ethnicity, and nature. Cultural images have a profound influence on associations between gender and other concepts based on binary relations such as culture and nature, movement and stasis, and thought and feeling. In addition, the relationships between ethnicity and nature can become highly mythologized, as Sherman Alexie points out in "What Sacagawea Means to Me" (Chapter 2). Ask students to examine the assumptions they bring to these relationships and to use this question to examine and dismantle those assumptions.

4. Students will find numerous sources online that discuss the gender gap in higher education. The student might also want to respond to this question by referring to Matthew B. Crawford's "The Case for Working with Your Hands" (Chapter 3) and Dave Leonhardt's "The College Dropout Boom" (Chapter 4) to consider why some men might not finish college or choose alternative professional and personal paths other than higher education.

Stanley Fish, Gerald Graff, James MacGregor Burns, and Nancy Hopkins, *College Advice, From People Who Have Been There Awhile* (p. 242)

1. This question asks students to prioritize the various demands involved in what Gerald Graff calls "a real socialization into the ways of intellectual culture" (2). Students might begin by listing the various goals they hope to achieve through higher education, such as exploring "the world at large" (Burns 1), learning "to write a clean English sentence" (Fish 3) and turn "stuff [...] into an argument" (Graff 4), and discovering a passion for a particular "intellectual vision of the future" (Hopkins 1). The instructor should encourage students to be as specific as possible when describing the appropriateness of these professors' advice. For example, have students had particular experiences with online evaluations of instructors? Do students feel uncomfortable asking professors about "their own intellectual interests" (Burns 5)? Have particular courses and instructors influenced their intellectual interests? Do they find it difficult to allocate time to nonrequired reading such as a newspaper?

2. and 3. In addition to Sedaris's speech, students can use as a model Alexie's "What Sacagawea Means to Me" (Chapter 2), which is less overtly comic and more satiric. Students may want to gear their advice toward technological issues such as those Nicholas Carr and Michael J. Bugeja raise in Chapter 5. For example, Carr describes how "reading and writing e-mails, scanning headlines and blog posts, watching videos and listening to podcasts, or just tripping from link to link" (3) is "chipping away my capacity for concentration and contemplation" (4), whereas Bugeja raises problems of privacy and student behavior (14) and issues of how technology is used in the classroom (22–23). Encourage students to be specific and explain their advice, or how they would change their advice, by referring to their learning experiences.

4. Encourage students to respond to this question by identifying clear themes that are relevant to the particular social demands they face, such as sexual relations, friendship, privacy, time management, and extracurricular activities.

David Sedaris, *What I Learned and What I Said at Princeton* (p. 246)

1. Sedaris is a well-known humorist, so his audience was probably already aware that he never attended Princeton and expected him to deliver a humorous speech. Even those who did not know what to expect would realize that the speech would be comic from Sedaris's first sentence: the phrase "when *I* went to Princeton" signals a cliché of nostalgic hindsight. Any residual doubts about whether Sedaris is serious or satirical are clearly demolished in the second sentence when he claims that he remembers when the chapel "was just a clearing, cordoned off with sharp sticks" (1). Sedaris goes on to satirize academic areas of study (2, 16, 24), legacy admissions (3), the elitism of Ivy League schools (4–15), parental ambitions (3, 15), the costs of college (19), the value of a liberal arts education (25, 28–30, 38, 39), eccentric professors (27), life's unexpected turns (30, 39), parental disappointments (34–36), and adult children living at home (30–37). It is important for the speaker to signal his intentions and for his audience to understand them so that they can enjoy hearing a satirical treatment of their college experience. To write their own satire, students can choose one of Sedaris's topics or some aspect of their experience of higher education that is more specific to their college or university.

2. Students can respond to this question by exploring the various aspects of the admissions process. They might explain what role parental, teacher, and peer expectations played in their decision-making process, and what types of admissions essays they wrote and how they tailored them to specific institutions. They can examine criteria such as geographical location and climate, choices of programs and majors, parents' experiences of higher education, academic prestige, and social life. More experienced students might compare their expectations to their experiences by making a list of each. Students should be as specific as possible.

3. Sedaris aims his humor at parental pride, particularly parents who have Ivy League connections: His father, he claims, has "the whole [Princeton] outfit" and bumper stickers (3). After Sedaris disappoints his parents by taking "a winding [path], with plenty of obstacles along the way" (30), they transfer their ambitions to the family dog (37). Sedaris implies that his audience will understand that some who leave Princeton will "[soar] like arrows into the bosoms of power and finance," whereas others take the "winding path" (30). His humorous narrative might either reassure or alarm some nervous graduates—depending on their own expectations.

4. Students may want to respond to this essay by referring to Matthew B. Crawford's "The Case for Working with Your Hands" (Chapter 3), which explores how graduates may not find life as a knowledge worker as fulfilling as they expect. Ask students to interview recent graduates or do some research on the professional and personal lives of recent graduates in particular fields. What does living at home signify in today's economic climate? What alternatives are graduates pursuing if they cannot find jobs in their fields?

5. This dialogue should take into account generational differences and how students today face a different set of choices than graduates did twenty years ago. Students might list and discuss the specific suggestions offered in "College Advice" as part of their discussion. They might use this opportunity to ask parents, grandparents, or others who are interested in their education about their own decision-making processes as young adults.

Charles M. Schulz, *Peanuts: Slow Reading* (p. 251)

1. Schulz's cartoon might be interpreted in light of the tendency to diagnose boys with ADHD far more than girls, who often find the classroom setting more congenial. Linus's explanation suggests that brains work and develop differently, which is the basis of Gardner's essay, "Who Owns Intelligence?" (Chapter 4) and of his theory of multiple intelligences. The National Institute of Mental Health is a good place for students to begin their research on ADHD: www.nimh.nih.gov/health/publications/attention-deficit-hyperactivity-disorder/complete-index.shtml.

2. Rodriguez and Kozol each point out that cultural and environmental factors influence student performance. Rodriguez describes living with parents who spoke "a hesitant, accented, and not always grammatical English" (8). He also describes his fear of the English-speaking classroom (20–21). Kozol points out that illiterate parents "cannot read the letters that their children bring home from their teachers" or "study school department circulars that tell them of the courses that their children must be taking if they hope to pass the SAT exams." Illiterate parents "cannot help with homework" or "write a letter to the teacher" (11). Children of illiterate parents are disadvantaged by their home environment

and are possibly less confident in school. Getting an eye test might be the initial response of a parent with a child who finds reading difficult and would be a logical first step.

3. Labels are weapons that can be damaging, even if they are sometimes humorous. Lucy's comment is funny because it contrasts with Linus's complicated explanation and because, as the regular reader of *Peanuts* knows, she and Charlie Brown have an ongoing feud. Lucy's name for Charlie Brown, "Blockhead," also implies stupidity. The perception of stupidity and intelligence often depends on context. Crawford's "The Case for Working with Your Hands," Gladwell's "The Physical Genius" (both in Chapter 3), Kozol's "The Human Cost of an Illiterate Society" and Rodriguez's "Aria" (both in Chapter 4), and Carr's "Is Google Making Us Stupid?" (Chapter 5) all explore the relationship between learning and the physical and cultural contexts in which we learn and are excellent companion readings.

4. Franklin shows that reading is a highly contextual activity. A consent form might be difficult to interpret for many reasons. The language is often "either too broad or amounts to a lawyer-driven list of everything that could possibly go wrong" (7). In addition, "relative risks and benefits can be very different for each patient depending on age, health and other factors" (8). Franklin reports that 21 percent of adults in the United States read at a sixth-grade level or below (13) and so are likely to find consent forms intimidating if not outright incomprehensible. Kozol describes the problems illiterates face in getting health care: For example, they cannot read health insurance forms or waivers that describe surgical procedures (13). The humor of Schulz's cartoon depends on the reader's ability to ignore some of these more serious social issues—humor often depends on maintaining a blind eye to suffering. However, the instructor might point out that that humor can also enlighten readers and make difficult subjects palatable.

Jonathan Kozol, *The Human Cost of an Illiterate Society* (p. 252)

1. Jonathan Kozol believes that questions of literacy are a moral issue because illiterate people cannot get accurate and sufficient information to act in their best interests when faced with a political decision such as voting. He agrees with James Madison about arming people with the power of knowledge, for "a popular government without popular information or the means of acquiring it, is but a prologue to a farce or a tragedy, or perhaps both" (3). Illiteracy threatens democracy because it endangers the "basic equity in the political construction" of our society.

Moreover, illiteracy makes every aspect of the life of an illiterate person difficult or even dangerous. Illiterate people are not able to read a product manual, a restaurant menu, or letters from their children; illiterate people may take the wrong amount or type of medication because they can't read the instructions on the bottle; illiterate people tend to spend more money on grocery shopping because their shopping decisions depend on the pictures that brand-name companies put on their products rather than on detailed information on the ingredients label. Thus Kozol thinks it is immoral for sixty million American citizens to be limited by illiteracy.

2. The label on the Drāno can is an eye-opening, worst-case-scenario response to the title. "I am going to tell you about the human cost of illiteracy," the title promises, then, bang! Here is a real-life case: Illiteracy can be deadly. This is a shocking but effective way to open an essay, and readers are compelled by a sense of moral responsibility to investigate the topic and therefore go on reading the body of the essay.

We can infer that Kozol's audience includes literate people. He wants to alert them to the moral complication of the questions of illiteracy so that they will support a truly democratic educational system, one that will reach out to the sixty million illiterate Americans. In addition, Kozol gives many lectures to promote literacy, and we should view his book as one instance of his work.

3. Repetition as a rhetorical device tends to lend emphasis to the message transmitted. Kozol's overwhelming use of repetition here is in keeping with the seriousness of his subject matter—the high cost of illiteracy in our society. As readers scan these parallel paragraphs, tension mounts as each cost is added. The effects of such repetition are not merely logical, however, and students should be encouraged to explore how these paragraphs affect their mind, feelings, senses, and heart.

The opening sentences are arranged in negative patterns to enhance the message: Illiteracy is an absolutely negative experience; it adversely affects every aspect of life.

4. Although responses to this writing assignment will vary, the instructor should encourage students to speculate freely and creatively. Students might explore how the absence of literacy could change our civilization and make it less complex. Isn't illiteracy—or different kinds of literacy—often an essential characteristic of Utopian stories? Why have so many talented writers and artists been fascinated by the dream of returning to a simpler—often illiterate—style of life?

In exploring the relationship between literacy and civilization, students should consider the role of oral traditions in illiterate and literate cultures. Rodriguez and Silko both suggest that oral traditions are important to the preservation of culture. Rodriguez argues that a child's "family language" is inseparable from the "intimate life" (4) of the home. He observes how family language evolves through oral communication: "At dinner we invented new words that sounded Spanish, but made sense only to us. We pieced together new words by taking, say, an English verb and giving it Spanish endings" (18). For Silko, written narrative cannot convey Pueblo tradition because the story is inseparable from the oral presentation of the story and its fluid structure (6), and from the particular storyteller and audience (8). Through stories, the individual "moves [...] from the idea of one's identity as a tribal person into clan identity, then to one's identity as a member of an extended family" (11). Thoreau emphasizes that the essential experience of life is found in what he calls a "Spartan simplicity of life and eleva- tion of purpose" (2). Thoreau links technological advancements and economic wealth with spiritual starvation (2–3) and suggests that communications, news- papers, and news (2–4) contribute to humanity's illusory belief that "that *is* which *appears* to be" (6).

5. This assignment allows students to examine the ramifications of illiteracy through an actual case study. Ask students how, specifically, the individuals in these situations were victimized by their illiteracy. Kozol writes that illiterates cannot understand the waivers they sign before surgery (13) and are "intimi- dated by the unfamiliar air of fear and atmosphere of ether [...] in the confines even of the most attractive and expensive medical facilities" (13). They cannot understand the risks of their choices and behaviors, such as smoking, and so make themselves "high-risk candidates for cancer" (19), and in fact do not enjoy the capacity to make choices about numerous small and large matters (26) or to challenge others (29). Franklin emphasizes the power that medical professionals have and how disadvantaged patients are: "[T]ruly informed consent" implies that the patient understands the "'risks, benefits, and alternatives' of a procedure" (5). How did these particular problems influence subjects such as Henrietta Lacks or the men who participated in the Tuskegee experiment? What are the consequences of depriving a segment of society of the capacity to make informed choices? Do students view the medical knowledge that these cases made possible as in any way justifiable?

Deborah Franklin, *"Informed Consent"—What Information? What Consent?* (p. 260)

1. The instructor should ask students to respond to this question by consid- ering the problems Franklin addresses. Franklin observes that "'truly informed consent'" requires the doctor to take the necessary time to ensure that the pa- tient understands the "'risks, benefits, and alternatives'" of the procedure (5–6). Students might consider whether they faced the problem that Franklin points out—that the language of the form "is usually either too broad or amounts to a lawyer-driven list of everything that could possibly go wrong" (7). Was the form "a one-size-fits-all form" (8)? Did the student ever want to walk away from a pro- cedure, as Franklin describes (9–11)? Ask the student to discuss any conversation with the health care provider, whether the student read the consent form, and whether the student understood the risks of the procedure.

2. Franklin quotes Dr. Manthous, who argues that the physician should take responsibility for the patient's understanding. Patients may be reluctant or scared to ask specific questions. Franklin asserts that it is the doctor who "must decide how much to tell a patient beforehand about the pros, cons, and alternatives" (2)

before a procedure. Franklin quotes a literacy advocate in support of her argument that the doctor bears the burden of ensuring that a patient is informed: "Unless they pay close attention, doctors may miss the signs that a patient is a poor reader" (14).

3. Students will find information at the Office of Human Subjects Research Web site: http://ohsr.od.nih.gov/guidelines/45cfr46.html. Students should consider what kinds of procedures their college or university uses, including whether, as Franklin suggests, they adapt consent forms for patients with poor literacy (14–16) or use interactive forms (16–17). Students should analyze the text of written forms and the complexity and level of the language used to decide how accessible the process actually is.

Social Psychology Network, *Tips on Informed Consent* (p. 262)

1. The U.S. Government Guidelines cover the eight elements of informed consent in the American Psychological Association Guidelines. In some respects, however, the U.S. Government Guidelines appear more comprehensive than those of the APA. For example:

- The government's guidelines require that research subjects receive a "disclosure of appropriate alternative procedures or courses of treatment, if any, that might be advantageous to the subject" (x). The APA Guidelines only address the prospective research participant's choice of "alternative activities" when "participation is a course requirement or an opportunity for extra credit" (x). The third element of the APA Guidelines, which require that the subject be informed of "the foreseeable consequences of declining or withdrawing" (x), could be interpreted as a similar requirement, but is rather vague.
- The government's guidelines require that the participant be informed "whether there are any treatments or compensation if injury occurs and, if so, what they consist of, or where further information may be obtained" (x). The APA Guidelines only require that the prospective subject be informed about any potential "adverse effects" (x).
- U.S. government guidelines require that the participants be given information on whom to contact "in the event of a research-related injury" (x), whereas APA guidelines only require that the subject be given contact information to ask "about the research and research participants' rights" (x).
- Government guidelines are more explicit about the language of consent forms than are the APA guidelines. The government guidelines require that consent forms not ask subjects "to waive (or appear to waive) any of their legal rights" or to release researchers or any affiliated institutions from liability (x).

However, the APA guidelines are more comprehensive than the U.S. government guidelines in that they explicitly address the situation of those who are "legally incapable of giving informed consent" (x).

Franklin appears to recommend that consent forms use simple, friendly language, with "a larger typeface" and "shorter paragraphs" than conventional consent forms, and use "illustrations and bulleted points" (16). However, Franklin's main goal is to emphasize the importance of "a candid, unhurried conversation between doctor and patient" (3). Franklin considers consent forms the "'last step'" in making a medical decision (4), rather than a substitute for that process. Franklin concludes that although the format and language of a good consent form are important, the form cannot "replace the bond of trust between doctor and patient" (19).

Franklin's description of patient-friendly consent forms is more explicit than the U.S. government guidelines' reference to "plain language that research subjects can understand" (x), in part because she investigates the recent introduction of interactive electronic consent forms (17–18). Guidelines such as those the U.S. Government and the APA issue are necessarily broad and do not address the many ways that, as Franklin points out, "the relative risks and benefits [of a procedure] can be very different for each patient depending on age, health, and other factors" (8). Franklin's goal is to educate readers about the limitations of consent forms as well as to stress the importance of "the bond of trust between doctor and patient" (19).

2. Students who have not been involved in a research study might respond to this question by imagining what kinds of risks they would be willing to assume and what kinds of benefits would encourage them to participate in a study. Would the student be willing to undergo some inconvenience or even assume a degree of personal risk to contribute to research that offers only abstract benefits to humankind?

Students who have been subjects in a research study might try to recall their experiences from memory and then find the guidelines that applied to that study. Does their memory of their experience tally with the guidelines? The instructor should ask students to discuss whether they paid much attention to the guidelines or consent forms they saw or signed, whether compensation influenced their decision to participate, whether they felt that they were truly and fully informed, and whether they see ways to improve how research subjects are treated.

Dave Leonhardt, *The College Dropout Boom* (p. 265)

1. Leonhardt presents evidence that, of the increasing number of Americans who drop out of college, "most are from poor and working-class families" (7). Thus, although college attendance has "become the norm throughout most of the United States" (8), college enrollments tend to "reinforce many of the advantages of birth" (9). Graduation rates at colleges that enroll poor students are "often low," and colleges with high graduation rates are increasingly populated by students "from the

top of the nation's income ladder" (9). More "high-income students" graduate from four-year colleges than "low-income students," and this gap is widening (10).

Thus, the "boom" that Leonhardt describes is predominantly one that affects lower-income students and has significant social effects. For example, Leonhardt argues that because college graduates earn more than nongraduates (12), the increasing likelihood that a low-income student will drop out of college creates a form of "inherited meritocracy": Children of college graduates tend to graduate, and so "success is largely being passed down from one generation to the next" (14). Lawrence H. Summers's argument that this "widening gap between the children of the rich and children of the poor" constitutes "the most serious domestic problem in the United States today" (10) suggests that a decrease in "economic mobility" (13) and economic diversity (15) is costly to society as a whole. An entrenched class of the poor and uneducated that cannot compete for a place in "today's globalized, computerized economy" (12) promotes a society of exclusion dominated by an educated elite.

2. Leanna realized that marriage would prevent her from acquiring a college degree. She also sees persistence as particularly key to completing a college degree for the low-income student (29). Thus, she might have encouraged her brother to delay marriage and finish his degree first. Leanna Blevins's institution, the New College Institute (www.newcollegeinstitute.org), describes its mission as "making education beyond the associate's degree level accessible and convenient to students of all ages in Southern Virginia." Its "Community Outreach" program seeks to help students who might be "intimidated" by higher education. Students such as Mr. Blevins also have the option of applying to universities that have broadened their admissions criteria; for example, the University of Virginia, under Mr. Casteen's leadership, has removed "'artificial barriers' to a college education" for "deserving students" (27).

3. Leonhardt points out that many race-based affirmative action programs have been banned and argues that "programs based on class backgrounds have wider [public] support than those based on race" (37). These developments have led some universities to "give weight to economic class in granting admissions" (35). Affirmative action programs were designed to rectify "specific kinds of discrimination" (35); Leonhardt suggests that these programs have done their job by "[swelling] the number of women, blacks, and Latinos on campuses" (34). Future programs will have to "address broad economic inequities" (34) to reduce the gap between high- and low-income students in higher education.

4. Students might begin thinking about this question by considering the advantages wealthier students have over low-income students. Leonhardt points out, of students who remain in college, "[t]heir parents, understanding the importance of a bachelor's degree, spent hours reading to them, researching school districts, and making it clear to them that they simply must graduate from college" (16). Leonhardt also offers evidence that "legacy applicants and minority students"

may have an advantage over poorer students with equivalent SAT scores (56). Ask students to consider how tutoring, prep courses for standardized tests such as the SAT, peer group pressure, and parental emotional and financial support can also give high-income students an advantage.

5. For this question students might consider the Blevins siblings' different views on their professional choices: Andy wanted to attend New College Institute, but Leanna "daydreamed about having a life that would seem as natural as her brother's, a life in which she would not feel like an outsider in her home town" (31). For Andy, higher education represents a promise of greater "control over his life" (33). In contrast, Crawford finds that his life as a mechanic gives him greater control compared to white-collar workers: "Like the mechanic, the manager faces the possibility of disaster at any time. But in his case, these disasters feel arbitrary; they are typically a result of corporate restructurings, not of physics" (24). Encourage students to consider the multiple dimensions of making a successful occupational choice. A great place to begin their research is the U.S. Department of Labor's Occupational Outlook Handbook available through the Bureau of Labor Statistics (www.bls.gov/oco/).

Richard Rodriguez, *Aria: A Memoir of a Bilingual Childhood* and Contexts (p. 275)

1. Richard Rodriguez uses "pretense to diversity" to refer to a false notion of multiculturalism: "What people mean by multiculturalism is different hues of themselves. They don't mean Islamic fundamentalists or skinheads. They mean other brown and black students who share opinions like theirs. It isn't diversity" ("Interview Excerpt" 2). Rodriguez, coming from a Chicano family, feels that he is expected to behave like a Chicano, assuming that certain qualities are exclusively Chicano. Although Rodriguez embraces the idea of a common human nature and resists being categorized as a Chicano or as anything other than "this man Rodriguez," in "Aria" he refers to qualities with which other Chicanos might tend to identify: "I was a bilingual child, but of a certain kind: 'socially disadvantaged,' the son of working-class parents, both Mexican immigrants" ("Aria" 5); and "enormous families of relatives" (7) visited and had great times together speaking Spanish, the sounds of which gave him an intimate feeling of being a member of a private circle.

However, Rodriquez's childhood was not like that of many Chicanos. He grew up in an affluent neighborhood and attended a white, middle-class school: "An accident of geography sent me to a school where all my classmates were white and many were the children of doctors and lawyers and business executives" (2). He thereby developed an idea about public and private languages that was different from both the Chicanos' and the whites', although he later admitted that the idea was wrong: "Because I wrongly imagined that English was intrinsically a public language and Spanish was intrinsically private, I easily noted the difference between classroom language and the language at home" (22). Had Rodriguez not been cut off, geographically and educationally, from the Chicano community in his childhood, he might have had experiences with Spanish on public occasions. Therefore, in this fundamental issue of language, he is neither typically Chicano nor typically white. He is just "*this man*" (1999 "Interview" 4).

Rodriguez and his family and relatives display qualities that are different than, or even opposite to, what Octavio Paz describes with sweeping generalization as the qualities of Mexicans: "The Mexican, whether young or old . . . general or laborer or lawyer, seems to me to be a person who shuts himself away to protect himself" (1). The Rodriguez family does not seem to be so reserved. The children laugh and scream when their father gets home, and "enormous families of relatives" (7) visited them regularly to have hearty parties together.

The intimacy and trust that Rodriguez's family enjoyed with one another during his childhood also seem at odds with Paz's characterization of the Mexican man who "builds a wall of indifference and remoteness between reality and himself" (1). However, Rodriguez seems conflicted as a result of his different experiences of Mexican masculinity. He longs for the "tender accents" of Spanish ("Aria" 33) and associates Spanish with "the golden age of my childhood" ("Aria" 37), but he dislikes "the tenderness of *Hunger of Memory*" ("Interview" 1). He describes his younger self as "too feminine, a little too American," and "too soft" ("Interview" 1) and would like to have been "tougher" and had the "spirit" of a Chicano, by which he appears to mean less "Anglo" and more rebellious. Rodriguez's experiences as a bilingual Chicano in America empower him to speak out on bilingual education and "the public uses of schooling" (4) and on "the value and necessity of assimilation" (38). He implies that by becoming "an American, no longer an alien in gringo society," he can represent the "dilemma" of the "socially disadvantaged" with more authority than "bilingualists" who believe that assimilation constitutes a loss of individuality (39).

2. Although he is from a Chicano family, Rodriguez defines individualism and America in Anglo-American or Protestant terms: "America is a Puritan country, Protestant baptized. It was Protestantism that taught Americans to fear the crowd and to believe in individualism" ("Slouching" 3). This individualism resists conformity, even in a "communal sense," and thus maintains the culture of an immigrant country, for "lacking a communal sense, how could Americans resist the coming of strangers?" (3). In this sense Rodriguez seems to suggest that new immigrants and their children are more American than those who can boast to be fifth-generation Americans. "Any immigrant kid could tell you that America exists. There is a culture. There is a shared accent, a shared defiance of authority, a shared skepticism about community" (5).

Rodriguez's theme in "Aria" advocates his own definition of individualism. As an adult Chicano, he speaks out against bilingual education because he believes "public individuality" is as important as "private" identity (38). As a child he wanted to be able to speak with a public language as soon as possible, and bilingual programs seem to him to delay that moment. He seems to be a true individualist in the sense he defines that term.

However, a critical reading of "Aria" reveals that it ironically offers many examples that challenge individualism. First, the young Richard enjoys a sense of belonging in his own house with his "enormous families of relatives." Second, if the true individualist resists conformity and crowds, why was the boy so determined to learn the "public language," rather than enjoy his private, native language? If the individualist defies authority, why did the boy accept the authority of the nuns so obediently? Students may find clues in the 1999 interview, in which Rodriguez refers to his younger self as "Bambi."

3. As a boy, Rodriguez began to wear masks to hide his "childhood fears" ("Aria" 12). At the gas station, embarrassed by his father's awkward English, the boy pretended not to hear his father's conversation with the employee, wearing a mask of nonchalance. At the first chance, he evaded his father's grasp on his shoulder and "ran on ahead into the dark, skipping with feigned boyish exuberance" (13). When he and his siblings became more fluent in English, they talked in English even at home. His mother, feeling left out, would wear the mask of an eager participant and ask "what?" so as to express her willingness to join the conversation. It was actually difficult for her to follow the spoken English and understand the content of her children's conversation. In order not to feel more alienated from her children than she already had, she put on the mask of an overly curious parent.

For the second part of this question, the instructor might point out that Rodriguez focuses on how he felt listening to Spanish and uses Spanish words sparingly. For example, the sounds of Spanish "embraced" him and set him apart from "*los otros*" (14). When he writes that his mother's words assured him "*You are home now*" (16), Rodriguez only provides the single Spanish word "*Sí*" (16). This stylistic technique allows Rodriguez to discuss his childhood linguistic experiences to the non-Spanish-speaking reader by giving a flavor of the way Spanish sounds and feels to him. Rodriguez also uses a phonetic representation of his name "*Rich-heard Road-ree-guess*" (3) to describe how American voices sounded to him as a child. Rodriguez's representations of language focus more on sound and the feelings that sounds convey than on grammar. For example, he describes his parents' agreement to speak English at home as the loss of "the language (the sounds)" (25) and uses a mixed Spanish and English sentence to convey the transition: "*Ahora*, speak to us only *en ingles*" (25).

4. Hoggart writes about "cultural change" through the experiences of the "working-class boy" who attends an upper-class school (1), focusing on the experiences of those boys who "have not sufficient [will] to resolve the complex tensions which their uprooting, the peculiar problems of their particular domestic setting . . . create" (3). Hoggart describes this boy as "progressively cut off from

the ordinary life of his group" (4). Although Rodriguez, similarly to Hoggart, describes the complex sociolinguistic tensions of his experience as the American child of immigrants, he differs from Hoggart's subject in that he grew up in an Anglo neighborhood and so was already cut off from the Mexican American community, except for his relatives. Also, although Rodriguez's position resembles that of the "working-class boy" on a scholarship in that he is culturally different, he finds himself the object of care and concern rather than, as Hoggart describes, one who is "marked out" by others as unusual (4); for example, the nuns who visit Rodriguez's parents do not discuss his unusual intelligence, but his poor English.

5. The National Association for Bilingual Education (www.nabe.org) is a good place for students to begin their research. The NABE has as its mission "to cultivate a multilingual multicultural society" through "linguistic diversity." Students will find through their research that those who oppose bilingual education point to Rodriguez as an example of a non-English speaker who learned to speak proficiently and become a successful, assimilated Mexican American. Others criticize Rodriguez's view because he had many advantages that non-English immigrants may not enjoy: Rodriguez grew up in an English-speaking community and school and was a talented reader and writer. Students will find that there is no consensus on whether a child's ability to read in his or her native language is helpful or necessary for the child to learn to read English. Children learning English, also called English Language Learners, may benefit from learning in their native language and transition more successfully into English; opponents of bilingual education say that letting children use their native languages too long hinders their transition to English. ESL refers to English-only classes taught at specific times with or without bilingual education courses. Bilingual education usually refers to programs that use both languages and transition the student to English-speaking classrooms.

Rodriguez emphasizes that he considers himself fortunate to have had teachers committed to teaching him "to speak public English" (21). However, that he was "dazed, diffident, afraid" in the face of his teachers' demands that he speak up might suggest that the process was traumatic and he might have benefited from a slower transition to English. He was required to attend daily tutoring (27), which might have been similar to an ESL class—one that focused on English. Richard experiences "unsounded grief" at hearing his parents switch to English when he enters their presence (27); the loss of family intimacy is a high price to pay for proficiency, an argument in favor of bilingual education.

Will Counts, *Central High School, Little Rock, Arkansas, September 4, 1957* (p. 294)

1. Counts's photograph contrasts the calm face and dignified bearing of the central figure with the angry faces of those who follow her. Although the soldiers

are evidently present to prevent violence, the crowd following the single, young woman could, the photograph implies, turn into a mob—with uncertain results. The main figure and the blonde woman to her right carry books, suggesting the context of this incident, namely, one involving access to education. Yet, the crowd consists not of students but primarily of older people, all white. The photograph implies that the young African American woman bears, at this moment, their fear and hatred for the African American community. The clothing styles suggest that the era is the 1950s.

2. The background information to this photograph helps the viewer to understand why Elizabeth Eckford was alone among the mob of hostile whites. Her calm seems to camouflage her fear—a reading that is supported by knowing that plans had been made for her to attend school accompanied by others. This background also helps the student to understand that interpretation is highly contextual. The instructor might want to have students use Niemeyer's "Picturing the Past Ten Years" (Chapter 1) or Boas and Hunt's photograph "An 'Authentic' Indian" (Chapter 2) as companion pieces in a discussion of how meaning is constructed.

3. Although responses will vary, the instructor may wish to point out to students that the Spingarn Medal was awarded a year after the desegregation of Central High School; Eckford did not receive the Congressional Gold Medal until more than forty years later. Is the reconciliation between Hazel Bryan Massery and Elizabeth Eckford part of the history of desegregation? How might Massery explain her reaction to Eckford at the time this photograph was taken? The instructor might ask students to consider how Hazel Bryan Massery illustrates Plato's depiction of prisoners who can see only "passing shadows" (9). The "reality" behind these shadows might be interpreted in the context of Counts's photograph, as the truth of our common humanity, and Massery's hatred as her entrapment in the "darkness" of ignorance and prejudice (29) and her reconciliation with Eckford as a "journey of the soul into the region of the intelligible" (31).

Plato, *The Allegory of the Cave* (p. 295)

Howard Gardner, *Who Owns Intelligence?* (p. 298)

1. Plato outlines "the degrees in which our nature may be enlightened or unenlightened" (1) as follows: At the unenlightened end of the continuum are the prisoners in the cave who see only the shadows directly in front of them. They "recognize as reality" (13) nothing but those shadows. As the freed prisoner begins to be enlightened, he is first too dazzled to see anything. He continues to recognize as reality only the shadows that he saw when confined. Once "hauled [...] into the sunlight" (19) of enlightenment, the prisoner begins to be able to see directly, apprehending first shadows, then reflections, and, penultimately, the sky by night. Ultimately, the prisoner can look at the sun directly "in its own do-

main" (23). The sequential order and upward motion indicate that the prisoner is becoming progressively less deceived and more knowing.

In contrast to Plato's hierarchical, linear, and progressive vision, Gardner's theory suggests that intelligence, the capacity to acquire and use knowledge, can assume different forms and progress along distinct and unique paths. The eight forms of intelligence, "linguistic and logical-mathematical [...], musical, spatial, bodily-kinesthetic, naturalist, interpersonal, and intrapersonal" (22), all have a place in human cognition. Although all *Homo sapiens* share these multiple forms of "mental representation" (23), Gardner argues, "no two of us exhibit the same intelligences in precisely the same proportions" (24). The idea of multiple intelligences suggests that each individual has a unique cognitive potential.

2. Gardner's eight forms of intelligence describe how humans process "the contents in the world" (35), by which he means "human information-processing and product-making capacities" (45). Thus, Gardner conceptualizes the individual as a curious being who interacts with the world. In contrast, Plato's allegory describes beings who have limited self-awareness, people who "have seen nothing of themselves or of one another, except the shadows thrown by the fire-light on the wall of the Cave facing them" (5). Plato's individual is helpless to process the images he sees until he is "set free and forced suddenly to stand up, turn his head, and walk with eyes lifted to the light" (15) and, after turning back, is dragged "away forcibly [...] into the sunlight" (19). Plato's representative individual only learns of the "upper world" by growing "accustomed" to seeing things as they really are (21) rather than creatively producing new knowledge. Once in the "upper world," the individual learns by observing empirical phenomena and slowly perceives higher forms of knowledge.

Plato's vision of learning corresponds most closely to what Gardner calls "logical-mathematical" intelligence. The individual learns by reasoning and thinking conceptually: For example, he first sees "the images of men and things reflected in water" and then realizes that these images are mere representations of "the things themselves" (21). The allegory relies less on the other forms of intelligence—the individual's environment ("visual-spatial"), body ("bodily-kinesthetic"), self-awareness ("intrapersonal"), relations with others ("interpersonal"), and speech ("linguistic")—as vehicles through which the individual perceives a transcendent Truth.

3. For Plato, the ultimate attainment of the truth seeker is to know Good: Goodness is "the last thing to be perceived and only with great difficulty" (31). In other words, Plato believes that Truth exists and can be discovered. In contrast, Gardner points out that "how intelligence is conceived" is a function of social needs and values: For example, the need for "people who are skilled symbol analysts [...] for enterprises ranging from business to science to war games" will help define intelligence and intelligence testing in the near future (27). Gardner argues that until recently, "the term 'intelligence' has been limited largely to

certain kinds of problem-solving involving language and logic" (34) and that "definitions of intelligence need to be expanded to include human skill" in other "kinds of content" such as "space, music, the psyches of other human beings" (34). For Gardner, intelligence is much more than "solving problems that have been posed by others"; it should include "the capacity of individuals to fashion products—scientific experiments, effective organizations" (34). Thus, Gardner implies that the importance of different kinds of intelligence depends on their cultural context. Because Gardner is interested in measuring intelligence for the purposes of measuring academic and professional aptitude, his focus implicitly considers "linguistic and logical-mathematical" intelligences (22) as cultural priorities. Even though Gardner separates intelligence from "traits such as creativity, morality, and emotional appropriateness" (44), he also suggests that cultural norms and needs will lead to an implicit ranking of each kind of intelligence.

For the second part of this question, the instructor should ask students to concentrate on an activity they know well and that requires multiple types of skills and knowledge, such as music or athletics, which require as much mental preparation as physical, or any academic subject that requires interpersonal and intrapersonal skills as well as linguistic skills.

4. Alchemy is a medieval form of chemistry that aims to transform base metals into gold and thereby to find a universal solvent and an elixir of life. People tend to regard alchemy as a pseudo-science and to use the term as a synonym for magic. Gardner uses the term to refer to purists' pursuit of an impossible measurement of "pure intelligence" that doesn't exist, because for Gardner all intelligences are displayed in real or virtual situations.

5. Acknowledging the importance of creativity, Gardner argues that it should not be conflated with intelligence. He defines creativity as persons or works and institutions that are "innovative" and their "innovations are eventually accepted by a relevant community" (36). According to Gardner, many intelligent people don't fit this definition:

> An expert may be intelligent in one or more domains but not necessarily inclined toward, or successful in, innovation. Similarly, although it is clear that the ability to innovate requires a certain degree of intelligence, we don't find a significant correlation between measures of intellect and of creativity. Indeed, creativity seems more dependent on a certain kind of temperament and personality—risk-taking, tough-skinned, persevering, above all having a lust to alter the status quo and leave a mark on society—than on efficiency in processing various kinds of information. (37)

Gardner's differentiation of morality from intelligence is based on two reasons. First, morality is culturally defined. What is held as moral in one culture may be held as immoral in another culture and amoral in a third culture. Second, Gardner distinguishes morality from intelligence by the same practical argument in which he distinguishes emotion from intelligence: "[O]ne must confront the fact that people who score high on tests of moral reasoning may act immorally outside the test situation" (38). Here is a great opportunity for instructors to help students develop critical thinking skills by asking them whether they agree with Gardner's practical separation of intelligence from morality and emotion. There may be an interesting self-contradiction in his argument: Using the same practical argument, we can challenge Gardner's definition of intelligence as well. Who can guarantee that people with high scores on logic-math tests will apply their logic-math ability in solving real-life problems? The gap between what we know and what we do, or between what we can do and what we actually do, remains the same with Gardner's own concepts of intelligence. Student responses to the latter part of this question will vary, but the instructor can encourage students to make connections between this essay and others in this anthology such as Walker's "In Search of Our Mothers' Gardens" and Malcolm Gladwell's "The Physical Genius," both in Chapter 3, Thoreau's "Where I Lived, and What I Lived For" in Chapter 8.

6. Plato's allegory invites readers to examine the assumptions and definitions through which they perceive reality. However, Plato's model also portrays knowledge as given and the learner as the receptacle that absorbs, with difficulty and reluctance, an objective truth. Thus, readers can use the allegory to examine their understanding of what constitutes knowledge. The instructor might ask students to compare Plato's model to Linda Simon's argument in "The Naked Source" (Chapter 4) that knowledge is not an objective set of "right answers" that the diligent student can learn (13). On the contrary, she argues that "the role of imagination and intuition in the telling of histories" is an essential part of knowledge (14). Can creativity be excluded from intelligence, as Gardner claims?

7. The student might approach this question by first devising a test that would measure the novice's state of knowledge and aptitude to learn. Then, the student might create a teaching plan that can be adapted to individuals with different kinds of intelligences. This question might form the basis of a discussion or activity on how individuals learn and which approaches seem most productive.

8. The metaphor of prisoners in a cave conveys the inferior and ignorant position that people who are without the resources of philosophy occupy. Without the benefit of higher-order thinking, people are limited to what they can know through their senses, information that is incomplete and indistinct. Their picture of reality is severely deficient. Only those who can look at a phenomenon directly and "contemplate its nature" (23) can attain the wisdom to assess true value. Since this capacity is reserved to a few, most people should defer to their wiser superiors for knowledge. Unfortunately, in Plato's view, people don't realize how unreliable their own sensory perceptions are. When an enlightened person attempts to describe reality to them, they reject this wisdom because they think their own perceptions are the truth. In fact, Plato believes that the unenlightened are so resistant to enlightenment that they might kill the messenger "who [is] trying to set them free and lead them up" (29).

9. In this Socratic dialogue, the "I" is Socrates and the "he" is his interlocutor, Glaucon. Socrates dominates the dialogue, while Glaucon is mostly limited to one-word answers, speaking only about seventy words during the dialogue. Glaucon's sole role in speaking is to agree with Socrates. Socrates has to provide his own apologia — "heaven knows whether it is true" (31) — because Glaucon never questions him. Dialogues are usually balanced conversations, in which each speaker contributes equally to an exchange of views. Socrates is lecturing to Glaucon. This Socratic dialogue encourages readers to seek knowledge from those who are wiser rather than to construct knowledge through their own thinking in dialogue with other thinkers. Such a model discourages readers from discovering the truth of their own ideas and perceptions or the truth of ideas that differ from wisdom received from authority figures. It accords well with Plato's model in this analogy of a few enlightened ones who should instruct and lead the unenlightened.

If Glaucon were given more to speech, he would interfere with Socrates' ability to enlighten his ignorant hearers for their own good. Glaucon's responses would shape the dialogue; what is said would no longer be completely under Socrates' control. Plato's view of who should speak and who can participate in the construction of knowledge is much in contrast with the contemporary efforts of women and people of color to break out of silences.

Marjane Satrapi, *The Convocation* (p. 312)

1. Satrapi depicts a university run on the basis of sexual segregation and an administration determined to control the female students' bodies and behavior. For example, Reza warns Satrapi that their relationship could lead to their expulsion from the university (panel 4); the university segregates students by gender (panels 5, 6, 21); and the administration imposes strict rules governing the women's clothing (panel 23). Despite these overt forms of control, the students subvert the administration's authority. They exchange "flirtatious looks" (panel 5); the women observe and comment on the men (panels 7–8); and the men appear to take any opportunity to observe the women (22). The women subvert the university's control over their appearance by arranging their head scarves to reveal part of their hair (panel 11), an arrangement that contrasts with the more severe appearance of the female university staff (panel 20).

2. Satrapi distinguishes each female character by individualizing her facial traits and body shapes (panels 5, 7–11). She helps the reader interpret women's different body shapes by showing how "you could guess their shape, the way they wore their hair, and even their political opinions" (panel 12). This inside peek under the uniform is also an insider's view into Iranian culture: Satrapi helps the reader to "see" the way Iranians "see" each other.

3. Satrapi characterizes herself as westernized and somewhat naïve when she asks Rezi whether they can announce their relationship to their fellow students

(panel 4). She presents herself as a sociable young woman who chats easily with the other female students (panels 9–10), as a warm and spontaneous daughter in the home (panels 1, 16), and as an honest narrator in her willingness to reveal her "cowardly act" (panel 14). She shows that she does not conceal her feelings well (panels 17–18) and that she has the courage to confront the university authorities by questioning their policies (panels 24–29). She also suggests that her sense of "self-esteem" and "dignity" are linked to her family's love and acceptance (panel 38). Students may condemn Satrapi's "cowardly act" as well as admire her willingness to speak out against what she sees as injustice. The instructor might point out that Satrapi's aim is to illustrate an individual woman's life within a hostile environment and how she learns to navigate that environment, in part, by making mistakes. Thus, her "cowardly act" might be read as the thoughtlessness of youth and her courageous speech on female dress as part of her personal development.

4. Satrapi uses a large, single panel (23) to show that the administration creates an intimidating presence and to suggest that the speaker's request that the women students change their appearance is, in fact, an order. Satrapi makes clear to the reader that the university has the power to expel students who do not conform to its code of sexual behavior (panel 4) and that the administration can compel students to attend meetings (panel 20).

5. Satrapi shocks her audience (panel 28), but the students do not boo her into submission, nor do the representatives of the administration order her to remain silent. The scene suggests that the authorities are prepared, within limits, to listen to a woman's opinion and, consequently, that conditions for women in Iran are changing. Instead of punishing her, the administration attempts to channel Satrapi's rebellion: The "true religious man" who speaks to her gives her the task of designing a "uniform adapted to the needs of the students" (panel 35).

6. Satrapi's grandmother reminds her granddaughter after the "cowardly act" that her husband had been imprisoned "for having defended some innocents" (p. 315). By arguing with the administration, Satrapi earns the respect she had lost in her grandmother's eyes.

7. Satrapi's simple style should encourage students who do not have drawing experience to try the graphic form. The instructor might ask students to consult Scott McCloud's "Reading the Comics" (Chapter 1) and Lynda Barry's "Hate" (Chapter 7) for alternative styles. McCloud's drawings range from the very simple to the elaborate, whereas Barry uses crude, childish figures that convey the primitive emotions of childhood. Whether students choose the graphic forms or a textual narrative, they should select specific personal information and traits that are relevant to their story. For example, Satrapi's anxiety over her grandmother's anger and her desire for reconciliation are important background for her decision to speak out against a stricter dress code. Similarly, Lynda Barry emphasizes her childish selfishness and anger to illustrate how she learns to define and manage her feelings.

Linda Simon, *The Naked Source* (p. 320)

1. Linda Simon is absolute. She claims that all U.S. students are ignorant of "a real sense of the past," that even the "bright and inquisitive" ones have only learned "names and dates" but "lack . . . a sense of historical-mindedness, a sense that lives were lived in a context, a sense that events had consequences, a sense that answers must generate questions, more questions, and still more subtle questions" (2, 9). This sweeping generalization is flawed, for some students can develop a more complex sense of history either on their own or with the help of inspiring teachers. After all, Simon was once a student. In addition, if Morison is correct in claiming that history is a "literary art" (24), then some students in English Departments must have a real sense of history to a certain extent.

With this concession in mind, one must acknowledge that what Simon says in this essay is true to a great extent. Her point is not to talk down to students (though she may sound that way to some readers) but to make readers aware of a flaw in the way history is taught. History is offered as a mass of facts rather than as a creative investigation. History curricula and exams tend to perpetuate the idea that history is a body of knowledge on which students will be tested, and thus overlooks the most exciting and challenging part of the historian's job—selecting, arranging, and interpreting events and teasing meaning out of an otherwise chaotic mass of facts. We learn from Simon's essay that history can never be purely objective; to the contrary, it is always subjective. Responses to the second part of this question will vary.

2.–4. Responses will vary. In order to help students develop a sense of history in which "lives were lived in a context . . . [and] answers must generate questions, more questions, and still more subtle questions" (9), these questions have been designed to offer students a "hands-on" opportunity to respond to Simon's argument through their own experience.

The instructor should encourage students to focus on a particular historical period or figure of interest. Ask students if there was a moment in a history class or in their reading that history came alive. Did they ever get "a sense of the historical method of inquiry" (14) during the writing of a paper or project by consulting primary texts, interviewing family members, or recording their own observations of places and objects? The instructor might ask students to refer to Philip Niemeyer's "Picturing the Past Ten Years" (Chapter 1), particularly Question 2, to understand how interpretation shapes historical narrative and that, consequently, "historical facts" are not "things out there, like seashells or autumn leaves" that look the same regardless of which historian has found them (13). The instructor could also ask students to imagine what kind of historian they themselves might make and what kinds of historical work they would most enjoy. Sherman Alexie's point in "What Sacagawea Means to Me" (Chapter 2) that "Lewis and Clark's story has never been just the triumphant tale of two white men, no matter what the white historians might need to believe" (3) might be instructive in encouraging students to consider historical narratives that they have found implausible or incomplete. Questions 3 and 4 ask students to connect the historian to history and could form part of a larger project. Orwell's "Shooting an Elephant" (Chapter 7) and Elie Wiesel's "Why I Write" (Chapter 1) are excellent companion readings.

5 WIRED — BE CAREFUL WHAT WE WISH FOR: WHAT ARE THE CONSEQUENCES OF LIFE IN THE HIGH-TECH FAST LANE?

Roz Chast, *The I.M.s of Romeo and Juliet* (p. 326)

1. Roz Chast's cartoon dialogue uses acronyms ("gtg," "btw"), simplified or abbreviated spelling ("purpl," "sci"), and numbers to represent sounds ("2day"). It also omits punctuation and capitalization. By using numbers and letters as phonetic symbols and ignoring conventional mechanics, I.M. mimics contemporary, informal American speech. One might argue that this form of writing is not a language in that the scope of its use is limited for the most part to electronic media. On the other hand, Chast's cartoon also demonstrates that the idiom of instant messaging can be read by a large group of English speakers, suggesting that informal electronic writing might constitute a type of dialect.

In exploring the question of the nature of informal electronic writing, students might extend their discussion to incorporate two readings from Chapter 1: Richard Wright's "Fighting Words," which illustrates writing as a political act, and Peter Elbow's "Freewriting," which emphasizes the development of a personal voice. Roz Chast's cartoon and these essays can form the basis of class discussion on how and when writing as a technical act (keyboarding, putting pencil or pen to paper) becomes writing as a culturally acknowledged text.

2. This question asks students to contextualize the dialogue in the cartoon by observing the furniture, posters, and consumer products in Juliet's room. The clutter around her contrasts with the pared-down language she uses to communicate with Romeo, while the electronic products and cordless telephone illustrate the dominant role consumer electronics and technology play in the typical American teenager's life. Juliet's apparent indifference to the clutter and to the spilled food and drink on the floor attests to the primacy of her computer as a social catalyst. On the other hand, the presence of books and other printed material in her room suggests that print coexists with electronic media in contemporary culture.

3. Chast's title, "The I.M.s of Romeo and Juliet," puts Shakespeare's play at the center of the cartoon and yet simultaneously undercuts its relevance. While

the cartoon asks the reader to reference the play, it also suggests that this Juliet is in charge of writing her own relationship with her Romeo. The modern Juliet has various forms of self-representation at her fingertips, forms that allow her to bypass or marginalize parental authority: This is exemplified in the shortening of the word "parents" to "rents." Romeo and Juliet's optimism and confidence in the cartoon also contrasts with the star-crossed path of their namesakes. On the other hand, this modern romance lacks the grand and powerful passion of Shakespeare's lovers. The simplified electronic symbols—a series of x's and o's—replace Shakespeare's dialogue, suggesting that computer language has come to define human emotions.

Dennis Baron, *The New Technologies of the Word* (p. 327)

1. and 2. Baron focuses on electronic media rather than the typewriter in order to trace "the impact of digital technology on our communication practices" (5). The typewriter merely mechanized the "literacy technology" of "uniform script" (9), whereas electronic technologies have created entirely new "linguistic genres" (10): E-mail has "carve[d] out its own communication space" (19), instant messaging represents "digital conversation" (23), and computers allow any writer "to claim public space and authority" (34). These questions ask students to examine their own communication practices, including handwriting and keyboarding, and to consider how electronic communication technologies bring with them new forms of linguistic and social organization.

3. This question asks students to consider Baron's argument that on the Internet "local forms and practices" coexist with standard language, transmitting "norms downward from the top," but also empowering individuals "to take control of authorship" (3). By researching a case in which the Internet has become a tool of the powerful or the powerless, students can explore how communication technology shapes and changes traditional hierarchies and social relationships and exploits its global reach.

Nicholas Carr, *Is Google Making Us Stupid?* (p. 336)

1. Carr argues that after years of surfing and searching on the Internet, he no longer finds reading an experience of deep immersion ("I was a scuba diver in a sea of words" [4]). Instead, he feels as though his mind "expects to take in information the way the Net distributes it: in a swiftly moving stream of particles" (4). Carr explains his experience by investigating how the brain adapts to technology. Because any form of reading "is not an instinctive skill for human beings," but must be acquired, "the media or other technologies we use in learning and practicing the craft of reading" shape "the neural circuits inside our brains" (9). And, because the brain is "almost infinitely malleable" (13), using computers to process information changes our brains "at a biological level" (16). Students may find Carr's argument persuasive, but they should also keep his caveat in mind:

"[W]e still await the long-term neurological and psychological experiments that will provide a definitive picture of how Internet use affects cognition" (7). The instructor might also point out to students that because the Internet and other new communications technologies are constantly changing, the practices of users are also still developing.

2. Carr points out that "[r]esearch that once required days in the stacks or periodical rooms of libraries can now be done in minutes" (3), a clear benefit. However, he also argues that our dependence on electronically delivered information has created the perception that "intelligence is the output of a mechanical process, a series of discrete steps that can be isolated, measured, and optimized" (28). Similarly, he is concerned that learning has come to be considered a process of processing data rather than one that involves "the fuzziness of contemplation" (28) or "leisurely reading or slow, concentrated thought" (29). The mind, Carr argues, is fundamentally different from a machine that collects information: "In the quiet spaces opened up by the sustained, undistracted reading of a book, or by any other act of contemplation, for that matter, we make our own associations, draw our own inferences and analogies, foster our own ideas" (32). Encourage students to dissect Carr's argument by exploring the types of learning that go on with or without electronic communications. Have them examine their own writing process: How do synthesizing and integrating information differ from extending that knowledge into an original argument?

3. This question asks students to study their own reading habits just as Frederick Winslow Taylor recorded factory workers' activities (21–22). By recording the electronic distractions and the time that passes without interruption, students can become more aware of their own interaction with what Carr calls the Internet's "info-thickets" (3). Can students glean from the data-rich environment of the Internet an experience of "intellectual discovery" (32)? Or do they find, as Carr argues, that electronic distractions "scatter our attention and diffuse our concentration" (18)? Do students find that these distractions affect their study habits?

4. Carr implies that, just as Socrates feared that widespread literacy would lead to a confusion of information with knowledge (30), our dependence on the Internet might endanger our complexity and creativity (32–33). Whether the changes wrought by the Internet will "flatten" our intelligence "into artificial intelligence" (34), Carr implies, largely depends on how human society employs "artificial" means. After all, as he points out, the "doomsayers" when the printing press was invented "were unable to imagine the myriad blessings that the printed word would deliver" (31). Ask students to consider whether human beings can be molded, as in the film *2001*, into "machinelike" creatures "who go about their business with an almost robotic efficiency" (34). How has Frederick Winslow Taylor's "tight industrial choreography" (21–23) influenced the lives of industrial workers? Are the lives of knowledge workers equally shaped by "computer

engineers and software coders" (23)? Is there any point in attempting to repress the relentless human urge to invent new ways to express and communicate? Students will find Matthew B. Crawford's "The Case for Working with Your Hands," Barbara Ehrenreich's "Serving in Florida," and Malcolm Gladwell's "The Physical Genius" (all in Chapter 3) helpful in discussing the relationships between the human spirit and work.

5. This question builds on Question 3 by asking students to compare their online reading practices with print reading. The instructor might begin this assignment by asking students to create a list of reading activities and the criteria by which to judge each reading experience. For example, we read to conduct research, for pleasure, or to inform ourselves; we read as part of professional and personal communications online and in print; and sometimes we read for deep understanding, and at other times we simply want to find an appropriate quote or a particular fact or nugget of information. How are our reading practices shaped by the purposes of reading? Students might consider also the context in which we read. How does reading in the library or outdoors or in bed, for example, shape the reading experience?

Ray Kurzweil, *Frontiers* (p. 345)

1. Kurzweil argues that readily available, inexpensive technology allows more people to create products, an activity once the province of a privileged few: "Individuals now have the tools to break new ground in every field" (2). The instructor might point out that Kurzweil's use of the term "democratized" is limited in that the individuals he refers to in his examples — "a musician in her dorm room" and "a couple of students at Stanford University" (2) — have access to such resources because they are part of a well-funded system of higher education. However, Kurzweil's argument that technology is democratizing creativity does seem to apply, albeit in a more limited way, to the ubiquitous technology of e-mail (3).

2. Kurzweil suggests that the "exponential growth of information technology" constitutes the ultimate form of democracy: His comment that "we'll finally be able to bury Karl Marx" implies that technology will create opportunities for greater self-determination to all (3–4). Thus, the characteristics needed in this economy, Kurzweil implies, include the ability to imagine ways to harness information technology and promote specific applications. Kurzweil implies that the personal characteristic necessary to make dreams a reality is entrepreneurial spirit: "[T]he American drive to push beyond frontiers is alive and well" (4). The instructor might ask students to research the financial backing required for a particular project and to explore how financing needs have changed since the early days of software development, when figures such as Bill Gates, Steve Jobs, and Sergey Brin and Larry Page, the founders of Google, revolutionized the information industry.

3. Students might consider the iPod, iPad, applications for cellphones, texting, Skype, and advanced forms of digital cameras, for example. Students can explore how these technological innovations have changed their daily lives, their relationships with family and friends, and their awareness of the world around them. Do they use these forms of technology for creative purposes?

4. Kurzweil's argument implies that biotechnology will increase human longevity through superior health care made possible by the immediate availability of life-saving information and through the transformation of research into beneficial products, medicines, and technologies. For example, his argument that products can be sent by e-mail using "nanotechnology assembly devices" (3) for immediate construction suggests that life-sustaining medical products could also be immediately available anywhere they are needed. If an individual has the capacity to "break new ground" by having access to a personal computer, then researchers and health care providers everywhere have the potential to create new medical products and applications, and the pace of medical breakthroughs should keep pace with exponentially increasing technologies.

Sherry Turkle, *How Computers Change the Way We Think* and Contexts (p. 347)

1. Because computer technology is rapidly diversifying and developing, students will be familiar with electronic products and tools other than those Turkle mentions: "e-mail, word processing, simulations, virtual communities, and Power-Point software" (8) as well as "online blogging, instant messaging, and Web browsing" (10). For example, there are dozens of computer games available aside from SimLife (26), both solo and online real-time played on proprietary systems such as Sony's PlayStation. Encourage students to list the features of the technologies they use by keeping in mind their social and psychological impacts. For example, Turkle argues that young people "are accustomed to electronic surveillance as part of their daily lives" (10) and are unconcerned with "safeguards" (11). On the other hand, Turkle sees a benefit in the capacity of "online worlds" to offer a place for "personal experimentation" (12). Ask students to discuss the effects of electronic technology on their lives and their dependence on technology by imagining a day without these devices or by recalling an experience in which they temporarily could not use them. This question would work well as a take-home assignment followed by classroom discussion of the ways we rely on electronic technology and whether, as Turkle argues in "The Human Spirit in a Computer Culture," that technology fosters an experience of "disconnection, of the unreality of self" (3).

2. Turkle argues that computer environments change "the way we see ourselves, our sense of human identity" (6), and that computers give us "new ways to think about what it means to know and understand" (8). Each author in this cluster of readings echoes and develops these ideas in different ways. For example,

Baron argues that even as electronic technologies reinforce the position of English as a dominant global language, they also provide spaces for "an infinite variety of local forms and practices" used by readers and writers of nondominant languages to flourish (3). Thus, Baron's argument that global technology brings with it "a new emphasis on the local" (2).

Similar to Turkle's notion that the computer changes "our sense of human identity," Carr's argument is that the "ubiquity of text on the Internet" creates "a different kind of reading, and behind it lies a different kind of thinking—perhaps even a new sense of the self" (8). Because the human brain adapts to the technologies it learns to use (9), Carr argues, and this adaptation affects not only the biology of the brain, but the language we use to "explain ourselves to ourselves" (16), the Internet is changing who we are and who we think we are.

Gleick shows how the Internet has accelerated the "boundlessness" (12) of language: "Cyberspace is an engine driving change in the language" (16). This expanding "universe of human discourse" (13), Gleick implies, transforms our identity because the Internet transmits language in a new way: All language, from the obscure to the popular, intermingles, "broadcasting to the millions, narrowcasting to groups, instant messaging one to one" (16).

Hockenberry argues that soldiers' ability to narrate their experiences to millions online has created "an oddball online Greek chorus narrating the conflict in Iraq" (6). Hockenberry quotes solider Chris Missick to show that the Internet has given the lone enlisted solider a global, potentially "explosive" (4) voice that may not serve the interests of the Department of Defense and challenges other media's representations of the conflict (6).

Ask students to examine how each author creates a different narrative of change, each of which defines specific intellectual and ethical issues. For example, Hockenberry's, Gleick's, and Baron's narratives tell stories of empowerment, whereas Turkle's and Carr's are more skeptical. Consequently, each essay suggests that different human qualities—independence, self-reliance, solidarity, or imagination, for example—are at stake in the debate and entail consideration of specific issues.

3. Turkle's concern that information technology must be embedded in cultural practices that support democratic ideals arises from the nature of computer environments, which tend to marginalize ambiguity and simplify the world by eliminating "shades of gray" (31). In "The Human Spirit in a Computer Culture," Turkle examines "the relationships between people and machines" (2), identifying a trend in which the user sees the computer as "a second self" (4). Ask students to examine what Turkle sees as the hacker's romantic relationship with the computer: Does the computer foster a fear of intimacy and a sense of "the unreality of the self" (3)? Might this detachment feed users' unwillingness to engage with the political dilemmas of "freedom of expression, tolerance, diversity, and complexity of opinion" ("How Computers Change the Way We Think" 32)? Does

electronic technology encourage a "culture of narcissism" ("The Human Spirit in a Computer Culture" 1)? Students may want to refer to Gorry's "Empathy in a Virtual World" for a similar argument.

4. Deresiewicz argues that Facebook invites us to believe in a false sense of "emotional proximity" (3); electronic relationships are simply "tokens of connection" rather than "an actual connection" (4). For Deresiewicz, social-networking sites foster the idea that "the instant disgorging of the self" constitutes intimacy: "[I]dentity is reducible to information" (8). Both Deresiewicz and Bugeja detect a tendency for users to think of themselves as products. Deresiewicz argues that social networking sites reduce identity to "consumer preferences" (8), whereas Bugeja observes that Facebook groups tend to resemble "advertisements for products or lifestyles" (11).

In describing MyLifeBits, Gordon Bell's digital life archive, Turkle argues that digital data collection flattens and eliminates texture: A digital archive "gives equal weight" to every aspect of life ("Inner History" 8). In "Logins R Us," Turkle suggests that users come to embrace various online personae, despite an initial "anguish at what they sense as a breakdown of identity" (6). Ask students whether Turkle's notion of "identity as multiplicity" ("Logins R Us" 10) applies to their different friendships. Encourage students to use in their discussion of the nature of friendship the different concepts that the authors in this cluster of readings employ to examine intimacy, connection, and autonomy.

5. Students can refer to Questions 1 and 3 following Solove's "The End of Privacy" to begin thinking about privacy issues. Encourage students to be specific in their concerns. For example, students might address information about their health and employment records or photographs they or others have posted. Ask students to review Solove's argument that the ease with which information spreads electronically has diminished the individual's ability "to protect reputation by shaping the image that is presented to others" (13). Encourage students to be as specific as possible in their answers and to use examples.

6. The instructor may want to use this question as the basis of a group exercise. After students rank the problems that electronic technology poses, they should categorize the problems and organize the groups accordingly. Each group should present an analysis and a solution to the class. Encourage each group to incorporate concepts in the essays by Turkle, Gleick, Deresiewicz, and Hockenberry, and, if relevant, those discussed by Bugeja, Carr, Dyson, and Solove.

7. The photograph might illustrate what Turkle calls "the instrumental and the subjective sides" of computer culture (6): Using electronic technology has personal and social effects and so changes the experience of being human. In this light, the subject of the photograph might be viewed as using technology as much as it is using him; he appears tangled up with the machines that surround him, as if they have become integral to his being and an extension of him. Has he become disengaged from his own humanity by becoming absorbed by the machinery of his life?

In the context of Carr's argument that the Internet is changing the way the mind takes in information, the photograph might illustrate a case of electronic technology "reprogramming" the user (20). For Gorry, the image might suggest that the user is "chained" to his machines much like Plato's prisoners (2). Guisewite's comic, like Deresiewicz's and Bugeja's essays, would suggest that the man has become detached from any authentic connection to places and other people. Finally, the image might, if embedded in Fuller's essay, illustrate the 2008 securities markets' "free fall" (3). Because this question invites students to explore the contexts in which we interpret images, the instructor might ask students to refer to other visual images in *The Arlington Reader*, such as Kim Warp's "Rising Sea Levels—An Alternative Theory" (Chapter 3) and Will Counts's "Central High School, Little Rock, Arkansas, September 4, 1957" (Chapter 4). Each of these images requires the viewer to participate actively in the construction of meaning, much as Scott McCloud's "Reading the Comics" (Chapter 1) explains and analyzes.

G. Anthony Gorry, *Empathy in the Virtual World* (p. 372)

1. Plato's allegory suggests that the capacity to perceive ultimate, transcendent truth requires the seeker to move beyond the illusory images that appear to constitute the observable world. On the basis of an analogy between the prisoners in Plato's allegory, who mistake "shadowy shapes" (2) for reality, Gorry offers us a cautionary tale for today's users of computers who are beguiled by "flickers on a screen" (3). Expanding on this idea, Gorry argues that the cost of "the magical garden of cyberspace" (5) is "a loss of empathy" because technology has the potential to "numb our emotions, distance us from our fellow humans, and attenuate our empathetic responses to their misfortunes" (5). He bases his argument on the idea that "strict social controls" are critical to keeping "brutish self-interest in check" (7). Technology overrides those controls and allows users to "present themselves as a blend of the actual and the fantasized"; as a result, we "alter our expectations of trustworthiness and reciprocity" (13).

Gorry's argument implies that "reality" consists of "traditional social structures of the face-to-face community" (13) and that the "false identities" that users post online will lead us to "pursue our own selfish interests more aggressively" (21). For Gorry, Plato's "shadows" correspond to the online personae that substitute for the physical and social experience of face-to-face relationships. Whether students find this argument persuasive may depend on their personal experience of technology and social interaction. Ask students to imagine being compelled to live without computers or electronic communications, as Plato imagines his prisoner compelled to confront the surface above them and the light of the sun. How would their social and family relationships change?

2. Gorry argues that computers offer users "a fantastic life in which we can indulge our interests with the click of a link, where we can be any place at any

time, where we can be who we want to be" (12). Because this technology is fluid and global, it overrides "the accountability of face-to-face interaction," makes "social conventions" unnecessary, and allows users to "invent themselves without regard for the concerns or needs of others" (13). Gorry's evidence for this argument is that the human brain adapts to its environment and, consequently, will "acclimate to digital technology" (9) by "seeking stimulation rather than knowledge" and finding "more engagement in a montage of simulated joys and agonies than in the lives of real people and events" (10).

3. Gorry seems uncertain whether the "ever-beguiling fabrications for entertainment and escape" (3) that the Internet makes available will "numb our emotions" (5) or "coax us to greater regard for the unfortunate and oppressed" (9). Does exposure to "streaming video, elaborate games, social networks, news reports, fiction, and gossip" encourage the viewer to feel compassion or to "tune in the emotional stimulation we crave and tune out what we find unpleasant or disturbing" (14)? The instructor might point out that a reader can just as easily put an unpleasant or a disturbing book down and then ask students to explore this question by comparing the imaginative experience reading offers with stories available online. Do both experiences "edify" the individual? In what ways?

4. Ask students to draw on their family traditions, religious or ethic heritage, and peer relations for their lists of social controls. These controls might include, for example, taboos on particular behaviors (violence or offensive language) and positive controls such as praise or other rewards for acceptable behavior. Students may want to explore Gorry's argument that such controls "keep our brutish self-interest in check" (7). How much self-interested behavior should be kept in check? Whose interests are served through the control of individuals' behavior? Students may also want to take a sociological approach to this question by considering how a peer group's standards might conflict with or reinforce familial influences in a specific setting, such as in high school, at a sports event, at work, or in living with others.

5. Students may want to research examples of online relationships that have helped or harmed others as well as drawing on their own experiences. Falsehood can be a form of confidentiality or a healthy way of exploring fantasies. Ask students whether the "rules" of online relationships between friends or acquaintances who do not have a face-to-face relationship or even know each other's names differ from the "rules" governing traditional social relations. Do students alter their expectations of others while online?

6. In addition to using Plato's allegory, Gorry makes abundant use of metaphors: the "magical garden" of cyberspace (3, 5), "shaping our brains" (9), "window to the world" (9), "technology's Muses" (9), "erasing the boundary between the magic and the mundane" (12), "chewing up books" (14), "cutting out pieces" (14), "grist for the mill of our emotions" (14), "shuttle from e-mail to hyperlinks to phone calls" (14), "tune in" and "tune out" (14), "profligate shoppers" (16),

"looking in the rearview mirror" while remembering "the road we have traveled" (23), and "anchors in the digital flood" (23). Students might explore how one or more of these help Gorry make a particular connection: For example, he uses "Muses" to emphasize the connection between the imaginative power of print fiction and that of various electronic narratives delivered over the Internet.

Esther Dyson, *Reflections on Privacy 2.0* (p. 378)

Daniel J. Solove, *The End of Privacy?* (p. 384)

1. Dyson distinguishes between "objective harms arising from the disclosure [of information]—fraud, denial of a service, denial of freedom," and "subjective privacy harms, in which the mere knowledge by a second or third party of one's private information is experienced as an injury" (7). Dyson implies that the boundary between these forms of privacy is clear, but her discussion of health insurance suggests that such a distinction is problematic. How much health information should be made available to insurance companies for the purposes of calculating "cost buckets with reasonable accuracy" (14)? As Dyson observes, "information opacity" is impossible (15). Rather, "society will have to decide, clearly and openly, which kinds of discrimination are acceptable and which are not" (15).

The instructor should encourage students to approach this question with a sense of the underlying social, legal, and ethical problem of developing a framework within which to make policy decisions regarding privacy in a world where, as Dyson points out, "the concept of privacy itself is changing" (24). What principles might govern such a framework? Must all policy decisions regarding privacy boil down to specific cases? Dyson concludes that "no single truth—or simple list of who is allowed to know what—exists" and that such ambiguity is a part of life (31). However, students might experiment with devising general principles and, from those, specific cases regarding, for example, health care and financial information, divorces and lawsuits, criminal cases, and employment records.

2. Solove implies that the major consequence of the Internet's global reach is that citizens, businesses, and governments must explicitly define the boundaries between private and public life: The Internet "raises the question of how much privacy people can expect—or even desire—in an age of ubiquitous networking" (6). Both Solove and Dyson recognize that electronic data collection and communications influence every aspect of our lives. Solove argues that one important part of this development is the difficulty individuals increasingly face in controlling their social, professional, and financial "reputation" (13). Both authors point out that government access to personal information represents a serious threat to the individual's privacy. Dyson argues that "[w]e should be able to monitor what the government does with our personal data and to audit (through representatives) the processes for managing the data and keeping them secure" (20). Solove

argues that the government "compromises privacy by assembling vast databases that can be searched for suspicious patterns of behavior" and that "[t]he National Security Agency listens [to] and examines the records of millions of telephone conversations" (12). Ask students to build on their responses to Question 1 by listing the types of their personal information that they believe are already stored electronically and which businesses, government agencies, institutions, or individuals have access to that information. Students might try to verify, as Dyson and Solove suggest, how secure that information actually is.

3. In response to this question, students might consider, as Dyson discusses, the extent to which they control their social information by using privacy settings (27) and services for sharing photographs (28), and by controlling their online posts and the ads accompanying those posts through "online-community services" (29). Students who are among the 90 percent who maintain accounts on social networking Web sites might consider how much information they have thus far made forever "accessible to this and future generations" (Solove 7). Do they have any regrets? Have any specific experiences led them to use privacy settings more stringently? Students might find a discussion of their responses to this question more comfortable in small groups than with the class as a whole.

4. This question builds on Questions 2 and 3 by asking students to explore more specifically the kind of personal information that is available to others and how much they control it. The instructor might use Questions 2 and 3 as the basis of class and peer-group discussion and assign this question as a take-home response paper.

5. This position paper expands on Question 1, which asks students to define "privacy." The instructor might ask each group to allocate aspects of this topic among the members. Alternatively, the instructor could assign each group an informational and privacy topic, such as health care and insurance, identity theft and encryption and other preventive measures, or issues related to anonymity and false or disguised identities. Encourage students to see the problem of control over personal information as a spectrum between "zero privacy" and total "transparency." Can an "ideal amount of control" be defined? What categories of personal information will form part of the position paper? What kinds of ethical, legal, and social issues will each group address? The instructor may ask each group to begin by submitting a list of sources and a methodological framework before beginning the paper to ensure that students have a clear idea of the group's goals.

Cathy Guisewite, *We Saw Paris* (p. 391)

1. Guisewite's cartoon suggests that the recording and presentation of an experience have become as important as the experience itself, or even more important. The technology that allows travelers to record and document their experience has redefined the nature of experience itself. An ideal vacation, her cartoon

implies, would be one in which the vacationers are not worried about recording or documenting it for future consumption.

2. Guisewite's travelers find themselves in a crisis not because they are lost or have been robbed or are ill—events that might be expected to complicate a trip—but because their laptop froze (panel 1). Her point is that technology makes the experience of travel more burdensome and detaches the travelers from making a sensual and immediate connection with the places, people, and objects they have come to see. Instead of exploring Paris, the travelers spend their time trying to download and e-mail their photos (panel 3). The speaker in the first three panels and her audience share the perception that finding a way to download and e-mail photographs constitutes "an adventure" (panel 3). They imply that the experience of travel is defined and dominated by the transformation of the trip into representations of the experience rather than, for example, by the transformation of the self.

3. The character who saw Paris does not interest what appear to be her co-workers because, apparently, the real experience of Paris cannot match the adventure of coping with a technological crisis. Guisewite might be suggesting here that memory and personal development or growth have become accessories, rather than the technological devices that were once additions to a trip. Ask students to compare these characters to the prisoners in Plato's "The Allegory of the Cave" (Chapter 4). Watching "the shadows thrown by the fire-light on the wall of the Cave facing them," Plato's prisoners honor "the man who had the keenest eye for the passing shadows and the best memory for the order in which they followed or accompanied one another" (27).

Amitai Etzioni with Radhika Bhat, *Social Chances, Social Forgiveness, and the Internet* (p. 391)

1. Etzioni and Bhat argue that the "idea that people deserve a second chance" reflects several cultural predispositions. First, immigrants to America often sought "to start a new life" (2). Second, the wave of settlers who moved into the American West found there "a second beginning" (2). Third, the "belief in a new beginning is a tenet of Christianity" (2). Fourth, "the secular, progressive, optimistic, therapeutic culture of today's America" promotes the idea that we can overcome our "failings" and "achieve a new start" (2). The instructor might point out to students that Etzioni and Bhat begin their essay with an example designed to persuade the reader of the reasonableness of such a point of view. The young man who is arrested in New York, reforms, and starts a new life in Oregon does not commit murder or rape or another serious felony. Rather, he "picks a fight" and "smashes up the bar" (1), inflicting property damage that can be repaired.

2. Dyson argues that debates over the erosion of privacy should distinguish between privacy and security: Sometimes "a breach of privacy is actually a breach of security or a financial harm" (7). Her argument suggests that in those cases

in which a convicted criminal poses a potential threat to others, privacy is not a right and security trumps the individual's desire to conceal his past. With respect to the control of the use of an individual's name or likeness, Solove argues that legal conceptions of privacy must create a balance between the "need to allow legitimate news gathering and dissemination of public information" (28). His argument implies that a clearer conception of the public interest is necessary to make policy decisions such as how much privacy a convicted criminal can expect: "[S]ociety must develop a new and more nuanced understanding of public and private life" (30). Solove implies that this understanding will limit people's ability to control their information: The most that can be expected is "some choice over how that information is shared" (30). Indeed, Solove observes, some technologists and legal scholars declare that "zero privacy" is the new paradigm: Privacy, such commentators maintain," is just not compatible with a world in which information flows so freely (17).

3. Etzioni and Bhat use the image of the "big bad wolf" to suggest that the Internet is preying on a "deeply entrenched narrative" based on the American belief in second chances. Internet databases make public information easily accessible nationally and globally (5). Etzioni and Bhat explain that the 1890 law review article by lawyers Samuel D. Warren and Louis D. Brandeis distinguished between gossip and the dispersion of information to people who are "unaware of the [...] 'whole story'" (5). They suggest that gossip that is spread through the print media takes information out of context. This form of gossip does not have the positive function of "[nudging] people to be better than they would otherwise be" (4), but simply exists to harm those being gossiped about. By extension, the Internet makes available information that does not promote social control but rather spreads selective information taken out of context.

4. Etzioni and Bhat offer anecdotal and statistical evidence that most criminals reoffend. However, the evidence that the authors present is rather narrow: The 67.5 percent of offenders who reoffend is based on data from fifteen states in a single year. Students may want to investigate recidivism by categories of crimes. Most of Etzioni and Bhat's evidence of high rates of recidivism concerns sex offenses (8, 10, 16). The instructor might point out that if such offenders are more likely to reoffend than other convicted criminals, then policy decisions about making such information available on the Internet should take such differences into account. In arguing that the dissemination of information about "wrongdoers" can offer "real benefits" (15), the authors focus on particularly egregious case of health care workers who harm patients (12–15). Encourage students to examine how such clear-cut examples may be persuasive but do not necessarily encourage a nuanced debate. Students might begin their research on publically available information on crime and convictions by consulting the Web sites of the U.S. Department of Justice (www.justice.gov) and the FBI (www.fbi.gov), both of which have links to information on crime registries.

5. The authors' argument that sealing the records of criminal convictions after a certain period of time suggests that such a policy would distinguish between those who need a second chance and those who reoffend (22). However, they point out earlier that "the majority of rapists and child molesters" admit "to having committed two to five as many sex crimes as were officially documented" (10), which suggests that a convicted sex offender who has not been caught has not necessarily reformed. Their argument that data on convictions should be restricted to "police authorities and educational institutions" (23) seems to contradict their earlier assertion that "we can show real benefits from the widespread dissemination of information about wrongdoers—for their potential victims" (15) and that "Registration and notification laws for sex offenders" support the argument in favor of the dissemination of information (16). The instructor might ask students, in light of these contradictions, to evaluate the article's conclusion that the "undesirable side effects" of "digitized transparency" "can be curbed" (27). Students might refer to Solove's "The End of Privacy?" in developing an argument about how privacy and public interests can be balanced in managing the public availability of such data.

6. This question asks students to take a multidisciplinary approach to the problem of distinguishing between the individual's right to privacy and the public's interest and safety. There is a wealth of information online and through academic databases on the social, ethical, moral, legal, and psychological aspects of privacy and electronic data. The instructor might make this a group project and ask each member to focus on a particular topic, such as the use of personal data for marketing purposes or how sensitive information such as an individual's finances or health records are stored securely. Particularly helpful companion readings would be Gorry's "Empathy in the Virtual World," Dyson's "Reflections on Privacy 2.0," Solove's "The End of Privacy?," and Bugeja's "Facing the Facebook."

Michael J. Bugeja, *Facing the Facebook* (p. 399)

1. Bugeja argues that Facebook may pressure academic institutions to invest in technology "rather than in tenure-track positions" (4); may be used to communicate unethical or illegal material (14); and, because it allows "high levels of surveillance" (13), provides parents, employers, and others access to students' accounts (4, 13, 14, 16). Facebook also offers a distraction in the classroom (4, 22) and fosters isolation rather than helping to expose students to challenging ideas (21). Facebook makes public behaviors that may violate university policies or laws, and thus threatening or injurious language and confessions of illegal behavior such as substance abuse expose students to the judgment of others and possibly to legal action.

2. Bugeja quotes an ethics specialist who points out that Facebook is "a public diary" and thus gives anybody with a computer access to information that some students may believe is restricted to "a vast network of peers" (13). Thus, students

may erroneously assume that their online activities remain beyond the reach of their educational institutions and parents and the criminal justice system. Although responses to this question will vary, instructors might initiate classroom discussion by obtaining the policy of their institution and by asking students to research other institutions to discover how many consider online activities among students subject to their conduct policies.

3. and 4. Student responses will vary, but the instructor can tailor these questions to meet specific pedagogical goals. For example, responses could take the form of a personal or argumentative essay or a sociological research study using case histories or a questionnaire. Although these questions emphasize researching students' own and their peers' use of online networking, the instructor might ask students to supplement their responses with research on ethical and privacy issues respecting the Internet. Turkle's "Logins R Us," Deresiewicz's "Faux Friendship," and Solove's "The End of Privacy?" will make excellent companion readings for this question.

Joseph Fuller, *The Terminator Comes to Wall Street* (p. 404)

1. Fuller likens the recent volatile U.S. financial markets to a Hollywood science-fiction movie in which technology "mutates into a catastrophic threat" (1). This story line reflects the anxiety that the future is unpredictable and that humankind cannot prepare for extraordinary events. Such films are often cautionary tales about humankind's arrogance, thoughtlessness, or enthrallment to the magic of technology. Similarly, in Fuller's narrative, the models designed for computer-based program trading "can have trouble responding to extraordinary or unprecedented events" (3) such as the 2008 panic he describes (3). The story line in both the Hollywood sci-fi techno thriller and Fuller's essay is one in which faulty or simplistic assumptions compounded by irresponsibility or a lack of accountability together create a crisis.

2. Computer-based trading is a form of securities trading driven by software programs created by quantitative analysts using "sophisticated data analytics and modeling skills to evaluate securities and develop portfolio-management theories" (2). These programs had come to account for nearly 17 percent of securities trading as of September 2008 (3). The computers execute trades "without specific human intervention"; the quantitative analysts who design the programs do not execute the trades themselves. The "blame" for volatility in securities markets is, as Fuller points out, a multidimensional problem. The computer modelers are often not experts in markets or trading, but in math, computer science, or physics (5). They tend to "think of markets as efficient abstractions" and use historical market data to create programs that exclude unusual or "unprecedented circumstances" (6). Fuller also points out that managers often do not have the background that allows them to "understand the nature of the risks underlying their trading strategies" or even to ask "the right questions" (10). Fuller goes on to

explain that preventing market volatility depends on the cooperation of managers, risk managers, boards, and regulatory authorities (10–17).

3. The disconnect between modelers' abstract view of markets and "unprecedented circumstances" such as the volatility in multiple markets seen in 2008 puts these markets at risk. As Fuller points out, computer-based trading programs have become a highly integrated part of capital markets (9). Consequently, given the limitations of existing trading programs and inadequate internal corporate governance and regulatory oversight, unusual events invariably increase market volatility.

4. Because managers don't understand the modelers, they "have difficulty framing the questions necessary to comprehend how the models might respond to different situations" (7), and they do not understand the risks that their firms incur (10). The case of Long-Term Capital Management might have grown out of such a scenario: "LTCM sold off assets in a frantic effort to cover its debts," which "depressed the market value of those assets" and led investors to liquidate their positions for cash (4). Fuller's argument implies that LTCM's managers did not fully understand the likely consequences of "a toxic mix of an aggressive strategy funded by high leverage"—and neither did regulators, who "ascribed the firm's collapse to a defective trading strategy" (5).

5. Because individual models do not take into account the effects of other models, "each program reacts almost in real time to the actions of other programs, potentially compounding volatility and leading to wild market swings" (8). As a result, in 2008, "models trading hundreds of millions of shares all tried to liquidate investments and move into cash," thus intensifying the market's fall (8).

6. Fuller argues that financial institutions need risk managers who can explain to bank executives "in plain English" the "logic of the models" the firm uses, the "nature of the risks underlying the firm's trading strategies," and the size and structure of the firm's trading positions (10). He argues that companies must oversee the firm's trading system and the work of modelers (11); that companies should "instill more discipline in the investing process" through a long-term, rather than short-term, compensation scheme (12); that boards and audit and risk-management committees should review "the models being employed to trade major positions" (14); and that regulators should set out better rules that hold managers and boards accountable for risk management (15). As in all recipes, the devil is in the details. The quality and thoroughness with which the industry carries out these recommendations will determine their success. If, as Fuller argues, some events simply cannot be anticipated, the oversight procedures he recommends will need to take such emergencies into account. Furthermore, Fuller's recommendation that "regulators and legislators design new regulatory structures to prevent future financial calamities" (14) can only be as effective as those authorities' powers of enforcement. Managers and boards are likely to comply with regulations if they face serious consequences for failing to do so.

7. Fuller points out that the models driving program trading "enable great market liquidity and permit firms to achieve a high level of productivity" (14). Consequently, the models themselves, Fuller argues, are only partially the problem. Fuller shows that the vulnerabilities of the U.S. financial system lie in gaps in accountability and argues that the solution consists of improving the interactions of those involved, including managers, risk management committees and auditors, boards, and regulatory authorities.

Fuller avoids complexities and details because his audience does not consist of experts in finance and because his readers do not need to know precisely how these models work in order to understand the overall argument. Fuller provides only a very brief argument about why computer-based trading programs will continue to drive trading: "It will not work for regulators to [...] curb the use of models" and "legislators cannot demand that managers cease to take imprudent risks if, in fact, the risks are being taken and magnified by the interplay of computers" (14). Instead, he points out that programs that "approximate the process of human reason" may be part of the solution (18): Current models are "relatively crude" and new "artificially intelligent models" will "consider numerous different data streams, interpret them, and look for patterns rather than simply trying to fit market behavior into a fixed algorithm"(19).

6 SCIENCE—DISCOVERY, INVENTION, CONTROVERSY: IF WE'RE SO SMART, WHY DON'T WE LIVE IN UTOPIA?

Henry Groskinsky, *Replaceable You* (p. 410)

1. The image implies that technology is taking over not only our lives, but our bodies. How much of our selfhood and our humanity do we lose when an artificial component replaces a physical one? The photograph suggests that at some point the self will become subordinate to the manufactured components that comprise the physical body.

2. Among the transplant advances since 1989 are lung transplants, stem-cell transplants, gene therapy, and liver transplants between individuals of different species. The advances in cloning during the time period are expected to have dramatic repercussions for body part replacement. Mechanical advances include the self-contained artificial hearts implanted at Jewish Hospital in Louisville, Kentucky. Researchers are working on an artificial substitute for human blood. The latter part of this question asks students to consider the costs and benefits of artificial body parts to the individual and to society. For example, artificial parts may enable an individual to remain economically and socially productive and prevent the immobility that often leads to more health problems. Although

longer life expectancy as a result of medical intervention places additional burdens on the health care and social welfare systems, healthy, long-lived citizens
bring great benefits to their families and to society as a whole.

Ellen Goodman, *Cure or Quest for Perfection?* (p. 411)

1. Goodman's title refers to one scientist's reading of "The Birthmark" as "a
cautionary moral tale about scientific hubris" (4). Her purpose in posing such
a question is to highlight how the issue of human cloning has become distorted
between two extreme poles. Arguing that the therapeutic cloning debate has become slanted by a fear of reproductive cloning, Goodman ultimately asserts that
using early-stage embryos for the treatment of serious diseases "passes the moral
threshold test" (15). Goodman uses rhetorical questions for a variety of purposes.
Her question "Is there a marriage counselor in the room?" provides a humorous,
alternative reading of the Hawthorne story and sets up her conclusion that "[i]f
Hawthorne's scientist had simply cured his wife's birthmark, I imagine he would
have found fault with her cooking" (16). The rhetorical question "The aspiration
for perfection?" directs the reader to share her surprise at Leon Kass's interpretation of "The Birthmark" (5) and join her in questioning the fallacy she sees in the
argument against therapeutic cloning. Some of her rhetorical questions replicate
the issues that are political hot potatoes and suggest that a total ban on cloning
will be ineffectual. For example, the question "Can we ban importing cures based
on cloning?" implies that a total ban on cloning will be ineffectual because other
countries will carry on such research, from which they will develop and sell medicines (13). The critical reader may find Goodman's argument circular: She argues
that therapeutic cloning "passes the moral threshold test" (15) because the cure
of serious diseases, such as cystic fibrosis and Parkinson's, do not represent "the
hubristic pursuit of perfection" (8). That the use of therapeutic cloning to cure
serious diseases is morally justifiable is both an assumption and the conclusion
of her argument.

2. Goodman argues that the "moral threshold test" is defined by the ability
of a therapy to relieve the "suffering of existing humans" (15). Hawthorne's story
suggests that the scientist overstepped a moral threshold because his obsession
with his wife's flaw leads to her death. Goodman objects to the interpretation of
"The Birthmark" as a tale of "scientific hubris" because curing serious diseases is
worthwhile and justifies human intervention while the elimination of a perceived
cosmetic flaw is frivolous by comparison.

3. Goodman uses several rhetorical strategies to garner the reader's support
and portray political radicalism as an inappropriate response to the therapeutic
cloning debate. She begins with an anecdote about a scientist whose "lit-crit" (7)
she easily discredits. She then suggests that the choice facing the reader is between
curing serious diseases and having scientific research held hostage by "religion
and prolife politics" (11). Goodman uses language that sounds scientific such as
"clusters of cells" to defuse the more charged language of the opponents of clon-

ing, who suggest that cloning advocates treat a potential child as "a mere piece of tissue" (15). She appeals to the reader's pragmatism by suggesting that a ban on cloning will allow other countries to overtake American research and product development. Her fundamental argument against the "prolife" (11) stance is that "a suffering adult" has as much "moral weight" as a "cluster of cells" (12).

Bill McKibben, *Designer Genes* (p. 413)

1. McKibben argues that parents are prepared "to spend virtually unlimited sums in pursuit of successful offspring" (14), as indicated by the sale of prenatal music system and audio tapes of foreign languages for babies. He also points to the market for growth hormones, HGH, that parents buy to make their children taller (15) and to the market for human eggs with specific features (16) in support of his assertion that "not to soup [your kids] up . . . could come to seem like child abuse" (17). Encourage students to ground their discussion of McKibben's predictions in the specific points underlying his argument. For example, to what extent does competition define our society, as McKibben claims (17)? How reasonable is it to argue that parents, generally speaking, want their child to be at "the top of the pack" (18)? Do people value their children according to their IQs, as McKibben implies (19)? Does McKibben distinguish between parents who "steer" their children "in particular directions" and those who try to get them "into the right schools, the right professions, the right income brackets" (23)? Does our genetic makeup ensure that we "behave in certain ways" throughout our lives (29)?

2. These questions ask students to consider the relationship of genetics and environment. McKibben argues that parents "engineer" their children by passing on "their prejudices, their politics, their attitude toward the world" (23) and yet, in American society, "kids eventually fight to determine their own destiny" (26), thus resisting their parents' efforts to shape their lives. The cultural pressure on every individual to join the "search for the 'authentic you'" (26) undercuts the certainty of genetic programming in determining behavior. McKibben also suggests that germline genetic engineering might complicate children's maturation by increasing and specifying parental expectations and undermining a child's sense of accomplishment. For the latter part of this question, the instructor might refer students to Sherman Alexie's "The Joy of Reading and Writing: Superman and Me" (Chapter 1), Eric Liu's "Notes of a Native Speaker," or Esmerelda Santiago's "Jibara" (both in Chapter 2), all of which examine the development of the individual in the context of cultural and familial influences.

3. McKibben argues that genetic enhancement engineering would "write" the "gap in power, wealth, and education that currently divides both our society and the world at large" into "our very biology" (39). Thus, this question asks students to consider how an elitist society run by a genetically superior class would affect democracy. To avoid simplistic responses, the instructor should encourage students to consider how genetic enhancement engineering might be regulated

if it were not prohibited, how improving access to medical care might change McKibben's argument, and the extent to which inequities in health care and education should determine collective decision making. The instructor might ask students to read the United Nations' "Universal Declaration of Human Rights" (Chapter 7) as a companion text. Which articles would address the inequities that genetic enhancement might produce? How would this Declaration have to change to accommodate a world in which, as McKibben claims, people consider their child "a product" (34)?

Freeman Dyson, *Our Biotech Future* (p. 423)

1. By the "domestication of biotechnology," Dyson means that "user-friendly" genetic engineering will become as much a part of our everyday lives as computers have (3). Just as computers are ubiquitous in the contemporary American household, biotechnology will become "small and domesticated rather than big and centralized" (4), providing the tools to create "an explosion of diversity of new living creatures" (6) in the home. Students' experiences of the domestication of the computer will vary, but the instructor might point out that computers have become more diversified, powerful, and smaller in recent years. Many households have multiple computers in the form of workstations, laptops, notebooks, and handheld computers handling complex jobs that once could only be performed by enormous and expensive hardware. Furthermore, computers are no longer luxuries, but are as necessary to everyday life as a telephone or kitchen appliances.

2. Dyson's series of questions implies that developments in biotechnology cannot be stopped: He moves from the open-ended question "Can it be stopped?" to the much more specific questions of how biotechnology can be regulated and how those regulations can be enforced. Although he cautions that the "dangers of biotechnology are real and serious" (7), he also suggests that regulation rather than prohibition will dictate the path these technological developments take. Students can begin to consider the various ways that such activities might be regulated and enforced by consulting the U.S. Regulatory Agencies Unified Biotechnology Web site (http://usbiotechreg.nbii.gov). Multiple state and federal government, university, and research institutes also have Web sites that provide excellent discussions of regulatory issues.

3. Dyson emphasizes the positive aspects of "open source" biotech such as "cheap and abundant solar energy" (18) and more efficient plants (20), although he points out that new biotech tools bring "new questions and new responsibilities" (21). These questions would have to address the types of animals and plants that might be created in the home. Since genetic engineering is a form of selective breeding, people would probably want domesticated animals with specific traits that suit their lifestyles. An example of such a genetically engineered pet is the GloFish, a fluorescent red zebrafish that is commercially available, but the sales of

which are restricted (see the University of California's "Genetic Engineering and Animal Agriculture" Fact Sheet at ucanr.org/freepubs/docs/8184.pdf).

An excellent companion reading for the latter part of this question is Bill McKibben's "Designer Genes," in which he argues that genetic engineering will soon allow biologists to manipulate the DNA of a human embryo, thus transforming parenthood into "'product development'" (14) and setting off a "biological arms race" (17) for the perfect child. Students can consult the Web site of Human Genome Project Information (www.ornl.gov/sci/techresources/Human_Genome/project/about.shtml) for resources on genetic research and engineering as well as links to information about related social, legal, and ethical issues. The USDA's National Institute of Food and Agriculture (www.csrees.usda.gov/nea/biotech/in_focus/biotechnology_if_animal.html) offers general information on animal biotechnology.

4. Dyson explains that green plants are relatively inefficient because they only "convert about 1 percent of the sunlight that falls onto them into chemical energy" (19). In contrast, plants with black silicon leaves would convert sunlight into electrical energy with "15 percent efficiency" (19). Creating genetically engineered plants with black silicon leaves would, however, create a number of environmental issues to be addressed: The plants would leave behind silicon "trash" (21), for example. This question asks students to consider how the benefits and costs of a technological advance, such as genetically engineered plants, might be compared with the benefits and costs of existing technology, such as traditional farming techniques. Can the potential impact of "a whole ecology of silicon-eating microbes and fungi and earthworms" be compared with the social and environmental problems that slash-and-burn and other agricultural practices produce? Remind students that any technological advance—not just genetic engineering—brings with it costs and benefits, and that implementation of such advances requires thoughtful assessment of that trade-off. Jared Diamond's "The World as Polder" (Chapter 8) discusses these issues.

5. Dyson uses the term "green technology" to refer to biology-based technology, as opposed to technology based on physics and chemistry, or "gray" technology (23). Gray technology has produced metal instruments, "wheeled vehicles and paved roads," "ships and war chariots," and "swords and guns and bombs" (24). It has also produced rural poverty by concentrating wealth in cities (23–25). Green technology could shift wealth back into rural areas by allowing agricultural producers to "breed new varieties of animals and plants" at a faster rate than ever known (26). Green technology could also replace "chemical industries and a large part of our mining and manufacturing industries" (27) with cleaner, cheaper methods of production. The latter part of this question asks students to research their local economies. Ask students to investigate some of the many resources on the Internet by using "green technology" as a search term.

6. Students might approach this question by focusing on one of the many topics Dyson discusses, including the engineering of new plants and animals (5–7,

19, 28), solar power (18), recycling (27), rural poverty and development (22–30), and political debate (28). Ask students to examine Dyson's assumptions closely. For example, when Dyson writes that his vision of the future implies that "every village in Africa could enjoy its fair share of the blessings of civilization" and that population movement would no longer occur out of "economic necessity" (31), what assumptions is he making about social, political, economic, and cultural factors and structures? How does his focus on the benefits of biotechnology tend to marginalize the complications of the implementation and application of such developments?

Lewis Thomas, *The Technology of Medicine* (p. 433)

1. Nontechnology consists of essential "supportive therapy" (5), including care for patients suffering from poorly understood diseases (5); "providing reassurance" for patients who are fearful but healthy (6); bedside care for illnesses that require observation, such as infectious diseases that are no longer widespread (7); "supportive medical care" for chronic or terminal diseases and mental disorders (8); and nursing and "nonmedical" professional care in and out of hospital (9). Nontechnology is costly because it involves a lot of time and "hard effort and skill on the part of physicians" (9). Thus, nontechnology absorbs a great deal of the energies and coping skills of expensive, highly trained medical professionals (9).

2. Halfway technology consists of "efforts to compensate for the incapacitating effects" of chronic or terminal illnesses and is thus "designed to make up for disease, or to postpone death" (10). Thomas considers halfway technology as temporary—"the kind of thing that one must continue to do until there is a genuine understanding of the mechanisms involved in disease" (12). A full understanding of a disorder leads to prevention and cure, making such interventions unnecessary. Halfway technology is costly because it can involve multiple resources, as in the case of the management of coronary heart disease (13) or treatment of the symptoms of a chronic disease such as cancer (14) and because it requires extensive hospital facilities and "highly trained people" (15).

3. Thomas argues that "the real high technology of medicine," which leads to a "genuine understanding of disease mechanisms" (17) and thus makes prevention or cure possible, is rare. Thomas provides several examples of such developments: certain immunizations; treatment for syphilis, tuberculosis, and endocrinologic disorders; prevention of hemolytic disease in newborns; and treatment and prevention of nutritional disorders (16). However, he also points out that "there are nothing like as many as the public has been led to believe" (16). The care of chronic and terminal conditions is far more costly than prevention or cure.

Thomas argues that "basic research in biologic science" would save money in the long term (20). His examples of poliomyelitis and pulmonary tuberculosis suggest why basic research does not receive as large a share of health care resources as he would like to see (18–19). In both cases, enormous resources were spent on caring for patients with these disorders because such care required costly intervention. Once the polio vaccine and, in the case of tuberculosis, INH (an antibacterial drug) and streptomycin (an antibiotic drug), were developed, these diseases were brought under control and expensive care regimes became for the most part obsolete.

As Freeman Dyson's "Our Biotech Future," published in 2007, suggests, biological sciences have come a long way since the 1970s. Advances in biotechnology, along with developments in information technology, have transformed the research milieu. Students interested in pursuing this question further might consult the National Center for Biotechnology Information (www.ncbi.nlm.nih.gov) and the National Science Foundation Directorate for Biological Sciences (www.nsf.gov/dir/index.jsp?org=BIO).

4. This question asks students to evaluate the trade-off between, on the one hand, complexity and completeness, and on the other, ease of comprehension and sustaining the reader's engagement with the text. Ask students to keep in mind as they analyze each author's stylistic devices and use of evidence how the context of the published text invites the reader to form particular expectations. For example, the article by Thomas first appeared as a monthly column in the *New England Journal of Medicine*, while Dyson's essay appeared originally in a book focused on the relationships among biology, philosophy, and religion. What kind of reader does each author address? Why might a reader of the *New England Journal of Medicine* enjoy a column that does not make use of detailed evidence and employs an accessible style? Do Thomas's readers know who he is? Who are Dyson's readers? Why might the same reader expect and desire different experiences from each author?

5. Students can use Thomas's examples of expensive "halfway technology" and the more efficient "real high technology of medicine" in their essays. Refer students to David Brown's "Science Reporting and Evidence-Based Journalism" (Chapter 1) as a model for using evidence to address a general audience. Encourage students to use what they have learned from Question 4 in developing their writing style. Another excellent model of writing for a general reader is Malcolm Gladwell's "The Physical Genius" (Chapter 3), which uses specific cases to draw larger conclusions.

Stephen Jay Gould, *Evolution as Fact and Theory* and Contexts (p. 437)

1. Gould defines "the mechanisms" through which evolution occurred as "theory" (7) and "facts" as "data" (5). Thus, natural selection represents Darwin's attempt to explain the data that indicates the "linking [of] all organisms by ties of genealogy" (9). This distinction between theory and fact enables Gould to argue

that the scientific debate over evolution is one in which scientists question "fundamental issues of theory" rather than the fact of evolution: "[N]o biologist has been led to doubt the fact that evolution occurred" (9). Gould bases the scientific consensus that evolution is a fact on "observational evidence of evolution in action, from both the field and the laboratory" (13); "the imperfections that record a history of descent," *imperfections* that many species share (16); and the "transitions [that] are often found in the fossil record" (17).

2. Gould assumes a public role as a scientist to influence the public's understanding of particular debates. In "Evolution as Fact and Theory," Gould characterizes the "debate" between Creationism and Evolution as "the resurgent evangelical right" versus "the mainstream" (2), by which he means the majority of the scientific community. Gould writes not only to discredit Creationism as science, but also to support the idea that scientific debate is "a sign of intellectual health" (9).

3. Huxley argues that the qualities that have helped mankind progress "throughout the savage state" are "his exceptional physical organization; his cunning, his sociability, his curiosity, and his imitativeness; his ruthless and ferocious destructiveness when his anger is roused by opposition" (1). Huxley implies that no behavior to which humans are biologically driven should be considered sinful. Huxley might redefine society's notion of sin as any effort to treat these qualities as "defects" and thereby "put an end to the survival of the fittest" (2). Gould would equate sin with ignorance or with the attempt to diminish free intellectual inquiry and the deliberate repression of knowledge. For example, Gould implies that the "wish to mute the healthy debate about theory" (25) is a kind of sin against science: "If we ever begin to suppress our search to understand nature, to quench our own intellectual excitement in a misguided effort to present a united front where it does not and should not exist, then we are truly lost" (26). While Gould would join Huxley in opposing the labeling of certain biologically driven behaviors as sinful, he also appreciates virtues that might not fall into Huxley's description of the qualities of "the ape and the tiger"—such as the respect for others' ideas (2).

4. The model of punctuated equilibrium theorizes that changes in species occur in relatively short bursts rather than gradually, as the traditional view envisions. The "punk eke" model (Gleick paragraph 2) suggests that new species might split off from existing species rather than progress in a continuous process. As Niles Eldredge explains, in "Stephen Jay Gould: Breaking Tradition with Darwin" (p. 448), the theory of punctuated equilibrium implies the mechanism of natural selection "at the species level" (7). Gould might conclude from Wilson's argument—that successful organisms can threaten the survival of their species—that competition tends to favor those species who demonstrate the ability to plan their consumption and husband their resources or to behave in an altruistic manner.

5. For Gould, "interesting ideas" are those that contribute to scientific debate. He excludes Scientific Creationism from the field of scientific debate because he categorizes it as "dogma" rather than science (12). Also, he charges Creationists

with "philosophical bankruptcy" and with relying on "distortion and innuendo to buttress their rhetorical claim" (18). In the case of the former, Gould argues that Creationism "attempt[s] to falsify evolution by presenting supposed contradictions among its supporters" (11), yet it does not present "an alternative system" that is also "falsifiable in principle" (11). In the case of the latter, Gould charges Creationists with using the "vernacular misunderstanding of the word 'theory'" (3) to suggest that the theory of evolution is a kind of "'imperfect fact'" (4), thereby confusing the fact of evolution with the debate on the mechanism by which evolution occurred.

6. While student responses will vary, the instructor should point out Gould's definition in "Evolution as Fact and Theory": "'Fact' can only mean 'confirmed to such a degree that it would be perverse to withhold provisional assent'" (6). Gould distinguishes between "facts" (e.g., apples fall to the ground when dropped) and "[t]heories," which are "structures of ideas that explain and interpret facts" (5).

The instructor can further help students respond to this question by reviewing the Popperian model in which "the primary criterion of science is the falsifiability of its theories" (10). Falsifiability is a product of the scientific method whereby a hypothesis is tested by seeking counterevidence, to find out where it will break down. Scientists advance hypotheses and then seek to prove or disprove them. Science can never say that a theory is absolutely true; it is always open to being disproved. To demand absolute proof from science is to fail to understand that science works by questioning and testing existing theories. Darwin follows this model of scientific inquiry when he writes, "What natural selection cannot do, is to modify the structure of one species, without giving it any advantage, for the good of another species; and though statements to this effect may be found in works of natural history, I cannot find one case which will bear investigation" (4). Darwin implies here that he has sought to prove or disprove a popular scientific assertion and has found no evidence to support it; on this basis he considers the assertion untrue until supporting evidence is brought forth.

For Phillip E. Johnson, the fact that a scientific theory can be tested and disproved in this way means that it is never proven at all. Johnson's attack on falsifiability is based on his insistence on absolute proof that establishes unshakeable truth, what Gould would call "sterile truth." The Book of Genesis is a narrative of the creation that one may choose to believe or disbelieve; it cannot, however, be tested and, therefore, cannot be proved or disproved. Gould asserts that "Evolutionists make no claim for perpetual truth" (6), but that does not mean that their explanations are not proven in the scientific definition of proof as "provisional assent" (6) until such time as the explanation may be refined or altered.

7. Examples of Gould's playful and approachable style in "Evolution as Fact and Theory" include many instances of colloquial language, including "rally round the flag" (25) and "brouhaha" (24). Many of these down-to-earth expressions are used to denigrate Creationists' ideas, characterized as "kooky" (2) and "nonsense" (12 and 22). Gould refers to shared knowledge of everyday things to

help readers to follow his explanations: Trends are "like climbing a flight of stairs" (20); if facts changed because theories changed, Newton's "apples might start to rise tomorrow" (6). Gould plays with religious language and ideas when he uses the image of a "straight and narrow path, surrounded by roads to perdition" (26).

Marisa Acocella Marchetto, *How Chemo Works* (p. 451)

1. This question asks students to evaluate how visual imagery enhances and helps to produce the meaning of text. Ask students to consider how each of these visual representations interacts with a specific reader in particular ways. For example, Marchetto's "How Chemo Works" is designed for a nonscientific, general audience, as is Groskinsky's "Replaceable You." In both cases, the images help transmit information to the reader. In contrast, McCloud's "Reading the Comics" explicitly teaches readers and creators of comics, as well as, perhaps, readers and creators of other narrative forms, how the reader participates in the construction of meaning. The content of McCloud's graphic essay is inseparable from its form. "Better Signs of Trouble" (Scher, Fogelson-Lubliner, and Brody and Knowles) uses the interaction of text and image to communicate a specific, immediate, and urgent message to the viewer.

2. Marchetto confines the scientific explanation of how chemo works in a narrative box and uses speech bubbles to animate the cancer cells. She explains that chemotherapy deprives both healthy and cancerous cells of the antioxidants they need to survive. As a result, the cells that make up hair die along with the cancer cells. The reader who does not have a scientific background might want to know how normal cells become cancerous, why they divide aggressively, how the body produces antioxidants, the role of antioxidants in sustaining life, and the chemical makeup of the chemotherapy medications that attack the cancer. However, the reader does not need a great deal of background to understand Marchetto's main point—that the cancerous cells reproduce rapidly and create chaos in the body.

3. This question is an opportunity to discuss how to evaluate information sources. Ask students to draw up a list of evaluative questions to ask. Who is the sponsor or publisher of the Web site? Who is the author of the text? Does the author provide contact information and credentials? Is the page updated regularly? Is the information intended to encourage users to buy a product or service? Has the information been cited correctly? Must the user register to use the site? The instructor can refer students to their university's or college's resources for help with composition and writing or to their library's resources for additional information. There are also multiple guides online through various colleges and universities and public libraries. Help students distinguish between browsing for general background and using sources for research assignments. This question also offers the instructor an opportunity to work with students on using library resources.

Charles Darwin, *Understanding Natural Selection* (p. 451)

1. Natural selection is the process by which new and better-adapted species are formed. Charles Darwin theorized that organisms that were less efficient at acquiring food, fighting off or escaping from predators, and resisting disease died off while those who survived were better adapted, on average, to their environment. According to Darwin these "improvements of each organic being" (1) occur over such a long time span that people cannot see natural selection at work over the course of a human lifetime. As Darwin explains with his example of evolution in wolves, "if any slight innate change of habit or of structure benefited an individual wolf" (10), that change would increase the wolf's chance of survival. Then the wolf would pass that change on to some of its offspring. Eventually, as the change was passed down through generations and animals with the change benefited and survived, their numbers would increase and "a new variety might be formed" (10). Some contemporary evolutionists, such as Stephen Jay Gould ("Evolution as Fact and Theory"), believe that evolutionary events occur more rapidly than Darwin's theory suggests. But still, Gould asserts that "major evolutionary change requires too much time for direct observation on the scale of recorded human history" (14).

2. Darwin explains that "in a state of nature, where the trees would have to struggle with other trees and with a host of enemies" (2), subtle differences in the color or texture of fruits make some varieties of the fruit less susceptible to certain insects or diseases while other varieties are less likely to survive because they are more susceptible to these enemies. The same is true of subtle differences within other species.

3. In sexual selection, the same principle underlying natural selection works to maximize the conditions under which more offspring will be produced. The males who are best equipped to successfully compete with other males for females with which to breed and/or to attract females are favored by sexual selection. In sexual selection variations that are "either useful to the males in battle or attractive to the females" (8) rather than the animal's ability to survive are selected. The selection depends on which males are selected to breed rather than on which species members survive. Sexual selection explains the more colorful or ornamented appearance of the males in comparison to the females in many species.

4. Darwin's evidence in support of his theory of natural selection includes examples of insects, grouse, fruit (2), pigeons (5), and wolves (9, 10). In "Evolution as Fact and Theory," Stephen Jay Gould helps readers to understand the difference between a fact (evolution) and a theory (natural selection). Although all biologists believe that evolution occurs, the mechanism that causes it to happen may not be precisely what Darwin describes. Gould references three arguments for the fact of evolution: abundant close observations of plants and animals, unneeded attributes in species that reveal descent from an ancestor in which those attributes had a function, and the fossil record showing the transitional life forms that appear as an evolutionary change occurs.

5. Student responses will vary. However, the instructor might point out that some of Darwin's paragraphs are rather long and he often uses complex sentences that begin with subordinate clauses (such as the first sentence). Darwin also uses qualifying parenthetical phrases such as "if not destroyed at some period of their lives" (1) and "as far as our ignorance permits us to judge" (2); adverbs ("assuredly" [1] and "conversely" [3]); and the passive voice ("they are known to suffer" [1], "natural selection will be enabled" [3], and "in this being effected" [3]). This question might form the basis of a discussion on how English has changed since Darwin wrote and even more so in recent years. The instructor will find Roz Chast's "The I.M.s of Romeo and Juliet," Dennis Baron's "The New Technologies of the Word," and James Gleick's "Cyber-Neologifération" (all in Chapter 5) excellent companion readings for such a discussion. In addition, the instructor might use this opportunity to explore with the class how written communication depends on a cooperative interaction between text and reader. Refer students to Peter Elbow's "Freewriting" and "Better Signs of Trouble" (Scher, Fogelson-Lubliner, and Brody and Knowles) in Chapter 1 to build on this discussion by exploring the writer's development of a personal voice and the reader's interpretive work.

Robert L. Park, *The Seven Warning Signs of Bogus Science* (p. 457)

Stanley Fish, *Academic Cross-Dressing: How Intelligent Design Gets Its Arguments from the Left* (p. 460)

1. Park gives several reasons why "spotting voodoo science" is a useful skill: Preposterous claims can "cost some gullible person or corporation a lot of money" (2); juries can be "bamboozled by technical gibberish they could not hope to follow, delivered by experts whose credentials they could not evaluate" (3); and, consumers' access to useful and safe medicines depend on the outcome of cases such as *Daubert v. Merrell Dow Pharmaceuticals, Inc.* Park also implies that the ability to evaluate scientific claims promotes a healthy public skepticism.

2. This question asks students to evaluate popular but questionable claims, such as the denial of the Holocaust, which Stanley Fish refers to in "Academic Cross-Dressing: How Intelligent Design Gets Its Arguments from the Left" (p. 460). An example of beliefs that are based on anecdotal evidence (4) and based on persistent myth (5) can be found in Natalie Angier's characterization of evolutionary psychology, which is based on a poorly supported belief in "male parental investment, the bedrock of so much of evolutionary psychology's theories" (32). Student responses to the latter part of this question will vary. However, the instructor might refer students to well-reasoned, persuasive essays designed to challenge entrenched beliefs such as Stephen J. Gould's "Evolution as Fact and Theory" or Martin Luther King's "Letter from Birmingham Jail" (Chapter 7).

3. This assignment asks students to apply Park's model of inquiry. Instruct students to address each of the seven "warning signs" that Park explains. Students may be interested in investigating semiscientific practices that are contested, such as homeopathy, or those that are becoming increasingly integrated into mainstream medicine, such as acupuncture.

4. Students might investigate, for example, Dr. Hwang Woo Suk's fraudulent stem cell claims in 2006; the 1989 "discovery" of cold fusion; Alfred Kinsey's dubious views of human sexuality in the 1950s; or any number of unsubstantiated claims for food and beauty products and vitamins. The instructor may want to refer students to David Brown's "Science Reporting and Evidence-Based Journalism" (Chapter 1) and Natasha Singer and Duff Wilson's "Medical Editors Push for Ghostwriting Crackdown" (Chapter 7) for examples that both model good writing and discuss the ethics of writing about science.

5. Fish makes the case that all arguments do not deserve equal treatment in the classroom because not all arguments concern "the underlying issues that structure academic discourse" (4) and because the validity of an argument depends on "the evidence one has, even if that evidence may be overtaken in the long run" (5). He also argues that diversity of opinion in debates has a legitimate place only when representing "persons who are committed to the protocols of rational inquiry" rather than "frivolous persons [...] who exploit those protocols or play with them to gain political ends" (7). Fish argues that the issue of fairness is a fraudulent one in the case of Intelligent Design: Like Holocaust deniers, proponents of Intelligent Design raise "issues that have been settled in the relevant academic departments—history and biology, respectively," which they then "[reopen] by reframing them as abstract questions about the value of debate as a moral good" (9). Fish implies that if arguments that perpetuate falsehood have a place, that place is not in the world of "scrupulous scholarship" (10).

6. Fish explains that the argument that multiculturalists "can defend gay marriage by challenging the right of a church or a state to define what marriage is" (2) is based on the idea that the stigma of homosexual behavior reflects the "interests and preferences of those in power" (2). The argument that Intelligent Design should have "equal time in the classroom by challenging the right of Ivy League professors to say what science is" is not based on an equivalent idea. Multiculturalism rejects the determination of knowledge on the basis of "prejudice and custom" (2), while Intelligent Design rejects the specific merits of canonic knowledge in the field of biology. Intelligent Design exploits "liberalism's privileging of tolerance over judgment" (6) by avoiding "questions about the qualifications necessary to be legitimate competitors in the competition" among ideas (9). The analogy is not valid because the premises of each argument differ. The premises that the church or state defines marriage and that such a definition is based on custom are true; the premises that Ivy League professors define what science is and do so based on the basis of custom is not true.

7. Fish characterizes Intelligent Design as the idea that "God [...] created the wonders of the physical world" (9). Proponents of Intelligent Design, Fish argues, charge the scientific community with marginalizing their ideas and demand that they be represented as a matter of "freedom and open inquiry" (2). The phrase "teach the controversy," (1) Fish argues, "takes the focus away from the scientific credibility of Intelligent Design" (2). Fish refutes the argument that all knowledge should be debated, regardless of the conclusions of the debate, by rejecting the position that values claims "simply because they are claims" (9).

8. Intelligent Design proponents and Holocaust deniers both argue that debate in and of itself is valuable "as a moral good" (9). Both equate orthodox knowledge with hegemonic institutions. Fish argues that for any claim the legitimacy of debate depends on the content of the ideas rather than on the basis that the idea has a "constituency" (2).

9. Fish would probably reject the suggestion of a rebuttal. In Fish's terms, the only rational and fruitful rebuttal would consist of scientific evidence in favor of Intelligent Design.

Natalie Angier, *Men, Women, Sex, and Darwin* (p. 466)

1. Examples of Natalie Angier's informality and humor include "rude little prods and jests" (2), "ego, if expressed as a vapor, would fill Biosphere II" (15), "we might want to sue for whiplash" (18), and "dashing breathlessly from sheet to sheet" (24). Sometimes her informal language is an expression of disdain, such as when she characterizes evolutionary psychologists as "types," "the evo-psycho set" (6), and "hard-cores" (9 and 10). Her tone becomes crisper and more businesslike when she provides evidence for her rebuttal of the evolutionary psychologists' theories, particularly where she gives evidence from female scholars documenting the persistent inequality of women (12 and 13).

2. Angier argues that a human sexual relationship, particularly marriage, is "a mutual bid between man and woman" to meet their own and each other's needs (35). Both men and women make choices in an effort to find "emotional parity" (36) and compatibility in a mate. Each party negotiates in the interest of getting his or her own needs met, but also in the hope of meeting the other person's needs. According to Angier, evolutionary psychologists construct men and women not as free agents making choices but as biologically driven: "Men can't help themselves" in their promiscuous attraction to nubile females (6) and "women's innate preference for a well-to-do man . . . can't be willed away" (8).

3. Responses will vary. Students are certainly familiar with the public confessions of philandering husbands who are in the public eye. Women's greater desire for commitment is a frequent topic on television sitcoms. The May–December romances of celebrities are also a frequent topic in the media.

4. Angier consistently argues that differences in male and female behavior are environmentally rather than biologically caused and are various and flexible. The

evolutionary psychologists she cites argue the opposite: Male and female behavior is determined by the biological imperatives required for successful evolution. Some evidence from primate studies seems to undermine the evolutionary psychologists' argument. It does not seem that evolutionary requirements are the basis for female primates' sexual behavior since there is no evolutionary need for female primates to seek out sex as often as primatologists report that they do (16 –17). Reported variations in male primate sexual behavior (30) contradict the evolutionary psychologists' claim that all males compete with other males for multiple female partners.

5. Evolutionary psychologists view this notion as fact and provide a theory to explain it. To support their claim, they use survey data showing that women rate ambition and financial success as important traits in a potential mate (11). Their theory is that women are evolutionarily programmed to seek a provider and protector even if modern conditions mean that they need one less than their cavewomen ancestors did. One of Angier's alternative theories is that women, recognizing that men's potential earning power is greater than women's due to sexual discrimination, seek financially stable men to compensate for their lower wages (12). Another alternative theory is that women hope that successful men will be more capable of an egalitarian relationship.

Edward O. Wilson, *Microbes 3, Humans 2* (p. 476)

1. Edward O. Wilson engages readers' attention by revising the expected expression. By doing so, he signals that in his discussion, he will not say what readers might expect. Readers tend to assume that humans are biologically superior in every aspect of existence. Wilson wants to challenge this conventional wisdom by surprising readers with zoological facts that confound their belief in human superiority.

2. Wilson gives two awards to humans, but the second, "our power of life and death over all other higher life forms" (10), is one we probably shouldn't be proud of because, as Wilson argues, we have yet to show that we can use this power in a positive way. Just as Wilson says he is an insect chauvinist (8), most people are human chauvinists, taking for granted that humans are the best in everything. As a result, we are not open-minded about learning from other species. Wilson wants to show that other species have much to teach us. He also wants us to consider that our assets for survival are more limited than we like to think.

3. Efficient use of an exhaustible resource is a success that ultimately becomes a failure when the resource runs out. In some ways, human intelligence is a short-term success that may become a long-term failure if humans continue to use their intelligence to think up new ways to exhaust natural resources or to kill each other.

4. Since humans are the most powerful species, we have the most impact on other species and, in that sense, are quite important. We are thus important because of our great potential for harm. Human intelligence equips us for "peering

into the future and understanding how the world works" (10), but we have yet to use our ability in a way that ensures the continuation of our own species, much less our peaceful coexistence with other species. Wilson clearly places himself in the camp of evolutionists along with Stephen J. Gould. For example, he writes, "All living species [...] have descended from early forms of life that originated more than 3.5 billion years ago" (6). Wilson treats evolution much as Gould does, who, in "Evolution as Fact and Theory," distinguishes between these two concepts: "Facts are the world's data. Theories are structures of ideas that explain and interpret facts" (5).

5. Wilson poses as an open question "whether we [humans] will choose life for them [other species] and ultimately for ourselves" (10). Clearly, he worries that human intelligence and power may lead us to destruction rather than to long-term success. Wilson seems to see human intelligence as a mixed blessing. More pessimistic, Rachel Carson is very clear that she sees the "disturbing magnitude" of human power as no blessing at all ("The Obligation to Endure" p. 612). By assaulting the environment with chemicals and making other changes at a recklessly rapid pace, humans have disturbed the balance of nature, putting all forms of life at risk.

7 ETHICS: WHAT PRINCIPLES DO—AND SHOULD— WE LIVE BY?

Leonard Freed, *Martin Luther King Jr. After Receiving the Nobel Peace Prize, Baltimore, 1964* (photograph) (p. 479)

1. and 2. Although responses will vary, many viewers may find that their eyes are drawn to King's face because it is so familiar. This is unexpected because King is not in the center of this photograph by Leonard Freed. The happy spirit captured in the photo can be located in King's quiet smile and in the broader proud grins of the women at the photo's center. As viewers continue looking at the photograph, the presence of the bodyguard seeking to shield King's body from the street may become more central. There may be irony in the presence of two white police officers in uniform who seem peripheral to the action in comparison to the African American bodyguard who occupies a crucial position for protecting King. These aspects of Freed's photograph seem to suggest King's impending violent death, but in this photograph, King is surrounded by African American well-wishers and is presumably in no danger.

3. The blurry face at the right of the scene suggests that the crowd reaching out toward King goes on and on, well beyond the frame of this photograph, bringing the view into the action of the photo.

4. King was awarded the Nobel Peace Prize in 1964 for his effective leadership of the civil rights movement. The award followed the success of the March on Washington and the passage of the Civil Rights Act. Like King, Al Gore and Wangari Maathai justify their political and personal leadership by emphasizing the urgency of the problems they address and the need for immediate action. Gore asserts in his Nobel Peace Prize speech that the "planetary emergency" we face requires us to act "boldly, decisively and quickly" (1). Similarly, in her speech, Maathai argues that the same environmental devastation that inspired the Green Belt Movement continues unabated: Humanity needs to act immediately to stop "threatening its life-support system" (21). King, too, demands immediate action: "For years now I have heart the word 'Wait!' It rings in the ear of every Negro with piercing familiarity. This 'Wait' has almost always meant 'Never.' We must come to see […] that 'justice too long delayed is justice denied'" (13).

Although Gore and Maathai differ from King in that they address environmental degradation—global warming and deforestation due to farming—they share with King a concern for the rights of individuals to participate fully and equitably in society. Gore points out that global warming threatens the world's political and social stability: "Climate refugees have migrated into areas already inhabited by people with different cultures, religions, and traditions, increasing the potential for conflict. […]. Millions have been displaced by massive flooding in South Asia, Mexico, and eighteen countries in Africa" (8). The "climate crisis," Gore argues, cannot be decoupled from "the afflictions of poverty, hunger, HIV-AIDS and other pandemics" (18). Maathai also speaks to the link between ecosystems and social systems: "[A] degraded environment leads to a scramble for scarce resources and may culminate in poverty and even conflict" (9). The management of environmental resources, she points out, is inseparable from the political participation of the communities who are part of the ecosystem they use: "[P]articipants [in the Greenbelt Movement] [have] come to recognize that they are the primary custodians and beneficiaries of the environment that sustains them" and thus must promote "justice, integrity and trust" in their leaders and themselves (12–13). The three speeches suggest that the Noble Peace Prize is intended to recognize matters of global urgency and human justice.

Jeffrey Wattles, *The Golden Rule—One or Many, Gold or Glitter?* (p. 480)

1. Jeffrey Wattles raises questions that challenge any easy assumptions of universalism for the golden rule. The questions he says readers should be asking are important to any analysis of rhetoric: What is the original context in which the words were used, and what is the present context in which they are being repeated? What is the place of this rule within the larger body of beliefs of a particular culture? Does the culture intend "others" to include all or only certain members of a particular group?

2. Like any ethical principle, the golden rule can be twisted and used as a rationale for misdeeds. A disingenuous user of the golden rule can twist its intention, seeking excuses to do what he or she wants at other people's expense. Wattles asserts in paragraph 14 that a person needs "a certain degree of maturity" in order to resist impulses to behave selfishly and to apply the rule in a sincere spirit of trying to do what is right.

3. Although responses will vary, students might feel that Wattles throws an overload of objections to the golden rule that complicate its application, seemingly beyond usefulness. On the other hand, as Wattles points out in paragraph 17, if individuals are unsure whether they are applying the golden rule in a way that truly benefits others, they have merely to ask themselves if they are taking into consideration the factors they would want someone else to take into consideration in determining conduct toward themselves.

4. Student responses will vary. However, the instructor can direct students to the answer to Question 1 for a discussion of the problems inherent in comparing moral precepts outside of their cultural contexts. With that proviso, what does seem universal in living by the rules is the effort to offer criteria to people on the basis of which they can make moral judgments. Many of these criteria specify moderation, in lifestyle and in ambition, as an important basis on which to judge what is moral.

John Donne, *Meditation 17 (For Whom the Bell Tolls)* (p. 486)

1. John Donne says that the bell calls the whole community, not just the immediate relations of the person who has died. If we believe, with Donne, that we are "involved in mankind," then we will be affected by the death-knell of someone we didn't know personally. If we are more than usually aware of our mortality, perhaps because, like Donne, we are ill or because we have suffered a recent loss, then we will be even more likely to feel involved in the bell's tolling.

2. Donne uses textual metaphors in the first section to highlight the unity of community members (we are all chapters in the same book by the same author). He uses the metaphor of translation to describe the transition from earthly life to heavenly life after death. He believes that death is an ending only of physical life; spiritual life continues, but in a transformed state. As St. Paul says in the New Testament, "Death is swallowed up in victory. O death, where is thy sting? O grave, where is thy victory?" (1 Corinthians 15:54–55).

3. Just as we are all chapters in one book in the first half, in the second half we are all pieces of one continent. Donne uses these geographical metaphors in the same way that he uses the textual metaphors: to suggest the unity of the community. While the textual metaphors focus on the continuation of life after death, albeit in another form, the geographical metaphors convey the loss to the community that accompanies death. The image of erosion, in which "a clod be

washed away by the sea," effectively conveys the idea of the diminishment of the community when a member dies.

4. As we have become aware of the size and diversity of the world in the centuries since Donne's "Meditation" was written, we have also come to feel that we cannot possibly be a part of "all mankind." While in one sense the media allow us to participate in events all around the world, in another sense our knowledge of the vastness of that world may result in a feeling that we are surrounded by strangers and are only connected to those we know well. Readers might also consider that Donne's "all mankind" is more limited than his rhetoric implies. He seems to limit his connectedness to those who are baptized and buried by the Catholic Church, far from "all mankind," even in his own time. He does not consider any who do not see God as their "Author" as part of his community.

United Nations, *Universal Declaration of Human Rights* (p. 488)

1. The Universal Declaration of Human Rights links the ideas of "the inherent dignity" and "the equal and inalienable rights" of all to "freedom, justice and peace" through the corresponding idea that such a foundation will prevent "barbarous acts" and grant all human beings "freedom of speech and belief" and "freedom from fear and want" (2). Also, the Declaration states that "inalienable human rights" promote political peace by making societies subject to "the rule of law" and by eliminating the need to resort to "rebellion against tyranny and oppression" (3). The legal protection of inalienable human rights, the Declaration suggests, will allow the citizens of a society to use the political process to effect change and, by assuring "the dignity and worth of the human person" and the "equal rights of men and women," will promote "social progress and better standards of life," which will, in turn, promote peace (5).

2. The list includes basic rights, such as equality "in dignity and rights" (Article 1); "the right to life, liberty, and security of person" (Article 3); freedom from slavery (Article 4); and freedom from torture (Article 5), as well as other, more ambiguous rights, such as freedom from "arbitrary interference with [...] privacy, family, home, or correspondence" (Article 12) and the right to "just and favorable conditions of work" and to "equal pay for equal work" (Article 23). The instructor might remind students that rights that are taken for granted in some societies—such as freedom from slavery—are neither accepted nor enforced in others and that basic rights, such as those that ensure equality of personhood in law (Articles 1–7), are interpreted differently in different cultures. Encourage students to determine which rights rely on or follow from foundational concepts in the Declaration.

3. The Declaration's ethical principles are based on equality of personhood and of opportunity; on the autonomy and dignity of individuals and families; political and economic security; and intellectual, social, and personal fulfillment.

These ideas imply universality of principles, a shared social and moral framework, and tolerance. They repudiate the notion of inherited or imposed social hierarchies and privilege merit, choice, and individuality.

4. This question asks students to explore the inherent difficulties that accompany the application of principles. What constitutes an attack on an individual's "honor and reputation" (Article 12)? How does a society define "family" (Article 16)? What is an "adequate" standard of living? Point out to students that social norms vary greatly not only among countries, but also among regions within countries. Moreover, the current generation of citizens who need "necessary social services" and should enjoy "the right to security" is also fiscally responsible for future generations. Encourage students to focus on a particular issue that engages them. The instructor might refer students to Dave Leonhardt's "The College Dropout Boom" (Chapter 4), which describes some of the problems involved in the implementation of equal access to higher education (Article 16); to Deirdre N. McCloskey's "Yes, Ma'am" (Chapter 2), which explores a particular form of sex discrimination (Article 2); Deborah Franklin's 'Informed Consent'—What Information? What Consent? (Chapter 4), which addresses unequal access to medical care (Article 25); and Wendell Berry's "Faustian Economics" (Chapter 8), which explores limits to the individual's right to resources (Articles 22–25).

5. The Preamble asserts that without the rights the Declaration enshrines, "man" may be "compelled to have recourse, as a last resort, to rebellion against tyranny and oppression" (3). Ethnic and religious conflicts, poverty and competition for resources, political and social turmoil, and poorly functioning social, economic, and legal structures are indisputably likely outcomes of arbitrary and egregious violations of human rights. Students can cite numerous instances of such conflicts as examples, including the massacre of Armenians (1915–1923); the Holocaust (1930s–40s); the Hungarian uprising of 1956; uprisings in Eastern Europe in the 1980s; ethnic conflict and massacres in Bosnia (1992–1995), Rwanda (1994), and the Sudan (1990s–present); and wars in the Congo (1998–2008). Encourage students to focus on a particular case and on specific violations of human rights that provoked political and social conflict and to trace the consequences of that conflict. Students will find the United Nations' Human Rights Web site helpful (www.un.org/en/rights/index.shtml) and can access additional resources through the Office of the High Commissioner for Human Rights (www.ohchr .org/EN/Pages/WelcomePage.aspx).

Martin Luther King Jr., *Letter from Birmingham Jail* and Contexts (p. 494)

1. and 3. Martin Luther King Jr. finds it rather ironic to be classified as extreme when he is trying so hard to stake out a moderate position within the African American community between the "opposing forces" (27) of complacency,

on the one hand, and the potentially violent resistance, on the other. He seeks to define a position that is "neither the 'do-nothingism' of the complacent nor the hatred and despair of the black nationalist" (28). Students might use the analogies of extreme sports, music, food, and products to explore the relationship between extreme and moderate versions of the same things or phenomena.

King goes on, however, to claim "extremist" as a desirable label, one to be shared with other "creative extremists" including Jesus, St. Paul, Thomas Jefferson, and Abraham Lincoln (31). Saying that he does not intend to be threatening, King points out the increasing power of more radical African American leaders, such as Elijah Muhammad and other Muslims and black nationalists. He fears that many will turn to these more radical movements if they continue to be frustrated by a lack of civil rights progress. Without the nonviolent movement, "many streets of the South would . . . be flowing with blood" (29).

2. These calls for moderation advocate for gradual changes over an extended time period and decry haste and impatience. In "A Southern Moderate Speaks," Hays objects to the *Brown v. Board of Education* (1954) Supreme Court decision on the basis of the South's "Constitutional right to dissent" (7). He attempted to dissuade the governor of Arkansas, Orville Faubus, from calling out the National Guard to oppose school desegregation in Little Rock. The Eight Clergymen from Birmingham criticize the civil rights movement's use of nonviolent demonstrations as "unwise and untimely" (paragraph 3 in "Eight Clergymen's Statement"). While acknowledging "the natural impatience" of African Americans, they also call for gradual changes. Patience is the hallmark of moderate courses of action.

For Hays and the Eight Clergymen, moderation means a desire for local solutions, not solutions coerced by court decisions and agitation coming from outside communities. Outsiders are seen as detrimental to the process; local leaders "with their knowledge and experience of the local situation" ("Eight Clergymen" 4) and using the moderate tactics of negotiation and committee meetings will move slowly toward change.

4. These *Time* and *Newsweek* photographs were taken on the same occasion, King's and Abernathy's arrests on April 12, 1963 (Good Friday), after they defied the injunction against further demonstrations in Birmingham. In the *Time* photo, King and Abernathy may be said to embody nonviolent protest in that they look calm, dignified, and solemn. Abernathy appears to carry a book, probably a Bible. King's face looks strained, and he appears to be walking with a cane. Both seem willing to "present our very bodies as a means of laying our case before the conscience of the local and national community" ("Letter from Birmingham Jail" 8). In the *Newsweek* photograph, which is shot from behind, the most striking visual elements are the blue jeans and work shirts that King and Abernathy have donned in preparation for their arrests. The two ministers have put themselves on the line dressed as working men; this is clearly not their everyday dress. King looks small and vulnerable in this photo, especially in comparison to Abernathy. While in

the *Time* photograph, the police officer seems to be treating the ministers with "hands-off" respect, here the officer has grabbed Abernathy by the back of his shirt. This aggressive move reminds us of King's description of the "process of self-purification" that nonviolent protesters should undergo in order to prepare themselves "to accept blows without retaliating" (8).

5. Both T. Olin Binkley (in "Southern Baptist Seminaries") and Will Herberg (in "A Religious 'Right' to Violate the Law?") equate Christian morality with following God's law. For Binkley, Christian morality is based in the revelations of the Holy Spirit: If one is open to the Holy Spirit's instruction and seeks to follow God's Word as revealed in the Bible, then one is acting as a moral Christian. Citing St. Paul and St. Augustine, Herberg argues that the Bible authorizes humans to break human law only when that law directly conflicts with God's commands, as for example, when a tyrant requires his subjects to worship him as if he is a god. Neither writer argues that humans should follow their individual consciences in isolation from God's teachings in the Bible, as interpreted in the Christian community. To set conscience up as divine, says Herberg, is to make it divine in denial of God's sole divinity. To refuse to obey unjust laws based on conscience (as King advocates) is not Christian morality. It is instead, according to Herberg, "deviant and heretical" (5).

6. Both preachers, King and John Donne display characteristics of oration in their writing. Oral expression is often characterized by repetition and by the juxtaposition of parallel or antithetical structures. Such devices bring a building of drama to a sermon and are an aid to memory, a holdover from a time when oral discourse existed only in memory. In "Letter from Birmingham Jail," King often employs the figure of speech called anaphora by repeating the same words at the start of successive clauses or sentences—for example, in the repetition of "I have" in "I have traveled the length and breadth of Alabama, Mississippi and all the other southern states. . . . I have looked at the South's beautiful churches with their lofty spires pointing heavenward. I have held the impressive outline of her massive religious education buildings" (38), as well as the repetition of "I doubt that" and "if you were to" (45). He frequently uses antithesis, juxtaposing contrasting ideas such as negative/positive and absence/presence in describing the white moderates' preference for "a negative peace which is the absence of tension to a positive peace which is the presence of justice" (23).

In "Meditation," Donne employs repetition and parallelism in similar ways; for example, by repeating "That action concerns me" and "some by" in the phrase "some by sickness, some by war, some by justice" in the beginning of the meditation. His repetition of the words "misery" and "miserable" in the sentence "[n]either can we call this a begging of misery or a borrowing of misery, as though we were not miserable enough of ourselves, but must fetch in more from the next house, in taking upon us the misery of our neighbors" is a good example of the way that repetition builds continuity in an oration through an accretion of similar words.

George Orwell, *Shooting an Elephant* and Contexts (p. 516)

1. Orwell's youth, bitterness, confusion, and feelings of helplessness are all crucial to his decision to shoot the elephant: "All I knew was that I was stuck between my hatred of the empire I served and my rage against the evil-spirited little beasts who tried to make my job impossible" (2). These emotions are compounded by his "intolerable sense of guilt" for being part of "the dirty work of Empire" (2). Even before he sees the elephant, Orwell is primed to take out his anger on what becomes a symbol of his entrapment. In addition, Orwell feels compelled to act without showing fear: "A white man mustn't be frightened in front of 'natives' [...]. The sole thought in my mind was that if anything went wrong those two thousand Burmans would see me pursued, caught, trampled on and reduced to a grinning corpse [...]" (9).

As Orwell looks back on his young self, his narrative assumes a tone of almost brutal detachment: "[A]fterwards I was very glad that the coolie had been killed; it put me legally in the right and it gave me a sufficient pretext for shooting the elephant" (14). This narrative voice is at odds with Orwell's earlier awareness of his situation and feelings, as if he has abandoned that self-awareness in order to describe precisely what he felt in the immediate aftermath of the shooting. In emphasizing his own brutishness, Orwell captures the effect on him of the empire in which he plays the part of "a sort of hollow, posing dummy, the conventionalized figure of a sahib" (7).

2. As Orwell prepares for the shooting, he becomes aware of the impossibility of his position: He is "only an absurd puppet pushed to and fro," trapped by the compulsion to "act like a sahib" and "impress the 'natives'" (7). Even though he knows "with perfect certainty that I ought not to shoot him" (6), he also knows that he must: "I had committed myself to doing it when I sent for the rifle" (7). Orwell's situation encapsulates his feelings about the British Empire: the cruelty he calls its "dirty work" (2) and "the futility of the white man's dominion in the East" (7). That Orwell bungles the shooting, inflicting on the elephant a slow, painful death, reinforces his guilt and sense of victimization. It is Orwell's experience as a cog in the wheel of the empire that the essay emphasizes, rather than the outcome. The incident of the elephant reveals to him "the real nature of imperialism" (2), not only because it reveals the relationship of the British to the Burmese, but because it shows Orwell's own participation in and powerlessness to resist the overwhelming presence of the empire.

3. Orwell might have refused to shoot the elephant because it was a valuable piece of property and belonged to somebody else, because it was unnecessary to kill an animal that might have been controlled, or because he did not want to be used by either the locals or the British as an instrument of destruction. Thus, he might have substituted the principles of respect for ownership rights, minimizing harm, or his own autonomy for the pragmatic reasons for shooting it, including

the need to demonstrate his authority and the possibility that it might kill more people or damage more property.

4. Orwell's story illustrates the paradox of tyranny: the despot sacrifices his own freedom. Consequently, this narrative might apply to any number of situations, including the French Revolution; Hitler's control of Germany through the Nazi Party; the takeover of Cambodia by Pol Pot, leader of the Khmer Rouge; Idi Amin's dictatorship of Uganda; or, more recently, Kim Jong Il's leadership of North Korea or Robert Mugabe's presidency of Zimbabwe.

5. This exercise works well when used in conjunction with Peter Elbow's "Freewriting" (Chapter 1). For Elbow, "The main thing is that a freewriting must never be evaluated in any way; in fact there must be no discussion or comment at all" (2). Freewriting about a painful or embarrassing incident can allow students to overcome anxiety and recollect their experiences more fully. Encourage students to write this first draft as a private exploration. In the second draft, students should avoid the temptation to give their narratives a neat resolution. Ask them to explore the ambiguity of their experience. Point out how Orwell's conclusion invites multiple readings of "Shooting an Elephant."

6. Students might consider several perspectives in their discussion of a particular action or decision, including how those involved were affected; the impact on society as a whole; the long-term consequences of the action or decision; how the action or decision violated laws, moral duties, or obligations based on friendship or family ties; considerations of justice; and protection of and respect for individuals' rights. Encourage students to keep their focus specific.

Lynda Barry, *Hate* (p. 522)

1. Lynda Barry portrays hate among young children as the expression of pure desire, such as for a toy, and motivated by childish egotism: "Although my first friendships were primitive, they certainly were honest" (panel 1). Later, Barry describes hate as a response to a physical threat: She hates kids who try to hurt her like Ronnie Delgado (panel 5). In exploring forms of hatred, Barry's friend argues that hating one's parents violates a "main rule of life" (panel 8), presumably because blood ties should be strong enough to transcend hate. Barry's new understanding that there might be limits to hatred suggests to her that hate may not always be an unmixed and overwhelming emotion. Yet, Barry finds her mother of little help in understanding her feelings: Her mother's language only thinly veils her own childish, primitive feelings (panel 4). For Barry, hate is defined in relation to love because learning to cope with strong emotions is part of her own and her peers' socialization. These children are learning how to differentiate their feelings for friends and for family, how to deal with those who might hurt them, how to control and express their feelings, and how to live with social conventions.

2. The distinction between "hate that has destructive intent" and hate as "a response to something destructive" (panel 17) helps Lynda understand that hate can be the source of irrational prejudice. Lynda's teacher helps her accept her feelings as rational and normal: She explains to her mother that she hates Ronnie "for shoving me" (panel 17). Lynda's note to her substitute teacher emphasizes with its punctuation the simplicity and transparency of her words and represents the clearness of her own feelings. Until she understands the distinction the teacher makes, Lynda searches for words that can "explain" hate (panel 12), none of which make sense or clarify her own emotions. Responses to the second part of this question will vary.

3. Barry's unattractive characters appeal to readers who experienced childhood as a time of rejection or insecurity, regardless of their physical or intellectual qualities. The characters are drawn to suggest more than their literal appearance—they convey to the reader Lynda's emotional experience of childhood. For example, Ronnie Delgado's spiky hair suggests aggression. The graphic art form allows Barry to exaggerate and simplify the appearance of the characters, which contributes to the interaction of text and image, and the spatial arrangement of the drawings and words in each panel in combination with their substance guide the reader in the construction of meaning. For example, in the first panel after the title panel, the two girls are placed in the center, are of similar size, and share the space equally, whereas in the second panel they are displayed to the left and a parent appears in a marginal role to intervene. The substitute teacher is the only adult to occupy a panel alone and facing the reader: She is the first authority figure that the children listen to and respect, her words incorporate the children's responses to her questions (panel 15), and, unlike the other adults portrayed, her body language parallels the children's in that she holds up her hand in panel 15, and the children hold up theirs in panel 16. The teacher should encourage students to examine how the graphic art form constructs meaning through the size and placement of the characters, the background of each frame, the positioning of the text, the presentation of characters' thoughts, and the use of extra authorial commentary (panels 11, 17) that support the narration.

4. and 5. Student responses will vary. However, the instructor should encourage students to examine how Barry's "Hate," like Spiegelman's "Mein Kampf" and Satrapi's "The Convocation," grounds its treatment of abstract concepts in a concrete narrative structure. For example, as Barry's younger self searches for language that might clarify her feelings, her teacher Mrs. Tink misinterprets the word "execrate" as "excrement" (panel 14). The narrator receives no help from adults in her search for self-understanding and self-expression, and those adults refuse to understand her efforts. Furthermore, most of the adults around her use obfuscating language to deny what the narrator experiences as real (panels 11–12). Similarly, Satrapi grounds her treatment of injustice in a specific issue—the dress code imposed on female students, Spiegelman develops the themes of childhood

fantasies and the problem of evil through his Cisco Kid outfit, his son's Superman pajamas, and his son's conflicted feelings toward King Kong (panels 9–end).

Michael Pollan, *An Ethic of Eating* (p. 533)
Barbara Kingsolver, *Home Cooking* (p. 541)

1. By advising readers to "just eat food," Pollan suggests that we should avoid the food products of our industrialized society, which he calls "foodlike substances" (1). For Kingsolver, dinner is "the cornerstone of our family's mental health" and the time at which "75 percent of my crucial parent effort" takes place (7). Kingsolver advises the reader to approach mealtimes "as a creative opportunity" that involves the entire family (13). Ask students to list the social, personal, practical, and cultural aspects of food. Does a meal offer the family a chance to participate in their cultural heritage? In their experience, what kinds of parenting and socializing go on at mealtime?

2. Following Pollan's advice would lead the reader to eliminate highly processed foods (7) and sugar. Gas stations, Pollan points out, stock "highly processed nonperishable snack foods" and soft drinks in "hefty twenty-ounce bottles" (22). Since drinks sweetened with high-fructose corn syrup are high in calories and low in nutritional value, eliminating them would immediately reduce calorie intake. Similarly, processed foods that are made with trans-fats, saturated fats, sodium, and sugar tend to be high in calories. Students can find many calorie counters online and information on nutrition at the Food and Nutrition site of the U.S. Department of Agriculture (www.usda.gov/wps/portal/usda/usdahome).

3. Kingsolver suggests that group participation can make cooking creative and fun. She uses the examples of pizza, which allows children to choose their toppings (16); having friends "share the work" of cooking (17); potlucks (17); and a "repertoire of unfussy recipes" that can be easily assembled (17). Kingsolver argues that cooking is "good citizenship" because it sustains local agriculture (22), teaches children "civility and practical skills" (22), and promotes good health (20, 23). Like Pollan, Kingsolver views meals as an important part of the human experience. Her argument supports Pollan's belief that one should "[s]hake the hand that feeds you (p. 160).

4. Students might include Pollan's advice that food should be unprocessed and thus perishable: "Don't eat anything incapable of rotting" is a simple but telling precept (5). Pollan's other precepts include: eat "ordinary food" (1), eat what your grandmother would recognize as food (2), avoid unfamiliar ingredients (9), and avoid complicated food (12). Kingsolver's advice includes developing simple, nutritious meals (15), cooking enough for more than one meal (15), sharing cooking knowledge (17), buying fresh ingredients (20), avoiding "corn syrup and added fats" (21), and buying locally grown foods (21).

5. Pollan and Kingsolver both strive to avoid preaching. Pollan injects humor into his advice, quotes experts, and provides the lists of ingredients from foods to allow the reader to see firsthand how artificial and complicated processed foods actually are (4–5). Pollan's main purpose is not to convert the reader to live or eat in specific ways, but to realize that "to reclaim [...] control over one's food" is to be part of a "large community to nourish and be nourished by" (30–31). Kingsolver acknowledges the busy lives that many people, especially working mothers, lead (9–12), and offers several practical suggestions on how to balance these demands with family meals (13–19). Both authors presume to advise the reader on the basis of their own experiences with food and because they consider the American diet to be an aspect of culture and potentially a serious social problem. Because they believe that eating is a community activity, not just a matter of fueling individual bodies, they speak out as part of their society.

Edward Hoagland, *Children Are Diamonds* (p. 547)

1. The various emergencies Hoagland describes include a group of hungry, armed children (1), pickpockets (3), "triaging kids who ought to go to the hospital" (4), AIDs (3–4, 20), a lack of supplies and medicines (5, 16), mechanical breakdowns (1, 6), ad hoc medical care (7, 13), malnutrition (9), warfare (11, 15), starvation (11, 14, 19), pillaging (14), widespread health problems (16), and displaced refugees (19). Hoagland characterizes "Africa" generally as a place of emergencies, but he also describes the particular problems each region or country faces: refugees in Kenya (2), Uganda's civil wars (10–11), tribal warfare in the Uganda-Sudan region (11–12, 14–15), and war in Sudan (20).

2. Hoagland performs triage when possible (4) and rations food (6) and medical care (7). Hoagland prioritizes the cases he faces on the basis of available resources and need. For example, in Kenya, he teaches the children who cannot go to school (4) and helps administer medical care "when nobody competent was around" (7). Hoagland's story about the lions that "have lost their sense of propriety" (19) illustrates how priorities shift in the chaotic world he describes. The lions normally avoid killing people and domestic animals to avoid "retaliation" (19), but their hunger and the wanton killing of lions by soldiers have broken down the boundaries that once allowed animal and human to coexist.

3. This chapter presents several different ethical principles that the student can use to discuss Hoagland's and other aid workers' efforts in Africa. For example, Peter Singer describes the utilitarian philosopher as "one who judges whether acts are right or wrong by their consequences" (5). Singer would probably see the work Hoagland describes as unambiguously good because that work prevents deaths and promotes the well-being of those who receive their aid. Jeffrey Wattles would probably consider Hoagland's work an unambiguous example of the golden rule insofar as one person can assume that an

act that sustains the life of another, especially a child, is the right thing to do. Hoagland's work recalls John Donne's declaration that we are all linked in our common humanity: "No man is an island, entire of itself," and thus "any man's death diminishes me, because I am involved in mankind." Martin Luther King offers a similar argument when he writes, "Injustice anywhere is a threat to justice everywhere" (4). In contrast, the "Eight Clergymen's Statement" ends with the appeal to civil rights protesters to "observe the principles of law and common sense" (7), a prescription that might seem ludicrous if applied to the circumstances Hoagland describes.

The Universal Declaration of Human Rights addresses nearly every aspect of the conditions Hoagland describes. The people he tries to help do not enjoy "the right to life, liberty and security of person" (Article 3) or freedom from being "arbitrarily deprived of [their] property (Article 17). The Declaration's concerns with standards of living, including the "right to work" (Article 23), "the right to rest and leisure" (Article 24), the "right to a standard of living adequate for the health and well-being of himself and of his family" (Article 25), and the "right to education" (Article 26), do not begin to address the basic survival issues Hoagland describes.

4. The lists convey the specificity of the needs of the people Hoagland seeks to help and the overwhelming nature of the situation. Also, the lists show that people's basic needs are not being met. For example, the street children need food and education (4) and the refugees face starvation (7). Hoagland also uses lists to convey the beauty of African nature and wildlife (12).

5. The phrase "nearer my God to thee" comes from a nineteenth-century Christian hymn by Sarah Flower Adams and is based on events in the book of Genesis. Hoagland adds to this phrase "without sectarianism" and thus implies that his use of "one Christ" should not be interpreted strictly as a reference to Christianity. Rather, he may be referring to the title "Christ," which is given to one who has transcended this world and attained enlightenment or a metaphysical illumination. Sectarianism refers to conflicts between groups on the basis of differing cultural beliefs and so may refer to both the religious and ethnic conflicts he witnesses in Africa.

Hoagland uses the metaphor of diamonds to convey the complexity of his experiences in Africa. Pressure and time transform carbon into translucent, strong, precious stones. Hoagland implies that his friend's experiences in Ethiopia, Somalia, and the Sudan have shown him that amid difficult and daunting conditions, he nevertheless witnesses and is sustained by the continent's endurance and beauty. Hoagland's final paragraph recalls his earlier statement that even amid "Christ's appalling work in the hinterlands" (6), facing "[h]undreds of passive, dying children" (7), the vitamins and food aid organizations hand out are a gesture of hope in the face of omnipresent death. The hardness of diamonds suggests that there is a material, real sense of God's presence in the midst of these horrors. For example, the nuns who are "seasoned heroes" who "don't believe that God is dead" (22), Hoagland suggests, have indelible faith and the tangible manifestations of that faith are the children who populate Africa.

Dorothea Lange, *Migrant Mother* (p. 556)

1. Lange directs the viewer's eye to the central figure, away from the three children. The soiled face of the sleeping baby is only partially visible, and the two other children lean on her for support, their faces turned away. The mother's frown suggests that she is stressed and anxious, and the furrows on her face give her the appearance of a woman older than her thirty-two years. Her posture suggests strength despite her exhaustion by the heavy burdens she bears. She appears both admirable and contemplative, as if thinking about how she will provide for her children. Her clothing is tattered and exposes the skin of her upper chest, reinforcing a sense of her maternity and vulnerability.

2. The composition suggests that the children trust and lean on their mother for survival and support. Like a conventional mother-and-child composition, the photograph encourages a sympathetic identification with the mother as a symbol of selfless love and courage. The children's anonymity encourages the viewer to imagine them as blanks upon which the face of any and every child may be projected. Thus, the intertwining of the figures has an archetypal significance. At the same time, the slightly disheveled state of mother and children and the mother's look of grave concern contrasts with the beatific image of a religious Madonna and child or a secular rendering of a mother and child, as for example, on a family's holiday card. This contrast invites the viewer to see the maternal figure as one of vulnerability and distress rather than one that sentimentalizes motherhood.

3. Lange's photograph represents maternal endurance at a pivotal moment in American history. The Great Depression had profound effects on the American psyche and "Migrant Mother" offers an intimate glimpse of that experience. The photograph also may embody for the viewer the qualities that American culture valorizes such as strength, self-reliance, and maternal devotion. Lange's description of the photo shoot suggests that she consciously shaped her subject, whose name was Florence Owens Thompson, into an archetype of a "hungry and desperate mother" (head notes). For example, Lange claims that she "did not ask her name or her history" and, given this limited contact, interprets her subject's thoughts for the reader of *Popular Photography*: "[She] seemed to know that my pictures might help her, so she helped me" (head notes). However, Lange does seem to have had enough conversation with Thompson to know her age, her husband's background, and how she and her children had been surviving. This context suggests that Lange sought to shape her subject and to present her relationship with her subject in a way that suited her artistic aims.

Peter Singer, *The Singer Solution to World Poverty* (p. 557)

1. Although responses will vary, students may want to consider the influence of being able to see and even to know the person or group who would be the recipient of the charity. Contributors often like to be able to picture the people who will benefit from their donations. This is the attraction of children's charities where the donor "adopts" a child and receives letters and a picture from the recipient. This may also be a factor when donors prefer local charities to those located far from home.

2. Peter Singer argues that the money we now spend on luxuries—anything over the $30,000 estimated to be needed for necessities—"should be given away" (22) to charity. His definition of "luxuries" is somewhat limited to a few leisure-related expenses (going out to dinner, vacationing, redecorating), though he also gives examples of buying expensive items when cheaper versions will do. The question of whether going to the movies is a luxury might depend on whether it is defined as a leisure activity or as a means of participating in cultural life. Readers might argue that going to see a film purely for entertainment is a luxury, whereas going to see what the filmmaker has to say in this form of artistic expression is not a luxury. This point of view relates to Berkowitz's critique of Singer mentioned in Question 4. Taking care of oneself and one's intellectual, physical, and emotional life, which Berkowitz terms "perfecting [one's] own talents," takes money. Some of the activities that Singer labels as "luxuries" may be necessities for nurturing oneself and maintaining one's productivity and creativity.

3. Among the reasons that people with the means to do so fail to donate to overseas children's charities, according to Singer, is the fear that the money will not be used for the intended purpose (11). Donors are discouraged by stories of corrupt governments and unreliable aid organizations diverting charitable donations to other uses rather than using the funds to feed the hungry. In addition, Singer says, people rationalize that someone else, perhaps someone else with more money, will donate, so that an individual's decision not to donate will not make an impact on the overall contribution (12). Within this rationale, an individual's decision not to donate does not mean that a child will starve because someone else will take care of it. The reverse of this rationale can also be a factor: Individuals may feel that since not enough others take responsibility, the burden should not fall disproportionately on them (19). Some potential donors may feel that their resources for donations are not infinite, necessitating a decision to limit the amount given and to give to some charities and not to others (15). Another reason is the belief that government should channel tax money to deal with the problem, not depend on private donations (20).

4. Student answers will vary. However, the instructor might encourage students to examine more complex scenarios than Bob's dilemma about whether to pull the switch or not. For example, many Americans give generously of their time and money to a variety of causes. As Berkowitz points out, the either/or reasoning

that Bob faces does not capture the many choices of those with extra disposable income. Nor does Singer address the financial pressures that middle-class families face to fund their children's education and provide them with culturally enriching experiences, to save for retirement and emergencies, and to pay for health care. Furthermore, Singer does not incorporate into his argument the important role consumption plays in sustaining the American economy and providing jobs. Berkowitz points out that moral choice often represents a "clash" between various needs and desires: Ask students whether it is more useful to discuss moral choices as points along a spectrum than as a simple choice between having and giving.

5. Relevant Web sites for this project include the following:

www.unicef.org
www.unicefusa.org
www.oxfam.org (the "Emergencies" link gives a list of current crises for children worldwide)
www.oxfamamerica.org
www.savethechildren.org
www.doctorswithoutborders.org.

Kelly Ritter, *The Economics of Authorship: Online Paper Mills, Student Writers, and First-Year Composition* (p. 563)

1. and 2. These questions ask students to analyze their writing process and thus promote a perception of "authorship as an intellectual, creative activity" (3). The instructor might remind students that research and revision are integral to authorship and that, as Ritter points out, "academic work itself is more than an economic means to an end" (4).

3. This question asks students to distinguish conventional research from primary and secondary sources, brainstorming, and the indiscriminate extraction from the Internet of any apparently relevant information. For most students, Ritter's survey indicates, research consists of reading secondary sources from the library. The instructor might ask students to read Linda Simon's "The Naked Source" (p. 320) for a discussion of writing history from primary sources. Classroom discussion of this question might also include how students can effectively use the Internet to do research by manipulating search engines and key words, by evaluating the credibility of Web sites, and by distinguishing among types of publications, including peer-reviewed journals. This question presents an opportunity to the instructor to help students use databases of academic and popular publications and of primary texts.

4. and 5. These questions ask students to consider how to develop what Ritter calls "the ethics of the writing classroom, and the larger university" (8) in the world of paper mills and multiple Internet sources. The instructor can help students respond to these questions by initiating classroom discussion of the

students' notions of themselves as "*consumers* . . . in a society defined by anonymity, convenience, and privacy" (3) and how "faculty definitions of authorship and intellectual property" conflict with some students' perception of writing "as an economic rather than an intellectual act" (4).

Natasha Singer and Duff Wilson, *Medical Editors Push for Ghostwriting Crackdown* (p. 570)

1. Singer and Wilson describe a specific kind of ghostwriting in which writers sponsored by drug companies make "extensive contributions" to a text that appears under the name of an academic author in a medical journal (1–4). Thus, these writers have an undisclosed conflict of interest. The International Committee of Medical Journal Writers defines an author "as a person who makes a substantial contribution to [...] a manuscript, and who approves the final version of an article"; the Committee wants authors to identify "other contributors to an article and their financing sources" (17). These stringent guidelines are appropriate for medical writing because published research on "life-and-death products like cancer and hematology drugs" (8) has a profound impact on people's lives. Decisions about health care should not, the authors point out, be based on research articles that are "skewed by the hidden influence of drug or medical device makers" (9). Ghostwritten autobiographies do not have an immediate or a profound impact on the welfare of the population, nor do they influence major policy decisions, such as those concerning health care.

2. "Scientific integrity" (1), the authors suggest, is compromised by undisclosed contributions to articles on medical research that are ostensibly authored by "independent academic authors" (1). Objective, unbiased research is important because health care policy and patient care decisions are often based on such research. For example, the drugs fen-phen and Vioxx, both of which were taken off the market (15), were the subjects of allegedly ghostwritten articles. Moreover, published research not only influences the use of a specific drug, it influences the "'direction of new investigation'" (26).

3. Published medical research that is biased violates the trust of patients, physicians, researchers, and government officials in the quality of scientific research and in the scientific community. Undisclosed bias violates patients' rights to good health care and diminishes their ability to make informed choices; it can lead to a misallocation of resources by channeling funds into inappropriate medicines and away from life-saving ones; it wastes researchers' and physicians' time and money; and it allows drug companies to manipulate markets and health care decisions and policies for profit.

4. Singer and Wilson suggest that the "honor system of disclosure" (1) has not been adequate: One study found a significant portion of ghostwritten articles in leading journals (20). In addition, the authors explain that policies that require

the disclosure of any contributing authors only asked for "incomplete informa-tion" and "typically had no teeth" (22). Ask students to examine this issue with respect to Ritter's "The Economics of Authorship." Do the pressures researchers face correspond to those of students who "believe that they can *and should* co-opt the accomplished authorship of others when necessary" (2)? How might research-ers experience, like the students Ritter discusses, a "cultural and ideological dis-connection from the system itself" (3)? Does the fact that the stakes are higher for medical publishing than for student writing make violations of an honor system more egregious?

5. Students might begin this assignment by referring to the Web sites of the International Committee of Medical Journal Editors (www.icmje.org) and the World Association of Medical Editors (www.wame.org). Students might consider defining an "author" and a "contributor," creating an objective review process for evaluating articles, listing disclosure guidelines, and establishing a process to investigate and respond to allegations of misconduct or plagiarism and a policy for publicizing the findings and decisions of that process.

8 THE ENVIRONMENT: WILL WE SAVE IT OR LOSE IT? WILL THIS BE THE END OF THE WORLD AS WE KNOW IT?

James P. Blair, *Haiti and the Dominican Republic* (p. 575)

1. The multiple impacts of environmental destruction that Diamond dis-cusses in "The World as Polder" suggest that poor environmental management policies have exacerbated the differences between Haiti and the Dominican Re-public. In Chapter 11 of *Collapse*, Diamond examines the contrasting countries in more detail, including differences in rainfall and water sources such as rivers, to-pography, soil, and population. The two countries also differ in culture, language, history, and socioeconomic development. For example, the Dominican Republic has strong European cultural roots and historical ties that have encouraged in-ternational investment, overseas trade, and the development of a strong middle class. In contrast, Haiti's population is dominated by former slaves who have received little help with economic development from European countries; Haiti's small farmers have relied on timber for fuel and intensive cultivation practices. In the Dominican Republic, per capita income is much higher than in Haiti, its population is less dense, and it has enjoyed greater political stability than Haiti. Encourage students to use Blair's photograph in their discussion of Diamond's treatment of the multiple dimensions of ecological systems and environmental problems. Diamond's two maps (p. 642) will also be useful in your discussion.

2. Blair's photograph might suggest two different scenarios to the readers of Gore's book: one in which their societies pursue sustainable environmental policies, and one in which undisciplined consumption leads to destruction. In addition to Diamond's "The World as Polder," Sandra Postel's "Troubled Waters" and William E. Rees's "Life in the Lap of Luxury as Ecosystems Collapse" would be excellent companion readings for this question. Encourage students to focus on how the political process, individual awareness, and education can reduce waste and promote good resource management.

3. Vaclav Havel, Jared Diamond, and Wendell Berry explore the problems that ecological crises pose for democracies; in contrast, Wangari Maathai bases her environmental activism on a grassroots movement. Ask students to examine these two approaches. What aspects of the political process promote or hinder sustainable resource management? Encourage students to be specific in their proposed policies by considering: the role of regulators, consumers, and local politicians; which industries would benefit from environmentally sound policies; whether schools, colleges, and universities could play a more active role in shaping issues and proposing solutions; and how international organizations such as the United Nations and the Intergovernmental Panel on Climate Change and environmental groups such as the World Wildlife Fund and Greenpeace help promote education and long-term solutions.

Terry Tempest Williams, *The Clan of One-Breasted Women* (p. 576)

1. Terry Tempest Williams chooses to identify herself with her grandmothers, mother, and aunts because she is a woman and she too has "a small tumor between my ribs diagnosed as 'borderline malignancy'" (1). Women in Utah, according to Williams, have been victimized by a male-dominated culture that conducted atomic-bomb experiments there in the 1950s and 1960s. Wanting to make women's voices heard, Williams appropriately chooses to identify with her female family members rather than the male members.

2. Williams ingeniously divides this piece into three sections, demarcated by the two dreams. The section preceding the first dream is the beginning, where she introduces her topic: nuclear victims, especially those in Utah in general and her female family members in particular. The first dream (or the haunting memory of a real horror) ushers in the next section, a brief history of nuclear testing and the awakening of the victims who eventually decide to resist the injustice and oppression imposed on them in the name of "patriotism or religion" (37). This section culminates in Williams's own awakening, her own decision to join "the clan of one-breasted women"—and to question authority. The second dream ushers in the third part of the essay, which includes her decision to take action (apparently imagined but probably real) against nuclear testing in Nevada and Utah. She is actually uttering a battle cry: "Women of all nations, unite!" The clan of one-

breasted women should not remain a "border tribe." They are "soul-centered and strong" (57).

3. Williams was brought up in a culture that respected authority: "For many years, I have . . . listened, observed, and quietly formed my own opinions, in a culture that rarely asks questions because it has all the answers" (32). Yet after many female family members die of cancer, she comes to realize that "the price of obedience has become too high" and that the "fear and inability to question authority that ultimately killed rural communities in Utah during atmospheric testing of atomic weapons is the same fear I saw in my mother's body. Sheep. Dead sheep. The evidence is buried" (32). Her essay (published as the epilogue to her 1991 book, *Refuge*) is a declaration of disobedience and, as living evidence to the victimization of Utah women, she wants to identify with the "buried evidence." She must question authority even if it means "becoming a border tribe among my own people," for "[t]olerating blind obedience . . . ultimately takes our lives" (37).

4. In the mid-nineteenth century, Horace Greeley evaluated the Humboldt watershed from an agro-business perspective: The desert lacked water and thus fertility, and its climate was severe; therefore, farming would not be profitable. In the mid-twentieth century, the Atomic Energy Commission looked at the desert from an urban-centric, Cold War perspective of geopolitics: The sparse population of the desert could not gather sufficient votes to challenge the policy of the power centers in big cosmopolitans; therefore, its residents were not significant politically. Their homeland thus was regarded as "virtually uninhabited" (38). The desert has been symbolized as a wasteland in Western literary tradition, while in the marginalized works of women, minorities, and environmentalists the desert vibrates with a life of its own. Williams is among the voices trying to correct people's erroneous impressions of the desert.

Responses to the latter part of this question will vary. The instructor might ask students to consider the spread of desert communities in terms of their costs and benefits to society and their impact on the ecosystem. Students will find Sandra Postel's discussion of "oasis cities" (8) in "Troubled Waters" useful in responding.

5. For Williams, writing as advocacy gives voice to those who lived through and suffered from atomic testing and its effects: contaminated milk as well as "burns, blisters, and nausea" (22). Her writing is also a protest of the "deceit" of the Atomic Energy Commission, which denied that radioactive fallout was harmful (22). Williams emphasizes that those for whom she decides to speak are "God-fearing" (26), patriotic, and religious (37), that is, those who do not "make waves" (30). Yet, her writing is also a form of civil disobedience, for writing about her "family nightmare" (36) is an act of defiance, one that makes her "a member of a border tribe among my own people" (37). Her act of trespassing along with other women on the military-owned Nevada Test Site is an extension of her writing: She refers to the pen and paper she carries to the protest as "weapons" (52).

6. This question asks students to consider the relationship between environment and cultural and personal values. Responses will vary, but the instructor should encourage students to use examples from these essays to support a particular stance. Ask students to keep in mind how Williams's willingness to become "a member of a border tribe among my own people" (37) suggests that she cannot abandon her culture even as she decides she must defy that culture's norms. In this sense, Williams's home determines her actions. Dillard seems to take the opposing view: Her life in the Virginia valley "is a fierce game I have joined because it is being played anyway, a game [...] in which the payoffs [...] might as well come to me as anyone else" (30). Dillard implies here that she has selected a particular place to glean its lessons for herself and thus that what she lives for has dictated her choice. Thoreau's advice to spend life "as deliberately as Nature" (7) might be interpreted in a number of ways: Ask students whether, for Thoreau, we can distinguish between who we are and the environment in which we live. Wangari Maathai suggests that individuals are inseparably shaped by where they live when she argues that individuals "are the primary custodians and beneficiaries of the environment that sustains them" (12). Encourage students to mine this vein by exploring their own relationships to their communities and culture.

Al Gore, *A Planetary Emergency* (p. 583)

1. The "planetary emergency" refers to the millions of tons of "global-warming pollution" that humans produce daily (3). Global warming, Gore argues, is endangering the North Polar ice cap (6), creating droughts and floods, and destroying farmland (8). Gore does not need to offer detailed evidence for his argument since the Peace Prize represents the recognition of his work along with that of the Intergovernmental Panel on Climate Change (head notes). The essays in this chapter by Havel, Rees, Carson, Postel, Diamond, and Berry offer abundant additional evidence that students can use to expand on Gore's discussion, and they can supplement this reading with their own research.

2. Gore declares that humanity's "war on the earth itself" has led to the threat of "'[m]utually assured destruction'" (13). The destruction that the earth and the life it supports now face has been produced by the long-term damage humans have inflicted on the atmosphere and climate. As a result of the heat trapped by our production of CO_2, we "are in danger of creating a permanent 'carbon summer'"(15), which would be as destructive as a "nuclear winter," in which nuclear explosions could "thrown so much debris and smoke into the air that it would block life-giving sunlight from our atmosphere" (14).

3. Gore suggests that solving the global warming problem requires the cooperation of governments: "We must begin by making the common rescue of the global environment the central organizing principle of the world community" (18). Vaclav Havel, William E. Rees, and Sandra Postel make similar arguments

about the necessity for collective action. For a different perspective, students should read Wangari Maathai's "The Green Belt Movement," which discusses the success of grassroots environmental activism. Wendell Berry's "Faustian Economics" also offers a contrasting approach: "The hope that we can cure the ills of industrialization by the homeopathy of more technology seems at last to be losing status" (10). For ideas on how students can evaluate their contributions to global warming and its management, see Questions 3–4 under Maathai, Question 3 under Saunders's "Kangerlua Glacier Melting," Question 5 under Diamond's "The World as Polder," and Question 6 under Berry's "Faustian Economics" in the *Instructor's Manual.*

4. Gore's plan involves understanding "the connections between the climate crisis and the afflictions of poverty, hunger, HIV-AIDS, and other pandemics" and "making the common rescue of the global environment the central organizing principle of the world community" (18). He also calls for an alliance among governments (19), particularly the governments of the United States and China, to act together (20).

5. Gore's plan calls for nations to "develop an agenda for mutual survival in a shared global environment" (50).

Wangari Maathai, *The Green Belt Movement* (p. 586)

1. Maathai started the Green Belt Movement in response to rural African women's needs for "firewood, clean drinking water, balanced diets, shelter, and income" (4). The movement began by organizing tree planting; trees were intended to provide "fuel, food, shelter, and income" to meet household needs and pay for children's schooling (8). The movement led to an educational program that helped the participants understand the relationship between "a degraded environment" and "poverty and even conflict" (9). Thus, this environmental work has had both political and social consequences: The participants "are empowered to overcome inertia and take action" (12) by working for democracy (14–15) and by promoting "good governance" (18). Maathai suggests that this model offers the potential to transform victims of poverty into politically active and responsible citizens: "Entire communities also come to understand that while it is necessary to hold their governments accountable, it is equally important that in their relationships with each other, they exemplify the leadership values they wish to see in their own leaders" (13). Although the world's regions have environmental needs, Maathai's model seems to offer an important lesson to any area where environmental damage exacerbates poverty.

2. Maathai argues that the poor African women she works with did not understand initially that environmental degradation produces, through competition for resources, "corruption, violence against women and children, disruption and breakdown of families, and disintegration of cultures and communities" (10).

Jared Diamond makes a similar argument (31), as does William R. Rees (12). The instructor might direct students to the two maps in Diamond's article (p. 642) to examine the coincidence of "political hot spots" and "environmental trouble spots" in the world: Diamond's point is that political instability and environmental destruction often go hand in hand.

3. and 4. Maathai emphasizes the link between the individual's willingness to act and the power of the community to effect change. She makes a powerful argument about education and the potential for individuals to change their lives. As she points out, the participants in the movement "come to recognize that they are the primary custodians and beneficiaries of the environment that sustains them" (12). Thus, each individual and the community as a whole are deeply invested in the local ecosystem. Ask students to compare different approaches to environmental management and activism: global versus local, individual versus collective, political versus educational. They might investigate how groups similar to the Green Belt Movement, those with a local focus and based on individual commitment, have brought about change in their own communities, cities, or states. Organizations such as the Sierra Club (www.sierraclub.org), Greenpeace (www.greenpeace.org), The Nature Conservancy (www.nature.org), and Grassroots Environmental Education (www.grassrootsinfo.org) are good places to start.

Vaclav Havel, *Our Moral Footprint* (p. 591)

1. Havel's title translates the idea of an "ecological footprint," which William E. Rees discusses in "Life in the Lap of Luxury as Ecosystems Collapse" (5–7), into an argument that humanity must take responsibility for climate change: "We can't endlessly fool ourselves that nothing is wrong and that we can go on cheerfully pursuing our wasteful lifestyles, ignoring the climate threats and postponing a solution" (7). Havel implies that each person on earth faces a moral choice by managing his or her consumption of the world's resources. Consumption is not, Havel implies, simply a matter of personal choice or income, but one that has moral ramifications for other people and for future generations.

2. Havel uses the metaphor of a loan to suggest that we do not "own" our planet in that we cannot use or waste its resources without regard to our own and others' well-being, and that using resources has consequences, like a debt that we must eventually repay. As several other authors in this chapter point out, the most significant contributors to this "debt" are wealthy, developed regions, such as the United States and Europe, and large cities. For example, as William E. Rees points out in "Life in the Lap of Luxury as Ecosystems Collapse," urbanization has accelerated per capita consumption of resources (5, 7–10), and the consumption levels of the wealthy nations of the world have led to massive resource depletion (12). Similarly, Sandra Postel, in "Troubled Waters," presents evidence that urbanization and industrialization are draining the world's sources of freshwater (14,

17–20). Jared Diamond echoes these concerns in "The World as Polder": "Our world society is presently on a non-sustainable course [...]. At current rates, we shall have depleted or destroyed most of the world's remaining marine fisheries, depleted clean or cheap or readily accessible reserves of oil and natural gas, and approached the photosynthetic ceiling within a few decades. Global warming is projected to have reached a degree Centigrade or more, and a substantial fraction of the world's wild animal and plant species are projected to be endangered or past the point of no return, within half a century" (30). Ask students to refer in their discussion to the photographs of the border of Haiti and the Dominican Republic (p. 575) and of the Kangerlua Glacier (p. 631), perhaps by exploring how these photographs illustrate Wendell Berry's argument in "Faustian Economics" that art deals "with the problem of limits" (30).

3. Havel suggests that political action and moral action should coincide: "[W]hat action is responsible or acceptable?" is the "moral question" that should guide our choices, "whether they concern the economy, society, culture, security, ecology, or civilization in general" (9). Havel also suggests that the trade-off between "civil freedoms" (8) and environmental management should be subjected to sober analysis and that we should focus on "practical policies" rather than make decisions on the basis of ideology (10). Thus, he argues that the political process should be harnessed to support sustainable environmental policies. Several of the essays in this chapter explore this connection between political action and environmental issues. For example, Al Gore, in "A Planetary Emergency," argues that the "world needs an alliance" of the "nations that weigh heaviest in the scales where earth is in balance" (19), focusing on the role of the United States, China, and India in reducing CO_2 levels (20). The essays by Wangari Maathai, William E. Rees, Sandra Postel, and Wendell Berry would make excellent companion readings for this question.

4. Havel enjoys a great deal of credibility with his audience because of his long political activism in support of democracy, his literary work, and his writing on human rights. He has earned the position of moral leader in contemporary society. By speaking out on climate change, he adds his voice to those of many others—scientists, economists, and politicians—who want to stop ecological destruction and bring about a sustainable relationship between humanity and nature.

5. The instructor may want to divide the class into groups, each of which focuses on a particular issue such as water management, energy resources, agriculture, CO_2 emissions, urbanization, pesticides, or demographics. Ask students to refer to relevant essays in this chapter, such as Postel's on water; Diamond's on energy, agriculture, and demographics; Carson's on pesticides; and Rees's on urbanization. The instructor may want to point out that practical solutions to the challenges Havel describes also entail an attitude shift, which several of these authors also explore. For example, in "Faustian Economics," Berry argues that

humans must give up the "fantasy of limitlessness," (6) whereas Carson points out "our distorted sense of proportion": "How could intelligent beings seek to control a few unwanted species by a method that contaminated the entire environment and brought the threat of disease and death even to their own kind?" (11).

Henry David Thoreau, *Where I Lived, and What I Lived For* (p. 594)

1. Students will recognize the distractions that Thoreau describes, such as the media (3), communications (4), and "routine and habit" (6). However, these demands on our time and energies are far greater today than in Thoreau's era and so more difficult to manage. The instructor may want to ask students to examine one or two thematically linked essays or images in *The Arlington Reader*, such as Heather King's "The Closest to Love We Ever Get" (Chapter 2), Simon McComb's "Education in Open Air" (Chapter 4), Nicholas Carr's "Is Google Making Us Stupid?" and Cathy Guisewite's "We Saw Paris" (Chapter 5), and Michael Pollan's "An Ethic of Eating" and Barbara Kingsolver's "Home Cooking" (Chapter 7). Students might focus their discussion of this question on technology, the demands of work and family, or urban life.

2. Thoreau's belief in minimal government would harmonize nicely with his faith in nature's instructive powers if everybody lived, as he suggests, with "simplicity," consumed only what food is "necessary," and avoided "luxury and heedless expense" (2). For Thoreau, government is part of an "unwieldy and over-grown establishment, cluttered with furniture and tripped up by its own traps, ruined by luxury and heedless expense, by want of calculation and a worthy aim" (2). Thus, Thoreau believes that political organization, like other expressions of modern material life such as railways and the post office, absorbs too much of our attention. The "great and worthy things" that he believes we should strive to know in preference to the "furniture" and "traps" that clutter our lives are not accessible through political activity, but through stillness, quiet, and openness to immediate experience: "In eternity there is indeed something true and sublime. But all these times and places and occasions are now and here. God himself culminates in the present moment, and will never be more divine in the lapse of all ages" (6). Ask students to consider how one might balance the practical realities of life with an awareness of what Thoreau calls "the reality that surrounds us" (6). Might this kind of balance resemble what Wendell Berry argues in "Faustian Economics" should be "our culture tradition," namely to define a credo according to which "we must do certain things and we must not do certain things" (20)? Can an active political consciousness and social life coexist with what Berry calls, in "A Secular Pilgrimage," the "eagerness to thrust through appearances toward a realization of the divine"? Are the political visions of Wangari Maathai, Rachel Carson, or Sandra Postel distinct from or compatible with the individual's pursuit of a "divine" relationship with the earth?

3. Students may want to set aside a particular time for this assignment, such as early in the morning or late at night, or when they are likely to be undisturbed. Ask students to forsake their electronic devices for the duration of the exercise. Many students will find that doing nothing can be quite difficult. Encourage them to persevere until, as Thoreau describes, they begin to see "the sun glimmer" (7) and to allow the mind to "mine and burrow" (8). Some students may find reading a poem such as Gerard Manley Hopkins's "God's Grandeur," which Berry excerpts in "A Secular Pilgrimage," helpful in calming the mind. Encourage students to use as a model one of the essays in *The Arlington Reader* in their writing. For example, students might want to study Annie Dillard's lively and precise observations in "Heaven and Earth in Jest," or emulate the spiritual focus and tone of N. Scott Momaday's "The Way to Rainy Mountain" or Heather King's "The Closest to Love We Ever Get" (Chapter 2), or the contemplative, reflective voice of E. B. White's "Once More to the Lake" (Chapter 3).

Annie Dillard, *Heaven and Earth in Jest* and Contexts (p. 599)

1. Annie Dillard and Henry David Thoreau (in "Journal") respond to and record their impressions of the natural world, bringing their concentrated attention to what they observe in their well-defined field of vision or "latitude" (Thoreau p. 608), just as astronomers train their telescopes on a particular point in the skies and watch patiently and carefully. Dillard and Thoreau see natural phenomena as holy in Thoreau's sense of coming from heaven—that is, related to fundamental questions of meaning in human life, such as the kinds of questions Dillard asks about the predominance of beauty or violence and about the presence or absence of God. Thoreau locates God in the steadily observed reality of the present moment. In his comparison of his own observations to an astronomer (meteorologist) watching a meteor, the meteor stands for a brief, fiery glimpse of that reality, similar to Dillard's experience of the world as "sparks and flames" (22).

In "Where I Lived, and What I Lived For" (p. 594) Thoreau calls his lifestyle "Spartan-like" (1), meaning that he aims to strip his lifestyle to the essentials so as to see life clearly. Others, according to Thoreau, live like ants or pygmies fighting with cranes, missing the essence of life in their routinized daily rounds and their attention to trivial matters (2). He uses a comparison to the German Confederacy to characterize a national life that is similarly focused on trivialities and materialist acquisitions (2). For Thoreau, a life focused on inessentials, such as the accumulation of wealth and technological advancement, is living like a baboon, whereas life focused on self-improvement is living like a man (2). Dillard emulates the life Thoreau describes in "Where I Lived, and What I Lived For": Thoreau's life at Walden is "unhurried and wise" and Spartan in its simplicity and allows him to focus on "great and worthy things that have . . . permanent and absolute existence" (6). Both writers try to live "as deliberately as Nature," seeking a natural pace of life that allows them to see beneath "the surface of things" (6). In addition, both are ready to see natural reality without blinders, to see both beauty and horror.

2. Dillard's allusions establish her as an educated person whose reading is wide and varied. She seems to be writing to a similarly well-educated audience. Her references to the Koran and to Blaise Pascal establish her right to discourse on theological matters. She is not just talking off the top of her head about the nature of God and his creation; she has studied both sacred and theological texts. With her more subtle allusions, those in which the author is not named, Dillard presupposes an erudite audience that is conversant enough with English literature to connect her glancing references to "fire" and "flames" (22) to Gerard Manley Hopkins's poem, "God's Grandeur."

3. and 4. The world Dillard describes is dynamic and vigorous. In a "continuous creation" (5), light pours down, the creeks reflect the blue sky, and her interaction with the plants, insects, and animals that inhabit the landscape creates its own en-ergy—an energy that manifests itself in the richness of her language. The narrator does not attempt to observe nature without disturbing it: She sees herself as part of the environment. Her experience is fully human; her presence, observations, and interactions are inseparable from her knowledge of the names and habits of the life forms around her. It is through this tangible, material experience, and her linguistic construction of that experience, that she captures the transcendence of nature. For example, the observation that the wind "crumples the water's skin" (33) represents an astute and concise use of language to depict a natural phenom-enon and forms part of a fleeting and yet profound experience, a "beautiful dream at the moment of being dreamed" (33).

5. The beauty of the world Dillard observes is "a grace wholly gratuitous" (18). By this, she means that "beauty and grace are performed whether or not we will or sense them" (19). We are only a small part of the mysterious beauty—and violence—that we observe in nature, and while we may not fully understand the world, we can observe it. Through understanding our own lives as "a faint tracing on the surface of mystery" (21), we begin to penetrate the darkness of that mystery.

6. Responses will vary, but the instructor should encourage students to em-ploy descriptive language to capture the quality of the places and objects they ob-serve, and to balance this with analytical language to give substance and discipline to their writing. A good example of such a balance is Dillard's observation of a frog collapsing "like a deflating football" (14) followed by her description of the giant water bug's method of attack (15).

Rachel Carson, *The Obligation to Endure* (p. 612)

1. You may want to encourage students to read Rachel Carson's piece to-gether with William E. Rees's "Life in the Lap of Luxury as Ecosystems Collapse," focusing on his argument about the Cartesian dualism that is "psychologically

separat[ing] humans from nature" in paragraph 2 and his quotation of William R. Catton about the "heady optimism of twentieth-century North America . . . sustained by a sense of unlimited abundance" in paragraph 10. Carson wrote "The Obligation to Endure" at the height of the "heady optimism"; therefore, many people in the United States, intoxicated by the "significant power" they had acquired, refused to imagine the kind of disaster that Carson depicts in the essay. Given her rhetorical situation, Carson chose the strategy of shock. Just as Henry David Thoreau did in the mid-nineteenth century, Carson tries to act as a "chanticleer in the morning, standing on his roost, if only to wake [her] neighbors up" (paragraph 7 in "Where I Lived, and What I Lived For").

Moreover, as a scientist, Carson added scientific evidence to her rhetorical statement: "The most alarming of all man's assaults upon the environment is the contamination of air, earth, rivers, and sea with dangerous and even lethal materials" (2). This human assault on nature would cause long-term and severe damage: "The rapidity of change and the speed with which new situations are created follow the impetuous and heedless pace of man rather than the deliberate pace of nature" (4). With the double power of science and rhetoric, Carson succeeds in alerting Americans who were previously unaware of how serious "contamination . . . could be" (2). Responses to the latter part of this question will vary. However, the instructor can pair Carson's essay with William E. Rees's "Life in the Lap of Luxury as Ecosystems Collapse," Jared Diamond's "The World as Polder," or Sandra Postel's "Troubled Waters," all of which incorporate abundant evidence of environmental degradation at the hands of human societies. Students could supplement their reading of one or more of these essays with independent research on a specific ecological topic.

2. Thoreau wants his fellow New Englanders to slow down and enjoy the finer fruits of life and Carson wants her neighbors to see that they are actually poisoning each other and the environment that sustains them: "Can anyone believe it is possible to lay down such a barrage of poisons on the surface of the earth without making it unfit for all life? They should not be called 'insecticides,' but 'biocides'" (7). Both might be considered ecological prophets in that both promote a philosophy of appreciating and preserving life. Thoreau focuses on the transcendent nature of reality and the conditions under which one might experience such transcendence, whereas Carson seeks to alert her readers of the real possibility of self-extinction. However, Carson's argument that humankind has "the obligation to endure" has an innate spirituality, for it suggests that life in itself is valuable.

3. Williams objects to language and policies that negate human life: She points out that the characterization of the Nevada Test Site as "virtually uninhabited desert terrain" makes her family and the wildlife that inhabited the area "virtual uninhabitants" (38). This question asks students to consider how cultural context determines the treatment and dissemination of scientific knowledge, as

Williams does when she describes the political environment during atomic test-ing: "The Korean War was raging. McCarthyism was rampant. Ike was it, and the cold war was hot" (20).

Although responses to the latter half of this question will vary, students should be encouraged to read Carson's piece together with related essays in this chapter: Sandra Postel's "Troubled Waters" (on the global water crisis) and Wil-liam E. Rees's "Life in the Lap of Luxury as Ecosystems Collapse" (on the ecologi-cal footprint of an urban society).

William E. Rees, *Life in the Lap of Luxury as Ecosystems Collapse* (p. 618)

Sandra Postel, *Troubled Waters* (p. 622)

1. According to William E. Rees, urban areas and high-income countries "use up to 9 hectares [22 acres] of productive land and water, [whereas] the earth contains only about 2 hectares of such ecosystems per capita" (9). In this sense, the "citizens of urban industrial societies" create a disproportionate drain on environmental resources, using up to more than four times their fair share of natural resources. It is hard for people, especially those who live in urban industrial societies, to realize that because "the Cartesian dualism . . . has been so successful in psychologically separating humans from nature that [people in Western civilization] simply don't conceive of [them]selves as ecological beings, as creatures of land" (2). Instead, they tend to regard "urbanization as further evidence of humanity's increasing technical prowess and independence from the land" (4). Once we perceive ourselves as above and beyond nature, we stop feeling responsible in our behavior for it and are thus blinded to the fact that we are actually using up other people's, including our grandchildren's, share of eco-logical resources. Rees's example is indeed shocking: "The ecological footprint of London, for example, is larger than the entire United Kingdom" (11).

2. Students should be encouraged to come up with their own definitions of "ecological footprint." However, you may find it helpful to have Rees's basic concept in mind: "[T]he ecological footprint of a population is the total area of land and water required to produce the resources that the population consumes, and to assimilate the wastes that the population generates, wherever on earth that land is located" (6). This concept is essential to Rees because it provides him with a foundation on which to reassess the role and responsibility of urban centers in the sustainable development of civilization. How long can we continue on this planet? Will our children and grandchildren be able to survive the aftermath of our luxurious lifestyle? We cannot start thinking constructively without first fac-ing the harsh principle that Rees offers in the concept of the ecological footprint.

Rees's tone is basically pessimistic, for he argues that our traditional optimism based on science and technology is misleading and dangerous. In a sense, Rees regards science and technology as the problem rather than the solution: "[O]ur ecological footprint is expanding, not decreasing, with increasing wealth and technological advances" (9). Quoting his colleague William R. Catton, Rees points out that we have been misled by a blind faith in science and technology and we will pay for it sooner or later: "[T]he heady optimism of twentieth-century North America, for example, has been sustained by a sense of unlimited abundance as we have exploited the continent's stocks of natural resources, particularly fossil fuels" (10). Rees's interpretation of that "temporary exuberance" is harsh: "[W]e have been consuming resources in this century that will therefore not be available in the next" (11). Unfortunately, many of us are still unaware of this urgent situation and still indulge in the fantasy of limitless development on the basis of unlimited resources. Consequently, "in many parts of the world, environmental degradation seems to have passed a threshold of irreversibility" and that "renewable resource scarcities of the next 50 years will probably occur with a speed, complexity, and magnitude unprecedented in history" (12).

Rees's statistics and argument are more than sufficient to alert readers to the urgency of understanding our behavior as environmental animals. Near the end of the essay, he offers reason for hope based on a big *if:*

> If we follow such ecological design principles, urban regions could gradually become not only more self-reliant, but also more socially rewarding and eco-logically benign. Through greater dependence on local ecosystems, city dwellers would become more aware of their connectedness to nature. As they became more conscientious stewards of the environment, their lives would become less materialistic; in turn, that change would reduce both cities' ecological footprints and the political tensions they would otherwise foster. (18)

3. Although responses to this writing project will vary, be sure to direct students to ground their responses in Rees's argument, citing his text as evidence. For example, Rees calculates the consumption level of an average person in terms of land and water usage (5) and the resources citizens of urban industrial countries use (9); he also discusses declining oil production (11), pressures on fisheries and forests (11–12), the importance of local recycling (14), and long-term urban planning (16–17).

4. The destruction of the Aral Sea is, as Postel explains, tragic in multiple ways. The "planned elimination" of the sea at the hands of "Moscow's central planners" and its "ongoing destruction" (2) led to the depopulation of the region, the loss of thousands of fishing jobs, and the spread of "toxic salt-dust chemical residue from the exposed seabed" on crops and villages (3). From a larger perspective, the destruction of the Aral Sea exemplifies "one of the greatest challenges facing humanity," satisfying the world's demand for water while preserving the "aquatic environment that sustains all terrestrial life" (4). Postel describes the many problems that high levels of consumption and government policies create for the management of water resources. Irrigation of dry areas to support crops has resulted in "[a]rtificial oasis cities" such as Phoenix (8); in addition, aquifers,

the source of much of the earth's "stable year-round water supply," are overdrawn in many places (10–12). The planned destruction of the Aral Sea for irrigating cotton in the central Asian desert illustrates the problems that competition for water presents worldwide (14–17). Just as the Aral Sea became the victim of what Postel describes as human arrogance (2), the Colorado River delta has been drained by the seven American states that share it with Mexico (18). Postel's argument that the world is overconsuming its water resources while depriving many of its people of safe drinking water (9) is supported by Rees's discussion of "the ecological footprint of a population" (5–6). Rees shows that increasing urbanization (3) has led to unsustainable levels of consumption of natural resources: "[C]ities typically impose an ecological footprint on the earth several hundred times larger than their political or geographic areas" (7). Specifically, although "the citizens of urban industrial societies use up to nine hectares of productive land and water, the earth contains only about two hectares of such ecosystems per capita. The consumer lifestyles of rich countries cannot be extended sustainably to the entire human population, using current technologies" (9).

Paul Saunders, *Kangerlua Glacier Melting* (p. 631)

1. As Jared Diamond explains, global warming will produce a "rise in global sea levels as a result of snow and ice melting," which "poses dangers of flooding and coastal erosion for densely populated low-lying coastal plans and river deltas" (20). Sandra Postel observes that the earth's supplies of freshwater are very small (6); because "rainfall and river flows are not distributed evenly throughout the year or across the continents" (7), melting glaciers will not necessarily add to those resources: "Every year two-thirds of the water in the earth's rivers rushes untapped to the seas in floods. An additional one-fifth flows in remote areas," including the Arctic (7). Melting glaciers are likely to add to rather than resolve the water management problems human societies currently face.

2. Rees, Carson, Postel, Diamond, and Berry draw attention to the economic costs of environmental mismanagement and destruction. Rees argues that the "consumer lifestyles of rich countries cannot be extended sustainably to the entire human population, using current technologies" (9). He supports this argument with evidence that agricultural and fisheries production is falling (11) and that resource depletion will worsen political and social conflict (12). Carson points to the costs of agricultural overproduction (11) and the economic and environmental consequences of excessive pesticide use (15–20). Postel shows that the destruction of water sources eliminates jobs and drives away local populations (3), creates enormous health costs (9), jeopardizes agriculture (11), and destroys wildlife habitats (20). As Diamond shows, all of these problems are linked (29); consequently environmental destruction, whether of water, land, fish, wildlife, or forests, and accelerated consumption of resources such as fossil fuels and

freshwater, will invariably create "a nonsustainable course" that will affect the socioeconomic conditions of all countries (30). Berry explicitly connects economic and environmental mismanagement: "[T]he economic fantasy of limitlessness in a limited world calls fearfully into question the value of our monetary wealth, which does not reliably stand for the real wealth of land, resources, and workmanship but instead wastes and depletes it" (9).

3. Students might read Wangari Maathai's "The Green Belt Movement" for an idea of how grassroots environmental activism can effect change. Question 6 for Annie Dillard's "Heaven and Earth in Jest" could offer a starting point for this assignment: Recording one's observations is the first step in identifying problems and proposing possible solutions. See also Question 3 for Rees's "Life in the Lap of Luxury as Ecosystems Collapse" in the *Instructor's Manual* for possible topics. Diamond's "The World as a Polder" is an excellent companion reading for this question. Wendell Berry refers to a specific problem that students may find useful to examine—the development of ostensibly "environmentally friendly" energy resources (4) in Kentucky. In the face of extensive support for programs such as he discusses ("Unbridled Energy"), might a grassroots response to a small environmental problem be not only more realistic but, in the long run, more effective? Ask students to consider whether individuals' choices can lead to national and global change. A good place to begin their research is the U.S. Environmental Protection Agency's Web site (www.epa.gov/climatechange/wyl.html).

Jared Diamond, *The World as a Polder* (p. 632)

1. This question helps students understand the intricate connections within an ecosystem and how environmental degradation is costly, diminishes our quality of life, and is unsustainable. Diamond points out, for example, that earthworms regenerate the soil, which helps sustain oxygen levels essential to human life (7). He also shows that the destruction of forests decreases the supply of raw materials such as timber, and also causes soil erosion (2), which reduces agricultural productivity (8). Moreover, forests provide other "ecosystem services," including the protection of watersheds (2), which are being increasingly depleted (12). Other examples are wetlands, the destruction of which endangers both "the quality of our water supplies" and "the existence of [...] freshwater fisheries" (3). The destruction of coral reefs affects the supply of saltwater fish (3), a major source of protein for humans (4).

2. Diamond's focus on the economic costs of environmental degradation gives students a specific way to analyze environmental problems and propose possible solutions. Encourage students to examine his arguments closely. For example, he argues that "at present conversion rates one-quarter of the forests that remain will become converted within the next half-century" (2). At current rates of coral reef damage, "about half of the remaining reefs would be lost by the year 2030" (3). He implies that we can protect resources through conservation

and management by controlling "conversion rates." Similarly, Diamond shows that citizens of rich, industrialized countries consume more scarce resources and produce more waste than inhabitants of developing countries (24). Diamond considers Western lifestyles an environmental problem not only because other countries' citizens aspire to those lifestyles (27), but because rich countries cannot sustain their current levels of consumption (28).

3. Diamond argues that demographic and consumption patterns are key factors in understanding the environmental problems we face. Diamond suggests that policy makers should focus on the "per capita impact" of consumption, which is highest in rich, industrialized countries (24). Other factors that affect population growth are public health (22), the age structure of the population (23), immigration patterns (25), and living standards (25–26). A workable solution would also have to take into account the cultural and social role of high living standards: Diamond argues that developed nations cannot hinder "the Third World's efforts to catch up" even though "First World living standards" are unsustainable across the globe (28). He also contends that the citizens of the developed world are unlikely to lower their consumption and rates of waste production (28). Encourage students to take a global, holistic approach to this question with a focus on long-term sustainability.

4. Diamond's two maps (p. 642) will help answer this question. Wealthy countries have largely avoided facing the worst consequences of environmental destruction because they have the economic resources to maintain high living standards in the face of rising costs of energy, water, and agriculture. Poorer countries have fewer resources with which to manage their industrial, agricultural, and social needs, which exacerbates environmental stress. Diamond argues that citizens of wealthy countries are unlikely to decrease their levels of consumption (28) and that refusing to make choices will inevitably spark crises: "The world's environmental problems *will* get resolved, in one way or another, within the lifetimes of the children and young adults alive today. The only question is whether they will become resolved in pleasant ways of our own choice, or in unpleasant ways not of our choice, such as warfare, genocide, starvation, disease epidemics, and collapses of societies" (31). Diamond suggests here that there cannot be an ideal world, such as the one the U.N.'s Universal Declaration of Human Rights envisions; rather, we must make realistic choices about global living standards and face up to the trade-offs between consumption and sustainability. Diamond's reference to the collapses of past societies suggests that human beings are loath to face such difficult decisions (2). His analysis also suggests that the difference between these past events and those we currently face lies in the global nature of the present crisis.

5. This question allows students to implement many of the concepts Diamond uses, as well as those in Rees's "Life in the Lap of Luxury as Ecosystems Collapse" and other essays in this chapter. Many online resources allow users to

evaluate the environmental impact of various consumer products. Students might begin with Good Guide (www.goodguide.com) and the U.S. Environmental Protection Agencys (www.epa.gov), including its "MyEnvironment" search engine, its link "EPA for Concerned Citizens" (www.epa.gov/epahome/citizen.htm), and the links under "Learn the Issues."

Wendell Berry, *Faustian Economics* (p. 644)

1. Berry begins with an anecdote to illustrate his claim that our belief in an "indestructible" (1) and "limitless" society is a "collective delusion of grandeur" (2)—an energy summit in Kentucky focused on the continued support of unlimited consumption and growth and ignored "temperance or thrift or the ecological law of return" (4). Berry's main purpose is not to present scientific evidence but to discuss how the consumption of global resources has become disconnected from "our cultural heritage" (18) and thus has led to an irresponsible relationship with our environment. He suggests that science cannot be relied upon to "'find an answer'" (1), because the problem of environmental degradation lies in our failure to understand ourselves as "limited creatures in a limited world" (10). With this goal in mind, Berry offers several supporting arguments that our culture fosters waste. He argues that "the commonly accepted basis of our economy is the supposed possibility of limitless wealth" (5), and that along with this idea has arisen the belief that "*all* are entitled to pursue without limit whatever they conceive as desirable" (5). He cites the coincidence of the industrial revolution with the "suddenly exploitable resources of the New World" (6) as one source of this misconceived optimism.

2. Berry argues that the credo of limitless consumption produces "a sort of moral minimalism" (8). This "desire to be efficient at any cost, to be unencumbered by complexity" (8) leads us, as if we are "spoiled children," to expect the fulfillment of our desires and to abandon "neighborliness, respect, reverence, responsibility, accountability, and self-subordination" (8). Thus, the fantasy of limitless consumption and growth comes at the inevitable cost of failure to recognize that the human condition is necessarily limited: We have "insistently" defined ourselves "as *limitless* animals—which is of course a contradiction in terms" (3). Diamond supports this argument by showing that undisciplined consumption leads to social conflict and even collapse. For example, he points out that deforestation "was a or *the* major factor in all the collapses of past societies described in this book" (2), that deaths from air pollution are estimated at over 130,000 a year (15), and that environmental contaminants are probably responsible for "the steep decline in sperm count in many human populations over the last several decades" (15). He also points out that environmental and population problems contributed to recent genocides, wars, starvation, and political instability (32).

3. Marlowe's Mephistopheles carries his hell with him: "[W]here we [the damned] are is hell" (14). Marlowe implies here that the experience of hell is not confined to a place, but consists of the suffering a being inflicts on himself and those who fall within his influence. Berry argues that Marlowe and Milton teach us that the inability to accept limits is a "fatal mistake" (26). Only by accepting limits can individuals sustain their society: "An ecosystem, even that of a working forest or farm, so long as it remains ecologically intact, is inexhaustible" (27). American society now must face the choice of accepting limits or self-destructing: "[W]e are entering a time of inescapable limits," and we must recognize that "science and technology" will not allow us to escape the consequences of "our economic stupidity" (10).

4. The Faustian bargain that contemporary society has made, Berry argues, is trading away our future for a temporary fantasy of absolute knowledge and power. "Faustian economics" describes the belief that we need not live within "natural limits" and self-imposed "cultural limits" (11). Berry's reader is likely to be receptive to his argument. This essay was first published in *Harper's*, a periodical that caters to an educated audience likely to be familiar with the literary sources Berry uses and with his work as a poet and essayist. In a sense, Berry's description of our insistence on thoughtless consumption also explains why it is so difficult to turn away from the destructive path he sees before us: The belief that "all of us are 'free' to be as conspicuously greedy and wasteful" as we like is ingrained in our culture (2). Although his argument is persuasive, his audience may be daunted by the strength of the ideology that Berry so effectively describes.

5. Berry argues that the "disease of limitlessness" is the product of our attitude toward ourselves as "*limitless* animals" (3); consequently, the solution lies in a shift of perspective: We must deal "with the problem of limits" (30). His belief that the arts are a source of cultural strength in this endeavor is based on the idea that it is "the artists, not the scientists, who have dealt unremittingly with the problem of limits" (30). Berry suggests here that cultural resources and thinkers from nonscientific areas of life can contribute to resolving the ecological crisis we face by creating a new understanding that we are "limited creatures in a limited world" (10). Students will find that each of the essays in this chapter is oriented toward attitudes (Terry Tempest Williams, Henry David Thoreau, Annie Dillard); scientific, economic, and political analysis (Al Gore, William E. Rees, Sandra Postel, Jared Diamond); or a combination of both approaches (Wangari Maathai, Vaclav Havel, Rachel Carson). Encourage students to choose readings from more than one camp to ensure a nuanced discussion.

6. Question 5 under Diamond's essay and Question 3 under Paul Saunders's photograph in the *Instructor's Manual* suggest how students can begin their research on environmental issues. In addition to these sources, students should look at the Division on Earth & Life Studies page of the National Academies' Web site (www.dels.nas.edu). This assignment is a great opportunity to help students ori-

ent themselves in their university or college library, learn to use data sources, and begin to evaluate the quality of Web sites. Students may need help in being as specific as possible in their plan and in using local resources. The U.S. Environmental Protection Agency (www.epa.gov) and Scorecard: The Pollution Information Site (www.scorecard.org) are good places to start.

PAIRED READINGS: BAD SCIENCE

ROBERT L. PARK

The Seven Warning Signs of Bogus Science

From the unverifiable claims of cold fusion experiments to plans for building a livable atmosphere on Mars, misleading, fallacious, and economically impractical ideas abound, masquerading as science, according to Robert L. Park. Labeling these claims "voodoo science," Park has devoted himself to informing and educating the public about scientific accuracy. Far from berating readers for being uninformed, however, his main target is bad information promulgated by government and media sources. Park's background is one of practical experience and theoretical depth. After serving as an electronics officer in the United States Air Force (1951–1956), he studied physics at the University of Texas (B.S., 1958; M.A., 1960) and Brown University (Ph.D., 1964). He worked at Sandia Laboratories for a decade until becoming a physics professor at the University of Maryland at College Park, where he continues to teach.

Park's writing in Voodoo Science: The Road from Foolishness to Fraud *(2000), ten essays for a lay audience, has been praised in* Science *as "an articulate and skeptical voice of reason about science," using "pathological science as a starting point for far-reaching discussions of science and society." Superstition: Belief in the Age of Science (2008) questions the continued existence of religion in the face of scientific discovery. "The Seven Warning Signs of Bogus Science," originally published in the* Chronicle of Higher Education *(January 31, 2003) offers policy makers and the general public a skeptic's guide to suspicious scientific claims.*

The National Aeronautics and Space Administration is investing close to a million dollars in an obscure Russian scientist's antigravity machine, although it has failed every test and would violate the most fundamental laws of nature. The Patent and Trademark Office recently issued Patent 6,362,718 for a physically impossible motionless electromagnetic generator, which is supposed to snatch free energy from a vacuum. And major power companies have sunk tens of millions of dollars into a scheme to produce energy by putting hydrogen atoms into a state below their ground state, a feat equivalent to mounting an expedition to explore the region south of the South Pole.

There is, alas, no scientific claim so preposterous that a scientist cannot be found to vouch for it. And many such claims end up in a court of law after they have cost some gullible person or corporation a lot of money. How are juries to evaluate them?

Before 1993, court cases that hinged on the validity of scientific claims were usually decided simply by which expert witness the jury found more credible. Expert testimony often consisted of tortured theoretical speculation with little or no supporting evidence. Jurors were bamboozled by technical gibberish they could not hope to follow, delivered by experts whose credentials they could not evaluate.

In 1993, however, with the Supreme Court's landmark decision in *Daubert* v. *Merrell Dow Pharmaceuticals, Inc.* the situation began to change. The case involved Bendectin, the only morning-sickness medication ever approved by the Food and Drug Administration. It had been used by millions of women, and more than 30 published studies had found no evidence that it caused birth defects. Yet eight so-called experts were willing to testify, in exchange for a fee from the Daubert family, that Bendectin might indeed cause birth defects.

In ruling that such testimony was not credible because of lack of supporting 5 evidence, the court instructed federal judges to serve as "gatekeepers," screening juries from testimony based on scientific nonsense. Recognizing that judges are not scientists, the court invited judges to experiment with ways to fulfill their gate-keeper responsibility.

Justice Stephen G. Breyer encouraged trial judges to appoint independent experts to help them. He noted that courts can turn to scientific organizations, like the National Academy of Sciences and the American Association for the Advance-ment of Science, to identify neutral experts who could preview questionable scien-tific testimony and advise a judge on whether a jury should be exposed to it. Judges are still concerned about meeting their responsibilities under the *Daubert* decision, and a group of them asked me how to recognize questionable scientific claims. What are the warning signs?

I have identified seven indicators that a scientific claim lies well outside the bounds of rational scientific discourse. Of course, they are only warning signs— even a claim with several of the signs could be legitimate.

1. **The discoverer pitches the claim directly to the media.** The integrity of sci-ence rests on the willingness of scientists to expose new ideas and findings to the scrutiny of other scientists. Thus, scientists expect their colleagues to reveal new findings to them initially. An attempt to bypass peer review by taking a new result directly to the media, and thence to the public, suggests that the work is unlikely to stand up to close examination by other scientists.

   One notorious example is the claim made in 1989 by two chemists from the University of Utah, B. Stanley Pons and Martin Fleischmann, that they had discovered cold fusion—a way to produce nuclear fusion without ex-pensive equipment. Scientists did not learn of the claim until they read re-ports of a news conference. Moreover, the announcement dealt largely with the economic potential of the discovery and was devoid of the sort of details that might have enabled other scientists to judge the strength of the claim or to repeat the experiment. (Ian Wilmut's announcement that he had success-fully cloned a sheep was just as public as Pons and Fleischmann's claim, but in the case of cloning, abundant scientific details allowed scientists to judge the work's validity.)

   Some scientific claims avoid even the scrutiny of reporters by appear-ing in paid commercial advertisements. A health-food company marketed a dietary supplement called Vitamin O in full-page newspaper ads. Vitamin O turned out to be ordinary saltwater.

2. **The discoverer says that a powerful establishment is trying to suppress his**   10
   or her work. The idea is that the establishment will presumably stop at nothing to suppress discoveries that might shift the balance of wealth and power in society. Often, the discoverer describes mainstream science as part of a larger conspiracy that includes industry and government. Claims that the oil companies are frustrating the invention of an automobile that runs on water, for instance, are a sure sign that the idea of such a car is baloney. In the case of cold fusion, Pons and Fleischmann blamed their cold reception on physicists who were protecting their own research in hot fusion.

3. **The scientific effect involved is always at the very limit of detection.** Alas, there is never a clear photograph of a flying saucer, or the Loch Ness monster. All scientific measurements must contend with some level of background noise or statistical fluctuation. But if the signal-to-noise ratio cannot be improved, even in principle, the effect is probably not real and the work is not science.

   Thousands of published papers in parapsychology, for example, claim to report verified instances of telepathy, psychokinesis, or precognition. But those effects show up only in tortured analyses of statistics. The researchers can find no way to boost the signal, which suggests that it isn't really there.

4. **Evidence for a discovery is anecdotal.** If modern science has learned anything in the past century, it is to distrust anecdotal evidence. Because anecdotes have a very strong emotional impact, they serve to keep superstitious beliefs alive in an age of science. The most important discovery of modern medicine is not vaccines or antibiotics, it is the randomized double-blind test, by means of which we know what works and what doesn't. Contrary to the saying, "data" is not the plural of "anecdote."

5. **The discoverer says a belief is credible because it has endured for centuries.** There is a persistent myth that hundreds or even thousands of years ago, long before anyone knew that blood circulates throughout the body, or that germs cause disease, our ancestors possessed miraculous remedies that modern science cannot understand. Much of what is termed "alternative medicine" is part of that myth.

   Ancient folk wisdom, rediscovered or repackaged, is unlikely to match the   15
   output of modern scientific laboratories.

6. **The discoverer has worked in isolation.** The image of a lone genius who struggles in secrecy in an attic laboratory and ends up making a revolutionary breakthrough is a staple of Hollywood's science-fiction films, but it is hard to find examples in real life. Scientific breakthroughs nowadays are almost always syntheses of the work of many scientists.

7. **The discoverer must propose new laws of nature to explain an observation.** A new law of nature, invoked to explain some extraordinary result, must not conflict with what is already known. If we must change existing laws of nature or propose new laws to account for an observation, it is almost certainly wrong.

I began this list of warning signs to help federal judges detect scientific nonsense. But as I finished the list, I realized that in our increasingly technological society, spotting voodoo science is a skill that every citizen should develop.

STANLEY FISH

Academic Cross-Dressing: How Intelligent Design Gets Its Arguments from the Left

Stanley Fish's prominence as a literary and cultural critic is intertwined with his reputation as an academic mover, shaker, and gadfly. This is seen in his administrative work as English Department head at Duke University and as dean of Liberal Arts and Sciences at the University of Illinois at Chicago. His writings, too, are provocative: Is There a Text in This Class? *(1986),* "The Unbearable Ugliness of Volvos" *(1994),* There's No Such Thing as Free Speech: And It's a Good Thing, Too *(1994), and* Save the World on Your Own Time *(2008).*

Born in 1939 in Providence, Rhode Island, Fish earned a Ph.D. in English from Yale (1962) and taught at the University of California, Berkeley, Johns Hopkins, as well as at Duke and Florida International University. Fish's work often focuses on "interpretive communities"—how and why readers accept a common set of foundational assumptions as the basis for interpreting what they read and think. This reader-response view undergirds his books on Milton, Surprised by Sin *(1967) and* How Milton Works *(2001), as well as his interpretation of the way people lock themselves into doctrinaire positions in "Academic Cross-Dressing: How Intelligent Design Gets Its Arguments from the Left," originally published in* Harper's Magazine *(December 2005).*

When George W. Bush said recently that evolution and Intelligent Design should be taught side by side, so that students "can understand what the debate is about," he probably didn't know that he was subscribing to the wisdom of Gerald Graff, a professor of English at the University of Illinois, Chicago, and a founder of Teachers for a Democratic Culture, an organization dedicated to "combating conservative misrepresentations" of what goes on in college classrooms. Graff and Intelligent Design are now a couple on the Internet; a Google search for both together will turn up more than 100,000 pages, even though Graff had never written a word on the subject until he wrote in protest against his having been "hijacked by the Christian Right." What the Christian Right took from him (without acknowledgment) was the idea that college instructors should "teach the conflicts" around academic issues so that students will learn that knowledge is neither inertly given nor merely a matter of personal opinion but is established in the crucible of controversy. What is ironic is that although Graff made his case for teaching the controversies in a book entitled *Beyond the Culture Wars,* the culture wars have now appropriated his thesis and made it into a weapon. In the Intelligent Design army, from Bush on down to every foot soldier, "teach the controversy" is the battle cry.

It is an effective one, for it takes the focus away from the scientific credibility of Intelligent Design—away from the question, "Why should it be taught in a biology class?"—and puts it instead on the more abstract issues of freedom and open inquiry. Rather than saying we're right, the other guys are wrong, and here are the scientific reasons why, Intelligent Design polemicists say that every idea should at least get a hearing; that unpopular or minority views should always be represented; that questions of right and wrong should be left open; that what currently counts as knowledge should always be suspect, because it will typically reflect the interests and preferences of those in power. These ideas have been appropriated wholesale from the rhetoric of multiculturalism—a school of thought, emerging from the 1960s left, that proceeds from the unimpeachable observation that there are many different standards of judgment in the world to the unwarranted conclusion that judgment should therefore be dethroned entirely. Multiculturalism's goal was to gain acceptance for practices ruled out of bounds by established authority; its strategy was not to put new forms of authority in place of the old ones (which would have required the constructing of arguments) but instead to render all authority illegitimate, by explaining it away as the accidental ascendancy of one tradition over its equally worthy rivals. Why should we accept a canon of literature put in place by dead white males? Why should we stigmatize homosexual behavior just because it is condemned by a few church fathers? Once questions like these are posed and the expected answer—there is no reason, just prejudice and custom—has been given, the way is open for any constituency to play the same game. If multiculturalists can defend gay marriage by challenging the right of a church or a state to define what marriage is, why can't Intelligent Design proponents demand equal time in the classroom by challenging the right of Ivy League professors to say what science is?

One needn't believe in this line of argument in order to employ it; it is purely a matter of tactics. Phillip E. Johnson, a leading Intelligent Design advocate, is quite forthright about this. "I'm no postmodernist," he declares in a 1996 interview with the sociologist Amy Binder, but "I've learned a lot" from reading them. What he's learned, he reports, is how to talk about "hidden assumptions" and "power relationships," and how to use those concepts to cast doubt on the authority of "science educators" and other purveyors of the reigning orthodoxy. His views, he says, "are considered outlandish in the academic world," but the strategy he borrows from the postmodernists—the strategy of claiming to have been marginalized by the powers that be—is, he boasts, "dead-bang mainstream academia these days."

This is nothing if not clever. In an academy where talk of "marginalization" and "hegemonic exclusion" is routine, Johnson and his friends can use that talk—in which they have no real stake—to gain a hearing for ideas that have failed to make their way in the usual give-and-take of the academic debates Graff celebrates. In Graff's book, "teach the controversy" is a serious answer to a serious question:

namely, how can we make students aware of the underlying issues that structure academic discourse? In the work of Johnson and other Intelligent Design proponents, "teach the controversy" is the answer to no question. Instead it is a wedge for prying open the doors of a world to which they have been denied access by gatekeepers—individual scientists, departments of biology, professional associations, editors of learned journals—who have found what they say unpersuasive. In their hands, the idea of teaching the controversies ceases to be an academic proposal directed at teachers and students and becomes a political proposal directed at legislators, school boards, and the general public.[1] They say "teach the controversy," but what they mean is that biology, having rejected Intelligent Design on scientific grounds, should nevertheless be forced to include it on the larger grounds of fairness.

The sleight of hand here is to deflect attention from the specific merits of one's claims by attaching them to some general truth or value that can then be piously affirmed. This is why Intelligent Design advocates so often urge a long view of history. Isn't it the case, they ask, that it was once evolutionary theory that was kept out of some classrooms in this country? That proved to be an error; isn't it possible that, someday, refusing to teach Intelligent Design in science classes will be thought to have been an error, too? After all, haven't many once-discredited theories been accepted by a later generation of scholars? And doesn't history show us that apparently settled wisdom is often kept in place by those whose careers are invested in it? Although the answer to all these questions is undeniably yes, the mistake—and it is one made by some postmodern thinkers and seized upon by conservative polemicists—is to turn the fact of past error into a reason for distrusting any and all conclusions reached in the present. The judgment of experts is not discredited generally because it has occasionally turned out to be wrong; one has to go with the evidence one has, even if that evidence may be overtaken in the long run. It is no method at all to say that given our uncertainty as to what might turn up in the distant future, we therefore should systematically distrust what now appears to us to be sound and true.

Unfortunately (or fortunately for the Intelligent Design agenda), this is precisely what is said by multiculturalists and some postmodernists; and in saying it they have merely drawn out the implications of one strain of liberalism, the strain that finds its source in John Stuart Mill. In *On Liberty*, Mill insists that knowledge not meeting the test of repeated challenge is not really knowledge; indeed, he goes so far as to recommend that when a settled conclusion seems to have no challengers, some must be invented, for in his view the process of debate and controversy is more important than any conclusions it might deliver. This is also the prevailing view of First Amendment doctrine, as articulated by *New York Times* v. *Sullivan* (1964), a case in which the values of truth and accuracy are subordinated to the supposedly greater value of "uninhibited, robust, and

[1]This is why they regard as evidence the fact that, according to a recent poll, 65 percent of the American population wants the creation account found in Genesis to be taught side by side with Darwinism; the scientific response to that—or any other—number is, "So what?"

wide-open" discussion. In its opinion the Court blurs the distinction between true and false statements by recharacterizing the latter (in a footnote that cites Mill) as a "valuable contribution to the public debate," thus paving the way for those who, like the advocates of Intelligent Design, assert that their views deserve to be considered (and taught), even when—especially when—the vast majority of authorities in the field have declared them to be without scientific merit. It is an assertion that liberals by and large resist when the message is racist or sexist, but it is a logical consequence of liberalism's privileging of tolerance over judgment.

Liberalism privileges tolerance because it is committed to fallibilism, the idea that our opinions about the world, derived as they are from the local, limited perspectives in which we necessarily live, are likely to be in error even when—again, especially when—we are wholly committed to them. If God or God's representative is removed as the guarantor of right judgment, all that remains is the judgment of fallible men and women who will be pretending to divinity whenever they confuse what seems to them to be true for what is really true. Because this mistake is natural to us, because the beliefs we acquire always seem to us to be perspicuous and indubitable, it is necessary, liberalism tells us, to put obstacles in the way of our assenting too easily to what are finally only our opinions. One way to do this is to institutionalize Mill's advice and to require, as a matter of principle, a diversity of views with respect to any question. The *New York Times* v. *Sullivan* decision quotes with approval Judge Learned Hand's declaration that in essence the First Amendment "presupposes that right conclusions are more likely to be gathered out of a multitude of tongues, than through any kind of authoritative selection." Typically, those who make pronouncements like this assume (without saying so) that the tongues making up the multitude will belong to persons who are committed to the protocols of rational inquiry; frivolous persons, persons who exploit those protocols or play with them to gain political ends, are not imagined. (When Graff counsels "teach the controversy," he means teach the real controversies, not the manufactured ones.) But nothing in a statement like Hand's rules them out, and once "authoritative selection" has been discounted and even rendered suspect because of its necessarily fallible origins, there is no reason at all for excluding any voice no matter how outlandish its assertions. After all, who's to say?

Intelligent Designers are not the first denizens of the right to borrow arguments and strategies from the liberal and postmodern left. In the early 1990s the Holocaust denier Bradley Smith was able to place an ad—actually an essay—in college student newspapers in part because he presented his ideas under the heading "The Holocaust Controversy: The Case for Open Debate." Not the case for why there was no campaign to exterminate the Jews, or for why the Nazis were innocent of genocidal thoughts, or for why Holocaust-promoting Jews are just trying to drum tip "financial support for Jewish causes"—though all these things were asserted in the body of the ad—but the case for open debate, and how could anyone, especially an academic, be against that? Ours is not a "radical point of view," Smith asserts. We are just acting on premises that "were worked out some time ago during a little something called the Enlightenment." In short, we are the true liberals, and it is the scholars who have become "Thought Police" either by actively working to exclude us or by sitting "dumbly by, allowing campus totalitarians to determine what can be said and what can be read on their campus."

Proponents of Intelligent Design are rightly outraged when their efforts are linked to the efforts of Holocaust deniers, for there is no moral equivalence between the two projects. One, after all, is in the business of whitewashing genocide, whereas the other wishes only to give God the credit for having created the wonders of the physical world. (I know that Intelligent Design literature stays away from the word "God," but no one, in or out of the movement, gives any other answer to the question, "Designed by whom?") There is, however, an equivalence of strategy that makes linking the two inevitable: in both cases, issues that have been settled in the relevant academic departments—history and biology, respectively—are reopened by reframing them as abstract questions about the value of debate as a moral good. When John West of the Discovery Institute (the Intelligent Design think tank) declares that "All Americans who cherish free speech" should reject any effort to exclude Intelligent Design from the classroom and invokes "the free marketplace of ideas" to clinch his case, his words could be incorporated wholesale into Bradley Smith's ad. Intelligent Designers and Holocaust deniers, despite the great differences between them, play the same shell game; they both say: Look here, in the highest reaches of speculation about inquiry in general, and not there, in the places where the particular, nitty-gritty work of inquiry is actually being done. They appeal to a higher value—the value of controversy as a good no matter what its content or who its participants—and thereby avoid questions about the qualifications necessary to be legitimate competitors in the competition. In the guise of upping the stakes, Intelligent Designers lower them, moving immediately to a perspective so broad and inclusive that all claims are valued not because they have proven out in the contest of ideas but simply because they are claims. When any claim has a right to be heard and taught just because it is one, judgment falls by the wayside and is replaced by the imperative to let a hundred (or a million) flowers bloom.

There's a word for this, and it's *relativism*. Polemicists on the right regularly 10 lambaste intellectuals on the left for promoting relativism and its attendant bad practices—relaxing or abandoning standards, opening the curriculum to any idea with a constituency attached to it, dismissing received wisdom by impugning the motives of those who have established it; disregarding inconvenient evidence and replacing it with grand theories supported by nothing but the partisan beliefs and desires of the theorizers. Whether or not this has ever been true of the right's targets, it is now demonstrably true of the right itself, whose members now recite the mantras of "teach the controversy" or "keep the debate open" whenever they find it convenient. They do so not out of a commitment to scrupulous scholarship (although that will be what is asserted) but in an effort to accomplish through misdirection and displacement what they cannot accomplish through evidence and argument.

QUESTIONS FOR DISCUSSION AND WRITING

1. Is "spotting voodoo science" a necessary survival skill for twenty-first-century citizens (Park, paragraph 18)? Why or why not? What are some bogus scientific claims, questionable "expert testimony," or problems with scientific accuracy that have caught your attention? How would Park's seven warning signs help in dealing with this problem?

2. To what extent could any of Park's seven warning signs be applied to fields besides science? Discuss questionable claims and "facts" from your experience or reading in nonscientific fields such as history, business, health, and Internet fraud. For example, what are some things that are accepted based mainly on anecdotal evidence (warning sign 4)? Have you encountered any questionable beliefs that are touted as true merely because they have endured for centuries (warning sign 5)? How would you reason with someone who holds these beliefs?

3. How might you test claims of folk medicine, miracle treatments and "cures," ESP, or other phenomena that depend on a person's willingness to believe? Pick something a person you know swears by. Interview the person (Why do you believe in this? What evidence do you have that it works? Always? How can its failures, if any, be explained?) and consult a library and the Internet for claims and counterclaims. Write up your results.

4. Write a case study of a piece of bogus science, using Park's warning signs to analyze how the claim was made and why it was ultimately rejected. Using library and Internet research, find the earliest newspaper or magazine reports of the claim, before it was debunked. Show how the warning sign appears in these reports. Then show how the fallacious claim was discredited.

5. Fish analyzes "the rhetoric of multiculturalism" to show how it proceeds from correctly observing "that there are many different standards of judgment in the world" to the "unwarranted conclusion" that renders "all authority illegitimate, by explaining it away as the accidental ascendancy of one tradition over its equally worthy rivals" (paragraph 2). Does Fish convince you that the claim that all arguments are equal is wrong? Do all arguments have to be fair, even if to be fair perpetuates falsehood?

6. Examine the analogy that Fish uses to explain the argument from Intelligent Design: "If multiculturalists can defend gay marriage by challenging the right of a state to define what marriage is, why can't Intelligent Design proponents demand equal time in the classroom by challenging the right of Ivy League professors to say what science is" (paragraph 2)? Is this a "manufactured controversy"? What's wrong with this analogy? What's wrong with arguing by analogy?

7. What do Intelligent Design proponents claim about evolution and the creation of the universe? How do they evade the argument by saying "Teach the controversy" (paragraph 4)? If evolutionists don't believe there is a controversy, are

they being co-opted into presenting the Intelligent Design argument by this exhortation? Must every claim on every subject be accompanied by information about alternative points of view even if they remain speculative or are largely discredited?

8. What parallels are there between the argumentative strategies of the Holocaust deniers and Intelligent Design proponents (paragraph 8)? If they argue in similar ways, must both be right? Or both be wrong?

9. Fish observes, Intelligent Designers and Holocaust deniers "play the same shell game. . . . They appeal to a higher value—the value of controversy as a good no matter what its content or who its participants—and thereby avoid questions about the qualifications necessary to be legitimate competitors in the competition" (paragraph 9). With a partner, evaluate the merits of Fish's analysis throughout the essay. Yes, he opposes the argumentative strategy of the Intelligent Designers. He offers detailed reasons. Must he give a rebuttal equal time?

NATALIE ANGIER

Men, Women, Sex, and Darwin

"It's bad luck to be born either sex" is Natalie Angier's favorite quotation (from anthropologist Sarah Hrdy). Angier (b. 1958) grew up in the Bronx, New York, and earned a bachelor's degree in physics and English from Barnard College (1978). In 1991 she received the Pulitzer Prize for her science writing in the New York Times, *where she has worked since 1990. Her books include* Natural Obsessions *(1988), on the world of cancer research;* The Beauty of the Beastly *(1995), on invertebrates; and* The Canon: A Whirligig Tour of the Beautiful Basics of Science *(2007). In* Woman: An Intimate Geography *(1999), Angier analyzes female genetics, anatomy, physiology, and endocrinology from the fetus to menopause, arguing that males and females are more androgynous than is often supposed. In the ongoing debate over whether genetics or culture more strongly influence the behavior of men and women, Angier favors "nurture" over "nature." In "Men, Women, Sex and Darwin," first published in the* New York Times Magazine *(February 1999), she provides evidence to contradict the psychologists who claim that sexual stereotypes have evolved over millions of years and are programmed into human genes.*

Life is short but jingles are forever. None more so, it seems, than the familiar ditty, variously attributed to William James, Ogden Nash and Dorothy Parker: "Hoggamus, higgamus, / Men are polygamous, / Higgamus, hoggamus, / Women monogamous."

Lately the pith of that jingle has found new fodder and new fans, through the explosive growth of a field known as evolutionary psychology. Evolutionary psychology professes to have discovered the fundamental modules of human nature, most notably the essential nature of man and of woman. It makes sense to be curious about the evolutionary roots of human behavior. It's reasonable to try to understand our impulses and actions by applying Darwinian logic to the problem. We're animals. We're not above the rude little prods and jests of natural and sexual selection. But evolutionary psychology as it has been disseminated across mainstream consciousness is a cranky and despotic Cyclops, its single eye glaring through an overwhelmingly masculinist lens. I say "masculinist" rather than "male" because the view of male behavior promulgated by hard-core evolutionary psychologists is as narrow and inflexible as their view of womanhood is.

I'm not interested in explaining to men what they really want or how they should behave. If a fellow chooses to tell himself that his yen for the fetching young assistant in his office and his concomitant disgruntlement with his aging wife make perfect Darwinian sense, who am I to argue with him? I'm only proposing here that the hard-core evolutionary psychologists have got a lot about women wrong—about some of us, anyway—and that women want more and deserve better than the cartoon *Olive Oyl* handed down for popular consumption.

The cardinal premises of evolutionary psychology of interest to this discussion are as follows: 1. Men are more promiscuous and less sexually reserved than women are. 2. Women are inherently more interested in a stable relationship than men are. 3. Women are naturally attracted to high-status men with resources. 4. Men are naturally attracted to youth and beauty. 5. Humankind's core preferences and desires were hammered out long, long ago, a hundred thousand years or more, in the legendary Environment of Evolutionary Adaptation, or E.E.A., also known as the ancestral environment, also known as the Stone Age, and they have not changed appreciably since then, nor are they likely to change in the future.

In sum: Higgamus, hoggamus, Pygmalionus, *Playboy* magazine, *eternitas*. 5 Amen.

Hard-core evolutionary psychology types go to extremes to argue in favor of the yawning chasm that separates the innate desires of women and men. They declare ringing confirmation for their theories even in the face of feeble and amusingly contradictory data. For example: Among the cardinal principles of the evo-psycho set is that men are by nature more polygamous than women are, and much more accepting of casual, even anonymous, sex. Men can't help themselves, they say: they are always hungry for sex, bodies, novelty and nubility. Granted, men needn't act on such desires, but the drive to sow seed is there nonetheless, satyric and relentless, and women cannot fully understand its force. David Buss, a professor of psychology at the University of Texas at Austin and one of the most outspoken of the evolutionary psychologists, says that asking a man not to lust after a pretty young woman is like telling a carnivore not to like meat.

At the same time, they recognize that the overwhelming majority of men and women get married, and so their theories must extend to different innate mate preferences among men and women. Men look for the hallmarks of youth, like smooth skin, full lips and perky breasts; they want a mate who has a long childbearing career ahead of her. Men also want women who are virginal and who seem as though they'll be faithful and not make cuckolds of them. The sexy, vampy types are fine for a Saturday romp, but when it comes to choosing a marital partner, men want modesty and fidelity.

Women want a provider, the theory goes. They want a man who seems rich, stable and ambitious. They want to know that they and their children will be cared for. They want a man who can take charge, maybe dominate them just a little, enough to reassure them that the man is genotypically, phenotypically, eternally, a king. Women's innate preference for a well-to-do man continues to this day, the evolutionary psychologists insist, even among financially independent and professionally successful women who don't need a man as a provider. It was adaptive in the past to look for the most resourceful man, they say, and adaptations can't be willed away in a generation or two of putative cultural change.

And what is the evidence for these male-female verities? For the difference in promiscuity quotas, the hard-cores love to raise the example of the differences between gay men and lesbians. Homosexuals are seen as a revealing population because they supposedly can behave according to the innermost impulses of their sex, untempered by the need to adjust to the demands and wishes of the opposite sex, as heterosexuals theoretically are. What do we see in this ideal study group? Just look at how gay men carry on! They are perfectly happy to have hundreds, thousands, of sexual partners, to have sex in bathhouses, in bathrooms, in Central Park. By contrast, lesbians are sexually sedate. They don't cruise sex clubs. They couple up and stay coupled, and they like cuddling and hugging more than they do serious, genitally based sex.

In the hard-core rendering of inherent male-female discrepancies in promiscuity, gay men are offered up as true men, real men, men set free to be men, while lesbians are real women, ultra-women, acting out every woman's fantasy of love and commitment. Interestingly, though, in many neurobiology studies gay men are said to have somewhat feminized brains, with hypothalamic nuclei that are closer in size to a woman's than to a straight man's, and spatial-reasoning skills that are modest and ladylike rather than manfully robust. For their part, lesbians are posited to have somewhat masculinized brains and skills—to be sportier, more mechanically inclined, less likely to have played with dolls or tea sets when young—all as an ostensible result of exposure to prenatal androgens. And so gay men are sissy boys in some contexts and Stone Age manly men in others, while lesbians are battering rams one day and flower into the softest and most sexually divested girlish girls the next.

On the question of mate preferences, evo-psychos rely on surveys, most of them compiled by David Buss. His surveys are celebrated by some, derided by others, but in any event they are ambitious—performed in 37 countries, he says, on six continents. His surveys, and others emulating them, consistently find that men rate youth and beauty as important traits in a mate, while women give comparatively greater weight to ambition and financial success. Surveys show that surveys never lie. Lest you think that women's mate preferences change with their own mounting economic clout, surveys assure us that they do not. Surveys of female medical students, according to John Marshall Townsend, of Syracuse University, indicate that they hope to marry men with an earning power and social status at least equal to and preferably greater than their own.

Perhaps all this means is that men can earn a living wage better, even now, than women can. Men make up about half the world's population, but they still own the vast majority of the world's wealth—the currency, the minerals, the timber, the gold, the stocks, the amber fields of grain. In her superb book *Why So Slow?* Virginia Valian, a professor of psychology at Hunter College, lays out the extent of lingering economic discrepancies between men and women in the United States. In 1978 there were two women heading Fortune 1000 companies; in 1994, there were still two; in 1996, the number had jumped all the way to four. In 1985, 2 percent of the Fortune 1000's senior-level executives were women; by 1992, that number had hardly budged, to 3 percent. A 1990 salary and compensation survey of 799 major companies showed that of the highest-paid officers and directors, less than one-half of 1 percent were women. Ask, and he shall receive. In the United States the possession of a bachelor's degree adds $28,000 to a man's salary but only $9,000 to a woman's. A degree from a high-prestige school contributes $11,500 to a man's income but *subtracts* $2,400 from a woman's. If women continue to worry that they need a man's money, because the playing field remains about as level as the surface of Mars, then we can't conclude anything about innate preferences. If women continue to suffer from bag-lady syndrome even as they become prosperous, if they still see their wealth as provisional and capsizable, and if they still hope to find a man with a dependable income to supplement their own, then we can credit women with intelligence and acumen, for inequities abound.

There's another reason that smart, professional women might respond on surveys that they'd like a mate of their socioeconomic status or better. Smart, professional women are smart enough to know that men can be tender of ego—is it genetic?—and that it hurts a man to earn less money than his wife, and that resentment is a noxious chemical in a marriage and best avoided at any price. "A woman who is more successful than her mate threatens his position in the male hierarchy," Elizabeth Cashdan, of the University of Utah, has written. If women could be persuaded that men didn't mind their being high achievers, were in fact pleased and proud to be affiliated with them, we might predict that the women would stop caring about the particulars of their mates' income. The anthropologist Sarah Blaffer Hrdy writes that "when female status and access to resources do not depend on her mate's status, women will likely use a range of criteria, not primarily or even necessarily prestige and wealth, for mate selection." She cites a 1996 *New York Times* story about women from a wide range of professions—bankers, judges, teachers, journalists—who marry male convicts.

The allure of such men is not their income, for you can't earn much when you make license plates for a living. Instead, it is the men's gratitude that proves irresistible. The women also like the fact that their husbands' fidelity is guaranteed. "Peculiar as it is," Hrdy writes, "this vignette of sex-reversed claustration makes a serious point about just how little we know about female choice in breeding systems where male interests are not paramount and patrilines are not making the rules."

Do women love older men? Do women find gray hair and wrinkles attractive on men—as attractive, that is, as a fine, full head of pigmented hair and a vigorous, firm complexion? The evolutionary psychologists suggest yes. They believe that women look for the signs of maturity in men because a mature man is likely to be a comparatively wealthy and resourceful man. That should logically include baldness, which generally comes with age and the higher status that it often confers. Yet, as Desmond Morris points out, a thinning hairline is not considered a particularly attractive state.

Assuming that women find older men attractive, is it the men's alpha status? Or could it be something less complimentary to the male, something like the following—that an older man is appealing not because he is powerful but because in his maturity he has lost some of his power, has become less marketable and desirable and potentially more grateful and gracious, more likely to make a younger woman feel that there is a balance of power in the relationship? The rude little calculation is simple: He is male, I am female—advantage, man. He is older, I am younger—advantage, woman. By the same token, a woman may place little value on a man's appearance because she values something else far more: room to breathe. Who can breathe in the presence of a handsome young man, whose ego, if expressed as a vapor, would fill Biosphere II? Not even, I'm afraid, a beautiful young woman.

In the end, what is important to question, and to hold to the fire of alternative interpretation, is the immutability and adaptive logic of the discrepancy, its basis in our genome rather than in the ecological circumstances in which a genome manages to express itself. Evolutionary psychologists insist on the essential discordance between the strength of the sex drive in males and females. They admit that many nonhuman female primates gallivant about rather more than we might have predicted before primatologists began observing their behavior in the field—more, far more, than is necessary for the sake of reproduction. Nonetheless, the credo of the coy female persists. It is garlanded with qualifications and is admitted to be an imperfect portrayal of female mating strategies, but then, that little matter of etiquette attended to, the credo is stated once again.

"Amid the great variety of social structure in these species, the basic theme . . . stands out, at least in minimal form: males seem very eager for sex and work hard to find it; females work less hard," Robert Wright says in *The Moral Animal.* "This isn't to say the females don't like sex. They love it, and may initiate it. And, intriguingly, the females of the species most closely related to humans—chimpanzees and bonobos—seem particularly amenable to a wild sex life, including a variety

15

of partners. Still, female apes don't do what male apes do: search high and low, risking life and limb, to find sex, and to find as much of it, with as many different partners, as possible; it has a way of finding them." In fact female chimpanzees do search high and low and take great risks to find sex with partners other than the partners who have a way of finding them. DNA studies of chimpanzees in West Africa show that half the offspring in a group of closely scrutinized chimpanzees turned out not to be the offspring of the resident males. The females of the group didn't rely on sex "finding" its way to them; they proactively left the local environs, under such conditions of secrecy that not even their vigilant human observers knew they had gone, and became impregnated by outside males. They did so even at the risk of life and limb—their own and those of their offspring. Male chimpanzees try to control the movements of fertile females. They'll scream at them and hit them if they think the females aren't listening. They may even kill an infant they think is not their own. We don't know why the females take such risks to philander, but they do, and to say that female chimpanzees "work less hard" than males do at finding sex does not appear to be supported by the data.

Evo-psychos pull us back and forth until we might want to sue for whiplash. On the one hand we are told that women have a lower sex drive than men do. On the other hand we are told that the madonna-whore dichotomy is a universal stereotype. In every culture, there is a tendency among both men and women to adjudge women as either chaste or trampy. The chaste ones are accorded esteem. The trampy ones are consigned to the basement, a notch or two below goats in social status. A woman can't sleep around without risking terrible retribution, to her reputation, to her prospects, to her life. "Can anyone find a single culture in which women with unrestrained sexual appetites *aren't* viewed as more aberrant than comparably libidinous men?" Wright asks rhetorically.

Women are said to have lower sex drives than men, yet they are universally punished if they display evidence to the contrary—if they disobey their "natural" inclination toward a stifled libido. Women supposedly have a lower sex drive than men do, yet it is not low enough. There is still just enough of a lingering female infidelity impulse that cultures everywhere have had to gird against it by articulating a rigid dichotomy with menacing implications for those who fall on the wrong side of it. There is still enough lingering female infidelity to justify infibulation, purdah, claustration. Men have the naturally higher sex drive, yet all the laws, customs, punishments, shame, strictures, mystiques and antimystiques are aimed with full hominid fury at that tepid, sleepy, hypoactive creature, the female libido.

"It seems premature . . . to attribute the relative lack of female interest in [20] sexual variety to women's biological nature alone in the face of overwhelming evidence that women are consistently beaten for promiscuity and adultery," the primatologist Barbara Smuts has written. "If female sexuality is muted compared to that of men, then why must men the world over go to extreme lengths to control and contain it?"

Why indeed? Consider a brief evolutionary apologia for President Clinton's adulteries written by Steven Pinker, of the Massachusetts Institute of Technology. "Most human drives have ancient Darwinian rationales," he wrote. "A prehistoric man who slept with fifty women could have sired fifty children, and would have been more likely to have descendants who inherited his tastes. A woman who slept with fifty men would have no more descendants than a woman who slept with one. Thus, men should seek quantity in sexual partners; women, quality." And isn't it so, he says, everywhere and always so? "In our society," he continues, "most young men tell researchers that they would like eight sexual partners in the next two years; most women say that they would like one." Yet would a man find the prospect of a string of partners so appealing if the following rules were applied: that no matter how much he may like a particular woman and be pleased by her performance and want to sleep with her again, he will have no say in the matter and will be dependent on her mood and good graces for all future contact; that each act of casual sex will cheapen his status and make him increasingly less attractive to other women; and that society will not wink at his randiness but rather sneer at him and think him pathetic, sullied, smaller than life? Until men are subjected to the same severe standards and threat of censure as women are, and until they are given the lower hand in a so-called casual encounter from the start, it is hard to insist with such self-satisfaction that, hey, it's natural, men like a lot of sex with a lot of people and women don't.

Reflect for a moment on Pinker's philandering caveman who slept with 50 women. Just how good a reproductive strategy is this chronic, random shooting of the gun? A woman is fertile only five or six days a month. Her ovulation is concealed. The man doesn't know when she's fertile. She might be in the early stages of pregnancy when he gets to her; she might still be lactating and thus not ovulating. Moreover, even if our hypothetical Don Juan hits a day on which a woman is ovulating, the chances are around 65 percent that his sperm will fail to fertilize her egg; human reproduction is complicated, and most eggs and sperm are not up to the demands of proper fusion. Even if conception occurs, the resulting embryo has about a 30 percent chance of miscarrying at some point in gestation. In sum, each episode of fleeting sex has a remarkably small probability of yielding a baby—no more than 1 or 2 percent at best.

And because the man is trysting and running, he isn't able to prevent any of his casual contacts from turning around and mating with other men. The poor fellow. He has to mate with many scores of women for his wham-bam strategy to pay off. And where are all these women to be found, anyway? Population densities during that purportedly all-powerful psyche shaper the "ancestral environment" were quite low, and long-distance travel was dangerous and difficult.

There are alternatives to wantonness, as a number of theorists have emphasized. If, for example, a man were to spend more time with one woman rather than dashing breathlessly from sheet to sheet, if he were to feel compelled to engage in what animal behaviorists call mate guarding, he might be better off, reproductively speaking, than the wild Lothario, both because the odds of impregnating the woman would increase and because he'd be monopolizing her energy and keeping her from the advances of other sperm bearers. It takes the average couple three to four months of regular sexual intercourse to become pregnant. That number of days is approximately equal to the number of partners our hypothetical libertine needs to sleep with to have one encounter result in a "fertility unit," that is, a baby. The two strategies, then, shake out about the same. A man can sleep with a lot of women — the quantitative approach — or he can sleep with one woman for months at a time, and be madly in love with her — the qualitative tactic.

It's possible that these two reproductive strategies are distributed in discrete 25
packets among the male population, with a result that some men are born philanderers and can never attach, while others are born romantics and perpetually in love with love; but it's also possible that men teeter back and forth from one impulse to the other, suffering an internal struggle between the desire to bond and the desire to retreat, with the circuits of attachment ever there to be toyed with, and their needs and desires difficult to understand, paradoxical, fickle, treacherous and glorious. It is possible, then, and for perfectly good Darwinian reason, that casual sex for men is rarely as casual as it is billed.

It needn't be argued that men and women are exactly the same, or that humans are meta-evolutionary beings, removed from nature and slaves to culture, to reject the perpetually regurgitated model of the coy female and the ardent male. Conflicts of interest are always among us, and the outcomes of those conflicts are interesting, more interesting by far than what the ultra-evolutionary psychology line has handed us. Patricia Gowaty, of the University of Georgia, sees conflict between males and females as inevitable and pervasive. She calls it sexual dialectics. Her thesis is that females and males vie for control over the means of reproduction. Those means are the female body, for there is as yet no such beast as the parthenogenetic man.

Women are under selective pressure to maintain control over their reproduction, to choose with whom they will mate and with whom they will not — to exercise female choice. Men are under selective pressure to make sure they're chosen or, barring that, to subvert female choice and coerce the female to mate against her will. "But once you have this basic dialectic set in motion, it's going to be a constant push-me, pull-you," Gowaty says. "That dynamism cannot possibly result in a unitary response, the caricatured coy woman and ardent man. Instead there are going to be some coy, reluctantly mating males and some ardent females, and any number of variations in between.

"A female will choose to mate with a male whom she believes, consciously or otherwise, will confer some advantage on her and her offspring. If that's the case, then her decision is contingent on what she brings to the equation." For example, she says, "the 'good genes' model leads to oversimplified notions that there is a 'best male' out there, a top-of-the-line hunk whom all females would prefer to mate with if they had the wherewithal. But in the viability model, a female brings her own genetic complement to the equation, with the result that what looks good genetically to one woman might be a clash of colors for another."

Maybe the man's immune system doesn't complement her own, for example, Gowaty proposes. There's evidence that the search for immune variation is one of the subtle factors driving mate selection, which may be why we care about how our lovers smell; immune molecules may be volatilized and released in sweat, hair, the oil on our skin. We are each of us a chemistry set, and each of us has a distinctive mix of reagents. "What pleases me might not please somebody else," Gowaty says. "There is no one-brand great male out there. We're not all programmed to look for the alpha male and only willing to mate with the little guy or the less aggressive guy because we can't do any better. But the propaganda gives us a picture of the right man and the ideal woman, and the effect of the propaganda is insidious. It becomes self-reinforcing. People who don't fit the model think, I'm weird, I'll have to change my behavior." It is this danger, that the ostensible "discoveries" of evolutionary psychology will be used as propaganda, that makes the enterprise so disturbing.

Variation and flexibility are the key themes that get set aside in the breathless 30 dissemination of evolutionary psychology. "The variation is tremendous, and is rooted in biology," Barbara Smuts said to me. "Flexibility itself is the adaptation." Smuts has studied olive baboons, and she has seen males pursuing all sorts of mating strategies. "There are some whose primary strategy is dominating other males, and being able to gain access to more females because of their fighting ability," she says. "Then there is the type of male who avoids competition and cultivates long-term relationships with females and their infants. These are the nice, affiliative guys. There's a third type, who focuses on sexual relationships. He's the consorter. . . . And as far as we can tell, no one reproductive strategy has advantages over the others."

Women are said to need an investing male. We think we know the reason. Human babies are difficult and time consuming to raise. Stone Age mothers needed husbands to bring home the bison. Yet the age-old assumption that male parental investment lies at the heart of human evolution is now open to serious question. Men in traditional foraging cultures do not necessarily invest resources in their offspring. Among the Hadza of Africa, for example, the men hunt, but they share the bounty of that hunting widely, politically, strategically. They don't deliver it straight to the mouths of their progeny. Women rely on their senior female kin to help feed their children. The women and their children in a gathering-hunting society clearly benefit from the meat that hunters bring back to the group. But they benefit as a group, not as a collection of nuclear family units, each beholden to the father's personal pound of wildeburger.

This is a startling revelation, which upends many of our presumptions about the origins of marriage and what women want from men and men from women. If the environment of evolutionary adaptation is not defined primarily by male parental investment, the bedrock of so much of evolutionary psychology's theories, then we can throw the door wide open and ask new questions, rather than endlessly repeating ditties and calling the female coy long after she has run her petticoats through the Presidential paper shredder.

For example: Nicholas Blurton Jones, of the University of California at Los Angeles, and others have proposed that marriage developed as an extension of men's efforts at mate guarding. If the cost of philandering becomes ludicrously high, the man might be better off trying to claim rights to one woman at a time. Regular sex with a fertile woman is at least likely to yield offspring at comparatively little risk to his life, particularly if sexual access to the woman is formalized through a public ceremony—a wedding. Looked at from this perspective, one must wonder why an ancestral woman bothered to get married, particularly if she and her female relatives did most of the work of keeping the family fed from year to year. Perhaps, Blurton Jones suggests, to limit the degree to which she was harassed. The cost of chronic male harassment may be too high to bear. Better to agree to a ritualized bond with a male and to benefit from whatever hands-off policy that marriage may bring, than to spend all of her time locked in one sexual dialectic or another.

Thus marriage may have arisen as a multifaceted social pact: between man and woman, between male and male and between the couple and the tribe. It is a reasonable solution to a series of cultural challenges that arose in concert with the expansion of the human neocortex. But its roots may not be what we think they are, nor may our contemporary mating behaviors stem from the pressures of an ancestral environment as it is commonly portrayed, in which a woman needed a mate to help feed and clothe her young. Instead, our "deep" feelings about marriage may be more pragmatic, more contextual and, dare I say it, more egalitarian than we give them credit for being.

If marriage is a social compact, a mutual bid between man and woman to 35 contrive a reasonably stable and agreeable microhabitat in a community of shrewd and well-armed members, then we can understand why, despite rhetoric to the contrary, men are as eager to marry as women are. A raft of epidemiological studies have shown that marriage adds more years to the life of a man than it does to that of a woman. Why should that be, if men are so "naturally" ill suited to matrimony?

What do women want? None of us can speak for all women, or for more than one woman, really, but we can hazard a mad guess that a desire for emotional parity is widespread and profound. It doesn't go away, although it often hibernates under duress, and it may be perverted by the restrictions of habitat or culture into something that looks like its opposite. The impulse for liberty is congenital. It is the ultimate manifestation of selfishness, which is why we can count on its endurance.

QUESTIONS FOR DISCUSSION AND WRITING

1. Throughout much of her article, Angier uses humorous words ("wildeburger") and phrases ("trysting and running") as well as informal words ("guy") and expressions ("hey"). With your classmates, gather other examples of such features. What kind of reader does Angier seem to be addressing? How do these expressions affect you as a reader? In what passages does she *avoid* using such expressions? Speculate on why she varies her style.

2. Angier writes that the "impulse for liberty is congenital" (paragraph 36). How do evolutionary psychologists explain the manifestations of this impulse? How does Angier explain them?

3. Which of the various stereotypical behaviors of men and women that Angier mentions have you seen or heard discussed in the press, in the media, or in conversation? What causes these behaviors, in your opinion—nature or culture?

4. What do primate studies reveal about the relative sexual activity of males and females? What implications for human beings are drawn by evolutionary psychologists and by Angier? Write an essay explaining why you find Angier's approach more or less persuasive than that of the evolutionary psychologists.

5. Write an essay comparing and contrasting the ways in which evolutionary psychologists and Angier view the notion that females choose males who can best care for them and their infants.

EDWARD O. WILSON

Microbes 3, Humans 2

Edward O. Wilson (b. 1929) is famed as an expert on insect societies and as a pioneer in sociobiological research (the biological bases of behavior). Many critics see Wilson's controversial Sociobiology: The New Synthesis *(1975), which argues that behavior—even altruism—is motivated by individuals' selfish need to propagate their own genes, as potentially arguing on behalf of racism and eugenics.*

As his autobiography Naturalist *(1994) relates, Wilson's boyhood interest in observing nature turned into a systematic study of insects. Educated at the University of Alabama (B.S., 1949; M.S., 1950) and at Harvard (Ph.D., 1955), he has taught zoology at Harvard since 1956. He was awarded the National Medal of Science, and has written two Pulitzer Prize–winning books,* On Human Nature *(1979) and* The Ants *(1990), followed in 2009 by* The Superorganism: The Beauty, Elegance and Strangeness of Insect Societies, *like* The Ants *coauthored with Bert Hölldobler. In* Consilience *(1998), he argues that all fields of knowledge—the sciences, humanities, and arts—are in search of fundamental order in the world.* The Future of Life *(2002) makes a plea for environmental sanity, while* From So

Simple a Beginning: Darwin's Four Great Books (2005) is a tribute to Darwin. "Microbes 3, Humans 2," originally published in the New York Times Magazine *(April 1999) addresses the complex question of which species are the "most abundant," the "most social," and the "most intelligent."*

Let us mince words. When we say "best," we mean some kind of success, implying the existence of goals, which in turn are the exclusive property of organisms and not of species. Where the goal of a runner in a track meet is to break the tape, where a dragonfly succeeds when it snatches a fly from the air for dinner, where even a colon bacterium reverses the spin of its flagella, causing it to tumble and depart in a new direction that leads to dissolved sugar, it takes an organism to have a best.

As a result of natural selection, species — or more precisely, the organisms composing species — generally perform brilliantly in the niche to which they are specialized. There are probably 10 million or more species alive on earth. Which are the best at filling their niches? All are, I guess. Consider this Zenlike question: Can a bird fly better than a fish can swim? Live species are by definition all successes, because the losers are extinct, having fallen victim to nature's equivalent of the Foreign Legion command, March or die.

Of course, success by organisms can ultimately be disastrous for their species. Browsing animals, like the American white-tailed deer, can be superlatively efficient and as a result wipe out the plants on which they depend, whereupon the species and the organisms it comprises plunge toward extinction. Or take the same principle in reverse: the most successful parasites are those that least harm their host. The champion human parasites may be the Demodex mites, microscopic spiderlike creatures that live unnoticed on the eyelashes and eyebrows of a large percentage of the human population.

That said, I am unwilling to give up entirely the quest for successful species. So let me use subjective, human-oriented criteria to pin some gold medals on members of the world's fauna and flora.

Most abundant. Bacterial species win this one easily. There are more *E. coli* 5 and other intestinal bacteria in your colon at this moment than there are human beings who have ever lived.

Longest lived. All living species are in a dead heat, since all have descended from early forms of life that originated more than 3.5 billion years ago. When biologists speak of ancient forms and living fossils, they really mean certain combinations of traits that have persisted for relatively long periods of time in certain lines of descent, like modern horseshoe crabs and coelacanth fish. But the direct ancestry of human beings goes back just as far as these living fossils, the only difference being that the traits that distinguish *Homo sapiens* as a species are less than one-hundredth as old.

Most likely to survive. Without doubt, bacteria and allied organisms known as archaea win again, especially the species that use photosynthesis or inorganic chemicals to grow and reproduce. If every kind of plant and animal on earth were destroyed, these hardy organisms would carry on. Even if the earth's surface were blasted to a cinder, the inorganic-energy extractors and petroleum feeders would continue their lives many kilometers below the surface of the earth. Given a few billion years, they might give rise to new higher life forms on the surface.

Most social. As an entomologist, I will be accused of insect chauvinism, but I say ants, termites and honeybees win hands down. That is, they win if we use the following criteria: altruism, the complexity of anatomy, instincts devoted to social life and the tightness of the bonds that turn colonies into virtual superorganisms.

Most intelligent. At last, a gold medal for humanity.

Most powerful. Human beings win again. Peering into the future and under- 10 standing how the world works, we have acquired the power of life and death over all other higher life forms. Whether we choose life for them and ultimately for ourselves is surely a valid criterion of success. To achieve that goal, however, requires wise management of the environment, an enterprise for which we have so far shown little dedication or talent.

QUESTIONS FOR DISCUSSION AND WRITING

1. In paragraph 1, Wilson inverts the familiar saying, "Let us not mince words." What might be his purpose in opening the essay this way?

2. Wilson's list of "gold medal" winners gives only two awards to humans; we aren't even the most social species, according to him. Why would Wilson want to demonstrate that humans aren't the best at everything?

3. Wilson explains that "success by organisms can ultimately be disastrous for their species" (paragraph 3). Why is abundance a "gold medal" for *E. coli* but not for white-tailed deer? In what ways could each of Wilson's "gold medals" turn into disasters for various species?

4. Considering that humans are not at the top of the animal kingdom in all categories (according to Wilson's analysis), write about the relative importance of the human race. How important is our species compared to other species, if we are not the most successful at everything? Where would Wilson stand in the debate between Stephen Jay Gould and creationists?

5. Wilson makes the paradoxical observation that an organism's success can jeopardize the survival of its species (see question 3). Are the success and intelligence of the human race similarly jeopardizing human survival? Write an essay using Wilson's model of perilous success, along with the ideas of Rachel Carson in "The Obligation to Endure" (p. 612), to discuss whether our impact on the environment (through pollution, war, and overdevelopment, for example) could render us extinct.

CHAPTER 7

Ethics: What Principles
Do — and Should — We Live By?

LEONARD FREED

Martin Luther King Jr. after Receiving the
Nobel Peace Prize, Baltimore, 1964

QUESTIONS FOR DISCUSSION AND WRITING

1. What is the central focus of this image? That is, where is your eye drawn as you look at it? What is the overall mood?

2. King is at the left of the photo, rather than at the center. What effect does his position have on this image? What do the expressions and body language of the people shown contribute to the overall effect?

3. Speculate on why Freed cropped the slightly blurry face at the right of the frame.

4. Based on your reading of "Letter from Birmingham Jail" (p. 494) and the Contexts that follow it, why do you think King received the Nobel Peace Prize? Amplify your answer with reference to the Nobel Peace Prize acceptance speeches of Al Gore (p. 583) and Wangari Maathai (p. 586).

JEFFREY WATTLES

The Golden Rule—One or Many, Gold or Glitter?

Jeffrey Wattles (b. 1945) received his bachelor's degree from Stanford University and his master's degree and doctorate from Northwestern. He is a professor of philosophy at Kent State University, where his research and teaching focus on ethics, comparative religious thought, and ways of integrating science, philosophy, and religion. He has written extensively about the golden rule in such journal articles as "Levels of Meaning in the Golden Rule" and "Plato's Brush with the Golden Rule." His book, The Golden Rule *(1996), is a detailed examination of the history, cultural variations, and interpretations of the classic moral dictum "Do to others as you want others to do to you."*

The following selection is from the opening chapter of The Golden Rule. *Here Wattles summarizes its themes, particularly his response to critics who argue that the golden rule fails to acknowledge differences among human beings, that it establishes a relatively low standard of morality, and that it encourages a simplistic moral outlook.*

Children are taught to respect parents and other authority figures. Adolescents are urged to control their impulses. Adults are told to conduct themselves in accord with certain moral and ethical standards. Morality, then, may seem to be just an affair of imposition, a cultural voice that says "no" in various ways to our desires. To be sure, there are times when the word "no" must be spoken and enforced. But, time and again, people have discovered something more to morality, something rooted in life itself. The "no" is but one word in the voice of life, a voice that has other words, including the golden rule: Do to others as you want others to do to you. This book is about the life in that principle.

THE UNITY OF THE RULE

What could be easier to grasp intuitively than the golden rule? It has such an immediate intelligibility that it serves as a ladder that anyone can step onto without a great stretch. I know how I like to be treated; and that is how I am to treat others. The rule asks me to be considerate of others rather than indulging in self-centeredness. The study of the rule, however, leads beyond conventional interpretation, and the practice of the rule leads beyond conventional morality.

The rule is widely regarded as obvious and self-evident. Nearly everyone is familiar with it in some formulation or other. An angry parent uses it as a weapon: "Is that how you want others to treat you?" A defense attorney invites the members of the jury to put themselves in the shoes of his or her client. Noting that particular rules and interpretations do not cover every situation, a manual of professional ethics exhorts members to treat other professionals with the same consideration and respect that they would wish for themselves. Formulated in one way or another, the rule finds its way into countless speeches, sermons, documents, and books on the assumption that it has a single, clear sense that the listener or reader grasps and approves of. In an age where differences so often occasion violence, here, it seems, is something that everyone can agree on.

Promoting the notion that the golden rule is "taught by all the world's religions," advocates have collected maxims from various traditions, producing lists with entries like the following: "Hinduism: 'Let no man do to another that which would be repugnant to himself.'" "Islam: 'None of you [truly] believes until he wishes for his brother what he wishes for himself.'" The point of these lists is self-evident. Despite the differences in phrasing, all religions acknowledge the same basic, universal moral teaching. Moreover, this principle may be accepted as common ground by secular ethics as well.

Under the microscope of analysis, however, things are not so simple. Different formulations have different implications, and differences in context raise the question of whether the same concept is at work in passages where the wording is nearly identical. Is the meaning of the rule constant whenever one of these phrases is mentioned? There is a persistent debate, for example, about the relative merit of the positive formulation versus the negative one, "Do not do to others what you do not want others to do to you." Nor can the full meaning of a sentence be grasped in isolation. For example, to point to "the golden rule in Confucianism" by quoting a fifteen-word sentence from the *Analects* of Confucius does not convey the historical dynamism of the rule's evolving social, ethical, and spiritual connotations. What do the words mean in their original context? How prominent is the rule within that particular tradition? Finally, how does the rule function in a given interaction between the speaker or writer and the listener or reader? The rule may function as an authoritative reproach, a pious rehearsal of tradition, a specimen for analytic dissection, or a confession of personal commitment. Is the rule one or many? Can we even properly speak of *the* golden rule at all? Some Hindus interpret the injunction to treat others as oneself as an invitation to identify with the divine spirit within each person. Some Muslims take the golden rule to apply primarily to the brotherhood of Islam. Some Christians regard the rule as a shorthand summary of the morality of Jesus's religion. And countless people think of the rule without any religious associations at all.

Raising the question about the meanings of the golden rule in different contexts is not intended to reduce similarities to dust and ashes merely by appealing to the imponderable weight of cultural differences. Context is not the last word on meaning; the sentence expressing the golden rule contributes meaning of its own to its context. Meaning does involve context, but the fact that contexts differ does not prove that there is no commonality of meaning. Language and culture, moreover, are not reliable clues for identifying conceptual similarity and difference, since conceptual harmony is experienced across these boundaries.

The golden rule, happily, has more than a single sense. It is not a static, one-dimensional proposition with a single meaning to be accepted or rejected, defended or refuted. Nor is its multiplicity chaotic. There is enough continuity of meaning in its varied uses to justify speaking of *the* golden rule. My own thesis is that the rule's unity is best comprehended not in terms of a single meaning but as a symbol of a process of growth on emotional, intellectual, and spiritual levels.

THE QUALITY OF THE RULE

"Gold is where you find it" runs a proverb coined by miners who found what they were seeking in unexpected places. So what sort of ore or alloy or sculpture is the teaching that, since the seventeenth century, has been called "the golden rule"? Is it gold or glitter? Certain appreciative remarks on the golden rule seem to bear witness to a discovery. "Eureka!" they seem to say. "There is a supreme principle of living! It *can* be expressed in a single statement!"

By contrast, theologian Paul Tillich found the rule an inferior principle. For him, the biblical commandment to love and the assurance that God *is* love "infinitely transcend" the golden rule. The problem with the rule is that it "does not tell us what we *should* wish."

Is the rule *golden*? In other words, is it worthy to be cherished as a rule of living or even as *the* rule of living? The values of the rule are as much in dispute as its meanings. Most people, it seems, intuitively regard the golden rule as a good principle, and some have spoken as though there is within the rule a special kind of agency with the power to transform humankind.

It is understandable that the golden rule has been regarded as *the* supreme moral principle. I do not want to be murdered; therefore I should not murder another. I do not want my spouse to commit adultery, my property to be stolen, and so forth; therefore I should treat others with comparable consideration. Others have comparable interests, and the rule calls me to treat the other as someone akin to myself. Moreover, I realize that I sometimes have desires to be treated in ways that do not represent my considered best judgment, and this reflection makes it obvious that reason is required for the proper application of the golden rule. Finally, in personal relationships, I want to be loved, and, in consequence, the rule directs me to be loving. From the perspective of someone simply interested in living right rather than in the construction and critique of theories, the rule has much to recommend it.

Some writers have put the rule on a pedestal, giving the impression that the rule is *sufficient* for ethics in the sense that no one could ever go wrong by adhering to it or in the sense that all duties may be inferred from it. Others have claimed that the rule is a *necessary* criterion for right action; in other words, an action must be able to pass the test of the golden rule if it is to be validated as right, and any action that fails the test is wrong. Some philosophers have hoped for an ethical theory that would be self-sufficient (depending on no controversial axioms), perfectly good (invulnerable to counterexamples), and all-powerful (enabling the derivation of every correct moral judgment, given appropriate data about the situation). They have dreamed of sculpting ethics into an independent, rational, deductive system, on the model of geometry, with a single normative axiom. However much reason may hanker for such a system, once the golden rule is taken as a candidate for such an axiom, a minor flexing of the analytic bicep is enough to humiliate it. A single counterexample suffices to defeat a pretender to this throne.

Many scholars today regard the rule as an acceptable principle for popular use but as embarrassing if taken with philosophic seriousness. Most professional ethicists rely instead on other principles, since the rule seems vulnerable to counterexamples, such as the current favorite, "What if a sadomasochist goes forth to treat others as he wants to be treated?"

Technically, the golden rule can defend itself from objections, since it contains within itself the seed of its own self-correction. Any easily abused interpretation may be challenged: "Would you want to be treated according to a rule construed in this way?" The recursive use of the rule—applying it to the results of its own earlier application—is a lever that extricates it from many tangles. Close examination of the counterexample of the sadomasochist . . . shows that to use the rule properly requires a certain degree of maturity. The counterexample does not refute the golden rule, properly understood; rather, it serves to clarify the interpretation of the rule—that the golden rule functions appropriately in a *growing* personality; indeed, the practice of the rule itself promotes the required growth. Since the rule is such a compressed statement of morality, it takes for granted at least a minimum sincerity that refuses to manipulate the rule sophistically to "justify" patently immoral conduct. Where that prerequisite cannot be assumed, problems multiply.

The objections that have been raised against the rule are useful to illustrate   15 misinterpretations of the rule and to make clear assumptions that must be satisfied for the rule to function in moral theory.

It has been objected that the golden rule assumes that human beings are basically alike and thereby fails to do justice to the differences between people. In particular, the rule allegedly implies that what we want is what others want. As George Bernard Shaw quipped, "Don't do to others as you want them to do unto you. Their tastes may be different." The golden rule may also seem to imply that what we want for ourselves is good for ourselves and that what is good for ourselves is good for others. The positive formulation, in particular, is accused of harboring the potential for presumption; thus, the rule is suited for immediate application only among those whose beliefs and needs are similar. In fact, however, the rule calls for due consideration for any relevant difference between persons—just as the agent would want such consideration from others.

Another criticism is that the golden rule sets too low a standard because it makes ordinary wants and desires the criterion of morality. On one interpretation, the rule asks individuals to do whatever they imagine they might wish to have done to them in a given situation; thus a judge would be obliged by the golden rule to sentence a convicted criminal with extreme leniency. As a mere principle of sympathy, therefore, it is argued, the rule is incapable of guiding judgment in cases where the necessary action is unwelcome to its immediate recipient.

A related problem is that the rule, taken merely as a policy of sympathy, amounts to the advice "Treat others as they want you to treat them," as in a puzzle from the opening chapter of Herman Melville's *Moby-Dick*, where Ishmael is invited by his new friend, Queequeg, to join in pagan worship. Ishmael pauses to think it over:

> But what is worship?—to do the will of God—*that* is worship. And what is the will of God?—to do to my fellow man what I would have my fellow man to do to me—*that* is the will of God. Now, Queequeg is my fellow man. And what do I wish that this Queequeg would do to me? Why, unite with me in my particular Presbyterian form of worship. Consequently, I must then unite with him in his; ergo, I must turn idolator.

If the golden rule is taken to require the agent to identify with the other in a simplistic and uncritical way, the result is a loss of the higher perspective toward which the rule moves the thoughtful practitioner.

The next clusters of objections have a depth that a quick, initial reply would betray, so I defer my response until later. If the rule is not to be interpreted as setting up the agent's idiosyncratic desires—or those of the recipient—as a supreme standard of goodness, then problems arise because the rule does not specify what the agent ought to desire. The rule merely requires consistency of moral judgment: one must apply the same standards to one's treatment of others that one applies to others' treatment of oneself. The lack of specificity in the rule, its merely formal or merely procedural character, allegedly renders its guidance insubstantial.

The rule seems to exhibit the limitations of any general moral principle: it does not carry sufficiently rich substantive implications to be helpful in the thicket of life's problems. Even though most people live with some allegiance to integrating principles, action guides, mottoes, proverbs, or commandments that serve to unify the mind, the deficiency of any principle is that it is merely a principle, merely a beginning; only the full exposition of a system of ethics can validate the place of an asserted principle. An appeal to a general principle, moreover, can function as a retreat and a refusal to think through issues in their concreteness.

There is also criticism of a practice widely associated with the rule—imagining oneself in the other person's situation. The charge is that this practice is an abstract, derivative, artificial, male, manipulative device, which can never compensate for the lack of human understanding and spontaneous goodness.

The rule has been criticized as a naïvely idealistic standard, unsuited to a world of rugged competition. The rule may seem to require that, if I am trustworthy and want to be trusted, I must treat everyone as being equally trustworthy. Furthermore, the broad humanitarianism of the golden rule allegedly makes unrealistic psychological demands; it is unfair to family and friends to embrace the universal concerns of the golden rule.

Last, some religious issues. The golden rule has been criticized for being a teaching that misleadingly lets people avoid confronting the higher teachings of religious ethics, for example, Jesus's commandment, "Love one another as I have loved you." Some find the rule of only intermediate usefulness, proposing that spiritual living moves beyond the standpoint of rules. Others have criticized the golden rule's traditional links to religion, arguing that moral intuition and moral reason can operate without reference to any religious foundation.

For responding to all these objections, there are three possible strategies: abandon the rule, reformulate it, or retain it as commonly worded, while taking advantage of objections to clarify its proper interpretation. I take the third way.

QUESTIONS FOR DISCUSSION AND WRITING

1. In paragraphs 4 and 5, Wattles offers variations on the golden rule, from Hinduism and Islam as well as the rule in its negative formulation. Do these variations state essentially the same moral precept, or are there subtle differences among them? Why do you think so?

2. Wattles writes that it is "obvious that reason is required for the proper application of the golden rule" (paragraph 11). What does he mean? How does this idea fit in with his point that the rule "takes for granted at least a minimum sincerity that refuses to manipulate the rule sophistically to 'justify' patently immoral conduct" (paragraph 14)?

3. Wattles raises objections that have been made regarding the usefulness of the golden rule, some of which he briefly responds to. His point, however, is that considering these various objections is "useful to illustrate misinterpretations of the rule and to make clear assumptions that must be satisfied for the rule to function in moral theory" (paragraph 15). Might this kind of thinking tend to make what is essentially a straightforward statement of moral principle into something too complicated to put into practice? Given the objections Wattles mentions, how would you go about interpreting the golden rule?

4. In an essay, consider the principles that you live by and explain whether they help you "in the thicket of life's problems." Do you ever use your principles "as a retreat and a refusal to think through issues in their concreteness" (paragraph 20)? Or do they provide you with a positive, adaptable, and useful set of guidelines for moral behavior?

JOHN DONNE

Meditation 17 (For Whom the Bell Tolls)

Poet and clergyman John Donne (1572–1631), like several famous poets of the English Renaissance, did not consider literature to be a career. Although he hoped for a place at the royal court, as a Catholic his career prospects were limited; Protestant England had been at war with Catholic Spain, and anti-Catholic sentiment was high. At Cambridge and Oxford Universities, Donne studied languages and science voraciously but never earned a degree because matriculation would have required him to convert to Protestantism. After abandoning Catholicism, studying law, and serving as a soldier, he won a promising appointment as secretary to a high government official, but his political hopes were dashed when he secretly married Ann More, his employer's seventeen-year-old niece. Ann's father saw to it that Donne was imprisoned briefly, and the couple lived in poverty. Only becoming an Anglican priest (1615) enabled him to win fame for his erudite, witty, and eloquent sermons and to become Dean of St. Paul's Cathedral (1621–1631). His poetry, on topics ranging from love to religion, displays brilliant metaphorical structure and verbal wit, but fell out of fashion until T. S. Eliot and other twentieth-century critics embraced Donne's fusion of emotion and intellect.

Donne wrote the following passage in response to Ann More's death in 1617 and his recovery from serious illness in 1623. It forms "Meditation 17" of Devotions upon Emergent Occasions *(1624), the most enduring of Donne's prose works because of its blend of private feeling and theological insight. Through a series of linked metaphors, Donne affirms each individual's integral place in the social community: "No man is an island."*

> Now, this bell tolling softly
> for another, says to me,
> Thou must die.

Perchance he for whom this bell tolls, may be so ill, as that he knows not it tolls for him; and perchance I may think myself so much better than I am, as that they who are about me, and see my state, may have caused it to toll for me, and I know not that. The Church is Catholic, universal, so are all her actions; all that she does belongs to all. When she baptizes a child, that action concerns me; for that child is thereby connected to that Head which is my Head too, and engrafted into that body, whereof I am a member. And when she buries a man, that action concerns me: all mankind is of one Author, and is one volume; when one man dies, one chapter is not torn out of the book, but translated into a better language; and every chapter must be so translated; God employs several translators; some pieces are translated by age, some by sickness, some by war, some by justice; but God's hand is in every translation; and his hand shall bind up all our scattered leaves again, for that Library where every book shall lie open to one another: As therefore the bell that rings to a sermon, calls not upon the preacher only, but upon the congregation to come; so this bell calls us all: but how much more me, who am brought so near the door by this sickness. There was a contention as far as a suit (in which both piety and dignity, religion and estimation, were mingled), which of the religious orders should ring to prayers first in the morning; and it was determined, that they should ring first that rose earliest. If we understand aright the dignity of this bell that tolls for our evening prayer, we would be glad to make it ours, by rising early, in that application, that it might be ours, as well as his, whose indeed it is. The bell doth toll for him that thinks it doth; and though it intermit again, yet from that minute, that that occasion wrought upon him, he is united to God. Who casts not up his eye to the sun when it rises? but who takes off his eye from a comet when that breaks out? Who bends not his ear to any bell, which upon any occasion rings? but who can remove it from that bell, which is passing a piece of himself out of this world? No man is an island, entire of itself; every man is a piece of the continent, a part of the main; if a clod be washed away by the sea, Europe is the less, as well as if a promontory were, as well as if a manor of thy friends or of thine own were; any man's death diminishes me, because I am involved in mankind; and therefore never send to know for whom the bell tolls; it tolls for thee. Neither can we call this a begging of misery or a borrowing of misery, as though we were not miserable enough of ourselves, but must fetch in more from the next house, in taking upon us the misery of our neighbors. Truly it were an excusable covetousness if we did; for affliction is a treasure, and scarce any man hath enough of it. No man hath affliction enough that is not matured, and ripened by it, and made fit for God by that affliction. If a man carry treasure in bullion, or in a wedge of gold, and have none coined into current monies, his treasure will not defray him as he travels. Tribulation is treasure in the nature of it, but it is not current money in the use of it, except we get nearer and nearer our home, Heaven, by it. Another man may be sick too, and sick to death, and this affliction may lie in his bowels, as gold in a mine, and be of no use to him; but this bell, that tells me of his affliction, digs out, and applies that gold to me; if by this consideration of another's danger I take mine own into contemplation, and so secure myself by making my recourse to my God, who is our only security.

QUESTIONS FOR DISCUSSION AND WRITING

1. How would this "bell tolling softly / for another" person affect you? Why?

2. Donne organizes the first half of his devotional meditation around a series of textual metaphors (author, volume, chapter, book, translation). Do these metaphors enhance his postulation that people are closely related? How so? What does he mean when he argues that death is merely a "translation"?

3. The second half of the meditation is held together by geographical metaphors (island, continent, main, promontory). How do they support his theme of universal connection? Are they consistent with the textual metaphors preceding them? Why or why not?

4. The first law of ecology is that everything is connected to everything else. Compare and contrast Donne's seventeenth-century religious vision of connectedness with the twenty-first-century environmental visions of it.

UNITED NATIONS

The Universal Declaration of Human Rights

After the cataclysm of World War II ended in 1945, the United Nations was founded to promote world peace and international cooperation in dealing with not only the immediate aftermath of the war, but with humanitarian, social, and economic issues more generally. Planning began in 1939 during U.S. President Franklin D. Roosevelt's administration, and the first session of the General Assembly was held on October 24, 1945, with 51 member nations participating. That number has increased to 192 nations today, virtually every sovereign state in the world. The work of the UN's major administrative bodies—the General Assembly, the Security Council, the Economic and Social Council, the Secretariat, and the International Court of Justice—has, like the rest of international politics, been full of controversy and disagreement throughout its nearly seventy-year history. Nevertheless, the members embraced the principle that the UN had a strong commitment to preventing a repetition of World War II's atrocities and genocide, "barbarous acts which have outraged the conscience of mankind" (Preamble). This consensus led the General Assembly to adopt the Universal Declaration of Human Rights on December 10, 1948, a major statement affirming UN principles to promote "a world in which human beings shall enjoy freedom of speech and belief and freedom from fear and want." Although not legally binding for the member nations, this document, reprinted in full below, is a simple, eloquent statement of the ideal principles of human relations and human rights, the foundational basis of individual, family, and social life which transcend time, nationality, and culture for the betterment of all.

PREAMBLE

Whereas recognition of the inherent dignity and of the equal and inalienable rights of all members of the human family is the foundation of freedom, justice and peace in the world,

Whereas disregard and contempt for human rights have resulted in barbarous acts which have outraged the conscience of mankind, and the advent of a world in which human beings shall enjoy freedom of speech and belief and freedom from fear and want has been proclaimed as the highest aspiration of the common people,

Whereas it is essential, if man is not to be compelled to have recourse, as a last resort, to rebellion against tyranny and oppression, that human rights should be protected by the rule of law,

Whereas it is essential to promote the development of friendly relations between nations,

Whereas the peoples of the United Nations have in the Charter reaffirmed their faith in fundamental human rights, in the dignity and worth of the human person and in the equal rights of men and women and have determined to promote social progress and better standards of life in larger freedom,

Whereas Member States have pledged themselves to achieve, in co-operation with the United Nations, the promotion of universal respect for and observance of human rights and fundamental freedoms,

Whereas a common understanding of these rights and freedoms is of the greatest importance for the full realization of this pledge,

Now, Therefore THE GENERAL ASSEMBLY proclaims THIS UNIVERSAL DECLARATION OF HUMAN RIGHTS as a common standard of achievement for all peoples and all nations, to the end that every individual and every organ of society, keeping this Declaration constantly in mind, shall strive by teaching and education to promote respect for these rights and freedoms and by progressive measures, national and international, to secure their universal and effective recognition and observance, both among the peoples of Member States themselves and among the peoples of territories under their jurisdiction.

Article 1.

All human beings are born free and equal in dignity and rights. They are endowed with reason and conscience and should act towards one another in a spirit of brotherhood.

Article 2.

Everyone is entitled to all the rights and freedoms set forth in this Declaration, without distinction of any kind, such as race, colour, sex, language, religion, political or other opinion, national or social origin, property, birth or other status. Furthermore, no distinction shall be made on the basis of the political, jurisdictional or international status of the country or territory to which a person belongs, whether it be independent, trust, non-self-governing or under any other limitation of sovereignty.

Article 3.

Everyone has the right to life, liberty and security of person.

Article 4.

No one shall be held in slavery or servitude; slavery and the slave trade shall be prohibited in all their forms.

Article 5.

No one shall be subjected to torture or to cruel, inhuman or degrading treatment or punishment.

Article 6.

Everyone has the right to recognition everywhere as a person before the law.

Article 7.

All are equal before the law and are entitled without any discrimination to equal protection of the law. All are entitled to equal protection against any discrimination in violation of this Declaration and against any incitement to such discrimination.

Article 8.

Everyone has the right to an effective remedy by the competent national tribunals for acts violating the fundamental rights granted him by the constitution or by law.

Article 9.

No one shall be subjected to arbitrary arrest, detention or exile.

Article 10.

Everyone is entitled in full equality to a fair and public hearing by an independent and impartial tribunal, in the determination of his rights and obligations and of any criminal charge against him.

Article 11.

(1) Everyone charged with a penal offence has the right to be presumed innocent until proved guilty according to law in a public trial at which he has had all the guarantees necessary for his defence.

(2) No one shall be held guilty of any penal offence on account of any act or omission which did not constitute a penal offence, under national or international law, at the time when it was committed. Nor shall a heavier penalty be imposed than the one that was applicable at the time the penal offence was committed.

Article 12.

No one shall be subjected to arbitrary interference with his privacy, family, home or correspondence, nor to attacks upon his honour and reputation. Everyone has the right to the protection of the law against such interference or attacks.

Article 13.

(1) Everyone has the right to freedom of movement and residence within the borders of each state.

(2) Everyone has the right to leave any country, including his own, and to return to his country.

Article 14.

(1) Everyone has the right to seek and to enjoy in other countries asylum from persecution.
(2) This right may not be invoked in the case of prosecutions genuinely arising from non-political crimes or from acts contrary to the purposes and principles of the United Nations.

Article 15.

(1) Everyone has the right to a nationality.
(2) No one shall be arbitrarily deprived of his nationality nor denied the right to change his nationality.

Article 16.

(1) Men and women of full age, without any limitation due to race, nationality or religion, have the right to marry and to found a family. They are entitled to equal rights as to marriage, during marriage and at its dissolution.
(2) Marriage shall be entered into only with the free and full consent of the intending spouses.
(3) The family is the natural and fundamental group unit of society and is entitled to protection by society and the State.

Article 17.

(1) Everyone has the right to own property alone as well as in association with others.
(2) No one shall be arbitrarily deprived of his property.

Article 18.

Everyone has the right to freedom of thought, conscience and religion; this right includes freedom to change his religion or belief, and freedom, either alone or in community with others and in public or private, to manifest his religion or belief in teaching, practice, worship and observance.

Article 19.

Everyone has the right to freedom of opinion and expression; this right includes freedom to hold opinions without interference and to seek, receive and impart information and ideas through any media and regardless of frontiers.

Article 20.

(1) Everyone has the right to freedom of peaceful assembly and association.
(2) No one may be compelled to belong to an association.

Article 21.

(1) Everyone has the right to take part in the government of his country, directly or through freely chosen representatives.

(2) Everyone has the right of equal access to public service in his country.

(3) The will of the people shall be the basis of the authority of government; this will shall be expressed in periodic and genuine elections which shall be by universal and equal suffrage and shall be held by secret vote or by equivalent free voting procedures.

Article 22.

Everyone, as a member of society, has the right to social security and is entitled to realization, through national effort and international co-operation and in accordance with the organization and resources of each State, of the economic, social and cultural rights indispensable for his dignity and the free development of his personality.

Article 23.

(1) Everyone has the right to work, to free choice of employment, to just and favourable conditions of work and to protection against unemployment.

(2) Everyone, without any discrimination, has the right to equal pay for equal work.

(3) Everyone who works has the right to just and favourable remuneration ensuring for himself and his family an existence worthy of human dignity, and supplemented, if necessary, by other means of social protection.

(4) Everyone has the right to form and to join trade unions for the protection of his interests.

Article 24.

Everyone has the right to rest and leisure, including reasonable limitation of working hours and periodic holidays with pay.

Article 25.

(1) Everyone has the right to a standard of living adequate for the health and well-being of himself and of his family, including food, clothing, housing and medical care and necessary social services, and the right to security in the event of unemployment, sickness, disability, widowhood, old age or other lack of livelihood in circumstances beyond his control.

(2) Motherhood and childhood are entitled to special care and assistance. All children, whether born in or out of wedlock, shall enjoy the same social protection.

Article 26.

(1) Everyone has the right to education. Education shall be free, at least in the elementary and fundamental stages. Elementary education shall be compulsory. Technical and professional education shall be made generally available and higher education shall be equally accessible to all on the basis of merit.

(2) Education shall be directed to the full development of the human personality and to the strengthening of respect for human rights and fundamental freedoms. It shall promote understanding, tolerance and friendship among all nations, racial or religious groups, and shall further the activities of the United Nations for the maintenance of peace.

(3) Parents have a prior right to choose the kind of education that shall be given to their children.

Article 27.

(1) Everyone has the right freely to participate in the cultural life of the community, to enjoy the arts and to share in scientific advancement and its benefits.

(2) Everyone has the right to the protection of the moral and material interests resulting from any scientific, literary or artistic production of which he is the author.

Article 28.

Everyone is entitled to a social and international order in which the rights and freedoms set forth in this Declaration can be fully realized.

Article 29.

(1) Everyone has duties to the community in which alone the free and full development of his personality is possible.

(2) In the exercise of his rights and freedoms, everyone shall be subject only to such limitations as are determined by law solely for the purpose of securing due recognition and respect for the rights and freedoms of others and of meeting the just requirements of morality, public order and the general welfare in a democratic society.

(3) These rights and freedoms may in no case be exercised contrary to the purposes and principles of the United Nations.

Article 30.

Nothing in this Declaration may be interpreted as implying for any State, group or person any right to engage in any activity or to perform any act aimed at the destruction of any of the rights and freedoms set forth herein.

QUESTIONS FOR DISCUSSION AND WRITING

1. The Preamble opens with the assertion that "the recognition of the inherent dignity and of the equal and inalienable rights of all members of the human family is the foundation of freedom, justice and peace in the world." What are the connections between fundamental human rights and "freedom, justice, and peace"?

2. The first twenty-nine articles of the Universal Declaration assert, in simple language, a comprehensive list of human rights. Identify some of the most significant. Or are they all of equal significance? Why are those you have chosen so important?

3. What ethical principles does the Universal Declaration of Human Rights embody?

4. In discussion and perhaps a paper written by yourself or with a partner, analyze the gap between the ideal of a human right and the reality of its application in a particular part of the world with which you are familiar, for instance, Article 25.1: "Everyone has the right to a standard of living adequate for the health and well-being of himself and of his family, including food, clothing, housing and medical care and necessary social services, and the right to security in the event of unemployment, sickness, disability, widowhood, old age or other lack of livelihood in circumstances beyond his control."

5. Imagine a worst-case scenario in which one of the human rights in this Declaration was absent, as in fact is often the case worldwide. What are the likely consequences, in political, economic, ethical, human terms?

MARTIN LUTHER KING JR.
Letter from Birmingham Jail

Martin Luther King Jr. (1929–1968) grew up listening to his father's and grandfather's sermons at Ebenezer Baptist Church in Atlanta. He earned a bachelor's degree in sociology at Morehouse College in 1948, a divinity degree at Crozer Theological Seminary in 1951, and a doctorate in theology at Boston University in 1955. When in December 1955 Rosa Parks refused to give up a "white" seat on a segregated bus, King became the eloquent and forceful leader of the subsequent Montgomery bus boycott. In 1957 he founded the Southern Christian Leadership Conference (SCLC) to challenge racial segregation in schools and public accommodations nationwide. King taught civil rights protesters how to practice the Gandhian doctrine of passive resistance in support of civil disobedience, a means of nonviolently breaking an unjust law in order to enact social change. King also reminded civil rights workers to protest with dignity and steady purpose in the face of segregationists' intimidation and violence.

In a letter published in the Birmingham Post-Herald, *eight white clergymen admonished King, the SCLC, and civil rights workers to wait peacefully for better conditions rather than persist in defying unjust laws. On April 12, 1963, Public Safety Commissioner Eugene "Bull" Connor arrested Dr. King for the thirteenth time, this time for "parading without a permit." From his jail cell, King wrote his "Letter from Birmingham Jail," ostensibly replying to the* Post-Herald *letter but actually addressing a national audience.*

"Letter from Birmingham Jail," revised and reprinted in King's Why We Can't Wait *(1964), is now taught not only for its ideas but also for its moving sermonic style,*

its sentence rhythms recalling those of Cicero and Donne, and its allusions to ideas gleaned from many cultures. The section that follows King's "Letter" focuses on how the terms law, justice, *and* extremism *were variously defined during the civil rights movement.*

April 16, 1963[1]

My Dear Fellow Clergymen:

While confined here in the Birmingham city jail, I came across your recent statement calling my present activities "unwise and untimely." Seldom do I pause to answer criticism of my work and ideas. If I sought to answer all the criticisms that cross my desk, my secretaries would have little time for anything other than such correspondence in the course of the day, and I would have no time for constructive work. But since I feel that you are men of genuine good will and that your criticisms are sincerely set forth, I want to try to answer your statement in what I hope will be patient and reasonable terms.

I think I should indicate why I am here in Birmingham, since you have been influenced by the view which argues against "outsiders coming in." I have the honor of serving as president of the Southern Christian Leadership Conference, an organization operating in every southern state, with headquarters in Atlanta, Georgia. We have some eighty-five affiliated organizations across the South, and one of them is the Alabama Christian Movement for Human Rights. Frequently we share staff, educational and financial resources with our affiliates. Several months ago the affiliate here in Birmingham asked us to be on call to engage in a nonviolent direct-action program if such were deemed necessary. We readily consented, and when the hour came we lived up to our promise. So I, along with several members of my staff, am here because I was invited here. I am here because I have organizational ties here.

But more basically, I am in Birmingham because injustice is here. Just as the prophets of the eighth century B.C. left their villages and carried their "thus saith the Lord" far beyond the boundaries of their home towns, and, just as the Apostle Paul left his village of Tarsus and carried the gospel of Jesus Christ to the far corners of the Greco-Roman world, so am I compelled to carry the gospel of freedom beyond my own home town. Like Paul, I must constantly respond to the Macedonian call for aid.

---

[1] This response to a published statement by eight fellow clergymen from Alabama (Bishop C. C. J. Carpenter, Bishop Joseph A. Durick, Rabbi Hilton L. Grafman, Bishop Paul Hardin, Bishop Holan B. Harmon, the Reverend George M. Murray, the Reverend Edward V. Ramage, and the Reverend Earl Stallings) was composed under somewhat constricting circumstances. Begun on the margins of the newspaper in which the statement appeared while I was in jail, the letter was continued on scraps of writing paper supplied by a friendly Negro trusty, and concluded on a pad my attorneys were eventually permitted to leave me. Although the text remains in substance unaltered, I have indulged in the author's prerogative of polishing it for publication.

Moreover, I am cognizant of the interrelatedness of all communities and states. I cannot sit idly by in Atlanta and not be concerned about what happens in Birmingham. Injustice anywhere is a threat to justice everywhere. We are caught in an inescapable network of mutuality, tied in a single garment of destiny. Whatever affects one directly, affects all indirectly. Never again can we afford to live with the narrow, provincial "outside agitator" idea. Anyone who lives inside the United States can never be considered an outsider anywhere within its bounds.

You deplore the demonstrations taking place in Birmingham. But your statement, I am sorry to say, fails to express a similar concern for the conditions that brought about the demonstrations. I am sure that none of you would want to rest content with the superficial kind of social analysis that deals merely with effects and does not grapple with underlying causes. It is unfortunate that demonstrations are taking place in Birmingham, but it is even more unfortunate that the city's white power structure left the Negro community with no alternative.

In any nonviolent campaign there are four basic steps: collection of the facts to determine whether injustices exist; negotiation; self-purification; and direct action. We have gone through all these steps in Birmingham. There can be no gainsaying the fact that racial injustice engulfs this community. Birmingham is probably the most thoroughly segregated city in the United States. An ugly record of brutality is widely known. Negroes have experienced grossly unjust treatment in the courts. There have been more unsolved bombings of Negro homes and churches in Birmingham than in any other city in the nation. These are the hard brutal facts of the case. On the basis of these conditions, Negro leaders sought to negotiate with the city fathers. But the latter consistently refused to engage in good-faith negotiation.

Then, last September, came the opportunity to talk with leaders of Birmingham's economic community. In the course of the negotiations, certain promises were made by the merchants—for example, to remove the stores' humiliating racial signs. On the basis of these promises, the Reverend Fred Shuttlesworth and the leaders of the Alabama Christian Movement for Human Rights agreed to a moratorium on all demonstrations. As the weeks and months went by, we realized that we were the victims of a broken promise. A few signs, briefly removed, returned; the others remained.

As in so many past experiences, our hopes had been blasted, and the shadow of deep disappointment settled upon us. We had no alternative except to prepare for direct action, whereby we would present our very bodies as a means of laying our case before the conscience of the local and the national community. Mindful of the difficulties involved, we decided to undertake a process of self-purification. We began a series of workshops on nonviolence, and we repeatedly asked ourselves: "Are you able to accept blows without retaliating?" "Are you able to endure the ordeal of jail?" We decided to schedule our direct-action program for the Easter season, realizing that except for Christmas, this is the main shopping period of the year. Knowing that a strong economic-withdrawal program would be the by-product of direct action, we felt that this would be the best time to bring pressure to bear on the merchants for the needed change.

Then it occurred to us that Birmingham's mayoral election was coming up in March, and we speedily decided to postpone action until after election day. When we discovered that the Commissioner of Public Safety, Eugene "Bull" Connor, had piled up enough votes to be in the run-off, we decided again to postpone action until the day after the run-off so that the demonstrations could not be used to cloud the issues. Like many others, we waited to see Mr. Connor defeated, and to this end we endured postponement after postponement. Having aided in this community need, we felt that our direct-action program could be delayed no longer.

You may well ask: "Why direct action? Why sit-ins, marches and so forth? Isn't negotiation a better path?" You are quite right in calling for negotiation. Indeed this is the very purpose of direct action. Nonviolent direct action seeks to create such a crisis and foster such a tension that a community which has constantly refused to negotiate is forced to confront the issue. It seeks so to dramatize the issue that it can no longer be ignored. My citing the creation of tension as part of the work of the nonviolent-resister may sound rather shocking. But I must confess that I am not afraid of the word "tension." I have earnestly opposed violent tension, but there is a type of nonviolent tension which is necessary for growth. Just as Socrates felt that it was necessary to create a tension in the mind so that individuals could rise from the bondage of myths and half-truths to the unfettered realm of creative analysis and objective appraisal, so must we see the need for nonviolent gadflies to create the kind of tension in society that will help men rise from the dark depths of prejudice and racism to the majestic heights of understanding and brotherhood. 10

The purpose of our direct-action program is to create a situation so crisis-packed that it will inevitably open the door to negotiation. I therefore concur with you in your call for negotiation. Too long has our beloved Southland been bogged down in a tragic effort to live in monologue rather than dialogue.

One of the basic points in your statement is that the action that I and my associates have taken in Birmingham is untimely. Some have asked: "Why didn't you give the new city administration time to act?" The only answer that I can give to this query is that the new Birmingham administration must be prodded about as much as the outgoing one, before it will act. We are sadly mistaken if we feel that the election of Albert Boutwell as mayor will bring the millennium to Birmingham. While Mr. Boutwell is a much more gentle person than Mr. Connor, they are both segregationists, dedicated to maintenance of the status quo. I have hope that Mr. Boutwell will be reasonable enough to see the futility of massive resistance to desegregation. But he will not see this without pressure from devotees of civil rights. My friends, I must say to you that we have not made a single gain in civil rights without determined legal and nonviolent pressure. Lamentably, it is an historical fact that privileged groups seldom give up their privileges voluntarily. Individuals may see the moral light and voluntarily give up their unjust posture; but, as Reinhold Niebuhr has reminded us, groups tend to be more immoral than individuals.

We know through painful experience that freedom is never voluntarily given by the oppressor; it must be demanded by the oppressed. Frankly, I have yet to engage in a direct-action campaign that was "well-timed" in the view of those who have not suffered unduly from the disease of segregation. For years now I have heard the word "Wait!" It rings in the ear of every Negro with piercing familiarity. This "Wait" has almost always meant "Never." We must come to see, with one of our distinguished jurists, that "justice too long delayed is justice denied."

We have waited for more than 340 years for our constitutional and God-given rights. The nations of Asia and Africa are moving with jetlike speed toward gaining political independence, but we still creep at horse-and-buggy pace toward gaining a cup of coffee at a lunch counter. Perhaps it is easy for those who have never felt the stinging darts of segregation to say, "Wait." But when you have seen vicious mobs lynch your mothers and fathers at will and drown your sisters and brothers at whim; when you have seen hate-filled policemen curse, kick, and even kill your black brothers and sisters; when you see the vast majority of your twenty million Negro brothers smothering in an airtight cage of poverty in the midst of an affluent society; when you suddenly find your tongue twisted and your speech stammering as you seek to explain to your six-year-old daughter why she can't go to the public amusement park that has just been advertised on television, and see tears welling up in her eyes when she is told that Funtown is closed to colored children, and see ominous clouds of inferiority beginning to form in her little mental sky, and see her beginning to distort her personality by developing an unconscious bitterness toward white people; when you have to concoct an answer for a five-year-old son who is asking: "Daddy, why do white people treat colored people so mean?"; when you take a cross-country drive and find it necessary to sleep night after night in the uncomfortable corners of your automobile because no motel will accept you; when you are humiliated day in and day out by nagging signs reading "white" and "colored"; when your first name becomes "nigger," your middle name becomes "boy" (however old you are), and your last name becomes "John," and your wife and mother are never given the respected title "Mrs."; when you are harried by day and haunted by night by the fact that you are a Negro, living constantly at tiptoe stance, never quite knowing what to expect next, and are plagued with inner fears and outer resentments; when you are forever fighting a degenerating sense of "nobodiness"—then you will understand why we find it difficult to wait. There comes a time when the cup of endurance runs over, and men are no longer willing to be plunged into the abyss of despair. I hope, sirs, you can understand our legitimate and unavoidable impatience.

You express a great deal of anxiety over our willingness to break laws. This 15 is certainly a legitimate concern. Since we so diligently urge people to obey the Supreme Court's decision of 1954 outlawing segregation in the public schools, at first glance it may seem rather paradoxical for us consciously to break laws. One may well ask: "How can you advocate breaking some laws and obeying others?"

The answer lies in the fact that there are two types of laws: just and unjust. I would be the first to advocate obeying just laws. One has not only a legal but a moral responsibility to obey just laws. Conversely, one has a moral responsibility to disobey unjust laws. I would agree with St. Augustine that "an unjust law is no law at all."

Now, what is the difference between the two? How does one determine whether a law is just or unjust? A just law is a man-made code that squares with the moral law or the law of God. An unjust law is a code that is out of harmony with the moral law. To put it in the terms of St. Thomas Aquinas: An unjust law is a human law that is not rooted in eternal law and natural law. Any law that uplifts human personality is just. Any law that degrades human personality is unjust. All segregation statutes are unjust because segregation distorts the soul and damages the personality. It gives the segregator a false sense of superiority and the segregated a false sense of inferiority. Segregation, to use the terminology of the Jewish philosopher Martin Buber, substitutes an "I-it" relationship for an "I-thou" relationship and ends up relegating persons to the status of things. Hence segregation is not only politically, economically, and sociologically unsound, it is morally wrong and sinful. Paul Tillich has said that sin is separation. Is not segregation an existential expression of man's tragic separation, his awful estrangement, his terrible sinfulness? Thus it is that I can urge men to obey the 1954 decision of the Supreme Court, for it is morally right; and I can urge them to disobey segregation ordinances, for they are morally wrong.

Let us consider a more concrete example of just and unjust laws. An unjust law is a code that a numerical or power majority group compels a minority group to obey but does not make binding on itself. This is *difference* made legal. By the same token, a just law is a code that a majority compels a minority to follow and that it is willing to follow itself. This is *sameness* made legal.

Let me give another explanation. A law is unjust if it is inflicted on a minority that, as a result of being denied the right to vote, had no part in enacting or devising the law. Who can say that the legislature of Alabama which set up that state's segregation laws was democratically elected? Throughout Alabama all sorts of devious methods are used to prevent Negroes from becoming registered voters, and there are some counties in which even though Negroes constitute a majority of the population, not a single Negro is registered. Can any law enacted under such circumstances be considered democratically structured?

Sometimes a law is just on its face and unjust in its application. For instance, I have been arrested on a charge of parading without a permit. Now, there is nothing wrong in having an ordinance which requires a permit for a parade. But such an ordinance becomes unjust when it is used to maintain segregation and to deny citizens the First-Amendment privilege of peaceful assembly and protest.

I hope you are able to see the distinction I am trying to point out. In no 20 sense do I advocate evading or defying the law, as would the rabid segregationist. That would lead to anarchy. One who breaks an unjust law must do so openly, lovingly, and with a willingness to accept the penalty. I submit that an individual who breaks a law that conscience tells him is unjust, and who willingly accepts the penalty of imprisonment in order to arouse the conscience of the community over its injustice, is in reality expressing the highest respect for the law.

Of course, there is nothing new about this kind of civil disobedience. It was evidenced sublimely in the refusal of Shadrach, Meshach, and Abednego to obey the laws of Nebuchadnezzar, on the ground that a higher moral law was at stake. It was practiced superbly by the early Christians, who were willing to face hungry lions and the excruciating pain of chopping blocks rather than submit to certain unjust laws of the Roman Empire. To a degree, academic freedom is a reality today because Socrates practiced civil disobedience. In our own nation, the Boston Tea Party represented a massive act of civil disobedience.

We should never forget that everything Adolf Hitler did in Germany was "legal" and everything the Hungarian freedom fighters did in Hungary was "illegal." It was "illegal" to aid and comfort a Jew in Hitler's Germany. Even so, I am sure that, had I lived in Germany at the time, I would have aided and comforted my Jewish brothers. If today I lived in a Communist country where certain principles dear to the Christian faith are suppressed, I would openly advocate disobeying that country's anti-religious laws.

I must make two honest confessions to you, my Christian and Jewish brothers. First, I must confess that over the past few years I have been gravely disappointed with the white moderate. I have almost reached the regrettable conclusion that the Negro's great stumbling block in his stride toward freedom is not the White Citizen's Counciler or the Ku Klux Klanner, but the white moderate, who is more devoted to "order" than to justice; who prefers a negative peace which is the absence of tension to a positive peace which is the presence of justice; who constantly says: "I agree with you in the goal you seek, but I cannot agree with your methods of direct action"; who paternalistically believes he can set the timetable for another man's freedom; who lives by a mythical concept of time and who constantly advises the Negro to wait for a "more convenient season." Shallow understanding from people of good will is more frustrating than absolute misunderstanding from people of ill will. Lukewarm acceptance is much more bewildering than outright rejection.

I had hoped that the white moderate would understand that law and order exist for the purpose of establishing justice and that when they fail in this purpose they become the dangerously structured dams that block the flow of social progress. I had hoped that the white moderate would understand that the present tension in the South is a necessary phase of the transition from an obnoxious negative peace, in which the Negro passively accepted his unjust plight, to a substantive and positive peace, in which all men will respect the dignity and worth of human personality. Actually, we who engage in nonviolent direct action are not the creators of tension. We merely bring to the surface the hidden tension that is already alive. We bring it out in the open, where it can be seen and dealt with. Like a boil that can never be cured so long as it is covered up but must be opened with all its ugliness to the natural medicines of air and light, injustice must be exposed, with all the tension its exposure creates, to the light of human conscience and the air of national opinion before it can be cured.

In your statement you assert that our actions, even though peaceful, must be condemned because they precipitate violence. But is this a logical assertion? Isn't this like condemning a robbed man because his possession of money precipitated the evil act of robbery? Isn't this like condemning Socrates because his unswerving commitment to truth and his philosophical inquiries precipitated the act by the misguided populace in which they made him drink hemlock? Isn't this like condemning Jesus because his unique God-consciousness and never-ceasing devotion to God's will precipitated the evil act of crucifixion? We must come to see that, as the federal courts have consistently affirmed, it is wrong to urge an individual to cease his efforts to gain his basic constitutional rights because the quest may precipitate violence. Society must protect the robbed and punish the robber.

I had also hoped that the white moderate would reject the myth concerning time in relation to the struggle for freedom. I have just received a letter from a white brother in Texas. He writes: "All Christians know that the colored people will receive equal rights eventually, but it is possible that you are in too great a religious hurry. It has taken Christianity almost two thousand years to accomplish what it has. The teachings of Christ take time to come to earth." Such an attitude stems from a tragic misconception of time, from the strangely irrational notion that there is something in the very flow of time that will inevitably cure all ills. Actually, time itself is neutral; it can be used either destructively or constructively. More and more I feel that the people of ill will have used time much more effectively than have the people of good will. We will have to repent in this generation not merely for the hateful words and actions of the bad people but for the appalling silence of the good people. Human progress never rolls in on wheels of inevitability; it comes through the tireless efforts of men willing to be co-workers with God, and without this hard work, time itself becomes an ally of the forces of social stagnation. We must use time creatively, in the knowledge that the time is always ripe to do right. Now is the time to make real the promise of democracy and transform our pending national elegy into a creative psalm of brotherhood. Now is the time to lift our national policy from the quicksand of racial injustice to the solid rock of human dignity.

You speak of our activity in Birmingham as extreme. At first I was rather disappointed that fellow clergymen would see my nonviolent efforts as those of an extremist. I began thinking about the fact that I stand in the middle of two opposing forces in the Negro community. One is a force of complacency, made up in part of Negroes who, as a result of long years of oppression, are so drained of self-respect and a sense of "somebodiness" that they have adjusted to segregation; and in part of a few middle-class Negroes who, because of a degree of academic and economic security and because in some ways they profit by segregation, have become insensitive to the problems of the masses. The other force is one of bitterness and hatred, and it comes perilously close to advocating violence. It is expressed in the various black nationalist groups that are springing up across the nation, the largest and best-known being Elijah Muhammad's Muslim movement. Nourished by the Negro's frustration over the continued existence of racial discrimination, this movement is made up of people who have lost faith in America, who have absolutely repudiated Christianity, and who have concluded that the white man is an incorrigible "devil."

I have tried to stand between these two forces, saying that we need emulate neither the "do-nothingism" of the complacent nor the hatred and despair of the black nationalist. For there is the more excellent way of love and nonviolent protest. I am grateful to God that, through the influence of the Negro church, the way of nonviolence became an integral part of our struggle.

If this philosophy had not emerged, by now many streets of the South would, I am convinced, be flowing with blood. And I am further convinced that if our white brothers dismiss as "rabble-rousers" and "outside agitators" those of us who employ nonviolent direct action, and if they refuse to support our nonviolent efforts, millions of Negroes will, out of frustration and despair, seek solace and security in black-nationalist ideologies—a development that would inevitably lead to a frightening racial nightmare.

Oppressed people cannot remain oppressed forever. The yearning for freedom eventually manifests itself, and that is what has happened to the American Negro. Something within has reminded him of his birthright of freedom, and something without has reminded him that it can be gained. Consciously or unconsciously, he has been caught up by the *Zeitgeist*, and with his black brothers of Africa and his brown and yellow brothers of Asia, South America, and the Caribbean, the United States Negro is moving with a sense of great urgency toward the promised land of racial justice. If one recognizes this vital urge that has engulfed the Negro community, one should readily understand why public demonstrations are taking place. The Negro has many pent-up resentments and latent frustrations, and he must release them. So let him march; let him make prayer pilgrimages to the city hall; let him go on freedom rides—and try to understand why he must do so. If his repressed emotions are not released in nonviolent ways, they will seek expression through violence; this is not a threat but a fact of history. So I have not said to my people: "Get rid of your discontent." Rather, I have tried to say that this normal and healthy discontent can be channeled into the creative outlet of nonviolent direct action. And now this approach is being termed extremist.

But though I was initially disappointed at being categorized as an extremist, as I continued to think about the matter I gradually gained a measure of satisfaction from the label. Was not Jesus an extremist for love: "Love your enemies, bless them that curse you, do good to them that hate you, and pray for them which despitefully use you, and persecute you." Was not Amos an extremist for justice: "Let justice roll down like waters and righteousness like an ever-flowing stream." Was not Paul an extremist for the Christian gospel: "I bear in my body the marks of the Lord Jesus." Was not Martin Luther an extremist: "Here I stand; I cannot do otherwise, so help me God." And John Bunyan: "I will stay in jail to the end of my days before I make a butchery of my conscience." And Abraham Lincoln: "This nation cannot survive half slave and half free." And Thomas Jefferson: "We hold these truths to be self-evident, that all men are created equal. . . ." So the question is not whether we will be extremists, but what kind of extremists we will be. Will we be extremists for hate or for love? Will we be extremists for the preservation of injustice or for the extension of justice? In that dramatic scene on Calvary's hill three men were crucified. We must never forget that all three were crucified for the same crime—the crime of extremism. Two were extremists for immorality, and thus fell below their environment. The other, Jesus Christ, was an extremist for love, truth, and goodness, and thereby rose above his environment. Perhaps the South, the nation, and the world are in dire need of creative extremists.

I had hoped that the white moderate would see this need. Perhaps I was too optimistic; perhaps I expected too much. I suppose I should have realized that few members of the oppressor race can understand the deep groans and passionate yearnings of the oppressed race, and still fewer have the vision to see that injustice must be rooted out by strong, persistent, and determined action. I am thankful, however, that some of our white brothers in the South have grasped the meaning of this social revolution and committed themselves to it. They are still all too few in quantity, but they are big in quality. Some—such as Ralph McGill, Lillian Smith, Harry Golden, James McBride Dabbs, Ann Braden, and Sarah Patton Boyle—have written about our struggle in eloquent and prophetic terms. Others have marched with us down nameless streets of the South. They have languished in filthy, roach-infested jails, suffering the abuse and brutality of policemen who view them as "dirty nigger-lovers." Unlike so many of their moderate brothers and sisters, they have recognized the urgency of the moment and sensed the need for powerful "action" antidotes to combat the disease of segregation.

Let me take note of my other major disappointment. I have been so greatly disappointed with the white church and its leadership. Of course, there are some notable exceptions. I am not unmindful of the fact that each of you has taken some significant stands on this issue. I commend you, Reverend Stallings, for your Christian stand on this past Sunday, in welcoming Negroes to your worship service on a nonsegregated basis. I commend the Catholic leaders of this state for integrating Spring Hill College several years ago.

But despite these notable exceptions, I must honestly reiterate that I have been disappointed with the church. I do not say this as one of those negative critics who can always find something wrong with the church. I say this as a minister of the gospel, who loves the church; who was nurtured in its bosom; who has been sustained by its spiritual blessings and who will remain true to it as long as the cord of life shall lengthen.

When I was suddenly catapulted into the leadership of the bus protest in 35 Montgomery, Alabama, a few years ago, I felt we would be supported by the white church. I felt that the white ministers, priests, and rabbis of the South would be among our strongest allies. Instead, some have been outright opponents, refusing to understand the freedom movement and misrepresenting its leaders; all too many others have been more cautious than courageous and have remained silent behind the anesthetizing security of stained-glass windows.

In spite of my shattered dreams, I came to Birmingham with the hope that the white religious leadership of this community would see the justice of our cause and, with deep moral concern, would serve as the channel through which our just grievances could reach the power structure. I had hoped that each of you would understand. But again I have been disappointed.

I have heard numerous southern religious leaders admonish their worshipers to comply with a desegregation decision because it is the law, but I have longed to hear white ministers declare: "Follow this decree because integration is morally right and because the Negro is your brother." In the midst of blatant injustices inflicted upon the Negro, I have watched white churchmen stand on the sideline and mouth pious irrelevancies and sanctimonious trivialities. In the midst of a mighty struggle to rid our nation of racial and economic injustice, I have heard many ministers say: "Those are social issues, with which the gospel has no real concern." And I have watched many churches commit themselves to a completely other-worldly religion which makes a strange, un-Biblical distinction between body and soul, between the sacred and the secular.

I have traveled the length and breadth of Alabama, Mississippi, and all the other southern states. On sweltering summer days and crisp autumn mornings I have looked at the South's beautiful churches with their lofty spires pointing heavenward. I have beheld the impressive outlines of her massive religious-education buildings. Over and over I have found myself asking: "What kind of people worship here? Who is their God? Where were their voices when the lips of Governor Barnett dripped with words of interposition and nullification? Where were they when Governor Wallace gave a clarion call for defiance and hatred? Where were their voices of support when bruised and weary Negro men and women decided to rise from the dark dungeons of complacency to the bright hills of creative protest?"

Yes, these questions are still in my mind. In deep disappointment I have wept over the laxity of the church. But be assured that my tears have been tears of love. There can be no deep disappointment where there is not deep love. Yes, I love the church. How could I do otherwise? I am in the rather unique position of being the son, the grandson, and the great-grandson of preachers. Yes, I see the church as the body of Christ. But, oh! How we have blemished and scarred that body through social neglect and through fear of being nonconformists.

There was a time when the church was very powerful—in the time when the 40 early Christians rejoiced at being deemed worthy to suffer for what they believed. In those days the church was not merely a thermometer that recorded the ideas and principles of popular opinion; it was a thermostat that transformed the mores of society. Whenever the early Christians entered a town, the people in power became disturbed and immediately sought to convict the Christians for being "disturbers of the peace" and "outside agitators." But the Christians pressed on, in the conviction that they were "a colony of heaven," called to obey God rather than man. Small in number, they were big in commitment. They were too God-intoxicated to be "astronomically intimidated." By their effort and example they brought an end to such ancient evils as infanticide and gladiatorial contests.

Things are different now. So often the contemporary church is a weak, ineffectual voice with an uncertain sound. So often it is an archdefender of the status quo. Far from being disturbed by the presence of the church, the power structure of the average community is consoled by the church's silent—and often even vocal—sanction of things as they are.

But the judgment of God is upon the church as never before. If today's church does not recapture the sacrificial spirit of the early church, it will lose its authenticity, forfeit the loyalty of millions, and be dismissed as an irrelevant social club with no meaning for the twentieth century. Every day I meet young people whose disappointment with the church has turned into outright disgust.

Perhaps I have once again been too optimistic. Is organized religion too inextricably bound to the status quo to save our nation and the world? Perhaps I must turn my faith to the inner spiritual church, the church within the church, as the true *ekklesia* and the hope of the world. But again I am thankful to God that some noble souls from the ranks of organized religion have broken loose from the paralyzing chains of conformity and joined us as active partners in the struggle for freedom. They have left their secure congregations and walked the streets of Albany, Georgia, with us. They have gone down the highways of the South on tortuous rides for freedom. Yes, they have gone to jail with us. Some have been dismissed from their churches, have lost the support of their bishops and fellow ministers. But they have acted in the faith that right defeated is stronger than evil triumphant. Their witness has been the spiritual salt that has preserved the true meaning of the gospel in these troubled times. They have carved a tunnel of hope through the dark mountain of disappointment.

I hope the church as a whole will meet the challenge of this decisive hour. But even if the church does not come to the aid of justice, I have no despair about the future. I have no fear about the outcome of our struggle in Birmingham, even if our motives are at present misunderstood. We will reach the goal of freedom in Birmingham and all over the nation, because the goal of America is freedom. Abused and scorned though we may be, our destiny is tied up with America's destiny. Before the pilgrims landed at Plymouth, we were here. Before the pen of Jefferson etched the majestic words of the Declaration of Independence across the pages of history, we were here. For more than two centuries our forebears labored in this country without wages; they made cotton king; they built the homes of their masters while suffering gross injustice and shameful humiliation—and yet out of a bottomless vitality they continued to thrive and develop. If the inexpressible cruelties of slavery could not stop us, the opposition we now face will surely fail. We will win our freedom because the sacred heritage of our nation and the eternal will of God are embodied in our echoing demands.

Before closing I feel impelled to mention one other point in your statement 45
that has troubled me profoundly. You warmly commended the Birmingham

police force for keeping "order" and "preventing violence." I doubt that you would have so warmly commended the police force if you had seen its dogs sinking their teeth into unarmed, nonviolent Negroes. I doubt that you would so quickly commend the policemen if you were to observe their ugly and inhumane treatment of Negroes here in the city jail; if you were to watch them push and curse old Negro women and young Negro girls; if you were to see them slap and kick old Negro men and young boys; if you were to observe them as they did on two occasions, refuse to give us food because we wanted to sing our grace together. I cannot join you in your praise of the Birmingham police department.

It is true that the police have exercised a degree of discipline in handling the demonstrators. In this sense they have conducted themselves rather "nonviolently" in public. But for what purpose? To preserve the evil system of segregation. Over the past few years I have consistently preached that nonviolence demands that the means we use must be as pure as the ends we seek. I have tried to make clear that it is wrong to use immoral means to attain moral ends. But now I must affirm that it is just as wrong, or perhaps even more so, to use moral means to preserve immoral ends. Perhaps Mr. Connor and his policemen have been rather nonviolent in public, as was Chief Pritchett in Albany, Georgia, but they have used the moral means of nonviolence to maintain the immoral end of racial injustice. As T. S. Eliot has said: "The last temptation is the greatest treason: To do the right deed for the wrong reason."

I wish you had commended the Negro sit-inners and demonstrators of Birmingham for their sublime courage, their willingness to suffer, and their amazing discipline in the midst of great provocation. One day the South will recognize its real heroes. They will be the James Merediths, with the noble sense of purpose that enables them to face jeering and hostile mobs, and with the agonizing loneliness that characterizes the life of the pioneer. They will be old, oppressed, battered Negro women, symbolized in a seventy-two-year-old woman in Montgomery, Alabama, who rose up with a sense of dignity and with her people decided not to ride segregated buses, and who responded with ungrammatical profundity to one who inquired about her weariness: "My feet is tired, but my soul is at rest." They will be the young high school and college students, the young ministers of the gospel and a host of their elders, courageously and nonviolently sitting in at lunch counters and willingly going to jail for conscience' sake. One day the South will know that when these disinherited children of God sat down at lunch counters, they were in reality standing up for what is best in the American dream and for the most sacred values in our Judaeo-Christian heritage, thereby bringing our nation back to those great wells of democracy which were dug deep by the founding fathers in their formulation of the Constitution and the Declaration of Independence.

Never before have I written so long a letter. I'm afraid it is much too long to take your precious time. I can assure you that it would have been much shorter if I had been writing from a comfortable desk, but what else can one do when he is alone in a narrow jail cell, other than write long letters, think long thoughts, and pray long prayers?

If I have said anything in this letter that overstates the truth and indicates an unreasonable impatience, I beg you to forgive me. If I have said anything that understates the truth and indicates my having a patience that allows me to settle for anything less than brotherhood, I beg God to forgive me.

I hope this letter finds you strong in faith. I also hope that circumstances 50 will soon make it possible for me to meet each of you, not as an integrationist or a civil-rights leader but as a fellow clergyman and a Christian brother. Let us all hope that the dark clouds of racial prejudice will soon pass away and the deep fog of misunderstanding will be lifted from our fear-drenched communities, and in some not too distant tomorrow the radiant stars of love and brotherhood will shine over our great nation with all their scintillating beauty.

Yours for the cause of Peace and Brotherhood,
Martin Luther King Jr.

CONTEXTS FOR "LETTER FROM BIRMINGHAM JAIL"

Eight Clergymen's Statement

King and his lieutenant, the Reverend Ralph Abernathy, led a series of demonstrations in Birmingham in April 1963. King was arrested on April 12 and while he was in jail he read the following statement in the Birmingham Post-Herald. *King then began his "Letter from Birmingham Jail," modeling it on thirteen biblical letters from Jesus's apostle Paul to the Corinthians, Ephesians, and others.*

We the undersigned clergymen are among those who, in January, issued "An Appeal for Law and Order and Common Sense," in dealing with racial problems in Alabama. We expressed understanding that honest convictions in racial matters could properly be pursued in the courts, but urged that decisions of those courts should in the meantime be peacefully obeyed.

Since that time there had been some evidence of increased forbearance and a willingness to face facts. Responsible citizens have undertaken to work on various problems which cause racial friction and unrest. In Birmingham, recent public events have given indication that we all have opportunity for a new constructive and realistic approach to racial problems.

However, we are now confronted by a series of demonstrations by some of our Negro citizens, directed and led in part by outsiders. We recognize the natural impatience of people who feel that their hopes are slow in being realized. But we are convinced that these demonstrations are unwise and untimely.

From the Birmingham *Post-Herald*, 13 April 1963, p. 10; reprinted in Martin Luther King Jr., *Why We Can't Wait* (New York: Harper, 1964).

We agree with certain local Negro leadership which has called for honest and open negotiations of racial issues in our area. And we believe this kind of facing of issues can best be accomplished by citizens of our town metropolitan area, white and Negro, meeting with their knowledge and experience of the local situation. All of us need to face that responsibility and find proper channels for its accomplishment.

Just as we formerly pointed out that "hatred and violence have no sanction in our religious and political traditions," we also point out that such actions as incite to hatred and violence, however technically peaceful actions may be, have not contributed to the resolution of our local problems. We do not believe that these days of new hope are days when extreme measures are justified in Birmingham.

We commend the community as a whole, and the local news media and law enforcement officials in particular, on the calm manner in which these demonstrations have been handled. We urge the public to continue to show restraint should the demonstrations continue, and the law enforcement officials to remain calm and continue to protect our city from violence.

We further strongly urge our own Negro community to withdraw support from these demonstrations, and to unite locally in working peacefully for a better Birmingham. When rights are consistently denied, a cause should be pressed in the courts and in negotiations among local leaders, and not in the streets. We appeal to both our white and Negro citizenry to observe the principles of law and order and common sense.

BROOKS HAYS

A Southern Moderate Speaks

The Supreme Court decision of May 17, 1954, is too well known to need extensive quotation. The Court swept aside completely the doctrine of "separate but equal" schools for Negro children, first enunciated in the *Plessy* v. *Ferguson* decision of 1896, with the words, "We conclude that in the field of public education the doctrine of 'separate but equal' has no place. Separate educational facilities are inherently unequal." Less well known, except for the phrase "with all deliberate speed," are the provisions to implement the Supreme Court's decision spelled out the following year. . . .

> [T]he courts will require that the defendants make a prompt and reasonable start toward full compliance with our May 17, 1954, ruling. Once such a start has been made, the courts may find that additional time is necessary to carry out the ruling in an effective manner. The burden rests upon the defendants to establish that such time is necessary in the public interest and is consistent with good faith compliance at the earliest practicable date. To that end,

From Brooks Hays, *A Southern Moderate Speaks* (Chapel Hill: University of North Carolina Press, 1959), 86–91, 189.

the courts may consider problems related to administration, rising from the physical condition of the school plant, the school transportation system, personnel, revision of school districts and attendance areas into compact units to achieve a system of determining admission to the public schools on a nonracial basis, and revision of local laws and regulations which may be necessary in solving the foregoing problems. They will also consider the adequacy of any plans the defendants may propose to meet these problems and to effectuate a transition to a racially nondiscriminatory school system. During this period of transition, the courts will retain jurisdiction of these cases.

The calm that initially prevailed in the South was eventually broken by the establishment of White Citizens Councils and the increased activity of the NAACP. . . . It was in this setting that the great majority of Southern congressmen and senators came together to issue the now-famous Declaration of Constitutional Principles or the so-called "Southern Manifesto." The declaration stated the views of over 100 members of the delegations of eleven Southern states as follows:

> In the case of *Plessy* v. *Ferguson* in 1896, the Supreme Court expressly declared that under the Fourteenth Amendment no person was denied any of his rights if the States provided separate but equal public facilities. This decision has been followed in many other cases. It is notable that the Supreme Court, speaking through Chief Justice Taft, a former President of the United States, unanimously declared in 1927 in *Lum* v. *Rice* that the "separate but equal principle is . . . within the discretion of the State in regulating its public schools and does not conflict with the Fourteenth Amendment."
>
> This interpretation, restated time and again, became a part of the life of the people of many of the States and confirmed their habits, customs, traditions, and way of life. It is founded on elemental humanity and common sense, for parents should not be deprived by government of the right to direct the lives and education of their own children. . . .
>
> We pledge ourselves to use all lawful means to bring about a reversal of this decision which is contrary to the Constitution and to prevent the use of force in its implementation.

I signed this declaration as a proper statement of the South's objections to the overthrow of the *Plessy* v. *Ferguson* decision and violation of the *stare decisis* principle in Constitutional law. While it contained items which to me would have been better omitted and expressed some sentiments in language not to my liking, I believed the declaration was an honest reaction to the injury the South believed had been done to its way of life. I joined with a number of other members of Congress who refused to sign the document unless it removed all mention of the doctrines of nullification and interposition. In this way, the Southern moderates hoped to preserve the Constitutional guarantee of the right to dissent without advocating measures which might do violence to the Constitution. . . .

King and Abernathy under arrest

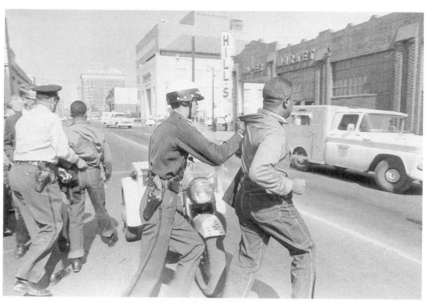

King (*left*) and Abernathy

Two Christians' Responses to King's Views

Immediately following the reprinting of King's "Letter" in a June 1963 issue of the Christian Century, T. Olin Binkley responded by advocating "[t]he exercise of truly responsible freedom in the pulpit and the classroom," but he stopped short of mentioning desegregation or civil rights.

Will Herberg rebutted Dr. King's differentiation of just from unjust laws and rejected the notion that individual conscience is a basis for civil disobedience. By basing his argument on a quotation from Paul's Epistle to the Romans, Herberg calls King's scholarly authority into question. Herberg restricts his definition of "authorities" to those who enforce local regulations against demonstrations; he omits mention of the U.S. Supreme Court's authority. He also defines justifiable disobedience as refusal to participate, not as the actions of civil disobedience such as demonstrations.

T. OLIN BINKLEY

Southern Baptist Seminaries

The exercise of truly responsible freedom in the pulpit and in the classroom is justified by the Christian doctrine of the Holy Spirit. The New Testament draws attention to three ways in which the Holy Spirit may be mistreated: he may be resisted, grieved, quenched. If Southern Baptists grieve and quench the Holy Spirit in their seminaries, the springs of Christian scholarship in those schools will dry up and the quality of Baptist witness and work will be diluted and seriously damaged. Such a course would be educationally inexcusable and spiritually disastrous. If, on the other hand, Southern Baptists submit themselves humbly and gratefully to correction and instruction by the Holy Spirit, he will lead them into a deeper knowledge of the mind of Christ; he will draw them together in a fellowship of faith and learning that will prove as strong as steel and as indestructible as truth; he will teach them to order their lives and their schools by what is "good, acceptable and perfect" in the sight of God. . . .

In all that we do in the churches and in the seminaries we are dependent on God who has committed to us the word and the ministry of reconciliation. The teachers and the graduates of Southern Baptist seminaries have their share of distractions and disappointments, but they understand the nature of the Christian ministry and the source of power for its fulfillment. On the most difficult assignments they are able to say with Paul, "Our sufficiency is from God, who has qualified us to be ministers of a new covenant."

From T. Olin Binkley, "Southern Baptist Seminaries," *Christian Century*, 12 June 1963, 774–775.

WILL HERBERG

A Religious "Right" to Violate the Law?

It is . . . of considerable interest to inquire a little more closely into Dr. King's notions of political responsibility and social order, particularly into his central contention that Christian principles permit, perhaps even require, the violation of laws the individual conscience may hold to be "unjust." . . .

But how does this position square with well-established Christian teaching on government, law, and civil obedience?

ST. PAUL'S TEACHING

The essential Christian teaching on government, law, and civil obedience is grounded on that celebrated Chapter XIII of Paul's Epistle to the Romans, which itself reflects earlier Jewish teaching. "Let every one be subject to the governing authorities," the Apostle enjoins. "For there is no authority except from God, and the existing authorities have been ordained by God. Therefore, he who resists the authorities resists what God has appointed, and those who resist will incur judgment. . . ." This is balanced in the New Testament by the conviction of Peter and the Apostles, "We must obey God rather than man" (Acts 5:29).

When does loyalty to God come into conflict with obedience to earthly rulers? When earthly rulers are insensate enough (as totalitarian states invariably are) to demand for themselves what is owing only to God—worship and ultimate allegiance. The classical Christian teaching emerges most profoundly perhaps in the writings of St. Augustine, whose position Professor Deane thus summarizes:

> When Augustine says that God's command overrules [human] laws and customs, it seems clear that he is referring to those commands of God that have been directly revealed to men in the Scriptures, such as the prohibition against idol-worship. . . . He does *not* say that if the ruler is unwise or evil, and fails to take the eternal law into account when he frames temporal laws, these laws have no validity, and the subjects have no obligation to obey them; nor does he say that the subjects have a right to determine for themselves, by reference to the natural or eternal law, whether or not such a temporal law is valid and is to be obeyed. (Herbert A. Deane, *The Political and Social Ideas of St. Augustine*, Columbia U.P., 1963, pp. 147, 89, 90; Dr. Deane is professor of government at Columbia)

This, in substance, early became the normative Christian doctrine, stated and   5 restated by Thomas Aquinas, Martin Luther, John Calvin, and every other great moralist and theologian of the Church. It is the standard by which the position advanced by Dr. King and U.S. Representative Adam Clayton Powell *as Christian*

From Will Herberg, "A Religious 'Right' to Violate the Law?" *National Review* 16 (July 1964): 579–580.

must be judged; and, judged by that standard, their position permitting the violation of any law disapproved of by the individual conscience as "unjust," must be judged as not Christian at all, but seriously deviant and heretical.

NO EARLY CHRISTIAN SIT-INS

The early Christians, under the teaching of the apostles, were enjoined to obey the laws of the state, a pagan state, mind you, whether they held these laws to be just or unjust—just so long as the state (the Emperor) did not claim for itself the worship and allegiance owing only to God. At that point, they knew how to draw the line. But even at that point, where they were compelled to disobey, their disobedience was limited to *refusal to participate* in the pagan abominations. The Christian refused, at the risk of life, to take part in the pagan cult, or to sacrifice to the Emperor; he did not set up mass picketing of the temples, or organize sit-ins in the public buildings in which the "blasphemies" (Tertullian) were being performed. . . .

STRANGE DOCTRINE

Would it not be well for Dr. King, as a responsible community leader honored with a Doctor of Laws by Yale University, to consider the consequences of his strange doctrine? Every man has his conscience; and if the individual conscience is absolutized (that is, divinized), and made the final judge of laws to be obeyed or disobeyed, nothing but anarchy and the dissolution of the very fabric of government would result. Thousands and thousands of Americans, eminent, respectable, and responsible, are convinced in their conscience that the new Civil Rights Act is utterly wrong, unjust, and unconstitutional; are they therefore entitled to disobey it, and to organize civil disobedience campaigns to impede its effectuation? Grant this "right" and there would be no law at all, nothing but a clash of "consciences" that could not hope to escape becoming a clash of raw power.[1] . . .

NOTES

1. One important exception must be noted. Under the American system of judicial review, the constitutionality, and therefore the legality, of a law, when challenged, cannot be finally determined until it comes to court; and, very frequently, it cannot come to court until it is somehow violated. Such technical violation for the sake of a *test case* is to be fundamentally distinguished from the mass civil disobedience advocated by Dr. King.

DEBATING "JUSTICE" AND INVOKING THE POWER OF BALLOTS AND BOYCOTTS

Perhaps realizing that ethical and religious debates defining *law* and *justice* could go on indefinitely, leaders of the civil rights movement soon augmented moral persuasion and civil disobedience with political and economic strategies, such as Negro voter registration, boycotts, entrepreneurship, and advocacy for public housing and school desegregation. . . .

While emphasizing the economic power of boycotts, King also expressed confidence that the white church and white community would support the civil rights bill (which President Lyndon Johnson signed into law on July 2, 1964) and that legislation would suppress racist behavior if not also racist attitudes.

Social movements often redefine old terms and coin new ones. Young civil rights leaders redefined *Negro* and *black* throughout the mid-1960s. *Negroes* had connoted respect but now began to mean conservative, even obsequious "Uncle Toms," who would await justice indefinitely. *Blacks* had connoted disrespect but now began to mean people ready to demonstrate, exert economic and political power, wear African dress and natural "Afro" hairstyles, and proclaim that "black is beautiful!" By 1967, King himself became a spokesman for "black power," a term he defined in an article for the *New York Times Magazine* in June of that year.

MARTIN LUTHER KING JR.

Boycotts Will Be Used

Q. Have you seen evidence that white resistance to demands of Negroes is stiffening—taking the form of bloc voting by whites?

A. I think some of this is inevitable in a period of social transition. Many people in the North have come to realize that they probably had much more deep-seated prejudices than they had been conscious of. It took the big push by the Negro community and the allies of the Negro in the white community to bring this whole issue to the surface in 1963.

I'm not at all discouraged. I think that this whole issue is out in the open now in a way that it has never been before. It's something like a boil, which, if kept covered up, will never be cured. It's only when you open it to air and light that it can be cured, even though it's ugly for the moment.

I think that we are bringing to the surface an issue that has been in the background all too long. We have tried to hide it. Now, it is out in the open, and this is the only way that it will be cured. . . .

Q. Why do Negro leaders place such heavy stress on the civil-rights bill? Do you feel that laws can solve the major problems that Negroes face? 5

A. I think laws are very important in getting to the major problems.

I'm not saying that the ultimate problem in human relations can be solved through legislation. You can't make a man, through legal strictures and judicial decrees or executive orders, love somebody else. But we aren't trying to legislate love. We are trying to legislate issues that regulate behavior.

Even though morality cannot be legislated, behavior can be regulated. While the law cannot change the heart, it can certainly restrain the heartless.

From Martin Luther King Jr., "Boycotts Will Be Used," *U.S. News and World Report*, 24 February 1964, 56–61.

QUESTIONS FOR DISCUSSION AND WRITING

1. In paragraphs 27–32 of "Letter from Birmingham Jail," King answers charges that his actions are "extreme." What does *extreme* mean for King in the context of civil rights demonstrations? Consider various contemporary connotations of *extreme*, as in extreme risk, extreme strength, extreme sports, extreme brutality. Is there a common core of the meaning of *extreme* in these contexts? Are there significant differences? In what ways do these definitions resemble or differ from Dr. King's usage?

2. Brooks Hays and the eight clergymen from Birmingham advocate moderation. What do their definitions of moderation have in common, and what differences can you identify?

3. On what grounds does King defend extremism (paragraphs 27–31), and how extreme does he think he actually is? Who is more radical than King, and in what ways?

4. What ethical and social values do the photographs of King and Abernathy from *Time* and *Newsweek* (p. 510) seem to represent? What do the photographs seem to be saying about the relative merits of moderation and extremism?

5. What are the hallmarks of "Christian morality" as T. Olin Binkley and Will Herberg understand it, and how does their version differ from King's?

6. The rhythm of King's sentences is often traced to the preaching style used to address many African American congregations. Read aloud John Donne's "Meditation" (p. 486), listening for the rhythm of the sentences. What features of Donne's sentences produce the rhythm? Which sentences in King's "Letter from Birmingham Jail" sound similar to Donne's, and which features produce the similarities?

GEORGE ORWELL

Shooting an Elephant

George Orwell (1903–1950) is best known for his anti-totalitarian novels, Animal Farm *(1945) and* 1984 *(1949). He was born Eric Arthur Blair in Bengal (now Bihar), India, where his father worked in the colonial civil service. Orwell was educated at Eton and served with the Indian Imperial Police in Burma, now Myanmar. Orwell writes of his frustration with racial and social barriers there in his novel* Burmese Days *(1934) and in his essay "Shooting an Elephant" (1936). In 1928 he committed himself to a life of hardship among Europe's poor and wrote* Down and Out in Paris and London *(1933) about his drudgery and near-starvation as a restaurant kitchen worker and as a tramp. In* The Road to Wigan Pier *(1937), he describes the harrowing lives of unemployed coal miners in Lancashire; and in* Homage to Catalonia *(1938), he writes of his fighting in 1936–1937 against the Communists in the Spanish Civil War. Rejected for military service in World War II, Orwell worked as a war correspondent for the BBC and the* Observer *until his death from tuberculosis in 1950. Orwell's political liberalism and his precise language and ability to tell vivid stories have made his essays widely anthologized. In "Shooting an Elephant," Orwell tells the story of how he, as an Imperial Police officer, for the wrong reasons killed a rambunctious but not enraged elephant to satisfy the Burmese crowd daring him to prove himself.*

In Moulmein, in lower Burma, I was hated by large numbers of people—the only time in my life that I have been important enough for this to happen to me. I was [a] sub-divisional police officer of the town, and in an aimless, petty kind of way anti-European feeling was very bitter. No one had the guts to raise a riot, but if a European woman went through the bazaars alone somebody would probably spit betel juice over her dress. As a police officer I was an obvious target and was baited whenever it seemed safe to do so. When a nimble Burman tripped me up on the football field and the referee (another Burman) looked the other way, the crowd yelled with hideous laughter. This happened more than once. In the end the sneering yellow faces of young men that met me everywhere, the insults hooted after me when I was at a safe distance, got badly on my nerves. The young Buddhist priests were the worst of all. There were several thousands of them in the town and none of them seemed to have anything to do except stand on street corners and jeer at Europeans.

All this was perplexing and upsetting. For at that time I had already made up my mind that imperialism was an evil thing and the sooner I chucked up my job and got out of it the better. Theoretically—and secretly, of course—I was all for the Burmese and all against their oppressors, the British. As for the job I was doing, I hated it more bitterly than I can perhaps make clear. In a job like that you see the dirty work of Empire at close quarters. The wretched prisoners huddling in the stinking cages of the lock-ups, the grey, cowed faces of the long-term convicts, the scarred buttocks of the men who had been flogged with bamboos — all these oppressed me with an intolerable sense of guilt. But I could get nothing into perspective. I was young and ill-educated and I had had to think out my problems in the utter silence that is imposed on every Englishman in the East. I did not even know that the British Empire is dying, still less did I know that it is a great deal better than the younger empires that are going to supplant it. All I knew was that I was stuck between my hatred of the empire I served and my rage against the evil-spirited little beasts who tried to make my job impossible. With one part of my mind I thought of the British Raj as an unbreakable tyranny, as something clamped down, *in saecula saeculorum*, upon the will of prostrate peoples: with another part I thought that the greatest joy in the world would be to drive a bayonet into a Buddhist priest's guts. Feelings like these are the normal by-products of imperialism; ask any Anglo-Indian official, if you can catch him off duty.

One day something happened which in a roundabout way was enlightening. It was a tiny incident in itself, but it gave me a better glimpse than I had had before of the real nature of imperialism — the real motives for which despotic governments act. Early one morning the sub-inspector at a police station the other end of the town rang me up on the 'phone and said that an elephant was ravaging the bazaar. Would I please come and do something about it? I did not know what I could do, but I wanted to see what was happening and I got on to a pony and started out. I took my rifle, an old .44 Winchester and much too small to kill an elephant, but I thought the noise might be useful *in terrorem*. Various Burmans stopped me on the way and told me about the elephant's doings. It was not, of course, a wild elephant, but a tame one which had gone "must." It had been chained up, as tame elephants always are when their attack of "must" is due, but on the previous night it had broken its chain and escaped. Its mahout, the only person who could manage it when it was in that state, had set out in pursuit, but had taken the wrong direction and was now twelve hours' journey away, and in the morning the elephant had suddenly reappeared in the town. The Burmese population had no weapons and were quite helpless against it. It had already destroyed somebody's bamboo hut, killed a cow and raided some fruit-stalls and devoured the stock; also it had met the municipal rubbish van and, when the driver jumped out and took to his heels, had turned the van over and inflicted violences upon it.

The Burmese sub-inspector and some Indian constables were waiting for me in the quarter where the elephant had been seen. It was a very poor quarter, a labyrinth of squalid bamboo huts, thatched with palm-leaf, winding all over a steep hillside. I remember that it was a cloudy, stuffy morning at the beginning of the rains. We began questioning the people as to where the elephant had gone and, as usual, failed to get any definite information. That is invariably the case in the East; a story always sounds clear enough at a distance, but the nearer you get to the scene of events the vaguer it becomes. Some of the people said that the elephant had gone in one direction, some said that he had gone in another, some professed not even to have heard of any elephant. I had almost made up my mind that the whole story was a pack of lies, when we heard yells a little distance away. There was a loud, scandalized cry of "Go away, child! Go away this instant!" and an old woman with a switch in her hand came round the corner of a hut, violently shooing away a crowd of naked children. Some more women followed, clicking their tongues and exclaiming; evidently there was something that the children ought not to have seen. I rounded the hut and saw a man's dead body sprawling in the mud. He was an Indian, a black Dravidian coolie, almost naked, and he could not have been dead many minutes. The people said that the elephant had come suddenly upon him round the corner of the hut, caught him with its trunk, put its foot on his back and ground him into the earth. This was the rainy season and the ground was soft, and his face had scored a trench a foot deep and a couple of yards long. He was lying on his belly with arms crucified and head sharply twisted to one side. His face was coated with mud, the eyes wide open, the teeth bared and grinning with an expression of unendurable agony. (Never tell me, by the way, that the dead look peaceful. Most of the corpses I have seen looked devilish.) The friction of the great beast's foot had stripped the skin from his back as neatly as one skins a rabbit. As soon as I saw the dead man I sent an orderly to a friend's house nearby to borrow an elephant rifle. I had already sent back the pony, not wanting it to go mad with fright and throw me if it smelt the elephant.

The orderly came back in a few minutes with a rifle and five cartridges, and 5 meanwhile some Burmans had arrived and told us that the elephant was in the paddy fields below, only a few hundred yards away. As I started forward practically the whole population of the quarter flocked out of the houses and followed me. They had seen the rifle and were all shouting excitedly that I was going to shoot the elephant. They had not shown much interest in the elephant when he was merely ravaging their homes, but it was different now that he was going to be shot. It was a bit of fun to them, as it would be to an English crowd; besides they wanted the meat. It made me vaguely uneasy. I had no intention of shooting the elephant—I had merely sent for the rifle to defend myself if necessary—and it is always unnerving to have a crowd following you. I marched down the hill, looking and feeling a fool, with the rifle over my shoulder and an ever-growing army of people jostling at my heels. At the bottom, when you got away from the huts, there was a metalled road and beyond that a miry waste of paddy fields a thousand yards across, not yet ploughed but soggy from the first rains and dotted with coarse grass. The elephant was standing eight yards from the road, his left side towards us. He took not the slightest notice of the crowd's approach. He was tearing up bunches of grass, beating them against his knees to clean them and stuffing them into his mouth.

I had halted on the road. As soon as I saw the elephant I knew with perfect certainty that I ought not to shoot him. It is a serious matter to shoot a working elephant—it is comparable to destroying a huge and costly piece of machinery—and obviously one ought not to do it if it can possibly be avoided. And at that distance, peacefully eating, the elephant looked no more dangerous than a cow. I thought then and I think now that his attack of "must" was already passing off; in which case he would merely wander harmlessly about until the mahout came back and caught him. Moreover, I did not in the least want to shoot him. I decided that I would watch him for a little while to make sure that he did not turn savage again, and then go home.

But at that moment I glanced round at the crowd that had followed me. It was an immense crowd, two thousand at the least and growing every minute. It blocked the road for a long distance on either side. I looked at the sea of yellow faces above the garish clothes—faces all happy and excited over this bit of fun, all certain that the elephant was going to be shot. They were watching me as they would watch a conjurer about to perform a trick. They did not like me, but with the magical rifle in my hands I was momentarily worth watching. And suddenly I realized that I should have to shoot the elephant after all. The people expected it of me and I had got to do it; I could feel their two thousand wills pressing me forward, irresistibly. And it was at this moment, as I stood there with the rifle in my hands, that I first grasped the hollowness, the futility of the white man's dominion in the East. Here was I, the white man with his gun, standing in front of the unarmed native crowd—seemingly the leading actor of the piece; but in reality I was only an absurd puppet pushed to and fro by the will of those yellow faces behind. I perceived in this moment that when the white man turns tyrant it is his own freedom that he destroys. He becomes a sort of hollow, posing dummy, the conventionalized figure of a sahib. For it is the condition of his rule that he shall spend his life in trying to impress the "natives," and so in every crisis he has got to do what the "natives" expect of him. He wears a mask, and his face grows to fit it. I had got to shoot the elephant. I had committed myself to doing it when I sent for the rifle. A sahib has got to act like a sahib; he has got to appear resolute, to know his own mind and do definite things. To come all that way, rifle in hand, with two thousand people marching at my heels, and then to trail feebly away, having done nothing—no, that was impossible. The crowd would laugh at me. And my whole life, every white man's life in the East, was one long struggle not to be laughed at.

But I did not want to shoot the elephant. I watched him beating his bunch of grass against his knees, with that preoccupied grandmotherly air that elephants have. It seemed to me that it would be murder to shoot him. At that age I was not squeamish about killing animals, but I had never shot an elephant and never wanted to. (Somehow it always seems worse to kill a *large* animal.) Besides, there was the beast's owner to be considered. Alive, the elephant was worth at least a hundred pounds; dead, he would only be worth the value of his tusks, five pounds, possibly. But I had got to act quickly. I turned to some experienced-looking Burmans who had been there when we arrived, and asked them how the elephant had been behaving. They all said the same thing: he took no notice of you if you left him alone, but he might charge if you went too close to him.

It was perfectly clear to me what I ought to do. I ought to walk up to within, say, twenty-five yards of the elephant and test his behavior. If he charged, I could shoot; if he took no notice of me, it would be safe to leave him until the mahout came back. But also I knew that I was going to do no such thing. I was a poor shot with a rifle and the ground was soft mud into which one would sink at every step. If the elephant charged and I missed him, I should have about as much chance as a toad under a steam-roller. But even then I was not thinking particularly of my own skin, only of the watchful yellow faces behind. For at that moment, with the crowd watching me, I was not afraid in the ordinary sense, as I would have been if I had been alone. A white man mustn't be frightened in front of "natives"; and so, in general, he isn't frightened. The sole thought in my mind was that if any-thing went wrong those two thousand Burmans would see me pursued, caught, trampled on and reduced to a grinning corpse like that Indian up the hill. And if that happened it was quite probable that some of them would laugh. That would never do. There was only one alternative. I shoved the cartridges into the maga-zine and lay down on the road to get a better aim.

The crowd grew very still, and a deep, low, happy sigh, as of people who see   10
the theatre curtain go up at last, breathed from innumerable throats. They were going to have their bit of fun after all. The rifle was a beautiful German thing with cross-hair sights. I did not then know that in shooting an elephant one would shoot to cut an imaginary bar running from ear-hole to ear-hole. I ought, there-fore, as the elephant was sideways on, to have aimed straight at his ear-hole; actu-ally I aimed several inches in front of this, thinking the brain would be further forward.

When I pulled the trigger I did not hear the bang or feel the kick—one never does when a shot goes home—but I heard the devilish roar of glee that went up from the crowd. In that instant, in too short a time, one would have thought, even for the bullet to get there, a mysterious, terrible change had come over the elephant. He neither stirred nor fell, but every line of his body had altered. He looked suddenly stricken, shrunken, immensely old, as though the frightful im-pact of the bullet had paralyzed him without knocking him down. At last, after what seemed a long time—it might have been five seconds, I dare say—he sagged flabbily to his knees. His mouth slobbered. An enormous senility seemed to have settled upon him. One could have imagined him thousands of years old. I fired again into the same spot. At the second shot he did not collapse but climbed with desperate slowness to his feet and stood weakly upright, with legs sagging and head drooping. I fired a third time. That was the shot that did for him. You could see the agony of it jolt his whole body and knock the last remnant of strength from his legs. But in falling he seemed for a moment to rise, for as his hind legs collapsed beneath him he seemed to tower upward like a huge rock top-pling, his trunk reaching skywards like a tree. He trumpeted, for the first and only time. And then down he came, his belly towards me, with a crash that seemed to shake the ground even where I lay.

I got up. The Burmans were already racing past me across the mud. It was obvious that the elephant would never rise again, but he was not dead. He was breath-ing very rhythmically with long rattling gasps, his great mound of a side painfully rising and falling. His mouth was wide open—I could see far down into caverns of pale pink throat. I waited a long time for him to die, but his breathing did not weaken. Finally I fired my two remaining shots into the spot where I thought his heart must be. The thick blood welled out of him like red velvet, but still he did not die. His body did not even jerk when the shots hit him, the tortured breathing continued without a pause. He was dying, very slowly and in great agony, but in some world remote from me where not even a bullet could damage him further. I felt that I had got to put an end to that dreadful noise. It seemed dreadful to see the great beast lying there, powerless to move and yet powerless to die, and not even to be able to finish him. I sent back for my small rifle and poured shot after shot into his heart and down his throat. They seemed to make no impression. The tortured gasps continued as steadily as the ticking of a clock.

In the end I could not stand it any longer and went away. I heard later that it took him half an hour to die. Burmans were bringing dahs and baskets even before I left, and I was told they had stripped his body almost to the bones by the afternoon.

Afterwards, of course, there were endless discussions about the shooting of the elephant. The owner was furious, but he was only an Indian and could do nothing. Besides, legally I had done the right thing, for a mad elephant has to be killed, like a mad dog, if its owner fails to control it. Among the Europeans opinion was divided. The older men said I was right, the younger men said it was a damn shame to shoot an elephant for killing a coolie, because an elephant was worth more than any damn Coringhee coolie. And afterwards I was very glad that the coolie had been killed; it put me legally in the right and it gave me a sufficient pretext for shooting the elephant. I often wondered whether any of the others grasped that I had done it solely to avoid looking a fool.

QUESTIONS FOR DISCUSSION AND WRITING

1. Why did Orwell shoot the elephant when in fact he "did not want to shoot the elephant" (paragraph 8)? Is the immediate cause of his action, crowd pressure (paragraphs 7–10), the *only* cause? Why was he receptive to this pressure? What did he come to believe, in retrospect, that he should have done with regard to the crowd? In regard to the elephant?

2. Why does Orwell devote so much space to the preparation for the shooting (paragraphs 7–9), and to the actual shooting (paragraphs 10–12)? And so little to the aftermath (paragraphs 13 and 14)?

3. If Orwell hadn't shot the elephant, what ethical principle would he have substituted for what pragmatic one? What might the ideal consequences have been? How likely would they have been to occur, given the tension between the Burmese and the British?

4. When Orwell wrote this essay he was a young, inexperienced British colonial officer in Burma (now Myanmar), a role he came to detest. "[W]hen the white man

turns tyrant it is his own freedom that he destroys" (paragraph 7). Explain the meaning of this in terms of "Shooting an Elephant." Is this principle applicable only to "white men" as tyrants? Examine recent wars and genocidal activities worldwide in your answer.

5. Write an essay in which you analyze an incident, event, or series of events, in which you—or someone you know well—acted contrary to your better judgment. In the process of showing why you acted as you did, disclose your current attitude toward your action. Are you proud of it? Ashamed? Ambivalent? Explain why. If you had it to do over again, what would you do? Based on what principles?

6. Pick a political action or decision either in America's history or in the current political climate that has made you angry. Analyze why it has angered you and identify one or more ethical principles that could have been applied to resolve it to your satisfaction.

LYNDA BARRY

Hate

Lynda Barry (b. 1956), daughter of a Filipino mother and an American father, grew up in an interracial Seattle neighborhood whose cultural mixture of languages, customs, wrong-side-of-the-tracks marginality, prejudices, shifting friendships, and antagonisms forms the matrix of many of the comics for which she is known. The life she depicts is harsh, tenuous, but with redeeming features and sparks of hope and love that shine, incandescent, through the dark. By the time she graduated from Evergreen State College (1978), she realized that her cartoons could make her friends laugh, and "Ernie Pook's Comeek"—now a widely syndicated strip—was born. Her course, "Writing the Unthinkable," may reflect her second novel, Cruddy *(1998).*

One! Hundred! Demons!, her autobiography in graphic form, was published in 2003. "Hate" is one chapter; there is no chapter on "Love," perhaps because Barry regards love as "an exploding cigar we willingly smoke."

QUESTIONS FOR DISCUSSION AND WRITING

1. What definitions of *hate* does Barry offer? Why does she use hearts to flank "hate" in the introductory panel? Why is it a "main rule of life" that "you can never hate your own parents. No matter what"—with the exception of stepparents (panel 8)? Are readers to believe this? How can her mother say someone "is pig vomit and should be eaten by snakes," and yet claim that she doesn't hate her (panel 10)? Why is hate defined throughout with relation to love?

2. What is the significance of distinguishing "between the kind of hate that has destructive intent and the kind that's a response to something destructive," as explained in panel 17? Why does the recognition of this distinction prompt the Lynda character to tell the substitute teacher "I. Love. You." (panel 18)? With a partner, arrive at a definition of hate and its antithesis, and write a paper arguing for your definition in comparison with alternative definitions, such as that offered by Art Spiegelman in "Mein Kampf " (p. 109).

3. What does graphic art enable Barry to accomplish that she couldn't do with words alone? How can her fairly unattractive (some might say ugly) characters be appealing?

4. Present a definition of an abstract concept (such as love, your own version of hate, fear, pleasure, rejection, acceptance) through a combination of words and drawings. If you're not an artist, team up with a classmate who is, or use existing cartoons, drawings, or other pictures and substitute your own captions.

5. By yourself or with a partner, write a paper in which you analyze and explain Barry's "Hate" in comparison with Spiegelman's "Mein Kampf" (p. 109) or Satrapi's "The Convocation" (p. 312).

PAIRED READINGS: ETHICS OF EATING AND COOKING

MICHAEL POLLAN

An Ethic of Eating

Pollan, born in 1955, is a journalism professor at the University of California, Berkeley, where he directs the Knight Program in Science and Environmental Journalism. He is also a contributing writer to the New York Times Magazine. *In addition to* The Botany of Desire: A Plant's-Eye View of the World *(2006), his work includes* The Omnivore's Dilemma: A Natural History of Four Meals *(2006) and* In Defense of Food: An Eater's Manifesto *(2008), which concludes with "An Ethic of Eating" (title supplied), reprinted here. His work presents a critical analysis of the ways American cooking, eating, and health have changed for the worse as a consequence of the dominance of industrial agriculture, which produces the high-fructose corn syrup added unobtrusively to many cheap and popular foods, with devastating high-calorie consequences. Pollan sums up his advice in seven simple words, offering simple and succulent ways to a healthful lifestyle: "Eat food. Not too much. Mostly plants."*

Pollan's precepts include: "Don't eat anything your great grandmother wouldn't recognize as food" (such as "Go-Gurt Portable Yogurt" with a dozen ingredients and "berry bubblegum bash" flavoring); "Avoid food products containing ingredients that are a) unfamiliar, b) unpronounceable, c) more than five in number, or that include d) high-fructose corn syrup." He also advises, "Avoid food products that make health claims," and "Shop the peripheries of the supermarket" (where the "real" fresh, natural foods are) and "stay out of the middle" (where the processed foods—"corn oil and chips and sugary breakfast foods"—lie in wait). For added resonance, read "An Ethic of Eating" in connection with Barbara Kingsolver's "Home Cooking" (p. 541).

The first time I heard the advice to "just eat food" it was in a speech by Joan Gussow, and it completely baffled me. Of course you should eat food—what else is there to eat? But Gussow, who grows much of her own food on a flood-prone finger of land jutting into the Hudson River, refuses to dignify most of the products for sale in the supermarket with that title. "In the thirty-four years I've been in the field of nutrition," she said in the same speech, "I have watched real food disappear from large areas of the supermarket and from much of the rest of the eating world." Taking food's place on the shelves has been an unending stream of foodlike substitutes, some seventeen thousand new ones every year—"products constructed largely around commerce and hope, supported by frighteningly little actual knowledge." Ordinary food is still out there, however, still being grown and even occasionally sold in the supermarket, and this ordinary food is what we should eat.

But given our current state of confusion and given the thousands of products scalling themselves food, this is more easily said than done. So consider these related rules of thumb. Each proposes a different sort of map to the contemporary food landscape, but all should take you to more or less the same place.

Don't Eat Anything Your Great Grandmother Wouldn't Recognize As Food.   Why your great grandmother? Because at this point your mother and possibly even your grandmother is as confused as the rest of us; to be safe we need to go back at least a couple generations, to a time before the advent of most modern foods. So depending on your age (and your grandmother), you may need to go back to your great- or even great-great grandmother. Some nutritionists recommend going back even further. John Yudkin, a British nutritionist whose early alarms about the dangers of refined carbohydrates were overlooked in the 1960s and 1970s, once advised, "Just don't eat anything your Neolithic ancestors wouldn't have recognized and you'll be ok."

What would shopping this way mean in the supermarket? Well, imagine your great grandmother at your side as you roll down the aisles. You're standing together in front of the dairy case. She picks up a package of Go-Gurt Portable Yogurt tubes—and has no idea what this could possibly be. Is it a food or a toothpaste? And how, exactly, do you introduce it into your body? You could tell her it's just yogurt in a squirtable form, yet if she read the ingredients label she would have every reason to doubt that that was in fact the case. Sure, there's some yogurt in there, but there are also a dozen other things that aren't remotely yogurtlike, ingredients she would probably fail to recognize as foods of any kind, including high-fructose corn syrup, modified corn starch, kosher gelatin, carrageenan, tricalcium phosphate, natural and artificial flavors, vitamins, and so forth. (And there's a whole other list of ingredients for the "berry bubblegum bash" flavoring, containing everything but berries or bubblegum.) How did yogurt, which in your great grandmother's day consisted simply of milk inoculated with a bacterial culture, ever get to be so complicated? Is a product like Go-Gurt Portable Yogurt still a whole food? A food of any kind? Or is it just a food product?

There are in fact hundreds of foodish products in the supermarket that your 5 ancestors simply wouldn't recognize as food: breakfast cereal bars transected by bright white veins representing, but in reality having nothing to do with, milk; "protein waters" and "nondairy creamer"; cheeselike foodstuffs equally innocent of any bovine contribution; cakelike cylinders (with creamlike fillings) called Twinkies that never grow stale. *Don't eat anything incapable of rotting* is another personal policy you might consider adopting.

There are many reasons to avoid eating such complicated food products beyond the various chemical additives and corn and soy derivatives they contain. One of the problems with the products of food science is that, as Joan Gussow has pointed out, they lie to your body; their artificial colors and flavors and synthetic sweeteners and novel fats confound the senses we rely on to assess new foods and prepare our bodies to deal with them. Foods that lie leave us with little choice but to eat by the numbers, consulting labels rather than our senses.

It's true that foods have long been processed in order to preserve them, as when we pickle or ferment or smoke, but industrial processing aims to do much more than extend shelf life. Today foods are processed in ways specifically designed to sell us more food by pushing our evolutionary buttons—our inborn preferences for sweetness and fat and salt. These qualities are difficult to find in nature but cheap and easy for the food scientist to deploy. with the result that processing induces us to consume much more of these ecological rarities than is good for us. "Tastes great, less filling!" could be the motto for most processed foods, which are far more energy dense than most whole foods: They contain much less water, fiber, and micronutrients, and generally much more sugar and fat, making them at the same time, to coin a marketing slogan. "More fattening, less nutritious!"

The great grandma rule will help keep many of these products out of your cart. But not all of them. Because thanks to the FDA's willingness, post–1973, to let food makers freely alter the identity of "traditional foods that everyone knows" without having to call them imitations, your great grandmother could easily be fooled into thinking that that loaf of bread or wedge of cheese is in fact a loaf of bread or a wedge of cheese. This is why we need a slightly more detailed personal policy to capture these imitation foods; to wit:

Avoid Food Products Containing Ingredients That Are A) Unfamiliar, B) Unpronounceable, C) More Than Five in Number, or That Include D) High-Fructose Corn Syrup.   None of these characteristics, not even the last one, is necessarily harmful in and of itself, but all of them are reliable markers for foods that have been highly processed to the point where they may no longer be what they purport to be. They have crossed over from foods to food products.

Consider a loaf of bread, one of the "traditional foods that everyone knows"   10 specifically singled out for protection in the 1938 imitation rule. As your grand-mother could tell you, bread is traditionally made using a remarkably small num-ber of familiar ingredients: flour, yeast, water, and a pinch of salt will do it. But industrial bread—even industrial whole-grain bread—has become a far more complicated product of modern food science (not to mention commerce and hope). Here's the complete ingredients list for Sara Lee's Soft & Smooth Whole Grain White Bread. (Wait a minute—isn't "Whole Grain White Bread" a contra-diction in terms? Evidently not any more.)

> Enriched bleached flour [wheat flour, malted barley flour, niacin, iron, thia-min mononitrate (vitamin B_1), riboflavin (vitamin B_2), folic acid], water, whole grains [whole wheat flour, brown rice flour (rice flour, rice bran)], high-fructose corn syrup [*hello!*], whey, wheat gluten, yeast, cellulose. Contains 2% or less of each of the following: honey, calcium sulfate, vegetable oil (soybean and/or cottonseed oils), salt, butter (cream, salt), dough conditioners (may contain one or more of the following: mono- and diglycerides, ethoxylated mono- and diglycerides, ascorbic acid, enzymes, azodicarbonamide), guar gum, calcium propionate (preservative), distilled vinegar, yeast nutrients (monocalcium phosphate, calcium sulfate, ammonium sulfate), corn starch, natural flavor, betacarotene (color), vitamin D_3, soy lecithin, soy flour.

There are many things you could say about this intricate loaf of "bread," but note first that even if it managed to slip by your great grandmother (because it is a loaf of bread, or at least is called one and strongly resembles one), the product fails every test proposed under rule number two: It's got unfamiliar ingredients (monoglycerides I've heard of before, but ethoxylated monoglycerides?); unpronounceable ingredients (try "azodicarbonamide"): it exceeds the maximum of five ingredients (by roughly thirty-six); and it contains high-fructose corn syrup. Sorry, Sara Lee, but your Soft & Smooth Whole Grain White Bread is not food and if not for the indulgence of the FDA could not even be labeled "bread."

Sara Lee's Soft & Smooth Whole Grain White Bread could serve as a monument to the age of nutritionism. It embodies the latest nutritional wisdom from science and government (which in its most recent food pyramid recommends that at least half our consumption of grain come from whole grains) but leavens that wisdom with the commercial recognition that American eaters (and American children in particular) have come to prefer their wheat highly refined—which is to say, cottony soft, snowy white, and exceptionally sweet on the tongue. In its marketing materials, Sara Lee treats this clash of interests as some sort of Gordian knot—it speaks in terms of an ambitious quest to build a "no compromise" loaf—which only the most sophisticated food science could possibly cut.

And so it has, with the invention of whole-grain white bread. Because the small percentage of whole grains in the bread would render it that much less sweet than, say, all-white Wonder Bread—which scarcely waits to be chewed before transforming itself into glucose—the food scientists have added high-fructose corn syrup and honey to to make up the difference; to overcome the problematic heft and toothsomeness of a real whole grain bread, they've deployed "dough conditioners," including guar gum and the aforementioned azodicarbonamide, to simulate the texture of supermarket white bread. By incorporating certain varieties of albino wheat, they've managed to maintain that deathly but apparently appealing Wonder Bread pallor.

Who would have thought Wonder Bread would ever become an ideal of aesthetic and gustatory perfection to which bakers would actually aspire—Sara Lee's Mona Lisa?

Very often food science's efforts to make traditional foods more nutritious 15 make them much more complicated, but not necessarily any better for you. To make dairy products low fat, it's not enough to remove the fat. You then have to go to great lengths to preserve the body or creamy texture by working in all kinds of food additives. In the case of low-fat or skim milk, that usually means adding powdered milk. But powdered milk contains oxidized cholesterol, which scientists believe is much worse for your arteries than ordinary cholesterol, so food makers sometimes compensate by adding antioxidants, further complicating what had been a simple one-ingredient whole food. Also, removing the fat makes it that much harder for your body to absorb the fat-soluble vitamins that are one of the reasons to drink milk in the first place.

All this heroic and occasionally counterproductive food science has been undertaken in the name of our health—so that Sara Lee can add to its plastic wrapper the magic words "good source of whole grain" or a food company can ballyhoo the even more magic words "low fat." Which brings us to a related food policy that may at first sound counterintuitive to a health-conscious eater:

Avoid Food Products That Make Health Claims.   For a food product to make health claims on its package it must first *have* a package, so right off the bat it's more likely to be a processed than a whole food. Generally speaking, it is only the big food companies that have the wherewithal to secure FDA-approved health claims for their products and then trumpet them to the world. Recently, however, some of the tonier fruits and nuts have begun boasting about their health-enhancing properties, and there will surely be more as each crop council scrounges together the money to commission its own scientific study. Because all plants contain antioxidants, all these studies are guaranteed to find *something* on which to base a health oriented marketing campaign.

But for the most part it is the products of food science that make the boldest health claims, and these are often founded on incomplete and often erroneous science—the dubious fruits of nutritionism. Don't forget that trans-fat-rich margarine, one of the first industrial foods to claim it was healthier than the traditional food it replaced, turned out to give people heart attacks. Since that debacle, the FDA, under tremendous pressure from industry, has made it only easier for food companies to make increasingly doubtful health claims, such as the one Frito-Lay now puts on some of its chips—that eating them is somehow good for your heart. If you bother to read the health claims closely (as food marketers make sure consumers seldom do), you will find that there is often considerably less to them than meets the eye.

Consider a recent "qualified" health claim approved by the FDA for (don't laugh) corn oil. ("Qualified" is a whole new category of health claim, introduced in 2002 at the behest of industry.) Corn oil, you may recall, is particularly high in the omega-6 fatty acids we're already consuming far too many of.

> Very limited and preliminary scientific evidence suggests that eating about one tablespoon (16 grams) of corn oil daily may reduce the risk of heart disease due to the unsaturated fat content in corn oil.

The tablespoon is a particularly rich touch, conjuring images of moms 20 administering medicine, or perhaps cod-liver oil, to their children. But what the FDA gives with one hand, it takes away with the other. Here's the small-print "qualification" of this already notably diffident health claim:

> [The] FDA concludes that there is little scientific evidence supporting this claim.

And then to make matters still more perplexing:

> To achieve this possible benefit, corn oil is to replace a similar amount of saturated fat and not increase the total number of calories you eat in a day.

This little masterpiece of pseudoscientific bureaucratese was extracted from the FDA by the manufacturer of Mazola corn oil. It would appear that "qualified" is an official FDA euphemism for "all but meaningless." Though someone might have let the consumer in on this game: The FDA's own research indicates that consumers have no idea what to make of qualified health claims (how would they?), and its rules allow companies to promote the claims pretty much any way they want—they can use really big type for the claim, for example, and then print the disclaimers in teeny-tiny rype. No doubt we can look forward to a qualified health claim for high-fructose corn syrup, a tablespoon of which probably does contribute to your health—as long as it replaces a comparable amount of, say, poison in your diet and doesn't increase the total number of calories you eat in a day.

When corn oil and chips and sugary breakfast cereals can all boast being good for your heart, health claims have become hopelessly corrupt. The American Heart Association currently bestows (for a fee) its heart-healthy seal of approval on Lucky Charms, Cocoa Puffs, and Trix cereals, Yoo-hoo lite chocolate drink, and Healthy Choice's Premium Caramel Swirl Ice Cream Sandwich—this at a time when scientists are coming to recognize that dietary sugar probably plays a more important role in heart disease than dietary fat. Meanwhile, the genuinely heart-healthy whole foods in the produce section, lacking the financial and political clout of the packaged goods a few aisles over, are mute. But don't take the silence of the yams as a sign that they have nothing valuable to say about health.

Bogus health claims and food science have made supermarkets particularly treacherous places to shop for real food, which suggests two further rules:

Shop the Peripheries of the Supermarket and Stay Out of the Middle.   Most supermarkets are laid out the same way: Processed food products dominate the center aisles of the store while the cases of ostensibly fresh food—dairy, produce, meat, and fish—line the walls. If you keep to the edges of the store you'll be that much more likely to wind up with real food in your shopping cart. The strategy is not foolproof, however, because things like high-fructose corn syrup have slipped into the dairy case under cover of Go-Gurt and such. So consider a more radical strategy:

Get Out of the Supermarket Whenever Possible.   You won't find *any* high-fructose corn syrup at the farmers' market. You also won't find any elaborately processed food products, any packages with long lists of unpronounceable ingredients or dubious health claims, nothing microwavable, and, perhaps best of all, no old food from far away. What you *will* find are fresh whole foods picked at the peak of their taste and nutritional quality—precisely the kind your great grandmother, or even your Neolithic ancestors, would easily have recognized as food.

Indeed, the surest way to escape the Western diet is simply to depart the realms it rules: the supermarket, the convenience store, and the fast-food outlet. It is hard to eat badly from the farmers' market, from a CSA box (community-supported agriculture, an increasingly popular scheme in which you subscribe to a farm and receive a weekly box of produce), or from your garden. The number of farmers' markets has more than doubled in the last ten years, to more than four thousand, making it one of the fastest-growing segments of the food marketplace. It is true that most farmers' markets operate only seasonally, and you won't find everything you need there. But buying as much as you can from the farmers' market, or directly from the farm when that's an option, is a simple act with a host of profound consequences for your health as well as for the health of the food chain you've now joined.

When you eat from the farmers' market, you automatically eat food that is in season, which is usually when it is most nutritious. Eating in season also tends to diversify your diet—because you can't buy strawberries or broccoli or potatoes twelve months of the year, you'll find yourself experimenting with other foods when they come into the market. The CSA box does an even better job of forcing you out of your dietary rut because you'll find things in your weekly allotment that you would never buy on your own. Whether it's a rutabaga or an unfamiliar winter squash, the CSA box's contents invariably send you to your cookbooks to figure out what in the world to do with them. Cooking is one of the most important health consequences of buying food from local farmers; for one thing, when you cook at home you seldom find yourself reaching for the ethoxylated diglycerides or high-fructose corn syrup. But more on cooking later.

To shop at a farmers' market or sign up with a CSA is to join a short food chain and that has several implications for your health. Local produce is typically picked ripe and is fresher than supermarket produce, and for those reasons it should be tastier and more nutritious. As for supermarket organic produce, it too is likely to have come from far away—from the industrial organic farms of California or, increasingly, China.[1] And while it's true that the organic label guarantees that no synthetic pesticides or fertilizers have been used to produce the food, many, if not most, of the small farms that supply farmers' markets are organic in everything but name. To survive in the farmers' market or CSA economy, a farm will need to be highly diversified, and a diversified farm usually has little need for pesticides; it's the big monocultures that can't survive without them.[2]

If you're concerned about chemicals in your produce, you can simply ask the farmer at the market how he or she deals with pests and fertility and begin the sort of conversation between producers and consumers that, in the end, is the best guarantee of quality in your food. So many of the problems of the industrial food chain stem from its length and complexity. A wall of ignorance intervenes between consumers and producers, and that wall fosters a certain carelessness on both sides. Farmers can lose sight of the fact that they're growing food for actual eaters rather than for middlemen, and consumers can easily forget that growing

---

[1] One recent study found that the average item of organic produce in the supermarket had actually traveled farther from the farm than the average item of conventional produce.

[2] Wendell Berry put the problem of monoculture with admirable brevity and clarity in his essay "The Pleasures of Eating": "But as scale increases, diversity declines; as diversity declines, so does health; as health declines, the dependence on drugs and chemicals necessarily increases."

good food takes care and hard work. In a long food chain, the story and identity of the food (Who grew it? Where and how was it grown?) disappear into the undifferentiated stream of commodities, so that the only information communicated between consumers and producers is a price. In a short food chain, eaters can make their needs and desires known to the farmer, and farmers can impress on eaters the distinctions between ordinary and exceptional food, and the many reasons why exceptional food is worth what it costs. Food reclaims its story, and some of its nobility, when the person who grew it hands it to you. So here's a subclause to the get-out-of-the-supermarket rule: *Shake the hand that feeds you.*

As soon as you do, accountability becomes once again a matter of relationships instead of regulation or labeling or legal liability. Food safety didn't become a national or global problem until the industrialization of the food chain attenuated the relationships between food producers and eaters. That was the story Upton Sinclair told about the Beef Trust in 1906, and it's the story unfolding in China today, where the rapid industrialization of the food system is leading to alarming breakdowns in food safety and integrity. Regulation is an imperfect substitute for the accountability, and trust, built into a market in which food producers meet the gaze of eaters and vice versa. Only when we participate in a short food chain are we reminded every week that we are indeed part of a food chain and dependent for our health on its peoples and soils and integrity—on its health.

"Eating is an agricultural act," Wendell Berry famously wrote, by which he meant that we are not just passive consumers of food but cocreators of the systems that feed us. Depending on how we spend them, our food dollars can either go to support a food industry devoted to quantity and convenience and "value" or they can nourish a food chain organized around *values*—values like quality and health. Yes, shopping this way takes more money and effort, but as soon you begin to treat that expenditure not just as shopping but also as a kind of vote—a vote for health in the largest sense—food no longer seems like the smartest place to economize.

BARBARA KINGSOLVER

Home Cooking

Barbara Kingsolver (b. 1955) grew up in rural Kentucky before attending DePauw University (B.S., 1977). Determined to save the world, though not exactly sure how, she traveled and worked in Greece, France, and England before earning her master's degree in ecology and evolutionary biology from the University of Arizona. She held a variety of jobs, ranging from x-ray technician to archaeologist, before becoming a science writer at that university, where she also published in scientific journals and the New York Times. *Insomnia during pregnancy led her to write her well-received*

first novel, The Bean Trees *(1988), followed by other riveting best-sellers, including* Pigs in Heaven *(1993),* The Poisonwood Bible *(1998; an Oprah selection),* The
Prodigal Summer *(2000), and* The Lacuna *(2009). Her nonfiction includes two
volumes of essays—* High Tide in Tucson *(1996) and* Small Wonder *(2003). Kingsolver's profound respect for nature and the land is evident in much of her work, and
has come to fruition in* Animal, Vegetable, Miracle: A Year of Food Life *(2007), in
which Kingsolver, her husband, and two daughters lived solely on what they could
raise (or barter) on their Virginia farm. Kingsolver explains, "This is the story . . .
of how our family was changed by our first year of deliberately eating food produced
from the same place where we worked, went to school, loved our neighbors, and
breathed the air." "Home Cooking," from this book, distills the essence of Kingsolver's
ethics, served up straight from the garden to the kitchen.*

When I was in college, living two states away from my family, I studied the map
one weekend and found a different route home from the one we usually traveled.
I drove back to Kentucky the new way, which did turn out to be faster. During my
visit I made sure all my relatives heard about the navigational brilliance that saved
me thirty-seven minutes.

"Thirty-seven," my grandfather mused. "And here you just used up fifteen of
them telling all about it. What's your plan for the other twenty-two?"

Good question, I'm still stumped for an answer, whenever the religion
of time-saving pushes me to zip through a meal or a chore, rushing everybody
out the door to the next point on a schedule. All that hurry can blur the truth
that life is a zero-sum equation. Every minute I save will get used on something
else, possibly no more sublime than staring at the newel post trying to remember what I just ran upstairs for. On the other hand, attending to the task in front
of me—even a quotidian chore—might make it into part of a good day, rather
than just a rock in the road to someplace else.

I have a farmer friend who would definitely side with my grandfather on the
subject of time's economies. He uses draft animals instead of a tractor. Doesn't it
take an eternity to turn a whole field with a horse-driven plow? The answer, he says,
is yes. *Eternal* is the right frame of mind. "When I'm out there cultivating the corn
with a good team in the quiet of the afternoon, watching the birds in the hedge-
rows, oh my goodness, I could just keep going all day. Kids from the city come out
here and ask," 'What do you do for fun around here?' I tell them, 'I cultivate.' "

Now that I'm decades older and much less clever than I was in college, I'm   5
getting better at facing life's routines the way my friend faces his cornfield. I
haven't mastered the serene mindset on all household chores (What do you do for
fun around here? *I scrub pots and pans, okay??*), but I might be getting there with
cooking. Eternal is the right frame of mind for making food for a family: cooking
down the tomatoes into a red-gold oregano-scented sauce for pasta. Before that,
harvesting sun-ripened fruits, pinching oregano leaves from their stems, growing
these things from seed—*yes.* A lifetime is what I'm after. Cooking is definitely

one of the things we do for fun around here. When I'm in a blue mood I head for the kitchen. I turn the pages of my favorite cookbooks, summoning the prospective joyful noise of a shared meal. I stand over a bubbling soup, close my eyes, and inhale. From the ground up, everything about nourishment steadies my soul.

Yes, I have other things to do. For nineteen years I've been nothing but a working mother, one of the legions who could justify a lot of packaged, precooked foods if I wanted to feed those to my family. I have no argument with convenience, on principle. I'm inordinately fond of my dishwasher, and I like the shiny tools that lie in my kitchen drawers, ready to make me a menace to any vegetable living or dead. I know the art of the quickie supper for after-a-long-day nights, and sometimes if we're too weary we'll go out to a restaurant, mainly to keep the kitchen clean.

But if I were to define my style of feeding my family, on a permanent basis, by the dictum, "Get it over with, *quick,*" something cherished in our family life would collapse. And I'm not just talking waistlines, though we'd miss those. I'm discussing dinnertime, the cornerstone of our family's mental health. If I had to quantify it, I'd say 75 percent of my crucial parenting effort has taken place during or surrounding the time our family convenes for our evening meal. I'm sure I'm not the only parent to think so. A survey of National Merit scholars—exceptionally successful eighteen-year-olds crossing all lines of ethnicity, gender, geography, and class—turned up a common thread in their lives: the habit of sitting down to a family dinner table. It's not just the food making them brilliant. It's probably the parents—their care, priorities, and culture of support. The words: "I'll except you home for dinner."

I understand that most U.S. citizens don't have room in their lives to grow food or even see it growing. But I have trouble accepting the next step in our journey toward obligate symbiosis with the packaged meal and takeout. Cooking is a dying art in our culture. *Why* is a good question, and an uneasy one, because I find myself politically and socioeconomically entangled in the answer. I belong to the generation of women who took as our youthful rallying cry: Allow us a good education so we won't have to slave in the kitchen. We recoiled from the proposition that keeping a husband presentable and fed should be our highest intellectual aspiration. We fought for entry as equal partners into every quarter of the labor force. We went to school, sweated those exams, earned our professional stripes, and we beg therefore to be excused from manual labor. Or else our full-time job is manual labor, we are carpenters or steelworkers, or we stand at a cash register all day. At the end of a shift we deserve to go home and put our feet up. Somehow, though, history came around and bit us in the backside: now most women have jobs *and* still find themselves largely in charge of the housework. Cooking at the end of a long day is a burden we could live without.

It's a reasonable position. But it got twisted into a pathological food culture. When my generation of women walked away from the kitchen we were escorted down that path by a profiteering industry that knew a tired, vulnerable marketing target when they saw it. "Hey, ladies," it said to us, "go ahead, get liberated. *We'll* take care of dinner." They threw open the door and we walked into a nutritional crisis and genuinely toxic food supply. If you think *toxic* is an exaggeration, read the package directions for handling raw chicken from a CAFO. We came a long way, baby, into bad eating habits and collaterally impaired family dynamics. No matter what else we do or believe, food remains at the center of every culture. Ours now runs on empty calories.

When we traded homemaking for careers, we were implicitly promised eco-   10
nomic independence and worldly influence. But a devil of a bargain it has turned out to be in terms of daily life. We gave up the aroma of warm bread rising, the measured pace of nurturing routines, the creative task of molding our families' tastes and zest for life; we received in exchange the minivan and the Lunchable. (Or worse, convenience-mart hot dogs and latchkey kids.) I consider it the great hoodwink of my generation.

Now what? Most of us, male or female, work at full-time jobs that seem organized around a presumption that some wifely person is at home picking up the slack—filling the gap between school and workday's end, doing errands only possible during business hours, meeting the expectation that we are *hungry* when we get home—but in fact June Cleaver has left the premises. Her income was needed to cover the mortgage and health insurance. Didn't the workplace organizers notice? In fact that gal Friday is *us*, both moms and dads running on overdrive, smashing the caretaking duties into small spaces between job and carpool and bedtime. Eating preprocessed or fast food can look like salvation in the short run, until we start losing what real mealtimes give to a family: civility, economy, and health. A lot of us are wishing for a way back home, to the place where care-and-feeding isn't zookeeper's duty but something happier and more creative.

"Cooking without remuneration"and "slaving over a hot stove" are activities separated mostly by a frame of mind. The distinction is crucial. Career women in many countries still routinely apply passion to their cooking, heading straight from work to the market to search out the freshest ingredients, feeding their loved ones with aplomb. In France and Spain I've sat in business meetings with female journalists and editors in which the conversation veered sharply from postcolonial literature to fish markets and the quality of this year's mushrooms or leeks. These women had no apparent concern about sounding unliberated; in the context of a healthy food culture, fish and leeks are as respectable as postcolonial literature. (And arguably more fun.)

Full-time homemaking may not be an option for those of us delivered without trust funds into the modern era. But approaching mealtimes as a creative opportunity rather than a chore, *is* an option. Required participation from spouse and kids is an element of the equation. An obsession with spotless collars, ironing, and kitchen floors you can eat off of—not so much. We've earned the right to forget about stupefying household busywork. But kitchens where food is cooked and eaten, those were really a good idea. We threw that baby out with the bathwater. It may be advisable to grab her by her slippery foot and haul her back in here before it's too late.

It's easy for any of us to claim no time for cooking; harder to look at what we're doing instead, and why every bit of it is presumed more worthy. Some people really do work double shifts with overtime and pursue no recreational activities, ever, or they are homeless or otherwise without access to a stove and refrigerator. But most are lucky enough to do *some* things for fun, or for self-improvement or family entertainment. Cooking can be one of those things.

Working people's cooking, of course, will develop an efficiency ethic. I'm shameless about throwing out the extraneous plot twists of a hoity-toity recipe and getting to its main theme. Or ignoring cookbooks altogether during the week, relying mostly on simple meals I've made a thousand times before, in endless variation: frittata, stir-fry, pasta with one protein and two vegetables thrown in. Or soups that can simmer unattended all day in our Crock-Pot, which is named Mrs. Cleaver. More labor-intensive recipes we save for weekends: lasagna, quiches, roasted chicken, desserts of any kind. I have another rule about complicated dishes: *always* double the recipe, so we can recoup the investment and eat this lovely thing again later in the week.

Routines save time, and tempers. Like a mother managing a toddler's mood swings, our family has built some reliable backstops for the times in our week when work-weary, low-blood-sugar blowouts are most likely. Friday nights are always pizza-movie nights. Friends or dates are welcome; we rent one PG feature and one for after small children go to bed. We always keep the basic ingredients for pizza on hand—flour and yeast for the dough, mozzarella, and tomatoes (fresh, dried, or canned sauce, depending on the season). All other toppings vary with the garden and personal tastes. Picky children get to control the toppings on their own austere quadrant, while the adventurous may stake out another, piling on anything from smoked eggplant to caramelized onions, fresh herbs, and spinach. Because it's a routine, our pizzas come together without any fuss as we gather in the kitchen to decompress, have a glass of wine if we are of age, and talk about everybody's week. I never have to think about what's for dinner on Fridays.

I like cooking as a social event. Friends always seem happy to share the work of putting together a do-it-yourself pizza, tacos, or vegetarian wraps. Potluck dinner parties are salvation. Takeout is not the only easy way out. With a basic repertoire of unfussy recipes in your head, the better part of valor is just turning on the burner and giving it a shot. With all due respect to Julia, I'm just thinking *Child* when I hazard a new throw-in-everything stew. I also have a crafty trick of inviting friends over for dinner whose cooking I admire, offering whatever ingredients they need, and myself as sous-chef. This is how I finally learned to make paella, pad Thai, and sushi, but the same scheme would work for acquiring basic skills and recipes. For a dedicated non-cook, the first step is likely the hardest: convincing oneself it's worth the trouble in terms of health and household economy, let alone saving the junked-up world.

It really is. Cooking is the great divide between good eating and bad. The gains are quantifiable: cooking and eating at home, even with quality ingredients, costs pennies on the dollar compared with meals prepared by a restaurant or factory. Shoppers who are most daunted by the high price of organics may be looking at bar codes on boutique-organic prepared foods, not actual vegetables.

A quality diet is not an elitist option for the do-it-yourselfer. Globally speaking, people consume more soft drinks and packaged foods as they grow more affluent; home-cooked meals of fresh ingredients are the mainstay of rural, less affluent people. This link between economic success and nutritional failure has become so widespread, it has a name: the nutrition transition.

In this country, some of our tired and poorest live in neighborhoods where groceries are sold only in gas station mini-marts. Food stamp allowances are in some cases as low as one dollar a person per meal, which will buy beans and rice with nothing thrown in. But many more of us have substantially broader food options than we're currently using to best advantage. Home-cooked, whole-ingredient cuisine *will* save money. It will also help trim off and keep off extra pounds, when that's an issue—which it is, for some two-thirds of adults in the U.S. Obesity is our most serious health problem, and our sneakiest, because so many calories slip in uncounted. Corn syrup and added fats have been outed as major ingredients in fast food, but they hide out in packaged foods too, even presumed-innocent ones like crackers. Cooking lets you guard the door, controlling not only what goes into your food, but what stays out.

Finally, cooking is good citizenship. It's the only way to get serious about 20 putting locally raised foods into your diet, which keeps farmlands healthy and grocery money in the neighborhood. Cooking and eating with children teaches them civility and practical skills they can use later on to save money and stay healthy, whatever may happen in their lifetimes to the gas-fueled food industry. Family time is at a premium for most of us, and legitimate competing interests can easily crowd out cooking. But if grabbing fast food is the only way to get the kids to their healthy fresh-air soccer practice on time, that's an interesting call. Arterial-plaque specials that save minutes now can cost years, later on.

Households that have lost the soul of cooking from their routines may not know what they're missing: the song of a stir-fry sizzle, the small talk of clinking measuring spoons, the yeasty scent of rising dough, the painting of flavors onto a pizza before it slides into the oven. The choreography of many people working in one kitchen is, by itself, a certain definition of family, after people have made their separate ways home to be together. The nurturing arts are more than just icing on the cake, insofar as they influence survival. We have dealt to today's kids the statistical hand of a shorter life expectancy than their parents, which would be *us*, the ones taking care of them. Our thrown-away food culture is the sole reason. By taking the faster drive, what did we save?

QUESTIONS FOR DISCUSSION AND WRITING

1. What does Pollan mean by "just eat food" (paragraph 1)? How would Kingsolver define food in "Home Cooking"? What's your personal definition of food? Does your definition agree with Pollan's? Kingsolver's? What are the main points on which you agree? Disagree? What sorts of ethical implications does "eat food" have for each definition?

2. What does Pollan mean by "Avoid food products containing ingredients that are a) unfamiliar, b) unpronounceable, c) more than five in number, or that include d) high-fructose corn syrup" (paragraph 9)? What sorts of food products would you eliminate from your diet if you followed this advice? What changes in your nutrition and calorie intake would this be likely to make?

3. Kingsolver makes the case for home cooking, "the great divide between good eating and bad" (paragraph 18). What evidence does she use to convince readers that even in a culture with "moms and dads running on overdrive" cooking can be "fun" (paragraph 12), "a creative opportunity, rather than a chore" (paragraph 13), efficient (paragraph 15), and "a social event" (paragraph 17)? Has her argument, her evidence, convinced you that "cooking is good citizenship" (paragraph 20)? Explain how Kingsolver's reasons reinforce Pollan's "Ethic of Eating."

4. By yourself or with partners, compose a five- to ten-item "Eater's Code of Ethics" based on Pollan's precepts and Kingsolver's advice, with a justification for each item.

5. What right, and on what authority, do Pollan or Kingsolver or anyone else have to tell you—and by extrapolation all Americans—how to eat, and when, what, and under what circumstances to do so? What obligation do you as a reader, as a person presumably in control of your own body, have to pay attention to Pollan's and Kingsolver's advice?

EDWARD HOAGLAND

Children Are Diamonds

Hoagland was born in New York City (1932) and grew up experiencing the bustle of the city as well as the beauty of rural Connecticut. He is best known for his distinguished nature writing, characterized by acute observation of wildlife in solitary settings, often remote. Hoagland's severe stammer has persisted throughout his life and profoundly influenced his writing. He explains: "Words are spoken at considerable cost to me, so a great value is placed on each one. That has had some effect on me as a writer. As a child, since I couldn't talk to people, I became close to animals. I became an observer, and in all my books, even the novels, witnessing things is what counts" as he characterizes them in evocative, sensory images.

For two summers (1951 and 1952) Hoagland joined the Ringling Brothers and Barnum and Bailey Circus where he took care of the big cats—the source of his first novel, Cat Man *(1955). After graduating from Harvard in 1954, he served two years in the army and published* The Circle Home *(1960), a novel about boxing. He has taught at Sarah Lawrence, CUNY, the University of Iowa, Columbia, Brown, and Bennington. His extensive travels in Africa and in the wilderness of Alaska, British*

Columbia, and Antarctica (among other places) provide the context for his metic-
ulous observations of nature and human nature in countless essays, stories, novels
and nonfiction books. Tigers & Ice *(1999),* Compass Points *(2001) and* Early in the
Season *(2008) are among the most recent of his twenty books. Fellow essayist John*
Updike called him "the best essayist of my generation," a judgment affirmed by the
selection of "Children Are Diamonds" for inclusion in The Best American Science
and Nature Writing 2008. *As you read, ponder the meaning of the title, whose bril-*
liant words do not appear until the last paragraph.

In Africa, everything is an emergency. Your radiator blows out, and as you solder
a repair job, kids emerge from the bush, belonging to a village that you'll never
see and reachable by a path you hadn't noticed. Though one of them has a
Kalashnikov, they aren't threatening, only hungry. Eight or ten of them, aged eight
or ten, they don't expect to be fed by you or any other strange adult. Although
you know some Swahili, you can't converse, not knowing Lango, but because
there is plenty of water in the streams roundabout, they are fascinated that you
choose to drink instead from bottles you have brought. Gradually growing bold
enough to peer into the open windows of your truck, they don't attempt to fiddle
with the door or reach inside, seeing no food or curious mechanical delectables.
The boxes packed there white-man-style are cryptically uninformative. Meningitis and polio vaccines, malaria meds, deworming pills, folic acid, vitamin A, and
similar famine fighters. However, the kids will remain as long as you do, and you
don't dare leave because this fabric of politesse would tear if you did, as it would
have already if they were five years older. You wish you could ask them if mines
have been laid in the road recently by either the rebels or the government forces.
Their fathers, the men of the village, haven't emerged because they're probably
off with the guerrillas, and the women would not show themselves in time of war
anyway. It's a balance you must maintain here: friendliness and mystery.

The city splits at the seams with squatter camps, swollen by an enormous flux of
displaced refugees from within hungry Kenya itself, not to mention all the illegals
from the civil wars afire in the countries that surround it: Somalia, Sudan, Ethiopia, Congo, Rwanda. Look on a map: dire suffering. Need I say more?

The joke, if you can call it that, among whites here is if you feel a hand grope for
your wallet, the second thing to do is try to save the life of the pickpocket. This is
a city veering into calamity, where transient whites like me still dribble in because
it's a hub for aid groups, and yet it's a traditional wash-up spot for Anglo ne'er-
do-wells who try to define themselves by where they have been. With the AIDS
pandemic, it will soon be too late for a number of things.

I help out in a place where we feed street kids and treat them with skin oint-
ments, antibiotics, inoculations, minerals, vitamins, whatever we happen to have.

Powdered milk, powdered eggs, surplus soups or porridges that another non-governmental organization may have given us. We have a basketball hoop up, and soccer balls, board games, playing cards, a tent fly hooked to the back wall in the courtyard with cots arranged underneath it as a shelter where the children can feel some safety in numbers at least. What makes you burn out are the ones dying visibly of AIDS. Yet you don't want to banish them again to the furnace of the streets or, on the other hand, specialize merely as a hospice, where salvageable kids aren't going to want to come. Many of them wish to go to school but have no home to go to school from or money for the fees. So I scrounged a blackboard and teach addition, subtraction, geography, the English alphabet, when I have a break from refereeing a gritty soccer game or supervising the dishwashing or triaging kids with fevers or contusions who ought to go to the hospital (not that that Dickensian trip is often in their best interest). We had artful dodgers eating our fruits and sandwiches between excursions into robbery, drugs, peddling—but also earnest tykes, plenty of them, whom your heart absolutely goes out to. Yet triage is frustrating.

You don't have to be a doctor to help people who have no aspirin or disinfectant 5 or pills for malaria, tuberculosis, dysentery, or epilepsy, no splints or bandaging, and no other nearby facility to walk to in the bush. No Kaopectate, cough suppressants, malnutrition supplements, antibiotics for bilharziasis or sleeping sickness or yaws. If you were a nurse, patients would be brought to you with these diseases or hepatitis or broken limbs. The old stone and concrete ruins of a Catholic chapel that has been forgotten since the colonial powers left could be reoccupied if you chased the leopards and the cobras out, because joy is what is partly needed, especially at first, and joy, I think, is, like photosynthesis for plants, an evidence of God. But joy, like beauty, is a continuum too, and in temperate climates it waxes with the sun somewhat as plants do.

I can do the basic mechanics if we break down on the road, and I know when to speed up or — equally important — slow down, when figures with guns appear to block our passage. (If it's soldiers, you never speed up, but the decision is not that easy because every male can look like a soldier in a war zone, and the soldiers look like civilians.) The big groups, such as Doctors Without Borders, CARE, Oxfam, Save the Children, have salaried international staff they can fly in from Honduras, Bangkok, or New Delhi to plug a momentary defection or a flip-out—dedicated career people, like the UN's ladies and gentlemen, with New York, Geneva, London, Paris, Rome behind them, who've been vetted: not much fooling around. But there are various smaller outfits, whose fliers you don't receive in the mail back home, that will hire "the spiritual drifter," as my friend Al put it to me, to haul pallets of plywood, bags of cement, first-aid kits in bulk, and bags of potatoes, bayou rice, cases of your basic tins, like corned beef, tuna, salmon, peas, what-have-you, and trunks of medicine to provision the solo picayune apostle out doing Christ's appalling work in the hinterlands.

You draw up lists of refugees so no one gets double their ration by coming through the corn queue twice. Use ink stamped on the wrists if you have to—if their names are always Mohammed or Josephine. And you census the children as well and weigh a sampling of them in a sling scale, plus measure their upper-arm fat, if they have any, with calipers to compile the ratio of malnutrition in the populace, severe versus moderate, and so on. I've helped inject against measles, tetanus, typhoid, when not enough licensed people were there, having been a vet's assistant at one point in my teens. I've powwowed with the traditional clan chiefs and tribal healers, the leopard-skin priests and village shamans and elders, or young militia commanders, and delivered babies when nobody competent was around. I've squeezed the rehydration salts into babies' mouths when they're at death's door, mixed the fortified formula that you spoon into them, and chalked the rows of little white squares in the dirt where you have all the children sit individually at their feeding hours so that every individual gets the same amount of protein, the same units of vitamins A, C, E, B, calcium, iron, phosphorus, out of the 55-gallon steel drum you're stewing the emergency preparation in. *Hundreds* of passive, dying children sitting cross-legged in the little squares, waiting for you to reach each of them. You don't think that breaks your heart? Chalk is never gonna look the same.

You meet many travelers: businessmen with attaché cases full of bank notes to persuade the bureaucrats in Government House to sign on to a certain project scheme; ecologists on a mission to save the chimpanzees; trust-fund hippies doing this route overland, now that you can't go from Istanbul into Afghanistan; specialists from one of the UN's many agencies studying a development proposal or transiting to the more difficult terrain of Rwanda, Zimbabwe, Somalia, then resting for a spell on the way back. The taxi stand is busy from sunrise to pitch dark, and the pool on the roof is patronized by African middle-class parents, some of whom are teaching their kids how to swim, as well as the KLM airline pilots and Swissair stewardesses, the Danish or USAID water-project administrators waiting for permanent housing, or bustling missionaries passing through.

Food is so central that you can't exaggerate the issue. My waitress, for example, was hungry for protein even though she worked in an expatriates' hotel. There was a pot of gruel in the kitchen for the help, but it wasn't nourishing enough for a lactating mother, and the chicken parts and fresh fruit, meat, and vegetables the guests ate were exactly inventoried each night to compare what remained in the refrigerator with the restaurant's orders. Nor did she eat leftovers from people's plates, because she'd heard that AIDS can be spread by saliva. And, although she wouldn't be robbed at night once she reached her bus station, she said that to get to it she needed to use her tips to take a taxi because men with clubs waited next to a corner between here and there.

The fabled "Cape to Cairo" artery from South Africa toward Khartoum and Egypt 10 is no more—a jaunt that was throttled first by Idi Amin and is now choked off again by the war in southern Sudan. Beyond the city's suburbs, indeed, signs of human occupancy almost disappear in the elephant grass and regrown jungle, because for the next eighty or a hundred miles all of this has been a triangle of death, incinerated in Uganda's own civil wars: Amin's eight years of butcheries and then, when he was overthrown, Obote, who in an ostensibly saner manner killed just as many until Museveni upended him. So many clanking tanks, half-tracks, and fearsome assault platoons crawled up this road, mowing down anything that moved, that even in the peace Museveni established, nobody wanted to take the chance of living anywhere that might be visible in the forest. Bower birds, sunbirds, bee-eaters, secretary birds, reedbucks, dik-diks, spitting cobras, and black mambas were about, but the people who had somehow survived on site or returned afterward were not going to trust the neighborhood of the road, except for bicycling quickly along the asphalt. And then the trick was to vanish imperceptibly when you reached your destination, with no path to a hidden village that soldiers rumbling by in a grisly truck would notice. Settlements had been scorched, torched, eviscerated horribly, the skulls piled up from the massacres. And women still sometimes flinched—broke into a run for the woods—at the sound of my motor.

In the sixties, after Uganda's independence from the British, it had been mainly these local forest tribes, such as the Baris and Acholis, who logically should have been part of Uganda to begin with anyway, fighting the Muslim government. Then in the seventies a new president of Sudan had made peace with them, with regional freedom of religion and cultural autonomy, until the eighties, when a new fundamentalist Sharia swing reignited the war, led now by the big plains tribes, Nuer and Dinka, pastoralists living between these mountains and forests and the vast Sahel of the Arabs. It was a more serious insurrection, with the southern black army officers defecting to command the rebels, and, on the government side, the Baggara Arab tribes armed for lethal, devastating cattle raids against their neighbors the Dinkas. The United States was allied with Khartoum for strategic reasons at the time—to harass Muammar al-Qaddafi on Libya's flank—and discouraged even food aid reaching the southerners. So a quarter of a million people starved.

One morning in Sudan I woke to a lovely morning sun and boundless rolling perspectives after I climbed to a viewpoint behind the church that overlooked the modest gorge of the Bahr el Jebel, the "Mountain Nile." It flows under the Imatong Range, Sudan's highest, its ridges behind me, all downstream from the Victoria and Albert sections of the Nile in Uganda's lake country. Near Malakal it is joined by the Bahr el Ghazal, the "Gazelle River," from the west, and the Sobat, from the east, to form the White Nile. Then at Khartoum, the Blue Nile, from Ethiopia, joins the White to constitute the famous Nile that flows to Shendi, Atbara, Wadi Haifa, Aswan, Luxor, Cairo, and the delta close to Alexandria: nowhere, though, is it more beautiful than around here. Beyond the gorge sit endless savanna grasslands, woodlands, parkland, in tropical, light-filled yellows and greens, where, although the hartebeests, kobs, buffalo, and reedbucks may already have been eaten and the rhinos and elephants shot for their horns or tusks to buy guns, the vistas remain primeval because for decades civil war has prevented any other kind of development, like logging, tourism, or mining. I had a spear-length stick in hand to defend myself afoot or keep the wildlife at bay and, more appropriately, to remind myself of how the Dinkas, as a cattle people from time immemorial, had been able to protect their herds and pasturage from the Baggara Arab tribes whose homelands adjoined theirs, even though the Baggara domesticated horses as well as cattle and rode into battle, instead of merely running. A Dinka, who could run for twenty miles with six spears in his free hand, attacking from the reeds and rushes of every river crossing, every hyacinth swamp, was not a foe whose cattle could be rustled and women stolen with impunity. But the equilibrium of spear versus spear had been skewed when Khartoum gave the Baggara guns and sent its army in motor vehicles and helicopter gunships to mow down the lumbering cattle who escaped the horses, driving the surviving herdsmen off their beloved prairies, steppes, swamps, and plains.

We were inoculating babies against measles before the dry ice that kept the vaccine fresh was gone. But an elephantiasis sufferer was in the line. How could she have survived this long? We gave her Cephalexin, for whatever that might be worth. The queue was checkered with people with rag-fashioned bandaging, wearing blue robes for one particular clan, red for another, with body paint, headcloths, loincloths, tribal scarifications on the forehead. One man had what was possibly a giraffe's scrotum as a carryall on a rawhide strap from his shoulder, yet he was wearing a garage-sale apron from Peoria.

As we drove north, the people walking were sparse, and mostly from the local Madi or Bari tribes, a foot shorter than the Dinkas and thicker-set, scrambling along like forest-and-mountain folk, not striding like cattle herders, plainsmen. As food got shorter again the next week, they would disappear into the woods, and gaunt Dinkas would take over the roads, famished, stalking something to eat. We saw a burly man with a bushbuck that he had snared slung over his shoulder, who started to run when he heard the motor, till he realized we were aid workers and not about to steal his meat, as guys in a Sudan People's Liberation Army vehicle would have. Another man, two miles on, was squatting on his heels, quietly collecting wood doves one by one every few minutes, when they fluttered down to drink at a roadside puddle he had poisoned with the juice of a certain plant that grew nearby. He too was frightened that this clutch of birds he had already caught might be snatched away, until white faces in the window proved we weren't hungry. He showed us the deadly root, and how pretty his half-dozen unplucked pigeons were, as well as a pumpkin he wanted to sell.

Close to the rope ferry from Kerripi to Kajo Kaja, we passed several Dinkas 15 with fishing nets and spears tall enough to fend off a crocodile or disable a hippo—which was what they were good at when not embedded in the intimacies of their cattle culture, with five hundred lowing beasts, and perhaps a lion outside the kraal to reason with; the rituals of manhood to observe; the myriad color con figurations and hieroglyphic markings of each man's or boy's special display ox or bull, for him to honor, celebrate, and sing to; and the sinuous, cultivated, choreographic eloquence of its individual horns, which he tied bells and tassels to. The colors were named after the fish eagle, ibis, bustard, leopard, brindled crocodile, mongoose, monitor lizard, goshawk, baboon, elephant ivory, and so on. Like the Nuer, who were so similar, the Dinka had been famous among anthropologists but were now shattered by the war. Adventure, marriage, contentment, art, and beauty had been marked and sculpted by the visual or intuitive impact of cattle, singly and in their wise and milling, rhythmic herds, as bride wealth and the principal currency, but also the coloring registering like impressionistic altarpieces, the scaffolding of clan relations and religion. A scorched-earth policy by the Arab army and militias needed only to wipe out their cattle to disorient and dishearten the Dinka. We stopped, and people emerged from the bush. One man was burdened by a goiter the size of a bagpipe's bladder; another, by a hernia bulging like an overnight bag. They were Madi, Bari, the so-called Juba peoples, displaced by the war and siege. We had palliatives like vitamins, acetaminophen, valium, cotrimoxazole, even some iodine pills for the goiter man, although, like the hernia character, he needed surgery.

There were patients with cataracts, VD, bronchitis, scabies, nosebleeds, chest pains, Parkinson's, thrush, cellulitis, breast tumors, colon troubles, a dislocated elbow, plus the usual heartbreaking woman whose urinary tract, injured in childbirth, dripped continuously, turning her into a pariah, although it would have been as easy as the hernia for a surgeon to fix. My friend could do the elbow, with my help, and knock back an infection temporarily, but not immunize the babies or anybody because our vaccines had had no refrigeration for so long. She bestowed her smile. The line that formed, the fact that she was going to finger and eyeball everybody, was reassuring.

One night in the sunset's afterglow a man with broken eyeglasses led us to the straw church he had built, quoting Isaiah, chapter 18, and Matthew, chapter 24: "For nation will go to war against nation, kingdom against kingdom; there will be famines." Ladoku was his name, and it's no exaggeration to say that his church was constructed mainly of straw or that any big drugstore would have had ten-dollar glasses that would have helped him a lot.

On the river herons, egrets, ibises, buzzards, guinea fowl, whale-headed storks flapped every which way over the dugouts of lanky men wielding fishing tridents. They stopped at hamlets of huts only a yard above the water to let people off or leave freight, with cattle browsing in the shallows, their left horn sometimes trained a certain way by the gradual application of weights. A herder, proudly dusted with ceremonial dung-ash, was poised upon one leg, the toes of the other hooking that knee so as to jut out quite jauntily as he leaned on the point of his fighting spear, with his fishing spear dandled in his free hand. Whether Nuer or Dinka, these were people of sufficient numbers that they hadn't needed to bother learning a common language like Arabic or English to speak with other tribes, and they stared with more interest at the cargo of goodies on the deck than at the foreign or inferior strangers. The captain, although he was ethnically an Arab, had been born to shopkeepers in Malakal and had gone onto the river as a boy with his uncle, who was a pilot during the British era, and then married a daughter of the king of the Shilluk. The Shilluk were a river tribe located just northward of the Nuer and Dinka, sharing Malakal with the others as a hub. Though less numerous, they were knit rather tighter as warriors, if only because they *had* a king, so that their tough neighbors seldom messed with them.

The lions here have lost their sense of propriety. They are rattled, eating human carrion like hyenas and hauling down live individual human beings, as if there hadn't been a truce in force between the local people and the local lions for eons. Before the war, lions always knew and taught their young where they would be trespassing—what domestic beasts they shouldn't kill unless they anticipated retaliation—and people, as well, knew where it was asking for trouble for them to go. Deliberately hunting a big black-maned male might be a manhood ritual, but it was never casually undertaken with a Kalashnikov, never meaningless. Neither species was a stranger to the other or its customary habitat—whereas many of these poor refugees had been on their last legs, eating lizards, drinking from muddy puddles, wandering displaced hundreds of miles from their home ground, where they belonged. And so, on the one hand, young lionesses grew up stalking staggering people, and, on the other, soldiers in jeeps were shooting lions that they ran across with Tommy guns, for fun. No rite of passage, no conversation or negotiation was involved: no spear in the teeth, which then became a cherished necklace worn at dances.

Back in Uganda I was back in the world of AIDS. Sudan's war had kept most infected people out of the zone we'd been in, but within a few minutes I noticed that several youngsters clustered around were not healthy. They weren't wasted from starvation or fascinated by a motor vehicle, like the crowds of kids where we'd come from. I couldn't tell whether they were orphans or belonged to someone, but their stumbling, discolored emaciation meant they were dying of AIDS.

Flying over Juba we saw muzzle flashes, burning huts, and a blackish tank askew on a roadway as we banked. Inside that broken circle of machine-gun sniping and mortar explosions nobody was moving as in a normal provincial city, just scurrying for bare essentials. From the air, you could spot the positions that were crumbling and who, hunkered there, was doomed.

I ran into a couple of gaunt, drained Maryknoll nuns recuperating on a two-week Christmas holiday from their current post at Chukudum, in the Didinga

Hills of borderline Sudan, where a pretty waterfall burbles down the rock bluff behind the garden of the priory, and Khartoum's Antonov bomber plane wheels over every morning looking for a target of opportunity. These nursing sisters are seasoned heroes. They're deep-dyed. You meet them on the hairiest road, coming or going from a posting, and they don't wilt. *They* don't believe that God is dead. They are wary but unflappable.

I load a truck with the standard fortified nutritional preparations and spare stethoscopes, blood-pressure cuffs, tourniquets, penlights, tongue depressors, tendon hammers, antimalarial amodiaquine, paracetamol, antibiotics such as amoxicillin, cotrimoxazole, ciprofloxacin, and doxycycline, mebendazole for worms, water purifiers, tetracycline eye ointment, ibuprofen, bandages in quantity and tape and nylon strapping, syringes and needles, scalpels, antiseptic for sterilizing, insecticide-treated mosquito netting for many people besides ourselves, IV cannulas, stitching needles and thread, umbrellas and tenting for the sun and rain, white coats for each of us to wear to give us an air of authority, and as much plastic sheeting as I have room for to shelter families in the coming rainy season. My friend Al says that children are diamonds, and he knew so from the front lines, having witnessed the successive Ethiopian and Somali famines and the Sahel droughts of the Kababish country in northern Sudan, knew that you can be nearer my God to thee without sectarianism. One Christ, many proxies.

QUESTIONS FOR DISCUSSION AND WRITING

1. Hoagland's opening statement, "In Africa, everything is an emergency," governs the entire essay. What emergencies does Hoagland identify? Do these pervade the entire African continent, or are they located in specific countries, regions?

2. Given the large number of emergencies, their severity, and the fact that they can't all be dealt with at once, how does Hoagland sort them out? Prioritize them? Because the people and politics are in flux, what causes the priorities to shift?

3. What ethical principles govern the behavior of Hoagland and others administering medical aid and providing food? What sections of the UN "Universal Declaration of Human Rights" (p. 488) are most applicable to the emergencies in Africa that Hoagland describes?

4. Hoagland's essay is full of lists; nearly every paragraph contains one or more lists. What's in these lists? Why does he use so many? Despite the lists, the essay reads like a narrative and the story moves right along. What's the essence of the story? Who are the main characters?

5. Hoagland concludes (paragraph 23) with his friend Al's observation that "children are diamonds." What does he mean by this? Explain your answer in terms of the entire essay, with particular emphasis on the two concluding sentences:

"he knew so from the front lines, having witnessed the successive Ethiopian and Somali famines and the Sahel droughts of the Kababish country in northern Sudan, knew that you can be nearer my God to thee without sectarianism. One Christ, many proxies."

DOROTHEA LANGE

Migrant Mother

The original caption on what has become the most iconic and widely reprinted photograph of the Great Depression in the United States read, "Nipomo, Calif. March 1936. Migrant agricultural worker's family. Seven hungry children and their mother,

aged 32. The father is a native Californian." Dorothea Lange, a photographer work-
ing for the Farm Security Administration to document working conditions of farm
laborers in hopes of improving them, explained in Popular Photography *(February*
1960): "I was following instinct, not reason; I drove into that wet and soggy camp
and parked my car like a homing pigeon. I saw and approached the hungry and des-
perate mother, as if drawn by a magnet. I do not remember how I explained my
presence or my camera to her but I do remember she asked me no questions. I made
five exposures, working closer and closer from the same direction. I did not ask her
name or her history. . . . She said that they had been living on frozen vegetables from
the surrounding fields, and birds that the children killed. She had just sold the tires
from her car to buy food. There she sat in that lean-to tent with her children huddled
around her, and seemed to know that my pictures might help her, and so she helped me."

QUESTIONS FOR DISCUSSION AND WRITING

1. "Read" the photograph. How many children do you see in the picture? Why
   aren't their faces exposed to the camera? What do the mother's face, clothing,
   posture tell viewers?

2. In this photograph all the human figures are intertwined. In what ways, and for
   what reasons? In discussion or an essay compare this with the conventional family photograph such as you might see on a Christmas card; identify some of the
   significant similarities and differences. In what ways does this analysis deepen
   your understanding of Lange's picture?

3. Why has this Depression era photograph remained so iconic for over seventy
   years, throughout good times and bad?

PETER SINGER

The Singer Solution to World Poverty

When Princeton University appointed Peter Singer to a new chair in bioethics in
1998, a New Yorker *profile hailed him as "the most influential living philosopher,"*
and the New York Times *as "perhaps the world's most controversial ethicist." Born*
in Melbourne, Australia (1946), Singer attended the University of Melbourne (B.A.,
1967; M.A., 1969) and Oxford (B. Phil., 1971). After teaching at Oxford and at New
York University, he led the Centre for Human Bioethics at Monash University
in Australia (1983–98). A vegetarian since college, Singer has devoted his career to
protecting animals from human "speciesism"—the valuing of human rights above
those of other species. In Animal Liberation: A New Ethics for Our Treatment of
Animals *(1975), he argues against redundant experimentation, advocates humane*

food production, and recommends that we consume more vegetable protein and less meat. Singer's work as coauthor and editor includes Making Babies: The New Science and Ethics of Conception *(1985), about ethical issues in human conception such as in vitro fertilization and surrogate motherhood;* Should the Baby Live? The Problem of Handicapped Infants *(1985); and* Rethinking Life and Death *(1995), about the quality-of-life issues raised by modern technology.*

In "The Singer Solution to World Poverty," originally published in the New York Times Magazine *(September 1999), Singer interrogates the ethics of affluence, arguing that because it is just as immoral to ignore the plight of sick and starving children overseas as it is to allow a child to be killed, we should willingly donate to charity the portion of our income not spent on necessities.*

In the Brazilian film *Central Station,* Dora is a retired schoolteacher who makes ends meet by sitting at the station writing letters for illiterate people. Suddenly she has an opportunity to pocket $1,000. All she has to do is persuade a homeless 9-year-old boy to follow her to an address she has been given. (She is told he will be adopted by wealthy foreigners.) She delivers the boy, gets the money, spends some of it on a television set and settles down to enjoy her new acquisition. Her neighbor spoils the fun, however, by telling her that the boy was too old to be adopted—he will be killed and his organs sold for transplantation. Perhaps Dora knew this all along, but after her neighbor's plain speaking, she spends a troubled night. In the morning Dora resolves to take the boy back.

Suppose Dora had told her neighbor that it is a tough world, other people have nice new TV's too, and if selling the kid is the only way she can get one, well, he was only a street kid. She would then have become, in the eyes of the audience, a monster. She redeems herself only by being prepared to bear considerable risks to save the boy.

At the end of the movie, in cinemas in the affluent nations of the world, people who would have been quick to condemn Dora if she had not rescued the boy go home to places far more comfortable than her apartment. In fact, the average family in the United States spends almost one-third of its income on things that are no more necessary to them than Dora's new TV was to her. Going out to nice restaurants, buying new clothes because the old ones are no longer stylish, vacationing at beach resorts—so much of our income is spent on things not essential to the preservation of our lives and health. Donated to one of a number of charitable agencies, that money could mean the difference between life and death for children in need.

All of which raises a question: In the end, what is the ethical distinction between a Brazilian who sells a homeless child to organ peddlers and an American who already has a TV and upgrades to a better one—knowing that the money could be donated to an organization that would use it to save the lives of kids in need?

Of course, there are several differences between the two situations that could support different moral judgments about them. For one thing, to be able to consign a child to death when he is standing right in front of you takes a chilling kind of heartlessness; it is much easier to ignore an appeal for money to help children you will never meet. Yet for a utilitarian philosopher like myself—that is, one who judges whether acts are right or wrong by their consequences—if the up-shot of the American's failure to donate the money is that one more kid dies on the streets of a Brazilian city, then it is, in some sense, just as bad as selling the kid to the organ peddlers. But one doesn't need to embrace my utilitarian ethic to see that, at the very least, there is a troubling incongruity in being so quick to condemn Dora for taking the child to the organ peddlers while, at the same time, not regarding the American consumer's behavior as raising a serious moral issue.

In his 1996 book, *Living High and Letting Die*, the New York University philosopher Peter Unger presented an ingenious series of imaginary examples designed to probe our intuitions about whether it is wrong to live well without giving substantial amounts of money to help people who are hungry, malnourished or dying from easily treatable illnesses like diarrhea. Here's my paraphrase of one of these examples:

Bob is close to retirement. He has invested most of his savings in a very rare and valuable old car, a Bugatti, which he has not been able to insure. The Bugatti is his pride and joy. In addition to the pleasure he gets from driving and caring for his car, Bob knows that its rising market value means that he will always be able to sell it and live comfortably after retirement. One day when Bob is out for a drive, he parks the Bugatti near the end of a railway siding and goes for a walk up the track. As he does so, he sees that a runaway train, with no one aboard, is running down the railway track. Looking farther down the track, he sees the small figure of a child very likely to be killed by the runaway train. He can't stop the train and the child is too far away to warn of the danger, but he can throw a switch that will divert the train down the siding where his Bugatti is parked. Then nobody will be killed—but the train will destroy his Bugatti. Thinking of his joy in owning the car and the financial security it represents, Bob decides not to throw the switch. The child is killed. For many years to come, Bob enjoys own-ing his Bugatti and the financial security it represents.

Bob's conduct, most of us will immediately respond, was gravely wrong. Unger agrees. But then he reminds us that we, too, have opportunities to save the lives of children. We can give to organizations like UNICEF or Oxfam Amer-ica. How much would we have to give one of these organizations to have a high probability of saving the life of a child threatened by easily preventable diseases? (I do not believe that children are more worth saving than adults, but since no one can argue that children have brought their poverty on themselves, focusing on them simplifies the issues.) Unger called up some experts and used the infor-mation they provided to offer some plausible estimates that include the cost of raising money, administrative expenses and the cost of delivering aid where it is most needed. By his calculation, $200 in donations would help a sickly 2-year-old transform into a healthy 6-year-old—offering safe passage through childhood's most dangerous years. To show how practical philosophical argument can be, Unger even tells his readers that they can easily donate funds by using their credit card and calling one of these toll-free numbers: (800) 367-5437 for UNICEF; (800) 693-2687 for Oxfam America.

Now you, too, have the information you need to save a child's life. How should you judge yourself if you don't do it? Think again about Bob and his Bugatti. Unlike Dora, Bob did not have to look into the eyes of the child he was sacrificing for his own material comfort. The child was a complete stranger to him and too far away to relate to in an intimate, personal way. Unlike Dora, too, he did not mislead the child or initiate the chain of events imperiling him. In all these respects, Bob's situation resembles that of people able but unwilling to donate to overseas aid and differs from Dora's situation.

If you still think that it was very wrong of Bob not to throw the switch that 10 would have diverted the train and saved the child's life, then it is hard to see how you could deny that it is also very wrong not to send money to one of the organizations listed above. Unless, that is, there is some morally important difference between the two situations that I have overlooked.

Is it the practical uncertainties about whether aid will really reach the people who need it? Nobody who knows the world of overseas aid can doubt that such uncertainties exist. But Unger's figure of $200 to save a child's life was reached after he had made conservative assumptions about the proportion of the money donated that will actually reach its target.

One genuine difference between Bob and those who can afford to donate to overseas aid organizations but don't is that only Bob can save the child on the tracks, whereas there are hundreds of millions of people who can give $200 to overseas aid organizations. The problem is that most of them aren't doing it. Does this mean that it is all right for you not to do it?

Suppose that there were more owners of priceless vintage cars—Carol, Dave, Emma, Fred and so on, down to Ziggy—all in exactly the same situation as Bob, with their own siding and their own switch, all sacrificing the child in order to preserve their own cherished car. Would that make it all right for Bob to do the same? To answer this question affirmatively is to endorse follow-the-crowd ethics—the kind of ethics that led many Germans to look away when the Nazi atrocities were being committed. We do not excuse them because others were behaving no better.

We seem to lack a sound basis for drawing a clear moral line between Bob's situation and that of any reader of this article with $200 to spare who does not donate it to an overseas aid agency. These readers seem to be acting at least as badly as Bob was acting when he chose to let the runaway train hurtle toward the unsuspecting child. In the light of this conclusion, I trust that many readers will reach for the phone and donate that $200. Perhaps you should do it before reading further.

Now that you have distinguished yourself morally from people who put their vin- 15 tage cars ahead of a child's life, how about treating yourself and your partner to dinner at your favorite restaurant? But wait. The money you will spend at the restaurant could also help save the lives of children overseas! True, you weren't planning to blow $200 tonight, but if you were to give up dining out just for one month, you would easily save that amount. And what is one month's dining out, compared to a child's life? There's the rub. Since there are a lot of desperately needy children in the world, there will always be another child whose life you could save for another $200. Are you therefore obliged to keep giving until you have nothing left? At what point can you stop?

Hypothetical examples can easily become farcical. Consider Bob. How far past losing the Bugatti should he go? Imagine that Bob had got his foot stuck in the track of the siding, and if he diverted the train, then before it rammed the car it would also amputate his big toe. Should he still throw the switch? What if it would amputate his foot? His entire leg?

As absurd as the Bugatti scenario gets when pushed to extremes, the point it raises is a serious one: only when the sacrifices become very significant indeed would most people be prepared to say that Bob does nothing wrong when he decides not to throw the switch. Of course, most people could be wrong; we can't decide moral issues by taking opinion polls. But consider for yourself the level of sacrifice that you would demand of Bob, and then think about how much money you would have to give away in order to make a sacrifice that is roughly equal to that. It's almost certainly much, much more than $200. For most middle-class Americans, it could easily be more like $200,000.

Isn't it counterproductive to ask people to do so much? Don't we run the risk that many will shrug their shoulders and say that morality, so conceived, is fine for saints but not for them? I accept that we are unlikely to see, in the near or even medium-term future, a world in which it is normal for wealthy Americans to give the bulk of their wealth to strangers. When it comes to praising or blaming people for what they do, we tend to use a standard that is relative to some conception of normal behavior. Comfortably off Americans who give, say, 10 percent of their income to overseas aid organizations are so far ahead of most of their equally comfortable fellow citizens that I wouldn't go out of my way to chastise them for not doing more. Nevertheless, they should be doing much more, and they are in no position to criticize Bob for failing to make the much greater sacrifice of his Bugatti.

At this point various objections may crop up. Someone may say: "If every citizen living in the affluent nations contributed his or her share I wouldn't have to make such a drastic sacrifice, because long before such levels were reached, the resources would have been there to save the lives of all those children dying from lack of food or medical care. So why should I give more than my fair share?" Another, related, objection is that the Government ought to increase its overseas aid allocations, since that would spread the burden more equitably across all taxpayers.

Yet the question of how much we ought to give is a matter to be decided in 20 the real world—and that, sadly, is a world in which we know that most people do not, and in the immediate future will not, give substantial amounts to overseas aid agencies. We know, too, that at least in the next year, the United States Government is not going to meet even the very modest United Nations–recommended target of 0.7 percent of gross national product; at the moment it lags far below that, at 0.09 percent, not even half of Japan's 0.22 percent or a tenth of Denmark's 0.97 percent. Thus, we know that the money we can give beyond that theoretical "fair share" is still going to save lives that would otherwise be lost. While the idea that no one need do more than his or her fair share is a powerful one, should it prevail if we know that others are not doing their fair share and that children will die preventable deaths unless we do more than our fair share? That would be taking fairness too far.

Thus, this ground for limiting how much we ought to give also fails. In the world as it is now, I can see no escape from the conclusion that each one of us with wealth surplus to his or her essential needs should be giving most of it to help people suffering from poverty so dire as to be life-threatening. That's right: I'm saying that you shouldn't buy that new car, take that cruise, redecorate the house or get that pricey new suit. After all, a $1,000 suit could save five children's lives.

So how does my philosophy break down in dollars and cents? An American household with an income of $50,000 spends around $30,000 annually on necessities, according to the Conference Board, a nonprofit economic research organization. Therefore, for a household bringing in $50,000 a year, donations to help the world's poor should be as close as possible to $20,000. The $30,000 required for necessities holds for higher incomes as well. So a household making $100,000 could cut a yearly check for $70,000. Again, the formula is simple: whatever money you're spending on luxuries, not necessities, should be given away.

Now, evolutionary psychologists tell us that human nature just isn't sufficiently altruistic to make it plausible that many people will sacrifice so much for strangers. On the facts of human nature, they might be right, but they would be wrong to draw a moral conclusion from those facts. If it is the case that we ought to do things that, predictably, most of us won't do, then let's face that fact head-on. Then, if we value the life of a child more than going to fancy restaurants, the next time we dine out we will know that we could have done something better with our money. If that makes living a morally decent life extremely arduous, well, then that is the way things are. If we don't do it, then we should at least know that we are failing to live a morally decent life—not because it is good to wallow in guilt but because knowing where we should be going is the first step toward heading in that direction.

When Bob first grasped the dilemma that faced him as he stood by that railway switch, he must have thought how extraordinarily unlucky he was to be placed in a situation in which he must choose between the life of an innocent child and the sacrifice of most of his savings. But he was not unlucky at all. We are all in that situation.

QUESTIONS FOR DISCUSSION AND WRITING

1. What types of charitable donations do you or people you know make? What are the reasons for supporting these particular causes? How do they stack up against Singer's cause?

2. Singer's article opens with reference to the film *Central Station*. Later he advocates that we avoid spending money on luxuries in order to donate it to save children's lives. Is going to the movies a luxury? To what extent is Singer being morally or logically inconsistent?

3. Singer considers some of the reasons people might give to justify their not reducing their consumption of "luxuries" in order to save poor children's lives. What are those reasons? What other reasons might you or people you know offer? Speculate on why Singer does not consider them. How does his neglect of those other reasons affect his ability to persuade you as a reader?

4. One critic, Peter Berkowitz, argues (in the *New Republic*, January 2000) that Singer's example of Bob is oversimplified through *either/or* reasoning (either Bob threw the switch or he did not), through "focusing on a single moral intuition" rather than "the clash between competing moral intuitions," and through neglecting such competing values as that of "perfecting [one's] own talents," which takes time and money. Write an essay that supports Berkowitz's charges or that defends Singer from them.

5. Learn about efforts to "save children's lives" in a particular situation abroad, such as in Darfur, Ethiopia, Somalia, Bangladesh, or elsewhere. In the situation you analyze, what are the meanings of the word *save*? Write an essay describing the relief agencies' goals and accomplishments as well as the factors that inhibit the agencies' effectiveness.

KELLY RITTER

The Economics of Authorship: Online Paper Mills, Student Writers, and First-Year Composition

Kelly Ritter is an English professor and coordinator of first-year composition at Southern Connecticut State University. "The Economics of Authorship" was published in College Composition and Communication *(2005), a journal for teachers of college writing. The abstract of the article explains: "Using sample student analyses of online paper mill Web sites, student survey responses, and existing scholarship on plagiarism, authorship, and intellectual property, this article examines how the consumerist rhetoric of the online paper mills construes academic writing as a commodity for sale, and why such rhetoric appeals to students in first-year composition, whose cultural disconnect from the academic system of authorship increasingly leads them to patronize these sites" (p. 601).*

The question of what constitutes plagiarism, let alone how to address its many permutations in this age of electronic cut-and-paste, has characterized much of the recent research into academic dishonesty both inside and outside composition studies. This scholarship promotes the notion that one egregious type of plagiarism—the patronage of online term-paper mills—is a willfully deceptive act that needs no further study against the less wholesale, more "complicated" forms that merit examination. Purchasing a term paper is engaging in "the plagiarism that approaches fraud"[1] and is the academic sin that we most dread our students' committing. I propose that online paper mills have thus been allowed to prosper in the absence of true critical reflection on their persuasive power, especially in composition studies, where definitions of authorship are the most contested and where student understanding of authorial agency is the most tenuous. There are compelling reasons that an examination of the consumer-driven discourse of on-line paper mills should be integrated into our research on student authorship, in the context of how it competes for, and often wins, our students' attention.

First-year composition students today carefully weigh interconnected economic, academic, and personal needs when choosing whether to do their own college writing and research or purchase it elsewhere. Instead of employing the World Wide Web to piece together a paper of their own, these students often are seeking out already-finished, available-for-purchase papers by nameless and faceless authors, so as to meet their academic ends more quickly and with more certainty of success (i.e., a finished paper is a better bet than a pieced-together product of unknown resulting quality). Without these students—who do not believe that they can or should be authors of their own academic work, but do believe that they can *and should* co-opt the accomplished authorship of others when necessary—the anonymous and powerful online paper-mill industry could not exist. First-year composition students are the most likely group to fall victim to this industry, as they are not only unfamiliar with the university and its discourse but also enrolled in a required course that emphasizes the development of intellectual identity through writing. Anxious about the course and sometimes even angry that a new form of writing is being foisted upon them, one that often contradicts or complicates what the time and space of their high school English curriculum allowed them to learn, first-year composition students may quite literally buy into the paper mills' rhetoric. In the process, they shape their lifelong perceptions of what authorship in academia really means.

---

[1]Rebecca Moore Howard, *Standing in the Shadow of Giants: Plagiarists, Authors, Collaborators* (Stamford, CT: Ablex, 1999).

These students patronize online paper mills not because of any desire to outwit the academic system of authorship, but because of their cultural and ideological disconnection from the system itself. The rhetoric present in online paper mills and in our students' support of them challenges our comfortable and traditional definition of plagiarism, which is predicated upon academia's intrinsic defense of authorship as an intellectual, creative activity. The paper-mill Web sites, in order to rationalize their existence, negate the academic value of authorship in their easy online commerce with our students, instantly changing that innocent eighteen-year-old in one's composition class from an author to a plagiarist, or, in the rhetoric of the paper-mill sites, from a student to a *consumer*. In order to truly understand how and why students continue to engage in dishonest practices in the composition classroom, we thus must seek to understand how and when students see themselves as authors; how students see themselves as *consumers*, not just in the purchase of a college education, but also in a society defined by anonymity, convenience, and privacy; and how students reconcile the warring concepts of author and consumer in the space of their own writing.

The composition-studies community has yet to tackle two important questions underlying these students' absent notions of authorship. First, what is the complicated relationship already in place between *student* authors and consumer culture that dictates the role that writing plays in one's college career? Second, how might this relationship explain why the online paper mills consistently, even exponentially, profit from our students' patronage? Since first-year students do not, and perhaps *cannot*, always share faculty definitions of authorship and intellectual property, they cannot always reconcile their personal and academic needs with our course standards, which reinforce the idea that authorship is valuable, and that academic work itself is more than an economic means to an end. Addressing these questions thus begins a necessary inquiry into how and why our students frequently see college writing — their own, their friends', that which is provided by the paper mills — as an economic rather than an intellectual act.

When considering whether, when, and how often to purchase an academic 5 paper from an online paper-mill site, first-year composition students therefore work with two factors that I wish to investigate here in pursuit of answering the questions posed above: the negligible desire to do one's own writing, or to be an author, with all that entails in this era of faceless authorship vis-à-vis the Internet; and the ever-shifting concept of "integrity," or responsibility when purchasing work, particularly in the anonymous arena of online consumerism. This latter concept is contingent upon the lure of a good academic/economic bargain — the purchased paper that might raise or solidify one's academic standing in the form of a "good" grade. To investigate these factors from a student standpoint, I will contextualize scholarly approaches to the notions of authorship, textual production, and academic dishonesty with not just samples of the discourse found on the paper-mill Web sites, but also select responses from both a coursewide student survey completed by 247 students enrolled in English 101 (research-based first-year composition) during one semester at my institution, and responses from an English 101 essay assignment, in which my own students (who have given me permission to cite their work here using pseudonyms) visited select paper-mill Web sites and analyzed the arguments put forth persuading students to buy their products. By privileging student responses in my study of the online paper mills and their antiacademic (and proeconomic) discourse, I hope to emphasize the important role that students themselves might play in our scholarship on this and allied subjects, as the responses articulate a compelling range of multilayered (and often internally competing) student perceptions of academic dishonesty and authorship. . . .

CONCLUSION: ASK THE AUTHOR(S)

Ed White, in "Student Plagiarism as an Institutional and Social Issue," warns:

> The response to theft cannot be merely individual [. . .]. Indeed, we should all expect that much plagiarism will naturally occur unless we help students understand what all the fuss is about; many students simply are clueless about the issue and many faculty think the issue is simpler than it is. Taking moral high ground is important and necessary, but, as with other moral is-sues, too many of the statements from that ground are hypocritical and not cognizant of the complex motives behind student actions. (207)[2]

White makes it clear that we must combat plagiarism from two sides, "prevention through education as well as punishment for violations" (p. 206). He believes that things will never change unless we help to change them by *educating* the "viola-tors," our students. Like White, I am not against punishment, nor do I believe that it alone will stop plagiarism, or that punishment, for some, teaches any long-term lessons. Those who do not *want* to learn how authorship builds and validates a writer's identity will find ways *not* to listen. Thus, while I agree with Wood-mansee's astute observation that "authorship does not exist to innocent eyes; they see only writing and texts" (p. 1), I also recognize that some students—including a few of my own—will remain willfully "innocent" unless, until, and sometimes in spite of having been proven "guilty."

Ultimately, I believe that what we have been doing thus far, particularly where online paper mills are concerned, is *not working*. We *do* have to take note of the now-slippery state of authorship vis-à-vis the expanding Internet, and be diligent about teaching our students that plagiarism is wrong and that academic ethics mean something. But let us not use the exponential—and seemingly un-stoppable—growth power of online paper mills as an excuse to give up on the idea of *singular student authorship* altogether; let us instead take this opportunity

---

[2]Edward M. White, "Student Plagiarism as an Institutional and Social Issue." *Perspectives on Plagia-rism and Intellectual Property in a Postmodern World.* Ed. Lise Buranen and Alice Roy (Albany: SUNY Press, 1999), 205–210.

to revisit theories of authorship with our students and reinforce the value of the writer-author. While cheating may arise from a complicated notion of personal worth and academic (in)ability, the purchase of essays from online companies strikes an even more basic chord in our students: the power to purchase this worth and ability, and by extension a new academic identity.

We should continue, in our battle against plagiarism, to see the composition classroom as a site for "responsible writing and learning" (White 210) on the part of teachers and students alike. Instead of further sublimating the author ourselves, we should work to solidify our students' ideas of authorship, and their identities as writers, so that if—or when—they visit an online paper mill, they will not be persuaded to erase their writing identity in favor of a good academic bargain. Students and teachers should work to find a way, together, to shape how the ethics of the writing classroom, and the larger university, should operate: not like a business, and not in the service of economics.

APPENDIX: SURVEY OF STUDENT OPINIONS ON ACADEMIC DISHONESTY IN ENGLISH 101

Please answer the following questions honestly. Your answers will become part of a study focusing on how students conceive of academic honesty and how these conceptions affect college professors who teach research-based writing.

Please circle *as many answers as are applicable* to your response for each question. Please use "*other*" if available to provide an answer that is not listed below. *Do not put your name on this survey*, as all survey responses will be kept anonymous.

1. When I hear the word "cheating" I think of:

   a. Copying answers from another student during an exam or in-class work (238; 96 percent)
   b. Copying lecture notes from another student when I have missed class, then using those notes in a paper or on an exam (27; 11 percent)
   c. Getting help outside of class from another student when writing a paper or take-home exam (30; 12 percent)
   d. Asking another student or a friend to write a paper for me (194; 79 percent)
   e. Buying a paper from an outside source, either a company or an individual (204; 83 percent)
   f. Taking source material from the Internet and using it as my own in a paper or take-home exam (175; 71 percent)
   g. Taking source material from books, magazines, or journals and using it as my own in a paper or take-home exam (169; 68 percent)
   h. Using a professor's lecture material as my own in a paper or take-home exam without naming my professor as a source (131; 53 percent)
   i. Bringing notes to a closed-book, in-class examination (180; 73 percent)
   j. Other (please specify): _____ (12; 5 percent)

2. In my experience, students I have known who have cheated in school have:

  a. Always been caught and punished by the teacher or professor (8; 3 percent)
  b. Always been caught and punished by someone outside the school (such as a parent) (4; 2 percent)
  c. Sometimes been caught and punished by the teacher or professor (97; 39 percent)
  d. Sometimes been caught and punished by someone outside the school (31; 13 percent)
  e. Seldom been caught or punished by the teacher or professor (126; 51 percent)
  f. Seldom been caught or punished by someone outside the school (38; 15 percent)
  g. Never been caught or punished by the teacher or professor (54; 22 percent)
  h. Never been caught or punished by anyone outside of school (55; 22 percent)
  i. I have never known anyone who has cheated in school (10; 4 percent)

3. The typical punishment for students I have known who have cheated has been:

  a. Failure of the paper or exam for which the cheating was done (206; 83 percent)
  b. Failure in the course in which the cheating was done (44; 18 percent)
  c. Higher disciplinary action (such as academic probation) or expulsion from school (34; 14 percent)
  d. No punishment, but the student has dropped the class or has dropped out of school (6; 2 percent)
  e. No punishment at all; no consequences for the student (31; 13 percent)

4. In my opinion, it is acceptable for me to cheat in school if:

  a. I am short on time and the assignment is due; if I don't cheat, I won't finish the work (24; 10 percent)
  b. I am under other personal stresses (such as relationship or family problems) that keep me from doing the work on my own (27; 11 percent)
  c. I am confused about the subject and can't do the work well on my own (32; 13 percent)
  d. I am uninterested in the subject and don't care if I do the work well, or if I do it myself (18; 7 percent)
  e. I will be punished by my parents or other authority if I do this work poorly (16; 6 percent)
  f. It is never acceptable for me to cheat (180; 73 percent)
  g. Other (please specify): _____ (10; 4 percent)

5. To me, being an "author" means:

  a. Writing a book or academic article (157; 64 percent)
  b. Writing anything, whether it is "academic" or not, that is then published (150; 61 percent)
  c. Writing anything, whether it is "academic" or not, and whether it is published or not (144; 58 percent)
  d. Writing material for the Internet (either a personal or business Web site) (96; 39 percent)

e. Writing a paper or a project for a college course (86; 35 percent)
f. Writing something for which one may become famous or well-known (112; 45 percent)
g. Co-writing a project of any kind with another person or persons (87; 35 percent)
h. Gathering different sources and pasting them together as a collection of writing, then putting your name on that collection (16; 6 percent)
i. Other (please specify): _____ (8; 3 percent)

6. Most of the papers I have written for college courses could best be defined as:

a. Material that has no use outside the particular course or area of study (82; 33 percent)
b. Material that may be used in other situations, such as a job or professional applications (63; 26 percent)
c. Material that represents who I am as a writer (110; 45 percent)
d. Material that in no way represents who I am as a writer (28; 11 percent)
e. Material that has required extensive research (84; 34 percent)
f. Material that has required moderate research (146; 59 percent)
g. Material that has required little to no research (45; 18 percent)

7. I would define "research" done for college papers as:

a. Going to the library and finding books and journal articles to use in my paper (214; 87 percent)
b. Going to a resource of some kind and learning more about a subject for my paper (172; 70 percent)
c. Going to the Internet and downloading any and all information that I can use in a paper (158; 64 percent)
d. Going to friends, family, or other persons and getting ideas or suggestions to use in my paper (129; 52 percent)
e. Other (please specify): _____ (9; 4 percent)

8. My opinion about the overall function or use of the Internet in college research is:

a. It is a very necessary and beneficial component of my research for college writing projects (132; 53 percent)
b. It is a somewhat necessary and beneficial component of my research for college writing projects (64; 26 percent)
c. It is an option for research in college writing projects; sometimes I use the Internet, sometimes I don't (109; 44 percent)
d. It is not an option for me, either because I don't have Internet access or don't like using the Internet (18; 7 percent)
e. Other (please specify): _____ (11; 4 percent)

Tallied results = (number of responses; percentage of total)
Total number of students surveyed = 247

QUESTIONS FOR DISCUSSION AND WRITING

1. What steps do you take to write a paper, and in what order?

2. When a paper is assigned, how far in advance of the due date do you begin to write it? How much time do you allow for investigating the subject? For writing a first draft? Do you consult outside sources? If so, how do you decide which ones to consult? Do you allow time to rethink your paper and to revise it before you turn it in?

3. How do you define "research" (see question 7 in the survey, p. 569)? In what ways is the Internet helpful in doing the type of research you need to do? Are there other equally or more useful ways to do research? Because the type of research depends, in part, on the problem at hand, you can identify a specific topic or issue to help you answer this question.

4. With a partner, answer survey question 1, including its subparts (p. 567): "When I hear the word 'cheating' I think of:" Or you could ask the same question to ten other students in different classes. Write a definition of "cheating" based on your survey results.

5. Answer survey question 4 (p. 568), "In my opinion, it is acceptable for me to cheat in school if:" and its subparts. Compare your answers with a partner's and write a code of ethics for student authors (for models, see the Ten Commandments and the code of ethics for the Society of Professional Journalists).

NATASHA SINGER AND DUFF WILSON

Medical Editors Push for Ghostwriting Crackdown

Natasha Singer graduated from Brown University with a degree in comparative literature and creative writing. Before joining the New York Times *in 2006, she covered the environment and biodiversity for* Outside *magazine. Singer has also been a health and beauty editor at* W *magazine, and worked in the fashion press in Russia. At the* Times *she developed the Skin Deep column, covering the beauty industry, and currently writes about the pharmaceutical and healthcare industries.*

Duff Wilson graduated from Western Washington University in Bellingham (1976) and from the Columbia University Graduate School of Journalism in New York (1982). After writing for the Seattle Times *(1989–2004), Wilson joined the* New York Times, *initially covering sports-related investigations and currently the pharmaceutical and tobacco industries. His reporting has received numerous awards, including the Harvard University Goldsmith Prize for Investigative Reporting (twice), two George Polk Awards, for medical and local reporting, and a Loeb Award for business reporting. His first nonfiction book,* Fateful Harvest: The True Story of a Small Town, a Global Industry, and a Toxic Secret, *was published in 2001.*

Throughout 2009, Singer and Wilson published a series of investigative articles on the ways pharmaceutical companies present and manipulate scientific evidence in order to represent their products to physicians and the public in the most favorable light. Their work is typified by "Menopause, as Brought to You by Big Pharma" (New York Times, 12 December 2009) and "Medical Editors Push for Ghostwriting Crackdown," in which scientific accuracy and crisp writing raise serious ethical issues.

The scientific integrity of medical research has been clouded in recent years by articles that were drafted by drug company–sponsored ghostwriters and then passed off as the work of independent academic authors.

Yet the leading medical journals have continued to rely largely on an honor system of disclosure to detect such potential bias, asking authors to voluntarily report any industry ties or contributors to their manuscripts.

But now, in light of recently released evidence that some drug makers have gone to great lengths to turn scientific articles into marketing vehicles for their products, some influential medical editors are cracking down on industry-financed ghostwriting. And they are getting help from some members of Congress.

These editors are demanding that journals impose tougher disclosure policies for academic authors and that the journals enforce their own rules by actively investigating the provenance of manuscripts and by punishing authors who play down extensive contributions by ghostwriters.

In medical journal circles, the exorcism of industry-financed editorial assis-   5
tance even has its own name: ghostbusting.

In an editorial last week calling for a zero tolerance policy, the editors of the medical journal *PLoS Medicine*, from the Public Library of Science, called for journals to identify and retract ghostwritten articles and banish their authors.

"Any papers where this breach is substantiated should be immediately retracted," the editors wrote. "Authors found to have not declared such interest should be banned from any subsequent publication in the journal and their misconduct reported to their institutions."

In the past, researchers have raised allegations of ghostwriting in articles about quality-of-life drugs like antidepressants, painkillers and diet pills. But the situation has become more serious this year after a few editors said they had discovered ghostwriting in manuscripts about life-and-death products like cancer and hematology drugs.

As Washington tries to revamp the health care system, concerns about ghostwriting are taking on new urgency. One of the underlying assumptions of the health care overhaul effort is that money can be saved and medical care improved by relying more heavily on research showing which drugs and procedures are the most effective. But experts fear that the process could be corrupted if research articles are skewed by the hidden influence of drug or medical device makers.

One senator on the trail of ghostwriting is Charles E. Grassley, a Republican   10
of Iowa and a member of the Senate Finance Committee, which has taken a leading role in the health overhaul effort.

In July, Mr. Grassley wrote letters asking eight leading medical journals about their ghostwriting policies. He also asked whether, since 2004, the journals had taken action against any author who had failed to report the involvement of a third party in the development of a manuscript.

None of the editors reported taking action against an author for ghostwriting. Their replies to the senator, obtained by *The New York Times*, varied from assurances of editorial diligence to the equivalent of "don't ask, don't tell." One editor in chief, for example, wrote that because his journal prohibited ghostwriting, the publication did not have a specific policy on the practice.

Journals without explicit ghostwriting rules can expect to hear more from the senator.

"Objective research is really at the heart of public trust in medicine," Mr. Grassley wrote in an e-mail message to a reporter last Friday.

Allegations of ghostwriting first surfaced several years ago in the promotion 15 of the diet drug combination fen-phen, which was taken off the market because of safety concerns in 1997, and the painkiller Vioxx, withdrawn in 2004. And last month, documents made public in litigation against the pharmaceutical giant Wyeth showed that the company had paid a medical writing firm to draft articles, published through 2005, favorable to its Premarin family of hormone drugs even as evidence mounted that certain hormone drugs could increase the risk of breast cancer.

Some researchers say industry ghostwriting is widespread and continuing. Even with disclosure policies already in effect at many publications, unnamed authors played a role in more than 40 articles published last year at six major medical journals, according to a study made public last week. That study, conducted by an editorial team at *The Journal of the American Medical Association*, or *JAMA*, defined ghostwriting broadly as any uncredited significant contribution to research or writing, regardless of whether it was financed by industry.

Over the last few years, international associations of medical journal editors have developed stricter disclosure criteria for authors of and contributors to scientific manuscripts. The International Committee of Medical Journal Editors, for example, defines an author as a person who makes a substantial contribution to developing a study or analyzing its results and in drafting a manuscript, and who approves the final version of an article. Authors should identify other contributors to an article and their financing sources, according to the group.

Drug companies say they are about to put these publication principles into effect for clinical trials.

"The pharmaceutical industry is moving in lock step with the editors of medical journals," Jeffrey K. Francer, assistant general counsel of the Pharmaceutical Research and Manufacturers of America, an industry trade group for drug makers, said in an interview last week. The new standards are to take effect in October, he said.

But even though disclosure policies are already in place at many journals, the 20 new *JAMA* study found a ghostwriting rate of more than 7 percent at *JAMA* and *PLoS Medicine*, and nearly 11 percent at *The New England Journal of Medicine*.

Joseph S. Wislar, who led the study, said in an interview last week that *The New England Journal of Medicine* may have had a higher rate because the journal did not require lead authors to list all other contributors.

Editors of *The New England Journal of Medicine* said that they were puzzled by and skeptical of the *JAMA* data, but confirmed that the publication left such disclosures to the discretion of authors.

Experts who study disclosure said authorship policies might be inadequate in part because they asked for incomplete information, but also because they typically had no teeth.

"Requiring someone to write a retraction or barring them from publishing in academic journals for some period of time—that would be an effective deterrent," said George Loewenstein, a professor of economics and psychology at Carnegie Mellon University in Pittsburgh who has conducted research on the effect of conflict-of-interest disclosures in medicine.

A few editors said they were already taking tougher stances after discovering their disclosure policies had allowed authors to acknowledge writers financed by drug companies without explaining that the paid writers played primary roles in creating the manuscripts.

The problem of incomplete disclosure is particularly worrisome for opinion 25 pieces like review articles, in which an author brings a personal perspective to a wide body of research, according to an editorial in *The Oncologist.*

"These articles are likely to influence the direction of new investigation as well as the practice of oncology," wrote Dr. Bruce A. Chabner, the clinical director of the cancer center at Massachusetts General Hospital and the editor in chief of *The Oncologist.* "It is critical that such articles represent the unbiased views of the authors, and not those of a ghostwriter or a drug's sponsor."

The Oncologist plans to continue publishing clinical trials sponsored by drug companies, Dr. Chabner wrote. But the journal no longer accepts opinion pieces that involve writers with ties to companies that have a commercial interest in an article's content—nor will its editors correspond with hired writers who are not named as the authors of manuscripts.

Mr. Francer, of the Pharmaceutical Research and Manufacturers of America, said such measures could be detrimental because they could "chill research and chill support for research."

But the trend may be too far along to deter.

In January, editors at *Blood*, the journal of the American Society of Hema- 30 tology, discovered that an unsolicited manuscript submitted by a prominent researcher involved significant contributions from a pharmaceutical company employee named in the acknowledgments—a major role in the manuscript that should have qualified the employee to be listed as an author of the paper. Further detective work quickly turned up two other ghostwritten manuscripts.

Editors decided to make their discoveries public in an editorial titled " 'Ghostbusting' at *Blood*" in which they wrote that the journal would henceforth reject opinion pieces that had industry ties.

In an interview last month, Dr. Cynthia E. Dunbar, the editor in chief of *Blood*, said that, in the future, the journal would consider a ban of several years for authors caught lying about ghostwriting, in addition to retracting their ghosted articles.

But, said Dr. Dunbar, who is a hematologist at the National Institutes of Health in Bethesda, "I hope we don't have to do that."

QUESTIONS FOR DISCUSSION AND WRITING

1. What is ghostwriting? Autobiographies of sports figures, such as Andre Agassiz, are often ghostwritten, with the ghostwriter acknowledged as a coauthor. What differences are there between such autobiographies and industry-financed ghost-written scientific articles?

2. Why is 'scientific integrity' so important not only in medical research but in writing about it? What might some of the consequences be if this integrity is violated (see, for instance, paragraphs, 15, 25, 26, 29)?

3. What ethical problems exist when scientific and medical journals publish "articles that were drafted by drug company–sponsored ghostwriters and then passed off as the work of independent academic authors" (paragraph 1)? Use the entire article to answer this question.

4. Should journal editors police authorship, or is it sufficient to rely on "an honor system of disclosure [of] . . . industry ties or contributors" to authors' manuscripts, as has been done for years? Is it appropriate to punish "authors who play down extensive contributions by ghostwriters" (paragraph 2)?

5. With a partner or team, draw up an honor code for authors of scientific articles with medical implications. What principles should it incorporate?

CHAPTER 8

The Environment:
Will We Save It or Lose It?
Will This Be the End of the World
As We Know It?

Haiti and the Dominican Republic

Border of Haiti and the Dominican Republic (south of Dajabon, Dominican Republic), 2001

James P. Blair/National Geographic/Getty Images

QUESTIONS FOR DISCUSSION AND WRITING

1. This photograph illustrates the effect of the very different histories and environmental management policies of Haiti and the Dominican Republic, adjacent countries on the Caribbean island of Hispaniola, six hundred miles off the Florida coast. As Jared Diamond points out in *Collapse,* whenever deforestation occurs, its consequences "include loss of timber and other forest building materials, soil erosion, loss of soil fertility, sediment loads in the rivers, loss of watershed protection and hence of potential hydroelectric power, and decreased rainfall" (p. 330). Using information from Diamond's "The World as a Polder" (p. 632) or his more extended discussion entitled "One Island, Two Peoples, Two Histories: The Dominican Republic and Haiti" (Chapter 11 of *Collapse*) explain why such remarkable environmental differences have occurred.

2. Al Gore used this striking photograph in his iconic book, *An Inconvenient Truth: The Planetary Emergency of Global Warming and What We Can Do About It* (2006) and the related film. What lessons is this picture intended to convey to a North American audience?

3. What can be done, at present or in the future, to rectify the environmental problems of the past and prevent them from happening in the future? Propose a policy that's feasible in a democracy.

TERRY TEMPEST WILLIAMS

The Clan of One-Breasted Women

When the U.S. government decided to test atomic weapons in a "virtually uninhabited" section of Utah in the 1950s, environmentalist Terry Tempest Williams's family was among the "virtual uninhabitants," as she puts it. In one of the most troubling episodes in U.S. history, Williams (b. 1955) and other Utah residents were being exposed to fallout while the federal government assured them that they were safe; thousands died of radiation-related diseases. As she watched the women in her family die of cancer, and as the government refused to acknowledge the claims of the test victims, she came to realize that "tolerating blind obedience in the name of patriotism or religion ultimately takes our lives." Williams earned degrees in English (B.S., 1979) and environmental education (M.S., 1984) at the University of Utah. All of her books — including The Secret Language of Snow *(1984), a children's book;* Pieces of White Shell: A Journey to Navajo Land *(1984); and* Leap *(2000) — reflect her belief in the vital link among human beings, animals, and the earth. These themes prevail in her best-known work,* Refuge: An Unnatural History of Family and Place *(1992). In "The Clan of One-Breasted Women" (1991), the epilogue to* Refuge, *Williams tells the story of her family's history with cancer. Her analysis becomes an emotional and ethical protest against the federal government's routine denial that anyone was harmed by the radioactive fallout.*

I belong to a Clan of One-Breasted Women. My mother, my grandmothers, and six aunts have all had mastectomies. Seven are dead. The two who survive have just completed rounds of chemotherapy and radiation.

I've had my own problems: two biopsies for breast cancer and a small tumor between my ribs diagnosed as a "borderline malignancy."

This is my family history.

Most statistics tell us breast cancer is genetic, hereditary, with rising percentages attached to fatty diets, childlessness, or becoming pregnant after thirty. What they don't say is living in Utah may be the greatest hazard of all.

We are a Mormon family with roots in Utah since 1847. The "word of wisdom"   5
in my family aligned us with good foods—no coffee, no tea, tobacco, or alcohol. For the most part, our women were finished having their babies by the time they were thirty. And only one faced breast cancer prior to 1960. Traditionally, as a group of people, Mormons have a low rate of cancer.

Is our family a cultural anomaly? The truth is, we didn't think about it. Those who did, usually the men, simply said, "bad genes." The women's attitude was stoic. Cancer was part of life. On February 16, 1971, the eve of my mother's surgery, I accidentally picked up the telephone and overheard her ask my grandmother what she could expect.

"Diane, it is one of the most spiritual experiences you will ever encounter."

I quietly put down the receiver.

Two days later, my father took my brothers and me to the hospital to visit her. She met us in the lobby in a wheelchair. No bandages were visible. I'll never forget her radiance, the way she held herself in a purple velvet robe, and how she gathered us around her.

"Children, I am fine. I want you to know I felt the arms of God around me."   10

We believed her. My father cried. Our mother, his wife, was thirty-eight years old.

A little over a year after Mother's death, Dad and I were having dinner together. He had just returned from St. George, where the Tempest Company was completing the gas lines that would service southern Utah. He spoke of his love for the country, the sandstone landscape, bare-boned and beautiful. He had just finished hiking the Kolob trail in Zion National Park. We got caught up in reminiscing, recalling with fondness our walk up Angel's Landing on his fiftieth birthday and the years our family had vacationed there.

Over dessert, I shared a recurring dream of mine. I told my father that for years, as long as I could remember, I saw this flash of light in the night in the desert—that this image had so permeated my being that I could not venture south without seeing it again, on the horizon, illuminating buttes and mesas.

"You did see it," he said.

"Saw what?"   15

"The bomb. The cloud. We were driving home from Riverside, California. You were sitting on Diane's lap. She was pregnant. In fact, I remember the day, September 7, 1957. We had just gotten out of the Service. We were driving north, past Las Vegas. It was an hour or so before dawn, when this explosion went off. We not only heard it, but felt it. I thought the oil tanker in front of us had blown up. We pulled over and suddenly, rising from the desert floor, we saw it, clearly, this golden-stemmed cloud, the mushroom. The sky seemed to vibrate with an eerie pink glow. Within a few minutes, a light ash was raining on the car."

I stared at my father.

"I thought you knew that," he said. "It was a common occurrence in the fifties."

It was at this moment that I realized the deceit I had been living under. Children growing up in the American Southwest, drinking contaminated milk from contaminated cows, even from the contaminated breasts of their mothers, my mother—members, years later, of the Clan of One-Breasted Women.

It is a well-known story in the Desert West, "The Day We Bombed Utah,"   20 or more accurately, the years we bombed Utah: aboveground atomic testing in Nevada took place from January 27, 1951, through July 11, 1962. Not only were the winds blowing north covering "low-use segments of the population" with fallout and leaving sheep dead in their tracks, but the climate was right. The United States of the 1950s was red, white, and blue. The Korean War was raging. McCarthyism was rampant. Ike was it, and the cold war was hot. If you were against nuclear testing, you were for a communist regime.

Much has been written about this "American nuclear tragedy." Public health was secondary to national security. The Atomic Energy Commissioner, Thomas Murray, said, "Gentlemen, we must not let anything interfere with this series of tests, nothing."

Again and again, the American public was told by its government, in spite of burns, blisters, and nausea, "It has been found that the tests may be conducted with adequate assurance of safety under conditions prevailing at the bombing reservations." Assuaging public fears was simply a matter of public relations. "Your best action," an Atomic Energy Commission booklet read, "is not to be worried about fallout." A news release typical of the times stated, "We find no basis for concluding that harm to any individual has resulted from radioactive fallout."

On August 30, 1979, during Jimmy Carter's presidency, a suit was filed, *Irene Allen* v. *The United States of America*. Mrs. Allen's case was the first on an alphabetical list of twenty-four test cases, representative of nearly twelve hundred plaintiffs seeking compensation from the United States government for cancers caused by nuclear testing in Nevada.

Irene Allen lived in Hurricane, Utah. She was the mother of five children and had been widowed twice. Her first husband, with their two oldest boys, had watched the tests from the roof of the local high school. He died of leukemia in 1956. Her second husband died of pancreatic cancer in 1978.

In a town meeting conducted by Utah Senator Orrin Hatch, shortly before the 25 suit was filed, Mrs. Allen said, "I am not blaming the government, I want you to know that, Senator Hatch. But I thought if my testimony could help in any way so this wouldn't happen again to any of the generations coming up after us . . . I am happy to be here this day to bear testimony of this."

God-fearing people. This is just one story in an anthology of thousands.

On May 10, 1984, Judge Bruce S. Jenkins handed down his opinion. Ten of the plaintiffs were awarded damages. It was the first time a federal court had determined that nuclear tests had been the cause of cancers. For the remaining fourteen test cases, the proof of causation was not sufficient. In spite of the split decision, it was considered a landmark ruling. It was not to remain so for long.

In April 1987, the Tenth Circuit Court of Appeals overturned Judge Jenkins's ruling on the ground that the United States was protected from suit by the legal doctrine of sovereign immunity, a centuries-old idea from England in the days of absolute monarchs.

In January 1988, the Supreme Court refused to review the Appeals Court decision. To our court system it does not matter whether the United States government was irresponsible, whether it lied to its citizens, or even that citizens died from the fallout of nuclear testing. What matters is that our government is immune: "The King can do no wrong."

In Mormon culture, authority is respected, obedience is revered, and inde- 30 pendent thinking is not. I was taught as a young girl not to "make waves" or "rock the boat."

"Just let it go," Mother would say. "You know how you feel, that's what counts."

For many years, I have done just that—listened, observed, and quietly formed my own opinions, in a culture that rarely asks questions because it has all the answers. But one by one, I have watched the women in my family die common, heroic deaths. We sat in waiting rooms hoping for good news, but always receiving the bad. I cared for them, bathed their scarred bodies, and kept their secrets. I watched beautiful women become bald as Cytoxan, cisplatin, and Adriamycin were injected into their veins. I held their foreheads as they vomited green-black bile, and I shot them with morphine when the pain became inhuman. In the end, I witnessed their last peaceful breaths, becoming a midwife to the rebirth of their souls.

The price of obedience has become too high.

The fear and inability to question authority that ultimately killed rural communities in Utah during atmospheric testing of atomic weapons is the same fear I saw in my mother's body. Sheep. Dead sheep. The evidence is buried.

I cannot prove that my mother, Diane Dixon Tempest, or my grandmothers, 35 Lettie Romney Dixon and Kathryn Blackett Tempest, along with my aunts developed cancer from nuclear fallout in Utah. But I can't prove they didn't.

My father's memory was correct. The September blast we drove through in 1957 was part of Operation Plumbbob, one of the most intensive series of bomb tests to be initiated. The flash of light in the night in the desert, which I had always thought was a dream, developed into a family nightmare. It took fourteen years, from 1957 to 1971, for cancer to manifest in my mother—the same time, Howard L. Andrews, an authority in radioactive fallout at the National Institutes of Health, says radiation cancer requires to become evident. The more I learn about what it means to be a "downwinder," the more questions I drown in.

What I do know, however, is that as a Mormon woman of the fifth generation of Latter-day Saints, I must question everything, even if it means losing my faith, even if it means becoming a member of a border tribe among my own people. Tolerating blind obedience in the name of patriotism or religion ultimately takes our lives.

When the Atomic Energy Commission described the country north of the Nevada Test Site as "virtually uninhabited desert terrain," my family and the birds at Great Salt Lake were some of the "virtual uninhabitants."

One night, I dreamed women from all over the world circled a blazing fire in the desert. They spoke of change, how they hold the moon in their bellies and wax and wane with its phases. They mocked the presumption of even-tempered beings and made promises that they would never fear the witch inside themselves. The women danced wildly as sparks broke away from the flames and entered the night sky as stars.

And they sang a song given to them by Shoshone grandmothers: 40

Ah ne nah, nah	Consider the rabbits
nin nah nah—	How gently they walk on the earth—
ah ne nah, nah	Consider the rabbits
nin nah nah—	How gently they walk on the earth—
Nyaga mutzi	We remember them
oh ne nay—	We can walk gently also—
Nyaga mutzi	We remember them
oh ne nay—	We can walk gently also—

The women danced and drummed and sang for weeks, preparing themselves for what was to come. They would reclaim the desert for the sake of their children, for the sake of the land.

A few miles downwind from the fire circle, bombs were being tested. Rabbits felt the tremors. Their soft leather pads on paws and feet recognized the shaking sands, while the roots of mesquite and sage were smoldering. Rocks were hot from the inside out and dust devils hummed unnaturally. And each time there was another nuclear test, ravens watched the desert heave. Stretch marks appeared. The land was losing its muscle.

The women couldn't bear it any longer. They were mothers. They had suffered labor pains but always under the promise of birth. The red hot pains beneath the desert promised death only, as each bomb became a stillborn. A contract had been made and broken between human beings and the land. A new contract was being drawn by the women, who understood the fate of the earth as their own.

Under the cover of darkness, ten women slipped under a barbed-wire fence and entered the contaminated country. They were trespassing. They walked toward the town of Mercury, in moonlight, taking their cues from coyote, kit fox, antelope squirrel, and quail. They moved quietly and deliberately through the maze of Joshua trees. When a hint of daylight appeared they rested, drinking tea and sharing their rations of food. The women closed their eyes. The time had come to protest with the heart, that to deny one's genealogy with the earth was to commit treason against one's soul.

At dawn, the women draped themselves in mylar, wrapping long streamers of silver plastic around their arms to blow in the breeze. They wore clear masks that became the faces of humanity. And when they arrived at the edge of Mercury, they carried all the butterflies of a summer day in their wombs. They paused to allow their courage to settle.

The town that forbids pregnant women and children to enter because of 45 radiation risks was asleep. The women moved through the streets as winged messengers, twirling around each other in slow motion, peeking inside homes and watching the easy sleep of men and women. They were astonished by such stillness and periodically would utter a shrill note or low cry just to verify life.

The residents finally awoke to these strange apparitions. Some simply stared. Others called authorities, and in time, the women were apprehended by wary soldiers dressed in desert fatigues. They were taken to a white, square building on the other edge of Mercury. When asked who they were and why they were there, the women replied, "We are mothers and we have come to reclaim the desert for our children."

The soldiers arrested them. As the ten women were blindfolded and handcuffed, they began singing:

> *You can't forbid us everything*
> *You can't forbid us to think —*
> *You can't forbid our tears to flow*
> *And you can't stop the songs that we sing.*

The women continued to sing louder and louder, until they heard the voices of their sisters moving across the mesa:

> *Ah ne nah, nah*
> *nin nah nah —*
> *Ah ne nah, nah*
> *nin nah nah —*
> *Nyaga mutzi*
> *oh ne nay —*
> *Nyaga mutzi*
> *oh ne nay —*

"Call for reinforcements," one soldier said.

"We have," interrupted one woman, "we have—and you have no idea of our numbers."

I crossed the line at the Nevada Test Site and was arrested with nine other Utahns for trespassing on military lands. They are still conducting nuclear tests in the desert. Ours was an act of civil disobedience. But as I walked toward the town of Mercury, it was more than a gesture of peace. It was a gesture on behalf of the Clan of One-Breasted Women.

As one officer cinched the handcuffs around my wrists, another frisked my 50 body. She found a pen and a pad of paper tucked inside my left boot.

"And these?" she asked sternly.

"Weapons," I replied.

Our eyes met. I smiled. She pulled the leg of my trousers back over my boot.

"Step forward, please," she said as she took my arm.

We were booked under an afternoon sun and bused to Tonopah, Nevada. It 55 was a two-hour ride. This was familiar country. The Joshua trees standing their ground had been named by my ancestors, who believed they looked like prophets pointing west to the Promised Land. These were the same trees that bloomed each spring, flowers appearing like white flames in the Mojave. And I recalled a full moon in May, when Mother and I had walked among them, flushing out mourning doves and owls.

The bus stopped short of town. We were released.

The officials thought it was a cruel joke to leave us stranded in the desert with no way to get home. What they didn't realize was that we were home, soul-centered and strong, women who recognized the sweet smell of sage as fuel for our spirits.

QUESTIONS FOR DISCUSSION AND WRITING

1. Terry Tempest Williams's family is prominent in Utah; her father was a member of the Stake High Council of the regional Mormon Church. Why does Williams define her "family history" (paragraph 3) in terms of women with breast cancer rather than men of power?

2. "The Clan of One-Breasted Women" is the ten-page epilogue to Williams's book *Refuge*. How many sections is the epilogue divided into? Why is it important to notice the demarcation of these sections? What is the significance—structurally and thematically—of the two "dreams" she describes (paragraphs 13 and 39)?

3. As a little girl, Williams was taught by her Mormon culture "not to 'make waves.'" As an adult woman, especially as a conscientious writer, she changed her behavior pattern: "[A]s a Mormon woman of the fifth generation of Latter-day Saints, I must question everything . . ." (paragraph 37). What is the significance of this change to her intellectual and spiritual growth?

4. According to Williams, the Atomic Energy Commission, which is made up of mostly male members, declared the "desert terrain" to be "virtually uninhabited" (paragraph 38). What factors (socioeconomic, geographic, political, psychological, cultural) might prompt continued disregard for the inhabitants? How does the existence of new, heavily populated desert communities in Arizona and Nevada (not to mention Middle Eastern countries) affect your answer?

5. What are the differences, for Terry Tempest Williams, between writing as a form of advocacy and the act of civil disobedience she describes in "The Clan of One-Breasted Women"? Consider in your response Martin Luther King Jr.'s advocacy of a "direct-action campaign" in support of civil rights and the role his "Letter from Birmingham Jail" (p. 494) played in influencing protesters' behavior.

6. Using Terry Tempest Williams, Henry David Thoreau (p. 594), and Annie Dillard (p. 599) as examples, write an essay in which you argue for or against the precept that where we live determines what we live for. Or argue the converse, that what we live for determines where and how we live, to whom we belong, and indeed, who we are.

AL GORE

A Planetary Emergency

Albert Arnold "Al" Gore Jr. (b. 1948), son of liberal Tennessee Senator Al Gore, graduated from Harvard in 1969, served in Vietnam although he opposed the war, and attended law school before dropping out to run for the U.S. House of Representatives, where he represented Tennessee for four terms, 1976–84. He then served in the U.S. Senate, 1985–93. As vice president under Bill Clinton, 1993– 2000, Gore continued the activities he had begun while in the Senate to develop national information infrastructure, "The Information Superhighway," and to promote environmental preservation. Although he received the popular vote for the presidency in 2000, a Supreme Court decision gave the Florida election recount to George W. Bush.

Gore and the Intergovernmental Panel on Climate Change (IPCC) shared the Nobel Peace Prize for 2007 for their efforts to inform the world "about man-made climate change," and their work to counteract such change. "A Planetary Emergency" is Gore's Nobel speech. The Nobel press release called Gore "probably the single individual who has done most to create greater worldwide understanding of the measures that need to be adopted" to strengthen "the struggle against climate change." His highly popular books on ecology are Earth in the Balance: Ecology and the Human Spirit *(1992) and* An Inconvenient Truth: The Planetary Emergency of Global Warming and What We Can Do About It *(2006); the movie version won an Oscar for Best Documentary. Gore is dedicated to warning people of the rapid climate changes causing world crisis, and to impel them to the "moral imperative to act."*

We, the human species, are confronting a planetary emergency—a threat to the survival of our civilization that is gathering ominous and destructive potential even as we gather here. But there is hopeful news as well: we have the ability to solve this crisis and avoid the worst—though not all—of its consequences, if we act boldly, decisively and quickly.

However, despite a growing number of honorable exceptions, too many of the world's leaders are still best described in the words Winston Churchill applied to those who ignored Adolf Hitler's threat: "They go on in strange paradox, decided only to be undecided, resolved to be irresolute, adamant for drift, solid for fluidity, all powerful to be impotent."

So today, we dumped another 70 million tons of global-warming pollution into the thin shell of atmosphere surrounding our planet, as if it were an open sewer. And tomorrow, we will dump a slightly larger amount, with the cumulative concentrations now trapping more and more heat from the sun.

As a result, the earth has a fever. And the fever is rising. The experts have told us it is not a passing affliction that will heal by itself. We asked for a second opinion. And a third. And a fourth. And the consistent conclusion, restated with increasing alarm, is that something basic is wrong.

We are what is wrong, and we must make it right.   5

Last September 21, as the Northern Hemisphere tilted away from the sun, scientists reported with unprecedented distress that the North Polar ice cap is "falling off a cliff." One study estimated that it could be completely gone during summer in less than 22 years. Another new study, to be presented by U.S. Navy researchers later this week, warns it could happen in as little as 7 years.

Seven years from now.

In the last few months, it has been harder and harder to misinterpret the signs that our world is spinning out of kilter. Major cities in North and South America, Asia and Australia are nearly out of water due to massive droughts and melting glaciers. Desperate farmers are losing their livelihoods. Peoples in the frozen Arctic and on low-lying Pacific islands are planning evacuations of places they have long called home. Unprecedented wildfires have forced a half million people from their homes in one country and caused a national emergency that almost brought down the government in another. Climate refugees have migrated into areas already inhabited by people with different cultures, religions, and traditions, increasing the potential for conflict. Stronger storms in the Pacific and Atlantic have threatened whole cities. Millions have been displaced by massive flooding in South Asia, Mexico, and 18 countries in Africa. As temperature extremes have increased, tens of thousands have lost their lives. We are recklessly burning and clearing our forests and driving more and more species into extinction. The very web of life on which we depend is being ripped and frayed.

We never intended to cause all this destruction. . . .

But unlike most other forms of pollution, CO_2 is invisible, tasteless, and   10
odorless—which has helped keep the truth about what it is doing to our climate
out of sight and out of mind. Moreover, the catastrophe now threatening us is
unprecedented—and we often confuse the unprecedented with the improbable.

We also find it hard to imagine making the massive changes that are now
necessary to solve the crisis. And when large truths are genuinely inconvenient,
whole societies can, at least for a time, ignore them. Yet as George Orwell reminds
us: "Sooner or later a false belief bumps up against solid reality, usually on a battlefield."

In the years since this prize was first awarded, the entire relationship between
humankind and the earth has been radically transformed. And still, we have
remained largely oblivious to the impact of our cumulative actions.

Indeed, without realizing it, we have begun to wage war on the earth itself.
Now, we and the earth's climate are locked in a relationship familiar to war planners: "Mutually assured destruction."

More than two decades ago, scientists calculated that nuclear war could
throw so much debris and smoke into the air that it would block life-giving sunlight from our atmosphere, causing a "nuclear winter." Their eloquent warnings
here in Oslo helped to galvanize the world's resolve to halt the nuclear arms race.

Now science is warning us that if we do not quickly reduce the global warm-   15
ing pollution that is trapping so much of the heat our planet normally radiates
back out of the atmosphere, we are in danger of creating a permanent "carbon
summer."

As the American poet Robert Frost wrote, "Some say the world will end in
fire; some say in ice." Either, he notes, "would suffice."

But neither need be our fate. It is time to make peace with the planet. . . .

We must understand the connections between the climate crisis and the
afflictions of poverty, hunger, HIV/AIDS and other pandemics. As these problems are linked, so too must be their solutions. We must begin by making the
common rescue of the global environment the central organizing principle of the
world community. . . .

The world needs an alliance—especially of those nations that weigh heaviest
in the scales where earth is in the balance. I salute Europe and Japan for the steps
they've taken in recent years to meet the challenge, and the new government in
Australia, which has made solving the climate crisis its first priority.

But the outcome will be decisively influenced by two nations that are now   20
failing to do enough: the United States and China. While India is also growing
fast in importance, it should be absolutely clear that it is the two largest CO_2
emitters—most of all, my own country—that will need to make the boldest
moves, or stand accountable before history for their failure to act.

Both countries should stop using the other's behavior as an excuse for
stalemate and instead develop an agenda for mutual survival in a shared global
environment. . . .

We have to expand the boundaries of what is possible. In the words of the Spanish poet, Antonio Machado, "Pathwalker, there is no path. You must make the path as you walk."

QUESTIONS FOR DISCUSSION AND WRITING

1. What is the "planetary emergency" (paragraph 8) to which Gore refers? Identify the evidence he offers (paragraphs 10–19) to characterize the emergency. Because the Nobel Prize address is necessarily brief, what sorts of additional evidence would a longer speech allow? Where could good evidence be found? (See pieces in this chapter by Havel, Rees, Carson, Postel, Diamond, and Berry, and Gore's own books.)

2. In what ways has the "entire relationship between humankind and the earth . . . been radically transformed"? If the changes are so great, why have we "remained largely oblivious to the impact of our cumulative actions" (paragraph 21)? What does Gore mean by the "'mutually assured destruction'" that will certainly occur if the world continues on its current trajectory (paragraph 22)? In contrast to a "nuclear winter," what is a "carbon summer" (paragraph 16)?

3. What might individuals do to help reduce global warming? Are you and your companions making conscious efforts to reduce global warming? If so, what are you doing? With what consequences? If not, why not?

4. Using other essays in this chapter and other sources of information as needed, pick a principle (such as the worldwide reduction of carbon emissions), research it, and present a plan to put it into effect. What consequences would you predict for your proposal?

5. What does Gore predict for the future if people combine to act to reduce global warming? And if they don't? Might you be living in the end of the world as you know it?

WANGARI MAATHAI

The Green Belt Movement

The Nobel Peace Prize was awarded in 2004 to Wangari Maathai for her "contribution to sustainable development, democracy and peace." The Awards Committee noted, "Peace on earth depends on our ability to secure our living environment. Maathai stands at the front of the fight to promote ecologically viable social, economic and cultural development in Kenya and in Africa. She has taken a holistic approach to sustainable development that embraces democracy, human rights and women's rights in particular. She thinks globally and acts locally." "The Green Belt Movement" is her Nobel Prize acceptance speech.

Maathai, born in Nyeri, Kenya, in 1940, earned degrees in biology from Mount St. Scholastica College in Atchison, Kansas (B.S., 1964), the University of Pittsburgh (M.S., 1966), and a Ph.D. from the University of Nairobi (1971), where she headed the Veterinary Anatomy Department. She introduced the idea of planting trees on farms and in school and church compounds. There she initiated what would become the Green Belt Movement, planting 30 million trees throughout Kenya to alleviate malnutrition, provide firewood, aid in cleaning up drinking water, and reforest the mountains. The movement spread to become the Pan African Green Belt Network, serving Zimbabwe, Ethiopia, Tanzania, Uganda, and other countries. Although her efforts on behalf of democracy and women's rights subjected her to beatings and imprisonment by Daniel arap Moi, Kenya's strong-man president, she was elected to Parliament in 2002 in Kenya's first free elections in a generation, and later appointed Kenya's Assistant Minister of Environment, Natural Resources, and Wildlife.

The Nobel Prize citation states, "Environmental protection has become yet another path to peace. . . . But where does tree-planting come in? When we analyze local conflicts, we tend to focus on their ethnic and religious aspects. But it is often the underlying ecological circumstances that bring the more readily visible factors to the flashpoint. Consider the conflict in Darfur in the Sudan. What catches the eye is that this is a conflict between Arabs and Africans, between the government, various armed militia groups, and civilians. Below this surface, however, lies the desertification that has taken place in the last few decades, especially in northern Darfur. The desert has spread southwards, forcing Arab nomads further and further south year by year, bringing them into conflict with African farmers. In the Philippines, uncontrolled deforestation has helped to provoke a rising against the authorities. In Mexico, soil erosion and deforestation have been factors in the revolt in Chiapas against the central government. In Haiti, in Amazonas, and in the Himalayas, deforestation and the resulting soil erosion have contributed to deteriorating living conditions and caused tension between population groups and countries. In many countries deforestation, often together with other problems, leads to migration to the big cities, where the lack of infrastructure is another source of further conflict. Can all this not be said more simply? Maathai herself has put it like this: "We are sharing our resources in a very inequitable way. We have parts of the world that are very deprived and parts of the world that are very rich. And that is partly the reason why we have conflicts."

In this year's prize, the Norwegian Nobel Committee has placed the critical issue of environment and its linkage to democracy and peace before the world. For their visionary action, I am profoundly grateful. Recognizing that sustainable development, democracy and peace are indivisible is an idea whose time has come. Our work over the past 30 years has always appreciated and engaged these linkages.

My inspiration partly comes from my childhood experiences and observations of Nature in rural Kenya. It has been influenced and nurtured by the formal education I was privileged to receive in Kenya, the United States and Germany. As I was growing up, I witnessed forests being cleared and replaced by commercial plantations, which destroyed local biodiversity and the capacity of the forests to conserve water.

Excellencies, ladies and gentlemen,

In 1977, when we started the Green Belt Movement, I was partly responding to needs identified by rural women, namely lack of firewood, clean drinking water, balanced diets, shelter and income.

Throughout Africa, women are the primary caretakers, holding significant responsibility for tilling the land and feeding their families. As a result, they are often the first to become aware of environmental damage as resources become scarce and incapable of sustaining their families. 5

The women we worked with recounted that unlike in the past, they were unable to meet their basic needs. This was due to the degradation of their immediate environment as well as the introduction of commercial farming, which replaced the growing of household food crops. But international trade controlled the price of the exports from these small-scale farmers and a reasonable and just income could not be guaranteed. I came to understand that when the environment is destroyed, plundered or mismanaged, we undermine our quality of life and that of future generations.

Tree planting became a natural choice to address some of the initial basic needs identified by women. Also, tree planting is simple, attainable and guarantees quick, successful results within a reasonable amount of time. This sustains interest and commitment.

So, together, we have planted over 30 million trees that provide fuel, food, shelter, and income to support their children's education and household needs. The activity also creates employment and improves soils and watersheds. Through their involvement, women gain some degree of power over their lives, especially their social and economic position and relevance in the family. This work continues.

Initially, the work was difficult because historically our people have been persuaded to believe that because they are poor, they lack not only capital, but also knowledge and skills to address their challenges. Instead they are conditioned to believe that solutions to their problems must come from 'outside.' Further, women did not realize that meeting their needs depended on their environment being healthy and well managed. They were also unaware that a degraded environment leads to a scramble for scarce resources and may culminate in poverty and even conflict. They were also unaware of the injustices of international economic arrangements.

In order to assist communities to understand these linkages, we developed a citizen education program, during which people identify their problems, the causes and possible solutions. They then make connections between their own personal actions and the problems they witness in the environment and in society. They learn that our world is confronted with a litany of woes: corruption, violence against women and children, disruption and breakdown of families, and 10 disintegration of cultures and communities. They also identify the abuse of drugs and chemical substances, especially among young people. There are also devastating diseases that are defying cures or occurring in epidemic proportions. Of particular concern are HIV/AIDS, malaria and diseases associated with malnutrition.

On the environment front, they are exposed to many human activities that are devastating to the environment and societies. These include widespread destruction of ecosystems, especially through deforestation, climatic instability, and contamination in the soils and waters that all contribute to excruciating poverty.

In the process, the participants discover that they must be part of the solutions. They realize their hidden potential and are empowered to overcome inertia and take action. They come to recognize that they are the primary custodians and beneficiaries of the environment that sustains them.

Entire communities also come to understand that while it is necessary to hold their governments accountable, it is equally important that in their own relationships with each other, they exemplify the leadership values they wish to see in their own leaders, namely justice, integrity and trust.

Although initially the Green Belt Movement's tree planting activities did not address issues of democracy and peace, it soon became clear that responsible governance of the environment was impossible without democratic space. Therefore, the tree became a symbol for the democratic struggle in Kenya. Citizens were mobilised to challenge widespread abuses of power, corruption and environmental mismanagement. In Nairobi's Uhuru Park, at Freedom Corner, and in many parts of the country, trees of peace were planted to demand the release of prisoners of conscience and a peaceful transition to democracy.

Through the Green Belt Movement, thousands of ordinary citizens were 15 mobilized and empowered to take action and effect change. They learned to overcome fear and a sense of helplessness and moved to defend democratic rights.

In time, the tree also became a symbol for peace and conflict resolution, especially during ethnic conflicts in Kenya when the Green Belt Movement used peace trees to reconcile disputing communities. During the ongoing re-writing of the Kenyan constitution, similar trees of peace were planted in many parts of the country to promote a culture of peace. Using trees as a symbol of peace is in keeping with a widespread African tradition. For example, the elders of the Kikuyu carried a staff from the thigi tree that, when placed between two disputing sides, caused them to stop fighting and seek reconciliation. Many communities in Africa have these traditions.

Such practises are part of an extensive cultural heritage, which contributes both to the conservation of habitats and to cultures of peace. With the destruction of these cultures and the introduction of new values, local biodiversity is no longer valued or protected and as a result, it is quickly degraded and disappears. For this reason, the Green Belt Movement explores the concept of cultural biodiversity, especially with respect to indigenous seeds and medicinal plants.

As we progressively understood the cause of environmental degradation, we saw the need for good governance. Indeed, the state of any county's environment is a reflection of the kind of governance in place, and without good governance there can be no peace. Many countries, which have poor governance systems, are also likely to have conflicts and poor laws protecting the environment.

In 2002, the courage, resilience, patience and commitment of members of the Green Belt Movement, other civil society organizations, and the Kenyan public culminated in the peaceful transition to a democratic government and laid the foundation for a more stable society.

Excellencies, friends, ladies and gentlemen,   20

It is 30 years since we started this work. Activities that devastate the environment and societies continue unabated. Today we are faced with a challenge that calls for a shift in our thinking, so that humanity stops threatening its life-support system. We are called to assist the Earth to heal her wounds and in the process heal our own—indeed, to embrace the whole creation in all its diversity, beauty and wonder. This will happen if we see the need to revive our sense of belonging to a larger family of life, with which we have shared our evolutionary process.

In the course of history, there comes a time when humanity is called to shift to a new level of consciousness, to reach a higher moral ground. A time when we have to shed our fear and give hope to each other.

That time is now.

QUESTIONS FOR DISCUSSION AND WRITING

1. What is the Green Belt Movement? Why was it started, and what have been its outcomes? Do you think the problems it responds to and the practices it employs are limited to Africa, or are there larger implications? If so, what are they?

2. The first paragraph of Maathai's speech links the environment with democracy and peace. Explain the link.

3. In what ways is the Green Belt Movement a movement of individual action and in what ways is it a movement of collective action? What do you see as the role of individual action in addressing global environmental issues? The role of collective action?

4. According to Maathai, the benefits of the Green Belt Movement go beyond improving the environment. She says, "Participants discover that they must be part of the solutions. They realize their hidden potential and are empowered to overcome inertia and take action" (paragraph 12). Explain how this realization and empowerment might come about. What would be the consequences?

5. Research the effects of deforestation and soil erosion. Are they of concern in your community, in the United States, throughout the world? What are the consequences of these processes? What can be done to stop them? What should be done?

6. Based on the evidence Maathai provides, how might you address the kinds of actions that could be undertaken based on your reading of Al Gore's "A Planetary

Emergency" (p. 583)? See in particular Questions for Discussion and Writing 3, 4, and 5 following the Gore selection (p. 586).

VACLAV HAVEL
Our Moral Footprint

Vaclav Havel (b. 1936 in Prague) is an internationally acclaimed playwright, essayist, political dissident, and human rights activist—a true Renaissance man. The elite status of his intellectual family and his outspoken anti-Communist stance provoked repeated conflict with the Czechoslovak Communist government during the 1970s and 1980s, and numerous arrests. Havel's first play, The Garden Party *(1963), received international acclaim, but after the Prague Spring in 1968, his plays (some featuring Ferdinand Vaněk, the revolutionary playwright's alter ego) were banned in his own country. Political harassment escalated as Havel became a leading dissident leader, promoting the human rights manifesto Charter 77 and cofounding the Committee for the Defense of the Unjustly Persecuted in 1979, for which he was imprisoned 1979–84.*

But sometimes justice is done. After the "Velvet Revolution," which resulted in the Communist downfall, Havel—who had steadfastly claimed he was uninterested in political office—was elected president of Czechoslovakia (1989–92). In 1993 he became the first president of the Czech Republic, and served for a decade. His widely translated work includes poetry; plays (Leaving, 2007, is reminiscent of King Lear*), nonfiction—on human rights, globalization, Czech and European culture, history, and politics, including a political autobiography,* To the Castle and Back *(2007); and collections of letters (many from prison). Through the European Council on Tolerance and Reconciliation he continues to fight racism, xenophobia, and anti-Semitism. The recipient of many awards, including the U.S. Presidential Medal of Freedom and the Ambassador of Conscience Award, Havel does not rest. In "Our Moral Footprint," first published in the* New York Times *(2007), he addresses our moral imperative to preserve the planet: "The moral order, our conscience and human rights—these are the most important issues at the beginning of the third millennium."*

Over the past few years the questions have been asked ever more forcefully whether global climate changes occur in natural cycles or not, to what degree we humans contribute to them, what threats stem from them and what can be done to prevent them. Scientific studies demonstrate that any changes in temperature and energy cycles on a planetary scale could mean danger for all people on all continents.

It is also obvious from published research that human activity is a cause of change; we just don't know how big its contribution is. Is it necessary to know that to the last percentage point, though? By waiting for incontrovertible precision, aren't we simply wasting time when we could be taking measures that are relatively painless compared to those we would have to adopt after further delays?

Maybe we should start considering our sojourn on earth as a loan. There can be no doubt that for the past hundred years at least, Europe and the United States have been running up a debt, and now other parts of the world are following their example. Nature is issuing warnings that we must not only stop the debt from growing but start to pay it back. There is little point in asking whether we have borrowed too much or what would happen if we postponed the repayments. Anyone with a mortgage or a bank loan can easily imagine the answer.

The effects of possible climate changes are hard to estimate. Our planet has never been in a state of balance from which it could deviate through human or other influence and then, in time, return to its original state. The climate is not like a pendulum that will return to its original position after a certain period. It has evolved turbulently over billions of years into a gigantic complex of networks, and of networks within networks, where everything is interlinked in diverse ways.

Its structures will never return to precisely the same state they were in 50 5 or 5,000 years ago. They will only change into a new state, which, so long as the change is slight, need not mean any threat to life.

Larger changes, however, could have unforeseeable effects within the global ecosystem. In that case, we would have to ask ourselves whether human life would be possible. Because so much uncertainty still reigns, a great deal of humility and circumspection is called for.

We can't endlessly fool ourselves that nothing is wrong and that we can go on cheerfully pursuing our wasteful lifestyles, ignoring the climate threats and postponing a solution. Maybe there will be no major catastrophe in the coming years or decades. Who knows? But that doesn't relieve us of responsibility toward future generations.

I don't agree with those whose reaction is to warn against restricting civil freedoms. Were the forecasts of certain climatologists to come true, our freedoms would be tantamount to those of someone hanging from a 20th-story parapet.

Whenever I reflect on the problems of today's world, whether they concern the economy, society, culture, security, ecology or civilization in general, I always end up confronting the moral question: what action is responsible or acceptable? The moral order, our conscience and human rights—these are the most important issues at the beginning of the third millennium.

We must return again and again to the roots of human existence and 10 consider our prospects in centuries to come. We must analyze everything open-mindedly, soberly, unideologically and unobsessively, and project our knowledge into practical policies. Maybe it is no longer a matter of simply promoting energy-saving technologies, but chiefly of introducing ecologically clean technologies, of diversifying resources and of not relying on just one invention as a panacea.

I'm skeptical that a problem as complex as climate change can be solved by any single branch of science. Technological measures and regulations are important, but equally important is support for education, ecological training and ethics—a consciousness of the commonality of all living beings and an emphasis on shared responsibility.

Either we will achieve an awareness of our place in the living and life-giving organism of our planet, or we will face the threat that our evolutionary journey may be set back thousands or even millions of years. That is why we must see this issue as a challenge to behave responsibly and not as a harbinger of the end of the world.

The end of the world has been anticipated many times and has never come, of course. And it won't come this time either. We need not fear for our planet. It was here before us and most likely will be here after us. But that doesn't mean that the human race is not at serious risk. As a result of our endeavors and our irresponsibility our climate might leave no place for us. If we drag our feet, the scope for decision-making—and hence for our individual freedom—could be considerably reduced.

QUESTIONS FOR DISCUSSION AND WRITING

1. Explain the meaning of Havel's title, "Our Moral Footprint."

2. Using other essays and photographs in this chapter for evidence, explain what Havel means when he says, "Maybe we should start considering our sojourn on earth as a loan. There can be no doubt that for the past hundred years at least, Europe and the United States have been running up a debt, and now other parts of the world are following their example" (paragraph 3). What other parts of the world are contributing to this debt? What other parts of the world are affected?

3. What connections are there between a life of political activism, such as Havel's, and a concern for ecological issues on a global scale, as expressed in this essay?

4. Writing this piece as an op-ed essay in the *New York Times*, Havel can be assured of a worldwide audience. Why is this important? Relevant?

5. Havel concludes, "Either we will achieve an awareness of our place in the living and life-giving organism of our planet, or we will face the threat that our evolutionary journey may be set back thousands or even millions of years. That is why we must see this issue as a challenge to behave responsibly and not as a harbinger of the end of the world." With a partner, discuss and write an essay on the implications of Havel's claims. What can people, nations do to avoid a doomsday scenario?

HENRY DAVID THOREAU

Where I Lived, and What I Lived For

"The mass of men lead lives of quiet desperation," wrote Henry David Thoreau (1817–1862) in Walden, *a book that taught the civilized world how to live closer to nature and eternal truth, or "reality," as he termed it. A poet, diarist, and essayist, his works are essential statements of American romantic idealism. After graduating from Harvard (1837), he worked intermittently as a teacher, gardener, and surveyor while doing his real work as an original thinker. As a transcendentalist, Thoreau believed that intuitive understanding transcends the limits of human experience and that ideas and the natural world are powerful—and more important than material goods. These views pervade his two major works,* A Week on the Concord and Merrimack Rivers *(1849) and* Walden, or Life in the Woods *(1854), the latter being Thoreau's interpretation of his two years at Concord's Walden Pond. There he lived frugally in the small cabin he built himself, feasting on the wonders of his natural surroundings, scarcely a mile from his Massachusetts birthplaces.*

"Where I Lived, and What I Lived For," from the second chapter of Walden, *gained worldwide renown as a philosophical manifesto and meditation on nature. Here Thoreau, in the guise of a rustic philosopher, spans the universe from earth to heaven, exploring what is essential to a good life well lived, and what is not. His mind having been shaped by classical learning and wide reading, he experienced modern life as frenetic, chaotic, and banal. He identifies the various enemies of self-knowledge—a preoccupation with speed (the railroad) and trivia (the latest news). "Our life is frittered away by detail," he boldly claims—then points the way back to genuine experience.*

I went to the woods because I wished to live deliberately, to front only the essential facts of life, and see if I could not learn what it had to teach, and not, when I came to die, discover that I had not lived. I did not wish to live what was not life, living is so dear; nor did I wish to practice resignation, unless it was quite necessary. I wanted to live deep and suck out all the marrow of life, to live so sturdily and Spartan-like as to put to rout all that was not life, to cut a broad swath and shave close, to drive life into a corner, and reduce it to its lowest terms, and, if it proved to be mean, why then to get the whole and genuine meanness of it, and publish its meanness to the world; or if it were sublime, to know it by experience, and be able to give a true account of it in my next excursion. For most men, it appears to me, are in a strange uncertainty about it, whether it is of the devil or of God, and have *somewhat hastily* concluded that it is the chief end of man here to "glorify God and enjoy him forever."

Still we live meanly, like ants; though the fable tells us that we were long ago changed into men; like pygmies we fight with cranes; it is error upon error, and clout upon clout, and our best virtue has for its occasion a superfluous and evitable wretchedness. Our life is frittered away by detail. An honest man has hardly need to count more than his ten fingers, or in extreme cases he may add his ten toes, and lump the rest. Simplicity, simplicity, simplicity! I say, let your affairs be as two or three, and not a hundred or a thousand; instead of a million count half a dozen, and keep your accounts on your thumb-nail. In the midst of this chopping sea of civilized life, such are the clouds and storms and quicksands and thousand-and-one items to be allowed for, that a man has to live, if he would not founder and go to the bottom and not make his port at all, by dead reckoning, and he must be a great calculator indeed who succeeds. Simplify, simplify. Instead of three meals a day, if it be necessary eat but one; instead of a hundred dishes, five; and reduce other things in proportion. Our life is like a German Confederacy, made up of petty states, with its boundary forever fluctuating, so that even a German cannot tell you how it is bounded at any moment. The nation itself, with all its so-called internal improvements, which, by the way are all external and superficial, is just such an unwieldy and overgrown establishment, cluttered with furniture and tripped up by its own traps, ruined by luxury and heedless expense, by want of calculation and a worthy aim, as the million households in the lands; and the only cure for it, as for them, is in a rigid economy, a stern and more than Spartan simplicity of life and elevation of purpose. It lives too fast. Men think that it is essential that the *Nation* have commerce, and export ice, and talk through a telegraph, and ride thirty miles an hour, without a doubt, whether *they* do or not; but whether we should live like baboons or like men, is a little uncertain. If we do not get out sleepers, and forge rails, and devote days and nights to the work, but go to tinkering upon our *lives* to improve *them*, who will build railroads? And if railroads are not built, how shall we get to heaven in season? But if we stay at home and mind our business, who will want railroads? We do not ride on the railroad; it rides upon us. Did you ever think what those sleepers are that underlie the railroad? Each one is a man, an Irishman, or a Yankee man. The rails are laid on them, and they are covered with sand, and the cars run smoothly over them. They are sound sleepers, I assure you. And every few years a new lot is laid down and run over; so that, if some have the pleasure of riding on a rail, others have the misfortune to be ridden upon. And when they run over a man that is walking in his sleep, a supernumerary sleeper in the wrong position, and wake him up, they suddenly stop the cars, and make a hue and cry about it, as if this were an exception. I am glad to know that it takes a gang of men for every five miles to keep the sleepers down and level in their beds as it is, for this is a sign that they may sometimes get up again.

Why should we live with such hurry and waste of life? We are determined to be starved before we are hungry. Men say that a stitch in time saves nine, and so they take a thousand stitches today to save nine to-morrow. As for *work*, we haven't any of any consequence. We have the Saint Vitus' dance, and cannot possibly keep our heads still. If I should only give a few pulls at the parish bell-rope, as for a fire, that is, without setting the bell, there is hardly a man on his farm in the outskirts of Concord, notwithstanding that press of engagements which was his excuse so many times this morning, nor a boy, nor a woman, I might almost say, but would foresake all and follow that sound, not mainly to save property from the flames, but, if we will confess the truth, much more to see it burn, since burn it must, and we, be it known, did not set it on fire,—or to see it put out, and have a hand in it, if that is done as handsomely; yes, even if it were the parish church itself. Hardly a man takes a half-hour's nap after dinner, but when he wakes he holds up his head and asks, "What's the news?" as if the rest of mankind had stood his sentinels. Some give directions to be waked every half-hour, doubtless for no other purpose; and then, to pay for it, they tell what they have dreamed. After a night's sleep the news is as indispensable as the breakfast. "Pray tell me anything new that has happened to a man anywhere on this globe,"—and he reads it over his coffee and rolls, that a man has had his eyes gouged out this morning on the Wachito River; never dreaming the while that he lives in the dark unfathomed mammoth cave of this world, and has but the rudiment of an eye himself.

For my part, I could easily do without the post-office. I think that there are very few important communications made through it. To speak critically, I never received more than one or two letters in my life—I wrote this some years ago—that were worth the postage. The penny-post is, commonly, an institution through which you seriously offer a man that penny for his thoughts which is so often safely offered in jest. And I am sure that I never read any memorable news in a newspaper. If we read of one man robbed, or murdered, or killed by accident, or one house burned, or one vessel wrecked, or one steamboat blown up, or one cow run over on the Western Railroad, or one mad dog killed, or one lot of grasshoppers in the winter,—we never need read of another. One is enough. If you are acquainted with the principle, what do you care for a myriad instances and applications? To a philosopher all *news,* as it is called, is gossip, and they who edit and read it are old women over their tea. Yet not a few are greedy after this gossip. There was such a rush, as I hear, the other day at one of the offices to learn the foreign news by the last arrival, that several large squares of plate glass belonging to the establishment were broken by the pressure,—news which I seriously think a ready wit might write a twelvemonth, or twelve years, beforehand with sufficient accuracy. As for Spain, for instance, if you know how to throw in Don Carlos and the Infanta, and Don Pedro and Seville and Granada, from time to time in the right proportions,—they may have changed the names a little since I saw the papers,—and serve up a bull-fight when other entertainments fail, it will be true to the letter, and give us as good an idea of the exact state or ruin of things in Spain as the most succinct and lucid reports under this head in the newspapers: and as for England, almost the last significant scrap of news from that quarter was the revolution of 1649; and if you have learned the history of her crops for an average year, you never need attend to that thing again, unless your speculations are of a merely pecuniary character. If one may judge who rarely looks into the newspapers, nothing new does ever happen in foreign parts, a French revolution not excepted.

What news! how much more important to know what that is which was never 5 old! "Kieou-he-yu (great dignitary of the state of Wei) sent a man to Khoung-tseu to know his news. Khoung-tseu caused the messenger to be seated near him, and questioned him in these terms: What is your master doing? The messenger answered with respect: My master desires to diminish the number of his faults, but he cannot come to the end of them. The messenger being gone, the philosopher remarked: What a worthy messenger! What a worthy messenger!" The preacher, instead of vexing the ears of drowsy farmers on their day of rest at the end of the week,—for Sunday is the fit conclusion of an ill-spent week, and not the fresh and brave beginning of a new one,—with this one other draggle-tail of a sermon, should shout with thundering voice, "Pause! Avast! Why so seeming fast, but deadly slow?"

Shams and delusions are esteemed for soundless truths, while reality is fabulous. If men would steadily observe realities only, and not allow themselves to be deluded, life, to compare it with such things as we know, would be like a fairy tale and the Arabian Nights Entertainments. If we respected only what is inevitable and has a right to be, music and poetry would resound along the streets. When we are unhurried and wise, we perceive that only great and worthy things have any permanent and absolute existence, that petty fears and petty pleasures are but the shadow of the reality. This is always exhilarating and sublime. By closing the eyes and slumbering, and consenting to be deceived by shows, men establish and confirm their daily life of routine and habit everywhere, which still is built on purely illusory foundations. Children, who play life, discern its true law and relations more clearly than men, who fail to live it worthily, but who think that they are wiser by experience, that is, by failure. I have read in a Hindoo book, that "there was a king's son, who, being expelled in infancy from his native city, was brought up by a forester, and, growing up to maturity in that state, imagined himself to belong to the barbarous race with which he lived. One of his father's ministers having discovered him, revealed to him what he was, and the misconception of his character was removed, and he knew himself to be a prince. "So soul," continues the Hindoo philosopher, "from the circumstances in which it is placed, mistakes its own character, until the truth is revealed to it by some holy teacher, and then it knows itself to be *Brahme*." I perceive that we inhabitants of New England live this mean life that we do because our vision does not penetrate the surface of things. We think that that *is* which *appears* to be. If a man should walk through this town and see only the reality, where, think you, would the "Mill-dam" go to? If he should give us an account of the realities he beheld there, we should not recognize the place in his description. Look at the meeting-house, or a court-house, or a jail, or a shop, or a dwelling-house, and say what that thing really is before a true gaze, and they would all go to pieces in your account of them. Men esteem truth remote, in the outskirts of the system, behind the farthest star, before Adam and after the last man. In eternity there is indeed something true and sublime. But all these times and places and occasions are now and here. God himself culminates in the present moment, and will never be more divine in the lapse of all the ages. And we are enabled to apprehend at all what is sublime and noble only by the perpetual instilling and drenching of the reality that surrounds us. The universe constantly and obediently answers to our conceptions; whether we travel fast or slow, the track is laid for us. Let us spend our lives in conceiving then. The poet or the artist never yet had so fair and noble a design but some of his posterity at least could accomplish it.

Let us spend one day as deliberately as Nature, and not be thrown off the track by every nutshell and mosquito's wing that falls on the rails. Let us rise early and fast, or breakfast, gently and without perturbation; let company come and let company go, let the bells ring and the children cry,—determined to make a day of it. Why should we knock under and go with the stream? Let us not be upset and overwhelmed in that terrible rapid and whirlpool called a dinner, situated in the meridian shallows. Weather this danger and you are safe, for the rest of the way is down hill. With unrelaxed nerves, with morning vigor, sail by it, looking another way, tied to the mast like Ulysses. If the engine whistles, let it whistle till it is hoarse for its pains. If the bell rings, why should we run? We will consider what kind of music they are like. Let us settle ourselves, and work and wedge our feet downward through the mud and slush of opinion, and prejudice, and tradition, and delusion, and appearance, that alluvion which covers the globe, through Paris and London, through New York and Boston and Concord, through Church and State, through poetry and philosophy and religion, till we come to a hard bottom and rocks in place, which we can call *reality,* and say, This is, and no mistake; and then begin, having a *point d'appui,* below freshet and frost and fire, a place where you might found a wall or a state, or set a lamppost safely, or perhaps a gauge, not a Nilometer, but a Realometer, that future ages might know how deep a freshet of shams and appearances had gathered from time to time. If you stand right fronting and face to face to a fact, you will see the sun glimmer on both its surfaces, as if it were a cimeter, and feel its sweet edge dividing you through the heart and marrow, and so you will happily conclude your mortal career. Be it life or death, we crave only reality. If we are really dying, let us hear the rattle in our throats and feel cold in the extremities; if we are alive, let us go about our business.

Time is but the stream I go a-fishing in. I drink at it; but while I drink I see the sandy bottom and detect how shallow it is. Its thin current slides away, but eternity remains. I would drink deeper; fish in the sky, whose bottom is pebbly with stars. I cannot count one. I know not the first letter of the alphabet. I have always been regretting that I was not as wise as the day I was born. The intellect is a cleaver; it discerns and rifts its way into the secret of things. I do not wish to be any more busy with my hands than is necessary. My head is hands and feet. I feel all my best faculties concentrated in it. My instinct tells me that my head is an organ for burrowing, as some creatures use their snout and fore paws, and with it I would mine and burrow my way through these hills. I think that the richest vein is somewhere hereabouts; so by the divining-rod and thin rising vapors I judge; and here I will begin to mine.

QUESTIONS FOR DISCUSSION AND WRITING

1. In "Where I Lived, and What I Lived For," Thoreau argues that "we are enabled to apprehend at all what is sublime and noble only by the perpetual instilling and drenching of the reality that surrounds us" (paragraph 6). In observing this reality, "we perceive that only great and worthy things have any permanent and absolute existence, that petty fears and petty pleasures are but the shadow of the reality." In a culture dominated by social networking and high technology, to what extent is it possible to live life focused on the sublime without being distracted by "petty fears and petty pleasure"? Explain.

2. Thoreau begins "Civil Disobedience" with the Jeffersonian sentiment, "That government is best which governs least" and follows it with the claim that the best government "governs not at all." How does this apparent support of political anarchy coexist with his claim in "Where I Lived, and What I Lived For" that nature can teach "the essential facts of life"? Does his belief that "only great and worthy things have any permanent and absolute existence" suggest that political organization is, as he argues in "Civil Disobedience," "at best but an expedient"?

3. After reading "Where I Lived, and What I Lived For," describe how Thoreau envisions the development of individual conscience. Consider Thoreau's challenge to "spend one day as deliberately as Nature, and not be thrown off the track by every nutshell and mosquito's wing that falls on the rails" (paragraph 7). Try doing so, and write a paper explaining and analyzing your experience. Would you ever repeat the experiment?

ANNIE DILLARD

Heaven and Earth in Jest

Annie Dillard was born (1945) and raised in Pittsburgh, where indulgent parents encouraged her interests in the natural world and art. In An American Childhood *(1987) she portrays herself as a curious, imaginative risk-taker, and ultimately a teenage rebel against her church (Presbyterian) but inspired by life's possibilities: "Why not . . . write an epic, become a medical missionary to the Amazon?" She studied creative writing at Hollins College (B.A., 1967; M.A., 1968) and quickly became a literary superstar, with the publication of Pulitzer Prize–winning* Pilgrim at Tinker Creek *(1974). In all of her works, whether poetry (*Tickets for a Prayer Wheel, *1974), commentary on writing (*The Writing Life, *1989), or fiction (*The Living, *1992), Dillard, sometimes labeled an* eco-theologist, *maintains her eclectic, impassioned, eloquent contemplation of God's presence — or absence.*

In Pilgrim at Tinker Creek, *from which the following selection is excerpted, Dillard's work is play. For a year in her cabin beside Tinker Creek, she plays Thoreau at Walden Pond (see p. 607). She takes on his character as a self-reliant, spiritually* oriented naturalist who finds transcendental meaning in all aspects of the natural world. She closely observes details: exactly how a giant water bug consumes a frog, how a frog consumes dragonflies. A stalker of animals, she also stalks and consumes ideas from the Koran to writings by Blaise Pascal and Nikos Kazantzakis. She stalks readers as well, embellishing her precisely detailed observations with both analyses and verbal cartoons: a panicked frog she startles emits "a froggy 'Yike!'" and splashes into the water. Indeed, the commentary following "Heaven and Earth in Jest" examines the workings of figurative language, such as metaphor and allusions to people, events, and other authors' works—ways of enriching the natural history, the theology.

I used to have a cat, an old fighting tom, who would jump through the open window by my bed in the middle of the night and land on my chest. I'd half-awaken. He'd stick his skull under my nose and purr, stinking of urine and blood. Some nights he kneaded my bare chest with his front paws, powerfully, arching his back, as if sharpening his claws, or pummeling a mother for milk. And some mornings I'd wake in daylight to find my body covered with paw prints in blood; I looked as though I'd been painted with roses.

It was hot, so hot the mirror felt warm. I washed before the mirror in a daze, my twisted summer sleep still hung about me like sea kelp. What blood was this, and what roses? It could have been the rose of union, the blood of murder, or the rose of beauty bare and the blood of some unspeakable sacrifice or birth. The sign on my body could have been an emblem or a stain, the keys to the kingdom or the mark of Cain. I never knew. I never knew as I washed, and the blood streaked, faded, and finally disappeared, whether I'd purified myself or ruined the blood sign of the passover. We wake, if we ever wake at all, to mystery, rumors of death, beauty, violence. . . . "Seem like we're just set down here," a woman said to me recently, "and don't nobody know why."

These are morning matters, pictures you dream as the final wave heaves you up on the sand to the bright light and drying air. You remember pressure, and a curved sleep you rested against, soft, like a scallop in its shell. But the air hardens your skin; you stand; you leave the lighted shore to explore some dim headland, and soon you're lost in the leafy interior, intent, remembering nothing.

I still think of that old tomcat, mornings, when I wake. Things are tamer now; I sleep with the window shut. The cat and our rites are gone and my life is changed, but the memory remains of something powerful playing over me. I wake expectant, hoping to see a new thing. If I'm lucky I might be jogged awake by a strange birdcall. I dress in a hurry, imagining the yard flapping with auks, or flamingos. This morning it was a wood duck, down at the creek. It flew away.

I live by a creek, Tinker Creek, in a valley in Virginia's Blue Ridge. An anchorite's hermitage is called an anchor-hold; some anchor-holds were simple sheds clamped to the side of a church like a barnacle to a rock. I think of this house clamped to the side of Tinker Creek as an anchor-hold. It holds me at anchor   5 to the rock bottom of the creek itself and it keeps me steadied in the current, as a sea anchor does, facing the stream of light pouring down. It's a good place to live; there's a lot to think about. The creeks—Tinker and Carvin's—are an active mystery, fresh every minute. Theirs is the mystery of the continuous creation and all that providence implies: the uncertainty of vision, the horror of the fixed, the dissolution of the present, the intricacy of beauty, the pressure of fecundity, the elusiveness of the free, and the flawed nature of perfection. The mountains—Tinker and Brushy, McAfee's Knob and Dead Man—are a passive mystery, the oldest of all. Theirs is the one simple mystery of creation from nothing, of matter itself, anything at all, the given. Mountains are giant, restful, absorbent. You can heave your spirit into a mountain and the mountain will keep it, folded, and not throw it back as some creeks will. The creeks are the world with all its stimulus and beauty; I live there. But the mountains are home.

The wood duck flew away. I caught only a glimpse of something like a bright torpedo that blasted the leaves where it flew. Back at the house I ate a bowl of oatmeal; much later in the day came the long slant of light that means good walking.

If the day is fine, any walk will do; it all looks good. Water in particular looks its best, reflecting blue sky in the flat, and chopping it into graveled shallows and white chute and foam in the riffles. On a dark day, or a hazy one, everything's washed-out and lackluster but the water. It carries its own lights. I set out for the railroad tracks, for the hill the flocks fly over, for the woods where the white mare lives. But I go to the water.

Today is one of those excellent January partly cloudies in which light chooses an unexpected part of the landscape to trick out in gilt, and then shadow sweeps it away. You know you're alive. You take huge steps, trying to feel the planet's roundness arc between your feet. Kazantzakis says that when he was young he had a canary and a globe. When he freed the canary, it would perch on the globe and sing. All his life, wandering the earth, he felt as though he had a canary on top of his mind, singing.

West of the house, Tinker Creek makes a sharp loop, so that the creek is both in back of the house, south of me, and also on the other side of the road, north of me. I like to go north. There the afternoon sun hits the creek just right, deepening the reflected blue and lighting the sides of trees on the banks. Steers from the pasture across the creek come down to drink; I always flush a rabbit or two there; I sit on a fallen trunk in the shade and watch the squirrels in the sun. There are two separated wooden fences suspended from cables that cross the creek just upstream from my tree-trunk bench. They keep the steers from escaping up or down the creek when they come to drink. Squirrels, the neighborhood children, and I use the downstream fence as a swaying bridge across the creek. But the steers are there today.

I sit on the downed tree and watch the black steers slip on the creek bottom. 10 They are all bred beef: beef heart, beef hide, beef hocks. They're a human product like rayon. They're like a field of shoes. They have cast-iron shanks and tongues like foam insoles. You can't see through to their brains as you can with other animals; they have beef fat behind their eyes, beef stew.

I cross the fence six feet above the water, walking my hands down the rusty cable and tightroping my feet along the narrow edge of the planks. When I hit the other bank and terra firma, some steers are bunched in a knot between me and the barbed-wire fence I want to cross. So I suddenly rush at them in an enthusiastic sprint, flailing my arms and hollering, "Lightning! Copperhead! Swedish meatballs!" They flee, still in a knot, stumbling across the flat pasture. I stand with the wind on my face.

When I slide under a barbed-wire fence, cross a field, and run over a sycamore trunk felled across the water, I'm on a little island shaped like a tear in the middle of Tinker Creek. On one side of the creek is a steep forested bank; the water is swift and deep on that side of the island. On the other side is the level field I walked through next to the steers' pasture; the water between the field and the island is shallow and sluggish. In summer's low water, flags and bulrushes grow along a series of shallow pools cooled by the lazy current. Water striders patrol the surface film, crayfish hump along the silt bottom eating filth, frogs shout and glare, and shiners and small bream hide among roots from the sulky green heron's eye. I come to this island every month of the year. I walk around it, stopping and staring, or I straddle the sycamore log over the creek, curling my legs out of the water in winter, trying to read. Today I sit on dry grass at the end of the island by the slower side of the creek. I'm drawn to this spot. I come to it as to an oracle; I return to it as a man years later will seek out the battlefield where he lost a leg or an arm.

A couple of summers ago I was walking along the edge of the island to see what I could see in the water, and mainly to scare frogs. Frogs have an inelegant way of taking off from invisible positions on the bank just ahead of your feet, in dire panic, emitting a froggy "Yike!" and splashing into the water. Incredibly, this amused me, and, incredibly, it amuses me still. As I walked along the grassy edge of the island, I got better and better at seeing frogs both in and out of the water. I learned to recognize, slowing down, the difference in texture of the light reflected from mudbank, water, grass, or frog. Frogs were flying all around me. At the end of the island I noticed a small green frog. He was exactly half in and half out of the water, looking like a schematic diagram of an amphibian, and he didn't jump.

He didn't jump; I crept closer. At last I knelt on the island's winterkilled grass, lost, dumbstruck, staring at the frog in the creek just four feet away. He was a very small frog with wide, dull eyes. And just as I looked at him, he slowly crumpled and began to sag. The spirit vanished from his eyes as if snuffed. His skin emptied and drooped; his very skull seemed to collapse and settle like a kicked tent. He was shrinking before my eyes like a deflating football. I watched the taut, glistening skin on his shoulders ruck, and rumple, and fall. Soon, part of his skin, formless as a pricked balloon, lay in floating folds like bright scum on top of the water: it was a monstrous and terrifying thing. I gaped bewildered, appalled. An oval shadow hung in the water behind the drained frog; then the shadow glided away. The frog skin bag started to sink.

I had read about the giant water bug, but never seen one. "Giant water bug" is really the name of the creature, which is an enormous, heavy-bodied brown bug. It 15 eats insects, tadpoles, fish, and frogs. Its grasping forelegs are mighty and hooked inward. It seizes a victim with these legs, hugs it tight, and paralyzes it with enzymes injected during a vicious bite. That one bite is the only bite it ever takes. Through the puncture shoot the poisons that dissolve the victim's muscles and bones and organs—all but the skin—and through it the giant water bug sucks out the victim's body, reduced to a juice. This event is quite common in warm fresh water. The frog I saw was being sucked by a giant water bug. I had been kneeling on the island grass; when the unrecognizable flap of frog skin settled on the creek bottom, swaying, I stood up and brushed the knees of my pants. I couldn't catch my breath.

Of course, many carnivorous animals devour their prey alive. The usual method seems to be to subdue the victim by downing or grasping it so it can't flee, then eating it whole or in a series of bloody bites. Frogs eat everything whole, stuffing prey into their mouths with their thumbs. People have seen frogs with their wide jaws so full of live dragonflies they couldn't close them. Ants don't even have to catch their prey: in the spring they swarm over newly hatched, featherless birds in the nest and eat them tiny bite by bite.

That it's rough out there and chancy is no surprise. Every live thing is a survivor on a kind of extended emergency bivouac. But at the same time we are also created. In the Koran, Allah asks, "The heaven and the earth and all in between, thinkest thou I made them *in jest*?" It's a good question. What do we think of the created universe, spanning an unthinkable void with an unthinkable profusion of forms? Or what do we think of nothingness, those sickening reaches of time in either direction? If the giant water bug was not made in jest, was it then made in earnest? Pascal uses a nice term to describe the notion of the creator's, once having called forth the universe, turning his back to it: *Deus Absconditus*. Is this what we think happened? Was the sense of it there, and God absconded with it, ate it, like a wolf who disappears round the edge of the house with the Thanksgiving turkey? "God is subtle," Einstein said, "but not malicious." Again, Einstein said that "nature conceals her mystery by means of her essential grandeur, not by her cunning." It could be that God has not absconded but spread, as our vision and understanding of the universe have spread, to a fabric of spirit and sense so grand and subtle, so powerful in a new way, that we can only feel blindly of its hem. In making the thick darkness a swaddling band for the sea, God "set bars and doors" and said, "Hitherto shalt thou come, but no further." But have we come even that far? Have we rowed out to the thick darkness, or are we all playing pinochle in the bottom of the boat?

Cruelty is a mystery, and the waste of pain. But if we describe a world to compass these things, a world that is a long, brute game, then we bump against another mystery: the inrush of power and light, the canary that sings on the skull. Unless all ages and races of men have been deluded by the same mass hypnotist (who?), there seems to be such a thing as beauty, a grace wholly gratuitous. About five years ago I saw a mockingbird make a straight vertical descent from the roof gutter of a four-story building. It was an act as careless and spontaneous as the curl of a stem or the kindling of a star.

The mockingbird took a single step into the air and dropped. His wings were still folded against his sides as though he were singing from a limb and not falling, accelerating thirty-two feet per second, through empty air. Just a breath before he would have been dashed to the ground, he unfurled his wings with exact, deliberate care, revealing the broad bars of white, spread his elegant, white-banded tail, and so floated onto the grass. I had just rounded a corner when his insouciant step caught my eye; there was no one else in sight. The fact of his free fall was like the old philosophical conundrum about the tree that falls in the forest. The answer must be, I think, that beauty and grace are performed whether or not we will or sense them. The least we can do is try to be there.

Another time I saw another wonder: sharks off the Atlantic coast of Florida. 20 There is a way a wave rises above the ocean horizon, a triangular wedge against the sky. If you stand where the ocean breaks on a shallow beach, you see the raised water in a wave is translucent, shot with lights. One late afternoon at low tide a hundred big sharks passed the beach near the mouth of a tidal river in a feeding frenzy. As each green wave rose from the churning water, it illuminated within itself the six- or eight-foot-long bodies of twisting sharks. The sharks disappeared as each wave rolled toward me; then a new wave would swell above the horizon, containing in it, like scorpions in amber, sharks that roiled and heaved. The sight held awesome wonders: power and beauty, grace tangled in a rapture with violence.

We don't know what's going on here. If these tremendous events are random combinations of matter run amok, the yield of millions of monkeys at millions of typewriters, then what is it in us, hammered out of those same typewriters, that they ignite? We don't know. Our life is a faint tracing on the surface of mystery, like the idle, curved tunnels of leaf miners on the face of a leaf. We must somehow take a wider view, look at the whole landscape, really see it, and describe what's going on here. Then we can at least wail the right question into the swaddling band of darkness, or, if it comes to that, choir the proper praise.

At the time of Lewis and Clark, setting the prairies on fire was a well-known signal that meant, "Come down to the water." It was an extravagant gesture, but we can't do less. If the landscape reveals one certainty, it is that the extravagant gesture is the very stuff of creation. After the one extravagant gesture of creation in the first place, the universe has continued to deal exclusively in extravagances, flinging intricacies and colossi down aeons of emptiness, heaping profusions on profligacies with ever-fresh vigor. The whole show has been on fire from the word go. I come down to the water to cool my eyes. But everywhere I look I see fire; that which isn't flint is tinder, and the whole world sparks and flames.

I have come to the grassy island late in the day. The creek is up; icy water sweeps under the sycamore log bridge. The frog skin, of course, is utterly gone. I have stared at that one spot on the creek bottom for so long, focusing past the rush of water, that when I stand, the opposite bank seems to stretch before my eyes and flow grassily upstream. When the bank settles down I cross the sycamore log and enter again the big plowed field next to the steers' pasture.

The wind is terrific out of the west; the sun comes and goes. I can see the shadow on the field before me deepen uniformly and spread like a plague.

Everything seems so dull I am amazed I can even distinguish objects. And suddenly the light runs across the land like a comber, and up the trees, and goes again in a wink: I think I've gone blind or died. When it comes again, the light, you hold your breath, and if it stays you forget about it until it goes again.

It's the most beautiful day of the year. At four o'clock the eastern sky is a 25
dead stratus black flecked with low white clouds. The sun in the west illuminates the ground, the mountains, and especially the bare branches of trees, so that everywhere silver trees cut into the black sky like a photographer's negative of a landscape. The air and the ground are dry; the mountains are going on and off like neon signs. Clouds slide east as if pulled from the horizon, like a tablecloth whipped off a table. The hemlocks by the barbed-wire fence are flinging themselves east as though their backs would break. Purple shadows are racing east; the wind makes me face east, and again I feel the dizzying, drawn sensation I felt when the creek bank reeled.

At four-thirty the sky in the east is clear; how could that big blackness be blown? Fifteen minutes later another darkness is coming overhead from the northwest; and it's here. Everything is drained of its light as if sucked. Only at the horizon do inky black mountains give way to distant, lighted mountains—lighted not by direct illumination but rather paled by glowing sheets of mist hung before them. Now the blackness is in the east; everything is half in shadow, half in sun, every clod, tree, mountain, and hedge. I can't see Tinker Mountain through the line of hemlock, till it comes on like a streetlight, ping, *ex nihilo*. Its sandstone cliffs pink and swell. Suddenly the light goes; the cliffs recede as if pushed. The sun hits a clump of sycamores between me and the mountains; the sycamore arms light up, and *I can't see the cliffs*. They're gone. The pale network of sycamore arms, which a second ago was transparent as a screen, is suddenly opaque, glowing with light. Now the sycamore arms snuff out, the mountains come on, and there are the cliffs again.

I walk home. By five-thirty the show has pulled out. Nothing is left but an unreal blue and a few banked clouds low in the north. Some sort of carnival magician has been here, some fast-talking worker of wonders who has the act backwards. "Something in this hand," he says, "something in this hand, something up my sleeve, something behind my back . . ." and abracadabra, he snaps his fingers, and it's all gone. Only the bland, blank-faced magician remains, in his unruffled coat, barehanded, acknowledging a smattering of baffled applause. When you look again the whole show has pulled up stakes and moved on down the road. It never stops. New shows roll in from over the mountains and the magician reappears unannounced from a fold in the curtain you never dreamed was an opening. Scarves of clouds, rabbits in plain view, disappear into the black hat forever. Presto chango. The audience, if there is an audience at all, is dizzy from head-turning, dazed.

Like the bear who went over the mountain, I went out to see what I could see. And, I might as well warn you, like the bear, all that I could see was the other side of the mountain: more of same. On a good day I might catch a glimpse of another wooded ridge rolling under the sun like water, another bivouac. I propose to keep here what Thoreau called "a meteorological journal of the mind," telling some tales and describing some of the sights of this rather tamed valley, and exploring, in fear and trembling, some of the unmapped dim reaches and unholy fastnesses to which those tales and sights so dizzyingly lead.

I am no scientist. I explore the neighborhood. An infant who has just learned to hold his head up has a frank and forthright way of gazing about him in bewilderment. He hasn't the faintest clue where he is, and he aims to learn. In a couple of years, what he will have learned instead is how to fake it: he'll have the cocksure air of a squatter who has come to feel he owns the place. Some unwonted, taught pride diverts us from our original intent, which is to explore the neighborhood, view the landscape, to discover at least *where* it is that we have been so startlingly set down, if we can't learn why.

So I think about the valley. It is my leisure as well as my work, a game. It is a 30 fierce game I have joined because it is being played anyway, a game of both skill and chance, played against an unseen adversary—the conditions of time—in which the payoffs, which may suddenly arrive in a blast of light at any moment, might as well come to me as anyone else. I stake the time I'm grateful to have, the energies I'm glad to direct. I risk getting stuck on the board, so to speak, unable to move in any direction, which happens enough, God knows; and I risk the searing, exhausting nightmares that plunder rest and force me face down all night long in some muddy ditch seething with hatching insects and crustaceans.

But if I can bear the nights, the days are a pleasure. I walk out; I see something, some event that would otherwise have been utterly missed and lost; or something sees me, some enormous power brushes me with its clean wing, and I resound like a beaten bell.

I am an explorer, then, and I am also a stalker, or the instrument of the hunt itself. Certain Indians used to carve long grooves along the wooden shafts of their arrows. They called the grooves "lightning marks," because they resembled the curved fissure lightning slices down the trunks of trees. The function of lightning marks is this: if the arrow fails to kill the game, blood from a deep wound will channel along the lightning mark, streak down the arrow shaft, and spatter to the ground, laying a trail dripped on broad-leaves, on stones, that the barefoot and trembling archer can follow into whatever deep or rare wilderness it leads. I am the arrow shaft, carved along my length by unexpected lights and gashes from the very sky, and this book is the straying trail of blood.

Something pummels us, something barely sheathed. Power broods and lights. We're played on like a pipe; our breath is not our own. James Houston describes two young Eskimo girls sitting cross-legged on the ground, mouth on mouth, blowing by turns each other's throat cords, making a low, unearthly music. When I cross again the bridge that is really the steers' fence, the wind has thinned to the delicate air of twilight; it crumples the water's skin. I watch the running sheets of light raised on the creek's surface. The sight has the appeal of the purely passive, like the racing of light under clouds on a field, the beautiful dream at the moment of being dreamed. The breeze is the merest puff, but you yourself sail headlong and breathless under the gale force of the spirit.

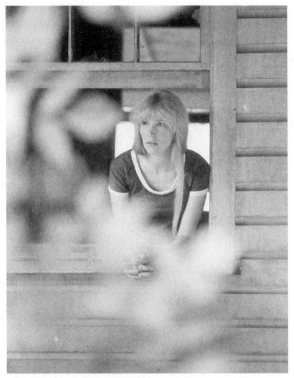

Annie Dillard in early 1974

CONTEXTS FOR "HEAVEN AND EARTH IN JEST"

HENRY DAVID THOREAU
From *Journal*

(For biography, see p. 594.) In the following journal entry for August 19, 1851, Thoreau wrote the passage that Dillard mentions in paragraph 28, where she

From Henry David Thoreau, *The Writings of Henry D. Thoreau: Journal*, vol. 3, *1848–1851*, ed. John C. Broderick, Robert Satelmeyer, Mark R. Patterson, and William Rossi (Princeton: Princeton University Press, 1990), 377.

defines the goal of her writing at Tinker Creek as keeping a " 'meteorological journal of the mind.' "

As travellers go round the world and report natural objects and phenomena—so faithfully let another stay at home and report the phenomena of his own life. Catalogue stars—those thoughts whose orbits are as rarely calculated as comets. It matters not whether they visit my mind or yours—whether the meteor falls in my field or in yours—only that it came from heaven. (I am not concerned to express that kind of truth which nature has expressed. Who knows but I may suggest some things to her. Time was when she was indebted to such suggestions from another quarter—as her present advancement shows. I deal with the truths that recommend themselves to me—please me—not those merely which any system has voted to accept.) A meteorological journal of the mind— You shall observe what occurs in your latitude, I in mine.

METAPHOR

A writer's deepest work is often play with metaphor, the assertion of identity between two different things. Metaphor is stronger than simile. Simile asserts mere likeness, *a ~ b:* the dying frog collapses "like a kicked tent . . . like a deflating football" (paragraph 14). Metaphor asserts identity between two different things. It equates, *a = b:* "I am the arrow shaft, . . . and this book is the straying trail of blood" (paragraph 32). As the poet Robert Frost observes, "all metaphor breaks down somewhere," because its two elements *are* different. Everybody knows that Dillard is not, literally, an arrow shaft. The playful work, then, is to figure out the ways in which Dillard and the arrow shaft *are* identical. Each way joins Dillard and the arrow shaft through a third term *with respect to* which they are identical: Dillard is the arrow shaft *with respect to* being an "instrument of the hunt" (for meaning in the natural world?), *with respect to* being "carved . . . by unexpected lights" (visions? intuitions?), *with respect to* bearing the gashes through which the game (meaning?) bleeds, leaving a trail (clues observable in language?) for the archer (a seeker after meaning? a reader?) to follow, and so on. When one metaphor leads into others (an archer is a reader *with respect to . . .* and *with respect to . . .* and so on), we call it an extended metaphor, an ancient figure of speech prominent in sacred writings and epic poetry. But our everyday language teems with metaphors, including those implied by concrete verbs: we *cover* a subject, *buttress* our arguments, *dig deeper* into our research, *stake out* our territory, and on and on. Playful work, words at play.

ALLUSION

An allusion is a casual reference to a well-known historical or literary text, figure, or event. The reference invites readers to compare and contrast the text, figure, or event alluded to with whatever subject the writer is addressing. It also invites readers to compare and contrast themselves with the writer. A writer alludes to something that the readers she has in mind are likely to understand with little or no explanation. Dillard's allusions help construct her persona: She is a person who reads the Koran, the *Pensées* of French mathematician Blaise Pascal (1623–1662), Thoreau's *Walden*, and so on. Allusions also help construct a writer's imagined readers and establish solidarity with them: "Dear Reader, you and I get this, but others don't." "Oh," we reply, "Pascal, of course." The catch, however, is that some readers reply, "Pascal, who?" The allusion then separates them from the writer, making the writer seem more learned or cosmopolitan than they. Even more subtle allusions withhold names and titles, relying on readers' attuned ears to catch echoes of other texts, as Dillard does in paraphrasing the British poet Gerard Manley Hopkins and her fellow American naturalist writer, Wendell Berry.

From *The Koran*

The divine reveals itself in and through its works: heaven and earth, or creation. The Koran often enjoins believers to recognize creation as a communication and a sign from Allah, and warns them not to take Allah's signs "in jest." The Bible similarly teaches Jews and Christians to see creation as evidence of God's existence and divinity, a view that many evolutionary biologists question (see Stephen Jay Gould's "Evolution as Fact and Theory" and its Contexts in Chapter 6). Dillard's allusion to the Koran in paragraph 17 may create solidarity with her Muslim readers, with those of other faiths who admire her as a reader of sacred texts, and with secular readers who admire a learned mind.

23. AL-MU'MENOON ("THE BELIEVERS"): VERSES 112–116

He will say: "What number of years did ye stay on earth?"

They will say: "We stayed a day or part of a day: but ask those who keep account."

He will say: "Ye stayed not but a little,—if ye had only known!

"Did ye then think that We had created you in jest, and that ye would not be brought back to Us (for account)?"

Therefore exalted be God, the King, the Reality: there is no god but He, the Lord   5
of the Throne of Honor!

BLAISE PASCAL

Pensées

Blaise Pascal (1623–1662), a devout Roman Catholic, was a precocious mathematician, a physicist, and a religious philosopher whose Pensées —*a collection of notes and manuscript fragments—presents his thoughts on Christian theology. In the passage that Dillard alludes to in paragraph 17, Pascal argues that if Christianity says that God is unknowable, then any deity whom Christians profess to know and understand cannot be God. By alluding to the Koran and to Pascal in almost the same breath, Dillard suggests that she is a learned reader of religious texts.*

194. . . . Let them at least learn what is the religion they attack, before attacking it. If this religion boasted of having a clear view of God, and of possessing it open and unveiled, it would be attacking it to say that we see nothing in the world which shows it with this clearness. But since, on the contrary, it says that men are in darkness and estranged from God, that He has hidden Himself from their knowledge, that this is in fact the name which He gives Himself in the Scriptures, *Deus absconditus*;[1] and finally, if it endeavors equally to establish these two things: that God has set up in the Church visible signs to make Himself known to those who should seek Him sincerely, and that He has nevertheless so disguised them that He will only be perceived by those who seek Him with all their heart; what advantage can they obtain, when, in the negligence with which they make profession of being in search of the truth, they cry out that nothing reveals it to them; and since that darkness in which they are, and with which they upbraid the Church, establishes only one of the things which she affirms, without touching the other, and, very far from destroying, proves her doctrine?

NIKOS KAZANTZAKIS

Report to Greco

Dillard alludes in paragraph 8 to Greek poet, novelist, playwright, and travel writer Nikos Kazantzakis (1885–1957), who wrote in his posthumously published autobiography, Report to Greco *(1961), about his ability to see the world from seemingly contradictory perspectives: the materialist and the spiritual. Like Kazantzakis, ever intent on discovering reciprocal illumination in the material and spiritual worlds, Dillard*

---

[1]"Thou art a God that hidest thyself."

From Blaise Pascal, *Pensées*, section 3, "The Necessity of the Wager," http://www.mala.bc.ca/~mcneil/PEN03.htm.

From Nikos Kazantzakis, *Report to Greco* (1961), trans. P. B. Bien (New York: Simon, 1965), 44.

paraphrases his story of the gift that—metaphysically and metaphorically—shaped his life.

I must have been four years old. On New Year's Day my father gave me a canary and a revolving globe as a handsel, "a good hand," as we say in Crete. Closing the doors and windows of my room, I used to open the cage and let the canary go free. It had developed the habit of sitting at the very top of the globe and singing for hours and hours, while I held my breath and listened.

This extremely simple event, I believe, influenced my life more than all the books and all the people I came to know afterwards. Wandering insatiably over the earth for years, greeting and taking leave of everything, I felt that my head was the globe and that a canary sat perched on the top of my mind, singing.

WENDELL BERRY

A Secular Pilgrimage

(For biography, see p. 644.)

Gerard Manley Hopkins, more conventionally religious than Wordsworth, had the same eagerness to thrust through appearances toward a realization of the divine. With Hopkins, this was not the anonymous Presence of Wordsworth's poems, but God, Jehovah, who broods over his creation in which his glory is manifest. But Hopkins was nevertheless a keener observer than Wordsworth; he loved the physical facts of nature, and took pains to capture their look and feel and movement. In the accuracy of his observation, and in the onomatopoeia of his diction and rhythms, he is clearly a forebear of the contemporary nature poets. "God's Grandeur" gives not only a sense of his technique but also of his critical values with respect to nature and civilization:

> The world is charged with the grandeur of God.
>   It will flame out, like shining from shook foil;
>   It gathers to a greatness like the ooze of oil
> Crushed. Why do men then now not reck his rod?
> Generations have trod, have trod, have trod;
>   And all is seared with trade; bleared, smeared with toil;
>   And wears man's smudge and shares man's smell: the soil
> Is bare now, nor can foot feel, being shod. . . .

From Wendell Berry, "A Secular Pilgrimage" (1970), in *A Continuous Harmony: Essays Cultural and Agricultural* (New York: Harcourt, 1975), 3–35.

QUESTIONS FOR DISCUSSION AND WRITING

1. Dillard borrows the simile of poet as astronomer from Thoreau. In what ways does the simile help explain her work at Tinker Creek? How are Thoreau's and Dillard's works alike? In the longer excerpt from Thoreau's *Walden* in this chapter ("Where I Lived, and What I Lived For," p. 594), what similes can you identify, how does each one affect you as a reader, and in what ways (if any) could they illuminate further aspects of Dillard's sojourn on Tinker Creek?

2. Read about allusion—in the "Reading in Context" section of the Introduction (p. 608)—as a way of defining one's intended reading audience and oneself. What kind of person do Dillard's allusions seem to add up to, and what type of audience does she seem to be writing for?

3. Dillard's "Heaven and Earth in Jest," like the writings of Thoreau, her model and source of inspiration (see "Where I Lived and What I Lived For," p. 594), conveys the impression that the author is an isolated individual, communing with the many facets of the natural world. Yet the author is hardly alone. What human, natural, and divine elements does her universe consist of? Why does it seem so full, so abundant?

4. The Tinker Creek environment is an energetic place; ducks fly, frogs jump, "the whole world sparks and flames" (paragraph 22). Identify the main manifestations of activity and energy—Dillard's own and those of animals and the environment, compounded by a spiritual energy. Why does she include all these?

5. The Tinker Creek environment is also a beautiful place, experienced on "the most beautiful day of the year" (paragraph 25). What makes it so beautiful?

6. Keep a daily journal about your environment for a week, and use it as the basis for an essay that is both descriptive and analytic of the place's characteristic energy and atmosphere. If it's beautiful, show why; if not, explain why not. Was it once beautiful but is no longer so? To what extent is this beauty in the eye of the beholder?

RACHEL CARSON

The Obligation to Endure

Before environmentalism was a movement—or even a common word—biologist Rachel Carson alerted us to the potentially fatal consequences of modern industrial pollution. Born in Pennsylvania in 1907, Carson attended Johns Hopkins University (M.A., 1932) and worked for the U.S. Fish and Wildlife Service as an aquatic biologist and publications editor-in-chief. Her works include Under the Sea-Wind *(1941);* The Sea around Us *(1951), a National Book Award winner and the basis for an Oscar-winning documentary;* The Edge of the Sea *(1955); and* The Sense of Wonder *(published posthumously in 1965). Carson died of cancer in 1964.*

"The Obligation to Endure" is the second chapter from Silent Spring *(1962), Carson's passionate and thoroughly researched demonstration that agricultural pesticides poison the environment, a radical argument for its time.*

The history of life on earth has been a history of interaction between living things and their surroundings. To a large extent, the physical form and the habits of the earth's vegetation and its animal life have been molded by the environment. Considering the whole span of earthly time, the opposite effect, in which life actually modifies its surroundings, has been relatively slight. Only within the moment of time represented by the present century has one species—man— acquired significant power to alter the nature of his world.

During the past quarter century this power has not only increased to one of disturbing magnitude but it has changed in character. The most alarming of all man's assaults upon the environment is the contamination of air, earth, rivers, and sea with dangerous and even lethal materials. This pollution is for the most part irrecoverable; the chain of evil it initiates not only in the world that must support life but in living tissues is for the most part irreversible. In this now universal contamination of the environment, chemicals are the sinister and little-recognized partners of radiation in changing the very nature of the world—the very nature of its life. Strontium 90, released through nuclear explosions into the air, comes to earth in rain or drifts down as fallout, lodges in soil, enters into the grass or corn or wheat grown there, and in time takes up its abode in the bones of a human being, there to remain until his death. Similarly, chemicals sprayed on croplands or forests or gardens lie long in soil, entering into living organisms, passing from one to another in a chain of poisoning and death. Or they pass mysteriously by underground streams until they emerge and, through the alchemy of air and sunlight, combine into new forms that kill vegetation, sicken cattle, and work unknown harm on those who drink from once pure wells. As Albert Schweitzer has said, "Man can hardly even recognize the devils of his own creation."

It took hundreds of millions of years to produce the life that now inhabits the earth—eons of time in which that developing and evolving and diversifying life reached a state of adjustment and balance with its surroundings. The environment, rigorously shaping and directing the life it supported, contained elements that were hostile as well as supporting. Certain rocks gave out dangerous radiation; even within the light of the sun, from which all life draws its energy, there were short-wave radiations with power to injure. Given time—time not in years but in millennia—life adjusts, and a balance has been reached. For time is the essential ingredient; but in the modern world there is no time.

The rapidity of change and the speed with which new situations are created follow the impetuous and heedless pace of man rather than the deliberate pace of nature. Radiation is no longer merely the background radiation of rocks, the bombardment of cosmic rays, the ultraviolet of the sun that have existed before there was any life on earth; radiation is now the unnatural creation of man's tampering with the atom. The chemicals to which life is asked to make its adjustment are no longer merely the calcium and silica and copper and all the rest of the minerals washed out of the rocks and carried in rivers to the sea; they are the synthetic creations of man's inventive mind, brewed in his laboratories, and having no counterparts in nature.

To adjust to these chemicals would require time on the scale that is nature's; 5
it would require not merely the years of a man's life but the life of generations. And even this, were it by some miracle possible, would be futile, for the new chemicals come from our laboratories in an endless stream; almost five hundred annually find their way into actual use in the United States alone. The figure is staggering and its implications are not easily grasped—500 new chemicals to which the bodies of men and animals are required somehow to adapt each year, chemicals totally outside the limits of biologic experience.

Among them are many that are used in man's war against nature. Since the mid-1940s over 200 basic chemicals have been created for use in killing insects, weeds, rodents, and other organisms described in the modern vernacular as "pests"; and they are sold under several thousand different brand names.

These sprays, dusts, and aerosols are now applied almost universally to farms, gardens, forests, and homes—nonselective chemicals that have the power to kill every insect, the "good" and the "bad," to still the song of birds and the leaping of fish in the streams, to coat the leaves with a deadly film, and to linger on in soil—all this though the intended target may be only a few weeds or insects. Can anyone believe it is possible to lay down such a barrage of poisons on the surface of the earth without making it unfit for all life? They should not be called "insecticides," but "biocides."

The whole process of spraying seems caught up in an endless spiral. Since DDT was released for civilian use, a process of escalation has been going on in which ever more toxic materials must be found. This has happened because insects, in a triumphant vindication of Darwin's principle of the survival of the fittest, have evolved super races immune to the particular insecticide used, hence a deadlier one has always to be developed—and then a deadlier one than that. It has happened also because, for reasons to be described later, destructive insects often undergo a "flareback," or resurgence, after spraying, in numbers greater than before. Thus the chemical war is never won, and all life is caught in its violent crossfire.

Along with the possibility of the extinction of mankind by nuclear war, the central problem of our age has therefore become the contamination of man's total environment with such substances of incredible potential for harm—substances that accumulate in the tissues of plants and animals and even penetrate the germ cells to shatter or alter the very material of heredity upon which the shape of the future depends.

Some would-be architects of our future look toward a time when it will be 10
possible to alter the human germ plasm by design. But we may easily be doing so now by inadvertence, for many chemicals, like radiation, bring about gene

mutations. It is ironic to think that man might determine his own future by something so seemingly trivial as the choice of an insect spray.

All this has been risked—for what? Future historians may well be amazed by our distorted sense of proportion. How could intelligent beings seek to control a few unwanted species by a method that contaminated the entire environment and brought the threat of disease and death even to their own kind? Yet this is precisely what we have done. We have done it, moreover, for reasons that collapse the moment we examine them. We are told that the enormous and expanding use of pesticides is necessary to maintain farm production. Yet is our real problem not one of *overproduction*? Our farms, despite measures to remove acreages from production and to pay farmers *not* to produce, have yielded such a staggering excess of crops that the American taxpayer in 1962 is paying out more than one billion dollars a year as the total carrying cost of the surplus-food storage program. And is the situation helped when one branch of the Agriculture Department tries to reduce production while another states, as it did in 1958, "It is believed generally that reduction of crop acreages under provisions of the Soil Bank will stimulate interest in use of chemicals to obtain maximum production on the land retained in crops."

All this is not to say there is no insect problem and no need of control. I am saying, rather, that control must be geared to realities, not to mythical situations, and that the methods employed must be such that they do not destroy us along with the insects.

The problem whose attempted solution has brought such a train of disaster in its wake is an accompaniment of our modern way of life. Long before the age of man, insects inhabited the earth—a group of extraordinarily varied and adaptable beings. Over the course of time since man's advent, a small percentage of the more than half a million species of insects have come into conflict with human welfare in two principal ways: as competitors for the food supply and as carriers of human disease.

Disease-carrying insects become important where human beings are crowded together, especially under conditions where sanitation is poor, as in time of natural disaster or war or in situations of extreme poverty and deprivation. Then control of some sort becomes necessary. It is a sobering fact, however, as we shall presently see, that the method of massive chemical control has had only limited success, and also threatens to worsen the very conditions it is intended to curb.

Under primitive agricultural conditions the farmer had few insect problems. 15 These arose with the intensification of agriculture—the devotion of immense acreages to a single crop. Such a system set the stage for explosive increases in specific insect populations. Single-crop farming does not take advantage of the principles by which nature works; it is agriculture as an engineer might conceive it to be. Nature has introduced great variety into the landscape, but man has displayed a passion for simplifying it. Thus he undoes the built-in checks and balances by which nature holds the species within bounds. One important natural check is a limit on the amount of suitable habitat for each species. Obviously then, an insect that lives on wheat can build up its population to much higher levels on a farm devoted to wheat than on one in which wheat is intermingled with other crops to which the insect is not adapted.

The same thing happens in other situations. A generation or more ago, the towns of large areas of the United States lined their streets with the noble elm tree. Now the beauty they hopefully created is threatened with complete destruction as disease sweeps through the elms, carried by a beetle that would have only limited chance to build up large populations and to spread from tree to tree if the elms were only occasional trees in a richly diversified planting.

Another factor in the modern insect problem is one that must be viewed against a background of geologic and human history: the spreading of thousands of different kinds of organisms from their native homes to invade new territories. This worldwide migration has been studied and graphically described by the British ecologist Charles Elton in his recent book *The Ecology of Invasions.* During the Cretaceous Period, some hundred million years ago, flooding seas cut many land bridges between continents and living things found themselves confined in what Elton calls "colossal separate nature reserves." There, isolated from others of their kind, they developed many new species. When some of the land masses were joined again, about 15 million years ago, these species began to move out into new territories—a movement that is not only still in progress but is now receiving considerable assistance from man.

The importation of plants is the primary agent in the modern spread of species, for animals have almost invariably gone along with the plants, quarantine being a comparatively recent and not completely effective innovation. The United States Office of Plant Introduction alone has introduced almost 200,000 species and varieties of plants from all over the world. Nearly half of the 180 or so major insect enemies of plants in the United States are accidental imports from abroad, and most of them have come as hitchhikers on plants.

In new territory, out of reach of the restraining hand of the natural enemies that kept down its numbers in its native land, an invading plant or animal is able to become enormously abundant. Thus it is no accident that our most troublesome insects are introduced species.

These invasions, both the naturally occurring and those dependent on 20 human assistance, are likely to continue indefinitely. Quarantine and massive chemical campaigns are only extremely expensive ways of buying time. We are faced, according to Dr. Elton, "with a life-and-death need not just to find new technological means of suppressing this plant or that animal"; instead we need the basic knowledge of animal populations and their relations to their surroundings that will "promote an even balance and damp down the explosive power of outbreaks and new invasions."

Much of the necessary knowledge is now available but we do not use it. We train ecologists in our universities and even employ them in our governmental agencies but we seldom take their advice. We allow the chemical death rain to fall as though there were no alternative, whereas in fact there are many, and our ingenuity could soon discover many more if given opportunity.

Have we fallen into a mesmerized state that makes us accept as inevitable that which is inferior or detrimental, as though having lost the will or the vision to demand that which is good? Such thinking, in the words of the ecologist Paul Shepard, "idealizes life with only its head out of water, inches above the limits of toleration of the corruption of its own environment. . . . Why should we tolerate a diet of weak poisons, a home in insipid surroundings, a circle of acquaintances who are not quite our enemies, the noise of motors with just enough relief to prevent insanity? Who would want to live in a world which is just not quite fatal?"

Yet such a world is pressed upon us. The crusade to create a chemically sterile, insect-free world seems to have engendered a fanatic zeal on the part of many specialists and most of the so-called control agencies. On every hand there is evidence that those engaged in spraying operations exercise a ruthless power. "The regulatory entomologists . . . function as prosecutor, judge and jury, tax assessor and collector and sheriff to enforce their own orders," said Connecticut entomologist Neely Turner. The most flagrant abuses go unchecked in both state and federal agencies.

It is not my contention that chemical insecticides must never be used. I do contend that we have put poisonous and biologically potent chemicals indiscriminately into the hands of persons largely or wholly ignorant of their potentials for harm. We have subjected enormous numbers of people to contact with these poisons, without their consent and often without their knowledge. If the Bill of Rights contains no guarantee that a citizen shall be secure against lethal poisons distributed either by private individuals or by public officials, it is surely only because our forefathers, despite their considerable wisdom and foresight, could conceive of no such problem.

I contend, furthermore, that we have allowed these chemicals to be used with 25 little or no advance investigation of their effect on soil, water, wildlife, and man himself. Future generations are unlikely to condone our lack of prudent concern for the integrity of the natural world that supports all life.

There is still very limited awareness of the nature of the threat. This is an era of specialists, each of whom sees his own problem and is unaware of or intolerant of the larger frame into which it fits. It is also an era dominated by industry, in which the right to make a dollar at whatever cost is seldom challenged. When the public protests, confronted with some obvious evidence of damaging results of pesticide applications, it is fed little tranquilizing pills of half truth. We urgently need an end to these false assurances, to the sugar coating of unpalatable facts. It is the public that is being asked to assume the risks that the insect controllers calculate. The public must decide whether it wishes to continue on the present road, and it can do so only when in full possession of the facts. In the words of Jean Rostand, "The obligation to endure gives us the right to know."

QUESTIONS FOR DISCUSSION AND WRITING

1. Why does Carson open her chapter with the disturbing claim that within a couple of decades in the mid-twentieth century, humans suddenly "acquired significant power" to disrupt the subtle balance "between living things and their surroundings" (paragraph 1)? What evidence does she cite? What has happened since then to corroborate her argument?

2. Thoreau asks in "Where I Lived and What I Lived For" (p. 594), "Why should we live with such hurry and waste of life?" Similarly, Carson urges us to follow "the deliberate pace of nature," not "the impetuous and heedless pace of man" (paragraph 4). How might both Thoreau and Carson be considered ecological prophets? Might Thoreau's and Carson's passion for nature represent, in part, an alternative to religious faith?

3. Compare Carson's notion of "little tranquilizing pills of half truth" (paragraph 26) with Williams's analysis in "The Clan of the One-Breasted Women" (p. 576) of the federal government's deceitful assurance during the decade of aboveground nuclear testing in Utah and Nevada, "'It has been found that the tests may be conducted with adequate assurance of safety'" (paragraph 22.). What hierarchy of values appears to govern the dissemination of scientific information to the general public by government and industry? How can the public influence or change that hierarchy of values?

PAIRED READINGS: TROUBLED ECOSYSTEMS

WILLIAM E. REES

Life in the Lap of Luxury as Ecosystems Collapse

William E. Rees received his doctorate in bioecology from the University of Toronto. Since 1969, he has been a professor at the University of British Columbia, where for many years he directed the School of Community and Regional Planning, a program that focuses on issues of environmentally sound global development. A founding member of Pollution Probe and a former president of the Canadian Society for Ecological Economics, Rees has focused much of his research and writing on sustainable socioeconomic development and on the public policy and planning implications of global environmental trends. He is the coauthor of Our Ecological Footprint: Reducing Human Impact on the Earth *(1995), which considers ways to measure area-based indicators of worldwide environmental sustainability. Rees has also argued extensively for limits on and alternatives to the industrial nations' use of dwindling reserves of fossil fuel and other resources. In the following essay from the* Chronicle of Higher Education *(July 30, 1999), Rees warns that growing urban centers increasingly drain worldwide ecological capacity, which could soon lead to environmental and political disaster.*

Have you ever asked yourself how much of the earth's surface is required to support you in the style to which you are accustomed? Every free-range dairy farmer knows, within a few square meters, how much pasture of a given quality is needed to support each of his cattle, and just how many head he can safely graze on the back forty. Similar questions, however, seldom come up in relation to people.

The Cartesian dualism that underpins Western philosophy and science has been so successful in psychologically separating humans from nature that we simply don't conceive of ourselves as ecological beings, as creatures of the land. Ignoring our dependence on our environment is a serious mistake.

In recent decades, the world has experienced an event of profound significance: the massive migration of people from the countryside to the city. In 1950, New York was the only city on the planet with 10 million or more inhabitants; by 2015, as many as 27 cities—most of them in the developing world—will be that large. In the 1990s alone, the population of the world's cities will increase by 50 per cent, to 3 billion people. The United Nations projects that an additional 2.1 billion people—which was roughly the population of the entire globe in the early 1930s—will be living in cities by 2025.

We usually think of urbanization mainly as a demographic or economic transition. Hardly anyone acknowledges it as a potential ecological problem. On the contrary, many observers interpret urbanization as further evidence of humanity's increasing technical prowess and independence from the land. Such technological hubris is an illusion. Separating billions of people from the land that sustains them is a giddy leap of faith with serious implications for ecological security.

For proof, let's explore the fundamental ecological question posed above. We   5 can analyze an average person's ecological footprint to estimate how much land people actually use. The analysis involves identifying and quantifying all significant categories of materials and energy appropriated from nature to support the consumption patterns of a defined group of people. We can then calculate the area of land and water required to supply the materials and energy. For example, about 25 square meters of former tropical forest are needed just to produce the coffee beans for the average java drinker in an industrialized country. We can also estimate the ecosystem area needed to absorb certain critical wastes. Heavy users of fossil fuels need 2 to 3 hectares (4.9 to 7.4 acres) of forest somewhere on the planet to absorb their carbon-dioxide emissions alone.

In summary, the ecological footprint of a population is the total area of land and water required to produce the resources that the population consumes, and to assimilate the wastes that the population generates, wherever on earth that land is located.

As Mathis Wackernagel and I have shown in *Our Ecological Footprint* (New Society, 1995), the residents of high-income countries typically need 4 to 9 hectares (10 to 22 acres) per capita to support their consumer life styles. That area seems large. However, since our calculations assume that all the land involved is being managed sustainably (which is rarely the case), our results actually underestimate the total demand. Thus, it is easy to see that cities typically impose an ecological footprint on the earth several hundred times larger than their political or geographic areas.

Most people think of cities as centers of culture and learning, and as the productive engines of economic growth. All that is true, but they also are sites of intense consumption of material and production of waste. As the well-known U.S. ecologist Eugene P. Odum recognized in *Fundamentals of Ecology*, "Great cities are planned and grow without any regard for the fact that they are parasites on the countryside which must somehow supply food, water, and air, and degrade huge quantities of waste." In short, far from signaling humanity's final separation from nature, urbanization merely removes people both spatially and psychologically from the land that sustains them.

In that light, consider the following additional dimensions of urban human ecology:

- The principal material effect of technology has been to extend the spatial scale and intensity of humans' capacity to exploit nature. Contrary to conventional views, our ecological footprint is expanding, not decreasing, with increasing wealth and technological advances.
- Many croplands and forests are being used more intensively than ever to sustain the world's burgeoning urban populations. In that sense, the great plains of North America are an essential component of the urban ecosystem.
- While the citizens of urban industrial societies use up to 9 hectares of productive land and water, the earth contains only about 2 hectares of such ecosystems per capita. The consumer life styles of rich countries cannot be extended sustainably to the entire human population, using current technologies.
- In a world of rapid change, no city can be truly sustainable unless the lands in its footprint are secure from ecological change and international hostilities.

Cities have been part of the human cultural landscape for thousands of years, 10 but only in recent decades has it become possible for the majority of people to live in cities. For better or worse, however, this phase of our development may be relatively short-lived. The recent explosive growth of the human population, our intensely material culture, and urbanization itself are all products of what the sociologist William R. Catton has called the "age of exuberance." In *Overshoot*, Catton explained that the heady optimism of twentieth-century North America, for example, has been sustained by a sense of unlimited abundance as we have exploited the continent's stocks of natural resources, particularly fossil fuels. But Catton recognized that that exuberance "had to be temporary, for [it leads] inexorably to a change in the environmental conditions that made [it] possible."

In short, we have been consuming resources in this century that will therefore not be available in the next. Global grain production per capita has been falling for more than a decade, the production of the world's fisheries peaked in the late 1980s, water supplies are stretched to the limit in many parts of the world, and global oil production will probably peak in the next decade. (The United States has been producing less and less oil for the past 30 years and now imports most of its petroleum.)

Although the world's wealthy nations have been protected so far from the consequences of such trends by their purchasing power in global markets, it is questionable whether that isolation can be maintained for long, in the face of growing demand and collapsing ecosystems. The political scientists Thomas Homer-Dixon, Jeffrey H. Boutwell, and George W. Rathjens directed a project on environmental change and acute conflict, sponsored by the University of Toronto and the American Academy of Arts and Sciences. In a 1993 article in *Scientific American*, they wrote that "in many parts of the world, environmental degradation seems to have passed a threshold of irreversibility" and that "renewable resource scarcities of the next 50 years will probably occur with a speed, complexity, and magnitude unprecedented in history." The authors made the case that the widespread loss of ecological stability—including the collapse of fisheries, deforestation, and chronic drought—is likely to lead to greater geopolitical strife and even war in the coming decades.

In an era of global change and increasing political uncertainty, should we not be developing strategies to insure the viability and sustainability of our cities? More fundamentally, should we encourage or resist further urbanization? In *Cities and Sustainable Development*, Diana Mitlin and David Satterthwaite stress that high urban-population densities produce the economies of scale needed for energy-saving strategies such as recycling and mass transit. However, their analysis implicitly assumes that the city enjoys a stable and predictable relationship with its hinterland. But can any city be viable, let alone sustainable, if its distant sources of supply are threatened by ecological change or international hostilities?

The perspectives and skills of many disciplines are required to assess the vulnerability of urban populations in the twenty-first century and to determine the measures needed to enhance their security. Perhaps most important, we must develop a holistic concept of the city-as-system. Urban planning should include as much as possible of the city's ecological footprint.

That would shift the focus of planning from mere growth management to   15
mechanisms to reduce the city's dependence on distant parts of the planet. I am not advocating self-sufficiency: Clearly, trade will continue to be important—and, despite global warming, it will be some time before we can grow coffee in the suburbs of Chicago. However, major cities should have secure access to food and other staples, preferably close at hand, and learn to recycle their wastes locally. Even this simpler goal is a daunting one at current levels of resource consumption and waste production. The ecological footprint of London, for example, is larger than the entire United Kingdom.

The time has come for us to take seriously the idea that each of us lives in a bioregion—a geographic area defined by both biophysical characteristics, including watershed boundaries, and patterns of occupancy by humans and other species—and that our urban ecological footprints should be contained as much as possible within our local bioregions. Ecologists and economists should work together to determine criteria for delineating bioregions. Geographers and urban planners might study such issues as the optimal pattern of human population distribution within various bioregions, and the appropriate size for cities. Political scientists should consider which powers federal and state or provincial governments might devolve to the local level, and which they should keep, to facilitate the planning that long-term urban sustainability will require.

In the long run, the most secure and sustainable cities may be those that succeed in reintegrating the geography of living and employment, of production and consumption, of city and hinterland. As Sim Van der Ryn and Peter Calthorpe wrote in *Sustainable Communities,* such a transformed city, "rather than being merely the site of consumption, might, through its very design, produce some of its own food and energy, as well as become the locus of work for its residents."

If we followed such ecological design principles, urban regions could gradually become not only more self-reliant, but also more socially rewarding and ecologically benign. Through greater dependence on local ecosystems, city dwellers would become more aware of their connectedness to nature. As they became more conscientious stewards of the environment, their lives would become less materialistic; in turn, that change would reduce both cities' ecological footprints and the political tensions they would otherwise foster.

To the upwardly mobile beneficiaries of the age of exuberance, all that may sound surreal, even ridiculous. We are accustomed to expecting a future of more and bigger, of freewheeling technological mastery over the natural world. But that road leads inevitably to a dead end. Accelerating global change has shown that the earth cannot keep an infinitely expanding population in the lap of luxury. Scholars should start looking for a new route now.

SANDRA POSTEL
Troubled Waters

Sandra Postel, whose graduate studies at Duke University were in resource economics and policy, is a leading expert on international water issues. Currently director of the Global Water Policy Project (in New Mexico), from 1988 to 1994 she served as vice president for research at the Worldwatch Institute, a Washington, D.C.–based environmental policy organization, and later directed Mount Holyoke College's Center for the Environment. In 1995 Postel was a Pew Scholar in Conservation and the Environment, and in 2002 was named by Scientific American *one of the "Scientific American 50."*

Her numerous scientific articles and books are dedicated, she says, "to the creation of a more environmentally secure world in which all people and living things may thrive." They include: Last Oasis: Facing Water Scarcity *(rev. 1997);* Pillar of Sand: Can the Irrigation Miracle Last? *(1999);* Rivers for Life: Managing Water for People and Nature *(2003); and* Liquid Assets: The Critical Need to Safeguard Freshwater Ecosystems *(2005). "Troubled Waters," reprinted below, was originally published in* The Sciences *(2000), then included in* Best American Science and Nature Writing *(2001). It focuses on the interrelationship between exploding world populations, the amount of freshwater available for human consumption, and the continued functioning of ecosystems.*

In June 1991, after a leisurely lunch in the fashionable Washington, D.C., neighborhood of Dupont Circle, Alexei Yablokov, then a Soviet parliamentarian, told me something shocking. Some years back he had had a map hanging on his office wall depicting Soviet central Asia without the vast Aral Sea. Cartographers had drawn it in the 1960s, when the Aral was still the world's fourth-largest inland body of water.

I felt for a moment like a cold war spy to whom a critical secret had just been revealed. The Aral Sea, as I knew well, was drying up. The existence of such a map implied that its ongoing destruction was no accident. Moscow's central planners had decided to sacrifice the sea, judging that the two rivers feeding it could be put to more valuable use irrigating cotton in the central Asian desert. Such a planned elimination of an ecosystem nearly the size of Ireland was surely one of humanity's more arrogant acts.

Four years later, when I traveled to the Aral Sea region, the Soviet Union was no more; the central Asian republics were now independent. But the legacy of Moscow's policies lived on: thirty-five years of siphoning the region's rivers had decreased the Aral's volume by nearly two thirds and its surface area by half. I stood on what had once been a seaside bluff outside the former port town of Muynak, but I could see no water. The sea was twenty-five miles away. A graveyard of ships lay before me, rotting and rusting in the dried-up seabed. Sixty thousand fishing jobs had vanished, and thousands of people had left the area. Many of those who remained suffered from a variety of cancers, respiratory ailments, and other diseases. Winds ripping across the desert were lifting tens of millions of tons of a toxic salt-dust chemical residue from the exposed seabed each year and dumping it on surrounding croplands and villages. Dust storms and polluted rivers made it hazardous to breathe the air and drink the water.

The tragedy of the Aral Sea is by no means unique. Around the world countless rivers, lakes, and wetlands are succumbing to dams, river diversions, rampant pollution, and other pressures. Collectively they underscore what is rapidly emerging as one of the greatest challenges facing humanity in the decades to come: how to satisfy the thirst of a world population pushing nine billion by the year 2050, while protecting the health of the aquatic environment that sustains all terrestrial life.

The problem, though daunting, is not insurmountable. A number of technologies and management practices are available that could substantially reduce the amount of water used by agriculture, industry, and households. But the sad reality is that the rules and policies that drive water-related decisions have not adequately promoted them. We have the ability to provide both people and eco-systems with the water they need for good health, but those goals need to be elevated on the political agenda.

Observed from space, our planet seems wealthy in water beyond measure. Yet most of the earth's vast blueness is ocean, far too salty to drink or to irrigate most crops. Only about 2.5 percent of all the water on earth is fresh water, and two thirds of that is locked away in glaciers and ice caps. A minuscule share of the world's water — less than one hundredth of 1 percent — is both drinkable and renewed each year through rainfall and other precipitation. And though that freshwater supply is renewable, it is also finite. The quantity available today is the same that was available when civilizations first arose thousands of years ago, and so the amount of water that should be allotted to each person has declined steadily with time. It has dropped by 58 percent since 1950, as the population climbed from 2.5 billion to 6 billion, and will fall an additional 33 percent within fifty years if our numbers reach 8.9 billion, the middle of the projected range.

Because rainfall and river flows are not distributed evenly throughout the year or across the continents, the task of adapting water to human use is not an easy one. Many rivers are tempestuous and erratic, running high when water is needed least and low when it is needed most. Every year two thirds of the water in the earth's rivers rushes untapped to the sea in floods. An additional one fifth flows in remote areas such as the Amazon basin and the Arctic tundra. In many developing countries monsoons bring between 70 and 80 percent of the year's rainfall in just three months, greatly complicating water management. When it comes to water, it seems, nature has dealt a difficult hand.

As a result, the history of water management has largely been one of striving to capture, control, and deliver water to cities and farms when and where they need it. Engineers have built massive canal networks to irrigate regions that are other-wise too dry to support the cultivation and growth of crops. The area of irrigated land worldwide has increased more than thirtyfold in the past two centuries, turning near-deserts such as southern California and Egypt into food baskets. Artificial oasis cities have bloomed. In Phoenix, Arizona, which gets about seven inches of rain a year, seemingly abundant water pours from taps. With a swimming pool, lawn, and an array of modern appliances, a Phoenix household can readily consume 700 gallons of water a day.

But while the affluent enjoy desert swimming pools, more than a billion of the world's people lack a safe supply of drinking water, and 2.8 billion do not have even minimal sanitation. The World Health Organization estimates that 250 million cases of water-related diseases such as cholera arise annually, resulting in between 5 and 10 million deaths. Intestinal worms infect some 1.5 billion people, killing as many as 100,000 a year. Outbreaks of parasitic diseases have sometimes followed the construction of large dams and irrigation systems, which create standing bodies of water where the parasites' hosts can breed. In sub-Saharan Africa, many women and girls walk several miles a day just to collect water for their families. Tens of millions of poor farm families cannot afford to irrigate their land, which lowers their crop productivity and leaves them vulnerable to droughts.

Even in countries in which water and sanitation are taken for granted, there [10] are disturbing trends. Much of the earth's stable year-round water supply resides underground in geologic formations called aquifers. Some aquifers are nonrenewable—the bulk of their water accumulated thousands of years ago and they get little or no replenishment from precipitation today. And though most aquifers are replenished by rainwater seeping into the ground, in a number of the world's most important food-producing regions farmers are pumping water from aquifers faster than nature can replace it. Aquifers are overdrawn in several key regions of the United States, including California's Central Valley, which supplies half of the nation's fruits and vegetables, and the southern Great Plains, where grain and cotton farmers are steadily depleting the Ogallala, one of the planet's greatest aquifers.

The problem is particularly severe in India, where a national assessment commissioned in 1996 found that water tables in critical farming regions were dropping at an alarming rate, jeopardizing perhaps as much as one fourth of the country's grain harvest. In China's north plain, where 40 percent of that nation's food is grown, water tables are plunging by more than a meter a year across a wide area.

On the basis of the best available data, I estimate that global groundwater overpumping totals at least 160 billion cubic meters a year, an amount equal to the annual flow of two Nile Rivers. Because it takes roughly 1,000 cubic meters of water to produce one ton of grain, some 160 million tons of grain—nearly 10 percent of the global food supply—depend on the unsustainable practice of depleting groundwater. That raises an unsettling question: If humanity is operating under such an enormous deficit today, where are we going to find the additional water to satisfy future needs?

Another harbinger of trouble is that many major rivers now run dry for large parts of the year. Five of Asia's great rivers—the Indus and the Ganges in southern Asia, the Yellow in China, and the Amu Darya and Syr Darya in the Aral Sea basin—no longer reach the sea for months at a time. The Chinese call the Yellow River their mother river, reflecting its role as the cradle of Chinese civilization. Today the Yellow River supplies water to 140 million people and 18 million acres of farmland. Yet it has run dry in its lower reaches almost every year of this past decade, and the dry section often stretches nearly 400 miles upstream from the river's mouth. In 1997 the dry spell lasted a record 226 days.

Not surprisingly, as water becomes scarce, competition for it is intensifying. Cities are beginning to divert water from farms in north-central China, southern India, the Middle East, and the western United States. Moreover, the world's urban population is expected to double to 5 billion by 2025, which will further increase the pressure to shift water away from agriculture. How such a shift will affect food production, employment in rural areas, rural-to-urban migration, and social stability are critical questions that have hardly been asked, much less analyzed.

Competition for water is also building in international river basins: 261 of   15
the world's rivers flow through two or more countries. In the vast majority of those cases there are no treaties governing how the river water should be shared. As demands tax the supply in those regions, tensions are mounting. In five water hot spots—the Aral Sea region, the Ganges, the Jordan, the Nile, and the Tigris-Euphrates—the population of the nations in each basin will probably increase by at least 30 percent and possibly by as much as 70 percent by 2025.

The plight of the Nile basin seems particularly worrisome. Last in line for Nile water, Egypt is almost entirely dependent on the river and currently uses two thirds of its annual flow. About 85 percent of the Nile's flow originates in Ethiopia, which to date has used little of that supply but is now constructing small dams to begin tapping the upper headwaters. Meanwhile, Egypt is pursuing two large irrigation projects that have put it on a collision course with Ethiopia. Although Nile-basin countries have been meeting regularly to discuss how they can share the river, no treaty that includes all the parties yet exists. Shortly after signing the historic peace accords with Israel in 1979, Egyptian president Anwar Sadat said that only water could make Egypt wage war again. He was referring not to another potential conflict with Israel but to the possibility of hostilities with Ethiopia over the Nile.

The story of the shrinking Aral Sea underscores another form of competition: the conflict between the use of water in agriculture and industry, on the one hand, and its ecological role as the basis of life and sustainer of ecosystem health, on the other. After I returned from the Aral Sea, I was tempted to view the sea and the communities around it as tragic victims of Communist central planning. A year later, however, in May 1996, I visited the delta of the Colorado River and found a depressingly similar story.

The Colorado delta had once been lush, supporting as many as 400 plant species and numerous birds, fish, and mammals. The great naturalist Aldo Leopold, who canoed through the delta in 1922, called it "a milk and honey wilderness," a land of "a hundred green lagoons." As I walked amid salt flats, mud-cracked earth, and murky pools, I could hardly believe I was in the same place that Leopold had described. The treaties that divide the Colorado River among seven U.S. states and Mexico had set aside nothing to protect the river system itself. More water was promised to the eight treaty parties than the river actually carries in an average year. As a result, the large dams and river diversions upstream now drain so much water that virtually nothing flows through the delta and out to the Gulf of California.

As in the Aral Sea basin, the Colorado predicament has caused more than an environmental tragedy. The Cocopa Indians have fished and farmed in the delta for more than 1,000 years. Now their culture faces extinction because too little river water makes it to the delta.

What was gained by despoiling such cultural and biological riches, by driving long-settled people from their homes and wildlife from its habitats? The answer seems to be more swimming pools in Los Angeles, more golf courses in Arizona, and more desert agriculture. To be sure, the tradeoff helped boost the U.S. gross national product, but at the untallied cost of irreplaceable natural and cultural diversity.

Given the challenges that lie ahead, how can the needs of an increasingly thirsty world be satisfied, without further destroying aquatic ecosystems? In my view, the solution hinges on three major components: allocating water to maintain the health of natural ecosystems, doubling the productivity of the water allocated to human activities, and extending access to a ready supply of water to the poor.

Just as people require a minimum amount of water to maintain good health, so do ecosystems—as the Aral Sea, the Colorado delta, and numerous other areas painfully demonstrate. As the human use of water nears the limits of the supply in many places, we must ensure the continued functioning of ecosystems and the invaluable services they perform. Providing that assurance will entail a major scientific initiative, aimed at determining safe limits of water usage from aquifers, rivers, lakes, and other aquatic systems. Laws and regulations, guaranteeing continued health of those ecosystems, must also be put in place.

Australia and South Africa are now leading the way in such efforts. Officials in Australia's Murray-Darling River basin have placed a cap on water extractions—a bold move aimed at reversing the decline in the health of the aquatic environment. South Africa's new water laws call for water managers to allocate water for the protection of ecological functions as well as for human needs.

The United States is also making efforts to heal some of its damaged aquatic environments. A joint federal-state initiative is working to restore the health of California's San Francisco Bay delta, which is home to more than 120 species of fish and supports 80 percent of the state's commercial fisheries. In Florida an $8 billion federal-state project is attempting to repair the treasured Everglades, the famed "river of grass," which has shrunk in half in the past century alone. And across the country a number of dams are slated for removal in an effort to restore fisheries and other benefits of river systems.

The second essential component in meeting water needs for the future will be to maximize the use of every gallon we extract. Because agriculture accounts for 70 percent of the world's water usage, raising water productivity in farming regions is a top priority. The bad news is that today less than half the water removed from rivers and aquifers for irrigation actually benefits a crop. The good news is that there is substantial room for improvement.

Drip irrigation ranks near the top of measures that offer great untapped potential. A drip system is essentially a network of perforated plastic tubing, installed on or below the soil surface, that delivers water at low volumes directly to the roots of plants. The loss to evaporation or runoff is minimal. When drip irrigation is combined with the monitoring of soil moisture and other ways of assessing a crop's water needs, the system delivers 95 percent of its water to the plant, compared with between 50 and 70 percent for the more conventional flood or furrow irrigation systems.

Besides saving water, drip irrigation usually boosts crop yield and quality, simply because it enables the farmer to maintain a nearly ideal moisture environment for the plants. In countries as diverse as India, Israel, Jordan, Spain, and the United States, studies have consistently shown that drip irrigation not only cuts water use by between 30 and 70 percent, but also increases crop yields by between 20 and 90 percent. Those improvements are often enough to double the water productivity. Lands watered by drip irrigation now account for a little more than 1 percent of all irrigated land worldwide. The potential, however, is far greater.

The information revolution that is transforming so many facets of society also promises to play a vital role in transforming the efficiency of water use. The state of California operates a network of more than a hundred automated and computerized weather stations that collect local climate data, including solar radiation, wind speed, relative humidity, rainfall, and air and soil temperature, and then transmit the data to a central computer in Sacramento. For each remote site, the computer calculates an evapotranspiration rate, from which farmers can then calculate the rate at which their crops are consuming water. In that way they can determine, quite accurately, how much water to apply at any given time throughout the growing season.

As urban populations continue expanding in the decades ahead, household consumption of water will also need to be made more efficient. As part of the National Energy Policy Act, which was signed into law in late 1992, the United States now has federal water standards for basic household plumbing fixtures—toilets, faucets, and showerheads. The regulations require that manufacturers of the fixtures meet certain standards of efficiency—thereby building conservation into urban infrastructure. Water usage with those fixtures will be about a third less in 2025 than it would have been without the new standards. Similar laws could also help rapidly growing Third World cities stretch their scarce water supplies. One of the most obvious ways to raise water productivity is to use water more than once. The Israelis, for instance, reuse two thirds of their municipal wastewater for crop production. Because both municipal and agricultural wastewater can carry toxic substances, reuse must be carefully monitored. But by matching appropriate water quality to various kinds of use, much more benefit can be derived from the fresh water already under human control. And that implies that more can remain in its natural state.

The third component of the solution to water security for the future is perhaps 30 also the greatest challenge: extending water and sanitation services to the poor.

Ensuring safe drinking water is one of the surest ways to reduce disease and death in developing countries. Likewise, the most direct way of reducing hunger among the rural poor is to raise their productive capacities directly. Like trickle-down economics, trickle-down food security does not work well for the poor. Greater corn production in Iowa will not alleviate hunger among the poor in India or sub-Saharan Africa. With access to affordable irrigation, however, millions of poor farmers who have largely been bypassed by the modern irrigation age can raise their productivity and incomes directly, reducing hunger and poverty at the same time.

In many cases the problem is not that the poor cannot afford to pay for water but that they are paying unfair prices — often more than do residents of developed nations. It is not uncommon for poor families to spend more than a quarter of their income on water. Lacking piped-in water, many must buy from vendors who charge outrageous prices, often for poor-quality water.

In Istanbul, Turkey, for instance, vendors charge ten times the rate paid by those who enjoy publicly supplied water; in Bombay, the overcharge is a factor of twenty. A survey of households in Port-au-Prince, Haiti, found that people connected to the water system pay about a dollar per cubic meter ($3.78 per 1,000 gallons), whereas the unconnected must buy water from vendors for between $5.50 and $16.50 per cubic meter — about twenty times the price typically paid by urban residents in the United States.

Cost estimates for providing universal access to water and sanitation vary widely. But even the higher-end estimates — some $50 billion a year — amount to only 7 percent of global military expenditures. A relatively minor reordering of social priorities and investments — and a more comprehensive definition of security — could enable everyone to share the benefits of clean water and adequate sanitation.

Equally modest expenditures could improve the lot of poor farmers. In recent years, for instance, large areas of Bangladesh have been transformed by a human-powered device called a treadle pump. When I first saw the pump in action on a trip to Bangladesh in 1998, it reminded me of a StairMaster exercise machine, and it is operated in much the same way. The operator pedals up and down on two long poles, or treadles, each attached to a cylinder. The upward stroke sucks shallow groundwater into one of the cylinders, while the downward stroke of the opposite pedal expels water from the other cylinder (that was sucked in on the preceding upward stroke) into a field channel.

The pump costs just thirty-five dollars, and with that purchase, farm families 35 that previously were forced to let their land lie fallow during the dry season — and go hungry for part of the year — can grow an extra crop of rice and vegetables and take the surplus to market. Each pump irrigates about half an acre, which is appropriate for the small plots that poor farmers generally cultivate. The average net annual return on the investment has been more than $100 per pump, enabling families to recoup their outlay in less than a year.

So far Bangladeshi farmers have purchased 1.2 million treadle pumps, thereby raising the productivity of more than 600,000 acres of farmland and injecting an additional $325 million a year into the poorest parts of the Bangladeshi economy. A private-sector network of 70 manufacturers, 830 dealers, and 2,500 installers supports the technology, creating jobs and raising incomes in urban areas as well.

The treadle pump is just one of many examples of small-scale, affordable irrigation technologies that can help raise the productivity and the income of poor farm families. In areas with no perennial source of water, as in the drylands of south Asia and sub-Saharan Africa, a variety of so-called water-harvesting techniques hold promise for capturing and channeling more rainwater into the soil. In parts of India, for instance, some farmers collect rainwater from the monsoon season in earth-walled embankments, then drain the stored water during the dry season. The method, known as *haveli,* enables farmers to grow crops when their fields would otherwise be barren. Israeli investigators have found that another simple practice—covering the soil between rows of plants with polyethylene sheets—helps keep rainwater in the soil by cutting down on evaporation. The method has doubled the yields of some crops.

To avert much misery in this new century, the ways water is priced, supplied, and allocated must be changed. Large government subsidies for irrigation, an estimated $33 billion a year worldwide, keep prices artificially low—and so fail to penalize farmers for wasting water. Inflexible laws and regulations discourage the marketing of water, leading to inefficient distribution and use. Without rules to regulate groundwater extractions, the depletion of aquifers persists. And the failure to place a value on freshwater ecosystems—their role in maintaining water quality, controlling floods, and providing wildlife habitats—has left far too little water in natural systems.

Will we make the right choices in the coming age of water scarcity? Our actions must ultimately be guided by more than technology or economics. The fact that water is essential to life lends an ethical dimension to every decision we make about how it is used, managed, and distributed. We need new technologies, to be sure, but we also need a new ethic: All living things must get enough water before some get more than enough.

QUESTIONS FOR DISCUSSION AND WRITING

1. Why, according to Rees, do urban areas and high-income countries create a disproportionate drain on worldwide environmental resources? Why is it so easy to overlook this fact?

2. In your own words, what is the "ecological footprint" of a population? In what ways is this concept central to Rees's argument here? Does Rees succeed in convincing you of the urgency of the problem he describes? Why or why not?

3. Based on Rees's argument here, what are some things that you could do to reduce your consumption of dwindling natural resources? With a partner, write a position paper offering advice to your peers, and perhaps to community planners, on how to shrink one's individual footprint.

4. What is "the tragedy of the Aral Sea" (Postel, paragraph 4)? In what ways is this representative of the larger problem of worldwide water consumption and governmental water policies? Relate the disappearance of the Aral Sea to the environmental problems Rees describes.

PAUL SOUDERS

Kangerlua Glacier Melting

© Paul Souders/Corbis

Water streaming from a melting iceberg carved from Kangerlua Glacier (Jakobshavn Icefjord) in Disko Bay, Ilulissat, Greenland, July 31, 2006.

QUESTIONS FOR DISCUSSION AND WRITING

1. Huge chunks of snow and ice, some compacted for one hundred fifty thousand years, break off from melting glaciers in the Arctic and Antarctic and crash into the warming ocean. Glaciers are melting from the Alps to the Andes to the snows of Kilimanjaro. The Intergovernmental Panel on Climate Change (a consensus of 2,000 scientists) says glaciers are expected to vanish entirely within three decades at the same time the oceans rise several feet. Rising water levels worldwide cause

floods, destruction of coral reefs, undrinkable salinated water, and higher temperatures that ultimately contribute to worldwide drought (see Postel, p. 622, and Diamond, p. 632). How and why can melting glaciers have effects worldwide? How can they produce both flooding and drought?

2. In *An Inconvenient Truth: The Planetary Emergency of Global Warming and What We Can Do About It* (2006), Al Gore presents several arguments to refute those who deny that global warming exists. He challenges the "misconception" that scientists disagree "about whether global warming is real"; shows that global warming is proceeding not gradually but at lightning speed; counters "the false belief that we have to choose between a healthy economy and a healthy environment"; and emphasizes that global warming is not too large to address on a global scale.[1] Discuss and analyze one of these points, using the pieces by Rees, Carson, Postel, Diamond, and Berry in this chapter.

3. Propose a realistic solution to one problem that contributes to global warming, however small or large. Begin locally (in your "backyard") but expand your discussion to include regional, national, even global implications.

JARED DIAMOND

The World as a Polder

Jared Diamond, born in Boston, 1937, earned a B.A. from Harvard (1958) and a Ph.D. from Cambridge (1961) in membrane biophysics and physiology. He then taught physiology at the UCLA Medical School for over twenty years, during the same period leading research expeditions to New Guinea to study ecology and avian evolution. His more recent work, now at UCLA as a professor of geography, draws on his extensive knowledge not only of physiology and evolutionary biology, but of anthropology and biogeography as well. He has been awarded a National Medal of Science; Guns, Germs, and Steel: The Fates of Human Societies *(1998) won a Pulitzer Prize. Diamond, who says this book's alternative title would be "a short history about everyone for the last 13,000 years," attempts to explain the survival and supremacy of Eurasian societies over the peoples they conquered. He denies that their success is due to any genetic, intellectual, or moral superiority, attributing gaps in power and technology instead to environmental differences in competing societies.*

In Collapse: How Societies Choose to Fail or Succeed *(2005), Diamond argues again that human mismanagement of natural resources has accounted for the failure of societies and civilizations as widely diverse as the Mayan and Easter Island cultures and the Nordic settlements in Greenland. Contemporary society, from Haiti and the Dominican Republic to Montana, is likewise seriously endangered by humans'*

---

[1]Al Gore, *An Inconvenient Truth: The Planetary Emergency of Global Warming and What We Can Do About It* (Emmans, PA: Rodale Press, 2006), 254–78.

inefficient and extravagant environmental exploitation. In "The World as a Polder," the book's concluding chapter, Diamond lists the world's current hot-button environmental problems, all interrelated. If they are not solved through coordinated efforts to prevent the earth's further depletion and degradation, the world will succumb to "warfare, genocide, starvation, disease epidemics, and collapses of societies."[1]

Let's begin with the natural resources that we are destroying or losing: natural habitats, wild food sources, biological diversity, and soil.

1. At an accelerating rate, we are destroying natural habitats or else converting them to human-made habitats, such as cities and villages, farmlands and pastures, roads, and golf courses. The natural habitats whose losses have provoked the most discussion are forests, wetlands, coral reefs, and the ocean bottom. . . . More than half of the world's original area of forest has already been converted to other uses, and at present conversion rates one-quarter of the forests that remain will become converted within the next half-century. Those losses of forests represent losses for us humans, especially because forests provide us with timber and other raw materials, and because they provide us with so-called ecosystem services such as protecting our watersheds, protecting soil against erosion, constituting essential steps in the water cycle that generates much of our rainfall, and providing habitat for most terrestrial plant and animal species. Deforestation was a or *the* major factor in all the collapses of past societies described. . . . In addition, . . . issues of concern to us are not only forest destruction and conversion, but also changes in the structure of wooded habitats that do remain. Among other things, that changed structure results in changed fire regimes that put forests, chaparral woodlands, and savannahs at greater risk of infrequent but catastrophic fires.

Other valuable natural habitats besides forests are also being destroyed. An even larger fraction of the world's original wetlands than of its forests has already been destroyed, damaged, or converted. Consequences for us arise from wetlands' importance in maintaining the quality of our water supplies and the existence of commercially important freshwater fisheries, while even ocean fisheries depend on mangrove wetlands to provide habitat for the juvenile phase of many fish species. About one-third of the world's coral reefs—the oceanic equivalent of tropical rainforests, because they are home to a disproportionate fraction of the ocean's species—have already been severely damaged. If current trends continue, about half of the remaining reefs would be lost by the year 2030. That damage and destruction result from the growing use of dynamite as a fishing method, reef over-growth by algae ("seaweeds") when the large herbivorous fish that normally graze on the algae become fished out, effects of sediment runoff and pollutants

---

[1]From Jared Diamond, *Collapse: How Societies Choose to Fail or Succeed* (London: Viking Penguin, 2005), 498.

from adjacent lands cleared or converted to agriculture, and coral bleaching due to rising ocean water temperatures. It has recently become appreciated that fishing by trawling is destroying much or most of the shallow ocean bottom and the species dependent on it.

2. Wild foods, especially fish and to a lesser extent shellfish, contribute a large fraction of the protein consumed by humans. In effect, this is protein that we obtain for free (other than the cost of catching and transporting the fish), and that reduces our needs for animal protein that we have to grow ourselves in the form of domestic livestock. About two billion people, most of them poor, depend on the oceans for protein. If wild fish stocks were managed appropriately, the stock levels could be maintained, and they could be harvested perpetually. Unfortunately, the problem known as the tragedy of the commons has regularly undone efforts to manage fisheries sustainably, and the great majority of valuable fisheries already either have collapsed or are in steep decline. Past societies that overfished included Easter Island, Mangareva, and Henderson.

Increasingly, fish and shrimp are being grown by aquaculture, which in prin-   5 ciple has a promising future as the cheapest way to produce animal protein. In several respects, though, aquaculture as commonly practiced today is making the problem of declining wild fisheries worse rather than better. Fish grown by aquaculture are mostly fed wild-caught fish and thereby usually consume more wild fish meat (up to 20 times more) than they yield in meat of their own. They contain higher toxin levels than do wild-caught fish. Cultured fish regularly escape, interbreed with wild fish, and thereby harm wild fish stocks genetically, because cultured fish strains have been selected for rapid growth at the expense of poor survival in the wild (50 times worse survival for cultured salmon than for wild salmon). Aquaculture runoff causes pollution and eutrophication. The lower costs of aquaculture than of fishing, by driving down fish prices, initially drive fishermen to exploit wild fish stocks even more heavily in order to maintain their incomes constant when they are receiving less money per pound of fish.

3. A significant fraction of wild species, populations, and genetic diversity has already been lost, and at present rates a large fraction of what remains will be lost within the next half-century. Some species, such as big edible animals, or plants with edible fruits or good timber, are of obvious value to us. . . .

But biodiversity losses of small inedible species often provoke the response, "Who cares? Do you really care less for humans than for some lousy useless little fish or weed, like the snail darter or Furbish lousewort?" This response misses the point that the entire natural world is made up of wild species providing us for free with services that can be very expensive, and in many cases impossible, for us to supply ourselves. Elimination of lots of lousy little species regularly causes big harmful consequences for humans, just as does randomly knocking out many of the lousy little rivets holding together an airplane. The literally innumerable examples include: the role of earthworms in regenerating soil and maintaining its texture (one of the reasons that oxygen levels dropped inside the Biosphere 2 enclosure, harming its human inhabitants and crippling a colleague of mine, was a lack of appropriate earthworms, contributing to altered soil/atmosphere gas exchange); soil bacteria that fix the essential crop nutrient nitrogen, which otherwise we have to spend money to supply in fertilizers; bees and other insect pollinators (they pollinate our crops for free, whereas it's expensive for us to pollinate every crop flower by hand); birds and mammals that disperse wild fruits (foresters still haven't figured out how to grow from seed the most important commercial tree species of the Solomon Islands, whose seeds are naturally dispersed by fruit bats, which are becoming hunted out); elimination of whales, sharks, bears, wolves, and other top predators in the seas and on the land, changing the whole food chain beneath them; and wild plants and animals that decompose wastes and recycle nutrients, ultimately providing us with clean water and air.

4. Soils of farmlands used for growing crops are being carried away by water and wind erosion at rates between 10 and 40 times the rates of soil formation, and between 500 and 10,000 times soil erosion rates on forested land. Because those soil erosion rates are so much higher than soil formation rates, that means a net loss of soil. For instance, about half of the topsoil of Iowa, the state whose agriculture productivity is among the highest in the U.S., has been eroded in the last 150 years. On my most recent visit to Iowa, my hosts showed me a churchyard offering a dramatically visible example of those soil losses. A church was built there in the middle of farmland during the 19th century and has been maintained continuously as a church ever since, while the land around it was being farmed. As a result of soil being eroded much more rapidly from fields than from the churchyard, the yard now stands like a little island raised 10 feet above the surrounding sea of farmland.

Other types of soil damage caused by human agricultural practices include salinization; . . . losses of soil fertility, because farming removes nutrients much more rapidly than they are restored by weathering of the underlying rock; and soil acidification in some areas, or its converse, alkalinization, in other areas. All of these types of harmful impacts have resulted in a fraction of the world's farmland variously estimated at between 20% and 80% having become severely damaged, during an era in which increasing human population has caused us to need more farmland rather than less farmland. Like deforestation, soil problems contributed to the collapses of all past societies discussed . . .

The next three problems involve ceilings—on energy, freshwater, and photosynthetic capacity. In each case the ceiling is not hard and fixed but soft: we can obtain more of the needed resource, but at increasing costs.   10

5. The world's major energy sources, especially for industrial societies, are fossil fuels: oil, natural gas, and coal. While there has been much discussion about how many big oil and gas fields remain to be discovered, and while coal reserves are believed to be large, the prevalent view is that known and likely reserves of readily accessible oil and natural gas will last for a few more decades. This view should not be misinterpreted to mean that all of the oil and natural gas within

the Earth will have been used up by then. Instead, further reserves will be deeper underground, dirtier, increasingly expensive to extract or process, or will involve higher environmental costs. Of course, fossil fuels are not our sole energy sources, and I shall consider problems raised by the alternatives below.

6. Most of the world's freshwater in rivers and lakes is already being utilized for irrigation, domestic and industrial water, and in situ uses such as boat transportation corridors, fisheries, and recreation. Rivers and lakes that are not already utilized are mostly far from major population centers and likely users, such as in Northwestern Australia, Siberia, and Iceland. Throughout the world, freshwater underground aquifers are being depleted at rates faster than they are being naturally replenished, so that they will eventually dwindle. Of course, freshwater can be made by desalinization of seawater, but that costs money and energy, as does pumping the resulting desalinized water inland for use. Hence desalinization, while it is useful locally, is too expensive to solve most of the world's water shortages. The Anasazi and Maya were among the past societies to be undone by water problems, while today over a billion people lack access to reliable safe drinking water.

7. It might at first seem that the supply of sunlight is infinite, so one might reason that the Earth's capacity to grow crops and wild plants is also infinite. Within the last 20 years, it has been appreciated that that is not the case, and that's not only because plants grow poorly in the world's Arctic regions and deserts unless one goes to the expense of supplying heat or water. More generally, the amount of solar energy fixed per acre by plant photosynthesis, hence plant growth per acre, depends on temperature and rainfall. At any given temperature and rainfall the plant growth that can be supported by the sunlight falling on an acre is limited by the geometry and biochemistry of plants, even if they take up the sunlight so efficiently that not a single photon of light passes through the plants unabsorbed to reach the ground. The first calculation of this photosynthetic ceiling, carried out in 1986, estimated that humans then already used (e.g., for crops, tree plantations, and golf courses) or diverted or wasted (e.g., light falling on concrete roads and buildings) about half of the Earth's photosynthetic capacity. Given the rate of increase of human population, and especially of population impact (see point 12 below), since 1986, we are projected to be utilizing most of the world's terrestrial photosynthetic capacity by the middle of this century. That is, most energy fixed from sunlight will be used for human purposes, and little will be left over to support the growth of natural plant communities, such as natural forests.

The next three problems involve harmful things that we generate or move around: toxic chemicals, alien species, and atmospheric gases.

8. The chemical industry and many other industries manufacture or release [15] into the air, soil, oceans, lakes, and rivers many toxic chemicals, some of them "unnatural" and synthesized only by humans, others present naturally in tiny

concentrations (e.g., mercury) or else synthesized by living things but synthesized and released by humans in quantities much larger than natural ones (e.g., hormones). The first of these toxic chemicals to achieve wide notice were insecticides, pesticides, and herbicides, whose effects on birds, fish, and other animals were publicized by Rachel Carson's 1962 book *Silent Spring*. Since then, it has been appreciated that the toxic effects of even greater significance for us humans are those on ourselves. The culprits include not only insecticides, pesticides, and herbicides, but also mercury and other metals, fire-retardant chemicals, refrigerator coolants, detergents, and components of plastics. We swallow them in our food and water, breathe them in our air, and absorb them through our skin. Often in very low concentrations, they variously cause birth defects, mental retardation, and temporary or permanent damage to our immune and reproductive systems. Some of them act as endocrine disruptors, i.e., they interfere with our reproductive systems by mimicking or blocking effects of our own sex hormones. They probably make the major contribution to the steep decline in sperm count in many human populations over the last several decades, and to the apparently increasing frequency with which couples are unable to conceive, even when one takes into account the increasing average age of marriage in many societies. In addition, deaths in the U.S. from air pollution alone (without considering soil and water pollution) are conservatively estimated at over 130,000 per year.

Many of these toxic chemicals are broken down in the environment only slowly (e.g., DDT and PCBs) or not at all (mercury), and they persist in the environment for long times before being washed out. Thus, cleanup costs of many polluted sites in the U.S. are measured in the billions of dollars (e.g., Love Canal, the Hudson River, Chesapeake Bay, the *Exxon Valdez* oil spill, and Montana copper mines). But pollution at those worst sites in the U.S. is mild compared to that in the former Soviet Union, China, and many Third World mines, whose cleanup costs no one even dares to think about.

9. The term "alien species" refers to species that we transfer, intentionally or inadvertently, from a place where they are native to another place where they are not native. Some alien species are obviously valuable to us as crops, domestic animals, and landscaping. But others devastate populations of native species with which they come in contact, either by preying on, parasitizing, infecting, or outcompeting them. The aliens cause these big effects because the native species with which they come in contact had no previous evolutionary experience of them and are unable to resist them (like human populations newly exposed to smallpox or AIDS). There are by now literally hundreds of cases in which alien species have caused one-time or annually recurring damages of hundreds of millions of dollars or even billions of dollars. Modern examples include Australia's rabbits and foxes, agricultural weeds like Spotted Knapweed and Leafy Spurge, pests and pathogens of trees and crops and livestock (like the blights that wiped out American chestnut trees and devastated American elms), the water hyacinth that chokes waterways, the zebra mussels that choke power plants, and the lampreys that devastated the former commercial fisheries of the North American Great Lakes.

Ancient examples include the introduced rats that contributed to the extinction of Easter Island's palm tree by gnawing its nuts, and that ate the eggs and chicks of nesting birds on Easter, Henderson, and all other Pacific islands previously without rats.

10. Human activities produce gases that escape into the atmosphere, where they either damage the protective ozone layer (as do formerly widespread refrigerator coolants) or else act as greenhouse gases that absorb sunlight and thereby lead to global warming. The gases contributing to global warming include carbon dioxide from combustion and respiration, and methane from fermentation in the intestines of ruminant animals. Of course, there have always been natural fires and animal respiration producing carbon dioxide, and wild ruminant animals producing methane, but our burning of firewood and of fossil fuels has greatly increased the former, and our herds of cattle and of sheep have greatly increased the latter.

For many years, scientists debated the reality, cause, and extent of global warming: are world temperatures really historically high now, and, if so, by how much, and are humans the leading cause? Most knowledgeable scientists now agree that, despite year-to-year ups and downs of temperature that necessitate complicated analyses to extract warming trends, the atmosphere really has been undergoing an unusually rapid rise in temperature recently, and that human activities are the or a major cause. The remaining uncertainties mainly concern the future expected magnitude of the effect: e.g., whether average global temperatures will increase by "just" 1.5 degrees Centigrade or by 5 degrees Centigrade over the next century. Those numbers may not sound like a big deal, until one reflects that average global temperatures were "only" 5 degrees cooler at the height of the last Ice Age.

While one might at first think that we should welcome global warming on   20 the grounds that warmer temperatures mean faster plant growth, it turns out that global warming will produce both winners and losers. Crop yields in cool areas with temperatures marginal for agriculture may indeed increase, while crop yields in already warm or dry areas may decrease. In Montana, California, and many other dry climates, the disappearance of mountain snowpacks will decrease the water available for domestic uses, and for irrigation that actually limits crop yields in those areas. The rise in global sea levels as a result of snow and ice melting poses dangers of flooding and coastal erosion for densely populated low-lying coastal plains and river deltas already barely above or even below sea level. The areas thereby threatened include much of the Netherlands, Bangladesh, and the seaboard of the eastern U.S., many low-lying Pacific islands, the deltas of the Nile and Mekong Rivers, and coastal and riverbank cities of the United Kingdom (e.g., London), India, Japan, and the Philippines. Global warming will also produce big secondary effects that are difficult to predict exactly in advance and that are likely to cause huge problems, such as further climate changes resulting from changes in ocean circulation resulting in turn from melting of the Arctic ice cap.

The remaining two problems involve the increase in human population:

11. The world's human population is growing. More people require more food, space, water, energy, and other resources. Rates and even the direction of human population change vary greatly around the world, with the highest rates of population growth (4% per year or higher) in some Third World countries, low rates of growth (1% per year or less) in some First World countries such as Italy and Japan, and negative rates of growth (i.e., decreasing populations) in countries facing major public health crises, such as Russia and AIDS-affected African countries. Everybody agrees that the world population is increasing, but that its annual percentage rate of increase is not as high as it was a decade or two ago. However, there is still disagreement about whether the world's population will stabilize at some value above its present level (double the present population?), and (if so) how many years (30 years? 50 years?) it will take for population to reach that level, or whether population will continue to grow.

There is long built-in momentum to human population growth because of what is termed the "demographic bulge" or "population momentum," i.e., a disproportionate number of children and young reproductive-age people in today's population, as a result of recent population growth. That is, suppose that every couple in the world decided tonight to limit themselves to two children, approximately the correct number of children to yield an unchanging population in the long run by exactly replacing their two parents who will eventually die (actually, around 2.1 children when one considers mortality, childless couples, and children who won't marry). The world's population would nevertheless continue to increase for about 70 years, because more people today are of reproductive age or entering reproductive age than are old and post-reproductive. The problem of human population growth has received much attention in recent decades and has given rise to movements such as Zero Population Growth, which aim to slow or halt the increase in the world's population.

12. What really counts is not the number of people alone, but their impact on the environment. If most of the world's 6 billion people today were in cryogenic storage and neither eating, breathing, nor metabolizing, that large population would cause no environmental problems. Instead, our numbers pose problems insofar as we consume resources and generate wastes. That per-capita impact — the resources consumed, and the wastes put out, by each person — varies greatly around the world, being highest in the First World and lowest in the Third World. On the average, each citizen of the U.S., western Europe, and Japan consumes 32 times more resources such as fossil fuels, and puts out 32 times more wastes, than do inhabitants of the Third World.

But low-impact people are becoming high-impact people for two reasons: rises in living standards in Third World countries whose inhabitants see and covet First World lifestyles; and immigration, both legal and illegal, of individual Third World inhabitants into the First World, driven by political, economic, and social problems at home. Immigration from low-impact countries is now the main contributor to the increasing populations of the U.S. and Europe. By the same token, the overwhelmingly most important human population problem for the world as a whole is not the high rate of population increase in Kenya, Rwanda, and some other poor Third World countries, although that certainly does pose a problem for Kenya and Rwanda themselves, and although that is the population problem most discussed. Instead, the biggest problem is the increase in total human impact, as the result of rising Third World living standards, and of Third World individuals moving to the First World and adopting First World living standards.

There are many "optimists" who argue that the world could support double its human population, and who consider only the increase in human numbers and not the average increase in per-capita impact. But I have not met anyone who seriously argues that the world could support 12 times its current impact, although an increase of that factor would result from all Third World inhabitants adopting First World living standards. (That factor of 12 is less than the factor of 32 that I mentioned in the preceding paragraph, because there are already First World inhabitants with high-impact lifestyles, although they are greatly outnumbered by Third World inhabitants.) Even if the people of China alone achieved a First World living standard while everyone else's living standard remained constant, that would double our human impact on the world.

People in the Third World aspire to First World living standards. They develop that aspiration through watching television, seeing advertisements for First World consumer products sold in their countries, and observing First World visitors to their countries. Even in the most remote villages and refugee camps today, people know about the outside world. Third World citizens are encouraged in that aspiration by First World and United Nations development agencies, which hold out to them the prospect of achieving their dream if they will only adopt the right policies, like balancing their national budgets, investing in education and infrastructure, and so on.

But no one in First World governments is willing to acknowledge the dream's impossibility: the unsustainability of a world in which the Third World's large population were to reach and maintain current First World living standards. It is impossible for the First World to resolve that dilemma by blocking the Third World's efforts to catch up: South Korea, Malaysia, Singapore, Hong Kong, Taiwan, and Mauritius have already succeeded or are close to success; China and India are progressing rapidly by their own efforts; and the 15 rich Western European countries making up the European Union have just extended Union membership to 10 poorer countries of Eastern Europe, in effect thereby pledging to help those 10 countries catch up. Even if the human populations of the Third World did not exist, it would be impossible for the First World alone to maintain its present course, because it is not in a steady state but is depleting its own resources as well as those imported from the Third World. At present, it is untenable politically for First World leaders to propose to their own citizens that they lower their living standards, as measured by lower resource consumption and waste production rates. What will happen when it finally dawns on all those people in the Third World that current First World standards are unreachable for them, and that the First World refuses to abandon those standards for itself? Life is full of agonizing choices based on trade-offs, but that's the cruelest trade-off that we shall have to resolve: encouraging and helping all people to achieve a higher standard of living, without thereby undermining that standard through overstressing global resources.

I have described these 12 sets of problems as separate from each other. In fact, they are linked: one problem exacerbates another or makes its solution more difficult. For example, human population growth affects all 11 other problems: more people means more deforestation, more toxic chemicals, more demand for wild fish, etc. The energy problem is linked to other problems because use of fossil fuels for energy contributes heavily to greenhouse gases, the combating of soil fertility losses by using synthetic fertilizers requires energy to make the fertilizers, fossil fuel scarcity increases our interest in nuclear energy which poses potentially the biggest "toxic" problem of all in case of an accident, and fossil fuel scarcity also makes it more expensive to solve our freshwater problems by using energy to desalinize ocean water. Depletion of fisheries and other wild food sources puts more pressure on livestock, crops, and aquaculture to replace them, thereby leading to more topsoil losses and more eutrophication from agriculture and aquaculture. Problems of deforestation, water shortage, and soil degradation in the Third World foster wars there and drive legal asylum seekers and illegal emigrants to the First World from the Third World.

Our world society is presently on a non-sustainable course, and any of our 12 problems of non-sustainability that we have just summarized would suffice to limit our lifestyle within the next several decades. They are like time bombs with fuses of less than 50 years. For example, destruction of accessible lowland tropical rainforest outside national parks is already virtually complete in Peninsular Malaysia, will be complete at current rates within less than a decade in the Solomon Islands, the Philippines, on Sumatra, and on Sulawesi, and will be complete around the world except perhaps for parts of the Amazon Basin and Congo Basin within 25 years. At current rates, we shall have depleted or destroyed most of the world's remaining marine fisheries, depleted clean or cheap or readily accessible reserves of oil and natural gas, and approached the photosynthetic ceiling within a few decades. Global warming is projected to have reached a degree Centigrade or more, and a substantial fraction of the world's wild animal and plant species are projected to be endangered or past the point of no return, within half a century. People often ask, "What is the single most important environmental/population problem facing the world today?" A flip answer would be, "The single most important problem is our misguided focus on identifying the single most important problem!" That flip answer is essentially correct, because any of the dozen problems if unsolved would do us grave harm, and because they all interact with each other. If we solved 11 of the problems, but not the 12th, we would still be

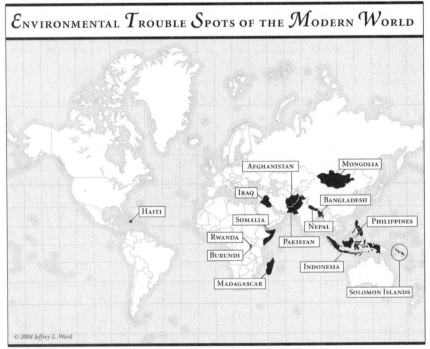

The World as a Polder, "maps" by Jeffrey L. Ward, copyright © 2004 by Jeffrey L. Ward, from *Collapse: How Societies Choose to Fail or Succeed* by Jared Diamond, copyright © 2005 by Jared Diamond. Used by permission of Viking Penguin, a division of Penguin Group (USA) Inc.

The black areas in each map indicate "trouble spots," political in the top map, environmental in the lower map. To what extent are these trouble spots the same? Identify some reasons why these are congruent.

in trouble, whichever was the problem that remained unsolved. We have to solve them all.

Thus, because we are rapidly advancing along this non-sustainable course, the world's environmental problems *will* get resolved, in one way or another, within the lifetimes of the children and young adults alive today. The only question is whether they will become resolved in pleasant ways of our own choice, or in unpleasant ways not of our choice, such as warfare, genocide, starvation, disease epidemics, and collapses of societies. While all of those grim phenomena have been endemic to humanity throughout our history, their frequency increases with environmental degradation, population pressure, and the resulting poverty and political instability.

Examples of those unpleasant solutions to environmental and population problems abound in both the modern world and the ancient world. The examples include the recent genocides in Rwanda, Burundi, and the former Yugoslavia; war, civil war, or guerrilla war in the modern Sudan, Philippines, and Nepal, and in the ancient Maya homeland; cannibalism on prehistoric Easter Island and Mangareva and among the ancient Anasazi; starvation in many modern African countries and on prehistoric Easter Island; the AIDS epidemic already in Africa, and incipiently elsewhere; and the collapse of state government in modern Somalia, the Solomon Islands, and Haiti, and among the ancient Maya. An outcome less drastic than a worldwide collapse might "merely" be the spread of Rwanda-like or Haiti-like conditions to many more developing countries, while we First World inhabitants retain many of our First World amenities but face a future with which we are unhappy, beset by more chronic terrorism, wars, and disease outbreaks. But it is doubtful that the First World could retain its separate lifestyle in the face of desperate waves of immigrants fleeing from collapsing Third World countries, in numbers much larger than the current unstoppable influx....

QUESTIONS FOR DISCUSSION AND WRITING

1. Diamond identifies a wide range of environmental problems: the destruction of habitats (paragraphs 2–3), wild species (paragraphs 4–7), farm soil erosion (paragraphs 8 and 9), depletion of freshwater aquifers (paragraph 12), toxic chemicals (paragraphs 15 and 16), atmospheric gases (paragraphs 18 and 19). Analyze these and explain how two or more problems are interrelated.

2. Investigate the possibilities of solutions to one or more of these problems (for starters, see the Nobel Peace Prize speeches of Al Gore and Wangari Maathai, pp. 583 and 586), and make a good case for your interpretation. You will need to take into account Diamond's cost/benefit analysis of the management of natural resources.

3. Diamond is extremely concerned about the rate of population growth and its relation to environmental degradation and the depletion of natural resources (paragraphs 22–27). What evidence does he present? Given that birthrates in the U.S.

and Europe are at an all-time low, from a perspective that includes birthrates in other heavily populated parts of the world, propose a potentially workable solution.

4. What evidence does Diamond offer to support his conclusion that global "society is presently on a non-sustainable course" (paragraph 30)? Why, in Diamond's view, are First World living standards unsustainable (paragraphs 29–32)? If the end of the world as we know it is really at hand, why don't Americans pay more attention to this doomsday scenario? How likely is it that the UN Declaration of Human Rights (p. 488) can be implemented in the twenty-first century? What effect have Al Gore's efforts to improve the environment had (see p. 583)?

5. Diamond says that each First World inhabitant "consumes 32 times more resources such as fossil fuels" (p. 639) than Third World dwellers. Study the environmental impact of your own consumption of, for example, water; processed foods; plastics and paper; fossil fuel; manufactured goods (cell phones, electronic equipment, clothing . . .). What is your environmental "footprint"? Pick several categories and identify ways in which you might reduce your use of resources. Then discuss how likely you are to actually put this into effect, and why. Are there any community, legal, or moral incentives to encourage your restraint? Explain.

WENDELL BERRY
Faustian Economics

Wendell Berry, a Kentuckian born (1934) and bred, has published over forty works of nonfiction, fiction, and poetry. His writing has been described in the New York Times Book Review *as "exquisitely constructed, suggesting the cyclic rhythms of his agrarian world." His work sustains the belief that one's work must be rooted in one's environment and responsive to it. He earned a B.A. (1956) and M.A. (1957) in English from the University of Kentucky, and in 1958 studied creative writing at Stanford. Although he taught creative writing at New York University, Stanford, Bucknell, and elsewhere, his roots remained at the University of Kentucky, where he taught 1964–1977, and again 1987–1993. Berry's latest works include* The Mad Farmer Poems *(2008) and a novel,* Whitefoot: A Story from the Center of the World *(2009).* The Unsettling of America: Culture and Agriculture *(1977, 1986) is a Sierra Club publication; his current nonfiction includes* Life Is a Miracle *(2000) and* The Way of Ignorance and Other Essays *(2005).*

"Faustian Economics" (Harper's, May 2008), with its evocative warning, "When there is, no more, our one choice is to make the most and the best of what we have," was selected for both Best American Essays 2009 *and* Best American Science and Nature Writing 2009. *For over half a century Berry and his wife have farmed "Lane's Landing" near Port Royal, Kentucky, "a small place that . . . can provide opportunities of work and learning, and a fund of beauty, solace, and pleasure—in addition to its difficulties—that cannot be exhausted in a lifetime or in generations."*

The general reaction to the apparent end of the era of cheap fossil fuel, as to other readily foreseeable curtailments, has been to delay any sort of reckoning. The strategies of delay so far have been a sort of willed oblivion, or visions of large profits to the manufacturers of such "biofuels" as ethanol from corn or switchgrass, or the familiar unscientific faith that "science will find an answer." The dominant response, in short, is a dogged belief that what we call the American Way of Life will prove somehow indestructible. We will keep on consuming, spending, wasting, and driving as before, at any cost to anything and everybody but ourselves.

This belief was always indefensible—the real names of global warming are Waste and Greed—and by now it is manifestly foolish. But foolishness on this scale looks disturbingly like a sort of national insanity. We seem to have come to a collective delusion of grandeur, insisting that all of us are "free" to be as conspicuously greedy and wasteful as the most corrupt of kings and queens. (Perhaps by devoting more and more of our already abused cropland to fuel production we will at last cure ourselves of obesity and become fashionably skeletal, hungry but—thank God!—still driving.)

The problem with us is not only prodigal extravagance but also an assumed limitlessness. We have obscured the issue by refusing to see that limitlessness is a godly trait. We have insistently, and with relief, defined ourselves as animals or as "higher animals." But to define ourselves as animals, given our specifically human powers and desires, is to define ourselves as *limitless* animals—which of course is a contradiction in terms. Any definition is a limit, which is why the God of Exodus refuses to define Himself: "I am that I am."

Even so, that we have founded our present society upon delusional assumptions of limitlessness is easy enough to demonstrate. A recent "summit" in Louisville, Kentucky, was entitled "Unbridled Energy: The Industrialization of Kentucky's Energy Resources." Its subjects were "clean-coal generation, biofuels, and other cutting-edge applications," the conversion of coal to "liquid fuels," and the likelihood that all this will be "environmentally friendly." These hopes, which "can create jobs and boost the nation's security," are to be supported by government "loan guarantees . . . investment tax credits and other tax breaks." Such talk we recognize as completely conventional. It is, in fact, a tissue of clichés that is now the common tongue of promoters, politicians, and journalists. This language does not allow for any computation or speculation as to the *net* good of anything proposed. The entire contraption of "Unbridled Energy" is supported only by a rote optimism: "The United States has 250 billion tons of recoverable coal reserves—enough to last 100 years even at double the current rate of consumption." We humans have inhabited the earth for many thousands of years, and now we can look forward to surviving for another hundred by doubling our consumption of coal? This is national security? The world-ending fire of industrial fundamentalism may already be burning in our furnaces and engines, but if it will burn for a hundred more years, that will be fine. Surely it would be better to intend straightforwardly to contain the fire and eventually put it out! But once greed has been made an honorable motive, then you have an economy without limits. It has no place for temperance or thrift or the ecological law of return. It will do anything. It is monstrous by definition.

In keeping with our unrestrained consumptiveness, the commonly accepted 5 basis of our economy is the supposed possibility of limitless growth, limitless wants, limitless wealth, limitless natural resources, limitless energy, and limitless debt. The idea of a limitless economy implies and requires a doctrine of general human limitlessness: *all* are entitled to pursue without limit whatever they conceive as desirable—a license that classifies the most exalted Christian capitalist with the lowliest pornographer.

This fantasy of limitlessness perhaps arose from the coincidence of the industrial revolution with the suddenly exploitable resources of the New World—though how the supposed limitlessness of resources can be reconciled with their exhaustion is not clear. Or perhaps it comes from the contrary apprehension of the world's "smallness," made possible by modern astronomy and high-speed transportation. Fear of the smallness of our world and its life may lead to a kind of claustrophobia and thence, with apparent reasonableness, to a desire for the "freedom" of limitlessness. But this desire, paradoxically, reduces everything. The life of this world is small to those who think it is, and the desire to enlarge it makes it smaller, and can reduce it finally to nothing.

However it came about, this credo of limitlessness clearly implies a principled wish not only for limitless possessions but also for limitless knowledge, limitless science, limitless technology, and limitless progress. And, necessarily, it must lead to limitless violence, waste, war, and destruction. That it should finally produce a crowning cult of political limitlessness is only a matter of mad logic.

The normalization of the doctrine of limitlessness has produced a sort of moral minimalism: the desire to be efficient at any cost, to be unencumbered by complexity. The minimization of neighborliness, respect, reverence, responsibility, accountability, and self-subordination—this is the culture of which our present leaders and heroes are the spoiled children.

Our national faith so far has been: "There's always more." Our true religion is a sort of autistic industrialism. People of intelligence and ability seem now to be genuinely embarrassed by any solution to any problem that does not involve high technology, a great expenditure of energy, or a big machine. Thus an X marked on a paper ballot no longer fulfills our idea of voting. One problem with this state of affairs is that the work now most needing to be done—that of neighborliness and caretaking—cannot be done by remote control with the greatest power on the largest scale. A second problem is that the economic fantasy of limitlessness in a limited world calls fearfully into question the value of our monetary wealth, which does not reliably stand for the real wealth of land, resources, and workmanship but instead wastes and depletes it.

That human limitlessness is a fantasy means, obviously, that its life expec- 10 tancy is limited. There is now a growing perception, and not just among a few experts, that we are entering a time of inescapable limits. We are not likely to be granted another world to plunder in compensation for our pillage of this one. Nor are we likely to believe much longer in our ability to outsmart, by means of science and technology, our economic stupidity. The hope that we can cure the ills of industrialism by the homeopathy of more technology seems at last to be losing status. We are, in short, coming under pressure to understand ourselves as limited creatures in a limited world.

This constraint, however, is not the condemnation it may seem. On the contrary, it returns us to our real condition and to our human heritage, from which our self-definition as limitless animals has for too long cut us off. Every cultural and religious tradition that I know about, while fully acknowledging our animal nature, defines us specifically as *humans*—that is, as animals (if the word still applies) capable of living not only within natural limits but also within cultural limits, self-imposed. As earthly creatures, we live, because we must, within natural limits, which we may describe by such names as "earth" or "ecosystem" or "watershed" or "place." But as humans, we may elect to respond to this necessary placement by the self-restraints implied in neighborliness, stewardship, thrift, temperance, generosity, care, kindness, friendship, loyalty, and love.

In our limitless selfishness, we have tried to define "freedom," for example, as an escape from all restraint. But, as my friend Bert Hornback has explained in his book *The Wisdom in Words*, "free" is etymologically related to "friend." These words come from the same Indo-European root, which carries the sense of "dear" or "beloved." We set our friends free by our love for them, with the implied restraints of faithfulness or loyalty. And this suggests that our "identity" is located not in the impulse of selfhood but in deliberately maintained connections.

Thinking of our predicament has sent me back again to Christopher Marlowe's *Tragical History of Doctor Faustus*. This is a play of the Renaissance; Faustus, a man of learning, longs to possess "all Nature's treasury," to "Ransack the ocean . . . / And search all corners of the new-found world." To assuage his thirst for knowledge and power, he deeds his soul to Lucifer, receiving in compensation for twenty-four years the services of the subdevil Mephistophilis, nominally Faustus's slave but in fact his master. Having the subject of limitlessness in mind, I was astonished on this reading to come upon Mephistophilis's description of hell. When Faustus asks, "How comes it then that thou art out of hell?" Mephistophilis replies, "Why, this is hell, nor am I out of it." And a few pages later he explains:

> Hell hath no limits, nor is circumscribed
> In one self place, but where we [the damned] are is hell,
> And where hell is must we ever be.

For those who reject heaven, hell is everywhere, and thus is limitless. For them, even the thought of heaven is hell.

It is only appropriate, then, that Mephistophilis rejects any conventional limit: "Tut, Faustus, marriage is but a ceremonial toy. If thou lovest me, think no more of it." Continuing this theme, for Faustus's pleasure the devils present a sort of pageant of the seven deadly sins, three of which—Pride, Wrath, and Gluttony—describe themselves as orphans, disdaining the restraints of parental or filial love.

Seventy or so years later, and with the issue of the human definition more than ever in doubt, John Milton in Book VII of *Paradise Lost* returns again to a consideration of our urge to know. To Adam's request to be told the story of Creation, the "affable Archangel" Raphael agrees "to answer thy desire / Of knowledge *within bounds* [my emphasis]," explaining that

> Knowledge is as food, and needs no less
> Her temperance over appetite, to know
> In measure what the mind may well contain;
> Oppresses else with surfeit, and soon turns
> Wisdom to folly, as nourishment to wind.

Raphael is saying, with angelic circumlocution, that knowledge without wisdom, limitless knowledge, is not worth a fart; he is not a humorless archangel. But he also is saying that knowledge without measure, knowledge that the human mind cannot appropriately use, is mortally dangerous.

I am well aware of what I risk in bringing this language of religion into what is normally a scientific discussion. I do so because I doubt that we can define our present problems adequately, let alone solve them, without some recourse to our cultural heritage. We are, after all, trying now to deal with the failure of scientists, technicians, and politicians to "think up" a version of human continuance that is economically probable and ecologically responsible, or perhaps even imaginable. If we go back into our tradition, we are going to find a concern with religion, which at a minimum shatters the selfish context of the individual life, and thus forces a consideration of what human beings are and ought to be.

This concern persists at least as late as our Declaration of Independence, which holds as "self-evident, that all men are created equal; that they are endowed by their Creator with certain unalienable rights." Thus among our political roots we have still our old preoccupation with our definition as humans, which in the Declaration is wisely assigned to our Creator; our rights and the rights of all humans are not granted by any human government but are innate, belonging to us by birth. This insistence comes not from the fear of death or even extinction but from the ancient fear that in order to survive we might become inhuman or monstrous.

And so our cultural tradition is in large part the record of our continuing effort to understand ourselves as beings specifically human: to say that, as humans, we must do certain things and we must not do certain things. We must have limits or we will cease to exist as humans; perhaps we will cease to exist, period. At times, for example, some of us humans have thought that human beings, properly so called, did not make war against civilian populations, or hold prisoners without a fair trial, or use torture for any reason.

Some of us would-be humans have thought too that we should not be free at anybody else's expense. And yet in the phrase "free market," the word "free" has come to mean unlimited economic power for some, with the necessary consequence of economic powerlessness for others. Several years ago, after I had spoken at a meeting, two earnest and obviously troubled young veterinarians approached me with a question: How could they practice veterinary medicine without serious economic damage to the farmers who were their clients? Underlying their question was the fact that for a long time veterinary help for a sheep or a pig has been likely to cost more than the animal is worth. I had to answer that, in my opinion, so long as their practice relied heavily on selling patented drugs, they had no choice, since the market for medicinal drugs was entirely controlled by the drug companies, whereas most farmers had no control at all over the market for agricultural products. My questioners were asking in effect if a predatory economy can have a beneficent result. The answer too often is no. And that is because there is an absolute discontinuity between the economy of the seller of medicines and the economy of the buyer, as there is in the health industry as a whole. The drug industry is interested in the survival of patients, we have to suppose, because surviving patients will continue to consume drugs.

Now let us consider a contrary example. Recently, at another meeting, I 20 talked for some time with an elderly, and some would say an old-fashioned, farmer from Nebraska. Unable to farm any longer himself, he had rented his land to a younger farmer on the basis of what he called "crop share" instead of a price paid or owed in advance. Thus, as the old farmer said of his renter, "If he has a good year, I have a good year. If he has a bad year, I have a bad one." This is what I would call community economics. It is a sharing of fate. It assures an economic continuity and a common interest between the two partners to the trade. This is as far as possible from the economy in which the young veterinarians were caught, in which the powerful are limitlessly "free" to trade, to the disadvantage, and ultimately the ruin, of the powerless.

It is this economy of community destruction that, wittingly or unwittingly, most scientists and technicians have served for the past two hundred years. These scientists and technicians have justified themselves by the proposition that they are the vanguard of progress, enlarging human knowledge and power, and thus they have romanticized both themselves and the predatory enterprises that they have served.

As a consequence, our great need now is for sciences and technologies of limits, of domesticity, of what Wes Jackson of the Land Institute in Salina, Kansas, has called "homecoming." These would be specifically human sciences and technologies, working, as the best humans always have worked, within self-imposed limits. The limits would be the accepted contexts of places, communities, and neighborhoods, both natural and human.

I know that the idea of such limitations will horrify some people, maybe most people, for we have long encouraged ourselves to feel at home on the "cutting edge" of knowledge and power or on some "frontier" of human experience. But I know too that we are talking now in the presence of much evidence that improvement by outward expansion may no longer be a good idea, if it ever was. It was not a good idea for the farmers who "leveraged" secure acreage to buy more during the 1970s. It has proved tragically to be a bad idea in a number of recent wars. If it is a good idea in the form of corporate gigantism, then we must ask, For whom? Faustus, who wants all knowledge and all the world for himself, is a man supremely lonely and finally doomed. I don't think Marlowe was kidding. I don't think Satan is kidding when he says in *Paradise Lost*, "Myself am Hell."

If the idea of appropriate limitation seems unacceptable to us, that may be because, like Marlowe's Faustus and Milton's Satan, we confuse limits with confinement. But that, as I think Marlowe and Milton and others were trying to tell us, is a great and potentially a fatal mistake. Satan's fault, as Milton understood it, and perhaps with some sympathy, was precisely that he could not tolerate his proper limitation; he could not subordinate himself to anything whatever. Faustus's error was his unwillingness to remain "Faustus, and a man." In our age of the world it is not rare to find writers, critics, and teachers of literature, as well as scientists and technicians, who regard Satan's and Faustus's defiance as salutary and heroic.

On the contrary, our human and earthly limits, properly understood, are 25 not confinements but rather inducements to formal elaboration and elegance, to *fullness* of relationship and meaning. Perhaps our most serious cultural loss in recent centuries is the knowledge that some things, though limited, are inexhaustible. For example, an ecosystem, even that of a working forest or farm, so long as it remains ecologically intact, is inexhaustible. A small place, as I know from my own experience, can provide opportunities of work and learning, and a fund of beauty, solace, and pleasure—in addition to its difficulties—that cannot be exhausted in a lifetime or in generations.

To recover from our disease of limitlessness, we will have to give up the idea that we have a right to be godlike animals, that we are potentially omniscient and omnipotent, ready to discover "the secret of the universe." We will have to start over, with a different and much older premise: the naturalness and, for creatures of limited intelligence, the necessity of limits. We must learn again to ask how we can make the most of what we are, what we have, what we have been given. If we always have a theoretically better substitute available from somebody or someplace else, we will never make the most of anything. It is hard to make the most of one life. If we each had two lives, we would not make much of either. Or as one of my best teachers said of people in general: "They'll never be worth a damn as long as they've got two choices."

To deal with the problems, which after all are inescapable, of living with limited intelligence in a limited world, I suggest that we may have to remove some of the emphasis we have lately placed on science and technology and have a new look at the arts. For an art does not propose to enlarge itself by limitless extension but rather to enrich itself within bounds that are accepted prior to the work.

It is the artists, not the scientists, who have dealt unremittingly with the problem of limits. A painting, however large, must finally be bounded by a frame or a wall. A composer or playwright must reckon, at a minimum, with the capacity of an audience to sit still and pay attention. A story, once begun, must end somewhere within the limits of the writer's and the reader's memory. And of course the arts characteristically impose limits that are artificial: the five acts of a play, or the fourteen lines of a sonnet. Within these limits artists achieve elaborations of pattern, of sustaining relationships of parts with one another and with the whole, that may be astonishingly complex. And probably most of us can name a painting, a piece of music, a poem or play or story that still grows in meaning and remains fresh after many years of familiarity.

We know by now that a natural ecosystem survives by the same sort of formal intricacy, ever changing, inexhaustible, and no doubt finally unknowable. We know further that if we want to make our economic landscapes sustainably and abundantly productive, we must do so by maintaining in them a living formal complexity something like that of natural ecosystems. We can do this only by raising to the highest level our mastery of the arts of agriculture, animal husbandry, forestry, and, ultimately, the art of living.

It is true that insofar as scientific experiments must be conducted within 30 carefully observed limits, scientists also are artists. But in science one experiment, whether it succeeds or fails, is logically followed by another in a theoretically infinite progression. According to the underlying myth of modern science, this progression is always replacing the smaller knowledge of the past with the larger knowledge of the present, which will be replaced by the yet larger knowledge of the future.

In the arts, by contrast, no limitless sequence of works is ever implied or looked for. No work of art is necessarily followed by a second work that is necessarily better. Given the methodologies of science, the law of gravity and the genome were bound to be discovered by somebody; the identity of the discoverer is incidental to the fact. But it appears that in the arts there are no second chances. We must assume that we had one chance each for *The Divine Comedy* and *King Lear*. If Dante and Shakespeare had died before they wrote those poems, nobody ever would have written them.

The same is true of our arts of land use, our economic arts, which are our arts of living. With these it is once-for-all. We will have no chance to redo our experiments with bad agriculture leading to soil loss. The Appalachian mountains and forests we have destroyed for coal are gone forever. It is now and forevermore too late to use thriftily the first half of the world's supply of petroleum. In the art of living we can only start again with what remains.

And so, in confronting the phenomenon of "peak oil," we are really confront- 35
ing the end of our customary delusion of "more." Whichever way we turn, from
now on, we are going to find a limit beyond which there will be no more. To
hit these limits at top speed is not a rational choice. To start slowing down, with
the idea of avoiding catastrophe, is a rational choice, and a viable one if we can
recover the necessary political sanity. Of course it makes sense to consider alternative energy sources, provided *they* make sense. But also we will have to reexamine the economic structures of our lives, and conform them to the tolerances and
limits of our earthly places. Where there is no more, our one choice is to make the
most and the best of what we have.

QUESTIONS FOR DISCUSSION AND WRITING

1. What evidence does Berry cite to support his claim that "what we call the American Way of Life will somehow prove indestructible," that "the real names of
   global warming are Waste and Greed. . . . The problem with us is not only prodigal extravagance but also an assumed limitlessness" (paragraphs 1–3)?

2. Berry asserts that "this credo of limitlessness clearly implies a principled wish not
   only for limitless possessions also but for limitless knowledge, limitless science,
   limitless technology, and limitless progress. And, necessarily, it must lead to limitless violence, waste, war, and destruction" (paragraph 7). What evidence does
   he cite to show that the apparently benign qualities in the first sentence "necessarily" result in the destructive phenomena of the second? With what information does Diamond (p. 632) support these views?

3. Faust, in Marlowe's *Doctor Faustus* and Milton's *Paradise Lost*, is a character "who
   wants all knowledge and all the world for himself, is a man supremely lonely
   and finally doomed." Milton's Satan, says Berry, is not "kidding when he says . . .
   'Myself am Hell'" (paragraphs 13, 14, 23, 24). Why can't Satan escape from himself and the consequences of his colossal ambition? In what ways, by implication,
   is American society in a comparable position?

4. If a "Faustian bargain" means that the bargainer sells his or her soul to the devil
   in exchange for a favor, what does Berry mean by the concept of "Faustian Economics" that governs this essay? Is it possible for Berry (or other writers in this
   chapter) to convince a nation of Faustian bargainers that they're wrong? Why or
   why not?

5. Why does Berry consider "limitlessness" a "disease" (paragraph 27)? "To recover,
   we will have to give up the idea that we have a right to be godlike animals, that we
   are potentially omniscient and omnipotent, ready to discover 'the secret of the
   universe' [and] start over, with a different and much older premise . . . the necessity of limits" (paragraph 26). Berry suggests how we can apply limits to "our arts
   of land use, our economic arts, which are our arts of living" (paragraphs 27–29).

Examine the feasibility of his solution, reinforcing your position with ideas from any or all of the essays in this chapter.

6. With reference to any or all of the essays in this chapter, with your fellow students work out a plan to save the environment. You could begin with a local plan — what can you, individually and collectively, do at home in the short and long run? At school? In your community? You could then expand your focus to the state, national, even international levels. Check relevant Web sites for more information. Charity Navigator, for instance, explains the focus and efforts of 337 organizations addressing environmental concerns, and rates their economic efficiency; you could then click on any of these organizations for more information. Good luck!

Acknowledgments

Marjorie Agosin. "Always Living in Spanish." Translated by Celeste Kostopulos-Cooperman. Used with permission of the author.

Sherman Alexie. "The Joy of Reading and Writing: Superman and Me." First published in *The Most Wonderful Books.* Copyright ©1992 by Sherman Alexie. Used with permission of Nancy Stauffer Associates as agent for the author. All rights reserved. "What Sacagawea Means to Me." From *Time*, July 8, 2002 issue. Copyright © 2002 Time, Inc. All rights reserved. Used by permission of Copyright Clearance Center via the format Textbook.

Paula Gunn Allen. "Three Voices." First published in *Voice of the Turtle: American Indian Literature, 1900–1970*, pp. 4-8. Used with permission.

Natalie Angier. "Men, Women, Sex, and Darwin." From *Woman: An Intimate Geography* by Natalie Angier. Copyright © 1999 by Natalie Angier. Adapted by permission of Houghton Mifflin Harcourt Publishing Company. All rights reserved.

Gloria Anzaldúa. "Beyond Traditional Notions of Identity." From *The Chronicle of Higher Education*, October 11, 2002, B11–13. A different version of this essay was originally published as "(Un)natural bridges, (Un)safe spaces" in *this bridge we call home: radical visions for transformation*, edited by Gloria E. Anzaldúa and AnaLouise Keating. Reprinted by permission of the Estate of Gloria E. Anzaldúa.

James Baldwin. "Stranger in the Village" and "Autobiographical Notes." From *Notes of a Native Son* by James Baldwin. Copyright © 1955, renewed 1983, by James Baldwin. Reprinted with permission of Beacon Press, Boston.

Denis Baron. "The New Technologies of the Word." From a speech given to the *International Association of World Englishes*, 2002. Used with permission of the author.

Lynda Barry. "Hate." Copyright © 2002 by Lynda Barry. Copyright © 2002 by Lynda Barry, originally published by Sasquatch Books and used courtesy of Darhansoff, Verrill, Feldman Literary Agents.

Wendell Berry. "Faustian Economics." Originally published in *Harper's*, May 2008. Copyright © 2010 by Wendell Berry from *What Matters?*. Reprinted by permission of Counterpoint.

Olin T. Binkley. "Southern Baptist Seminaries." First published in the June 12, 1963 issue of *Christian Century*. Copyright © 1963 Christian Century. Reprinted with permission of the publisher. Subscriptions: $49/yr., POB 378, Mt. Morris, IL 61054, 1-800-208-4097.

David Brown. "Science Reporting and Evidence-Based Journalism." Remarks to University of Iowa on October 8, 2008, for the Project on Rhetoric of Inquiry.

Michael J. Bugeia. "Facing the Facebook." First published in *The Chronicle of Higher Education*, January 27, 2006, C1, 4. Copyright © 2006 by Michael J. Bugeia. Used with permission of the author.

James MacGregor Burns. "Off-Campus Life." From *The New York Times*, Editorial Section, September 6, 2009 issue, page 10. Copyright © 2009 The New York Times. All rights reserved. Used by permission and protected by the Copyright Laws of the United States. The printing, copying, redistribution, or retransmission of the Material without experss written permission is prohibited.

Nicholas Carr. "Is Google Making Us Stupid?" First published in *The Atlantic*, July/August 2008, pp. 56–57, 59–63. Copyright © 2008 by Nicholas Carr. All rights reserved. Reprinted with the author's permission.

Rachel Carson. "The Obligation to Endure." From *Silent Spring* by Rachel Carson. Copyright © 1962 by Rachel L. Carson. Renewed 1990 by Roger Christie. Reprinted by permission of Houghton Mifflin Harcourt Publishing Company. All rights reserved.

Michael Crawford. First published as "The Case for Working with Your Hands." Published in *The New York Times*, May 21, 2009. Adapted from *Shop Class as Soulcraft* by Michael Crawford. Copyright © 2009 by Michael B. Crawford. Penguin USA. Reprinted by permission of the author.

William Deresiewicz. "Faux Friendship." First published in *The Chronicle of Higher Education*, December 6, 2009. Reprinted with permission of the author.

Jared Diamond. "The World as a Polder." From *Collapse: How Societies Choose to Fail or Succeed* by Jared Diamond. Copyright © 2005 by Jared Diamond. Used by permission of Viking Penguin, a division of Penguin Group (USA) Inc.

Joan Didion. "On Keeping a Notebook." From *Slouching Towards Bethlehem* by Joan Didion. Copyright © 1966, 1968, renewed 1996 by Joan Didion. Reprinted by permission of Farrar, Straus and Giroux, LLC.

Joan Didion. "Why I Write." Originally published in *The New York Times Book Review*, December 5, 1976. Copyright © 1976 by Joan Didion. Reprinted by permission of the author. "Last Words." Originally published in *The New Yorker*, November 9, 1998, p. 74. Copyright © 1998 by Joan Didion. Reprinted by permission of the author.

Annie Dillard. "Heaven and Earth in Jest." From pages 1–13 in *Pilgrim at Tinker Creek* by Annie Dillard. Copyright © 1974 by Annie Dillard. Reprinted by permission of HarperCollins Publishers.

Brian Doyle. "Joyas Voladoras." Reprinted from *The American Scholar*, Volume 73, No. 4, Autumn 2004. Used with permission.

Esther Dyson. "Reflections on Privacy 2.0." First published in *Scientific American*, September 2008, pp. 50–55. Reprinted with permission of the author.

Freeman Dyson. "Our Biotech Future." From *The New York Review of Books*, July 19, 2007, Volume 54, Number 12. Reprinted with permission from *The New York Review of Books*.

Barbara Ehrenreich. "Serving in Florida." From the book *Nickel and Dimed: On (Not) Getting By in America* by Barbara Ehrenreich. Copyright © 2001 by Barbara Ehrenreich. Reprinted by arrangement with Henry Holt and Company, LLC.

Peter Elbow. "Freewriting Exercises." From *Twenty-fifth Anniversary Edition, Writing Without Teachers*, pages 3–7. Copyright © 1978, 1998 by Oxford University Press, Inc. Reprinted by permission of Oxford University Press, Inc.

Amitai Etzioni. "Second Chances, Social Forgiveness, and the Internet." First published in *The American Scholar*, Spring 2009. Reprinted with permission.

Stanley Fish. "Academic Cross-Dressing: How Intelligent Design Gets Its Arguments from the Left." Copyright © 2005 by *Harper's Magazine*. Reprinted from the December issue by special permission. All rights reserved.

"College Advice, from People Who Have Been There Awhile." From *The New York Times*, September 6, 2009 issue, This Week In Review Section, page 20. Copyright © 2009 The New York Times. All rights reserved. Used by permission and protected by the Copyright Laws of the United States. The printing, copying, redistribution, or retransmission of the Material without express written permission is prohibited.

Deborah Franklin. "Informed Consent." Originally titled, "Come Again? Good Medicine Requires Clarity," from *The New York Times*, Health Section, January 24, 2006 issue. Copyright © 2006 by The New York Times. All rights reserved. Used by permission and protected by the Copyright Laws of the United States. The printing, copying, redistribution, or retransmission of the Material without express written permission is prohibited.

Lewis Burke Frumkes. Excerpt from "A Conversation with Joan Didion." Originally published in *The Writer*, March 1999, pp. 14–15. Published by The Writing Center. Copyright © 1999 by Lewis Burke Frumkes. Reprinted with permission of the author.

Joseph Fuller. "The Terminator Comes to Wall Street." Reprinted from *The American Scholar*, Volume 78, No. 2, Spring 2009. Copyright © 2009 by Joseph Fuller. Used with permission of The American Scholar.

Howard Gardner. "Who Owns Intelligence?" First published in *The Atlantic Monthly*, February 1999. Copyright © 1999 by Howard Gardner. Used by permission of the author.

Nick Gillespie and Virginia I. Postrel. Excerpt from "The New, New World" interview with Richard Rodriguez. From the August/September 1994 issue of *Reason Magazine*. Copyright © 2002 by Reason Magazine. Reprinted with permission.

Al Gore. "A Planetary Emergency." Nobel Peace Prize Speech, 2007. Copyright © 2007 The Nobel Foundation. Reprinted with permission.

James Gleick. "Cyber-Neologoliferation." Originally published in *The New York Times*, November 5, 2006 issue. James Gleick © 2006. Reprinted with permission of Inkwell Management, LLC, as agent for James Gleick. "Stephen Jay Gould, Breaking Tradition with Darwin." Originally published in *The New York Times Magazine*, November 20, 1983, pp. 54–56. James Gleick © 1983. Reprinted with permission of Carlisle & Company, as agent for James Gleick.

Sandra Postel. "Troubled Waters." Originally published in the March/April 2000 issue of *The Sciences.* Copyright © 2000 by Sandra Postel. Reprinted with permission of The New York Academy of Sciences.

Anna Quindlen. "Anniversary." From *Loud and Clear,* published by Random House, Inc. Copyright © 2004 by Anna Quindlen. First published in *Newsweek,* 1997. Reprinted by permission of International Creative Management, Inc.

William E. Rees. "Life in the Lap of Luxury as Ecosystems Collapse." First published in *The Chronicle of Higher Education,* July 30, 1999. Copyright © 1999 by William E. Rees. Reprinted with permission of the author.

Richard Rodriguez. "Aria: A Memoir of a Bilingual Childhood." Interview Excerpt, "Slouching towards Los Angeles." Copyright © 1993 by Richard Rodriguez. Originally appeared in *The Los Angeles Times,* April 11, 1993. Reprinted by permission of Georges Borchardt, Inc., on behalf of Richard Rodriguez.

Scott Russell Sanders. "Under the Influence." Copyright © 1986 by Scott Russell Sanders. First appeared in *The North American Review;* later published in *The Paradise of Bombs;* reprinted by permission of the author and the author's agents, the Virginia Kidd Agency, Inc.

Esmeralda Santiago. "Jibara." Excerpt from *When I Was Puerto Rican.* Copyright © 1993 Esmeralda Santiago. Reprinted by permission of Da Capo Press, a member of the Perseus Books Group.

Marjane Satrapi. "The Convocation." From *The Story of a Childhood* by Marjane Satrapi, translated by Mattias Ripa & Blake Ferris. Translation copyright © 2003 by L'Association, Paris, France. Used by permission of Pantheon Books, a division of Random House, Inc.

David Sedaris. "What I Learned and What I Said at Princeton." From *When You Are Engulfed in Flames* by David Sedaris. Copyright © 2008 by David Sedaris. By permission of Little, Brown and Company.

Timothy S. Sedore. "Violating the Boundaries: An Interview with Richard Rodriguez." Originally published in *Michigan Quarterly Review,* Summer 1999, pages 425–446.

Leslie Marmon Silko. "Language and Literature from a Pueblo Indian Perspective." From *Yellow Woman and a Beauty of the Spirit* by Leslie Marmon Silko. Copyright © 1996 by Leslie Marmon Silko. Reprinted with the permission of Simon & Schuster, Inc. All rights reserved.

Linda Simon. "The Naked Source." First published in *Michigan Quarterly Review,* 1998. Used with permission of the author.

Natasha Singer and Duff Wilson. "Medical Editors Push for Ghostwriting Crackdown." From *The New York Times,* Business Section, September 18, 2009 issue. Copyright © 2009 The New York Times. All rights reserved. Used by permission and protected by the Copyright Laws of the United States. The printing, copying, redistribution, or retransmission of the Material without express written permission is prohibited.

Peter Singer. "The Singer Solution to World Poverty." Originally published by *The New York Times,* Magazine Section, September 5, 1999. Reprinted with permission of the author.

Social Psychology Network. "Tips on Informed Consent." www.socialpsychology.org. Reprinted courtesy of Social Psychology Network. All rights reserved.

Daniel Solove. "The End of Privacy?" First published in *Scientific American,* September 2006, pp. 101–104, 106. Copyright © 2006 by Daniel Solove. Used by permission of the author.

Art Spiegelman. "Mein Kampf." Originally published in *The New York Times Magazine.* Copyright © 1996 by Art Spiegelman. Reprinted with permission of The Wylie Agency, LLC.

Amy Tan. "Mother Tongue." First appeared in *Threepenny Review.* Copyright © 1989. Reprinted by permission of the author and the Sandra Dijkstra Literary Agency.

Lewis Thomas. "The Technology of Medicine." From *The Lives of a Cell* by Lewis Thomas. Copyright © 1971 by The Massachusetts Medical Society. Used by permission of Viking Penguin, a division of Penguin Group (USA) Inc.

Sherry Turkle. "How Computers Change the Way We Think." Originally published in *The Chronicle Review,* January 30, 2004, Volume 50, Issue 21, B26. Used with permission of the author. "The Human Spirit in a Computer Culture," pages 279–280 from *The Second Self, Twentieth Anniversary Edition: Computers and the Human Spirit.* Copyright © 2005 Massachusetts Institute of Technology. By permission of The MIT Press. "Logins R Us." "Identity and Multiplicity" (1.5 pp); "Inner History: Collection and ReCollection in the Digital Archive," from *The Inner History of*

Rhetorical Index

Argument and Persuasion

Autobiography

Cause and Effect

Classification and Division

Comparison/Contrast

Definition

Description

Editorial, Column, and Op-Ed

Graphic Selections

Humor and Satire

Illustration

Implied Argument

Interview

Lists and Guidelines

Index of Titles and Authors